THE ROCK SONG

INDEX

ESSENTIAL INFORMATION ON THE 7,500 MOST IMPORTANT SONGS OF ROCK AND ROLL

BRUCE POLLOCK

SCHIRMER BOOKS
An Imprint of Simon & Schuster Macmillan
New York

Prentice Hall International
London   Mexico City   New Delhi   Singapore   Sydney   Toronto

Schirmer Books
An Imprint of Simon & Schuster Macmillan
1633 Broadway
New York, NY 10019

Printed in the United States of America

Printing number
1   2   3   4   5   6   7   8   9   10

Library of Congress Cataloging-in-Publication Data:

Pollock, Bruce.
    Rock songs index / Bruce Pollock.
        p.   cm.
    Includes index.
    ISBN 0-02-8720687 (alk. paper)
    1. Rock music—Bibliography. I. Title.
ML128.R6P65 1997
016.78242166—dc20   96-31950

The paper used in this publication meets the requirements of ANSI/NISO Z39.48-1992 (Permanence of Paper).

THE ROCK SONG INDEX

Acknowledgments

A book of this magnitude and complexity is never the product of one person alone. For helping me bring this epic tome to completion I would like to thank the scrupulous editorial staff at Schirmer Books—Richard, Andy, Barry, Dan, Robert, and Kerry. I would also like to give special mention to Bob "Macro" Swain, my invaluable behind-the-scenes computer specialist. Another acknowledgment is needed for the talented team of trainers, masseuses, chiropractors, and other assorted physical therapists, whose 'round-the-clock efforts enabled me to become "the Indiana Jones of typing." Finally, to my endlessly tolerant family—Barbara, Lisa, and Becky—the greatest praise, for bravely manning the fort while I plunged ever onward toward the conclusion of this monumental project.

Though the Rock and Roll repertoire now numbers well into the hundreds of thousands of titles, multiplying daily, the task of collecting virtually everything under one or several covers (and/or CD-ROM file) has already been attempted several times. In the new Internet-inspired information age, undifferentiated raw data abounds about every track by every artist imaginable—every single, every album cut, every chart record, every non-album B-side of interest only to the particular artist's friends, family, and fan club president. This book seeks to accomplish the estimable, if not quixotic feat, of making sense of it all, by editing this number down to a usable figure of only the worthiest works.

This figure would have to be large enough to encompass the depth and sweep of Rock and Roll from its inception in the '40s to its dominant place in today's mainstream, yet small enough to reward those included with a measure of exclusivity. A hundred titles or even 1,000 would not suffice to represent the intricacies of the mass and cult tastes that have shaped this rough beast over the last fifty years. 10,000 would be too indiscriminate a sum, precluding the tough if not heartbreaking decisions upon which the framework of this book depends. 7,500 titles, however, seemed right, giving each year a chance to showcase not only its popular hits most often dismissed by critics, but its myriad underground gems cherished mainly by the avant-garde and dismissed by Top-40 chartaholics and the similarly radio addled. While avoiding the suffocating minutiae of the more inclusive tomes, there is still room to study artists with all their significant singles and album cuts, cutting-edge trends as they emerged from underground and merged with the mainstream, the ineffable one-shot, the in-concert perennial, the legendary obscurity discovered by a cult band in England.

Ultimately, the purpose of this book is to celebrate the lowly and often forgotten linchpin around which the whole ball of wax revolves, the song. Supplanted over the years in primacy by artist, image, performance, record, mix, video, genre battles, internecine demographic face-offs, societal upheavals, and regional turf wars, the song has nevertheless survived and transcended the volatile, ever-changing landscape of Rock and Roll, as derivative and incessant as an advertising jingle, as powerful and cathartic as poetry. While hardly neglecting the impact of performing artists, and the underground scenes that regularly energize the mainstream, this work reveals the true legacy of Rock and Roll through its collected songs, each one summing up its moment, all 7,500 forming an awesome fantasy radio station that every true fan carries around in his or her head.

As a significant added attraction, this context provides a new way to view the history of Rock and Roll: by its songwriters. Leading the pack, not unexpectedly, is Paul McCartney, accounting for a massive 162 titles, 135 of which were written with John Lennon for the Beatles, making Lennon & McCartney by far the greatest songwriting team in Rock and Roll history. (With twenty-seven non-Beatles titles, even a post-Beatles Paul would have made #25 on the list. The post-Beatles Lennon, his career cut short by tragedy, notched another twenty-three solo titles). Showing just how closely songwriting and performance go together in Rock and Roll, the second-place songwriting team is Mick Jagger & Keith Richards of the inexhaustible Rolling Stones, with a total of sixty-four—less than half of Lennon & McCartney's prodigious output. In third place is arguably the team most responsible for Rock and Roll's initial crossover into mass consciousness, Jerry Leiber & Mike Stoller, with forty-one classics. The Holland-Dozier-Holland combine out of Motown are next, with thirty-nine titles (Eddie Holland's grand total is forty-three), edging out their modern-day counterparts, Kenny "Babyface" Edmunds—whose total of thirty-seven includes twenty-six with frequent partners Antonio "L.A." Reid and Daryl Simmons— and James Harris III and Terry Lewis, who clocked thirty-three. Philly soul stalwarts Kenny Gamble and Leon Huff wind up in a dead heat with England's Elton John and Bernie Taupin, with thirty (although Elton was the featured artist on all of his tunes). Broadway legends Gerry Goffin and Carole King account for twenty-eight untarnished gems, giving them sole possession of eighth place (adding other collaborations and solo efforts to the scrolls, Carole King comes up with a grand total of thirty-nine, Gerry Goffin thirty-six). Ninth position would have to go to Madonna Ciccone and her various collaborators, who have placed twenty-six titles on the list (only two of which were written by Madonna alone). The final slot belongs to the blooze-heavy tandem of Jimmy Page and Robert Plant, with twenty-two titles (with eight more Page compositions elsewhere bringing his grand total to thirty on the Big 7,500).

The individual songwriters in this book were invariably performers, most often in bands, but whose songs were so influential and pervasive and consistently excellent that they either defined a genre, dominated the record charts, and/or captivated a generation with a body of work equal to the greatest of lyric poets. Bob Dylan is far and away the leader of this group, with 108 titles, more than twice as many as Bruce Springsteen's forty-nine. In third place is Pete Townshend, of whose forty-three titles only one was written with Who cohort Roger Daltrey (their initial hit, "Anyway, Anyhow, Anywhere"). Fourth place belongs to Paul Simon, with forty-two titles, only two of which were written with Art Garfunkel (including their first hit, "Hey Schoolgirl") and one under the pseudonym Paul Kane ("He Was My Brother"). Perhaps surprisingly, the top black solo songwriter of the Rock and Roll era is Prince, with forty-two memorable and often outrageous tunes, edging Chuck Berry by one and Smokey Robinson by two. Brian Wilson follows, with thirty-six entries (mostly written with and for the Beach Boys). Neil Young's thirty-five titles includes many Buffalo-Springfield and CSNY selections, and Lou Reed's thirty-five includes many with the Velvet Underground. Stevie Wonder (thirty-five) rounds out the list.

Taking note of—but not including—two major artists who specialized in interpreting material with groundbreaking performances (Elvis Presley, sixty-one; Aretha Franklin, twenty-six), we wind up with an all-time songwriter-driven Top-25 list that is not unlike many a Rock and Roll Hall of Fame pantheon (except for the already-noted omission of Elvis and Aretha).

1.	**Lennon & McCartney**	**135**
2.	**Bob Dylan**	**108**
3.	**Jagger & Richards**	**64**
4.	**Bruce Springsteen**	**49**
5.	**Pete Townshend**	**43**
6.	**Prince Rogers Nelson**	**42**
6.	**Paul Simon**	**42**
8.	**Leiber & Stoller**	**41**
9.	**Chuck Berry**	**39**
9.	**Holland-Dozier-Holland**	**39**
11.	**Smokey Robinson**	**38**
12.	**Kenny "Babyface" Edmunds**	**37**
13.	**Brian Wilson**	**36**
14.	**Lou Reed**	**35**
14.	**Neil Young**	**35**
14.	**Stevie Wonder**	**35**

The songs themselves are less easily quantified. In putting together a list that includes all the hits along with all important B-sides and album tracks, obviously chart positions have had to be a consideration, even though it is by now common knowledge that the charts, no matter what magazine provided the numbers, are a deceptive and problematic realm, where any given #5 could have been a #1 but for the grace of enough payola. When you factor in the systematic blindness to the early R&B classics, and who knows what other untold artistic betrayals over the years, it's easy to see why successive generations have chosen to assemble fairly complete Rock and Roll libraries without ever knowing or caring that Gary Lewis & the Playboys or the New Kids on the Block were releasing hit after hit after hit. (And there's many a lifelong chart-watcher who has conceded that everything charted in the '90s should be regarded with the baseball equivalent of an asterisk!) In this very book—one of the sacred hallmarks of Rock and Roll veracity—a song that scored a #1 R&B/#1 R&R crossover has to answer for the fact that such unlikely bellwether acts as Lesley Gore ("It's My Party"), Danny & the Juniors ("At the Hop"), Paul Anka ("Diana"), and the Four Seasons ("Sherry" *and* "Big Girls Don't Cry"), have all achieved that feat. On the other hand, when you stop to consider that Lesley Gore was produced by Quincy Jones, Danny & the Juniors were celebrating a new Disco age, and the Four Seasons were routinely mistaken for black, you can see that, for all their problems—like Paul Anka—the charts have maintained a kind of skewed integrity, bestowing their rewards more often than not on worthy recipients. And besides, after a slew of white records topped the R&B charts in the early '60s, changes were finally made to the system to prevent such an embarrassment from ever occurring again, with fairly successful results. Meanwhile, since 1956, R&B records have crossed over to the mass market R&R charts with a historic consistency that has been both numerically and stylistically rewarding. Though ironically, again in the '90s, the preponderance of rap-/hip-hop-influenced tunes on the charts has caused music fans to be more alienated from the Pop Top-40 than at any time since the pre-rock 1940s, when R&B represented the first underground movement.

The Country charts are another matter. Having shut the barn door on Rock and Roll shortly after Elvis Presley escaped in '56, they've been a world unto themselves, allowing only the rare crossover to spoil their purity ever since. Just ask Brenda Lee, who never had a Country hit during the height of her Rock and Roll career (she did, however, cross over to the R&B charts). Thus, even a #1 Country crossover is not an automatic add in this book, especially one from the last thirty years, when it seemed that half of all songs released on the Country charts peaked at #1. On the other hand, there was indeed a time in the '80s when most popular Country tunes sounded a lot like the Rock and Roll of the early '60s.

And then there's Pop music. By establishing as its generational credo the breaking away from their parents' music of the '30s and '40s—only to then one by one bring the standards (along with a batch of slick Tin Pan Alley-esque ballads) back into the literature— Rock and Roll has always taken a schizophrenic stance toward Pop music, as exemplified today in the pejorative use of the term "Pop" when applied to a Rock and Roll song or artist. When is Rock and Roll Pop, when is it Pop/Rock, technically or emotionally? Is all Pop since 1958 or so actually a form of Rock and Roll (even rock), except for Frank Sinatra, Percy Faith, and Mr. Acker Bilk? Or is Rock and Roll only to be considered in its faster and louder abject Punk attitude? In the latter case, half of what fans and even critics think of as Rock and Roll would have to be thrown out. But if all easy listening had to be thought of as Rock and Roll, then half the titles included in this book would also have to be thrown out just to squeeze in every hit by Whitney Houston and Mariah Carey, to say nothing of Connie Francis, the Bobbys Vinton and Goldsboro, and the dreaded Air Supply.

To prevent any further psychic damage, I gave myself the option of eliminating from contention anything that failed to break into the R&R Top-10 (and even a few redundant #9s and #8s, if a particularly stern mood gripped me). Deciding what, for the purposes of this book, was too R&B or C&W or Pop to include was an even more emotionally draining assignment. But it was nothing compared to fleshing out the book with quality tracks from among the hundreds of thousands of singles and album cuts to emerge from the plenteous undergrounds that have at times warred with and at other times dominated the mainstream, especially when you take into account a post-Beatles generational bias of ignoring the individual song in favor of entire albums viewed as single entities—along with the universal disdain for the cover song. In order to ferret out the one or two songs that really made that classic album classic, or the influential sides that first brought national attention to a scene or made a crucial difference to the career of an artist, I depended on aspects of the Rock and Roll experience other than mass market airplay, as they have evolved over the years.

Invented in the '60s, the rock press has spawned a number of publications and important critics, most of whom are themselves at war not only with the mainstream but also with each other. Yet, there are the odd instances in which *Rolling Stone* and *Spin, the Village Voice, Trouser Press* and the *Alternate Press* come to the same conclusions, even if for opposite reasons. Among the several diehards who've made a business out of listening to virtually every release to come down the Rock and Roll pike, the trilogy of Dave Marsh, Robert Christgau, and Ira Robbins have to rank as the most perspicacious and opinionated of the bylined regulars. Each has their genre biases and blindspots, but their commitment to the endurance of Rock and Roll as an artform, a parlor game, and a way of life is undeniable. For filling in various research blanks and deadlocks there was none better than Charlie Gillette's '50s, Lillian Roxon's '60s, Christgau's '70s, Robbins's '80s, and AP's '90s. The Marsh 1001 was an admirable personal compendium; the Rock and Roll Hall of Fame 500 an obviously *Rolling Stone* derived but useful academic framework.

But just as Rock and Roll does not exist by lyric alone, the lit-crit accolades of journalists are only a part of the picture. Another element is the players themselves. Usually the worst judge of their own material, many bands proved to be positively brilliant in their choice of cover tunes, often discovering songs way before even their hippest audience members (who also became part of the process with their response to said tunes in concert, and support of said cult bands when they finally emerged with record deals). Live albums were another indicator as to which tunes the band as well as their management, their label, and their fans considered essential. Lately, the boxed set and the tribute album have become another valued resource in assessing a band's ultimate repertoire, mainly for unearthing the obscure B-side and the buried gem of an anecdote.

College radio has been the voice of the underground for twenty years, taking up the cause of leading-edge Rock and Roll where FM radio failed after its brief '60s heyday. Unfortunately, just as the college experience is often one of wild, eclectic experimentalism, exhaustively detailed documentation and unparalleled accuracy of the sort that made the *Billboard* charts the industry Bible fails to exist in college radio to any great degree.

On another grassroots level, the deejay, once considered an integral part of the taste-making/hit-making continuum, then relegated to toneless cog in the corporate spinning wheel, re-emerged as a major player during the Disco craze of the '70s, and evolved into full-fledged cult hero status with the arrival of rap in the '80s. Though also not fully documented, the modern art of sampling bits and pieces of R&B history into current hit records is an amazing cross-generational educational process. Rap has certainly taken its lumps from its elders (R&B, doo-wop, soul) for its negative attitude (not unlike Punk/rock, not unlike Rock and Roll, not unlike early R&B), but for bringing back the deejay's art alone, its contribution is immense.

For a certain generation the video of a song is routinely its first exposure to it, but for this book, the rock video played almost no role in the selection process, except in the cases where the TV airplay of a certain hot video was directly responsible for a song's ascension on the charts—which could nevertheless mean nine out of ten hit songs circa 1982 onward. A song included in a movie, especially in an opening or closing credit slot, has been judged to have made a greater impact. In this era of compilation albums run rampant, movie scores composed of tracks barely heard in the film still dominate the landscape. And cult directors slipping a Tom Waits ("Downtown Train") or a Joy Division ("Love Will Tear Us Apart") track subliminally into a scene have made their mark as the hippest program directors around.

Another adage that invariably stood me in good stead was: When in doubt, look to the R&B charts or England, both fertile watering grounds for future Rock and Roll standards. Many tracks deemed critical to the evolution of Rock and Roll established their credibility in one of these historical off-off radio ghettos (but certainly not in both).

In assembling the data, I have tried to locate the first appearance of a given song, as opposed to its more famous cover version, noting the cover version in the commentary section. While this approach is bound to cause confusion to some at first (expecting to see "Louie Louie," for instance, listed under the Kingsmen instead of its originator, Richard Berry, or "Midnight Train to Georgia" under Gladys Knight & the Pips instead of its writer Jim Weatherly—who recorded it by its given name of "Midnight Plane to Houston"—just to cite two of the hundreds of such occasions), the decision was necessary in order to maintain the book's primary focus on songs—and the artist's role in introducing them. For those unable or unwilling to consult the song title index in these cases, I have provided a chart of the one hundred most significant examples, including the name of the originator as well as the artist who made the song famous.

TITLE	ORIGINAL, YEAR	COVER, YEAR
Air That I Breathe, The	Albert Hammond, '72	The Hollies, '74
All the Man (That) I Need	Sister Sledge, '82	Whitney Houston, '91
Always on My Mind	Elvis Presley, '72	Willie Nelson, '82; Pet Shop Boys, '88
Babe I'm Gonna Leave You	Joan Baez, '62	Led Zeppelin, '69
Before You Accuse Me	Bo Diddley, '57	Eric Clapton, '89
Bette Davis Eyes	Jackie DeShannon, '75	Kim Carnes, '81
Bottle of Wine	Tom Paxton, '63	The Fireballs, '68
Brandy (Mandy)	Scott English, '72	Barry Manilow, '75
Brother Louie	Hot Chocolate, '73	Stories, '73
Burning Love	Arthur Alexander, '72	Elvis Presley, '72
Busted	Johnny Cash, '63	Ray Charles, '63
Cherry Pie	Marvin and Johnny, '54	Skip and Flip, '60

Midnight Plane to Houston (Midnight Train to Georgia)	Jim Weatherly, '71	Gladys Knight & the Pips, '75
Mr. Bojangles	Jerry Jeff Walker, '68	Nitty Gritty Dirt Band, '71
MTA	Will Holt, '57	The Kingston Trio, '59
Mustang Sally	Sir Mack Rice,'65	Wilson Pickett, '66
My Prayer	The Ink Spots, '39	Platters, '56
Mystery Train	Little Jr. Parker, '53	Elvis Presley, '55
Night They Drove Old Dixie Down, The	The Band, '69	Joan Baez, '71
Not Fade Away	Buddy Holly, '57	The Rolling Stones, '64
Passionate Kisses	Lucinda Williams, '88	Mary Chapin Carpenter, '93
Piece of My Heart	Garnett Mimms & the Enchanters, '67	Big Brother & the Holding Co., '68
Police and Thieves	Junior Murvin, '76	The Clash, '79
Put Your Hand in the Hand	Anne Murray, '70	Ocean, '71
Red Red Wine	Neil Diamond, '68	UB'40, '88
Respect	Otis Redding, '65	Aretha Franklin, '67
Rose Garden	Joe South, '69	Lynn Anderson, '71
Saving All My Love for You	Billy Davis and Marilyn McCoo, '78	Whitney Houston, '85
See You Later, Alligator	Bobby Charles, '56	Bill Haley & the Comets, '56
Someone (Somebody) to Love	The Great Society, '65	The Jefferson Airplane, '67
Still Alive and Well	Hoodoo Rhythm Devils, '72	Johnny Winter, '73
Sun Ain't Gonna Shine Anymore, The	Frankie Valli, '67	The Walker Brothers, '66
Sweet and Innocent	Roy Orbison, '58	The Osmonds, '71
Tainted Love	Gloria Jones, '64	Soft Cell, '82
Take Good Care of My Baby	Dion, '61	Bobby Vee, '61
That's All Right Mama	Arthur Big Boy Crudup, '47	Elvis Presley, '54
Thing Called Love	John Hiatt, '87	Bonnie Raitt, '89
Think	The 5 Royals, '57	James Brown, '60
Those Were the Days	The Limeliters, '62	Mary Hopkin, '68
Tide Is High, The	Paragons, '63	Blondie, '81
Time Is on My Side	Irma Thomas, '64	The Rolling Stones, '64
Train Kept a Rollin'	Johnny Burnette & the Rock and Roll Trio, '56	The Yardbirds, '65; Aerosmith, '74
Turn Turn Turn	Pete Seeger, '62	The Byrds, '65
Twist, The	Hank Ballard, '59	Chubby Checker, '60
Walk Don't Run	Chet Atkins, '57	The Ventures, '60
Walk on By	Leroy Van Dyke, '61	Dionne Warwick, '64
Walking on Sunshine	Eddy Grant, '79	Katrina & the Waves, '81
Wedding Bell Blues	Laura Nyro, '67	The 5th Dimension, '69
White Rabbit	The Great Society, '65	The Jefferson Airplane, '67
Wimoweh (Lion Sleeps Tonight, The)	The Weavers, '51	The Tokens, '61
Whole Lotta Shakin Goin On	Big Maybelle, '55	Jerry Lee Lewis, '57

Wishin' and Hopin'	Dionne Warwick, '64	Dusty Springfield, '64
Wishing on a Star	Rose Royce, '76	The Cover Girls, '92
Without You	Badfinger, '70	Nilsson, '72
Wonder of You, The	Ray Peterson, '59	Elvis Presley, '64
Wreck of the John B. (Sloop John B.)	The Weavers, '50	The Beach Boys, '66
You Are So Beautiful	Billy Preston, '74	Joe Cocker, '75
You Can't Sit Down	Phil Upchurch, '61	The Dovells, '63
You Were on My Mind	Ian and Sylvia, '64	We Five, '65
Younger Girl	The Lovin' Spoonful, '65	The Critters, '66

The commentary section, with a nod to the inspired brevity of *The New York Times* TV-movie review, is the only forum I've allowed myself for editorialization. For the most part my comments speak to the main reason for a song's inclusion in the book, among them significant cover versions, movie usages, and chart success, especially if the song crossed over, that is, achieved great success in more than one genre of record chart. In listing songwriter names, I have provided the writer's given name and, when appropriate, the pseudonym a particular song was written under in parentheses. In certain obvious cases—Madonna and Prince come to mind—I have chosen to omit the parenthetical identification, even though these two did in fact write under their first names only. I have also tried to list the first album a song appeared on, rather than the *Greatest Hits* album ten years later, or its current CD incarnation—along with that album's original producer (some producer credits are totally unknown, or at least unavailable; some artists produce and write songs under different names or different versions of their name; I have tried to keep these mentions separate but consistent). And, with every boxed set liner note booklet and new exhaustive Rock and Roll tome and CD-ROM/Internet web-site configuration carrying at least two or three credit line twists the lawyers as well as ASCAP and BMI only recently signed off on, keeping up to date has been a problematic task. The record companies in question cannot be counted on to provide accurate details, as album credits are often riddled with errors; the artists themselves are the most unreliable sources of all.

Yet, is there anything to delight the career researcher more than learning that Paul Anka's theme for *The Johnny Carson Show* was originally recorded by Annette Funicello as "It's Really Love" in 1960? That Wanda Jackson introduced "Silver Threads and Golden Needles" on the B-side of her 1956 single "Hot Dog! That Made Him Mad"; and "I Fought the Law" was introduced by the Crickets, and not the Bobby Fuller Four? Clive Davis's tinkering with "Brandy" to become Barry Manilow's first hit "Mandy" (the last hit on Bell records, and the tune that launched Clive's Arista label) is well known, but what about his other song selection coups? For instance, the Captain & Tennille recorded "I Write the Songs" six months before Barry Manilow's hit record. Sister Sledge had a minor R&B hit with "He's All the Man That I Need" a decade before Whitney Houston made it a #1 tune. George Benson introduced "The Greatest Love of All," as did Dolly Parton "I Will Always Love You." Ace of Base's hit "Don't Turn Around" had already been #1 in England, as done by Aswad, who may have gotten it from a rare Tina Turner B-side, released only in England. Which is where Bryan Ferry heard the Everly Brothers doing "Price of Love." But it was R&B obscurities that particularly enchanted the British: from the Moody Blues co-opting Bessie Banks's "Go Now" to Soft Cell's cover of Gloria Jones's "Tainted Love." The Shirelles were favorites of the Beatles ("Boys," "Baby It's You") and Manfred Mann ("Sha La La"), who were also partial to Bob Dylan ("Just Like a Woman") and Bruce Springsteen ("Blinded by the Light"). The Rolling Stones preferred Howling Wolf ("Little Red Rooster"), but both the Who ("Young Man Blues") and the Yardbirds' ("I'm Not Talking") were big fans of Mose Allison.

These 7,500 songs can be looked at not only by artist but also by year, by songwriter or producer, or even by record label, with each new view hopefully offering another distinct and yet complementary picture of the whole—the trends as they emerged, the great years for Rock and Roll indisputably standing up to be counted and revered, the influential classics taking their place alongside the artists who recorded them. From Charlie Christian's 1940 electric guitar break-through "Solo Flight" to Louis Jordan's fully populated world of the "Saturday Night Fish Fry" of 1949, that decade was filled with harbingers of the revolution to come, including a decade-ending dance craze with "The Hucklebuck," later covered by Chubby Checker. Early '50s R&B benchmarks "Sixty Minute Man" by the Dominoes and "Work with Me Annie" by the Midnighters seem paeans to romantic innocence in contrast to rap's new anti-euphemistic worldview. But back then you'd have thought they were salacious enough to corrupt the morals of a generation (and they probably were). Much has been made of Pop music's mid-'50s plundering of the R&B market for many of its biggest hits, with Gene & Eunice's "Ko Ko Mo" (covered by Perry Como), Fats Domino's "Ain't It a Shame" (covered by Pat Boone), and the pioneering "Earth Angel" by the Penguins and "Sh-Boom" by the Chords (both covered by the Crew Cuts) leading the way. But you have to consider that the movers and shakers of the Pop sphere had also been routine-ly pilfering from the Country market as well, with Patty Page's cover of Pee Wee King's "Tennessee Waltz," Tony Bennett's cover of Hank Williams's "Cold Cold Heart," and Guy Mitchell's humongous Pop interpretation of Marty Robbins's "Singin' the Blues," to say nothing of the Weavers' and Gordon Jenkins's transformation of Leadbelly's "Goodnight Irene." Then again, both of Baltimore's earliest doo-wop groups (and future sports teams), the Ravens ("Old Man River") and the Orioles ("Crying in the Chapel") made their breakthroughs covering a Broadway ballad and a Country weeper, respectively. Anyway, once Chuck Berry crashed the party with "Maybellene" and the Platters came about with "Only You" (within a week of each other), the question became largely moot.

Elvis Presley broke through first on the C&W charts with "Baby Let's Play House," written by R&B stalwart Arthur Gunter (not to be confused with Eddy Arnold's C&W hit, "I Wanna Play House with You"). After three straight #1 C&W hits, his cover of Leiber & Stoller's previous #1 R&B tune "Hound Dog" was the first #1 C&W/R&B/R&R triple crossover in history (Louis Jordan and Nat King Cole had come close in '44 with "Is You Is or Is You Ain't My Baby" and "Straighten up and Fly Right," respectively). Sam Phillips knew a good thing when he heard one. He imme-diate did for Jerry Lee Lewis what he'd done for Elvis, rescuing Big Maybelle's "Whole Lotta Shakin' Goin' On" (written by a couple of C&W writers) from the R&B market, for another early Rock and Roll defining hit. Another one, "Rock Around the Clock" was written by a pair of veter-an Tin Pan Alley tunesmiths for a Hollywood movie. By 1957 Rock and Roll had achieved such a stranglehold on the music scene that one week in May the Everly Brothers' "All I Have to Do Is Dream" topped all seven of Billboard's then-operating charts. By the decade's end, everyone was dancing again, especially in Philadelphia, "At the Hop." Hank Ballard's meal ticket, "The Twist," officially brought the new dance era to New York City in 1962 when it hit #1 for an unprecedented second time in two years. Of course, it was Chubby Checker doing the singing and not Hank (in some sort of retribution, no doubt, for Hank's having spawned the notorious "Annie" records).

New York City was where the Brill Building generation flourished, mainly across the street, at 1650 Broadway—one hundred hits from eight writers in four cubicles, the best of them by Goffin & King ("Will You Love Me Tomorrow" by the Shirelles, "Up on the Roof" by the Drifters). Leiber & Stoller moved there from L.A. ("On Broadway"). Phil Spector completed the same West to East journey ("Be My Baby"). Doc Pomus wrote his best songs for the former Bronx gang member, Dion DiMucci, and his Belmont Avenue pals ("Teenager in Love"). Further downtown Bob Dylan either bought or wrote "Blowin' in the Wind" and then went on to rewrite the *Childe's Book of*

English Ballads as well as the history of his generation. Many of his anthems were considered folk music, but only because such molten verbiage as "A Hard Rain's a-Gonna Fall" and "Masters of War" had never been heard by his young Elvis-educated followers, and also because *Rolling Stone* magazine had not as yet come into existence to claim them. Meanwhile, in Detroit, Berry Gordy Jr. and Smokey Robinson found their life's work after writing "Got a Job" in answer to the Silhouettes' more negative attitude in "Get a Job." Motown would rescue a lot of people from the mailroom and the typing pool (and the Detroit bar scene), including Eddie and Brian Holland, Lamont Dozier, James Jamerson, Stevie Wonder, Marvin Gaye, Norman Whitfield, and Nolan Strong's cousin Barrett. Back in Elvis's Memphis, Isaac Hayes & David Porter were inventing soul music ("Soul Man"), along with Otis Redding ("Respect") and Aretha Franklin ("I Never Loved a Man") and Dan Penn ("You Left the Water Running").

Meanwhile, in England, the Beatles had been emulating Buddy Holly & the Crickets as far back as 1958, when, under the name of the Quarrymen, they recorded "That'll Be the Day" as their first single. Five years and many personnel changes later they had their first UK #1 with "Please Please Me." A year later they'd be occupying positions #1-5 on the *Billboard* charts. Del Shannon was the first American to recognize their songwriting talents (although Brenda Lee claims to have introduced them to her record company, Decca), covering "From Me to You" on a single that stiffed over here. The Stones, of course, were more into Muddy Waters and Howling Wolf, but their first hit was a Buddy Holly tune, "Not Fade Away." The Beatles, widely considered to be named in honor of Holly's crickets, only recorded one of his songs, "Words of Love," in 1965. (Elvis, in his vast repertoire, claims three Beatles tunes, two Dylan cuts, including the almost inexplicable "Tomorrow Is a Long Time" from the movie *Spinout,* and no—count 'em— no Motown tunes. The Yardbirds, in the persons of their soon-to-be-legendary guitarists, Jeff Beck, Jimmy Page, and Eric Clapton, were in the process of spinning the Blues into Heavy Metal, notably on their cover of the classic Rock and Roll Trio cover of Tiny Bradshaw's R&B epic, "Train Kept a Rollin'." Clapton would move on to Robert Johnson ("Crossroads"), Beck to Charlie Mingus ("Pork Pie Hat"), Page to Led Zeppelin ("Dazed and Confused"). Jimi Hendrix would soon join the triumvirate, leaving Joey Dee's Starlighters and moving to England ("The Wind Cries Mary") before he returned to Greenwich Village in New York a conquering guitar hero.

As much as it has become politically correct—as well as expedient—to decry Rap's use of profanity—the legendary reputation of the Fugs is primarily based on the choice expletives not deleted from their most famous works. Of course the Fugs were operating in the more academically accepted tradition of satire when they wrote "Boobs a Lot," "Saran Wrap" and "Coca Cola Douche." As musicians, however, they were certainly on a par with most rappers. This led to the Mothers of Invention, Frank Zappa's high concept, where the music, Spike Jones spiked with Edgard Varèse, was as outrageous as the words. Satire flourished in the sixties with Dylan ("Leopard Skin Pillbox Hat"), Phil Ochs ("Love Me, I'm a Liberal"), Country Joe & the Fish ("The Fish Cheer"), the Byrds ("So You Wanna Be a Rock and Roll Star"), and Randy Newman ("Mama Told Me Not to Come"). But it was John Sebastian's effervescent "Do You Believe in Magic" that put the Village underground on the Rock and Roll map, just after the Byrds with "Mr. Tambourine Man" and Dylan with "Like a Rolling Stone" had christened it folk/rock city. At just about this time John Phillips was writing "California Dreaming" and Joni Mitchell the similarly themed "Urge for Going," which George Hamilton IV would turn into a C&W hit in 1967.

In California, psychedelia was changing the inner landscape of songwriting: Janis Joplin pondered the infinite ("I Got Dem Ol Kosmic Blues, Mama"), the Jefferson Airplane prepared for space flight ("Wooden Ships"), the Grateful Dead embarked upon their endless jam with a remake of Gus Cannon & the Jug Stompers "New Minglewood Blues." Sly Stone provided the ultimate party ("Dance to the Music") before he began to get angry ("Don't Call Me Nigger, Whitey"). Creedence Clearwater Revival's John Fogerty wrote with a survivalist's dementia ("Who'll Stop the Rain"). In L.A. he was matched only by Jim Morrison's demonic fatalism ("The End"). Just about then, Brian Wilson and the Beach Boys went into hiding ("I Just Wasn't Made for These Times"). But P. F. Sloan ("Eve of Destruction") thought he could be the West Coast Brill Building answer to Bob Dylan, leading Gerry Goffin to decide he could be the East Coast Brill Building answer to Bob Dylan ("I Wasn't Born to Follow," heard in the film *Easy Rider* by the Byrds). However he and Carole King had already relocated to L.A. to write for the Monkees ("Pleasant Valley Sunday"). Soon Carole and Gerry would be divorced. Carole wrote "Goin' Back" for Dusty Springfield; Neil Young wrote "Sugar Mountain," which Joni Mitchell answered with "The Circle Game," but there was no going back; everyone was turning twenty, then thirty, then dying. The Band tried to get back to the garden ("The Weight"), Dylan tried to go to Nashville ("Lay Lady Lay"), the Beatles broke up ("Let It Be"). Heavier Metal loomed on the horizon ("Paranoid" by Black Sabbath), Punk/Rock threatened the hinterlands ("Anarchy in the UK" by the Sex Pistols), another Disco phase awaited. Soon Peter Tork of the Monkees would be living on the floor of the mansion he once owned.

Sexually, Disco-era landmarks like Donna Summer's breathy "Love to Love You Baby" and Andrea True's insatiable "More More More," stand as rap equivalents to the earlier feminine paragons of "Be My Baby," "My Boyfriend's Back," and "It's My Party." In England, Punk/Rockers studied the Reggae scriptures as handed down by Bob Marley ("One Love") and Jimmy Cliff ("Many Rivers to Cross"), Toots & the Maytals ("Kingston Town"), Desmond Dekker ("You Can Get It If You Really Want"), and Junior Murvin ("Police and Thieves") just like the previous generation studied rare R&B B-sides. Back to us came a new energized Rock and Roll in the process (though no Punk/rocker ever made the American R&B charts): the Police ("Driven to Tears"), the Clash ("White Man in Hammersmith Palais"), the Specials ("Gangsters"), New York Anglophiles Blondie ("The Tide Is High"). In the U.S., black musicians responded with rap ("Rapper's Delight" by the Sugar Hill Gang, the more pointed "The Message" and "New York, New York" by Grandmaster Flash & the Furious Five, "The Breaks" by Curtis Blow).

In the '70s we suffered through a glut of singer/songwriteritis, an outgrowth of the laid-back folk/rock acoustic guitar scare/boom of the sixties—and the Elton John ("Your Song")/Carole King ("So Far Away") mellow piano man/woman sound of the seventies (epitomized by Billy Joel's "Piano Man"). Anguished poetic sorts like Laura Nyro ("Been on a Train"), Jackson Browne ("These Days"), John Lennon ("Working Class Hero" and a batch of similar personal exorcisms), and Joni Mitchell ("Blue") were as dark as James Taylor ("Sweet Baby James") and Paul McCartney ("Silly Love Songs" and a batch of similar jaunty ditties) were light. The Rock and Roll antidote was provided by the Velvet Underground ('Heroin") and their decadent brethren, David Bowie ("Changes"), Mott the Hoople ("All the Young Dudes"), the New York Dolls ("Trash"), and the post-Velvet Lou Reed ("Walk on the Wild Side"). On the same emotional side of the street, a few blocks down and a few years later, Television brought a new generation into the alternative camps ("Little Johnny Jewel"), Patti Smith resurrected "Gloria" as a demonic white witch of lust, the Talking Heads made alienation fashionable again ("Once in a Lifetime"), the Ramones just wanted to rock ("Rockaway Beach"). From nearby New Jersey, Bruce Springsteen's prodigious output stood in contrast to both the singer/songwriter and the decadent Punk ethos; "Spirit in the Night," "Rosalita," and "Born to Run" were nothing less than fully Spectorized new all-American Rock and Roll romances, with a touch of Otis and James Brown (and his own Daddy Gee on the sax). John Mellencamp ("Pink Houses") and Bob Seger ("Night Moves") entered the main street mainstream from the Midwest; Elvis Costello ("Alison") strapped on his word machine in England. In Florida, Tom Petty ("American Girl") found the Dylan/Byrds jangly guitar niche temporarily abandoned. In California, Randy Newman's terse verseplay ("Political Science," "Sail Away") found its stinging voice.

While we were still mourning John Lennon, MTV claimed the airwaves in the '80s, promising that the rest of the Rock and Roll revolution would indeed be televised. Yet new undergrounds emerged in defiance to this slick pronouncement, with no commercial potential and decidedly not ready for prime time. Former Box Top Alex Chilton became a cult hero ("September Gurls"), deified by the Replacements ("Alex Chilton"). Kate Bush gave new meaning to the term thrush ("Wuthering Heights"). Metallica raised the thrash and burn credo of Sabbath up a few more decibels ("Kill Em All"). The otherwise obscure X-Ray Specs raised their single anthem like a middle finger at the smug establishment ("Oh Bondage, up Yours!"). Public Enemy brought Rap's emerging street culture fully into modern reality ("Bring the Noise"). Sonic Youth began their feverish guitar explorations ("Teenage Riot"). Camper Van Beethoven went beyond the third world (and this world) for their influences ("Take the Skinheads Bowling"). George Clinton upped both James Brown's and Sly Stone's timeless funk ante ("One Nation under a Groove"). Michael Jackson made his run for King credible with the aid of guitar god Eddie Van Halen ("Beat It"). Prince, the anti-Michael, started to parade his "Dirty Mind." The sounds of a new jangly guitar alternative percolated up from the static, featuring "Radio Free Europe" by REM, and "Mexican Radio" by Wall of Voodoo. U2 resurrected Queen-size Arena-Rock with a cause ("Sunday Bloody Sunday"). Rappers Run-DMC resurrected the fallen Aerosmith, with a cover of "Walk This Way," creating two new careers in the process. From the hardcore anger of Fugazi ("Repeater") to the low-fi angst of Sebadoah ("Freed Pig"), the underground of the '90s continued to churn out defining moments. But it was Kurt Cobain's melancholy "Feels Like Teen Spirit" that truly opened the gates for the mid-decade alternative onslaught, flush in the middle of yet another Disco era ("Vogue" by Madonna, "Just Another Night" by Real McCoy).

Although this book has primarily been a solitary effort, in fact it owes a debt to all the research that's come before it. In that sense, it's more like a tribute to the landmark works already mentioned, and dozens of others, combining the most salient features of each into one volume in order to take in the measure of such a rich and diverse literature—a volume that contains both singles *and* album cuts, but only the best of each; one that is complete with writers *and* producers (where available), original versions, original albums and labels, the most revealing detail, the choicest anecdote—so that future generations of archaeologists may come to know and understand just what it was we were listening to and singing here during the age of Rock and Roll.

A

AALIYAH
1994

BACK AND FORTH
Producer: Robert Kelly
Album: Age Ain't Nothin' but a Number
Record Label: Blackground
Songwriter: Robert Kelly

Junior high-school hip-hop.

ABBA
1974

WATERLOO
Producers: Benny Andersson, Bjorn Ulvaeus
Album: Waterloo
Record Label: Atlantic
Songwriters: Benny Andersson, Bjorn Ulvaeus, Stig Anderson

Eurovision-winning international Folk Rock introduces the Swedish answer to the Mamas & the Papas and Fleetwood Mac.

1977

DANCING QUEEN
Producers: Benny Andersson, Bjorn Ulvaeus
Album: Arrival
Record Label: Atlantic
Songwriters: Benny Andersson, Bjorn Ulvaeus, Stig Anderson

#1 U.S./U.K. Atlantic crossover. Their biggest international hit—frothy and incessant.

KNOWING ME, KNOWING YOU
Producers: Benny Andersson, Bjorn Ulvaeus
Album: Arrival
Record Label: Atlantic
Songwriters: Benny Andersson, Stig Anderson, Bjorn Ulvaeus

U.K. record of the year, Top-20 in the U.S.

TAKE A CHANCE ON ME
Producers: Benny Andersson, Bjorn Ulvaeus
Album: The Album
Record Label: Atlantic
Songwriters: Benny Andersson, Bjorn Ulvaeus

The formula returns.

1980

WINNER TAKES IT ALL
Producers: Benny Andersson, Bjorn Ulvaeus
Album: Super Trooper
Record Label: Atlantic
Songwriters: Benny Andersson, Bjorn Ulvaeus

Abba cashes in and goes home.

GREGORY ABBOTT
1986

SHAKE YOU DOWN
Producer: Gregory Abbott
Album: Shake You Down
Record Label: Columbia
Songwriter: Gregory Abbott

#1 R&R/R&B crossover Soul-man ballad.

ABC
1982

LOOK OF LOVE (PART I)
Producer: Martin Rushent
Album: The Lexicon of Love
Record Label: Mercury
Songwriters: Martin Fry, Mark Lickley, Stephen Singleton, David Palmer

Bowie-esque Synth Rock.

1985

BE NEAR ME
Producer: Martin Rushent
Album: how to be a . . . Zillionaire
Record Label: Mercury
Songwriters: Martin Fry, Mark White

Glossy post-Disco romantic posturing.

1987

WHEN SMOKEY SINGS
Producer: Martin Rushent
Album: Alphabet City
Record Label: Mercury
Songwriters: Martin Fry, Mark White

Blue-eyed English studio Soul. Their biggest hit.

PAULA ABDUL
1988

COLD-HEARTED
Producers: Elliot Wolff, K. Cohen
Album: Forever Your Girl
Record Label: Virgin
Songwriter: Elliot Wolff

It began as the B-side of her second single, "Straight Up," *and became her third #1 when it was released as an A-side.*

FOREVER YOUR GIRL
Producer: Oliver Leiber
Album: Forever Your Girl
Record Label: Virgin
Songwriter: Oliver Leiber

Perfect top of the Top-40 sentiments—a hummable #1 follow-up to a #1.

(IT'S JUST) THE WAY THAT YOU LOVE ME
Producer: Oliver Leiber
Album: Forever Your Girl
Record Label: Virgin
Songwriter: Oliver Leiber

Debut neo-Disco single for Janet Jackson's award-winning choreographer. It stiffed in '88, but hit Top-10 when re-released in '89.

OPPOSITES ATTRACT
Producer: Oliver Leiber
Album: Forever Your Girl
Record Label: Virgin
Songwriter: Oliver Leiber

Typifying the dearth of quality Top-40 options in the early '90s, Abdul had a virtually uncontested run to her fourth #1 from the same album.

STRAIGHT UP
Producer: Elliot Wolff
Album: Forever Your Girl
Record Label: Virgin
Songwriter: Elliott Wolff

Instant MTV icon.

1991

PROMISE OF A NEW DAY
Producer: Peter Lord
Album: Spellbound
Record Label: Virgin
Songwriters: Peter Lord, Sondra St. Victor, V. Jeffrey Smith, Paula Abdul

New album, new formula Pop Rock teen love ballad; her fifth #1.

RUSH, RUSH
Producer: Peter Lord
Album: Spellbound
Record Label: Virgin
Songwriter: Peter Lord

Shortly after her sixth #1 perfect Pop rocker, Abdul retired to the courtroom to defend herself from a Milli Vannilli—the charge that she didn't really sing on all, some, or at least one of her records. She eventually prevailed.

AC/DC
1977

WHOLE LOTTA ROSIE
Producers: Harry Vanda, George Young
Album: Let There Be Rock
Record Label: Atco
Songwriters: Angus Young, Malcolm Young

Song of the Year in "Kerrang," the British Heavy Metal bible.

1979

HIGHWAY TO HELL
Producer: Mutt Lange
Album: Highway to Hell
Record Label: Atlantic
Songwriters: Malcolm Young, Angus Young, Bon Scott

Their last big hit before the death of Bon Scott.

1980

BACK IN BLACK
Producer: Mutt Lange
Album: Back in Black
Record Label: Atlantic
Songwriters: Angus Young, Malcolm Young, Brian Johnson

A tribute to the departed Bon—sung by the highly-charged Brian, backed by Angus, Malcolm, their preppies-on-acid Bermuda shorts, and orchestra.

HELL'S BELLS
Producer: Mutt Lange
Album: Back in Black
Record Label: Atlantic
Songwriters: Angus Young, Malcolm Young, Brian Johnson

Your basic Metal maelstrom.

YOU SHOOK ME ALL NIGHT LONG
Producer: Mutt Lange
Album: Back in Black
Record Label: Atlantic
Songwriters: Angus Young, Malcolm Young, Brian Johnson

Essential fantasy anthem of the Metal age.

1981

DIRTY DEEDS DONE DIRT CHEAP
Producers: Harry Vanda, George Young
Album: Dirty Deeds Done Dirt Cheap
Record Label: Atlantic
Songwriters: Angus Young, Malcolm Young

From '76, this was Bon Scott revisited in all his vile glory. Covered by Joan Jett (Blackheart, '90).

FOR THOSE ABOUT TO ROCK (WE SALUTE YOU)
Producer: Mutt Lange
Album: For Those About to Rock (We Salute You)
Record Label: Atlantic
Songwriters: Angus Young, Malcolm Young, Brian Johnson

Blatant self- and audience-aggrandizement.

1986

WHO MADE WHO
Album: Who Made Who
Record Label: Atlantic
Songwriters: Malcolm Young, Angus Young, Brian Johnson

From the Stephen King movie Maximum Overdrive, which also features their "Hell's Bells" and "You Shook Me All Night Long."

1990

MONEYTALKS
Producer: Bruce Fairbairn
Album: The Razors Edge
Record Label: Atco
Songwriters: Angus Young, Malcolm Young

Breaking Top-25. Their biggest hit.

ACE
1975

HOW LONG
Producer: John Anthony
Album: Five-a-Side (An Ace Album)
Record Label: Anchor
Songwriter: Paul Carrack

U.K. balladeer, Carrack, would return with Squeeze, and Mike & the Mechanics.

ACE OF BASE
1993

ALL THAT SHE WANTS
Producers: Joker, Buddha, Denniz PoP
Album: The Sign
Record Label: Arista
Songwriters: Jonas Berggren (Joker), Ulf Edberg (Buddha), Jennie Berggren, Maria Berggren

Easy-listening Pop Reggae hit—Abba meets "Sally Go Round the Roses."

THE SIGN
Producers: Joker, Carr, Denniz PoP
Album: The Sign
Record Label: Arista
Songwriter: Jonas Berggren (Joker)

Top-40 dance track with a marathon chart run.

JOHNNY ACE
1952

MY SONG
Album: Memorial Album: For Johnny Ace
Record Label: Duke
Songwriters: John Alexander (Johnny Ace), David Mattis

First #1 R&B hit for the great pre-Soul crooner, covered by Aretha Franklin on the B-side of "See Saw" (Atlantic, '68).

1953

THE CLOCK
Album: Memorial Album: For Johnny Ace
Record Label: Duke
Songwriter: David Mattis

First R&B hit for the Charles Brown-influenced crooner.

1954

PLEDGING MY LOVE
Album: Memorial Album: For Johnny Ace
Record Label: Duke
Songwriters: Ferdinand Washington, Don D. Robey

The chilling and mournful Ace sings his own epitaph.

DAVID ACKLES
1968

DOWN RIVER
Producers: David Anderle, Russ Miller
Album: David Ackles
Record Label: Elektra
Songwriter: David Ackles

Evocative keyboard ballad of lost love. Elvis Costello selected it in a magazine as the song that changed his life.

ROAD TO CAIRO
Producers: David Anderle, Russ Miller
Album: David Ackles
Record Label: Elektra
Songwriter: David Ackles

Rock ballad of a deadbeat dad and his thwarted attempts at reconciliation. Covered by Howard Jones (Elektra, '90).

BARBARA ACKLIN
LOVE MAKES A WOMAN
Producer: Eugene Record
Record Label: Brunswick
Songwriters: Carl Davis, Eugene Record, William Sanders, George Sims

Classic and classy R&B. Covered by Phoebe Snow (Columbia, '78).

BRYAN ADAMS
1983

CUTS LIKE A KNIFE
Producers: Bryan Adams, Bob Clearmountain
Album: Cuts Like a Knife
Record Label: A&M
Songwriters: Bryan Adams, Jim Vallance

From Canada, the new Neil Young, but without the angst or verisimilitude.

STRAIGHT FROM THE HEART
Producers: Bryan Adams, Bob Clearmountain
Album: Cuts Like a Knife
Record Label: A&M
Songwriters: Bryan Adams, Eric Kagna

Establishing his Rock ballad persona.

1984

HEAVEN
Producers: Bryan Adams, Bob Clearmountain
Album: Reckless
Record Label: A&M
Songwriters: Bryan Adams, Jim Vallance

His personal best and first #1. From the movie A Night in Heaven.

RUN TO YOU
Producers: Bryan Adams, Bob Clearmountain
Album: Reckless
Record Label: A&M
Songwriters: Bryan Adams, Jim Vallance

Upping his rock credentials.

SUMMER OF '69
Producers: Bryan Adams, Bob Clearmountain

Album: Reckless
Record Label: A&M
Songwriters: Bryan Adams, Jim Vallance

Biographically fraudulent tale of Adams's early years became his most recurrent anthem.

1987

HEAT OF THE NIGHT
Producers: Bryan Adams, Bob Clearmountain
Album: Into the Fire
Record Label: A&M
Songwriters: Bryan Adams, Jim Vallance

1991

(EVERYTHING I DO) I DO IT FOR YOU
Producer: Mutt Lange
Album: *Robin Hood: Prince of Thieves* Soundtrack
Record Label: Morgan Creek
Songwriters: Bryan Adams, Robert John "Mutt" Lange, Michael Kamen

Big movie ballad.

CAN'T STOP THIS THING WE STARTED
Producer: Mutt Lange
Album: Waking up the Neighbors
Record Label: A&M
Songwriters: Bryan Adams, Robert John "Mutt" Lange

1993

PLEASE FORGIVE ME
Producer: Mutt Lange
Album: So Far So Good
Record Label: A&M
Songwriters: Bryan Adams, Robert John "Mutt" Lange

Easy-listening Lite Rock staple.

ALL FOR LOVE
Producer: Mutt Lange
Album: *Three Musketeers* Soundtrack
Record Label: Hollywood/A&M
Songwriters: Bryan Adams, Robert John "Mutt" Lange, Michael Kamen

Adams' big movie ballad times three, with his middle-of-the-road musketeers—Rod Stewart and Sting.

FAYE ADAMS
1953

SHAKE A HAND
Producer: Al Silver
Album: Shake a Hand
Record Label: Herald
Songwriter: Joe Morris

This influential singer launched her, as well as Al Silver's, career at Herald with this #1 R&B shouter. Covered by LaVern Baker (Atlantic, '60), Ruth Brown (Phillies, '62), Jackie Wilson and Linda Hopkins (Brunswick, '63).

1954

HURTS ME TO MY HEART
Producer: Al Silver
Record Label: Herald
Songwriters: Charles Singleton, Rose Marie McCoy

#1 R&B from a stellar songwriting team.

MARIE ADAMS
1952

I'M GONNA PLAY THE HONKY TONKS
Producer: Don Robey
Record Label: Peacock
Songwriters: Don Robey, Marie Adams

Top-10 R&B standard. Suggested segue: "It Wasn't God Who Made Honky Tonk Angels" by Kitty Wells.

OLETA ADAMS
1991

GET HERE
Album: Circle of One
Record Label: Fontana
Songwriter: Brenda Russell

#1 R&B/Top-10 R&R crossover.

JOHNNY ADAMS
1991

PRISONER OF LIFE
Album: Johnny Adams Sings Doc Pomus
Record Label: Rounder
Songwriters: Doc Pomus, Mack Rebennack

Covered by Annie Ross in the '93 Robert Altman movie Short Cuts.

CANNONBALL ADDERLY
1967

MERCY, MERCY, MERCY

Producer: David Adderly
Album: Mercy, Mercy, Mercy
Record Label: Capitol
Songwriter: Joe Zawinul

Early Jazz Rock. Covered by the Buckinghams (Columbia, '67).

THE AD LIBS
1964

THE BOY FROM NEW YORK CITY

Producers: Jerry Leiber, Mike Stoller
Record Label: Blue Cat
Songwriter: John Taylor

Sprightly, post-Chiffons, Brill Building factory second.

AEROSMITH
1973

DREAM ON

Producer: Adrian Barber
Album: Aerosmith
Record Label: Columbia
Songwriter: Steven Tallarico (Steven Tyler)

With the power chords to build a dream on, this was what every Heavy Metal arena band aspired toward—the Top-40 Rock ballad. Looming just out of earshot were Journey, Boston, Foreigner, and Styx.

MAMA KIN

Producer: Adrian Barber
Album: Aerosmith
Record Label: Columbia
Songwriter: Steven Tyler

Covered by Guns N' Roses (Geffen, '88).

WALK THIS WAY

Producer: Jack Douglas
Album: Toys in the Attic
Record Label: Columbia
Songwriters: Joe Perry, Steven Tyler

Considered semi-lewd in its day, this ode to the Three Stooges, and high-school making out eventually crossed over from the arena underground to FM Top-10 status, marking the creative summit of corporate rock. By this time, Tyler was bankrupt—emotionally if not financially, or vice-versa—and the band was kaput. Covered by Run DMC (Priority, '86), with contributions by Steven and Joe, leading to a new commercial visibility for the rappers from Queens, as well

as a clean and sober return to the charts for Aerosmith.

1974

SEASONS OF WITHER

Producers: Jack Douglas, Ray Colcord
Album: Get Your Wings
Record Label: Columbia
Songwriter: Steven Tyler

Plodding toward the grail of the new Rolling Stones.

1975

SWEET EMOTION

Producer: Jack Douglas
Album: Toys in the Attic
Record Label: Columbia
Songwriters: Steven Tyler, Tom Hamilton

With this, Tyler gained his arena wings.

1976

BACK IN THE SADDLE

Producers: Jack Douglas, Aerosmith
Album: Rocks
Record Label: Columbia
Songwriters: Steven Tyler, Joe Perry

An enduring Metal war-horse.

LAST CHILD

Producers: Jack Douglas, Aerosmith
Album: Rocks
Record Label: Columbia
Songwriters: Steven Tyler, Brad Whitford

This concert favorite hit Top-25.

1987

ANGEL

Producer: Bruce Fairbairn
Album: Permanent Vacation
Record Label: Geffen
Songwriters: Steven Tyler, Desmond Child

The biggest hit from their comeback album was—what else—a ballad.

DUDE (LOOKS LIKE A LADY)

Producer: Bruce Fairbairn
Album: Permanent Vacation
Record Label: Geffen
Songwriters: Steven Tyler, Joe Perry, Desmond Child

Suggested segue: "Are You a Boy or Are You a Girl" by the Barbarians.

RAG DOLL

Producer: Bruce Fairbairn
Album: Permanent Vacation
Record Label: Geffen
Songwriters: Steven Tyler, Joe Perry, Jim Vallance, Holly Knight

Arena Rock with corporate consultation.

1989

JANIE'S GOT A GUN

Producer: Bruce Fairbairn
Album: Pump
Record Label: Geffen
Songwriters: Steven Tyler, Tom Hamilton

Their most provocative and unique single—sinuous, sinister, with a '90s twist.

LOVE IN AN ELEVATOR

Producer: Bruce Fairbairn
Album: Pump
Record Label: Geffen
Songwriters: Steven Tyler, Joe Perry

An anthem for the 60-second man.

WHAT IT TAKES

Producer: Bruce Fairbairn
Album: Pump
Record Label: Geffen
Songwriters: Steven Tyler, Joe Perry, Desmond Child

Aerosmith ventures into Heavy Metal country.

1993

AMAZING

Producer: Bruce Fairbairn
Album: Get a Grip
Record Label: Geffen
Songwriters: Steven Tyler, Richard Supa

A toned and tuneful hit-bound, autobiographical career summation.

CRYIN'

Producer: Bruce Fairbairn
Album: Get a Grip
Record Label: Geffen
Songwriters: Steven Tyler, Joe Perry, Taylor Rhodes

A timeless ode to the yin and yang of the old in and out.

LIVIN' ON THE EDGE

Producer: Bruce Fairbairn
Album: Get a Grip
Record Label: Geffen
Songwriters: Steven Tyler, Joe Perry, Mark Hudson

Archetypal Lite Metal number was one of the form's best swansongs.

AFGHAN WHIGS
1990

I KNOW YOUR LITTLE SECRET
Producer: Jack Endino
Album: Up in It
Record Label: Sub Pop
Songwriter: Greg Dulli

The sound of the new underground—part Replacements, part Johnny Thunders.

AFTER 7
1989

CAN'T STOP
Producers: Babyface, L.A. Reid
Album: After 7
Record Label: Virgin
Songwriters: Kenny Edmunds (Babyface), Antonio Reid (L.A. Reid)

A #1 R&B/Top-10 R&R notch for the dominant songwriting team of the '90s.

READY OR NOT
Producers: Babyface, L.A. Reid
Album: After 7
Record Label: Virgin
Songwriters: Kenny Edmunds (Babyface), Antonio Reid (L.A. Reid)

AFTER THE FIRE
1983

DER KOMMISSAR
Producer: John Eden
Album: ATF
Record Label: Epic
Songwriters: Falco (Johann Hoelzel), Andrew Piercy, Robert Ponger

Falco had the original hit in Germany.

A-HA
1985

TAKE ON ME
Producer: Alan Tarney
Album: Hunting High and Low
Record Label: Warner Brothers
Songwriters: Pal Weaktaar, Mags Furuholem, Marten Harket

Soaring Norwegian psychedelia.

AHMAD
1994

BACK IN THE DAY
Producer: Ahmad
Album: Ahmad
Record Label: Giant
Songwriters: Ahmad Lewis, Stefan Gordy

A catalogue of urban nostalgia for the mid-'80s.

AIR SUPPLY
1983

MAKING LOVE OUT OF NOTHING AT ALL
Producer: Jim Steinman
Album: Greatest Hits
Record Label: Arista
Songwriter: Jim Steinman

Three-day-old meatloaf.

JEWEL AKENS
1964

THE BIRDS & THE BEES
Album: The Birds & the Bees
Record Label: Era
Songwriter: Herb Newman

Post-Rockabilly one-shot from Texas.

ALABAMA
1981

LOVE IN THE FIRST DEGREE
Producers: Harold Shedd, Alabama
Album: Feels So Right
Record Label: RCA
Songwriters: Jim Hurt, James Dubois

#1 C&W/Top-20 R&R is the biggest crossover hit for the predominant Country harmony group of the '80s.

THE ALARM
1989

SOLD ME DOWN THE RIVER
Producer: Tony Visconti
Album: Change
Record Label: IRS
Songwriters: Eddie Macdonald, Mike Peters

The rebel intensity of U2, without the cause.

ALCATRAZZ
1984

EVIL EYE
Album: Live Sentence
Record Label: Rocshire
Songwriter: Yngwie Malmsteen

Introduced a new guitar god in the classically-oriented Malmsteen.

ARTHUR ALEXANDER
1962

YOU BETTER MOVE ON
Album: You Better Move On
Record Label: Dot
Songwriter: Arthur Alexander

Classic R&B/Soul ballad. Covered by the Rolling Stones (London, '65).

1962

A SHOT OF RHYTHM & BLUES
Album: You Better Move On
Record Label: Dot
Songwriter: Terry Thompson

B-side of "You Better Move On." This one was covered by the Beatles.

SOLDIER OF LOVE
Album: You Better Move On
Record Label: Dot
Songwriters: Buzz Cason, Tony Moon

Another early Beatles performing favorite. Covered by Marshall Crenshaw, who played John Lennon in Beatlemania (Reprise, '82).

1963

ANNA (GO TO HIM)
Record Label: Dot
Songwriter: Arthur Alexander

Top-10 R&B/R&R crossover. Covered by the Beatles (Vee-Jay, '63).

1969

BURNING LOVE
Record Label: Dot
Songwriter: Dennis Linde

Cover by Elvis Presely (RCA, '69) was his 38th and last Top-10 single. Also covered by Dr. & the Medics (IRS, '87).

ALIAS
1990

MORE THAN WORDS CAN SAY
Album: Alias
Record Label: EMI

Songwriters: Freddy Curci, Steve DeMarchi

Mainstream Rock.

ALICE IN CHAINS
1992

WOULD
Producer: Alice in Chains
Album: Dirt
Record Label: Columbia
Songwriter: Jerry Cantrell

The Metal edge of '92 Seattle Grunge.

1994

NO EXCUSES
Producer: Alice in Chains
Album: Jar of Flies
Record Label: Columbia
Songwriter: Jerry Cantrell

The Metal edge of '94 Seattle Grunge goes commercial.

ALIVE AND KICKING
1970

TIGHTER TIGHTER
Producer: Tommy James
Album: Alive and Kicking
Record Label: Roulette
Songwriters: Tommy James, Bob King

Joplin-esque bubble Pop.

ALL
1988

JUST PERFECT
Album: Allroy Sez
Record Label: Cruz
Songwriter: Bill Stephenson

Pop Punk descendants go to Metal beach.

ALL-4-ONE
1994

I SWEAR
Producer: David Foster
Album: All-4-One
Record Label: Blitz/Atlantic
Songwriters: Frank Myers, Gerry Baker

This Country cover by an interracial R&B group was a left-field harmony hit. John Montgomery had the original (Atlantic, '92), which won a Grammy for Country Song of the Year in '94.

TONY ALLEN
1955

NITE OWL
Producer: Bumps Blackwell
Album: Rock and Roll with Tony Allen
Record Label: Specialty
Songwriter: Tony Allen

Suggested segue: "In the Still of the Night," by the Five Satins, for its shoo-doot'n shoo be doo's.

MOSE ALLISON
1958

THE SEVENTH SON
Album: Creek Bank
Record Label: Prestige
Songwriter: Willie Dixon

From the noted Jazz/Blues satirist ("Your Mind Is on Vacation but Your Mouth Is Working Overtime"), the classic rendition of the Willie Dixon epic. Covered by Johnny Rivers (Imperial, '65), John Hammond Jr. (Vanguard, '66), Willie Dixon (Columbia, '70).

THE ALLMAN BROTHERS
1970

IN MEMORY OF ELIZABETH REED
Producer: Adrian Barber
Album: Idlewild South
Record Label: Atco
Songwriter: Dickie Betts

Betts' grade school music teacher would be proud. Epic instrumental.

MIDNIGHT RIDER
Producer: Adrian Barber
Album: Idlewild South
Record Label: Capricorn
Songwriters: Greg Allman, Kim Payne

This essential blues rocker was recorded by both Duane and Greg on early solo albums.

WHIPPING POST
Producer: Adrian Barber
Album: The Allman Brothers Band
Record Label: Atco
Songwriter: Greg Allman

Inevitable concert favorite became the wounded battle cry of a-thousand-and-one Fillmore nights (where is that hoarse and weary trooper now?).

1971

STATESBORO BLUES
Producer: Tom Dowd
Album: Live at Fillmore East
Record Label: Capricorn
Songwriter: Blind Willie McTell

Showpiece number introduced by the great bluesman in 1928.

1972

AIN'T WASTIN' TIME NO MORE
Producer: Tom Dowd
Album: Eat a Peach
Record Label: Capricorn
Songwriter: Greg Allman

The epitome of the barn-burnin' Blues 'n' boogie paradise called Southern Rock.

BLUE SKY
Producer: Tom Dowd
Album: Eat a Peach
Record Label: Capricorn
Songwriter: Dickie Betts

Betts's lilting signature piece.

LITTLE MARTHA
Producer: Tom Dowd
Album: Eat a Peach
Record Label: Capricorn
Songwriter: Greg Allman

Enchanted, acoustic guitar/dobro passing of the torch from the departed Duane to Dicky B.

MELISSA
Producer: Tom Dowd
Album: Eat a Peach
Record Label: Capricorn
Songwriters: Greg Allman, Stephen Alaimo

Greg's tortured ode to his late brother.

1973

JESSICA
Producers: Jerry Sandlin, Allman Brothers Band
Album: Brothers and Sisters
Record Label: Capricorn
Songwriter: Dickie Betts

Betts took over, with laid-back southern preserves.

RAMBLIN' MAN
Producers: Jerry Sandlin, Allman Brothers Band
Album: Brothers and Sisters
Record Label: Capricorn
Songwriter: Dickie Betts

What they will be remembered for—lots of layered Rock guitar at the top of the charts. The Eagles were taking notes for "Hotel California."

ALTERED IMAGES
1981

HAPPY BIRTHDAY
Producer: Martin Rushent
Album: Happy Birthday
Record Label: Portrait
Songwriter: Altered Images

Early video age romp from England. In America, Patty Smyth was in the wings.

DAVE ALVIN
1987

FOURTH OF JULY
Producer: Steve Berlin
Album: Romeo's Escape
Record Label: Epic
Songwriter: Dave Alvin

Landmark of the '80s American Roots revival. Covered by X (Elektra, '87).

THE AMBOY DUKES
1968

JOURNEY TO THE CENTER OF THE MIND
Producer: Bob Shad
Album: Journey to the Center of the Mind
Record Label: Mainstream
Songwriters: Ted Nugent, Steve Farmer

Motor City Garage Band psychedelia by the avid deer hunter and gonzo guitarist Nugent.

AMBROSIA
1975

NICE, NICE, VERY NICE
Producer: Freddie Piro
Album: Ambrosia
Record Label: 20th Century
Songwriters: David Pack, Kurt Vonnegut Jr., Joseph Puerta Jr., Christopher North, Burleigh Drummond

From the Kurt Vonnegut novel, Cat's Cradle. Suggested segue: "Eyes of a New York Woman" by Insect Trust (lyrics from Thomas Pynchon's V).

1978

HOW MUCH I FEEL
Producers: Freddie Piro, Ambrosia
Album: Life Beyond L.A.

Record Label: Warner Brothers
Songwriter: David Pack

L.A. mellow prototype.

1980

BIGGEST PART OF ME
Producers: Freddie Piro, Ambrosia
Album: One Eighty
Record Label: Warner Brothers
Songwriter: David Pack

Their biggest hit.

AMERICA
1972

HORSE WITH NO NAME
Producer: Ian Samwell
Album: America
Record Label: Warner Brothers
Songwriter: Lee Bunnell

Neil Youngian Folk Rock.

I NEED YOU
Producer: Ian Samwell
Album: America
Record Label: Warner Brothers
Songwriter: Gerry Beckley

Defining the sunny Folk-Rock, Top-10 style of the miserable early '70s.

VENTURA HIGHWAY
Producer: America
Album: Homecoming
Record Label: Warner Brothers
Songwriter: Lee Bunnell

More of their patented formula.

1974

LONELY PEOPLE
Producer: George Martin
Album: Holiday
Record Label: Warner Brothers
Songwriters: Catherine Peek, Dan Peek

Beatles producer Martin attempts to recreate "Eleanor Rigby."

TIN MAN
Producer: George Martin
Album: Holiday
Record Label: Warner Brothers
Songwriter: Lee Bunnell

In evoking the Land of Oz, they may have inadvertently awakened the sensibilities of Australia's Little River Band.

1975

SISTER GOLDEN HAIR
Producer: George Martin
Album: Hearts
Record Label: Warner Brothers
Songwriter: Gerry Beckley

Approaching Folk Rock heaven with their second #1.

1982

YOU CAN DO MAGIC
Producer: Russ Ballard
Album: View from the Ground
Record Label: Capitol
Songwriter: Russ Ballard

Their last big hit.

AMERICAN BREED
1967

BEND ME, SHAPE ME
Producer: Bill Traut
Album: Bend Me, Shape Me
Record Label: Acta
Songwriters: Scott English, Laurence Weiss

Good-time Frat Rock one-shot. English would be back with "Mandy."

TORI AMOS
1992

CRUCIFY
Producer: Davitt Sigerson
Album: Little Earthquakes
Record Label: Atlantic
Songwriter: Tori Amos

Tortured Alternative confessional from the Laura Nyro of the '90s.

ME AND A GUN
Producer: Ian Stanley
Album: Little Earthquakes
Record Label: Atlantic
Songwriter: Tori Amos

Her first solo single plumbs remarkable autobiographical depths detailing a rape.

SILENT ALL THESE YEARS
Producer: Davitt Sigerson
Album: Little Earthquakes
Record Label: Atlantic
Songwriter: Tori Amos

Powerful tale of a female coming of age in the '90s.

WINTER
Producer: Davitt Sigerson
Album: Little Earthquakes
Record Label: Atlantic
Songwriter: Tori Amos

Career-making reflection on the pains of growing up.

1994

GOD
Producers: Eric Rosse, Tori Amos
Album: Under the Pink
Record Label: Atlantic
Songwriter: Tori Amos

Outrageously calculated.

ERIC ANDERSEN
1968

TIN CAN ALLEY
Producer: Al Gorgoni
Album: More Hits from Tin Can Alley
Record Label: Vanguard
Songwriter: Eric Andersen

All-inclusive, antiurban Folk Rock from the recovered romantic balladeer.

1989

GHOSTS UPON THE ROAD
Producers: Steve Addabo, Eric Andersen
Album: Ghosts Upon the Road
Record Label: Gold Castle
Songwriter: Eric Andersen

Reflecting on '60s bohemia, with an agonized, '90s-talking Blues from his home in Norway.

BILL ANDERSON
1963

(I LOVE YOU) STILL
Album: Still
Record Label: Decca
Songwriter: Bill Anderson

#1 C&W/Top-10 R&R crossover.

LAURIE ANDERSON
1982

O SUPERMAN
Producers: Roma Baran, Laurie Anderson
Album: Big Science
Record Label: Warner Brothers
Songwriter: Laurie Anderson

This epic-length performance art tone poem was a major smash in England.

1984

SHARKEY'S DAY
Producers: Laurie Anderson, Bill Laswell
Album: Mister Heartbreak
Record Label: Warner Brothers
Songwriter: Laurie Anderson

A cross-generational, multi-media, universal day-in-the-life of the bohemian, a la Joni Mitchell-meets-Gertrude-Stein. Narrative by William Burroughs, and guitar by Adrian Belew.

LEE ANDREWS AND THE HEARTS
1957

LONG LONELY NIGHTS
Album: Main Line
Record Label: Chess
Songwriters: Lee Andrews, Roquel Davis (Tyran Carlo), Douglas Henderson, Mimi Uniman

Influenced by Nat King Cole, this post Doo-Wop ballad was an early harbinger of Philly Soul.

TEARDROPS
Album: Main Line
Record Label: Chess
Songwriters: Edwin Charles, Helen Stanley, Roy Calhoun

Their biggest hit.

THE ANGELS
1963

I ADORE HIM
Producers: Richard Gottehrer, Robert Feldman, Jerry Goldstein
Album: My Boyfriend's Back
Record Label: Smash
Songwriters: Jan Berry, Art Kornfeld

Subversive '60s subservience.

MY BOYFRIEND'S BACK
Producers: Richard Gottehrer, Robert Feldman, Jerry Goldstein
Album: My Boyfriend's Back
Record Label: Smash
Songwriters: Richard Gottehrer, Robert Feldman, Jerry Goldstein

Eau-de-girl-group single that hit in a time when such female anthems were written and directed by men.

THANK YOU AND GOODNIGHT
Producers: Richard Gottehrer, Robert Feldman, Jerry Goldstein
Album: My Boyfriend's Back
Record Label: Smash
Songwriters: Richard Gottehrer, Robert Feldman, Jerry Goldstein

Concert-closing comments from the ultimate of supportive girlfriends.

ANGRY SAMOANS
1980

RIGHT SIDE OF MY BRAIN
Album: Inside My Brain
Record Label: Bad Trip
Songwriter: Todd Homer

Punk in-joke for the L.A. Rock critic league.

THE ANIMALS
1964

THE HOUSE OF THE RISING SUN
Producer: Mickie Most
Album: The Animals
Record Label: MGM
Songwriter: Traditional (arr. Alan Price)

The Animals' cover of the legendary American Folk classic performed by Bob Dylan on his debut album (Columbia, '61) laid the early foundations for Folk Rock.

1965

DON'T LET ME BE MISUNDERSTOOD
Producer: Mickie Most
Album: Animal Tracks
Record Label: MGM
Songwriters: Benny Benjamin, Gloria Caldwell, Sol Marcus

Bridging the gap between Folk Rock and Garage Punk.

IT'S MY LIFE
Producer: Mickie Most
Album: Best of the Animals
Record Label: MGM
Songwriters: Roger Atkins, Carl D'Errico

The existential howl of the Garage Band era. In the '70s, it was a Bruce-Springsteen-in-concert peak.

WE GOTTA GET OUTA THIS PLACE
Producer: Mickie Most
Album: Animal Tracks
Record Label: MGM
Songwriters: Barry Mann, Cynthia Weil

Under-class/working-class Folk Rock anthem. Covered by Katrina & the Waves on the China Beach *Soundtrack album (Capitol, '90).*

1966

DON'T BRING ME DOWN
Producer: Mickie Most
Album: Animalization
Record Label: MGM
Songwriters: Gerry Goffin, Carole King

Essential Brill Building angst.

1967

MAMA TOLD ME NOT TO COME
Producer: Mickie Most
Album: Eric Is Here
Record Label: MGM
Songwriter: Randy Newman

Newman's ultimate anti-party song is introduced by the ultimate party Animal, Eric Burdon. Newman's own version is on Reprise, *'68. Cover by Three Dog Night (Dunhill, '70) went to #1.*

MONTEREY
Producer: Tom Wilson
Album: The Twain Shall Meet
Record Label: MGM
Songwriters: Eric Burdon, Victor Briggs, John Weider, Barry Jenkins, Denny McCulloch

With Bob Dylan's producer, Burdon recalls one of the Rock Generation's high points, with a stirring sitar intro.

SAN FRANCISCAN NIGHTS
Producer: Mickie Most
Album: Winds of Change
Record Label: MGM
Songwriters: Eric Burdon, Victor Briggs, John Weider, Barry Jenkins, Denny McCulloch

Tribute to the Summer of Love. Suggested segue: "San Francisco (Wear Some Flowers in Your Hair)" by Scott McKenzie.

SKY PILOT
Producer: Tom Wilson
Album: The Twain Shall Meet
Record Label: MGM
Songwriters: Eric Burdon, Victor Briggs, John Weider, Barry Jenkins, Denny McCulloch

Recalling the Rock Generation's lowest point, with a Vietnam War story.

ANIMOTION

1985

OBSESSION
Producer: J. Ryan
Album: Animotion
Record Label: Mercury
Songwriters: Holly Knight, Michael Desbarres

Corporate Synth Pop.

1989

ROOM TO MOVE
Producers: Steve Barri, Tony Peluso
Album: Animotion
Record Label: Polydor
Songwriters: Simon Climie, Roger Fisher, Dennis Morgan

PAUL ANKA

1957

DIANA
Producer: Don Costa
Album: Diana
Record Label: ABC-Paramount
Songwriter: Paul Anka

This quintessential #1 R&R/R&B tale of adolescent yearning was the product of the first of the new breed of Tin Pan Alley rock and rollers, who could not only write the lyrics and the music, but also sing the songs, and balance the books. Anka had an office in the Brill Building. The song was the first by a teenager to go #1 U.K.

1958

(ALL OF A SUDDEN) MY HEART SINGS
Producer: Don Costa
Album: Paul Anka Sings His Big 15
Record Label: ABC-Paramount
Songwriters: Harold Rome, Henri Herpin

No less intrigued by the evergreens than his Doo-Wop brethren, Anka chose a tune introduced by Kathryn Grayson in the '45 film, Anchors Aweigh, *for his last release of '58.*

YOU ARE MY DESTINY
Producer: Don Costa
Album: Paul Anka Sings His Big 15
Record Label: ABC-Paramount
Songwriter: Paul Anka

For his second major hit, Anka adopted the quasi-operatic mode that moved him out of Rock and into Pop.

1959

LONELY BOY
Producer: Don Costa
Album: Lonely Boy
Record Label: ABC-Paramount
Songwriter: Paul Anka

Teen depression, introduced in the 1959 film Girls Town.

PUT YOUR HEAD ON MY SHOULDER
Producer: Don Costa
Album: Paul Anka Sings His Big 15
Record Label: ABC-Paramount
Songwriter: Paul Anka

The follow up to "Lonely Boy."

1960

IT'S TIME TO CRY
Producer: Don Costa
Album: Paul Anka Sings His Big 15 (Vol. II)
Record Label: ABC-Paramount
Songwriter: Paul Anka

PUPPY LOVE
Producer: Don Costa
Album: Paul Anka Sings His Big 15
Record Label: ABC-Paramount
Songwriter: Paul Anka

A sedated take on a traditional theme. Suggested segues: "Only Sixteen" by Sam Cooke, and "Born Too Late" by the Ponitails. Covered by Donny Osmond (MGM, '72).

1976

TIMES OF YOUR LIFE
Album: The Times of Your Life
Record Label: United Artists
Songwriters: William M. Lane, Roger S. Nichols

Vegas TV commercial. Suggested segue: "Kodachrome" by Paul Simon.

ANNETTE

1959

TALL PAUL
Producer: Tutti Camarata
Album: Annette: The Story of My Teens
Record Label: Disneyland
Songwriters: Bob Roberts, Bob Sherman, Dick Sherman

This teen queen of the beach for the baby-boom crowd was manufactured by Walt Disney. Her ode to the short Paul Anka was appropriately scripted by Disney's house writers, the Sherman Brothers, for Annette's sister Mouseketeer, Judy Harriet; but Annette ultimately got the hit and the movies.

1960

O DIO MIO

Album: Italianette
Record Label: Buena Vista
Songwriters: Al Hoffman, Dick Manning

Suggested 1960 segue: "Mama" by Connie Francis, the East Coast Annette.

1960

IT'S REALLY LOVE

Album: Annette Sings Anka
Record Label: Buena Vista
Songwriter: Paul Anka

As Judy Collins was to Leonard Cohen (as the Byrds were to Bob Dylan, as Nilsson was to Randy Newman), Annette was to her favorite poet. This tune would later earn Anka a whole lot more money as the theme to "The Johnny Carson Show."

ANNISTEEN ALLEN
1955

FUJIYAMA MAMA

Record Label: Capitol
Songwriter: Earl Burrows

Rockabilly landmark, covered by Wanda Jackson, in one of her most incendiary performances (Capitol, '56).

ANOTHER BAD CREATION
1991

IESHA

Producer: Dallas Austin
Album: Coolin' at the Playground Ya' Know
Record Label: Motown
Songwriters: Dallas Austin, Michael Bivens

Urban renewal.

PLAYGROUND

Producer: Dallas Austin
Album: Coolin' at the Playground Ya' Know
Record Label: Motown
Songwriters: Dallas Austin, Michael Bivens, Kevin Wales

Austin would become a major producer of '90s R&B.

ADAM ANT
1982

GOODY TWO SHOES

Producers: Adam Ant, Marco Pironi
Album: Friend or Foe
Record Label: Epic
Songwriters: Stuart Goddard (Adam Ant), Marco Pirroni

Made-for-MTV, dance Rock with a bad attitude.

ANTHRAX
1986

A.D.I./THE HORROR OF IT ALL

Album: *Return of the Living Dead, Part II* Soundtrack
Record Label: Island
Songwriter: Anthrax

Comic-book, horror-movie Metal.

THE AQUATONES
1958

YOU

Album: The Aquatones Sing
Record Label: Fargo
Songwriter: Larry Vanatta

A glorious East Coast harmony one-shot; Lynn Nixon was the Rosie Hamlin of Long Island.

ARCADIA
1985

ELECTION DAY

Producer: Alex Sadkin
Album: So Red the Rose
Record Label: Capitol
Songwriters: Nick Rhodes, Roger Taylor, Simon LeBon

What Duran Duran hath wrought (with the voice of supermodel Grace Jones).

TASMIN ARCHER
1992

SLEEPING SATELLITE

Producer: John Hughes
Album: Great Expectations
Record Label: SBK
Songwriters: Tasmin Archer, John Beck, John Hughes

#1 U.K./Top-40 U.S. crossover.

THE ARCHIES
1969

SUGAR SUGAR

Producer: Jeff Barry
Album: Everything's Archie
Record Label: Calendar
Songwriters: Jeff Barry, Andy Kim

Ultimate bubblegum creation by studio singer Ron Dante. Covered by Wilson Pickett (Atlantic, '70).

ARGENT
1969

LIAR

Producer: Argent
Album: Argent
Record Label: Epic
Songwriter: Russ Ballard

Covered by Three Dog Night (Dunhill, '71).

1972

HOLD YOUR HEAD UP

Producer: Argent
Album: All Together Now
Record Label: Epic
Songwriters: Rod Argent, Chris White

Ex-Zombie leader espouses a new cause. Edited from the original 6-plus-minute version.

1973

GOD GAVE ROCK AND ROLL TO YOU

Producer: Argent
Album: In Deep
Record Label: Epic
Songwriter: Rod Argent

Suggested alternate anthems: "It Will Stand" by the Showmen, "Rock and Roll Is Here to Stay" by Danny & the Juniors, and "(Rock and Roll) I Gave You the Best Years of My Life" by Kevin Johnson.

JOAN ARMATRADING
1976

LOVE AND AFFECTION

Producer: Glyn Johns
Album: Joan Armatrading
Record Label: A&M
Songwriter: Joan Armatrading

The Tracy Chapman of the '70s, without a fast car.

LOUIS ARMSTRONG
1956

MACK THE KNIFE
Album: Mack the Knife
Record Label: Columbia
Songwriters: Berthold Brecht, Kurt Weill, Marc Blitzstein

One quintessential character introduces another to the rock and roll sphere. Bobby Darin's version of the tune from The Threepenny Opera, *lifted from his album* That's All *(Atlantic, '59), spent 9 weeks at #1.*

ARRESTED DEVELOPMENT
1992

MR. WENDALL
Producer: Speech
Album: 3 Years 5 Months and 2 Days in the Life Of
Record Label: Chrysalis
Songwriter: Todd Thomas (Speech)

PEOPLE EVERYDAY
Producer: Speech
Album: 3 Years 5 Months and 2 Days in the Life Of
Record Label: Chrysalis
Songwriter(s): Todd Thomas (Speech)

A play on Sly & the Family Stone.

REVOLUTION
Producer: Speech
Album: *Malcolm X* Soundtrack
Record Label: Chrysalis/EMI
Songwriter: Todd Thomas (Speech)

Speech got a dream assignment in the Spike Lee film Malcolm X. *Arrested Development quickly moved to the bottom of the Hip-Hop playlist.*

TENNESSEE
Producer: Speech
Album: 3 Years 5 Months and 2 Days in the Life Of
Record Label: Chrysalis
Songwriter: Todd Thomas (Speech)

The Roots-meets-Rap breakthrough single that briefly united the warring camps of Rap and Alternative music under the world-beat banner, giving rise to the Jazz/Rock/Rap fusions of Digable Planets, Rusted Root, and Zap Mama.

ARTISTS UNITED AGAINST APARTHEID
1985

SUN CITY
Producers: Steve Van Zandt, Arthur Baker
Album: Sun City
Record Label: Manhattan
Songwriter: Steve Van Zandt

The superstar concept of "We Are the World" as applied to artists protesting apartheid in South Africa, spearheaded by a New Jersey guitar hero/activist/former-Springsteen sideman.

DANIEL ASH
1992

GET OUT OF CONTROL
Album: Foolish Thing Desire
Record Label: Columbia
Songwriter: Daniel Ash

A rocker from the ashes of Bauhaus and Love and Rockets.

ASHFORD AND SIMPSON
1978

IS IT STILL GOOD TA YA
Producers: Nick Ashford, Valerie Simpson
Album: Is It Still Good ta Ya
Record Label: Warner Brothers
Songwriters: Nick Ashford, Valerie Simpson

1984

SOLID
Producers: Nick Ashford, Valerie Simpson
Album: Solid
Record Label: Capitol
Songwriters: Nick Ashford, Valerie Simpson

By far, the biggest hit as artists for these prolific songwriters: #1 R&B/Top-20 R&R.

ASIA
1982

HEAT OF THE MOMENT
Producer: Mike Stone
Album: Asia
Record Label: Geffen
Songwriters: John Wetton, Geoffrey Downes

Former giants of the Progressive genre, from Yes, King Crimson and Emerson, Lake & Palmer, labor to produce a pygmy.

ONLY TIME WILL TELL
Producer: Mike Stone
Album: Asia
Record Label: Geffen
Songwriters: John Wetton, Geoffrey Downes

All the pomp of Art Rock, but without the circumstance.

THE ASSOCIATION
1966

ALONG COMES MARY
Producer: Kurt Boettcher
Album: & then . . . Along Comes the Association
Record Label: Warner Brothers
Songwriter: Tandyn Almer

This was Folk Rock's first alleged marijuana reference (Mary=Maryjane) to become a hit single, and to be selected Record of the Year by the Sisters of Marymount College.

CHERISH
Producer: Kurt Boettcher
Album: & then . . . Along Comes the Association
Record Label: Warner Brothers
Songwriter: Terry Kirkman

#1 Soft Rock classic.

1967

NEVER MY LOVE
Producer: Bones Howe
Album: Greatest Hits
Record Label: Warner Brothers
Songwriters: Don Addrisi, Dick Addrisi

An enduring Pop Rock ballad.

WINDY
Producer: Bones Howe
Album: Insight Out
Record Label: Warner Brothers
Songwriter: Ruthann Friedman

Creating a '60s female stereotype—breezy, blowsy, and a little spaced-out. Suggested segues: "Ruby Tuesday," by Linda Ronstadt, "Suzanne" by Leonard Cohen, "We'll Sing in the Sunshine" by Gale Garnett, "Angel of the Morning" by Merilee Rush, and "Arizona" by Mark Lindsay.

RICK ASTLEY

1987

NEVER GONNA GIVE YOU UP

Producers: Mike Stock, Matt Aitken, Pete Waterman
Album: Whenever You Need Somebody
Record Label: RCA
Songwriters: Mike Stock, Matt Aitken, Pete Waterman

This top U.K. single of '87 became the best-selling dance disc in the U.S. in '88.

1988

IT WOULD TAKE A STRONG STRONG MAN

Producers: Mike Stock, Matt Aitken, Pete Waterman
Album: Whenever You Need Somebody
Record Label: RCA
Songwriters: Mike Stock, Matt Aitken, Pete Waterman

A third-time visit to the dancehall well.

TOGETHER FOREVER

Producers: Mike Stock, Matt Aitken, Pete Waterman
Album: Whenever You Need Somebody
Record Label: RCA
Songwriters: Mike Stock, Matt Aitken, Pete Waterman

Teenybop dance groove redux; his second straight #1 in the U.S.

1989

SHE WANTS TO DANCE WITH ME

Album: Hold Me in Your Arms
Record Label: RCA
Songwriter: Rick Astley

1991

CRY FOR HELP

Producers: Gary Stevenson, Rick Astley
Album: Free
Record Label: RCA
Songwriters: Rick Astley, Rob Fisher

CHET ATKINS

1957

WALK, DON'T RUN

Album: Hi-Fi in Focus
Record Label: RCA
Songwriter: John H. Smith Jr.

Legendary guitar instrumental was turned into a twangy surf classic by the West Coast group the Ventures (Dolton, '60).

1959

LET IT BE ME

Album: Chet Atkins in Hollywood
Record Label: RCA
Songwriters: Mann Curtis (English words), Pierre Delanoe (French words), Gilbert Becaud

Introduced by Gilbert Becaud in France in 1955. Sung by Jill Corey on the TV show "Climax" and released on Columbia, '57. The Everly Brothers heard Chet's version and recorded the tune in New York, their first session outside of Nashville (Cadence, '60). Also covered by Betty Everett and Jerry Butler (Vee Jay, '64).

ATLANTA RHYTHM SECTION

1976

SO IN TO YOU

Producer: Buddy Buie
Album: A Rock and Roll Alternative
Record Label: Polydor
Songwriters: Buddy Buie, Dean Daughtry, Robert Nix

Epitomizing the homogenized sound of the New South.

1978

IMAGINARY LOVER

Producer: Buddy Buie
Album: Champagne Jam
Record Label: Polydor
Songwriters: Buddy Buie, Dean Daughtry, Robert Nix

ATLANTIC STARR

1986

SECRET LOVERS

Producers: David Lewis, Wayne Lewis
Album: As the Band Turns
Record Label: A&M
Songwriters: David Lewis, Wayne Lewis

1987

ALWAYS

Producers: David Lewis, Wayne Lewis
Album: All in the Name of Love
Record Label: Warner Brothers
Songwriters: David Lewis, Wayne Lewis, Jonathan Lewis

Their all-time best-selling wedding song.

1992

MASTERPIECE

Album: Love Crazy
Record Label: Reprise
Songwriter: Kenny Nolan

#1 R&B/Top-10 R&R crossover.

PATTI AUSTIN

BABY, COME TO ME

Producer: Quincy Jones
Album: Every Home Should Have One
Record Label: Qwest
Songwriter: Rod Temperton

Benefitting from airplay on "General Hospital," this ballad with James Austin made it to #1 two years after it was released.

FRANKIE AVALON

1958

DEDE DINAH

Producers: Pete DeAngelis, Bob Marcucci
Album: A Whole Lotta Frankie
Record Label: Chancellor
Songwriters: Bob Marcucci, Pete DeAngelis

First hit for the first in the questionable line of manufactured superstars, born and bred on Dick Clark's "American Bandstand."

GINGERBREAD

Producers: Pete DeAngelis, Bob Marcucci
Album: A Whole Lotta Frankie
Record Label: Chancellor
Songwriters: Clint Ballard Jr., Hank Hunter

1959

BOBBY SOX TO STOCKINGS

Producers: Pete DeAngelis, Bob Marcucci
Album: A Whole Lotta Frankie
Record Label: Chancellor
Songwriters: Russell Faith, Clarence Kehner, R. diCicco

As a follow up to "Venus," Avalon (all of 19 years old by then) waxed philosophic. Suggested segue: Pat Boone's book Twixt Twelve and Twenty.

JUST ASK YOUR HEART

Producers: Pete DeAngelis, Bob Marcucci
Album: A Whole Lotta Frankie

Record Label: Chancellor
Songwriters: Pete Damato, Joe Ricci, Diane De Nota

VENUS

Producers: Pete DeAngelis, Bob Marcucci
Album: A Whole Lotta Frankie
Record Label: Chancellor
Songwriter: Ed Marshall

Avalon's crowning moment of pristine balladry.

WHY

Producers: Pete DeAngelis, Bob Marcucci
Album: A Whole Lotta Frankie
Record Label: Chancellor
Songwriters: Pete DeAngelis, Bob Marcucci

Why indeed? Covered by Donny Osmond (MGM, '72).

THE AVERAGE WHITE BAND

1974

PICK UP THE PIECES

Producer: Arif Mardin
Album: AWB
Record Label: Atlantic
Songwriters: Roger Ball, Malcolm Duncan, Alan Garrie, Robbie McIntosh, Owen McIntyre, Jamie (Hamish) Stuart

Soul instrumental from Scotland.

1975

CUT THE CAKE

Producer: Arif Mardin
Album: Cut the Cake
Record Label: Atlantic
Songwriters: Roger Ball, Malcolm Duncan, Alan Gorrie, Robbie McIntosh, Owen McIntyre, Jamie (Hamish) Stuart

AZTEC TWO-STEP

1972

THE PERSECUTION AND RESTORATION OF DEAN MORIARTY (ON THE ROAD)

Producer: Jerry Yester
Album: Aztec Two-Step
Record Label: Elektra
Songwriter: Rex Fowler

This influential acoustic duo salutes a beat legend.

B

THE B-52'S

1979

DANCE THIS MESS AROUND

Producer: Chris Blackwell
Album: The B-52's
Record Label: Warner Brothers
Songwriter: The B-52's

Opening the incipient Athens, Georgia college scene to inquiring minds, the original queens of hairspray chic reinvent grassroots boogie. Michael Stipe stopped applying to out-of-town colleges.

ROCK LOBSTER

Producer: Chris Blackwell
Album: The B-52's
Record Label: Warner Brothers
Songwriters: Fred Schneider, Ricky Wilson

Punk goes Disco, with a cheeky attitude. Featured in Paul Simon's movie, One Trick Pony.

1980

PARTY OUT OF BOUNDS

Producers: Rhett Davis, the B-52's
Album: Wild Planet
Record Label: Warner Brothers
Songwriters: Fred Schneider, Ricky Wilson, Cindy Wilson, Cindy Strickland, Kate Pierson

The battle cry for a new decade's new dance generation.

PRIVATE IDAHO

Producers: Rhett Davies, the B-52's
Album: Wild Planet
Record Label: Warner Brothers
Songwriters: Fred Schneider, Ricky Wilson, Cindy Wilson, Keith Strickland, Kate Pierson

Advancing their kitschy Disco vision with an all-purpose metaphor.

1983

SONG FOR A FUTURE GENERATION

Producer: Steven Starley
Album: Whammy
Record Label: Warner Brothers
Songwriters: Fred Schneider, Ricky Wilson, Cindy Wilson, Julie Strickland, Kate Pierson

1989

LOVE SHACK

Producer: Don Was
Album: Cosmic Thing
Record Label: Reprise
Songwriter: The B-52's

A blissful return to the frat house of long ago. Suggested segue: "Sugar Shack" by Jimmy Gilmer & the Fireballs

ROAM

Producer: Nile Rodgers
Album: Cosmic Thing
Record Label: Reprise
Songwriters: The B-52's, Robert Waldrop

The B-52's cling to their manic groove despite the AIDS-related death of their founding guitarist, Ricky Wilson.

BABES IN TOYLAND

1990

BRUISED VIOLET

Producer: Lee Ranaldo
Album: Fontanelle
Record Label: Reprise
Songwriter: Babes in Toyland

The Riot Grrrrl sound with an Alternative pedigree. See "Violet" by Hole, "Flower" by Liz Phair.

BABYFACE

1989

IT'S NO CRIME

Producers: Babyface, L.A. Reid
Album: Tender Lover
Record Label: Solar
Songwriters: Kenny Edmunds (Babyface), Antonio Reid (L.A. Reid), Daryl Simmons

This '80s songwriting and producing giant (with co-partners and fellow members of Deele, Reid, and Simmons) achieved his first Top-10 hit with this ballad.

TENDER LOVER

Producers: Babyface, L.A. Reid
Album: Tender Lover
Record Label: Solar
Songwriters: Kenny Edmunds (Babyface), Antonio Reid (L.A. Reid), Pete Q. Smith

WHIP APPEAL

Producers: Babyface, L.A. Reid
Album: Tender Lover
Record Label: Solar

Songwriters: Kenny Edmunds (Babyface), Perri Alette McKissack (Pebbles)

Top-10 R&B/R&R crossover.

1994

WHEN CAN I SEE YOU

Producer: Babyface
Album: For the Cool in You
Record Label: Epic
Songwriter: Kenny Edmunds (Babyface)

His biggest hit thus far.

BACHMAN TURNER OVERDRIVE

1973

TAKIN' CARE OF BUSINESS

Producer: Randy Bachman
Album: Bachman Turner Overdrive II
Record Label: Mercury
Songwriter: Randy Bachman

Roadhouse Metal by a Guess Who graduate.

1974

YOU AIN'T SEEN NOTHIN' YET

Producer: Randy Bachman
Album: Not Fragile
Record Label: Mercury
Songwriter: Randy Bachman

Epitomizing the bravado of the big guitar bands of the '70s. Covered by a solo Burton Cummings (Portrait, '76). Suggested segue: Roger Daltrey's stuttering "My Generation."

BAD BRAINS

1980

PAY TO CUM

Producer: Jimmy Quidd
Record Label: X
Songwriters: Gary Miller (Dr. Know), Daryl Jenifer, Paul Hudson

A landmark indie single, this fusion of Metal, Punk, and Reggae launched the career of this Jazz-influenced, speedcore band from D.C.

1986

INTRO

Album: I Against I
Record Label: SST
Songwriters: Gary Miller (Dr. Know), Daryl Jenifer

A Van Halen-esque Speed Metal eruption.

BAD COMPANY

1974

CAN'T GET ENOUGH

Producer: Bad Company
Album: Bad Co.
Record Label: Swan Song
Songwriter: Mick Ralphs

Biggest hit for the workmanlike arena Metal band.

MOVIN' ON

Producer: Bad Company
Album: Bad Co.
Record Label: Swan Song
Songwriter: Mick Ralphs

From their #1 LP.

1975

FEEL LIKE MAKING LOVE

Producer: Bad Company
Album: Straight Shooter
Record Label: Swan Song
Songwriters: Paul Rodgers, Mick Ralphs

Mellow Metal offspring of Free and Mott the Hoople was their only other Top-10 hit.

1979

ROCK `N' ROLL FANTASY

Producer: Bad Company
Album: Desolation Angels
Record Label: Swan Song
Songwriter: Paul Rodgers

BAD ENGLISH

1989

WHEN I SEE YOU SMILE

Producer: Ritchie Zito
Album: Bad English
Record Label: Epic
Songwriter: Diane Warren

Inheriting the mantle from Carole King (princess of Pop Rock songwriting), Warren dispensed hits throughout the '80s and '90s to a variety of deserving and undeserving clients—from Cher to Bon Jovi to Michael Bolton to these post-Journey offshoots, who benefitted with an instant #1.

BADFINGER

1969

COME AND GET IT

Producer: Paul McCartney
Album: Magic Christian Music
Record Label: Apple
Songwriter: Paul McCartney

Their first hit, from the movie The Magic Christian, *starring Ringo Starr and Peter Sellers.*

1970

NO MATTER WHAT

Producer: Paul McCartney
Album: No Dice
Record Label: Apple
Songwriter: William Peter Ham

WITHOUT YOU

Producer: Paul McCartney
Album: No Vice
Record Label: Apple

Cover by Nilsson was #1 U.S./U.K. (RCA, '71). Covered by Mariah Carey (Columbia, '94).

1971

DAY AFTER DAY

Producers: Todd Rundgren, George Harrison
Album: Straight Up
Record Label: Apple
Songwriter: William Peter Ham

Beatle-esque in extremis.

BAD RELIGION

1994

21ST CENTURY DIGITAL BOY

Producer: Andy Wallace
Album: Stranger Than Fiction
Record Label: Atlantic
Songwriter: Brett Gurewitz

Breakthrough anthem for this veteran hardcore band.

JOAN BAEZ

1962

BABE, I'M GONNA LEAVE YOU

Record Label: Vanguard
Songwriter: Anne Bredon

Covered by Quicksilver Messenger Service in the hippie movie Revolution *(United Artists, '69). Was also one of the earliest influences on the eclectic Folk/Rock/Blues direction pursued by Led Zeppelin, who covered it on their first album (Atlantic, '69).*

1964

BIRMINGHAM SUNDAY

Album: Joan Baez/5
Record Label: Vanguard
Songwriter: Richard Fariña

About the bombing of a black church in Alabama, written by her sister's husband—

Richard Fariña. It was based on the English Folk tune, "I Loved a Lass."

1965

DADDY YOU BEEN ON MY MIND
  Producer: Maynard Solomon
  Album: Farewell Angelina
  Record Label: Vanguard
  Songwriter: Bob Dylan

Recorded first by Dylan as "Mama You Been on My Mind," one of the many unreleased Dylan masterpieces that would make up several albums 20 and 30 years down the line.

FAREWELL ANGELINA
  Producer: Maynard Solomon
  Album: Farewell Angelina
  Record Label: Vanguard
  Songwriter: Bob Dylan

As Annette did for Anka, Baez gave Dylan's poetry a quintessential female voice.

1967

LOVE IS JUST A FOUR-LETTER WORD
  Producer: Maynard Solomon
  Album: Any Day Now
  Record Label: Vanguard
  Songwriter: Bob Dylan

Another Dylan anthem of disaffection.

SAIGON BRIDE
  Album: Children of Darkness
  Record Label: Vanguard
  Songwriters: Joan Baez, Nina Dusheck

1975

DIAMONDS AND RUST
  Producer: David Kershenbaum
  Album: Diamonds and Rust
  Record Label: A&M
  Songwriter: Joan Baez

Joannie and Bobby, from Joannie's point of view. Bobby's point of view is allegedly stated in "Queen Jane Approximately," but probably boils down to "Love Is Just a Four-Letter Word." Covered by Judas Priest (Columbia, '79).

1992

STONES IN THE ROAD
  Producers: Wally Wilson, Kenny Greenberg
  Album: Play Me Backwards
  Record Label: Virgin
  Songwriter: Mary Chapin-Carpenter

Previewing a Folk Rock classic written and

later performed by Carpenter, a Princeton-graduate-turned-new-Country superstar (Columbia, '94).

PHILIP BAILEY
1985

EASY LOVER
  Producers: Philip Bailey, Phil Collins
  Album: Chinese Wall
  Record Label: Columbia
  Songwriters: Philip Bailey, Phil Collins, Nathan East

A pair of solo drummers—Bailey from Earth, Wind, and Fire, joined by Collins from Genesis—with a #2 U.S. and #1 U.K. smash.

ANITA BAKER
1986

CAUGHT UP IN THE RAPTURE
  Producer: Michael Powell
  Album: Rapture
  Record Label: Elektra
  Songwriters: Garry Glenn, Diane Quander

Inspired by Sarah Vaughan, a new Soul diva arrives on the scene.

SWEET LOVE
  Producer: Michael Powell
  Album: Rapture
  Record Label: Elektra
  Songwriters: Anita Baker, Louis Johnson, Gary Bias

Her ballad breakthrough.

1988

GIVING YOU THE BEST THAT I GOT
  Producer: Michael Powell
  Album: Giving You the Best That I Got
  Record Label: Elektra
  Songwriters: Anita Baker, Skip Scarborough, Randy Holland

JUST BECAUSE
  Producer: Michael Powell
  Album: Giving You the Best That I Got
  Record Label: Elektra
  Songwriters: Michael O'Hara, Sami McKinney, Alex Brown

LAVERN BAKER
1953

SOUL ON FIRE
  Producers: Ahmet Ertegun, Jerry Wexler
  Record Label: Atlantic
  Songwriters: Ahmet Ertegun, Jerry Wexler, LaVern Baker

The incomparable production team of Wexler and Ertegun enter the Rock and Roll era with the former Little Miss Sharecropper's first recording for the new Atlantic label.

1954

TWEEDLEE DEE
  Producers: Ahmet Ertegun, Jerry Wexler
  Record Label: Atlantic
  Songwriter: Winfield Scott

Top-10 R&B/Top20 R&R crossover. The Pop cover by Georgia Gibbs went to #2 (Mercury, '54).

1955

BOP-TING-A-LING
  Producers: Ahmet Ertegun, Jerry Wexler
  Album: LaVern Baker
  Record Label: Atlantic
  Songwriter: Winfield Scott

Top-10 R&B example of Baker's rockin' Soul, which owned the '50s.

1957

JIM DANDY
  Producers: Ahmet Ertegun, Jerry Wexler
  Record Label: Atlantic
  Songwriter: Lincoln Chase

A likeable, upbeat, heroic kind of Rock and Roll model, Top-10 R&B/Top-20 R&R.

JIM DANDY GOT MARRIED
  Producers: Ahmet Ertegun, Jerry Wexler
  Record Label: Atlantic
  Songwriters: Lincoln Chase, Roquel Davis (Tyrone Carlo), Alonzo Tucker, Al Green

The sequel; three new writers, and a big two weeks on the charts.

1959

I CRIED A TEAR
  Record Label: Atlantic
  Songwriters: Al Julia, Fred Jay

Her biggest hit—#2 R&B/Top-10 R&R.

1961

SAVED
Producers: Jerry Leiber, Mike Stoller
Album: Saved
Record Label: Atlantic
Songwriters: Jerry Leiber, Mike Stoller

Covered by Elvis Presley (RCA, '68).

LONG JOHN BALDRY
1971

DON'T TRY TO LAY NO BOOGIE WOOGIE ON THE KING OF ROCK AND ROLL
Producer: Rod Stewart
Album: It Ain't Easy
Record Label: Warner Brothers
Songwriter: Jeff Thomas

Stewart's production of his Steampacket bandmate.

MARTY BALIN
1981

HEARTS
Producer: John Balin
Album: Balin
Record Label: EMI-America
Songwriter: Jesse Barish

Airplane's Balin takes off for Journey territory.

BALTIMORA
1986

TARZAN BOY
Producer: Maurizio Bassi
Album: Living in the Background
Record Label: Capitol
Songwriters: Naimy Hackett, Maurizio Bassi

Italian novelty hit.

AFRIKA BAMBAATAA AND SOULSONIC FORCE
1982

PLANET ROCK
Producer: Arthur Baker
Album: Planet Rock—The Album
Record Label: Tommy Boy
Songwriters: Arthur Baker, Ellis Williams, John Miller, Bhambatta Aasim, Robert Allen, John Robie

A trailblazing Rap/Disco synthesis mixed by the future legend, Jellybean Benitez. Soon the mixer would be up there with the producer as the key song-shaper of the '90s.

1986

LOOKING FOR THE PERFECT BEAT
Producer: Arthur Baker
Album: Planet Rock—The Album
Record Label: Tommy Boy
Songwriters: Arthur Baker, John Robie

A mastery of sampling art—part computer, part deejay scratch.

BANANARAMA
1984

CRUEL SUMMER
Producers: Tony Swain, Steve Jolley
Album: Bananarama
Record Label: London
Songwriters: Tony Swain, Steve Jolley

An incessantly infectious summmertime U.K./U.S. Top-10 that established this droll British girlgroup as instant soul-sisters of the Go-Gos and the Bangles.

1987

I HEARD A RUMOUR
Producers: Mike Stock, Matt Aitken, Pete Waterman
Album: Wow
Record Label: London
Songwriters: Matt Aitken, Pete Waterman, Mike Stock, Sarah Dallin, Siobhan Fahey, Keren Woodward,

U.K. factory dance groove. Featured in the movie Disorderlies.

THE BAND
1968

ACROSS THE GREAT DIVIDE
Producers: John Simon, the Band
Album: The Band
Record Label: Capitol
Songwriter: Robbie Robertson

Bedrock Americana—the root of the coming Roots Rock movement.

CHEST FEVER
Producers: John Simon, the Band
Album: Music from Big Pink
Record Label: Capitol
Songwriter: Robbie Robertson

More organic rock.

I SHALL BE RELEASED
Producers: John Simon, the Band
Album: Music From Big Pink
Record Label: Capitol
Songwriter: Bob Dylan

Superior version of one of Dylan's most transcendent ballads, covered by the Box Tops (Mala, '69) and Joe Cocker (A&M, '69).

KING HARVEST (HAS SURELY COME)
Producers: John Simon, the Band
Album: The Band
Record Label: Capitol
Songwriter: Robbie Robertson

Suggested segue "Dancing in the Moonlight" by King Harvest.

THE NIGHT THEY DROVE OLD DIXIE DOWN
Producers: John Simon, the Band
Album: The Band
Record Label: Capitol
Songwriter: Robbie Robertson

Both Country covers by Don Rich & the Buckaroos (Capitol, '70) and Alice Creech (Target, '71) stiffed. The R&R (Yankee) version by Joan Baez (Vanguard, '71) was her biggest hit.

RAG, MAMA, RAG
Producers: John Simon, the Band
Album: The Band
Record Label: Capitol
Songwriter: Robbie Robertson

Cajun jug-band music.

TEARS OF RAGE
Producers: John Simon, the Band
Album: Music from Big Pink
Record Label: Capitol
Songwriters: Bob Dylan, Richard Manuel

A recovery ballad, co-written by one who did (Dylan), and one who didn't (Manuel).

THIS WHEEL'S ON FIRE
Producers: John Simon, the Band
Album: Music from Big Pink
Record Label: Capitol
Songwriter: Bob Dylan

An epic of coiled frustration, written during Dylan's post-Blonde-on-Blonde creative ferment at Big Pink, and performed by the house Band there in an album that could have been titled (or subtitled) The Basement Tapes, Volume II (or I, as the case may be). It was covered by the only other band as suited to interpreting Dylan's work—the Byrds (Columbia, '69).

TO KINGDOM COME
Producers: John Simon, the Band
Album: Music from Big Pink

Record Label: Capitol
Songwriter: Robbie Robertson

Paved the way for a back-to-the-soil revolution of the late '60s.

UP ON CRIPPLE CREEK
Producers: John Simon, the Band
Album: The Band
Record Label: Capitol
Songwriter: Robbie Robertson

Their biggest R&R hit on the charts. Under the calming influence of the Band, Bob Dylan would travel up that creek to Nashville, without a paddle.

THE WEIGHT
Producers: John Simon, the Band
Album: The Band
Record Label: Capitol
Songwriter: Robbie Robertson

Their most famous song. Covered by Aretha Franklin (Atlantic, '69). Used in the classic counter-culture film Easy Rider. *Has most recently shown up in a soda commercial.*

1970

THE SHAPE I'M IN
Producer: The Band
Album: Stage Fright
Record Label: Capitol
Songwriter: Robbie Robertson

A recovery from their Woodstock non-appearance.

STAGE FRIGHT
Producer: The Band
Album: Stage Fright
Record Label: Capitol
Songwriter: Robbie Robertson

Expounding upon the possible reason for it.

1971

LIFE IS A CARNIVAL
Producer: The Band
Album: Cahoots
Record Label: Capitol
Songwriters: Robbie Robertson, Levon Helm, Rick Danko

Prelude to the '80 Jodie Foster movie Carny, *which Robertson starred in and scored.*

1975

OPHELIA
Producer: The Band
Album: Northern Lights/Southern Cross

Record Label: Capitol
Songwriter: Robbie Robertson

The last waltz.

BAND-AID
1984

DO THEY KNOW IT'S CHRISTMAS?
Record Label: Columbia
Songwriters: Bob Geldof, Midge Ure

An all-star charity jam for Ethiopian relief that launched Geldof toward knighthood. This #1 U.K. single was the biggest seller in U.K. history, and hit Top-20 in the U.S. It led to the famous Live Aid concert, as well as a spate of Rock aid events. Covered in '89 on PWL by a new set of all-stars.

THE BANGLES
1984

GOIN' DOWN TO LIVERPOOL
Producer: David Kahne
Album: All over the Place
Record Label: Columbia
Songwriter: Kimberly Rew

A venture to the Liverpool home of their biggest influence—the Beatles. Covered by Rew's band, Katrina & the Waves (Capitol, '85).

JAMES
Producer: David Kahne
Album: All over the Place
Record Label: Columbia
Songwriter: Vicki Peterson

Beatle-esque harmonies, girl-group attitude, contemporary bite.

1986

IF SHE KNEW WHAT SHE WANTS
Producer: David Kahne
Album: Different Light
Record Label: Columbia
Songwriter: Jules Shear

This wise, witty, and complex soft album rocker stiffed as a single.

MANIC MONDAY
Producer: David Kahne
Album: Different Light
Record Label: Columbia
Songwriter: Prince Rogers Nelson

An irresistible rendezvous with the master of salacious Funk in the backyard of the Mamas & the Papas, and a trans-Atlantic #2 U.S./#2 U.K. crossover.

WALK LIKE AN EGYPTIAN
Producer: David Kahne
Album: Different Light
Record Label: Columbia
Songwriter: Liam Sternberg

The Paisley Underground of San Francisco meets the collegiate Funk of Athens, Georgia, as the Bangles temporarily out-kitsch the B-52's for their first #1. Later parodied as "Walk With an Erection."

WALKING DOWN YOUR STREET
Producer: David Kahne
Album: Different Light
Record Label: Columbia
Songwriters: Susannah Hoffs, Louis Gutierrez, David Kahne

1988

IN YOUR ROOM
Producer: Davitt Sigerson
Album: Everything
Record Label: Columbia
Songwriters: Billy Steinberg, Tom Kelly, Susannah Hoffs

As Patty Smyth had before her, another winsome waif succumbs to the starmaking machine, in a co-scripted, conscripted, deleterious fantasy package.

1989

ETERNAL FLAME
Producer: Davitt Sigerson
Album: Everything
Record Label: Columbia
Songwriters: Billy Steinberg, Tom Kelly, Susannah Hoffs

Susannah goes out on a corporate high note with a #1 U.S./#1 U.K smash. Later she'd be making movies directed by her mother.

BESSIE BANKS
1963

GO NOW
Producers: Jerry Leiber, Mike Stoller
Record Label: Red Bird
Songwriters: Larry Banks, Milton Bennett

R&B tune covered by the Moody Blues (London, '65), whose future work would be nothing like this.

THE BAR-KAYS
1984

FREAKSHOW ON THE DANCEFLOOR
Producer: Allen A. Jones
Album: Dangerous
Record Label: Mercury
Songwriters: James Alexander, Michael Beard, Mark Bynum, Larry Dodson, Harvey Henderson, Lloyd Smith, Winston Stewart, Frank Thompson, Allen A. Jones

Disco redux.

THE BARBARIANS
1965

ARE YOU A BOY OR ARE YOU A GIRL?
Producer: Robert Schwartz
Album: Are You a Boy or Are You a Girl
Record Label: Laurie
Songwriters: Doug Morris, Elliot Greenberg, Barbara Baer, Robert Schwartz

A classic Garage-Band-era, working-class protest that appeared when long hair on men was strictly a middle-class fad.

1966

MOULTY
Producer: Robert Schwartz
Record Label: Laurie
Songwriters: Doug Morris, Elliot Greenberg, Barbara Baer, Robert Schwartz

The ultimate Frat Punk tragicomedy of a one-armed drummer and his desire to play. Life would imitate art-imitating-life again, when something similar happened to the drummer in Def Leppard.

THE BARBUSTERS
1987

LIGHT OF DAY
Producer: Jimmy Iovine
Album: *Light of Day* Soundtrack
Record Label: Blackheart
Songwriter: Bruce Springsteen

A Rock band grows in Cleveland, courtesy of a New Jersey bard and a Philadelphia babe, Joan Jett.

BOBBY BARE
1963

500 MILES AWAY FROM HOME
Producer: Chet Atkins
Album: 500 Miles Away from Home
Record Label: RCA
Songwriters: Bobby Bare, Charlie Williams, Hedy West

His second Countrypolitan hit with Folk roots.

DETROIT CITY
Producer: Chet Atkins
Album: Detroit City and Other Hits by Bobby Bare
Record Label: RCA
Songwriter: Bobby Bare

Introducing the Countrypolitan Sound—a natural outgrowth of the Everly Brothers' trip to the Brill Building. Soon Nashville would be awash in strings, and staff songwriters there would have their own cafes.

BARENAKED LADIES
1992

BE MY YOKO ONO
Producers: Scott Dibbie, Barenaked Ladies
Album: Gordon
Record Label: Sire
Songwriters: Stephen Page, Ed Robertson

Canadian Folk Rock mythologizing.

BRIAN WILSON
Producer: Michael Philip-Wojewoda
Album: Gordon
Record Label: Sire
Songwriter: Stephen Page

Satirizing the deleterious effects of hero worship.

SYD BARRETT
1974

TERRAPIN
Producer: Malcolm Jones
Album: The Madcap Laughs/Syd Barrett
Record Label: Harvest
Songwriter: Syd Barrett

Pink Floyd co-founder-cum-acid-casualty becomes the psychedelic Metal answer to Jonathan Richman.

LEN BARRY
1965

ONE, TWO, THREE (1-2-3)
Producer: Leon Huff
Album: 1-2-3
Record Label: Decca
Songwriters: John Madara, David White, Leonard Borisoff

Good-time, blue-eyed Soul.

ROB BASE AND DJ E-Z ROCK
1988

IT TAKES TWO
Producers: Rob Base, William Hamilton
Album: It Takes Two
Record Label: Profile
Songwriter: Rob Base

Moving Hip-Hop several hops toward its eventual mainstream takeover, this track was named as the #1 single of all time by Spin magazine. Suggested segue: "It Takes Two" by Marvin Gaye and Kim Weston (Motown, '68).

BASEHEAD
1992

PLAY WITH TOYS
Album: Plays with Toys
Record Label: Imago
Songwriter: Michael Ivey

Moody Hip-Hop/Rap fusion.

TONI BASIL
1982

MICKEY
Producers: Greg Mathieson, Trevor Veitch
Album: Word of Mouth
Record Label: Chrysalis
Songwriters: Mike Chapman, Nicky Chinn

Female football Pop Rock anthem for the noted choreographer of the pioneering '60s TV rock and roll show "Shindig"). Originated in England as "Kitty" by the Chapman and Chinn group Racey in '79.

FONTELLA BASS
1965

RESCUE ME
Album: The 'New' Look
Record Label: Checker

Songwriters: Carl William Smith,
Raymond Miner
#1 R&B/Top-10 R&R crossover.

BAUHAUS

1979

BELA LUGOSI'S DEAD

Record Label: Small Wonder (U.K.)
Songwriter: Bauhaus

Debut single for the progenitors of Gothic Rock (David J., Kevin Haskins, and Daniel Ash would move on to Love and Rockets) and future stalwarts of the clinical-depressive market. The Jam, the Cure, New Order, the Jesus and Mary Chain, and the Smiths would mine the turf.

1981

KICK IN THE EYE

Album: The Mask
Record Label: Beggar's Banquet
Songwriter: Bauhaus

Their first U.K. Alternative hit.

THE BAY CITY ROLLERS

1975

MONEY HONEY

Producers: Phil Coulter, William
MacPherson
Album: Rock and Roll Love Letter
Record Label: Arista
Songwriters: Eric Faulkner, Stuart
Woods

In the shank of rollermania, their eighth U.K. hit became their second U.S. Top-10.

ROCK AND ROLL LOVE LETTER

Producers: Phil Coulter, William
MacPherson
Album: Rock and Roll Love Letter
Record Label: Arista
Songwriter: Timothy Moore

These Beatles clones tap out their adieu.

SATURDAY NIGHT

Producers: Phil Coulter, William
MacPherson
Album: Rock and Roll Love Letter
Record Label: Arista
Songwriters: Phil Coulter, William
MacPherson

This '73 U.K. flop went straight to #1 in the U.S. after auspiciously kicking off Howard Cosell's "Saturday Night" TV variety show, which subsequently went straight into the dumper. Revived in Mike Myers' heavily

Scots-flavored soundtrack to So I Married an Axe Murderer, in '93.

THE BEACH BOYS

1961

SURFIN'

Producer: Hite Morgan
Album: Surfin' Safari
Record Label: X/Candix
Songwriter: Brian Wilson

Mixing the urban soul of white doo-wop and the white-bucked suburban Pop of the Four Freshmen with the sound of the surf, the Beach Boys officially opened the gates to Rock and Roll's new frontier—the teen dream of California in the '60s.

1962

409

Producer: Nik Venet
Album: Surfin' Safari
Record Label: Capitol
Songwriters: Brian Wilson, Gary
Usher

The B-side of "Surfin' Safari" and the Beach Boys' first major label classic car song hit—classic car: the 409 Chevy. The stereo version was produced by Brian Wilson and included on Little Deuce Coupe *(Capitol, '62).*

SURFIN' SAFARI

Producer: Nik Venet
Album: Surfin' Safari
Record Label: Capitol
Songwriters: Brian Wilson, Mike
Love

Offering a West-Coast Brill Building pop alternative: dancing on the waves.

1963

BE TRUE TO YOUR SCHOOL

Producer: Brian Wilson
Album: Little Deuce Coupe
Record Label: Capitol
Songwriter: Brian Wilson

Branching out from the beach, this single contains a bit of "On Wisconsin."

FARMER'S DAUGHTER

Producer: Nik Venet
Album: Surfin' USA
Record Label: Capitol
Songwriter: Brian Wilson

Covered by Fleetwood Mac (Reprise, '81): Lindsay Buckingham was a big Beach Boys fan.

IN MY ROOM

Producer: Brian Wilson
Album: Surfer Girl
Record Label: Capitol
Songwriters: Brian Wilson, Gary
Usher

B-side of "Be True to Your School." Maureen Love on harp.

SHUT DOWN

Producer: Brian Wilson
Album: Shut Down
Record Label: Capitol
Songwriters: Brian Wilson, Roger
Christian

Nod to the hot rod market.

SURFER GIRL

Producer: Brian Wilson
Album: Surfer Girl
Record Label: Capitol
Songwriter: Brian Wilson

The Four Freshmen meet Walt Disney at Muscle Beach. The first song Brian ever wrote.

SURFIN' USA

Producer: Nik Venet
Album: Surfin' USA
Record Label: Capitol
Songwriters: Brian Wilson, Chuck
Berry

Revisiting the original R&R icon—"Sweet Little Sixteen." Later listing notices would give Berry the full credit he deserved, though the Beach Boys had done their part as well in resurrecting his career (along with, of course, all those British invasion acts).

1964

ALL SUMMER LONG

Producer: Brian Wilson
Album: All Summer Long
Record Label: Capitol
Songwriter: Brian Wilson

Beach music in its original form.

CALIFORNIA GIRLS

Producer: Brian Wilson
Album: Shutdown (Vol. II)
Record Label: Capitol
Songwriter: Brian Wilson

Their ultimate picture postcard. Covered by the ultimate California man, David Lee Roth (Warner Brothers, '85).

DANCE, DANCE, DANCE

Producer: Brian Wilson
Album: Beach Boys Today
Record Label: Capitol
Songwriters: Brian Wilson, Dennis Wilson

The Beach Boys bring their surfing act to dry land. Brian could dance as well as he surfed.

DON'T WORRY BABY

Producer: Brian Wilson
Album: Shut Down (Vol. II)
Record Label: Capitol
Songwriters: Brian Wilson, Roger Christian

This B-side of their biggest hit, "I Get Around," has aged more gracefully than most of their rock and roll fantasies. Covered by the Beach Boys and the Everly Brothers in the '89 movie, Tequila Sunrise.

FUN FUN FUN

Producer: Brian Wilson
Album: Shut Down (Vol. II)
Record Label: Capitol
Songwriters: Brian Wilson, Mike Love

Car classic—classic car: the T-Bird. Released a week after the Beatles arrived in the U.S.

I GET AROUND

Producer: Brian Wilson
Album: All Summer Long
Record Label: Capitol
Songwriter: Brian Wilson

Their biggest all-time hit and first #1. Even Mick Jagger liked it.

THE WARMTH OF THE SUN

Producer: Brian Wilson
Album: Shut Down (Vol. II)
Record Label: Capitol
Songwriters: Brian Wilson, Mike Love

Written a few hours after John F. Kennedy was assassinated.

WENDY

Producer: Brian Wilson
Album: All Summer Long
Record Label: Capitol
Songwriter: Brian Wilson

Originally in the EP Four by the Beach Boys along with "Little Honda." Covered by the Hondells (Mercury, '64).

WHEN I GROW UP TO BE A MAN

Producer: Brian Wilson
Album: Beach Boys Today
Record Label: Capitol
Songwriters: Brian Wilson, Roger Christian

The B-side of "Dance, Dance, Dance." Suggested segue: "Sugar Mountain" by Neil Young.

1965

HELP ME, RHONDA

Producer: Brian Wilson
Album: Beach Boys Today
Record Label: Capitol
Songwriter: Brian Wilson

Their second #1.

PLEASE LET ME WONDER

Producer: Brian Wilson
Album: Beach Boys Today
Record Label: Capitol
Songwriters: Brian Wilson, Mike Love

The B-side of "Help Me, Rhonda."

1966

CAROLINE, NO

Producer: Brian Wilson
Album: Pet Sounds
Record Label: Capitol
Songwriters: Brian Wilson, Tony Asher

Beautiful and anguished, like its composer, who, years later in an interview, suggested that his intended title was "Carol I Know."

GOD ONLY KNOWS

Producer: Brian Wilson
Album: Pet Sounds
Record Label: Capitol
Songwriters: Brian Wilson, Tony Asher

Reported to be Paul McCartney's favorite song, which inspired Brian to go head-to-head with the Beatles in a creative/ego battle he could never win or recover from.

GOOD VIBRATIONS

Producer: Brian Wilson
Album: Smiley Smile
Record Label: Capitol
Songwriters: Brian Wilson, Mike Love

Years in the making and yet eerily at one with the times, this would be Brian's last #1 with the Beach Boys and the best rock and roll moment for the theramin, aside from the career of Lothar & the Hand People.

I JUST WASN'T MADE FOR THESE TIMES

Producer: Brian Wilson
Album: Pet Sounds
Record Label: Capitol
Songwriter: Brian Wilson

Brian succumbs to a general and generational malaise. Revived as the title of a '95 documentary on his life.

WOULDN'T IT BE NICE

Producer: Brian Wilson
Album: Pet Sounds
Record Label: Capitol
Songwriters: Brian Wilson, Tony Asher

Brian visits Fantasyland. Used in the '75 film Shampoo.

1967

DARLIN'

Producer: The Beach Boys
Album: 20/20
Record Label: Capitol
Songwriters: Brian Wilson, Mike Love

HEROES AND VILLAINS

Producers: Brian Wilson, Van Dyke Parks
Album: Smiley Smile
Record Label: Brother
Songwriters: Brian Wilson, Van Dyke Parks

Beginning to sense he "just wasn't made for these times," Brian found a soul brother to collaborate with on an all-time epic that was never completed.

1968

DO IT AGAIN

Producer: Brian Wilson
Album: 20/20
Record Label: Capitol
Songwriters: Brian Wilson, Mike Love

Re-recorded by Brian and his daughter Carnie for the documentary I Just Wasn't Made for These Times, and its soundtrack album (MCA, '95).

1970

ADD SOME MUSIC TO YOUR DAY

Producer: Brian Wilson
Album: Sunflower
Record Label: Reprise
Songwriters: Brian Wilson, Mike Love, Joe Knott

In the autumn of their career.

1973

CALIFORNIA SAGA (BIG SUR)
Producer: Brian Wilson
Album: Holland
Record Label: Brother
Songwriter: Mike Love

A Brian-less opus.

SAIL ON SAILOR
Producer: Brian Wilson
Album: Holland
Record Label: Brother
Songwriters: Jack Rieley, Ray Kennedy, Brian Wilson, Tandyn Almer

Off the surfboard and onto the yacht.

1988

KOKOMO
Producer: Terry Melcher
Album: *Cocktail* Soundtrack
Record Label: Elektra
Songwriters: Mike Love, Terry Melcher, John Phillips, Scott Mackenzie

Catching one last perfect wave; revisiting #1 for the first time in over 20 years with another sailing yarn.

EDWARD BEAR

1973

LAST SONG
Producer: Gene Martynec
Album: Edward Bear
Record Label: Capitol
Songwriter: Lawrence Wayne Evoy

Folk/rock.

THE BEASTIE BOYS

1986

(YOU GOTTA) FIGHT FOR YOUR RIGHT TO PARTY
Producer: Rick Rubin
Album: Licensed to Ill
Record Label: Def Jam
Songwriters: Adam Horovitz, Adam Yauch, Michael Diamond, Rick Rubin

White Hip-Hop anthem for rebellious youth who wanted to act black.

BRASS MONKEY
Producer: Rick Rubin
Album: Licensed to Ill
Record Label: Def Jam
Songwriters: The Beastie Boys, Rick Rubin

From the album that established the Beastie Boys as the complete Beatles-meets-Sha-Na-Na of the post-Punk/post-Rap era.

NO SLEEP TILL BROOKLYN
Producer: Rick Rubin
Album: Licensed to Ill
Record Label: Def Jam
Songwriters: The Beastie Boys, Rick Rubin

Establishing Brooklyn as the center of Rap America. In L.A., Compton would be the left of center.

1989

HEY LADIES
Producer: Dust Brothers
Album: Paul's Boutique
Record Label: Capitol
Songwriters: Adam Horovitz, Adam Yauch, Michael Diamond, the Dust Brothers

No longer new kids in Rap's bad neighborhood.

1992

PASS THE MIC
Producer: Mario Caldato Jr.
Album: Check Your Head
Record Label: Capitol
Songwriters: The Beastie Boys, Mario Caldato Jr.

A mild return to form.

SO WHAT'CHA WANT
Producer: Mario Caldato Jr.
Album: Check Your Head
Record Label: Capitol
Songwriter: The Beastie Boys

BEAT HAPPENING

1988

INDIAN SUMMER
Producers: Mark Lanegan, Gary Lee Connor
Album: Jamboree
Record Label: K/Sub Pop
Songwriter: Beat Happening

A Jonathan-Richman-influenced, Velvet Underground-tempered drone. Covered by the obscure underground bands Luna and Spectrum.

THE BEATLES

1963

DO YOU WANT TO KNOW A SECRET
Producer: George Martin
Album: Introducing the Beatles
Record Label: Vee Jay
Songwriters: John Lennon, Paul McCartney

A hit in England for Billy J. Kramer & the Dakotas (Parlaphone, '63), which they later sang in the '74 movie Stardust. The Beatles' '64 U.S. version was George's biggest vocal hit. Suggested segue: "I Really Love You" by the Stereos.

FROM ME TO YOU
Producer: George Martin
Album: Jolly What! The Beatles and Frank Ifield
Record Label: Vee Jay
Songwriters: John Lennon, Paul McCartney

England's top song of '63. Del Shannon (Big Top, '63) was the first American to cover a Beatle tune. It stiffed at lucky #77. Re-released as the B-side of "Please Please Me" (Vee-Jay, '64).

I SAW HER STANDING THERE
Producer: George Martin
Album: Meet the Beatles
Record Label: Capitol
Songwriters: John Lennon, Paul McCartney

The B-side of "I Wanna Hold Your Hand." Covered by Tiffany (MCA, '88).

I WANNA HOLD YOUR HAND
Producer: George Martin
Album: Meet the Beatles
Record Label: Capitol
Songwriters: John Lennon, Paul McCartney

#1 in the U.K., December '63, and first #1 in the U.S. (Capitol, '64).

I'LL GET YOU
Producer: George Martin
Album: The Beatles Second Album
Record Label: Capitol
Songwriters: John Lennon, Paul McCartney

The B-side of "She Loves You."

LOVE ME DO
Producer: George Martin
Album: Introducing the Beatles

Record Label: Vee Jay
Songwriters: John Lennon, Paul McCartney

From the album that stiffed when it was released in July in the U.S. (recorded with "(P.S.) I Love You" at their first recording session in '62), this was one of the many undeniable singles rescued in the wake of '64. Recycling Brill Building and Motown sounds with a Little-Richard-esque vengeance and an Everly-Brothers-esque harmony, they went on to display Chuck Berry-esque verbal wit and acuity, in a tight Buddy-Holly-and-the-Crickets-esque Rock and Roll combo setting. A couple of years later John Lennon would become infatuated with Bob Dylan. A couple of years after that, they would take up with the Mahareeshi. And there you have the '60s.

PLEASE PLEASE ME

Producer: George Martin
Album: Introducing the Beatles
Record Label: Vee Jay
Songwriters: John Lennon, Paul McCartney

Their first hit in England, a year before their ultimate crossover to the U.S.

(P.S.) I LOVE YOU

Producer: George Martin
Album: Introducing the Beatles
Record Label: Vee Jay
Songwriters: John Lennon, Paul McCartney

The B-side of "Love Me Do," recorded at their first session in '62.

SHE LOVES YOU

Producer: George Martin
Album: The Beatles Second Album
Record Label: Swan/Capitol
Songwriters: John Lennon, Paul McCartney

The third of their four #1 U.K. singles in '63, and #1 in the U.S. in '64, by which time a new American teenage market had come out of the woodwork, soon to be followed by a horde of homegrown Rock bands (first from England, and then out of every other hinterland's garage, rec room, and cellar).

THANK YOU GIRL

Producer: George Martin
Album: Jolly What! the Beatles and Frank Ifield
Record Label: Vee Jay
Songwriters: John Lennon, Paul McCartney

The B-side of the original release of "From Me to You."

THERE'S A PLACE

Producer: George Martin
Album: Introducing the Beatles
Record Label: Vee Jay
Songwriters: John Lennon, Paul McCartney

Pristine ballad from the '63 LP that also contains "Twist and Shout."

1964

ALL MY LOVING

Producer: George Martin
Album: Meet the Beatles
Record Label: Capitol
Songwriters: John Lennon, Paul McCartney

Featured in their groundbreaking, image-making docu-farce, A Hard Day's Night.

AND I LOVE HER

Producer: George Martin
Album: A Hard Day's Night
Record Label: Capitol
Songwriters: John Lennon, Paul McCartney

Pure McCartney ballad formula that would age but never change. Sung in A Hard Day's Night.

ANY TIME AT ALL

Producer: George Martin
Album: A Hard Day's Night
Record Label: Capitol
Songwriters: John Lennon, Paul McCartney

Patented rocker.

CAN'T BUY ME LOVE

Producer: George Martin
Album: A Hard Day's Night
Record Label: Capitol
Songwriters: John Lennon, Paul McCartney

The third of their six #1 singles of '64 from A Hard Day's Night.

DON'T BOTHER ME

Producer: George Martin
Album: Meet the Beatles
Record Label: Capitol
Songwriter: George Harrison

The quiet Beatle finally gets a copyright all his own. Note how even the title suggests how the reclusive George would develop in the future.

A HARD DAY'S NIGHT

Producer: George Martin
Album: A Hard Days Night
Record Label: United Artists
Songwriters: John Lennon, Paul McCartney

Title song from the movie that established the Beatles as worthy of attention from the cynical Folk-Rock-leaning/Jean-Luc-Godard-enthralled intelligentsia.

I FEEL FINE

Producer: George Martin
Album: Beatles '65
Record Label: Capitol
Songwriters: John Lennon, Paul McCartney

Their sixth and last #1 of '64.

I SHOULD HAVE KNOWN BETTER

Producer: George Martin
Album: A Hard Day's Night
Record Label: United Artists
Songwriters: John Lennon, Paul McCartney

Found on the B-side of "A Hard Day's Night" and in the film.

I'LL CRY INSTEAD

Producer: George Martin
Album: A Hard Day's Night
Record Label: United Artists
Songwriters: John Lennon, Paul McCartney

On the album, but not in the original movie. Inserted in a later version of the film (1982). Covered by Joe Cocker (Decca, '64) as his first single release in the U.K.

I'M HAPPY JUST TO DANCE WITH YOU

Producer: George Martin
Album: A Hard Day's Night
Record Label: United Artists
Songwriters: John Lennon, Paul McCartney

The B-side of "I Should Have Known Better."

IF I FELL

Producer: George Martin
Album: A Hard Day's Night
Record Label: United Artists
Songwriters: John Lennon, Paul McCartney

The B-side of "And I Love Her."

IT WON'T BE LONG

Producer: George Martin
Album: Meet the Beatles

Record Label: Capitol
Songwriters: John Lennon, Paul McCartney

Album rocker.

SHE'S A WOMAN

Producer: George Martin
Album: Beatles '65
Record Label: Capitol
Songwriters: John Lennon, Paul McCartney

This B-side of "I Feel Fine" was their nod to and approval of the girl-group mentality of the early '60s.

TELL ME WHY

Producer: George Martin
Album: A Hard Day's Night
Record Label: United Artists
Songwriters: John Lennon, Paul McCartney

THINGS WE SAID TODAY

Producer: George Martin
Album: Something New
Record Label: Capitol
Songwriters: John Lennon, Paul McCartney

One of their finest melodies. Preponderance of album cuts such as this—on a format usually tailor-made for throwaways—precipitated the advent of FM radio (so they could play non-single releases) and the album market (so people could buy them). This soon gave rise to album artists—with the Beatles first and foremost in the Rock and Roll arena—who thought of the album as the primary artistic creation rather than a collection of singles. Concept albums, twenty-minute songs, long jams, psychedelic mind excursions, and FM radio stations that would play them all were just around the bend.

THIS BOY (RINGO'S THEME)

Producer: George Martin
Album: A Hard Day's Night
Record Label: United Artists
Songwriters: John Lennon, Paul McCartney

The B-side of "All My Lovin," included in A Hard Day's Night during the Ringo showcase sequence, from which all of his subsequent commercial endorsement sprang.

YOU CAN'T DO THAT

Producer: George Martin
Album: The Beatles' Second Album
Record Label: Capitol

Songwriters: John Lennon, Paul McCartney

Album rocker.

1965

ANOTHER GIRL

Producer: George Martin
Album: Help!
Record Label: Capitol
Songwriters: John Lennon, Paul McCartney

From their second movie, this was a neo-psychedelic stiff.

BABY'S IN BLACK

Producer: George Martin
Album: Beatles '65
Record Label: Capitol
Songwriters: John Lennon, Paul McCartney

DAY TRIPPER

Producer: George Martin
Album: Yesterday and Today
Record Label: Capitol
Songwriters: John Lennon, Paul McCartney

The B-side of "We Can Work It Out." In their own optimistic way, the Beatles were slowly turning on their Berry-esque powers of observation.

DRIVE MY CAR

Producer: George Martin
Album: Yesterday and Today
Record Label: Capitol
Songwriters: John Lennon, Paul McCartney

Classic car song—classic car: probably a Bentley.

EIGHT DAYS A WEEK

Producer: George Martin
Album: Beatles VI
Record Label: Capitol
Songwriters: John Lennon, Paul McCartney

EVERY LITTLE THING

Producer: George Martin
Album: Beatles VI
Record Label: Capitol
Songwriters: John Lennon, Paul McCartney

GIRL

Producer: George Martin
Album: Rubber Soul
Record Label: Capitol

Songwriters: John Lennon, Paul McCartney

Expanding into new terrains of complexity.

HELP!

Producer: George Martin
Album: Help!
Record Label: Capitol
Songwriters: John Lennon, Paul McCartney

Movie theme song in which Lennon begins expressing some previously unexpressible angst. Suggested segue: "Problems" by the Everly Brothers.

I DON'T WANT TO SPOIL THE PARTY

Producer: George Martin
Album: Beatles VI
Record Label: Capitol
Songwriters: John Lennon, Paul McCartney

In a rare somber mood. Covered by Rosanne Cash (Columbia, '89).

I NEED YOU

Producer: George Martin
Album: Help!
Record Label: Capitol
Songwriter: George Harrison

George admits the possibility of sustaining a relationship.

I'LL FOLLOW THE SUN

Producer: George Martin
Album: Beatles '65
Record Label: Capitol
Songwriters: John Lennon, Paul McCartney

Peter-and-Gordon-esque Folk Rock.

I'M A LOSER

Producer: George Martin
Album: Beatles '65
Record Label: Capitol
Songwriters: John Lennon, Paul McCartney

John goes back to the couch, foretelling more agonized confessions to come.

I'M LOOKING THROUGH YOU

Producer: George Martin
Album: Rubber Soul
Record Label: Capitol
Songwriters: John Lennon, Paul McCartney

Having passed through the doors of perception, there was no turning back to the days of wide-eyed Brill Building innocence.

I'VE JUST SEEN A FACE
Producer: George Martin
Album: Rubber Soul
Record Label: Capitol
Songwriters: John Lennon, Paul McCartney

Irresistible album rocker.

IF I NEEDED SOMEONE
Producer: George Martin
Album: Yesterday and Today
Record Label: Capitol
Songwriter: George Harrison

IN MY LIFE
Producer: George Martin
Album: Rubber Soul
Record Label: Capitol
Songwriters: John Lennon, Paul McCartney

A Lennon art film. One of his best. Covered by Judy Collins (Elektra, '67).

IT'S ONLY LOVE
Producer: George Martin
Album: Rubber Soul
Record Label: Capitol
Songwriters: John Lennon, Paul McCartney

Looking at their favorite subject from a 90-degree angle, probably provided by John.

MICHELLE
Producer: George Martin
Album: Rubber Soul
Record Label: Capitol
Songwriters: John Lennon, Paul McCartney

A McCartney lullabye, with French subtitles.

THE NIGHT BEFORE
Producer: George Martin
Album: Help!
Record Label: Capitol
Songwriters: John Lennon, Paul McCartney

Rocker from the film Help!

NORWEGIAN WOOD (THIS BIRD HAS FLOWN)
Producer: George Martin
Album: Rubber Soul
Record Label: Capitol
Songwriters: John Lennon, Paul McCartney

Lennon's coming-of-age song. The sitar joins the autoharp as prime '60s stringed alternatives to the guitar.

NOWHERE MAN
Producer: George Martin
Album: Yesterday and Today
Record Label: Capitol
Songwriters: John Lennon, Paul McCartney

Venturing into Kinksian social satire.

RUN FOR YOUR LIFE
Producer: George Martin
Album: Rubber Soul
Record Label: Capitol
Songwriters: John Lennon, Paul McCartney

The natural follow-up to "Help!"

THINK FOR YOURSELF
Producer: George Martin
Album: Rubber Soul
Record Label: Capitol
Songwriter: George Harrison

Stentorian George at the podium undermining any further chances for a relationship.

TICKET TO RIDE
Producer: George Martin
Album: Help!
Record Label: Capitol
Songwriters: John Lennon, Paul McCartney

Or, as latter day Beatleologists suggest, was the title referring to the English red light town of Rye? The cover by the Carpenters (A&M, '70) was their debut single.

WE CAN WORK IT OUT
Producer: George Martin
Album: Yesterday and Today
Record Label: Capitol
Songwriters: John Lennon, Paul McCartney

Closing out '65 on a more hopeful note than much of the year's and their own output. Covered by Stevie Wonder (Tamla, '70).

THE WORD
Producer: George Martin
Album: Rubber Soul
Record Label: Capitol
Songwriters: John Lennon, Paul McCartney

The Mahareeshi was listening.

YES IT IS
Producer: George Martin
Album: Beatles VI
Record Label: Capitol
Songwriters: John Lennon, Paul McCartney

The B-side of "Ticket to Ride."

YESTERDAY
Producer: George Martin
Album: Yesterday and Today
Record Label: Capitol
Songwriters: John Lennon, Paul McCartney

Blinking in the face of an uncertain future, this is their most covered classic, virtually all of them superfluous.

YOU WON'T SEE ME
Producer: George Martin
Album: Rubber Soul
Record Label: Capitol
Songwriters: John Lennon, Paul McCartney

YOU'RE GONNA LOSE THAT GIRL
Producer: George Martin
Album: Help!
Record Label: Capitol
Songwriters: John Lennon, Paul McCartney

Another winning rocker from the movie. Comparing the Beatles' movie songs to Elvis's movie songs might be an interesting endeavor, if the Beatles had made upwards of 30 movies, or if all of Elvis' movie songs were written by Leiber and Stoller.

YOU'VE GOT TO HIDE YOUR LOVE AWAY
Producer: George Martin
Album: Help!
Record Label: Capitol
Songwriters: John Lennon, Paul McCartney

Turning 180 degrees away from their favorite topic. Covered by the Silkie (Fontana, '65) on a hit single produced by Lennon and McCartney.

1966

ELEANOR RIGBY
Producer: George Martin
Album: Revolver
Record Label: Capitol
Songwriters: John Lennon, Paul McCartney

A love song of a more humanitarian sort—to "all the lonely people." Covered by Ray Charles (ABC/Paramount, '68) and Aretha Franklin (Atlantic, '69).

FOR NO ONE
Producer: George Martin
Album: Revolver

Record Label: Capitol
Songwriters: John Lennon, Paul McCartney

One of their most melancholy gems.

GOOD DAY SUNSHINE

Producer: George Martin
Album: Revolver
Record Label: Capitol
Songwriters: John Lennon, Paul McCartney

The antidote to "For No One."

GOT TO GET YOU INTO MY LIFE

Producer: George Martin
Album: Revolver
Record Label: Capitol
Songwriters: John Lennon, Paul McCartney

HERE, THERE AND EVERYWHERE

Producer: George Martin
Album: Revolver
Record Label: Capitol
Songwriters: John Lennon, Paul McCartney

One of their most captivating melodies. Covered by Emmylou Harris (Reprise, '76) and George Benson (Warner Brothers, '89).

I WANT TO TELL YOU

Producer: George Martin
Album: Revolver
Record Label: Capitol
Songwriter: George Harrison

Enough of George.

PAPERBACK WRITER

Producer: George Martin
Album: Hey Jude
Record Label: Capitol
Songwriters: John Lennon, Paul McCartney

More Kinks-style pop sociology.

RAIN

Producer: George Martin
Album: Hey Jude
Record Label: Capitol
Songwriters: John Lennon, Paul McCartney

TAXMAN

Producer: George Martin
Album: Revolver
Record Label: Capitol
Songwriter: George Harrison

George at his most intense.

TOMORROW NEVER KNOWS

Producer: George Martin
Album: Revolver
Record Label: Capitol
Songwriters: John Lennon, Paul McCartney

Into the sitar-based void.

YELLOW SUBMARINE

Producer: George Martin
Album: Yellow Submarine
Record Label: Capitol
Songwriters: John Lennon, Paul McCartney

Future Saturday morning cartoon.

1967

ALL YOU NEED IS LOVE

Producer: George Martin
Album: Magical Mystery Tour
Record Label: Capitol
Songwriters: John Lennon, Paul McCartney

Opening with the strains of the French National Anthem, this best-selling credo of '68 stood in blissful opposition to the many ringing declamations of the counterculture, of which the Beatles were de-facto titular heads. Featured in the last episode of the cult TV classic "The Prisoner."

BABY, YOU'RE A RICH MAN

Producer: George Martin
Album: Magical Mystery Tour
Record Label: Capitol
Songwriters: John Lennon, Paul McCartney

The B-side of "All You Need Is Love," written for their manager, Brian Epstein.

BEING FOR THE BENEFIT OF MR. KITE

Producer: George Martin
Album: Sgt. Pepper's Lonely Hearts Club Band
Record Label: Capitol
Songwriters: John Lennon, Paul McCartney

From the concept album to begin all concept albums.

BLUE JAY WAY

Producer: George Martin
Album: Magical Mystery Tour
Record Label: Capitol
Songwriter: George Harrison

Entering Mr. Harrison's quasi-spiritual neighborhood.

A DAY IN THE LIFE

Producer: George Martin
Album: Sgt. Pepper's Lonely Hearts Club Band
Record Label: Capitol
Songwriters: John Lennon, Paul McCartney

Their major existential statement: the beckoning void of its final endless note closes the album and opens a new era in album Rock.

FIXING A HOLE

Producer: George Martin
Album: Sgt. Pepper's Lonely Hearts Club Band
Record Label: Capitol
Songwriters: John Lennon, Paul McCartney

Fixing their relationship.

THE FOOL ON THE HILL

Producer: George Martin
Album: Magical Mystery Tour
Record Label: Capitol
Songwriters: John Lennon, Paul McCartney

Indian pop philosophy. Covered by Sergio Mendes and Brazil 66 (A&M, '68).

GETTING BETTER

Producer: George Martin
Album: Sgt. Pepper's Lonely Hearts Club Band
Record Label: Capitol
Songwriters: John Lennon, Paul McCartney

A rebound from the unpleasantness of their Revolver era, packed with plenty of optimistic homilies.

GOOD MORNING, GOOD MORNING

Producer: George Martin
Album: Sgt. Pepper's Lonely Hearts Club Band
Record Label: Capitol
Songwriters: John Lennon, Paul McCartney

As cheery as "A Day in the Life" was dour.

HELLO, GOODBYE

Producer: George Martin
Album: Magical Mystery Tour
Record Label: Capitol
Songwriters: John Lennon, Paul McCartney

Closing out '67 with their third straight #1. Although this was their fifteenth #1 single, it was only their fifth since '65: beginning in

'66, the Beatles were content to limit their AM output (ie, they didn't release any singles from Sgt. Pepper's). and devote most of their time to the newly minted FM radio, which proved much more able to air the bulk of their album cuts.

I AM THE WALRUS
Producer: George Martin
Album: Magical Mystery Tour
Record Label: Capitol
Songwriters: John Lennon, Paul McCartney

John's most literary affectation and the B-side of "Hello, Goodbye."

LOVELY RITA
Producer: George Martin
Album: Sgt. Pepper's Lonely Hearts Club Band
Record Label: Capitol
Songwriters: John Lennon, Paul McCartney

Portrayal of one of their more obscure characters: Rita the meter maid.

LUCY IN THE SKY WITH DIAMONDS
Producer: George Martin
Album: Sgt. Pepper's Lonely Hearts Club Band
Record Label: Capitol
Songwriters: John Lennon, Paul McCartney

Considered a thinly-veiled celebration of LSD-inspired imagery by everyone but its writer, John Lennon, it was never released as a single by the Beatles. Cover by Elton John (Rocket, '75), went to #1.

MAGICAL MYSTERY TOUR
Producer: George Martin
Album: Magical Mystery Tour
Record Label: Capitol
Songwriters: John Lennon, Paul McCartney

Title tune to the album and TV special.

PENNY LANE
Producer: George Martin
Album: Magical Mystery Tour
Record Label: Capitol
Songwriters: John Lennon, Paul McCartney

An ethereal and compelling vision, complete with a string of classical trumpets.

SGT. PEPPER'S LONELY HEARTS CLUB BAND
Producer: George Martin
Album: Sgt. Pepper's Lonely Hearts Club Band

Record Label: Capitol
Songwriters: John Lennon, Paul McCartney

The title tune from their legendary concept album, reportedly inspired by the Who's mini opera, "A Quick One."

SHE'S LEAVING HOME
Producer: George Martin
Album: Sgt. Pepper's Lonely Hearts Club Band
Record Label: Capitol
Songwriters: John Lennon, Paul McCartney

"Sweet Little Sixteen" meets the '60s.

STRAWBERRY FIELDS FOREVER
Producer: George Martin
Album: Magical Mystery Tour
Record Label: Capitol
Songwriters: John Lennon, Paul McCartney

The B-side of "Penny Lane." Lennon's enduring epitaph.

WHEN I'M SIXTY-FOUR
Producer: George Martin
Album: Sgt. Pepper's Lonely Hearts Club Band
Record Label: Capitol
Songwriters: John Lennon, Paul McCartney

Amiable McCartney predicts his friendly fate.

WITH A LITTLE HELP FROM MY FRIENDS
Producer: George Martin
Album: Sgt. Pepper's Lonely Hearts Club Band
Record Label: Capitol
Songwriters: John Lennon, Paul McCartney

All-time communal anthem. Covered by Joe Cocker (A&M, '69).

WITHIN YOU, WITHOUT YOU
Producer: George Martin
Album: Sgt. Pepper's Lonely Hearts Club Band
Record Label: Capitol
Songwriter: George Harrison

George gets earnestly mystical.

YOUR MOTHER SHOULD KNOW
Producer: George Martin
Album: Magical Mystery Tour
Record Label: Capitol
Songwriters: John Lennon, Paul McCartney

Suggested segue: "Stray Cat Blues" by the Rolling Stones.

1968

ALL TOGETHER NOW
Producer: George Martin
Album: Yellow Submarine
Record Label: Apple
Songwriters: John Lennon, Paul McCartney

The Beatles as a barbershop quartet.

BIRTHDAY
Producer: George Martin
Album: The Beatles
Record Label: Apple
Songwriters: John Lennon, Paul McCartney

One of their loudest rockers.

BLACKBIRD
Producer: George Martin
Album: The Beatles
Record Label: Apple
Songwriters: John Lennon, Paul McCartney

Unplugged.

THE CONTINUING STORY OF BUNGALOW BILL
Producer: George Martin
Album: The Beatles
Record Label: Apple
Songwriters: John Lennon, Paul McCartney

A cartoon for British TV.

CRY BABY CRY
Producer: George Martin
Album: The Beatles
Record Label: Apple
Songwriters: John Lennon, Paul McCartney

Melancholy rocker. Covered by Richard Barone (Passport, '87).

DEAR PRUDENCE
Producer: George Martin
Album: The Beatles
Record Label: Apple
Songwriters: John Lennon, Paul McCartney

Dedicated to Mia Farrow's sister Prudence. Covered by the Five Stairsteps on the B-side of "O-o-h Child." (Buddah, '70). Also a big U.K. hit for Siouxsie & the Banshees (Wonderland, '83; Geffen, '84).

DON'T PASS ME BY
Producer: George Martin
Album: The Beatles
Record Label: Apple
Songwriter: Richard Starkey (Ringo Starr)

Ringo's first cut.

EVERYBODY'S GOT SOMETHING TO HIDE EXCEPT ME AND MY MONKEY
Producer: George Martin
Album: The Beatles
Record Label: Apple
Songwriters: John Lennon, Paul McCartney

The legendary monkey motif gets the Beatle treatment.

GLASS ONION
Producer: George Martin
Album: The Beatles
Record Label: Apple
Songwriters: John Lennon, Paul McCartney

HAPPINESS IS A WARM GUN
Producer: George Martin
Album: The Beatles
Record Label: Apple
Songwriters: John Lennon, Paul McCartney

Subversive gem from Lennon. Covered by the Breeders (4AD, '90) and Karl Wallinger (Chrysalis, '92).

HELTER SKELTER
Producer: George Martin
Album: The Beatles
Record Label: Apple
Songwriters: John Lennon, Paul McCartney

Inalterably connected to the Sharon Tate murders as a purported Charles Manson influence. Covered by Siouxsie & the Banshees (Polydor, '79).

HEY JUDE
Producer: George Martin
Album: Hey Jude
Record Label: Capitol
Songwriters: John Lennon, Paul McCartney

Their all-time best-seller and the #1 song of '68. This cautionary ode to Lennon's son scaled the charts in the waning months of a scathing year of political backlash against Rock and its musicians—the assassinations of Martin Luther King and Robert Kennedy,

the riots in the streets of Chicago at the Democratic National Convention, and the continued escalation of the war in Vietnam—peaking in time to be the song coming on right after the newscast announcing the election of Richard M. Nixon and the beginning of the end of the alternate culture. Covered by Wilson Pickett (Atlantic, '69).

HONEY PIE
Producer: George Martin
Album: The Beatles
Record Label: Apple
Songwriters: John Lennon, Paul McCartney

I WILL
Producer: George Martin
Album: The Beatles
Record Label: Apple
Songwriters: John Lennon, Paul McCartney

THE INNER LIGHT
Producer: George Martin
Album: Rarities
Record Label: Capitol
Songwriter: George Harrison

JULIA
Producer: George Martin
Album: The Beatles
Record Label: Apple
Songwriters: John Lennon, Paul McCartney

Lennon to his mother.

LADY MADONNA
Producer: George Martin
Album: Hey Jude
Record Label: Capitol
Songwriters: John Lennon, Paul McCartney

The cover by Fats Domino (Reprise, '68) was his first chart single since '64.

MARTHA MY DEAR
Producer: George Martin
Album: The Beatles
Record Label: Apple
Songwriters: John Lennon, Paul McCartney

MOTHER NATURE'S SON
Producer: George Martin
Album: The Beatles
Record Label: Apple
Songwriters: John Lennon, Paul McCartney

OB-LA-DI, OB-LA-DA
Producer: George Martin
Album: The Beatles
Record Label: Apple
Songwriters: John Lennon, Paul McCartney

Their latter-day TV theme song.

PIGGIES
Producer: George Martin
Album: The Beatles
Record Label: Apple
Songwriter: George Harrison

Quintessential George.

REVOLUTION
Producer: George Martin
Album: The Beatles
Record Label: Apple
Songwriters: John Lennon, Paul McCartney

The B-side of "Hey Jude."

REVOLUTION 9
Producer: George Martin
Album: The Beatles
Record Label: Apple
Songwriters: John Lennon, Paul McCartney

Overtly detaching themselves from the counterculture they had set in motion, as said counterculture hurtled toward its Armageddon.

ROCKY RACOON
Producer: George Martin
Album: The Beatles
Record Label: Apple
Songwriters: John Lennon, Paul McCartney

In which Paul offers his apologies to Bob Dylan. Covered by Richie Havens (Stormy Forest, '72).

SAVOY TRUFFLE
Producer: George Martin
Album: The Beatles
Record Label: Apple
Songwriter: George Harrison

A George trifle.

SEXY SADIE
Producer: George Martin
Album: The Beatles
Record Label: Apple
Songwriters: John Lennon, Paul McCartney

WHILE MY GUITAR GENTLY WEEPS

Producer: George Martin
Album: The Beatles
Record Label: Apple
Songwriter: George Harrison

Essential George philosophy, magical Eric Clapton guitar.

WHY DON'T WE DO IT IN THE ROAD?

Producer: George Martin
Album: The Beatles
Record Label: Apple
Songwriters: John Lennon, Paul McCartney

One of Paul's silliest love songs.

WILD HONEY PIE

Producer: George Martin
Album: The Beatles
Record Label: Apple
Songwriters: John Lennon, Paul McCartney

Sequel to "Honey Pie."

YER BLUES

Producer: George Martin
Album: The Beatles
Record Label: Apple
Songwriters: John Lennon, Paul McCartney

Heavy Metalesque.

1969

THE BALLAD OF JOHN AND YOKO

Producer: George Martin
Album: Hey Jude
Record Label: Apple
Songwriters: John Lennon, Paul McCartney

Establishing their cause as modern Folk heroes.

BECAUSE

Producer: George Martin
Album: Abbey Road
Record Label: Apple
Songwriters: John Lennon, Paul McCartney

In the midst of turmoil, another effortless love ballad.

CARRY THAT WEIGHT

Producer: George Martin
Album: Abbey Road
Record Label: Apple
Songwriters: John Lennon, Paul McCartney

Part of the legendary "Medley" that begins with "Her Majesty's a pretty nice girl . . ." and concludes with "and in the end the love you make/is equal to the love you take."

COME TOGETHER

Producer: George Martin
Album: Abbey Road
Record Label: Apple
Songwriters: John Lennon, Paul McCartney

Restating their ultimate theme for their eighteenth #1. Covered by Aerosmith (Columbia, '78).

DON'T LET ME DOWN

Producer: George Martin
Album: Hey Jude
Record Label: Apple
Songwriters: John Lennon, Paul McCartney

The B-side of "Get Back."

THE END

Producer: George Martin
Album: Abbey Road
Record Label: Apple
Songwriters: John Lennon, Paul McCartney

Concluding the medley, before their understated tribute to the Queen. Suggested segues for contrast: "The End" by the Doors, "God Save the Queen," by the Sex Pistols.

GET BACK

Producer: George Martin
Album: Let It Be
Record Label: Apple
Songwriters: John Lennon, Paul McCartney

Their biggest hit of '69.

GOLDEN SLUMBERS

Producer: George Martin
Album: Abbey Road
Record Label: Apple
Songwriters: John Lennon, Paul McCartney

Beautiful fragment that starts the famous Medley.

HERE COMES THE SUN

Producer: George Martin
Album: Abbey Road
Record Label: Apple
Songwriter: George Harrison

George finally takes off his shades. Covered by Richie Havens (Stormy Forest, '71).

HEY BULLDOG

Producer: George Martin
Album: Yellow Submarine
Record Label: Apple
Songwriters: John Lennon, Paul McCartney

Album rock commentary on the enduring dog motif.

I WANT YOU (SHE'S SO HEAVY)

Producer: George Martin
Album: Abbey Road
Record Label: Apple
Songwriters: John Lennon, Paul McCartney

Heavy Metal-ish.

IT'S ALL TOO MUCH

Producer: George Martin
Album: Yellow Submarine
Record Label: Apple
Songwriter: George Harrison

George puts his sunglasses back on.

MAXWELL'S SILVER HAMMER

Producer: George Martin
Album: Abbey Road
Record Label: Apple
Songwriters: John Lennon, Paul McCartney

Paul gets cutesy.

MEAN MR. MUSTARD

Producer: George Martin
Album: Abbey Road
Record Label: Apple
Songwriters: John Lennon, Paul McCartney

The band has been playing too much Clue in the studio.

OCTOPUS'S GARDEN

Producer: George Martin
Album: Abbey Road
Record Label: Apple
Songwriter: Richard Starkey (Ringo Starr)

Ringo stakes out his own cartoon turf.

OH! DARLING

Producer: George Martin
Album: Abbey Road
Record Label: Apple
Songwriters: John Lennon, Paul McCartney

POLYTHENE PAM

Producer: George Martin
Album: Abbey Road

Record Label: Apple
Songwriters: John Lennon, Paul McCartney

A connecting link in the magical medley.

SHE CAME IN THROUGH THE BATHROOM WINDOW

Producer: George Martin
Album: Abbey Road
Record Label: Apple
Songwriters: John Lennon, Paul McCartney

McCartney at his most Lennon-esque (or was it vice versa?). Covered by Joe Cocker (A&M, '70).

SOMETHING

Producer: George Martin
Album: Abbey Road
Record Label: Apple
Songwriter: George Harrison

George's shining ballad moment on the B-side of "Come Together." Covered by Frank Sinatra (Reprise, '72)!

YOU NEVER GIVE ME YOUR MONEY

Producer: George Martin
Album: Abbey Road
Record Label: Apple
Songwriters: John Lennon, Paul McCartney

Quintessential rocker.

1970

FOR YOU BLUE

Producer: Phil Spector
Album: Let It Be
Record Label: Apple
Songwriter: George Harrison

LET IT BE

Producer: George Martin
Album: Let It Be
Record Label: Apple
Songwriters: John Lennon, Paul McCartney

R.I.P.

THE LONG AND WINDING ROAD

Producers: George Martin, Phil Spector
Album: Let It Be
Record Label: Apple
Songwriters: John Lennon, Paul McCartney

Phil Spector, who arguably launched the jangly rock alternative '60s with his flashy productions, winds up with the Beatles'

abandoned rooftop tapes and nowhere to go.

THE BEAU BRUMMELS
1964

LAUGH, LAUGH

Producer: Sly Stone
Album: Best of the Beau Brummels
Record Label: Autumn
Songwriter: Ronald C. Elliot

The San Francisco sound when it was not yet a scene.

1965

JUST A LITTLE

Producer: Sly Stone
Album: Introducing the Beau Brummels
Record Label: Autumn
Songwriters: Ronald C. Elliott, Robert Durand

San Francisco in the days when the Grateful Dead were still the Warlocks.

THE BEAUTIFUL SOUTH
1990

I'LL SAIL THIS SHIP ALONE

Producer: Mike Hedges
Album: Welcome to the Beautiful South
Record Label: Elektra
Songwriters: Paul Heaton, David Rotheray

Edgy Mope Rock, from the former Housemartins.

BEAVIS AND BUTT-HEAD
1993

COME TO BUTT-HEAD

Producer: Nile Rodgers
Album: Beavis and Butt-Head Experience
Record Label: Geffen
Songwriters: Mike Judge, Nile Rodgers

The '90s experience: dumb and dumber.

BECK
1993

LOSER

Producers: Karl Stephenson, Tom Rothrock
Album: Mellow Gold
Record Label: Geffen

Songwriters: Beck Hansen, Karl Stephenson

Literate anti-folk, low-fi harangue, defining the slacker essence of a new Beat Generation.

JEFF BECK
1976

FREEWAY JAM

Producer: Jan Hammer
Album: Jeff Beck with the Jan Hammer Group
Record Label: Epic
Songwriter: Max Middleton

Signature guitar epic from the man who wouldn't be God.

GOODBYE PORK PIE HAT

Producers: George Martin, Jan Hammer
Album: Wired
Record Label: Epic
Songwriter: Charles Mingus

Jeff takes on a Jazz standard.

THE JEFF BECK GROUP
1968

PLYNTH (WATER DOWN THE DRAIN)

Producer: Mickie Most
Album: Beck-ola
Record Label: Epic
Songwriters: Rod Stewart, Nicky Hopkins, Ron Wood

High spot of their second and last album.

ROCK MY PLIMSOUL

Producer: Mickie Most
Album: Truth
Record Label: Epic
Songwriter: Jeff Beck

Introducing Rock's British odd couple—the reclusive guitar star, Jeff Beck, and the effusive front man, Rod "the Mod" Stewart.

THE BEE GEES
1967

(THE LIGHTS WENT OUT IN) MASSACHUSETTS

Producer: Robert Stigwood
Album: Horizontal
Record Label: Atco
Songwriters: Barry Gibb, Robin Gibb, Maurice Gibb

This anguished folkie lament was their #1 U.K. debut single.

NEW YORK MINING DISASTER 1941 (HAVE YOU SEEN MY WIFE MR. JONES)

Producer: Ossie Byrne
Album: Bee Gee's First
Record Label: Atco
Songwriters: Barry Gibb, Robin Gibb, Maurice Gibb

Late entry in the Beatles-influenced British invasion. After all, they were coming by way of Australia.

TO LOVE SOMEBODY

Producer: Robert Stigwood
Album: Horizontal
Record Label: Atco
Songwriters: Barry Gibb, Robin Gibb, Maurice Gibb

Torchy Pop Rock. Covered by Janis Joplin (Columbia, '69).

1968

I STARTED A JOKE

Producer: Robert Stigwood
Album: Idea
Record Label: Atco
Songwriters: Barry Gibb, Robin Gibb, Maurice Gibb

I'VE GOT TO GET A MESSAGE TO YOU

Producer: Robert Stigwood
Album: Idea
Record Label: Atco
Songwriters: Barry Gibb, Robin Gibb, Maurice Gibb

Their first U.S. Top-10 was their second U.K. #1.

1970

LONELY DAYS

Producer: Robert Stigwood, the Bee Gees
Album: 2 Years On
Record Label: Atco
Songwriters: Barry Gibb, Robin Gibb, Maurice Gibb

The Beatles are dead; long live the Beatles sound.

1971

HOW CAN YOU MEND A BROKEN HEART

Producers: Robert Stigwood, the Bee Gees
Album: Trafalgar
Record Label: Atco
Songwriters: Barry Gibb, Robin Gibb

Their first #1 U.S. single.

1975

JIVE TALKIN'

Producer: Arif Mardin
Album: Main Course
Record Label: RSO
Songwriters: Barry Gibb, Robin Gibb, Maurice Gibb

Learning the new language of R&B. Covered by the Blenders (Orchard Lane, '95).

NIGHTS ON BROADWAY

Producer: Arif Mardin
Album: Main Course
Record Label: RSO
Songwriters: Barry Gibb, Robin Gibb, Maurice Gibb

Moving toward their blue-eyed Soul crescendo.

1976

LOVE SO RIGHT

Producers: Robert Stigwood, the Bee Gees
Album: Children of the World
Record Label: RSO
Songwriters: Barry Gibb, Robin Gibb, Maurice Gibb

YOU SHOULD BE DANCING

Producer: Arif Mardin
Album: Main Course
Record Label: RSO
Songwriters: Barry Gibb, Robin Gibb, Maurice Gibb

1977

HOW DEEP IS YOUR LOVE

Producers: Albhy Galutin, Karl Richardson, the Bee Gees
Album: Saturday Night Fever
Record Label: RSO
Songwriters: Barry Gibb, Robin Gibb, Maurice Gibb

From the classic soundtrack that brought Disco home to middle America, this was their fourth #1.

NIGHT FEVER

Producers: Albhy Galutin, Karl Richardson, the Bee Gees
Album: Saturday Night Fever
Record Label: RSO
Songwriters: Barry Gibb, Robin Gibb, Maurice Gibb

Their biggest hit; defining the dread disease of Disco.

1975

STAYIN' ALIVE

Producers: Albhy Galutin, Karl Richardson, the Bee Gees
Album: Saturday Night Fever
Record Label: RSO
Songwriters: Barry Gibb, Robin Gibb, Maurice Gibb

Enduring anthem of the '70s Disco Age.

1978

TOO MUCH HEAVEN

Producers: Albhy Galutin, Karl Richardson, the Bee Gees
Album: Spirits Having Flown
Record Label: RSO
Songwriters: Barry Gibb, Robin Gibb, Maurice Gibb

Luxuriating in their Miami period.

TRAGEDY

Producers: Albhy Galutin, Karl Richardson, the Bee Gees
Album: Spirits Having Flown
Record Label: RSO
Songwriters: Barry Gibb, Robin Gibb, Maurice Gibb

Reviving the spirit of "Massachusetts."

1979

LOVE YOU INSIDE OUT

Producers: Albhy Galutin, Karl Richardson, the Bee Gees
Album: Spirits Having Flown
Record Label: RSO
Songwriters: Barry Gibb, Robin Gibb, Maurice Gibb

Their ninth and last #1.

1989

ONE

Album: One
Record Label: Warner Brothers
Songwriters: Barry Gibb, Robin Gibb, Maurice Gibb

BELL BIV DEVOE

1990

DO ME!

Producers: Carl Bourelly, Dr. Freeze
Album: Poison
Record Label: MCA
Songwriters: Carl Bourelly, Michael Bivens, Ronnie Devoe, Ricky Bell

Post-high school New Edition.

POISON

Producers: Carl Bourelly, Dr. Freeze
Album: Poison

Record Label: MCA
Songwriter: Elliot Straite

The '50s harmony ethos meets the '90s street.

THE BELL NOTES
1958

I'VE HAD IT
Record Label: Time
Songwriters: Ray Ceroni, Carl Bonura

From the mean streets of Long Island, this song was used to spectacular effect in Martin Scorsese's first film, Who's That Knocking? *Suggested segue: "Cynical Girl" by Marshall Crenshaw (Warner Brothers, '82).*

ARCHIE BELL AND THE DRELLS
1968

I CAN'T STOP DANCING
Producers: Kenny Gamble, Leon Huff
Record Label: Atlantic
Songwriters: Kenny Gamble, Leon Huff

Top-10 R&B/Top-10 R&R crossover.

TIGHTEN UP
Producer: Skipper Lee Frazier
Album: Tighten Up
Record Label: Atlantic
Songwriters: Billy Buttier, Archie Bell

#1 R&B/R&R crossover and beach-music classic.

1969

THERE'S GONNA BE A SHOWDOWN
Producers: Kenny Gamble, Leon Huff
Album: There's Gonna Be a Showdown
Record Label: Atlantic
Songwriters: Kenny Gamble, Leon Huff

Covered by the New York Dolls (Mercury, '74).

WILLIAM BELL
1962

YOU DON'T MISS YOUR WATER
Producer: Chips Moman
Album: The Soul of a Bell

Record Label: Stax
Songwriter: William Bell

1968

I FORGOT TO BE YOUR LOVER
Producer: Booker T. Jones
Record Label: Stax
Songwriters: William Bell, Booker T. Jones

Top-10 R&B/R&R crossover. Covered by Billy Idol (Chrysalis, '86).

TRIBUTE TO A KING
Producer: Booker T. Jones
Record Label: Stax
Songwriters: William Bell, Booker T. Jones

1977

TRYIN' TO LOVE TWO
Album: Coming Back for More
Record Label: Mercury
Songwriters: William Bell, Paul Mitchell

His last and biggest hit.

REGINA BELLE
1989

BABY, COME TO ME
Producers: Narada Michael Walden, Barry Eastmond
Album Title: Stay with Me
Record Label: Columbia
Songwriters: Narada Michael Walden, Jeffrey Cohen

#1 R&B/Bottom-40 crossover.

MAKE IT LIKE IT WAS
Producers: Narada Michael Walden, Barry Eastmond
Album Title: Stay with Me
Record Label: Columbia
Songwriter: Ce Ce Winans

Her biggest hit. #1 R&B/Top-50 crossover.

THE BELLS
1971

STAY AWHILE
Producer: Cliff Edwards
Album: Fly Little White Dove Fly
Record Label: Polydor
Songwriter: Ken Tobias

Big-time border crossover: Top-10 R&R in the U.S., and #1 in Canada.

BELLY
1993

FEED THE TREE
Producer: Tracy Chisholm
Album: Star
Record Label: Sire
Songwriter: Tanya Donelly

Post-Bangles Folk Rock allegory by a veteran new scenestress.

JOHN BELUSHI
1973

LONELY AT THE BOTTOM
Producer: Tony Hendra
Album: *Lemmings* Original Cast Album
Record Label: Banana
Songwriters: Paul Jacobs, John Belushi

Future stalwart of "Saturday Night Live," John Belushi, perfects his Joe Cocker imitation in a Greenwich Village musical that helped shape the comedy of the Classic Rock generation.

JESSE BELVIN
1951

GOODNIGHT MY LOVE
Producer: George Motola
Record Label: Modern
Songwriters: George Motola, Jesse Belvin

Out of L.A.'s Compton section—a generation away from spawning Gangsta Rap—Belvin's ballad would become DJ Alan Freed's closing theme in New York. Belvin's other masterwork, "Earth Angel," would become a Doo-Wop anthem.

PAT BENATAR
1980

HIT ME WITH YOUR BEST SHOT
Producer: Keith Olson
Album: Crimes of Passion
Record Label: Chrysalis
Songwriter: Eddie Schwartz

The histrionic belter tempts fate.

1983

LOVE IS A BATTLEFIELD
Producers: Peter Coleman, Neil Giraldo
Album: Live from Earth
Record Label: Chrysalis

Songwriters: Mike Chapman, Holly Knight

Benatar returns to her favorite theme.

1984

WE BELONG
Producers: Peter Coleman, Neil Giraldo
Album: Tropico
Record Label: Chrysalis
Songwriters: David Lowen, Daniel Navarro

Arena anthem.

1985

INVINCIBLE (THEME FROM *THE LEGEND OF BILLIE JEAN*)
Producer: Mike Chapman
Album: Seven the Hard Way
Record Label: Chrysalis
Songwriters: Holly Knight, Simon Climie

A title song as invincible as Benatar when she ruled the '80s.

BOYD BENNETT
1955

SEVENTEEN
Album: Boyd Bennett
Record Label: King
Songwriters: John Young Jr., Chuck Gorman, Boyd Bennett

A Rockabilly crossover.

JOE BENNETT AND THE SPARKLETONES
1957

BLACK SLACKS
Record Label: ABC Paramount
Songwriters: Joe Bennett, Jimmy Denton

Essential Rock and Roll attire.

GEORGE BENSON
1977

THE GREATEST LOVE OF ALL
Producer: Michael Masser
Album: Weekend in L.A.
Record Label: Warner Brothers
Songwriters: Linda Creed, Michael Masser

Philly Soul theme from Muhammed Ali's biopic—The Greatest. Covered by Whitney Houston (Arista, '85). It peaked at #1 while Linda Creed was dying of cancer.

1980

GIVE ME THE NIGHT
Producer: Quincy Jones
Album: Give Me the Night
Record Label: Warner Brothers
Songwriter: Rod Temperton

The biggest Wonder-esque hit for the former jazz guitarist.

BROOK BENTON
1959

ENDLESSLY
Producer: Clyde Otis
Album: Brook Benton
Record Label: Mercury
Songwriters: Clyde Otis, Brook Benton

Written by the same team that gave Nat Cole his classic, "Looking Back," and Clyde McPhatter his durable, "A Lover's Question."

IT'S JUST A MATTER OF TIME
Producer: Clyde Otis
Album: Golden Hits
Record Label: Mercury
Songwriters: Clyde Otis, Brook Benton, Belford Hendricks

Cool Soul in the Nat Cole manner.

THANK YOU, PRETTY BABY
Producer: Clyde Otis
Record Label: Mercury
Songwriters: Clyde Otis, Brook Benton

#1 R&B/Top-20 R&R crossover.

1963

HOTEL HAPPINESS
Album: Golden Hits, Volume 2
Record Label: Mercury
Songwriters: Earl Shuman, Leon Carr

1970

A RAINY NIGHT IN GEORGIA
Producer: Arif Mardin
Album: Brook Benton Today
Record Label: Cotillion
Songwriter: Tony Joe White

A #1 R&B/Top-10 R&R crossover.

BROOK BENTON AND DINAH WASHINGTON
1960

BABY (YOU'VE GOT WHAT IT TAKES)
Producer: Clyde Otis
Album: The Two of Us
Record Label: Mercury
Songwriters: Clyde Otis, Murray Stein

A classic Soul duet that was the #1 R&B song of the year and a Top-10 R&R crossover. Marvin and Tammy were listening.

BERLIN
1983

SEX (I'M A)
Producers: Daniel Van Patten, Maomen
Album: Pleasure Victim
Record Label: Warner Brothers
Songwriters: John Crawford, David Diamond, Terri Nunn

A Debbie Harry/Blondie pretender, creates a one-shot photo opportunity.

1986

TAKE MY BREATH AWAY (LOVE THEME FROM *TOP GUN*)
Producer: Giorgio Moroder
Album: Count Three and Pray
Record Label: Columbia
Songwriters: Giorgio Moroder, Tom Whitlock.

Big movie ballad from Top Gun.

CHUCK BERRY
1955

MAYBELLENE
Producers: Leonard Chess, Phil Chess
Album: Chuck Berry Is on Top
Record Label: Chess
Songwriter: Chuck Berry

Establishing the Rock and Roll essentials—fast cars and loose women—and introducing the Louis Jordan of the teen set. Original writer credits include Russ Fratto and Alan Freed.

THIRTY DAYS
Producers: Leonard Chess, Marshall Chess
Album: Greatest Hits
Record Label: Chess

Songwriter: Chuck Berry

Presaging Berry's future run-ins with the law.

1957

BROWN EYED HANDSOME MAN

Producers: Leonard Chess, Phil Chess
Album: After School Sessions
Record Label: Chess
Songwriter: Chuck Berry

Not above self-promotion, Berry was just better at it than most.

NO MONEY DOWN

Producers: Leonard Chess, Phil Chess
Album: After School Sessions
Record Label: Chess
Songwriter: Chuck Berry

A look through Chuck's legendary, jaundiced eye at life as a used car lot.

ROCK AND ROLL MUSIC

Producers: Leonard Chess, Phil Chess
Album: One Dozen Berrys
Record Label: Chess
Songwriter: Chuck Berry

His first of many anthems dedicated to the proposition—"Rock and Roll is here to stay." Covered by the Beatles (Capitol, '65) and the Archies (Calendar, '69).

SCHOOL DAY

Producers: Leonard Chess, Phil Chess
Album: After School Sessions
Record Label: Chess
Songwriter: Chuck Berry

A teenage day-in-the-life.

TOO MUCH MONKEY BUSINESS

Producers: Leonard Chess, Phil Chess
Album: After School Sessions
Record Label: Chess
Songwriter: Chuck Berry

Chronicling the life and times of his neighborhood like a duck-walking Nelson Algren. Covered by Tom Rush (Elektra, '65), the Kinks (Capitol, '65), Elvis Presley (RCA Camden, '69).

WEE WEE HOURS

Producers: Leonard Chess, Phil Chess
Album: After School Sessions
Record Label: Chess
Songwriter: Chuck Berry

A slow Blues from his original demo tape, which also contained "Maybellene."

1958

BEAUTIFUL DELILAH

Producers: Leonard Chess, Phil Chess
Album: Chuck Berry's Golden Decade (Vol. III)
Record Label: Chess
Songwriter: Chuck Berry

CAROL

Producers: Leonard Chess, Phil Chess
Album: Chuck Berry Is on Top
Record Label: Chess
Songwriter: Chuck Berry

One of his hardest rocking hits. Covered by the Rolling Stones (London, '64).

JOHNNY B. GOODE

Producers: Leonard Chess, Phil Chess
Album: One Dozen Berrys
Record Label: Chess
Songwriter: Chuck Berry

The creation of a character and guitar figure that would transcend their time and place, even while defining it in wonderfully choice details in all its innocence and ambition, raw talent, and relentless exploitation. Covered by the royalty of rock and roll: Jerry Lee Lewis (Mercury, '65), Elvis Presley (RCA, '69), Johnny Winter (Columbia, '69), the Grateful Dead (Warner Brothers, '71), Jimi Hendrix (Reprise, '72), and even Judas Priest (Columbia, '88). Michael J. Fox played it in Back to the Future. Bobby Bare tried to satirize it as early as '59 in "The All American Boy."

MERRY CHRISTMAS BABY

Producers: Leonard Chess, Phil Chess
Album: St. Louis to Liverpool
Record Label: Chess
Songwriters: Lou Baxter, Johnny Moore

#1 R&B holiday tidings, Berry Style. Covered by James Brown, Elvis Presley, Ike and Tina Turner, the Beach Boys, Bruce Springsteen.

OH BABY DOLL

Producers: Leonard Chess, Phil Chess
Album: One Dozen Berrys
Record Label: Chess
Songwriter: Chuck Berry

REELIN' AND ROCKIN'

Producers: Leonard Chess, Phil Chess
Album: One Dozen Berrys
Record Label: Chess
Songwriter: Chuck Berry

Re-released in '73, his last chart item.

RUN RUDOLPH RUN

Producers: Leonard Chess, Phil Chess
Album: Golden Decade (Vol. II)
Record Label: Chess
Songwriter: Chuck Berry

Covered by Keith Richards (Rolling Stones, '78).

SWEET LITTLE SIXTEEN

Producers: Leonard Chess, Phil Chess
Album: One Dozen Berrys
Record Label: Chess
Songwriter: Chuck Berry

In a genre rapidly becoming obsessed with "the self," this was the most self-aware song yet, promoting not only the inevitability of Rock and Roll, but the mundane actuality thereof.

1959

ALMOST GROWN

Producers: Leonard Chess, Phil Chess
Album: Chuck Berry Is on Top
Record Label: Chess
Songwriter: Chuck Berry

Typically cogent, wise, empathetic, and uplifting analysis of the eternal adolescent experience: in its subtle way, it was more penetrating than many of the works of Leiber and Stoller, his chief rivals in mining this turf, whose "Yakety Yak" was released a month later.

AROUND AND AROUND

Producers: Leonard Chess, Phil Chess
Album: Chuck Berry Is on Top
Record Label: Chess
Songwriter: Chuck Berry

Exemplary album rocker. Covered by the Animals (MGM, '64) and the Rolling Stones (London, '64) in their legendary appearance on the T.A.M.I Show music documentary.

BACK IN THE U.S.A.

Producers: Leonard Chess, Phil Chess
Album: Twist
Record Label: Chess

Songwriter: Chuck Berry

Covered by the Beatles as "Back in the USSR" (Apple, '68).

JO JO GUNNE

Producers: Leonard Chess, Phil Chess

Album: Chuck Berry Is on Top

Record Label: Chess

Songwriter: Chuck Berry

Inspired Jay Ferguson to name his post-Spirit Rock band after it. Unfortunately, Jo Jo Gunne (the band) produced nothing up to the level of its namesake.

LITTLE QUEENIE

Producers: Leonard Chess, Phil Chess

Album: Chuck Berry Is on Top

Record Label: Chess

Songwriter: Chuck Berry

B-side of "Almost Grown" and one of his great live numbers. Covered in '62 concert performance by the Beatles at the Star Club in Germany (Lingasong, '77), the Rolling Stones at Madison Square Garden (London, '70), and Rod Stewart, "Absolutely Live" (Warner Brothers, '82).

MEMPHIS

Producers: Leonard Chess, Phil Chess

Album: Chuck Berry's Greatest Hits

Record Label: Chess

Songwriter: Chuck Berry

In classic Country territory, this B-side of "Back in the U.S.A" introduced the lovelorn 6-year-old Marie to a moist-eyed America, unaccustomed then to the ravages of divorce. Covered by Lonnie Mack (Fraternity, '63).

ROLL OVER BEETHOVEN

Producers: Leonard Chess, Phil Chess

Album: Chuck Berry Is on Top

Record Label: Chess

Songwriter: Chuck Berry

One of his best celebrations. Covered by the Beatles (Capitol, '64) to effectively return Berry to the spotlight, and then by Electric Light Orchestra (United Artists, '73).

SWEET LITTLE ROCK AND ROLLER

Producers: Leonard Chess, Phil Chess

Album: Chuck Berry Is on Top

Record Label: Chess

Songwriter: Chuck Berry

One of his more moving tributes. Covered by Rod Stewart (Mercury, '74).

1960

BYE, BYE, JOHNNY

Producers: Leonard Chess, Phil Chess

Album: Rockin' at the Hops

Record Label: Chess

Songwriter: Chuck Berry

A live staple of the early Rolling Stones (London, '72).

LET IT ROCK

Producers: Leonard Chess, Phil Chess

Album: Rockin' at the Hops

Record Label: Chess

Songwriter: Chuck Berry

B-side of "Too Pooped to Pop," originally accredited to E. Anderson.

TOO POOPED TO POP

Producers: Leonard Chess, Phil Chess

Album: Rockin' at the Hops

Record Label: Chess

Songwriter: Chuck Berry

Too pooped to partake of the dance crazes of the early '60s, and in the pen by '62, this was Chuck's only chart record until the Beatles and the Stones restored him to his place of esteem in '64.

1961

13 QUESTION METHOD

Producers: Leonard Chess, Phil Chess

Album: New Jukebox Hits

Record Label: Chess

Songwriter: Chuck Berry

COME ON

Producers: Leonard Chess, Phil Chess

Album: Twist

Record Label: Chess

Songwriter: Chuck Berry

First U.K. single for the Rolling Stones (London, '64).

I'M TALKING ABOUT YOU

Producers: Leonard Chess, Phil Chess

Album: New Jukebox Hits

Record Label: Chess

Songwriter: Chuck Berry

Covered by the Rolling Stones (London, '64).

1964

C'EST LA VIE (YOU NEVER CAN TELL)

Producers: Leonard Chess, Phil Chess

Album: St. Louis to Liverpool

Record Label: Chess

Songwriter: Chuck Berry

Covered by Emmylou Harris (Warner Brothers, '77).

LITTLE MARIE

Producers: Leonard Chess, Phil Chess

Album: St. Louis to Liverpool

Record Label: Chess

Songwriter: Chuck Berry

Catching up with the girl from Memphis, Tennessee.

LIVERPOOL DRIVE

Producers: Leonard Chess, Phil Chess

Album: Two Great Guitars

Record Label: Chess

Songwriter: Chuck Berry

From his famed guitar duel album with Bo Diddley.

NADINE (IS IT YOU?)

Producers: Leonard Chess, Phil Chess

Album: Chuck Berry's Greatest Hits

Record Label: Chess

Songwriter: Chuck Berry

NO PARTICULAR PLACE TO GO

Producers: Leonard Chess, Phil Chess

Album: St. Louis to Liverpool

Record Label: Chess

Songwriter: Chuck Berry

By virtue of his rediscovery by the Beatles and the Stones, Chuck Berry returned to the Top-10 after an absence of seven years. The message, the equanimity, and the humor remained the same, especially considering the fact that this tune, like "Nadine," was written while Chuck was in prison, ostensibly for violating the Mann Act.

PROMISED LAND

Producers: Leonard Chess, Phil Chess

Album: St. Louis to Liverpool

Record Label: Chess

Songwriter: Chuck Berry

Closing out '64 with his fifth chart record of the year.

1967

YOU CAN'T CATCH ME
Producers: Leonard Chess, Phil Chess
Album: Chuck Berry's Golden Decade
Record Label: Chess
Songwriter: Chuck Berry

Car classic—classic car: the Airmobile. Performed by Chuck in the '57 movie Rock, Rock, Rock. Covered by the Rolling Stones (London, '65) and the Blues Project (Verve Forecast, '67).

1970

HAVE MERCY JUDGE
Producers: Leonard Chess, Phil Chess
Album: Back Home
Record Label: Chess
Songwriter: Chuck Berry

Introduced as a Bluesman to Chess records by Muddy Waters, Berry finally displayed his chops.

TULANE
Producers: Leonard Chess, Phil Chess
Album: Back Home
Record Label: Chess
Songwriter: Chuck Berry

Berry's look at the '60s.

1972

MY DING-A-LING
Producer: Esmond Edwards
Album: London Chuck Berry Sessions
Record Label: Chess
Songwriter: Chuck Berry

An aged throwaway ditty that was, unfortunately, his biggest hit, as caught live in England. Written in '58, when it was considered risque, as "My Tambourine." Suggested segue: Dave Bartholomew's similar version of "My Ding-a-Ling" (Imperial, '52).

DAVE BERRY

1965

THE CRYING GAME
Record Label: Decca
Songwriter: Geoff Stephens

U.K. hit in '64. Covered by Brenda Lee (Decca, '65) and revived by Boy George for the film, The Crying Game (SBK, '93).

RICHARD BERRY

1956

LOUIE, LOUIE
Record Label: Flip
Songwriter: Richard Berry

Introduced by Richard Berry, voice of "Riot in Cell Block #9" by the Robins. Popularized for eternity by the Kingsmen (Wand, '63). For a generation of Garage Band hopefuls, this would be their three-chord primer. For the FBI, this would conclusively define them for the same generation as latter-day Keystone Kops, as they sought to find obscenities hidden in the mix, an endeavor far more obscene than anything they were able to discern.

BIG AUDIO DYNAMITE

1991

RUSH
Producers: Mick Jones, Climax, D. J. Shappe
Album: The Globe
Record Label: Columbia
Songwriter: Mick Jones

An outgrowth of the Clash.

BIG BLACK

1986

KEROSENE
Producer: Steve Albini
Album: Atomizer
Record Label: Touch and Go
Songwriter: Steve Albini

Punk Rock redux—louder, faster, angrier.

THE BIG BOPPER

1958

CHANTILLY LACE
Album: Chantilly Lace
Record Label: Mercury
Songwriter: J. P. Richardson

Early novelty Rap: how Wolfman Jack would have sounded had he decided to cut a record of his act.

BIG BROTHER AND THE HOLDING COMPANY

1968

ALL IS LONELINESS
Producer: Bob Shad
Album: Big Brother and the Holding Company
Record Label: Mainstream
Songwriter: Louis Hardin

San Francisco psychedelic Blues, courtesy of Austin's Janis Joplin.

BALL AND CHAIN
Producer: John Simon
Album: Cheap Thrills
Record Label: Columbia
Songwriter: Willa Mae Thornton

Janis Joplin's Monterey signature. Introduced by Big Mama Thorton.

BYE BYE BABY
Producer: John Riney
Album: Big Brother and the Holding Company
Record Label: Mainstream
Songwriter: R. Powell St. John

COMBINATION OF THE TWO
Producer: John Simon
Album: Cheap Thrills
Record Label: Columbia
Songwriter: Sam Andrew

Kicking off their overground career at the Monterey Rock and Pop Festival.

COO COO
Producer: Bob Shad
Album: Big Brother and the Holding Company
Record Label: Mainstream
Songwriter: Pete Albin

Propelled by a wailing Joplin.

DOWN ON ME
Producer: Bob Shad
Album: Big Brother and the Holding Company
Record Label: Mainstream
Songwriter: Janis Joplin

Updated white-woman Blues that packs an emotional and sexual double whammy.

FAREWELL SONG
Producer: John Simon
Record Label: Columbia
Songwriter: Sam Andrew

First released on the album Farewell Song (Columbia, '82).

WOMEN IS LOSERS
Producer: Bob Shad
Album: Big Brother and the Holding Company
Record Label: Mainstream
Songwriter: Janis Joplin

The twisted roots of Joplin's upbringing.

BIG COUNTRY

1983

IN A BIG COUNTRY
Producer: Steve Lillywhite
Album: The Crossing
Record Label: Mercury
Songwriter: Big Country

Loping Scottish Folk Rock and their biggest hit.

1984

FIELDS OF FIRE
Producer: Steve Lillywhite
Album: The Crossing
Record Label: Mercury
Songwriter: Big Country

First U.K./U.S. crossover for the Scottish band. The Proclaimers were listening.

BIG FUN

1989

TEENAGE SUICIDE (DON'T DO IT)
Album: *Heathers* Soundtrack
Songwriter: Don Dixon

The big song from the movie Heathers, sung by the Athens Mafia—Mitch Easter, Don Dixon, Marti Jones, and Angie Carlson.

BIG MAYBELLE

1954

ONE MONKEY DON'T STOP NO SHOW
Producer: Larry Kirkland
Album: Big Maybelle Sings Blues . . . and Big Maybelle
Record Label: Okeh
Songwriters: Charlie Singleton, Rose Marie McCoy

Choice bit of R&B wisdom, with "Whole Lotta Shakin' Goin' On" on the B-side. Covered by Joe Tex (Dial, '65) and Honey Cone (Hot Wax, '71).

1955

WHOLE LOTTA SHAKIN' GOIN' ON
Producer: Quincy Jones
Record Label: Okeh
Songwriters: Dave Williams, Sunny David (Roy Hall)

Big Maybelle's biggest B-side. Jerry Lee Lewis's #1 C&W/#1 R&B/Top-5 R&R triple crossover cover marked his hystrionic entrance into Rock and Roll, with one foot on the keyboard and one foot in the Hall of Fame.

BIG STAR

1972

DON'T LIE TO ME
Album: #1 Record
Record Label: Ardent
Songwriters: Alex Chilton, Chris Bell

The birth of a critics' darling: Chilton graduates from the Box Tops, but never fulfills his yearbook predictions.

1974

BACK OF A CAR
Album: Radio City
Record Label: Ardent
Songwriter: Alex Chilton

Make-out music for Generation X.

SEPTEMBER GURLS
Album: Radio City
Record Label: Ardent
Songwriter: Alex Chilton

Chilton's most accessibly haunting post-Box Tops tune. Covered by the Searchers (Sire, '81) and the Bangles (Columbia, '86).

1978

HOLOCAUST
Album: 3rd
Record Label: PVC
Songwriter: Alex Chilton

BIKINI KILL

1970

DOUBLE DARE YA
Producer: Ian Mackaye
Album: Bikini Kill
Record Label: Kill Rock Stars
Songwriter: Bikini Kill

The antifeminity movement in its purest, most explosive Riot Grrrl form.

BILLY AND THE BEATERS

1981

AT THIS MOMENT
Producer: Jeff Baxter
Album: Billy and the Beaters
Record Label: Alfa/Rhino
Songwriter: Billy Vera

An archetype R&B-influenced slow dance number that was revived on the TV show, "Family Ties," in 1986, five years after it originally flopped as a single. Shown twice in one season as Alex's (played by Michael J. Fox) wedding song, this Billy Vera number was the #1 sentimental comeback story of the year.

BILLY AND LILLIE

1958

LA DEE DAH
Record Label: Swan
Songwriters: Frank C. Slay Jr., Bob Crewe

The Philly sound in its earliest dance incarnation.

JANE BIRKIN AND SERGE GAINSBOURG

1970

JE T'AIME . . . MOI NON PLUS
Record Label: Fontana
Songwriter: Serge Gainsbourg

Heavy-breathing pre-disco hit that influenced Donna Summer.

ELVIN BISHOP

1976

FOOLED AROUND AND FELL IN LOVE
Producers: Bill Szymczyk, Allen Blazek
Album: Struttin' My Stuff
Record Label: Capricorn
Songwriter: Elvin Bishop

Mike Bloomfield's one-time guitar mate in the Butterfield Blues Band creates a middling, noodling Southern Rock hit.

STEPHEN BISHOP

1982

IT MIGHT BE YOU
Producer: Dave Grusin
Album: *Tootsie* Soundtrack
Record Label: Warner Brothers
Songwriters: Alan Bergman, Marilyn Bergman, Dave Grusin

Haunting big movie ballad from Tootsie.

BIZ MARKIE

1989

JUST A FRIEND
Producer: Marcel Hall
Album: The Biz Never Sleeps
Record Label: Cold Chillin'
Songwriter: Marcel Hall

Novelty Rap.

BJÖRK
1993

HUMAN BEHAVIOUR
Producer: Nellee Hooper
Album: Debut
Record Label: Elektra
Songwriters: Nellee Hooper, Bjork Gudmundsdottir

Former lead singer of the Sugarcubes as a decidedly off-kilter Swedish Melanie.

BLACK 47
1992

FUNKY CEILI (BRIDIE'S SONG)
Producers: Ric Okasek, Larry Kirwan
Album: Black 47
Record Label: SBK/ERG
Songwriter: Larry Kirwan

Rousing Irish bar-band romantic anthem.

BLACK BOX
1989

RIDE ON TIME
Producer: Groove Groove Melody
Album: Dreamland
Record Label: RCA
Songwriters: Mirko Limoni, Daniele Davoli, Valerio Semplici, Dan Hartman

#1 U.K. debut with vocals sampled from Loleatta Holloway's "Love Sensation."

1990

EVERYBODY EVERYBODY
Producer: Groove Groove Melody
Album: Dreamland
Record Label: RCA
Songwriters: Mirko Limoni, Daniele Davoli, Valerio Semplici

Dance sensation from Italy, featuring the uncredited voice of U.S. diva, Martha Wash.

STRIKE IT UP
Producer: Groove Groove Melody
Album: Dreamland
Record Label: RCA
Songwriters: Mirko Limoni, Daniele Davoli, Valerio Semplici

Big dance hit that established Martha Wash as the Darlene Love of the '90s.

THE BLACK CROWES
1990

SHE TALKS TO ANGELS
Producers: Rich Rubin, George Drakoulias
Album: Shake Your Moneymaker
Record Label: Def American
Songwriters: Rich Robinson, Chris Robinson

Smouldering neo-Blues Rock.

BLACK FLAG
1978

WASTED
Album: Nervous Breakdown
Record Label: SST
Songwriters: Greg Ginn, Keith Morris

Covered by Camper Van Beethoven (Independent Project, '85).

1981

RISE ABOVE
Producers: Spot, Black Flag
Album: Damaged
Record Label: SST
Songwriter: Greg Ginn

Hardcore's first poet manque, Henry Rollins, debuted as a singer with this Punk Rock classic.

TV PARTY
Producers: Spot, Black Flag
Album: Damaged
Record Label: SST
Songwriter: Greg Ginn

What might have happened if the Sex Pistols had a sense of humor and came from the vast wasteland of suburban L.A.

BLACK SABBATH
1970

PARANOID
Producer: Rodger Rain
Album: Paranoid
Record Label: Warner Brothers
Songwriters: Tony Iommi, Geezer Butler, Ozzy Osbourne, Bill Butler

Introducing John "Ozzy" Osbourne, the original behemoth of Heavy Metal (with the notable exception of Ian "Lemmy" Kilmeister) arising from the sludge of Birmingham, England. With four-fingered Tony Iommi on guitar, Sabbath's first chart single defined their lumbering, mouldering attitude.

1971

BLACK SABBATH
Producer: Rodger Rain
Album: Black Sabbath
Record Label: Warner Brothers
Songwriters: Tony Iommi, Geezer Butler, Ozzy Osbourne, Bill Ward

Perennially indomitable sludge personified.

CHILDREN OF THE GRAVE
Producer: Rodger Rain
Album: Master of Reality
Record Label: Warner Brothers
Songwriters: Tony Iommi, Geezer Butler, Ozzy Osbourne, Bill Ward

Covered by Ozzy Osbourne (Jet, '82) and on his tribute album to his legendary late guitarist Randy Rhoads (CBS Associated, '87).

IRON MAN
Producer: Rodger Rain
Album: Paranoid
Record Label: Warner Brothers
Songwriters: Tony Iommi, Geezer Butler, Ozzy Osbourne, Bill Ward

Metal monster.

BILL BLACK'S COMBO
1959

SMOKIE (PART II)
Record Label: Hi
Songwriter: Bill Black

#1 R&B/Top-20 R&R crossover instrumental by Elvis's bassman, in a prototypical Rock-n-Soul combo setting (see Booker T. and the MGs) that would result in four more Top-20 hits for him in the next year, including the #1 R&B/Top-10 R&R crossover, "White Silver Sands," a cover of Don Rondo's '57 Pop hit.

CILLA BLACK
1964

IT'S FOR YOU
Album: Is It Love
Record Label: Capitol
Songwriters: John Lennon, Paul McCartney

Big hit in England for the Cavern Club's former hat-check girl.

BLACKBYRDS
1975

WALKING IN RHYTHM
Album: Flyin' Start
Record Label: Fantasy
Songwriter: Barney Perry

BLACKSTREET

1994

BEFORE I LET YOU GO
Producer: Teddy Riley
Album: This is Me
Record Label: Warner Brothers
Songwriters: Teddy Riley, Leon Sylvers, Melvin Riley, Chauncey Hannibal, Dave Hollister
Another undeniable Riley production.

BILLY BLAND

1960

LET THE LITTLE GIRL DANCE
Record Label: Old Town
Songwriters: Henry Glover, Carl Spencer
Anticipation of the coming dance wave.

BOBBY BLAND

1957

FARTHER UP THE ROAD
Producer: Joe Scott
Record Label: Duke
Songwriters: J. Veasey, Don Robey
His first hit—a Top-5 R&B/Top-50 R&R crossover.

1960

I'LL TAKE CARE OF YOU
Producer: Joe Scott
Album: Together for the First Time . . . Live
Record Label: Duke
Songwriter: Brook Benton
#2 R&B/Bottom-20 R&R crossover for the great R&B/Soul belter.

1961

I PITY THE FOOL
Producer: Joe Scott
Album: 2 Steps from the Blues
Record Label: Duke
Songwriter: Deadric Malone
One of his bluesiest refrains. #1 R&B/Top-50 R&R crossover. Covered by Ann Peebles (Hi, '71).

TURN ON YOUR LOVE LIGHT
Producer: Joe Scott
Album: Here's the Man
Record Label: Duke
Songwriters: Deadric Malone, Joseph Scott
His most revered rockin' Soul and a Top-10 R&B/Top-30 R&R crossover.

1963

THAT'S THE WAY LOVE IS
Record Label: Duke
Songwriter: Deadric Malone
#1 R&B/Top-40 crossover.

1964

AIN'T NOTHIN' YOU CAN DO
Producer: Joe Scott
Album: Ain't Nothin' You Can Do
Record Label: Duke
Songwriters: Deadric Malone, Joe Scott
Top-20 R&R hit.

MARCIE BLANE

1962

BOBBY'S GIRL
Producer: Marv Holtzman
Record Label: Seville
Songwriters: Henry Hoffman, Gary Klein
Quintessential teen lament. Covered in England by Susan Maugham (Phillips, '62).

FREDDIE BLASSIE

1977

PENCIL NECK GEEK
Album: King of Men
Record Label: Rhino
Songwriters: Martin Margulies, Peter Cicero
The Rock and wrestling connection comes together on this entirely convincing, threatening oddity/novelty, more fist-in-cheek than tongue-in-cheek. Blassie once appeared on "The Dick Van Dyke Show," doing the Twazzle.

THE BLASTERS

1980

AMERICAN MUSIC
Producer: Ron Weiser
Album: American Music
Record Label: Slash
Songwriter: Dave Alvin
Roots Rock anthem and cause.

MARIE MARIE
Producer: Ron Weiser
Album: American Music
Record Label: Rolling Rock
Songwriter: Dave Alvin
Chuck Berry, squared.

1963

BORDER RADIO
Album: The Blasters
Record Label: Slash
Songwriter: Dave Alvin
Suggested segue: "Mexican Radio" by Wall of Voodoo.

1983

LONG WHITE CADILLAC
Producer: The Blasters
Album: Non Fiction
Record Label: Slash
Songwriter: Dave Alvin
Tribute to Hank Williams.

1985

COMMON MAN
Album: Hard Line
Record Label: Slash
Songwriter: Dave Alvin
Lighting out for John Cougar Mellencamp territory.

MARY J. BLIGE

1992

REAL LOVE
Producer: Dave Hall
Album: What's the 411?
Record Label: Uptown
Songwriters: Mark Rooney, Mark Morales
New Soul temptress.

YOU REMIND ME
Album: Strictly Business Soundtrack
Record Label: Uptown
Songwriters: Dave Hall, Eric Militeer
#1 R&B/Top-30 crossover.

BLIND FAITH

1969

CAN'T FIND MY WAY HOME
Producer: Jimmy Miller
Album: Blind Faith
Record Label: Atco
Songwriter: Steve Winwood
Top track for the British supergroup (Clapton, Winwood, Baker, Grech).

PRESENCE OF THE LORD
Producer: Jimmy Miller
Album: Blind Faith
Record Label: Atco
Songwriter: Eric Clapton

Cream meets Traffic at the crossroads of Progressive Rock and Gospel.

BLIND MELON

1993

NO RAIN
Producers: Rich Parashar, Blind Melon
Album: Blind Melon
Record Label: Capitol
Songwriter: Blind Melon

Updated psychedelia-lite.

BLONDIE

1976

X-OFFENDER
Producers: Richard Gottehrer, Craig Leon
Album: Blondie
Record Label: Private Stock
Songwriters: Deborah Harry, Gary Valentine

Their legendary first single.

1977

IN THE SUN
Producers: Richard Gottehrer, Craig Leon
Album: Blondie
Record Label: Private Stock
Songwriter: Chris Stein

Fresh and weathered, unworldly and wise, this B-side of "X-Offender" was a postmodern girl-group tribute to the memory of quintessential Disney girl Annette. Suggested segues: "Under the Boardwalk" by the Drifters, "California Sun" by the Beach Boys, and "California Sun" by the Ramones .

1978

HEART OF GLASS
Producer: Mike Chapman
Album: Parallel Lines
Record Label: Chrysalis
Songwriters: Deborah Harry, Chris Stein

#1 U.S./#1 U.K. crossover; the one-time Max's Kansas City waitress became the sensuously cynical voice of a generation's ennui.

ONE WAY OR ANOTHER
Producer: Mike Chapman
Album: Parallel Lines
Record Label: Chrysalis

Songwriters: Nigel Harrison, Deborah Harry

Somewhere the Shangri-las were smiling.

1979

DREAMING
Producer: Mike Chapman
Album: Eat to the Beat
Record Label: Chrysalis
Songwriters: Deborah Harry, Chris Stein

Punk Rock pin-up girl achieves Pop perfection.

SUNDAY GIRL
Producer: Mike Chapman
Album: Parallel Lines
Record Label: Chrysalis
Songwriter: Chris Stein

#1 in the U.K. Harriet Gavurin, to say nothing of Hope Sandoval, was listening.

1980

CALL ME
Producer: Giorgio Moroder
Album: The Best of Blondie
Record Label: Chrysalis
Songwriters: Giorgio Moroder, Deborah Harry

Debbie does Disco. From the Richard Gere movie, American Gigolo.

1981

RAPTURE
Producer: Mike Chapman
Album: Autoamerican
Record Label: Chrysalis
Songwriters: Deborah Harry, Chris Stein

Dancehall staple.

BLOOD, SWEAT, AND TEARS

1968

I CAN'T QUIT HER
Producer: John Simon
Album: Child Is Father to the Man
Record Label: Columbia
Songwriters: Al Kooper, Irwin Levine

Dylan collaborator and former Royal Teen, Al Kooper reached a white Blues epiphany, with the help of future co-writer of "Tie a Yellow Ribbon Round the Old Oak Tree."

I LOVE YOU MORE THAN YOU'LL EVER KNOW
Producer: John Simon
Album: Child Is Father to the Man

Record Label: Columbia
Songwriter: Al Kooper

Blue-eyed Soul standard. Covered by Donnie Hathaway (Atco, '73).

1969

SPINNING WHEEL
Producer: James William Guercio
Album: Blood, Sweat, and Tears
Record Label: Columbia
Songwriter: David Clayon Thomas

This second, more successful and less-interesting incarnation of Blood, Sweat, and Tears finds Guercio practicing for Chicago.

BLOODSTONE

1973

NATURAL HIGH
Producer: Mike Vernon
Album: Natural High
Record Label: London
Songwriter: Charles E. McCormick

Like Hendrix a decade earlier, and Suzi Quatro the year before, this U.S. act went to England to establish a career, though not quite as formidable as the former, nor as snazzy as the latter.

BOBBY BLOOM

1970

MONTEGO BAY
Producer: Jeff Barry
Album: Bobby Bloom Album
Record Label: LTR
Songwriters: Jeff Barry, Bobby Bloom

Reggae Lite escapism.

BLOTTO

1980

I WANNA BE A LIFEGUARD
Album: Hello! My Name's Blotto, What's Yours?
Record Label: Blotto
Songwriters: Bob Rothberg, Sammy Timberg

The Ramones go to community college.

KURTIS BLOW

1980

THE BREAKS
Producers: James Moore, Robert Ford
Album: Kurtis Blow
Record Label: Mercury

Songwriters: James Moore, Lawrence Smith, Kurt Walker, Robert Ford Jr., Russell Simmons

Classic Rap track, opening the voice of the inner city to the minds of its young inhabitants.

1986

STREET ROCK
Album: Kingdom Blow
Record Label: Polygram
Songwriters: Kurtis Blow, Bill Black, Tashim

With Bob Dylan doing his first Rap song since "Talking World War III."

BLUE MAGIC
1974

SIDESHOW
Producer: Norman Harris
Album: Blue Magic
Record Label: Atco
Songwriters: Vinnie Barrett, Bobby Eli

#1 R&B/Top-10 R&R crossover.

BLUE OYSTER CULT
1972

CITIES ON FLAME WITH ROCK AND ROLL
Producer: Sandy Pearlman
Album: Blue Oyster Cult
Record Label: Columbia
Songwriters: Sandy Pearlman, Donald Roeser (Buck Dharma), Jack Bouchard

Opening Heavy Metal's door to the literati. The New York Dolls would shortly tramp on through.

SHE'S AS BEAUTIFUL AS A FOOT
Producer: Sandy Pearlman
Album: Blue Oyster Cult
Record Label: Columbia
Songwriters: Richard Meltzer, Jack Bouchard, Allen Lanier

The Rock critic's revenge; the noted author, Meltzer, earns more in royalties writing for these post-hippies from Long Island than he could ever expect from epic tomes like The Aesthetics of Rock. *John ("I have seen the future of Rock and Roll") Landau was listening and learning.*

1976

(DON'T FEAR) THE REAPER
Producer: Sandy Pearlman
Album: Agents of Fortune

Record Label: Columbia
Songwriter: Donald Roeser (Buck Dharma)

Joining the corporate arena crowd with a crowd-pleaser about death.

1977

GODZILLA
Producer: Sandy Pearlman
Album: Spectres
Record Label: Columbia
Songwriter: Donald Roeser (Buck Dharma)

Establishing the natural creative leap between Heavy Metal and horror movies. The various members of Anthrax, Slayer, and White Zombie were captivated by this scintillating premise.

1979

IN THEE
Producer: Sandy Pearlman
Album: Mirrors
Record Label: Columbia
Songwriter: Allen Lanier

A tribute to East Village Rock-poet manque, Patti Smith.

1981

BURNIN' FOR YOU
Producer: Martin Birch
Album: Fire of Unknown Origin
Record Label: Columbia
Songwriters: Donald Roeser (Buck Dharma), Richard Meltzer

Completing their journey to the mainstream.

JOAN CRAWFORD
Producer: Martin Birch
Album: Fire of Unknown Origin
Record Label: Columbia
Songwriters: Albert Bouchard, David R. Ruter, John Lennert Rigg

Cult goes Hollywood.

DAVID BLUE
1968

THESE 23 DAYS IN SEPTEMBER
Producer: Gabriel Mekler
Album: These 23 Days in September
Record Label: Asylum
Songwriter: David Blue

Advancing from Dylanology to Jackson-Brownean singer/songwriterism.

THE BLUEBELLES
1962

I SOLD MY HEART TO THE JUNKMAN
Producer: Bobby Martin
Album: Apollo Presents the Bluebelles
Record Label: Newton
Songwriters: Otis Rene Jr., Leon Rene

Originated by Steve Gibson and the Redcaps, with vocals by Damita Jo. Sung by the Starlets, but mistakenly accredited to the Bluebelles.

BLUES IMAGE
1970

RIDE CAPTAIN RIDE
Producer: Richard Polodor
Album: Open
Record Label: Atco
Songwriters: Frank Konte, Carlos Pinera

The beginning of Classic Rock; the beginning of the end of FM radio.

THE BLUES MAGOOS
1966

WE AIN'T GOT NOTHING YET
Producer: Wyld & Polhemus
Album: Psychedelic Lollipop
Record Label: Mercury
Songwriters: Emil Thielhelm, Michael Esposito, Ralph Scala, Ronald Gilbert

Elucidating the Garage Punk agenda.

THE BLUES PROJECT
1966

VIOLETS OF DAWN
Producer: Jerry Schoenbaum
Album: The Blues Project Live at Cafe Au Go Go
Record Label: Verve/Folkways
Songwriter: Eric Andersen

Post-coital or post-acid trip: the legendary Greenwich Village Blues Project at their folkiest.

1967

NO TIME LIKE THE RIGHT TIME
Producer: Tom Wilson
Album: Blues Project Live at Town Hall
Record Label: Verve/Forecast

Songwriter: Al Kooper

Early Kooper Blues rouser.

WAKE ME, SHAKE ME

Producer: Tom Wilson
Album: Projections
Record Label: Verve/Forecast
Songwriter: Al Kooper

Also known as "Don't Let Me Sleep Too Long," as covered by the Myddle Class (Kama Sutra, '67) and produced by Carole King.

BLUES TRAVELER

1994

RUN AROUND

Producers: S. Thompson, M. Barbiero
Album: Four
Record Label: A&M
Songwriter: John Popper

The return of the Rock harmonica, in an advanced Springsteenian boogie setting that would have made Rosalita as well as Paul Butterfield smile.

BLUR

1994

GIRLS AND BOYS

Producer: Stephen Street
Album: Parklife
Record Label: ERG/SBK
Songwriters: Damon Albarn, Graham Coxon, Alex James, Dave Rountree

Big in the U.K. Blurring the sexuality of the English dancehall of the '90s. Suggested segue: "Lola" by the Kinks.

BOB AND EARL

1964

HARLEM SHUFFLE

Album: Harlem Shuffle
Record Label: Marc
Songwriters: Bob Reig, Earl Nelson

Top-50 R&R classic. Covered by the Rolling Stones (Rolling Stones, '91).

THE BOBBETTES

1957

MR. LEE

Record Label: Atlantic
Songwriters: Heather Dixon, Helen Gathers, Emma Ruth Pought, Laura Webb, Janine Pought

The real-life principal of New York's P.S. 109 becomes the stuff of teenage girl-group history. Three years later, the Bobbettes would finish him off in "I Shot Mr. Lee," on Triple X.

THE BODEANS

1987

FOREVER YOUNG (THE WILD ONES)

Producers: Jerry Harrison, He and He
Album: Outside Looking In
Record Label: Slash
Songwriters: Sammy Llanas, Kurt Neumann

Propulsive neo-Folk Rock with updated Everly Brothers harmonies.

BODY COUNT

1992

COP KILLER

Producers: Ernie C., Lee T.
Album: Body Count
Record Label: Warner Brothers
Songwriter: Tracy Morrow (Ice T)

More explicit than "I Fought the Law" and "I Shot the Sherrif" (and "I Shot Mr. Lee") combined, this track came to symbolize Gangsta Rap as an anti-authoritarian genre glorifying violence and espousing anarchy under the guise of merely describing it.

MICHAEL BOLTON

1990

HOW CAN WE BE LOVERS

Producers: Desmond Child, Michael Bolton
Album: Soul Provider
Record Label: Columbia
Songwriters: Diane Warren, Desmond Child, Michael Bolton

Corporate Rock of the '90s.

1991

LOVE IS A WONDERFUL THING

Producers: Walter Afanasieff, Michael Bolton
Album: Time, Love and Tenderness
Record Label: Columbia
Songwriters: Michael Bolton, Andy Goldmark

BON JOVI

1984

RUNAWAY

Producers: Tony Bongiovi, Lance Quinn
Album: Bon Jovi
Record Label: Mercury
Songwriters: Jon Bon Jovi, George Karak

Streetwise Arena Rock; their first angst-ridden hit.

1986

YOU GIVE LOVE A BAD NAME

Producer: Bruce Fairbairn
Album: Slippery When Wet
Record Label: Polygram
Songwriters: Jon Bon Jovi, Richie Sambora, Desmond Child

#1 R&R Arena Metal monster. Song-doctor Child tweaks his magic twanger.

1987

LIVIN' ON A PRAYER

Producer: Bruce Fairbairn
Album: Slippery When Wet
Record Label: Polygram
Songwriters: Jon Bon Jovi, Richie Sambora, Desmond Child

With characters straight from Springsteen's Greasy Lake, the Desmond Child-guided writing team follows up "You Give Love a Bad Name" with an even bigger #1 hit.

WANTED DEAD OR ALIVE

Producer: Bruce Fairbairn
Album: Slippery When Wet
Record Label: Polygram
Songwriters: Jon Bon Jovi, Richie Sambora

Mining the Rock-star-as-gunslinger motif originated by Bo Diddley.

1988

BAD MEDICINE

Producer: Bruce Fairbairn
Album: New Jersey
Record Label: Mercury
Songwriters: Jon Bon Jovi, Richie Sambora, Desmond Child

Representing the apex of the second great corporate Arena Metal heyday.

1989

BORN TO BE MY BABY

Producer: Bruce Fairbairn
Album: New Jersey
Record Label: Mercury

Songwriters: Jon Bon Jovi, Richie Sambora, Desmond Child

Typical pseduo-Springsteenian, Spectoresque overstated smash.

I'LL BE THERE FOR YOU
Producer: Bruce Fairbairn
Album: New Jersey
Record Label: Mercury/Polygram
Songwriters: Jon Bon Jovi, Richie Sambora

The glossy idealized romantic Rock ballad strikes again.

1992

BED OF ROSES
Producer: Bob Rock
Album: Keep the Faith
Record Label: Mercury
Songwriter: Jon Bon Jovi

Typical New Jersey dramaturg.

1994

ALWAYS
Producer: Peter Collins
Album: Cross Roads
Record Label: Mercury
Songwriter: Jon Bon Jovi

Opening with six cliches in a row, including major chart success.

JON BON JOVI

1990

BLAZE OF GLORY
Producers: Danny Kortchmar, Jon Bon Jovi
Album: *Blaze of Glory* Soundtrack
Record Label: Polygram
Songwriter: Jon Bon Jovi

Returning to the gunslinger motif.

JOHNNY BOND

1955

HOT ROD LINCOLN
Record Label: Souvenir
Songwriters: Charlie Ryan, W. S. Stevenson

This trusty Rockabilly vehicle was originated by Tiny Hill. Covered by author Charlie Ryan (4-Star, '60), Johnny Bond (Republic, '60), and Commander Cody (Paramount, '72).

GARY U.S. BONDS

1960

(DOWN IN) NEW ORLEANS
Producer: Frank J. Guida
Album: Dance Til Quarter to Three

Record Label: LeGrand
Songwriter: Frank J. Guida

Gary's debut hit, among the many celebrations of one of Rock and Roll's first cities.

1961

DEAR LADY TWIST
Producer: Frank J. Guida
Album: Dance 'Til Quarter to Three
Record Label: LeGrand
Songwriter: Frank J. Guida

A twist on the Twist.

QUARTER TO THREE
Producer: Frank J. Guida
Album: Dance 'Til Quarter to Three
Record Label: LeGrand
Songwriters: Frank J. Guida, Gene Barge, Joe Royster, Gary Anderson (U.S. Bonds)

Stoking the relentless dance groove of '61. Gene Barge on sax is Daddy Gee; the rhythm track, entitled "A Night with Daddy Gee," rewritten by Bonds, was provided by the very Church Street Five mentioned in the lyrics.

SCHOOL IS OUT
Producer: Frank J. Guida
Album: Dance Til Quarter to Three
Record Label: LeGrand
Songwriters: Gary Anderson (U.S. Bonds), Gene Barge

Suggested segue: "School's Out" by Alice Cooper.

1962

SEVEN-DAY WEEKEND
Producer: Frank J. Guida
Album: Twist up Calypso
Record Label: LeGrand
Songwriters: Doc Pomus, Mort Shuman

TWIST, TWIST SENORA
Producer: Frank J. Guida
Album: Twist up Calypso
Record Label: LeGrand
Songwriters: Frank J. Guida, Joseph Royster, Gene Barge

Combining two early-'60s dance beats— the Twist and Calypso.

1981

THIS LITTLE GIRL
Producers: Bruce Springsteen, Steve Van Zandt
Album: Dedication
Record Label: EMI-America

Songwriter: Bruce Springsteen

Comeback hit for the noted East Coast rocker.

1982

OUT OF WORK
Producers: Bruce Springsteen, Steve Van Zandt
Album: On the Line
Record Label: EMI-America
Songwriter: Bruce Springsteen

Working class meets middle class with the help of the Boss, who also wrote about this kind of situation.

KARLA BONOFF

1977

I CAN'T HOLD ON
Producer: Kenny Edwards
Album: Karla Bonoff
Record Label: Columbia
Songwriter: Karla Bonoff

Nasal West-coast lite-rocker, with plenty to say about getting and keeping love.

IF HE'S EVER NEAR
Producer: Kenny Edwards
Album: Karla Bonoff
Record Label: Columbia
Songwriter: Karla Bonoff

The poet laureate of the singles bar set. Covered by Linda Ronstadt (Asylum, '76).

BOOGIE DOWN PRODUCTIONS

1988

STOP THE VIOLENCE
Producer: KNS-One
Album: By All Means Necessary
Record Label: Jive
Songwriter: Lawrence Parker

Civic-minded Rap classic by a major artist in the genre of heavy street poetics. Led to the all-star Self-Destruction EP (Jive, '89).

BOOKER T. AND THE MG'S

1962

GREEN ONIONS
Producer: Jim Stewart
Album: Green Onions
Record Label: Stax
Songwriters: Steve Cropper, Booker T. Jones, Al Jackson Jr., Lewis Steinberg.

Soul food by the house band at Stax.

1968

HANG 'EM HIGH

Producer: Booker T. and the MG's
Album: Soul Limbo
Record Label: Stax
Songwriters: Jack Gold, Phil Zeller, Dominic Frontiere

Spaghetti Soul, from the film.

1969

TIME IS TIGHT

Producer: Booker T. Jones
Album: Uptight
Record Label: Stax
Songwriters: Steve Cropper, Booker T. Jones, Al Jackson Jr., Donald V. Dunn

Still tight after all those years.

CHUCKII BOOKER

1989

TURNED AWAY

Album: Chuckii
Record Label: Atlantic
Songwriter: Chuck Booker

#1 R&B/Top-50 crossover.

1992

GAMES

Album: Nice n' Wild
Record Label: Atlantic
Songwriters: Gerald Levert, Chuckii Booker, C. J. Anthony

#1 R&B/Bottom-40 crossover.

THE BOOMTOWN RATS

1979

I DON'T LIKE MONDAYS

Album: The Fine Art of Surfacing
Record Label: Columbia
Songwriter: Bob Geldof

#1 U.K./U.S. crossover; post-Punk Rock journalism based on the true story of the mass-murderer Brenda Spencer, who offered the immortal title phrase to explain why she gunned down eleven people.

PAT BOONE

1956

DON'T FORBID ME

Album: Pat's Great Hits
Record Label: Dot
Songwriter: Charlie Singleton

Covered by Elvis Presley with the Million Dollar Quartet: Carl Perkins, Jerry Lee Lewis, and Johnny Cash (Sun, '56).

1958

(EVERYBODY'S GONNA HAVE) A WONDERFUL TIME UP THERE (GOSPEL BOOGIE)

Record Label: Dot
Songwriter: Lee Roy Abernethy

B-side of his cover of the Orioles' "It's Too Soon to Know," was a cover of Leroy Abernethy's Gospel classic from 1947.

1961

MOODY RIVER

Album: Moody River
Record Label: Dot
Songwriter: Gary Bruce

One of his rare non-cover hits.

BOOTSY'S RUBBER BAND

1978

BOOTZILLA

Producer: George Clifton
Album: Bootsy? Player of the Year
Record Label: Warner Brothers
Songwriters: George Clinton, William Collins

Kiddie Funk, from James Brown's famous bassist, William "Bootsy" Collins.

BOSTON

1976

LONG TIME

Producers: Tom Scholz, John Boylan
Album: Boston
Record Label: Epic
Songwriter: Tom Scholz

Ushering in the first heyday of corporate Rock since the Brill Building/Motown '60s.

MORE THAN A FEELING

Producers: Tom Scholz, John Boylan
Album: Boston
Record Label: Epic
Songwriter: Tom Scholz

Heavy Metal-processed landmark; Scholz went on to found a company to keep him in electronic devices.

1978

DON'T LOOK BACK

Producers: Tom Scholz, Dave Butler
Album: Don't Look Back
Record Label: Epic
Songwriter: Tom Scholz

Speedy followup of the inspired Arena formula.

1986

AMANDA

Producer: Tom Scholz
Album: Third Stage
Record Label: MCA
Songwriter: Tom Scholz

Still masters of high-tech, corporate Arena Rock after all those lawsuits.

WE'RE READY

Producer: Tom Scholz
Album: Third Stage
Record Label: MCA
Songwriter: Tom Scholz

Corporate Metal swansong.

BOW WOW WOW

1980

LOUIS QUATORZE

Producer: Malcolm McLaren
Album: Your Cassette Pet
Record Label: EMI (Import)
Songwriters: Malcolm McLaren, Mathew Ashman, David Della Barbarrosa, Leigh Roy Gorman

Jailbait rocker, by the fabricated British group more famous for their cover of "I Want Candy" (RCA, '82).

JIMMY BOWEN

1957

I'M STICKIN' WITH YOU

Producer: Norman Petty
Album: Triple D
Record Label: Roulette
Songwriters: Jimmy Bowen, Buddy Knox

Exploiting the massive clout of Rockabilly, the Rhythm Orchids spawned a double A-sided hit for two of its members. The guitarist, Buddy Knox, beat the bass player, Jimmy Bowen, by a country mile, hitting #1 with "Party Doll." Bowen, however, would have his retribution, as he would eventually climb the rungs of the music business ladder to a comparable position.

DAVID BOWIE

1968

SPACE ODDITY

Producer: Mike Vernon
Album: Man of Words—Man of Music

Record Label: Mercury
Songwriter: David Bowie

An English music-hall original, formerly known as Davy Jones, re-invents himself for the space age with a tune inspired by Stanley Kubrick's 2001: A Space Odyssey. *Written for the film* Love You Till Tuesday, *it was a hit in England in '69; re-released, it was a hit in the U.S. (RCA, '73). Suggested segue: "Major Tom (Coming Home)" by Peter Schilling.*

1970

THE MAN WHO SOLD THE WORLD

Producer: Tony Visconti
Album: The Man Who Sold the World
Record Label: Mercury
Songwriter: David Bowie

Protoypically arch early track from the chameleonic superstar who influenced a generation of British Rock styles, from glam to gloom, pomp to Punk. Covered by Nirvana (DGC, '94).

1971

CHANGES

Producer: Ken Scott
Album: Hunky Dory
Record Label: RCA
Songwriter: David Bowie

Rock's first fashion guru identifies change as a concept, a niche, a trend, a market, with a stutter borrowed from Roger Daltrey.

1972

JEAN GENIE

Producer: David Bowie
Album: Aladdin Sane
Record Label: RCA
Songwriter: David Bowie

Title derived from the name of French poet, Jean Genet, and inspired by Iggy Pop.

SUFFRAGETTE CITY

Producers: Ken Scott, David Bowie
Album: The Rise and Fall of Ziggy Stardust and the Spiders from Mars
Record Label: RCA
Songwriter: David Bowie

One of his best rockers.

1973

ALADDIN SANE

Producers: Ken Scott, David Bowie
Album: Aladdin Sane
Record Label: RCA
Songwriter: David Bowie

Pouty pyrotechnics, a battle plan for Mope Rock. Covered by Bauhaus (4AD, '80).

1974

REBEL REBEL

Producer: David Bowie
Album: Diamond Dogs
Record Label: RCA
Songwriter: David Bowie

Deca-Rock companion piece to "All the Young Dudes."

1975

FAME

Producers: Harry Maslin, David Bowie
Album: Young Americans
Record Label: RCA
Songwriters: John Lennon, David Bowie, Carlos Alomar

His first U.S. #1. Suggested segue: "Hot" by James Brown.

YOUNG AMERICANS

Producers: Harry Maslin, David Bowie
Album: Young Americans
Record Label: RCA
Songwriter: David Bowie

Bowie records in and is inspired by Philadelphia.

1976

GOLDEN YEARS

Producers: Harry Maslin, David Bowie
Album: Station to Station
Record Label: RCA
Songwriter: David Bowie

Flirting with Soul.

TVC 15

Producers: Harry Maslin, David Bowie
Album: Station to Station
Record Label: RCA
Songwriter: David Bowie

Disco-age experimentalism.

1977

HEROES

Producers: Tony Visconti, David Bowie
Album: Heroes
Record Label: RCA
Songwriter: David Bowie

Venturing into Kraftwerk territory.

1980

ASHES TO ASHES

Producers: Tony Visconti, David Bowie
Album: Scary Monsters
Record Label: RCA
Songwriter: David Bowie

#1 U.K. hit, collected on six different album anthologies; comes with a trend-setting and very expensive pre-MTV music video.

FASHION

Producers: Tony Visconti, David Bowie
Album: Scary Monsters
Record Label: RCA
Songwriter: David Bowie

Return to his favorite topic.

1983

LET'S DANCE

Producers: Nile Rodgers, David Bowie
Album: Let's Dance
Record Label: EMI-America
Songwriter: David Bowie

#1 U.S./U.K. smash introduced the world outside of Austin, Tex., to Stevie Ray Vaughan on guitar.

MODERN LOVE

Producers: Nile Rodgers, David Bowie
Album: Let's Dance
Record Label: EMI-America
Songwriter: David Bowie

Bowie at his most accessible, danceable.

1984

BLUE JEAN

Producers: Nile Rodgers, David Bowie
Album: Tonight
Record Label: EMI-America
Songwriter: David Bowie

Typifying his commercial heyday.

1986

ABSOLUTE BEGINNERS

Producers: Clive Langer, David Bowie, Alan Winstanley
Album: *Absolute Beginners* Soundtrack
Record Label: EMI-America
Songwriter: David Bowie

Title tune.

DAY IN—DAY OUT

Producers: D. Richards, David Bowie
Album: Never Let Me Down
Record Label: EMI
Songwriter: David Bowie

Bowie's take on Arena Rock. Later he would create Tin Men to partake of this experience.

THE BOX TOPS

1967

BREAK MY MIND

Producer: Dan Penn
Album: The Box Tops
Record Label: Bell
Songwriter: Gram Parsons

Launching the career of two legends in the making. Gram Parsons would join the Byrds the following year and help create Country Rock. Alex Chilton would graduate from the Box Tops into cult status and influence almost all of Alternative Rock, starting with the Replacements. Dan Penn, meanwhile, would become one of Soul's top songwriters. Covered by Parsons' band, the Flying Burrito Brothers (A&M, '72).

THE LETTER

Producer: Dan Penn
Album: The Box Tops: "The Letter"/"Neon Rainbow"
Record Label: Mala
Songwriter: Wayne Carson Thompson

One of the more perfect singles of '67. Covered by Joe Cocker (A&M, '70).

NEON RAINBOW

Producer: Dan Penn
Album: The Box Tops: "The Letter"/"Neon Rainbow"
Record Label: Mala
Songwriter: Wayne Carson Thompson

Following up "The Letter" with the same team, but less-than-perfect results.

1968

CRY LIKE A BABY

Producer: Dan Penn
Album: Cry Like a Baby
Record Label: Mala
Songwriters: Dan Penn, Spooner Oldman

Blue-eyed Memphis Soul. Their second biggest hit.

I MET HER IN CHURCH

Producer: Dan Penn
Album: Non Stop
Record Label: Mala
Songwriters: Dan Penn, Spooner Oldman

Memphis Gospel.

1969

CHOO CHOO TRAIN

Producer: Dan Penn
Album: Box Tops' Super Hits
Record Label: Bell
Songwriters: Eddie Hinton, Donnie Fritts

Their version of Soul train.

SOUL DEEP

Producers: Chips Moman, Tommy Cogbill
Album: Soul Deep
Record Label: Mala
Songwriter: Wayne Carson Thompson

Their last big hit.

BOY MEETS GIRL

1988

WAITING FOR A STAR TO FALL

Producer: Arif Mardin
Album: Reel Life
Record Label: RCA
Songwriters: Gary Merrill, Shannon Rubicam

Alterna-pop hit from the songwriting team that wrote "How Will I Know" for Whitney Houston.

TOMMY BOYCE AND BOBBY HART

1967

I WONDER WHAT SHE'S DOING TONIGHT?

Producers: Tommy Boyce, Bobby Hart
Album: I Wonder What She's Doing Tonight?
Record Label: A&M
Songwriters: Tommy Boyce, Bobby Hart

Post Doo-Wop flashback.

EDDIE BOYD

1952

FIVE LONG YEARS

Record Label: J.O.B.
Songwriter: Eddie Boyd

#1 R&B hit was a Yardbirds concert staple. Covered by Eric Clapton (Warner Brothers, '94).

THE BOYS

1988

DIAL MY HEART

Producers: Babyface, L. A. Reid
Album: Messages from the Boys
Record Label: Motown
Songwriters: Kenny Edmunds (Babyface), Antonio Reid (L. A. Reid, Daryl Simmons

#1 R&B/Top-20 R&R crossover.

1989

LUCKY CHARM

Producer: Babyface
Album: Messages from the Boys
Record Label: Motown
Songwriters: Kenny Edmunds (Babyface), Greg Scelsa, Daryl Simmons

As a writer/singer/producer, Babyface would rule the '90s.

1990

CRAZY

Album: The Boys
Record Label: Motown
Songwriters: Hakeem Abdulsamad, Khlry Abdulsamad

#1 R&B/Top-30 R&R crossover.

BOYS CLUB

1988

I REMEMBER HOLDING YOU

Producers: David Cole, Joe Pasquale
Album: Boys Club
Record Label: MCA
Songwriter: Joe Pasquale

BOYZ II MEN

1991

IT'S SO HARD TO SAY GOODBYE TO YESTERDAY

Producer: Dallas Austin
Album: Cooleyhighharmony
Record Label: Motown
Songwriters: Freddie Perren, Christine Yarian

Exemplary vocal harmony, featured in the movie Lethal Weapon III.

MOTOWNPHILLY

Producer: Dallas Austin
Album: Cooleyhighharmony
Record Label: Motown
Songwriters: Dallas Austin, Michael Bivins, Nathan Morris, Shawn Stockman

Tribute to the roots of '90s harmony Hip-Hop revival.

UHH-AHH

Producer: Dallas Austin
Album: Cooleyhighharmony
Record Label: Motown
Songwriters: Nathan Morris, Wayna Morris, Michael Bivins

1992

END OF THE ROAD

Producers: Babyface, L. A. Reid
Album: *Boomerang* Soundtrack
Record Label: Gee Street/LaFace
Songwriters: Kenny Edmunds (Babyface), Antonio Reid (L.A. Reid), Daryl Simmons

High harmony history; was #1 R&B and briefly the longest-running #1 R&R single of all-time, until Whitney Houston swept by it with "I Will Always Love You." (But were either of them rock and roll?)

1994

I'LL MAKE LOVE TO YOU

Producer: Babyface
Album: II
Record Label: Motown
Songwriter: Kenny Edmunds (Babyface)

#1 R&B/R&R crossover; a gentlemanly seduction.

ON BENDED KNEE

Producer: Babyface
Album: II
Record Label: Motown
Songwriters: James Harris III, Terry Lewis

More Doo-Wop redux in a politically and sexually-correct context.

JAN BRADLEY

1963

MAMA DIDN'T LIE

Producer: Curtis Mayfield
Record Label: Chess
Songwriter: Curtis Mayfield

Low-key Soul tribute to the one who really knows best. Suggested segue: "Mama

Said" by the Shirelles, "Mama" by Connie Francis, "Shop Around" by the Miracles, and "Tell Mama" by Etta James.*

BILLY BRAGG

1983

A NEW ENGLAND

Album: Life's a Riot
Record Label: Utility/Go Discs
Songwriter: Billy Bragg

The Woody Guthrie-inspired Folk singer's debut U.K. single established his two major themes: sex and politics, not necessarily in that order. Covered by Kristy MacColl (Stiff, '85).

1991

SEXUALITY

Producer: Johnny Marr
Album: Don't Try This at Home
Record Label: Elektra
Songwriters: Billy Bragg, Johnny Marr

Refining his sexual politics for his U.S. alternative breakthrough.

THE BRAINS

1980

MONEY CHANGES EVERYTHING

Producer: Steve Lillywhite
Album: The Brains
Record Label: Mercury
Songwriter: Tom Gray

Remake of their inspired Indie Rock single. Covered in equally inspired fashion by Cyndi Lauper (Portrait, '84).

BRANDY

1994

I WANNA BE DOWN

Producer: Keith Crouch
Album: Brandy
Record Label: Atlantic
Songwriters: Keith Crouch, Kipper Jones

Pre-teen bubblegum Hip-Hop is a #1 R&B/R&R crossover.

LAURA BRANIGAN

1982

GLORIA

Producer: Greg Mathieson
Album: Branigan
Record Label: Atlantic
Songwriters: Trevor Veitch, Giancarlo Bigazzi, Umberto Tozzi

The schizoid '80s, "Gloria" was a big hit in Italy by Bigazzi.

1983

HOW AM I SUPPOSED TO LIVE WITHOUT YOU?

Producer: Jack White
Album: Branigan 2
Record Label: Atlantic
Songwriters: Michael Bolton, Doug James

First major hit for the aspiring R&B songwriter, Bolton. Covered by Michael Bolton (Columbia, '89).

SOLITAIRE

Producer: Jack White
Album: Branigan 2
Record Label: Atlantic
Songwriters: Diane Warren, Martine Clemenceau

1984

SELF CONTROL

Producers: Jack White, Robbie Buchanon
Album: Self Control
Record Label: Atlantic
Songwriters: Steve Piccolo, Giancarlo Bigazzi, Raffaele Riefolo

BRASS CONSTRUCTION

1976

MOVIN'

Album: Brass Construction
Record Label: United Artists
Songwriters: Randy Muller, Wade Williamston

TONI BRAXTON

1993

ANOTHER SAD LOVE SONG

Producer: Babyface
Album: Toni Braxton
Record Label: LaFace/Arista
Songwriters: Kenny Edmunds (Babyface), Daryl Simmons

Prime R&B ballad from the prolific team.

BREATHE AGAIN

Producer: Babyface
Album: Toni Braxton
Record Label: LaFace/Arista
Songwriter: Kenny Edmunds (Babyface)

A new Soul diva emerges.

YOU MEAN THE WORLD TO ME

Producer: Babyface
Album: Toni Braxton
Record Label: LaFace/Arista
Songwriters: Kenny Edmunds (Babyface), Antonio Reid (L.A. Reid), Daryl Simmons

Upbeat, responsible message to go with the unstoppable ballad groove.

BREAD
1970

IT DON'T MATTER TO ME

Producers: David Gates, Robb Royer, James Grafton
Album: On the Waters
Record Label: Elektra
Songwriter: David Gates

MAKE IT WITH YOU

Producers: David Gates, Robb Royer, James Grafton
Album: On the Waters
Record Label: Elektra
Songwriter: David Gates

The L.A. session sound survives in the starched perfection of the anti-Randy Newman. Richard Marx sees an eventual niche.

1971

BABY I'M-A-WANT YOU

Producer: David Gates
Album: Baby I'm-a-Want You
Record Label: Elektra
Songwriter: David Gates

Fluff.

IF

Producer: David Gates
Album: Manna
Record Label: Elektra
Songwriter: David Gates

Covered by Telly Savalas (MCA, '75).

1972

EVERYTHING I OWN

Producer: David Gates
Album: Baby I'm-a-Want You
Record Label: Elektra
Songwriter: David Gates

Exemplary Pop Rock product.

1976

LOST WITHOUT YOUR LOVE

Producer: David Gates
Album: Lost Without Your Love

Record Label: Elektra
Songwriter: David Gates

Previewing Lite-Rock

THE BREAKFAST CLUB
1987

RIGHT ON TRACK

Producer: Jimmy Iovine
Album: The Breakfast Club
Record Label: MCA
Songwriters: Steve Bray, Steve Gilroy

Madonna's old band.

BREATHE
1986

DON'T TELL ME LIES

Producer: Bob Sergeant
Album: All That Jazz
Record Label: A&M
Songwriters: Dave Glaspar, Marcus Lillington

First release for the British Dance Rock crooners became a hit when re-released in '89.

1988

HANDS TO HEAVEN

Producer: Bob Sergeant
Album: All That Jazz
Record Label: A&M
Songwriters: Dave Glaspar, Marcus Lillington

In the Paul Weller/Spandau Ballet neo-Soul groove, this plaintive ballad was their biggest hit.

HOW CAN I FALL?

Producer: Bob Sergeant
Album: All That Jazz
Record Label: A&M
Songwriters: Dave Glaspar, Marcus Lillington

More of their breathless, blue-eyed British Soul.

THE BREEDERS
1990

OPENED

Producer: Steve Albini
Album: Pod
Record Label: 4AD
Songwriter: Kim Deal

The first alterna-femme supergroup of the '90s—with Kim Deal from the Pixies and

Tanya Donnelly from Throwing Muses— proves itself with this "History of Utah" for girls.

1993

CANNONBALL

Producer: Kim Deal
Album: Last Splash
Record Label: 4AD/Elektra
Songwriter: Kim Deal

Typifying the hard edge and the soft center of the neo-Folk Rock sound of the '90s girl-group.

SAINTS

Producer: Kim Deal
Album: Last Splash
Record Label: 4AD/Elektra
Songwriter: Kim Deal

JACKIE BRENSTON AND HIS DELTA CATS
1951

ROCKET 88

Producer: Sam Phillips
Record Label: Chess
Songwriter: Jackie Brenston

Elvis Presley's mentor, Phillips, gets the Rock and Roll bug. With Ike Turner on keyboards evoking Jerry Lee Lewis, and Jackie Brenston on sax and vocals, this presages a sound still four years from taking over the planet. Immediately covered by Bill Haley and His Saddlemen (Holiday, '51). The first classic car song of the Rock and Roll era— classic car: the Olds 88. Suggested segue: "Cadillac Boogie" by Jimmy Liggins (Specialty, '47).

BREWER AND SHIPLEY
1971

ONE TOKE OVER THE LINE

Producer: Nick Gravenites
Album: Tarkio
Record Label: Kama Sutra
Songwriters: Michael Brewer, Thomas Shipley

Requiem for an over-indulgent age.

BRICK
1977

DAZZ

Producers: Jim Healy, Johnny Duncan, Robert Lee, Brick
Album: Good High
Record Label: Bang

Songwriters: Reginald Hargis, Edward Irons, Ray Ransom Jr.

Mating Disco and Jazz for a #1 R&B/Top-10 R&R crossover.

EDIE BRICKELL AND NEW BOHEMIANS
1988

CIRCLE

Producer: Pat Moran
Album: Shooting Rubberbands at the Stars
Record Label: Geffen
Songwriters: Edie Brickell, Kenny Withrow

Jazz Rock-flavored introversion, recorded in Wales.

WHAT I AM

Producer: Pat Moran
Album: Shooting Rubberbands at the Stars
Record Label: Geffen
Songwriters: Edie Brickell, Kenny Withrow

Austin-based post-hippie dogma.

ALICIA BRIDGES
1977

I LOVE THE NIGHTLIFE (DISCO ROUND)

Producer: Steve Buckingham
Album: Alicia Bridges
Record Label: Polydor
Songwriters: Alicia Bridges, Susan Hutcheson

Nasal Disco one-shot.

LILLIAN BRIGGS
1956

I WANT YOU TO BE MY BABY

Record Label: Epic
Songwriter: John Hendricks

The signature tune of this white, trombone-playing, laundry truck driver routinely brought the house down at the Apollo Theatre in Harlem.

MARTIN BRILEY
1983

THE SALT IN MY TEARS

Producer: Peter Coleman
Album: One Night with a Stranger
Record Label: Mercury
Songwriter: Martin Briley

British drollery.

BRINZLEY SCHWARZ
1974

(WHAT'S SO FUNNY 'BOUT) PEACE, LOVE, AND UNDERSTANDING

Album: New Favourites of Brinzley Schwarz
Record Label: United Artists
Songwriter: Nick Lowe

Future pure-Pop peacenik classic, covered by Elvis Costello (Columbia, '79).

JOHNNY BRISTOL
1974

HANG ON IN THERE BABY

Producer: Johnny Bristol
Album: Hang on in There Baby
Record Label: MGM
Songwriter: Johnny Bristol

Best-selling solo effort from the former Motown producer/writer.

BRONSKI BEAT
1985

SMALL TOWN BOY

Producer: Mike Thorne
Album: The Age of Consent
Record Label: MCA
Songwriters: Jimmy Somerville, Larry Steinbachek, Steve Bronski

Alternative dancehall falsetto.

DONNIE BROOKS
1960

MISSION BELL

Album: The Happiest
Record Label: Era
Songwriter: William Michael

A big year for Country crossovers.

BROTHERHOOD OF MAN
1970

UNITED WE STAND

Producer: Tony Hiller
Album: United We Stand
Record Label: Deram
Songwriters: Tony Hiller, Peter Simons

Uplifting British Soul commodity.

THE BROTHERS FIGARO
1990

1959

Producer: Pat Moran
Album: Gypsy Beat
Record Label: Geffen
Songwriter: Bill Bonk

Retro-Folk harmonizing.

THE BROTHERS FOUR
1960

GREENFIELDS

Album: The Brothers Four
Record Label: Columbia
Songwriters: Terry Gilkyson, Rick Dehr, Frank Miller

Future Folk standard, written by Terry Gilkyson and the Easy Riders, of "Marianne" fame.

THE BROTHERS JOHNSON
1976

I'LL BE GOOD TO YOU

Producer: Quincy Jones
Album: Look out for #1
Record Label: A&M
Songwriters: Louis Johnson, George Johnson, Senora Sam

#1 R&B/Top-10 R&R crossover. Covered by Quincy Jones (with Chaha Kahn) was a #1 R&B/Top-20 R&R crossover.

1977

STRAWBERRY LETTER 23

Producer: Quincy Jones
Album: Right on Time
Record Label: A&M
Songwriter: Shuggie Otis

#1 R&B/Top-10 R&R crossover.

1979

STOMP

Producer: Quincy Jones
Album: Light up the Night
Record Label: A&M
Songwriters: Louis Johnson, George Johnson, Rod Temperton, Valerie Johnson

#1 R&B/Top-10 R&R crossover.

ARTHUR BROWN

1968

FIRE!

Producer: Kit Lambert
Album: The Crazy World of Arthur Brown
Record Label: Atlantic
Songwriters: Arthur Brown, Vincent Crane, Peter Ker, Finesilver

Fire-breathing progressive rock one-shot.

BOBBY BROWN

1986

GIRLFRIEND

Producer: Larry White
Album: King of Stage
Record Label: MCA
Songwriters: Larry White, Lee Peters, Kirk Crumpler

#1 R&B debut for the former New Edition heartthrob.

1988

DON'T BE CRUEL

Producers: Babyface, L. A. Reid
Album: Don't Be Cruel
Record Label: MCA
Songwriters: Kenny Edmunds (Babyface), Antonio Reid (L.A. Reid), Daryl Simmons

#1 R&B/R&R crossover launched his Pop Soul career.

MY PREROGATIVE

Producer: Gene Griffen
Album: Don't Be Cruel
Record Label: MCA
Songwriters: Gene Griffin, Bobby Brown

#1 R&B/R&R crossover.

ROCK WIT'CHA

Producers: Babyface, L. A. Reid
Album: Don't Be Cruel
Record Label: MCA
Songwriters: Babyface (Kenny Edmunds), Daryl Simmons

1989

EVERY LITTLE STEP

Producers: Babyface, L. A. Reid
Album: Don't Be Cruel
Record Label: MCA
Songwriters: Kenny Edmunds (Babyface), Antonio Reid (L.A. Reid)

ON OUR OWN (FROM *GHOSTBUSTERS II*)

Producers: Babyface, L. A. Reid
Album: *Ghostbusters II* Soundtrack
Record Label: Warner Brothers
Songwriters: Kenny Edmunds (Babyface), Antonio Reid (L.A. Reid), Daryl Simmons

Hit single in the U.K.

RONI

Producers: Babyface, L. A. Reid
Album: Don't Be Cruel
Record Label: MCA
Songwriter: Kenny Edmunds (Babyface)

1992

GOOD ENOUGH

Producers: Babyface, L. A. Reid
Album: Bobby
Record Label: MCA
Songwriters: Kenny Edmunds (Babyface), Antonio Reid (L.A. Reid), Daryl Simmons

HUMPIN' AROUND

Producers: Babyface, L. A. Reid
Album: Bobby
Record Label: MCA
Songwriters: Kenny Edmunds (Babyface), Antonio Reid (L.A. Reid), Daryl Simmons

Blowing all his fame and money in the process.

BUSTER BROWN

1960

FANNIE MAE

Album: The New King of the Blues
Record Label: Fire
Songwriter: Waymon Glasco

#1 R&B.

CHARLES BROWN

1947

GLORIA

Record Label: Exclusive
Songwriter: Leon Rene

Cover by the Mills Brothers (Decca, '48), stiffed at #18. Other, more rocking Glorias would follow.

1949

TROUBLE BLUES

Record Label: Deluxe
Songwriter: Roy Brown

Mournful #1 R&B ballad, covered by Sam Cooke (RCA, '63).

1951

BLACK NIGHT

Album: Mood Music
Record Label: Aladdin
Songwriter: Jessie Mae Robinson

Third and final segment of Brown's dark trilogy of the Urban Blues that began with "Drifting Blues." Covered by Bobby Bland (Duke, '65).

1961

PLEASE COME HOME FOR CHRISTMAS

Album: Charles Brown Sings Christmas Songs
Record Label: King
Songwriters: Charles Brown, Gene Redd

Seasonal classic.

CHUCK BROWN AND THE SOUL SEARCHERS

1978

BUSTIN' LOOSE (PART I)

Album: Bustin' Loose
Record Label: Source
Songwriter: Chuck Brown

Soulful Funk.

JAMES BROWN AND THE FAMOUS FLAMES

1956

PLEASE, PLEASE, PLEASE

Producer: Ralph Bass
Album: Please, Please, Please
Record Label: Federal
Songwriters: James Brown, Johnny Terry

Archetypal Rock and Roll with an epic Rhythm and Blues groove, massive amounts of blood, sweat, soul, intensity, and integrity: James Brown begins a thirty-year career on the charts.

1958

TRY ME

Producer: Andy Gibson
Album: Try Me
Record Label: Federal
Songwriter: James Brown

His first Pop crossover; #1 R&B.

1961

BABY YOU'RE RIGHT

Producer: James Brown
Record Label: King
Songwriters: James Brown, Joe Tex

#2 R&B/Top-50 R&R crossover.

1963

PRISONER OF LOVE

Producer: James Brown
Album: Prisoner of Love
Record Label: King
Songwriters: Leo Robin, Russ
Columbo, Clarence Gaskill

Brown's eighteenth R&B hit was his first Top-20 R&R. Originated by Russ Columbo in '31.

1965

I GOT YOU (I FEEL GOOD)

Producer: James Brown
Album: I Got You (I Feel Good)
Record Label: King
Songwriter: James Brown

Defining the electric essence of the moment, James connects with the youth culture; his biggest hit, a #1 R&B/Top-5 R&R crossover.

PAPA'S GOT A BRAND NEW BAG

Producer: James Brown
Album: Papa's Got a Brand New
Bag
Record Label: King
Songwriter: James Brown

The dance of the blood personified: some would get it and move into Soul, others would stay seated, preferring Folk Rock.

1966

DON'T BE A DROP-OUT

Producer: James Brown
Album: Raw Soul
Record Label: King
Songwriters: James Brown, Nat
Jones

Public service announcement as crossover hit.

IT'S A MAN'S, MAN'S, MAN'S WORLD (BUT IT WOULDN'T BE NOTHING WITHOUT A WOMAN OR GIRL)

Producer: James Brown
Album: It's a Man's, Man's, Man's
World
Record Label: King
Songwriters: James Brown, Betty
Jean Newsome

The awesome, naked intensity of everyday yearning.

1967

COLD SWEAT

Producers: James Brown, Alfred
Ellis
Album: Cold Sweat
Record Label: King
Songwriters: James Brown, Alfred
Ellis

Funk personified; #1 R&B/Top-10 R&R.

1968

I GOT THE FEELIN'

Producer: James Brown
Album: I Got the Feelin'
Record Label: King
Songwriter: James Brown

#1 R&B/Top-10 R&R; his second biggest all-time hit.

SAY IT LOUD—I'M BLACK AND I'M PROUD

Producer: James Brown
Album: Say It Loud—I'm Black and
I'm Proud
Record Label: King
Songwriters: James Brown, Alfred
Ellis

#1 R&B/Top-10 R&R crossover, released five months after the assassination of Martin Luther King Jr.

JAMES BROWN

1969

GIVE IT UP OR TURN IT LOOSE

Producer: James Brown
Album: Ain't It Funky
Record Label: King
Songwriter: James Brown

#1 R&B/Top-20 R&R crossover.

MOTHER POPCORN (YOU GOT TO HAVE A MOTHER FOR ME) (PART I)

Producer: James Brown
Album: The Popcorn
Record Label: King
Songwriters: James Brown, Alfred
Ellis

Fifth of ten single releases in '69 (nine of which crossed over Top-40, three of which were instrumentals), his second #1 R&B/Top-20 R&R crossover, and biggest hit of the year.

THE POPCORN

Producer: James Brown
Album: The Popcorn
Record Label: King
Songwriter: James Brown

Instrumental mother of "Mother Popcorn" and all subsequent Popcorns, including "Lowdown Popcorn," and "Let a Man Come in and Do the Popcorn (Parts I and II)."

1970

SEX MACHINE

Producer: James Brown
Album: Sex Machine
Record Label: King
Songwriter: James Brown

The hardest-working man in show business. Shows no signs of flagging.

SUPER BAD

Producer: James Brown
Album: Super Bad
Record Label: King
Songwriter: James Brown

Michael Jackson was taking notes.

1971

HOT PANTS (SHE GOT TO USE WHAT SHE GOT TO GET WHAT SHE WANTS)

Producer: James Brown
Album: Hot Pants
Record Label: People
Songwriters: James Brown, Fred
Wesley

#1 R&B/Top-20 R&R crossover.

MAKE IT FUNKY (PART I)

Producer: James Brown
Album: Revolution of the Mind: Live
at the Apollo (Vol. II)
Record Label: Polydor
Songwriter: James Brown

#1 R&B/Top-25 R&R crossover.

1972

GET ON THE GOOD FOOT, PT. 1

Producer: James Brown
Album: Get on the Good Foot
Record Label: Polydor
Songwriters: James Brown, Fred
Wesley, Joe Mims

#1 R&B/Top-20 R&R. Off the king-of-rhythm assembly line, a million-selling single.

TALKING LOUD AND SAYIN' NOTHING (PART II)
Producer: James Brown
Album: There It Is
Record Label: Polydor
Songwriters: James Brown, Bobby Byrd
#1 R&B/Top-30 R&R.

1973

THE PAYBACK
Producer: James Brown
Album: The Payback
Record Label: Polydor
Songwriters: James Brown, Fred Wesley, John Starks
From the movie The Payback. *The second of his two million-selling singles. Covered by Big Black (Homestead, '84).*

1974

MY THANG
Producer: James Brown
Album: Hell
Record Label: Polydor
Songwriter: James Brown
#1 R&B/Top-30 R&R crossover.

PAPA DON'T TAKE NO MESS
Producer: James Brown
Album: Hell
Record Label: Polydor
Songwriters: James Brown, Fred Wesley, John Starks, Charles Bobbit
#1 R&B/Top-40 R&R crossover.

1986

LIVING IN AMERICA
Producer: Charlie Midnight
Album: Gravity
Record Label: Scotti Brothers
Songwriters: Dan Hartman, Charlie Midnight
From the soundtrack of Rocky IV.

JULIE BROWN

1987

THE HOMECOMING QUEEN'S GOT A GUN
Album: Trapped in the Body of a White Girl
Record Label: Sire
Songwriters: Julie Brown, Terrence McNally, Charlie Coffey, Ray Colcord
Suburban satire. Suggested segue: "The Sweater" by Meryn Cadell.

MAXINE BROWN

1961

ALL IN MY MIND
Producer: Leroy Kirkland
Record Label: Nomar
Songwriters: Leroy Kirkland, Fred Johnson, Maxine Brown
Her biggest hit.

1964

OH! NO, NOT MY BABY
Record Label: Wand
Songwriters: Gerry Goffin, Carole King
Brill Building Soul, written across the street, at 1650 Broadway. Covered by Rod Stewart (Mercury, '73).

PETER BROWN

1977

DANCE WITH ME
Album: A Fantasy Love Affair
Record Label: Drive
Songwriters: Peter Brown, Robert Rans
Home-made Disco smash, with Betty Wright.

ROY BROWN

1947

GOOD ROCKIN' TONIGHT
Record Label: DeLuxe
Songwriter: Roy Brown
Cover by Wynonie Harris went to #1 R&B (King, '48). Cover by Elvis Presley (Sun, '54) was the gateway to an era and the realization of Sam Phillips' dream of putting an acceptable white image on black music.

1949

ROCKIN' AT MIDNIGHT
Record Label: De Luxe
Songwriter: Roy Brown
Covered by the Honeydrippers (Es Paranza, '84).

1957

LET THE FOUR WINDS BLOW
Producer: Dave Bartholomew
Record Label: Imperial
Songwriters: Dave Bartholomew, Fats Domino
First and only Top-40 hit by the legendary Soul crooner. Covered by Fats Domino, who had an R&B hit with it (Imperial, '61).

RUTH BROWN AND HER RHYTHM MAKERS

1950

TEARDROPS FROM MY EYES
Record Label: Atlantic
Songwriter: Rudolph Toombs
#1 R&B smash by former Lucky Millinder front woman, from the pen of one of the genre's finest writers.

1952

5-10-15 HOURS
Record Label: Atlantic
Songwriter: Rudolph Toombs
#1 R&B.

RUTH BROWN

1953

MAMA (HE TREATS YOUR DAUGHTER MEAN)
Producers: Ahmet Ertegun, Jerry Wexler, Herb Abrahmson
Album: The Best of LaVern Baker
Record Label: Atlantic
Songwriters: Johnny Wallace, Herb Lance
Her third #1 R&B; crossed over to Pop, for a week (Phillips, '62).

1954

MAMBO BABY
Record Label: Atlantic
Songwriters: Charles Singleton, Rose Marie McCoy
Her fifth #1 R&B hit; the most by a solo female artist, save Aretha Franklin (until the Janet/Whitney/Mariah era of the asterisk).

OH WHAT A DREAM
Record Label: Atlantic
Songwriter: Chuck Willis
As she did in '53, Brown would spend 26 weeks on the R&B charts in '54: 16 of them with this Chuck Willis original—the tune Alan Freed used to introduce his "Moondog/Rock and Roll Party" radio show to the listeners of 1010 WINS in New York.

1955

WILD, WILD YOUNG MEN
Record Label: Atlantic
Songwriter: Ahmet Ertegun

1957

LUCKY LIPS
Record Label: Atlantic
Songwriters: Jerry Leiber, Mike Stoller

After 11 Top-10 R&B tunes, her first R&R crossover hit. Covered by Cliff Richard (Epic, '63).

1958

THIS LITTLE GIRL'S GONE ROCKIN'
Record Label: Atlantic
Songwriters: Bobby Darin, Mann Curtis

Her biggest R&R hit.

SHIRLEY BROWN

1974

WOMAN TO WOMAN
Producer: Al Jackson
Album: Woman to Woman
Record Label: Truth
Songwriters: Homer Banks, Fred Marvin, Bobby Thigpen

Aretha-esque #1 R&B/Top-25 R&R crossover from the point of view of the other woman. Suggested segue: "From His Woman to You" by Barbara Mason.

JACKSON BROWNE

1972

DOCTOR MY EYES
Producer: Richard Orshoff
Album: Saturate Before Using
Record Label: Asylum
Songwriter: Jackson Browne

In the mellowing year of California Folk Rock, Browne's laid-back philosophizing was an R&R hit.

MY OPENING FAREWELL
Producer: Richard Orshoff
Album: Saturate Before Using
Record Label: Asylum
Songwriter: Jackson Browne

A major Folk Rock artist stakes out his poetic turf, somewhere west of Eric Anderson, east of Tim Buckley. Covered by Bonnie Raitt (Warner Brothers, '77).

ROCK ME ON THE WATER
Producer: Richard Orshoff
Album: Saturate Before Using
Record Label: Asylum
Songwriter: Jackson Browne

The second single from the Folk Rock album of the year also hits Top-50.

SONG FOR ADAM
Producer: Richard Orshoff
Album: Saturate Before Using
Record Label: Asylum
Songwriter: Jackson Browne

Quintessential '60s character portrait. Suggested segue: "Stoney" by Jerry Jeff Walker.

1973

FOR EVERYMAN
Producer: Jackson Browne
Album: For Everyman
Record Label: Asylum
Songwriter: Jackson Browne

Browne moves from singer/songwriter to Folk oracle.

READY OR NOT
Producer: Jackson Browne
Album: For Everyman
Record Label: Asylum
Songwriter: Jackson Browne

She's havin' his baby. Browne's coming-of-age saga.

REDNECK FRIEND
Producer: Jackson Browne
Album: For Everyman
Record Label: Asylum
Songwriter: Jackson Browne

One of Browne's subtler metaphors.

1974

BEFORE THE DELUGE
Producers: Jackson Browne, Al Schmidt
Album: Late for the Sky
Record Label: Asylum
Songwriter: Jackson Browne

This '60s survival anthem may be his finest work.

FOR A DANCER
Producers: Jackson Browne, Al Schmidt
Album: Late for the Sky
Record Label: Asylum
Songwriter: Jackson Browne

Contemplating his first wife's suicide.

FOUNTAIN OF SORROW
Producers: Jackson Browne, Al Schmidt
Album: Late for the Sky
Record Label: Asylum

Songwriter: Jackson Browne
Exquisitely painful self-examination.

1976

THE FUSE
Producer: Jon Landau
Album: The Pretender
Record Label: Asylum
Songwriter: Jackson Browne

From a critically-lauded album.

HERE COME THOSE TEARS AGAIN
Producer: Jon Landau
Album: The Pretender
Record Label: Asylum
Songwriters: Jackson Browne, Nancy Farnsworth

THE PRETENDER
Producer: Jon Landau
Album: The Pretender
Record Label: Asylum
Songwriter: Jackson Browne

Attempted epic statement falls short.

1977

THE LOAD OUT
Producer: Jackson Browne
Album: Running on Empty
Record Label: Asylum
Songwriters: Jackson Browne, Bryan Garufalo

Tales from the road crew. Hit medley with cover of Maurice Williams and the Zodiacs' "Stay."

RUNNING ON EMPTY
Producer: Jackson Browne
Album: Running on Empty
Record Label: Asylum
Songwriter: Jackson Browne

A virtual auto biography.

1982

SOMEBODY'S BABY
Album: *Fast Times at Ridgemont High* Soundtrack
Record Label: Asylum
Songwriters: Jackson Browne, Danny Kortchmar

From Cameron Crowe's movie of his book.

1983

LAWYERS IN LOVE
Producers: Jackson Browne, Greg Ladanyi
Album: Lawyers in Love
Record Label: Asylum

Songwriter: Jackson Browne
Upper-middle-class angst.

1986

LIVES IN THE BALANCE
Producer: Jackson Browne
Album: Lives in the Balance
Record Label: Asylum
Songwriter: Jackson Browne
One of his most powerful global protest tunes.

THE BROWNS
1959

THE THREE BELLS
Producer: Chet Atkins
Album: Sweet Sounds by the Browns
Record Label: RCA
Songwriters: Bert Reisfeld, Jean Villard
Country & Western mortality tale from 1946, by way of France.

BROWNSVILLE STATION
1973

SMOKIN' IN THE BOYS ROOM
Album: Yeah!
Record Label: Big Tree
Songwriters: Cub Koda, Michael Lutz
A teen pre-dropout Metal anthem. Covered by Mötley Crüe (Elektra, '85).

PEABO BRYSON
1984

IF EVER YOU'RE IN MY ARMS AGAIN
Producer: Michael Masser
Album: Straight from the Heart
Record Label: Elektra
Songwriters: Cynthia Weil, Michael Masser, Tom Snow
Smooth Soul ballad.

CAN YOU STOP THE RAIN
Album: Can You Stop the Rain
Record Label: Columbia
Songwriters: John Bettis, Walter Afanasieff
#1 R&B/Top-60 R&R crossover.

B.T. EXPRESS
1974

DO IT ('TIL YOU'RE SATISFIED)
Album: Do It ('Til You're Satisfied)
Record Label: Roadshow
Songwriter: Billy Nichols
#1 R&B/Top-10 R&R disco crossover.

EXPRESS
Album: Do It ('Til You're Satisfied)
Record Label: Roadshow
Songwriters: Louis Risbrook, Barbara Lomas, William Risbrook, Orlando Woods, Richard Thompson, Carlos Ward, Dennis Rowe
Disco instrumental; #1 R&B/Top-10 R&R crossover.

ROY BUCHANON
1972

THE MESSIAH WILL COME AGAIN
Album: Roy Buchanon
Record Label: Polydor
Songwriter: Roy Buchanon
Blistering guitar Blues. Covered by Gary Moore (Virgin, '93).

LINDSAY BUCKINGHAM
1982

TROUBLE
Producers: Richard Dashut, Lindsay Buckingham
Album: Law and Order
Record Label: Asylum
Songwriter: Lindsay Buckingham
His first post-Fleetwood Mac success.

THE BUCKINGHAMS
1966

KIND OF A DRAG
Producer: Dan Belloc
Album: Kind of a Drag
Record Label: U.S.A.
Songwriter: James Holvay
Jazz-inflected Pop Rock.

1967

DON'T YOU CARE?
Producer: James William Guercio
Album: Time and Changes
Record Label: Columbia
Songwriters: Gary Beisbier, Jim Holvay
Their signature blue-eyed, elevator Jazz.

JEFF BUCKLEY
1994

LAST GOODBYE
Producer: Andy Wallace
Album: Grace
Record Label: Columbia
Songwriter: Jeff Buckley
Second-generation ethereality from the son of the late Tim.

TIM BUCKLEY
1967

GOODBYE AND HELLO
Producer: Jerry Lester
Album: Goodbye and Hello
Record Label: Elektra
Songwriter: Tim Buckley
The dawning of the singer/songwriter age. Jackson Browne was listening.

ONCE I WAS
Producer: Jerry Lester
Album: Goodbye and Hello
Record Label: Elektra
Songwriter: Tim Buckley
Morose Folk/Jazz/Rock gem from the star-crossed California singer/songwriter who died of a heroin overdose. The B-side of his first single, "Morning Glory," it was featured to bone-chilling effect at the end of the '78 movie Coming Home, *when the character played by Bruce Dern drowns himself in the Pacific.*

1968

VALENTINE MELODY
Producers: Paul Rothchild, Jac Holzman
Album: Tim Buckley
Record Label: Elektra
Songwriter: Tim Buckley

1969

BUZZIN' FLY
Producer: Jerry Lester
Album: Happy/Sad
Record Label: Elektra
Songwriter: Tim Buckley
Sparkling Jazz/Rock/Folk/Blues fusion.

STRANGE FEELING
Producer: Jerry Lester
Album: Happy/Sad
Record Label: Elektra
Songwriter: Tim Buckley

BUFFALO SPRINGFIELD

1967

BLUEBIRD

Producer: Turk-Pila
Album: Buffalo Springfield Again
Record Label: Atco
Songwriter: Stephen Stills

Influential Folk Rock, laying the groundwork for Crosby, Stills, Nash and Young; Souther, Hillman and Furay; and Poco, Firefall, et al.

BROKEN ARROW

Producer: Turk-Pila
Album: Buffalo Springfield Again
Record Label: Atco
Songwriter: Neil Young

Neil's earthly poetics find their early form.

EXPECTING TO FLY

Producer: Turk-Pila
Album: Buffalo Springfield Again
Record Label: Atco
Songwriter: Neil Young

One of Young's most poignant efforts.

FOR WHAT IT'S WORTH

Producers: Charles Greene, Brian Stone
Album: Buffalo Springfield
Record Label: Atco
Songwriter: Stephen Stills

This classic protest song about an L.A.-police-vs.-hippie confrontation over loitering on the streets in front of several Rock and Roll night clubs became the anthem for all such spectacles of youth taking the law into their own hands and getting their heads handed to them, of which the later '60s would be rife.

MR. SOUL

Producer: Turk-Pila
Album: Buffalo Springfield Again
Record Label: Atco
Songwriter: Neil Young

Neil's head was the event of the season and many seasons to come. Suggested segue: "So You Wanna Be a Rock and Roll Star" by the Byrds.

NOWADAYS CLANCY CAN'T EVEN SING

Producers: Charles Greene, Brian Stone
Album: Buffalo Springfield
Record Label: Atco
Songwriter: Neil Young

FM staple in the earliest days of FM.

1968

FOUR DAYS GONE

Producers: Charles Greene, Brian Stone
Album: Last Time Around
Record Label: Atco
Songwriter: Stephen Stills

I AM A CHILD

Producers: Charles Greene, Brian Stone
Album: Last Time Around
Record Label: Atco
Songwriter: Neil Young

Young and innocent.

KIND WOMAN

Producers: Charles Greene, Brian Stone
Album: Last Time Around
Record Label: Atco
Songwriter: Richie Furay

Country-oriented Folk Rock. Presages the middle-of-the-dirt-road singer/songwriter era of the '70s.

ON THE WAY HOME

Producers: Charles Greene, Brian Stone
Album: Last Time Around
Record Label: Atco
Songwriter: Neil Young

BUFFALO TOM

1994

I'M ALLOWED

Producers: The Robb Brothers, Buffalo Tom
Album: Big Red Letter Day
Record Label: East/West
Songwriter: Buffalo Tom

JIMMY BUFFETT

1974

COME MONDAY

Producer: D. Gant
Album: Living and Dying in 3/4 Time
Record Label: Dunhill
Songwriter: Jimmy Buffett

Welcome to Margaritaville, the lazy, hazy Key West of the mind that Jimmy Buffett populated and popularized like Springsteen did New Jersey.

A PIRATE LOOKS AT FORTY

Album: A1A
Record Label: Dunhill

Songwriter: Jimmy Buffett

From a Key West good-time vantage point—over a tall, cool beverage.

1977

MARGARITAVILLE

Producer: Norbert Putnam
Album: Changes in Latitudes, Changes in Attitudes
Record Label: ABC
Songwriter: Jimmy Buffett

Buffett's biggest hit and biggest problem.

1978

CHEESEBURGER IN PARADISE

Producer: Norbert Putnam
Album: Son of a Son of a Sailor
Record Label: ABC
Songwriter: Jimmy Buffett

Celebrating the simple joys of sloth.

THE BUGGLES

1979

VIDEO KILLED THE RADIO STAR

Album: The Age of Plastic
Record Label: Island
Songwriters: Geoffrey Downs, Trevor Horn, Bruce Woolley

This #1 U.K. Techno prophecy was the first video played on MTV in '81; the second was "Time Heals," by Todd Rundgren.

SOLOMON BURKE

1961

CRY TO ME

Producers: Bert Berns, Jerry Wexler
Album: Best of Solomon Burke
Record Label: Atlantic
Songwriter: Bert Berns (Bert Russell)

Soul gem, covered by Betty Harris (Jubilee, '63), Garnett Mimms and the Enchanters (United Artists, '65), the Rolling Stones (London, '65), and Freddy Scott (Shout, '67).

JUST OUT OF REACH (OF MY TWO OPEN ARMS)

Producers: Bert Berns, Jerry Wexler
Record Label: Atlantic
Songwriter: V. F. Stewart

Top-10 R&B/Top-30 R&R crossover with a country tune.

1965

GOT TO GET YOU OFF MY MIND

Album: Best of Solomon Burke
Record Label: Atlantic

Songwriters: Solomon Burke, Delores Burke, J. B. Moore

#1 R&B/Top-25 R&R crossover; his biggest hit.

TONIGHT'S THE NIGHT
Album: Best of Solomon Burke
Record Label: Atlantic
Songwriters: Solomon Burke, Don Covay

#2 R&B/Top-30 R&R.

1966

TAKE ME (JUST AS I AM)
Album: Best of Solomon Burke
Record Label: Atlantic
Songwriters: Dan Penn, Spooner Oldham

Early classic from the classic Memphis songwriting team.

1968

I WISH I KNEW (HOW IT WOULD FEEL TO BE FREE)
Producer: Tom Dowd
Album: I Wish I Knew
Songwriters: Billy Taylor, Dick Dallas

Stirring anthem of Black pride. Performed by Nina Simone (RCA, '67).

JOHNNY BURNETTE AND THE ROCK AND ROLL TRIO

1956

ROCKABILLY BOOGIE
Producer: Owen Bradley
Album: Johnny Burnette and the Rock and Roll Trio
Record Label: Decca
Songwriters: Johnny Burnette, Dorsey Burnette, Henry Jerome, G. Hawkins

Establishing Memphis as the first Rock and Roll underground scene, with the Elvis Presley Band—Scotty Moore, Bill Black, D. J. Fontana; and the Rockabilly Trio— Johnny and Dorsey Burnette, and Paul Burlison. Johnny and Elvis went to the same high school, Humes High (as did Thomas Wayne, whose records were produced by Scotty Moore) and worked for the same electric company, which explains their high-voltage performances.

ROCK THERAPY
Producer: Owen Bradley
Album: Johnny Burnette and the Rock and Roll Trio

Record Label: Liberty
Songwriters: Len Moore, Alice Bayer, Mort Subotsky

Covered by the Stray Cats (EMI, '86).

TEAR IT UP
Producer: Owen Bradley
Album: Johnny Burnette and the Rock and Roll Trio
Record Label: Coral
Songwriters: Johnny Burnette, Dorsey Burnette, Paul Burlison

The first release by the first underground Rock and Roll band. Covered by the Cramps (IRS, '80) and Rod Stewart (Warner Brothers, '81).

THE TRAIN KEPT A-ROLLIN'
Producer: Owen Bradley
Album: Johnny Burnette and the Rock and Roll Trio
Record Label: Coral
Songwriters: Tiny Bradshaw, Syd Nathan (Lois Mann), Howie Kay

A Tiny Bradshaw R&B tune, transformed by Paul Burlison's accidental fuzztone experiments into the first guitar classic of the Rock and Roll era. Covered by (actor) Jim (not surf guitarist Dick) Dale in the '57 movie The 6.5 Special, the Yardbirds (Epic, '69), Aerosmith (Columbia, '74), and Jeff Beck in the '89 movie, Twins.

JOHNNY BURNETTE

1960

DREAMIN'
Producer: Snuff Garrett
Album: Dreamin'
Record Label: Liberty
Songwriters: Ted Ellis, Barry DeVorzon

Softening Rockabilly into Country Rock.

YOU'RE SIXTEEN, YOU'RE BEAUTIFUL, AND YOU'RE MINE
Producer: Snuff Garrett
Album: Johnny Burnette
Record Label: Liberty
Songwriters: Dick Sherman, Bob Sherman

The Disney version of young love (rumored to have once been entitled "You're 13," undoubtedly for a Hayley Mills movie). Covered by Ringo Starr (Apple, '74).

ROCKY BURNETTE

1980

TIRED OF TOEIN' THE LINE
Producers: Jim Seiter, Bill House
Album: The Son of Rock and Roll
Record Label: EMI-America
Songwriters: Rocky Burnette, Ron Coleman

The son of Johnny, with a faux-rockabilly one-shot.

T-BONE BURNETTE

1983

BABY FALL DOWN
Producer: Jeff Eyrich
Album: Proof Through the Night
Record Label: Warner Brothers
Songwriter: T-Bone Burnette

No relation to Johnny, Dorsey, or Rocky. Folk Rock morality tale.

BUSH

1994

EVERYTHING ZEN
Producers: Clive Langer, Alan Winstanley, Bush
Album: Sixteen Stone
Record Label: Capitol
Songwriter: Gavin Rossdale

Leaders of the latest British invasion, with Oasis.

KATE BUSH

1978

THE MAN WITH THE CHILD IN HIS EYES
Producer: Andrew Powell
Album: The Kick Inside
Record Label: EMI-America
Songwriter: Kate Bush

The song she sang on her only "Saturday Night Live" appearance.

THEM HEAVY PEOPLE
Producer: Andrew Powell
Album: The Kick Inside
Record Label: EMI-America
Songwriter: Kate Bush

Future queen of the Fairlight synthesizer exercises her extraordinary vocal and instrumental chops.

WUTHERING HEIGHTS
Producer: Andrew Powell
Album: The Kick Inside

Record Label: EMI-America
Songwriter: Kate Bush

Dense and mysterious as the moors, the witchy child-woman who both wrote and sang this classic storysong (based on Bronte's classic novel) was the first female to top the U.K. charts with a self-penned tune. A post-Joni Mitchell generation, led by Tori Amos and Natalie Merchant, were listening.

1980

BABOOSHKA

Producers: Kate Bush, Jon Kelly
Album: Never Forever
Record Label: EMI-America
Songwriter: Kate Bush

Suggested segue: "Escape (the Pina Colada Song)" by Rupert Holmes.

BREATHING

Producers: Kate Bush, Jon Kelly
Album: Never Forever
Record Label: EMI-America
Songwriter: Kate Bush

A passionate ode to the life-force on the morning after annihilation.

OH ENGLAND MY LIONHEART

Producer: Andrew Powell
Album: Lionheart
Record Label: EMI-America
Songwriter: Kate Bush

New English anthem.

WOW

Producer: Andrew Powell
Album: Lionheart
Record Label: EMI-America
Songwriter: Kate Bush

Rousing burst of girlish glee; unbelievable!

1982

THE DREAMING

Producer: Kate Bush
Album: The Dreaming
Record Label: EMI-America
Songwriter: Kate Bush

Kate discovers the Fairlight (also the digeridu), and England would never be the same.

SAT IN YOUR LAP

Producer: Kate Bush
Album: The Dreaming
Record Label: EMI-America
Songwriter: Kate Bush

In quest of the unknowable. Suggested segue: "I Am the Walrus" by the Beatles.

SUSPENDED IN GAFFA

Producer: Kate Bush
Album: The Dreaming
Record Label: EMI-America
Songwriter: Kate Bush

1985

THE BIG SKY

Producer: Kate Bush
Album: Hounds of Love
Record Label: EMI-America
Songwriter: Kate Bush

CLOUDBUSTING

Producer: Kate Bush
Album: Hounds of Love
Record Label: EMI-America
Songwriter: Kate Bush

Deep in the web of her unique technology, something good is preparing to happen. Sampled by the Utah Saints (London/PLG, '93).

RUNNING UP THAT HILL

Producer: Kate Bush
Album: Hounds of Love
Record Label: EMI-America
Songwriter: Kate Bush

A personal and artistic peak; her only U.S. Top-40.

1988

THIS WOMAN'S WORK

Producer: Kate Bush
Album: The Sensual World
Record Label: Columbia
Songwriter: Kate Bush

From the waiting-room scene in the movie She's Having a Baby, *one of Bush's most magnificent performances.*

1989

LOVE AND ANGER

Producer: Kate Bush
Album: The Sensual World
Record Label: Columbia
Songwriter: Kate Bush

New complexity and maturity.

1993

THE RED SHOES

Producer: Kate Bush
Album: The Red Shoes
Record Label: Columbia
Songwriter: Kate Bush

Spinning her own mystical take on the famous ballet film.

RUBBERBAND GIRL

Producer: Kate Bush
Album: The Red Shoes
Record Label: Columbia
Songwriter: Kate Bush

Re-establishing herself as the reigning queen of Alternative rock.

JERRY BUTLER AND THE IMPRESSIONS

1958

FOR YOUR PRECIOUS LOVE

Producer: Calvin Carter
Record Label: Abner
Songwriters: Arthur Brooks, Richard Brooks, Jerry Butler

Introducing the gospelized Soul of the original Impressions, with Jerry Butler and Curtis Mayfield. Covered by Garnett Mimms and the Enchanters (United Artists, '63) and Jackie Wilson and Count Basie (Brunswick, '68).

JERRY BUTLER

1960

HE WILL BREAK YOUR HEART

Producer: Calvin Carter
Album: Jerry Butler's Golden Hits
Record Label: Vee Jay
Songwriters: Curtis Mayfield, Jerry Butler, Calvin Carter

Also known as "He Don't Love You (Like I Love You)." Butler's first post-Impressions hit as a Soul solo, written and performed with his old collaborator, Curtis Mayfield. Covered by Tony Orlando and Dawn (Elektra, '75).

1961

MOON RIVER

Album: Jerry Butler's Golden Hits
Songwriters: Henry Mancini, Johnny Mercer

Soul version of the theme from the Audrey Hepburn movie Breakfast at Tiffany's. *Also an instrumental hit for Henry Mancini (RCA, '61).*

1962

MAKE IT EASY ON YOURSELF

Album: Jerry Butler's Golden Hits
Record Label: Vee Jay
Songwriters: Burt Bacharach, Hal David

Covered by the Walker Brothers (Smash, '65) and Dionne Warwick (Scepter, '67).

1967

MR. DREAM MERCHANT

Producer: Jerry Ross
Album: Mr. Dream Merchant
Record Label: Mercury
Songwriters: Larry Weiss, Jerry Ross

Cover by New Birth (Buddah, 76) went #1 R&B.

1968

HEY, WESTERN UNION MAN

Producers: Kenny Gamble, Leon Huff
Album: The Ice Man Cometh
Record Label: Mercury
Songwriters: Kenny Gamble, Leon Huff, Jerry Butler

His first #1 R&B since '60, forecasts Philly Soul.

1969

ONLY THE STRONG SURVIVE

Producers: Kenny Gamble, Leon Huff
Album: The Ice Man Cometh
Record Label: Mercury
Songwriters: Kenny Gamble, Leon Huff, Jerry Butler

A Philly Soul showpiece; #1 R&B/Top-10 R&R. Butler's biggest all-time hit.

THE PAUL BUTTERFIELD BLUES BAND

1965

BORN IN CHICAGO

Producer: Paul Rothchild
Album: The Paul Butterfield Blues Band
Record Label: Elektra
Songwriter: Nick Gravenites

Heartland Blues Rock with a feeling . . . and several stellar instrumentalists, including Paul Butterfield on the amplified harp, and Mike Bloomfield and Elvin Bishop on guitars. Like the Yardbirds and the Rolling Stones over in England, they covered Muddy Waters and Willie Dixon tunes with gusto, dexterity, passion, and aplomb. But lacking their teenybop sex appeal, they failed to become America's answer to either of them, thus making Cream and the Jimi Hendrix Experience necessary and Led Zeppelin inevitable.

SHAKE YOUR MONEY MAKER

Producer: Paul Rothchild
Album: The Paul Butterfield Blues Band

Record Label: Elektra
Songwriter: Elmore James

Paying tribute to a master blues guitar influence on Michael Bloomfield as well as many other members of Rock's guitaristocracy.

1966

EAST-WEST

Producers: Paul Rothchild, Mark Abramson
Album: East West
Record Label: Elektra
Songwriters: Mark Naftalin, Nick Gravenites

Bloomfield's transcontinental transcendental magnum opus.

PAUL BUTTERFIELD'S BETTER DAYS

1973

SMALL TOWN TALK

Album: It All Comes Back
Record Label: Bearsville
Songwriter: Robert Guidry (Bobby Charles)

Woodstock Valley PTA, as sung by Maria Muldaur's ex, Geoff. Covered by Rick Danko (Capitol, '77).

BUTTHOLE SURFERS

1983

THE SHAH SLEEPS IN LEE HARVEY OSWALD'S GRAVE

Album: Butthole Surfers
Record Label: Alternative Tentacles
Songwriter: Gibby Hayes

Stretching the Alternative envelope.

1993

WHO WAS IN MY ROOM LAST NIGHT

Producers: John Paul Jones, Butthole Surfers
Album: Independent Worm Saloon
Record Label: Capitol
Songwriter: Butthole Surfers

Crashing the R&R party.

THE BUZZCOCKS

1977

ORGASM ADDICT

Producer: Martin Rushent
Album: Singles Going Steady
Record Label: IRS

Songwriters: Pete Shelley, Howard DeVoto

Early influential and inflammatory British single, released after DeVoto left the band; collected in the U.S. (IRS, '79).

1978

EVERYBODY'S HAPPY NOWADAYS

Producer: Martin Rushent
Album: Singles Going Steady
Record Label: IRS
Songwriter: Pete Shelley

Power Punk.

BREAKDOWN

Producer: Martin Rushent
Album: Spiral Scratch
Record Label: New Hormones
Songwriters: Pete Shelley, Howard DeVoto

Landmark effort from the first U.K. Indie Punk Rock band. Influenced by the Sex Pistols.

EVER FALLEN IN LOVE (WITH SOMEONE YOU SHOULDN'T HAVE FALLEN IN LOVE WITH)

Producer: Martin Rushent
Album: Love Bites
Record Label: United Artists
Songwriter: Pete Shelley

Classic early Punk Rock single shows a Pop attitude. Covered by the Fine Young Cannibals (Island, '87) in the Jonathan Demme film Something Wild.

1979

I BELIEVE

Producer: Martin Rushent
Album: A Different Kind of Tension
Record Label: United Artists
Songwriter: Pete Shelley

A mini Rock opera of affirmations.

YOU SAY YOU DON'T LOVE ME

Producer: Martin Rushent
Album: A Different Kind of Tension
Record Label: IRS
Songwriter: Pete Shelley

Shelley at his Byronic best.

DONALD BYRD

1963

CHRISTO REDENTOR

Album: A New Perspective
Record Label: Blue Note
Songwriter: Duke Pearson

Introduced by Jazz pianist Duke Pearson.

Byrd's version was used in the Robert De Niro film A Bronx Tale in 1993. Covered by Charlie Mussel White (Vanguard, '67), Harvey Mandel (Philips, '69).

THE BYRDS

1965

I'LL FEEL A WHOLE LOT BETTER
Producer: Terry Melcher
Album: Mr. Tambourine Man
Record Label: Columbia
Songwriter: Gene Clark

Jangling toward Country Rock.

IT WON'T BE WRONG
Producer: Terry Melcher
Album: Turn! Turn! Turn!
Record Label: Columbia
Songwriters: Jim McGuinn (Roger McGuinn), Harvey Gerst

Why they were known as the American Beatles.

SET YOU FREE THIS TIME
Producer: Terry Melcher
Album: Turn! Turn! Turn!
Record Label: Columbia
Songwriter: Jim McGuinn (Roger McGuinn)

B-side of "I'll Feel a Whole Lot Better."

1966

EIGHT MILES HIGH
Producer: Allen Stanton
Album: 5D (Fifth Dimension)
Record Label: Columbia
Songwriters: Jim McGuinn (Roger McGuinn), Gene Clark, David Crosby

Post-flyte fantasy, inspired by John Coltrane, retired by the U.S. Government. Suggested segues: "Along Comes Mary" by the Association and "I Couldn't Get High" by the Fugs.

FIVE D (FIFTH DIMENSION)
Producer: Allen Stanton
Album: 5D (Fifth Dimension)
Record Label: Columbia
Songwriter: Jim McGuinn (Roger McGuinn)

HAVE YOU SEEN HER FACE?
Producer: Gary Usher
Album: Younger Than Yesterday
Record Label: Columbia
Songwriter: Chris Hillman

Suggested segue: "I've Just Seen a Face" by the Beatles.

MR. SPACEMAN
Producer: Allen Stanton
Album: 5D (Fifth Dimension)
Record Label: Columbia
Songwriter: Jim McGuinn (Roger McGuinn)

Suggested segue: "Mr. Bassman" by Johnny Cymbal.

1967

EVERYBODY'S BEEN BURNED
Producer: Allen Stanton
Album: 5D (Fifth Dimension)
Record Label: Columbia
Songwriter: David Crosby

In the American Beatles, Crosby quit before he could become their obligatory George.

SO YOU WANNA BE A ROCK AND ROLL STAR
Producer: Gary Usher
Album: Younger Than Yesterday
Record Label: Columbia
Songwriters: Roger McGuinn, Chris Hillman

A cautionary tale. Suggested segue: "Johnny B. Goode" by Chuck Berry.

TRIAD
Producer: Gary Usher
Record Label: Columbia
Songwriter: David Crosby

Crosby's attempt at making trouble, with his band, and with the opposite sex. Covered in the female version by Grace Slick with the Jefferson Airplane (RCA, '68).

1968

HICKORY WIND
Producer: Gary Usher
Album: Sweetheart of the Rodeo
Record Label: Columbia
Songwriters: Gram Parsons, Bob Bucannan

Introducing their drugstore-cowboy legend, Gram Parsons, one of the prime motivating forces behind the return-to-your-Country-roots-Rock revolution espoused by the Byrds and instigated by Bob Dylan's earthy collaborations with the Band at Big Pink. Revived by Gram Parsons (Reprise, '74) and covered by Gram's soulmate, Emmylou Harris (Warner Brothers, '79).

I WASN'T BORN TO FOLLOW
Producer: Gary Usher
Album: The Notorious Byrd Brothers
Record Label: Columbia
Songwriters: Carole King, Gerry Goffin

Prodded by the poetry of Folk Rock, the Brill Building era's finest chronicler of teen dreams, Gerry Goffin, goes pyschedelic. Included in the film Easy Rider. Revived by Carole King in her first band, the City (Ode, '70).

LADY FRIEND
Producer: Gary Usher
Album: The Notorious Byrd Brothers
Record Label: Columbia
Songwriter: David Crosby

Crosby's favorite topic.

NOTHING WAS DELIVERED
Producer: Gary Usher
Album: Sweetheart of the Rodeo
Record Label: Columbia
Songwriter: Bob Dylan

Another anthem of frustration by Dylan and the Band, unreleased by them until "The Basement Tapes" (Columbia, '75).

YOU AIN'T GOIN' NOWHERE
Producer: Gary Usher
Album: Sweetheart of the Rodeo
Record Label: Columbia
Songwriter: Bob Dylan

Out of traction and longing to be back in action, Dylan turns to Country Rock and the Band for release.

1969

BALLAD OF AN EASY RIDER
Producer: Terry Melcher
Album: Easy Rider Soundtrack
Record Label: Columbia
Songwriter: Roger McGuinn

With help from an uncredited Bob Dylan, the waning counter culture, Phil Spector, Peter Fonda, and Jack Nicholson, who came to Easy Rider right after making the equally ineffable films Psych-Out and Head!

DRUG STORE TRUCK DRIVIN' MAN
Producer: Gary Usher
Album: Dr. Byrds and Mr. Hyde
Record Label: Columbia
Songwriters: Roger McGuinn, Gram Parsons

More Country train Rock

1969

YOU SHOWED ME
Album: PreFlyte
Record Label: Together
Songwriters: Gene Clark, Jim McGuinn

Recorded by the Byrds in '64 but not released for five years. Covered by the Turtles (White Whale, '69).

1970

CHESTNUT MARE
Producers: Terry Melcher, Jim Dickson
Album: The Byrds (Untitled)
Record Label: Columbia
Songwriters: Roger McGuinn, Jacques Levy

A hootenanny hoe down. Levy would collaborate with Dylan and Leonard Cohen.

JESUS IS JUST ALRIGHT
Album: Ballad of Easy Rider
Record Label: Warner Brothers
Songwriter: Arthur Reynolds

Deeper into the Christian life. Covered by the non-denominational Doobie Brothers (Warner Brothers, '73).

DAVID BYRNE AND CELIA CRUZ
1986

LOCO DE AMOR (CRAZY FOR LOVE)
Album: *Something Wild* Soundtrack
Record Label: MCA
Songwriter: David Byrne

The King of spastic Soul with the Queen of Salsa.

JERRY BYRNE
1958

LIGHTS OUT
Producer: Harold Battiste
Record Label: Specialty
Songwriters: Seth David, Mack Rebennack

New Orleans Rockabilly romp, composed by the once and future Dr. John.

EDWARD BYRNES AND CONNIE STEVENS
1959

KOOKIE, KOOKIE, LEND ME YOUR COMB
Producer: Karl Engemann
Album: Kookie, Kookie, Lend Me Your Comb
Record Label: Warner Brothers
Songwriter: Irving Taylor

Fashion advice via the co-star of the '59 detective show "77 Sunset Strip."

C

MERYN CADELL
1992

THE SWEATER
Producers: John Tucker, Meryn Cadell
Album: Angel Food for Thought
Record Label: Reprise
Songwriter: Meryn Cadell

Plundering the depths of the pre-teen female psyche in the guise of a suburban tone poem.

THE CADETS
1956

STRANDED IN THE JUNGLE
Album: Rockin' 'n' Reelin'
Record Label: Modern
Songwriters: Ernestine Smith, James Johnson

The Leiber and Stoller storyline goes Doo-Wop. Covered by another R&B group, the Jayhawks (Flash, '56).

THE CADILLACS
1954

GLORIA
Producer: Esther Navarro
Record Label: Josie
Songwriter: Esther Navarro

The all-time Doo-Wop neighborhood girl arrives in this tune, written about singer Gloria Smith. Covered by the Passions (Audicon, '60). Many singers and groups knew her in slightly different accents, clothes, attitudes.

1955

SPEEDOO
Album: The Fabulous Cadillacs
Record Label: Josie
Songwriter: Esther Navarro

Introducing Mr. Earl, as in Earl Carroll, lead singer of the Cadillacs.

JOHN CAFFERTY AND THE BEAVER BROWN BAND
1984

ON THE DARK SIDE
Album: *Eddie and the Cruisers* Soundtrack
Record Label: Scotti Brothers
Songwriter: John Cafferty

Theme from the nearly credible Springsteen-does-an-Elvis cult film.

J. J. CALE
1972

CALL ME THE BREEZE
Album: Naturally
Record Label: Shelter
Songwriter: John J. Cale

Covered by Lynyrd Skynyrd (MCA, '74)

CRAZY MAMA
Producer: Audie Ashworth
Album: Naturally
Record Label: Shelter
Songwriters: Mick Jagger, Keith Richards

Covered by the Rolling Stones (Rolling Stones, '76).

JOHN CALE
1974

FEAR IS A MAN'S BEST FRIEND
Producer: John Cale
Album: Fear
Record Label: Island
Songwriter: John Cale

Disturbing rocker from the co-founder of the Velvet Underground, at the peak of his disturbed form.

BOBBY CALDWELL
1978

WHAT YOU WON'T DO FOR LOVE
Album: Bobby Caldwell
Record Label: Clouds
Songwriters: Bobby Caldwell, Al Kettner

CALLOWAY
1990

I WANNA BE RICH
Producers: Reggie Calloway, Vincent Calloway
Album: All the Way
Record Label: Epic
Songwriters: Reggie Calloway, Vincent Calloway, Melvin Gentry, Belinda Lipscomb

Modern R&B answer to "Money" by Barrett Strong.

CAMEO

1981

FREAKY DANCIN'
Producer: Larry Blackmon
Album: Knights of the Sound Table
Record Label: Chocolate City
Songwriters: Larry Blackmon, Tomi Jenkins

1984

SHE'S STRANGE
Producer: Larry Blackmon
Album: She's Strange
Record Label: Atlanta Artists
Songwriters: Larry Blackmon, Tomi Jenkins, Charles Singleton, Nathan Leftenant

Their #1 R&B/Top-50 R&R breakthrough.

1985

THE SINGLE LIFE
Producer: Larry Blackmon
Album: Single Life
Record Label: Atlanta Artists
Songwriters: Larry Blackmon, Tomi Jenkins

One of Blackmon's best party records.

1986

BACK AND FORTH
Producer: Larry Blackmon
Album: Word Up
Record Label: Atlanta Artists
Songwriters: Larry Blackmon, Tomi Jenkins, Kevin Kendricks, Nathan Leftenant

CANDY
Producer: Larry Blackmon
Album: Word Up
Record Label: Atlanta Artists
Songwriters: Larry Blackmon, Tomi Jenkins

#1 R&B/Top-25 R&R single from their best-selling of fourteen albums.

WORD UP
Producer: Larry Blackmon
Album: Word Up
Record Label: Atlanta Artists
Songwriters: Larry Blackmon, Tomi Jenkins

Glomming onto one of the decade's catchphrases, Blackmon's troupe gains their funky peak; #1 R&B/Top-10 R&R.

GLEN CAMPBELL

1967

BY THE TIME I GET TO PHOENIX
Producer: Al DeLory
Album: By the Time I Get to Phoenix
Record Label: Capitol
Songwriter: Jimmy Webb

Part of the essential cabaret repertoire.

1968

WICHITA LINEMAN
Producer: Al DeLory
Album: Wichita Lineman
Record Label: Capitol
Songwriter: Jimmy Webb

An American classic. First of two Webb-authored #1 C&W/Top-10 R&R crossovers for Campbell.

1969

GALVESTON
Producer: Al DeLory
Album: Galveston
Record Label: Capitol
Songwriter: Jimmy Webb

Searching anti-war ballad. His second straight #1 C&W/Top-10 R&R crossover.

JO-ANN CAMPBELL

1957

COME ON, BABY
Record Label: Eldorado
Songwriter: Jo-Ann Campbell

For the offending phrase "drive on baby," Alan Freed's "Blonde Bombshell" was denied a chance for a hit single.

JO-ANN (CAMPBELL) AND TROY

1965

I FOUND A LOVE, OH WHAT A LOVE
Record Label: Atlantic
Songwriter: Jo-Ann Campbell

Two months pregnant after this was released, Jo-Ann and husband Troy Seals miss their last chance to become Sonny and Cher.

TEVIN CAMPBELL

1992

ALONE WITH YOU
Producer: Narada Michael Walden
Album: T.E.V.I.N.
Record Label: Qwest
Songwriters: Al B. Sure, Kyle West

New subteen voice on the Hip-Hop crooning circuit debuts with a #1 R&B hit.

TELL ME WHAT YOU WANT ME TO DO
Producer: Narada Michael Walden
Album: T.E.V.I.N.
Record Label: Qwest
Songwriters: Narada Michael Walden, Tevin Campbell, Sally Jo Dakota

#1 R&B/Top-10 R&R crossover.

1993

CAN WE TALK
Producers: Babyface, Daryl Simmons
Album: I'm Ready
Record Label: Qwest
Songwriters: Kenny Edmunds (Babyface), Daryl Simmons

Sophomore year. Not a blemish in sight.

CAMPER VAN BEETHOVEN

1985

BAD TRIP
Producer: Camper Van Beethoven
Album: Telephone Free Landslide Victory
Record Label: Independent Project
Songwriter: Camper Van Beethoven

Just your typical Southern California cowboys on acid.

TAKE THE SKINHEADS BOWLING
Producer: Camper Van Beethoven
Album: Telephone Free Landslide Victory
Record Label: Independent Project
Songwriter: Camper Van Beethoven

The Rock critic track (or at least title) of the year.

1986

HISTORY OF UTAH
Producer: Camper Van Beethoven
Album: Camper Van Beethoven
Record Label: Pitch a Tent
Songwriter: David Lowery

Lowery steps forth to take the claim for this epic Roots Rock anthem, the roots of which plunge to the depths of the American experience: the pilgrims, the Apaches, "Apache" by the Shadows, gypsies, peyote, and the campfire stories of sixth graders everywhere. An alternative world culture was tuned in.

JOE STALIN'S CADILLAC
Producer: Camper Van Beethoven
Album: Camper Van Beethoven
Record Label: Pitch a Tent
Songwriter: David Lowery

Revealing Lowery's winsomely warped post-Folk world view.

1988

EYE OF FATIMA (PARTS I AND II)
Producer: Dennis Herring
Album: Our Beloved Revolutionary Sweetheart
Record Label: Virgin
Songwriter: Camper Van Beethoven

Gussied up for corporate approval the Campers camp out on the fine line between whimsy and AOR.

1989

ALL HER FAVORITE FRUIT
Producer: Dennis Herring
Album: Key Lime Pie
Record Label: Virgin
Songwriters: David Lowery, Victor Krummenacher, Greg Lisher, Chris Pedersen

Powered by Lowery's loopy conviction, these moderately happy Campers finish their legendary Alternative careers in typically elliptical Bakerstown-on-downs fashion.

BORDERLINE
Producer: Dennis Herring
Album: Key Lime Pie
Record Label: Virgin
Songwriters: David Lowery, Victor Krummenacher, Greg Lisher, Chris Pedersen

Obliterating the borders between cow-Punk and anti-Folk, a new world beat for a new flannel world.

SWEETHEARTS
Producer: Dennis Herring
Album: Key Lime Pie
Record Label: Virgin
Songwriters: David Lowery, Victor Krummenacher, Greg Lisher, Chris Pedersen

Saying farewell to the most repressive decade for original Rock and Roll—and to Camper Van Beethoven as we know it. Lowery would show up forthwith in the only slightly warped, but much more successful, guitar band, Cracker.

WHEN I WIN THE LOTTERY
Producer: Dennis Herring
Album: Key Lime Pie
Record Label: Virgin
Songwriters: David Lowery, Victor Krummenacher, Greg Lisher, Chris Pedersen

Sassy essay on trailer-park culture features a killer Rock fiddle part.

CANDLEBOX
1993

FAR BEHIND
Producers: K. Gray, Candlebox
Album: Candlebox
Record Label: Maverick/Warner Brothers
Songwriter: Kevin Martin

Where Alternative meets Hard Rock: at the tombstone of a friend.

CANDYMAN
1990

KNOCKIN' BOOTS
Album: Ain't No Shame in My Game
Record Label: Epic
Songwriters: Candyman, Betty Wright, E. Hamilton, A. Hamilton, R. Wylie, W. Clarke

Euphemistic Hip-Hop ditty.

CANNED HEAT
1968

GOING UP THE COUNTRY
Producer: Skip Taylor
Album: Living the Blues
Record Label: Liberty
Songwriters: Al Wilson, Canned Heat

Your basic boogie.

ON THE ROAD AGAIN
Producer: Dallas Smith
Album: Boogie with Canned Heat
Record Label: Liberty
Songwriters: Al Wilson, Floyd Jones

Your basic boogie makes the charts.

ACE CANNON
1961

TUFF
Album: Tuff-Sax
Record Label: Hi
Songwriter: Ace Cannon

Sax instrumental.

FREDDY CANNON
1959

TALLAHASSEE LASSIE
Album: The Explosive Freddy Cannon
Record Label: Swan
Songwriters: Frank Slay, Bob Crewe, Frederick A. Picariello (Freddy Cannon)

The Philly sound in its Rock and Roll incarnation.

1960

WAY DOWN YONDER IN NEW ORLEANS
Album: Solid Gold Hits
Record Label: Swan
Songwriters: Henry Creamer, Turner Layton

Initiating the year's belated salute to New Orleans. Introduced in '22 by the writers.

1962

PALISADES PARK
Album: Freddy Cannon at Palisades Park
Record Label: Kapp
Songwriter: Chuck Barris

It was no Disneyland; it wasn't even Action Park.

THE CAPITOLS
1966

COOL JERK
Producer: Ollie McLaughlin
Album: Dance the Cool Jerk
Record Label: Karen
Songwriter: Donald Storball

What came after the Frug.

THE CAPRIS
1961

THERE'S A MOON OUT TONIGHT
Album: There's a Moon out Tonight
Record Label: Old Town
Songwriters: Al Striano, Al Gentile

Essence of Italian Soul.

THE CAPTAIN AND TENNILLE
1975

I WRITE THE SONGS
Album: Love Will Keep Us Together
Record Label: A&M
Songwriter: Bruce Johnston

Covered by Barry Manilow (Arista, '76).

CAPTAIN BEEFHEART

1966

YELLOW BRICK ROAD

Album: Safe As Milk
Record Label: Buddah
Songwriters: Don Van Vliet, Herb Bermann

His first single release after the failed "Diddy Wah Diddy" is a psychedelic bubblegum trifle. Buddah would shortly own this niche. The Captain would move into another psychedelic dimension entirely.

1969

WELL

Producer: Frank Zappa
Album: Trout Mask Replica
Record Label: Straight
Songwriter: Van Don Vliet

Eerie and hypnotic poetry from the edge introduced on a revered cult album.

WILD LIFE

Producer: Frank Zappa
Album: Trout Mask Replica
Record Label: Straight
Songwriter: Van Don Vliet

Defining the new underground. Dave Thomas of Pere Ubu was listening.

1972

BIG EYED BEANS FROM VENUS

Album: Clear Spot
Record Label: Reprise
Songwriter: Van Don Vliet

Rocks out.

1982

ICE CREAM FOR CROW

Album: Ice Cream for Crow
Record Label: Virgin
Songwriter: Van Don Vliet

One of his finest efforts, the video of which was shown at the Museum of Modern Art.

CAPTAIN HOLLYWOOD PROJECT

1993

MORE AND MORE

Producers: Cyborg, Dip
Album: Love Is Not Sex
Record Label: Imago
Songwriters: Gora Schein, Oliver Reinecke, Juergen Katzmann, Tony Dawson-Harrison

Euro-dance sensation.

IRENE CARA

1980

FAME

Producer: Michael Gore
Album: Fame
Record Label: RSO
Songwriters: Dean Pitchford, Michael Gore

Title theme about New York's High School of the Performing Arts.

OUT HERE ON MY OWN

Producer: Michael Gore
Album: Fame
Record Label: RSO
Songwriters: Michael Gore, Leslie Gore

The obligatory big ballad from the movie.

1983

FLASHDANCE . . . WHAT A FEELING

Producer: Giorgio Moroder
Album: Flashdance
Record Label: Casablanca
Songwriters: Keith Forsey, Irene Cara, Giorgio Moroder

Title tune from the attempted Saturday Night Fever *of the '80s.*

1984

BREAKDANCE

Producer: Giorgio Moroder
Album: What a Feelin'
Record Label: Geffen
Songwriters: Irene Cara, Bunny Hull, Giorgio Moroder

What Michael Jackson's Moonwalk hath wrought.

THE CARDINALS

1955

THE DOOR IS STILL OPEN TO MY HEART

Record Label: Atlantic
Songwriter: Chuck Willis

Covered by Dean Martin (Reprise, '64).

MARIAH CAREY

1990

VISION OF LOVE

Producer: David Lawrence
Album: Mariah Carey
Record Label: Columbia
Songwriters: Ben Margulies, Mariah Carey

#1 R&B/R&R crossover establishes an ethereal new voice; Pop Soul of the spheres and the marketplace.

LOVE TAKES TIME

Producer: David Lawrence
Album: Mariah Carey
Record Label: Columbia
Songwriters: Ben Margulies, Mariah Carey

1991

EMOTIONS

Producers: David Cole, Rob Clivilles
Album: Emotions
Record Label: Columbia
Songwriters: Dave Hall, Mariah Carey

#1 R&B/R&R crossover.

1993

HERO

Producer: Walter Afanasieff
Album: Music Box
Record Label: Columbia
Songwriters: Walter Afanasieff, Mariah Carey

Affirmative pop psychology.

MARIAH CAREY AND BOYZ II MEN

1995

ONE SWEET DAY

Producers: Walter Afanasieff, Mariah Carey
Album: Fantasy
Record Label: Columbia
Songwriters: Mariah Carey, Michael McCary, Nathan Morris, Wayna Morris, Shawn Stockman, Walter Afanasieff

Recording setting multi-Grammy nominated #1 R&B/R&R crossover. But all you had to do was see Mariah's face at the telecast to know it didn't win any.

TONY CAREY

1984

A FINE FINE DAY

Producer: Peter Hauke
Album: Some Tough City
Record Label: MCA
Songwriter: Tony Carey

One of the year's best story-songs.

BELINDA CARLISLE

1986

MAD ABOUT YOU
Producer: Rick Nowels
Album: Belinda Carlisle
Record Label: MCA
Songwriters: Paula Brown, James Whelan, Mitchell Young Evans
Post Go-Gos Valley Pop ballad.

1987

HEAVEN IS A PLACE ON EARTH
Producer: Rick Nowels
Album: Heaven on Earth
Record Label: MCA
Songwriters: Rick Nowels, Ellen Shipley
#1 U.S./U.K. crossover.

1988

CIRCLE IN THE SAND
Producer: Rick Nowels
Album: Heaven on Earth
Record Label: MCA
Songwriter: Ellen Shipley
Beach music in the tradition of Annette.

I GET WEAK
Producer: Rick Nowels
Album: Heaven on Earth
Record Label: MCA
Songwriter: Diane Warren
Succumbing in a moment of professional drought to the undeniable Warren catalogue.

CARL CARLTON

1981

SHE'S A BAD MAMA JAMA
Producer: Leon Haywood
Album: Carl Carlton
Record Label: 20th Century Fox
Songwriter: Leon Haywood

ERIC CARMEN

1976

ALL BY MYSELF
Producer: Jimmy Ienner
Album: Eric Carmen
Record Label: Arista
Songwriter: Eric Carmen
First solo effort from the former Raspberry.

1988

HUNGRY EYES
Producer: Jimmy Ienner
Album: *Dirty Dancing* Soundtrack
Record Label: RCA
Songwriters: John Nicola, Franke Previte
Pop Rock ballad from the monster soundtrack of the year.

MAKE ME LOSE CONTROL
Album: Best of Eric Carmen
Record Label: Arista
Songwriters: Eric Carmen, Dean Pitchford
Capitalizing on his movie exposure to revitalize his moribund career.

KIM CARNES

1988

SPEED OF THE SOUND OF LONELINESS
Album: View from the House
Record Label: MCA
Songwriter: John Prine
Covered by Nanci Griffith (Elektra, '93).

MARY CHAPIN CARPENTER

1992

I AM A TOWN
Producers: John Jennings, Mary Chapin Carpenter
Album: Come on, Come on
Record Label: Columbia
Songwriter: Mary Chapin Carpenter
A tour de force through a sleepy Southern town, establishing Carpenter as the voice of the new adult album alternative radio format: middle-of-the-dirt-road music for the college sensibility.

THE CARPENTERS

1970

WE'VE ONLY JUST BEGUN
Producer: Jack Daugherty
Album: Close to You
Record Label: A&M
Songwriters: Paul Williams, Roger Nichols
All white lace and promises unkept, the voice of Karen Carpenter inherits the bittersweet, suburban legacy of Brian Wilson.

1971

FOR ALL WE KNOW
Producer: Jack Daugherty
Album: The Carpenters
Record Label: A&M
Songwriters: Fred Carlin, Robb Royer, James Griffin
Theme from the classic Renee Taylor/Joe Bologna movie Lovers and Other Strangers.

RAINY DAYS AND MONDAYS
Producer: Jack Daugherty
Album: The Carpenters
Record Label: A&M
Songwriters: Paul Williams, Roger Nichols
Melodious and melancholy.

SUPERSTAR
Producer: Jack Daugherty
Album: Now and Then
Record Label: A&M
Songwriters: Leon Russell, Bonnie Bramlett
"Sweet Little Sixteen" from the girl's point of view.

1972

GOODBYE TO LOVE
Album: A Song for You
Record Label: A&M
Songwriters: John Bettis, Richard Carpenter

1973

TOP OF THE WORLD
Producers: Jack Daugherty, Richard Carpenter, Karen Carpenter
Album: A Song for You
Record Label: A&M
Songwriters: John Bettis, Richard Carpenter
Their biggest hit since their cover of "Close to You," in 1970.

JAMES CARR

1967

THE DARK END OF THE STREET
Producers: Quinton Claunch, Doc Russell
Record Label: Goldwax
Songwriters: Dan Penn, Chips Moman
An all-time cheatin' classic. Covered by Clarence Carter as "Making Love (at the Dark End of the Street)" (Atlantic, '69), the Flying Burrito Brothers (A&M, '69), and Aretha Franklin (Atlantic, '70).

PAUL CARRACK
1988

DON'T SHED A TEAR
Producer: Christopher Neil
Album: One Good Reason
Record Label: Chrysalis
Songwriters: Eddie Schwartz, Rob Freidman

The voice of Ace and Mike and the Mechanics attains his only Top-10 R&R solo hit. Eddie Schwartz wrote "Hit Me with Your Best Shot" for Pat Benatar.

KEITH CARRADINE
1975

I'M EASY
Producer: Richard Baskin
Album: *Nashville* Soundtrack
Record Label: ABC
Songwriter: Keith Carradine

Proto-typical coffee house ballad from the classic Altman film won the Oscar for Best Song.

THE JIM CARROLL BAND
1980

PEOPLE WHO DIED
Producers: Bob Clearmountain, Earl McGrath
Album: Catholic Boy
Record Label: Atco
Songwriter: Jim Carroll

Fevered junkie prose/poetry eulogy. Suggested segue: "88 Lines About 44 Women" by the Nails.

THE CARS
1978

GOOD TIMES ROLL
Producer: Roy Thomas Baker
Album: The Cars
Record Label: Elektra
Songwriter: Ric Ocasek

Synthesized Rockabilly with a Boston accent.

JUST WHAT I NEEDED
Producer: Roy Thomas Baker
Album: The Cars
Record Label: Elektra
Songwriter: Ric Ocasek

Their first single; Top-40 goes New Wave.

MY BEST FRIEND'S GIRL
Producer: Roy Thomas Baker
Album: The Cars
Record Label: Elektra
Songwriter: Ric Ocasek

Catchy, punchy, nervy and nervous smash in England, where the album was recorded.

YOU'RE ALL I'VE GOT TONIGHT
Producer: Roy Thomas Baker
Album: The Cars
Record Label: Elektra
Songwriter: Ric Ocasek

1979

LET'S GO
Producer: Roy Thomas Baker
Album: Candy-O
Record Label: Elektra
Songwriter: Ric Ocasek

Critically lauded hit single.

1982

SHAKE IT UP
Producer: Ray Thomas Baker
Album: Shake It Up
Record Label: Elektra
Songwriter: Ric Ocasek

Punk-lite.

SINCE YOU'RE GONE
Producer: Ray Thomas Baker
Album: Shake It Up
Record Label: Elektra
Songwriter: Ric Ocasek

With their New Wave career at a plateau, the Cars turn to video to make their mark, where they quickly outdo Nesmith and Rundgren.

1984

DRIVE
Producer: Mutt Lange
Album: Heartbeat City
Record Label: Elektra
Songwriter: Ric Ocasek

One of their more perfect ballads.

YOU MIGHT THINK
Producer: Mutt Lange
Album: Heartbreak City
Record Label: Elektra
Songwriter: Ric Ocasek

Their best video yet.

1985

TONIGHT SHE COMES
Producers: M. Shipley, the Cars
Album: Greatest Hits
Record Label: Elektra
Songwriter: Ric Ocasek

Pure Pop payoff.

CLARENCE CARTER
1967

SLIP AWAY
Producer: Rick Hall
Album: This Is Clarence Carter
Record Label: Atlantic
Songwriters: William Armstrong, Wilbur Terrell, Marcus Daniel

A classic cheating song, Muscle-Shoals style.

1969

SNATCHING IT BACK
Producer: Rick Hall
Album: Testifying
Record Label: Atlantic
Songwriters: George Jackson, Clarence Carter

TOO WEAK TO FIGHT
Producer: Rick Hall
Album: Dynamic Clarence Carter
Record Label: Atlantic
Songwriters: John Keyes, Clarence Carter, Rick Hall, George Jackson

THE CASCADES
1963

RHYTHM OF THE RAIN
Album: Rhythm of the Rain
Record Label: Valiant
Songwriter: John Gummoe

One-shot thunderbolt.

PETER CASE
1989

HIDDEN LOVE
Album: The Man with the Blue, Postmodern, Fragmented, Neotraditionalist Guitar
Record Label: Geffen
Songwriter: Peter Case

Post-modern Folk Rock from a former Plimsoul.

ALVIN CASH AND THE CRAWLERS

1965

TWINE TIME

Record Label: Mar-V-Lus
Songwriters: Andre Williams, Verlie Rice

After the Jerk and before the Hustle.

JOHNNY CASH

1956

FOLSOM PRISON BLUES

Producer: Sam Phillips
Album: Johnny Cash with His Red and Blue Guitar
Record Label: Sun
Songwriter: Johnny Cash

The Rockabilly rebellion moves forward, with a tale told by an outlaw, in a voice that'd been to Hell and back.

I WALK THE LINE

Producer: Sam Phillips
Album: Johnny Cash with His Red and Blue Guitar
Record Label: Sun
Songwriter: Johnny Cash

Cash's profound bass could also cut to the quick in the service of an up tune, relatively speaking.

1958

BALLAD OF A TEENAGE QUEEN

Producer: Sam Phillips
Album: Johnny Cash Sings the Songs That Made Him Famous
Record Label: Sun
Songwriter: Jack Clement

Of all the uncle figures in Rock and Roll, Cash was the most convincingly empathetic; #1 C&W/Top-15 R&R crossover.

GUESS THINGS HAPPEN THAT WAY

Producer: Sam Phillips
Album: Johnny Cash Sings the Songs That Made Him Famous
Record Label: Sun
Songwriter: Jack Clement

As a Rock and Roll attitude, Cash's mid-tempo resignation was ages beyond the audience. His second straight #1 C&W/Top-15 R&R crossover.

1959

FIVE FEET HIGH AND RISING

Producer: Sam Phillips
Album: Songs of Our Soul
Record Label: Columbia
Songwriter: Johnny Cash

Along with A-side "I Got Stripes," a rare example of C&W protest music.

1961

TENNESSEE FLAT-TOP BOX

Producers: Don Law, Frank Jones
Album: Ring of Fire: The Best of Johnny Cash
Record Label: Columbia
Songwriter: Johnny Cash

Covered by daughter Rosanne (Columbia, '87).

1963

BUSTED

Producers: Don Law, Frank Jones
Album: Blood, Sweat and Tears
Record Label: Columbia
Songwriter: Harlan Howard

Top-20 C&W hit by Cash. Cover by Ray Charles (ABC-Paramount, '63). Went Top-10 R&B/R&R.

RING OF FIRE

Producers: Don Law, Frank Jones
Album: Ring of Fire: The Best of Johnny Cash
Record Label: Columbia
Songwriters: Merle Kilgore, June Carter

#1 C&W/Top-20 R&R crossover. Rock and Roll attitude, Country retribution.

1964

BALLAD OF IRA HAYES

Producers: Don Law, Frank Jones
Album: Bitter Tears
Record Label: Columbia
Songwriter: Peter LaFarge

Folk tune about the downfall of a Native-American vet.

UNDERSTAND YOUR MAN

Producers: Don Law, Frank Jones
Album: I Walk the Line
Record Label: Columbia
Songwriter: Johnny Cash

#1 C&W/Top-40 R&R crossover.

1969

WANTED MAN

Producer: Bob Johnston
Album: Johnny Cash at San Quentin
Record Label: Columbia
Songwriter: Bob Dylan

Perfect match of singer, songwriter, song, and venue.

ROSANNE CASH

1981

MY BABY THINKS HE'S A TRAIN

Producer: Rodney Crowell
Album: Seven Year Ache
Record Label: Columbia
Songwriter: Rosanne Cash

On the rocking edge of new Country. #1 C&W.

SEVEN YEAR ACHE

Producer: Rodney Crowell
Album: Seven Year Ache
Record Label: Columbia
Songwriter: Rosanne Cash

On the confessional edge of Country Folk. Her first # 1C&W; her only R&R crossover (Top-25).

1987

IF YOU CHANGE YOUR MIND

Producer: Rodney Crowell
Album: King's Record Shop
Record Label: Columbia
Songwriters: Rosanne Cash, Hank Devito

THE WAY WE MAKE A BROKEN HEART

Producer: Rodney Crowell
Album: King's Record Shop
Record Label: Columbia
Songwriter: John Hiatt

Tapping the prime purveyor of soulful twisted Folk Rock, John Hiatt, for a #1 Country hit.

CASHMAN AND WEST

1972

AMERICAN CITY SUITE

Producers: Terry Cashman, Tommy West
Album: A Song or Two
Record Label: Dunhill
Songwriters: Dennis Minogue (Terry Cashman), Thomas Picardo (Tommy West)

As opposed to their paean to baseball ("Whitey, Mickey and the Duke"), this three-part opus casts a jaundiced eye on its equally declining subject. Consists of "Sweet City Song," "All Around the Town" and "A Friend Is Dying."

THE CASINOS
1967

THEN YOU CAN TELL ME GOODBYE

    Producer: Gene Hughes
    Album: Then You Can Tell Me Goodbye
    Record Label: Fraternity
    Songwriter: John D. Loudermilk

The C&W reaction to a year of R&B cheating songs: a fidelity song. The Casino's version went R&R in '67. Cover by Eddy Arnold went #1 C&W (RCA, '68).

MAMA CASS
1970

NEW WORLD COMING

    Producers: Steve Barri, Joel Sill
    Album: Mama's Big Ones
    Record Label: Dunhill
    Songwriters: Barry Mann, Cynthia Weil

Mama's big solo effort fell flat, prediction-wise.

SHAUN CASSIDY
1977

THAT'S ROCK 'N' ROLL

    Producer: Michael Lloyd
    Album: Shaun Cassidy
    Record Label: Warner Brothers
    Songwriter: Eric Carmen

Teenybop Pop by David's brother.

1978

HEY DEANNIE

    Producer: Michael Lloyd
    Album: Born Late
    Record Label: Warner/Curb
    Songwriter: Eric Carmen

The teen idol trip, scripted by someone who'd been there.

THE CASTAWAYS
1965

LIAR, LIAR

    Record Label: Soma
    Songwriter: James J. Donna

Garage classic, covered by Debbie Harry in Married to the Mob (Reprise, '88).

THE CASTELLS
1961

SACRED

    Album: So This Is Love
    Record Label: Era
    Songwriter: William Landau

California sound, before the surf came in.

THE JIMMY CASTOR BUNCH
1972

TROGLODYTE (CAVE MAN)

    Producer: Castor-Pruit Productions
    Album: It's Just Begun
    Record Label: RCA
    Songwriters: Harry Jensen, Gerald Thomas, Douglas Gibson, Robert Manigault, James Castor, Langdon Fridie

Novelty.

BERNADETTE CASTRO
1964

HIS LIPS GOT IN THE WAY

    Record Label: Colpix
    Songwriters: Howard Greenfield, Helen Miller

Did the girl on the Castro convertible commercial actually inspire the Four Tops' "Bernadette"? Not really.

VINCE CASTRO
1958

BONG BONG I LOVE YOU MADLY

    Record Label: ABC-Paramount
    Songwriters: Vince Castro Jr., Charles Merenstein

Cited by Stormy Weather magazine as one of the greatest Rock and Roll achievements. Go figure.

CAT MOTHER AND THE ALL NIGHT NEWSBOYS
1969

GOOD OLD ROCK AND ROLL

    Producer: Jimi Hendrix
    Album: Street Giveth . . . and the Street Taketh Away
    Record Label: Polydor
    Songwriter: Various

Medley of '50s Rock and Roll by Hendrix's East Village neighbors. He had more presence as a producer with Eire Apparent.

CATHY JEAN AND THE ROOMMATES
1961

PLEASE LOVE ME FOREVER

    Album: At the Hop
    Record Label: Valmor
    Songwriters: Johnny Malone, Ollie Blanchard

White Doo-Wop, girl-group style.

C&C MUSIC FACTORY
1991

GONNA MAKE YOU SWEAT

    Producers: Rob Clivilles, David Cole
    Album: Gonna Make You Sweat
    Record Label: Columbia
    Songwriters: Rob Clivilles, Freedom Williams

The '90s formula: Heavy MTV dance rotation = #1 R&B/R&R crossover.

HERE WE GO

    Producers: Rob Clivilles, David Cole
    Album: Gonna Make You Sweat
    Record Label: Columbia
    Songwriters: Rob Clivilles, Freedom Williams

Featuring Freedom Williams and Zelma Davis.

1991

THINGS THAT MAKE YOU GO HMMMM

    Producers: Rob Clivilles, David Cole
    Album: Gonna Make You Sweat
    Record Label: Columbia
    Songwriters: Rob Clivilles, Freedom Williams

PETER CETERA
1986

THE GLORY OF LOVE (THEME FROM *THE KARATE KID II*)

    Producer: Michael Omartian
    Album: Solitude/Solitare
    Record Label: Warner Brothers
    Songwriters: Peter Cetera, David Foster

Big movie song for the former lead singer for Chicago.

THE NEXT TIME I FALL

    Producer: Michael Omartian
    Album: Solitude/Solitaire

Record Label: Warner Brothers
Songwriters: Robert Caldwell, Paul Gordon

Big follow-up ballad, with Amy Grant.

1988

ONE GOOD WOMAN
Album: One More Story
Record Label: Full Moon
Songwriters: Peter Cetera, Patrick Leonard

CHAD AND JEREMY
1966

A SUMMER SONG
Album: Best of Chad and Jeremy
Record Label: World s
Songwriters: Clive Metcalfe, Keith Noble, David Stuart

Breezy Folk Rock. Seals and Crofts were listening.

THE CHAIRMEN OF THE BOARD
1970

GIVE ME JUST A LITTLE MORE TIME
Producer: The Staff
Album: Give Me Just a Little More Time
Record Label: Invictus
Songwriters: Brian Holland, Edythe Wayne

Featuring General Johnson, first heard on "It Will Stand" by the Showmen.

PATCHES (I'M DEPENDING ON YOU)
Producer: Rick Hall
Album: Give Me Just a Little More Time
Record Label: Invictus
Songwriters: General Johnson, Ronald Dunbar

Covered by Clarence Carter (Atlantic, '70).

THE CHAMBERS BROTHERS
1967

TIME HAS COME TODAY
Producer: David Robinson
Album: The Time Has Come
Record Label: Columbia
Songwriters: Joseph Chambers, Willie Chambers

One of the most enduring '60s chants, primarily by virtue of its inclusion in several period films, including Coming Home *('78), and Oliver Stone's treatise,* The Doors *('91).*

CHAMPAIGN
1981

HOW 'BOUT US
Producer: Leo Graham
Album: How 'bout Us
Record Label: Columbia
Songwriter: Dana Walden

THE CHAMPS
1958

TEQUILA
Producer: Joe Johnson
Album: Go Champs Go
Record Label: Challenge
Songwriter: Chuck Rio

Rock and Roll's best-known homage to drink, for a generation still too young to do so, legally.

1962

LIMBO ROCK
Record Label: Challenge
Songwriters: Kal Mann (Jon Sheldon), William Strange

Covered by Chubby Checker (Parkway, '62)— how low could he go in his battles with Hank Ballard to remain Dance King of the early '60s?

JAMES CHANCE
1979

CONTORT YOURSELF
Album: Buy Contortions
Record Label: Ze
Songwriter: James Chance

Snarling post Punk anthem.

GENE CHANDLER
1961

DUKE OF EARL
Producer: Carl Davis
Album: The Duke of Earl
Record Label: Vee Jay
Songwriters: Earl Edwards, Eugene Dixon, Bernie Williams

One of the ultimate Doo-Wop R&B statements, #1 R&B/R&R crossover.

CHANGIN' TIMES
1965

THE PIED PIPER
Record Label: Philips
Songwriters: Artie Kornfeld, Steve Duboff

Covered by Crispian St. Peters (Laurie, '66).

CHANGING FACES
1994

STROKE YOU UP
Producer: Robert Kelly
Album: Changing Faces
Record Label: Big Beat/Atlantic
Songwriter: Robert Kelly

An R&B homage to foreplay in the post-erotic era.

BRUCE CHANNEL
1962

HEY! BABY
Producer: Mayor Bill Smith
Songwriter: Marvin Montgomery
Album: Hey! Baby (and 11 Other Songs About Your Baby)
Record Label: Smash
Songwriters: Margaret Cobb, Bruce Channel

Delbert McClinton's harmonica part reportedly inspired John Lennon's harp solo in "Love Me Do."

THE CHANNELS
1956

THE CLOSER YOU ARE
Record Label: Whirlin' Disc
Songwriters: Earle Lewis, Morgan C. Robinson

New York Doo-Wop standard.

THE CHANTAYS
1963

PIPELINE
Producer: Art Wenzel
Album: Pipeline
Record Label: Dot
Songwriters: Bob Spickard, Brian Carman

Bubbling surf signature.

THE CHANTELS
1957

HE'S GONE
    Producer: George Goldner
    Album: We Are the Chantels
    Record Label: End
    Songwriter: Arlene Smith
Featuring Arlene singing lead—one of the golden voices of the first Rock and Roll era.

THE PLEA
    Producer: George Goldner
    Album: We Are the Chantels
    Record Label: End
    Songwriter: Arlene Smith
Another reason why the Chantels challenge the Shirelles in the memory of Doo-Wop historians as the ultimate East-coast girl-group.

1958

MAYBE
    Producer: George Goldner
    Album: We Are the Chantels
    Record Label: End
    Songwriter: Richard Barrett
Their emotional peak; Top-5 R&B/Top-20 R&R.

1961

LOOK IN MY EYES
    Producer: Richard Barrett
    Songwriter: George Goldner
    Album: There's Our Song Again
    Record Label: Carlton
    Songwriter: Richard Barrett
Spurred by the success of the Shirelles, the original girl group returns with their biggest comeback hit, without Arlene.

HARRY CHAPIN
1972

TAXI
    Producer: Paul Leka
    Album: Heads and Tails
    Record Label: Elektra
    Songwriter: Harry Chapin
Former filmmaker spins an epic length saga, redeemed by the cello solo.

1974

CAT'S IN THE CRADLE
    Producer: Paul Leka
    Album: Verities and Balderdash
    Record Label: Elektra
    Songwriters: Harry Chapin, Sandra Chapin

A made-for-TV morality tale. Covered by Ugly Kid Joe (Mercury, '94).

TRACY CHAPMAN
1988

BEHIND THE WALL
    Producer: David Kershenbaum
    Album: Tracy Chapman
    Record Label: Elektra
    Songwriter: Tracy Chapman
Urban folktale of domestic violence.

FAST CAR
    Producer: David Kershenbaum
    Album: Tracy Chapman
    Record Label: Elektra
    Songwriter: Tracy Chapman
Classic car song of the post-car-song era; restless youth approaching a dead end. The debut left field folkie smash of the year.

MOUNTAINS O' THINGS
    Producer: David Kershenbaum
    Album: Tracy Chapman
    Record Label: Elektra
    Songwriter: Tracy Chapman
Postmodern reaction to "Material Girl" by Madonna.

THE CHARLATANS U.K.
1992

WEIRDO
    Album: Between 10th and 11th
    Record Label: Beggar's
       Banquet/BMG
    Songwriter: Charlatans U.K.
English New Rave synth band takes on the timeless theme of low self esteem.

CHARLES AND EDDIE
1992

WOULD I LIE TO YOU
    Producer: J. Deutsch
    Album: Duophonic
    Record Label: Capitol
    Songwriters: Mike Leeson, Pete Vale
Hip-Hop Doo-Wop.

BOBBY CHARLES
1955

SEE YOU LATER, ALLIGATOR
    Record Label: Chess
    Songwriter: Robert Guidry
Covered by Bill Haley and His Comets (Decca, '56).

JIMMY CHARLES
1960

A MILLION TO ONE
    Record Label: Promo
    Songwriter: Phil Medley
Frankie Lymon redux.

RAY CHARLES
1952

SINNER'S PRAYER
    Record Label: Atlantic
    Songwriter: Lowell Fulson
The former Fulson sideman steps out of the Blues.

1954

COME BACK BABY
    Producers: Ahmet Ertegun, Jerry
       Wexler
    Album: The Ray Charles Story
    Record Label: Atlantic
    Songwriter: Ray Charles

DON'T YOU KNOW
    Producers: Ahmet Ertegun, Jerry
       Wexler
    Album: The Ray Charles Story
    Record Label: Atlantic
    Songwriter: Ray Charles
Covered by Fats Domino (Imperial, '55).

HEARTBREAKER
    Producers: Ahmet Ertegun, Jerry
       Wexler
    Album: Yes Indeed
    Record Label: Atlantic
    Songwriter: Ahmet Ertegun

MESS AROUND
    Producer: Jerry Wexler
    Album: Ray Charles
    Record Label: Atlantic
    Songwriter: Ahmet Ertegun

1955

A FOOL FOR YOU
    Producers: Ahmet Ertegun, Jerry
       Wexler
    Album: Ray Charles
    Record Label: Atlantic
    Songwriter: Ray Charles
Widely regarded as one of his finest Blues performances, especially at the '58 Newport Jazz Festival. Turned into a ballet by the New York City Ballet Company in '89.

I GOT A WOMAN (I GOT A SWEETIE)

Producers: Ahmet Ertegun, Jerry Wexler

Album: Do the Twist

Record Label: Atlantic

Songwriters: Ray Charles, Renald Richard

One of his most enduring classics, based on an Alex Bradford hymn. Marked the first instance of gospel soul mixing with R&B roots. Covered by Elvis Presley on his first RCA album in '56. Recorded by the Beatles, July '63, but not released until '95, on Capitol.

THIS LITTLE GIRL OF MINE

Producers: Ahmet Ertegun, Jerry Wexler

Album: Ray Charles

Record Label: Atlantic

Songwriter: Ray Charles

Based on the gospel "This Little Light of Mine." Covered by the Everly Brothers (Cadence, '58).

1956

DROWN IN MY TEARS

Producers: Ahmet Ertegun, Jerry Wexler

Album: Ray Charles

Record Label: Atlantic

Songwriter: Henry Glover

Covered by Richie Havens (Douglas, '66).

HALLELUJAH, I LOVE HER SO

Producers: Ahmet Ertegun, Jerry Wexler

Album: Ray Charles

Record Label: Atlantic

Songwriter: Ray Charles

One of the great modern gospel performances. Covered by Peggy Lee (Capitol, '59) and the Quarrymen (Lost Gold, '60).

LONELY AVENUE

Producers: Ahmet Ertegun, Jerry Wexler

Album: The Ray Charles Story

Record Label: Atlantic

Songwriter: Doc Pomus

First R&B hit for the future Rock and Roll Hall of Fame songwriter. Early Beatles favorite, covered by the Everly Brothers (Warner Brothers, '65), Los Lobos (Rhino, '95). Suggested segue: "I've Got a New Home," by the Pilgrim Travelers (Specialty, '53).

1958

LEAVE MY WOMAN ALONE

Album: Yes, Indeed

Record Label: Atlantic

Songwriter: Ray Charles

Legendary album cut, covered by the Everly Brothers (Cadence, '58), Dave Edmunds (RCA, '75).

(NIGHT TIME IS THE) RIGHT TIME

Producers: Ahmet Ertegun, Jerry Wexler

Album: Ray Charles in Person

Record Label: Atlantic

Songwriter: Lew Herman

Top-5 R&B hit.

SWEET SIXTEEN BARS

Producers: Ahmet Ertegun, Jerry Wexler

Album: Great Ray Charles

Record Label: Atlantic

Songwriter: Ray Charles

In the tradition of Amos Milburn's "One Scotch, One Bourbon, One Beer."

1959

WHAT'D I SAY

Producers: Ahmet Ertegun, Jerry Wexler

Album: What'd I Say

Record Label: Atlantic

Songwriter: Ray Charles

Ultimate merger of Soul and raunch, street and Gospel, making it a Rock and Roll classic, and Ray's biggest hit of the '50s (his first #1 R&B, first Top-10 R&R). Covered by the Beatles with Tony Sheridan (Polydor, '60), Jerry Lee Lewis (Sun, '61), Bobby Darin (Atco, '62), Elvis Presley (RCA, '64, and in the film Viva Las Vegas*), Etta James (Argo, '64), and the Righteous Brothers (Philles, '65).*

1960

GEORGIA ON MY MIND

Producer: Sid Feller

Album: Ray Charles' Greatest Hits

Record Label: ABC-Paramount

Songwriters: Hoagy Carmichael, Stuart Gorrell

Ray's first #1 R&R/Top-5 R&B. Introduced by Mildred Bailey in '30.

UNCHAIN MY HEART

Producer: Sid Feller

Album: Ray Charles' Greatest Hits

Record Label: ABC-Paramount

Songwriters: Agnes Jones, Freddy James

Ray on a roll. #1 R&B/Top-10 R&R.

1961

HIT THE ROAD, JACK

Producer: Sid Feller

Album: Ray Charles' Greatest Hits

Record Label: ABC-Paramount

Songwriter: Percy Mayfield

His first #1 R&B/R&R crossover, written by a great poet of the Blues.

1962

YOU DON'T KNOW ME

Producer: Sid Feller

Album: Modern Sounds in Country and Western Music

Record Label: ABC-Paramount

Songwriters: Cindy Walker, Eddy Arnold

Top-5 R&R/R&B hit. Introduced as a Top-10 C&W hit by Eddy Arnold (RCA, '56). Covered by Lenny Welch (Cadence, '60) and Elvis Presley (RCA, '67).

1966

I DON'T NEED NO DOCTOR

Producer: TRC

Album: A Man and His Soul

Record Label: ABC

Songwriters: Nick Ashford, Valerie Simpson

Covered by Humble Pie (A&M, '71).

LET'S GO GET STONED

Producer: Joe Adams

Album: Let's Go Get Stoned

Record Label: ABC

Songwriters: Nick Ashford, Valerie Simpson, Josie Armstead

Ray's seventh and last #1 R&B. Suggested segues: "Rainy Day Women #12 and 35" by Bob Dylan, "Eight Miles High" by the Byrds, "Along Comes Mary" by the Association, and "Mellow Yellow" by Donovan.

1984

SEVEN SPANISH ANGELS

Album: Friendship

Record Label: Columbia

Songwriters: Troy Seals, Eddie Setser

His first #1 C&W hit, with help from Willie Nelson.

SONNY CHARLES AND THE CHECKMATES, LTD.
1969

BLACK PEARL
Producer: Phil Spector
Record Label: A&M
Songwriters: Irwin Levine, Toni Wine, Phil Spector

Spector comes out of retirement with a Top-20 hit.

THE CHARMS
1954

HEARTS OF STONE
Record Label: De Luxe
Songwriters: Rudy Jackson, Eddie Ray

#1 R&B. Covered by the Fontane Sisters (Dot, '55).

THE CHARTS
1957

DESERIE
Producers: Bobby Robinson, Danny Robinson
Record Label: Everlast
Songwriters: Joseph Grier, Danny Robinson

In Doo-Wop 101, the final exam.

CHEVY CHASE
1973

COLORADO
Producer: Tony Hendra
Album: *Lemmings* Original Cast Album
Record Label: Banana
Songwriters: Christopher Guest, Sean Kelly, Tony Hendra

Chevy perfects his John Denver, in the musical that spawned all those National Lampoon movies.

CHEAP TRICK
1976

SURRENDER
Producer: Tom Werman
Album: Heaven Tonight
Record Label: Epic
Songwriter: Rick Nielsen

Good-time Arena Rock.

1977

I WANT YOU TO WANT ME
Producer: Cheap Trick
Album: In Color
Record Label: Epic
Songwriter: Rick Nielsen

Touted as the Beatles of the Arena age, Cheap Trick updated "I Want to Hold Your Hand."

1988

THE FLAME
Producer: Ritchie Zito
Album: Lap of Luxury
Record Label: Epic
Songwriters: Robert Mitchell, Dick Graham

Aided by a slick production, Rick Neilsen and crew finally scale the commercial heights, sounding just like any other corporate Arena band.

CHUBBY CHECKER
1961

THE FLY
Producer: Kal Mann
Album: For Teen Twisters Only
Record Label: Parkway
Songwriters: John Madara, Dave White

By the writers of "At the Hop."

LET'S TWIST AGAIN
Producer: Kal Mann
Album: Let's Twist Again
Record Label: Parkway
Songwriters: Kal Mann, Dave Appell

Keeping the Twist alive.

SLOW TWISTIN'
Producer: Kal Mann
Album: For Teen Twisters Only
Record Label: Parkway
Songwriter: John Sheldon (Kal Mann)

Seemingly endless variations on the perfect Philadelphia theme. Sung with stablemate Dee Dee Sharp.

1962

POPEYE THE HITCHHIKER
Producer: Kal Mann
Album: All the Hits (for Your Dancin' Party)
Record Label: Parkway
Songwriters: Kal Mann, Dave Appel

Another new dance, but no Twist.

THE CHEERS
1955

BLACK DENIM TROUSERS AND MOTORCYCLE BOOTS
Producers: Jerry Leiber, Mike Stoller
Record Label: Capitol
Songwriters: Jerry Leiber, Mike Stoller

The patented Leiber and Stoller patter, adapted for a white audience fearful of the impending Rock and Roll onslaught, typified, at the time, by Marlon Brando and his denim-and-leather brethren.

CHER
1966

BANG BANG (MY BABY SHOT ME DOWN)
Producer: Sonny Bono
Album: The Sonny Side of Cher
Record Label: Imperial
Songwriter: Sonny Bono

Prophetic role reversal.

1967

YOU BETTER SIT DOWN KIDS
Producer: Sonny Bono
Album: With Love
Record Label: Imperial
Songwriter: Sonny Bono

Las Vegas Country.

1971

GYPSIES, TRAMPS AND THIEVES
Producer: Snuff Garrett
Album: Gypsies, Tramps and Thieves
Record Label: Kapp
Songwriter: Robert Stone

One of Garrett's favorite productions.

1973

HALF-BREED
Producer: Snuff Garrett
Album: Half-Breed
Record Label: MCA
Songwriters: Mary Dean, Al Capps

Her biggest hit, sans Sonny.

1974

DARK LADY
Producer: Snuff Garrett
Album: Dark Lady
Record Label: MCA
Songwriter: John Durrill

Her third solo #1 R&R about gypsies, tramps, thieves, or Sonny.

1987

I FOUND SOMEONE
Producer: Michael Bolton
Album: Cher
Record Label: Geffen
Songwriters: Michael Bolton, Mark Mangold

Cher returns as a Middle of the Road Madonna.

1988

WE ALL SLEEP ALONE
Producers: Desmond Child, Jon Bon Jovi, Richie Sambora
Album: Cher
Record Label: Geffen
Songwriters: Jon Bon Jovi, Richie Sambora, Desmond Child

From the New Jersey song bag.

1989

AFTER ALL (LOVE THEME FROM CHANCES ARE)
Producer: Peter Asher
Album: Heart of Stone
Record Label: Geffen
Songwriters: Tom Snow, Dean Pitchford

A big movie ballad, sung with Peter Cetera.

IF I COULD TURN BACK TIME
Producers: Diane Warren, G. Roche
Album: Heart of Stone
Record Label: Geffen
Songwriter: Diane Warren

With the memorably explicit video.

JUST LIKE JESSE JAMES
Producer: Desmond Child
Album: Heart of Stone
Record Label: Geffen
Songwriters: Diane Warren, Desmond Child

From the ultimate hired guns of '80s Pop-Rock songwriting.

CHERRELLE

1984

I DIDN'T MEAN TO TURN YOU ON
Producers: Jimmy Jam, Terry Lewis
Album: Fragile
Record Label: Tabu
Songwriters: James Harris III, Terry Lewis

Covered by Robert Palmer (Atlantic, '86).

1988

EVERYTHING I MISS AT HOME
Producers: Jimmy Jam, Terry Lewis
Album: Affair
Record Label: Tabu
Songwriters: James Harris III, Terry Lewis

#1 R&B.

NENEH CHERRY

1989

BUFFALO STANCE
Producers: T. Simenon, M. Saunders
Album: Raw like Sushi
Record Label: Virgin
Songwriters: Neneh Cherry, Booga Bear, Phil Ramacon, Jamie Morgan

Originated in the U.K. by Morgan McVey. Remixed by Bomb the Bass. Featured in the '89 movie Slaves of New York.

KISSES ON THE WIND
Producers: N. Plytas, Dynamic Duo
Album: Raw Like Sushi
Record Label: Virgin
Songwriters: Neneh Cherry, Cameron McVey

The hip dance alternative to Paula Abdul.

THE CHI-LITES

1971

(FOR GOD'S SAKE) GIVE MORE POWER TO THE PEOPLE
Producer: Eugene Record
Album: (For God's Sake) Give More Power to the People
Record Label: Brunswick
Songwriter: Eugene Record

Part of a significant early '70s black social protest movement. Suggested segues: "Inner City Blues" by Marvin Gaye, "Bring the Boys Home" by Freda Payne, "Respect Yourself" by the Staple Singers, "Ball of Confusion" by the Temptations, "Express Yourself" by the Watts 103rd St. Band, and "The Revolution Will Not Be Televised" by the Last Poets.

HAVE YOU SEEN HER
Producer: Eugene Record
Album: (For God's Sake) Give More Power to the People
Record Label: Brunswick
Songwriters: Eugene Record, Barbara Acklin

#1 R&B/Top-10 R&R crossover.

1972

OH GIRL
Producer: Eugene Record
Album: A Lonely Man
Record Label: Brunswick
Songwriter: Eugene Record

Smokey Soul, in the vulnerable Robinson style, with a sweet, funky harp.

CHIC

1977

DANCE, DANCE, DANCE (YOWSAH, YOWSAH, YOWSAH)
Producers: Nile Rodgers, Bernard Edwards
Album: Chic
Record Label: Atlantic
Songwriters: Nile Rodgers, Bernard Edwards, Kenny Lehman

Evoking a bygone Disco era, Chic clicks.

1978

I WANT YOUR LOVE
Producers: Nile Rodgers, Bernard Edwards
Album: C'est Chic
Record Label: Atlantic
Songwriters: Nile Rodgers, Bernard Edwards

Establishing a higher Disco standard.

LE FREAK
Producers: Nile Rodgers, Bernard Edwards
Album: C'est Chic
Record Label: Atlantic
Songwriters: Nile Rodgers, Bernard Edwards

#1 R&B/R&R crossover; at the time the best-selling single in Atlantic Records' venerable history.

1979

GOOD TIMES
Producers: Nile Rodgers, Bernard Edwards
Album: Risque
Record Label: Atlantic
Songwriters: Nile Rodgers, Bernard Edwards

#1 R&B/R&R crossover. Sampled on "Rapper's Delight" by the Sugarhill Gang (Sugarhill, '79), the first Rap hit.

CHICAGO

1969

BEGINNINGS
Producer: James William Guercio
Album: Chicago Transit Authority
Record Label: Columbia
Songwriter: Robert Lamm

The Chicago ersatz Jazz sound wafts in off the lake.

1970

25 OR 6 TO 4
Producer: James William Guercio
Album: Chicago II
Record Label: Columbia
Songwriter: Robert Lamm

Lamm establishes Chicago's early voice; the first big Rock band of the big Rock band era.

DOES ANYBODY REALLY KNOW WHAT TIME IT IS
Producer: James William Guercio
Album: Chicago Transit Authority
Record Label: Columbia
Songwriter: Robert Lamm

Answering the question posed by the earlier "25 or 6 to 4."

MAKE ME SMILE
Producer: James William Guercio
Album: Chicago II
Record Label: Columbia
Songwriter: James Pankow

The band's first Top-10 R&R.

1972

SATURDAY IN THE PARK
Producer: James William Guercio
Album: Chicago V
Record Label: Columbia
Songwriter: Robert Lamm

Mainstream Jazz-flavored Pop is Lamm's last big hit.

1973

JUST YOU 'N' ME
Producer: James William Guercio
Album: Chicago VI
Record Label: Columbia
Songwriter: James Pankow

Just Pankow and Cetera trading the hits now.

1974

(I'VE BEEN) SEARCHIN' SO LONG
Producer: James William Guercio
Album: Chicago VII
Record Label: Columbia
Songwriter: James Pankow

Pankow proves himself as accomplished at easy-listening, semi-orchestral Jazz as Lamm.

CALL ON ME
Producer: James William Guercio
Album: Chicago VII
Record Label: Columbia
Songwriter: Lee Loughrane

Who let the trumpet player have some?

1975

OLD DAYS
Producer: James William Guercio
Album: Chicago VIII
Record Label: Columbia
Songwriter: James Pankow

Pankow's fourth Top-10.

1976

IF YOU LEAVE ME NOW
Producer: James William Guercio
Album: Chicago X
Record Label: Columbia
Songwriter: Peter Cetera

Cetera's writing debut: their biggest all-time hit, #1 U.S./U.K.

1977

BABY, WHAT A BIG SURPRISE
Producer: James William Guercio
Album: Chicago XI
Record Label: Columbia
Songwriter: Peter Cetera

Cetera's follow-up goes Top-5.

1978

ALIVE AGAIN
Producer: James William Guercio
Album: Hot Streets
Record Label: Columbia
Songwriter: James Pankow

Pankow wrests a single from Cetera's grasp.

1982

HARD TO SAY I'M SORRY
Producer: David Foster
Album: 16
Record Label: Full Moon
Songwriters: Peter Cetera, David Foster

A #1 R&R mini-comeback for Cetera (and Chicago), with a new partner. From the film Summer Lovers.

1984

HARD HABIT TO BREAK
Producer: David Foster
Album: 17
Record Label: Full Moon
Songwriters: Stephen Kipner, John Parker

The hit habit.

1985

YOU'RE THE INSPIRATION
Producer: David Foster
Album: 17
Record Label: Full Moon
Songwriters: Peter Cetera, David Foster

Cetera/Foster in stride.

1987

WILL YOU STILL LOVE ME?
Album: Chicago 18
Record Label: Warner Brothers
Songwriters: David Foster, Tom Keane, Richard Baskin

1988

I DON'T WANNA LIVE WITHOUT YOUR LOVE
Producer: Ron Nevison
Album: 19
Record Label: Reprise
Songwriters: Diane Warren, Albert Hammond

Cetera having departed for a solo career, Chicago seeks professional help.

LOOK AWAY
Producer: Ron Nevison
Album: 19
Record Label: Reprise
Songwriter: Diane Warren

#1 R&R hit of the year from the pen of Brill building throwback Warren.

1989

YOU'RE NOT ALONE
Producer: Ron Nevison
Album: 19
Record Label: Reprise
Songwriter: Jim Scott

WHAT KIND OF MAN WOULD I BE
Producer: Ron Nevison
Album: Greatest Hits 1982–1989
Record Label: Reprise
Songwriters: Bobby Caldwell, Charles Sandford, Jason Scheff

The end of a golden era of schmaltz.

THE CHIFFONS
1963

HE'S SO FINE
Producers: Mitch Margo, Phil
Margo, Hank Medress, Jay Siegel
Album: He's So Fine
Record Label: Laurie
Songwriter: Ronnie Mack

#1 R&B/R&R. Mid-tempo, girl-group frosting on the Brill Building male ego of the pre-Beatles '60s.

ONE FINE DAY
Producers: Mitch Margo, Phil
Margo, Hank Medress, Jay Siegel
Album: One Fine Day
Record Label: Laurie
Songwriters: Gerry Goffin, Carole
King

More hero worship from one of the more restrained of the girl-groups.

1966

SWEET TALKIN' GUY
Producer: Bright Tunes
Album: Sweet Talkin' Guy
Record Label: Laurie
Songwriters: Doug Morris, Elliot
Greenberg, Barbara Baer, Robert
Schwartz

From the authors of "Are You a Boy or Are You a Girl?"

JANE CHILD
1990

DON'T WANNA FALL IN LOVE
Producer: Jane Child
Album: Jane Child
Record Label: Warner Brothers
Songwriter: Jane Child

Dance groove.

THE CHILLS
1990

EFFLOURESCE AND DELIQUESCE
Producer: Gary Smith
Album: Submarine Bells
Record Label: Slash
Songwriter: Martyn Phillips

Haunting psychedelic gem from New Zealand.

ALEX CHILTON
1985

THANK YOU JOHN
Producer: Alex Chilton
Album: Feudalist Tarts
Record Label: Big Time
Songwriter: Willie Turbington

A critical cult hero returns to the fold with a great song, not his own.

THE CHIPS
1956

RUBBER BISCUIT
Record Label: Josie
Songwriter: Charles Johnson

Novelty R&B with profound implications, subverted by the Blues Brothers (Atlantic, '79).

CHOCOLATE WATCHBAND
1966

LET'S TALK ABOUT GIRLS
Producer: Ed Cobb
Album: No Way Out
Record Label: Tower
Songwriter: M. Freiser

Garage band nugget.

THE CHORDS
1954

SH-BOOM (LIFE COULD BE A DREAM)
Producers: Ahmet Ertegun, Jerry
Wexler
Record Label: Cat
Songwriters: James Keyes, Claude
Feaster, Carl Feaster, Floyd F.
McRae, James Edwards

B-side of "Cross over the Bridge" is the first R&B record to cross over to the Top-10 R&R, marking a turning point in the history of race music. Crewcuts cover went to #1 R&R (Mercury, '54).

CHARLIE CHRISTIAN
1944

SOLO FLIGHT
Album: Genius of the Electric Guitar
Record Label: Columbia
Songwriters: Charlie Christian,
Benny Goodman, Jimmy Mundy

Posthumous hit for Benny Goodman's legendary electric guitarist, recorded in 1941,

was a #1 R&B/Top-20 crossover, influencing a generation of players.

FRANK CHRISTIAN
1988

THREE FLIGHTS UP
Album: Fast Folk Sixth Anniversary
Issue
Record Label: Fast Folk
Songwriter: Frank Christian

Evocative Urban Folk lament. Covered by Nanci Griffith (Elektra, '92) with Christian reprising his wonderful guitar part.

THE CHRISTIANS
1988

IDEAL WORLD
Producer: Laurie Latham
Album: The Christians
Record Label: Island
Songwriters: Henry Priestman, Mark
Herman

Mellifluous U.K. Soul with a poignant, pointed message.

LOU CHRISTIE
1963

TWO FACES HAVE I
Producer: Nick Cenci
Album: Lou Christie
Record Label: Roulette
Songwriters: Twyla Herbert, Lou
Sacco (Lou Christie)

Two faces, four voices, and a pseudonym; Lou Sacco comes clean.

1966

LIGHTNIN' STRIKES
Producer: Charlie Calello
Album: Lightnin' Strikes
Record Label: MGM
Songwriters: Twyla Herbert, Lou
Sacco (Lou Christie)

The male libido as an uncontrollable force of nature. Gary Puckett was listening.

EUGENE CHURCH
1959

PRETTY GIRLS EVERYWHERE
Record Label: Class
Songwriters: Eugene Church,
Thomas Williams

Top-10 R&B/Top-40 R&R crossover.

THE CHURCH
1988

REPTILE
Producers: Greg Ladanyi, Waddy
Wachtel, the Church
Album: Starfish
Record Label: Arista
Songwriters: Steve Kilbey, the
Church
Slithery Rave Rock; the early years.

UNDER THE MILKY WAY
Producers: Greg Ladanyi, Waddy
Wachtel, the Church
Album: Starfish
Record Label: Arista
Songwriters: Steve Kilbey, Karin
Jannson
*The '80s jangly ethereal answer to
"Daydream" by the Lovin' Spoonful and
"Waterloo Sunset" by the Kinks.*

CINDERELLA
1987

NOBODY'S FOOL
Producer: A. Johns
Album: Night Songs
Record Label: Mercury
Songwriter: Tom Keifer
Heavy Metal in glass slippers.

THE CIRCLE JERKS
1980

GROUP SEX
Producers: Cary Markoff, Circle
Jerks
Album: Group Sex
Record Label: Frontier
Songwriters: Jeffrey Pierce, Greg
Hetson, Keith Lehrer, Keith Morris,
Roger Downing
L.A. Punk confidential.

CIRCUS MAXIMUS
1967

WIND
Album: Circus Maximus
Record Label: Vanguard
Songwriter: Jerry Jeff Walker
*Early FM radio Art Rock forerunner, by the
house band at the Electric Circus just before
the Velvet Underground moved in.*

THE CITY
1968

SNOW QUEEN
Producer: Lou Adler
Album: Now That Everything's Been
Said
Record Label: Ode
Songwriters: Gerry Goffin, Carole
King
*Elaborate writer's demo from Carole King's
pre-solo days, with Danny Kortchmar on
guitar. Covered by the Assocation
(Columbia, '72).*

THAT OLD SWEET ROLL
Producer: Lou Adler
Album: Now That Everything's Been
Said
Record Label: Ode
Songwriters: Carole King, Gerry
Goffin
*Transplanted Broadway Jazz. Covered by
Blood, Sweat, and Tears (Columbia, '71) as
"Hi De Ho."*

JIMMY CLANTON
1958

JUST A DREAM
Producer: Johnny Vincent
Album: Just a Dream
Record Label: Ace
Songwriters: Jimmy Clanton,
Cosimo Matassa
*Blue-eyed New Orleans Soul, influenced by
Earl King, leader of the band for which
Clanton labelmate Huey Smith played piano.*

1959

GO, JIMMY, GO
Producer: Johnny Vincent
Record Label: Ace
Songwriters: Doc Pomus, Mort
Shuman
*As an example of the interchangeability of
Rock and Roll parts in the Bobby & Jimmy
& Johnny "Bandstand" era, before Clanton
heard this Top-5 tune it was entitled "Go,
Bobby, Go" and pitched by the writers to
Bobby Rydell. It was Jimmy's second
biggest hit.*

1959

SHIP ON A STORMY SEA
Producer: Johnny Vincent
Record Label: Ace
Songwriters: Jimmy Clanton,
Cosimo Matassa, Seth David, Mack
Rebennack

*The cream of New Orleans musical society
gave Clanton this obscure companion to
"Sea of Love."*

1961

VENUS IN BLUE JEANS
Producer: Johnny Vincent
Album: Venus in Blue Jeans
Record Label: Ace
Songwriters: Howard Greenfield,
Jack Keller
Imported from 1650 Broadway.

ERIC CLAPTON
1970

AFTER MIDNIGHT
Producer: Delaney Bramlett
Album: Eric Clapton
Record Label: Atco
Songwriter: John J. Cale
*Defining the mid-tempo blues that would
define much of Clapton's post-God singing
career. Covered by J. J. Cale (Shelter, '72).*

LET IT RAIN
Producer: Delaney Bramlett
Album: Eric Clapton
Record Label: Atco
Songwriter: Richard Martin

1977

COCAINE
Producer: Jon Astley
Album: Slowhand
Record Label: RSO
Songwriter: John J. Cale
Enduring signature rocker.

LAY DOWN SALLY
Producer: Glyn Johns
Album: Slowhand
Record Label: RSO
Songwriters: Eric Clapton, Marcy
Levy, George Terry
*So mellow it crossed over to the Country
charts.*

WONDERFUL TONIGHT
Producer: Glyn Johns
Album: Slowhand
Record Label: RSO
Songwriter: Eric Clapton
*A classic Clapton caption of English parlor
life, capturing an almost New Yorker-esque
repression; included on two best-of albums
and two live sets.*

1978

PROMISES
Producer: Glyn Johns
Album: Backless
Record Label: RSO
Songwriters: Richard Feldman, Roger Linn
Top-10 tune done in Tulsa time.

TULSA TIME
Producer: Jon Astley
Album: Backless
Record Label: RSO
Songwriter: Danny Flowers
Originated on the Country charts by Don Williams.

1980

BLUES POWER
Producer: Jon Astley
Album: Blues Power
Record Label: RSO
Songwriters: Eric Clapton, Leon Russell
Still his defining credo.

1981

I CAN'T STAND IT
Producer: Tom Dowd
Album: Another Ticket
Record Label: RSO
Songwriter: Eric Clapton
Blues powerless.

1983

I'VE GOT A ROCK AND ROLL HEART
Producer: Tom Dowd
Album: Money and Cigarettes
Record Label: Duck/Warner Brothers
Songwriters: Troy Seals, Eddie Setser, Steve Diamond
Suggested segue: "Rock and Roll Heart" by Lou Reed.

1985

FOREVER MAN
Producers: Ted Templeman, Lenny Waronker
Album: Behind the Sun
Record Label: Duck
Songwriter: Jerry Williams
"God" in his descendancy.

1986

IT'S IN THE WAY YOU USE IT
Producers: Tom Dowd, Phil Collins
Album: August

Record Label: Duck
Songwriters: Eric Clapton, Robbie Robertson
Featured in the '86 film The Color of Money.

1989

BAD LOVE
Producer: Mick Jones
Album: Journeyman
Record Label: Duck
Songwriters: Eric Clapton, Mick Jones
A latter-day guitar highlight.

1991

TEARS IN HEAVEN
Producer: Russ Titelman
Album: *Rush* Soundtrack
Record Label: Reprise
Songwriters: Eric Clapton, Will Jennings
This exquisite soundtrack ballad from a film about drug addicts enabled Clapton to express his grief over losing his young son in a tragic fall.

CLAUDINE CLARK

1962

PARTY LIGHTS
Producers: Claudine Clark, Marcucci and Faith
Album: Party Lights
Record Label: Chancellor
Songwriter: Claudine Clark
B-side of "Disappointed." True essence of the teenage dilemma in one of the all-time-great girl-group era one-shots.

THE DAVE CLARK FIVE

1964

BECAUSE
Producer: Dave Clark
Album: American Tour
Record Label: Epic
Songwriter: Dave Clark
The poppiest of the Invasion army.

BITS AND PIECES
Producer: Dave Clark
Album: Coast to Coast
Record Label: Epic
Songwriters: Dave Clark, Mike Smith
Their biggest rocker.

CAN'T YOU SEE THAT SHE'S MINE
Producer: Dave Clark
Album: Dave Clark Five Return
Record Label: Epic
Songwriters: Dave Clark, Mike Smith

GLAD ALL OVER
Producer: Dave Clark
Album: Glad All Over
Record Label: Epic
Songwriters: Dave Clark, Mike Smith
They had their moment. This was it.

1965

CATCH US IF YOU CAN
Producer: Dave Clark
Album: Having a Wild Weekend
Record Label: Epic
Songwriters: Dave Clark, Lenny Davidson
From the film.

DEE CLARK

1959

HEY, LITTLE GIRL
Album: Dee Clark
Record Label: Abner
Songwriters: Otis Blackwell, Bobby Stevenson
In the Clyde McPhatter mold.

1961

RAINDROPS
Record Label: Vee Jay
Songwriter: Dee Clark
A fertile motif for sad songs.

PETULA CLARK

1964

DOWNTOWN
Producer: Tony Hatch
Album: Downtown
Record Label: Warner Brothers
Songwriter: Tony Hatch
A generation on the edge of a night life were pushed over by this exhilarating Pop rocker; #1 U.S./#2 U.K.

1965

I KNOW A PLACE
Producer: Tony Hatch
Album: I Know a Place
Record Label: Warner Brothers
Songwriter: Tony Hatch

YOU'RE THE ONE
Producer: Tony Hatch
Album: I Know a Place
Record Label: Warner Brothers
Songwriters: Tony Hatch, Petula Clark

Covered by the Vogues (Co and Ce, '65).

SANFORD CLARK
1956

THE FOOL
Producer: Lee Hazelwood
Record Label: Dot
Songwriter: Lee Hazelwood

Covered by the Gallahads (Jubilee, '56). A double one-shot: two groups, no follow-ups, except for producer/author Hazelwood, who would move on to Duane Eddy.

THE CLASH
1977

1977
Producer: Mickey Foote
Album: The Clash
Record Label: Epic
Songwriters: John Mellor (Joe Strummer), Mick Jones

The B-side of "White Riot," and conclusive proof that the Clash were "No Elvis, No Beatles, No Rolling Stones." The Sex Pistols, maybe.

CLASH CITY ROCKERS
Producer: Mickey Foote
Album: The Clash
Record Label: Epic
Songwriters: John Mellor (Joe Strummer), Mick Jones

What could a poor boy in London do in the late '70s except to sing in a Reggae-influenced band? This single was added to the U.S. version of their first album when it was finally released in '79, after their second.

COMPLETE CONTROL
Producer: Lee Perry
Album: The Clash
Record Label: Epic
Songwriters: John Mellor (Joe Strummer), Mick Jones

Fierce autobiographical single was produced by Reggae legend Lee Perry and added to the U.S. version of their U.K. album.

I'M SO BORED WITH THE U.S.A
Producer: Mickey Foote
Album: The Clash

Record Label: Epic
Songwriters: John Mellor (Joe Strummer), Mick Jones

Signature Punk Rock track from a band whose scrawled signature was often seen on their T-shirts reading "Passion Is a Fashion," "Creative Violence," and "Pure Energy."

LONDON'S BURNING
Producer: Mickey Foote
Album: The Clash
Record Label: Epic
Songwriters: John Mellor (Joe Strummer), Mick Jones

Some of the most incendiary licks Rock and Roll has ever heard.

WHITE RIOT
Producer: Mickey Foote
Album: The Clash
Record Label: Epic
Songwriters: John Mellor (Joe Strummer), Mick Jones

Their first single became one of the key songs in establishing Punk Rock as a vital movement and moment in Britian and throughout the world; its elemental heat and anger helped the original LP become the biggest selling import album in U.S. history. Every angry young man within earshot was influenced.

1978

JULIE'S IN THE DRUG SQUAD
Producer: Sandy Pearlman
Album: Give 'Em Enough Rope
Record Label: Epic
Songwriters: John Mellor (Joe Strummer), Mick Jones

A post-hippie vision redefined, cops on acid for Operation Julie.

SAFE EUROPEAN HOME
Producer: Sandy Pearlman
Album: Give 'Em Enough Rope
Record Label: Epic
Songwriters: John Mellor (Joe Strummer), Mick Jones

Written in the Pegasus Hotel, Kingston, Jamaica, one of the best from their second album, the first to be released in the U.S.; newfound studio sophstication took them out of garageland forever.

STAY FREE
Producer: Sandy Pearlman
Album: Give 'Em Enough Rope
Record Label: Epic
Songwriters: John Mellor (Joe

Strummer), Mick Jones

Ballad about a real-life rude boy.

TOMMY GUN
Producer: Sandy Pearlman
Album: Give 'Em Enough Rope
Record Label: Epic
Songwriters: John Mellor (Joe Strummer), Mick Jones

Their first hit single.

WHITE MAN IN HAMMERSMITH PALAIS
Producer: The Clash
Album: The Clash
Record Label: Epic
Songwriters: John Mellor (Joe Strummer), Mick Jones

Inspired post-debut LP track. This U.K. single (with "I Fought the Law") was added to the U.S. album called by many the best of the year and maybe of all time (turning rebellion into money indeed).

1979

LONDON CALLING
Producer: Guy Stevens
Album: London Calling
Record Label: Epic
Songwriters: John Mellor (Joe Strummer), Mick Jones

Stevens had produced their early demos.

LOST IN THE SUPERMARKET
Producer: Guy Stevens
Album: London Calling
Record Label: Epic
Songwriters: John Mellor (Joe Strummer), Mick Jones

The Taj Mahal influence.

TRAIN IN VAIN (STAND BY ME)
Producer: Guy Stevens
Album: London Calling
Record Label: Epic
Songwriters: John Mellor (Joe Strummer), Mick Jones

Punk Rock's next last best hope marked the end of a decade of recession and repression in England with their first hit in the U.S.

WRONG 'EM BOYO
Producer: Guy Stevens
Album: London Calling
Record Label: Epic
Songwriters: John Mellor (Joe Strummer), Mick Jones

Another highlight from their double LP.

1980

BANK ROBBER
Producer: Mikey Dread
Album: Black Market Clash
Record Label: Epic/Nu Disc
Songwriters: John Mellor (Joe Strummer), Mick Jones

Flipside of "Train in Vain" in Holland. The record company said it sounded like "all of David Bowie's records played backwards at once." Eventually became a big hit in England.

1982

ROCK THE CASBAH
Producer: Glyn Johns
Album: Combat Rock
Record Label: Epic
Songwriters: John Mellor (Joe Strummer), Mick Jones, Paul Simonon, Topper Headon

Their only U.S. Top-40.

SHOULD I STAY OR SHOULD I GO
Producer: Glyn Johns
Album: Combat Rock
Record Label: Epic
Songwriters: John Mellor (Joe Strummer), Mick Jones

Their last chart single.

THE CLASSICS IV AND DENNIS YOST
1968

SPOOKY
Producer: Buddy Buie
Album: Spooky
Record Label: Imperial
Songwriters: Harvey Middlebrooks, Mike Shapiro

Consummate easy-listening. Covered by the Atlanta Rhythm Section (Polydor, '79).

STORMY
Producer: Buddy Buie
Album: Mamas and Papas/Soul Train
Record Label: Imperial
Songwriters: Buddy Buie, James B. Cobb

Suggested segue: "Raindrops" by Dee Clark.

1969

TRACES
Producer: Buddy Buie
Album: Traces

Record Label: Imperial
Songwriters: Buddy Buie, James B. Cobb Jr., Emory Gordy Jr.

OTIS CLAY
1972

TRYING TO LIVE MY LIFE WITHOUT YOU
Producer: Willie Mitchell
Record Label: Hi
Songwriter: Eugene Williams

Revered R&B cut. Covered by Bob Seger (Capitol, '81). Suggested segue: "The Long Run" by the Eagles.

THE CLEFTONES
1956

CAN'T WE BE SWEETHEARTS
Producer: George Goldner
Album: Teenage Party
Record Label: Gee
Songwriters: George Goldner, Herbert Cox

Classic New York Doo-Wop.

LITTLE GIRL OF MINE
Producer: George Goldner
Album: Teenage Party
Record Label: Gee
Songwriters: George Goldner, Herbert Cox

Their first R&B hit, cowritten by lead singer, Cox.

1961

HEART AND SOUL
Producer: George Goldner
Album: Heart and Soul
Record Label: Gee
Songwriters: Hoagy Carmichael, Frank Loesser

A scenic highlight along the Doo-Wop to standards route. Introduced by Larry Clinton and his Orchestra, in the '38 movie, A Song Is Born.

JIMMY CLIFF
1970

MANY RIVERS TO CROSS
Record Label: Mango
Songwriter: Jimmy Cliff

Reggae classic. Covered by Nilsson (RCA, 74), Linda Ronstadt (Asylum, '75), and UB40 (A&M, '83). Included in the soundtrack LP, The Harder They Come (Mango, '72).

VIET NAM
Producer: Jimmy Cliff
Album: Wonderful World, Beautiful People
Record Label: A&M
Songwriter: Jimmy Cliff

Bob Dylan called this the best protest song he'd ever heard. Paul Simon went to Jamaica and used Cliff's rhythm section to record "Mother and Child Reunion" in '72.

WONDERFUL WORLD, BEAUTIFUL PEOPLE
Producer: Jimmy Cliff
Album: Wonderful World, Beautiful People
Record Label: A&M
Songwriter: Jimmy Cliff

His first big Reggae hit.

1972

THE HARDER THEY COME
Producer: Jimmy Cliff
Album: *The Harder They Come* Soundtrack
Record Label: Mango
Songwriter: Jimmy Cliff

Underclass anthem from the classic Reggae movie and sampler.

SITTING IN LIMBO
Producer: Jimmy Cliff
Album: *The Harder They Come* Soundtrack
Record Label: Mango
Songwriters: Jimmy Cliff, Gilly Bright-Plummer

Covered by Three Dog Night (Dunhill, '73).

YOU CAN GET IT IF YOU REALLY WANT
Producer: Jimmy Cliff
Album: *The Harder They Come* Soundtrack
Record Label: Mango
Songwriter: Jimmy Cliff

Suggested segue: "You Can't Always Get What You Want" by the Rolling Stones, "You Can't Get What You Want Until You Know What You Want" by Joe Jackson.

BUZZ CLIFFORD
1961

BABY SITTIN' BOOGIE
Record Label: Columbia
Songwriter: Johnny Parker

CLIMAX
1972

PRECIOUS AND FEW
Producer: Larry Cox
Album: Climax
Record Label: Carousel
Songwriter: Walter Nims

Featuring the voice of Sonny Geraci, last heard on "Time Won't Let Me" by the Outsiders.

CLIMAX BLUES BAND
1977

COULDN'T GET IT RIGHT
Producer: Mike Vernon
Album: Gold Plated
Record Label: Sire
Songwriters: Derek Holt, Colin Cooper, John Cuffley, Peter Haycock, Derek Holt, Frederick Jones

Southern-fried Pop Rock, with an unstoppable hook.

1981

I LOVE YOU
Album: Flying the Flag
Record Label: Warner Brothers
Songwriter: Derek Holt

Legendary wedding song, long out of print.

PATSY CLINE
1956

WALKING AFTER MIDNIGHT
Producer: Owen Bradley
Album: Patsy Cline Showcase
Record Label: Decca
Songwriters: Don Hecht, Alan Block

Classic Country Blues in a Pop Rock setting.

1961

CRAZY
Producer: Owen Bradley
Album: Patsy Cline Showcase
Record Label: Decca
Songwriter: Willie Nelson

One of the all-time Country jukebox classic weepers; #2 C&W/Top-10 R&R crossover. Ross Perot's '92 presidential theme song.

I FALL TO PIECES
Album: Patsy Cline Showcase
Record Label: Decca
Songwriters: Hank Cochran, Harlan Howard

Defining classic Cline. #1 C&W/Top-15 R&R crossover.

1962

SHE'S GOT YOU
Producer: Owen Bradley
Album: The Patsy Cline Story
Record Label: Decca
Songwriter: Hank Cochran

#1 C&W/Top-20 R&R crossover.

GEORGE CLINTON
1983

ATOMIC DOG
Producer: George Clinton
Album: Computer Games
Record Label: Capitol
Songwriters: George Clinton, Garry Shider, David Spradley

From the first solo effort by the legendary producer of Funkadelic.

1986

DO FRIES GO WITH THAT SHAKE?
Producer: George Clinton
Album: R&B Skeletons in the Closet
Record Label: Capitol
Songwriters: George Clinton, Sheila Washington, Stephen Washington

THE CLIQUE
1968

SUPERMAN
Album: The Clique
Record Label: White Whale
Songwriters: Gary Zekely, Mitch Bottler

Legendary B-side of "Sugar on Sunday." Covered by R.E.M. (IRS, '86).

THE CLOVERS
1951

DON'T YOU KNOW I LOVE YOU
Producers: Ahmet Ertegun, Herb Abramson
Record Label: Atlantic
Songwriter: Ahmet Ertegun

#1 R&B out of the Mills Brothers and the Ink Spots. The Clovers helped to establish the Doo-Wop ballad as the primary form of black romance in the '50s.

FOOL, FOOL, FOOL
Producers: Ahmet Ertegun, Herb Abramson
Record Label: Atlantic
Songwriter: Ahmet Ertegun

Their second #1 R&B hit.

1952

ONE MINT JULEP
Producers: Ahmet Ertegun, Herb Abramson
Record Label: Atlantic
Songwriter: Rudolph Toombs

Another masterpiece from Toombs. Covered by Ray Charles (ABC-Paramount, '61).

TING-A-LING
Producers: Ahmet Ertegun, Herb Abramson
Record Label: Atlantic
Songwriter: Ahmet Ertegun

#1 R&B, up tempo.

1953

GOOD LOVIN'
Producers: Ahmet Ertegun, Herb Abramson
Record Label: Atlantic
Songwriters: Ahmet Ertegun, Jesse Stone (Charles Calhoun), Leroy Kirkland, Danny Taylor

Competition for Leiber and Stoller. Covered by the Young Rascals (Atlantic, '66).

1954

LITTLE MAMA
Producers: Ahmet Ertegun, Jerry Wexler
Record Label: Atlantic
Songwriters: Ahmet Ertegun, Jerry Wexler, Carmen Taylor, Willis Carroll

B-side of "Lovey Dovey."

YOUR CASH AIN'T NOTHIN' BUT TRASH
Producers: Ahmet Ertegun, Jerry Wexler
Record Label: Atlantic
Songwriter: Jesse Stone (Charles Calhoun)

Their fiercest commentary; covered by the Steve Miller Band (Capitol, '74).

1955

BLUE VELVET
Producers: Ahmet Ertegun, Jerry Wexler
Record Label: Atlantic
Songwriters: Bernie Wayne, Lee Morris

Introduced by Tony Bennett (Columbia, '51), popularized by Bobby Vinton (Epic, '63), but tailor-made for Doo-Wop legendhood by the Clovers.

DEVIL OR ANGEL

Producers: Ahmet Ertegun, Jerry Wexler
Record Label: Atlantic
Songwriter: Blanche Carter

Covered by Bobby Vee (Liberty, '60).

LOVEY DOVEY

Producers: Ahmet Ertegun, Jerry Wexler
Record Label: Atlantic
Songwriters: Ahmet Ertegun, Memphis Curtis

Producers' choice: covered by Clyde McPhatter (Atlantic, '59), Buddy Knox (Liberty, '60), and Otis and Carla (Stax, '68).

1956

LOVE, LOVE, LOVE

Producers: Ahmet Ertegun, Jerry Wexler
Record Label: Atlantic
Songwriters: Teddy McRae, Sid Wyche, Sunny David

Covered by the Diamonds (Mercury, '56).

1959

LOVE POTION NUMBER NINE

Producers: Jerry Leiber, Mike Stoller
Album: Love Potion Number Nine
Record Label: United Artists
Songwriters: Jerry Leiber, Mike Stoller

Way past their prime, their biggest hit. Covered by the Searchers (Kapp, '65).

CLUB NOUVEAU

1987

WHY YOU TREAT ME SO BAD

Producers: Thom McElroy, Denzil Foster, Jay King
Album: Life, Love, and Pain
Record Label: Tommy Boy
Songwriters: Thom McElroy, Jay King

Dancehall tableau. Foster and McElroy would be back with En Vogue.

THE COASTERS

1956

DOWN IN MEXICO

Producers: Jerry Leiber, Mike Stoller
Album: The Coasters
Record Label: Atco
Songwriters: Jerry Leiber, Mike Stoller

Their first R&B hit.

ONE KISS LED TO ANOTHER

Producers: Jerry Leiber, Mike Stoller
Record Label: Atco
Songwriters: Jerry Leiber, Mike Stoller

One week on the charts for their first Rock and Roll crossover.

1957

(WHEN SHE WANTS GOOD LOVIN) MY BABY COMES TO ME

Producers: Jerry Leiber, Mike Stoller
Album: The Coasters
Record Label: Atco
Songwriters: Jerry Leiber, Mike Stoller

Covered by Tom Rush (Elektra, '65). Suggested segue: "Good Lovin'" by the Clovers.

SEARCHIN'

Producers: Jerry Leiber, Mike Stoller
Album: The Coasters
Record Label: Atco
Songwriters: Jerry Leiber, Mike Stoller

Calling on a lineup of detective super-heroes, in one of their more perfect novelty conceits. #1 R&B/Top-10 R&R.

YOUNG BLOOD

Producers: Jerry Leiber, Mike Stoller
Album: The Coasters
Record Label: Atco
Songwriters: Jerry Leiber, Mike Stoller, Doc Pomus

Early R&B-flavored effort by Doc Pomus, one of the most beloved figures in Rock and Roll songwriting history.

1958

YAKETY YAK

Producers: Jerry Leiber, Mike Stoller
Album: The Coasters
Record Label: Atco
Songwriters: Jerry Leiber, Mike Stoller

Beyond novelty, this was worthy of an entire issue of "Archie" comics; only there were no black Archie comics equivalents in those days, except for the Coasters. Most radio listeners didn't necessarily think of the Coasters as black, merely teenagers, expressing the previously expressable (but by now virtually inexhaustible) rage at their semi-indentured (that is, teenage) condition. Their only #1 R&B/R&R crossover.

1959

ALONG CAME JONES

Producers: Jerry Leiber, Mike Stoller
Record Label: Atco
Songwriters: Jerry Leiber, Mike Stoller

More of the good-natured novelty formula; not as biting as some others.

CHARLIE BROWN

Producers: Jerry Leiber, Mike Stoller
Album: Yakety Yak
Record Label: Atco
Songwriters: Jerry Leiber, Mike Stoller

Perhaps their most enduring novelty; certainly their most cartoonish.

POISON IVY

Producers: Jerry Leiber, Mike Stoller
Album: Yakety Yak
Record Label: Atco
Songwriters: Jerry Leiber, Mike Stoller

Their third Top-10 hit of '59 (#1 R&B). Covered by the Kingsmen (Wand, '65) and the Rolling Stones (London, '72).

THAT IS ROCK AND ROLL

Producers: Jerry Leiber, Mike Stoller
Record Label: Atco
Songwriters: Jerry Leiber, Mike Stoller

Critically revered B-side of "Along Came Jones." Covered by Sylvester and the Hot Band (Blue Thumb, '73).

WHAT ABOUT US

Producers: Jerry Leiber, Mike Stoller
Album: Coast Along with the Coasters
Record Label: Atco
Songwriters: Jerry Leiber, Mike Stoller

Couched in their usual humor, a rare note of real outrage.

1960

SHOPPING FOR CLOTHES

Producers: Jerry Leiber, Mike Stoller
Record Label: Atco
Songwriters: Jerry Leiber, Mike Stoller

1961

LITTLE EGYPT

Producers: Jerry Leiber, Mike Stoller
Album: Coast Along with the Coasters

Record Label: Atco
Songwriters: Jerry Leiber, Mike Stoller

The saga of a fan dancer borrowed from the Coasters by Elvis Presley for use in Roustabout (1964), his sixteenth movie, co-starring Barbara Stanwyck.

EDDIE COCHRAN

1956

PINK PEGGED SLACKS

Producers: Snuff Garrett, Eddie Cochran, Jerry Capeheart
Album: Singin' to My Baby
Record Label: United Artists
Songwriters: Eddie Cochran, Hank Cochran, Jerry Capeheart

First single for the stylish rocker.

TWENTY FLIGHT ROCK

Producers: Snuff Garrett, Eddie Cochran, Jerry Capeheart
Album: Singin' to My Baby
Record Label: Liberty
Songwriters: Eddie Cochran, Ned Fairchild

Introduced in a scintillating cameo in the movie, The Girl Can't Help It. Early indication of the power of the music video.

1957

DRIVE-IN SHOW

Producers: Snuff Garrett, Eddie Cochran, Jerry Capeheart
Album: Eddie Cochran
Record Label: Liberty
Songwriters: Fred Dexter, Clare Kane

Calculated follow-up to "Sittin' in the Balcony."

SITTIN' IN THE BALCONY

Producers: Snuff Garrett, Eddie Cochran, Jerry Capeheart
Album: Singin' to My Baby
Record Label: Liberty
Songwriter: John Loudermilk

An L.A. leather rocker singing about the movies. Introduced by the pseudonymous author, Johnny Dee (Colonial, '57).

1958

C'MON EVERYBODY

Producers: Eddie Cochran, Jerry Capeheart
Album: Eddie Cochran
Record Label: Liberty
Songwriters: Eddie Cochran, Jerry Capeheart

One of Cochran's most convincing rockers; a much bigger hit in the U.K., where he was touring when he was killed in a car crash.

CUT ACROSS SHORTY

Producer: Snuff Garrett
Record Label: Liberty
Songwriters: Wayne Walker, Marijohn Wilkin

Carl Smith had the Country hit (Columbia, '60). Also covered by Rod Stewart (Mercury, '70), and with the Faces (Warner Brothers, '74).

LOVE AGAIN

Album: Never to be Forgotten
Record Label: Liberty
Songwriter: Sharon Sheeley

Early songwriting effort by Eddie's legendary L.A. girlfriend, author of "Poor Little Fool."

SUMMERTIME BLUES

Producers: Eddie Cochran, Jerry Capeheart
Album: Summertime Blues
Record Label: Liberty
Songwriters: Eddie Cochran, Jerry Capeheart

Timeless essay on the teenage condition exacerbated by the season itself—oppressive idleness, endless, sunbaked alienation. As a black-leather, James Dean biker type in a Los Angeles on the edge of the Beach Boys, no one could have been more out of place or out of time than Cochran, whose time would soon run out. Covered by Blue Cheer (Phillips, '68) and the Who (Decca, '70).

1959

SOMETHIN' ELSE

Album: Eddie Cochran
Record Label: Liberty
Songwriters: Sharon Sheeley, Eddie Cochran

Cochran's second most enduring rocker. Covered in an appropriately stomping rendition by the duo of Tanya Tucker and Little Richard (MCA, '94) on a concept album uniting C&W and R&B superstars (occasionally with R&R material) as they haven't been united since Elvis left for Germany.

TEENAGE HEAVEN

Record Label: Liberty
Songwriters: Eddie Cochran, Jerry Capeheart

Pre-posthumous tribute/prophecy was his last chart single.

THREE STARS

Record Label: Liberty
Songwriter: Tommy Dee

Fixated by the deaths of three contemporaries, Cochran introduces this memorial. Covered by Dee, with Carol Kay (Crest, '59).

1960

THREE STEPS TO HEAVEN

Producers: Eddie Cochran, Jerry Capeheart
Album: Eddie Cochran
Record Label: Liberty
Songwriters: Eddie Cochran, Bob Cochran

His biggest U.K. hit, stiffed in the U.S.

1961

NERVOUS BREAKDOWN

Producers: Eddie Cochran, Jerry Capeheart
Album: Cherished Memories of Eddie Cochran
Record Label: London
Songwriters: Mario Roccuzzo, Eddie Cochran

WAYNE COCHRAN

1961

LAST KISS

Record Label: Gala
Songwriter: Wayne Cochran

Classic car (crash) song—classic car: '54 Chevy Impala. Covered by J. Frank Wilson with the Cavaliers (Josie, '64).

TOM COCHRANE

1992

LIFE IS A HIGHWAY

Producers: Joe Hardy, Tom Cochrane
Album: Mad Mad World
Record Label: Capitol
Songwriter: Tom Cochrane

Watered-down Springsteenian traveling song from the former leader of Red Rider.

COCK ROBIN

1985

WHEN YOUR HEART IS WEAK

Producer: Steve Hillage
Album: Cock Robin
Record Label: Columbia
Songwriter: Peter Kingsbery

Lush Art-Rock ballad.

BRUCE COCKBURN
1979

WONDERING WHERE THE LIONS ARE
Producer: Gene Martynec
Album: Dancing in the Dragon's Jaw
Record Label: Millennium
Songwriter: Bruce Cockburn

Canadian acoustic singer/songwriter's most commercial effort.

1985

IF I HAD A ROCKET LAUNCHER
Producers: J. Goldsmith, K. Crawford
Album: Stealing Fire
Record Label: Gold Mountain
Songwriter: Bruce Cockburn

Unplugging his social conscience.

JOE COCKER
1969

DELTA LADY
Producer: Denny Cordell
Album: Joe Cocker
Record Label: A&M
Songwriter: Leon Russell

That was no lady, that was Rita Coolidge. FM perennial, recorded by Russell (Shelter, '70).

1971

HIGH TIME WE WENT
Album: Joe Cocker
Record Label: A&M
Songwriters: Chris Stainton, Joe Cocker

1976

CATFISH
Album: Stingray
Record Label: A&M
Songwriter: Bob Dylan

An ode to baseball's Catfish Hunter. Recorded by Dylan (Columbia, '91).

JEALOUS KIND
Album: Stingray
Record Label: A&M
Songwriter: Robert Guidry (Bobby Charles)

Covered by Ray Charles (ABC, '76).

JOE COCKER AND JENNIFER WARNES
1982

UP WHERE WE BELONG
Producer: Stewart Levine
Album: *An Officer and a Gentleman* Soundtrack
Record Label: Island
Songwriters: Will Jennings, Jack Nitzsche, Buffy Sainte-Marie

This #1 R&R ballad from the Richard Gere/Debra Winger movie won the Oscar for Best Song.

COCTEAU TWINS
1990

CHERRY-COLOURED FUNK
Producer: Cocteau Twins
Album: Heaven or Las Vegas
Record Label: 4AD/Capitol
Songwriter: Cocteau Twins

A breath of artistic life into this moody, meandering band that previously made the Cowboy Junkies seem like speedcore thrashers.

LEONARD COHEN
1968

HEY, THAT'S NO WAY TO SAY GOODBYE
Producer: John Simon
Album: Songs of Leonard Cohen
Record Label: Columbia
Songwriter: Leonard Cohen

Song/poetry as a concept and a reality; brooding, Country-sounding sing-along dirge. Covered by the Vogues (Reprise, '70).

SO LONG, MARIANNE
Producer: John Simon
Album: Songs of Leonard Cohen
Record Label: Columbia
Songwriter: Leonard Cohen

A simple ditty from the author of the novel Beautiful Losers. *Covered by the group James (Atlantic, '91).*

STRANGER SONG
Producer: John Simon
Album: Songs of Leonard Cohen
Record Label: Columbia
Songwriter: Leonard Cohen

Literary and morose Folk Rock perfectly placed by Robert Altman in his movie McCabe and Mrs. Miller.

WINTER LADY
Producer: John Simon
Album: Songs of Leonard Cohen
Record Label: Columbia
Songwriter: Leonard Cohen

Trancelike doom and gloom by the master of the genre. Another reason for renting the video of McCabe and Mrs. Miller.

1969

SEEMS SO LONG AGO, NANCY
Producer: Bob Johnston
Album: Songs from a Room
Record Label: Columbia
Songwriter: Leonard Cohen

Sad tale of a party girl in the era of sad parties.

1971

FAMOUS BLUE RAINCOAT
Producer: John Simon
Album: Songs of Love and Hate
Record Label: Columbia
Songwriter: Leonard Cohen

A letter from Clinton Street, Cohen at his most divinely melancholy. Covered by Jennifer Warnes, along with an entire album of others (Cypress, '87).

1974

CHELSEA HOTEL #2
Producers: Leonard Cohen, John Lissauer
Album: New Skin for an Old Ceremony
Record Label: Columbia
Songwriter: Leonard Cohen

Evoking the bohemian ghost of the '60s, when poets briefly ruled, and Janis Joplin and Leonard Cohen made the Chelsea New York's version of the Sunset Marquis in Hollywood. Covered by Lloyd Cole (Atlantic, '91).

TAKE THIS LONGING
Producers: Leonard Cohen, John Lissauer
Album: New Skin for an Old Ceremony
Record Label: Columbia
Songwriter: Leonard Cohen

Deep in the maw of desire/depression.

1977

DON'T GO HOME WITH YOUR HARD-ON
Producer: Phil Spector
Album: Death of a Ladies Man

Record Label: Warner Brothers
Songwriters: Leonard Cohen, Phil Spector

Best results of a legendary mismatch of artist and producer.

1979

HUMBLED IN LOVE
Producers: Leonard Cohen, Henry Lewy
Album: Recent Songs
Record Label: Columbia
Songwriter: Leonard Cohen

In his most favorite position.

1985

THE CAPTAIN
Album: Various Positions
Record Label: PVC
Songwriter: Leonard Cohen

1988

I CAN'T FORGET
Album: I'm Your Man
Record Label: Columbia
Songwriter: Leonard Cohen

From a best-selling album in Europe. Covered by the Pixies (Atlantic, '91).

I'M YOUR MAN
Album: I'm Your Man
Record Label: Columbia
Songwriter: Leonard Cohen

The first Alternative Rock tribute package to the grand old man of Rock poetry was entitled "I'm Your Fan."

TOWER OF SONG
Album: I'm Your Man
Record Label: Columbia
Songwriter: Leonard Cohen

The second, more mainstream tribute album was called Tower of Song. Covered by Nick Cave and the Bad Seeds (Atlantic, '91).

1992

CLOSING TIME
Producers: Steve Lindsay, Bill Ginn, Leanne Ungar, Rebecca DeMornay, Yoav Goren
Album: The Future
Record Label: Virgin
Songwriter: Leonard Cohen

Bestowing a producer credit on close friend DeMornay is just one example of the undimmed romanticism that continues to make Cohen an idol in Europe and a cult figure in the U.S., though he's never had a hit single in either place.

MARC COHN

1991

WALKING IN MEMPHIS
Producers: Marc Cohn, Ben Wisch
Album: Marc Cohn
Record Label: Atlantic
Songwriter: Marc Cohn

Bruce Hornsby-esque Folk Jazz tribute to the ghost of Elvis Presley. Crossed over to the country chart.

COZY COLE

1958

TOPSY (PART II)
Record Label: Love
Songwriters: Edgar Battle, Edward Durham

The original "Topsy" was released by Benny Goodman (Victor, '38).

NAT KING COLE

1944

GEE BABY, AIN'T I GOOD TO YOU
Record Label: Capitol
Songwriters: Andy Razaf, Don Redman

#1 R&B/Top-20 Pop crossover. Covered by Ray Charles (ABC/TRC, '67).

STRAIGHTEN UP AND FLY RIGHT
Record Label: Capitol
Songwriters: Nat Cole, Irving Mills

Written in 1937, this landmark #1 C&W/#1 R&B/#2 Pop crossover was reportedly sold to Irving Mills for $50. In any event, it would launch the King Cole Trio as a big influence on Johnny Moore's Three Blazers, with Charles Brown, Ray Charles, Sam Cooke, and many others listening. Covered by Linda Ronstadt (Asylum, '86).

1946

(GET YOUR KICKS ON) ROUTE 66
Record Label: Capitol
Songwriter: Bobby Troup

Top-20 Pop. Covered by the Rolling Stones (London, '64), Them (Parrot, '65), Depeche Mode (Sire, '87).

1947

(I LOVE YOU) FOR SENTIMENTAL REASONS
Album: Unforgettable
Songwriters: Deek Watson, William Best

His first #1 Pop hit, with the Trio. Covered by Sam Cooke (Keen, '57), the Cleftones

(Gee, '61), James Brown (King, '69), Linda Ronstadt (Asylum, '86).

1951

MONA LISA
Album: Unforgettable
Record Label: Capitol
Songwriters: Jay Livingston, Ray Evans

First #1 Pop/Top-10 R&B crossover for the silken Blues balladeer and bandleader. Covered by Moon Mullican (King, '50), Conway Twitty (Mercury, '59), and Kal Mann (Phillips, '59).

TOO YOUNG
Album: Unforgettable
Record Label: Capitol
Songwriters: Sylvia Dee, Sid Lippman

Cole's second #1 Pop/Top-10 R&B crossover. Covered by Donny Osmond (MGM, '72).

NATALIE COLE

1975

THIS WILL BE
Producers: Chuck Jackson, Marvin Yancey
Album: Inseparable
Record Label: Capitol
Songwriters: Charles Jackson Jr., Marvin Yancy

#1 R&B/Top-10 R&R; after briefly vying for Aretha's Queen of Soul crown, she settled for Roberta Flack's stylish Pop chapeau.

1977

I GOT LOVE ON MY MIND
Producers: Chuck Jackson, Marvin Yancey
Album: Unpredictable
Record Label: Capitol
Songwriters: Charles Jackson Jr., Marvin Yancy

#1 R&B/Top-10 R&R; biggest hit for Nat's daughter, except for her cover of Bruce Springsteen's "Pink Cadillac" in '87.

OUR LOVE
Producers: Chuck Jackson, Marvin Yancey
Album: Thankful
Record Label: Capitol
Songwriters: Charles Jackson Jr., Marvin Yancy

#1 R&B/Top-10 R&R.

1989

MISS YOU LIKE CRAZY
Producer: Michael Masser
Album: Good to Be Back
Record Label: EMI
Songwriters: Michael Masser, Gerry Goffin, Preston Glass

A big ballad return to the Top-10 for Carole King's former collaborator and husband, Gerry Goffin.

COLLECTIVE SOUL

1994

SHINE
Producer: Ed Roland
Album: Hints, Allegations and Things Left Unsaid
Record Label: Atlantic
Songwriter: Ed Roland

Uplifting modified Southern rocker.

THE COLLEGE BOYZ

1992

VICTIM OF THE GHETTO
Album: Radio Fusion Radio
Record Label: Virgin
Songwriters: Eric Johnson, Rom, Tony Joseph

Rap commentary on urban devastation.

JUDY COLLINS

1965

CARRY IT ON
Producers: Mark Abramson, Jac Holzman
Album: 5th
Record Label: Elektra
Songwriter: Gil Turner

Civil-rights-era Folk standard.

EARLY MORNING RAIN
Producers: Mark Abramson, Jac Holzman
Album: 5th
Record Label: Elektra
Songwriter: Gordon Lightfoot

Ian-and-Sylvia-influenced Folk. Covered by Peter, Paul and Mary (Warner Brothers, '65) and Ian and Sylvia (Vanguard, '65).

ME AND MY UNCLE
Producers: Mark Abramson, Jac Holzman
Album: 5th
Record Label: Elektra

Songwriter: Billy Edd Wheeler
Almost Bluegrass. Covered by the Grateful Dead (Warner Brothers, '71).

RAMBLING BOY
Producers: Mark Abramson, Jac Holzman
Album: 5th
Record Label: Elektra
Songwriter: Tom Paxton
Fireside Folk favorite.

THIRSTY BOOTS
Producers: Mark Abramson, Jac Holzman
Album: 5th
Record Label: Elektra
Songwriter: Eric Andersen
Classic peace marching song.

1966

DRESS REHEARSAL RAG
Producer: Mark Abramson
Album: In My Life
Record Label: Elektra
Songwriter: Leonard Cohen

Collins puts her art-theatre stamp of approval on the Canadian novelist/poet/singer/songwriter.

I THINK IT'S GONNA RAIN TODAY
Producer: Mark Abramson
Album: In My Life
Record Label: Elektra
Songwriter: Randy Newman

Randy Newman reaches the Folk intelligentsia with one of his most straightforward and moving ballads. Covered by Newman (Reprise, '68) and Bette Midler in the movie Beaches (Atlantic, '83).

SUZANNE
Producer: Mark Abramson
Album: In My Life
Record Label: Elektra
Songwriter: Leonard Cohen

One of the most indelible character portraits of the decade, by Canada's past master of melancholy. Released by Leonard Cohen on his first album (Columbia, '68). A single by Noel Harrison stiffed (Reprise, '67).

1968

BIRD ON THE WIRE
Producer: David Anderle
Album: Who Knows Where the Time Goes
Record Label: Elektra
Songwriter: Leonard Cohen

Recorded by Cohen (Columbia, '69): Covered by Joe Cocker (A&M, '70).

MY FATHER
Producer: David Anderle
Album: Who Knows Where the Time Goes
Record Label: Elektra
Songwriter: Judy Collins

Autobiographical Folk Rock from the era's prime interpreter.

SISTERS OF MERCY
Album: Wildflowers
Record Label: Elektra
Songwriter: Leonard Cohen

On Cohen's first album (Columbia, '68) and featured in McCabe & Mrs. Miller. Covered by Sting (A&M, '95).

1975

THE MOON IS A HARSH MISTRESS
Album: Judith
Record Label: Elektra
Songwriter: Jimmy Webb.
Covered by Linda Ronstadt (Asylum, '82).

PHIL COLLINS

1981

IN THE AIR TONIGHT
Producer: Phil Collins
Album: Face Value
Record Label: Atlantic
Songwriter: Phil Collins

Atmospheric English Art Rock semi-classic gained massive credibility for Collins through its use in the background of the climactic train scene in the Tom Cruise/Rebecca De Mornay film Risky Business, and in an early episode of the high-gloss, scene-making, TV drama, "Miami Vice."

1984

AGAINST ALL ODDS (TAKE A LOOK AT ME NOW)
Producer: Arif Mardin
Album: *Against All Odds* Soundtrack
Record Label: Atlantic
Songwriter: Phil Collins

Capping Collins's ascent to the peak of the middle-of-the-road.

1985

DON'T LOSE MY NUMBER
Producers: Hugh Padgham, Phil Collins
Album: No Jacket Required

Record Label: Atlantic
Songwriter: Phil Collins

ONE MORE NIGHT

Producers: Hugh Padgham, Phil Collins
Album: No Jacket Required
Record Label: Atlantic
Songwriter: Phil Collins

His second #1.

SUSSUDIO

Producers: Hugh Padgham, Phil Collins
Album: No Jacket Required
Record Label: Atlantic
Songwriter: Phil Collins

Third #1.

TAKE ME HOME

Producers: Hugh Padgham, Phil Collins
Album: No Jacket Required
Record Label: Atlantic
Songwriter: Phil Collins

Fourth Top-10 from the same LP.

1988

TWO HEARTS

Producer: Phil Collins
Album: *Buster* Soundtrack
Record Label: Atlantic
Songwriters: Phil Collins, Lamont Dozier

Written with the great Motown collaborator. Phil's cover of Dozier's Supremes tune, "You Can't Hurry Love," went #1 U.K. in '83.

1989

ANOTHER DAY IN PARADISE

Producers: Hugh Padgham, Phil Collins
Album: . . . But Seriously Folks
Record Label: Atlantic
Songwriter: Phil Collins

Taking on homelessness, with a middle-of-the-road backbeat, Collins garners his sixth #1 song and a recurring part on "Miami Vice" and MTV as the aging, everyman Bob Hoskins of Rock and Roll.

I WISH IT WOULD RAIN DOWN

Producers: Hugh Padgham, Phil Collins
Album: . . . But Seriously Folks
Record Label: Atlantic
Songwriter: Phil Collins

SOMETHING HAPPENED ON THE WAY TO HEAVEN

Producers: Hugh Padgham, Phil Collins
Album: . . . But Seriously Folks
Record Label: Atlantic
Songwriter: Phil Collins

1990

DO YOU REMEMBER

Producers: Hugh Padgham, Phil Collins
Album: . . . But Seriously Folks
Record Label: Atlantic
Songwriter: Phil Collins

1993

BOTH SIDES OF THE STORY

Producer: Phil Collins
Album: Both Sides of the Story
Record Label: Atlantic
Songwriter: Phil Collins

EVERYDAY

Producer: Phil Collins
Album: Both Sides of the Story
Record Label: Atlantic
Songwriter: Phil Collins

COLOR ME BADD

1991

ALL 4 LOVE

Producers: Hamza Lee, Royal Bayyan
Album: C.M.B.
Record Label: Giant
Songwriters: Howard Thompson, Color Me Badd

#1 R&B/Top-10 R&R crossover; four-part harmony for the mall culture.

I ADORE MI AMOR

Producers: Hamza Lee, Royal Bayyan
Album: C.M.B.
Record Label: Giant
Songwriters: Hamza Lee, Color Me Badd

#1 R&B/R&R crossover blend. Boyz II Men were in the wings.

I WANNA SEX YOU UP

Producers: Hamza Lee, Royal Bayyan
Album: *New Jack City* Soundtrack
Record Label: Giant
Songwriter: Elliot Straite (Dr. Freeze)

A new low in innuendo.

THE COMMODORES

1974

MACHINE GUN

Producers: James Carmichael, the Commodores
Album: Machine Gun
Record Label: Motown
Songwriter: Milan Williams

Debuting on the charts with an instrumental.

1975

SLIPPERY WHEN WET

Producers: James Carmichael, the Commodores
Album: Caught in the Act
Record Label: Motown
Songwriters: Lionel B. Richie Jr., Ronald La Pread, Thomas McClary, Walter Orange, William King Jr., Milan Williams

#1 R&B/Top-20 R&R.

SWEET LOVE

Producers: James Carmichael, the Commodores
Album: Movin' On
Record Label: Motown
Songwriters: Lionel B. Richie Jr., Ronald La Pread, Thomas McClary, Walter Orange, William King Jr., Milan Williams

Lionel Richie displays an early ear for the Top-10.

1976

JUST TO BE CLOSE TO YOU

Producers: James Carmichael, the Commodores
Album: Hot on the Tracks
Record Label: Motown
Songwriter: Lionel B. Richie Jr.

Warm ballad; #1 R&B/Top-10 R&R.

1977

BRICK HOUSE

Producers: James Carmichael, the Commodores
Album: Commodores
Record Label: Motown
Songwriters: Lionel B. Richie Jr., Ronald La Pread, Thomas McClary, Walter Orange, William King Jr., Milan Williams

Returning to their Funk roots.

EASY

Producers: James Carmichael, the Commodores

Album: Commodores
Record Label: Motown
Songwriter: Lionel B. Richie Jr.
Mellow #1 R&B/Top-10 R&R.

TOO HOT TA TROT

Album: Commodores Live
Record Label: Motown
Songwriters: Lionel B. Richie Jr.,
Ronald La Pread, Thomas McClary,
Walter Orange, William King Jr.,
Milan Williams
Featured in the film Thank God It's Friday.

1978

THREE TIMES A LADY

Producers: James Carmichael, the
Commodores
Album: Natural High
Record Label: Motown
Songwriter: Lionel B. Richie Jr.
#1 R&B/R&R crossover.

1979

SAIL ON

Producers: James Carmichael, the
Commodores
Album: Midnight Magic
Record Label: Motown
Songwriter: Lionel B. Richie Jr.
Veering into a Country groove.

STILL

Producers: James Carmichael, the
Commodores
Album: Midnight Magic
Record Label: Motown
Songwriter: Lionel B. Richie Jr.
Quiet.

1981

LADY YOU BRING ME UP

Album: In the Pocket
Record Label: Motown
Songwriters: William King, Howard
Hudson, S. King

OH NO

Album: In the Pocket
Record Label: Motown
Songwriter: Lionel B. Richie Jr.

1985

NIGHTSHIFT

Producer: Dennis Lambert
Album: Nightshift
Record Label: Motown
Songwriters: Dennis Lambert,
Frannie Golde, Walter Orange

*A tribute to Marvin Gaye and Jackie Wilson
in R&B heaven.*

COMPTON'S MOST WANTED

1991

GROWIN' UP IN THE HOOD

Producer: Big Beat Productions
Album: Straight Checkn Em
Record Label: Orpheus/Epic
Songwriters: Terry Allen, Andre
Manuel, Joe Simon, Aaron Tyler

*The voice of urban America, Gangsta Rap,
gets national visibility in the movie* Boyz in
the Hood, *the 'hood in question, the
Compton section of L.A.*

CON FUNK SHUN

1977

FFUN

Producer: Con Funk Shun
Album: Secrets
Record Label: Mercury
Songwriter: Michael Cooper
#1 R&B/Top-25 R&R Funk stalwart.

1981

TOO TIGHT

Producer: Con Funk Shun
Album: Touch
Record Label: Mercury
Songwriter: Michael Cooper

1983

BABY I'M HOOKED (RIGHT INTO YOUR LOVE)

Producers: Cedric Martin, Van Ross
Redding
Album: Fever
Record Label: Mercury
Songwriters: Cedric Martin, Van
Ross Redding

ARTHUR CONLEY

1967

SWEET SOUL MUSIC

Producer: Otis Redding
Album: Sweet Soul Music
Record Label: Atco
Songwriters: Otis Redding, Arthur
Conley

*In the heyday of Soul; this R&B/R&R
crossover classic just missed the top on
both charts. Suggested segue: "Yeah Man"
by Sam Cooke (RCA, '65).*

THE CONTOURS

1962

DO YOU LOVE ME?

Producer: Berry Gordy Jr.
Album: Do You Love Me
Record Label: Gordy
Songwriter: Berry Gordy Jr.

*Early Motown dance groove; #1 R&B/Top-
10 R&R. Covered by the Dave Clark Five
(Epic, '64). Featured in the '87 film* Dirty
Dancing.

1965

FIRST I LOOK AT THE PURSE

Producer: Berry Gordy Jr.
Record Label: Tamla
Songwriter: Smokey Robinson

*Streetwise advice from Gordy's main man,
Smokey. Covered by the J. Geils Band
(Atlantic, '71).*

SAM COOKE

1957

I'LL COME RUNNING BACK TO YOU

Producer: Art Rupe
Album: The Man and His Music
Record Label: Specialty
Songwriter: Sam Cooke (Charles
Cooke)

*Working from an old existing track, Rupe
fashioned this Cooke follow-up to "You
Send Me," a #1 R&B/Top-20 R&R
crossover.*

LONELY ISLAND

Record Label: Keen
Songwriter: Eden Ahbez

*By the author of "Nature Boy," recorded by
Sam's idol, Nat King Cole.*

YOU SEND ME

Producer: Art Rupe
Record Label: Keen
Songwriter: Sam Cooke (Charles
Cooke)

*Groundbreaking merger of Pop, R&B and
Gospel in #1 R&B/R&R crossover. The
tune was the first by a black Rock and Roll
solo artist to reach number one (the next
one, the remake of "It's All in the Game" by
Tommy Edwards, came almost ten months
later). Marked turning point in Cooke's
career, toward the secular and away from
the church. Otis Redding, Marvin Gaye, Al
Green were all listening. Little Richard was
preparing to go in the opposite direction.*

1958

WIN YOUR LOVE FOR ME
Producer: Bumps Blackwell
Record Label: Keen
Songwriter: Sam Cooke (Charles Cooke)

1959

ONLY SIXTEEN
Producer: Bumps Blackwell
Record Label: Keen
Songwriter: Sam Cooke (Charles Cooke)

In one of the year's most soulful Pop rockers, Cooke defined a fantasy. Covering it, Dr. Hook (Capitol, '76), sounded like just another dirty old man.

1960

(WHAT A) WONDERFUL WORLD
Record Label: Keen
Songwriters: Barbara Campbell, Herb Alpert, Lou Adler

An unintentional stay-in-school anthem. Covered by Herman's Hermits (MGM, '65) and Art Garfunkel, James Taylor, and Paul Simon (Columbia, '78).

1961

CUPID
Producer: Hugo and Luigi
Album: The Best of Sam Cooke
Record Label: RCA Victor
Songwriter: Sam Cooke

Finally writing under his own name, Sam offers a tribute to the first Love Man. Future successors, from Smokey Robinson to Babyface, might refer to this as chapter one in the Book of Love.

1962

BRING IT ON HOME TO ME
Producer: Hugo and Luigi
Album: The Best of Sam Cooke
Record Label: RCA Victor
Songwriter: Sam Cooke

Covered by the Animals (MGM, '65) and was Eddie Floyd's biggest hit (Stax, '68). Suggested segue: "I Want to Go Home" by Charles Brown and Amos Milburn (Ace, '59).

HAVING A PARTY
Producer: Hugo and Luigi
Album: The Best of Sam Cooke
Record Label: RCA Victor
Songwriter: Sam Cooke

B-side of "Bring It on Home to Me." Covered by Rod Stewart (Warner Brothers, '94).

TWISTIN' THE NIGHT AWAY
Producer: Hugo and Luigi
Album: Twistin' the Night Away
Record Label: RCA Victor
Songwriter: Sam Cooke

#1 R&B/Top-10 R&R crossover with a little twist of Soul.

1963

ANOTHER SATURDAY NIGHT
Producer: Hugo and Luigi
Album: Ain't That Good News
Record Label: RCA Victor
Songwriter: Sam Cooke

#1 R&B/Top-10 R&R. Typifying his sad-edged crooning style. Covered by Cat Stevens (A&M, '74).

1965

A CHANGE IS GONNA COME
Producer: Hugo and Luigi
Album: Ain't That Good News
Record Label: RCA Victor
Songwriter: Sam Cooke

The B-side of "Shake." His enduring anthem: a soulful, pointed response to "Blowin' in the Wind." Covered by Aretha Franklin (Atlantic, '67).

SHAKE
Producer: Sam Cooke
Album: Shake
Record Label: RCA
Songwriter: Sam Cooke

Cooke's last hit, a momentous one. Covered by Otis Redding (Volt, '65).

THE COOKIES

1962

CHAINS
Producer: Gerry Goffin
Record Label: Dimension
Songwriters: Gerry Goffin, Carole King

Covered by the Beatles (Veejay, '64) as a token of their Brill Building esteem.

1963

DON'T SAY NOTHIN' BAD (ABOUT MY BABY)
Producer: Gerry Goffin
Record Label: Dimension
Songwriters: Gerry Goffin, Carole King

Aggressively defending her man.

ALICE COOPER

1971

EIGHTEEN
Producers: Bob Ezrin, Jack Richardson
Album: Love It to Death
Record Label: Straight
Songwriters: Vincent Furnier (Alice Cooper), Michael Bruce, Glen Buxton, Dennis Dunaway, Neal Smith

Frank Zappa's bizarre protege Vincent Furnier creates a legendary nom de plume and a teenage anthem.

1972

ELECTED
Producer: Bob Ezrin
Album: Billion Dollar Babies
Record Label: Warner Brothers
Songwriters: Vincent Furnier (Alice Cooper), Michael Bruce, Glen Buxton, Dennis Dunaway, Neal Smith

From the tour on which columnist Bob Greene played Santa Claus (and was beheaded a hundred times, more or less).

SCHOOL'S OUT
Producer: Bob Ezrin
Album: School's Out
Record Label: Warner Brothers
Songwriters: Vincent Furnier (Alice Cooper), Michael Bruce

The "Summertime Blues" of the '70s. But not the "Summertime Summertime."

1974

NO MORE MR. NICE GUY
Producer: Bob Ezrin
Album: Billion Dollar Babies
Record Label: Warner Brothers
Songwriters: Vincent Furnier (Alice Cooper), Michael Bruce

Extending the one-joke theme.

1975

ONLY WOMEN (BLEED)
Producer: Bob Ezrin
Album: Welcome to My Nightmare
Record Label: Atlantic
Songwriters: Vincent Furnier (Alice Cooper), Dick Wagner

The man with the woman's name walks a mile (or three and a half minutes) in her shoes.

WELCOME TO MY NIGHTMARE

Producer: Bob Ezrin
Album: Welcome to My Nightmare
Record Label: Atlantic
Songwriters: Vincent Furnier (Alice Cooper), Dick Wagner

Flaying the formula.

1976

I NEVER CRY

Producer: Bob Ezrin
Album: Alice Cooper Goes to Hell
Record Label: Warner Brothers
Songwriters: Vincent Furnier (Alice Cooper), Dick Wagner

A million-selling single.

1977

YOU AND ME

Producer: Bob Ezrin
Album: Lace and Whiskey
Record Label: Warner Brothers
Songwriters: Vincent Furnier (Alice Cooper), Dick Wagner

A new mellow Alice lights out for barroom country territory and achieves his biggest hit since "School's Out" in '72.

1989

POISON

Producer: Desmond Child
Album: Trash
Record Label: Epic
Songwriters: Vincent Furnier (Alice Cooper), Desmond Child, John McCurry

Return to the corporate fold.

CORINA

1991

TEMPTATION

Album: Corina
Record Label: Atco
Songwriters: Corina, Franc Reyes, Carlos Berrios, Luis Capri Duprey

Latino dance sensation.

THE CORNELIUS BROTHERS AND SISTER ROSE

1971

TREAT HER LIKE A LADY

Producer: Bob Archibald
Album: The Cornelius Brothers and Sister Rose
Record Label: United Artists
Songwriter: Eddie Cornelius

1972

TOO LATE TO TURN BACK NOW

Producer: Bob Archibald
Album: The Cornelius Brothers and Sister Rose
Record Label: United Artists
Songwriter: Eddie Cornelius

CORONA

1994

THE RHYTHM OF THE NIGHT

Producers: Checco, Soul Train
Record Label: East/West
Songwriters: Francisco Bontempi, Annehly Gordon, Giorgio Spagna, Michael Gaffey, Peter Glenister

Big dance groove in the Euro-Disco central casting mold of Real McCoy, Haddaway, et al.

THE CORSAIRS

1961

SMOKEY PLACES

Record Label: Tuff
Songwriter: Abner Spector

In the moody, misty mold of the Impressions' "Gypsy Woman."

DAVE "BABY" CORTEZ

1959

THE HAPPY ORGAN

Producer: Dave "Baby" Cortez
Album: Dave "Baby" Cortez and the Happy Organ
Record Label: Clock
Songwriters: Ken Wood, David Clowney

Celebrating the Hammond B-3 sound that would influence a generation of suburban garage bands on two continents.

BILL COSBY

1967

LITTLE OLE MAN (UPTIGHT EVERYTHING'S ALRIGHT)

Producer: Fred Smith
Album: Bill Cosby Sings/Silver Throat
Record Label: Warner Brothers
Songwriters: Stevie Wonder, Sylvia Moy, Henry Cosby

Stevie Wonder parody gave Cosby a Top-10 R&R/Top-20 R&B hit. But the bigger question is, is Henry related to Bill?

ELVIS COSTELLO

1977

(ANGELS WANNA WEAR MY) RED SHOES

Producer: Nick Lowe
Album: My Aim Is True
Record Label: Columbia
Songwriter: Declan McManus (Elvis Costello)

The advent of Nerd Rock disguised as Pub Rock.

ALISON

Producer: Nick Lowe
Album: My Aim Is True
Record Label: Columbia
Songwriter: Declan McManus (Elvis Costello)

Rapier wordplay, Costello at his caustic best. Covered by Linda Ronstadt (Asylum, '80).

LESS THAN ZERO

Producer: Nick Lowe
Album: My Aim Is True
Record Label: Columbia
Songwriter: Declan McManus (Elvis Costello)

His first single; eloquent New Wave rage.

WATCHING THE DETECTIVES

Producer: Nick Lowe
Album: My Aim Is True
Record Label: Columbia
Songwriter: Declan McManus (Elvis Costello)

His first U.K. hit.

WELCOME TO THE WORKING WEEK

Producer: Nick Lowe
Album: My Aim Is True
Record Label: Columbia
Songwriter: Declan McManus (Elvis Costello)

Leaving his job in computers.

1978

LIPSTICK VOGUE

Producer: Nick Lowe
Album: This Year's Model
Record Label: Columbia
Songwriter: Declan McManus (Elvis Costello)

Introducing the Attractions with one of his hardest, angriest rockers.

PUMP IT UP

Producer: Nick Lowe
Album: This Year's Model
Record Label: Columbia
Songwriter: Declan McManus (Elvis Costello)

One of his most enduring verbal flights. Suggested segue: "Subterranean Homesick Blues" by Bob Dylan.

RADIO RADIO

Producer: Nick Lowe
Album: This Year's Model
Record Label: Columbia
Songwriter: Declan McManus (Elvis Costello)

An anthem for anyone who's ever bitten the hand that feeds them. Costello sang this anti-media/anti-audience song during his first appearance on "Saturday Night Live," in defiance of the producer, and was banned from further shows forthwith.

1979

ACCIDENTS WILL HAPPEN

Producer: Nick Lowe
Album: Armed Forces
Record Label: Columbia
Songwriter: Declan McManus (Elvis Costello)

A cynical mouthful from the guy who once insulted Ray Charles and slugged Bonnie Bramlett in the same evening.

OLIVER'S ARMY

Producer: Nick Lowe
Album: Armed Forces
Record Label: Columbia
Songwriter: Declan McManus (Elvis Costello)

His biggest U.K. hit.

1980

(I DON'T WANT TO GO TO) CHELSEA

Producer: Nick Lowe
Album: Taking Liberties
Record Label: Columbia
Songwriter: Declan McManus (Elvis Costello)

More compulsive nihilism for Now people.

GIRLS TALK

Producer: Nick Lowe
Album: Taking Liberties
Record Label: Columbia
Songwriter: Declan McManus (Elvis Costello)

The last word on the opposite sex. Covered by Linda Ronstadt (Asylum, '80).

HOOVER FACTORY

Producer: Nick Lowe
Album: Taking Liberties
Record Label: Columbia
Songwriter: Declan McManus (Elvis Costello)

Buddy Holly with an Uzi.

TALKING IN THE DARK

Album: Taking Liberties
Record Label: Columbia
Songwriter: Declan McManus (Elvis Costello)

Covered by Linda Ronstadt (Asylum, '80).

1982

BOY WITH A PROBLEM

Producer: Geoff Emerich
Album: Imperial Bedroom
Record Label: Columbia
Songwriters: Declan McManus (Elvis Costello), Chris Difford

A U.K. songwriting super session.

KID ABOUT IT

Producer: Geoff Emerich
Album: Imperial Bedroom
Record Label: Columbia
Songwriter: Declan McManus (Elvis Costello)

Pub Rock visits the boite.

THE LONG HONEYMOON

Producer: Geoff Emerich
Album: Imperial Bedroom
Record Label: Columbia
Songwriter: Declan McManus (Elvis Costello)

One of his finest lyrics.

1983

EVERY DAY I WRITE THE BOOK

Producers: Clive Langer, Alan Winstanley
Album: Punch the Clock
Record Label: Columbia
Songwriter: Declan McManus (Elvis Costello)

Winsome Motown-flavored rocker nets him his first U.S. Top-40. People started to get him confused with John Hiatt.

SHIPBUILDING

Producers: Clive Langer, Alan Winstanley
Album: Punch the Clock
Record Label: Columbia

Songwriters: Declan McManus (Elvis Costello), Clive Langer

Evocative anti-war scenario.

1984

THE ONLY FLAME IN TOWN

Producers: Clive Langer, Alan Winstanley
Album: Goodbye Cruel World
Record Label: Columbia
Songwriter: Declan McManus (Elvis Costello)

The other voice is Daryl Hall.

PEACE IN OUR TIME

Producers: Clive Langer, Alan Winstanley
Album: Goodbye Cruel World
Record Label: Columbia
Songwriter: Declan McManus (Elvis Costello)

Post-nuclear protest.

1986

HOME IS ANYWHERE YOU HANG YOUR HEAD

Album: Blood and Chocolate
Record Label: Columbia
Songwriter: Declan McManus (Elvis Costello)

One of his best titles.

LOVABLE

Producers: T-Bone Burnette, Declan McManus (Elvis Costello)
Album: King of America
Record Label: Columbia
Songwriters: Declan McManus (Elvis Costello), Cait O'Riordan

Writing against type.

1989

BABY PLAYS AROUND

Producers: T-Bone Burnette, Kevin Killen
Album: Spike
Record Label: Warner Brothers
Songwriters: Declan McManus (Elvis Costello), Cait O'Riordan

Supper club infidelity.

DEEP DARK TRUTHFUL MIRROR

Producers: T-Bone Burnette, Kevin Killen
Album: Spike
Record Label: Warner Brothers
Songwriter: Declan MacManus (Elvis Costello)

Almost Folk.

GOD'S COMIC

Producers: T-Bone Burnette, Kevin Killen
Album: Spike
Record Label: Warner Brothers
Songwriter: Declan McManus (Elvis Costello)

Cosmic in-joke.

TRAMP THE DIRT DOWN

Producers: T-Bone Burnette, Kevin Killen
Album: Spike
Record Label: Warner Brothers
Songwriter: Declan McManus (Elvis Costello)

Anti-Thatcher diatribe.

VERONICA

Producers: Kevin Killen, T-Bone Burnett
Album: Spike
Record Label: Warner Brothers
Songwriters: Declan McManus (Elvis Costello), Paul McCartney

McCartney finally finds his new Lennon. Perhaps his most perfect single.

1991

THE OTHER SIDE OF SUMMER

Producers: Mitchell Froom, Kevin Killen
Album: Mighty Like a Rose
Record Label: Columbia
Songwriter: Declan McManus (Elvis Costello)

Costello adds to the canon of summer songs his decidedly skewed view.

1993

I ALMOST HAD A WEAKNESS

Producers: Elvis Costello, Kevin Killen
Album: The Juliet Letters
Record Label: Warner Brothers
Songwriters: Declan McManus (Elvis Costello), Michael Thomas

Completing the journey from the garage to the front parlor, with the world famous classical musicians, the Brodsky Quartet.

1994

JUST ABOUT GLAD

Producers: Mitchell Froom, Declan McManus (Elvis Costello)
Album: Brutal Youth
Record Label: Warner Brothers

Songwriter: Declan McManus (Elvis Costello)

Still sarcastic after all those songs.

THIRTEEN STEPS LEAD DOWN

Producers: Mitchell Froom, Declan McManus (Elvis Costello)
Album: Brutal Youth
Record Label: Warner Brothers
Songwriter: Declan McManus (Elvis Costello)

When last seen on American TV (perhaps for the first time since being banned from "SNL") he was singing this tune on "The Larry Sanders Show," and trashing his dressing room in a thoroughly satisfying performance.

JOSIE COTTON

1981

JOHNNY ARE YOU QUEER

Producers: Bobby Paine, Larson Paine
Album: *Valley Girl* Soundtrack
Record Label: Bomp
Songwriters: Bobby Paine, Larson Paine

Valley Punk classic.

THE COUNT FIVE

1966

PSYCHOTIC REACTION

Producers: Joe Hooven, Hal Wynn
Album: Psychotic Reaction
Record Label: Double Shot
Songwriters: Ken Ellner, Roy Chaney, Craig Atkinson, John Byrne, John Michalski

Garage band psychedelia.

COUNTING CROWS

1993

MR. JONES

Producer: T-Bone Burnette
Album: August and Everything After
Record Label: DGC
Songwriters: Adam Duritz, David Bryson, Counting Crows

Updating the same mix of influences that brought Bruce Springsteen to the Rock forefront (Van Morrison, Bob Dylan, the Band), including Springsteen himself, this San Francisco mystery figure named after Dylan's "Thin Man" led an Alternative Rock crusade onto the record charts of '93–'94.

Never released as a single, it was nonetheless played (to death) as regularly on hit radio as if it were.

ROUND HERE

Producers: T-Bone Burnette, Counting Crows
Album: August and Everything After
Record Label: DGC
Songwriter: Adam Duritz

Earnest Frat Rock of the '90s, presaging Hootie, and the Dave Matthews Band.

1994

EINSTEIN ON THE BEACH (FOR AN EGGMAN)

Producer: Counting Crows
Album: DGC Rarities (Vol. I)
Record Label: DGC
Songwriters: Adam Duritz, David Bryson, Charlie Gillingham, Matt Malloy, Steve Bowman

Maintaining their Alternative chic in the face of massive success.

COUNTRY JOE AND THE FISH

1967

I-FEEL-LIKE-I'M-FIXIN'-TO-DIE RAG

Producer: Sam Charters
Album: I-Feel-Like-I'm-Fixin'-to-Die
Record Label: Vanguard
Songwriter: Joe McDonald

Folk Rock anthem from the barricades of Berkeley.

JANIS

Producer: Sam Charters
Album: I-Feel-Like-I'm-Fixin'-to-Die
Record Label: Vanguard
Songwriter: Joe McDonald

About Joe's San Francisco sweetheart, Janis Joplin, about to go national with Big Brother and the Holding Company.

NOT SO SWEET MARTHA LORRAINE

Producer: Sam Charters
Album: Electric Music for the Mind and Body
Record Label: Vanguard
Songwriter: Joe McDonald

Riding the crest of the San Francisco scene, on the wings of a Farfisa. Crash-landed after two weeks on the charts, a few weeks after the Jefferson Airplane skied into the Top-10. Suggested segue: "Like a Rolling Stone" by Bob Dylan.

DON COVAY

1961

PONY TIME

Record Label: Arnold
Songwriters: Don Covay, John Berry

Six months after "The Twist" and four months after his cover of "The Hucklebuck" merely dented the Top-20, Chubby Checker was back at the top covering a newer dance (Parkway, '62), this one created by Covay's group, the Goodtimers.

1965

SEESAW

Record Label: Atlantic
Songwriters: Don Covay, Steve Cropper

Top-10 R&B/Top-50 R&R crossover. Covered by Aretha Franklin (Atlantic, '68).

THE COVER GIRLS

1990

WE CAN'T GO WRONG

Album: We Can't Go Wrong
Record Label: Capitol
Songwriters: Andy Tripoli, Tony Moran, Gardner Cole

#1 R&B/Top-10 R&R crossover.

DAVID COVERDALE AND JIMMY PAGE

1993

PRIDE AND JOY

Album: Coverdale/Page
Record Label: Geffen
Songwriters: Jimmy Page, David Coverdale

Metal throwback.

THE COWSILLS

1967

THE RAIN, THE PARK AND OTHER THINGS

Producers: Bill Cowsill, Bob Cowsill
Album: The Cowsills
Record Label: MGM
Songwriters: Artie Kornfeld, Steve Duboff

Their first and biggest hit; in Hollywood, The Partridge Family was being created in their image.

1968

INDIAN LAKE

Producers: Bill Cowsill, Bob Cowsill
Album: Captain Sad and His Ship of Fools

Record Label: MGM
Songwriter: Tony Romeo

1969

HAIR

Producers: Bill Cowsill, Bob Cowsill
Album: Cowsills in Concert
Record Label: MGM
Songwriters: James Rado, Gerome Ragni, Galt MacDermot

Performed in Hair and on the original cast album by James Rado, Gerome Ragni and Company (RCA, '69). One of five hit songs to emerge in '69 from the '67 Rock musical about a generation's refusal to come of age.

CRACKER

1991

TEEN ANGST (WHAT THE WORLD NEEDS NOW)

Producer: Don Smith
Album: Kerosene Hat
Record Label: Virgin
Songwriter: David Lowery

Lowery leavens his Acid Punk vision with Alternative Hard Rock.

1993

GET OFF THIS

Producer: Don Smith
Album: Kerosene Hat
Record Label: Virgin
Songwriters: David Lowery, David Faragher, John Hickman

Leader of Camper Van Beethoven goes relatively straight.

LOW

Producer: Don Smith
Album: Kerosene Hat
Record Label: Virgin
Songwriters: David Lowery, David Faragher, John Hickman

The highbrow Hard Rock alternative: for free-thinking junkie cosmonauts everywhere.

FLOYD CRAMER

1960

LAST DATE

Producer: Chet Atkins
Album: Last Date
Record Label: RCA Victor
Songwriter: Floyd Cramer

Countrified Pop instrumental and vice versa.

THE CRAMPS

1979

HUMAN FLY

Producer: Alex Chilton
Album: Gravest Hits
Record Label: IRS
Songwriters: Kirsty Wallace (Ivy Rorsach), Erick Purkhiser (Lux Interior)

Punk everygroup reinvents sci-fi hi-fi with a monster track produced by a minor living legend.

1981

GOO GOO MUCK

Album: Psychedelic Jungle
Record Label: I.R.S.
Songwriters: Ronnie Cook, Edgar James

THE CRANBERRIES

1993

DREAMS

Producer: Stephen Street
Album: Everybody Else Is Doing It, So Why Can't We?
Record Label: Island
Songwriters: Noel Hogan, Dolores O'Riordan

Ethereal Pop Rock.

LINGER

Producer: Stephen Street
Album: Everybody Else Is Doing It, So Why Can't We?
Record Label: Island
Songwriters: Noel Hogan, Dolores O'Riordan

In the neo girl-group groove of the '90s, from Ireland.

1994

ZOMBIE

Producer: Stephen Street
Album: No Need to Agree
Record Label: Island
Songwriters: Noel Hogan, Dolores O'Riordan

Leaving their pristine image behind, with a strong anti-war message.

CRASH TEST DUMMIES

1994

MMM MMM MMM MMM

Producers: Jerry Harrison, Crash Test Dummies

Album: God Shuffled His Feet
Record Label: Arista
Songwriter: Brad Roberts
Campy New-age philosophizing hits the top of the charts.

JOHNNY CRAWFORD
1962

CINDY'S BIRTHDAY
Record Label: Del-Fi
Songwriters: Jeff Hooven, Hal Wynn

ROBERT CRAY
1983

BAD INFLUENCE
Album: Bad Influence
Record Label: Hightone
Songwriters: Robert Cray, Mike Vannice
The emergence of a new Blues guitar hero. Covered by Eric Clapton (Duck, '86).

1986

I GUESS I SHOWED HER
Producers: Bruce Bromberg, Dennis Walker
Album: Strong Persuader
Record Label: Mercury
Songwriter: Dennis Walker
Evoking the vocal legend of Tyrone Davis.

1987

SMOKING GUN
Producers: Bruce Bromberg, Dennis Walker
Album: Strong Persuader
Record Label: Mercury
Songwriters: Bruce Bromberg (D. Amy), Robert Cray, Richard Cousins
The bluesiest cut to hit Top-30 since B. B. was King.

CRAZY HORSE
1971

BEGGAR'S DAY
Producer: Jack Nitzsche, Bruce Botnick
Album: Crazy Horse
Record Label: Reprise
Songwriter: Nils Lofgren
From the legendary Danny Whitten-era version of Neil Young's once-and-future backing band, a great Lofgren cut, covered by Nils (A&M, '77).

I DON'T WANT TO TALK ABOUT IT
Producers: Jack Nitzsche, Bruce Botnick
Album: Crazy Horse
Record Label: Warner Brothers
Songwriter: Danny Whitten
Whitten's enduring legacy. Covered by Rod Stewart (Warner Brothers, '75).

CREAM
1967

I FEEL FREE
Producer: Robert Stigwood
Album: Fresh Cream
Record Label: Atco
Songwriters: Jack Bruce, Pete Brown
Clapton's post-Yardbirds/Mayall, pre-Derek and the Dominoes supergroup debut.

I'M SO GLAD
Producer: Robert Stigwood
Album: Fresh Cream
Record Label: Atco
Songwriter: Nehemiah "Skip" James
Metalizing the Blues.

STRANGE BREW
Producer: Felix Pappalardi
Album: Disraeli Gears
Record Label: Atco
Songwriters: Eric Clapton, Felix Pappalardi, Gail Collins
Fermented psychedelia with a Blues chaser.

TOAD
Producer: Robert Stigwood
Album: Fresh Cream
Record Label: Atco
Songwriter: Ginger Baker
Drum showpiece.

1968

CROSSROADS
Producer: Felix Pappalardi
Album: Wheels of Fire
Record Label: Atco
Songwriter: Robert Johnson
Clapton guitar standard. Originated by legendary bluesman Robert Johnson (Vocalion, '36); Johnson's "Cross Road Blues" released on CD (Columbia, '90).

POLITICIAN
Producer: Felix Pappalardi
Album: Wheels of Fire
Record Label: Atco

Songwriters: Jack Bruce, Pete Brown
Suggested segues: "Taxman" by George Harrison and "So You Wanna Be a Rock and Roll Star" by the Byrds.

SUNSHINE OF YOUR LOVE
Producer: Felix Pappalardi
Album: Disraeli Gears
Record Label: Atco
Songwriters: Eric Clapton, Jack Bruce, Peter Brown
Their best-selling single, a Top-10 U.S./Top-30 U.K. high-powered R&R Blues blast, covered by every nascent bar band on two continents.

TALES OF BRAVE ULYSSES
Producer: Felix Pappalardi
Album: Disraeli Gears
Record Label: Atco
Songwriter: Eric Clapton
Joycean psychedelica.

WHITE ROOM
Producer: Felix Pappalardi
Album: Wheels of Fire
Record Label: Atco
Songwriters: Jack Bruce, Pete Brown
Their second and last Top-10 R&R.

1969

BADGE
Producer: Felix Pappalardi
Album: Goodbye
Record Label: RSO
Songwriters: Eric Clapton, George Harrison
Clapton rocks out and moves on.

CREEDENCE CLEARWATER REVIVAL
1969

BAD MOON RISING
Producer: John C. Fogerty
Album: Green River
Record Label: Fantasy
Songwriter: John C. Fogerty
Forecasting the new political climate, without a weatherman.

BORN ON THE BAYOU
Producer: John C. Fogerty
Album: Bayou Country
Record Label: Fantasy
Songwriter: John C. Fogerty
Staking out their Swamp Rock turf.

DOWN ON THE CORNER
Producer: John C. Fogerty
Album: Willy and the Poor Boys
Record Label: Fantasy
Songwriter: John C. Fogerty

Convincing New Orleansiana, by way of Northern California.

EFFIGY
Producer: John C. Fogerty
Album: Willy and the Poor Boys
Record Label: Fantasy
Songwriter: John C. Fogerty

Covered by Uncle Tupelo (Arista, '93).

FORTUNATE SON
Producer: John C. Fogerty
Album: Willy and the Poor Boys
Record Label: Fantasy
Songwriter: John C. Fogerty

B-side of "Down on the Corner." Rage returns to Rock and Roll in the voice of the draftee and the volunteer; freedom of choice as a class issue.

GREEN RIVER
Producer: John C. Fogerty
Album: Green River
Record Label: Fantasy
Songwriter: John C. Fogerty

Choogling boogie.

IT CAME OUT OF THE SKY
Producer: John C. Fogerty
Album: Willy and the Poor Boys
Record Label: Fantasy
Songwriter: John C. Fogerty

A close encounter of the Rock and Roll kind.

LODI
Producer: John C. Fogerty
Album: Green River
Record Label: Fantasy
Songwriter: John C. Fogerty

B-side of "Bad Moon Rising." A day in the life of Rock and Roll has never been better told or sung. Suggested segue: "Rock and Roll (I Gave You the Best Years of My Life)" by Kevin Johnson.

PROUD MARY
Producer: John C. Fogerty
Album: Bayou Country
Record Label: Fantasy
Songwriter: John C. Fogerty

First of three amazing singles to peak at #2 in '69. Country cover by Anthony Armstrong Jones (Chart, '69). Top-5 R&B/R&R crossover hit by Ike and Tina Turner (Liberty, '71).

HAVE YOU EVER SEEN THE RAIN?
Producer: John C. Fogerty
Album: Pendulum
Record Label: Fantasy
Songwriter: John C. Fogerty

Biblical Rock.

LONG AS I CAN SEE THE LIGHT
Producer: John C. Fogerty
Album: Cosmo's Factory
Record Label: Fantasy
Songwriter: John C. Fogerty

B-side of "Looking out My Back Door."

LOOKIN' OUT MY BACK DOOR
Producer: John C. Fogerty
Album: Cosmo's Factory
Record Label: Fantasy
Songwriter: John C. Fogerty

Their fifth career #2 single without ever having achieved a #1.

RUN THROUGH THE JUNGLE
Producer: John C. Fogerty
Album: Cosmo's Factory
Record Label: Fantasy
Songwriter: John C. Fogerty

Back to their swampy roots.

TRAVELIN' BAND
Producer: John C. Fogerty
Album: Cosmo's Factory
Record Label: Fantasy
Songwriter: John C. Fogerty

Suggested segues: "Band on the Run" by Wings, "Homeward Bound" by Simon and Garfunkel, "Jukebox Hero" by Foreigner, and "You're Probably Wondering Why I'm Here" by the Mothers of Invention.

UP AROUND THE BEND
Producer: John C. Fogerty
Album: Cosmo's Factory
Record Label: Fantasy
Songwriter: John C. Fogerty

WHO'LL STOP THE RAIN
Producer: John C. Fogerty
Album: Cosmo's Factory
Record Label: Fantasy
Songwriter: John C. Fogerty

Rain of bullets, blood, terror, propaganda. A companion piece to "Blowin' in the Wind."

SWEET HITCH-HIKER
Producer: John C. Fogerty
Album: Mardi Gras
Record Label: Fantasy
Songwriter: John C. Fogerty

Their ninth and last Top-10 single (including two two-sided hits).

SOMEDAY NEVER COMES
Producer: John C. Fogerty
Album: Mardi Gras
Record Label: Fantasy
Songwriter: John C. Fogerty

Going out on a down note.

MARSHALL CRENSHAW

CYNICAL GIRL
Producer: Richard Gottehrer
Album: Marshall Crenshaw
Record Label: Warner Brothers
Songwriter: Marshall Crenshaw

Buddy Holly goes to college, looks for his dreamgirl. Suggested segue: "I've Had It" by the Bellnotes.

YOU'RE MY FAVORITE WASTE OF TIME
Producers: Marshall Crenshaw, Will Schillinger
Album: Marshall Crenshaw
Record Label: Warner Brothers
Songwriter: Marshall Crenshaw

Initial attention getter for the man who played John Lennon in Beatlemania, *the movie, and "Sorry (I Ran All the Way Home)" in* Peggy Sue Got Married. *With the Handsome, Ruthless and Stupid Band. Covered by Bette Midler (Atlantic, '83). Matthew Sweet was listening.*

WHENEVER YOU'RE ON MY MIND
Producer: Steve Lillywhite
Album: Field Day
Record Label: Warner Brothers
Songwriters: Marshall Crenshaw, Bill Teeley

America's finest pure Pop of the '80s was created in New York; in the heartland and in England, the notion of Alternative Rock was born.

1985

I'M SORRY (BUT SO IS BRENDA LEE)
Album: Downtown
Record Label: Warner Brothers
Songwriter: Ben Vaughan

Covered by Ben Vaughan (Fever/Restless, '86).

LITTLE WILD ONE (NO. 5)
Producer: T-Bone Burnette
Album: Downtown
Record Label: Warner Brothers
Songwriter: Marshall Crenshaw

Return to Rockabilly.

TERRIFYING LOVE
Producer: T-Bone Burnette
Album: Downtown
Record Label: Warner Brothers
Songwriter: Marshall Crenshaw

Buddy Holly graduates, moves in with his dreamgirl, turns out to be a nightmare.

YVONNE
Producer: Mitch Easter
Album: Downtown
Record Label: Warner Brothers
Songwriter: Marshall Crenshaw

Neighbor of Gloria, Blanche, Sherry, et al.

1989

SHE HATES TO GO HOME
Album: Good Evening
Record Label: Warner Brothers
Songwriters: Marshall Crenshaw, Leroy Preston

SOMEPLACE WHERE LOVE CAN'T FIND ME
Album: Good Evening
Record Label: Warner Brothers
Songwriter: John Hiatt

YOU SHOULDA BEEN THERE
Album: Good Evening
Record Label: Warner Brothers
Songwriters: Marshall Crenshaw, Leroy Preston

Still casting pearls at the swinish '80s era of radio repression.

THE CRESCENDOS

1958

OH JULIE
Album: Oh Julie
Record Label: Nasco
Songwriters: Ken Moffitt, Noel Ball

THE CRESTS

1957

MY JUANITA
Record Label: Joyce
Songwriters: Johnny Mastroangelo, Al Browne

Their legendary first release.

1959

16 CANDLES
Producer: Luther Dixon
Album: The Crests Sing All the Biggies
Record Label: Coed
Songwriters: Luther Dixon, Allyson Khent

Originally titled "21 Candles," and the B-side of "Beside You," this tune encapsulates the essence of city Soul and marks the ascent of Johnny Maestro and the arrival of Luther Dixon. Against a backdrop of the Buddy Holly crash the week the song peaked on the radio, they were memorial candles too. Suggested segue: "Molly" by Sponge (Work, '95), which contains the haunting chorus: "16 candles down the drain."

THE ANGELS LISTENED IN
Album: The Angels Listened In
Record Label: Coed
Songwriters: Billy Dawn Smith, Sid Faust

Essential blue-eyed Doo-Wop, otherwise known as Italian Soul.

SIX NIGHTS A WEEK
Album: The Angels Listened In
Record Label: Coed
Songwriter: Billy Dawn Smith

Attempting to follow up "Sixteen Candles."

1960

STEP BY STEP
Album: The Best of the Crests
Record Label: Coed
Songwriters: Billy Dawn Smith, Ollie Jones

Their second biggest hit.

THE CRICKETS

1957

AN EMPTY CUP (AND A BROKEN DATE)
Producer: Norman Petty
Album: The Chirpin' Crickets
Record Label: Brunswick
Songwriter: Roy Orbison

Early obscure Roy and Buddy Holly.

I'M LOOKING FOR SOMEONE TO LOVE
Producer: Norman Petty
Album: The Chirpin' Crickets
Record Label: Brunswick
Songwriters: Buddy Holly, Norman Petty

Legendary album cut from their first album.

MAYBE BABY
Producer: Norman Petty
Album: The Chirpin' Crickets
Record Label: Brunswick
Songwriters: Buddy Holly, Norman Petty

With three hits under his belt, Holly entertains some healthy Rockabilly aggression to augment his endearing hillbilly nervousness. In Minnesota, Bob Dylan was listening. In Liverpool, so were the Beatles, who named themselves after the Crickets (and recorded a Holly tune as their first single as the Quarrymen in '58), and the Hollies, who co-opted Buddy.

NOT FADE AWAY
Producer: Norman Petty
Album: The Chirpin' Crickets
Record Label: Brunswick
Songwriters: Buddy Holly, Norman Petty

B-side of "Oh Boy," covered by the Rolling Stones (London, '64) as their first single.

OH BOY
Producer: Norman Petty
Album: The Chirpin' Crickets
Record Label: Brunswick
Songwriters: Sunny West, Bill Tilgham, Norman Petty

The second hit by the Crickets. Planting the Pop Rockabilly root from which Roots Rock would flower two decades later.

THAT'LL BE THE DAY
Producer: Norman Petty
Album: The Chirpin' Crickets
Record Label: Brunswick
Songwriters: Buddy Holly, Norman Petty, Jerry Allison

Inspired by Norman Petty's production of "Party Doll" by fellow Texan and fellow buddy, Knox, Holly brought his band and their John Wayne-inspired lyric to Clovis, New Mexico, to introduce the Tex-Mex element to the Rockabilly brush fire. Like the Rockabilly Trio (already defunct) and the Blue Caps (peaked), the Crickets were a band: unlike the others, and more like the Beatles, they had Buddy Holly, the first great Rock and Roll singer/songwriter/musician, who had a catalogue of future standards in his head and in his heart, just waiting to be unloaded. Covered by the Quarrymen (the future Beatles) in '58.

1958

IT'S SO EASY
Producer: Norman Petty
Album: In Style with the Crickets
Record Label: Brunswick
Songwriters: Buddy Holly, Norman Petty

Covered by Linda Ronstadt (Asylum, '77).

THINK IT OVER
Producer: Norman Petty
Album: The Buddy Holly Story
Record Label: Brunswick
Songwriters: Buddy Holly, Norman Petty, Jerry Allison

1959

I FOUGHT THE LAW
Producer: Norman Petty
Album: In Style with the Crickets
Record Label: Brunswick
Songwriter: Sonny Curtis

Last blast of Rockabilly from the post-Buddy Crickets, featuring the guitar of Sonny Curtis, who would go on to write "The Mary Tyler Moore Show" theme (covered by Husker Du). Covered by the Bobby Fuller Four (Mustang, '66); and the Clash, for whom it was their first U.S. single, backed with "(White Man) In Hammersmith Palais" (Epic, '79).

LOVE'S MADE A FOOL OF YOU
Producer: Norman Petty
Album: In Style with the Crickets
Record Label: Brunswick
Songwriters: Buddy Holly, Bob Montgomery

Released by the Crickets as their first post-Buddy single. Covered by Tom Rush (Elektra, '64), the Bobby Fuller Four (Mustang, '66).

MORE THAN I CAN SAY
Producer: Norman Petty
Album: In Style with the Crickets
Record Label: Coral
Songwriters: Sonny Curtis, Jerry Allison.

Stiffed as a single. Cover by Bobby Vee (Liberty, '61) also stiffed. Cover by Leo Sayer (Warner Brothers, '80) reached Top-10.

JIM CROCE

1972

TIME IN A BOTTLE
Producer: Terry Cashman
Album: You Don't Mess Around with Jim
Record Label: ABC
Songwriters: Jim Croce, Tommy West

Poignant, posthumous #1 easy listening Folk hit.

YOU DON'T MESS AROUND WITH JIM
Producers: Terry Cashman, Tommy West
Album: You Don't Mess Around with Jim
Record Label: ABC
Songwriter: Jim Croce

Defining the '70s singer/songwriter.

1973

BAD, BAD LEROY BROWN
Producers: Terry Cashman, Tommy West
Album: Life and Times
Record Label: ABC
Songwriter: Jim Croce

Chicago's mean streets, the unplugged rendition. Covered by Frank Sinatra (Reprise, '74).

I GOT A NAME
Producers: Terry Cashman, Tommy West
Album: I Got a Name
Record Label: ABC
Songwriters: Norman Gimbel, Charles Fox

Theme from the film, The Last American Hero.

I'LL HAVE TO SAY I LOVE YOU IN A SONG
Producers: Terry Cashman, Tommy West
Album: I Got a Name
Record Label: ABC
Songwriter: Jim Croce

Used as the theme for the TV movie She Lives, this became a hit posthumously.

CROSBY, STILLS AND NASH

1969

MARRAKESH EXPRESS
Producer: Crosby, Stills and Nash
Album: Crosby, Stills and Nash
Record Label: Atlantic
Songwriter: Graham Nash

Anthem for rich hippies everywhere.

SUITE: JUDY BLUE EYES
Producer: Crosby, Stills and Nash
Album: Crosby, Stills and Nash
Record Label: Atlantic
Songwriter: Stephen Stills

Guitar tribute to Judy Collins.

WOODEN SHIPS
Producer: Crosby, Stills and Nash
Album: Crosby, Stills and Nash
Record Label: Atlantic
Songwriters: David Crosby, Stephen Stills, Paul Kantner

Sci-fi brain-child of future Starship pilot Kantner, this was covered by the Jefferson Airplane (RCA, '69) a few months later.

1977

JUST A SONG BEFORE I GO
Producer: Crosby, Stills and Nash
Album: CSN
Record Label: Atlantic
Songwriter: Graham Nash

Their biggest hit.

1982

SOUTHERN CROSS
Producers: Crosby, Stills and Nash, Stanley Johnson, Steve Gursky
Album: Daylight Again
Record Label: Atlantic
Songwriters: Stephen Stills, Richard Curtis, Michael Curtis

Life in semi-retirement; Stills's version of a sailing song.

WASTED ON THE WAY
Producers: Crosby, Stills and Nash, Stanley Johnson, Steve Gursky
Album: Daylight Again
Record Label: Atlantic
Songwriter: Graham Nash

Summing up the faded hopes and dashed dreams of the generation that made them famous. Suggested segue: "Before the Deluge" by Jackson Browne.

CROSBY, STILLS, NASH AND YOUNG

1970

HELPLESS
Producer: Crosby, Stills, Nash and Young
Album: Deja Vu

Record Label: Atlantic
Songwriter: Neil Young

Primordial Neilsian angst. Re-recored by Young (Reprise, '77).

OHIO

Producer: Crosby, Stills, Nash and Young
Album: So Far
Record Label: Atlantic
Songwriter: Neil Young

Rock as journalism. Written by Young in response to the murder in Ohio of four students by the National Guard at a protest rally at Kent State in May. Recorded, released, and actually played on the radio a month later. But not as much as "Ride, Captain, Ride" by Blues Image, or 122 other songs that year.

OUR HOUSE

Producer: Crosby, Stills, Nash and Young
Album: Deja Vu
Record Label: Atlantic
Songwriter: Graham Nash

Contemplating hippie domesticity, in a Laurel Canyon mansion.

TEACH YOUR CHILDREN

Producer: Crosby, Stills, Nash and Young
Album: Deja Vu
Rccord Label: Atlantic
Songwriter: Graham Nash

Has since become a theme song for various educational and social public service organizations.

WOODSTOCK

Producer: Crosby, Stills, Nash and Young
Album: Deja Vu
Record Label: Atlantic
Songwriter: Joni Mitchell

Idealized title tune for the counter-cultural commencement concert written by someone who was three thousand miles away at the time, and, everything considered, pretty glad to be there. Covered by Mitchell on the B-side of "Big Yellow Taxi" (Reprise, '70) and by Matthews Southern Comfort (Decca, '71).

CHRISTOPHER CROSS
1980

RIDE LIKE THE WIND

Producer: Michael Omartian
Album: Christopher Cross

Record Label: Warner Brothers
Songwriter: Christopher Geppert

Formula L.A. corporate mellowness.

SAILING

Producer: Michael Omartian
Album: Christopher Cross
Record Label: Warner Brothers
Songwriter: Christopher Geppert

Typifying the stultifying drift the '80s would have on the radio, this song peaked at #1. Cross won five Grammies in '81, including Best New Artist and Album of the Year; "Sailing" won Song of the Year and Record of the Year.

SHERYL CROW
1994

ALL I WANNA DO

Producer: Bill Bottrell
Album: Tuesday Night Music Club
Record Label: A&M
Songwriters: Sheryl Crow, Bill Bottrell, David Baerwald, Kevin Gilbert, Wyn Cooper

Picturesque and picaresque multi-Grammy winner.

LEAVING LAS VEGAS

Producer: Bill Bottrell
Album: Tuesday Night Music Club
Record Label: A&M
Songwriters: Sheryl Crow, Bill Bottrell, David Baerwald, Kevin Gilbert, David Ricketts

Rickie Lee Jones meets Carole King at a Sunset Strip piano bar.

CROWDED HOUSE
1987

DON'T DREAM IT'S OVER

Producer: Mitchell Froom
Album: Crowded House
Record Label: Capitol
Songwriter: Neil Finn

Soulful easy listening from Australia.

SOMETHING SO STRONG

Producer: Mitchell Froom
Album: Crowded House
Record Label: Capitol
Songwriters: Neil Finn, Mitchell Froom

Their initial single, which became their second Top-10 when it was re-released after the success of the first.

1991

CHOCOLATE CAKE

Producers: Mitchell Froom, Crowded House
Album: Woodface
Record Label: Capitol
Songwriters: Neil Finn, Tim Finn

THE CROWS
1954

GEE!

Producer: George Goldner
Record Label: Rama
Songwriters: Viola Watkins, Daniel Norton, William Davis

Early R&B standard bearer, hit the R&R charts a year later.

JULEE CRUISE
1990

FALLING

Album: Floating into the Night
Record Label: Warner Brothers
Songwriters: Angelo Badalamenti, David Lynch

Appropriately eerie theme for the cult TV classic "Twin Peaks."

ARTHUR BIG BOY CRUDUP
1947

THAT'S ALL RIGHT, MAMA

Album: That's All Right, Mama
Record Label: RCA
Songwriter: Arthur Crudup

Essential Mississippi bar band blues. Covered by Elvis Presley in his first historic Sun session in Memphis, July 7, 1954, and released two weeks later.

1950

MY BABY LEFT ME

Record Label: RCA
Songwriter: Arthur Crudup

Covered by Elvis Presley (RCA, '56).

BILLY CRYSTAL
1985

YOU LOOK MAHVELOUS

Producers: A. Baker, B. Tischler
Album: You Look Marvelous
Record Label: A&M
Songwriters: Billy Crystal, Paul Shaffer

Las Vegas schtick. Shaffer's best collaboration since "Honey (Touch Me with My Clothes On)" by Gilda Radner.

THE CRYSTALS
1961

THERE'S NO OTHER
Producer: Phil Spector
Album: He's a Rebel
Record Label: Philles
Songwriters: Phil Spector, Leroy Bates

B-side of their first release, "Oh Boy Maybe Baby"; preview of Spectorian girl-group greatness to come.

1962

HE'S A REBEL
Producer: Phil Spector
Album: He's a Rebel
Record Label: Philles
Songwriter: Gene Pitney

Recreating the sensitive outsider for a new Rock and Roll generation. Another hit for the great uncredited girl group lead singer of the '60s, Darlene Love.

HE'S SURE THE BOY I LOVE
Producer: Phil Spector
Album: He's a Rebel
Record Label: Philles
Songwriters: Barry Mann, Cynthia Weil

Stellar Darlene Love vocal.

UPTOWN
Producer: Phil Spector
Album: He's a Rebel
Record Label: Philles
Songwriters: Barry Mann, Cynthia Weil

For the staff writers at the Brill Building in '62, uptown meant 1650 Broadway, where this and many more of the hits were written. For the Crystals, uptown was a decidedly different place.

1963

DA DOO RON RON
Producer: Phil Spector
Album: The Crystals Sing the Greatest Hits
Record Label: Philles
Songwriters: Jeff Barry, Ellie Greenwich, Phil Spector

Borrowing the days of the week motif as well as the tag line from the Shirelles' "I Met Him on a Sunday."

HE HIT ME (AND IT FELT LIKE A KISS)
Producer: Phil Spector
Album: He's a Rebel
Record Label: Philles
Songwriters: Gerry Goffin, Carole King

In the deified male-dominated atmosphere of "My Boyfriend's Back" and "Don't Say Nothing Bad (About My Baby)" a song like this seems less unforgivable than inevitable. Covered by Hole (DGC, '95).

THEN HE KISSED ME
Producer: Phil Spector
Album: Uptown Twist
Record Label: Philles
Songwriters: Jeff Barry, Ellie Greenwich, Phil Spector

Brill brilliance.

1964

ALL GROWN UP
Producer: Phil Spector
Album: Uptown Twist
Record Label: Philles
Songwriters: Jeff Barry, Ellie Greenwich, Phil Spector

The girl-group swan song—nowhere to go but middle class. Suggested segue: "Almost Grown" by Chuck Berry.

THE CUCUMBERS
1983

MY BOYFRIEND
Album: Fresh Cucumbers
Record Label: Fake Doom
Songwriters: Jon Fried, Deena Shoskes

The great girl-group sound returns; but where Deena Shoskes failed to crack the airwaves of '83, Cyndi Lauper, the Bangles, and later Madonna would plow over her tracks by the end of the year. Re-recorded on Profile, '87, by which time the latest girl-group moment would have passed, not to return again until '93–'94.

1987

MY TOWN
Album: The Cucumbers
Record Label: Profile
Songwriters: John Fried, Deena Shoskes

An ode to Hoboken. Suggested segues: "I'm from New Jersey" by John Gorka, "Jersey Girl" by Tom Waits, and "The Eyes of a New York Woman" by Insect Trust.

THE CUFF LINKS
1969

TRACY
Producer: Paul Vance
Album: Tracy
Record Label: Decca
Songwriters: Paul Vance, Lee Pockriss

A day's work for studio singer Ron Dante.

THE CULT
1985

SHE SELLS SANCTUARY
Album: Love
Record Label: Sire
Songwriters: Ian Astbury, Billy Duffy

Alternative smash for an otherwise typical Generation X Hard Rock band.

CULTURE BEAT
1993

MR. VAIN
Album: Serenity
Record Label: 550 Music
Songwriters: Steven Levis, Josie Katzmann, Jay Supreme

Euro-Disco refuses to die.

CULTURE CLUB
1983

CHURCH OF THE POISON MIND
Producer: Steve Levene
Album: Colour by Numbers
Record Label: Epic
Songwriters: Roy Hay, Jon Moss, Michael Craig, George O'Dowd

DO YOU REALLY WANT TO HURT ME?
Producer: Steve Levene
Album: Kissing to Be Clever
Record Label: Epic
Songwriters: Roy Hay, Jon Moss, Michael Craig, George O'Dowd

Catchy British Soul in lite Reggae drag was their first transAtlantic hit.

I'LL TUMBLE 4 YA
Producer: Steve Levene
Album: Kissing to be Clever
Record Label: Epic
Songwriters: Roy Hay, Jon Moss, Michael Craig, George O'Dowd

KARMA CHAMELEON
Producer: Steve Levene
Album: Colour by Numbers
Record Label: Epic
Songwriters: Jon Moss, Roy Hay, Michael Craig, George O'Dowd, Phil Pickett

Their only #1 single, an irresistible Folk Rock melange, with a hidden tribute to Jamaica.

TIME (CLOCK OF THE HEART)
Producer: Steve Levene
Album: Kissing to Be Clever
Record Label: Epic
Songwriters: Roy Hay, Jon Moss, Michael Craig

Third biggest hit.

1984

MISS ME BLIND
Producer: Steve Levene
Album: Colour by Numbers
Record Label: Epic
Songwriters: Jon Moss, Roy Hay, Michael Craig, George O'Dowd

1986

MOVE AWAY
Producers: Arif Mardin, L. Hahn
Album: From Luxury to Heartache
Record Label: Virgin
Songwriters: Culture Club, Phil Pickett

Their last hit single.

BURTON CUMMINGS
1976

STAND TALL
Producer: Richard Perry
Album: Burton Cummings
Record Label: Portrait
Songwriter: Burton Cummings

Suggested segue: "Hold Your Head Up" by Argent.

THE CURE
1979

BOYS DON'T CRY
Producer: Chris Parry
Album: Boys Don't Cry
Record Label: Fiction/PVC
Songwriters: Robert Smith, Laurence Tolhurst, Michael Dempsey

Their first critical success; Gloom Rock awaits.

JUMPING SOMEONE ELSE'S TRAIN
Producer: Chris Parry
Album: Boys Don't Cry
Record Label: Fiction/PVC
Songwriters: Robert Smith, Laurence Tolhurst, Michael Dempsey

KILLING AN ARAB
Producer: Chris Parry
Album: Boys Don't Cry
Record Label: Small Wonder/Fiction/PVC
Songwriters: Robert Smith, Laurence Tolhurst, Michael Dempsey

Led by the ghostly Robert Smith, Nerd Rock goes to Oxford. Morrissey's appropriately named Smiths were listening.

1983

LET'S GO TO BED
Producers: Robert Smith, Dave Allen
Album: The Walk
Record Label: Sire
Songwriters: Robert Smith, Laurence Tolhurst

The notoriously dour and Byronic Smith's idea of a good-time single.

1985

IN BETWEEN DAYS (WITHOUT YOU)
Producers: Robert Smith, Dave Allen
Album: The Head on the Door
Record Label: Elektra
Songwriter: Robert Smith

Alternative classic on the order of New Order.

1987

JUST LIKE HEAVEN
Producers: Robert Smith, Dave Allen
Album: Kiss Me, Kiss Me, Kiss Me
Record Label: Elektra
Songwriters: Robert Smith, Laurence Tolhurst, Simon Gallup, Purl Thompson, Boris Williams

WHY CAN'T I BE YOU
Producers: Robert Smith, Dave Allen
Album: Kiss Me, Kiss Me, Kiss Me
Record Label: Elektra
Songwriters: Robert Smith, Laurence Tolhurst, Simon Gallup, Purl Thompson, Boris Williams

A love song.

1989

LOVE SONG
Producers: Robert Smith, Dave Allen
Album: Disintegration
Record Label: Elektra
Songwriters: Robert Smith, Laurence Tolhurst, Simon Gallup, Purl Thompson, Boris Williams, Roger O'Donnell

Their first and only U.S. Top-10.

LULLABYE
Producers: Robert Smith, Dave Allen
Album: Disintegration
Record Label: Elektra
Songwriters: Robert Smith, Laurence Tolhurst, Simon Gallup, Boris Williams, Purl Thompson, Roger O'Donnell

Great video.

1992

FRIDAY I'M IN LOVE
Producers: The Cure, Dave Allen
Album: Wish
Record Label: Elektra
Songwriters: Robert Smith, Simon Gallup, Boris Williams, Purl Thompson, Perry Bamonte

Closest thing to an up tune.

TIM CURRY
1979

I DO THE ROCK
Album: Fearless
Record Label: A&M
Songwriters: Tim Curry, Michael Kamen

Underground treatise by star of cult classic The Rocky Horror Picture Show.

CUTTING CREW
1987

(I JUST) DIED IN YOUR ARMS
Producers: T. Brown, J. Jansen, Cutting Crew
Album: Broadcast
Record Label: Virgin
Songwriter: Nick Eede

Synth Pop hit.

I'VE BEEN IN LOVE BEFORE
Producers: T, Brown, J. Jansen, Cutting Crew
Album: Broadcast
Record Label: Virgin
Songwriter: Nick Eede

CYPRESS HILL
1993

I AIN'T GOIN' OUT LIKE THAT
Producer: T-Ray
Album: Black Sunday
Record Label: Ruffhouse
Songwriters: Louis Freese (Dr. Freeze), Larry Muggurud, T. Ray
Rugged Rap sentiments.

INSANE IN THE BRAIN
Producer: D. J. Muggs
Album: Black Sunday
Record Label: Ruffhouse
Songwriters: Louis Freese (Dr. Freeze), Senen Reyes, Larry Muggurud
A paean to cannabis.

THE CYRCLE
1966

RED RUBBER BALL
Producer: John Simon
Album: Red Rubber Ball
Record Label: Columbia
Songwriters: Paul Simon, Bruce Woodley
Simon reverts to earlier Brill Building form. Further attesting to the notion that he would never get the Brill Building out of his blood, Paul would one day open his own publishing company there.

BILLY RAY CYRUS
1992

ACHY BREAKY HEART
Producers: Jim Cotton, Joe Scaife
Album: Some Gave All
Record Label: Mercury
Songwriter: Don Von Tress
#1 C&W/Top-5 R&R crossover, a rarity in the '90s. Briefly sparked an interest in country line-dancing.

D

TERENCE TRENT D'ARBY
1987

DANCE LITTLE SISTER
Producers: Martyn Ware, Terence Trent D'Arby
Album: The Hardline According to Terence Trent D'Arby
Record Label: Columbia
Songwriter: Terence Trent D'Arby

SIGN YOUR NAME
Producer: Martyn Ware
Album: The Hardline According to Terence Trent D'Arby
Record Label: Columbia
Songwriter: Terence Trent D'Arby
Modernized Al Green/Smokey Robinson.

WISHING WELL
Producer: Martyn Ware
Album: The Hardline According to Terence Trent D'Arby
Record Label: Columbia
Songwriters: Terence Trent D'Arby, Sean Oliver
#1 R&R/R&B/Top-10 U.K. breakthrough British-influenced Pop Soul single.

D. J. JAZZY JEFF AND THE FRESH PRINCE
1988

A NIGHTMARE ON MY STREET
Producers: D. J. Jazzy Jeff, the Fresh Prince, Pete Q. Harris, N. Green
Album: He's the D.J., I'm the Rapper
Record Label: Jive
Songwriters: Will Smith, Jeff Townes, Pete Q. Harris
Teen Rap on the horror movie tip.

1989

PARENTS JUST DON'T UNDERSTAND
Producers: D. J. Jazzy Jeff, the Fresh Prince, Pete Q. Harris, N. Green
Album: He's the D.J., I'm the Rapper
Record Label: Jive
Songwriters: Will Smith, Jeff Townes, Pete Q. Harris
Urban sitcom rap, rated PG-13.

1991

SUMMERTIME
Album: Homebase
Record Label: Jive
Songwriters: Kool and the Gang, Will Smith, Fingers, Hula
Celebratory Rap concoction with a Kool groove sampled from "Summer Madness;" #1 R&B/Top-10 R&R.

D.R.S.
1993

GANGSTA LEAN
Producers: Chris Jackson, Delaney McGil
Album: 51
Record Label: Capitol
Songwriters: Chris Jackson, E. Jay Turner, Tracy Carter
Chilling and compelling Gangsta Rap ballad.

DA BRAT
1994

FUNKDAFIED
Producer: Jermaine Dupri
Album: Funkdafied
Record Label: So So Def
Songwriters: Jermaine Dupri, Da Brat
The '90s Rap/Hip-Hop fusion groove personified.

DADA
1992

DIZZ KNEE LAND
Producers: Kenn Scott, dada
Album: Puzzle
Record Label: I.R.S.
Songwriters: Joie Alio, Michael Gorley
Alternative whimsy with a cutting edge.

DICK DALE
1961

LET'S GO TRIPPING
Producer: Jim Monsour
Album: Surfer's Choice
Record Label: Deltone
Songwriter: Dick Dale
Defining the rippling sound of the king of the surf guitar. Covered by the Beach Boys (Capitol, '63).

MISERLOU
Producer: Jim Monsour
Album: Surfer's Choice
Record Label: Deltone
Songwriters: N. Roubanis, Milton Leeds, Fred Wise, S. K. Russell
Surf treatment for the '34 Greek classic.

1964

SURFER'S HOLIDAY
Album: *Surfer's Holiday* Soundtrack
Record Label: AIP

Songwriter: Brian Wilson

Before New Wave there was only one kind of wave.

ROGER DALTREY
1973

GIVING IT ALL AWAY
Album: Daltrey
Record Label: Track
Songwriters: David Courtney, Leo Sayer

First hit for the Who frontman. Covered by Leo Sayer (Warner Brothers, '75).

1985

UNDER A RAGING MOON
Album: Under a Raging Moon
Record Label: Atlantic
Songwriters: John Parr, Julia Downes

Dedicated to his former Who bandmate, the late Keith Moon.

DAMN YANKEES
1990

HIGH ENOUGH
Producer: Ron Nevison
Album: Damn Yankees
Record Label: Warner Brothers
Songwriters: Ted Nugent, Tommy Shaw, Jack Blades

Exemplary corporate Rock of the '90s.

THE DAMNED
1976

NEW ROSE
Producer: Nick Lowe
Album: The Damned
Record Label: Stiff
Songwriter: Brian James

Generally regarded as the first single from England's first Punk Rock band. Covered by Guns N' Roses (Geffen, '89).

CHARLIE DANIELS
1973

UNEASY RIDER
Producer: Charlie Daniels
Album: Honey in the Rock
Record Label: Kama Sutra
Songwriter: Charlie Daniels

A displaced hippie in the post-Easy Rider South.

1979

THE DEVIL WENT DOWN TO GEORGIA
Producer: Charlie Daniels
Album: Million Mile Reflections
Record Label: Epic
Songwriters: Charlie Daniels, Tommy Crain, Taz DiGregorio, Fred Edwards, Charles Hayward, Jim Marshall

#1 C&W/Top-10 R&R crossover story song with Biblical implications. In the similarly themed movie about legendary bluesman Robert Johnson, Crossroads, *the boy was played by Ralph Maccio, the devil's guitar by Steve Vai.*

1982

STILL IN SAIGON
Producer: John Boylan
Album: Windows
Record Label: Epic
Songwriter: Dan Daley

Country/Rock tale of a returning Viet Nam vet is one of the best post-war, anti-war songs ever.

THE DANLEERS
1958

ONE SUMMER NIGHT
Record Label: AMP
Songwriter: Danny Webb

A Doo-Wop treasure under the moon of love.

DANNY AND DUSTY
1985

SONG FOR THE DREAMERS
Producer: Paul Cutter
Album: The Lost Weekend
Record Label: A&M
Songwriters: Steve Wynn, Dan Stuart

A hopeful Cow Punk drinking song; dedicated to baseball's fabulous Rynes, Duren and Sandberg.

DANNY AND THE JUNIORS
1957

AT THE HOP
Producer: Arthur Singer
Record Label: ABC Paramount
Songwriters: Artie Singer, John Medora, Dave White

Dick Clark-inspired anthem of the "American Bandstand" generation, originally entitled "Do the Bop," represented the first acknowledgment of Rock and Roll's first dance era. Extolling the virtues of the Lindy, the Slop, the Bop, the Stroll, the Chicken, the Calypso, etc, it went to #1 R&B/R&R.

1958

ROCK AND ROLL IS HERE TO STAY
Producer: Arthur Singer
Record Label: ABC
Songwriter: Dave White

Early celebratory anthem. Suggested segues: "It Will Stand" by the Showmen, "Roll Over Beethoven" by Chuck Berry.

DANZIG
1988

MOTHER
Album: Danzig
Record Label: Def American
Songwriter: Glenn Danzig

If Jim Morrison had survived, he might have sued the perpetrators of this thundering Metal monsterpiece for co-opting his act. Revived by Danzig (American/WB, '93).

BOBBY DARIN
1958

QUEEN OF THE HOP
Producer: Ahmet Ertegun
Album: The Bobby Darin Story
Record Label: Atco
Songwriters: Woody Harris, Bobby Darin

SPLISH SPLASH
Producer: Ahmet Ertegun
Album: The Bobby Darin Story
Record Label: Atco
Songwriters: Bobby Darin, Murray Kaufman (Jean Murray)

Darin's embarrassing R&R breakthrough is a teenybop ditty. Compounding the embarrassment, the tub was in the kitchen. In the tradition of Alan Freed (and Elvis), DJ Murray the K took a writing credit. In the Good Son tradition, he gave his mother all the credit.

1959

DREAM LOVER
Producer: Ahmet Ertegun
Ibum Title: The Bobby Darin Story
Record Label: Atco

Songwriter: Bobby Darin

Hall of fame soft rocker (dedicated to studio backup and future Angels' lead singer, Peggy Santiglia, whom Darin mentions by name in the closing moments of the outro).

PLAIN JANE
Producer: Ahmet Ertegun
Album: The Bobby Darin Story
Record Label: Atco
Songwriters: Doc Pomus, Mort Shuman

Creating the archetype of the '60s earth mother.

1960

BEYOND THE SEA
Producer: Ahmet Ertegun
Album: That's All
Record Label: Atco
Songwriters: Jack Lawrence, Charles Trenet

Introduced by Charles Trenet in France, '47. Darin makes his Pop move, formalized by "Mack the Knife" in '59. The Copa beckoned.

1962

THINGS
Album: Things and Other Things
Record Label: Atco
Songwriter: Bobby Darin

Breezy Pop rocker.

1963

YOU'RE THE REASON I'M LIVING
Album: You're the Reason I'm Living
Record Label: Capitol
Songwriter: Bobby Darin

JAMES DARREN
1963

GOODBYE CRUEL WORLD
Album: Teenage Triangle
Record Label: Colpix
Songwriter: Gloria Shayne

On some surveys, the worst Top-10 record of all time.

HER ROYAL MAJESTY
Album: Teenage Triangle
Record Label: Colpix
Songwriters: Gerry Goffin, Carole King

One of Rock's best teams' contribution to a dubious career.

THE DARTELLS
1963

HOT PASTRAMI
Album: Hot Pastrami
Record Label: Dot
Songwriter: Dessie Rozier

Twisting to the deli.

DAVID AND DAVID
1986

WELCOME TO THE BOOMTOWN
Producer: Davitt Sigerson
Album: Boomtown
Record Label: A&M
Songwriters: David Baerwald, David Ricketts

'80s L.A. anti-mellow singer/songwriting answer to Steely Dan.

MAC DAVIS
1972

BABY DON'T GET HOOKED ON ME
Producer: Rick Hall
Album: Baby Don't Get Hooked on Me
Record Label: Columbia
Songwriter: Mac Davis

Preening Country Pop. Kenny Rogers would perfect this groove.

PAUL DAVIS
1978

I GO CRAZY
Producer: Paul Davis
Album: Singer of Songs—Teller of Tales
Record Label: Bang
Songwriter: Paul Davis

Country-esque Pop Rock ditty was so mellow it took more than six months to peak on the charts.

1981

'65 LOVE AFFAIR
Producers: Paul Davis, Ed Seay
Album: Cool Night
Record Label: Arista
Songwriter: Paul Davis

Calculated nostalgia with a nod toward England Dan and John Ford Coley. Suggested segue: "The Summer of '69" by Bryan Adams.

SKEETER DAVIS
1963

THE END OF THE WORLD
Producer: Chet Atkins
Album: The End of the World
Record Label: RCA Victor
Songwriters: Sylvia Dee, Arthur Kent

Rare Top-10 R&B/C&W/R&R crossover reflected Davis's feelings after losing her best friend and former singing partner Betty Jack Davis in a car crash.

I CAN'T STAY MAD AT YOU
Producer: Chet Atkins
Record Label: RCA Victor
Songwriters: Gerry Goffin, Carole King

Broadway Pop Rock; Top-15 C&W/Top-10 R&R crossover. Her only other Top-10 item.

SPENCER DAVIS GROUP
1967

GIMME SOME LOVIN'
Producers: Jimmy Miller, Chris Blackwell
Album: Gimme Some Lovin'
Record Label: United Artists
Songwriters: Steve Winwood, Muff Winwood, Spencer Davis

The heavy organ sound provides the basis for their biggest hit; Top-10 U.S./#2 U.K.

I'M A MAN
Producer: Jimmy Miller
Album: I'm a Man
Record Label:United Artists
Songwriters: Steve Winwood, Jimmy Miller

Signature number for the Progressive Blues Supergroup. Winwood would move into Traffic; Miller would produce the Rolling Stones.

TYRONE DAVIS
1968

CAN I CHANGE MY MIND
Producer: Willie Henderson
Album: Can I Change My Mind?
Record Label: Dakar
Songwriters: Barry Despenza, Carl Wolfolk

#1 R&B/Top-10 R&R crossover. Robert Cray was listening.

TURN BACK THE HANDS OF TIME
Producer: Willie Henderson
Album: Turn Back the Hands of Time
Record Label: Dakar
Songwriters: Jack Daniels, Bonnie Thompson
The mid-tempo groove of the year; #1 R&B/R&R crossover.

DAWN

1970

CANDIDA
Producers: Hank Medress, Dave Appell
Album: Candida
Record Label: Bell
Songwriters: Irwin Levine, Tony Wine
Probably not about Candida Donadio, legendary literary agent for Thomas Pynchon, Don Delillo, and others.

KNOCK THREE TIMES
Producer: Hank Medress
Album: Candida
Record Label: Bell
Songwriters: L. Russell Brown, Irwin Levine, Dave Appell
An ode to apartment house living.

1973

SAY, HAS ANYBODY SEEN MY SWEET GYPSY ROSE
Album: Dawn's New Ragtime Follies
Record Label: Bell
Songwriters: Irwin Levine, L. Russell Brown
Ragtime folly.

STEPPIN' OUT (GONNA BOOGIE TONIGHT)
Album: Dawn's New Ragtime Follies
Record Label: Bell
Songwriters: Irwin Levine, L. Russell Brown

TIE A YELLOW RIBBON ROUND THE OLD OAK TREE
Producers: Irwin Levine, L. Russell Brown
Album: Tuneweaving
Record Label: Bell
Songwriters: Irwin Levine, L. Russell Brown
Based on a true story, this semi-contagious slice of life imitated reality when the tune

was used to welcome back the hostages from Tehran.

BOBBY DAY

1957

LITTLE BITTY PRETTY ONE
Record Label: Class
Songwriter: Robert Byrd
Covered by Thurston Harris (Aladdin, '57).

1958

OVER AND OVER
Producer: Leon Rene
Album: Rockin' with Robin
Record Label: Class
Songwriter: Robert Byrd
B-side of "Rockin' Robin," covered by the Dave Clark Five (Epic, 64).

ROCKIN' ROBIN
Producer: Leon Rene
Album: Rockin' with Robin
Record Label: Class
Songwriter: Leon Rene (Jimmie Thomas)
Written under a pseudonym by the author of "When the Swallows Come Back to Capistrano." Covered by Michael Jackson (Epic, 70).

MORRIS DAY

1988

FISHNET
Producer: Morris Day
Album: Daydreaming
Record Label: Warner Brothers
Songwriters: James Harris III, Terry Lewis
#1 R&B hit reunites the members of Prince's backing band, the Time. Influential songwriter/producers, Harris and Lewis named their publishing company Flyte Tyme.

TAYLOR DAYNE

1987

TELL IT TO MY HEART
Album: Tell It to My Heart
Record Label: Arista
Songwriters: Seth Swirsky, Ernie Gold
Top-10 R&R Bar-Mitzvah dance groove.

THE DAZZ BAND

1982

LET IT WHIP
Producer: Reggie Andrews
Album: Keep It Live
Record Label: Motown
Songwriters: Reggie Andrews, Leon Chancler
Disco Jazz; #1 R&B/Top-10 R&R crossover.

THE DBS

1981

LIVING A LIE
Producer: Scott Litt
Album: Repercussion
Record Label: Albion/IRS
Songwriters: Chris Stamey, Peter Holsapple
From the early pioneers of low-fi, the return of the folkie sensibility in Rock drag. R.E.M. was waiting to co-opt it; Litt would help them.

1984

LOVE IS FOR LOVERS
Album: Like This
Record Label: Bearsville
Songwriters: Peter Holsapple, Darby Hall
Defining the emerging Folk Rock Zeitgeist of '84.

DE LA SOUL

1989

ME MYSELF AND I
Producer: Paul Husten
Album: 3 Feet High and Rising
Record Label: Tommy Boy
Songwriters: Paul Husten, Kevin Mercer, Dave Jolicoeur, Vincent Mason, George Clinton
Self-aware R&B Rap, with a sense of history and Funkadelic's "(Not Just) Knee Deep."

TERI DESARIO WITH K. C.

1979

PLEASE DON'T GO
Producer: Harry Casey
Album: Do You Wanna Go Party
Record Label: Casablanca
Songwriters: Harry Casey, Richard Finch
One-shot for the Sunshine side girl.

WILLIAM DEVAUGHN
1974

BE THANKFUL FOR WHAT YOU GOT
Producer: Frank Fioavanti
Album: Be Thankful for What You Got
Record Label: Roxbury
Songwriter: William DeVaughn

#1 R&B/Top-10 R&R crossover bedroom ballad.

THE DEAD BOYS
1977

SONIC REDUCER
Producer: Genya Raven
Album: Young Loud and Snotty
Record Label: Sire
Songwriters: Steve Bators (Stiv Bators), Cheetah Chrome, David Thomas, Johnny Blitz, Jeff Magnum, Jimmy Zero

Punk anthem of ear-challenging intensity.

1978

AIN'T IT FUN
Producer: Felix Pappalardi
Album: We Have Come for Your Children
Record Label: Sire
Songwriters: Cheetah Chrome, Peter Laughner

Composed with a prime instigator of the mid-'70s Akron Indie Punk Rock scene; Laughner played in Pere Ube before it was Pere Ubu.

THE DEAD KENNEDYS
1980

CALIFORNIA ÜBER ALLES
Album: Fresh Fruit for Rotting Vegetables
Record Label: I.R.S./Cherry Red
Songwriters: Eric Boucher (Jello Biafra), John Greenway, Michael Franti, Gene Pistel

First single for the San Francisco hardcore legends; an attack on California governor Jerry Brown.

HOLIDAY IN CAMBODIA
Album: Fresh Fruit for Rotting Vegetables
Record Label: I.R.S./Cherry Red
Songwriters: Eric Boucher (Jello Biafra), East Bay Ray, Klaus Flouride, Bruce Slesinger

U.S. hardcore answer to the Sex Pistols' "Holidays in the Sun." Lead singer/actor/poet Biafra came in fourth out of ten candidates in a San Francisco mayoralty run off in '79 to elect a successor to the murdered Harvey Milk.

DEAD MILKMEN
1989

PUNK ROCK GIRL
Album: Beezlebubba
Record Label: Enigma
Songwriter: Dead Milkmen

Leaders of the suburban Punk Garage movement of the '80s finally achieve a semi-classic.

DEAD OR ALIVE
1985

YOU SPIN ME ROUND (LIKE A RECORD)
Producer: Pete Waterman
Album: Youthquake
Record Label: Epic
Songwriters: Peter Burns, Michael Percy, Timothy Lever, Steven Coy

Dance record of the year; #1 U.K.

1986

BRAND NEW LOVER
Producers: Mike Stock, Matt Aitken, Pete Waterman
Album: Mad, Bad, and Dangerous to Know
Record Label: Epic
Songwriters: Peter Burns, Michael Percy, Timothy Lever, Steven Coy

Another dance sensation.

DEADEYE DICK
1994

NEW AGE GIRL
Producer: F. LeBlanc
Album: A Different Story
Record Label: Ichaban
Songwriter: Caleb Guillotte

"Punk Rock Girl" five years later. Featured in the Jim Carrey movie Dumb and Dumber.

JIMMY DEAN
1961

BIG BAD JOHN
Producer: Don Law
Album: Big Bad John and Other Fabulous Songs and Tales
Record Label: Columbia
Songwriter: Jimmy Dean

One of the year's top-selling Country story-songs; a #1 C&W/R&R crossover.

1962

P.T. 109
Album: Portrait of Jimmy Dean
Record Label: Columbia
Songwriters: Marijohn Wilkins, Fred Burch

Another story-song; in this case the mythical John in question is purportedly JFK.

DEBARGE
1983

TIME WILL REVEAL
Producer: Eldra DeBarge
Album: In a Special Way
Record Label: Gordy
Songwriters: Bunny DeBarge, Eldra DeBarge

Searching, soft Soul.

1985

RHYTHM OF THE NIGHT
Producer: Richard Perry
Album: Rhythm of the Night
Record Label: Motown
Songwriter: Diane Warren

From the movie The Last Dragon.

WHO'S HOLDING DONNA NOW
Producer: Jay Graydon
Album: Rhythm of the Night
Record Label: Motown
Songwriters: David Foster, Jay Graydon, Randy Goodrum

Chicago-esque middle-of-the-road R&B.

YOU WEAR IT WELL
Producer: Eldra DeBarge
Album: Rhythm of the Night
Record Label: Motown
Songwriters: Chico DeBarge, Eldra DeBarge

Top-10 R&B/Top-50 R&R crossover, featuring El Debarge singing lead.

1986

WHO'S JOHNNY? (*SHORT CIRCUIT* THEME)
Album: El Debarge
Record Label: Motown
Songwriters: Peter Wolf, Ina Wolf

From the movie Short Circuit.

CHRIS DEBURGH
1983

DON'T PAY THE FERRYMAN
Producer: Rupert Hine
Album: The Getaway
Record Label: A&M
Songwriter: Chris DeBurgh
British progressive Art rocker.

1986

THE LADY IN RED
Album: Into the Night
Record Label: A&M
Songwriter: Chris DeBurgh
#1 U.K./Top-10 U.S. ballad.

JOEY DEE AND THE STARLIGHTERS
1961

PEPPERMINT TWIST
Producer: Henry Glover
Album: Doin' the Twist at the Peppermint Lounge
Record Label: Roulette
Songwriter: Henry Glover
Having failed to note the historic potential of Hank Ballard's "The Twist," when he first encountered it, on the B-side of his own "Teardrops on Your Letter," Henry Glover redeemed himself by shepherding Joey Dee's celebration of "The Peppermint Twist" to the top of the charts in January of '62, knocking off the second coming of the selfsame "The Twist" in the bargain. In fact, it was the popularity of the Twist at New York's Peppermint Lounge among the Jet Set glitterati in attendance (Dee led the house band) that pushed the dance into headline news as a Baby Boom phenomenon, making Chubby's historic return to the top inevitable (aided by a key Ed Sullivan appearance).

KIKI DEE
1974

I'VE GOT THE MUSIC IN ME
Producer: Gus Dudgeon
Album: I've Got the Music in Me
Record Label: Rocket
Songwriter: Bias Boshell
Elton John protege earned her right to sing Pop Rock as the first U.K. act to sign with Motown in '70 ("Love Makes the World Go Round" peaked at #87 in '71).

KOOL MOE DEE
1989

KNOWLEDGE IS KING
Producers: Teddy Riley, P. Q. Harris, Lavalba, Moe Dewese
Album: Knowledge Is King
Record Label: Jive
Songwriter: P. Q. Harris, Moe Dewese
Heavy Rapper Kool Moe challenges his streetwise cronies to raise their level of discourse.

DEEE-LITE
1990

GROOVE IS IN THE HEART
Producer: Deee-Lite
Album: World Clique
Record Label: Elektra
Songwriters: Deee-Lite, Herbie Hancock, John Davis
B-52's of the '90s, transplanted to New York's high-Disco society.

THE DEELE
1987

TWO OCCASIONS
Producers: Babyface, L. A. Reid
Album: Eyes of a Stranger
Record Label: Solar
Songwriters: Kenny Edmunds (Babyface), Antonio Reid (L. A. Reid), Darnell Johnson
#1 R&B/Top-10 R&R hit for the superstar writing/production team of the '90s and their first band.

DEEP FOREST
1994

SWEET LULLABYE
Producer: Dan Laxman
Album: Deep Forever
Record Label: 550 Music
Songwriters: Eric Mouquet, Miguel Sanchez
Defining New Age world music; a pygmy ballet from Australia.

DEEP PURPLE
1972

HIGHWAY STAR
Producer: Deep Purple
Album: Machine Head
Record Label: Warner Brothers
Songwriters: Ritchie Blackmore, Ian Gillan, Roger Glover, Jon Lord, Ian Paice
Blackmore's Metal guitar triumph.

SMOKE ON THE WATER
Producer: Deep Purple
Album: Machine Head
Record Label: Warner Brothers
Songwriters: Ritchie Blackmore, Ian Gillan, Roger Glover, Jon Lord, Ian Paice
Celebrating a hot night in Montreaux, opening for Frank Zappa.

SPACE TRUCKIN'
Producer: Deep Purple
Album: Machine Head
Record Label: Warner Brothers
Songwriters: Ritchie Blackmore, Ian Gillan, Roger Glover, Jon Lord, Ian Paice
Another metal showpiece.

1973

WOMAN FROM TOKYO
Producer: Deep Purple
Album: Who Do You Think We Are?
Record Label: Warner Brothers
Songwriters: Ritchie Blackmore, Ian Gillian, Roger Glover, Jon Lord, Ian Paice
Taking the edge off their sonic explorations in the service of a hit single.

1974

BURN
Producer: Deep Purple
Album: Burn
Record Label: Warner Brothers
Songwriters: Ritchie Blackmore, David Coverdale, Jon Lord, Ian Paice
Blackmore burns again.

1985

KNOCKING AT YOUR BACK DOOR
Producers: Deep Purple, Roger Glover
Album: Perfect Stranger
Record Label: Mercury
Songwriters: Ritchie Blackmore, Ian Gillan, Roger Glover
Searching for an FM formula in the midst of a Folk Roots revival and an English Synth invasion.

DEF LEPPARD

1981

BRINGIN' ON THE HEARTBREAK
Producers: Steve Clark, Joe Elliott, Pete Willis
Album: High N' Dry
Record Label: Mercury
Songwriters: Steve Clark, Joe Elliott, Pete Willis

Scions of Zeppelin start a new Metal Age in England with Iron Maiden, Judas Priest, and Motorhead.

1983

FOOLIN'
Producer: Mutt Lange
Album: Pyromania
Record Label: Mercury
Songwriters: Steve Clark, Joe Elliott, Robert John "Mutt" Lange

Processed Metal studiocraft.

PHOTOGRAPH
Producer: Mutt Lange
Album: Pyromania
Record Label: Mercury
Songwriters: Steve Clark, Joe Elliott, Robert John "Mutt" Lange, Pete Willis, Rick Savage

Presaging the advent of Lite Metal, which would dominate AOR radio for the remainder of the decade.

ROCK OF AGES
Producer: Mutt Lange
Album: Pyromania
Record Label: Mercury
Songwriters: Steve Clark, Joe Elliott, Robert John "Mutt" Lange

Out of the hockey rinks and into the football stadiums.

1987

ARMEGEDDON IT
Producer: Mutt Lange
Album: Hysteria
Record Label: Mercury
Songwriters: Steve Clark, Joe Elliott, Robert John "Mutt" Lange, Phil Collen, Rick Savage

Lite-metal explodes, their fourth Top-10 hit from the monster LP.

HYSTERIA
Producer: Mutt Lange
Album: Hysteria
Record Label: Mercury
Songwriters: Steve Clark, Joe Elliot, Robert John "Mutt" Lange, Phil Collen, Rick Savage

The metal formula back in platinum, giving them their first Top-10 hit.

LOVE BITES
Producer: Mutt Lange
Album: Hysteria
Record Label: Mercury
Songwriters: Steve Clark, Joe Elliott, Robert John "Mutt" Lange, Phil Collen, Rick Savage

Their first and only #1 single, from the largest-selling album ever recorded by a U.K. group.

1988

POUR SOME SUGAR ON ME
Producer: Mutt Lange
Album: Hysteria
Record Label: Mercury
Songwriters: Steve Clark, Joe Elliott, Robert John "Mutt" Lange, Phil Collen, Rick Savage

Sweet taste of success; second Top-10 hit from the album.

1992

STAND UP (KICK LOVE INTO MOTION)
Producer: Mutt Lange
Album: Adrenalize
Record Label: Mercury
Songwriters: Steve Clark, Joe Elliot, Robert John "Mutt" Lange, Phil Collen

AOR's new dinosaurs in the age of Grunge.

THE DEFRANCO FAMILY

1973

HEARTBEAT—IT'S A LOVEBEAT
Producer: Walt Meskell
Album: Heartbeat—It's a Lovebeat
Record Label: 20th Century
Songwriters: William Gregory Hudspeth, Michael Kennedy

Manufactured bubble opus for the pre-teen set.

DESMOND DEKKER AND THE ACES

1969

ISRAELITES
Producer: Leslie Kong
Album: Israelites
Record Label: Uni
Songwriters: Desmond Dekker, Leslie Kong

First Reggae artist to hit the Top-10 U.S./#1 U.K.

1970

YOU CAN GET IT IF YOU REALLY WANT
Record Label: Trojan
Songwriter: Jimmy Cliff

Reggae classic was a smash in England. Covered by Jimmy Cliff on the legendary Reggae soundtrack to The Harder They Come *(Mango, '72).*

DEL AMITRI

1990

KISS THIS THING GOODBYE
Producer: M. Freegard
Album: Waking Hours
Record Label: A&M
Songwriter: Justin Currie

Scottish Folk Rock.

THE DEL FUEGOS

1985

DON'T RUN WILD
Producer: Mitchell Froom
Album: Boston, Mass
Record Label: Slash
Songwriters: Dan Zanes, Tom Lloyd, James Ralston

The Garage Band sound of New England.

THE DEL LORDS

1988

CHEYENNE
Producer: Neil Giraldo
Album: Based on a True Story
Record Label: Enigma
Songwriter: Scott Kempner

The Garage Band sound of New York City.

THE DELL VIKINGS

1957

COME GO WITH ME
Producer: Joe Averbach
Album: Come Go with the Dell Vikings
Record Label: Dot
Songwriter: C. E. Quick

Interracial harmony at its finest; Top-10 R&B/R&R crossover.

WHISPERING BELLS
Producer: Joe Averbach
Album: Come Go with the Dell
  Vikings
Record Label: Dot
Songwriter: C. E. Quick

Their second and last Top-10 R&B/R&R.

DELANEY AND BONNIE
1970

FREE THE PEOPLE
Producer: Delaney Bramlett
Album: To Bonnie from Delaney
Record Label: Atco
Songwriter: Barbara Keith

Folk Gospel sing-along.

1971

NEVER ENDING SONG OF LOVE
Producer: Delaney Bramlett
Album: Motel Shot
Record Label: Atco
Songwriter: Delaney Bramlett

A rustic acoustic favorite.

THE DELFONICS
1968

LA LA LA (MEANS I LOVE YOU)
Producers: Stan Watson, Thom Bell
Album: La La La (Means I Love You)
Record Label: Philly Groove
Songwriters: Thom Bell, William
  Hart

#2 R&B/#4 R&R Philly Soul crossover; their first, and best-selling single.

1970

DIDN'T I (BLOW YOUR MIND THIS TIME)
Producers: Stan Watson, Thom Bell
Album: The Delfonics
Record Label: Philly Groove
Songwriters: Thom Bell, William
  Hart

Defining Philly groove. A Top-10 R&B/R&R crossover.

THE DELLS
1956

OH WHAT A NIGHT
Producer: Bobby Miller
Album: Love Is Blue
Record Label: VeeJay
Songwriters: Marvin Junior, Johnny
  Funches

Their first #1 R&B/Top-10 R&R crossover, re-recorded on Cadet in '69.

1965

STAY IN MY CORNER
Producer: Bobby Miller
Album: There Is
Record Label: Vee-Jay/Cadet
Songwriters: Wade Flemons, Bobby
  Miller, Barrett Strong

Re-recorded version was a #1 R&B/Top-10 R&R crossover (Cadet, '68) and is included on the album.

CAROLE DEMAS AND BARRY BOSTWICK
1972

SUMMER NIGHTS
Album: *Grease* Original Cast Album
Record Label: MGM
Songwriters: Jim Jacobs, Warren
  Casey

A convincingly dumb and innocent summer song, from the musical that brought back the sturm of the '50s, stripped of all its redeeming drang. Covered in the movie version, which stripped even the relatively meager sturm from the questionable concept, by John Travolta and Olivia Newton-John (RSO, '78).

IRIS DEMENT
1994

MY LIFE
Producer: Jim Rooney
Album: My Life
Record Label: Warner Brothers
Songwriter: Iris DeMent

Confessional Folk Rock goes Appalachian.

CATHY DENNIS
1990

C'MON AND GET MY LOVE
Producer: Danny D.
Album: A Little Bit of This, a Little Bit
  of That
Record Label: Polygram
Songwriters: Danny Poku, Cathy
  Dennis

Dance groove.

JUST ANOTHER DREAM
Producer: Danny D.
Album: Move to This
Record Label: Polydor
Songwriters: Cathy Dennis, Danny
  Poku

TOO MANY WALLS
Producer: Danny D.
Album: Move to This
Record Label: Polydor
Songwriters: Cathy Dennis, Anne
  Dudley

SANDY DENNY
1971

CRASH ON THE LEVEE (DOWN IN THE FLOOD)
Producer: Bob Johnston
Album: Northstar Grass Man and the
  Raven
Record Label: A&M
Songwriter: Bob Dylan

Covered by Bob Dylan (Columbia, '72).

1974

SOLO
Producer: Trevor Lucas
Album: Like an Old Fashioned Waltz
Record Label: Island
Songwriter: Sandy Denny

The legendary Folk voice from Fairport Convention; her opening farewell.

JOHN DENVER
1971

TAKE ME HOME, COUNTRY ROAD
Producer: Milt Okun
Album: Poems, Prayers and
  Promises
Record Label: RCA
Songwriters: H. J. Deutschendorf Jr.
  (John Denver), Taffy Nivert, Bill
  Danoff

Chad Mitchell trio leader graduates from Folk to Folk Rock with a rambling classic. Covered by Olivia Newton-John (MCA, '73), Toots and the Maytals (Island, '75).

1973

ROCKY MOUNTAIN HIGH
Producer: Milt Okun
Album: Rocky Mountain High
Record Label: RCA
Songwriters: H. J. Deutschendorf Jr.
  (John Denver), Michael Taylor

Answering "I Am, I Said" with a Midwestern accent.

1974

ANNIE'S SONG
Producer: Milt Okun
Album: Back Home Again
Record Label: RCA

Songwriter: H. J. Deutschendorf Jr.
(John Denver)

Pristine Folk Rock smash dedicated to his then-wife was his second #1 R&R.

BACK HOME AGAIN

Producer: Milt Okun
Album: Back Home Again
Record Label: RCA
Songwriter: H. J. Deutschendorf Jr.
(John Denver)

Returning to a familiar theme for a #1 C&W/Top-5 R&R crossover.

SUNSHINE ON MY SHOULDERS

Producer: Milt Okun
Album: Poems, Prayers and
Promises
Record Label: RCA
Songwriters: H. J. Deutschendorf Jr.
(John Denver), Michael Taylor,
Richard Kniss

His first #1 R&R. Defining the year's sun-drenched, rose-colored Folk Rock motif.

THANK GOD I'M A COUNTRY BOY

Producer: Milt Okun
Album: Back Home Again
Record Label: RCA
Songwriter: John Sommers

#1 C&W/R&R crossover. A hoot.

1975

I'M SORRY

Producer: Milt Okun
Album: Windsong
Record Label: RCA
Songwriter: H. J. Deutschendorf Jr.
(John Denver)

#1 C&W/R&R crossover; his most heartfelt song.

DEPECHE MODE

1981

JUST CAN'T GET ENOUGH

Producers: Daniel Miller, Depeche
Mode
Album: Speak and Spell
Record Label: Sire/Mute
Songwriter: Vince Clarke

Modern dance in the age of the synthesizer; their first U.K. hit.

NEW LIFE

Producers: Daniel Miller, Depeche
Mode
Album: Speak and Spell
Record Label: Sire/Mute

Songwriter: Vince Clarke

Presaging the U.K. synth invasion of the mid-'80s.

1984

PEOPLE ARE PEOPLE

Producers: Depeche Mode, Daniel
Miller
Album: People Are People
Record Label: Sire
Songwriter: Martin Gore

Leading the U.K. Synth invasion of the mid-'80s, with a Top-20 hit.

1985

MASTER AND SERVANT

Producers: Depeche Mode, Daniel
Miller, G. Jones
Album: Some Great Reward
Record Label: Sire
Songwriter: Martin Gore

Dominating the world's dance charts.

1990

ENJOY THE SILENCE

Producers: Depeche Mode, Flood
Album: Violator
Record Label: Sire
Songwriter: Martin Gore

Their fashionable angst achieves its antiseptic peak; their first and only Top-10 hit.

PERSONAL JESUS

Producers: Depeche Mode, Flood
Album: Violator
Record Label: Sire
Songwriter: Martin Gore

POLICY OF TRUTH

Producers: Depeche Mode, Flood
Album: Violator
Record Label: Sire
Songwriter: Martin Gore

DEREK AND THE DOMINOES

1970

BELL BOTTOM BLUES

Producer: Tom Dowd
Album: Layla
Record Label: Atco
Songwriters: Eric Clapton, Derek
and the Dominoes

Easy Blues listening.

WHY DOES LOVE GOT TO BE SO SAD

Producers: Tom Dowd, Derek and
the Dominoes
Album: Layla
Record Label: Atco
Songwriters: Eric Clapton, Bobby
Whitlock

A major Clapton Blues Rock guitar highlight.

LAYLA

Producer: Tom Dowd
Album: Layla
Record Label: Atco
Songwriters: Eric Clapton, Jim
Gordon, Derek and the Dominos

The ultimate guitarists' guitar cut; opened the door for the long-jam style of Southern Rock when it charted in '71 (featuring Duane Allman's blistering sidemanship). The Allman Brothers would dominate FM playlists in '72, when "Layla" returned to the charts, this time peaking in the Top-10. "Bell Bottom Blues," from the same album, would hit the charts in '71 and '73. Much later, and beside the point, Clapton would cover a completely remodeled "Layla" again (Duck, '94).

DES'REE

1994

YOU GOTTA BE

Producers: Ashley Ingram, Des'ree
Album: I Ain't Movin'
Record Label: 550 Music/Epic
Songwriters: Ashley Ingram, Des'ree

Lilting Pop R&B anthem of affirmations.

JACKIE DESHANNON

1963

NEEDLES AND PINS

Producers: Jack Nitzsche, Jackie
DeShannon
Album: Breaking It up on the
Beatles' Tour
Record Label: Liberty
Songwriters: Sonny Bono, Jack
Nitzsche

Anxious epic. Covered by Cher (Imperial, '64) and the Searchers (Pye, '65).

1964

WHEN YOU WALK IN THE ROOM

Producers: Jack Nitzsche, Jackie
DeShannon
Album: Breaking It up on the
Beatles' Tour

Record Label: Liberty
Songwriter: Jackie DeShannon

The essence of Beatle-esque. Covered by the Searchers (Kapp, '64).

1965

WHAT THE WORLD NEEDS NOW IS LOVE

Producers: Burt Bacharach, Hal David
Album: This Is Jackie DeShannon
Record Label: Imperial
Songwriters: Burt Bacharach, Hal David

Jackie does Dionne.

1969

PUT A LITTLE LOVE IN YOUR HEART

Producer: VME
Album: Put a Little Love in Your Heart
Record Label: Imperial
Songwriters: Jimmy Holiday, Randy Myers, Jackie DeShannon

Her biggest hit. Covered by the Circle Jerks (Faulty Products, '82) and Annie Lennox and Al Green in the '88 movie Scrooged.

1972

VANILLA OLAY

Producers: Tom Dowd, Jerry Wexler, Arlf Mardin
Album: Jackie
Record Label: Atlantic
Songwriter: Jackie DeShannon

A woman's coming-of-age saga. Covered by Marianne Faithful (Immediate, '77).

1975

BETTE DAVIS EYES

Album: New Arrangement
Record Label: Columbia
Songwriters: Jackie DeShannon, Donna Weiss

Portrait of a modern she-devil. Cover by Kim Carnes (EMI-America, '81) was the top song of '75—except for "Physical" by Olivia Newton-John—winning Grammys for both Song and Record of the Year.

THE DETERGENTS

1964

LEADER OF THE LAUNDROMAT

Producers: Paul Vance, Lee Pockriss
Album: The Many Faces of the Detergents

Record Label: Roulette
Songwriters: Paul Vance, Lee Pockriss

Parody of "Leader of the Pack" by the Shangri-Las.

DEVO

1978

MONGOLOID

Producer: Brian Eno
Album: Are We Not Men? We Are Devo
Record Label: Warner Brothers
Songwriters: Gerald Casale, Mark Mothersbaugh

Akron assembly-line parodists' post-Punk thesis.

1980

WHIP IT

Producer: Devo
Album: Freedom of Choice
Record Label: Warner Brothers
Songwriters: Mark Mothersbaugh, Gerald Casale

Devo takes on Disco and positive thinking.

1981

THROUGH BEING COOL

Producer: Devo
Album: New Traditionalists
Record Label: Warner Brothers
Songwriters: Mark Mothersbaugh, Bob Mothersbaugh, Gerald Casale

Revenge of the nerds.

DEVONSQUARE

1992

RAINING DOWN ON BLEECKER STREET

Producer: Shane Reisher
Album: If You Could See Me Now
Record Label: Atlantic
Songwriters: Tom Dean, Alana MacDonald, Herb Ludwig

Retro Folk Rock lamenting the end of the bohemian dream. Suggested segue: "Hey, Jack Kerouac" by 10,000 Maniacs, "Cassady" by Bob Weir.

DEXY'S MIDNIGHT RUNNERS

1983

COME ON EILEEN

Producers: Clive Langer, Alan Winstanley

Album: Too-Rye-Ay
Record Label: Mercury
Songwriters: Kevin Rowland, Jim Paterson, Kevin Adams

One-shot #1 U.S./U.K. crossover.

THE DIABLOS

1954

THE WIND

Producers: Jack Brown, DeVora Brown
Record Label: Fortune
Songwriters: Nolan Strong, Quentin Eubank, Willie Hunter, Juan Guiterriez, Bob Edwards

Might be the greatest Doo-Wop performance of all-time, certainly the most chilling. Frankie Lymon was listening. So was cousin Barrett Strong, who went on to a lucrative songwriting career at Motown. But ethereal Nolan disappeared with the wind.

NEIL DIAMOND

1966

CHERRY, CHERRY

Producers: Jeff Barry, Ellie Greenwich
Album: The Feel of Neil Diamond
Record Label: Bang
Songwriter: Neil Diamond

His first big hit; the missing link between the Garys, Lewis and Puckett.

SOLITARY MAN

Producers: Jeff Barry, Ellie Greenwich
Album: The Feel of Neil Diamond
Record Label: Bang
Songwriter: Neil Diamond

Brooding introductory classic by the last of the Brill Building Rock generation. Covered by Chris Isaak (Warner Brothers, '92).

1967

GIRL, YOU'LL BE A WOMAN SOON

Producers: Jeff Barry, Ellie Greenwich
Album: Neil Diamond's Greatest Hits
Record Label: Bang
Songwriter(s): Neil Diamond

Suggested segues: "This Girl Is a Woman Now" by Gary Puckett and the Union Gap, "Younger Girl" by the Lovin' Spoonful, "Don't Stand So Close to Me" by the Police. Covered by Urge Overkill on the Pulp Fiction *Soundtrack (MCA, '94).*

KENTUCKY WOMAN

Producers: Jeff Barry, Ellie Greenwich
Album: Neil Diamond's Greatest Hits
Record Label: Bang
Songwriter: Neil Diamond

Covered by Deep Purple (Tetragrammaton, '68).

RED RED WINE

Producers: Jeff Barry, Ellie Greenwich
Album: Just for You
Record Label: Bang
Songwriter: Neil Diamond

Originally a Top-40 stiff. Cover by UB40 (A&M, '84) was #1 U.K., and #1 U.S. when re-released in '88.

SHILO

Producers: Jeff Barry, Ellie Greenwich
Album: Just for You
Record Label: Bang
Songwriter: Neil Diamond

Neil's in-concert autobiographical favorite.

1969

BROTHER LOVE'S TRAVELING SALVATION SHOW

Producer: Tom Catalano
Album: Brother Love's Traveling Salvation Show
Record Label: Uni
Songwriter: Neil Diamond

The Gospel according to Las Vegas. Suggested segue: "Say Has Anybody Seen My Sweet Gypsy Rose" by Dawn.

HOLLY HOLY

Producer: Tom Catalano
Album: Touching You, Touching Me
Record Label: Uni
Songwriter: Neil Diamond

SWEET CAROLINE

Producer: Tom Catalano
Album: Gold
Record Label: Uni
Songwriter: Neil Diamond

His biggest hit of the '60s.

1970

CRACKLIN' ROSIE

Producer: Tom Catalano
Album: Tap Root Manuscript
Record Label: Uni
Songwriter: Neil Diamond

Pursuing the ghost of Tommy James.

1971

I AM . . . I SAID

Producer: Tom Catalano
Album: Stones
Record Label: Uni
Songwriter: Neil Diamond

Battling his lack of critical esteem, and other mid-century maladies.

1972

SONGS SUNG BLUE

Producer: Tom Catalano
Album: Moods
Record Label: Uni
Songwriter: Neil Diamond

His second of three #1 tunes.

1974

LONGFELLOW SERENADE

Producer: Bob Catalano
Album: Serenade
Record Label: Columbia
Songwriter: Neil Diamond

His last big hit of the '70s, aside from "You Don't Bring Me Flowers," his duet with former Brooklyn neighbor Barbra Streisand (Columbia, '78).

1981

LOVE ON THE ROCKS

Producer: Bob Gaudio
Album: *The Jazz Singer* Soundtrack
Record Label: Capitol
Songwriters: Neil Diamond, Gilbert Becaud

From his magnificently miscast performance as Sir Laurence Olivier's son, the young Al Jolson.

YESTERDAY'S SONGS

Producer: Neil Diamond
Album: On the Way to the Sky
Record Label: Columbia
Songwriter: Neil Diamond

Preparing for the oldies circuit on the grandest possible scale.

THE DIAMONDS

1957

THE STROLL

Producer: David Carroll
Album: Collection of Golden Hits
Record Label: Mercury
Songwriters: Clyde Otis, Nancy Lee

The infamous Canadian Cover Kings sing a Clyde Otis tune. But it was Chuck Willis who was the "King of the Stroll."

DICK AND DEEDEE

1961

THE MOUNTAIN'S HIGH

Producers: Don Rafkine, Wilder Bros.
Album: The Mountain's High
Record Label: Liberty
Songwriter: Dick Gosting

Classic west-coast, white Doo-Wop in the age of surf. The Beach Boys paid attention.

DICTATORS

1975

I LIVE FOR CARS AND GIRLS

Producers: Sandy Pearlman, Murray Krugman
Album: The Dictators Go Girl Crazy
Record Label: Epic
Songwriter: Andy Shernoff

Pre-Glam tongue-in-chic rocker. Pearlman would move on to more fertile pastures with another New York band, Blue Oyster Cult. Soon the Clash would also be on his resume.

TWO TUB MAN

Producers: Sandy Pearlman, Murray Krugman
Album: The Dictators Go Girl Crazy
Record Label: Epic
Songwriter: Andy Shernoff

The New York Dolls redux, only dryer.

BO DIDDLEY

1955

BO DIDDLEY

Producer: Willie Dixon
Album: Bo Diddley's a Twister
Record Label: Checker
Songwriter: Ellas McDaniel (Bo Diddley)

Introducing the beat that would infiltrate the repertoires of a thousand frat-house Rock bands.

DIDDLEY DADDY

Producer: Leonard Chess
Album: Bo Diddley's 16 All-Time Greatest Hits
Record Label: Checker
Songwriter: Ellas McDaniel (Bo Diddley)

Bo knew Blues.

HERE 'TIS

Producer: Willie Dixon
Album: Bo Diddley's a Twister
Record Label: Chess
Songwriter: Ellas McDaniel (Bo Diddley)

Covered by the Yardbirds (Epic, '65).

I'M A MAN

Producer: Leonard Chess
Album: Bo Diddley's 16 All-Time Greatest Hits
Record Label: Checker
Songwriter: Ellas McDaniel (Bo Diddley)

Primordial boasting, covered by the Yardbirds (Epic, '65) in a groundbreaking Heavy Metal rendition.

WHO DO YOU LOVE?

Producer: Willie Dixon
Album: Bo Diddley's a Twister
Record Label: Checker
Songwriter: Ellas McDaniel (Bo Diddley)

Primordial boasting taken to grandiose extremes. Covered by John Hammond Jr., (Vanguard, '63), the Blues Project (MCA, '66), Quicksilver Messenger Service (Capitol, '69), Tom Ruth (Elektra, '71), George Thorogood (MCA, '78), Santana (Columbia, '83), and the Jesus and Mary Chain in the '89 movie Earth Girls Are Easy.

YOU CAN'T JUDGE A BOOK BY LOOKING AT THE COVER

Producer: Willie Dixon
Album: Bo Diddley
Record Label: Chess
Songwriter: Ellas McDaniel (Bo Diddley)

Not merely a man in eternal search of respect, love, and lost royalties, Bo is a down home philosopher of the first rank. This hit the R&B/R&R charts in '62. Covered by Stevie Wonder (Tamla, '70) and Wilson Pickett (Atlantic, '71).

1957

BEFORE YOU ACCUSE ME

Producer: Willie Dixon
Album: Bo Diddley
Record Label: Checker
Songwriter: Ellas McDaniel (Bo Diddley)

Covered by Eric Clapton (Duck, '89).

DIDDEY WAH DIDDEY

Producer: Willie Dixon
Album: Bo Diddley
Record Label: Checker
Songwriters: Ellas McDaniel (Bo Diddley), Willie Dixon

The title phrase has a place in the language of Folk music equaled only by "Guabi Guabi." Covered by Captain Beefheart as his first single (A&M, '66).

HEY BO DIDDLEY

Album: Road Runner
Record Label: Checker
Songwriter: Ellas McDaniel (Bo Diddley)

Classic call and response.

MONA

Record Label: Checker
Songwriter: Ellas McDaniel (Bo Diddley)

Pastoral and provocative neighborhood girl. Covered by the Rolling Stones (London, '64).

1958

PRETTY THING

Producer: Willie Dixon
Album: Bo Diddley
Record Label: Checker
Songwriter: Willie Dixon

1959

CRACKIN' UP

Producer: Leonard Chess
Album: Go Bo Diddley
Record Label: Chess
Songwriter(s): Ellas McDaniel (Bo Diddley)

Covered by the Gants (Liberty, '66).

SAY MAN

Producer: Leonard Chess
Album: Have Guitar Will Travel
Record Label: Checker
Songwriters: Ellas McDaniel (Bo Diddley), Jerome Green

Off-the-cuff studio version of the dozens gave Bo his biggest chart success. Three months later "Say Man Back Again" was a bomb.

DIDJETS

1990

KILLBOY POWERHEAD

Album: Hornet Pinata
Record Label: Touch and Go

Songwriter: Rick Sims

Anarchic Power Metal rant. Covered by Offspring (Epitaph, '94).

DIESEL

1981

SAUSALITO SUMMERNIGHT

Album: Watts in a Tank
Record Label: Regency
Songwriter: Marc Boon Lucian, Robert Vundernik

Middle of the road.

DIGABLE PLANETS

1993

REBIRTH OF SLICK (COOL LIKE DAT)

Producer: Butterfly
Album: Reachin' (a New Refutation of Time and Space)
Record Label: Pendulum
Songwriter: Digable Planets

Establishing a new Jazz Rap fusion.

WHERE I'M FROM

Producer: Butterfly
Album: Reachin' (a New Refutation of Time and Space)
Record Label: Pendulum
Songwriter: Digable Plancts

Be-bop Hip-Hop; the Jazz poetry of the '90s.

DIGITAL UNDERGROUND

1990

THE HUMPTY DANCE

Producer: Shock G.
Album: Sex Packets
Record Label: Tommy Boy
Songwriters: Edward Humphries, Greg Jacobs

Novelty Rap dance groove.

MARK DINNING

1959

TEEN ANGEL

Producer: Jim Vinneau
Album: Teen Angel
Record Label: MGM
Songwriter: Jean Dinning Surrey

Chart-topping weeper, exploiting the somber mood of a generation still mourning their first Rock and Roll casualties.

DINO
1989

I LIKE IT
Album: 24/7
Record Label: 4th & B'way
Songwriter: Dino Esposito
Frankie Avalon Jr.

1990

ROMEO
Producer: Dino
Album: Swingin'
Record Label: Island
Songwriter: Dino Esposito
Teenie ballad.

KENNY DINO
1961

YOUR MA SAID YOU CRIED IN YOUR SLEEP LAST NIGHT
Record Label: Musicor
Songwriters: Steve Schlaks, Robert Glaser
Covered by Robert Plant (Es Peranza, '90).

DINOSAUR JR.
1987

FREAK SCENE
Producer: J. Mascis
Album: Bug
Record Label: SST
Songwriter: Joseph Mascis
Career-establishing classic.

YOU'RE LIVING ALL OVER ME
Producer: J. Mascis
Album: You're Living All over Me
Record Label: SST
Songwriter: Joseph Mascis
Influential Alternative Rock classic ignited a new East-coast bohemian scene including the Lemonheads, Throwing Muses, Sebadoah, et al.

1994

FEEL THE PAIN
Producer: J. Mascis
Album: Without a Sound
Record Label: Sire
Songwriter: Joseph Mascis
Edgy Folk Rock breakthrough to the larger college audience of the '90s.

I DON'T THINK SO
Producer: J. Mascis
Album: Without a Sound

Record Label: Sire
Songwriter: Joseph Mascis
Anti-Folk/Rock à la Paul Westerberg.

DIO
1983

RAINBOW IN THE DARK
Album: Holy Diver
Record Label: Warner Brothers
Songwriters: Ronnie Dio, Vivian Campbell
Arena Metal heroics from a former Elf.

1984

THE LAST IN LINE
Album: Last in Line
Record Label: Warner Brothers
Songwriters: Ronnie Dio, Vivian Campbell
Dio's Metal signature.

DION (AND THE BELMONTS)
1958

I WONDER WHY
Producer: Gene Schwartz
Record Label: Laurie
Songwriters: Ricardo Weeks, Melvin Anderson
Headed by Dion DiMucci, the Elvis of white Doo-Wop, Dion and the Belmonts spawned a uniquely city-bred sound and image: the sensitive tough guy.

NO ONE KNOWS
Producer: Gene Schwartz
Record Label: Laurie
Songwriters: Ken Hecht, Ernie Maresca
A bigger hit than "I Wonder Why," but not as influential; here Dion is more pitiful than cool.

1959

A TEENAGER IN LOVE
Producer: Gene Schwartz
Album: A Teenager in Love
Record Label: Laurie
Songwriters: Doc Pomus, Mort Shuman
His second biggest hit, behind the standard "Where or When."

1960

WHERE OR WHEN
Producer: Gene Schwartz
Album: Dion Sings His Greatest Hits
Record Label: Laurie

Songwriters: Richard Rodgers, Lorenz Hart
A promising Doo-Wop career ends in a predictable pair of standards. This one, from the '37 musical Babes in Arms was the Belmonts' biggest hit. Following it, "When You Wish upon a Star" was a stiff. Dion was well on his way to solo stardom; the Belmonts went back to the corner. They never even played the Copa.

DION
1960

LONELY TEENAGER
Producer: Gene Schwartz
Album: Dion Sings His Greatest Hits
Record Label: Laurie
Songwriters: Salvatore Pippa, Silvio Faraci, Paolo Di Alfred
Describing Dion's condition on his first effort without the Belmonts.

1961

RUNAROUND SUE
Producer: Gene Schwartz
Album: Runaround Sue
Record Label: Laurie
Songwriters: Dion DiMucci, Ernie Maresca
His biggest, and one of his best. He would follow it up with his own answer song, "The Wanderer."

TAKE GOOD CARE OF MY BABY
Producer: Gene Schwartz
Album: Runaround Sue
Record Label: Laurie
Songwriters: Gerry Goffin, Carole King
Cover by Bobby Vee (Liberty, '61) was his biggest hit, a Holly-esque #1.

1962

LITTLE DIANE
Producer: Gene Schwartz
Album: Lovers Who Wander
Record Label: Laurie
Songwriter: Dion DiMucci
Noted for its kazoo solo.

LOVE CAME TO ME
Producer: Gene Schwartz
Album: Dion Sings to Sandy (and All His Other Girls)
Record Label: Laurie
Songwriters: Dion DiMucci John Falbo
In Bobby Darin territory.

LOVERS WHO WANDER

Producer: Gene Schwartz
Album: Lovers Who Wander
Record Label: Laurie
Songwriters: Dion DiMucci, Ernie Maresca

Trying out for Atlantic City, Dion made it as far as Palisades Park.

THE WANDERER

Producer: Gene Schwartz
Album: Runaround Sue
Record Label: Laurie
Songwriter: Ernest Maresca

No longer a teenager, no longer in love; perhaps his most famous number.

1963

DONNA THE PRIMA DONNA

Producer: Robert Mersey
Album: Donna the Prima Donna
Record Label: Columbia
Songwriters: Dion DiMucci, Ernie Maresca

She was no "Runaround Sue."

1968

ABRAHAM MARTIN AND JOHN

Album: Dion
Record Label: Laurie
Songwriter: Dick Holler

Poignant easy listening Top-40 reflection. Covered by Smokey Robinson and the Miracles (Tamla, '69).

1970

YOUR OWN BACK YARD

Record Label: Warner Brothers
Songwriters: Dion DiMucci, Tony Fasce

Dion's soul-baring anti-drug anthem. Covered by Mott the Hoople (Columbia, '74).

1989

KING OF THE NEW YORK STREET

Producer: Dave Edmunds
Album: Yo Frankie
Record Label: Arista
Songwriters: Dion DiMucci, Bill Tuohy

Earning his long-overdue solid gold Spauldeen.

DIRE STRAITS

1979

SULTANS OF SWING

Producer: Muff Winwood
Album: Dire Straits

Record Label: Warner Brothers
Songwriter: Mark Knopfler

Guitar-powered return to the days of Hank Marvin and the Shadows.

1980

ROMEO AND JULIET

Producers: Mark Knopfler, Jimmy Iovine
Album: Making Movies
Record Label: Warner Brothers
Songwriter: Mark Knopfler

Tortured love song. Covered by the Indigo Girls (Epic, '93).

TUNNEL OF LOVE

Producers: Mark Knopfler, Jimmy Iovine
Album: Making Movies
Record Label: Warner Brothers
Songwriter: Mark Knopfler

Knopfler's finest guitar moments.

1985

BROTHERS IN ARMS

Producers: Neil Dorfsman, Mark Knopfler
Album: Brothers in Arms
Record Label: Warner Brothers
Songwriter: Mark Knopfler

Acoustic anthem.

1985

MONEY FOR NOTHING

Producers: Neil Dorfsman, Mark Knopfler
Album: Brothers in Arms
Record Label: Warner Brothers
Songwriters: Mark Knopfler, Gordon Sumner (Sting)

Getting back at MTV for dropping him from the playlist.

1985

WALK OF LIFE

Producers: Neil Dorfsman, Mark Knopfler
Album: Brothers in Arms
Record Label: Warner Brothers
Songwriter: Mark Knopfler

Moving into his soundtrack phase.

1985

WHY WORRY

Producers: Neil Dorfsman, Mark Knopfler
Album: Brothers in Arms
Record Label: Warner Brothers

Songwriter: Mark Knopfler

Unplugged lament. Covered by the Everly Brothers (Mercury, '85).

DISCO TEX AND THE SEX-O-LETTES

1974

GET DANCIN'

Producer: Bob Crewe
Album: Disco Tex and the Sex-o-Lettes
Record Label: Chelsea
Songwriters: Bob Crewe, Kenny Nolan Helfman

The continuing adventures of Monte Rock III, the self-made, self-promoting hairdresser, who wound up with a cameo in Saturday Night Fever.

1975

I WANNA DANCE WIT' CHOO (DOO DAT DANCE) (PART I)

Producer: Bob Crewe
Album: Disco Tex and the Sex-o-Lettes
Record Label: Chelsea
Songwriters: Bob Crewe, Denny Randell

What Disco hath wrought? Or where have you gone Monte Rock III?

DISPOSABLE HEROES OF HIPHOPRISY

1992

LANGUAGE OF VIOLENCE

Album: Hypocrisy Is the Greatest Luxury
Record Label: 4th and Broadway
Songwriters: Michael Franti, Mark Pistel

Dead Kennedys survivors keep on griping.

DIVINYLS

1991

I TOUCH MYSELF

Producers: David Tickle, Divinyls
Album: Divinyls
Record Label: Virgin
Songwriters: Billy Steinberg, Tom Kelly, Christina Amphlett, Mark McEntee

Playful U.S. Top-10 breakthrough for the Australian Punk band. Suggested segues: "She Bop" by Cyndi Lauper and "Secret" by Madonna.

THE DIXIE CUPS

1964

CHAPEL OF LOVE

Producers: Jerry Leiber, Mike Stoller, Jeff Barry
Album: Chapel of Love
Record Label: Red Bird
Songwriters: Jeff Barry, Ellie Greenwich, Phil Spector

Grasping the last Brill Building sure thing: girl-group innocence and wedded bliss.

1965

IKO IKO

Producers: Jerry Leiber, Mike Stoller
Album: Chapel of Love
Record Label: Red Bird
Songwriters: Marylin Jones, Sharon Jones, Joe Jones, Jessie Thomas

The voice of New Orleans, undimmed by era. Featured in the soundtrack for The Big Easy *(Antilles, '87) and* Rain Man *(Capitol, '89).*

THE DIXIE DREGS

1980

TWIGGS APPROVED

Album: Dregs of the Earth
Record Label: Arista
Songwriter: Steve Morse

Progressive Southern Rock guitar classic.

THE DIXIEBELLES

1963

(DOWN AT) POPPA JOE'S

Producer: Bill Justis
Album: Down at Poppa Joe's
Record Label: Sound Stage 7
Songwriter: Jerry Dean Smith

Shindig south of "Sugar Shack."

CARL DOBKINS JR.

1957

MY HEART IS AN OPEN BOOK

Album: Carl Dobkins Jr.
Record Label: Decca
Songwriters: Lee Pockriss, Hal David

The essence of Pat Boone-inspired Pop Rock. David Gates may have already been tuned in on his first transistor radio.

BONNIE DOBSON

1964

MORNING DEW

Album: Bonnie Dodson
Record Label: RCA
Songwriters: Bonnie Dobson, Tim Rose

Anti-war, post-bomb standard. Covered by the Grateful Dead (Warner Brothers, '67); Lulu (Epic, '68), and the Jeff Beck Group (Epic, '68).

SNOOP DOGGY DOGG

1993

GIN AND JUICE

Producer: Dr. Dre
Album: Doggy Style
Record Label: Death Row/Interscope
Songwriter: Calvin Broadus (Snoop Doggy Dogg)

Verbal ghetto riff of the year.

WHAT'S MY NAME?

Producer: Dr. Dre
Album: Doggy Style
Record Label: Death Row/Interscope
Songwriter: Calvin Broadus (Snoop Doggy Dogg)

Gangsta Rap personified, with a rap sheet to boot.

1995

MURDER WAS THE CASE

Producer: Dr. Dre
Album: Murder Was the Case
Record Label: Death Row/Interscope
Songwriters: Calvin Broadus (Snoop Doggy Dogg), Andre Young (Dr. Dre), Delmic Arnaud (Dat Nigga Daz), Warren Griffin (Warren G.)

Gangsta Rap, the movie; answering Michael Jackson's "Thriller" a decade later.

BILL DOGGETT

1956

HONKY TONK

Producer: Henry Glover
Record Label: King
Songwriters: Henry Glover, Bill Doggett, Billy Butler, Shape Sheppard, Clifford Scott

#1 R&B/#2 R&R sax instrumental crossover.

DOKKEN

1987

MR. SCARY

Producer: Neil Kirwin
Album: Back for the Attack
Record Label: Elektra
Songwriter: George Lynch

Massive guitar solo from L.A. virtuouso George Lynch.

THOMAS DOLBY

1983

SHE BLINDED ME WITH SCIENCE

Producers: Thomas Dolby, Tim Greene
Album: Blinded by Science
Record Label: Capitol
Songwriters: Thomas Dolby, Joe Kerr

Synth Rock with a pen-holder, defining the year's British Techno invasion.

DOMINO

1993

GHETTO JAM

Producer: D. J. Battlecat
Album: Domino
Record Label: RAL/Chaos
Songwriters: Kevin Gilliam, Domino

Gangsta Rap for Sunday morning confession.

FATS DOMINO

1950

THE FAT MAN

Producer: Dave Bartholomew
Album: Rock and Rollin' with Fats Domino
Record Label: Imperial
Songwriter: Dave Bartholomew

Influenced by Amos Milburn, the Fat Man arrives upon the scene in New Orleans, with his first R&B hit.

1952

GOIN' HOME

Producer: Dave Bartholomew
Album: Rock and Rollin' with Fats Domino
Record Label: Imperial
Songwriters: Fats Domino, Alvin Young

His first #1 R&B song.

1953

GOIN' TO THE RIVER
Producer: Dave Bartholomew
Album: Rock and Rollin' with Fats Domino
Record Label: Imperial
Songwriters: Dave Bartholmew, Fats Domino

The biggest R&B hit of '53.

1955

AIN'T IT A SHAME
Producer: Dave Bartholomew
Album: Rock and Rollin' with Fats Domino
Record Label: Imperial
Songwriters: Fats Domino, Dave Bartholomew

Domino's first crossover hit, after eleven R&B hits in five years; gentleman crooner Pat Boone had the bigger cover (Dot, '55). For the next two years, Fats' tunes would spend a total of 153 weeks on the R&B charts (41 at #1).

1956

BLUEBERRY HILL
Producer: Dave Bartholomew
Album: This Is Fats Domino
Record Label: Imperial
Songwriters: Al Lewis, Larry Stock, Vincent Rose

Fats' Pop breakthrough after twenty R&B hits; #1 R&B/#2 R&R. Initially a cowboy song, popularized by Gene Autry in the '41 movie The Singing Hills.

I'M IN LOVE AGAIN
Producer: Dave Bartholomew
Album: Rock and Rollin' with Fats Domino
Record Label: Imperial
Songwriters: Fats Domino, Dave Bartholomew

Having opened the commercial door with "Blueberry Hill," Fats took up semi-permanent residence on the Top-10, starting with this sashaying original. Covered by Ricky Nelson (Imperial, '58).

1957

BLUE MONDAY
Producer: Dave Bartholomew
Album: This Is Fats Domino
Record Label: Imperial
Songwriters: Fats Domino, Dave Bartholomew

From the motion picture The Girl Can't Help It, his fifth #1 R&B, fourth Top-10 R&R crossover.

I'M WALKIN'
Producer: Dave Bartholomew
Album: Here Stands Fats Domino
Record Label: Imperial
Songwriters: Fats Domino, Dave Bartholomew

Third straight #1 R&B/Top-10 R&R crossover for Fats, completing an incredible run of five months at #1 on the R&B charts. Covered by Rick Nelson (Imperial, '57), who went Top-10 R&R.

1958

THE BIG BEAT
Producer: Dave Bartholomew
Record Label: Imperial
Songwriters: Fats Domino, Dave Bartholomew

Title song of the film, co-starring Gogi Grant.

WHOLE LOTTA LOVING
Producer: Dave Bartholomew
Record Label: Imperial
Songwriters: Fats Domino, Dave Bartholomew

Prime Fats in his prime, Top-10 R&B/Top-10 R&R crossover.

1959

BE MY GUEST
Producer: Dave Bartholomew
Record Label: Imperial
Songwriters: Fats Domino, Tommy Boyce, John Marascalco

I WANT TO WALK YOU HOME
Producer: Dave Bartholomew
Album: Fats Domino Sings Million Record Hits
Record Label: Imperial
Songwriter: Fats Domino

His seventh and last #1 R&B, his ninth Top-10 R&R.

I'M GONNA BE A WHEEL SOMEDAY
Producer: Dave Bartholomew
Album: Let's Play Fats Domino
Record Label: Imperial
Songwriters: Fats Domino, Dave Bartholomew

B-side of "I Want to Walk You Home."

I'M READY
Producer: Dave Bartholomew
Album: Fats Domino Sings Million Record Hits
Record Label: Imperial
Songwriters: Fats Domino, Al Lewis, Sylvester Bradford

Fats rocks.

1960

WALKING TO NEW ORLEANS
Producer: Dave Bartholomew
Album: Million Sellers by Fats
Record Label: Imperial
Songwriters: Fats Domino, Dave Bartholomew, Robert Guidry (Sonny Charles)

Capitalizing on the attention drawn to his rockin' headquarters that year, Fats has his last and biggest hit of the '60s.

THE DOMINOES

1951

SIXTY MINUTE MAN
Producer: Ralph Bass
Record Label: Federal
Songwriters: Billy Ward, Rose Marks

The advent of Lovin' Dan, the first black man to cross over to the white charts, where he spent a full sixty minutes in the bedrooms of the middle class, thereby changing the sexual rhythms of popular music forever.

1952

HAVE MERCY BABY
Record Label: Federal
Songwriter: Billy Ward

From the stars of Alan Freed's early ground-breaking Cleveland soirees, this #1 R&B hit was the biggest of '52, kicking off a decade of Disco mania, culminating in the gyrations of "At the Hop" in '58 and "The Twist," '60–'62, which launched the first interracial dance craze of the Postwar era. Covered by James Brown (King, '65).

DON AND DEWEY

1957

I'M LEAVING IT UP TO YOU
Producer: Sonny Bono
Album: Jungle Hop
Record Label: Specialty
Songwriters: Don Harris, Dewey Terry

Important R&B songwriting/performing duo who never hit the charts, but influenced some other legendary duos, like the Righteous Brothers, and Sam and Dave; and some others that were not so legendary, like Dale and Grace, who turned this into a #1 hit (Montel, '63). Tune actually hit number one the week JFK was assassinated, while Dale and Grace were on tour in Dallas. Covered by the Righteous Brothers (Verve, '66); producer Bono's duo Sonny and Cher (Atco, '66), Linda Ronstadt (Capitol, '70), Donny and Marie Osmond (MGM, '74).

1958

JUSTINE
Producer: Art Rupe
Album: Jungle Hop
Record Label: Specialty
Songwriters: Don Harris, Dewey Terry

More in their classic Rock and Roll duo style. Covered by the Righteous Brothers (Moonglow, '65) and in the film A Swingin' Summer, *with Raquel Welch.*

KOKO JOE
Producer: Sonny Bono
Album: Jungle Hop
Record Label: Specialty
Songwriter: Sonny Bono

Sonny in his pre-Spector, pre-Cher mode.

THE LETTER
Producer: Sonny Bono
Record Label: Specialty
Songwriters: Don Harris, Dewey Terry

Covered by Sonny and Cher (aka Caesar and Cleo), as their first single (Vault, '65).

1959

BIG BOY PETE
Producer: Harold Battiste
Album: Jungle Hop
Record Label: Specialty
Songwriters: Don Harris, Dewey Terry

Covered by the Olympics (Arvee, '60); Top-10 R&B/R&R crossover.

FARMER JOHN
Producer: Harold Battiste
Album: Jungle Hop
Record Label: Specialty
Songwriters: Don Harris, Dewey Terry

Covered by the Premiers (Warner Brothers, '64).

DON AND JUAN
1961

WHAT'S YOUR NAME?
Record Label: Big Top
Songwriter: Claude Johnson

Popping the existential Doo-Wop question.

BO DONALDSON AND THE HEYWOODS
1974

BILLY, DON'T BE A HERO
Producer: Steve Barri
Album: Bo Donaldson and the Heywoods
Record Label: ABC
Songwriters: Peter Callendar, Mitch Murray

Anti-war ditty was a trans-Atlantic #1 crossover; U.K. version was by Paper Lace (Bus Stop, '74), whose U.S. release on Mercury stiffed.

ERIC DONALDSON
1971

CHERRY OH BABY
Producers: Tommy Cowan, Bunny Lee
Record Label: Trojan
Songwriter: Eric Donaldson

Reggae classic, covered by the Rolling Stones (Rolling Stones, '76) and UB40 (A&M, '83).

THE DONAYS
1962

DEVIL IN HIS HEART
Record Label: Brent
Songwriter: Richard Drapkin

Classic girl-group obscurity, covered by the Beatles (Capitol, '65).

LONNIE DONEGAN
1959

DOES YOUR CHEWING GUM LOSE ITS FLAVOR ON THE BEDPOST OVERNIGHT?
Record Label: Dot
Songwriters: Billy Rose, Marty Bloom, Ernest Breuer

Pre-Beatles England skiffle standard, originated by Harry Richman in '24.

JAMIE DONNELLY
1974

SCIENCE FICTION DOUBLE FEATURE
Album: *The Rocky Horror Picture Show* Cast Album
Record Label: Ode
Songwriter: Richard O'Brien

From the cult musical that became a midnight cult film. Over the film's opening credits.

RAL DONNER
1961

YOU DON'T KNOW WHAT YOU'VE GOT
Record Label: Gone
Songwriters: Paul Hampton, George Burton

Formulaic but inspired Elvis imitation was his biggest hit.

DONOVAN
1965

CATCH THE WIND
Producer: Steve Hoffman
Album: Catch the Wind
Record Label: Hickory
Songwriter: Donovan Leitch

Gossamer Folk Rock, covered by the Blues Project at their most gossamer (Verve/Folkways, '66).

SEASON OF THE WITCH
Producer: Steve Hoffman
Album: Catch the Wind
Record Label: Hickory
Songwriter: Donovan Leitch

The other side of Donovan, nearly Zombie-esque. Covered by Al Kooper (Columbia, '68) and Vanilla Fudge (Atco, '68).

SUNNY GOODGE STREET
Album: Fairy Tales
Record Label: Hickory
Songwriter: Donovan Leitch

Fey travelogue. Covered by Judy Collins (Elektra, '67).

TO SING FOR YOU
Producer: Steve Hoffman
Album: Catch the Wind
Record Label: Hickory
Songwriter: Donovan Leitch

Introducing "the English Dylan" to Bob, his audience and entourage, in the classic documentary Don't Look Back; *with this song, Donovan joins Tommy Sands on "The Les Crane Show," and the reporter from* Time, *in the movie, as another Dylan media victim.*

1966

MELLOW YELLOW
Producer: Mickie Most
Album: Mellow Yellow
Record Label: Epic
Songwriter: Donovan Leitch
Instigating a brief banana-smoking craze.

SUNSHINE SUPERMAN
Producer: Mickie Most
Album: Sunshine Superman
Record Label: Epic
Songwriter: Donovan Leitch
Often considered a druggy ode. His only #1.

TURQUOISE
Producer: Mickie Most
Album: Real Donovan
Record Label: Hickory
Songwriter: Donovan Leitch
Suggested segue: "Mama You Been on My Mind" by Bob Dylan. Covered by Joan Baez (Vanguard, '67).

1967

THERE IS A MOUNTAIN
Producer: Mickie Most
Album: Donovan in Concert
Record Label: Epic
Songwriter: Donovan Leitch
Pop mysticism.

WEAR YOUR LOVE LIKE HEAVEN
Producer: Mickie Most
Album: Gift from a Flower to a Garden
Record Label: Epic
Songwriter: Donovan Leitch
In which Donovan becomes the original flower child; Melanie was listening.

1968

HURDY GURDY MAN
Producer: Mickie Most
Album: Hurdy Gurdy Man
Record Label: Epic
Songwriter: Donovan Leitch
Practicing for Kiddie Rock.

1969

ATLANTIS
Producer: Mickie Most
Album: Barabajagal
Record Label: Epic
Songwriter: Donovan Leitch
Typical other-worldly Folk Rock from the crown prince of the genre.

DICKEY DOO AND THE DON'TS

1959

TEARDROPS WILL FALL
Record Label: Swan
Songwriters: Marion Smith, Dickey Doo
Rescued from terminal obscurity by Ry Cooder (Reprise, '72).

THE DOOBIE BROTHERS, JOHN HALL AND JAMES TAYLOR

1979

POWER
Producer: John Hall
Album: No Nukes
Record Label: Asylum
Songwriters: John J. Hall, Johanna Hall
Anti-nuke Folk Rock.

THE DOOBIE BROTHERS

1972

LISTEN TO THE MUSIC
Producer: Ted Templeman
Album: Talouse Street
Record Label: Warner Brothers
Songwriter: Tom Johnston
The advent of Southern Folk Rock, by way of San Jose, CA.

1973

CHINA GROVE
Producer: Ted Templeman
Album: What Were Once Vices Are Now Habits
Record Label: Warner Brothers
Songwriter: Tom Johnston
Pastoral Arena Rock: call it ballpark Metal.

LONG TRAIN RUNNING
Producer: Ted Templeman
Album: The Captain and Me
Record Label: Warner Brothers

Songwriter: Tom Johnston
Progressive FM perennial.

1974

BLACK WATER
Producer: Ted Templeman
Album: What Were Once Vices Are Now Habits
Record Label: Warner Brothers
Songwriter: Pat Simmons
B-side of "Another Park, Another Sunday" was their biggest hit. Suggested Mississippi River segue: "Proud Mary" by Creedence Clearwater Revival.

1976

TAKIN' IT TO THE STREETS
Producer: Ted Templeman
Album: Takin' It to the Streets
Record Label: Warner Brothers
Songwriter: Michael McDonald
Suggested segue: "Street Fighting Man" by the Rolling Stones.

1977

ECHOES OF LOVE
Producer: Ted Templeman
Album: Livin' on the Fault Line
Record Label: Warner Brothers
Songwriters: Willie Mitchell, Earl Randle, Pat Simmons
Their ineffable essay on classic neo Doo-Wop. Covered by the Pointer Sisters (Planet, '78).

YOU BELONG TO ME
Producer: Ted Templeman
Album: Livin' on the Fault Line
Record Label: Warner Brothers
Songwriters: Michael McDonald, Carly Simon
Their single stiffed, but Carly's cover was Top-10 R&R (Elektra, '78).

1978

MINUTE BY MINUTE
Producer: Ted Templeman
Album: Minute by Minute
Record Label: Warner Brothers
Songwriters: Michael McDonald, Lester Abrams
Mainstay of the mellow McDonald era.

1979

WHAT A FOOL BELIEVES
Producer: Ted Templeman
Album: Minute by Minute
Record Label: Warner Brothers

Songwriters: Michael McDonald, Kenny Loggins

A double dose of mellow; double Grammy winner.

1980

REAL LOVE

Producer: Ted Templeman
Album: One Step Closer
Record Label: Warner Brothers
Songwriters: Michael McDonald, Patrick Henderson

1989

THE DOCTOR

Producers: Charlie Midnight, Eddie Schwartz
Album: Cycles
Record Label: Capitol
Songwriters: Tom Johnston, Charlie Midnight, Eddie Schwartz

After a decade off, just what the doctor ordered, a hit single.

THE DOORS

1967

20TH CENTURY FOX

Producer: Paul Rothchild
Album: The Doors
Record Label: Elektra
Songwriters: Jim Morrison, Ray Manzarek

Film students, a decade before MTV, move over to the then more relevant generational art form of the moment—the Rock and Roll album cut.

BREAK ON THROUGH

Producer: Paul Rothchild
Album: Strange Days
Record Label: Elektra
Songwriters: Jim Morrison, Robbie Krieger, John Densmore

Their first single, inspired by Aldous "Doors of Perception" Huxley, an organ propelled rush.

CRYSTAL SHIP

Producer: Paul Rothchild
Album: Strange Days
Record Label: Elektra
Songwriters: Jim Morrison, Robbie Krieger, John Densmore

B-side of "Light My Fire," a comparatively tranquil ride.

THE END

Producer: Paul Rothchild
Album: The Doors
Record Label: Elektra
Songwriters: Jim Morrison, Robbie Krieger, John Densmore, Ray Manzarek

Morrisonian epic centerpiece: contorted, disturbed, and disturbing poetics. Remixed for use in the film and soundtrack Apocalypse Now *(Elektra, '79).*

LIGHT MY FIRE

Producer: Paul Rothchild
Album: The Doors
Record Label: Elektra
Songwriters: Jim Morrison, Robbie Krieger, John Densmore, Ray Manzarek

Igniting the summer of love with Manzarek's organ pyrotechnics, Morrison chewing the scenery. Covered by Jose Feliciano (RCA, '68).

LOVE ME TWO TIMES

Producer: Paul Rothchild
Album: Strange Days
Record Label: Elektra
Songwriters: Jim Morrison, Robbie Krieger, John Densmore, Ray Manzarek

Frat Rock sentiments, fraught with Hollywood angst.

MOONLIGHT DRIVE

Producer: Paul Rothchild
Album: Strange Days
Record Label: Elektra
Songwriters: Jim Morrison, Robbie Krieger, John Densmore

B-side of "Love Me Two Times." Loopy lunar guitar by Krieger.

PEOPLE ARE STRANGE

Producer: Paul Rothchild
Album: Strange Days
Record Label: Elektra
Songwriters: Jim Morrison, Robbie Krieger, John Densmore, Ray Manzarek

Chart-ready alienation.

WHEN THE MUSIC'S OVER

Producer: Paul Rothchild
Album: Strange Days
Record Label: Elektra
Songwriters: Jim Morrison, Robbie Krieger, John Densmore

Another stentorian tone poem that left nothing on the cutting room floor.

1968

FIVE TO ONE

Producer: Paul Rothchild
Album: Waiting for the Sun
Record Label: Elektra
Songwriters: Jim Morrison, Robbie Krieger, John Densmore, Ray Manzarek

Their best bar-room rocker.

HELLO, I LOVE YOU

Producer: Paul Rothchild
Album: Waiting for the Sun
Record Label: Elektra
Songwriters: Jim Morrison, Robbie Krieger, John Densmore, Ray Manzarek

At their teeny boppiest.

UNKNOWN SOLDIER

Producer: Paul Rothchild
Album: Waiting for the Sun
Record Label: Elektra
Songwriters: Jim Morrison, Robbie Krieger, John Densmore, Ray Manzarek

Opus from the poet manqué.

1969

TOUCH ME

Producer: Paul Rothchild
Album: The Soft Parade
Record Label: Elektra
Songwriters: Jim Morrison, Robbie Krieger, John Densmore, Ray Manzarek

Their last visit to the Top-10.

WISHFUL, SINFUL

Producer: Paul Rothchild
Album: The Soft Parade
Record Label: Elektra
Songwriters: Jim Morrison, Robbie Krieger, John Densmore, Ray Manzarek

Follow up to "Touch Me" didn't even make Top-40. But the wishful, sinful Morrison got plenty of press nonetheless, most of it for allegedly taking his song "Touch Me" far too literally (and literally too far).

1970

ROADHOUSE BLUES

Producer: Paul Rothchild
Album: Morrison Hotel/Hard Rock Cafe
Record Label: Elektra

Songwriters: Jim Morrison, Robbie Krieger, John Densmore, Ray Manzarek

From whence emerged the prophetic: No one here gets out alive.

1971

L.A. WOMAN
Producer: Paul Rothchild
Album: L.A. Woman
Record Label: Elektra
Songwriters: Jim Morrison, Robbie Krieger, John Densmore, Ray Manzarek

LOVE HER MADLY
Producer: Paul Rothchild
Album: L.A. Woman
Record Label: Elektra
Songwriters: Robbie Krieger, Ray Manzarek, John Densmore

RIDERS ON THE STORM
Producer: Paul Rothchild
Album: L.A. Woman
Record Label: Elektra
Songwriters: Jim Morrison, Robbie Krieger, John Densmore, Ray Manzarek

Riding the storm to the end of the line. Song peaked on the charts a month after Morrison's death in Paris. But the Doors' catalogue would sell steadily for the next twenty years.

HAROLD DORMAN
1960

MOUNTAIN OF LOVE
Producer: Roland James
Record Label: Rita
Songwriter: Harold Dorman

Covered by Johnny Rivers (Imperial, '64)

LEE DORSEY
1961

YA YA
Producer: Allen Toussaint
Album: Ya Ya
Record Label: Fury
Songwriters: Lee Dorsey, Morgan Robinson, Clarence Lewis

Easy New Orleans listening #1 R&B/Top-10 R&R crossover.

1965

GET OUT OF MY LIFE WOMAN
Producer: Allen Toussaint
Album: The New Lee Dorsey

Record Label: Amy
Songwriter: Allen Toussaint

Not so mellow any more.

HOLY COW
Producer: Allen Toussaint
Album: The New Lee Dorsey
Record Label: Amy
Songwriter: Allen Toussaint

RIDE YOUR PONY
Producer: Allen Toussaint
Album: The New Lee Dorsey
Record Label: Amy
Songwriter: Allen Toussaint (Naomi Neville)

New Orleans meets Soul.

WORKING IN THE COAL MINE
Producer: Allen Toussaint
Album: The New Lee Dorsey
Record Label: Amy
Songwriter: Allen Toussaint

His biggest international hit.

DOUBLE DEE AND STEINSKI
1985

THE PAYOFF MIX
Producers: Double Dee, Steinski
Album: The Payoff Mix/Lesson Two/Lesson 3
Record Label: Tommy Boy
Songwriters: Various

Subtitled: Mastermix of G.L.O.B.E. and Whiz Kid's "Play That Beat Mr. DJ," an ingenious cult classic of the splice and dice school of DJ multi-media art for the junk culture generation.

CARL DOUGLAS
1974

KUNG FU FIGHTING
Producer: Biddu
Album: Kung Fu Fighting and Other Great Love Songs
Record Label: 20th Century
Songwriter: Carl Douglas

Topical kick dance number; #1 R&B/R&R/U.K.

THE DOVELLS
1961

THE BRISTOL STOMP
Album: The Bristol Stomp
Record Label: Parkway

Songwriter: Dave Appell

Another twist in the continuing saga of the baby boom's first dance craze. Before it was through, a solid couple of years of this groove would all but shake out the remaining original R&B pioneers, paving the way for a new jangly guitar sound and white hope to replace Elvis Presley, called the Beatles.

1962

DOIN' THE NEW CONTINENTAL
Album: Don't Knock the Twist Soundtrack
Record Label: Parkway
Songwriters: Kal Mann, Bernie Lowe

Nifty, but no Twist.

LAMONT DOZIER
1974

TRYING TO HOLD ON TO MY WOMAN
Album: Out Here on My Own
Record Label: ABC
Songwriters: McKinley Jackson, James Reddick

Sprung from the Motown confines of the Holland Brothers, Dozier returns to his singing roots.

DR. BUZZARD'S ORIGINAL SAVANNAH BAND
1976

I'LL PLAY THE FOOL
Producer: Tommy Motolla
Album: Dr. Buzzard's Original Savannah Band
Record Label: RCA
Songwriters: August Darnell, Jerry Seleen

Big R&B hit.

WHISPERING/CHERCHEZ LA FEMME/C'EST SI BON
Producer: Tommy Motolla
Album: Dr. Buzzard's Original Savannah Band
Record Label: RCA
Songwriters: John Schonberger, Richard Coburn, Vincent Rose, August Darnell, Stoney Browder Jr., Henri Betti, Andy Horvez, Jerry Seleen.

Topical Disco medley. Motolla would go on to become president of Columbia records. Darnell would go on to become Kid Creole.

DR. DRE

1992

DRE DAY
Producer: Dr. Dre
Album: The Chronic
Record Label: Death Row
Songwriters: Andre Young (Dr. Dre), Calvin Broadus (Snoop Doggy Dogg), Colin Wolfe

Defining urban culture in the '90s.

1993

LET ME RIDE
Producer: Dr. Dre
Album: The Chronic
Record Label: Death Row
Songwriters: Andre Young (Dr. Dre), Calvin Broadus (Snoop Doggy Dogg)

A trip to the bad neighborhood, but safe enough for good kids to enjoy (on record, at least).

NUTHIN' BUT A "G" THANG
Producer: Dr. Dre
Album: The Chronic
Record Label: Death Row
Songwriter: Calvin Broadus (Snoop Doggy Dogg)

Evoking a furor reminiscent of "Annie Had a Baby" and other early pre-Rock and Roll classics of R&B three decades before, this updated version of life in the '90s ghetto came under attack from all manner of definers and defenders of traditional morality and manners.

DR. HOOK

1972

SYLVIA'S MOTHER
Producer: Ron Haffkine
Album: Dr. Hook and the Medicine Show
Record Label: Columbia
Songwriter: Shel Silverstein

Playboy magazine's best songwriting cartoonist finds a Pop Folk Rock group with similar sensibilities. Their biggest hit, and among their straighter efforts.

1973

THE COVER OF ROLLING STONE
Producer: Ron Haffkine
Album: Sloppy Seconds
Record Label: Columbia
Songwriter: Shel Silverstein

Poking fun at the careerist lust that dominated the mid-'70s Rock and Roll business, written by someone who knew a thing or two about lust.

1978

SHARING THE NIGHT TOGETHER
Producer: Ron Haffkine
Album: Pleasure and Pain
Record Label: Capitol
Songwriters: Ava Alderidge, Edward Struzick

Suggested segues: "Let's Spend the Night Together" by the Rolling Stones, "Wouldn't It Be Nice" by the Beach Boys, and "Flower" by Liz Phair.

1979

SEXY EYES
Producer: Ron Haffkine
Album: Sometimes You Win
Record Label: Capitol
Songwriters: Christopher Dunn, Robert Mather, Keith Stegall

WHEN YOU'RE IN LOVE WITH A BEAUTIFUL WOMAN
Producer: Ron Haffkine
Album: Pleasure and Pain
Record Label: Capitol
Songwriter: Even Stevens

#1 U.K. Suggested segue: "If You Wanna Be Happy" by Jimmy Soul.

DR. JOHN

1968

WALK ON GILDED SPLINTERS
Album: Gris Gris
Record Label: Atlantic
Songwriter: Mac Rebennack

Psychedelic parody from the debut album of the quintessential New Orleans Soul/Groove/gris gris/session man, Dr. John, aka Mac Rebennack. Covered in a masterful guitar performance by Duane Allman (Capricorn, '72).

1973

RIGHT PLACE WRONG TIME
Producer: Allen Toussaint
Album: In the Right Place
Record Label: Atco
Songwriter: Mac Rebennack

Fronting the classic New Orleans house band, the Meters.

DR. WEST'S MEDICINE SHOW AND JUNK BAND

1966

THE EGG PLANT (THAT ATE CHICAGO)
Producer: T. Mazer
Record Label: GoGo
Songwriter: Norman Greenbaum

Not to be confused with "The Night Chicago Died" by Paper Lace. Greenbaum would recover to write "Spirit in the Sky."

NICK DRAKE

1969

WAY TO BLUE
Producer: Joe Boyd
Album: Five Leaves Left
Record Label: Hannibal
Songwriter: Nick Drake

Big track from the quintessentially depressive English singer/songwriter.

DRAMARAMA

1989

LAST CIGARETTE
Album: Stuck in Wonderamaland
Record Label: Chameleon
Songwriter: Jon Easdale

In the midst of modernism a Rock and Roll voice that harkened back to the Stones and the NY Dolls.

1993

WORK FOR FOOD
Producers: Chris Carter, Jon Easdale
Album: Hi-Fi Sci-Fi
Record Label: Chameleon
Songwriter: Jon Easdale

Ultimate statement of artistic purpose; a rollicking Rock and Roll alternative to Grunge despair.

THE DRAMATICS

1971

IN THE RAIN
Producer: Tony Hester
Album: Whatcha See Is What You Get
Record Label: Volt
Songwriter: Tony Hester

Lush and evocative #1 R&B/Top-10 R&R crossover.

WHATCHA SEE IS WHAT YOU GET
Producer: Tony Hester
Album: Whatcha See Is What You Get
Record Label: Volt
Songwriter: Tony Hester
Capitalizing on current slang.

RUSTY DRAPER
1957

FREIGHT TRAIN
Record Label: Mercury
Songwriter: Elizabeth Cotten
Classic folktune, originated by Elizabeth Cotton at the turn of the century and recorded by her (Folkways, '58).

THE DREAM ACADEMY
1985

LIFE IN A NORTHERN TOWN
Producers: Nick Laird-Clowes, David Gilmour, George Nicholson
Album: The Dream Academy
Record Label: Warner Brothers
Songwriters: Nick Laird-Clowes, Gilbert Gabriel
Lulling Folk Rock pastorale.

DREAM SYNDICATE
1988

LOVING THE SINNER, HATING THE SIN
Producer: Elliot Mazur
Album: Ghost Stories
Record Label: Enigma
Songwriter: Steve Wynn
Edgy West-coast paisley classic.

THE DREAMLOVERS
1961

WHEN WE GET MARRIED
Album: The Bird and Other Golden Dancing Grooves
Record Label: Heritage
Songwriter: Donald Hogan
Doo-Wop from Philly.

THE DRIFTERS
1953

MONEY HONEY
Producers: Ahmet Ertegun, Jerry Wexler
Record Label: Atlantic
Songwriter: Jesse Stone (Charles Calhoun)

The first virtual R&B supersession of the Rock era: kingpin producers (Wexler and Ertegun), writer (the prolific Stone, also known as Charles Calhoun), artist (McPhatter, with his new band after leaving the Dominos) and subject matter. The result, the #1 R&B hit of '53. Covered by Ella Mae Morse (Capitol, '54).

WHATCHA GONNA DO
Producers: Ahmet Ertegun, Jerry Wexler
Album: Their Greatest Recordings— The Early Years
Record Label: Atlantic
Songwriter: Ahmet Ertegun
Their last hit with Clyde McPhatter as lead singer. Suggested segues: "The Twist," by Hank Ballard and/or Chubby Checker.

1954

HONEY LOVE
Producers: Ahmet Ertegun, Jerry Wexler
Record Label: Atlantic
Songwriters: Clyde McPhatter, J. Gerald
#1 R&B despite (or because of) being banned around the country for suggestive lyrics.

SUCH A NIGHT
Producers: Ahmet Ertegun, Jerry Wexler
Record Label: Atlantic
Songwriter: Lincoln Chase
Another tune that sparked record burning and witch hunts among the populace when it was released. Covered by Johnny Ray (Columbia, '54) and Elvis Presley (RCA, '60).

1955

ADORABLE
Producer: Neshui Ertegun
Record Label: Atlantic
Songwriter: Buck Ram
Easing the transition from Doo-Wop to R&B with a lilting ballad. Ram would perfect this niche with the Platters.

WHITE CHRISTMAS
Producers: Ahmet Ertegun, Jerry Wexler
Record Label: Atlantic
Songwriter: Irving Berlin
As reviled as they may have been by the high-minded members of black and white society, the Drifters' transcendently poignant version of this American classic was one of the best it has yet received.

1956

RUBY BABY
Producer: Neshui Ertegun
Album: Rockin' and Driftin'
Record Label: Atlantic
Songwriters: Jerry Leiber, Mike Stoller
Covered by Dion (Columbia, '63).

1957

HYPNOTIZED
Record Label: Atlantic
Songwriters: Terry Noland, Norman Petty
Originated by Noland, whose version of the tune was never released.

1958

DRIP DROP
Album: Rockin' and Driftin'
Record Label: Atlantic
Songwriters: Jerry Leiber, Mike Stoller
Covered by Dion (Columbia, '63).

1959

DANCE WITH ME
Producers: Jerry Leiber, Mike Stoller
Album: Drifters' Greatest Hits
Record Label: Atlantic
Songwriters: Jerry Leiber (Lewis Lebish), Mike Stoller (Elmo Glick), Irv Nahan, George Treadwell
Advancing the Pop R&B formula of the new Drifters.

THERE GOES MY BABY
Producers: Jerry Leiber, Mike Stoller
Album: Drifters' Greatest Hits
Record Label: Atlantic
Songwriters: Benjamin Nelson, Lover Patterson, George Treadwell
Drifting along with the year's prevailing softening of Rock and Roll, the new Drifters add strings to their patented sound; for their efforts gaining a #1 R&B/#2 R&R crossover.

1960

SAVE THE LAST DANCE FOR ME
Producers: Jerry Leiber, Mike Stoller
Album: Up on the Roof, the Best of the Drifters
Record Label: Atlantic
Songwriters: Doc Pomus, Mort Shuman
In capable Brill Building hands, the Drifters partake of the second great dance era with their only #1 R&B/R&R hit.

THIS MAGIC MOMENT

Producers: Jerry Leiber, Mike Stoller
Album: Up on the Roof, the Best of the Drifters
Record Label: Atlantic
Songwriters: Doc Pomus, Mort Shuman

Morty and Doc on a Top-10 R&B/Top-20 R&R roll.

1961

I COUNT THE TEARS

Producers: Jerry Leiber, Mike Stoller
Album: Save the Last Dance for Me
Record Label: Atlantic
Songwriters: Doc Pomus, Mort Shuman

Classic Brill Building Soul; another Top-10 R&B/Top-20 R&R crossover.

SOME KIND A WONDERFUL

Producers: Jerry Leiber, Mike Stoller
Album: Save the Last Dance for Me
Record Label: Atlantic
Songwriters: Jerry Leiber, Mike Stoller

Another stellar songwriting team, another Top-10 R&B/Top-40 R&R crossover.

SWEETS FOR MY SWEET

Producers: Jerry Leiber, Mike Stoller
Album: Up on the Roof, the Best of the Drifters
Record Label: Atlantic
Songwriters: Doc Pomus, Mort Shuman

Regaining their songwriting hold on the fortunes of the new Drifters hit machine, Pomus and Shuman provide the Drifters with their third straight Top-10 R&R/Top-20 R&B crossover.

1962

UP ON THE ROOF

Producers: Jerry Leiber, Mike Stoller
Album: Up on the Roof, the Best of the Drifters
Record Label: Atlantic
Songwriters: Gerry Goffin, Carole King

The essential City Soul classic from a classic candystore tandem—with Rudy Lewis on vocals; a Top-5 R&B/R&R crossover. Unforgettably covered by Laura Nyro (Columbia, '70).

1963

ON BROADWAY

Producers: Jerry Leiber, Mike Stoller
Album: Under the Boardwalk
Record Label: Atlantic
Songwriters: Jerry Leiber, Mike Stoller, Barry Mann, Cynthia Weil

Brill Building Top-10 R&B/R&R conference call crossover, with Phil Spector sitting in on guitar. Covered by George Benson (Warner Brothers, '78).

1964

UNDER THE BOARDWALK

Producer: Bert Berns
Album: Under the Boardwalk
Record Label: Atlantic
Songwriters: Artie Resnick, Kenny Young

Prime summertime escapism was the last Drifters Top-10 hit; concocted by yet another conscripted songwriting team (who would also write the follow up, "I've Got Sand in My Shoes," which stiffed in the fall). Covered by the Rolling Stones (London, '64).

THE DU DROPPERS

1954

BOOT EM UP

Record Label: RCA
Songwriters: Charlie Singleton, Rose Marie McCoy

Prime rhythm rocker, following up their revealing chartmakers of '53: April's "I Wanna Know," succeeded by June's "I Found Out."

THE DUBS

1957

COULD THIS BE MAGIC

Record Label: Gone
Songwriters: Richard Blandon, Hiram Johnson

Classic Doo-Wop ballad that never charted R&B.

DON'T ASK ME TO BE LONELY

Album: Meet the Shells
Record Label: Gone
Songwriter: Richard Blandon

George Goldner took a belated writing credit when the tune was re-released on Gone.

DUCKS DELUXE

1974

DON'T MIND ROCKIN' TONIGHT

Producer: Dave Bloxham
Album: Don't Mind Rockin' Tonight
Record Label: RCA

Songwriters: Martin Belmont, Nick Garvey

Fevered retro Rockabilly boogie from the pubs of England. The Motors evolved from this band, as did Sean Tyla. Graham Parker was listening.

DAVE DUDLEY

1963

SIX DAYS ON THE ROAD

Record Label: Golden Wing
Songwriters: Earl Green, Carl Montgomery

#2 C&W/Top-40 R&R crossover establishes the trucker school of alternative country Rock.

PATTY DUKE

1964

DON'T JUST STAND THERE (WHAT'S ON YOUR MIND)

Album: Don't Just Stand There
Record Label: United Artists
Songwriters: Lor Crane, Bernice Ross

On the pop princess scale, closer to Leslie Gore than Shelley Fabares.

ROBBIE DUPREE

1979

STEAL AWAY

Producers: Peter Bunetta, Rick Chudacoff
Album: Robbie Dupree
Record Label: Elektra
Songwriters: Robbie Dupuis, Rick Chudacoff

The England Dan and John Ford Coley sound transplanted to the East coast.

1980

HOT ROD HEARTS

Producers: Peter Bunetta, Rick Chudacoff
Album: Robbie Dupree
Record Label: Elektra
Songwriters: Bill LaBounty, Stephen Geyer

Springsteenian take-off on "Hungry Heart."

DURAN DURAN

1981

GIRLS ON FILM

Producer: Colin Thurston
Album: Duran Duran
Record Label: Harvest/EMI

Songwriters: Andy Taylor, John Taylor, Roger Taylor, Simon LeBon, Nick Rhodes

Must-see video.

1983

HUNGRY LIKE THE WOLF
Producer: Colin Thurston
Album: Rio
Record Label: Capitol
Songwriter: Duran Duran

The international playboy on vacation, taking along a synthesizer.

IS THERE SOMETHING I SHOULD KNOW
Producers: Duran Duran, Ian Little
Album: Arena
Record Label: Capitol
Songwriter: Duran Duran

Their first #1 U.K.

NEW MOON ON MONDAY
Producers: Duran Duran, Alex Sadkin, Ian Little
Album: Seven and the Ragged Tiger
Record Label: Capitol
Songwriter: Duran Duran

THE REFLEX
Producers: Duran Duran, Alex Sadkin, Ian Little
Album: Seven and the Ragged Tiger
Record Label: Capitol
Songwriter: Duran Duran

Their commercial peak; #1 U.S./U.K.

RIO
Producer: Colin Thurston
Album: Rio
Record Label: Capitol
Songwriter: Duran Duran

Honing their jet set image.

UNION OF THE SNAKE
Producers: Duran Duran, Alex Sadkin, Ian Little
Album: Seven and the Ragged Tiger
Record Label: Capitol
Songwriter: Duran Duran

The image wearing thin.

1984

THE WILD BOYS
Producers: Nile Rodgers, Duran Duran
Album: Arena
Record Label: Capitol
Songwriter: Duran Duran

1985

A VIEW TO A KILL
Producers: Bernard Edwards, Duran Duran, J. Corsaro
Album: *A View to a Kill* Soundtrack
Record Label: Capitol
Songwriters: Duran Duran, John Barry

From the James Bond film.

1988

I DON'T WANT YOUR LOVE
Producers: Duran Duran, J. Elias, D. Abraham
Album: Big Thing
Record Label: Capitol
Songwriters: John Taylor, Nick Rhodes, Simon Lebon

1993

COME UNDONE
Producer: Duran Duran
Album: Duran Duran
Record Label: Capitol
Songwriter: Duran Duran

Veterans of early-'80s English Synth invasion return to influence an early '90s invasion with a Top-10 R&R hit.

ORDINARY WORLD
Producers: Duran Duran, John Jones
Album: Duran Duran
Record Label: Capitol
Songwriter: Duran Duran

Totally '80s. The first nostalgia act for the MTV generation.

IAN DURY AND THE BLOCKHEADS

1977

SWEET GENE VINCENT
Producers: Laurie Latham, Peter Jenner, Rick Walton
Album: New Boots and Panties
Record Label: Stiff
Songwriters: Ian Dury, Chaz Jankel

Poignant ballad from the gimpy pub-rocking gnome, about a man after his own gnarled heart.

1978

SEX AND DRUGS AND ROCK 'N' ROLL
Producers: Laurie Latham, Peter Jenner, Rick Walton
Album: New Boots and Panties

Record Label: Stiff
Songwriters: Ian Dury, Chaz Jankel

New Wave anthem for the anti-Disco crowd.

1979

HIT ME WITH YOUR RHYTHM STICK
Album: Do It Yourself
Record Label: Stiff
Songwriters: Ian Dury, Chaz Jankel

Bonus 45 on the album; #1 in the U.K.

DYKE & THE BLAZERS

1967

FUNKY BROADWAY (PART 1)
Album: The Funky Broadway
Record Label: Original Sound
Songwriter: Arlester Christian

After the original was a moderate stiff, Pickett's version went #1 R&B/Top-10 R&R and was his biggest hit except for "Land of a Thousand Dances" in '66.

BOB DYLAN

1962

BABY LET ME FOLLOW YOU DOWN
Producer: John Hammond
Album: Bob Dylan
Record Label: Columbia
Songwriter: Bob Dylan (Arranged)

Borrowing freely from Folk and Blues (and in this case, Westport, Conn., folk artist Eric Von Schmidt), Dylan would represent a reaction not only against the Pop operatics of the post-Army Elvis, but of the collegiate harmonies of the Kingston Trio and their homogenized ilk. Covered by Jackie DeShannon (Liberty, '63).

SONG TO WOODY
Producer: John Hammond
Album: Bob Dylan
Record Label: Columbia
Songwriter: Bob Dylan

The very first thing he wanted to do was to acknowledge his debt to Woody Guthrie and simultaneously break away.

TOMORROW IS A LONG TIME
Producer: John Hammond
Album: The Freewheelin' Bob Dylan
Record Label: Columbia
Songwriter: Bob Dylan

A quintessential rambling song. Covered by Elvis Presley in the movie Spinout *('66); his only other cover of a Dylan song was "Don't Think Twice" (RCA, '73). Also covered by Sandy Denny (A&M, '72).*

1963

BLOWIN' IN THE WIND

Producer: John Hammond
Album: The Freewheelin' Bob Dylan
Record Label: Columbia
Songwriter: Bob Dylan

Like Shakespeare before him, the Bard of his generation, Bob Dylan, has been accused of not writing some of his most famous works, most notably this anthem of the Civil Rights Era. When you consider that Hank Ballard has been accused of not writing "The Twist" and Freddy Paris of not writing "(I'll Remember) In the Still of the Nite," both Bards are in fairly good company. Especially in the case of Dylan, what remains to be researched is what other songs the supposed real writer of "Blowin' in the Wind" has written—as compared to Dylan's output over the next thirty or so years. Covered by Peter, Paul and Mary (Warner Brothers, '63) in the career-launching version, and Stevie Wonder, in the #1 R&B version (Tamla, '69).

BOOTS OF SPANISH LEATHER

Producer: John Hammond
Album: The Freewheelin' Bob Dylan
Record Label: Columbia
Songwriter: Bob Dylan

An international rambling song. In this case, however, it's the girl who's rambling, by boat.

DON'T THINK TWICE, IT'S ALL RIGHT

Producer: John Hammond
Album: The Freewheelin' Bob Dylan
Record Label: Columbia
Songwriter: Bob Dylan

Country-flavored cynicism, seeing beneath the surface sweetness of all those coy girl-groups. Covered by Peter, Paul and Mary (Warner Brothers, '63), the Wonder Who (aka the Four Seasons) (Philips, '65), and Elvis Presley (RCA, '73).

GIRL FROM THE NORTH COUNTRY

Producer: John Hammond
Album: The Freewheelin' Bob Dylan
Record Label: Columbia
Songwriter: Bob Dylan

In an era of "Bandstand" dancers from Philly, candystore girl-groups from New York City and Detroit, surfing sun goddesses in L.A. (and Mandy Rice Davies scandalizing England), Dylan defies the stereotypes to extol a decidedly different locale and female persona.

A HARD RAIN'S A-GONNA FALL

Producer: John Hammond
Album: The Freewheelin' Bob Dylan
Record Label: Columbia
Songwriter: Bob Dylan

About as rabid and riotous (and boisterous and Biblical) a departure from the Pop (and anti-war Folk singing) norm as you could hear before 1964. Covered by Bryan Ferry (Reprise, '89) and Edie Brickell in the movie Born on the 4th of July (MCA, '89).

HE WAS A FRIEND OF MINE

Producer: John Hammond
Album: The Freewheelin' Bob Dylan
Record Label: Columbia
Songwriter: Bob Dylan

Covered by the Byrds (Columbia, '65).

LET ME DIE IN MY FOOTSTEPS

Producer: John Hammond
Album: The Freewheelin' Bob Dylan
Record Label: Columbia
Songwriter: Bob Dylan

Anti-bomb-shelter song was contained on early pressings of this album, before being deleted.

MASTERS OF WAR

Producer: John Hammond
Album: The Freewheelin' Bob Dylan
Record Label: Columbia
Songwriter: Bob Dylan

One of his most cogent anti-war diatribes. Covered by Pearl Jam's Eddie Vedder at the Thirtieth Anniversary Dylan "Bobfest" broadcast in '93.

PLAYBOYS AND PLAYGIRLS

Album: Newport, '63
Record Label: Vanguard
Songwriter: Bob Dylan

Defying the social order, at the hallowed Newport Folk Festival in '63.

WITH GOD ON OUR SIDE

Producer: John Hammond
Album: The Freewheelin' Bob Dylan
Record Label: Columbia
Songwriter: Bob Dylan

Anti-war polemic, based on "The Patriot Game," by Dominic Behan.

1964

ALL I REALLY WANT TO DO

Producer: Tom Wilson
Album: Another Side of Bob Dylan

Record Label: Columbia
Songwriter: Bob Dylan

Dylan at his most accommodating, during his least-accommodating phase. Lent itself well to more commercially viable versions by the obligatory Byrds (Columbia, '65) and the surprising Cher (Imperial, '65).

CHIMES OF FREEDOM

Producer: Tom Wilson
Album: Another Side of Bob Dylan
Record Label: Columbia
Songwriter: Bob Dylan

A freedom song, of a personal sort. Covered by the Byrds (Columbia, '65) and Bruce Springsteen (Columbia, '86).

I DON'T BELIEVE YOU (SHE ACTS LIKE WE NEVER HAVE MET)

Producer: Tom Wilson
Album: Another Side of Bob Dylan
Record Label: Columbia
Songwriter: Bob Dylan

In the age of the dysfunctional relationship, Dylan was its Rube Goldberg.

IT AIN'T ME, BABE

Producer: Tom Wilson
Album: Another Side of Bob Dylan
Record Label: Columbia
Songwriter: Bob Dylan

Reviving the Punk attitude smoothed over by the Brill Building and Motown. Unconvinced by girl-group homilies of matrimonial bliss or Smokey Robinson-induced visions of eternal ecstasy, Dylan would lead a new brigade of alienated free thinkers into the depths of the tortured '60s. Covered in a trailblazing Surf Garage hit by the Turtles (White Whale, '65).

LAY DOWN YOUR WEARY TUNE

Producer: Tom Wilson
Record Label: Columbia
Songwriter: Bob Dylan

Treasured bootlegged obscurity, covered by the Byrds (Columbia, '65).

MAMA YOU BEEN ON MY MIND

Producer: Tom Wilson
Record Label: Columbia
Bob Dylan

Preparing for "She Belongs to Me" and "Just like a Woman." Covered by Joan Baez as "Daddy You Been on My Mind" (Vanguard, '65).

MY BACK PAGES (I'M YOUNGER THAN THAT NOW)

Producer: Tom Wilson
Album: Another Side of Bob Dylan
Record Label: Columbia
Songwriter: Bob Dylan

Embracing the new consciousness. Covered by the Byrds (Columbia, '65) and revived by Dylan and a backup cast of famous friends at the Bobfest (Columbia, '94).

ONE TOO MANY MORNINGS

Producer: Tom Wilson
Album: The Times They Are A-Changin'
Record Label: Columbia
Songwriter: Bob Dylan

Ultimate rambler's lament. Covered by Ian and Sylvia (Vanguard, '64) and the Beau Brummels (Warner Brothers, '66).

ONLY A PAWN IN THEIR GAME

Producer: Tom Wilson
Album: The Times They Are A-Changin'
Record Label: Columbia
Songwriter: Bob Dylan

Memorial to civil rights casualty Medgar Evers, slain in Mississippi in '64.

SPANISH HARLEM INCIDENT

Producer: Tom Wilson
Album: Another Side of Bob Dylan
Record Label: Columbia
Songwriter: Bob Dylan

Dylan's raggedly rhapsodic answer to "Spanish Harlem." Covered by the Byrds (Columbia, '65).

THE TIMES THEY ARE A-CHANGIN'

Producer: Tom Wilson
Album: The Times They Are A-Changin'
Record Label: Columbia
Songwriter: Bob Dylan

Putting the post-Kennedy generational malaise into counter-cultural perspective.

WHEN THE SHIP COMES IN

Producer: Tom Wilson
Album: The Times They Are A-Changin'
Record Label: Columbia
Songwriter: Bob Dylan

Talking about a revolution, metaphorically speaking. Covered by Peter, Paul and Mary (Warner Brothers, '65).

1965

BALLAD OF A THIN MAN

Producer: Tom Wilson
Album: Highway 61 Revisited
Record Label: Columbia
Songwriter: Bob Dylan

Introducing the anti-bohemian everyman, Mr. Jones, later to reappear in "Mr. Jones" by Counting Crows. When Dylan sang this at the Newport Folk Festival, everyone thought he was talking about them—and he was.

CAN YOU PLEASE CRAWL OUT YOUR WINDOW?

Producer: Tom Wilson
Record Label: Columbia
Songwriter: Bob Dylan

The Dylan approach to anti-romance, released as a single, which naturally stiffed. First recorded by the Vacels (Kama Sutra, '65), which didn't do half as well.

DESOLATION ROW

Producer: Tom Wilson
Album: Highway 61 Revisited
Record Label: Columbia
Songwriter: Bob Dylan

Postcards of the hanging, East Village style.

FROM A BUICK 6

Producer: Tom Wilson
Album: Highway 61 Revisited
Record Label: Columbia
Songwriter: Bob Dylan

Dylanized car classic—classic car: a Buick 6.

GATES OF EDEN

Producer: Tom Wilson
Album: Bringing It All Back Home
Record Label: Columbia
Songwriter: Bob Dylan

Dylan's sermon of the moment: there are no truths, except his.

HIGHWAY 61 REVISITED

Producer: Tom Wilson
Album: Highway 61 Revisited
Record Label: Columbia
Songwriter: Bob Dylan

Dylan in a Biblical frame of mind and reference again; blistering Rock for the (and all) ages. Covered by Johnny Winter (Columbia, '69) and P. J. Harvey (Island, '94).

IT TAKES A LOT TO LAUGH, IT TAKES A TRAIN TO CRY

Producer: Tom Wilson
Album: Highway 61 Revisited
Record Label: Columbia
Songwriter: Bob Dylan

A yearning Country Blues Rock orgasm. When Dylan was booed off the stage at Newport that year, for the sin of becoming a rock and roller, this was one of the three tunes he played, before returning for an acoustic set. Covered by his guitarist for the night, Mike Bloomfield, in his supersession set with Al Kooper and Steve Stills (Columbia, '68) and Tracy Nelson (Atlantic, '74).

IT'S ALL OVER NOW, BABY BLUE

Producer: Tom Wilson
Album: Bringing It All Back Home
Record Label: Columbia
Songwriter: Bob Dylan

Love was a four-letter word to Dylan; relationships were worth at least four minutes. Covered in a bravura performance by Van Morrison with Them (Parrot, '66).

IT'S ALRIGHT, MA (I'M ONLY BLEEDING)

Producer: Tom Wilson
Album: Bringing It All Back Home
Record Label: Columbia
Songwriter: Bob Dylan

Nothing to live up to, in approximately eight minutes of righteous wrath.

JUST LIKE TOM THUMB'S BLUES

Producer: Tom Wilson
Album: Highway 61 Revisited
Record Label: Columbia
Songwriter: Bob Dylan

Lost in the rain in Juarez.

LIKE A ROLLING STONE

Producer: Tom Wilson
Album: Highway 61 Revisited
Record Label: Columbia
Songwriter: Bob Dylan

Verbose and incandescent, Dylan skewers every frugging go-go girl on "Hullabaloo" and "Shindig," and with the help of Al Kooper's thrilling organ part, establishes the musical direction home for the remainder of the '60s as Stones-inspired Folk Rock. Middle-class white collegiate rage has its transcendent moment at the top of the charts. Covered, at long last, by the Rolling Stones (Virgin, '95).

LOVE MINUS ZERO/NO LIMIT

Producer: Tom Wilson
Album: Bringing It All Back Home
Record Label: Columbia
Songwriter: Bob Dylan

His tenderest love song.

MAGGIE'S FARM

Producer: Tom Wilson
Album: Bringing It All Back Home
Record Label: Columbia
Songwriter: Bob Dylan

An earthly companion piece to "Subterreanean Homesick Blues." Covered by the Specials (2Tone, '81). Performed with absurdist perfection in the Marlon Brando/Matthew Broderick film, The Freshman, *by Bert Parks backed by Was (Not Was).*

MR. TAMBOURINE MAN

Producer: Tom Wilson
Album: Bringing It All Back Home
Record Label: Columbia
Songwriter: Bob Dylan

Dylan goes to the Mardi Gras under the influence of Jack Kerouac. With just one of its verses covered by the Byrds (Columbia, '65) this tune launched the '60s jingle-jangle white alternative known as Folk Rock, one part Beach Boys "Don't Worry Baby," three parts Creative Writing 101.

POSITIVELY 4TH STREET

Producer: Bob Johnston
Album: Bob Dylan's Greatest Hits
Record Label: Columbia
Songwriter: Bob Dylan

A new-fashioned tongue lashing directed at his cronies from the old neighborhood. Covered by Victoria Williams (Razor & Tie, '93) and the Beat Farmers (Sector 2, '95).

QUEEN JANE APPROXIMATELY

Producer: Tom Wilson
Album: Highway 61 Revisited
Record Label: Columbia
Songwriter: Bob Dylan

Reverential reference to his one-time bene-factress Baez.

SHE BELONGS TO ME

Producer: Tom Wilson
Album: Bringing It All Back Home
Record Label: Columbia
Songwriter: Bob Dylan

B-side of "Subterranean Homesick Blues." Covered by Rick Nelson (Decca, '69).

SUBTERRANEAN HOMESICK BLUES

Producer: Tom Wilson
Album: Bringing It All Back Home
Record Label: Columbia
Songwriter: Bob Dylan

Dylan's first music video, co-starring Allen Ginsberg, opened the classic documentary Don't Look Back. *From whence came the radical slogan: You don't need a weather-man to know which way the wind blows. Covered by Harry Nilsson (RCA, '74). Suggested segues: "Too Much Monkey Business," by Chuck Berry, "It's the End of the World As We Know It (and I Feel Fine")" by R.E.M., "We Didn't Start the Fire" by Billy Joel.*

1966

I WANT YOU

Producer: Bob Johnston
Album: Blonde on Blonde
Record Label: Columbia
Songwriter: Bob Dylan

Rare instance of unrequited lust.

I'LL KEEP IT WITH MINE

Producer: Tom Wilson
Record Label: Columbia
Songwriter: Bob Dylan

One of the legendary early outtakes, which went uncollected by Dylan for twenty years. Wilson had Nico cover it on her solo album, which he also produced (Verve, '67).

JUST LIKE A WOMAN

Producer: Bob Johnston
Album: Blonde on Blonde
Record Label: Columbia
Songwriter: Bob Dylan

Painting his masterpiece. U.K. Top-10 hit for Manfred Mann (Fontana, '66). Covered by Richie Havens (Verve Folkways, '66), Joe Cocker (A&M, '69), and Rod Stewart (Warner Brothers, '81).

LEOPARD-SKIN PILL-BOX HAT

Producer: Bob Johnston
Album: Blonde on Blonde
Record Label: Columbia
Songwriter: Bob Dylan

Apt commentary on fickle fashions. Stiffed as a single.

MOST LIKELY YOU GO YOUR WAY (AND I'LL GO MINE)

Producer: Bob Johnston
Album: Blonde on Blonde
Record Label: Columbia
Songwriter: Bob Dylan

For a while Dylan's concert-opening dia-logue with his audience.

ONE OF US MUST KNOW (SOONER OR LATER)

Producer: Bob Johnston
Album: Blonde on Blonde
Record Label: Columbia
Songwriter: Bob Dylan

His logical melodic successor to "Like a Rolling Stone."

RAINY DAY WOMEN #12 AND 35

Producer: Bob Johnston
Album: Blonde on Blonde
Record Label: Columbia
Songwriter: Bob Dylan

Treatise on the various meanings of getting stoned.

SAD-EYED LADY OF THE LOWLANDS

Producer: Bob Johnston
Album: Blonde on Blonde
Record Label: Columbia
Songwriter: Bob Dylan

All of side IV.

STUCK INSIDE OF MOBILE WITH THE MEMPHIS BLUES AGAIN.

Producer: Bob Johnston
Album: Blonde on Blonde
Record Label: Columbia
Songwriter: Bob Dylan

One of his greatest verbal challenges, baf-fling Dylanographers and Dylanologists to this day.

VISIONS OF JOHANNA

Producer: Bob Johnston
Album: Blonde on Blonde
Record Label: Columbia
Songwriter: Bob Dylan

His most tangled urban psychodrama, as directed by Fellini.

1968

ALL ALONG THE WATCHTOWER

Producer: Bob Johnston
Album: John Wesley Harding
Record Label: Columbia
Songwriter: Bob Dylan

One of the few echoes of the volatile and metaphorically abundant "old" Dylan on this spare and severe album. Covered in typically incendiary fashion by Jimi Hendrix (Reprise, '68).

DEAR LANDLORD

Producer: Bob Johnston
Album: John Wesley Harding
Record Label: Columbia
Songwriter: Bob Dylan

Compared to the pre-motorcycle accident, mid-'60s Dylan, this was virtually a haiku. Covered by Joe Cocker (A&M, '70).

I'LL BE YOUR BABY TONIGHT
Producer: Bob Johnston
Album: John Wesley Harding
Record Label: Columbia
Songwriter: Bob Dylan

As a pure Country throwaway tagged onto the arid western orientation of the album, this prelude to Bob's full conversion to Nashville was seen by many as the beginning of the end of Dylanology as a legitimate career choice for the downwardly mobile college dropout. For others it was a sign of Roots Rock to come. Covered by Marianne Faithfull (Immediate, '77).

JOHN WESLEY HARDING
Producer: Bob Johnston
Album: John Wesley Harding
Record Label: Columbia
Songwriter: Bob Dylan

Veering to the western half of C&W, this brief tune (and album) was reportedly named after Blues singer Tim Hardin's great grandfather.

1969

LAY, LADY, LAY
Producer: Bob Johnston
Album: Nashville Skyline
Record Label: Columbia
Songwriter: Bob Dylan

A simple Country love song, rejected by the Everly Brothers, this was Dylan's biggest single in three years. Dylanologists and Dylanographers despaired of finding hidden meanings. Covered by Ministry (Warner Brothers, '96).

TONIGHT I'LL BE STAYING HERE WITH YOU
Producer: Bob Johnston
Album: Nashville Skyline
Record Label: Columbia
Songwriter: Bob Dylan

Thoroughly Nashville Bob.

1970

DAY OF THE LOCUSTS
Producer: Bob Johnston
Album: New Morning
Record Label: Columbia
Songwriter: Bob Dylan

Dr. Bob accepts his honorary degree at Princeton.

IF NOT FOR YOU
Producer: Bob Johnston
Album: New Morning
Record Label: Columbia

Songwriter: Bob Dylan

Country pie in the sky. Covered by George Harrison (Apple, '70) and Olivia Newton-John (Uni, '71) for her first U.K. and U.S. hit.

SIGN ON THE WINDOW
Producer: Bob Johnston
Album: New Morning
Record Label: Columbia
Songwriter: Bob Dylan

Thoroughly domesticated Bob, surrounded by wife and kids, holed up in a remote cabin in Utah; what's that all about?

TIME PASSES SLOWLY
Producer: Bob Johnston
Album: New Morning
Record Label: Columbia
Songwriter: Bob Dylan

Bob returns to his Country and Northern roots.

WENT TO SEE THE GYPSY
Producer: Bob Johnston
Album: New Morning
Record Label: Columbia
Songwriter: Bob Dylan

Reputedly about a meeting with Elvis Presley.

1971

GEORGE JACKSON
Record Label: Columbia
Songwriter: Bob Dylan

Dylan finds a new lost cause. It would do until a better one came along (Hurricane Carter).

WATCHING THE RIVER FLOW
Producer: Leon Russell
Album: Bob Dylan's Greatest Hits (Vol. II)
Record Label: Columbia
Songwriter: Bob Dylan

Celebrating the inevitable ennui of the living legend. Spiritual cousin to "Watching the Wheels" by John Lennon.

WHEN I PAINT MY MASTERPIECE
Producer: Leon Russell
Album: Bob Dylan's Greatest Hits (Vol. II)
Record Label: Columbia
Songwriter: Bob Dylan

Another side of Bob Dylan: self-mocking humor. Recorded by the Band (Capitol, '71).

1973

FOREVER YOUNG
Producer: Bob Dylan
Album: Planet Waves
Record Label: Asylum
Songwriter: Bob Dylan

One of his more accessible and moving messages.

KNOCKIN' ON HEAVEN'S DOOR
Producer: Gordon Carroll
Album: *Pat Garrett and Billy the Kid* Soundtrack
Record Label: Columbia
Songwriter: Bob Dylan

Written for the film, a pure emotional highlight. Covered by Guns N' Roses (Geffen, '91).

1974

IDIOT WIND
Producers: Phil Ramone, Bob Dylan
Album: Blood on the Tracks
Record Label: Columbia
Songwriter: Bob Dylan

Long-winded post-domestic diatribe.

SHELTER FROM THE STORM
Producers: Phil Ramone, Bob Dylan
Album: Blood on the Tracks
Record Label: Columbia
Songwriter: Bob Dylan

Best of the "new" Dylan.

SIMPLE TWIST OF FATE
Producers: Phil Ramone, Bob Dylan
Album: Blood on the Tracks
Record Label: Columbia
Songwriter: Bob Dylan

Twisted story/song. But it was no "Visions of Johanna."

TANGLED UP IN BLUE
Producers: Phil Ramone, Bob Dylan
Album: Blood on the Tracks
Record Label: Columbia
Songwriter: Bob Dylan

Another convoluted gem from the comeback album. But he would never come all the way back, and neither would the sound, the fury, or the dreams he inspired.

YOU ANGEL YOU
Producer: Bob Dylan
Album: Planet Waves
Record Label: Asylum
Songwriter: Bob Dylan

B-side of "On a Night Like This."

1975

HURRICANE (PART I)
Producer: Don DeVito
Album: Desire
Record Label: Columbia
Songwriters: Bob Dylan, Jacques Levy

Helping to set Rubin Hurricane Carter free, with a quintessential folk/rock beat.

JOEY
Producer: Don DeVito
Album: Desire
Record Label: Columbia
Songwriters: Bob Dylan, Jacques Levy

Deifying mobster Joey Gallo cost Dylan two-thirds of his remaining critical credibility. Co-writer Jacques Levy wrote "Chestnut Mare" with Roger McGuinn.

MILLION DOLLAR BASH
Producers: Bob Dylan, the Band
Album: The Basement Tapes
Record Label: Columbia
Songwriter: Bob Dylan

Freewheeling fun and games from the post-accident '60s. The first of many gems released from the vaults.

1976

SARA
Producer: Don DeVito
Album: Desire
Record Label: Columbia
Songwriter: Bob Dylan

A mere song for his wife where once he wrote an entire side of an album for her. Soon they would be divorced.

1978

BABY STOP CRYING
Producer: Don Devito
Album: Street Legal
Record Label: Columbia
Songwriter: Bob Dylan

Song to himself.

WHERE ARE YOU TONIGHT
Producer: Don Devito
Album: Street Legal
Record Label: Columbia
Songwriter: Bob Dylan

Song to his lost '60s audience.

1979

GOTTA SERVE SOMEBODY
Producers: Jerry Wexler, Barry Beckett

Album: Slow Train Coming
Record Label: Columbia
Songwriter: Bob Dylan

Entering his controversial religious phase. But it was only relatively controversial. With Dylanology a moribund industry, his every move and verbal nuance no longer caused the world to instantly react and ponder.

WHEN YOU GONNA WAKE UP
Producers: Bob Dylan, Chuck Plotkin
Album: Slow Train Coming
Record Label: Columbia
Songwriter: Bob Dylan

The wrath of Bob.

1981

EVERY GRAIN OF SAND
Album: Shot of Love
Record Label: Columbia
Songwriter: Bob Dylan

One of his finest songs of any era. Covered by Emmylou Harris (Reprise, '95).

THE GROOM'S STILL WAITING AT THE ALTAR
Producers: Chuck Plotkin, Bob Dylan
Record Label: Columbia
Songwriter: Bob Dylan

Obscure non-album cut is the nearest thing to Dylan heaven since "Highway 61 Revisited."

LENNY BRUCE
Producers: Chuck Plotkin, Bob Dylan
Album: Shot of Love
Record Label: Columbia
Songwriter: Bob Dylan

Song to a soul mate. Suggested segue: "Lenny's Song" by Tim Hardin.

1983

DON'T FALL APART ON ME TONIGHT
Producers: Bob Dylan, Mark Knopfler
Album: Infidels
Record Label: Columbia
Songwriter: Bob Dylan

Song to Ramona's younger sister. Dylan's first appearance on MTV.

JOKERMAN
Producers: Bob Dylan, Mark Knopfler
Album: Infidels
Record Label: Columbia

Songwriter: Bob Dylan

Into the raging inferno.

1985

EMOTIONALLY YOURS
Album: Empire Burlesque
Record Label: Columbia
Songwriter: Bob Dylan

Covered by the O' Jays (EMI, '91).

TIGHT CONNECTION TO MY HEART (HAS ANYBODY SEEN MY LOVE)
Album: Empire Burlesque
Record Label: Columbia
Songwriter: Bob Dylan

1986

BROWNSVILLE GIRL
Album: Knocked out Loaded
Record Label: Columbia
Songwriters: Bob Dylan, Sam Shepard

Artistically natural collaboration of two bohemian giants at the end of their era.

UNDER YOUR SPELL
Album: Knocked out Loaded
Record Label: Columbia
Songwriters: Bob Dylan, Carole Bayer Sager

Artistically unnatural collaboration of two cold songwriters looking for a hook.

1987

HAD A DREAM ABOUT YOU, BABY
Album: *Hearts of Fire* Soundtrack
Record Label: Columbia
Songwriter: Bob Dylan

Artistically ludicrous collaboration with the rocker Fiona in his worst movie since Renaldo and Clara.

1988

SILVIO
Producer: Bob Dylan
Album: Down in the Groove
Record Label: Columbia
Songwriters: Bob Dylan, Robert Hunter

Artistically confused collaboration with the Dead's head writer. Dylanologists might have had a field day with it, had there been any left in the field.

1989

EVERYTHING IS BROKEN
Producer: Daniel Lanois
Album: Oh Mercy
Record Label: Columbia

Songwriter: Bob Dylan

Dylan's state of the decade address. In the '90s this function would be served by his cryptic comments accepting a Lifetime Achievement Grammy Award on TV.

RONNIE DYSON

1970

(IF YOU LET ME MAKE LOVE TO YOU) WHY CAN'T I TOUCH YOU

Producer: Billy Jackson
Album: *Salvation* (Musical)
Record Label: Columbia
Songwriters: C.C. Courtney, Peter Link

From the other Rock musical.

1973

JUST DON'T WANT TO BE LONELY TONIGHT

Album: One Man Band
Record label: Columbia
Songwriters: Vinnie Barrett, Bobby Eli, John Freeman

Covered by the Main Ingredient (RCA, '74).

E

E.U.

1988

DA BUTT

Producer: Marcus Miller
Album: *School Daze* Soundtrack
Record Label: EMI-Manhattan
Songwriters: Marcus Miller, Mark Stevens

Short-lived new dance craze from the Spike Lee film.

THE EAGLES

1972

PEACEFUL EASY FEELING

Producer: Glyn Johns
Album: The Eagles
Record Label: Asylum
Songwriter: Jack Tempchin

In the heart of Folk Rock country.

TAKE IT EASY

Producer: Glyn Johns
Album: The Eagles
Record Label: Asylum
Songwriters: Jackson Browne, Glenn Frey

Defining the sunbaked Country Folk Soul of Winslow, Ariz., Jackson Browne makes it big in L.A.

WITCHY WOMAN

Producer: Glyn Johns
Album: The Eagles
Record Label: Asylum
Songwriters: Don Henley, Bernie Leadon

Stating their attitude about the opposite sex.

1973

DESPERADO

Producer: Glyn Johns
Album: Desperado
Record Label: Asylum
Songwriters: Don Henley, Glenn Frey

Moving Country Rock lament. Covered by Linda Ronstadt (Asylum, '73).

TEQUILA SUNRISE

Producer: Glyn Johns
Album: Desperado
Record Label: Asylum
Songwriters: Don Henley, Glenn Frey

A parched anthem for the fern-bar crowd.

1974

ALREADY GONE

Producer: Bill Szymczyk
Album: On the Border
Record Label: Asylum
Songwriters: Bob Strandlund, Jack Tempchin

Celebrating the commitment-phobic male.

BEST OF MY LOVE

Producer: Bill Szymczyk
Album: On the Border
Record Label: Asylum
Songwriters: Don Henley, Glenn Frey, John David Souther

First of their five #1s.

JAMES DEAN

Producer: Bill Szymczyk
Album: On the Border
Record Label: Asylum
Songwriters: Don Henley, Glenn Frey, Jackson Browne, John David Souther

Identifying with the Hollywood anti-hero. Suggested segue: "James Dean of Indiana" by Phil Ochs, "A Young Man Is Gone" by the Beach Boys.

1975

LYIN' EYES

Producer: Bill Szymczyk
Album: One of These Nights
Record Label: Asylum
Songwriters: Don Henley, Glenn Frey

On the attack.

ONE OF THESE NIGHTS

Producer: Bill Szymczyk
Album: One of These Nights
Record Label: Asylum
Songwriters: Don Henley, Glenn Frey

Chart-topping Country Folk/Rock.

1976

TAKE IT TO THE LIMIT

Producer: Bill Szymczyk
Album: One of These Nights
Record Label: Asylum
Songwriters: Don Henley, Randy Meisner

Hollywood Country.

1977

HOTEL CALIFORNIA

Producer: Bill Szymczyk
Album: Hotel California
Record Label: Asylum
Songwriters: Don Henley, Glenn Frey, Don Felder

All-purpose metaphor serves as the vehicle for their most enduring classic guitar cut (classic guitarist: Joe Walsh).

LIFE IN THE FAST LANE

Producer: Bill Szymczyk
Album: Hotel California
Record Label: Asylum
Songwriters: Don Henley, Glenn Frey, Joe Walsh

Crafty ode to their chosen lifestyle.

NEW KID IN TOWN

Producer: Bill Szymczyk
Album: Hotel California
Record Label: Asylum
Songwriters: Don Henley, Glenn Frey, John David Souther

Country Soul-less.

1979

HEARTACHE TONIGHT

Producer: Bill Szymczyk
Album: The Long Run
Record Label: Asylum

Songwriters: Don Henley, Glenn Frey, Bob Seger, John David Souther
Their hardest rocking #1.

I CAN'T TELL YOU WHY

Producer: Bill Szymczyk
Album: The Long Run
Record Label: Asylum
Songwriters: Don Henley, Glenn Frey, Timothy Schmit

Patented ballad.

EARL-JEAN
1964

I'M INTO SOMETHING GOOD

Producers: Gerry Goffin, Carole King
Record Label: Colpix
Songwriters: Gerry Goffin, Carole King

Covered by Herman's Hermits (MGM, '64).

STEVE EARLE
1986

GUITAR TOWN

Producers: Tony Brown, Emory Gordy Jr.
Album: Guitar Town
Record Label: MCA
Songwriter: Steve Earle

Hard-hitting Alternative Country Rock.

1988

COPPERHEAD ROAD

Producers: Tony Brown, Steve Earle
Album: Copperhead Road
Record Label: Uni
Songwriter: Steve Earle

Runs parallel to his "Nowhere Road" and cuts through "Guitar Town."

THE EARLS
1962

REMEMBER THEN

Album: Remember Me, Baby
Record Label: Old Town
Songwriters: Stan Vincent, Tony Powers, Beverly Ross

End of an era anthem.

EARTH OPERA
1969

THE REDSOX ARE WINNING

Producer: Peter K. Siegel
Album: Earth Opera
Record Label: Elektra

Songwriter: Peter Rowan

Early psychedelic Bluegrass. Seigel was once a member of the Even Dozen Jugband, to which Rowan obviously listened. The members of Camper Van Beethoven would have listened to Earth Opera, if anyone played them on the West coast.

EARTH, WIND AND FIRE
1975

REASONS

Producer: Maurice White
Album: That's the Way of the World
Record Label: Columbia
Songwriters: Maurice White, Philip Bailey, Verdine White

Early enduring classic.

SING A SONG

Producers: Maurice White, Charles Stepney
Album: Gratitude
Record Label: Columbia
Songwriters: Maurice White, Albert McKay

Their first #1 R&B/Top-10 R&R crossover. The world beat Beatles to George Clinton's Rolling Stones.

THAT'S THE WAY OF THE WORLD

Producers: Maurice White, Charles Stepney
Album: That's the Way of the World
Record Label: Columbia
Songwriters: Maurice White, Philip Bailey, Larry Dunn

Title tune from their movie debut.

SHINING STAR

Producers: Maurice White, Charles Stepney
Album: That's the Way of the World
Record Label: Columbia
Songwriters: Maurice White, Philip Bailey, Larry Dunn

Their shining moment; #1 R&B/R&R crossover. A Tribe Called Quest paid attention.

1976

GETAWAY

Producers: Maurice White, Charles Stepney
Album: Spirit
Record Label: Columbia
Songwriters: Peter Cor, Beloyd Taylor

Sophisticated Funk. #1 R&B/Top-20 R&R. The title track of this album is dedicated to Stepney, who died of a heart attack during production.

1977

SERPENTINE FIRE

Producer: Maurice White
Album: All 'N' All
Record Label: Columbia
Songwriters: Maurice White, Reginald Burke, Verdine White

#1 R&B/Top-20 R&R crossover. The Brazilian influence.

1979

AFTER THE LOVE HAS GONE

Producer: Maurice White
Album: I Am
Record Label: ARC
Songwriters: David Foster, Jay Graydon, Bill Champlin

#2 R&B/#2 R&R Pop Funk crossover, presages New Jack Swing.

BOOGIE WONDERLAND

Producers: Maurice White, Al McKay
Album: I Am
Record Label: ARC
Songwriters: John Lind, Allee Willis

With the Emotions. A Top-5 R&B/Top-10 R&R Disco anthem.

SEPTEMBER

Producer: Maurice White
Album: Best of Earth, Wind and Fire (Vol. I)
Record Label: Arc
Songwriters: Maurice White, Allee Willis, Albert McKay

#1 R&B/Top-10 R&R crossover.

1981

LET'S GROOVE

Producer: Maurice White
Album: Raise!
Record Label: Arc/Columbia
Songwriters: Maurice White, Wayne Vaughn, Wanda Vaughn

#1 R&B/Top-10 R&R world dance groove supreme.

SHEENA EASTON
1981

MORNING TRAIN

Producer: Christopher Neil
Album: Sheena Easton

Record Label: EMI-America
Songwriter: Florrie Palmer

Scottish Pop/Rock. Suggested segue: "Uptown" by the Crystals, "9 to 5" by Dolly Parton.

1984

STRUT
Producer: Greg Mathieson
Album: A Private Heaven
Record Label: EMI-America
Songwriters: Charlene Dore, Julian Littman

SUGAR WALLS
Producer: Greg Mathieson
Alexander Nevermind
Album: A Private Heaven
Record Label: EMI-America
Songwriter: Alexander Nevermind (Prince)

Sexual innuendo hit of the year. Top-10 R&B/R&R crossover. Easton would soon show up on "Miami Vice" as Don Johnson's doomed love interest.

THE EASYBEATS

1966

FRIDAY ON MY MIND
Producer: Shel Talmy
Album: Friday on My Mind
Record Label: United Artists
Songwriters: Harry Vanda, George Young

Undeniable working class Folk Rock by the Goffin & King of Australia.

ECHO AND THE BUNNYMEN

1980

ALL THAT JAZZ
Producers: David Balse, Bill Drummond
Album: Crocodiles
Record Label: Sire
Songwriters: Jamie McCullough, Leslie Pattinson, Will Sergeant, Pete De Freitas

2nd wave Punk protest with a Reggae lilt.

THE ECHOES

1961

BABY BLUE
Producer: Jack Gold
Record Label: Seg-Way

Songwriters: Val Lageux, Sam Guilino

Farewell to Italian Soul's Golden Era.

DUANE EDDY

1957

RAMROD
Producer: Lee Hazelwood
Album: Have Twangy Guitar Will Travel
Record Label: Jamie
Songwriter: Al Casey

1st release originally as Duane Eddy and His Rocka-Billies (Ford). Re-released in 1958.

1958

CANNONBALL
Producer: Lee Hazelwood
Album: Have Twangy Guitar Will Travel
Record Label: Jamie
Songwriters: Lee Hazelwood, Duane Eddy

Early guitar heroics. Al Caiola was listening.

MOVIN' 'N GROOVIN'
Producer: Lee Hazelwood
Album: Have Twangy Guitar, Will Travel
Record Label: Jamie
Songwriters: Al Casey, Duane Eddy

Introducing the "Twangy" guitar, a Gretsch 6120. Suggested segue: "Surfin' U.S.A." by the Beach Boys.

REBEL ROUSER
Producers: Lee Hazelwood, Lester Sill
Album: Have Twangy Guitar Will Travel
Record Label: Jamie
Songwriters: Duane Eddy, Lee Hazelwood

B-side of "Stalkin'" was his first smash, establishing the solo guitar hero as a genuine Rock and Roll animal. Just up the road, waiting to be aroused, the next rebel guitar music, tied to the rhythms of the surf.

1959

FORTY MILES OF BAD ROAD
Producer: Lee Hazelwood
Album: $1,000,000.00 Worth of Twang
Record Label: Jamie
Songwriters: Al Casey, Duane Eddy

One of twenty-eight instrumentals to hit the Top-40 in '59.

1960

BECAUSE THEY'RE YOUNG
Producer: Lee Hazelwood
Album: $1,000,000.00 Worth of Twang
Record Label: Jamie
Songwriters: Aaron Schroeder, Don Costa, Wally Gold

His biggest hit, title tune from the Dick Clark/Tuesday Weld film, Because They're Young, in which James Darren sings a vocal version.

1962

(DANCE WITH THE) GUITAR MAN
Producer: Lee Hazelwood
Album: Dance with the Guitar Man
Record Label: RCA
Songwriters: Duane Eddy, Lee Hazelwood

EDISON LIGHTHOUSE

1970

LOVE GROWS (WHERE MY ROSEMARY GOES)
Record Label: Bell
Songwriters: Tony Macaulay, Barry Mason

#1 U.K./Top-10 U.S. crossover. Lite-Rock perfection.

DAVE EDMUNDS

1979

QUEEN OF HEARTS
Album: Repeat When Necessary
Record Label: Swan Song
Songwriter: Hank DeVito

Cover by Juice Newton (Capitol, '81) was #1 C&W/Top-10 R&R crossover, produced by Edmunds.

1982

FROM SMALL THINGS (BIG THINGS ONE DAY COME)
Record Label: Columbia
Songwriter: Bruce Springsteen

A Boss cover.

1985

HIGH SCHOOL NIGHTS
Producer: Dave Edmunds
Album: *Porky's Revenge* Soundtrack
Record Label: Columbia
Songwriters: Dave Edmunds, Sam Gould, John David

Highlight of the raunchy movie.

THE EDSELS
1958

RAMA LAMA DING DONG (LAMA RAMA DING DONG)
Record Label: Dub/Twin
Songwriter: George Jones Jr.

Essential Doo-Wop hit originally listed as "Lama Rama Ding Dong." Re-released in '61 with a corrected title.

EDWARD BEAR
1973

LAST SONG
Producer: Gene Martynec
Album: Edward Bear
Record Label: Capitol
Songwriter: Lawrence Wayne Evoy.

Standard issue Folk/Rock.

TOMMY EDWARDS
1951

IT'S ALL IN THE GAME
Producer: Harry Myerson
Album: It's All in the Game
Record Label: M-G-M
Songwriters: Carl Sigman, General Charles Gates Dawes

Top R&B hit. Sigman wrote "Ebb Tide" as well as the Louis Jordan hit, "That Chick's Too Young to Fry." Melody was by former U.S. Vice-President Dawes. Song became a #1 R&B/#1 R&R crossover when released in '58.

JONATHAN EDWARDS
1972

SUNSHINE
Producer: Peter Casperson
Album: Jonathan Edwards
Record Label: Capricorn
Songwriter: Andy Yoakim (Andy Kim)

Exploiting the year's predominating metaphor, as the Alternate culture packed up and went home.

WALTER EGAN
1977

MAGNET AND STEEL
Producers: Richard Dashut, Lindsay Buckingham, Walter Egan
Album: Not Shy
Record Label: Columbia
Songwriter: Walter Egan

Using the Fleetwood Mac production team as well as Stevie Nicks and Lindsay Buckingham on backing vocal for an L.A. one-shot.

808 STATE
1989

PACIFIC
Album: Quadrastate
Record Label: Creed (U.K.)
Songwriter: 808 State

Influenced by Brian Eno, Rick Wakeman and Kraftwerk, this breakthrough British dance instrumental commentary on the likes of middle-of-the-road sax god Kenny G. created a splinter form known as New Age House.

THE EL DORADOS
1955

AT MY FRONT DOOR (CRAZY LITTLE MAMA SONG)
Album: Crazy Little Mama
Record Label: Vee Jay
Songwriters: John C. Moore, Ewart Abner

Groundbreaking Top-10 R&B/Top-20 R&R crossover. Covered by Pat Boone (Dot, '55). Pat would take six more R&B tunes Top-10 R&R through the '50s. The El Dorados would have an oldies magazine named after their only other semi-hit, "Bim Bam Boom."

ELECTRIC FLAG
1968

GROOVIN' IS EASY
Producer: John Court
Album: A Long Time Comin'
Record Label: Columbia
Songwriters: Nick Gravenites, Ron Polte

Led by ex-Paul Butterfield blues guitarist, Mike Bloomfield, some prime Chicago noodling. Polte is credited, Gravenites is the actual writer.

SITTIN' IN CIRCLES
Producer: John Court
Album: A Long Time Comin'
Record Label: Columbia
Songwriter: Barry Goldberg

American Blues supergroup as hard rock AM/FM stiff.

ELECTRIC LIGHT ORCHESTRA (ELO)
1974

CAN'T GET IT OUT OF MY HEAD
Producer: Jeff Lynne
Album: Eldorado
Record Label: United Artists
Songwriter: Jeff Lynne

First Top-10 U.S. by the progenitors of England's Hard Rock Heroes, the Move.

1975

EVIL WOMAN
Producer: Jeff Lynne
Album: Face the Music
Record Label: United Artists
Songwriter: Jeff Lynne

Classic Classic Rock.

STRANGE MAGIC
Producer: Jeff Lynne
Album: Face the Music
Record Label: United Artists
Songwriter: Jeff Lynne

Perfecting their Beatles-esque studio Rock craft.

1976

LIVIN' THING
Producer: Jeff Lynne
Album: A New World Record
Record Label: United Artists
Songwriter: Jeff Lynne

TELEPHONE LINE
Producer: Jeff Lynne
Album: A New World Record
Record Label: United Artists/Jet
Songwriter: Jeff Lynne

1977

SWEET TALKIN' WOMAN
Producer: Jeff Lynne
Album: Out of the Blue
Record Label: Jet
Songwriter: Jeff Lynne

Hard-Rock lite.

1979

DON'T BRING ME DOWN
Album: Discovery
Record Label: Jet
Songwriter: Jeff Lynne

SHINE A LITTLE LOVE
Album: Discovery
Record Label: Jet
Songwriter: Jeff Lynne

1980

XANADU
Producer: Jeff Lynne
Album: *Xanadu* Soundtrack
Record Label: MCA
Songwriter: Jeff Lynne

From the Olivia Newton-John movie, their only #1 U.K. (performed with Newton-John).

1981

HOLD ON TIGHT
Producer: Jeff Lynne
Album: Time
Record Label: Jet
Songwriter: Jeff Lynne

Their last U.S./U.K. hit. Lynne would move on to the Traveling Wilburys.

1983

ROCK 'N' ROLL IS KING
Producer: Jeff Lynne
Album: Secret Messages
Record Label: A&M
Songwriter: Jeff Lynne

Suggested segue: "Sweet Little Rock and Roll" and "Roll Over Beethoven" by Chuck Berry.

ELECTRIC PRUNES
1967

I HAD TOO MUCH TO DREAM (LAST NIGHT)
Producer: Damo Productions
Album: Electric Prunes
Record Label: Reprise
Songwriters: Nancie Mantz, Annette Tucker

Prime exponent of the ill-fated pseudo-psychedelic, Boss-town sound.

THE ELEGANTS
1958

LITTLE STAR
Record Label: Hull/Apt
Songwriters: Vito Picone, Arthur Venosa

Proving the old adage, "be careful what you wish for, it might come true," the Elegants hit number one with their first release, this wishful nursery rhyme disguised as white Doo-Wop, and never returned to the charts again.

JIMMY ELLEDGE
1961

FUNNY HOW TIME SLIPS AWAY
Producer: Chet Atkins
Record Label: RCA
Songwriter: Willie Nelson

Poignant Willie classic. Covered by Johnny Tillotsen (Cadence, '63), Joe Hinton (Back Beat, '64), Willie Nelson (RCA, '65), Al Green (Hi, '73). The country hit was by Billy Walker (Columbia, '61).

YVONNE ELLIMAN
1971

EVERYTHING'S ALRIGHT
Producers: Tim Rice, Andrew Lloyd Webber
Album: Jesus Christ Superstar
Record Label: Decca
Songwriters: Tim Rice, Andrew Lloyd Webber

Mid-tempo secular love song from the legendary Rock opera.

I DON'T KNOW HOW TO LOVE HIM
Producers: Tim Rice, Andrew Lloyd Webber
Album: Jesus Christ Superstar
Record Label: Decca
Songwriters: Tim Rice, Andrew Lloyd Webber

Love song (of the physical kind) sung by Mary to Jesus on Broadway via England.

1977

IF I CAN'T HAVE YOU
Producer: Freddie Perren
Album: Love Me
Record Label: RSO
Songwriters: Barry Gibb, Robin Gibb, Maurice Gibb

#1 soulful rocker from the movie Saturday Night Fever.

SHIRLEY ELLIS
1963

THE NITTY GRITTY
Record Label: Congress
Songwriter: Lincoln Chase

The phrase has endured longer than the song.

1964

THE NAME GAME
Producer: Charlie Calello
Album: The Name Game
Record Label: Congress

Songwriters: Shirley Elliston, Lincoln Chase

Fun and games.

1965

THE CLAPPING SONG (CLAP PAT CLAP SLAP)
Record Label: Congress
Songwriter: Lincoln Chase

Last of a productive series.

LORRAINE ELLISON
1966

STAY WITH ME
Producer: Jerry Ragovoy
Record Label: Warner Brothers
Songwriters: Jerry Ragovoy, George David Weiss

Essential Soul thriller. Covered by Bette Midler's Janis Joplin in The Rose *in '79.*

JOE ELY
1978

BOXCARS
Producer: Chip Young
Album: Honky Tonk Masquerade
Record Label: MCA
Songwriters: Butch Hancock, Joe Ely

Haunting Austin-bred Country Rock, written with Joe's favorite hometown collaborator.

HONKY TONK MASQUERADE
Producer: Chip Young
Album: Honky Tonk Masquerade
Record Label: MCA
Songwriters: Butch Hancock, Joe Ely

The missing link between Buddy Holly and Tom Petty.

1981

MUSTA NOTTA GOTTA LOTTA
Producers: Michael Brovsky, Joe Ely
Album: Musta Notta Gotta Lotta
Record Label: SouthCoast
Songwriter: Joe Ely

Hard-hitting autobiographical alternative Country standard.

1994

WHISKEY AND WOMEN AND MONEY TO BURN
Album: *Chippy* Original Cast Album
Record Label: Hollywood
Songwriter: Joe Ely

From the latter-day Austin horse opera.

EMERSON LAKE AND PALMER (ELP)

1971

LUCKY MAN
Producer: Greg Lake
Album: Emerson Lake and Palmer
Record Label: Cotillion
Songwriter: Greg Lake

FM Progressive Rock perennial: King Crimson lite.

1972

FROM THE BEGINNING
Producer: Greg Lake
Album: Emerson Lake and Palmer
Record Label: Cotillion
Songwriter: Greg Lake

Forming the keyboard basis of Classic(al) Rock.

1973

KARN EVIL 9
Producer: Greg Lake
Album: Brain Salad Surgery
Record Label: Manticore
Songwriters: Greg Lake, Keith Emerson, Pete Sinfield

Clocking in at just under a lifetime (nearly 30 minutes for all three parts), more Progressive Rock than a body, a band, or a nation should be expected to endure at one sitting.

STILL . . . YOU TURN ME ON
Producer: Greg Lake
Album: Brain Salad Surgery
Record Label: Manticore
Songwriter: Greg Lake

EMF

1991

UNBELIEVABLE
Producers: EMF, Ralph Jezzard
Album: Schubert Dip
Record Label: EMI
Songwriters: James Atkin, Ian Dench, Zak Foley, Mark Decloedt, Derry Brownson

#1 R&R breakthrough for the British post-psychedelic Rave sound.

THE EMOTIONS

1977

BEST OF MY LOVE
Producer: Maurice White
Album: Rejoice

Record Label: Columbia
Songwriters: Maurice White, Albert McKay

#1 R&B/R&R crossover for the former Earth, Wind and Fire backing group.

EN VOGUE

1990

HOLD ON
Producers: Thomas McElroy, Denzil Foster
Album: Born to Sing
Record Label: Atlantic
Songwriters: Thomas McElroy, Denzil Foster, En Vogue

Modern R&B-oriented dance Pop.

LIES
Producers: Denzil Foster, Thom McElroy
Album: Born to Sing
Record Label: Atlantic
Songwriters: Denzil Foster, Thom McElroy, Khayree Shaheed, En Vogue

YOU DON'T HAVE TO WORRY
Producers: Denzil Foster, Thom McElroy
Album Title: Born to Sing
Record Label: Atlantic
Songwriters: Denzil Foster, Thom McElroy

1992

FREE YOUR MIND
Producers: Thomas McElroy, Denzil Foster
Album: Funky Divas of Soul
Record Label: Atco/East West
Songwriters: Thom McElroy, Denzil Foster

Tip of the verbal hat to George Clinton's "Free Your Mind and Your Ass Will Follow" turns into a Curtis-Mayfield-meets-the-Supremes plea for color-blindness.

MY LOVIN' (YOU'RE NEVER GONNA GET IT)
Producers: Thomas McElroy, Denzil Foster
Album: Funky Divas of Soul
Record Label: Atco/East West
Songwriters: Thom McElroy, Denzil Foster

Ultimate R&B partygirl putdown.

ENCHANTMENT

1978

IT'S YOU THAT I NEED
Album: Once upon a Dream
Record Label: Roadshow
Songwriters: Verdell Lanier, Michael Stokes

#1 R&B/Top-40 crossover.

ENGLAND DAN AND JOHN FORD COLEY

1975

I'D REALLY LOVE TO SEE YOU TONIGHT
Producer: Kyle Lehning
Album: Nights Are Forever
Record Label: Big Tree
Songwriter: Parker McGee

Defining the popular '70s middle-of-the-dirt-road genre.

1976

NIGHTS ARE FOREVER WITHOUT YOU
Producer: Kyle Lehning
Album: Nights Are Forever
Record Label: Big Tree
Songwriter: Parker McGee

The Seals and Crofts of the '70s is actually (Dan) Seals and Coley.

1978

WE'LL NEVER HAVE TO SAY GOODBYE AGAIN
Producer: Kyle Lehning
Album: Some Things Don't Come Easy
Record Label: Big Tree
Songwriter: Jeff Comanor

Big with adults.

THE ENGLISH BEAT

1980

TWIST AND CRAWL
Producer: Bob Sergeant
Album: I Just Can't Stop It
Record Label: Sire
Songwriter: English Beat

Riding the Rock and Reggae wave of the late '70s.

1982

SAVE IT FOR LATER
Producer: Bob Sergeant
Album: Special Beat Service
Record Label: I.R.S.

Songwriter: The English Beat

Enduring Reggae-esque anthem.

SCOTT ENGLISH
1972

BRANDY (MANDY)
Record Label: Janus
Songwriters: Scott English, Richard Kerr

Three years later, Clive Davis chose this former stiff to launch Barry Manilow (Bell, '75) and his new record label, Arista.

ENIGMA
1991

SADENESS (PART I)
Album: MCMXC A.D.
Record Label: Charisma
Songwriters: M. C. Curly, F. Gregorian, David Fairstein

Nailing the Gregorian mood of the '90s dance crowd.

1994

RETURN TO INNOCENCE
Album: Cross of Changes
Record Label: Charisma/Virgin
Songwriter: Michael Cretu

Greek songwriter samples Native-American flavors.

BRIAN ENO
1977

CINDY TELLS ME
Producer: Brian Eno
Album: Here Come the Warm Jets
Record Label: Antilles
Songwriter: Brian Eno

Brainy, quirky Pop Rock for the progressive sound painter.

ENYA
1988

ORINOCO FLOW (SAIL AWAY)
Album: Watermark
Record Label: Geffen
Songwriters: Enya, Roma Ryan

With a wash of hypnotic sound, Enya creates the spiritual elevator music of the '80s, called New Age.

PRESTON EPPS
1959

BONGO ROCK
Album: Bongo, Bongo, Bongo
Record Label: Original Sound
Songwriters: Preston Epps, Arthur Egnoian

Most famous use of bongos in Pop history, outside of an early Ricky Ricardo performance on "I Love Lucy." Maynard G. Krebs was listening.

ERASURE
1987

VICTIM OF LOVE
Producer: Stephen Hague
Album: The Circus
Record Label: Sire
Songwriters: Vince Clarke, Andy Bell

Big U.K./ U.S. Techno Dance crossover.

1989

A LITTLE RESPECT
Producer: Stephen Hague
Album: The Innocents
Record Label: Sire
Songwriters: Vince Clarke, Andy Bell

Their biggest hit.

ROKY ERICKSON AND THE ALIENS
1982

DON'T SHAKE ME LUCIFER
Album: The Evil One
Record Label: 415
Songwriter: Roky Erickson

Wigged-out, erstwhile Texas Acid Rock from the leader of the 13th Floor Elevators.

THE ESCAPE CLUB
1988

WILD, WILD WEST
Producer: Chris Kimsey
Album: Wild, Wild West
Record Label: Atlantic
Songwriter: The Escape Club

Dance groove, '80s style.

THE ESQUIRES
1967

GET ON UP
Producer: Bill Sheppard
Album: Get on up and Get Away
Record Label: Bunky

Songwriters: Gilbert Moorer, Johnny Taylor, Bill Sheppard

Dance groove, '60s style.

DAVID ESSEX
1973

ROCK ON
Producer: Jeff Wayne
Album: Rock On
Record Label: Columbia
Songwriter: David Essex

Leather rocker from the angry young British film That'll Be the Day.

THE ESSEX
1963

EASIER SAID THAN DONE
Producer: Henry Glover
Album: Easier Said Than Done
Record Label: Roulette
Songwriters: William Linton, Larry Huff

Responding with rare honesty to the advice dispensed in "Tell Him" by the Exciters earlier in the year.

GLORIA ESTEFAN
1991

COMING OUT OF THE DARK
Producer: Emilio Estefan
Album: Into the Light
Record Label: Epic
Songwriters: Gloria Estefan, Emilio Estefan, Jon Secada

Gloria's Pop crossover move.

DEON ESTUS
1989

HEAVEN HELP ME
Producer: George Michael
Album: Spell
Record Label: Mika/Polydor
Songwriters: Deon Estus, George Michael

R&B from Britain.

THE ETERNALS
1959

BABALU'S WEDDING DAY
Record Label: Hollywood
Songwriters: Charlie Girona, Bill Martin, Alex Miranda

More of the Ricky Ricardo influence that pervaded '59.

ETHEL AND THE SHAMELESS HUSSIES
1988

ONE NITE STAN
Album: Born to Burn
Record Label: MCA
Songwriters: Kacey Jones, Jon Iger

Suggested segues: "The Homecoming Queen's Got a Gun" by Julie Brown, "The Sweater" by Meryn Cadell, "Victims of Their Hair" by Christine Lavin, "Valley Girl" by Moon Zappa.

MELISSA ETHERIDGE
1988

LIKE THE WAY I DO
Album: Melissa Etheridge
Record Label: Island
Songwriter: Melissa Etheridge

Revived in '95.

1993

I'M THE ONLY ONE
Producers: Hugh Padgham, Melissa Etheridge
Album: Yes I Am
Record Label: Island
Songwriter: Melissa Etheridge

Defining female Rock in the moribund post-Joan Lett, pre-Liz Phair/P. J. Harvey/Courtney Love mini-era.

1994

COME TO MY WINDOW
Producers: Hugh Padgham, Melissa Etheridge
Album: Yes I Am
Record Label: Island
Songwriter: Melissa Etheridge

Tortured love relationship. Suggested segue: "Can You Please Crawl Out Your Window" by Bob Dylan.

EUROPE
1986

CARRIE
Producer: Kevin Elson
Album: The Final Countdown
Record Label: Epic
Songwriters: Joey Tempest, Mic Michaeli

Bouffant Metal.

THE FINAL COUNTDOWN
Producer: Kevin Elson
Album: The Final Countdown

Record Label: Epic
Songwriter: Joey Tempest
#1 U.K./Top-10 U.S.

EURYTHMICS
1983

SWEET DREAMS (ARE MADE OF THIS)
Producer: Dave Stewart
Album: Sweet Dreams (Are Made of This)
Record Label: RCA
Songwriters: Annie Lennox, Dave Stewart

#1 U.S./#2 U.K. crossover established their Synth-laden New Wave/New Age existential harmony.

1984

HERE COMES THE RAIN AGAIN
Producer: Dave Stewart
Album: Touch
Record Label: RCA
Songwriters: Annie Lennox, Dave Stewart

Essential mover in the British Synth-wave invasion of the mid-'80s.

1985

SISTERS ARE DOIN' IT FOR THEMSELVES
Producer: Dave Stewart
Album: Be Yourself Tonight
Record Label: RCA
Songwriters: Annie Lennox, Dave Stewart

Twin divas Lennox and guest Aretha Franklin with an uplifting contemporary message. Suggested segue: La Streisand and Donna Summer's "No More Tears."

WOULD I LIE TO YOU
Producer: Dave Stewart
Album: Be Yourself Tonight
Record Label: RCA
Songwriters: Annie Lennox, Dave Stewart

1986

MISSIONARY MAN
Producer: Dave Stewart
Album: Revenge
Record Label: MCA
Songwriters: Dave Stewart, Annie Lennox

PAUL EVANS
1959

SEVEN LITTLE GIRLS (SITTING IN THE BACK SEAT)
Album: Fabulous Teens
Record Label: Guaranteed
Songwriters: Bob Hilliard, Lee Pockriss

Novelty sound from the co-author of Bobby Vinton's "Roses Are Red" and "When" by the Kalin Twins.

1960

HAPPY GO LUCKY ME
Record Label: Guaranteed
Songwriters: Al Byron, Paul Evans

BETTY EVERETT
1963

YOU'RE NO GOOD
Record Label: Vee Jay
Songwriter: Clint Ballard Jr.

Soul ballad. Covered by Linda Ronstadt (Capitol, '75) for her biggest hit.

1964

THE SHOOP, SHOOP SONG (IT'S IN HIS KISS)
Producer: Calvin Carter
Album: It's in His Kiss
Record Label: Vee Jay
Songwriter: Rudy Clark

Winsome Pop Soul philosophy. Covered by Cher in the film Mermaids (Geffen, '91).

THE EVERLY BROTHERS
1957

BYE BYE LOVE
Producer: Archie Bleyer
Album: The Everly Brothers
Record Label: Cadence
Songwriters: Boudleaux Bryant, Felice Bryant

Pristine Country harmonies in Rockabilly drag; a perfect fit for the new Rock and Roll market. After dozens of rejections, both the Everly Brothers and this endearing Felice and Boudleaux Bryant tune make the big time.

I WONDER IF I CARE AS MUCH
Producer: Archie Bleyer
Album: The Everly Brothers
Record Label: Cadence
Songwriter: Don Everly

B-side of "Bye Bye Love." Don's emergence as a writer.

WAKE UP, LITTLE SUSIE

Producer: Archie Bleyer
Album: The Everly Brothers
Record Label: Cadence
Songwriters: Boudleaux Bryant,
   Felice Bryant

#1 C&W/R&R crossover with subject matter that was regarded as risque for Nashville.

1958

ALL I HAVE TO DO IS DREAM

Producer: Archie Bleyer
Album: The Everly Brothers Best
Record Label: Cadence
Songwriter: Boudleaux Bryant

In the blissful heyday of their ethereal harmonies, they accomplished the rare triple #1 R&R/C&W/R&B crossover. In fact, on the morning of May 4, 1957, this tune topped all seven of Billboard's *then-operating charts, the only time this has ever been done.*

BIRD DOG

Producer: Archie Bleyer
Album: The Everly Brothers Best
Record Label: Cadence
Songwriter: Boudleaux Bryant

Their most overt country lyric still went #3 R&B. It would take several years for the R&R charts to be revised to prevent this kind of thing from happening too often.

DEVOTED TO YOU

Producer: Archie Bleyer
Album: The Everly Brothers Best
Record Label: Cadence
Songwriter: Boudleaux Bryant

B-side of "Bird Dog."

PROBLEMS

Producer: Archie Bleyer
Album: The Everly Brothers Best
Record Label: Cadence
Songwriters: Boudleaux Bryant,
   Felice Bryant

Suggested segue: "Help" by the Beatles, "19th Nervous Breakdown" by the Rolling Stones, "They're Coming to Take Me Away, Ha Ha" by Napoleon XIV, "At Seventeen" by Janis Ian.

SHOULD WE TELL HIM

Producer: Archie Bleyer
Album: The Everly Brothers
Record Label: Cadence
Songwriters: Don Everly, Phil Everly

The B-side of "This Little Girl of Mine" was their first brotherly hit.

1959

'TIL I KISSED YOU

Producer: Archie Bleyer
Album: The Fabulous Style of the
   Everly Brothers
Record Label: Cadence
Songwriter: Don Everly

Adding a drumbeat by Cricket Jerry Allison, the Everlys produce their last Top-5 hit for Cadence (accompanied by the rest of the Crickets).

POOR JENNY

Producer: Archie Bleyer
Album: The Fabulous Style of the
   Everly Brothers
Record Label: Cadence
Songwriters: Boudleaux Bryant,
   Felice Bryant

B-side of "Take a Message to Mary."

TAKE A MESSAGE TO MARY

Producer: Archie Bleyer
Album: The Fabulous Style of the
   Everly Brothers
Record Label: Cadence
Songwriters: Boudleaux Bryant,
   Felice Bryant

Country Rock lament. Suggested segue: "I've Got to Get a Message to You" by the Bee Gees. Covered by Bob Dylan (Columbia, '69).

1960

CATHY'S CLOWN

Producer: Wesley Rose
Album: A Date with the Everly
   Brothers
Record Label: Warner Brothers
Songwriters: Don Everly, Phil Everly

After signing with Warner Brothers for a cool million, they have the biggest hit of their career with Don's version of "The Grand Canyon Suite," inspired, of course, by an old girlfriend.

LIKE STRANGERS

Producer: Archie Bleyer
Album: The Fabulous Style of the
   Everly Brothers
Record Label: Cadence
Songwriters: Felice Bryant,
   Boudleaux Bryant

Mining the Cadence catalogue for an appropriate farewell to the Bryants' best clients.

LOVE HURTS

Producer: Wesley Rose
Album: A Date with the Everly
   Brothers

Record Label: Warner Brothers
Songwriter: Boudleaux Bryant

Everly album cut is one of Boudleaux Bryant's most enduring classics of the Rock era. Covered by Roy Orbison on the B-side of "Running Scared" (Monument, '62), Gram Parsons (Reprise, '74), and Nazareth (A&M, '76).

SO SAD (TO WATCH GOOD LOVE GO BAD)

Producer: Wesley Rose
Album: It's Everly Time
Record Label: Warner Brothers
Songwriter: Don Everly

WALK RIGHT BACK

Producer: Wesley Rose
Album: Golden Hits of the Everly
   Brothers
Record Label: Warner Brothers
Songwriter: Sonny Curtis

Effective rocker by the man who wrote "I Fought the Law" and "The Mary Tyler Moore Show" theme.

WHEN WILL I BE LOVED

Producer: Archie Bleyer
Album: The Fabulous Style of the
   Everly Brothers
Record Label: Cadence
Songwriter: Phil Everly

Their ultimate Bluegrass Gospel harmony ballad. Covered by Dave Edmunds and the Stray Cats in the '74 film Stardust *and Linda Ronstadt (Capitol, '75).*

1961

EBONY EYES

Producer: Wesley Rose
Album: The Golden Hits of the
   Everly Brothers
Record Label: Warner Brothers
Songwriter: John D. Loudermilk

1962

CRYING IN THE RAIN

Producer: Wesley Rose
Album: Golden Hits of the Everly
   Brothers
Record Label: Warner Brothers
Songwriters: Howard Greenfield,
   Carole King

In '62 the Everly Brothers once again invaded New York, home of the much-despised Brill Building (as well as 1650 Broadway, a few blocks to the north). Perhaps it was to pay their grudging respects (the Beatles, after all, were in awe of the Brill Building/staff-songwriter sound). More likely, it was in an attempt to stave off the inevitable changing of the guard. The results were less than inspiring: "Crying in the Rain" fell short of the Top-5 in March; "That's Old Fashioned" hit the bottom of the Top-10 in June; and "Don't Ask Me to Be Friends" failed to even dent the Top-40 in November. While the Beatles were recycling the Everly sound in England, 1963 would produce no hits for the Brothers. While the Beatles dominated the American charts, minds, and radio waves, the Everly Brothers best effort of '64 was called "Gone Gone Gone."

DON'T ASK ME TO BE FRIENDS

Producer: Wesley Rose
Record Label: Warner Brothers
Songwriters: Gerry Goffin, Jack Keller

If the Everly Brothers couldn't crack the top of the charts with the best minds of New York Rock and Roll on the case, then more than one era was ending. Prescient publishers in that vaunted edifice began shipping their best material overseas, where Herman's Hermits and Manfred Mann, among others, would do it more justice.

HOW CAN I MEET HER?

Producer: Wesley Rose
Album: The Golden Hits of the Everly Brothers
Record Label: Warner Brothers
Songwriters: Gerry Goffin, Jack Keller

B-side of "That's Old Fashioned."

THAT'S OLD FASHIONED

Producer: Wesley Rose
Album: The Golden Hits of the Everly Brothers
Record Label: Warner Brothers
Songwriters: Bill Giant, Bernie Baum, Florence Kaye

Their last appearance on the Top-10.

1965

PRICE OF LOVE

Album: In Our Image
Record Label: Warner Brothers
Songwriters: Don Everly, Phil Everly

One of their favorite concert openers, this was a #2 hit in England, where it was heard and eventually covered by Bryan Ferry (Polydor, '77).

1968

SING ME BACK HOME

Album: Roots
Record Label: Warner Brothers
Songwriter: Gram Parsons

#1 C&W hit by Merle Haggard (Capitol, '67). Covered by the Flying Burrito Brothers (A&M, '72). They also recorded Merle's "White Line Fever" in '80, after Gram was gone, and it became their first C&W hit.

1972

THE STORIES WE COULD TELL

Producer: Paul Rothchild
Album: The Stories We Could Tell
Record Label: RCA
Songwriter: John Sebastian

Revived by Sebastian (Shanachie, '93).

1984

ON THE WINGS OF A NIGHTINGALE

Producer: Dave Edmunds
Album: EB84
Record Label: Mercury
Songwriter: Paul McCartney

Never saying never again, the Everly Brothers reunite. Produced by one of their biggest British fans.

EVERY MOTHER'S SON

1966

COME ON DOWN TO MY BOAT

Producer: Wes Farrell
Album: Every Mother's Son
Record Label: MGM
Songwriters: Wes Farrell, Jerry Goldstein

Good-time rocker.

EVERYTHING IS EVERYTHING

1969

WITCHI-TAI-TO

Record Label: Vanguard Apostolic
Songwriter: Jim Pepper

3,000-year-old Indian peace chant, covered by Brewer and Shipley in their first album, Weeds (Kama Sutra, '70).

THE EXCELLENTS

1962

CONEY ISLAND BABY

Producer: Vinny Catalano
Record Label: Blast
Songwriters: Vinny Catalano, Peter Alonzo

Legendary tale of urban fantasy by a Bronx group who'd never seen the Parachute Jump in person. Big winner on deejay Murray the K's Boss-Record-of-the-Week contest in New York City.

THE EXCITERS

1963

DO WAH DIDDY

Producers: Jeff Barry, Ellie Greenwich
Album: Tell Him
Record Label: United Artists
Songwriters: Jeff Barry, Ellie Greenwich

Covered by Manfred Mann as "Do Wah Diddy Diddy" (Ascot, '64), that added "Diddy" propelling the previous stiff to #1 U.S./U.K.

TELL HIM

Producers: Jerry Leiber, Mike Stoller
Album: Tell Him
Record Label: United Artists
Songwriter: Bert Burns (Bert Russell)

Aggressive girl-group advice in the Brill Building/R&B mode.

EXILE

1978

KISS YOU ALL OVER

Producer: Mike Chapman
Album: Mixed Emotions
Record Label: Warner/Curb
Songwriters: Mike Chapman, Nicky Chinn

#1 R&R, and then the entire group crossed over to Country.

EXPOSE

1987

COME GO WITH ME

Producer: Lewis Martinee
Album: Exposure
Record Label: Arista
Songwriter: Lewis Martinee

Debut groove for the Miami-based Dance Rock specialists.

LET ME BE THE ONE

Producer: Lewis Martinee
Album: Exposure
Record Label: Arista
Songwriter: Lewis Martinee

POINT OF NO RETURN

Producer: Lewis Martinee
Album: Exposure
Record Label: Arista
Songwriter: Lewis Martinee

SEASONS CHANGE

Producer: Lewis Martinee
Album: Exposure
Record Label: Arista
Songwriter: Lewis Martinee

Their first #1 R&R and fourth Top-10 R&R from the same album.

1989

TELL ME WHY

Producer: Lewis Martinee
Album: What You Don't Know
Record Label: Arista
Songwriter: Lewis Martinee

WHAT YOU DON'T KNOW

Producer: Lewis Martinee
Album: What You Don't Know
Record Label: Arista
Songwriter: Lewis Martinee

1993

I'LL NEVER GET OVER YOU (GETTING OVER ME)

Album: Expose
Record Label: Arista
Songwriter: Diane Warren

Crossing over into corporate Top-40 territory, via Warren.

EXTREME

1990

HOLE HEARTED

Producer: Michael Wagener
Album: Pornograffiti II
Record Label: A&M
Songwriters: Nuno Bettencourt, Gary Cherone

Scions of Aerosmith tune down for radio consumption.

MORE THAN WORDS

Producer: Michael Wagener
Album: Pornograffiti II
Record Label: A&M
Songwriters: Nuno Bettencourt, Gary Cherone

Unplugged Beatles-esque departure from their Metal norm was their biggest hit.

1992

REST IN PEACE

Producers: Nuno Bettencourt, Bob St. John
Album: III Sides to Every Story
Record Label: A&M

Songwriters: Gary Cherone, Nuno Bettencourt

Getting back to Metal business.

F

SHELLEY FABARES

1962

JOHNNY ANGEL

Producer: Stu Phillips
Album: Shelley!
Record Label: Colpix
Songwriters: Lyn Duddy, Lee Pockriss

In the waifish Debbie Reynolds mold, Donna Reed's TV daughter steps forth, bolstered by the Blossoms on backing vocals, featuring Darlene Love.

FABIAN

1958

I'M A MAN

Producer: Pete D'Angelis
Album: The Fabulous Fabian
Record Label: Chancellor
Songwriters: Doc Pomus, Mort Shuman

Off the Philadelphia assembly line.

1959

HOUND DOG MAN

Producer: Pete D'Angelis
Album: Hound Dog Man
Record Label: Chancellor
Songwriters: Doc Pomus, Mort Shuman

From the film of the same name, starring Stuart Whitman.

TIGER

Producer: Pete D'Angelis
Album: Hold That Tiger
Record Label: Chancellor
Songwriter: Ollie Jones

His biggest hit.

TURN ME LOOSE

Producer: Pete D'Angelis
Record Label: Chancellor
Songwriters: Doc Pomus, Mort Shuman

Teen idle.

BENT FABRIC

1962

ALLEY CAT

Album: Alley Cat
Record Label: Atco
Songwriters: Jack Harlen, Frank Bjorn

Instrumental from wonderful Copenhagen.

THE FABULOUS THUNDERBIRDS

1986

TUFF ENUFF

Producer: Dave Edmunds
Album: Tuff Enuff
Record Label: Epic
Songwriter: Kim Wilson

Rockabilly, with horns, breaks into the Top-10.

TOMMY FACENDA

1959

HIGH SCHOOL U.S.A.

Record Label: Atlantic
Songwriter: Frank J. Guida

Sparing no expense or effort, approximately 28 separate versions of this high school-ography were tailored to specific markets around the U.S.A, a lot of work for a mere Top-30 showing.

THE FACES

1972

STAY WITH ME

Producers: Glyn Johns, Faces
Album: A Nod Is As Good As a Wink to a Blind Horse
Record Label: Warner Brothers
Songwriters: Rod Stewart, Ron Wood

One of Rod's early seduction anthems. Revived by Stewart and his erstwhile guitar-mate Wood during Rod's later, acoustically sedate period (Warner Brothers, '94).

1973

CINDY INCIDENTALLY

Producer: Glyn Johns
Album: Ooh La La
Record Label: Warner Brothers
Songwriters: Rod Stewart, Ron Wood, Ian McLachan

Smiling Faces.

DONALD FAGEN
1982

I.G.Y. (WHAT A BEAUTIFUL WORLD)
Producer: Gary Katz
Album: The Nightfly
Record Label: Warner Brothers
Songwriter: Donald Fagen

A cool flashback by an ex-Steely Dan founder.

1993

TEAHOUSE ON THE TRACKS
Producer: Walter Becker
Album: Kamakiriad
Record Label: Reprise
Songwriter: Donald Fagen

Noodling toward the apocalypse, with an old partner in Steely Dan.

FAIRPORT CONVENTION
1968

MEET ON THE LEDGE
Producer: Joe Boyd
Album: Fairport Convention
Record Label: A&M
Songwriter: Richard Thompson

A beer-drinking anthem, on the edge of doom.

1969

CAJUN GIRL
Producers: Joe Boyd, Simon Nicol
Album: Unhalfbricking
Record Label: A&M
Songwriter: Richard Thompson

Introducing Richard Thompson, a major new songwriting and guitar-playing talent, soon to be a cult hero to dispossessed folkies the world over.

CRAZY MAN MICHAEL
Producer: Joe Boyd
Album: Liege & Lief
Record Label: A&M
Songwriters: Richard Thompson, Dave Swarbrick

PERCY'S SONG
Producers: Joe Boyd, Simon Nicol
Album: Unhalfbricking
Record Label: A&M
Songwriter: Bob Dylan

This epic, early-Dylan ramble on injustice was performed by Joan Baez in the '67 documentary Don't Look Back.

WHO KNOWS WHERE THE TIME GOES
Producers: Joe Boyd, Simon Nicol
Album: Unhalfbricking
Record Label: A&M
Songwriter: Sandy Denny

Spotlighting Sandy Denny, a striking new singer/songwriter in the traditional English Folk mold. Covered by Judy Collins (Elektra, '69). Featured in the movie The Subject Was Roses. Suggested segues: "The Circle Game" by Joni Mitchell and "Sugar Mountain" by Neil Young.

FAITH NO MORE
1990

EPIC
Producers: Matt Wallace, Faith No More
Album: The Real Thing
Record Label: Slash/Reprise
Songwriter: Faith No More

Their sobering rebuke to the ghost of Jim Morrison—"You want it all and you can't have it"—hit a nerve in the nervous '90s.

1992

MIDLIFE CRISIS
Producers: Matt Wallace, Faith No More
Album: Angel Dust
Record Label: Island
Songwriter: Faith No More

Too old to mosh, too young to matriculate.

FAITH, HOPE AND CHARITY
1975

TO EACH HIS OWN (THAT'S MY PHILOSOPHY)
Producer: Van McCoy
Album: Faith, Hope and Charity
Record Label: RCA
Songwriter: Van McCoy

#1 R&B/Top-50 R&R crossover.

MARIANNE FAITHFULL
1964

AS TEARS GO BY
Producer: Andrew Loog-Oldham
Album: Marianne Faithfull
Record Label: London
Songwriters: Mick Jagger, Andrew Loog-Oldham, Keith Richards

Delicate Pop Rock semi-hit would define

Faithfull as the ultimate lost-waif R&R groupie of the decade. Covered by its authors, the Rolling Stones (London, '64), it became an even bigger hit in '66.

1965

COME AND STAY WITH ME
Producer: Tony Calder
Album: Marianne Faitfull
Record Label: London
Songwriter: Jackie De Shannon

Covered by Cher (Imperial, '65), Jackie De Shannon (Imperial, '67).

THIS LITTLE BIRD
Producer: Tony Calder
Album: Marianne Faithfull
Record Label: London
Songwriter: John D. Loudermilk

Also recorded by Loudermilk (Decca, '65).

1980

BALLAD OF LUCY JORDAN
Producer: Mark Miller Mundy
Album: Broken English
Record Label: Island
Songwriter: Shel Silverstein

From the pen of another raspy soulmate. Featured in the '91 movie Thelma and Louise.

1986

THE HAWK (EL GAVILAN)
Album: Trouble in Mind
Record Label: Island
Songwriter: Kris Kristofferson

Anguished lament from the movie is a career peak for the singer and the author.

1987

HELLO STRANGER
Producer: Mark Miller Mundy
Album: Strange Weather
Record Label: Island
Songwriters: Doc Pomus, Mac Rebennack

A scintillating match of composer, lyricist, song, and performer.

STRANGE WEATHER
Producer: Mark Miller Mundy
Album: Strange Weather
Record Label: Island
Songwriters: Tom Waits, Kathleen Brennan

Waits finds his female voice. Covered by Waits Big Time (Island, '88).

FALCO
1986

ROCK ME AMADEUS
Producers: Rob Bolland, Ferdi
Bolland
Album: Falco 3
Record Label: A&M
Songwriters: Rob Bolland, Ferdi
Bolland, Hans Hoelzl (Falco)

German novelty song.

THE FALCONS
1959

YOU'RE SO FINE
Producer: Bob West
Record Label: Unart
Songwriters: Lance Finney, Willie
Schofield

*From the Detroit school of R&B, prefiguring
the later '60s emanations of Motown and
Soul. Group included future stalwarts, Mack
Rice ("Mustang Sally") and Eddie Floyd
("Knock on Wood").*

1962

I FOUND A LOVE
Record Label: Lupine
Songwriters: Willie Schofield, Robert
West, Wilson Pickett

*Covered by former group member, Wilson
Pickett (Atlantic, '67).*

THE FALL
1977

REPETITION
Album: Early Years, '77–'79
Record Label: Faulty Productions
Songwriter: Mark E. Smith

*Experimentalist noise; influenced Public
Image.*

GEORGIE FAME
1968

THE BALLAD OF BONNIE
AND CLYDE
Album: The Ballad of Bonnie and
Clyde
Record Label: Epic
Songwriters: Mitch Murray, Peter
Callender

*Suggested segue: "The Ballad of John and
Yoko" by the Beatles.*

THE FAMILY STAND
1990

GHETTO HEAVEN
Producers: Jeffrey Smith, Peter Lord
Album: Chain
Record Label: Atlantic
Songwriters: Peter Lord, V. Jeffrey
Smith, Sandra St. Victor

*The writing trio would move on to Paula
Abdul.*

THE FAMILY
1985

NOTHING COMPARES 2 U
Producer: Prince
Album: The Family
Record Label: Paisley Park
Songwriter: Prince Rogers Nelson

*Career-making cover by Sinead O'Connor
(Chrysalis, '90).*

FANNY
1971

CHARITY BALL
Producer: Richard Perry
Album: Charity Ball
Record Label: Reprise
Songwriters: June Millington, Jean
Millington, Alice DeBuhe

Femme Rock with balls.

FANTASTIC JOHNNY C.
1967

BOOGALOO DOWN BROADWAY
Producer: Jesse James
Album: Boogaloo down Broadway
Record Label: Phil L.A. of Soul
Songwriter: Jesse James

*Still dancing, while the rest of the Youth
Culture was nodding off.*

DON FARDON
1968

(THE LAMENT OF THE CHEROKEE)
INDIAN RESERVATION
Producer: Mike Dalcon
Record Label: GNP Crescendo
Songwriter: John D. Loudermilk

*Big hit in England in 1970. Covered by Paul
Revere and the Raiders (Columbia, '71).*

RICHARD AND MIMI
FARIÑA
1965

MICHAEL, ANDREW AND JAMES
Album: Celebrations for a Grey Day
Record Label: Vanguard
Songwriter: Richard Fariña

*Written about three civil rights workers slain
in Mississippi. Suggested segue: "He Was
My Brother" by Simon and Garfunkel.*

PACK UP YOUR SORROWS
Album: Celebrations for a Grey Day
Record Label: Vanguard
Songwriters: Pauline Marden,
Richard Fariña

*Bridging the gap from Folk to Folk Rock.
Popularized by Joan Baez (Vanguard, '64).*

RENO, NEVADA
Album: Celebrations for a Grey Day
Record Label: Vanguard
Songwriter: Richard Fariña

Their only single.

V
Album: Celebrations for a Grey Day
Record Label: Vanguard
Songwriter: Richard Fariña

*Dedicated to Fariña's college buddy
Thomas Pynchon's epic novel "V."
Suggested segue: "The Eyes of a New York
Woman" by Insect Trust, from the same
book, with lyrics by Pynchon.*

1966

HARD LOVIN' LOSER
Album: Reflections in a Crystal Wind
Record Label: Vanguard
Songwriter: Richard Fariña

*The only chart record for the author of the
black humor (Pynchon-esque) novel, Been
Down So Long It Looks Like Up to Me,
arrived for a cup of coffee on the charts
courtesy of Judy Collins (Elektra, '67) about
a year after Fariña had been killed in a
motorcycle accident coming home from his
book publication party.*

MAINLINE PROSPERITY BLUES
Album: Reflections in a Crystal Wind
Record Label: Vanguard
Songwriter: Richard Fariña

*Depicting a generation's symbolic and
actual attraction to drugs.*

CHRIS FARLOWE
1966

OUT OF TIME
Record Label: Immediate
Songwriters: Mick Jagger, Keith Richards

#1 in the U.K., a stiff in the States. Stones released it on Flowers *(London, '67), and put it out as a single themselves in '75, whereupon it stiffed again.*

THE FAT BOYS
1985

JAILHOUSE RAP
Album: Fat Boys
Record Label: Sutra
Songwriters: Kurtis Blow, Larry Smith, Mark Morales, Darren Robinson, Damon Wimbley, David Reeve, Sal Abbatiello

Rap answer to Elvis Presley's "Jailhouse Rock" introduces a new force in urban mythology. The Boys would go on to cover "The Twist" and "Wipeout."

CHARLIE FEATHERS
1955

DEFROST YOUR HEART
Producer: Sam Phillips
Record Label: Sun
Songwriters: Quinton Flaunch, William Cantrell

The legendary Rockabilly sideman, Feathers, wrote the famous Presley #1 C&W B-side, "I Forgot to Remember to Forget."

THE FEELIES
1988

AWAY
Album: Only Life
Record Label: A&M
Songwriter: Glen Mercer

Critic/cult band classic from classic critic's cult album.

THE FENDERMEN
1960

MULE SKINNER BLUES (BLUE YODEL #8)
Album: Muleskinner Blues
Record Label: Soma
Songwriters: Jimmie Rodgers, George Vaughan

Introduced by Country music pioneer Jimmie Rodgers (Victor, '31).

JAY FERGUSON
1977

THUNDER ISLAND
Producer: Bill Szymczyk
Album: Thunder Island
Record Label: Asylum
Songwriter: Jay Ferguson

One-shot single for the former co-leader of Spirit.

FERRON
1990

STAND UP
Album: Phantom Center
Record Label: Chameleon
Songwriter: Ferron

Feminist folkie anthem, influenced the Indigo Girls.

BRYAN FERRY
1985

SLAVE TO LOVE
Album: Boys and Girls
Record Label: Warner Brothers
Songwriter: Bryan Ferry

Reinventing Frank Sinatra-style romantic Pop in England in the '80s just as the Beatles reinvented Rock and Roll in England in the '60s.

FEVER TREE
1968

SAN FRANCISCO GIRLS (THE RETURN OF THE NATIVE)
Producers: Scott Holtzman, Vivian Holtzman
Album: Fever Tree
Record Label: Uni
Songwriters: Scott Holtzman, Vivian Holtzman, Michael Knust

Atmospheric FM nostalgia for the days of hippie splendor and grass.

THE FIESTAS
1959

SO FINE
Record Label: Old Town
Songwriter: John Veliotis (Johnny Otis)

Evocative post-Doo-Wop, pre-R&B standard. Sounds like it was recorded in a men's room.

THE FIFTH DIMENSION
1967

UP-UP AND AWAY
Producer: Johnny Rivers
Album: Up-Up and Away
Record Label: Soul City
Songwriter: Jimmy Webb

Flighty Pop Rock standard introduces one of the '60s most distinctive voices, that of songwriter Jimmy Webb.

WORST THAT COULD HAPPEN
Producer: Bones Howe
Album: Magic Garden
Record Label: Soul City
Songwriter: Jimmy Webb

Doo-Wop redux. Covered by Johnny Maestro with the Brooklyn Bridge (Buddah, '69).

1969

AQUARIUS (LET THE SUN SHINE IN)
Producer: Bones Howe
Album: Age of Aquarius
Record Label: Soul City
Songwriters: Gerome Ragni, James Rado, Galt MacDermot

#1 R&R/Top-10 R&B crossover. Introduced in the musical Hair *in '67 and in the original cast album by Ronnie Dyson (RCA, '70). Medley with "The Flesh Failures (Let the Sunshine In)," sung in the show by Melba Moore and Broadway hippies James Rado and Gerome Ragni.*

FINE YOUNG CANNIBALS
1989

DON'T LOOK BACK
Producers: David Steele, Roland Gift, Andy Cox
Album: The Raw and the Cooked
Record Label: IRS
Songwriters: David Steele, Roland Gift

Commercializing the Reggae Soul of London.

GOOD THING
Producers: David Steele, Roland Gift
Album: The Raw and the Cooked
Record Label: IRS
Songwriters: David Steele, Roland Gift

Used in the movies Scandal *and* Tin Men.

SHE DRIVES ME CRAZY
Producers: David Z., Fine Young Cannibals, Andy Cox

Album: The Raw and the Cooked
Record Label: IRS
Songwriters: David Steele, Roland Gift

Their biggest hit.

LARRY FINNEGAN
1962

DEAR ONE
Record Label: Old Town
Songwriters: John Lawrence Finneran, Vincent Finneran

In the agonized Del-Shannon mode.

FIRE, INC.
1984

TONIGHT IS WHAT IT MEANS TO BE YOUNG
Producer: Jim Steinman
Album: *Streets of Fire* Soundtrack
Record Label: MCA
Songwriter: Jim Steinman

Between courses of Meatloaf.

FIREFALL
1976

YOU ARE THE WOMAN
Producer: Jim Mason
Album: Firefall
Record Label: Atlantic
Songwriter: Rick Roberts

L.A. Folk Rock lite.

THE FIREFLIES
1959

YOU WERE MINE
Album: You Were Mine
Record Label: Ribbon
Songwriter: Paul Giacalone

Long Island mellow.

fIREHOSE
1986

THINGS COULD TURN AROUND
Producers: Ethan James, Mike Watt
Album: Ragin', Full On
Record Label: SST
Songwriters: Kira Roessler, Mike Watt

From the ashes of the Minutemen, an Alternative survivor emerges.

1991

FLYIN' THE FLANNEL
Producer: Paul Q. Kolderie, fIREHOSE
Album: Flyin' the Flannel
Record Label: Columbia
Songwriter: Mike Watt

Watt's major label debut.

FIREHOUSE
1991

LOVE OF A LIFETIME
Producer: David Prater
Album: Firehouse
Record Label: Epic
Songwriters: Bill Leverty, C. J. Snare

Pop/Rock.

1992

WHEN I LOOK IN YOUR EYES
Album: Hold Your Fire
Record Label: Epic
Songwriters: Bill Leverty, C. J. Snare

FIRETOWN
1987

HEART COUNTRY
Producer: Butch Vig
Album: In the Heart of the Heart Country
Record Label: Atlantic
Songwriters: Paul Davis, Doug Erikson

Inspired Roots Rock one-shot.

THE GOOD LIFE
Producer: Butch Vig
Album: In the Heart of the Heart Country
Record Label: Atlantic
Songwriters: Phil Davis, Doug Erikson

Vig would move on to produce Nirvana.

LISA FISCHER
1991

HOW CAN I EASE THE PAIN
Producer: Narada Michael Walden
Album: So Intense
Record Label: Elektra
Songwriters: Lisa Fischer, Narada Michael Walden

#1 R&B/Top-15 R&R crossover.

MISS TONI FISCHER
1959

THE BIG HURT
Album: The Big Hurt
Record Label: Signet
Songwriter: Wayne Shanklin

This early example of the popular phasing guitar effect gave Miss Fischer her biggest hit. With Mr. Acker Bilk, the only Miss and Mr. ever on the charts (Mr. Mister doesn't count). The New York Times would have approved.

FISHBONE
1985

? (MODERN INDUSTRY)
Album: Fishbone
Record Label: Columbia
Songwriters: David Kahne, Kendall Jones

Urban Ska fusion.

THE FIVE AMERICANS
1967

WESTERN UNION
Producer: Dale Hawkins
Album: Western Union
Record Label: Abnak
Songwriters: Mike Rabon, Norman Ezell, John Durrill

THE FIVE KEYS
1951

THE GLORY OF LOVE
Record Label: Aladdin
Songwriter: Billy Hill

The other-side-of-the-cover syndrome; black groups of the Doo-Wop era, seeking both harmony and assimilation, attacked the Pop classics with reverence and hunger. This '36 standard was also devoured by Otis Redding (Volt, '67).

1954

LING TING TONG
Record Label: Capitol
Songwriter: Mable Godwin

Novelty R&B, covered by the Charms (DeLuxe, '55).

1955

CLOSE YOUR EYES
Record Label: Capitol
Songwriter: Chuck Willis

One of their finest moments of Doo-Wop

perfection. *Covered by Peaches and Herb (Polydor, '67).*

FIVE MAN ELECTRICAL BAND

1971

SIGNS

Producer: Dallas Smith
Album: Goodbyes and Butterflys
Record Label: Lionel
Songwriter: Arthur Thomas

Muted protest. Covered by Tesla (Geffen, '90).

THE 5 ROYALES

1953

BABY, DON'T DO IT

Album: The Rockin' 5 Royales
Record Label: Apollo
Songwriter: Lowman Pauling

Their first R&B hit and the advent of a major force in '50s writing, playing, and producing, Lowman Pauling.

HELP ME SOMEBODY

Album: The Rockin' Five Royals
Record Label: King
Songwriter: Lowman Pauling

#1 R&B smash for the prototypical rock 'n' rhythm group. B-side "Crazy Crazy Crazy" was a Lowman Pauling guitar showcase.

1957

TELL THE TRUTH

Record Label: King
Songwriter: Lowman Pauling

Covered by Ray Charles (Atlantic, '60), Ike and Tina Turner (Warner Brothers, '65).

THINK

Record Label: King
Songwriter: Lowman Pauling

Covered by James Brown (Federal, '60).

1958

DEDICATED TO THE ONE I LOVE

Producer: Ralph Bass
Album: Dedicated to You
Record Label: King
Songwriters: Lowman Pauling, Ralph Bass

Inspired by the notion of Rock and Roll as the first true medium of teenage connection, the radio DJ litany of dedications preceeding each sacred tune was like a manic reading of a holy scroll, the ultimate reaching out for the unattainable oneness of harmony, leading to the inevitability of teenage

separation and abandonment. Pauling and Bass were undoubtedly thinking of none of this when they wrote this tune. Covered by the Shirelles (Scepter, '61) and the Mamas and the Papas (Dunhill, '67).*

THE FIVE SATINS

1956

I'LL REMEMBER (IN THE STILL OF THE NIGHT)

Producer: Freddy Parris
Album: The Five Satins Sing
Record Label: Standord/Ember
Songwriter: Freddy Parris

B-side of "The Jones Girl" became one of the most cherished and popular Doo-Wop classics of all-time, though not necessarily the most lucrative.

1957

TO THE AISLE

Album: The Five Satins Sing
Record Label: Ember
Songwriters: Billy Dawn Smith, Stuart Wiener

Classic Doo-Wop ballad, espousing harmony and monogamy. The subsequent career of the Five Satins espoused anything but.

THE FIVE SCAMPS

1949

RED HOT

Record Label: Okeh/Columbia
Songwriters: Earl Robinson, James Whitcomb

Seminal R&B rocker. Covered by Billy Lee Riley (Sun, '57), Sam the Sham and the Pharoahs (MGM, '65) and Robert Gordon with Link Wray (RCA, '77).

THE FIVE STAIRSTEPS

1970

O-O-H CHILD

Producer: Stan Vincent
Album: Stairsteps
Record Label: Buddah
Songwriter: Stan Vincent

A tonic for the troops, after the scathing '60s, soothing and soulful. The B-side was their cover of the Beatles' "Dear Prudence."

THE FIXX

1982

STAND OR FALL

Producer: Rupert Hine
Album: Shuttered Rooms

Record Label: MCA
Songwriters: Cy Curnin, Adam Woods, Jamie West-Oram, Peter Greenall, Charles Barrett

Video-age anxiety, presages a new British invasion. Thomas Dolby was in synch.

1983

ONE THING LEADS TO ANOTHER

Producer: Rupert Hine
Album: Reach the Beach
Record Label: MCA
Songwriters: Cy Curnin, Adam Woods, Jamie West-Oram, Rupert Greenall, Alfred Agius

Their biggest hit. Human League, the Eurhythmics, and Duran Duran were on the way.

ROBERTA FLACK

1972

WHERE IS THE LOVE

Producer: Joel Dorn
Album: Roberta Flack and Donny Hathaway
Record Label: Atlantic
Songwriters: Ralph MacDonald, William Slater

#1 R&B/Top-10 R&R; crossover ballad with Donny Hathaway.

1974

FEEL LIKE MAKIN' LOVE

Producer: Roberta Flack
Album: Feel Like Makin' Love
Record Label: Atlantic
Songwriters: Roberta Flack, Peabo Bryson

#1 R&B/R&R crossover; her Soul peak, again with Donny Hathaway.

FLAMIN' GROOVIES

1971

TEENAGE HEAD

Producer: Richard Robinson
Album: Teenage Head
Record Label: Buddah
Songwriters: Roy A. Loney, Cyril Jordan

Anti-Beach Boys return to the East Coast. Covered by Ducks Deluxe (RCA, '75).

1972

SLOW DEATH

Producer: Dave Edmunds
Album: Slow Death

Record Label: United Artists
Songwriters: Roy A. Loney, Cyril Jordan

Quintessential Punk Rockabilly track, released in the U.K. as a single. Covered by the Dictators (Epic, '78).

1976

SHAKE SOME ACTION
Producer: Dave Edmunds
Album: Shake Some Action
Record Label: Sire
Songwriters: Chris Wilson, Cyril Jordan

Returning to their retro roots.

THE FLAMING LIPS

1987

ONE MILLION BILLIONTH OF A MILLISECOND ON A SUNDAY MORNING
Album: Oh My Gawd! . . . the Flaming Lips
Record Label: Restless
Songwriter: Flaming Lips

The new garage era begins in college towns across the land.

THE FLAMINGOS

1956

I'LL BE HOME
Producer: Leonard Chess
Album: The Flamingos
Record Label: Chess
Songwriters: Ferdinand Washington, Stan Lewis

The flowering of Doo-Wop as urban romance. Covered by Pat Boone (Dot, '56).

THE VOW
Producer: Leonard Chess
Album: The Flamingos
Record Label: Checker
Songwriters: George Motola, Zeke Carey, Danny Webb

Family values.

1959

I ONLY HAVE EYES FOR YOU
Producer: George Goldner
Album: Flamingo's Serenade
Record Label: End
Songwriters: Harry Warren, Al Dubin

Achieving the pinnacle of the reverse-cover sound with a tune originated by Dick Powell and Ruby Keeler in the '34 film, Dames.

LOVERS NEVER SAY GOODBYE
Producer: George Goldner
Album: Battle of the Groups
Record Label: End
Songwriters: Terry Johnson, Paul Wilson

Not their biggest hit, but probably their best remembered. Also known as "Please Wait for Me."

1970

BUFFALO SOLDIER
Record Label: Polydor
Songwriters: David Barnes, Myra Smith, Margaret Lewis

About a legendary brigade of black soldiers.

FLEETWOOD MAC

1968

GOT TO MOVE
Producers: Keith Olson, Fleetwood Mac
Album: Fleetwood Mac
Record Label: Reprise
Songwriters: Elmore James, Marshall Sehorn

Cover of a Blues tune by the influential guitarist James, best-known for "The Sky Is Crying" and "I Believe I'll Dust My Broom."

1969

ALBATROSS
Album: English Rose
Record Label: Epic
Songwriter: Peter Green

Instrumental hit in England.

BLACK MAGIC WOMAN
Album: English Rose
Record Label: Epic
Songwriter: Peter Green

Showcasing Peter Green, one of the finest English Blues guitarists. Covered by Santana (Columbia, '71).

LOVE THAT BURNS
Album: English Rose
Record Label: Epic
Songwriter: Peter Green

OH WELL (PART I)
Producer: Fleetwood Mac
Album: Then Play On
Record Label: Reprise
Songwriter: Peter Green

Fleetwood Mac's only U.S. chart appearance in their bluesy Peter Green incarnation; in the U.K. they were the #1 band of '69.

RATTLESNAKE SHAKE
Album: Then Play On
Record Label: Reprise
Songwriter: Peter Green

A Fleetwood fixture until Green followed Syd Barrett into the Rock and Roll void.

1972

SENTIMENTAL LADY
Producer: Fleetwood Mac
Album: Bare Trees
Record Label: Warner Brothers
Songwriter: Bob Welch

The California Folk Blues, laid back and mellow. Covered by Bob Welch (Capitol, '77).

1975

LANDSLIDE
Producers: Keith Olson, Fleetwood Mac
Album: Fleetwood Mac
Record Label: Reprise
Songwriter: Stephanie Nicks

Ethereal Nicks at her spaciest. Covered by Olivia Newton-John (MCA, '81) and Smashing Pumpkins (Virgin, '84).

OVER MY HEAD
Producers: Keith Olson, Fleetwood Mac
Album: Fleetwood Mac
Record Label: Reprise
Songwriter: Christine McVie

A reminder of their Blues heritage.

RHIANNON (WILL YOU EVER WIN)
Producers: Keith Olson, Fleetwood Mac
Album: Fleetwood Mac
Record Label: Reprise
Songwriter: Stephanie Nicks

The Eagles' "Witchy Woman" personified.

SAY YOU LOVE ME
Producers: Keith Olson, Fleetwood Mac
Album: Fleetwood Mac
Record Label: Reprise
Songwriter: Christine McVie

Closer to perfect.

1977

THE CHAIN
Producers: Richard Dashut, Ken Caillat, Fleetwood Mac
Album: Rumours
Record Label: Warner Brothers

Songwriters: Lindsay Buckingham, Stephanie Nicks, Christine McVie, John McVie, Mick Fleetwood

From their double breakup breakout album, a dire chant.

DON'T STOP
Producers: Richard Dashut, Ken Caillat, Fleetwood Mac
Album: Rumours
Record Label: Warner Brothers
Songwriter: Christine McVie

McVie turns into Linda Thompson. Or is it vice versa?

DREAMS
Producers: Richard Dashut, Ken Caillat, Fleetwood Mac
Album: Rumours
Record Label: Warner Brothers
Songwriter: Stephanie Nicks

Their biggest thoroughly L.A. hit.

GO YOUR OWN WAY
Producers: Richard Dashut, Ken Caillat, Fleetwood Mac
Album: Rumours
Record Label: Warner Brothers
Songwriter: Lindsay Buckingham

Autobiographical Folk Rock soap operatics from their monster album.

YOU MAKE LOVING FUN
Producers: Richard Dashut, Ken Caillat, Fleetwood Mac
Album: Rumours
Record Label: Warner Brothers
Songwriter: Christine McVie

An ironic face on the intramural coed skirmishes within, or a clue to their inception?

1979

SARA
Producer: Fleetwood Mac
Album: Tusk
Record Label: Warner Brothers
Songwriter: Stephanie Nicks

Her trademark Folk swirl.

TUSK
Producer: Fleetwood Mac
Album: Tusk
Record Label: Warner Brothers
Songwriter: Lindsay Buckingham

White elephant.

1982

GYPSY
Producers: Richard Dashut, Lindsay Buckingham, Ken Caillet, Fleetwood Mac
Album: Mirage
Record Label: Warner Brothers
Songwriter: Stephanie Nicks

Her defining metaphor.

HOLD ME
Producers: Richard Dashut, Lindsay Buckingham, Ken Caillet, Fleetwood Mac
Album: Mirage
Record Label: Warner Brothers
Songwriters: Christine McVie, Robbie Patton

1987

BIG LOVE
Producers: Richard Dashut, Lindsay Buckingham
Album: Tango in the Night
Record Label: Warner Brothers
Songwriter: Lindsay Buckingham

LITTLE LIES
Producers: Richard Dashut, Lindsay Buckingham
Album: Tango in the Night
Record Label: Warner Brothers
Songwriters: Christine McVie, Eddy Quintela

Their last big hit.

THE FLEETWOODS
1959

COME SOFTLY TO ME
Producer: Bob Reisdorff
Album: Come Softly to Me
Record Label: Dolton
Songwriters: Gary Troxel, Gretchen Christopher, Barbara Ellis

The leading edge of the new Soft Rock sound.

MR. BLUE
Producer: Bob Reisdorff
Album: Mr. Blue
Record Label: Dolton
Songwriter: DeWayne Blackwell

Their second straight #1, closing out '59 on the note that once-feared Rock and Roll had been vanquished at last.

FLESH FOR LULU
1987

I GO CRAZY
Album: Long Live the New Flesh
Record Label: Beggars' Banquet/Capitol
Songwriters: James Mitchell, Kevin Mills, Nick Marsh, Rocco Barker

Gothic glamsters go commercial with this tune from the soundtrack of the film Some Kind of Wonderful.

THE FLESHTONES
1979

AMERICAN BEAT
Album: Blast Off
Record Label: RIOR
Songwriter: Peter Zaremba

Critically regarded as his best work with this underground Roots Rock band.

FLO AND EDDIE
1971

MARMENDY MILL
Producer: Bob Ezrin
Album: Flo and Eddie
Record Label: Reprise
Songwriters: Howard Kaylan, Mark Volman, Jim Pons, Al Nichol, John Seiter

A seven-minute biographical opus by the ex-Turtles part-time Mothers, containing one of the great Rock and Roll screams.

THE FLOATERS
1977

FLOAT ON
Producer: Woody Wilson
Album: Floaters
Record Label: ABC
Songwriters: Arnold Ingram, James Mitchell Jr., Marvin Willis

#1 R&B/Top-5 R&R crossover.

A FLOCK OF SEAGULLS
1982

I RAN
Producer: Mike Howlett
Album: A Flock of Seagulls
Record Label: Jive
Songwriters: Ali Score, Paul Reynolds, Mike Score, Frank Maudley

Perhaps the most annoying of artsy British Synth Rock invasion artifacts.

EDDIE FLOYD

1966

KNOCK ON WOOD

Producer: Jim Stewart
Album: Knock on Wood
Record Label: Stax
Songwriters: Eddie Floyd, Steve Cropper

#1 R&B/Top-30 R&R Soul classic. Covered by Wilson Pickett (Atlantic, '67), King Curtis (Atco, '67), Otis and Carla (Stax '67), Archie Bell and the Drells (Atlantic, '68), and Eric Clapton (Duck, '85).

THE FLYING BURRITTO BROTHERS

1969

HOT BURRITO #1

Album: The Gilded Palace of Sin
Record Label: A&M
Songwriter: Gram Parsons

Their signature anthem. Covered by Emmylou Harris (Warner Brothers, '81).

SIN CITY

Album: The Gilded Palace of Sin
Record Label: A&M
Songwriter: Gram Parsons

From one of the most influential Country Rock albums of the '60s. Covered by Parsons' soulmate, Emmylou Harris (Reprise, '76).

1971

COLORADO

Album: Flying Burrito Brothers
Record Label: Asylum
Songwriter: Rick Roberts

Moving into a more recognizably Folk Rock bag. Covered by Linda Ronstadt (Asylum, '73).

FOCUS

1973

HOCUS POCUS

Producer: Mike Vernon
Album: Moving Waves
Record Label: Sire
Songwriters: Jan Akkerman, Theis Van Leen

Instrumental from the Dutch guitar hero, Akkerman.

DAN FOGELBERG

1975

PART OF THE PLAN

Producer: Joe Walsh
Album: Souvenirs
Record Label: Full Moon
Songwriter: Dan Fogelberg

Jackson Browneian philosophizing.

1978

POWER OF GOLD

Album: Twin Sons of Different Mothers
Record Label: Full Moon
Songwriter: Dan Fogelberg

New Age Folk Rock.

1979

LONGER

Producers: Dan Fogelberg, Marty Lewis, Norbert Putnam
Album: Phoenix
Record Label: Full Moon
Songwriter: Dan Fogelberg

Achieving easy-listening nirvana.

1980

SAME OLD LANG SYNE

Producers: Dan Fogelberg, Marty Lewis
Album: The Innocent Age
Record Label: Full Moon
Songwriter: Dan Fogelberg

Harry Chapin-esque champagne commercial.

1981

HARD TO SAY

Album: The Innocent Age
Record Label: Full Moon
Songwriter: Dan Fogelberg

LEADER OF THE BAND

Producers: Dan Fogelberg, Marty Lewis
Album: The Innocent Age
Record Label: Full Moon
Songwriter: Dan Fogelberg

Jim Croceian reminiscence.

1982

RUN FOR THE ROSES

Producers: Dan Fogelberg, Marty Lewis
Album: The Innocent Age
Record Label: Full Moon
Songwriter: Dan Fogelberg

Could be the national anthem of Kentucky.

JOHN FOGERTY

1975

ALMOST SATURDAY NIGHT

Producer: John C. Fogerty
Album: John Fogerty
Record Label: Asylum
Songwriter: John C. Fogerty

Rockabilly-esque charmer from the former Creedence frontman. Covered by Dave Edmunds (Swan Song, '81).

ROCKIN' ALL OVER THE WORLD

Producer: John C. Fogerty
Album: John Fogerty
Record Label: Asylum
Songwriter: John C. Fogerty

Suggested segue: "Rockin' in the Free World" by Neil Young, "Back in the U.S.A." by Chuck Berry.

1985

BIG TRAIN FROM MEMPHIS

Producer: John C. Fogerty
Album: Centerfield
Record Label: Warner Brothers
Songwriter: John C. Fogerty

Squarely in the tradition. Covered by Class of '55 (American, '86).

CENTERFIELD

Producer: John C. Fogerty
Album: Centerfield
Record Label: Warner Brothers
Songwriter: John C. Fogerty

The antidote to Cashman and West's baseball odes. Fit perfectly into the Bull Durham Soundtrack.

THE OLD MAN DOWN THE ROAD

Producer: John C. Fogerty
Album: Centerfield
Record Label: Warner Brothers
Songwriter: John C. Fogerty

His biggest solo hit reputedly about Ronald Reagan.

ROCK AND ROLL GIRLS

Producer: John C. Fogerty
Album: Centerfield
Record Label: Warner Brothers
Songwriter: John C. Fogerty

The Northern California answer to Brian's L.A.-oriented "California Girls."

ZANZ CAN'T DANCE (VANZ CAN'T DANCE)

Producer: John C. Fogerty
Album: Centerfield
Record Label: Warner Brothers

Songwriter: John C. Fogerty

Sparked a lawsuit from the owner of Fogerty's then-disputed previous copyrights, the coincidentally named Saul Zaentz.

FOGHAT
1976

SLOW RIDE
Producer: Nick Jameson
Album: Fool for the City
Record Label: Bearsville
Songwriter: Dave Peverett

Indominable boogie.

WAYNE FONTANA AND THE MINDBENDERS
1964

THE GAME OF LOVE
Album: The Game of Love
Record Label: Fontana
Songwriter: Clint Ballard Jr.

Re-asserting the verities, under assault from sixties Folk singers like Gale Garnett and her flower-child ilk.

FOO FIGHTERS
1995

I'LL STICK AROUND
Album: Foo Fighters
Record Label: Rosswell/Capitol
Songwriter: Dave Grohl

Reassuring legions of Nirvana fans, drummer Dave Grohl formed the Foo Fighters.

STEVE FORBERT
1979

GOIN' DOWN TO LAUREL
Producer: John Simon
Album: Alive on Arrival
Record Label: Nemperor
Songwriter: Steve Forbert

Neo-Dylanizing travelogue.

ROMEO'S TUNE
Producer: John Simon
Album: Jackrabbit Slim
Record Label: Nemperor
Songwriter: Steve Forbert

A fresh new Folk Rock fluke hit.

THE FORCE M.D.'S
1985

ITCHIN' FOR A SCRATCH
Producers: Jimmy Jam, Terry Lewis
Album: Love Letters
Record Label: T-Boy
Songwriters: Robin Halpin, Steve Stein, Doug Wimbish, Keith LeBlanc, the Force M.D.'s

Featured in the movie Rappin'.

1986

TENDER LOVE
Producers: Jimmy Jam, Terry Lewis
Album: Chillin'
Record Label: Warner Brothers
Songwriters: James Harris III, Terry Lewis

Evoking the great Doo-Wop ballads of old, in the film Krush Groove.

1987

LOVE IS A HOUSE
Producers: Martin Lascelles, Geoff Gurd
Album: Touch and Go
Record Label: Tommy Boy
Songwriters: Martin Lascelles, Geoff Gurd, G. Foster

#1 R&B/Bottom-20 crossover.

FRANKIE FORD
1959

SEA CRUISE
Producer: Johnny Vincent
Album: Let's Take a Sea Cruise
Record Label: Ace
Songwriter: Huey Smith

His first and biggest hit, with Huey Piano Smith providing the song, and his band, the Clowns, the backing tracks.

LITA FORD
1988

KISS ME DEADLY
Producer: Mike Chapman
Album: Lita
Record Label: RCA
Songwriter: Mick Smiley

Former runaway guitar queen follows in the Chapman-polished footsteps of leatherette goddesses Suzi Quatro and Debbie Harry.

1989

CLOSE MY EYES FOREVER
Producer: Mike Chapman
Album: Lita

Record Label: RCA
Songwriters: Lita Ford, Ozzy Osbourne

With Ozzie Osbourne; the king and queen of hell's senior prom.

FOREIGNER
1977

COLD AS ICE
Producers: John Sinclair, Gary Lyons, Mick Jones
Album: Foreigner
Record Label: Atlantic
Songwriters: Lou Grammatico (Lou Gram), Mick Jones

Arena natural.

FEELS LIKE THE FIRST TIME
Producers: John Sinclair, Gary Lyons
Album: Foreigner
Record Label: Atlantic
Songwriter: Mick Jones

Their first big Metal hit.

1978

DOUBLE VISION
Producer: Keith Olson
Album: Double Vision
Record Label: Atlantic
Songwriters: Lou Grammatico (Lou Gram), Mick Jones

HOT BLOODED
Producers: Keith Olson, Mick Jones
Album: Double Vision
Record Label: Atlantic
Songwriter: Lou Grammatico (Lou Gram)

Inheriting the Kiss flair for the double-entendre.

1981

JUKE BOX HERO
Producer: Mutt Lange
Album: 4
Record Label: Atlantic
Songwriters: Lou Grammatico (Lou Gram), Mick Jones

A cogent look at the exigencies of the rock star's life. But it was no "Lodi."

URGENT
Producers: Mutt Lange, Mick Jones
Album: 4
Record Label: Atlantic
Songwriter: Mick Jones

Becoming the Chicago of Heavy Metal yearning. Michael Bolton was listening.

WAITING FOR A GIRL LIKE YOU
Producers: Mutt Lange, Mick Jones
Album: 4
Record Label: Atlantic
Songwriters: Lou Grammatico (Lou Gram), Mick Jones

Trying to renounce their sexist ways, with ten weeks at #2 as delayed gratification.

1984

I WANT TO KNOW WHAT LOVE IS
Producers: Alex Sadkin, Mick Jones
Album: Agent Provocateur
Record Label: Atlantic
Songwriter: Mick Jones

Their biggest hit; thoroughly renouncing their sexist ways, with a church choir as witness.

1988

I DON'T WANT TO LIVE WITHOUT YOU
Album: Inside Information
Record Label: Atlantic
Songwriter: Mick Jones

Their last big hit.

SAY YOU WILL
Album: Inside Information
Record Label: Atlantic
Songwriters: Lou Grammatico (Lou Gram), Mick Jones

JIMMY FORREST
1952

NIGHT TRAIN
Record Label: United
Songwriters: Oscar Washington, Lewis Simpkins, Jimmy Forrest

Smokin' Jazz-flavored single. Covered by the Viscounts (Madison, '60) and James Brown (King, '62).

THE FORTUNES
1965

YOU'VE GOT YOUR TROUBLES
Producers: Roger Greenaway, Roger Cook
Album: The Fortunes
Record Label: Press
Songwriters: Roger Greenaway, Roger Cook

The British Garage Band sound.

1971

HERE COMES THAT RAINY DAY FEELING AGAIN
Producers: Roger Greenaway, Roger Cook
Album: Here Comes That Rainy Day Feeling Again
Record Label: Capitol
Songwriters: Roger Greenaway, Roger Cook, Gordon Anthony Instone

Vintage Invasion Pop.

THE FOUNDATIONS
1967

BABY, NOW THAT I'VE FOUND YOU
Producer: Tony Macaulay
Album: Baby, Now That I've Found You
Record Label: Uni
Songwriters: John Macleod, Tony Macaulay

Multi-racial British Soul group was the first to crossover to the U.S. R&B charts with this #1 U.K./#33 R&B/Top-15 R&R breakthrough. Prelude to the British Invasion of the '70s and '80s, featuring the Soul- and Reggae-influenced stylings of the Clash, Elvis Costello, Roxy Music, the Jam, the Style Council, Culture Club, Spandau Ballet, Simply Red, and the Christians.

1969

BUILD ME UP, BUTTERCUP
Producer: Tony Macaulay
Album: Build Me up, Buttercup
Record Label: Uni
Songwriters: Tony Macaulay, Michael D'Abo, John McLeod

Their biggest Pop Soul hit.

THE FOUR DEUCES
1955

WPLJ
Producer: Luther McDaniel
Record Label: Music City
Songwriter: Ray Dobard

Covered by Frank Zappa (Bizarre, '70). Later became the call letters of a New York radio station (stands for White Port and Lemon Juice).

THE FOUR FLAMES
1952

WHEEL OF FORTUNE
Producer: Art Rupe
Record Label: Specialty

Songwriters: Bennie Benjamin, George Weiss

Covered by the Cardinals (Atlantic, '52). Pop version by Kaye Starr (Capitol, '52). The Four Flames would become the Hollywood Flames.

THE FOUR FRESHMEN
1956

GRADUATION DAY
Album: Freshman Favorites
Record Label: Capitol
Songwriters: Joe Sherman, Noel Sherman

Approaching their various graduation days, in high school and junior high school in Hawthorne, California, the Wilson family, aka the Beach Boys, would soon reinvent these ethereal harmonies to apply to the '60s teen dream of surf and turf. Covered by the Arbors (Date, '67).

FOUR NON BLONDES
1993

WHAT'S UP
Producer: David Tickle
Album: Bigger, Better, Faster, More!
Record Label: Interscope
Songwriter: Linda Perry

The Angry Young Woman of Art Rock arrives. She would be followed by Courtney Love, P. J. Harvey, Liz Phair, and Alanis Morissette.

THE FOUR PREPS
1958

26 MILES
Album: The Things We Did Last Summer
Record Label: Capitol
Songwriters: Glen Larson, Bruce Belland

Previewing the sunny sound of Southern California.

BIG MAN
Album: The Things We Did Last Summer
Record Label: Capitol
Songwriters: Glen Larson, Bruce Belland

Straddling the surf and collegiate markets.

THE FOUR SEASONS
1962

BIG GIRLS DON'T CRY
Producer: Bob Crewe
Album: Sherry and 11 Others

Record Label: Vee Jay
Songwriters: Bob Gaudio, Bob Crewe

Following "Sherry," their biggest hit and their second straight #1 R&B/R&R.

SHERRY

Producer: Bob Crewe
Album: Sherry and 11 Others
Record Label: Vee Jay
Songwriter: Bob Gaudio

#1 R&B/R&R crossover, recorded at the session that also produced "Big Girls Don't Cry." Italian Soul at its commercial peak, in the anguished falsetto of New Jersey's Frankie Valli.

1963

CANDY GIRL

Producer: Bob Crewe
Album: Ain't That a Shame and 11 Others
Record Label: Vee Jay
Songwriter: Larry Santos

Suggested segue: "I Want Candy" by the Strangeloves.

WALK LIKE A MAN

Producer: Bob Crewe
Album: Big Girls Don't Cry and Twelve Others
Record Label: Vee Jay
Songwriters: Bob Gaudio, Bob Crewe

Their third #1. Suggested segue: "Mama Said" by the Shirelles.

1964

BIG MAN IN TOWN

Producer: Bob Crewe
Album: Rag Doll
Record Label: Philips
Songwriter: Bob Gaudio

Sadness behind the high-pitched bravado.

DAWN (GO AWAY)

Producer: Bob Crewe
Album: Dawn (Go Away) and 11 Other Great Songs
Record Label: Philips
Songwriters: Bob Gaudio, Sandy Linzer

Inaugurating Frankie Valli's holier-than-thou persona.

RAG DOLL

Producer: Bob Crewe
Album: Rag Doll
Record Label: Philips

Songwriters: Bob Gaudio, Bob Crewe

Defining the quintessential New Jersey attraction for the underdog.

RONNIE

Producer: Bob Crewe
Album: Rag Doll
Record Label: Philips
Songwriters: Bob Crewe, Bob Gaudio

Another girl, another heartache.

SAVE IT FOR ME

Producer: Bob Crewe
Album: Rag Doll
Record Label: Philips
Songwriters: Bob Gaudio, Bob Crewe

Traditional arrangement.

1965

LET'S HANG ON (TO WHAT WE'VE GOT)

Producer: Bob Crewe
Album: Four Seasons Gold Vault of Hits
Record Label: Philips
Songwriters: Bob Crewe, Sandy Linzer, Denny Randell

1966

TELL IT TO THE RAIN

Producer: Bob Crewe
Album: New Gold Hits
Record Label: Phillips
Songwriters: Mike Petrillo, Chubby Cifelli

WORKIN' MY WAY BACK TO YOU

Producer: Bob Crewe
Album: Workin' My Way Back to You
Record Label: Philips
Songwriters: Sandy Linzer, Denny Randell

Covered by the Spinners (Atlantic, '80).

1967

C'MON MARIANNE

Producer: Bob Crewe
Album: Four Seasons New Gold Hits
Record Label: Philips
Songwriters: L. Russell Brown, Raymond Bloodworth

Their last Top-10 hit for eight years.

1975

DECEMBER 1963 (OH WHAT A NIGHT)

Producer: Bob Gaudio
Album: Who Loves You
Record Label: Warner Brothers
Songwriters: Bob Gaudio, Judy Parker

Their biggest international hit, #1 U.S./U.K. Remixed version became another international monster in '94.

WHO LOVES YOU

Producer: Bob Crewe
Album: Who Loves You
Record Label: Warner Brothers
Songwriters: Bob Gaudio, Judy Parker

Singles-bar anthem, based on a Telly Savalas catch phrase from "Kojak."

THE FOUR TOPS

1964

BABY, I NEED YOUR LOVING

Producers: Brian Holland, Lamont Dozier
Album: Four Tops
Record Label: Motown
Songwriters: Eddie Holland, Lamont Dozier, Brian Holland

First chart single for the Detroit veterans.

1965

I CAN'T HELP MYSELF (SUGAR PIE, HONEY BUNCH)

Producers: Brian Holland, Lamont Dozier
Album: Four Tops Second Album
Record Label: Motown
Songwriters: Eddie Holland, Lamont Dozier, Brian Holland

Their biggest hit; a #1 R&B/R&R crossover.

IT'S THE SAME OLD SONG

Producers: Brian Holland, Lamont Dozier
Album: Four Tops Second Album
Record Label: Motown
Songwriters: Eddie Holland, Lamont Dozier, Brian Holland

Unintentionally revealing followup.

1966

REACH OUT, I'LL BE THERE

Producers: Brian Holland, Lamont Dozier

Album: Reach Out
Record Label: Motown
Songwriters: Eddie Holland, Lamont Dozier, Brian Holland
Their second #1 R&B/R&R crossover.

SHAKE ME, WAKE ME (WHEN IT'S OVER)
Producers: Brian Holland, Lamont Dozier
Album: On Top
Record Label: Motown
Songwriters: Eddie Holland, Lamont Dozier, Brian Holland

STANDING IN THE SHADOWS OF LOVE
Producers: Brian Holland, Lamont Dozier
Album: Reach Out
Record Label: Motown
Songwriters: Eddie Holland, Lamont Dozier, Brian Holland
Typical dramatics from the Supremes' emotional soul brothers.

1967

BERNADETTE
Producers: Brian Holland, Lamont Dozier
Album: Reach Out
Record Label: Motown
Songwriters: Eddie Holland, Lamont Dozier, Brian Holland
More overacting.

SEVEN ROOMS OF GLOOM
Producers: Brian Holland, Lamont Dozier
Album: Reach Out
Record Label: Motown
Songwriters: Eddie Holland, Lamont Dozier, Brian Holland
The Tops' formula wearing thin.

1972

KEEPER OF THE CASTLE
Producers: Dennis Lambert, Brian Potter
Album: Keeper of the Castle
Record Label: Dunhill
Songwriters: Dennis Lambert, Brian Potter
Continuing a mini-'70s comeback for their bombastic R&B. Levi Stubbs would later find himself perfectly cast as the voice of the man-eating plant in the movie version of the musical Little Shop of Horrors.

1973

AIN'T NO WOMAN (LIKE THE ONE I GOT)
Producers: Dennis Lambert, Brian Potter
Album: Keeper of the Castle
Record Label: Dunhill
Songwriters: Dennis Lambert, Brian Potter
Best-selling comeback effort.

1981

WHEN SHE WAS MY GIRL
Album: Tonight
Record Label: Casablanca
Songwriters: Marc Blatte, Larry Gottlieb
#1 R&B/Top-15 R&R crossover.

THE FOUR TUNES
1954

I UNDERSTAND JUST HOW YOU FEEL
Album: 12 x 4
Record Label: Jubilee
Songwriter: Pat Best
Covered by the G-Clefs (Terrace, '61).

KIM FOWLEY
1969

BUBBLEGUM
Album: Outrageous
Record Label: Imperial
Songwriter: Kim Fowley
Legendary track from the quintessential rock and roll character. Covered by Sonic Youth (SST, '86).

INEZ FOXX
1963

MOCKINGBIRD
Album: Mockingbird
Record Label: Symbol
Songwriters: Inez Foxx, Charlie Foxx
Covered by James Taylor and Carly Simon (Elektra, '74).

NORMAN FOX AND THE ROB ROYS
1957

TELL ME WHY
Record Label: Back Beat
Songwriters: Marshall Helfand, Don Carter

Doo-wop gem, covered by the Dion-less Belmonts (Sabrina, '61).

SAMANTHA FOX
1987

TOUCH ME (I WANT YOUR BODY)
Producers: J. Astrop, Pete Q. Harris
Album: Touch Me
Record Label: Jive
Songwriters: Michael Shreeve, J. Astrop, Pete Q. Harris
As a trailblazing icon for horny young boys, Samantha took off her top several years before Madonna took it all off.

1988

NAUGHTY GIRLS NEED LOVE TOO
Producer: Full Force
Album: Samantha Fox
Record Label: Jive
Songwriter: Full Force
As a dancehall chanteuse, Samantha was more of a tease than a talent.

1989

I WANNA HAVE SOME FUN
Producer: Full Force
Album: I Wanna Have Some Fun
Record Label: Jive
Songwriter: Full Force
In the absence of a picture disc, her allure wore thin.

FOXY
1978

GET OFF
Producer: Cory Wade
Album: Get Off
Record Label: Dash
Songwriters: Carlos Driggs, Ishmael Ledesma
#1 R&B/Top-10 R&R crossover.

PETER FRAMPTON
1975

BABY I LOVE YOUR WAY
Producer: Peter Frampton
Album: Frampton
Record Label: A&M
Songwriter: Peter Frampton
Lite Metal from the former Humble Pie front man. Covered by Big Mountain in the movie Reality Bites *(RCA, '94).*

SHOW ME THE WAY
Producer: Peter Frampton
Album: Frampton Comes Alive

Record Label: A&M
Songwriter: Peter Frampton

Featuring his trademark Wah Wah sound.

1976

DO YOU FEEL LIKE WE DO?

Producer: Peter Frampton
Album: Frampton's Camel
Record Label: A&M
Songwriters: Peter Frampton,
   Michael Gallagher, John Sidmos,
   Rick Wills

Big Arena favorite.

1977

I'M IN YOU

Producer: Peter Frampton
Album: I'm in You
Record Label: A&M
Songwriter: Peter Frampton

His biggest hit, courtesy of the infernal squawk box.

CONNIE FRANCIS

1958

STUPID CUPID

Album: Connie's Greatest Hits
Record Label: MGM
Songwriters: Howard Greenfield,
   Neil Sedaka

Kicking Don Kirshner's and Al Nevins's Broadway publishing empire into high gear, the Brighton Beach duo of Sedaka and Greenfield contributed this Top-20 Pop Rock ditty to New Jersey's aspiring diva, Connie Francis, just coming off "Who's Sorry Now." Soon thereafter, Connie would be on her way to Atlantic City; Sedaka and Greenfield would sign a songwriting deal for $50 a week.

WHO'S SORRY NOW?

Album: Connie's Greatest Hits
Record Label: MGM
Songwriters: Bert Kalmer, Harry
   Ruby, Ted Snyder

Connie's first hit. Introduced by the Original Memphis Five (Victor, '23).

1959

FRANKIE

Album: Connie's Greatest Hits
Record Label: MGM
Songwriters: Howard Greenfield,
   Neil Sedaka

Annette having copped "Tall Paul" (Anka) in February, Kirshner conscripts Sedaka and

Greenfield served up the requisite "Frankie" (Avalon) as the B-side of "Lipstick on Your Collar" in time for release in May.

LIPSTICK ON YOUR COLLAR

Album: Connie's Greatest Hits
Record Label: MGM
Songwriters: Edna Lewis, George
   Goehring

An almost-Country Connie with a classic Country theme.

MY HAPPINESS

Album: Connie's Greatest Hits
Record Label: MGM
Songwriters: Betty Peterson, Borney
   Bergantine

This '33 tune was popularized by John and Sandra Steele (Damon, '48). Legendary as the first demo Elvis recorded for his mom at Sam Phillips' Sun studios.

1960

EVERYBODY'S SOMEBODY'S FOOL

Album: More Greatest Hits
Record Label: MGM
Songwriters: Howard Greenfield,
   Jack Keller

Connie goes Country, New York style, for her biggest hit, Top-20 C&W/#1 R&R.

MY HEART HAS A MIND OF ITS OWN

Producer: Connie Francis
Album: More Greatest Hits
Record Label: MGM
Songwriters: Howard Greenfield,
   Jack Keller

Same team as "Everybody's Somebody's Fool," same formula, same #1 R&R result. But no Country crossover.

TEDDY

Album: Teddy
Record Label: MGM
Songwriter: Paul Anka

B-side of "Mama." But who was Teddy (Randazzo)?

1961

WHERE THE BOYS ARE

Album: More Greatest Hits
Record Label: MGM
Songwriters: Howard Greenfield,
   Neil Sedaka

Theme from Connie's beach movie. But she was no Annette.

1962

BREAKING IN A BRAND NEW BROKEN HEART

Album: Connie Francis Sings
Record Label: MGM
Songwriters: Howard Greenfield,
   Jack Keller

DON'T BREAK THE HEART THAT LOVES YOU

Producer: Connie Francis
Album: Connie Francis Sings
Record Label: MGM
Songwriters: Benny Davis, Ted
   Murry

Her third #1.

SECOND HAND LOVE

Producer: Phil Spector
Album: Connie Francis Sings
Record Label: MGM
Songwriters: Hank Hunter, Phil
   Spector

Rare Spector collaboration and production.

V-A-C-A-T-I-O-N

Album: The Very Best of Connie
   Francis
Record Label: MGM
Songwriters: Hank Hunter, Gary
   Weston, Connie Francis

FRANKE AND THE KNOCKOUTS

1981

SWEETHEART

Producer: Jimmy Ienner
Album: Franke and the Knockouts
Record Label: Millenium
Songwriters: Franke Previtte, William
   Ellworthy

Previtte would return as author of "(I've Had) The Time of My Life" from Dirty Dancing.

FRANKIE GOES TO HOLLYWOOD

1984

RELAX

Producer: Trevor Horn
Album: Welcome to the Pleasure
   Dome
Record Label: Island
Songwriters: Peter Gill, William
   Johnson, Mark O'Toole

#1 U.K./Bottom-40 U.S. crossover. English dancehall Synth flavor of the month.

TWO TRIBES

Producer: Trevor Horn
Album: Welcome to the Pleasure Dome
Record Label: Island
Songwriters: Peter Gill, William Johnson, Mark O'Toole

#1 U.K./Top-50 U.S. crossover.

WELCOME TO THE PLEASURE DOME

Producer: Trevor Horn
Album: Welcome to the Pleasure Dome
Record Label: Island
Songwriters: Peter Gill, William Johnson, Mark O'Toole, Brian Nash

Supposedly decadent British pleasures were lost on the U.S. audience, though almost everything else with an accent and a synthesizer achieved unprecedented chart success during this period.

ARETHA FRANKLIN

1967

(YOU MAKE ME FEEL LIKE) A NATURAL WOMAN

Producer: Jerry Wexler
Album: Lady Soul
Record Label: Atlantic
Songwriters: Gerry Goffin, Carole King, Jerry Wexler

Definitive star performance, a Top-10 R&R/R&B crossover classic. Covered by Carole King (Ode, '71).

AIN'T NO WAY

Producer: Jerry Wexler
Album: Lady Soul
Record Label: Atlantic
Songwriter: Carolyn Franklin

B-side of "(Sweet Sweet Baby) Since You've Been Gone."

BABY I LOVE YOU

Producer: Jerry Wexler
Album: Aretha Arrives
Record Label: Atlantic
Songwriter: Ronnie Shannon

Her third #1 R&B/Top-10 R&R crossover of the year.

CHAIN OF FOOLS

Producer: Jerry Wexler
Album: Lady Soul
Record Label: Atlantic
Songwriter: Don Covay

Her fourth #1 R&B/Top-10 R&R crossover of the year.

DO RIGHT WOMAN, DO RIGHT MAN

Producer: Jerry Wexler
Album: I Never Loved a Man
Record Label: Atlantic
Songwriters: Dan Penn, Chips Moman

B-side of "I Never Loved a Man (the Way I Love You)" and one of her greatest all-time performances. Covered by the Flying Burrito Brothers (A&M, '69).

I NEVER LOVED A MAN (THE WAY I LOVE YOU)

Producer: Jerry Wexler
Album: I Never Loved a Man
Record Label: Atlantic
Songwriter: Ronny Shannon

Starting off her career on Atlantic, under the wing of Jerry Wexler, with a #1 R&B/Top-10 R&R classic.

(SWEET, SWEET BABY) SINCE YOU'VE BEEN GONE

Producer: Jerry Wexler
Album: Lady Soul
Record Label: Atlantic
Songwriters: Aretha Franklin, Ted White

Her fourth #1 R&B/Top-10 R&R crossover, from her breakthrough Soul album.

1968

THE HOUSE THAT JACK BUILT

Producer: Jerry Wexler
Album: Aretha's Gold
Record Label: Atlantic
Songwriters: Bobby Lance, Fran Robbins

Top-10 R&B/R&R crossover.

THINK

Producer: Jerry Wexler
Album: Aretha Now
Record Label: Atlantic
Songwriters: Aretha Franklin, Ted White

Sixth out of last seven singles to reach #1 R&B/Top-10 R&R (discounting B-sides).

1969

CALL ME

Producers: Tom Dowd, Jerry Wexler, Arif Mardin
Album: This Girl's in Love with You
Record Label: Atlantic
Songwriter: Aretha Franklin

#1 R&B/Top-20 R&R crossover. Covered by Phil Perry (Capitol, '91).

SHARE YOUR LOVE WITH ME

Producers: Tom Dowd, Jerry Wexler, Arif Mardin
Album: This Girl's in Love with You
Record Label: Atlantic
Songwriters: Deadric Malone, Al Braggs

#1 R&B/Top-20 R&R crossover. Malone's major credits are with Bobby Bland.

1970

SPIRIT IN THE DARK

Producers: Jerry Wexler, Tom Dowd, Arif Mardin
Album: Spirit in the Dark
Record Label: Atlantic
Songwriter: Aretha Franklin

1971

ROCK STEADY

Producers: Tom Dowd, Jerry Wexler, Arif Mardin
Album: To Be Young, Gifted and Black
Record Label: Atlantic
Songwriter: Aretha Franklin

Top-10 R&B/R&R crossover.

TO BE YOUNG, GIFTED AND BLACK

Producers: Tom Dowd, Jerry Wexler, Arif Mardin
Album: To Be Young, Gifted and Black
Record Label: Atlantic
Songwriters: Nina Simone, Weldon Irvine Jr.

Topping off a positive year for R&B songwriting. Introduced by Jazz singer Nina Simone (RCA, '69).

1972

DAY DREAMING

Producers: Tom Dowd, Jerry Wexler, Arif Mardin
Album: To Be Young, Gifted and Black
Record Label: Atlantic
Songwriter: Aretha Franklin

Another #1 R&B/Top-10 R&R Soul classic.

1973

ANGEL

Producer: Quincy Jones
Album: Hey Now Hey (The Other Side of the Sky)
Record Label: Atlantic
Songwriters: Rory Bourke, Gayle Barnhill

#1 R&B/Top-20 R&R.

UNTIL YOU COME BACK TO ME (THAT'S WHAT I'M GONNA DO)

Producers: Tom Dowd, Jerry Wexler
Album: Let Me in Your Life
Record Label: Atlantic
Songwriters: Stevie Wonder, Clarence Paul, Morris Broadnax

#1 R&B/#3 R&R crossover. Written and recorded by Stevie Wonder in '67, but not released on an album of his until '77.

1976

SOMETHING HE CAN FEEL

Producer: Curtis Mayfield
Album: Sparkle
Record Label: Atlantic
Songwriter: Curtis Mayfield

#1 R&B/Top-30 R&R crossover. Introduced by Irene Cara and Lonette McKee in the film Sparkle. Covered by En Vogue (Atlantic, '92).

1977

BREAK IT TO ME GENTLY

Album: Sweet Passion
Record Label: Atlantic
Songwriters: Marvin Hamlisch, Carole Bayer Sager

Aretha gives M.O.R.'s leading songwriting couple their first #1 R&B/Bottom-30 R&R crossover.

1982

JUMP TO IT

Producer: Luther Vandross
Album: Jump to It
Record Label: Arista
Songwriters: Luther Vandross, Marcus Miller

#1 R&B/Top-25 R&R crossover.

JUST MY DAYDREAM

Producer: Luther Vandross
Album: Jump to It
Record Label: Arista
Songwriter: Smokey Robinson

1983

GET IT RIGHT

Producer: Luther Vandross
Album: Get It Right
Record Label: Arista
Songwriters: Luther Vandross, Marcus Miller

#1 R&B/Bottom-40 R&R crossover.

1985

FREEWAY OF LOVE

Producer: Narada Michael Walden
Album: Who's Zoomin' Who?
Record Label: Arista
Songwriters: Narada Michael Walden, Jeffrey Cohen

#1 R&B/Top-10 R&R crossover. Her biggest hit in over ten years.

WHO'S ZOOMIN' WHO?

Producer: Narada Michael Walden
Album: Who's Zoomin' Who?
Record Label: Arista
Songwriters: Narada Michael Walden, Preston Glass, Aretha Franklin

Top-10 R&B/R&R followup to "Freeway of Love."

1986

JIMMY LEE

Producer: Narada Michael Walden
Album: Aretha
Record Label: Arista
Songwriters: Jeffrey Cohen, Preston Glass, Narada Michael Walden

1987

I KNEW YOU WERE WAITING (FOR ME)

Producer: Narada Michael Walden
Album: Aretha
Record Label: Arista
Songwriters: Simon Climie, Dennis Morgan

#1 U.K./U.S. Her biggest international hit.

1989

THROUGH THE STORM

Producer: Narada Michael Walden
Album: Through the Storm
Record Label: Arista
Songwriters: Diane Warren, Albert Hammond

With Elton John.

GIMME YOUR LOVE

Producer: Narada Michael Walden
Album: Gimme Your Love
Record Label: Arista
Songwriters: Narada Michael Walden, Jeffrey Cohen

A duet with the godfather of Soul, James Brown, who is the only artist with more #1 R&B hits than Aretha.

FRATERNITY OF MAN

1968

DON'T BOGART ME

Producer: Kim Fowley
Album: Fraternity of Man
Record Label: ABC
Songwriters: Elliot Ingber, Stash Wagner

Classic '60s period piece featured in the movie Easy Rider. Covered by Little Feat (Warner Brothers, '78) under its more appropriate title "Don't Bogart That Joint."

DALLAS FRAZIER

1966

ELVIRA

Producer: Marvin Hughes
Record Label: Capitol
Songwriter: Dallas Frazier

Cover by the Oak Ridge Boys was #1 C&W/Top-5 R&R (MCA, '81).

JOHN FRED AND HIS PLAYBOY BAND

1967

JUDY IN DISGUISE (WITH GLASSES)

Producers: John Fred, Andrew Bernard
Album: John Fred and His Playboy Band
Record Label: Paula
Songwriters: John Fred, Andrew Bernard

Psychedelic bubblegum.

FREDDIE AND THE DREAMERS

1963

I'M TELLING YOU NOW

Album: Frantic Freddie
Record Label: Tower
Songwriters: Freddy Garrity, Mitch Murray

Pop rocker that stiffed in '63; went to #1 in '65.

FREE

1970

ALL RIGHT NOW

Producers: John Kelly, Free
Album: Fire and Water
Record Label: Atlantic
Songwriters: Paul Rodgers, Andy Fraser

Out of Bad Company, Free's melodic Metal reigned briefly, as a sophisticated respite to Zeppelin's mainstream frenzy.

FIRE AND WATER
Producers: John Kelly, Free
Album: Fire and Water
Record Label: A&M
Songwriters: Paul Rodgers, Andy Fraser

FM Metal staple.

I'M A MOVER
Producers: John Kelly, Free
Album: Tons of Sobs
Record Label: A&M
Songwriters: Paul Rodgers, Andy Fraser

One of their more raging slabs.

FREE MOVEMENT
1971

I'VE FOUND SOMEONE OF MY OWN
Album: I've Found Someone of My Own
Record Label: Decca
Songwriter: Frank K. Robinson

California one-shot.

BOBBY FREEMAN
1958

DO YOU WANT TO DANCE?
Album: Do You Want to Dance
Record Label: Josie
Songwriter: Bobby Freeman

An anthem of the sock-hop era, with a false ending that drove deejays mad.

1964

C'MON AND SWIM
Producer: Cougar Productions
Album: C'mon and S-w-i-m
Record Label: Autumn
Songwriter: Sylvester Stewart

Later, Sly would provide much more energizing music to dance to, with his Family Stone.

ACE FREHLEY
1979

NEW YORK GROOVE
Producers: Eddie Kramer, Ace Frehley
Album: Ace Frehley
Record Label: Casablanca
Songwriter: Russ Ballard

Relatively mellow outing for the legendary Kiss axeman, temporarily solo.

FRENCH FRITH KAISER THOMPSON
1990

NOW THAT I AM DEAD
Producer: Henry Kaiser
Album: Invisible Means
Record Label: Windham Hill
Songwriters: Donna Blair, John French

From the quintessentially eccentric progressive alternative supergroup, possibly the only real challenger to "Lodi" on the verities of the musician's lifestyle.

DOUG E. FRESH AND THE GET FRESH CREW
1985

THE SHOW
Album: Rap's Greatest Hits
Record Label: Reality/Danga
Songwriters: Douglas David, Ricky Walters

One of Rap's earliest and greatest poems.

GLENN FREY
1985

THE HEAT IS ON
Producers: Keith Forsey, Harold Faltermeyer
Album: *Beverly Hills Cop* Soundtrack
Record Label: MCA
Songwriters: Keith Forsey, Harold Faltermeyer

Frey begins his multimedia comeback blitz with a movie song.

SMUGGLER'S BLUES
Producers: Glenn Frey, Allen Blazek
Album: The Allnighter
Record Label: MCA
Songwriters: Glenn Frey, Jack Tempchin

Frey continues his multi-media comeback with a TV song, from an episode of "Miami Vice," in which he had a major supporting role.

YOU BELONG TO THE CITY
Producer: Glenn Frey
Album: *Miami Vice* Soundtrack
Record Label: MCA
Songwriter: Glenn Frey

Cementing his multi-media comeback with a song that opened an entire season of "Miami Vice." A decade later Frey's multimedia comeback would achieve its ultimate fruition and devastation, when he would star

in the televised equivalent of a one-shot single, the series "Miami Heat," which was cancelled after one show.

DEAN FRIEDMAN
1977

ARIEL
Producer: Rob Stevens
Album: Dean Friedman
Record Label: Lifesong
Songwriter: Dean Friedman

Deft and ineffable portrait of latter-day hippie love affair is one of the cutest songs ever to hit Top-40.

KINKY FRIEDMAN
1973

SOLD AMERICAN
Producer: Chuck Glaser
Album: Sold American
Record Label: Vanguard
Songwriter: Kinky Friedman

Mellow Cow-Punk satire from the future detective novelist.

1976

MEN'S ROOM L.A.
Album: Lasso from El Paso
Record Label: Epic
Songwriter: Kinky Friedman

FRIEND AND LOVER
1968

REACH OUT OF THE DARKNESS
Producers: Joe South, Bill Lowery
Record Label: Verve Forecast
Songwriter: Jim Post

Revealingly needy Folk Rock one-shot.

THE FRIENDS OF DISTINCTION
1969

GOING IN CIRCLES
Album: Grazin' Peters
Record Label: RCA
Songwriters: Jerry Peters, Anita Poree

1970

LOVE OR LET ME BE LONELY
Producer: Ray Cork Jr.
Album: Real Friends
Record Label: RCA
Songwriters: Anita Poree, C. "Skip" Scarborough

Middle-of-the-R&B-road.

FU-SCHNICKENS WITH SHAQUILLE O'NEAL
1993

WHAT'S UP DOC? (CAN WE ROCK)
Album: Shaq Deisel
Record Label: Jive
Songwriters: Kevin KcKenzie, Shaquille O'Neal, R. Roachford, J. Jones, L. Maturine

The Rap equivalent of a slam dunk.

FUGAZI
1988

WAITING ROOM
Album: Fugazi
Record Label: Dischord
Songwriter: Ian MacKaye

Hardcore Punk revisited: faster and louder.

1990

REPEATER
Album: Repeater
Record Label: Dischord
Songwriters: Ian MacKaye, Guy Picciato, Joe Lally, Brendan Cauty

THE FUGS
1965

BOOBS A LOT
Producer: Harry Smith
Album: First Album
Record Label: ESP
Songwriter: Peter Stampfel

Stretching the envelope on Pop propriety, the Fugs briefly gave scatology a good name.

COCA COLA DOUCHE
Album: Virgin Fugs
Record Label: ESP
Songwriters: Tuli Kupferberg, Ed Sanders

Bringing a poetic eye and a tin ear to the camps of Rock and Roll decadence. For a time in '67 they played in the same neighborhood (actual and metaphorical) as Frank Zappa's Mothers of Invention.

FRENZY
Album: The Fugs
Record Label: ESP
Songwriters: Tuli Kupferberg, Ed Sanders

Tame enough to be released as a single, naturally it stiffed.

I COULDN'T GET HIGH
Producer: Harry Smith
Album: First Album
Record Label: ESP
Songwriters: Tuli Kupferberg, Ed Sanders

Pungent satire.

I SAW THE BEST MINDS OF MY GENERATION ROT
Album: Virgin Fugs
Record Label: ESP
Songwriters: Tuli Kupferberg, Ed Sanders

Where Allen Ginsberg left off, the Fugs prevailed, merging the poetic with the puerile, the sacred with the profane, "The Swinburne Stomp" with "Group Grope."

KILL FOR PEACE
Album: The Fugs
Record Label: ESP
Songwriters: Tuli Kupferberg, Ed Sanders

Satiric polemic was actually adopted as serious slogan by soldiers in Viet Nam.

MORNING MORNING
Album: The Fugs
Record Label: ESP
Songwriter: Tuli Kupferberg

His most simple, poignant, and profound lyric. Covered by Richie Havens (Verve/ Folkways, '66).

SARAN WRAP
Album: Virgin Fugs
Record Label: ESP
Songwriters: Tuli Kupferberg, Ed Sanders

Safe sex in the era of free love.

SLUM GODDESS
Producer: Harry Smith
Album: First Album
Record Label: ESP
Songwriters: Tuli Kupferberg, Ed Sanders

When the Fugs sang to the various slum goddesses in attendance at the Dom on St. Marks Place on the Lower East Side of New York, among those taking notice was the artist Andy Warhol. Soon an alternative to Folk Rock would arise, in the repertoire of the Velvet Underground, Andy's house band at the Dom when it reopened as the Electric Circus.

SUPERGIRL
Producer: Harry Smith
Album: First Album
Record Label: ESP
Songwriters: Tuli Kupferberg, Ed Sanders

Rampant sexism, hippie-style.

1968

EXORCISING THE EVIL SPIRITS FROM THE PENTAGON, OCT. 21, 1967
Album: Tenderness Junction
Record Label: ESP
Songwriters: Tuli Kupferberg, Ed Sanders

Levitating the Pentagon, during a high point in the '60s protest movement.

JESSE FULLER
1954

SAN FRANCISCO BAY BLUES
Record Label: World Song
Songwriter: Jesse Fuller

A classic of the coming Folk scare, chronicling the appeal of the incipient bohemian nexus, San Francisco, where Jerry Garcia was only a few years away from forming Mother Macree's Uptown Jug Champions. Covered by Peter, Paul, and Mary (Warner Brothers, '65), Richie Havens (Verve, '66), and Rambling Jack Elliot. Fuller recorded this again on Good Time Jazz in '58, Folk Lyric in '62, Folk Lore in '63, Vanguard in '64, and Fontana in '65.

JOHNNY FULLER
1959

HAUNTED HOUSE
Record Label: Specialty
Songwriter: Robert Geddins

Covered by Jumping Gene Simmons (Hi, '64).

LOWELL FULSON
1948

3 O'CLOCK BLUES
Producer: Bob Geddins
Record Label: Down Town
Songwriter: Lowell Fulson

Early L.A. blues poetry. Cover by B. B. King (RPM, '51) was the legendary Bluesman's first #1 R&B hit.

1950

BLUE SHADOWS
Album: Hung down Head
Record Label: Swing Time
Songwriter: Lloyd Glenn

First hit for the L.A. Bluesman and Ray Charles' employer.

EVERY DAY I HAVE THE BLUES
Record Label: Swingtime
Songwriter: Peter Chatman

Memphis Slim Blues standard, covered by Johnny Raye (Okeh, '52) Big Joe Williams with the Count Basie Orchestra (Clef, '55), B. B. King on the legendary Live at the Regal (RPM, '65: an album that launched a generation of white electric Blues guitarists), James Brown (King, '70), Fleetwood Mac (Blue Horizon, '71), and Chuck Berry (Chess, '72).

1954

RECONSIDER BABY
Record Label: Checker
Songwriter: Lowell Fulson

Covered by Elvis Presley (RCA, '60) and B. B. King (ABC, '75).

1967

TRAMP
Producer: Lowell Fulson
Album: The Tramp
Record Label: Kent
Songwriters: Lowell Fulson, Jimmy McCracklin

Covered by Otis and Carla (Stax, '67).

FUN BOY THREE

1983

THE FARM YARD CONNECTION
Album: Waiting
Record Label: Chrysalis
Songwriter: Fun Boy Three

Late Reggae entry caught between invasions.

FUNKADELIC

1971

MAGGOT BRAIN
Producer: George Clinton
Album: Maggot Brain
Record Label: Westbound
Songwriters: George Clinton, Eddie Hazel

Taking Funk to the next level of intensity and anger.

1973

COSMIC SLOP
Producer: George Clinton
Album: Cosmic Slop
Record Label: Westbound
Songwriter: George Clinton

1978

ONE NATION UNDER A GROOVE
Producer: George Clinton
Album: One Nation under a Groove
Record Label: Warner Brothers
Songwriters: George Clinton, Gary Shider, Walter Morrison

#1 R&B/Top-30 R&R crossover; future Funk standard was their biggest hit. Re-interpreted by Ice-T in '94 as "Bop Gun (One Nation)."

1979

(NOT JUST) KNEE DEEP
Producer: George Clinton
Album: Uncle Jam Wants You
Record Label: Warner Brothers
Songwriters: George Clinton, Philippe Wynn

#1 R&B/Bottom-20 R&R crossover.

THE FUNKY KINGS

1975

SLOW DANCING
Record Label: Arista
Songwriter: Jack Tempchin

Belated prom classic when it was covered by Johnny Rivers (Big Tree, '75) as "Swayin' to the Music."

G

PETER GABRIEL

1977

SOLSBURY HILL
Producer: Bob Ezrin
Album: Peter Gabriel
Record Label: Atco
Songwriter: Peter Gabriel

Artistic voice of Genesis goes solo with this melancholy rocker about leaving Genesis.

1980

BIKO
Producer: Steve Lillywhite
Album Title: Peter Gabriel

Record Label: Mercury
Songwriter: Peter Gabriel

Tribute to the South African martyr Stephen Biko brings Gabriel into the worldbeat arena. Covered by Joan Baez (Gold Castle, '87).

GAMES WITHOUT FRONTIERS
Producer: Steve Lillywhite
Album: Peter Gabriel
Record Label: Mercury
Songwriter: Peter Gabriel

Expanding his progressive world vision.

1982

SHOCK THE MONKEY
Producers: David Lord, Peter Gabriel
Album: Peter Gabriel (Security)
Record Label: Geffen
Songwriter: Peter Gabriel

Even better in its original German version, entitled "Schock den Affen" (Warner Brothers, '83). Suggested segues: "99 Luftbalons" by Nena; "Morgen" by Ivo Robic.

1986

BIG TIME
Producers: Peter Gabriel, Daniel Lanois
Album: Birdy
Record Label: Geffen
Songwriter: Peter Gabriel

His first Top-10 hit.

DON'T GIVE UP
Producers: Peter Gabriel, Daniel Lanois
Album: So
Record Label: Geffen
Songwriter: Peter Gabriel

Plaintive duet with techno-soulmate, Kate Bush.

IN YOUR EYES (THEME FROM *SAY ANYTHING*)
Producers: Peter Gabriel, Daniel Lanois
Album: So
Record Label: Geffen
Songwriters: Peter Gabriel, Bill Laswell

Featured in the soundtrack to Cameron Crowe's miniature coming-of-age film Say Anything.

MERCY STREET
Producers: Peter Gabriel, Daniel Lanois

Album: So
Record Label: Geffen
Songwriter: Peter Gabriel

Covered by Black Uhuru (Mesa, '93).

RED RAIN
Producers: Peter Gabriel, Daniel Lanois
Album: So
Record Label: Geffen
Songwriter: Peter Gabriel

Intense ecological rocker kicks off his most celebrated album.

SLEDGEHAMMER
Producers: Peter Gabriel, Daniel Lanois
Album: So
Record Label: Geffen
Songwriter: Peter Gabriel

His biggest hit.

1992

STEAM
Producers: Peter Gabriel, Daniel Lanois
Album: US
Record Label: Geffen
Songwriter: Peter Gabriel

Great video.

REG E. GAINES
1993

PLEASE DON'T TAKE MY AIR JORDANS
Producer: Philip Damien
Album: Please Don't Take My Air Jordans
Record Label: Mercury
Songwriters: Reg E. Gaines, Philip Damien

Where Rap meets poetry on the urban streets of upward mobility.

GALLERY
1972

NICE TO BE WITH YOU
Producer: Dennis Coffey
Album: Nice to Be with You
Record Label: Sussex
Songwriter: Jim Gold

Exemplary sunny Pop Rock of the post-apocalyptic, everything-is-beautiful singles era of the early '70s.

THE GAMBLERS
1959

MOON DAWG
Producer: Nik Venet
Record Label: World Pacific
Songwriter: Derry Weaver

Considered to be the first surf record. Covered by the Beach Boys (Capitol, '62), the Ventures (Dolton, '62), as well as the Surfaris and the Challengers.

GANG OF FOUR
1980

ANTHRAX
Producers: Andy Gill, Jon King, Rob Warr
Album: Entertainment
Record Label: Warner Brothers
Songwriters: Jon King, Andy Gill, Hugo Burnham

Doctrinaire Rock tract from England. Lines like "Feel like a beetle on its back" spoke to collegiate rockers on both sides of the Atlantic who wanted to break from the influence of the Fab Four.

I FOUND THAT ESSENCE RARE
Producer: Andy Gill
Album: Entertainment
Record Label: Warner Brothers
Songwriters: Jon King, Andy Gill, Hugo Burnham, Rob Warr

Essential listening for alternative alphabet bands, U2, R.E.M., INXS.

1982

TO HELL WITH POVERTY
Album: Another Day/Another Dollar
Record Label: Warner Brothers
Songwriters: Andy Gill, Hugo Burnham, Jon King

Their classic single.

GANG STARR
1990

A JAZZ THING
Album: *Mo' Better Blues* Soundtrack
Producers: Branford Marsalis, DJ Premier
Record Label: Columbia
Songwriters: Branford Marsalis, Chris Martin, Keith Elam, L. E. Elie

From the Spike Lee film. Using the form and function of Rap to illustrate the history of jazz.

THE GAP BAND
1982

BURN RUBBER ON ME (WHY YOU WANNA HURT ME)
Producer: Lonnie Simmons
Album: The Gap Band IV
Record Label: Total Experience
Songwriters: Lonnie Simmons, Charles Wilson, Rudolph Taylor

A hunka hunka burning Funk.

EARLY IN THE MORNING
Producer: Lonnie Simmons
Album: The Gap Band IV
Record Label: Total Experience
Songwriters: Lonnie Simmons, Charles Wilson, Rudolph Taylor, Robert Palmer

Their Jazz Funk breakthrough crosses over from #1 R&B to Top-25 R&R.

OUTSTANDING
Producer: Lonnie Simmons
Album: The Gap Band IV
Record Label: Total Experience
Songwriters: Lonnie Simmons, Ray Calhoun.

#1 R&B/Top-50 R&R. Used by Shaquille O'Neal as part of "I'm Outstanding" (Jive, '93).

YOU DROPPED A BOMB ON ME
Producer: Lonnie Simmons
Album: The Gap Band IV
Record Label: Total Experience
Songwriters: Lonnie Simmons, Charles Wilson, Rudolph Taylor

1985

BEEP A FREAK
Producer: Lonnie Simmons
Album: Gap Band VI
Record Label: Total Experience
Songwriters: Lonnie Simmons, Charles Wilson, Rudolph Taylor

JERRY GARCIA
1972

SUGAREE

Producers: Bob Matthews, Betty Cantor, Ramrod
Album: Garcia
Record Label: Warner Brothers
Songwriters: Jerry Garcia, Robert Hunter

The Bluegrass side of Captain Trips resurfaces, epitomizing the Country Folk Rock sound of '72. Recorded live by the full band (Warner Brothers, '76).

ART GARFUNKEL
1973

ALL I KNOW

Producers: Roy Halee, Art Garfunkel
Album: Angel Clare
Record Label: Columbia
Songwriter: Jimmy Webb

His solo best-seller.

GALE GARNETT
1964

WE'LL SING IN THE SUNSHINE

Producer: Andy Wiswell
Album: My Kind of Folk Songs
Record Label: RCA Victor
Songwriter: Gale Garnett

Advancing the decidedly un-girl-group notion of serial monogamy, wins a '64 Grammy for Folk song of the year. Around the corner was emancipation, liberation, the topless bathing suit, Carole Doda, group sex, Janis Joplin, and Grace Slick. Gale Garnett, meanwhile, disappeared, later to re-emerge in a cabaret performance of the songs of Leonard Cohen.

LEIF GARRETT
1979

I WAS MADE FOR DANCIN'

Producer: Michael Lloyd
Album: Feel the Need
Record Label: Scotti Brothers
Songwriter: Michael Lloyd

Aspiring teen idol Garrett would achieve a more lasting fame as Felix Unger's son on the TV version of "The Odd Couple," in which he wasn't that good either, except on the episode when Felix nurses his frog back to racing health.

MARVIN GAYE
1962

STUBBORN KIND OF FELLOW

Producer: William Stevenson
Album: Marvin Gaye/Greatest Hits
Record Label: Tamla
Songwriters: William Stevenson, George Gordy, Marvin Gaye

Introducing Motown session drummer Marvin Gaye, in his early backwoodsy incarnation.

1963

CAN I GET A WITNESS

Producers: Brian Holland, Lamont Dozier
Album: Marvin Gaye/Greatest Hits
Record Label: Tamla
Songwriters: Eddie Holland, Lamont Dozier, Brian Holland

Gaye's raw Soul triumphs, as always, over the Motown machine. Covered by the Rolling Stones (London, '64) and Lee Michaels (A&M, '69).

PRIDE AND JOY

Producer: William Stevenson
Album: Marvin Gaye/Greatest Hits
Record Label: Tamla
Songwriters: Marvin Gaye, Norman Whitfield, William Stevenson

1964

BABY DON'T YOU DO IT

Producers: Brian Holland, Lamont Dozier
Album: How Sweet It Is (to Be Loved by You)
Record Label: Tamla
Songwriters: Eddie Holland, Lamont Dozier, Brian Holland

Covered by the Band as "Don't Do It" (Capitol, '72).

HITCH HIKE

Producer: William Stevenson
Album: Marvin Gaye/Greatest Hits
Record Label: Tamla
Songwriters: Clarence Paul, William Stevenson

New dance sensation, briefly.

HOW SWEET IT IS (TO BE LOVED BY YOU)

Producers: Brian Holland, Lamont Dozier
Album: How Sweet It Is to Be Loved by You

Record Label: Tamla
Songwriters: Eddie Holland, Lamont Dozier, Brian Holland

Covered by Junior Walker (Soul, '66) and James Taylor (Warner Brothers, '75).

TRY IT BABY

Producers: Brian Holland, Lamont Dozier
Album: How Sweet It Is to Be Loved by You
Record Label: Tamla
Songwriter: Berry Gordy Jr.

YOU'RE A WONDERFUL ONE

Producers: Brian Holland, Lamont Dozier
Album: Marvin Gaye/Greatest Hits
Record Label: Tamla
Songwriters: Eddie Holland, Lamont Dozier, Brian Holland

Gaye swings. Hits another home run.

1965

AIN'T THAT PECULIAR

Producer: Smokey Robinson
Album: Greatest Hits (Vol. 2)
Record Label: Tamla
Songwriters: Smokey Robinson, Warren Moore, Marv Tarplin, Robert Rogers

Gaye's second #1 R&B/Top 10 R&R.

I'LL BE DOGGONE

Producer: Smokey Robinson
Album: Moods of Marvin Gaye
Record Label: Tamla
Songwriters: Smokey Robinson, Warren Moore, Marv Tarplin

Under the calming influence of Smokey, Gaye creates a gem of folksy Soul; his first #1 R&B/Top-10 R&R crossover.

1969

IT'S A BITTER PILL TO SWALLOW

Producer: Smokey Robinson
Album: M.P.G.
Record Label: Tamla
Songwriter: Smokey Robinson

By this time Marvin was serving as Smokey's surrogate sufferer.

THAT'S THE WAY LOVE IS

Producer: Norman Whitfield
Album: M.P.G.
Record Label: Tamla
Songwriters: Norman Whitfield, Barrett Strong

TOO BUSY THINKING ABOUT MY BABY

Producer: Norman Whitfield
Album: M.P.G.
Record Label: Tamla
Songwriters: Norman Whitfield, Barrett Strong, Janie Bradford

His fourth #1 R&B/Top-10 R&R crossover, second in a row, following up his version of "I Heard It through the Grapevine."

1971

INNER CITY BLUES (MAKE ME WANNA HOLLER)

Producer: Marvin Gaye
Album: What's Goin' On
Record Label: Tamla
Songwriters: Marvin Gaye, James Myx Jr.

Presaging a message that would dominate the R&B sensibility by the end of the decade. #1 R&B/Top-10 R&R crossover.

MERCY MERCY ME (THE ECOLOGY)

Producer: Marvin Gaye
Album: What's Goin' On
Record Label: Tamla
Songwriter: Marvin Gaye

His newfound activist period resulted in another #1 R&B/Top-10 R&R crossover.

WHAT'S GOIN' ON

Producer: Marvin Gaye
Album: What's Goin' On
Record Label: Tamla
Songwriters: Al Cleveland, Marvin Gaye, Renauldo Benson

The politics of being Gaye; three straight #1 R&B/Top-10 R&R crossovers in '71, detailing Marvin's new aware stance. Covered by Cyndi Lauper (Portrait, '86).

1972

THEME FROM TROUBLE MAN

Producer: Marvin Gaye
Album: Trouble Man
Record Label: Tamla
Songwriter: Marvin Gaye

Outlaw R&B, a few years before Rap.

1973

LET'S GET IT ON

Producers: Marvin Gaye, Ed Townshend
Album: Let's Get It On
Record Label: Tamla
Songwriters: Marvin Gaye, Edward Townshend

Leaving the barricades and going back to the bedroom, Gaye scores another #1 R&B/R&R crossover.

1976

I WANT YOU

Album: I Want You
Record Label: Tamla
Songwriters: Leon Ware, Anita Ross

#1 R&B/Top-20 R&R crossover. Covered by Madonna and Material Issue (Sire, '95).

1977

GOT TO GIVE IT UP (PART I)

Producer: Art Stewart
Album: Marvin Gaye Live at the London Palladium
Record Label: Tamla
Songwriter: Marvin Gaye

#1 R&B/R&R crossover.

1982

SEXUAL HEALING

Producer: Marvin Gaye
Album: Midnight Love
Record Label: Columbia
Songwriters: Marvin Gaye, Odell Brown, David Ritz

Perhaps his crowning achievement, the bedroom ballad as more than just a service contract. The profane made as sacred as it was in the days of the Ravens and the Orioles, if not the Dominoes and the Five Royals.

1985

SANCTIFIED LADY

Producers: Brian Holland, Lamont Dozier
Album: Dream of a Lifetime
Record Label: Columbia
Songwriters: Marvin Gaye, Gordon Banko

Funk from over the edge, posthumously released after Gaye was shot to death by his father in '84.

MARVIN GAYE AND TAMMI TERRELL

1967

AIN'T NO MOUNTAIN HIGH ENOUGH

Producers: Harvey Fuqua, Johnny Bristol
Album: United
Record Label: Tamla
Songwriters: Nick Ashford, Valerie Simpson

Motown inspirational peak, great career move for two of the label's more perfect couples. Cover by Diana Ross went #1 R&B.

IF I COULD BUILD MY WHOLE WORLD AROUND YOU

Producers: Harvey Fuqua, Johnny Bristol
Album: United
Record Label: Tamla
Songwriters: Harvey Fuqua, Johnny Bristol, Vernon Bullock

YOUR PRECIOUS LOVE

Producers: Johnny Bristol, Harvey Fuqua
Record Label: Tamla
Songwriters: Nick Ashford, Valerie Simpson

Their biggest R&R hit together.

1968

AIN'T NOTHING LIKE THE REAL THING

Producers: Nick Ashford, Valerie Simpson
Album: You're All I Need
Record Label: Tamla
Songwriters: Nick Ashford, Valerie Simpson

Their first #1 R&B/Top-10 R&R crossover. Covered by Aretha Franklin (Atlantic, '74). Later an anthem for Coca-Cola.

YOU'RE ALL I NEED TO GET BY

Producers: Nick Ashford, Valerie Simpson
Album: You're All I Need
Record Label: Tamla
Songwriters: Nick Ashford, Valerie Simpson

Second straight #1 R&B/Top-10 R&R crossover for both couples.

1969

GOOD LOVIN' AIN'T EASY TO COME BY

Producers: Nick Ashford, Valerie Simpson
Album: Marvin Gaye and His Girls
Record Label: Tamla
Songwriters: Nick Ashford, Valerie Simpson

Tammi Terrell died in '70. Marvin also sang with Diana Ross, Mary Wells, Kim Weston, and Martha Reeves.

MARVIN GAYE AND KIM WESTON

1969

IT TAKES TWO
Producer: William Stevenson
Album: Marvin Gaye and His Girls
Record Label: Tamla
Songwriters: Sylvia Moy, William Stevenson

Another promising pair, but she was no Tammi.

CRYSTAL GAYLE

1977

DON'T IT MAKE MY BROWN EYES BLUE
Album: We Must Believe in Magic
Record Label: United Artists
Songwriter: Richard Leigh

In the footsteps of Olivia Newton-John, Loretta Lynn's youngest sister goes Pop for a rare #1 C&W/Top-10 R&R crossover.

BILLY GAYLES

1956

I'M TORE UP
Producer: Ike Turner
Record Label: Federal
Songwriter: Ike Turner

Classic Ike in his R&B session salad days with Ike Turner's Rhythm Rockers.

GLORIA GAYNOR

1978

I WILL SURVIVE
Producers: Freddie Perren, Dino Fekaris
Album: Love Tracks
Record Label: Polydor
Songwriters: Freddie Perren, Dino Fekaris

#1 U.S./U.K. Disco anthem, anticipating the coming plague years ahead, the closing of Studio 54, and the advent of MTV, which Gaynor herself failed to survive. Covered by Chantay Savage (RCA, '96).

THE J. GEILS BAND

1973

GIVE IT TO ME
Producer: Bill Szymczyk
Album: Bloodshot
Record Label: Atlantic
Songwriters: Seth Justman, Peter Wolf

Following Springsteen and Southside Johnny to the great American East coast bar-band trough.

1974

MUST OF GOT LOST
Album: Nightmares . . . and Other Tales from the Vinyl Jungle
Record Label: Atlantic
Songwriters: Seth Justman, Peter Wolf

From Boston, they never quite located the trough.

1977

YOU'RE THE ONLY ONE
Producer: J. Geils Band
Album: Monkey Island
Record Label: Atlantic
Songwriters: Seth Justman, Peter Wolf

Still cranking out gin-soaked, harp-driven R&B gems, while Boston brethren Aerosmith took the masses with them to the Heavy Metal arena.

1979

LOVE STINKS
Producer: Seth Justman
Album: Love Stinks
Record Label: EMI-America
Songwriters: Seth Justman, Peter Wolf

An apt career summation at that point in time, almost Punk in its negative ardor.

1982

CENTERFOLD
Producer: Seth Justman
Album: Freeze-Frame
Record Label: EMI-America
Songwriter: Seth Justman

Hitting a long-awaited #1 in the video age with a perfectly adaptable if patently unbelievable storyline.

FREEZE-FRAME
Producer: Seth Justman
Album: Freeze-Frame
Record Label: EMI-America
Songwriters: Seth Justman, Peter Wolf

Another slick hit, exploiting the terminology of the new video age.

GENE AND EUNICE

1955

KO KO MO (I LOVE YOU SO)
Record Label: Combo
Songwriters: Forrest Wilson, Jake Porter, Eunice Levy

Seminal R&B rocker achieves the distinction of garnering two Pop covers: Perry Como (RCA, '55) and the Crewcuts (Mercury, '55). RCA would gain enough confidence in the teen market through Perry's performance to sign Elvis Presley.

GENERATION X

1978

YOUR GENERATION
Album: Generation X
Record Label: Chrysalis
Songwriters: William Broad (Billy Idol), Tony James

Early Punk single by the archetype poseur, Idol.

GENESIS

1972

SUPPER'S READY
Producers: Dave Hitchcock
Album: Foxtrot
Record Label: Charisma
Songwriters: Peter Gabriel, Tony Banks

Genesis in the beginning, with Peter Gabriel's fabled classical Rock operetta

1973

CINEMA SHOW
Producers: John Burns, Genesis
Album: Selling England by the Pound
Record Label: Charisma
Songwriters: Peter Gabriel, Tony Banks, Phil Collins, Steve Hackett

Burnishing their Art Rock legend.

1974

THE LAMB LIES DOWN ON BROADWAY
Producer: Brian Eno
Album: The Lamb Lies down on Broadway
Record Label: Atco
Songwriter: Genesis

Their progressive Rock apex.

1977

YOUR OWN SPECIAL WAY
Album: Wind and Wuthering
Record Label: Atco
Songwriter: Mike Rutherford

A progessive Rock breakthrough Bottom-40 single.

1978

FOLLOW YOU FOLLOW ME
Producers: D. Hentschel, Genesis
Album: And Then There Were Three
Record Label: Atlantic
Songwriters: Phil Collins, Tony Banks, Mike Rutherford

Minus their founding artists, Gabriel and Hackett, Genesis begins to proceed without impediment toward the land of the Top-10. This one breaks Top-25.

1980

MISUNDERSTANDING
Producers: D. Hentschel, Genesis
Album: Duke
Record Label: Atlantic
Songwriter: Phil Collins

Paying their commercial dues, with a Top-20 R&R.

1981

ABACAB
Album: Abacab
Record Label: Atlantic
Songwriters: Phil Collins, Tony Banks, Mike Rutherford

Essential progressive rhyme scheme.

1983

THAT'S ALL
Producers: Hugh Padgham, Genesis
Album: Genesis
Record Label: Atlantic
Songwriters: Phil Collins, Tony Banks, Mike Rutherford

Paydirt. Their first Top-10 R&R.

1986

IN TOO DEEP
Producers: Hugh Padgham, Genesis
Album: Invisible Touch
Record Label: Atlantic
Songwriters: Phil Collins, Tony Banks, Mike Rutherford

Suddenly the Chicago of England.

INVISIBLE TOUCH
Producers: Hugh Padgham, Genesis
Album: Invisible Touch

Record Label: Atlantic
Songwriters: Phil Collins, Mike Rutherford

Their first and only #1 R&R.

LAND OF CONFUSION
Producers: Hugh Padgham, Genesis
Album: Invisible Touch
Record Label: Atlantic
Songwriters: Phil Collins, Tony Banks, Mike Rutherford

THROWING IT ALL AWAY
Producers: Hugh Padgham, Genesis
Album: Invisible Touch
Record Label: Atlantic
Songwriters: Phil Collins, Tony Banks, Mike Rutherford

1987

TONIGHT, TONIGHT, TONIGHT
Producers: Hugh Padgham, Genesis
Album: Invisible Touch
Record Label: Atlantic
Songwriters: Phil Collins, Tony Banks, Mike Rutherford

Moving to the next level with a future beer commercial.

1991

I CAN'T DANCE
Producers: Nick Davis, Genesis
Album: We Can't Dance
Record Label: Genesis
Songwriters: Phil Collins, Tony Banks, Mike Rutherford

The theme song of progressive rockers everywhere.

NO SON OF MINE
Producers: Nick Davis, Genesis
Album: We Can't Dance
Record Label: Atlantic
Songwriters: Phil Collins, Tony Banks, Mike Rutherford

An attempt at social realism. Collins would exploit this vein further as a solo act. Suggested segue: Rutherford's "The Living Years."

BOBBIE GENTRY

1967

ODE TO BILLIE JOE
Producers: Gordon Kelly, Bobby Paris
Album: Ode to Billy Joe
Record Label: Capitol
Songwriter: Bobbie Gentry

C&W narrative landmark went #1 R&R but barely grazed the Country Top-20. It served as the basis for the Robbie Benson movie, thus leading to the commercial inevitability of "Harper Valley PTA," "The Night the Lights went out in Georgia," "The Gambler," and "The Devil went down to Georgia," which were also made into full-length films.

THE GENTRYS

1965

KEEP ON DANCING
Producer: Chips Moman
Album: Keep on Dancing
Record Label: MGM
Songwriter: Willie David Young

Anticipating the rise of Frat Rock, the subliterate, beer-swilling, party side of R&R.

BARBARA GEORGE

1961

I KNOW (YOU DON'T LOVE ME NO MORE)
Album: I Know You Don't Love Me No More
Record Label: AFO
Songwriter: Barbara George

New Orleans R&R Soul, didn't make the R&B charts.

GEORGIA SATELLITES

1986

KEEP YOUR HANDS TO YOURSELF
Album: Georgia Satellites
Record Label: Elektra
Songwriter: Don Baird

Rockabilly in the age of Safe Sex.

GERARDO

1991

RICO SUAVE
Producer: Michael Sembello
Album: Mo' Ritmo
Record Label: Interscope
Songwriters: Gerardo Mejia, Christian Carlos Warren

Latino posturing that defines the Hip-Hop '90s urban cultural mix.

THE GERMS

1980

MANIMAL
Album: The Decline and Fall of Western Civilization
Record Label: Slash

Songwriters: Paul Beahm (Darby Crash), George Rothenberg
Hard-core legends in their filmic glory.

GERRY AND THE PACEMAKERS
1964

DON'T LET THE SUN CATCH YOU CRYING
Producer: George Martin
Album: Don't Let the Sun Catch You Crying
Record Label: Laurie
Songwriter: Gerry Marsden
First and biggest hit for Brian Epstein's other clients.

FERRY CROSS THE MERSEY
Producer: George Martin
Album: Ferry Cross the Mersey
Record Label: Laurie
Songwriter: Gerry Marsden
Elegiac snapshot of the land from whence the first British Invasion was plotted and launched.

HOW DO YOU DO IT
Producer: George Martin
Album: Don't Let the Sun Catch You Crying
Record Label: Laurie
Songwriter: Mitch Murray
#1 U.K./Top-10 U.S. tune was turned down by the Beatles.

ANDY GIBB
1977

I JUST WANT TO BE YOUR EVERYTHING
Producers: Karl Richardson, Albhy Galuten, Barry Gibb
Album: Flowing Rivers
Record Label: RSO
Songwriter: Barry Gibb
In the family tradition, Gibb sibling's debut single hits #1 R&R.

1978

AN EVERLASTING LOVE
Producers: Karl Richardson, Albhy Galuten, Barry Gibb
Album: Shadow Dancing
Record Label: RSO
Songwriter: Barry Gibb
After leaping into Pop Rock history with three straight #1 R&R singles, this middling hit started the youngest Gibb's inex-

orable decline toward Broadway, Victoria Principal, bankruptcy, and early death.

SHADOW DANCING
Producers: Karl Richardson, Albhy Galuten, Barry Gibb
Album: Shadow Dancing
Record Label: RSO
Songwriters: Barry Gibb, Robin Gibb, Maurice Gibb, Andy Gibb
A family affair; #1 R&R single of the year.

(LOVE IS) THICKER THAN WATER
Producers: Karl Richardson, Albhy Galuten, Barry Gibb
Album: Shadow Dancing
Record Label: RSO
Songwriters: Barry Gibb, Andy Gibb
But nothing is as thick as blood.

DEBBIE GIBSON
1987

FOOLISH BEAT
Producers: Fred Zarr, Debbie Gibson
Album: Out of the Blue
Record Label: Atlantic
Songwriter: Debbie Gibson
Pubescent prodigy achieves Pop perfection.

ONLY IN MY DREAMS
Producers: Fred Zarr, Debbie Gibson
Album: Out of the Blue
Record Label: Atlantic
Songwriter: Debbie Gibson
New teen triple threat thrush in the Carole King writer/producer/singer mode.

OUT OF THE BLUE
Producers: Fred Zarr, Debbie Gibson
Album: Out of the Blue
Record Label: Atlantic
Songwriter: Debbie Gibson
In the suburban sweetheart sweepstakes of '87, her only competition came from the street-smart mallrat, Tiffany.

SHAKE YOUR LOVE
Producers: Fred Zarr, Debbie Gibson
Album: Out of the Blue
Record Label: Atlantic
Songwriter: Debbie Gibson
Closest thing to a rocker.

1989

LOST IN YOUR EYES
Producer: Debbie Gibson
Album: Electric Youth

Record Label: Atlantic
Songwriter: Debbie Gibson
Nothing as stale as yesterday's teen idol. Her second straight #1 R&R would be her last Top-10 hit. Soon she would be following Carole King and Helen Reddy (to say nothing of Andy Gibb) to Broadway obscurity.

DON GIBSON
1958

I CAN'T STOP LOVING YOU
Album: Oh Lonesome Me
Record Label: RCA
Songwriter: Don Gibson
#1 C&W B-side of "Oh Lonesome Me," which went #1 C&W/Top-10 R&R. Cover by Ray Charles (ABC-Paramount, '62) was the #1 R&B/R&R single of the year.

OH LONESOME ME
Album: Oh Lonesome Me
Record Label: RCA
Songwriter: Don Gibson
His biggest hit, #1 C&W/Top-10 R&R crossover.

1960

SWEET DREAMS
Producer: Chet Atkins
Album: Sweet Dreams
Record Label: RCA
Songwriter: Don Gibson
Covered by Patsy Cline (Decca, '63).

NICK GILDER
1978

HOT CHILD IN THE CITY
Producer: Mike Chapman
Album: City Nights
Record Label: Chrysalis
Songwriters: James McColloch, Nick Gilder
Chart-topping one-shot from England.

JOHNNY GILL
1990

MY MY MY
Producers: L.A. Reid, Babyface
Album: Johnny Gill
Record Label: Motown
Songwriters: Kenny Edmunds (Babyface), Daryl Simmons
#1 R&B/Top-10 R&R crossover for the New Edition graduate.

RUB YOU THE RIGHT WAY
Producers: Jimmy Jam, Terry Lewis
Album: Johnny Gill
Record Label: Motown
Songwriters: James Harris III, Terry Lewis

His biggest hit.

WRAP MY BODY TIGHT
Producers: Jimmy Jam, Terry Lewis
Album: Johnny Gill
Record Label: Motown
Songwriters: James Harris III, Terry Lewis

#1 R&B.

JIMMY GILMER AND THE FIREBALLS
1963

SUGAR SHACK
Producer: Norman Petty
Album: Sugar Shack
Record Label: Dot
Songwriters: Keith McCormack, Faye Voss

White post-Rockabilly tune would peak at #1 R&B/R&R, causing a wholesale re-evaluation of the credibility of the R&B charts.

JIMMIE DALE GILMORE AND THE FLATLANDERS
1972

TONIGHT I THINK I'M GONNA GO DOWNTOWN
Album: One More Road
Record Label: Charly
Songwriters: Jimmie Dale Gilmore, John Reed

Legendary Alternative Country track, introduced by Gilmore's short-lived but long-remembered band with Joe Ely and Butch Hancock, the Flatlanders, whose only album was released on cassette (like most of Hancock's other product) by a small Nashville label run by Shelby Singleton. Release on vinyl didn't come until 1980. Re-released by Rounder in 1990. Covered by Joe Ely (MCA, '78), Nanci Griffith (Philo, '85), Jimmy Dale Gilmore (Nonesuch, '91).

THE GIN BLOSSOMS
1992

FOUND OUT ABOUT YOU
Producers: John Hampton, the Gin Blossoms
Album: New Miserable Experience
Record Label: A&M
Songwriter: Doug Hopkins

Bringing jangly Rock back to the charts, and with it an onslaught of '90s Alternative bands, which, like the Gin Blossoms, were all second-generation versions of the Grass Roots.

HEY JEALOUSY
Producers: John Hampton, the Gin Blossoms
Album: New Miserable Experience
Record Label: A&M
Songwriter: Doug Hopkins

First posthumous hit for the band's former guitarist, whose suicide earlier in the year was overshadowed by the verbiage following Nirvana leader Kurt Cobain's self-inflicted death.

THE GLADIOLAS
1957

LITTLE DARLIN'
Record Label: Excello
Songwriter: Maurice Williams

Classic early rocker by the author of "Stay." Covered by the Diamonds (Mercury, '57) and Dustin Hoffman and Warren Beatty in the film Ishtar (Capitol, '87).

GLASS TIGER
1986

DON'T FORGET ME (WHEN I'M GONE)
Producer: Jim Vallance
Album: The Thin Red Line
Record Label: Manhattan
Songwriters: Alan Frew, Jim Vallance, Sam Reid

Canadian smash, produced by Bryan Adams' partner in Corporate Rock.

GARY GLITTER
1972

ROCK AND ROLL (PART II)
Producer: Mike Leander
Album: Glitter
Record Label: Bell
Songwriters: Gary Glitter, Mike Leander

Trans-Atlantic instrumental hit.

1973

DO YOU WANNA TOUCH ME
Producer: Mike Leander
Record Label: Bell
Songwriters: Gary Glitter, Mike Leander

Arena rocker eventually covered by Joan Jett (Boardwalk, '82).

GO WEST
1990

KING OF WISHFUL THINKING
Album: Pretty Woman Soundtrack
Record Label: EMI
Songwriters: Peter Cox, Richard Drummie, Martin Page

Pop Rock from the Julia Roberts fantasy film Pretty Woman.

THE GO-GO'S
1981

OUR LIPS ARE SEALED
Producer: Richard Gottehrer
Album: Beauty and the Beat
Record Label: I.R.S.
Songwriters: Jane Weidlin, Terry Hall

Teen beat with angst, from the West-coast Blondie. Covered by Fun Boy Three (Chrysalis, '83).

1982

VACATION
Producer: Richard Gottehrer
Album: Vacation
Record Label: I.R.S.
Songwriters: Kathy Valentine, Charlotte Caffey, Jane Wiedlin

Answering Blondie's "In the Sun" with a Busby Berkeley-esque twist on beach movie choreography and a tip of the swim cap to Esther Williams.

WE GOT THE BEAT
Producer: Richard Gottehrer
Album: Beauty and the Beat
Record Label: I.R.S.
Songwriter: Charlotte Caffey

Making radio safe for the Bangles, as well as solo hits from Go-Gos Wiedlen and Belinda Carlisle.

THE GODFATHERS
1988

BIRTH, SCHOOL, WORK, DEATH
Producer: Vic Maile
Album: Birth, School, Work, Death
Record Label: Epic
Songwriter: The Godfathers

Gangsta Rock, the working-class white British version of Gangsta Rap.

GODLEY AND CREME
1985

CRY
Producers: Trevor Horn, Lol Creme, Kevin Godley
Album: The History Mix Volume I
Record Label: Polygram
Songwriters: Lawrence Creme, Kevin Godley

Post 10 c.c. transfusion.

CAST OF *GODSPELL*
1971

DAY BY DAY
Producer: Stephen Schwartz
Album: *Godspell* Original Cast
Record Label: Bell
Songwriters: John-Michael Tebelak, Stephen Schwartz

Spirit on the stage.

GERRY GOFFIN
1973

IT'S NOT THE SPOTLIGHT
Producer: Tom Dowd
Album: It Ain't Exactly Entertainment
Record Label: Warner Brothers
Songwriters: Gerry Goffin, Barry Goldberg

Gerry's solo excursion featured material that was not as good as ex-spouse Carole King's, but not that much worse than the best by contemporaries like Barry Mann ("The Princess and the Punk") and Jimmy Webb ("P. F. Sloan"). Covered by Rod Stewart (Warner Brothers, '75).

ANDREW GOLD
1977

LONELY BOY
Producer: Peter Asher
Album: What's Wrong with This Picture?
Record Label: Asylum
Songwriter: Andrew Gold

Ubiquitous L.A. session man, whose band with Karla Bonoff, Bryndle, finally surfaced in '95.

1978

THANK YOU FOR BEING A FRIEND
Producers: Andrew Gold, Brock Walsh
Album: All This and Heaven Too
Record Label: Asylum
Songwriter: Andrew Gold

Resurfaced as the theme song for the TV show "The Golden Girls."

GOLDEN EARRING
1974

RADAR LOVE
Producer: Shell Schellekens
Album: Moontan
Record Label: Track
Songwriters: Barry Hays, George Kooymans

Euro-Metal highway classic. Covered by White Lion (Atlantic, '89).

1983

TWILIGHT ZONE
Producers: Fred Hadyen, Golden Earring
Album: Cut
Record Label: 21 Records
Songwriter: George Kooymans

In another Metal world.

BOBBY GOLDSBORO
1968

HONEY
Producers: Bob Montgomery, Bobby Goldsboro
Album: Honey
Record Label: United Artists
Songwriter: Bobby Russell

#1 C&W/#1 R&R weeper.

GOO GOO DOLLS
1993

WE ARE THE NORMAL
Producer: Gavin MacKillop
Album: Superstar Carwash
Record Label: Metal Blade
Songwriters: Paul Westerberg, John Rzeznick, Robert Takac, George Tususka

Written with one of their idols/influences, Paul Westerberg of the Replacements, a hard-core rocker from the days before they had a "name."

1995

NAME
Producer: Lou Giordano
Album: A Boy Named Goo
Record Label: Metal Blade/Warner Brothers
Songwriter: Johnny Rzeznick

Their breakthrough hit is something familiar, an Arena Rock Alternative ballad.

DICKIE GOODMAN
1956

THE FLYING SAUCER
Record Label: Luniverse
Songwriter: Mae Boren Axton

Novelty collage of current popular songs, taking off where even Orson Welles dared not follow—presaging the technique of sampling, but not its intent.

STEVE GOODMAN
1970

THE DUTCHMAN
Producer: Arif Mardin
Album: Somebody Else's Troubles
Record Label: Buddah
Songwriter: Michael Smith

Poignant Folk Rock character portrait.

YOU NEVER EVEN CALLED ME BY MY NAME
Producer: Arif Mardin
Album: Somebody Else's Troubles
Record Label: Buddah
Songwriters: Steve Goodman, John Prine

Classic spoof of C&W form and function. Covered by David Allen Coe (Epic, '73) and Doug Kershaw (Mercury, '94).

1971

THE CITY OF NEW ORLEANS
Producers: Norbert Putnam, Kris Kristofferson
Album: Steve Goodman
Record Label: Buddah
Songwriter: Steve Goodman

A vivid cross-country American traveling anthem. Covered by Arlo Guthrie (Reprise, '72) and Willie Nelson (Columbia, '84).

ROBERT GORDON
1978

FIRE
Album: Fresh Fish Special
Record Label: Private Stock
Songwriter: Bruce Springsteen

Catch of the day, Rockabilly à la Boss. Covered by the Pointer Sisters (Planet, '79) and Bruce Springsteen (Columbia, '86).

1981

SOMEDAY, SOMEWAY
Album: Are You Gonna Be the One
Record Label: RCA
Songwriter: Marshall Crenshaw

Quintessential neo-Rockabilly. Covered by Crenshaw (Warner Brothers, '82).

LESLEY GORE
1963

IT'S MY PARTY
Producer: Quincy Jones
Album: I'll Cry If I Want To
Record Label: Mercury
Songwriters: Herb Wiener, John Gluck Jr., Wally Gold

While all the girls of the era were catering to their guys, they were not necessarily as kind to other girls, a fact Lesley Gore was daring enough to admit, if not wallow in.

JUDY'S TURN TO CRY
Producer: Quincy Jones
Album: I'll Cry If I Want To
Record Label: Mercury
Songwriters: Edna Lewis, Beverly Ross

Proving herself not above entering the cat fight, Lesley sets out for revenge on the girl who stole her guy in "It's My Party."

SHE'S A FOOL
Producer: Quincy Jones
Album: Lesley Gore Sings of Mixed up Hearts
Record Label: Mercury
Songwriters: Ben Raleigh, Mark Barkan

By now Lesley's suburban princess persona has been defined.

YOU DON'T OWN ME
Producer: Quincy Jones
Album: Lesley Gore Sings of Mixed up Hearts
Record Label: Mercury
Songwriters: John Madara, David White

By the end of a tortuous '63, in which she'd been raked over the emotional coals by assorted boyfriends and girlfriends, Lesley finally finds herself a relationship (as well as an anthem). But that doesn't mean she's about to lose her essential Goryness. Written by the authors of "At the Hop" and "The Dawn of Correction." Covered by Blow Monkeys in Dirty Dancing *(RCA, '87).*

1964

LOOK OF LOVE
Producer: Quincy Jones
Album: Girl Talk
Record Label: Mercury

Songwriters: Jeff Barry, Ellie Greenwich

Gore playing against type.

MAYBE I KNOW
Producer: Quincy Jones
Album: Golden Hits of Lesley Gore
Record Label: Mercury
Songwriters: Jeff Barry, Ellie Greenwich

One of her more perceptive and reasoned (and rocking) efforts, enabling many of us, for the first time, to actually sympathize with (as well as dance to) her.

1965

SUNSHINE, LOLLIPOPS AND RAINBOWS
Producer: Quincy Jones
Album: Golden Hits of Lesley Gore
Record Label: Mercury
Songwriters: Howard Liebling, Marvin Hamlisch

Gore at her most uncharacteristically winsome. Hamlisch would move on from her to another suburban princess, Carole Bayer Sager.

JOHN GORKA
1992

THE GYPSY LIFE
Producers: Dawn Atkinson, Steven Miller
Album: Temporary Road
Record Label: High Street
Songwriter: John Gorka

Folk Rock rambling gem, defining the new Adult Alternative radio format of the '90s.

GQ
1979

DISCO NIGHTS (ROCK FREAK)
Album: Disco Nights
Record Label: Arista
Songwriters: Emmanuel Le Blanc, Herbert Lane, Keith Crier, Paul Service

CHARLIE GRACIE
1957

BUTTERFLY
Record Label: Cameo
Songwriters: Cal Mann, Bernie Lowe

Philly dance groove, from the dance capitol of '50s America, the land of Dick Clark's "American Bandstand."

GRAHAM CENTRAL STATION
1975

YOUR LOVE
Producer: Larry Graham
Album: Ain't No 'Bout-a-Doubt It
Record Label: Warner Brothers
Songwriter: Larry Graham

#1 R&B/Top-40 R&R crossover for the Sly Stone bass man Larry Graham.

LARRY GRAHAM
1980

ONE IN A MILLION YOU
Producer: Larry Graham, Ron Nadel
Album: One in a Million You
Record Label: Warner Brothers
Songwriter: Sam Dees

Middle-of-the-R&B-road.

LOU GRAMM
1987

MIDNIGHT BLUE
Producers: Pat Moran, Lou Gramm
Album: Ready or Not
Record Label: Atlantic
Songwriters: Lou Grammatico (Lou Gramm), Bruce Turgon

Former lead singer utilizes the Foreigner formula.

1990

JUST BETWEEN YOU AND ME
Album: Long Hard Look
Record Label: Atlantic
Songwriter: Lou Grammatico (Lou Gramm)

GERRY GRANAHAN
1958

NO CHEMISE, PLEASE!
Record Label: Sunbeam
Songwriters: Gerry Granahan, Jodi D'Amour, Arnold Goland

Important fashion commentary by the former leader of Dickie Doo and the Don'ts.

GRAND FUNK RAILROAD
1970

CLOSER TO HOME
Producer: Terry Knight
Album: Closer to Home
Record Label: Capitol

Songwriter: Mark Farner

Breakthrough R&R hit for the American Metal mongers.

1973

WE'RE AN AMERICAN BAND
Producer: Todd Rundgren
Album: We're an American Band
Record Label: Capitol
Songwriter: Don Brewer

Their signature Hard Rock anthem.

1975

BAD TIME
Producer: Jimmy Ienner
Album: All the Girls in the World Beware
Record Label: Capitol
Songwriter: Mark Farner

Their last big hit.

GRANDMASTER FLASH AND THE FURIOUS FIVE

1980

THE ADVENTURES OF GRANDMASTER FLASH ON THE WHEELS OF STEEL
Producers: Sylvia Robinson, Joey Robinson Jr.
Album: The Great Rap Hits
Record Label: Sugarhill
Songwriter: Various

Epic and pioneering demonstration of the fine art of sampling in a Rap context; as usual, misunderstood, reviled, ridiculed, rebuked, and scorned at first.

1982

THE MESSAGE
Producers: Melvin Glover, Sylvia Robinson, Clifton Chase
Album: Grandmaster Flash
Record Label: Sugarhill
Songwriter: Duke Bootee

Outlining the precepts of the basic Rap worldview, in a raw epic of rhythm and poetry.

1983

NEW YORK, NEW YORK
Record Label: Sugarhill
Songwriters: Melvin Glover, Sylvia Robinson, Edward Fletcher, Reginald Griffin

No fun city.

1984

BEATSTREET
Album: Beatstreet
Record Label: Sugarhill
Songwriters: Melvin Glover, Reggie Griffin

From the breakdance movie, Beatstreet, *with Mr. Ness and Cowboy.*

GRANDMASTER FLASH AND MELLE MEL

1983

WHITE LINES (DON'T DO IT)
Producers: Melle Mel, Sylvia Robinson, Joey Robinson Jr.
Record Label: Sugar Hill
Songwriters: Sylvia Robinson, Melvin Glover

A Rap treatise on cocaine; Top-10 U.K.

EARL GRANT

1958

(AT) THE END (OF A RAINBOW)
Record Label: Decca
Songwriters: Jimmy Krondes, Sid Jacobsen

A hit in the sound/image of Brook Benton.

EDDY GRANT

1979

WALKING ON SUNSHINE
Producer: Eddy Grant
Album: Walking on Sunshine
Record Label: Epic
Songwriter: Kimberly Rew

Legendary U.K. production, covered by Rockers Revenge (London, '82) and Rew's Band and by Katrina and the Waves (Capitol, '85).

1983

ELECTRIC AVENUE
Producer: Eddy Grant
Album: Killer on the Rampage
Record Label: Portrait
Songwriter: Eddy Grant

Trans-Atlantic #2 U.K./R&R crossover.

GRASS ROOTS

1967

LET'S LIVE FOR TODAY
Producer: Steve Barri
Album: Let's Live for Today
Record Label: Dunhill

Songwriters: Michael Julien, Mogol (Guilio Rapetti), Shel Shapiro, Mike Shepstone

Based on the Italian hit, "Piangi Con Mi," a Top-10 R&R Folk Rocker.

MIDNIGHT CONFESSIONS
Producer: Steve Barri
Album: Golden Grass
Record Label: Dunhill
Songwriter: Lou Josie

Commercial Folk Rock; the Gin Blossoms were listening.

1971

SOONER OR LATER
Producer: Steve Barri
Album: Their 16 Greatest
Record Label: Dunhill
Songwriters: Gary Zekley, Mitch Bottler, Adeneyi Paris, Ted McNamara, Ekundayo Paris

THE GRATEFUL DEAD

1967

GOOD MORNING, LITTLE SCHOOL GIRL
Producer: The Grateful Dead
Album: The Grateful Dead
Record Label: Warner Brothers
Songwriter: H. G. Demarais

The ultimate school-boy Blues Rock fantasy, derived from the '37 original by Sonny Boy Williamson. Covered by Rod Stewart in '64, the Yardbirds (Epic, '69), Ten Years After (Deram, '69), and Muddy Waters (Blue Sky, '78).

NEW NEW MINGLEWOOD BLUES
Producer: The Grateful Dead
Album: The Grateful Dead
Record Label: Warner Brothers
Songwriters: Jerry Garcia, Robert Hunter

With Gus Cannon's Jug Stompers' "Minglewood Blues" (RCA '28) in mind, the legendary touring institution and traveling hippie circus and museum first known as Mother Mcree's Uptown Jug Champions, and then as the Warlocks, begin their reign as house band at Ken Kesey's Trips Festivals, led by Captain Trips himself, otherwise known as Jerry Garcia.

1968

DARK STAR
Album: Live/Dead
Record Label: Warner Brothers

Songwriter: Jerry Garcia

Jerry's solo, captured in Antonioni's 1970 ersatz psychedelic commentary Zabriskie Point.

1969

CHINA CAT SUNFLOWER

Producers: Bob Matthew, Betty Cantor
Album: Aoxomoxoa
Record Label: Warner Brothers
Songwriters: Jerry Garcia, Robert Hunter

A mystical, translucent ball of twine.

ST. STEPHEN

Producers: Bob Matthew, Betty Cantor
Album: Aoxomoxoa
Record Label: Warner Bros.
Songwriters: Jerry Garcia, Bob Hunter, Phil Lesh

A concert favorite, collected on five different label compilations, and probably 50 million bootleg tapes.

1970

ATTICS OF MY LIFE

Producer: The Grateful Dead
Album: American Beauty
Record Label: Warner Brothers
Songwriters: Jerry Garcia, Robert Hunter

Early psychedelic Bluegrass.

BOX OF RAIN

Producers: Bob Matthews, Betty Cantor, the Grateful Dead
Album: Workingman's Dead
Record Label: Warner Brothers
Songwriters: Jerry Garcia, Robert Hunter

From their most profound and prolific period.

CASEY JONES

Producers: Bob Matthews, Betty Cantor, the Grateful Dead
Album: Workingman's Dead
Record Label: Warner Brothers
Songwriter: Jerry Garcia

Updating an epic American cautionary folk tale. Suggested segue: "Casey Jones" by Billy Murray and the American Quartet (Victor, '10).

FRIEND OF THE DEVIL

Producer: The Grateful Dead
Album: American Beauty

Record Label: Warner Brothers
Songwriters: Jerry Garcia, Robert Hunter, John Dawson

Outlaw Bluegrass.

RIPPLE

Producer: The Grateful Dead
Album: American Beauty
Record Label: Warner Brothers
Songwriters: Jerry Garcia, Robert Hunter

Traveling through the mystic waters of life, aided by Jerry's guitar and David Grisman's mandolin.

SUGAR MAGNOLIA

Producer: The Grateful Dead
Album: American Beauty
Record Label: Warner Brothers
Songwriters: Bob Weir, Robert Hunter

TRUCKIN'

Producer: The Grateful Dead
Album: American Beauty
Record Label: Warner Brothers
Songwriters: Robert Hunter, Jerry Garcia, Philip Lesh, Bob Weir, Billy Kreutzmann

Detailing a long, strange trip that would only get longer and stranger, eventually logging more miles and reels of tape than any Rock band before or since.

UNCLE JOHN'S BAND

Producers: Bob Matthews, Betty Cantor, the Grateful Dead
Album: Workingman's Dead
Record Label: Warner Brothers
Songwriters: Robert Hunter, Jerry Garcia

The unalloyed hippie ethos in a rare chart single.

1975

FRANKLIN'S TOWER

Producer: The Grateful Dead
Album: Blues for Allah
Record Label: Grateful Dead
Songwriters: Jerry Garcia, Robert Hunter, Billy Kreutzmann

Recorded at the Sphinx in Egypt.

1987

TOUCH OF GREY

Producers: Jerry Garcia, J. Cutler
Album: In the Dark
Record Label: Arista

Songwriters: Jerry Garcia, Robert Hunter

After twenty years, a Top-10 R&R single.

1994

DAYS BETWEEN

Record Label: Arista
Songwriters: Jerry Garcia, Robert Hunter

One of the last tunes Garcia completed before his death in '95.

DOBIE GRAY

1964

THE IN CROWD

Producer: Fred Darian
Album: Dobie Gray Sings for the In Crowd
Record Label: Charger
Songwriter: Billy Page

His biggest hit.

1973

DRIFT AWAY

Producer: Mentor Williams
Album: Drift Away
Record Label: Decca
Songwriter: Mentor Williams

Pining for the lost magic of Rock and Roll.

THE GREAT SOCIETY

1965

SOMEONE TO LOVE

Album: Conspicuous Only in Its Absence
Record Label: Columbia
Songwriter: Darby Slick.

Local anthem was covered by Grace Slick's new band, the Jefferson Airplane, as "Somebody to Love" (RCA, '67), which became the first national hit from psychedelic San Francisco. The Great Society album, meanwhile, would sit in the can until 1968.

WHITE RABBIT

Album: Conspicuous Only in Its Absence
Record Label: Columbia
Songwriter: Grace Slick

Talk about being a head of your time. The Great Society's version of this tune, written in '65, wouldn't be released until '68, by which time the Jefferson Airplane would be the apparent heirs to psychedelia's fortune, spurred by Grace taking her song with her, for inclusion on their second album (RCA, '67). Covered by the Muffs (MCA, '95).

R. B. GREAVES
1969

TAKE A LETTER, MARIA
Producer: Ahmet Ertegun
Album: R. B. Greaves
Record Label: Atco
Songwriter: Ronald Bertram Greaves
(Sonny Childe)

Top-10 R&B/R&R one-shot crossover. Covered by Anthony Armstrong Jones on the Country Chart (Chart, '70).

CYNDI GRECCO
1976

MAKING OUR DREAMS COME TRUE
Producers: Charles Fox, James Feliciano
Album: Laverne and Shirley
Record Label: Private Stock
Songwriters: Norman Gimbel, Charles Fox

From the mid-'70s heyday of the TV sitcom theme song.

GREEN DAY
1991

GREEN DAY
Producers: Andy Ernst, Green Day
Album: 1039/Smoothed Out
Record Label: Lookout
Songwriters: Billy Joe Armstrong, Green Day

1992

WELCOME TO PARADISE
Producers: Andy Ernst, Green Day
Album: Ker-Plunk
Record Label: Lookout
Songwriters: Billie Joe Armstrong, Green Day

Espousing the new slacker style of Power Punk. Re-released on their breakthrough album Dookie (Reprise, '94).

1994

BASKET CASE
Producers: Rob Cavallo, Green Day
Album: Dookie
Record Label: Reprise
Songwriters: Billy Joe Armstrong, Green Day

Making Punk rebellion palatable for the suburban subteens of the '90s.

LONGVIEW
Producers: Rob Cavallo, Green Day
Album: Dookie
Record Label: Reprise
Songwriters: Billy Joe Armstrong, Green Day

New neurotic Rock for the pre-teen set.

WHEN I COME AROUND
Producers: Rob Cavallo, Green Day
Album: Dookie
Record Label: Reprise
Songwriters: Billy Joe Armstrong, Green Day

GREEN JELLY
1993

THREE LITTLE PIGS
Producers: S. Massey, C. J. Buscaglia
Album: *Cereal Killer* Soundtrack
Record Label: Zoo
Songwriters: William Manspeaker, Marc Levinthal

Teenybop video cartoon crosses over to radio.

AL GREEN
1967

BACK UP, TRAIN
Producer: Willie Mitchell
Album: Al Green
Record Label: Hot Line
Songwriters: Curtis Rogers, Palmer E. James

Introducing the heir apparent to Sam Cooke, Otis Redding and Smokey Robinson (with the Soul Mates).

1971

TIRED OF BEING ALONE
Producer: Willie Mitchell
Album: Al Green Gets Next to You
Record Label: Hi
Songwriter: Al Green

His patented crooning breakthrough.

1972

I'M STILL IN LOVE WITH YOU
Producer: Willie Mitchell
Album: I'm Still in Love with You
Record Label: Hi
Songwriters: Al Green, Willie Mitchell, Al Jackson

Hitting his Soulful stride, #1 R&B/Top-10 R&R.

LET'S STAY TOGETHER
Producer: Willie Mitchell
Album: Let's Stay Together
Record Label: Hi
Songwriters: Al Green, Willie Mitchell, Al Jackson

The smoothest of Green's smooth Soul sound that owned '72, starting out with this #1 R&B/R&R crossover. Covered by Isaac Hayes (Enterprise, '72) and Tina Turner (Capitol, '83).

LOOK WHAT YOU DONE FOR ME
Producer: Willie Mitchell
Album: I'm Still in Love with You
Record Label: Hi
Songwriters: Al Green, Willie Mitchell, Al Jackson

Second big crossover hit of '72.

YOU OUGHTA BE WITH ME
Producer: Willie Mitchell
Album: Call Me
Record Label: Hi
Songwriters: Al Green, Willie Mitchell, Al Jackson

His third #1 R&B/Top-10 R&R crossover of the year.

1973

CALL ME (COME BACK HOME)
Producer: Willie Mitchell
Album: Call Me
Record Label: Hi
Songwriters: Al Green, Willie Mitchell, Al Jackson

After a banner '72, Green's effortless Soul reaches a creative peak that would not be reflected on the singles chart, which had him moving downhill from there.

HERE I AM (COME AND TAKE ME)
Producer: Willie Mitchell
Album: Call Me
Record Label: Hi
Songwriters: Chuck Jackson, Marvin Yancy Jr., Lee Charles

Jackson and Yancy would move on to Natalie Cole.

LIVIN' FOR YOU
Producer: Willie Mitchell
Album: Livin' for You
Record Label: Hi
Songwriters: Al Green, Willie Mitchell

#1 R&B/Top-20 R&R.

TAKE ME TO THE RIVER
Producer: Willie Mitchell
Album: Al Green Explores Your Mind
Record Label: Hi
Songwriters: Al Green, Mabon Hodges

His Gospel imagery attracts the Rock crowd with a cover by Talking Heads (Sire, '78).

1974

SHA-LA-LA (MAKE ME HAPPY)
Producer: Willie Mitchell
Album: Al Green Explores Your Mind
Record Label: Hi
Songwriter: Al Green

1975

FULL OF FIRE
Producer: Willie Mitchell
Album: Full of Fire
Record Label: Hi
Songwriters: Al Green, Willie Mitchell, Mabon Hodges

#1 R&B/Top-30 R&R crossover.

L-O-V-E (LOVE)
Producer: Willie Mitchell
Album: Al Green Is Love
Record Label: Hi
Songwriters: Al Green, Willie Mitchell, Mabon Hodges

#1 R&B/Top-20 R&R crossover.

1977

BELLE
Producer: Willie Mitchell
Album: The Belle Album
Record Label: Hi
Songwriters: Al Green, Fred Jordan, Reuben Fairfax Jr.

I FEEL GOOD
Producer: Willie Mitchell
Album: The Belle Album
Record Label: Hi
Songwriter: Al Green

Like James Brown knew he would.

NORMAN GREENBAUM
1970

SPIRIT IN THE SKY
Album: Spirit in the Sky
Record Label: Reprise
Songwriter: Norman Greenbaum

Echoing the era's Pop spiritual sound ("Instant Karma," " Put Your Hand in the Hand," "Oh Happy Day") the writer of "The

Eggplant That Ate Chicago" had a true religious experience when Dorothy Morrison's cover of this tune (Buddah, '70) won a Grammy for best Gospel performance.

ELLEN GREENE AND LEE WILKOFF
1982

SUDDENLY SEYMOUR
Producer: Phil Ramone
Album: Little Shop of Horrors
Record Label: Warner Brothers
Songwriters: Howard Ashman, Alan Menken

Key ballad from the hip musical by the future Disney ("Under the Sea," "Kiss the Girl") stalwarts. Reprised by Greene and Rick Moranis in the movie (Geffen, '86).

ELLIE GREENWICH
1985

WE'RE GONNA MAKE IT (AFTER ALL)
Album: Leader of the Pack
Record Label: Elektra/Asylum
Songwriter: Ellie Greenwich

Preceding Leiber and Stoller and Carole King but not Leonard Cohen to the cabaret showcase production, the other side of the tribute album.

NANCI GRIFFITH
1987

FROM A DISTANCE
Producers: Tony Breen, Nanci Griffith
Album: Lone Star State of Mind
Record Label: MCA
Songwriter: Julie Gold

Ecumenical anthem discovered and published by renegade Country Folk artist Griffith. Popularized by Bette Midler (Atlantic, '90).

1988

GULF COAST HIGHWAY
Album: Little Love Affairs
Record Label: MCA
Songwriters: Nanci Griffith, James Hooker, Danny Flowers

Poignant Country Folk ballad, paving the way for Mary Chapin Carpenter, and a radio format based on the advanced Folk Rock sound. Covered by Evangeline (Margaritaville, '92).

1989

IT'S A HARD LIFE WHEREVER YOU GO
Producer: Glyn Johns
Album: Storms
Record Label: MCA
Songwriter: Nanci Griffith

Carrying the torch of Protest Folk Rock into the '90s.

YOU MADE THIS LOVE A TEARDROP
Producer: Glyn Johns
Album: Storms
Record Label: MCA
Songwriter: Nanci Griffith

Perfect Folk Pop rocker, with Phil Everly on backing vocal.

LARRY GROCE
1976

JUNK FOOD JUNKIE
Producer: Randolph Nauert
Album: Junk Food Junkie
Record Label: Warner Brothers
Songwriter: Larry Groce

Novelty one-shot.

HENRY GROSS
1976

SHANNON
Producers: Terry Cashman, Tommy West
Album: Release
Record Label: Lifesong
Songwriter: Henry Gross

Brooklyn-born Henry's answer to "Old Shep."

VINCE GUARALDI TRIO
1962

CAST YOUR FATE TO THE WIND
Album: Jazz Impressions of *Black Orpheus*
Record Label: Fantasy
Songwriter: Vince Guaraldi

Jazz Rock ramblin' classic.

THE GUESS WHO
1969

LAUGHING
Producer: Jack Richardson
Album: Canned Wheat Packed by the Guess Who

Record Label: RCA
Songwriter: Randall Bachman

The Canadian Gary Puckett and the Union Gap.

NO TIME
Producer: Jack Richardson
Album: Canned Wheat Packed by the Guess Who
Record Label: RCA
Songwriters: Randall Bachman, Burton Cummings

Their answer to Chicago's "Does Anybody Really Know What Time It Is?".

THESE EYES
Producer: Jack Richardson
Album: Wheatfield Soul
Record Label: RCA
Songwriters: Randall Bachman, Burton Cummings

First big hit for the Canadian Arena rockers.

1970

AMERICAN WOMAN
Producer: Jack Richardson
Album: American Woman
Record Label: RCA
Songwriters: Randall Bachman, Burton Cummings, Garry Peterson, Jim Kale

This anti-female anti-American rockin' rant from Canada went to #1 R&R; possibly inspiring the #1 Pop/Rock answer song, "I Am Woman" by Australia's Helen Reddy, two years later.

SHARE THE LAND
Producer: Jack Richardson
Album: Share the Land
Record Label: RCA
Songwriter: Burton Cummings

1974

CLAP FOR THE WOLFMAN
Producer: Jack Richardson
Album: Road Food
Record Label: RCA
Songwriters: Burton Cummings, Bill Wallace, Kurt Winter

Their last big hit.

CHRISTOPHER GUEST
1973

HIGHWAY TOES
Producer: Tony Hendra
Album: *Lemmings* Original Cast Album
Record Label: Banana

Songwriters: Christopher Guest, Sean Kelly

Guest dusts off his James Taylor for the landmark Rock satire of the Woodstock Generation. Rob Reiner was laughing: his This Is Spinal Tap was only a decade away, starring Guest (and Hendra).

GUIDED BY VOICES
1994

I AM A SCIENTIST
Album: Bee Thousand
Record Label: Scat/Matador
Songwriter: Robert Pollard

Out of obscurity, a gift from the prolific mad scientist of low-fi, the sound of the '90s anti-techno rebellion.

GUNS N' ROSES
1987

PATIENCE
Producer: Mike Clink
Album: G N' R Lies
Record Label: Geffen
Songwriter: Guns N' Roses

Mid-tempo ballad returned to the airwaves after the band's massive breakthrough.

WELCOME TO THE JUNGLE
Producer: Mike Clink
Album: Appetite for Destruction
Record Label: Geffen
Songwriter: Guns N' Roses

Defining Heavy Metal's last bombastic '80s gasp. Featured in the movie The Dead Pool.

1988

SWEET CHILD O' MINE
Producer: Mike Clink
Album: Appetite for Destruction
Record Label: Geffen
Songwriter: Guns N' Roses

The Heavy Metal ballad refuses to die as a radio-friendly introduction to an inherently unfriendly genre. Suggested segues: "More Than Words" by Extreme; "To be with You" by Mr. Big; "High Enough" by Damn Yankees; and "Wait" by White Lion, and all the way back to the granddaddies of the form: "More Than a Feeling" by Boston, and "Dream On" by Aerosmith, to say nothing of the mother of them all, "Stairway to Heaven" by Led Zeppelin.

1989

PARADISE CITY
Producer: Mike Clink
Album: Appetite for Destruction

Record Label: Geffen
Songwriter: Guns N' Roses

Wearing out their welcome on the Top-10, but not before establishing a new level of bad-boy bravado.

1991

CIVIL WAR
Producers: Mike Clink, Guns N' Roses
Album: Use Your Illusion II
Record Label: Geffen
Songwriter: Guns N' Roses

Previewing their double-price-tag double-album set.

DON'T CRY
Producers: Mike Clink, Guns N' Roses
Album: Use Your Illusion II
Record Label: Geffen
Songwriters: Axl Rose, Izzy Stradlin

Another Rock ballad. But it was no "Sweet Child O' Mine."

NOVEMBER RAIN
Producers: Mike Clink, Guns N' Roses
Album: Use Your Illusion I
Record Label: Geffen
Songwriter: Axl Rose

Axl shows off his misunderstood, sensitive, River Phoenix-ian side with this brooding magnum opus.

ARTHUR GUNTER
1954

BABY LET'S PLAY HOUSE
Record Label: Excello
Songwriters: Knox Phillips, Jerry Phillips

Covered by Elvis, for his first appearance on the country charts (Sun, '54). Suggested segue: "I Wanna Play House with You," by Eddy Arnold (RCA, '51).

HARD ROCK GUNTER AND THE PEBBLES
1950

BIRMINGHAM BOUNCE
Record Label: Bama
Songwriter: Sid Gunter

Ushering in another early '50s mini-dance craze. Covered by Amos Milburn (Aladdin, '50) and Red Foley (Decca, '50).

SHIRLEY GUNTER AND THE QUEENS

1954

OOP SHOOP
Album: Black and Blues
Record Label: Flair
Songwriter: Joe Josea

First R&B girl-group to hit the charts. The Teen Queens were listening.

ARLO GUTHRIE

1967

ALICE'S RESTAURANT
Producers: Van Dyke Parks, Lenny Waronker
Album: Alice's Restaurant
Record Label: Reprise
Songwriter: Arlo Guthrie

The epic endless Folkie tone poem of the alternate culture, basis for the Arthur Penn movie Alice's Restaurant *and still played religiously by certain FM stations every Christmas.*

1969

COMING INTO LOS ANGELES
Album: Running down the Road
Record Label: Reprise
Songwriter: Arlo Guthrie

Essential Folk Rock subversion.

DEPORTEES (THE PLANE WRECK AT LOS GATOS)
Album: Arlo Guthrie
Record Label: Reprise
Songwriters: Woody Guthrie, Martin Hoffman

Tapping into the Folk tradition of his father, Woody.

1976

VICTOR JARA
Producer: John Pilla
Album: Amigo
Record Label: Reprise
Songwriter: Arlo Guthrie

Celebrating the South American singer/songwriter and revolutionary.

GWEN GUTHRIE

1986

AIN'T NOTHIN' GOIN' ON BUT THE RENT
Producer: Gwen Guthrie
Album: Good to Go Lover
Record Label: Polydor

Songwriter: Gwen Guthrie
Critically lauded maximum R&B.

WOODY GUTHRIE

1941

PASTURES OF PLENTY
Record Label: Library of Congress
Songwriter: Woody Guthrie

Pioneering Folk balladeer's classic American anthem, written while he was under the employ of the Bonneville Power Administration. Adapting the ballad "Pretty Polly," Guthrie's celebration of freedom, the land, and the outlaws, outcasts, and outsiders who labored to maintain these precious gifts, influenced a nascent generation of peaceniks, pacificists, and protesters, from Bob Dylan to the Clash. Originally published in the first issue of Pete Seeger's magazine Sing Out! *Covered by Cisco Houston (Vanguard, '60).*

1942

PRETTY BOY FLOYD
Record Label: Library of Congress
Songwriter: Woody Guthrie

Advancing the radical notion of the noble outlaw as common man and the system as villain, from which the cause of Rock and Roll, Punk Rock, outlaw Country, and Rap will prove inextricable. Covered by Joan Baez (Vanguard, '62); the Byrds (Columbia, '68); Melanie (Neighborhood, '73), and Bob Dylan (Columbia, '88).

GUY

1988

I LIKE
Producers: Teddy Riley, Gene Griffin
Album: Guy
Record Label: Uptown
Songwriters: Teddy Riley, Gene Griffin, Aaron Hall, Timothy Gatling

#1 R&B.

MY FANTASY
Producers: Teddy Riley, Gene Griffin
Album: Do the Right Thing Soundtrack
Record Label: Motown
Songwriters: Gene Griffin, William Aquart

#1 R&B/Bottom-40 R&R crossover from Spike Lee's Do the Right Thing.

H

H-TOWN

1993

KNOCKIN' DA BOOTS
Producer: Bishop Burrell
Album: Fever for Da Flavor
Record Label: Luke
Songwriters: Shazam, Dino Conner, Bishop (Stick) Burrell, Roger Troutman

#1 R&B/Top-10 R&R; sporting the year's Hip-Hop flavor.

HADDAWAY

1993

WHAT IS LOVE?
Album: Haddaway
Record Label: Arista
Songwriters: Dee Dee Halligan, Junior Torello

New Euro-Disco sound.

SAMMY HAGAR

1982

FAST TIMES AT RIDGEMONT HIGH
Album: Fast Times at Ridgemont High *Soundtrack*
Record Label: Full Moon
Songwriter: Sammy Hagar

From the influential post-Slacker, pre-Generation X movie.

1983

YOUR LOVE IS DRIVING ME CRAZY
Producer: Keith Olsen
Album: Three-Lock Box
Record Label: Geffen
Songwriter: Sammy Hagar

Biggest hit for the future Van Halen frontman.

1984

I CAN'T DRIVE 55
Album: VOA
Record Label: Geffen
Songwriter: Sammy Hagar

Rock as social protest; eventually the speed limits in many states were rolled back to '65.

MERLE HAGGARD

1970

OKIE FROM MUSKOGEE

Album: Okie from Muskogee
Record Label: Capitol
Songwriters: Merle Haggard, Roy Edward Burris

#1 C&W/Top-50 R&R crossover has come to define, if not deify, the red-necked, hippie-baiting, soul of middle America, if not Haggard himself, who has done many other, less contentious Country songs.

BILL HALEY AND HIS COMETS

1952

ROCK A-BEATING BOOGIE

Producer: Milt Gabler
Album: Rock Around the Clock
Record Label: Essex
Songwriter: Bill Haley

Introducing the first C&W/R&R (Rock and Roll) dance band, trying to exploit the rhythms of "The Hucklebuck" for a new generation. Song was previously released by Haley guitarist Danny Cedrone's first group, the Esquire Boys.

1953

(WE'RE GONNA) ROCK AROUND THE CLOCK

Producer: Milt Gabler
Album: Rock Around the Clock
Record Label: Decca
Songwriters: Max C. Freedman, Jimmy Myers (Jimmy DeKnight)

Perhaps the most significant career move of early Rock and Roll history occured when Jimmy DeKnight was appointed music director of the movie Blackboard Jungle. In his first official act, he ordered "Rock Around the Clock," the Bill Haley B-side that had already flopped twice (once for Bill, once for its originator, Sunny Doe (Impact, '53), to be used behind the opening credits. Thus, when the single hit #1 in 1955, Rock and Roll, as a song and an image, officially crossed over into mainstream America. It's too bad Danny Cedrone, who took the quintessential Rockabilly guitar solo, never lived to see it, having died in a fall sometime shortly after the record's original release.

CRAZY MAN, CRAZY

Producer: Milt Gabler
Record Label: Essex
Songwriter: Bill Haley

Killing time between the release and reissue of "Rock Around the Clock."

1954

DIM, DIM THE LIGHTS (I WANT SOME ATMOSPHERE)

Producer: Milt Gabler
Album: Rock Around the Clock
Record Label: Decca
Songwriters: Julius Dixon, Beverly Ross

Making the world a safer place for Rock and Roll, Haley charts his first R&B/R&R crossover.

1955

BURN THAT CANDLE

Producer: Milt Gabler
Album: Rock Around the Clock
Record Label: Decca
Songwriter: Winfield Scott

From one of the genre's best writers, Haley snags a Top-10 R&R hit.

1958

SKINNY MINNIE

Producer: Milt Gabler
Record Label: Decca
Songwriters: Bill Haley, Arrett "Rusty" Keefer, Catherine Cafra, Milt Gabler

Plainly out of steam by now, Bill and the gang were determined to go down swinging. They followed this up with "Lean Jean," which was an even bigger bomb.

HALF JAPANESE

1984

SECRET SHARER

Album: Sing No Evil
Record Label: Iridescence
Songwriter: Jad Fair

Jonathan Richman innocence, squared.

HALL AND OATES

1974

SHE'S GONE

Producer: Arif Mardin
Album: Abandoned Luncheonette
Record Label: Atlantic
Songwriters: Daryl Hall, John Oates

Philly Soul with a New York accent. Cover by Tavares (Capitol, '73) went #1 R&B. Hall and Oates' version hit Top-10 R&R when re-released in '76.

1975

CAMELLIA

Producer: Chris Bond
Album: Daryl Hall and John Oates

Record Label: RCA
Songwriters: Daryl Hall, John Oates

Early highlight and still one of their all-time best tracks.

SARA SMILE

Producer: Chris Bond
Album: Daryl Hall and John Oates
Record Label: RCA
Songwriters: Daryl Hall, John Oates

Their first big hit, dedicated to future collaborator Sara Allen.

1976

RICH GIRL

Producer: Chris Bond
Album: Bigger Than the Both of Us
Record Label: RCA
Songwriter: Daryl Hall

Finding their true subject matter—the suburban princess—and achieving their first #1 R&R.

1981

DID IT IN A MINUTE

Producer: Hall and Oates
Album: Private Eyes
Record Label: RCA
Songwriters: Daryl Hall, Janna Allen, Sara Allen

Sara and her sister cement their writing relationship with the duo.

I CAN'T GO FOR THAT (NO CAN DO)

Producer: Hall and Oates
Album: Private Eyes
Record Label: RCA
Songwriters: Daryl Hall, John Oates, Sara Allen

On their way toward eclipsing the Everly Brothers—in the record books, if not in the eyes of the critical community—with their fourth #1 R&R (also a #1 R&B crossover; the first all-white act to accomplish this feat since Jimmy Gilmer and the Fireballs in '63).

KISS ON MY LIST

Producer: Hall and Oates
Album: Voices
Record Label: RCA
Songwriters: Daryl Hall, Janna Allen

Starting off a massive year ('81) and album with their second biggest all-time hit.

PRIVATE EYES

Producer: Hall and Oates
Album: Private Eyes
Record Label: RCA

Songwriters: Daryl Hall, Janna Allen, Sara Allen, Warren Pash

New album, same sound, same result—their second #1 of '81.

YOU MAKE MY DREAMS

Producer: Hall and Oates
Album: Voices
Record Label: RCA
Songwriters: Daryl Hall, John Oates, Sara Allen

Mining their favorite Philly Pop dance groove.

1982

MANEATER

Producer: Hall and Oates
Album: H2O
Record Label: RCA
Songwriters: Daryl Hall, John Oates, Sara Allen

Returning to their favorite subject for their biggest all-time hit.

1983

FAMILY MAN

Producer: Hall and Oates
Album: H2O
Record Label: RCA
Songwriters: Mike Oldfield, Morris Pert, Tim Cross, Rick Fenn, Mike Frye

ONE ON ONE

Producer: Hall and Oates
Album: H2O
Record Label: RCA
Songwriter: Daryl Hall

Their brand of sophisticated blue-eyed Soul at its finest: Top-10 R&B/R&R.

SAY IT ISN'T SO

Producer: Hall and Oates
Album: Rock 'N Soul (Part I)
Record Label: RCA
Songwriter: Daryl Hall

1984

ADULT EDUCATION

Producers: Hall and Oates, Bob Clearmountain
Album: Rock 'N Soul (Part I)
Record Label: RCA
Songwriters: Daryl Hall, John Oates, Sara Allen

OUT OF TOUCH

Producers: Hall and Oates, Bob Clearmountain
Album: Big Bam Boom

Record Label: RCA
Songwriters: Daryl Hall, John Oates

Philly-Souled out; their sixth and last #1 R&R.

1985

EVERY TIME YOU GO AWAY

Producer: Hall & Oates
Album: Voices
Record Label: RCA
Songwriter: Daryl Hall

Covered by Paul Young (Columbia, '85).

METHOD OF MODERN LOVE

Producers: Hall and Oates, Bob Clearmountain
Album: Big Bam Boom
Record Label: RCA
Songwriters: Daryl Hall, Janna Allen

1988

EVERYTHING YOUR HEART DESIRES

Album: ooh yeah
Record Label: Arista
Songwriter: Daryl Hall

After a long layoff, they come back with their sixteenth and last Top-10 R&R hit.

AARON HALL

1991

DON'T BE AFRAID

Album: *Juice* Soundtrack
Record Label: Soul
Songwriters: Hank Shocklee, Gary G. Wiz, Floyd Fisher, Aaron Hall

From the soundtrack of the Rap movie, a #1 R&B/Top-50 R&R crossover

DARYL HALL

1986

DREAMTIME

Album: Three Hearts and the Happy Ending Machine
Record Label: RCA
Songwriters: Daryl Hall, John Beeby

Blue-eyed solo.

TOM T. HALL

1971

THE YEAR THAT CLAYTON DELANEY DIED

Album: In Search of a Song
Record Label: Mercury
Songwriter: Tom T. Hall

#1 C&W/Top-50 R&R crossover from one of Country music's finest writers, who also wrote "Harper Valley PTA."

GEORGE HAMILTON IV

1956

A ROSE AND A BABY RUTH

Album: George Hamilton IV on Campus
Record Label: ABC Paramount
Songwriter: John D. Loudermilk

First Pop Rockabilly hit for the prolific Country writer, John D. Loudermilk.

1957

WHY DON'T THEY UNDERSTAND?

Album: George Hamilton IV on Campus
Record Label: ABC Paramount
Songwriters: Jack Fishman, Joe Henderson

Essential teen lament.

1963

ABILENE

Album: Abilene
Record Label: RCA
Songwriters: John D. Loudermilk, Bob Gibson, Lester Brown, Albert Stanton

#1 C&W/Top-20 R&R crossover indicating Hamilton's drift from Rockabilly to Country music, a sojourn many original and/or played-out rockers would be taking in the decades to come.

1967

URGE FOR GOING

Album: Folky
Record Label: RCA
Songwriter: Joni Mitchell

Mitchell crosses over to the Country top 20 with the first song she ever wrote, a landmark ode to rolling with the emotional and seasonal changes. Covered in the definitive Folk Rock version by Tom Rush (Elektra, '68), which Hamilton actually heard in pre-release form on a Boston radio station. Recorded by Mitchell as the B-side of "You Turn Me On, I'm a Radio" (Asylum, '73).

HAMILTON, JOE FRANK, AND REYNOLDS

1971

DON'T PULL YOUR LOVE

Producers: Dennis Lambert, Brian Potter
Album: Hamilton, Joe Frank, and Reynolds
Record Label: Dunhill
Songwriters: Dennis Lambert, Brian Potter

The Country Folk Rock formula of '71.

FALLIN' IN LOVE (AGAIN)

1975

Producer: Jim Price
Album: Fallin' in Love
Record Label: Playboy
Songwriters: Danny Hamilton, Ann Hamilton

Their peak.

ROY HAMILTON

1954

EBB TIDE

Record Label: Epic
Songwriters: Carl Sigman, Robert Maxwell

Dramatic Top-10 R&B ballad given the appropriate gospel feel by Hamilton, whose previous "You'll Never Walk Alone" topped the R&B charts earlier that year. Introduced by Frank Chacksfield (London, '53). Covered by the Righteous Brothers (Philles, '65).

HURT

Record Label: Epic
Songwriters: Jimmie Crane, Al Jacobs

Closing out '54 with another Top-10 R&B. Cover by Timi Yuro (Liberty, '62) went Top-10 R&R.

1955

UNCHAINED MELODY

Record Label: Epic
Songwriters: Alex North, Hy Zaret

This intense ballad from the movie Unchained *gives Hamilton his biggest hit, a #1 R&B/Top-10 R&R crossover. Covered by Al Hibbler (Decca, '55) and the Righteous Brothers (Philles, '65).*

1958

DON'T LET GO

Record Label: Epic
Songwriter: Jesse Stone

Covered by Commander Cody (Warner Brothers, '75).

1961

YOU CAN HAVE HER

Record Label: Epic
Songwriter: Bill Cook

His last big crossover hit.

JAN HAMMER

1985

MIAMI VICE THEME

Producer: Jan Hammer
Album: *Miami Vice* Soundtrack

Record Label: MCA
Songwriter: Jan Hammer

As musical director of the stylish TV drama, Hammer was briefly the most important A&R man in showbiz.

M. C. HAMMER

1990

PRAY

Producer: Hammer
Album: Please Hammer Don't Hurt 'Em
Record Label: Capitol
Songwriters: Prince Rogers Nelson, M. C. Hammer (Stanley Burrell)

U CAN'T TOUCH THIS

Producer: Hammer
Album: Please Hammer Don't Hurt 'Em
Record Label: Capitol
Songwriters: Rick James, M. C. Hammer (Stanley Burrell), James Miller

James's "Super Freak" sparks Hammer's rise to #1 R&B/Top-10 R&R.

1991

2 LEGIT TO QUIT

Producers: Hammer, Felton Pilate
Album: 2 Legit to Quit
Record Label: Capitol
Songwriters: Felton Pilate, M. C. Hammer (Stanley Burrell), James Earley, Michael Kelly, Louis Burrell

Amid rumors that he wasn't so legit after all, a defensive posture.

ADDAMS' GROOVE

Producers: Hammer, Felton Pilate
Album: 2 Legit to Quit
Record Label: Capitol
Songwriters: Felton Pilate, M. C. Hammer (Stanley Burrell), Vic Mizzy

From the '92 film The Addams Family. *Mizzy wrote the original TV theme.*

ALBERT HAMMOND

1972

THE AIR THAT I BREATHE

Producers: Don Altfeld, Albert Hammond
Album: It Never Rains in Southern California
Record Label: Mums
Songwriters: Albert Hammond, Mike Hazelwood

Covered by the Hollies (Epic, '74).

IT NEVER RAINS IN SOUTHERN CALIFORNIA

Producers: Don Altfeld, Albert Hammond
Album: It Never Rains in Southern California
Record Label: Mums
Songwriters: Albert Hammond, Mike Hazelwood

Sunny L.A. state-of-the-art-of-'70s studiocraft. Covered by the Hollies (Epic, '74).

HERBIE HANCOCK

1983

ROCKIT

Producers: Herbie Hancock, Material
Album: Future Shock
Record Label: Columbia
Songwriters: Herbie Hancock, Bill Laswell, Michael Beinhorn

Pop Funk novelty breakthrough for the veteran Jazz keyboardist.

PAUL HARDCASTLE

1985

19

Producer: Paul Hardcastle
Record Label: Chrysalis
Songwriters: Paul Hardcastle, W. Coutourie, J. McCord

Vietnam war commentary.

TIM HARDIN

1966

REASON TO BELIEVE

Album: Tim Hardin
Record Label: Verve/Forecast
Songwriter: Tim Hardin

One of his most enduring and fragile Folk Blues rockers. Covered by Bobby Darin (Atlantic, '67) and Rod Stewart (Warner Brothers, '94).

1967

IF I WERE A CARPENTER

Album: Tim Hardin (Vol. II)
Record Label: Verve/Forecast
Songwriter: Tim Hardin

Classic Folk Rock ballad. Covered, if not cloned, by Bobby Darin (Atlantic, '66) and the Four Tops (Motown, '68).

THE LADY CAME FROM BALTIMORE

Album: Tim Hardin (Vol. II)
Record Label: Verve/Forecast

Songwriter: Tim Hardin
Covered by Bobby Darin (Atlantic, '67).

HARPER'S BIZARRE
1966

COME TO THE SUNSHINE
Producer: Lenny Waronker
Album: Feelin' Groovy
Record Label: Warner Brothers
Songwriter: Van Dyke Parks

Showcasing the work of the noted L.A. eccentric and friend of Brian Wilson, Van Dyke Parks.

SIMON SMITH AND THE AMAZING DANCING BEAR
Producer: Lenny Waronker
Album: Feelin' Groovy
Record Label: Warner Brothers
Songwriter: Randy Newman

Quirky Warner Brothers' house songwriter begins to get weird. Covered in England by Alan Price (Decca, '67). Newman recorded his own version (Reprise, '72).

1967

HIGH COIN
Producer: Lenny Waronker
Album: Anything Goes
Record Label: Warner Brothers
Songwriter: Van Dyke Parks

Big-Surian extravaganza previews Parks' lush epics to come. Covered by the Charlatans (Philips, '69).

THE BIGGEST NIGHT OF HER LIFE
Producer: Lenny Waronker
Album: Anything Goes
Record Label: Warner Brothers
Songwriter: Randy Newman

Another early-teen dream epic from Newman's days as a relatively sincere senior-prom advocate.

BEN HARPER
1993

I'LL RISE
Album: Welcome to the Cruel World
Record Label: Virgin
Songwriter: Ben Harper

Gospel-inflected modern Folk Blues.

SLIM HARPO
1957

I'M A KING BEE
Producer: Jay Miller
Record Label: Excello

Songwriter: James Moore (Slim Harpo)

Rootsy Blues classic, covered by the Rolling Stones (London, '64).

1966

BABY, SCRATCH MY BACK
Producer: Jay Miller
Album: Baby, Scratch My Back
Record Label: Excello
Songwriter: James Moore (Slim Harpo)

#1 R&B/Top-20 R&R crossover, in the days when a true Blues could still make either chart.

THE HARPTONES
1953

A SUNDAY KIND OF LOVE
Producer: George Goldner
Record Label: Bruce
Songwriters: Barbara Belle, Anita Leonard, Stan Rhodes, Louis Prima

The ultimate version of this fine ballad, which failed to score on either the R&R or the R&B chart. Introduced in 1947 by Jo Stafford.

1954

LIFE IS BUT A DREAM
Producer: Rauol Cita
Record Label: Paradise
Songwriters: Rauol Cita, Hy Weiss

More of their patented Doo-Wop escapism.

BARBARA HARRIS
1975

IT DON'T WORRY ME
Producer: Richard Baskin
Album: *Nashville* Soundtrack
Record Label: ABC
Songwriter: Keith Carradine

Ersatz Country anthem from the Robert Altman masterwork Nashville.

MAJOR HARRIS
1975

LOVE WON'T LET ME WAIT
Album: My Way
Record Label: Atlantic
Songwriters: Bobby Eli, Vinnie Barrett

#1 R&B/Top-10 R&R crossover for a Philly Soul veteran.

PEPPERMINT HARRIS
1951

I GOT LOADED
Record Label: Aladdin
Songwriter: Harrison Nelson

Crucial #1 R&B ode to the joys of getting plastered. Covered by Los Lobos (Slash, '84) and Robert Cray (Hightone, '87). Suggested segues: "Drinkin' Wine Spoo-De-o-Dee" by Stick McGhee, "One Scotch, One Bourbon, One Beer" by Amos Milburn, "Let's Go Get Stoned" by Ray Charles.

RICHARD HARRIS
1968

MACARTHUR PARK
Producer: Jimmy Webb
Album: A Tramp Shining
Record Label: Dunhill
Songwriter: Jimmy Webb

Webb's lovelorn epiphanies get the standard Pop treatment. Fabled now for the improbable "someone left a cake out in the rain" image. Covered for the Disco set by Donna Summer (Casablanca, '78).

WYNONIE HARRIS
1949

ALL SHE WANTS TO DO IS ROCK
Record Label: King
Songwriters: Teddy McRea, Beatrice Harris

The first #1 R&B hit of the Rock and Roll era Harris helped create with his version of Roy Brown's "Good Rockin' Tonight."

GEORGE HARRISON
1970

ISN'T IT A PITY
Producer: Phil Spector
Album: All Things Must Pass
Record Label: Apple
Songwriter: George Harrison

The inevitable solo George.

MY SWEET LORD
Producer: Phil Spector
Album: All Things Must Pass
Record Label: Apple
Songwriters: George Harrison, Ronald Mack

The pious Beatle is nailed for unconsciously plagiarizing "He's So Fine" by the Chiffons.

WHAT IS LIFE?

Producer: Phil Spector
Album: All Things Must Pass
Record Label: Apple
Songwriter: George Harrison

More of George's eternal quest for meaning.

1971

BANGLA-DESH

Producers: Phil Spector, George Harrison
Album: Concert for Bangala-Desh
Record Label: Apple
Songwriter: George Harrison

Theme song for the first of the all-world, Rock-charity-song events.

1973

GIVE ME LOVE (GIVE ME PEACE ON EARTH)

Producer: George Harrison
Album: Living in the Material World
Record Label: Apple
Songwriter: George Harrison

Harrison would one day produce a movie starring the material girl, Madonna.

1976

CRACKERBOX PALACE

Producers: Tom Scott, George Harrison
Album: Thirty-Three and 1/3
Record Label: Dark House
Songwriter: George Harrison

One of his more spirited rockers.

THIS SONG

Producer: George Harrison
Album: Thirty-Three and 1/3
Record Label: Dark Horse
Songwriter: George Harrison

Responding with notable, if not previously noticeable, humor about the "My Sweet Lord" fiasco.

1981

ALL THOSE YEARS AGO

Producers: Ray Cooper, George Harrison
Album: Somewhere in England
Record Label: Dark Horse
Songwriter: George Harrison

In the wake of the John Lennon tragedy, Harrison took a turn at summing things up, from a considerable distance.

1987

WHEN WE WAS FAB

Producers: Jeff Lynne, George Harrison
Album: Cloud Nine
Record Label: Dark Horse
Songwriters: George Harrison, Jeff Lynne

Another career summation, presaging his future collaboration with Lynne in the Traveling Wilburys, and in the mid-'90s, on several 3/4 of the Beatles reunion tunes.

WILBERT HARRISON

1969

LET'S WORK TOGETHER (PART 1)

Producer: Juggy Murray
Album: Let's Work Together
Record Label: Sue
Songwriter: Wilbert Harrison

A decade after "Kansas City," Harrison returns to the charts. Covered by Canned Heat (Liberty, '70).

COREY HART

1984

SUNGLASSES AT NIGHT

Producers: Jon Astley, Corey Hart
Album: First Offense
Record Label: EMI-America
Songwriter: Corey Hart

Bryan Adamsish rocker.

1985

NEVER SURRENDER

Album: Boy in the Box
Record Label: EMI-America
Songwriter: Corey Hart

JOHN HARTFORD

1967

GENTLE ON MY MIND

Album: Gentle on My Mind
Record Label: RCA
Songwriter: John Hartford

Country Folk rambling standard. Covered by Glen Campbell (Capitol, '67).

DAN HARTMAN

1984

I CAN DREAM ABOUT YOU

Producers: Jimmy Iovine, Dan Hartman
Album: I Can Dream About You

Record Label: MCA
Songwriter: Dan Hartman

From the movie Streets of Fire.

P. J. HARVEY

1992

DRESS

Producer: P. J. Harvey
Album: Dry
Record Label: Indigo/Island
Songwriters: Polly Jean Harvey, Robert Ellis

Low-fi feminist rage from England.

1993

50 FT. QUEENIE

Producer: P. J. Harvey
Album: Rid of Me
Record Label: Island
Songwriter: Polly Jean Harvey

Ingeniously amateurish Hard-Rock demo indicates why Harvey has since become a leading figure in the anti-thrush movement of the early '90s.

1995

DOWN BY THE WATER

Producers: Flood, P. J. Harvey, John Parish
Album: To Bring You My Love
Record Label: Island
Songwriter: Polly Jean Harvey

Establishing herself as the most unique female Blues rocker since Janis Joplin.

THE JULIANA HATFIELD THREE

1993

MY SISTER

Producer: Scott Litt
Album: Become What You Are
Record Label: Mammoth
Songwriter: Juliana Hatfield

The girl-group sound with a feminist perspective, female sensibility, and alternative cache.

SPIN THE BOTTLE

Producer: Scott Litt
Album: Become What You Are
Record Label: Mammoth
Songwriter: Juliana Hatfield

Featured in the movie Reality Bites.

DONNIE HATHAWAY
1973

SOMEDAY WE'LL ALL BE FREE
Album: Extension of a Man
Record Label: Atco
Songwriters: Donnie Hathaway,
    Edward Howard

Career song for the R&B crooner. Covered by Aretha Franklin on the Malcolm X Soundtrack (Qwest/Warner Brothers, '92).

RICHIE HAVENS
1967

FOLLOW
Producer: Jerry Schoenbaum
Album: Mixed Bag
Record Label: Verve/Folkways
Songwriter: Jerry Merrick

Early in-concert show-stopper; a ten minute stream of new consciousness, raised to a higher level by Richie's booming voice.

HANDSOME JOHNNY
Producer: Jerry Schoenbaum
Album: Mixed Bag
Record Label: Verve/Forecast
Songwriters: Richie Havens, Lou
    Gossett

Cogent antiwar song. Brought the house to its feet when he sang it on "The Johnny Carson Show."

HIGH FLYING BIRD
Producer: Jerry Schoenbaum
Album: Mixed Bag
Record Label: Verve/Folkways
Songwriter: Billy Edd Wheeler

Folk Rock's greatest Soul man mines a Country gem. Performed by the Jefferson Airplane at the Monterey Rock and Pop Festival in '67; released on Grunt, '74. Covered by Lovecraft (Philips, '68).

1968

THE KLAN
Album: Something Else Again
Record Label: Verve/Forecast
Songwriters: D. Grey, A. Grey

Powerful civil-rights era dirge. Covered by Gil Scott-Heron (Arista, '80).

1970

FREEDOM
Album: *Woodstock* Soundtrack
Record Label: Cotillion
Songwriter: Richie Havens

Composed on stage at the Woodstock Festival, waiting for the other acts to arrive.

CHESNEY HAWKES
1991

THE ONE AND ONLY
Album: *Doc Hollywood* Soundtrack
Record Label: Chrysalis
Songwriter: Nick Kershaw

Obligatory closing credits ballad.

DALE HAWKINS
1957

SUZIE Q
Album: Suzie Q.
Record Label: Checker
Songwriters: Dale Hawkins, Stanley
    Lewis, Eleanor Broadwater

Blistering Rockabilly classic. Covered by Creedence Clearwater Revival (Fantasy, '68).

EDWIN HAWKINS SINGERS
1969

OH HAPPY DAY
Producer: Lamont Beech
Album: Let Us Go into the House of
    the Lord
Record Label: Pavilion
Songwriter: Edwin Hawkins

Hawkins arranged this old Gospel favorite, Dorothy Morrison sang lead. In the waning days of the Mahareeshi, it foretold a new spiritual direction/need and sold a couple of million copies.

RONNIE HAWKINS
1959

FORTY DAYS
Album: Ronnie Hawkins
Record Label: Roulette
Songwriter: Bernie Roth

With Levon Helms, later of his backup band, the Hawks, on drums.

SCREAMING JAY HAWKINS
1956

I PUT A SPELL ON YOU
Producer: Leroy Kirkland
Album: I Put a Spell on You
Record Label: Okeh
Songwriter: Jay Hawkins

Stark raving 1st Rock single on Okeh. Covered by Creedence Clearwater Revival (Fantasy, '68), Arthur Brown (Track, '68).

SOPHIE B. HAWKINS
1992

DAMN, I WISH I WAS YOUR LOVER
Producers: Rick Chertoff, Ralph
    Schukett
Album: Tongues and Tails
Record Label: Columbia
Songwriter: Sophie B. Hawkins

This Pop Rock hit updates the Lesley Gore persona.

HAWKWIND
1972

SILVER MACHINE
Record Label: United Artists
Songwriters: Dave Brock, Robert
    Calvert

English relic of the psychedelic era was their biggest U.K. hit—charting again in '78 and '83.

1974

LOST JOHNNY
Album: Hall of the Mountain Grill
Record Label: United Artists
Songwriters: Ian Kilmeister
    (Lemmy), Mick Farren

Kilmeister would emerge again in the raging Metal monster, Motorhead.

ISAAC HAYES
1971

THEME FROM *SHAFT* (WHO SHAFT WHERE)
Producer: Isaac Hayes
Album: Shaft
Record Label: Enterprise
Songwriter: Isaac Hayes

The seductive sound of blaxploitation, one part Disco, two parts R&B, that would soon engulf the community, the airwaves, the nation, and the film industry, to say nothing of the NBA.

LEON HAYWOOD
1975

I WANT'A DO SOMETHING FREAKY TO YOU
Producer: Leon Haywood
Album: Come and Get Yourself
    Some
Record Label: 20th Century
Songwriter: Leon Haywood

His first hit.

1980

DON'T PUSH IT DON'T FORCE IT
Producer: Leon Haywood
Album: Naturally
Record Label: 20th Century
Songwriter: Leon Haywood

ROBERT HAZARD
1982

GIRLS JUST WANT TO HAVE FUN
Record Label: RCA
Songwriter: Robert Hazard
Covered by Cyndi Lauper (Portrait, '84).

MURRAY HEAD
1970

JESUS CHRIST SUPERSTAR
Producers: Tim Rice, Andrew Lloyd
   Webber
Album: Jesus Christ Superstar
Record Label: Decca
Songwriters: Tim Rice, Andrew
   Lloyd Webber

In a karma-conscious, guru-heavy musical period, the future Broadway icons snag a record deal for their Broadway-bound Rock opera with this title track.

ROY HEAD
1965

TREAT HER RIGHT
Album: Treat Me Right
Record Label: Back Beat
Songwriter: Roy Head
His first and biggest hit, a #2 R&B/R&R crossover

THE JEFF HEALEY BAND
1989

ANGEL EYES
Producer: Greg Ladanyi
Album: See the Light
Record Label: Arista
Songwriters: John Hiatt, Fred Koller

Blues rocking ballad hit; an anomaly in the catalogue of its mondo quirky writers as well as the Canadian, heavy-Blues, bar band performing it.

1992

CRUEL LITTLE NUMBER
Album: Feel This
Record Label: Arista

Songwriters: Jeff Healey, Joe
   Rockman, Tom Stephen, Carl Marsh,
   Justis Walker
Rock track from the blind, Blues-guitar phenom Healey.

HEAR 'N' AID
1986

STARS
Producer: Ronnie James Dio
Album: Hear 'n' Aid
Record Label: Mercury
Songwriters: Ronnie Dio, Vivian
   Campbell, Jimmy Bain
Heavy Metal charity rocker, with a slew of featured solos.

HEART
1976

CRAZY ON YOU
Producer: Mike Flicker
Album: Dreamboat Annie
Record Label: Mushroom
Songwriters: Ann Wilson, Nancy
   Wilson, Roger Fisher
Top-40 breakthrough for the Zeppelin-esque girl-group, fronted by the Wilson sisters.

MAGIC MAN
Producer: Mike Flicker
Album: Dreamboat Annie
Record Label: Mushroom
Songwriters: Ann Wilson, Nancy
   Wilson
Second single is their biggest hit of the '70s.

1977

BARRACUDA
Producer: Mike Flicker
Album: Little Queen
Record Label: Portrait/CBS
Songwriters: Ann Wilson, Nancy
   Wilson, Michael Derosier, Roger
   Fisher
A rocker with teeth.

1978

STRAIGHT ON
Producer: Mike Flicker
Album: Dog and Butterfly
Record Label: Portrait
Songwriters: Ann Wilson, Nancy
   Wilson
Straight-ahead rocker.

1980

EVEN IT UP
Producers: Mike Flicker, Gonnie and
   Howie
Album: Bebe Le Strange
Record Label: Portrait
Songwriters: Ann Wilson, Nancy
   Wilson, Sue Ennis
Last hit from their Arena Rock period.

1983

HOW CAN I REFUSE
Album: Passionworks
Record Label: Epic
Songwriters: Ann Wilson, Howard
   Leese, Sue Ennis, Mark Andes,
   Denny Carmassi
Big transitional track on their comeback trail.

1985

NEVER
Producer: Ron Nevison
Album: Heart
Record Label: Capitol
Songwriters: Holly Knight, Walter
   Bloch, Ann Wilson
Returning to the tiles with the first of six Top-10 R&R Lite Metal ballads.

WHAT ABOUT LOVE?
Producer: Ron Nevison
Album: Heart
Record Label: Capitol
Songwriters: Sheron Alton, Jim
   Vallance, Brian Allan
In conjunction with Bryan Adams' renowned collaborator, Vallance.

1986

NOTHIN' AT ALL
Producer: Ron Nevison
Album: Heart
Record Label: Capitol
Songwriter: Mark Mueller

THESE DREAMS
Producer: Ron Nevison
Album: Heart
Record Label: Capitol
Songwriters: Bernie Taupin, Martin
   Page
With Elton's word man, Bernie, Heart achieves their first #1 R&R.

1987

ALONE
Producer: Ron Nevison
Album: Bad Animals

Record Label: Capitol
Songwriters: Billy Steinberg, Tom Kelly

In capable corporate hands, they reach the peak of their well-earned formula.

WHO WILL YOU RUN TO

Producer: Ron Nevison
Album: Bad Animals
Record Label: Capitol
Songwriter: Diane Warren

Only a matter of time before they would pluck a winner from the massive Warren archive.

1990

ALL I WANNA DO IS MAKE LOVE TO YOU

Album: Brigade
Record Label: Capitol
Songwriter: Robert John "Mutt" Lange

Launching Lange's superstar-'90s period. But by now this band knows their soap-opera formula by heart.

THE HEARTBEATS
1956

A THOUSAND MILES AWAY

Album: A Thousand Miles Away
Record Label: Hull/Rama
Songwriters: James Sheppard, William H. Miller

B-side of "Oh Baby Don't." Another one-shot Doo-Wop standard.

THE HEARTBREAKERS
1977

BORN TO LOSE

Album: L.A.M.F.
Record Label: Track
Songwriter: John Genzale (Johnny Thunders)

Signature number for the former New York Doll and his band.

CHINESE ROCKS

Album: L.A.M.F.
Record Label: Track
Songwriter: Douglas Colvin (Dee Dee Ramone), Richard Meyer (Richard Hell)

Documenting the heyday of American Glam, written by two Punk legends.

THE HEARTS
1955

LONELY NIGHTS

Record Label: Baton
Songwriter: Zell Sanders

The essence of New York Doo-Wop.

HEATWAVE
1977

BOOGIE NIGHTS

Producer: Barry Blue
Album: Too Hot to Handle
Record Label: Epic
Songwriter: Rod Temperton

Big Disco hit.

1978

THE GROOVE LINE

Producer: Barry Blue
Album: Central Heating
Record Label: Epic
Songwriter: Rod Temperton

HEAVEN 17
1982

TEMPTATION

Producers: Greg Walsh, B.E.F.
Album: The Luxury Gap
Record Label: Sire
Songwriters: Glenn Gregory, Ian Craig Marsh, Martyn Ware

Riding the British Techno wave.

WE LIVE SO FAST

Producers: Greg Walsh, B.E.F.
Album: The Luxury Gap
Record Label: Sire
Songwriters: Glenn Gregory, Ian Craig Marsh, Martyn Ware

Ware and Marsh co-founded the Human League.

HEAVY D AND THE BOYS
1994

GOT ME WAITING

Album: Nuttin' But Love
Record Label: Uptown/MCA
Songwriters: Heavy D, Luther Vandross, Pete Rock, C. L. Smooth.

NUTTIN' BUT LOVE

Album: Nuttin' but Love
Record Label: Uptown/MCA
Songwriters: Dwight Meyers (Heavy D), Kid Capri

Breakthrough hit for the New York rapper.

BOBBY HEBB
1966

SUNNY

Album: Sunny
Record Label: Philips
Songwriter: Bobby Hebb

Lilting Pop Rock gem was written the morning after the assassination of JFK.

THE HEIGHTS
1992

HOW DO YOU TALK TO AN ANGEL

Producer: Steve Tyrell
Album: The Heights
Record Label: Capitol
Songwriters: Steve Tyrell, Stephanie Tyrell, Barry Coffing

From the failed TV series about Rock stardom this was a lesson in one-shot Rock balladry. Lead singer Jamie Walters would move to a lot across the compound, for a recurring role on "Beverly Hills 90120," and several more innocuous singles.

RICHARD HELL AND THE VOIDOIDS
1976

BLANK GENERATION

Album: Blank Generation
Record Label: ORK
Songwriter: Michael Meyers (Richard Hell)

From the CBGB's proving ground that spawned New York's version of Punk Rock, this was an anthem for post-flower-power youth derived from the repertoire of Hell's first band, Television. Hell would eventually overcome his own malaise enough to marry the quintessentially funky Patti Smyth.

HELMET
1992

UNSUNG

Album: Meantime
Record Label: Interscope
Songwriter: Page Hamilton

Hard Rock exponent from the experimental Band of Susans.

BOBBY HELMS
1957

JINGLE-BELL ROCK

Record Label: Decca
Songwriters: Joe Beal, Jim Boothe

Timeless rocking classic of the season.

MY SPECIAL ANGEL
Album: To My Special Angel
Record Label: Decca
Songwriter: Jimmy Duncan

*Johnny Ray-influenced rocker. #1
C&W/Top-10 R&B/R&R crossover.*

JOE HENDERSON
1962

SNAP YOUR FINGERS
Album: Snap Your Fingers
Record Label: Todd
Songwriters: Grady Martin, Alex
Zanetis

*Jazz-influenced Top-10 R&B/R&R
crossover.*

JIMI HENDRIX
1967

ARE YOU EXPERIENCED?
Producer: Chas Chandler
Album: Are You Experienced?
Record Label: Reprise
Songwriter: Jimi Hendrix

*Electric, space-age Blues: amplified, psy-
chedelicized, and funkafied. Every guitarist
within earshot went back to the woodshed
demoralized.*

FIRE
Producer: Chas Chandler
Album: Are You Experienced?
Record Label: Reprise
Songwriter: Jimi Hendrix

*A favorite concert opener, evoking the fire-
breathing guitar pyrotechnics of his
Monterey-closing "Wild Thing."*

FOXY LADY
Producer: Chas Chandler
Album: Are You Experienced?
Record Label: Reprise
Songwriter: Jimi Hendrix

*A salacious come-on for the sexual revolu-
tion, unaccountably passed over by the R&B
charts.*

I DON'T LIVE TODAY
Producer: Chas Chandler
Album: Are You Experienced?
Record Label: Reprise
Songwriter: Jimi Hendrix

*One of the first black artists to cover the
white genre of psychedelic Rock, which was
itself second-generation B. B. King, as
processed through Owsley Stanley. See
Arthur Lee. Sly Stone was already on the
scene. Ernie Isley was listening in his crib.*

MANIC DEPRESSION
Producer: Chas Chandler
Album: Are You Experienced?
Record Label: Reprise
Songwriter: Jimi Hendrix

*A Seattle native previews the indigenous
Grunge attitude.*

MAY THIS BE LOVE
Producer: Chas Chandler
Album: Are You Experienced?
Record Label: Reprise
Songwriter: Jimi Hendrix

*Featured in the soundtrack to the Seattle
tribute movie* Singles.

PURPLE HAZE
Producer: Chas Chandler
Album: Are You Experienced?
Record Label: Reprise
Songwriter: Jimi Hendrix

*The aural equivalent of the acid experience:
life-changing, life-threatening, and revealingly unreal.*

THE WIND CRIES MARY
Producer: Chas Chandler
Album: Are You Experienced?
Record Label: Reprise
Songwriter: Jimi Hendrix

*For those who have always thought his
lyrics needed work—especially in this
song—it has recently come to light that this
particular lyric was written soon after Jimi
had been hit on the head with a frying pan
by a girlfriend.*

1968

CASTLES MADE OF SAND
Producer: Chas Chandler
Album: Axis: Bold as Love
Record Label: Reprise
Songwriter: Jimi Hendrix

Unplugged.

CROSSTOWN TRAFFIC
Producer: Jimi Hendrix
Album: Electric Ladyland
Record Label: Reprise
Songwriter: Jimi Hendrix

*His second biggest hit after "All Along the
Watchtower."*

IF 6 WAS 9
Producer: Chas Chandler
Album: Axis: Bold as Love
Record Label: Reprise
Songwriter: Jimi Hendrix

*Enacting the apocalypse, sexual and instru-
mental. Featured in the film* Easy Rider.

LITTLE WING
Producer: Chas Chandler
Album: Axis: Bold as Love
Record Label: Reprise
Songwriter: Jimi Hendrix

*In an acoustic mode. Covered by Sting
(A&M, '87) and Stevie Ray Vaughan (Epic,
'91).*

STONE FREE
Producer: Jimi Hendrix
Album: Smash Hits
Record Label: Reprise
Songwriter: Jimi Hendrix

The ultimate fusion of man and guitar.

VOODOO CHILE (SLIGHT RETURN)
Producer: Jimi Hendrix
Album: Electric Ladyland
Record Label: Reprise
Songwriter: Jimi Hendrix

*Perhaps his most famous composition, his
first posthumous hit, which went to #1 in
the U.K., where they were always more
amenable to the extravagant gesture.
Covered by Stevie Ray Vaughan (Epic, '84).*

YOU GOT ME FLOATIN'
Producer: Chas Chandler
Album: Axis: Bold as Love
Record Label: Reprise
Songwriter: Jimi Hendrix

Wah-wah heaven.

1969

RED HOUSE
Producer: Jimi Hendrix
Album: Smash Hits
Record Label: Reprise
Songwriter: Jimi Hendrix

*Out of T-Bone Walker by way of Pharoah
Sanders, this quintessential Blues extravaganza was recorded on at least six different
albums.*

1971

DOLLY DAGGER
Producer: Jimi Hendrix
Album: Rainbow Bridge
Record Label: Reprise
Songwriter: Jimi Hendrix

*Last posthumous single, before the deluge
of reissues by the infamous Hendrixologist
Alan Douglas.*

FREEDOM
Producer: Jimi Hendrix
Album: The Cry of Love
Record Label: Reprise
Songwriter: Jimi Hendrix

HEAR MY TRAIN A-COMING
Producer: Jimi Hendrix
Album: Rainbow Bridge
Record Label: Reprise
Songwriter: Jimi Hendrix

One of his great performances.

NIGHT BIRD FLYING
Producers: Jimi Hendrix, Mitch Mitchell, Eddie Kramer
Album: The Cry of Love
Record Label: Reprise
Songwriter: Jimi Hendrix

Inspired improvisation. First of a virtual warehouse full of posthumous noodling.

ROOM FULL OF MIRRORS
Album: Rainbow Bridge
Record Label: Reprise
Songwriter: Jimi Hendrix

Saves the epic hippie movie Rainbow Bridge. Covered by the Pretenders (Sire, '86).

DON HENLEY
1982

DIRTY LAUNDRY
Producers: Don Henley, Danny Kortchmar
Album: I Can't Stand Still
Record Label: Asylum
Songwriters: Don Henley, Danny Kortchmar

First solo hit for the former Eagle.

1985

ALL SHE WANTS TO DO IS DANCE
Producers: Don Henley, Danny Kortchmar, Greg Ladanyi
Album: Building the Perfect Beast
Record Label: Geffen
Songwriter: Danny Kortchmar

Typical Henley-esque vitriol.

THE BOYS OF SUMMER
Producers: Don Henley, Danny Kortchmar, Greg Ladanyi
Album: Building the Perfect Beast
Record Label: Geffen
Songwriters: Don Henley, Mike Campbell

Evocative modern Folk rocker is Henley's

most perfect achievement, as is Campbell's opening guitar figure.

1989

THE END OF THE INNOCENCE
Producers: Don Henley, Bruce Hornsby
Album: The End of the Innocence
Record Label: Geffen
Songwriters: Don Henley, Bruce Hornsby

This eloquent diatribe defines Henley's post-Eagles renaissance.

THE HEART OF THE MATTER
Producers: Don Henley, Danny Kortchmar, Mike Campbell
Album: The End of the Innocence
Record Label: Geffen
Songwriters: Don Henley, Mike Campbell, J. D. Souther

It's all about forgiveness. His second finest work.

CLARENCE "FROGMAN" HENRY
1956

AIN'T GOT NO HOME
Producer: Paul Gayten
Record Label: Argo
Songwriter: Clarence Henry

Deep-throated New Orleans R&B novelty, literally earning Henry his nickname.

1960

BUT I DO
Album: You Always Hurt the One You Love
Record Label: Argo
Songwriters: Robert Guidry, Paul Gayten

Top-10 R&B/R&R crossover.

HERMAN'S HERMITS
1965

CAN'T YOU HEAR MY HEARTBEAT?
Producer: Mickie Most
Album: Hold On
Record Label: MGM
Songwriters: John Carter, Ken Lewis

Coming in on the Beatles' coattails.

I'M HENRY VIII, I AM
Producer: Mickie Most
Album: Herman's Hermits on Tour
Record Label: MGM

Songwriters: Fred Murray, R. P. Weston

Music Hall standard, introduced in '11, by English comedian Harry Champion.

JUST A LITTLE BIT BETTER
Producer: Mickie Most
Album: The Best of Herman's Hermits
Record Label: MGM
Songwriter: Kenny Young

Sampling American Pop.

MRS. BROWN, YOU'VE GOT A LOVELY DAUGHTER
Producer: Mickie Most
Album: Introducing
Record Label: MGM
Songwriter: Trevor Peacock

Skiffle-inspired classic introduced in '63 by Tom Courtenay in a British TV play, was their first #1 U.S. and their biggest hit.

A MUST TO AVOID
Producer: Mickie Most
Album: Hold On
Record Label: MGM
Songwriters: Steve Barri, P. F. Sloan

Sampling West coast staff songwriting at its best. Featured in Hold On, the Hermits' version of A Hard Day's Night.

LEANING ON THE LAMP POST
Producer: Mickie Most
Album: Hold On
Record Label: MGM
Songwriter: Noel Gay

Another music hall favorite, introduced in the '37 musical "Feather Your Nest."

1966

DANDY
Producer: Mickie Most
Album: Best of Herman's Hermits (Vol. II)
Record Label: MGM
Songwriter: Ray Davies

Reverting to more modern homegrown product, with this Ray Davies character portrait.

LISTEN PEOPLE
Producer: Mickie Most
Album: Best of Herman's Hermits (Vol. II)
Record Label: MGM
Songwriter: Graham Gouldman

From the film When the Boys Meet the Girls. Gouldman would move on to the Yardbirds and 10 c.c.

1967

THERE'S A KIND OF HUSH (ALL OVER THE WORLD)
Producer: Mickie Most
Album: There's a Kind of a Hush
Record Label: MGM
Songwriters: Les Reed, Geoff Stevens

Their last big hit.

HI-FIVE

1990

I LIKE THE WAY (THE KISSING GAME)
Producer: Teddy Riley
Album: Hi-Five
Record Label: Jive
Songwriters: Teddy Riley, Bernard Belle, David Way

Teenybop Hip-Hop chart topper.

1991

I CAN'T WAIT ANOTHER MINUTE
Producer: Eric Foster White
Album: Hi-Five
Record Label: Jive
Songwriter: Eric Foster White

#1 R&B/Top-10 R&R crossover.

1992

SHE'S PLAYING HARD TO GET
Producer: Timmy Allen
Album: Keep It Goin' On
Record Label: Jive
Songwriters: Timmy Allen, William Walton

JOHN HIATT

1979

PINK BEDROOM
Producer: Denny Bruce
Album: Slug Line
Record Label: MCA
Songwriter: John Hiatt

Introducing the anti-Mellencamp, the song-writing voice of the maladjusted middle-American. Covered by Lou Ann Barton, an Austin Blues-Rock protege of Stevie Ray Vaughan's (Spindletop, '86).

YOU'RE MY LOVE INTEREST
Producer: Denny Bruce
Album: Slug Line
Record Label: MCA
Songwriter: John Hiatt

1983

RIDING WITH THE KING
Producer: Nick Lowe
Album: Riding with the King
Record Label: Geffen
Songwriter: John Hiatt

Fixating on our Elvis fixation.

SHE LOVES THE JERK
Producers: Ron Nagle, Scott Matthews
Album: Riding with the King
Record Label: Geffen
Songwriter: John Hiatt

As opposed to Randy Newman, Hiatt's losers are merely average-guys suffering fools with everyday Midwestern stoicism.

1985

LIVING A LITTLE, LAUGHING A LITTLE
Producer: Norbert Putnam
Album: Warming up to the Ice Age
Record Label: Geffen
Songwriter: John Hiatt

A duet with soundalike, Elvis Costello.

SHE SAID THE SAME THINGS TO ME
Producer: Norbert Putnam
Album: Warming up to the Ice Age
Record Label: Λ&M
Songwriter: John Hiatt

More of Hiatt's epic struggle to comprehend the opposing sex.

THE USUAL
Producer: Norbert Putnam
Album: Warming up to the Ice Age
Record Label: A&M
Songwriter: John Hiatt

Covered by Bob Dylan and Fiona in the film Hearts on Fire.

WHEN WE RAN
Producer: Norbert Putnam
Album: Warming up to the Ice Age
Record Label: Geffen
Songwriter: John Hiatt

His most poignant love song.

1987

LEARNING HOW TO LOVE YOU
Producer: John Chelew
Album: Bring the Family
Record Label: A&M
Songwriter: John Hiatt

According to Hiatt, the emotional highpoint of the album.

THING CALLED LOVE
Producer: John Chelew
Album: Bring the Family
Record Label: A&M
Songwriter: John Hiatt

Mild, mid-tempo. Cover by Bonnie Raitt (Capitol, '89) helped to save her mouldering career.

1988

DRIVE SOUTH
Producer: Glyn Johns
Album: Slow Turning
Record Label: A&M
Songwriter: John Hiatt

#2 C&W hit for Suzy Bogguss (Mercury, '93).

1990

THROUGH YOUR HANDS
Producer: Glyn Johns
Album: Stolen Moments
Record Label: A&M
Songwriter: John Hiatt

One of his more pointed, poignant messages, verging on Folk Rock. Covered by David Crosby (Atlantic, '92).

BERTIE HIGGINS

1982

KEY LARGO
Producers: Sonny Limbo, Scott MacLellan
Album: Just Another Day in Paradise
Record Label: Kat Family
Songwriters: Sonny Limbo, Bertie Higgins

The best promotion for Key Largo since Bogie.

HIGH INERGY

1977

YOU CAN'T TURN ME OFF (IN THE MIDDLE OF TURNING ME ON)
Album: Turnin' On
Record Label: Gordy
Songwriters: Marolyn McLeod, Pam Sawyer

Top-10 R&B/Top-20 R&R crossover.

THE HIGHWAYMEN
1961

COTTONFIELDS
    Producer: Dave Fisher
    Album: Standing Room Only
    Record Label: United Artists
    Songwriter: Huddie Ledbetter
        (Leadbelly)
The pasteurized sound of early '60s Folk harmony.

DAN HILL
1977

SOMETIMES WHEN WE TOUCH
    Producers: Matthew McCauley, Fred
        Mollin
    Album: Longer Fuse
    Record Label: 20th Century
    Songwriters: Barry Mann, Dan Hill
An arena ballad for the coffee house.

1987

CAN'T WE TRY
    Album: Dan Hill
    Record Label: Columbia
    Songwriters: Dan Hill, Beverly
        Chapin-Hill
Duet with Country singer Vonda Shepherd.

JESSIE HILL
1960

OOH POO PAH DOO (PART I)
    Producer: Allen Toussaint
    Record Label: Minit
    Songwriter: Jessie Hill
Instrumental version on the flip side. Some of New Orleans' finest minutes. Covered by Ike and Tina Turner (United Artists, '71).

Z. Z. HILL
1981

CHEATING IN THE NEXT ROOM
    Album: Down Home
    Record Label: Malaco
    Songwriters: George Jackson,
        Robert Alton Miller
Bluesy R&B breakthrough nearly 20 years later.

DOWN HOME BLUES
    Album: Down Home
    Record Label: Malaco
    Songwriter: George Jackson
Classic bar band Blues.

ROBYN HITCHCOCK
1989

MADONNA OF THE WASPS
    Album: Queen Elvis
    Record Label: A&M
    Songwriter: Robyn Hitchcock
Solo effort from the offbeat British singer/songwriter and former member of the Undertones.

1990

QUEEN ELVIS
    Album: Eye
    Record Label: Twin/Tone
    Songwriter: Robyn Hitchcock
More of his quirky English drollery.

RON HOLDEN
1960

LOVE YOU SO
    Record Label: Donne
    Songwriter: Ron Holden

HOLE
1991

BABYDOLL
    Producers: Kim Gordon, Don
        Fleming
    Album: Pretty on the Inside
    Record Label: Caroline
    Songwriter: Hole
In the nascent era of the Riot Grrrl, Courtney Love is the prototype.

PRETTY ON THE INSIDE
    Producers: Kim Gordon, Don
        Fleming
    Album: Pretty on the Inside
    Record Label: Caroline
    Songwriter: Hole
Hoisting a glass to the Punk poet Patty Smith.

1994

DOLL PARTS
    Producers: Paul Q. Kolderie, Sean
        Slade
    Album: Live Through This
    Record Label: DGC
    Songwriters: Courtney Love, Kristen
        Pfaff, Eric Erlandson, Patty Schemel
Commercial breakthrough for Kurt Cobain's feisty widow.

MISS WORLD
    Producers: Paul Q. Kolderie, Sean
        Slade
    Album: Live Through This
    Record Label: DGC
    Songwriters: Courtney Love, Kristen
        Pfaff, Eric Erlandson, Patty Schemel
From Rolling Stone's album of the year for 1994.

VIOLET
    Producers: Paul Q. Kolderie, Sean
        Slade
    Album: Live Through This
    Record Label: DGC
    Songwriters: Courtney Love, Kristen
        Pfaff, Eric Erlandson, Patty Schemel
Suggested segue: "Bruised Violet" by Babes in Toyland.

EDDIE HOLLAND
1961

JAMIE
    Producer: William Stevenson
    Album: Eddie Holland
    Record Label: Motown
    Songwriters: William Stevenson,
        Barrett Strong
Introducing one-third of Motown's legendary Holland-Dozier-Holland songwriting combine.

JENNIFER HOLLIDAY
1982

AND I'M TELLING YOU
I'M NOT GOING
    Producer: David Foster
    Album: *Dreamgirls* Original Cast LP
        Album
    Record Label: Geffen
    Songwriters: Tom Eyen, Henry
        Krieger
This booming ballad from the Supremes-esque musical was a #1 R&B/Top-25 R&R crossover.

THE HOLLIES
1966

BUS STOP
    Producer: Ron Richards
    Album: Stop, Stop, Stop
    Record Label: Imperial
    Songwriter: Graham Gouldman
One of the ubiquitous Gouldman's best, this Pop rocker is their second biggest hit.

I CAN'T LET GO
Producer: Ron Richards
Album: Beat Group
Record Label: Imperial
Songwriters: Chip Taylor, Al Gorgoni

Covered by Linda Ronstadt (Asylum, '80).

STOP, STOP, STOP
Producer: Ron Richards
Album: Stop, Stop, Stop
Record Label: Imperial
Songwriters: Allan Clarke, Graham Nash, Tony Hicks

1967

CARRIE-ANNE
Producer: Ron Richards
Album: Evolution
Record Label: Epic
Songwriters: Allan Clarke, Graham Nash, Tony Hicks

ON A CAROUSEL
Producer: Ron Richards
Album: Greatest Hits
Record Label: Imperial
Songwriters: Allan Clarke, Graham Nash, Tony Hicks

Their patented harmonies reach a professional peak.

1970

HE AIN'T HEAVY . . . HE'S MY BROTHER
Producer: Ron Richards
Album: He Ain't Heavy . . . He's My Brother
Record Label: Epic
Songwriters: Bob Russell, Bobby Scott

Flowery post-'60s anthem.

1972

LONG COOL WOMAN (IN A BLACK DRESS)
Producer: Ron Richards
Album: Distant Light
Record Label: Epic
Songwriters: Roger Greenaway, Roger Cook, Harold Clarke

Their biggest hit is a return to their AM-radio, Invasion roots.

BRENDA HOLLOWAY

1964

WHEN I'M GONE
Producer: Smokey Robinson
Album: Every Little Bit Hurts
Record Label: Tamla
Songwriter: Smokey Robinson

Her biggest R&B/R&R crossover.

1967

YOU'VE MADE ME SO VERY HAPPY
Producer: Berry Gordy Jr.
Record Label: Tamla
Songwriters: Frank Wilson, Berry Gordy Jr., Brenda Holloway, Patrice Holloway

Top-40 R&B/R&R crossover. Covered by Blood, Sweat, and Tears (Columbia, '69).

HOLLY AND THE ITALIANS

1981

TELL THAT GIRL TO SHUT UP
Producer: Chris Butler
Album: The Right to Be Italian
Record Label: Virgin
Songwriter: Holly Vincent

The voice of the beehive, from the hairdresser's mouth.

BUDDY HOLLY

1956

ROCK AROUND WITH OLLIE VEE
Producer: Owen Bradley
Album: The Nashville Sessions
Record Label: Coral
Songwriter: Sonny Curtis

Buddy's first solo single.

1957

PEGGY SUE
Producer: Norman Petty
Album: The Buddy Holly Story
Record Label: Coral
Songwriters: Buddy Holly, Jerry Allison, Norman Petty

His first solo hit, written with and backed by the Crickets, epitomizing not only the self-contained group concept that would flourish with the Beatles in the '60s, but the jangly guitar essence of all alternative Rock movements ever since, from Bob Dylan and the Byrds to Joe Ely to Tom Petty & the Heartbreakers to R.E.M. to the Gin Blossoms.

EVERYDAY
Producer: Norman Petty
Album: The Buddy Holly Story
Record Label: Coral
Songwriter: Buddy Holly

B-side of "Peggy Sue."

1958

HEARTBEAT
Producer: Norman Petty
Album: The Buddy Holly Story
Record Label: Coral
Songwriter: Buddy Holly

I'M GONNA LOVE YOU TOO
Producer: Norman Petty
Album: Buddy Holly
Record Label: Coral
Songwriters: Joe Mauldin, Norman Petty, Niki Sullivan

RAVE ON
Producers: Norman Petty, Bob Thiele
Album: Buddy Holly
Record Label: Coral
Songwriters: Sunny West, Norman Petty, Bill Tilghman

One of his best rockers. Covered by Marshall Crenshaw (Warner Brothers, '84).

TRUE LOVE WAYS
Producer: Bob Thiele
Album: The Buddy Holly Story
Record Label: Coral
Songwriters: Buddy Holly, Norman Petty

Covered by Peter and Gordon (Capitol, '65), and performed by Trent Reznor in the '75 Michael J. Fox/Joan Jett film Light of Day.

WELL ALL RIGHT
Producer: Norman Petty
Album: The Buddy Holly Story
Record Label: Coral
Songwriters: Buddy Holly, Norman Petty, Jerry Allison, Joe B. Mauldin

B-side of "Heartbeat."

WORDS OF LOVE
Producer: Norman Petty
Album: Buddy Holly
Record Label: Coral
Songwriter: Buddy Holly

Classic album cut, covered by the Beatles (Capitol, '65) and the Mamas and the Papas (Dunhill, '67).

1959

IT DOESN'T MATTER ANY MORE
Producer: Bob Thiele
Album: The Buddy Holly Story
Record Label: Coral
Songwriter: Paul Anka

His last hit, released the month he died, went to #1 U.K. Covered by Paul Anka (RCA, '63).

RAINING IN MY HEART

Producer: Norman Petty
Album: The Buddy Holly Story
Record Label: Coral
Songwriter: Buddy Holly

B-side of "It Doesn't Matter Anymore." Covered by Bobby Vee (Liberty, '62).

THE HOLLYWOOD ARGYLES

1960

ALLEY OOP

Producers: Gary Paxton, Kim Fowley
Album: Hollywood Argyles
Record Label: Lute
Songwriter: Dallas Frazier

The endearing comic-book dinosaur comes to Rock and Roll life in a legendary one-shot. Several of the Hollywood Argyles went on to future careers in the music business, including Gary Paxton and Kim Fowley; the competing (and more authentic) Dante and the Evergreens (Madison) as well as the Dyno-Sores (Rendezvous) went nowhere.

THE HOLLYWOOD FLAMES

1957

BUZZ BUZZ BUZZ

Record Label: Ebb
Songwriters: J. Gray, Robert Byrd

Bobby Day's backup band on their only national hit.

CLINT HOLMES

1973

PLAYGROUND IN MY MIND

Producer: Paul Vance
Album: Playground in My Mind
Record Label: Epic
Songwriters: Paul Vance, Lee Pockriss

Sophisticated bubblegum Pop one-shot.

RUPERT HOLMES

1979

ESCAPE (THE PINA COLADA SONG)

Producers: Rupert Holmes, Jom Boyer
Album: Partners in Crime
Record Label: Infinity
Songwriter: Rupert Holmes

O'Henry-esque story song. Suggested segue: the far more haunting "Babooshka" by Kate Bush.

HIM

Producers: Rupert Holmes, Jim Boyer
Album: Partners in Crime
Record Label: Infinity
Songwriter: Rupert Holmes

Exemplary David Gatesian Pop Rock.

WILL HOLT

1957

THE M.T.A.

Album: The World of Will Holt
Record Label: Coral
Songwriters: Jacqueline Steiner, Bess Hawes

Social satire presaging the coming Folk scare. Based on "The Wreck of the Old 97," it was written in 1948 about the Boston political campaign of Walter F. O' Brien. Covered by the Kingston Trio (Capitol, '59).

THE HOLY MODAL ROUNDERS

1965

HALF A MIND

Album: Moray Eels Eat the Holy Modal Rounders
Record Label: Elektra
Songwriter: Peter Stampfel

Legendary old-time good-time folkies' most dangerous concept.

IF YOU WANNA BE A BIRD

Producer: Peter Stampfel
Album: Moray Eels Eat the Holy Modal Rounders
Record Label: Elektra
Songwriter: Antonia

Jug band revisionaries achieve generational immortality in the '69 film Easy Rider.

WEREWOLF

Album: Moray Eels Eat the Holy Modal Rounders
Record Label: Elektra
Songwriter: Michael Hurley

Exemplary backwoods howl. Warren Zevon was listening. Covered by Michael Hurley (Raccoon, '71).

1967

EUPHORIA

Album: Moray Eels Eat the Holy Modal Rounders
Record Label: Elektra
Songwriter: Robin Remaily

Epitomizing their subversive Acid Bluegrass; Camper Van Beethoven were probably reared on it. Covered by the Nitty Gritty Dirt Band (Liberty, '67) and the Youngbloods (RCA, '70).

HOMBRES

1967

LET IT OUT (LET IT ALL HANG OUT)

Producer: Huey Meaux
Album: Let It Out (Let It All Hang Out)
Record Label: Verve/Forecast
Songwriters: B. B. Cunningham, Jerry Lee Masters, Gary Wayne McEwen, Johnny Will Hunter

Loopy Southern Rock one-shot with a nasal twang.

THE HONDELLS

1964

LITTLE HONDA

Album: Go Little Honda
Record Label: Mercury
Songwriter: Brian Wilson

Surfing the Asphalts—introducing the Honda motorbike.

HONEY CONE

1971

STICK UP

Producer: Greg S. Perry
Album: Soulful Tapestry
Record Label: Hot Wax
Songwriters: General Johnson, Greg S. Perry, Angelo Bond

Glomming the Jacksons' teen dance groove.

WANT-ADS

Producer: Greg S. Perry
Album: Sweet Replies
Record Label: Hot Wax
Songwriters: General Johnson, Greg S. Perry, Barney Perkins

This "Stick Up" rewrite stiffed for Glass House and Freda Payne, before Honey Cone took it to #1 R&R/R&B.

THE HONEYCOMBS
1965

HAVE I THE RIGHT?
Album: Here Come the Honeycombs
Record Label: Interphon
Songwriters: Alan Blaikley, Harold Blaikley

THE HOODOO GURUS
1987

WHAT'S MY SCENE
Producers: Mark Opitz, Hoodoo Gurus
Album: Blow Your Cool
Record Label: Elektra
Songwriter: Dave Faulkner

Aussie Power Pop with a vengeance.

HOODOO RHYTHM DEVILS
1972

STILL ALIVE AND WELL
Record Label: Capitol
Songwriter: Rick Derringer

Covered by Johnny Winter, his classic Blues Rock signature tune (Columbia, '73).

JOHN LEE HOOKER
1949

BOOGIE CHILLEN
Record Label: Modern
Songwriter: John Lee Hooker

#1 R&B tune; led to the chooglin' boogie Blues groove favored by the Creedence Clearwater Revival and Canned Heat.

1951

I'M IN THE MOOD
Producer: Ralph Bass
Record Label: Modern
Songwriters: John Lee Hooker, Bernard Besman

His basic down and dirty boogie, that would last a lifetime.

1962

BOOM BOOM
Record Label: VeeJay
Songwriter: John Lee Hooker

Covered by the Animals (MGM, '65).

THE HOOTERS
1985

WHERE DO THE CHILDREN GO
Producer: Rick Chertoff
Album: Nervous Night
Record Label: Columbia
Songwriters: Rob Hyman, Eric Bazilian

Introducing the mellodica into the Folk Rock canon. Distinguished by the throaty moan of Patty Smyth at her most scandalous. Hyman collaborated with Cyndi Lauper on "Time After Time" and later wrote Joan Osborne's "One of Us."

HOOTIE AND THE BLOWFISH
1994

HOLD MY HAND
Producer: Don Gehman
Album: Cracked Rear View
Record Label: Atlantic
Songwriters: Mark Bryan, Dean Felber, Darius Rucker, Jim Sonefeld

The bar-band ethos of the New South: white rhythm section, black lead singer.

LET HER CRY
Producer: Don Gehman
Album: Cracked Rear View
Record Label: Atlantic
Songwriters: Mark Bryan, Dean Felber, Darius Rucker, Jim Sonefeld

The sensitive side of '90s Frat Rock.

BRUCE HORNSBY AND THE RANGE
1986

EVERY LITTLE KISS
Producers: E. Scheiner, Bruce Hornsby
Album: The Way It Is
Record Label: RCA
Songwriter: Bruce Hornsby

New Age Jazz Rock, with a touch of Country Soul.

MANDOLIN RAIN
Producers: E. Scheiner, Bruce Hornsby
Album: The Way It Is
Record Label: RCA
Songwriters: Bruce Hornsby, John Hornsby

Suggested segue: "Mandolin Wind" by Rod Stewart.

THE WAY IT IS
Producer: Bruce Hornsby
Album: The Way It Is
Record Label: RCA
Songwriter: Bruce Hornsby

Anthemic post-civil rights era Jazz Rock dirge went to #1 R&R.

1988

THE VALLEY ROAD
Producers: Neil Dorfsman, Bruce Hornsby
Album: Scenes from the Southside
Record Label: RCA
Songwriters: Bruce Hornsby, John Hornsby

Southern-flavored Folk Pop strikes a country chord.

JOHNNY HORTON
1956

HONKY TONK MAN
Record Label: Columbia
Songwriters: Johnny Horton, Tillman Franks, Howard Hausey

His first Country hit in '56 was his last Pop hit in '62.

1959

THE BATTLE OF NEW ORLEANS
Record Label: Columbia
Songwriter: Jimmy Driftwood

Based on a Folk tune from the War of 1812, with lyrics added by Country singer Driftwood (RCA, '59). Horton's version was a rare #1 C&W/R&R crossover.

1960

NORTH TO ALASKA
Album: Johnny Horton's Greatest Hits
Record Label: Columbia
Songwriter: Mike Phillips

Title song from the movie, a #1 C&W/Top-10 R&R crossover.

SINK THE BISMARCK
Album: Johnny Horton's Greatest Hits
Record Label: Columbia
Songwriters: Tillman Franks, Johnny Horton

Based on but not in the movie.

HOT
1977

ANGEL IN YOUR ARMS
Producers: Clayton Ivey, Terry Woodford
Album: Hot
Record Label: Big Tree
Songwriters: Herbert Ivey, Terry Woodford, Thomas Brasfield

One shot trans-Atlantic Disco smash.

HOT CHOCOLATE
1973

BROTHER LOUIE
Producer: Mickie Most
Album: Cicero Park
Record Label: Big Tree
Songwriters: Errol Brown, Anthony Wilson

This Pop Reggae story of interracial romance was a big U.K. hit. The cover by Stories (Kama Sutra, '73) went to #1.

1975

EMMA
Producer: Mickie Most
Album: Cicero Park
Record Label: Big Tree
Songwriters: Errol Brown, Anthony Wilson

Previewing the upcoming British Soul invasion.

YOU SEXY THING
Producer: Mickie Most
Album: Hot Chocolate
Record Label: Big Tree
Songwriters: Errol Brown, Anthony Wilson

Their biggest state-side hit.

1977

SO YOU WIN AGAIN
Producer: Mickie Most
Album: 10 Greatest Hits
Record Label: Big Tree
Songwriter: Glen Ballard

#1 in England.

1979

EVERY 1'S A WINNER
Producer: Mickie Most
Album: Every 1's a Winner
Record Label: Infinity
Songwriter: Errol Brown

HOUSE OF PAIN
1992

JUMP AROUND
Album: House of Pain
Record Label: Tommy Boy
Songwriters: Larry Muggerud, Everlast Schrody

THE HOUSEMARTINS
1986

HAPPY HOUR
Producer: John Williams
Album: London O Hull 4
Record Label: Elektra
Songwriters: Paul D. Heaton, Stan Cullimore

First U.K. hit for the literate popsters, spiritual cousins of XTC, Prefab Sprout, and the Christians.

FLAG DAY
Producer: Flag Day
Album: London O Hull 4
Record Label: Elektra
Songwriters: Paul D. Heaton, Stan Cullimore

Re-released from their initial U.K. LP. A Pop Rock look at Punk England.

THELMA HOUSTON
1977

DON'T LEAVE ME THIS WAY
Producer: Hal Davis
Album: Any Way You Like It
Record Label: Tamla
Songwriters: Kenny Gamble, Leon Huff, Cary Gilbert

#1 R&B/R&R crossover.

WHITNEY HOUSTON
1985

HOW WILL I KNOW
Producer: Narada Michael Walden
Album: Whitney Houston
Record Label: Arista
Songwriters: Gary Merrill, Shannon Rubicam, Narada Michael Walden

#1 R&B/R&R crossover for the new middle-of-the-road Pop sensation.

YOU GIVE GOOD LOVE
Producer: Narada Michael Walden
Album: Whitney Houston
Record Label: Arista
Songwriter: LaForest (La La) Cope

Her first hit single.

1987

I WANNA DANCE WITH SOMEBODY (WHO LOVES ME)
Producer: Narada Michael Walden
Album: Whitney Houston
Record Label: Arista
Songwriters: Gary Merrill, Shannon Rubicam

Her fourth #1 R&R.

1990

I'M YOUR BABY TONIGHT
Producers: Babyface, L. A. Reid
Album: I'm Your Baby Tonight
Record Label: Arista
Songwriters: Kenny Edmunds (Babyface), Antonio Reid (L. A. Reid)

Flirting with the best of the R&R/R&B crossover breed.

HOWLIN' WOLF
1950

DOWN IN THE BOTTOM
Album: Tune Box
Record Label: Chess
Songwriter: Chester Burnette (Howlin' Wolf)

Introducing the bottomless voice that would entrance a generation of young British Chicago Blues fanatics.

1951

HOW MANY MORE YEARS
Album: Moaning in the Moonlight
Record Label: Chess
Songwriter: Chester Burnette (Howlin' Wolf)

From his first session at Chess; his first entry on the R&B charts.

1954

EVIL
Album: Moaning in the Moonlight
Record Label: Chess
Songwriter: Willie Dixon

Naming and personifying a music that would move inexorably from Blues to R&B to R&R, with all the sinful promise such a Soul-shaking upheaval would imply.

1956

SMOKESTACK LIGHTNING
Album: Moaning in the Moonlight
Record Label: Chess
Songwriter: Chester Burnette (Howling Wolf)

His second big R&B hit.

1961

LITTLE RED ROOSTER
Album: Tune Box
Record Label: Chess
Songwriter: Willie Dixon

Wolf earns his place in the Rock pantheon; so does Dixon. Covered by Sam Cooke (RCA, '63) and the Rolling Stones (London, '65).

SPOONFUL
Record Label: Chess
Songwriter: Willie Dixon

Remake of the Charlie Patton 1929 original. Covered by the Allman Joys (Deal, '67).

1962

I AIN'T SUPERSTITIOUS
Record Label: Chess
Songwriter: Willie Dixon

Covered by the Jeff Beck Group (Epic, '68).

1966

KILLING FLOOR
Producer: Marshall Chess
Album: Real Folk Blues
Record Label: Chess
Songwriter: Chester Burnette
(Howling Wolf)

Another quintessential down and dirty Blues. Covered by the Electric Flag (Columbia, '68).

THE HUES CORPORATION
1974

ROCK THE BOAT
Producer: John Florez
Album: Freedom for the Stallion
Record Label: RCA
Songwriter: Waldo Holmes

Disco hit.

JIMMY HUGHES
1964

STEAL AWAY
Album: Steal Away
Record Label: Fame
Songwriter: Jimmy Hughes

Soul chestnut covered by Johnnie Taylor (Stax, '70).

HUMAN LEAGUE
1982

DON'T YOU WANT ME
Producers: Martin Rushent, Human
League

Album: Dare
Record Label: A&M/Virgin
Songwriters: Jo Callis, Phil Oakey,
Adrian Wright

First of the mid-'80s British Techno-invasion, synthesized alienation bands; #1 U.K. (#1 U.S. six months later).

1983

(KEEP FEELING) FASCINATION
Producers: Martin Rushent, Human
League
Album: Fascination
Record Label: A&M
Songwriters: Phil Oakey, Jo Callis

Definitive Synth Rock.

1986

HUMAN
Producers: Jimmy Jam, Terry Lewis
Album: Crash
Record Label: A&M
Songwriters: James Harris III, Terry
Lewis

Miscast collaborators give this anti-Soul band another #1 R&R.

HUMBLE PIE
1972

HOT N' NASTY
Producer: Humble Pie
Album: Smokin'
Record Label: A&M
Songwriters: Steve Marriott, Greg
Ridley, Jerry Shirley, Clem Clempson

Arena dandy Steve Marriott in an R&B groove. They also covered "I Don't Need No Doctor" (A&M, '71) and "I Walk on Gilded Splinters" (A&M, '71).

IAN HUNTER
1975

I GET SO EXCITED
Producer: Mick Ronson
Album: Ian Hunter
Record Label: Columbia
Songwriter: Ian Hunter

The voice of Mott the Hoople, without the hoopla.

ONCE BITTEN, TWICE SHY
Producer: Mick Ronson
Album: Ian Hunter
Record Label: Columbia
Songwriter: Ian Hunter

Covered by Great White (Capitol, '89).

1979

CLEVELAND ROCKS
Producers: Mick Ronson, Ian Hunter
Album: You're Never Alone with a
Schizophrenic
Record Label: Chrysalis
Songwriter: Ian Hunter

Featured in the '87 Cleveland movie Light of Day.

SHIPS
Producers: Mick Ronson, Ian Hunter
Album: You're Never Alone with a
Schizophrenic
Record Label: Chrysalis
Songwriter: Ian Hunter

Covered by Barry Manilow (Arista, '79).

IVORY JOE HUNTER
1950

I ALMOST LOST MY MIND
Record Label: MGM
Songwriter: Ivory Joe Hunter

#1 R&B hit, from the L.A. jump school.

1956

SINCE I MET YOU BABY
Producers: Ahmet Ertegun, Jerry
Wexler
Album: 16 of His Greatest Hits
Record Label: Atlantic
Songwriter: Ivory Joe Hunter

His defining Rock and Roll moment.

HÜSKER DÜ
1984

TURN ON THE NEWS
Producers: Spot, Hüsker Dü
Album: Zen Arcade
Record Label: SST
Songwriter: Grant Hart

Essential speedcore anthem from the Minneapolis anti-Prince rockers, cohorts of the Replacements and Soul Asylum.

1985

CELEBRATED SUMMER
Album: New Day Rising
Record Label: SST
Songwriter: Bob Mould

Midwestern Sonic Youth, with a Dead Boys attitude, and Richard Thompson leanings.

1986

SORRY SOMEHOW

Producers: Bob Mould, Grant Hart
Album: Candy Apple Grey
Record Label: Warner Brothers
Songwriter: Grant Hart

Grant Hart explains his divorce, in this first overground release.

1987

NO RESERVATIONS

Producers: Bob Mould, Grant Hart
Album: Warehouse Songs and Stories
Record Label: Warner Brothers
Songwriter: Bob Mould

Mould would graduate to Alternative legendhood.

DANNY HUTTON

1966

BEACH BABY

Record Label: HBR
Songwriters: John Carter, Gil Shakespeare

Covered by First Class (U.K., '74).

BRIAN HYLAND

1960

ITSY BITSY TEENIE WEENIE YELLOW POLKADOT BIKINI

Producer: Richard Wolfe
Album: The Bashful Blonde
Record Label: Leader/Kapp
Songwriters: Paul Vance, Lee Pockriss

Summertime teen exploitation. But it was no "One Piece Topless Bathing Suit" by the Ripchords.

1962

SEALED WITH A KISS

Producer: Snuff Garrett
Album: Sealed with a Kiss
Record Label: ABC-Paramount
Songwriters: Peter Udell, Gary Geld

Summer standard.

1963

SAVE YOUR HEART FOR ME

Producer: Snuff Garrett
Record Label: ABC-Paramount
Songwriters: Gary Geld, Peter Udell

Covered by Gary Lewis and the Playboys (Imperial, '65).

I

IAN AND SYLVIA

1964

FOUR STRONG WINDS

Album: Four Strong Winds
Record Label: Vanguard
Songwriter: Ian Tyson

The romance of drifting has never been so eloquently stated, by popster or folkie. Covered by George Hamilton IV (RCA, '66) and Neil Young (Reprise, '78).

SOMEDAY SOON

Album: Northern Journey
Record Label: Vanguard
Songwriter: Ian Tyson

Cowboy Folk Rock from the Canadian Northwest. Covered by Judy Collins (Elektra, '68).

YOU WERE ON MY MIND

Album: Northern Journey
Record Label: Vanguard
Songwriter: Sylvia Fricker

Folk Rock standard. Covered by We Five (A&M, '65).

JANIS IAN

1967

SOCIETY'S CHILD (BABY, I'VE BEEN THINKING)

Producer: Shadow Morton
Album: Janis Ian
Record Label: Verve/Forecast
Songwriter: Janis Fink (Janis Ian)

Travails of an interracial teen relationship; outspoken for its time. Covered by Spooky Tooth (A&M, '71). Suggested segues: "Brother Louie" by Stories, "I Believe" by Soul for Real.

1975

AT SEVENTEEN

Producer: Brooks Arthur
Album: Between the Lines
Record Label: Columbia
Songwriter: Janis Ian

Nerd Rock standard of the self-absorbed confessional mode, culminating Ian's career as a protest singer.

ICE CUBE

1992

CHECK YO SELF

Producer: DJ Pooh
Album: The Predator
Record Label: Priority
Songwriter: O' Shea Jackson (Ice Cube)

#1 R&B/Top-20 R&R statement of Rap priorities from the founding lyricist of N.W.A., one of the most outspoken of Gangsta Rap groups.

1993

IT WAS A GOOD DAY

Producer: DJ Pooh
Album: The Predator
Record Label: Priority
Songwriter: O' Shea Jackson (Ice Cube)

ICE-T

1988

COLORS

Producers: Ice-T, Africa Islam
Album: *Colors* Soundtrack
Record Label: Warner Brothers
Songwriters: Tracy Morrow (Ice-T), Africa Islam

1991

NEW JACK HUSTLER (NINO'S THEME)

Album: *New Jack City* Soundtrack
Record Label: Giant
Songwriter: Tracy Morrow (Ice-T)

From the '90s-era blaxploitation model film, depicting life in the urban ghetto.

ICEHOUSE

1988

ELECTRIC BLUE

Producer: D. Lord
Album: Man of Colours
Record Label: Chrysalis
Songwriters: Iva Davies, John Oates

THE IDES OF MARCH

1970

VEHICLE

Producer: Lee Productions
Album: Vehicle
Record Label: Warner Brothers
Songwriter: James M. Peterik

Peterik would return with Survivor.

BILLY IDOL

1981

DANCING WITH MYSELF

Album: Don't Stop
Record Label: Chrysalis
Songwriters: William Broad (Billy Idol), Tony James

Last hit with the influential Punk Rock band, Generation X.

1982

HOT IN THE CITY

Producer: Keith Forsey
Album: Billy Idol
Record Label: Chrysalis
Songwriter: William Broad (Billy Idol)

Joining the retro Rockabilly ranks (X, the Blasters) for his first U.S. hit.

1983

WHITE WEDDING

Producer: Keith Forsey
Album: Billy Idol
Record Label: Chrysalis
Songwriter: William Broad (Billy Idol)

Powerful postmodern anthem. Suggested segue: "Love Stinks" by the J. Geils Band.

1984

EYES WITHOUT A FACE

Producer: Keith Forsey
Album: Rebel Yell
Record Label: Chrysalis
Songwriters: William Broad (Billy Idol), Steve Stevens

Continuing his Bowie-esque denunciations.

REBEL YELL

Producer: Keith Forsey
Album: Rebel Yell
Record Label: Chrysalis
Songwriters: William Broad (Billy Idol), Steve Stevens

Eddie Cochran as Jim Morrison.

1990

CRADLE OF LOVE

Producer: Keith Forsey
Album: Charmed Life
Record Label: Chrysalis
Songwriters: William Broad (Billy Idol), David Werner

His biggest hit; from the Andrew Dice Clay movie Ford Fairlane.

FRANK IFIELD

1962

I REMEMBER YOU

Album: Jolly What! The Beatles and Frank Ifield
Record Label: VeeJay
Songwriters: Johnny Mercer, Victor Schertzinger

A one-man (yodeling) British invasion, a year too soon. Introduced by Dorothy Lamour in the '42 film The Fleet's In. *Suggested segue: "Lovesick Blues" by Hank Williams.*

THE IKETTES

1961

I'M BLUE (THE GONG GONG SONG)

Record Label: Atco
Songwriter: Ike Turner

Ike's backup singers step out on an Ike original, featuring Tina Turner on lead vocals.

IMMATURE

1994

NEVER LIE

Album: Playtyme Is Over
Record Label: MCA
Songwriters: Chris Stokes, Claudio Cuen

More teenybop Hip-Hop, a Boyz II Men for the junior high set.

THE IMPALAS

1959

SORRY, I RAN ALL THE WAY HOME

Producer: Leroy Holmes
Album: Sorry, I Ran All the Way Home
Record Label: Cub
Songwriters: Harry Giosasi, Artie Zwirn

Late Italian Soul era lament. Revived by Marshall Crenshaw in the '86 movie Peggy Sue Got Married.

THE IMPRESSIONS

1961

GYPSY WOMAN

Album: The Impressions
Record Label: ABC-Paramount
Songwriter: Curtis Mayfield

Their first R&B/R&R crossover, inspired by the Ink Spots. Covered by Brian Hyland (Uni, '70).

1963

IT'S ALL RIGHT!

Album: The Impressions
Record Label: ABC-Paramount
Songwriter: Curtis Mayfield

Their best-selling single; a #1 R&B/Top-10 R&R crossover.

1964

AMEN

Album: Keep on Pushing
Record Label: ABC-Paramount
Songwriters: Curtis Mayfield, John W. Pate Sr.

With their Gospel fervor and flavor intact, the Impressions pre-Soul civil rights anthem.

I'M SO PROUD

Album: The Never Ending Impressions
Record Label: ABC-Paramount
Songwriter: Curtis Mayfield

Another of their consistently soul-stirring efforts. Revived on the soundtrack to A Bronx Tale *(Epic Soundtrax, '94).*

KEEP ON PUSHING

Album: Keep on Pushing
Record Label: ABC-Paramount
Songwriter: Curtis Mayfield

Their third and last Top-10 hit.

1965

PEOPLE GET READY

Producer: Curtis Mayfield
Album: People Get Ready
Record Label: ABC-Paramount
Songwriter: Curtis Mayfield

Their most famous Gospel-influenced anthem. Covered by Rod Stewart and Jeff Beck (Epic, '85).

WOMAN'S GOT SOUL

Producer: Curtis Mayfield
Album: People Get Ready
Record Label: ABC-Paramount
Songwriter: Curtis Mayfield

1967

WE'RE A WINNER

Producer: Johnny Pate
Album: We're a Winner
Record Label: ABC
Songwriter: Curtis Mayfield

#1 R&B/Top-20 R&R crossover.

1968

THIS IS MY COUNTRY
Producer: Curtis Mayfield
Album: This Is My Country
Record Label: Curtom
Songwriter: Curtis Mayfield

Curtis paves the way for Marvin Gaye's chart-topping social commentaries, with this Top-10 R&B/Top-25 R&R crossover.

1969

CHOICE OF COLORS
Producer: Curtis Mayfield
Album: Young Mods' Forgotten Story
Record Label: Curtom
Songwriter: Curtis Mayfield

#1 R&B/Top-20 R&R crossover.

1974

FINALLY GOT MYSELF TOGETHER (I'M A CHANGED MAN)
Producer: Ed Townshend
Album: Finally Got Myself Together
Record Label: Curtom
Songwriter: Edward Townshend

Their fourth and last #1 R&B/Top-20 R&R crossover, first sans Curtis.

THE INCREDIBLE STRING BAND

1967

THE FIRST GIRL I LOVED
Album: Spirits (Layers of the Onion)
Record Label: Elektra
Songwriter: Robin Williamson

Existential Folk Rock, twisted and haunting. Female version by Judy Collins (Elektra, '68).

THE INDEPENDENTS

1973

LEAVIN' ME
Producers: Chuck Jackson, Marvin Yancey Jr.
Album: First Time We Met
Record Label: Wand
Songwriters: M. Barge, Jimmy Giles

#1 R&B/Top-40 R&R crossover.

THE INDIGO GIRLS

1989

CLOSER TO FINE
Producer: Scott Litt
Album: Indigo Girls

Record Label: Epic
Songwriter: Emily Saliers

New Age Folk harmony duo's breakthrough effort.

1992

GALILEO
Producer: Peter Collins
Album: Rites of Passage
Record Label: Epic
Songwriter: Emily Saliers

Thrilling Folk Rock contemplation of reincarnation.

1994

POWER OF TWO
Producer: Peter Collins
Album: Swamp Ophelia
Record Label: Epic
Songwriter: Emily Saliers

The Simon and Garfunkel of the '90s, transmogrified, with a great song about togetherness.

INFORMATION SOCIETY

1988

WALKING AWAY
Producer: F. Maher
Album: Information Society
Record Label: Tommy Boy
Songwriter: Paul Robb

Techno groove.

WHAT'S ON YOUR MIND (PURE ENERGY)
Producer: F. Maher
Album: Information Society
Record Label: Tommy Boy
Songwriters: Paul Robb, Kurt Valaquen

JAMES INGRAM

1983

YAH MO B THERE
Producer: Quincy Jones
Album: It's Your Night
Record Label: Qwest
Songwriters: James Ingram, Michael McDonald, Rod Temperton, Quincy Jones

Soul hit with Michael McDonald.

1990

I DON'T HAVE THE HEART
Producers: Thom Bell, James Ingram

Album: It's Real
Record Label: Warner Brothers
Songwriters: Allen Rich, Judd Friedman

His biggest solo hit, a middle-of-the-Soul-road classic.

LUTHER INGRAM

1971

IF LOVING YOU IS WRONG, I DON'T WANT TO BE RIGHT
Producer: Johnny Baylor
Album: If Loving You Is Wrong, I Don't Want to Be Right
Record Label: Koko
Songwriters: Homer Banks, Raymond Jackson, Carl Hampton

#1 R&B/Top-10 R&R crossover is a classic cheating song.

THE INK SPOTS

1939

MY PRAYER
Record Label: Decca
Songwriters: Jimmy Kennedy, Georges Boulanger

Borrowing from their mentors in Soul harmony, the Platters turned this Pop hit into the stuff of anguished teen dramatics in the final thrilling notes, for their second #1 tune (Mercury, '56).

1946

THE GYPSY
Record Label: Decca
Songwriter: Billy Reid

Ten weeks at #1 Pop for the harmony group that would influence a Doo-Wop generation. Taking special note of Jerry Daniels lead singing were Jimmy Ricks of the Ravens, and Sonny Til of the Orioles. An entire ASCAP library of Pop standards were waiting to be attacked. Covered by Sam Cooke (RCA, '65).

INNER CIRCLE

1993

BAD BOYS
Producer: Ian Lewis
Album: Inner Circle
Record Label: Big Beat/Atlantic
Songwriter: Inner Circle

Reggae-influenced theme from the TV show "Cops."

INSECT TRUST
1970

EYES OF A NEW YORK WOMAN
Producer: Steve Duboff
Album: Hoboken Saturday Night
Record Label: Atco
Songwriters: Thomas Pynchon, Jeff Ogden

A (middle) Eastern hoedown, with lyrics taken straight out of Pynchon's epic literary novel of 1963, "V.," as sung in the book by Benny Profane. Richard Fariña would have been proud. The Holy Modal Rounders couldn't believe they didn't think of doing it first.

INSPIRAL CARPETS
1990

COMMERCIAL RAIN
Album: Life
Record Label: Elektra
Songwriter: Inspiral Carpets

Big on the incipient Rave scene in England.

INSTANT FUNK
1979

I GOT MY MIND MADE UP (YOU CAN GET IT GIRL)
Album: Instant Funk
Record Label: Salsoul
Songwriters: Ray Earl, Scottie Miller, Kevin Miller

#1 R&B/Top-20 R&R; Philly Funk.

INTRO
1993

COME INSIDE
Producer: Nevelle Hodge
Album: Intro
Record Label: Atlantic
Songwriters: Kenny Greene, Clint Wike, Nevelle Hodge

All vestiges of subtlety leave the Pop and Hip-Hop oriented '90s Top-40, perhaps for good.

THE INTRUDERS
1968

COWBOYS TO GIRLS
Producers: Kenny Gamble, Leon Huff
Album: Cowboys to Girls
Record Label: Gamble
Songwriters: Kenny Gamble, Leon Huff

#1 R&B/Top-10 R&R crossover puts Philly Soul on the map, reaffirming Philadelphia as the dance capitol of America.

1973

I'LL ALWAYS LOVE MY MAMA
Producers: Kenny Gamble, Leon Huff
Album: Save the Children
Record Label: TSOP
Songwriters: Kenny Gamble, Leon Huff, John Whitehead, Vic Carstarphen

INXS
1986

WHAT YOU NEED
Producer: Chris Thomas
Album: Listen Like Thieves
Record Label: Atlantic
Songwriters: Andrew Farriss, Michael Hutchence

First big hit for the Australian modern rockers.

1987

DEVIL INSIDE
Producer: Chris Thomas
Album: Kick
Record Label: Atlantic
Songwriters: Andrew Farriss, Michael Hutchence

Following up a #1 single with a #2 single.

NEED YOU TONIGHT
Producer: Chris Thomas
Album: Kick
Record Label: Atlantic
Songwriters: Andrew Farriss, Michael Hutchence

Their biggest hit.

NEVER TEAR US APART
Producer: Chris Thomas
Album: Kick
Record Label: Atlantic
Songwriters: Andrew Farriss, Michael Hutchence

Their fourth Top-10 R&R from the album.

NEW SENSATION
Producer: Chris Thomas
Album: Kick
Record Label: Atlantic
Songwriters: Andrew Farriss, Michael Hutchence

Following up a #2 single with a #3 single.

1990

DISAPPEAR
Album: X
Record Label: Atlantic
Songwriters: Jon Farriss, Michael Hutchence

SUICIDE BLONDE
Album: X
Record Label: Atlantic
Songwriters: Andrew Farriss, Michael Hutchence

THE IRISH ROVERS
1968

THE UNICORN
Producer: Charles Dant
Album: The Unicorn
Record Label: Decca
Songwriter: Shel Silverstein

Standard kiddie Folk Rock tale from the pen of the Playboy cartoonist. Suggested segues: "Puff the Magic Dragon" by Peter, Paul and Mary, "The House at Pooh Corners" by Loggins and Messina.

IRON BUTTERFLY
1968

IN-A-GADDA-DA-VIDA
Producer: Jim Hinton
Album: In-a-Gadda-Da-Vida
Record Label: Atco
Songwriter: Doug Ingle

Epitomizing—or unintentionally parodying—the wretched excess of the FM psychedelic/progressive Rock as Jazz improvisation era (with half an era left to go). Covered by archetypal death Metal band, Slayer, in the wasted youth epic Less Than Zero (Def Jam, '87).

THE IRON CITY HOUSE ROCKERS
1980

JUNIOR'S BAR
Album: Have a Good Time (But Get out Alive)
Record Label: MCA
Songwriters: Joe Grushecky, Gil Snyder, Eddie Britt

Defining track from the Boss of Pittsburgh.

IRON MAIDEN

1981

WRATHCHILD
Producer: Martin Birch
Album: Killers
Record Label: Harvest
Songwriter: Steve Harris

The new wave of British Heavy Metal. Metallica was listening. Judas Priest was oiling their gears. But Def Leppard would get all the girls.

1982

NUMBER OF THE BEAST
Producer: Martin Birch
Album: Number of the Beast
Record Label: Harvest
Songwriter: Steve Harris

The number, of course, was 666, the devil's 411.

RUN TO THE HILLS
Producer: Martin Birch
Album: Number of the Beast
Record Label: Harvest
Songwriter: Steve Harris

First U.K. hit for the modern Megalometalheads, known for their seven-minute epics.

1983

THE TROOPER
Producer: Martin Birch
Album: Piece of Mind
Record Label: Harvest
Songwriter: Steve Harris

Another blast from Harris' monster bass.

CHRIS ISAAK

1987

BLUE HOTEL
Producer: Erik Jacobsen
Album: Chris Isaak
Record Label: Warner Brothers
Songwriter: Chris Isaak

The man with the studied Orbisonian twang takes a walk down Lonely Street.

1989

WICKED GAME
Producer: Erik Jacobsen
Album: Heart Shaped World
Record Label: Reprise
Songwriter: Chris Isaak

From the film Wild at Heart, *one of the sexiest videos of the year.*

THE ISLEY BROTHERS

1959

SHOUT (PARTS I AND II)
Producer: Hugo and Luigi
Album: Shout
Record Label: RCA
Songwriters: Ronald Isley, Rudolph Isley, O' Kelly Isley

Deep into Rock and Roll's softest year, a cry in the wilderness, "A little bit louder now!" Prelude to the original party rave-up of "Part II," their first of many.

1962

TWIST AND SHOUT
Album: Twist and Shout
Record Label: Wand
Songwriters: Bert Berns (Bert Russell), Phil Medley

Out of the '57 Twist varieties, the one true enduring classic, Chubby Checker and Hank Ballard notwithstanding. Covered by the Beatles (Tollie/Capitol, '64).

1963

NOBODY BUT ME
Record Label: Wand
Songwriters: Ronald Isley, Rudolph Isley, O' Kelly Isley

Covered by the Human Beinz (Capitol, '68).

1966

THIS OLD HEART OF MINE (IS WEAK FOR YOU)
Producers: Brian Holland, Lamont Dozier
Album: This Old Heart of Mine
Record Label: Tamla
Songwriters: Eddie Holland, Lamont Dozier, Brian Holland, Sylvia Moy

Exemplary R&B. Covered by Rod Stewart (Warner Brothers, '75).

1969

IT'S YOUR THING
Producer: Isley Brothers
Album: It's Our Thing
Record Label: T-Neck
Songwriters: Ronald Isley, Rudolph Isley, O' Kelly Isley

Their biggest hit; #1 R&B/#2 R&R crossover

1972

WORK TO DO
Producer: Isley Brothers
Album: Brother, Brother, Brother
Record Label: T-Neck

Songwriters: Ronald Isley, Rudolph Isley, O' Kelly Isley

Suggested segue: "Take a Letter Maria" by R. B. Greaves.

1973

THAT LADY
Producer: Isley Brothers
Album: 3 + 3
Record Label: T-Neck
Songwriters: Ernie Isley, Marvin Isley, Chris Jasper

Funk Rock Classic began life as "Who's That Lady" (United Artists, '64); updated by the younger generation (with cousin Chris) for their last Top-10 R&R hit, courtesy of Ernie's ineffable wah.

1975

FIGHT THE POWER (PART I)
Producers: Isley Brothers, Chris Jasper
Album: The Heat Is On
Record Label: T-Neck
Songwriters: Ronald Isley, Rudolph Isley, O' Kelly Isley, Ernest Isley, Marvin Isley

#1 R&B/Top-10 R&R crossover. Their second-biggest hit.

FOR THE LOVE OF YOU (PARTS 1 AND 2)
Producer: Isley Brothers
Album: The Heat Is On
Record Label: T-Neck
Songwriters: Ronald Isley, Rudolph Isley, O' Kelly Isley, Ernest Isley, Marvin Isley

1976

AT YOUR BEST YOU ARE LOVE
Producers: Isley Brothers, Chris Jasper
Album: Harvest for the World
Record Label: T-Neck
Songwriters: Ronald Isley, Rudolph Isley, O' Kelly Isley, Ernest Isley, Marvin Isley, Chris Jasper

Covered by Aaliyah (Blackground, '94).

1977

THE PRIDE (PART I)
Producers: Isley Brothers, Chris Jasper
Album: Go for Your Guns
Record Label: T-Neck
Songwriters: Ronald Isley, Rudolph Isley, O' Kelly Isley, Ernest Isley, Marvin Isley, Chris Jasper

#1 R&B/Bottom-40 R&R crossover.

1980

DON'T SAY GOODNIGHT (IT'S TIME FOR LOVE) (PARTS I AND II)
Producers: Isley Brothers, Chris Jasper
Album: Go All the Way
Record Label: T-Neck
Songwriters: Ronald Isley, Rudolph Isley, O' Kelly Isley, Ernest Isley, Marvin Isley

#1 R&B/Top-40 R&R crossover.

ISLEY/JASPER/ISLEY
1985

CARAVAN OF LOVE
Producers: Ernest Isley, Marvin Isley, Chris Jasper
Album: Caravan of Love
Record Label: CBS Associated
Songwriters: Ernest Isley, Marvin Isley, Chris Jasper

#1 R&B/Top-10 R&R crossover. Cover by the Housemartins went to #1 U.K. (Elektra, '86).

IVAN (JERRY ALLISON)
1958

REAL WILD CHILD
Record Label: Coral
Songwriters: John O' Keefe, John Greenan, David Owens

Rockabilly one-off by the Crickets' drummer. Covered by Jerry Lee Lewis (Sun, '58), Iggy Pop (A&M, '87). O' Keefe's original stiffed.

THE IVY THREE
1960

YOGI
Producers: Lou Stallman, Sid Jacobsen
Record Label: Shell
Songwriters: Lou Stallman, Sid Jacobson, Charles Koppelman

Celebrating neither Berra nor Mahareeshi; the Huckleberry Hound co-star earns this one-shot Rock and Roll asterisk.

J

THE JACKS
1955

WHY DON'T YOU WRITE ME
Album: Jumpin' with the Jacks
Record Label: RPM
Songwriter: Laura Hollins

Classic Doo-Wop. Original by the Feathers. The Jacks also recorded as the Cadets.

THE JACKSON 5
1967

MICHAEL THE LOVER
Record Label: Steel Town
Songwriters: Larry Brownlee, Charles Matthews

Recently unearthed Jackson tracks from the Gary, Indiana, days (Inverted/Brunswick, '96) finds the pre-Gloved-one in "ABC" form.

1969

I WANT YOU BACK
Producers: Freddie Perren, Berry Gordy Jr., Deke Richards, Fonce Mizell
Album: Diana Ross Presents the Jackson Five
Record Label: Motown
Songwriters: Freddie Perren, Berry Gordy Jr., Deke Richards, Fonce Mizell

With a pre-pubescent Michael in the lead, this infectious dance track #1 R&B/R&R crossover started off the most impressive debut in R&B/R&R history.

1970

ABC
Producers: Freddie Perren, Berry Gordy Jr., Deke Richards, Fonce Mizell
Album: ABC
Record Label: Motown
Songwriters: Freddie Perren, Berry Gordy Jr., Deke Richards, Fonce Mizell

Frankie Lymon and the Teenagers redux. Their second of four straight #1 R&B/R&R smashes. An impressive enough debut to start, in and of itself, a new dance era, perfectly timed to the start of a new decade.

I'LL BE THERE
Producer: Hal Davis
Album: Third Album

Record Label: Motown
Songwriters: Bob West, Berry Gordy Jr., Willie Hutch, Hal Davis

Their fourth straight #1 R&B/R&R crossover. Covered by Mariah Carey unplugged (Columbia, '92).

THE LOVE YOU SAVE
Producers: Freddie Perren, Berry Gordy Jr., Deke Richards, Fonce Mizell
Album: ABC
Record Label: Motown
Songwriters: Freddie Perren, Berry Gordy Jr., Deke Richards, Fonce Mizell

An irresistible dance groove. #1 R&B/R&R crossover.

MAMA'S PEARL
Producers: Freddie Perren, Berry Gordy Jr., Deke Richards, Fonce Mizell
Album: Third Album
Record Label: Motown
Songwriters: Freddie Perren, Berry Gordy Jr., Deke Richards, Fonce Mizell

The ballad side of Michael.

NEVER CAN SAY GOODBYE
Album: Maybe Tomorrow
Record Label: Motown
Songwriter: Clifton Davis

Future Disco standard, covered by Isaac Hayes (Enterprise, '71) and Gloria Gaynor (MGM, '75).

1971

SUGAR DADDY
Producers: Freddie Perren, Berry Gordy Jr., Deke Richards, Fonce Mizell
Album: Jackson 5 Greatest Hits
Record Label: Motown
Songwriters: Freddie Perren, Berry Gordy Jr., Deke Richards, Fonce Mizell

1974

DANCING MACHINE
Album: Get It Together
Record Label: Motown
Songwriters: Weldon Parks, Hal Davis, Donald Fletcher

The unstoppable beat goes on.

THE JACKSONS
1976

ENJOY YOURSELF
Producers: Kenny Gamble, Leon Huff
Album: The Jacksons
Record Label: Epic
Songwriters: Kenny Gamble, Leon Huff

First hit as the Jacksons; post-pubescent, post-Motown dance groove eternal.

1978

SHAKE YOUR BODY (DOWN TO THE GROUND)
Producer: The Jacksons
Album: Destiny
Record Label: Epic
Songwriters: Stephen Jackson, Michael Jackson

Presiding over yet another Disco era.

1980

HEARTBREAK HOTEL
Producer: The Jacksons
Album: Triumph
Record Label: Epic
Songwriter: Michael Jackson

Even before he became the King of Pop, and way before he married the King of Rock and Roll's daughter, Michael was brazen enough to appropriate a hallowed Presley title.

1984

STATE OF SHOCK
Album: Victory
Record Label: Epic
Songwriters: Michael Jackson, Randy Hansen

Mike meets Mick Jagger in a danceoff reminiscent of the great Gene Kelly–Fred Astaire battles of old.

ALAN JACKSON
1993

CHATTAHOOCHIE
Producer: Keith Stegall
Album: A Lot About Livin' (and a Little 'Bout Love)
Record Label: Arista
Songwriters: Alan Jackson, Jim McBride

Rockin' #1 C&W/Top-50 R&R flashback epitomizes the slick crossover style of the '90s.

CHUCK JACKSON
1962

ANY DAY NOW
Producer: Luther Dixon
Album: Greatest Hits
Record Label: Wand
Songwriters: Bob Hilliard, Burt Bacharach

His biggest R&B/R&R crossover ballad.

FREDDIE JACKSON
1985

ROCK ME TONIGHT (FOR OLD TIMES SAKE)
Producer: Paul Laurence
Album: Rock Me Tonight
Record Label: Capitol
Songwriter: Paul Laurence

First Top-20 R&R crossover for the New Jack swinger.

YOU ARE MY LADY
Producer: Barry Eastmond
Album: Rock Me Tonight
Record Label: Capitol
Songwriter: Barry Eastmond

The '80s R&B bedroom ballad at its smoothest.

1986

HAVE YOU EVER LOVED SOMEBODY
Producer: Barry Eastmond
Album: Just Like the First Time
Record Label: Capitol
Songwriters: Barry Eastmond, Terry Skinner

#1 R&B/Bottom-40 R&R crossover.

JAM TONIGHT
Producer: Paul Laurence
Album: Just Like the First Time
Record Label: Capitol
Songwriters: Paul Laurence, Freddie Jackson

#1 R&B/Top-40 R&R crossover.

TASTY LOVE
Album: Just like the First Time
Record Label: Capitol
Songwriters: Freddie Jackson, Paul Laurence

#1 R&B/Top-40 R&R crossover.

1988

NICE 'N' SLOW
Producer: Barry Eastmond
Album: Don't Let Love Slip Away

Record Label: Capitol
Songwriters: Barry Eastmond, Jolyon Skinner

#1 R&B/Bottom-40 R&R crossover.

JANET JACKSON
1986

LET'S WAIT AWHILE
Producers: Jimmy Jam, Terry Lewis, Janet Jackson
Album: Control
Record Label: A&M
Songwriters: James Harris III, Terry Lewis, Janet Jackson, Reginald Andrews

On her third album, Michael's younger sister breaks into the dance arena on a cautionary note with a #1 R&B/Top-10 R&R crossover.

NASTY
Producers: Jimmy Jam, Terry Lewis
Album: Control
Record Label: A&M
Songwriters: James Harris III, Terry Lewis, Janet Jackson

Going against type, she's already more believable than big brother. Another #1 R&B/Top-10 R&R crossover.

THE PLEASURE PRINCIPLE
Producer: Monte Moir
Album: Control
Record Label: A&M
Songwriter: Monte Moir

#1 R&B/Top-20 R&R crossover.

WHAT HAVE YOU DONE FOR ME LATELY
Producers: Jimmy Jam, Terry Lewis
Album: Control
Record Label: A&M
Songwriters: James Harris III, Terry Lewis

Her first #1 R&B/Top-10 crossover establishes Jackson's persona as a black Lesley Gore, who can dance.

WHEN I THINK OF YOU
Producers: Jimmy Jam, Terry Lewis
Album: Control
Record Label: A&M
Songwriters: James Harris III, Terry Lewis, Janet Jackson

First #1 R&R.

ALRIGHT

Producers: Jimmy Jam, Terry Lewis
Album: Rhythm Nation 1814
Record Label: A&M
Songwriters: James Harris III, Terry Lewis, Janet Jackson

More of Jackson's patented teenybop Hip-Hop, a genre she helped make the dominant chartbeat of the late-'80s/early-'90s.

BLACK CAT

Producers: Jimmy Jam, Terry Lewis
Album: Rhythm Nation 1814
Record Label: A&M
Songwriter: Janet Jackson

#1 R&R hit from the monster album.

COME BACK TO ME

Producers: Jimmy Jam, Terry Lewis
Album: Rhythm Nation 1814
Record Label: A&M
Songwriters: James Harris III, Terry Lewis, Janet Jackson

ESCAPADE

Producers: Jimmy Jam, Terry Lewis
Album: Rhythm Nation 1814
Record Label: A&M
Songwriters: James Harris III, Terry Lewis, Janet Jackson

Her most successful single thus far; a #1 R&B/R&R crossover.

LOVE WILL NEVER DO WITHOUT YOU

Producers: Jimmy Jam, Terry Lewis
Album: Rhythm Nation 1814
Record Label: A&M
Songwriters: James Harris III, Terry Lewis

MISS YOU MUCH

Producers: Jimmy Jam, Terry Lewis
Album: Rhythm Nation 1814
Record Label: A&M
Songwriters: James Harris III, Terry Lewis

#1 R&B/R&R crossover.

RHYTHM NATION

Producers: Jimmy Jam, Terry Lewis
Album: Rhythm Nation 1814
Record Label: A&M
Songwriters: James Harris III, Terry Lewis, Janet Jackson

#1 R&B/Top-10 R&R crossover.

THE BEST THINGS IN LIFE ARE FREE

Producers: Jimmy Jam, Terry Lewis
Album: *Mo' Money* Soundtrack
Record Label: Perspective/A&M
Songwriters: James Harris III, Terry Lewis, Tresvant, Ralph, Bivins, Michael, DeVoe, Ronnie

With Luther Vandross, Bell Biv Devoe, and Ralph Tresvant, a #1 R&B/Top-10 R&R crossover from the film Mo' Money.

AGAIN

Producers: James Harris III, Terry Lewis, Janet Jackson
Album: janet
Record Label: A&M
Songwriters: James Harris III, Terry Lewis, Janet Jackson

An actress/singer now, in the Diana Ross mold, this is Janet's Oscar-nominated breathless and deathless ballad from the breathless and deathless film Poetic Justice, *co-starring Tupac Shakur.*

ANYTIME, ANY PLACE

Producers: James Harris III, Terry Lewis, Janet Jackson
Album: janet
Record Label: Virgin
Songwriters: James Harris III, Terry Lewis, Janet Jackson

#1 R&B/Top-10 R&R crossover, with "And On and On" on the B-side.

BECAUSE OF LOVE

Producers: James Harris III, Terry Lewis, Janet Jackson
Album: janet
Record Label: Virgin
Songwriters: James Harris III, Terry Lewis, Janet Jackson

IF

Producers: James Harris III, Terry Lewis, Janet Jackson
Album: janet
Record Label: Virgin
Songwriters: James Harris III, Terry Lewis, Janet Jackson

Jackson at her most salacious. Madonna wasn't worried.

THAT'S THE WAY LOVE GOES

Producers: James Harris III, Terry Lewis, Janet Jackson
Album: janet

Record Label: Virgin
Songwriters: James Harris III, Terry Lewis, Janet Jackson

A #1 R&B/R&R crossover.

YOU WANT THIS

Producers: James Harris III, Terry Lewis, Janet Jackson
Album: janet
Record Label: Virgin
Songwriters: James Harris III, Terry Lewis, Janet Jackson

Another #1 R&B/Top-10 R&R crossover, giving Jackson the most #1 R&B hits of any solo female performer aside from Aretha Franklin.

JERMAINE JACKSON

LET'S GET SERIOUS

Producer: Stevie Wonder
Album: Let's Get Serious
Record Label: Motown
Songwriters: Stevie Wonder, Lee Garrett

His biggest hit; #1 R&B/Top-10 R&R crossover.

CLOSEST THING TO PERFECT

Producer: Michael Omartian
Album: *Perfect* Soundtrack
Record Label: Arista
Songwriters: Michael Omartian, Bruce Sudano, Jermaine Jackson

From the John Travolta movie Perfect.

WORD TO THE BADD

Producers: Babyface, L. A. Reid
Album: You Said
Record Label: LaFace
Songwriters: Kenny Edmunds (Babyface), Antonio Reid (L.A. Reid), Daryl Simmons, Jermaine Jackson, Lisa Lopes

Exploiting the Michael madness of the early '90s, with his own superfluous message.

JOE JACKSON

IS SHE REALLY GOING OUT WITH HIM

Producer: David Kershenbaum
Album: Look Sharp!
Record Label: A&M
Songwriter: Joe Jackson

Exemplary pub-rocker placed Jackson briefly in the company of the new English brat pack, along with Graham Parker, Brinsley Schwarz, Nick Lowe, Dave Edmunds, and Elvis Costello.

1982

STEPPIN' OUT

Producers: David Kershenbaum, Joe Jackson
Album: Night and Day
Record Label: A&M
Songwriter: Joe Jackson

Jackson steps out of the pack, moves back into the shadows of '40s Jazz.

1984

YOU CAN'T GET WHAT YOU WANT (TILL YOU KNOW WHAT YOU WANT)

Producers: Joe Jackson, David Kershenbaum
Album: Body and Soul
Record Label: A&M
Songwriter: Joe Jackson

One of his best titles. Suggested segue: "You Can't Always Get What You Want" by the Rolling Stones.

MICHAEL JACKSON

1971

GOT TO BE THERE

Producers: Freddie Perren, Berry Gordy Jr., Deke Richards, Fonce Mizell
Album: Got to Be There
Record Label: Motown
Songwriter: Elliot Willensky

Michael goes solo with a Top-5 R&B/Top-5 R&R crossover.

1972

BEN

Producers: Freddie Perren, Berry Gordy Jr., Deke Richards, Fonce Mizell
Album: Ben
Record Label: Motown
Songwriters: Walter Scharf, Don Black

Before Willy the whale, there was Ben the rat. Michael's first big movie ballad.

1979

DON'T STOP 'TIL YOU GET ENOUGH

Producer: Quincy Jones
Album: Off the Wall
Record Label: Epic

Songwriter: Michael Jackson

The unstoppable dance groove, ten years later, and another #1 R&B/R&R crossover.

OFF THE WALL

Producer: Quincy Jones
Album: Off the Wall
Record Label: Epic
Songwriter: Rod Temperton

#1 R&B/Top-10 R&R crossover.

ROCK WITH YOU

Producer: Quincy Jones
Album: Off the Wall
Record Label: Epic
Songwriter: Rod Temperton

#1 R&B/R&R crossover.

SHE'S OUT OF MY LIFE

Producer: Quincy Jones
Album: Off the Wall
Record Label: Epic
Songwriter: Tom Bahler

His tenderest ballad.

1983

BEAT IT

Producers: Quincy Jones, Michael Jackson
Album: Thriller
Record Label: Epic
Songwriter: Michael Jackson

A #1 R&B/R&R crossover from Jackson's mega-selling mega-opus album and video, launching the MTV-era as a major factor in the marketplace of ideas and dollars. Title taken from the first words in the musical West Side Story, *which also formed the basis of the video concept. Guitar solo taken by Eddie Van Halen left Michael a wide window of Rock Scene credibility.*

BILLIE JEAN

Producers: Quincy Jones, Michael Jackson
Album: Thriller
Record Label: Epic
Songwriter: Michael Jackson

First #1 R&B/R&R crossover from the all-time top-selling album. Jackson emerges as a mysterious, sylph-like, ambisexual figure in a great hat.

THE GIRL IS MINE

Producers: Quincy Jones, Michael Jackson
Album: Thriller
Record Label: Epic
Songwriter: Michael Jackson

Duet with Paul McCartney launches the historic album, with the help of MTV.

HUMAN NATURE

Producers: Quincy Jones, Michael Jackson
Album: Thriller
Record Label: Epic
Songwriters: John Bettis, Jeffrey Porcaro

Smooth mid-tempo groove. Covered by S.W.V. (RCA, '93).

P.Y.T. (PRETTY YOUNG THING)

Producers: Quincy Jones, Michael Jackson
Album: Thriller
Record Label: Epic
Songwriters: James Ingram, Quincy Jones

THRILLER

Producers: Quincy Jones, Michael Jackson
Album: Thriller
Record Label: Epic
Songwriter: Rod Temperton

The seventh Top-10 hit from the album: Michael meets the freaks in a 20-minute video, wherein he confides the immortal line "I'm not like the other boys."

WANNA BE STARTIN' SOMETHING

Producers: Quincy Jones, Michael Jackson
Album: Thriller
Record Label: Epic
Songwriter: Michael Jackson

1987

ANOTHER PART OF ME

Producer: Quincy Jones
Album: Bad
Record Label: Epic
Songwriter: Michael Jackson

#1 R&B/Top-20 R&R crossover.

BAD

Producer: Quincy Jones
Album: Bad
Record Label: Epic
Songwriter: Michael Jackson

First of four #1 R&B/R&R crossovers from the Thriller *followup, as Michael enters his King of Pop phase.*

DIRTY DIANA

Producer: Quincy Jones
Album: Bad

Record Label: Epic
Songwriter: Michael Jackson

A #1 R&B/R&R crossover, with Steve Stevens playing the Eddie Van Halen part on guitar.

I JUST CAN'T STOP LOVING YOU
Producer: Quincy Jones
Album: Bad
Record Label: Epic
Songwriter: Michael Jackson

#1 R&B/R&R crossover.

MAN IN THE MIRROR
Producer: Quincy Jones
Album: Bad
Record Label: Epic
Songwriters: Siedah Garrett, Greg Ballard

One of his best ballads, peaked at #1.

SMOOTH CRIMINAL
Producer: Quincy Jones
Album: Bad
Record Label: Epic
Songwriter: Michael Jackson

THE WAY YOU MAKE ME FEEL
Producer: Quincy Jones
Album: Bad
Record Label: Epic
Songwriter: Michael Jackson

#1 R&B/R&R crossover.

1991

BLACK OR WHITE
Producers: Michael Jackson, Bill Bottrell
Album: Dangerous
Record Label: Epic
Songwriters: Michael Jackson, Bill Bottrell

A socially minded message from Michael; #1 R&R.

IN THE CLOSET
Producers: Michael Jackson, Bill Bottrell
Album: Dangerous
Record Label: Epic
Songwriters: Michael Jackson, Teddy Riley

Attempting to undeify the King of Pop.

REMEMBER THE TIME
Producers: Michael Jackson, Bill Bottrell
Album: Dangerous
Record Label: Epic

Songwriters: Michael Jackson, Teddy Riley, Bernard Belle

#1 R&B/Top-10 R&R crossover.

WILL YOU BE THERE
Producers: Michael Jackson, Bill Bottrell
Album: Dangerous
Record Label: Epic
Songwriter: Michael Jackson

Used in the film Free Willy in '93.

STONEWALL JACKSON
1959

WATERLOO
Record Label: Columbia
Songwriters: John D. Loudermilk, Marijohn Wilkins

A #1 C&W/Top-10 R&R crossover.

WANDA JACKSON
1956

SILVER THREADS AND GOLDEN NEEDLES
Producer: Ken Nelson
Album: Wanda Jackson
Record Label: Capitol
Songwriters: Dick Reynolds, Jack Rhodes

Introduced by the Rockabilly raver as the B-side of "Hot Dog! That Made Him Mad." Covered by the Springfields (Philips, '62), Linda Ronstadt (Capitol, '74).

JADE
1993

DON'T WALK AWAY
Producer: Vassal Benford
Album: Jade to the Max
Record Label: Giant
Songwriters: Vassal Benford, Ron Spearman

MICK JAGGER
1970

MEMO FROM TURNER
Producer: Jack Nitzsche
Album: Metamorphosis
Record Label: Abkco
Songwriters: Mick Jagger, Keith Richards

As a Rolling Stones record, this is Jagger's most scary, convincing, and lethal performance. From his starring role in the cult film Performance.

1985

JUST ANOTHER NIGHT
Producers: Mick Jagger, Bill Laswell
Album: She's the Boss
Record Label: Columbia
Songwriter: Mick Jagger

As a solo artist, Jagger was merely fodder for the aerobics mill.

THE JAGGERZ
1970

THE RAPPER
Album: We Went to Different Schools Together
Record Label: Kama Sutra
Songwriter: Donnie Iris

When rapping was only the inevitable result of too much speed instead of an urban lifestyle commentary.

THE JAM
1977

ALL AROUND THE WORLD
Album: This Is the Modern World
Record Label: Polydor
Songwriter: Paul Weller

Steller single from these post-mod, pre-modern English rockers.

IN THE CITY
Album: In the City
Record Label: Polydor
Songwriter: Paul Weller

Debut release from a second generation Who. Suggested segue: "Holidays in the Sun" by the Sex Pistols.

1979

ETON RIFLES
Producer: Vic Coppersmith-Heaven
Album: Setting Sons
Record Label: Polydor
Songwriter: Paul Weller

Their first U.K. hit; powerful post-war protest.

GOING UNDERGROUND
Producer: Vic Coppersmith-Heaven
Album: Setting Sons
Record Label: Polydor
Songwriter: Paul Weller

Their first #1 U.K.

1982

BEAT SURRENDER
Album: Beat Surrender
Record Label: Polydor

Songwriter: Paul Weller

Their last record together was their third and last #1 U.K. Weller would move on to the more soulful Style Council.

THE BITTEREST PILL (I EVER HAD TO SWALLOW)

Album: The Bitterest Pill
Record Label: Polydor
Songwriter: Paul Weller

One of Weller's best vocals.

JAMES

1994

LAID

Producer: Brian Eno
Album: Laid
Record Label: Mercury
Songwriters: Tim Booth, Larry Gott, Saul Davies, Mark Hunter, Jim Glennie, David Bayton-Power

Invoking the ghost of Folk Rock past. Suggested segue: Like a Rolling Stone" by Bob Dylan.

THE JAMES GANG

1970

FUNK #49

Producer: Bill Szymczyk
Album: James Gang Rides Again
Record Label: ABC
Songwriters: Joe Walsh, Jim Fox, Dale Peters

Launching Walsh's classic Rock guitar career.

ELMORE JAMES

1952

I BELIEVE I'LL DUST MY BROOM

Album: Blues After Hours
Record Label: Trumpet
Songwriter: Robert Johnson

Originated by Robert Johnson (Vocalion, '36) an essential Blues cover in the Rock and Roll repertoire. Elmore James' dusty slide guitar style was a major influence on Eric Clapton, Billy Gibbons, and Stevie Ray Vaughan.

1960

THE SKY IS CRYING

Producer: Bobby Robinson
Record Label: Fire
Songwriter: Elmore James

In the days when a hair-raising Blues tune could still make the R&B charts. Covered by Stevie Ray Vaughan (Epic, '90).

ETTA JAMES

1955

DANCE WITH ME HENRY (THE WALLFLOWER)

Record Label: Modern
Songwriters: Johnny Otis, Hank Ballard, Etta James

Part of the "Annie" franchise, also known as "Roll with Me Henry." It was written, largely by the same crew, in answer to "Work with Me Annie." Etta had her biggest R&B hit with it. Covered by Georgia Gibbs (Mercury, '55). Featured prominently in the past part of the '85 film Back to the Future.

1960

ALL I COULD DO WAS CRY

Album: At Last
Record Label: Argo
Songwriters: Gwen Gordy, Berry Gordy Jr., Roquel Davis (Tyran Carlo)

Etta's first Top-10 R&B/Top-40 R&R crossover. More money in the bank toward the Gordy's future Detroit startup, Motown.

MY DEAREST DARLING

Album: At Last
Record Label: Argo
Songwriters: Paul Gayton, Edwin Bocage

Top-10 R&B/Top-40 R&R crossover.

1961

AT LAST

Album: At Last
Record Label: Argo
Songwriters: Mack Gordon, Harry Warren

Etta's signature ballad, a Top-10 R&B/Top-50 crossover, received new life when it was used at a climactic moment in the '89 Dustin Hoffman/Tom Cruise film Rain Man. Subsequently immortalized in a Cadillac commercial as the ultimate high-class luxury car song. Introduced by Glenn Miller in the '42 film Orchestra Wives.

1962

SOMETHING'S GOT A HOLD ON ME

Album: Etta James' Top Ten
Record Label: Argo
Songwriters: Pearl Woods, Leroy Kirkland, Etta James

Top-10 R&B/Top-40 R&R crossover.

1963

PUSHOVER

Album: Etta James' Top Ten
Record Label: Argo
Songwriters: Roquel Davis (Tyran Carlo), Tony Clarke

Top-10 R&B/Top-30 R&R crossover.

1967

TELL MAMA

Producer: Rick Hall
Album: Tell Mama
Record Label: Cadet
Songwriters: Clarence Carter, Marcus Daniel, Wilbur Terrell

Her biggest crossover hit; Top-10 R&B/Top-25 R&R.

RICK JAMES

1978

YOU AND I

Producers: Rick James, Art Stewart
Album: Come Get It!
Record Label: Gordy
Songwriter: James Johnson Jr.

Launching an influential Funk career with a #1 R&B/ Top-20 R&R crossover, his biggest hit.

1979

BUSTIN' OUT

Producers: Rick James, Art Stewart
Album: Bustin' out of L Seven
Record Label: Gordy
Songwriter: James Johnson Jr.

HIGH ON YOUR LOVE SUITE

Producer: Rick James
Album: Bustin' out of L Seven
Record Label: Gordy
Songwriter: James Johnson Jr.

1981

GIVE IT TO ME BABY

Producer: Rick James
Album: Street Songs
Record Label: Gordy
Songwriter: James Johnson Jr.

#1 R&B/Top-40 R&R crossover.

SUPER FREAK

Producer: Rick James
Album: Street Songs
Record Label: Gordy
Songwriter: James Johnson Jr.

His defining groove.

1983

COLD BLOODED
Producer: Rick James
Album: Cold Blooded
Record Label: Motown
Songwriter: James Johnson Jr.
#1 R&B/Top-40 crossover.

1984

17
Producer: Rick James
Album: Reflections
Record Label: Gordy
Songwriter: James Johnson Jr.

1988

LOOSEY'S RAP
Album: Wonderful
Record Label: Reprise
Songwriter: James Johnson Jr.
With Roxanne Shante.

SONNY JAMES

1956

YOUNG LOVE
Producer: Ken Nelson
Record Label: Capitol
Songwriters: Ric Cartey, Carole Joyner

Early easy-listening Country rocker. Originally released by co-writer Ric Cartey (RCA, '56). James' version was a #1 C&W/R&R crossover. Covered by Pop singer/movie star, Tab Hunter (Dot, '56), whose version raced James' up the charts.

TOMMY JAMES AND THE SHONDELLS

1967

I THINK WE'RE ALONE NOW
Producers: Bo Gentry, Ritchie Cordell
Album: I Think We're Alone Now
Record Label: Roulette
Songwriters: Ritchie Cordell, Bo Gentry

In the midst of the pyschedelic revolution, the new sound of bubblegum emerges. Covered by Lene Lovich (Stiff, '79) and Tiffany (MCA, '87).

MIRAGE
Producers: Bo Gentry, Ritchie Cordell
Album: I Think We're Alone Now
Record Label: Roulette
Songwriters: Ritchie Cordell, Bo Gentry

1968

MONY MONY
Producers: Bo Gentry, Ritchie Cordell
Album: Crimson and Clover
Record Label: Roulette
Songwriters: Ritchie Cordell, Bo Gentry, Bobby Bloom, Tommy James

A bubblegum epiphany, inspired by the insurance company, Mutual of New York. Covered by Billy Idol (Chrysalis, '87).

1969

CRIMSON AND CLOVER
Producer: Tommy James
Album: Crimson and Clover
Record Label: Roulette
Songwriters: Tommy James, Pete Lucia

His biggest hit since "Hanky Panky," in 1966.

CRYSTAL BLUE PERSUASION
Producer: Tommy James
Album: Crimson and Clover
Record Label: Roulette
Songwriters: Tommy James, Mike Vale, Ed Gray

Best known example of pyschedelic bubblegum.

SWEET CHERRY WINE
Producer: Tommy James
Album: Cellophane Symphony
Record Label: Roulette
Songwriters: Tommy James, Richie Grass

Suggested segue: "Red Red Wine" by Neil Diamond.

1971

DRAGGIN' THE LINE
Producer: Tommy James
Album: Christian of the World
Record Label: Roulette
Songwriters: Tommy James, Robert L. King

Frothy summertime tune was his biggest solo hit.

1980

THREE TIMES IN LOVE
Producer: Tommy James
Album: Three Times in Love
Record Label: Millennium
Songwriters: Tommy James, Rick Serota

Still blowing bubbles after all these years.

THE JAMIES

1958

SUMMERTIME, SUMMERTIME
Record Label: Epic
Songwriters: Tom Jameson, Sherm Feller

The ultimate song of summer freedom, played every June on the last day of school. Suggested segues: "One Summer Night" by the Danleers, for the ultimate summer fantasy expectation and "Summertime Blues" by Eddie Cochran for the more probable painful reality. Featured in the '78 Harvey Keitel cult movie Fingers.

JAN AND ARNIE

1958

JENNY-LEE
Album: Jan and Dean's Golden Hits
Record Label: Arwin
Songwriters: Jan Berry, Arnie Ginsburg

California blue-eyed Soul, pre-Spector, pre-surf, recorded in Jan's garage with Dean sitting in.

JAN AND DEAN

1958

BABY TALK
Producers: Lou Adler, Herb Albert
Album: Jan and Dean's Golden Hits
Record Label: Dore
Songwriter: Melvin H. Schwartz

Post Doo-Wop beach music from California.

1963

DRAG CITY
Producer: Jan Berry
Album: Drag City
Record Label: Liberty
Songwriters: Brian Wilson, Jan Berry, Roger Christian

Racing in the streets of American Graffitiville.

SURF CITY
Producer: Jan Berry
Album: Surf City and Other Swingin' Cities
Record Label: Liberty
Songwriters: Brian Wilson, Jan Berry

Their biggest hit, their biggest fantasy: two girls for every boy.

1964

DEAD MAN'S CURVE

Producer: Jan Berry

Album: Surf City and Other Swingin' Cities

Record Label: Liberty

Songwriters: Brian Wilson, Jan Berry, Roger Christian, Artie Kornfeld

Classic (and prophetic) car song: classic cars, Stingray and Jaguar XKE.

THE LITTLE OLD LADY (FROM PASADENA)

Producer: Jan Berry

Album: The Little Old Lady from Pasadena

Record Label: Liberty

Songwriters: Roger Christian, Don Altfeld

Car classic—classic car line: "only driven once by a little old lady from Pasadena."

THE NEW GIRL IN SCHOOL

Album: Dead Man's Curve/The New Girl in School

Record Label: Liberty

Songwriters: Brian Wilson, Jan Berry, Roger Christian, Bob Norman

Covered by Alex Chilton (Ardent, '95).

RIDE THE WILD SURF

Album: *Ride the Wild Surf* Soundtrack

Record Label: Liberty

Songwriters: Brian Wilson, Jan Berry, Roger Christian

Theme from the classic beach movie.

1965

(HERE THEY COME) FROM ALL OVER THE WORLD

Producer: Jan Berry

Album: From All over the World

Record Label: Liberty

Songwriters: Steve Barri, P. F. Sloan

Theme from the legendary youth cult concert film, The T.A.M.I. Show, *which starred James Brown, the Rolling Stones, Jan and Dean, Ike and Tina, and others.*

JANE'S ADDICTION

1991

BEEN CAUGHT STEALING

Producers: Dave Jerden, Perry Farrell

Album: Ritual de lo Habitual

Record Label: Warner Brothers

Songwriter: Jane's Addiction

Breakthrough Rock track for the semi-outrageous L.A. band.

BERT JANSCH

1965

ANJI

Album: Lucky Thirteen

Record Label: Vanguard

Songwriter: Davey Graham

Acoustic guitar instrumental by a major influence on Jimmy Page. Jansch went on to form Pentacle with John Renbourn. Covered by Simon and Garfunkel (Columbia,'65).

THE JARMELS

1961

A LITTLE BIT OF SOAP

Record Label: Laurie

Songwriter: Bert Berns (Bert Russell)

The essence of early '60s Uptown R&B.

JAY AND THE AMERICANS

1962

SHE CRIED

Producers: Jerry Leiber, Mike Stoller

Album: She Cried

Record Label: United Artists

Songwriters: Ted Daryll, Greg Richards

Eternal teen soap operatics, covered by the Shangri-Las in the equal opportunity "He Cried" (Redbird, '66).

1963

ONLY IN AMERICA

Producers: Jerry Leiber, Mike Stoller

Album: Come a Little Bit Closer

Record Label: United Artists

Songwriters: Jerry Leiber, Mike Stoller, Barry Mann, Cynthia Weil

Cut by the Drifters but not released. Jay and the Americans, with David Black singing lead, recorded their version over the Drifters' arrangement.

1964

COME A LITTLE BIT CLOSER

Album: Come a Little Bit Closer

Record Label: United Artists

Songwriters: Tommy Boyce, Bobby Hart, Wes Farrell

Biggest hit for the semi-operatic New Yorkers.

1965

CARA MIA

Album: Blockbusters

Record Label: United Artists

Songwriters: Bunny Lewis (Tulio Tropani), Annunzio Mantovani (Lee Lange)

Introduced in England by David Whitfield and Mantovani (Decca/London, '54). Buoyed by Elvis' and Jackie Wilson's forays into the light-opera realms, Jay Black plumbs to the roots of Italian soul with this cover of Whitfield's British million seller.

JAY AND THE TECHNIQUES

1967

APPLES, PEACHES, PUMPKIN PIE (READY OR NOT)

Producer: Jerry Ross

Album: Apples, Peaches, Pumpkin Pie

Record Label: Smash

Songwriter: Maurice Irby Jr.

Feel good Top-10 R&B/R&R one-shot.

THE JAYNETTES

1963

SALLY GO 'ROUND THE ROSES

Producer: Abner Spector

Album: Sally Go 'Round the Roses

Record Label: Tuff

Songwriters: Zell Sanders, Lona Stevens

An eerie, foreboding tale that seemed to forecast the end of the girl-group era.

JB'S

1973

DOIN' IT TO DEATH

Producer: James Brown

Album: Doin' It to Death

Record Label: People

Songwriter: James Brown

#1 R&B/Top-30 crossover for Brown's backup band.

THE JEFFERSON AIRPLANE

1966

IT'S NO SECRET

Producers: Matthew Katz, Tony Oliver

Album: Takes Off

Record Label: RCA

Songwriter: Marty Balin

Pre-flyte Folk Rock from San Francisco's nascent psychedelic scenemakers.

1967

EMBRYONIC JOURNEY
Producer: Rick Jarrard
Album: Surrealistic Pillow
Record Label: RCA
Songwriter: Jorma Kaukonen

Classic early instrumental, revealing Jorma's Reverend Gary Davis proclivities.

1968

WON'T YOU TRY/ SATURDAY AFTERNOON
Producer: Al Schmitt
Album: After Bathing at Baxter's
Record Label: RCA
Songwriter: Paul Kantner

Conjuring a perfect San Francisco weekend in the late '60s. Utopian idealism at the corner of Love and Haight, complete with acid, incense, and balloons. Pyschedelic optimism almost too sad to contemplate in retrospect.

1968

GREASY HEART
Producer: Al Schmitt
Album: Crown of Creation
Record Label: RCA
Songwriter: Grace Slick

LATHER
Producer: Al Schmitt
Album: Crown of Creation
Record Label: RCA
Songwriter: Grace Slick

Chronicling the end of the innocence, '60s style.

1969

HAVE YOU SEEN THE SAUCERS?
Album: Thirty Seconds over Winterland
Record Label: Grunt
Songwriter: Paul Kantner

Paul introduces an enduring obsession on a classic single. Suggested segue: "It Came out of the Sky" by Creedence Clearwater Revival.

MEXICO
Album: Early Flight
Record Label: Grunt
Songwriter: Grace Slick

B-side of "Have You Seen the Saucers?" or maybe the A-side.

WE CAN BE TOGETHER/VOLUNTEERS
Producer: Al Schmitt
Album: Volunteers of America
Record Label: RCA
Songwriters: Marty Balin, Paul Kantner

Doomed anthem of a counter culture, up against the wall.

1971

PRETTY AS YOU FEEL
Producer: Jefferson Airplane
Album: Bark
Record Label: Grunt
Songwriters: Joey Covington, Jack Casady, Jorma Kaukonen

Presaging the coming of the "Me" generation.

THIRD WEEK AT THE CHELSEA
Producer: Jefferson Airplane
Album: Bark
Record Label: Grunt
Songwriter: Jorma Kaukonen

Jorma's eminently hummable Folk Rock-cum-psychedelic-Bluegrass farewell to the Sunshine era. Hot Tuna was in the wings.

THE JEFFERSON STARSHIP

1975

MIRACLES
Producers: Larry Cox, Jefferson Starship
Album: Red Octopus
Record Label: Grunt
Songwriter: Martyn Buchwald (Marty Balin)

New name, new era, same psychedelic harmonies.

1978

COUNT ON ME
Producers: Larry Cox, Jefferson Starship
Album: Earth
Record Label: Grunt
Songwriter: Jesse Barish

Entering the Arena Rock arena.

1980

JANE
Producer: Ron Nevison
Album: Freedom at Point Zero
Record Label: Grunt

Songwriters: David Friedberg, Paul Kantner, Jim McPherson, Craig Chaquico

Jefferson now in name only. The rest was Starship.

GARLAND JEFFREYS

1977

COOL DOWN BOY
Producers: David Spinozza, Garland Jeffreys
Album: Ghost Writer
Record Label: A&M
Songwriter: Garland Jeffreys

Lou Reed meets Gil Scott-Heron.

I MAY NOT BE YOUR KIND
Producers: David Spinozza, Garland Jeffreys
Album: Ghost Writer
Record Label: A&M
Songwriter: Garland Jeffreys

WILD IN THE STREETS
Producers: David Spinozza, Garland Jeffreys
Album: Ghost Writer
Record Label: A&M
Songwriter: Garland Jeffreys

The angry American young man's answer to Graham Parker.

1991

HAIL, HAIL ROCK 'N' ROLL
Producer: Garland Jeffreys
Album: Don't Call Me Buckwheat
Record Label: RCA
Songwriter: Garland Jeffreys

One man's history of Rock and Roll, and race relations.

THE JOE JEFFREY GROUP

1969

MY PLEDGE OF LOVE
Record Label: Wand
Songwriter: Joe Stafford Jr.

Mellow Jazz Rock groove.

THE JELLY BEANS

1964

I WANNA LOVE HIM SO BAD
Producer: Jeff Barry
Record Label: Red Bird
Songwriters: Jeff Barry, Ellie Greenwich

Brill Building studio Soul.

JELLYBEAN

1985

SIDEWALK TALK
Producer: Jellybean Benitez
Record Label: EMI-America
Songwriter: Madonna Ciccone
Dance hit written by a former protege.

WAYLON JENNINGS

1967

THE CHOKIN' KIND
Record Label: RCA
Songwriter: Harlan Howard
Top-10 C&W hit for the former Cricket turned Country outlaw. Cover by Joe Simon was his first #1 R&B/Top-20 R&R crossover (Sound Stage 7, '69).

1975

ARE YOU SURE HANK DONE IT THIS WAY?
Producers: Jack Clement, Waylon Jennings
Album: Dreaming My Dreams
Record Label: RCA
Songwriter: Waylon Jennings
Buddy Holly's former bassman turns to C&W with a touch of Rockabilly attitude: #1 C&W/Bottom-40 R&R.

A GOOD-HEARTED WOMAN
Album: Waylon Live
Record Label: RCA
Songwriters: Willie Nelson, Waylon Jennings
Willie & Waylon, the Frank and Jesse James of outlaw country, with their masterwork; #1 C&W/Top-30 R&R.

THE JESUS AND MARY CHAIN

1984

UPSIDE DOWN
Record Label: Creation
Songwriters: James Reid, William Reid
First indie hit for the Scottish Velvet Underground of the '80s.

1986

JUST LIKE HONEY
Producer: The Jesus and Mary Chain
Album: Psychocandy
Record Label: Reprise
Songwriter: James Reid
College radio track of the year.

1987

HAPPY WHEN IT RAINS
Producers: William Reid, Bill Price
Album: Darklands
Record Label: Warner Brothers
Songwriters: James Reid, William Reid
From their acclaimed neo-psychedelic album.

JESUS JONES

1991

REAL REAL REAL
Producer: Jesus Jones
Album: Doubt
Record Label: SBK
Songwriter: Jesus Jones

RIGHT HERE, RIGHT NOW
Producer: Jesus Jones
Album: Doubt
Record Label: SBK
Songwriter: Mike Edwards
International smash written about the razing of the Berlin Wall. Suggested segue: "Winds of Change," by the Scorpions.

1993

THE DEVIL YOU KNOW
Producers: Mike Edwards, Wayne Livesy
Album: Perverse
Record Label: SBK
Songwriter: Mike Edwards

JETHRO TULL

1971

AQUALUNG
Producers: Ian Anderson, Terry Ellis
Album: Aqualung
Record Label: Reprise
Songwriter: Ian Anderson
Ian Anderson's flute-driven thing; the ultimate progressive FM radio twisted standard.

CROSS-EYED MARY
Producers: Ian Anderson, Terry Ellis
Album: Aqualung
Record Label: Reprise
Songwriter: Ian Anderson
Classic of Classic Rock.

1972

LIVING IN THE PAST
Producer: Terry Ellis
Album: Living in the Past

1987

Record Label: Chrysalis
Songwriter: Ian Anderson
Their biggest hit.

THICK AS A BRICK
Producers: Ian Anderson, Terry Ellis
Album: Thick as a Brick
Record Label: Chrysalis
Songwriter: Ian Anderson

1974

BUNGLE IN THE JUNGLE
Album: War Child
Record Label: Chrysalis
Songwriter: Ian Anderson
Their second biggest hit.

1976

TOO OLD TO ROCK 'N' ROLL: TOO YOUNG TO DIE
Producer: Ian Anderson
Album: Too Old to Rock 'N' Roll: Too Young to Die
Record Label: Chrysalis
Songwriter: Ian Anderson
Their defining credo; in '89 these progressive folkies won a Hard Rock Grammy.

THE JETS

1986

CRUSH ON YOU
Producers: Dan Powell, D. Rivkin, Jerry Knight, Aaron Zigman
Album: The Jets
Record Label: MCA
Songwriters: Jerry Knight, Aaron Zigman
New generation Osmond family from Tonga by way of Minneapolis, with appropriately Osmond-flavored teeny dance Pop.

1987

CROSS MY BROKEN HEART
Producers: Steve Bray, M. Verdick
Album: Magic
Record Label: MCA
Songwriters: Steve Bray, Tony Pierce
From the soundtrack of Beverly Hills Cop II.

MAKE IT REAL
Producers: Dan Powell, M. Verdick, Rich Kelly
Album: Magic
Record Label: MCA
Songwriters: Linda Mallah, Rich Kelly, Dan Powell

YOU GOT IT ALL
Producer: Dan Powell
Album: The Jets
Record Label: MCA
Songwriters: Rupert Holmes, D. Rivkin

The author's best Pop rocker since "Escape (The Pina Colada Song)."

1988

ROCKET 2 U
Producer: Robert Nunn
Album: Magic
Record Label: MCA
Songwriter: Robert Nunn

JOAN JETT

1981

BAD REPUTATION
Producers: Ritchie Cordell, Kenny Laguna
Album: Joan Jett
Record Label: Blackheart/Ariola
Songwriters: Joan Jett, Kenny Laguna, Ritchie Cordell, Martin Kupersmith

Former teeny Punk goddess with the Runaways burnishes her image.

1982

I LOVE ROCK AND ROLL
Producers: Ritchie Cordell, Kenny Laguna
Album: I Love Rock and Roll
Record Label: Boardwalk
Songwriters: Jake Hooker, Alan Merrill

Year's #1 American bedrock manifesto was previously a stiff as a U.K. single for the Arrows, consisting of its expatriate authors, and a B-side of Jett's cover of "You Don't Own Me" (Boardwalk, '81).

1984

I GOT NO ANSWERS
Album: Glorious Results of a Misspent Youth
Record Label: Boardwalk
Songwriters: Joan Jett, Kenny Laguna

Critically regarded as her ultimate achievement.

1988

I HATE MYSELF FOR LOVING YOU
Producers: Kenny Laguna, Desmond Child
Album: Up Your Alley
Record Label: CBS Associated

Songwriters: Joan Jett, Desmond Child

Visiting the noted song doctor for another Top-10 fix.

JIGSAW

1975

SKY HIGH
Producer: Chas Peate
Album: Sky High
Record Label: Chelsea
Songwriters: Des Dyer, Clive Scott

From the movie The Dragon Flies.

THE JIVE FIVE

1961

MY TRUE STORY
Album: The Jive Five
Record Label: Beltone
Songwriters: Eugene Pitt, Oscar Waltzer

#1 R&B/Top-10 R&R crossover.

1965

I'M A HAPPY MAN
Record Label: United Artists
Songwriter: Casey Spencer

Happy to be virtually Doo-Wop's lone representative on the Top-40 of '65.

JO JO GUNNE

1972

RUN, RUN, RUN
Album: Jo Jo Gunne
Record Label: Asylum
Songwriter: Jay Ferguson

Spiritless.

JODECI

1991

COME AND TALK TO ME
Producers: Andre Harrell, Steve Lucas
Album: Forever My Lady
Record Label: Uptown
Songwriter: Devante Swing

#1 R&B/Top-20 R&R in the modern back to Doo-Wop mode.

STAY
Producers: Andre Harrell, Steve Lucas
Album: Forever My Lady
Record Label: Uptown
Songwriter: Devante Swing

#1 R&B/Top-50 R&R.

1993

CRY FOR YOU
Producer: DeVante Swing
Album: Diary of a Mad Band
Record Label: Uptown/MCA
Songwriter: DeVante Swing

#1 R&B/Top-20 R&R crossover for the newest of the new Jacks on the block.

JOE PUBLIC

1992

LIVE AND LEARN
Producers: Lionel Job, Joe Public
Album: Joe Public
Record Label: Columbia
Songwriters: Joe Carter, Joseph Sayles, Kev Scott, Dew Wyatt

Hip-Hop with a down-to-earth message.

BILLY JOEL

1971

CAPTAIN JACK
Producer: Phil Ramone
Album: Billy Joel
Record Label: Columbia
Songwriter: Billy Joel

The angry young man from Long Island: a New York FM staple.

PIANO MAN
Producer: Michael Stewart
Album: Billy Joel
Record Label: Columbia
Songwriter: Billy Joel

His autobiographical piano bar claim to fame.

1974

THE ENTERTAINER
Producer: Michael Stewart
Album: Streetlife Serenader
Record Label: Columbia
Songwriter: Billy Joel

Self-absorbed confessional from the pen and piano of the former L.A. lounge lizard Bill Martin.

1976

MIAMI 2017 (SEEN THE LIGHTS GO OUT ON BROADWAY)
Producer: Phil Ramone
Album: Turnstiles
Record Label: Columbia
Songwriter: Billy Joel

From the piano bar to the airport lounge.

NEW YORK STATE OF MIND

Producer: Phil Ramone
Album: Turnstiles
Record Label: Columbia
Songwriter: Billy Joel

Homegrown city anthem achieved a Long Island boy epiphany, a cover version by Brooklyn princess Barbra Streisand (Columbia, '77).

SAY GOODBYE TO HOLLYWOOD

Producer: Phil Ramone
Album: Turnstiles
Record Label: Columbia
Songwriter: Billy Joel

Suggested segue: "I Love L.A." by Randy Newman. Covered by Ronnie Spector & the E Street Band (Cleveland International, '77).

1977

JUST THE WAY YOU ARE

Producer: Phil Ramone
Album: The Stranger
Record Label: Columbia
Songwriter: Billy Joel

His crowning lounge ballad. Covered by Frank Sinatra (Reprise, '80).

MOVING OUT (ANTHONY'S SONG)

Producer: Phil Ramone
Album: The Stranger
Record Label: Columbia
Songwriter: Billy Joel

Symbolically moving into his own as a top singer/songwriter.

ONLY THE GOOD DIE YOUNG

Producer: Phil Ramone
Album: The Stranger
Record Label: Columbia
Songwriter: Billy Joel

Easily his most heartfelt and profound personal protest song. Banned by the Catholic Church, which immediately established Joel as a Rock and Roll hero.

SCENES FROM AN ITALIAN RESTAURANT

Producer: Phil Ramone
Album: The Stranger
Record Label: Columbia
Songwriter: Billy Joel

The Long Island yuppie version of "The Way We Were" by Barbra Streisand.

SHE'S ALWAYS A WOMAN

Producer: Phil Ramone
Album: The Stranger
Record Label: Columbia

Songwriter: Billy Joel

The Long Island hippie version of "She Belongs to Me" by Bob Dylan.

1978

BIG SHOT

Producer: Phil Ramone
Album: 52nd Street
Record Label: Columbia
Songwriter: Billy Joel

Perhaps his most revealing hit.

MY LIFE

Producer: Phil Ramone
Album: 52nd Street
Record Label: Columbia
Songwriter: Billy Joel

The middle-class answer to "It's My Life" by the Animals.

1980

YOU MAY BE RIGHT

Producer: Phil Ramone
Album: Glass Houses
Record Label: Columbia
Songwriter: Billy Joel

Entering a Rocking phase, rocks in hand.

IT'S STILL ROCK AND ROLL TO ME

Producer: Phil Ramone
Album: Glass Houses
Record Label: Columbia
Songwriter: Billy Joel

The still angry young man answers his critics with his first #1.

1982

ALLENTOWN

Producer: Phil Ramone
Album: The Nylon Curtain
Record Label: Columbia
Songwriter: Billy Joel

Entering his Woody Guthrie phase. Suggested Guthrian segue: "Youngstown" by Bruce Springsteen.

GOODNIGHT SAIGON

Producer: Phil Ramone
Album: The Nylon Curtain
Record Label: Columbia
Songwriter: Billy Joel

Suggested segue: "Still in Saigon" by the Charlie Daniels Band.

1983

AN INNOCENT MAN

Producer: Phil Ramone
Album: An Innocent Man
Record Label: Columbia

Songwriter: Billy Joel

One of the highlights of his album-length tribute to the Soul-based Rock of the mid-'60s—and his newfound teenage requited lust for the model Christie Brinkley.

THE LONGEST TIME

Producer: Phil Ramone
Album: An Innocent Man
Record Label: Columbia
Songwriter: Billy Joel

TELL HER ABOUT IT

Producer: Phil Ramone
Album: An Innocent Man
Record Label: Columbia
Songwriter: Billy Joel

Revisiting Motown by way of the Brill Building, out of his Long Island home studio.

UPTOWN GIRL

Producer: Phil Ramone
Album: An Innocent Man
Record Label: Columbia
Songwriter: Billy Joel

The perfect Four Seasons song, twenty years later.

1985

YOU'RE ONLY HUMAN (SECOND WIND)

Album: Greatest Hits (Vols. I and II)
Record Label: Columbia
Songwriter: Billy Joel

1986

BIG MAN ON MULBERRY STREET

Producer: Phil Ramone
Album: The Bridge
Record Label: Columbia
Songwriter: Billy Joel

Served as the basis for an episode of the TV series "Moonlighting."

A MATTER OF TRUST

Producer: Phil Ramone
Album: The Bridge
Record Label: Columbia
Songwriter: Billy Joel

MODERN WOMAN (FROM *RUTHLESS PEOPLE*)

Producer: Phil Ramone
Album: The Bridge
Record Label: Epic
Songwriter: Billy Joel

From the soundtrack of the Bette Midler comedy Ruthless People.

THIS IS THE TIME

Producer: Phil Ramone
Album: The Bridge
Record Label: Columbia
Songwriter: Billy Joel

His wedding/sweet-sixteen/bar-mitzvah standard.

1989

I GO TO EXTREMES

Producers: Mick Jones, Billy Joel
Album: Storm Front
Record Label: Columbia
Songwriter: Billy Joel

Follow-up to "You May Be Right."

LENINGRAD

Producers: Mick Jones, Billy Joel
Album: Storm Front
Record Label: Columbia
Songwriter: Billy Joel

Pre-Glasnost ballad.

WE DIDN'T START THE FIRE

Producers: Mick Jones, Billy Joel
Album: Storm Front
Record Label: Columbia
Songwriter: Billy Joel

The three-minute MTV version of Pop Culture 101. Suggested segues: "It's the End of the World as We Know It (and I Feel Fine)" by R.E.M.; "Subterranean Homesick Blues" by Bob Dylan.

1993

RIVER OF DREAMS

Producers: Mick Jones, Billy Joel
Album: River of Dreams
Record Label: Columbia
Songwriter: Billy Joel

DAVID JOHANSEN

1977

FRENCHETTE

Producers: Richard Robinson, David Johansen
Album: David Johansen
Record Label: Blue Sky
Songwriters: David Johansen, Syl Sylvain

FUNKY BUT CHIC

Producers: Richard Robinson, David Johansen
Album: David Johansen
Record Label: Blue Sky
Songwriters: David Johansen, Syl Sylvain

Statement of purpose from the ex-New York Doll. But not as purposeful as his amazing '82 cover of "It's My Life" by the Animals.

1978

COOL METRO

Producers: Richard Robinson, David Johansen
Album: David Johansen
Record Label: Blue Sky
Songwriters: David Johansen, Syl Sylvain

The roots of Buster Poindexter.

ELTON JOHN

1970

BORDER SONG (HOLY MOSES)

Producer: Gus Dudgeon
Album: Elton John
Record Label: MCA
Songwriters: Elton John, Bernie Taupin

Crossing the border to the lucrative U.S. market, on the brink of a singer/song-writer/piano man resurgence. Covered by Aretha Franklin (Atlantic, '70).

TAKE ME TO THE PILOT

Producer: Gus Dudgeon
Album: Elton John
Record Label: MCA
Songwriters: Elton John, Bernie Taupin

Prelude to "Rocket Man."

YOUR SONG

Producer: Gus Dudgeon
Album: Elton John
Record Label: MCA
Songwriters: Elton John, Bernie Taupin

Epitomizing the nascent singer-songwriter era with a perfect take on American diction ("Anyway, the thing is . . . what I really mean . . . .")

1971

LEVON

Producer: Gus Dudgeon
Album: Madman Across the Water
Record Label: Uni
Songwriters: Elton John, Bernie Taupin

Listening to a lot of Leon Russell and the Band.

1972

CROCODILE ROCK

Producer: Gus Dudgeon
Album: Don't Shoot Me, I'm Only the Piano Player
Record Label: MCA
Songwriters: Elton John, Bernie Taupin

Retro rocker was his first #1.

DANIEL

Producer: Gus Dudgeon
Album: Don't Shoot Me, I'm Only the Piano Player
Record Label: MCA
Songwriters: Elton John, Bernie Taupin

One of his strongest Rock ballads.

HONKY CAT

Producer: Gus Dudgeon
Album: Honky Chateau
Record Label: Uni
Songwriters: Elton John, Bernie Taupin

And his pumping piano.

ROCKET MAN (I THINK IT'S GONNA BE A LONG LONG TIME)

Producer: Gus Dudgeon
Album: Honky Chateau
Record Label: Uni
Songwriters: Elton John, Bernie Taupin

Suggested segues: "Starman" by David Bowie, "Major Tom" by Peter Schilling. Covered by Kate Bush (MCA, '93).

SATURDAY NIGHT'S ALRIGHT (FOR FIGHTING)

Producer: Gus Dudgeon
Album: Don't Shoot Me, I'm Only the Piano Player
Record Label: MCA
Songwriters: Elton John, Bernie Taupin

More of his Jerry Lee Lewis groove.

1973

BENNIE AND THE JETS

Producer: Gus Dudgeon
Album: Goodbye Yellow Brick Road
Record Label: MCA
Songwriters: Elton John, Bernie Taupin

His second #1 R&R and biggest R&B crossover.

CANDLE IN THE WIND
Producer: Gus Dudgeon
Album: Goodbye Yellow Brick Road
Record Label: MCA
Songwriters: Elton John, Bernie Taupin

Elton and Bernie's Hollywood Fixation Part I. Live version released as a single (MCA, '87).

GOODBYE YELLOW BRICK ROAD
Producer: Gus Dudgeon
Album: Goodbye Yellow Brick Road
Record Label: MCA
Songwriters: Elton John, Bernie Taupin

Elton and Bernie's Hollywood fixation, Part II.

LOVE LIES BLEEDING
Producer: Gus Dudgeon
Album: Goodbye Yellow Brick Road
Record Label: MCA
Songwriters: Elton John, Bernie Taupin

One of his toughest rockers. In an 11-minute medley with "Funeral for a Friend."

1974

THE BITCH IS BACK
Producer: Gus Dudgeon
Album: Caribou
Record Label: MCA
Songwriters: Elton John, Bernie Taupin

DON'T LET THE SUN GO DOWN ON ME
Producer: Gus Dudgeon
Album: Caribou
Record Label: MCA
Songwriters: Elton John, Bernie Taupin

Elton compares himself to the British Empire. Revived by Elton and George Michael (MCA, '90).

I FEEL LIKE A BULLET (IN THE GUN OF ROBERT FORD)
Producer: Gus Dudgeon
Album: Rock of the Westies
Record Label: MCA
Songwriters: Elton John, Bernie Taupin

One of Bernie's best metaphors, reminiscent of Dylan's "I might look like Robert Ford but I feel just like Jesse James," from "Outlaw Blues."

1975

ISLAND GIRL
Producer: Gus Dudgeon
Album: Rock of the Westies
Record Label: MCA
Songwriters: Elton John, Bernie Taupin

His biggest solo hit of the '70s.

PHILADELPHIA FREEDOM
Producer: Gus Dudgeon
Album: Elton John's Greatest Hits (Vol. II)
Record Label: MCA
Songwriters: Elton John, Bernie Taupin

Named after Billie Jean King's pro tennis team.

SOMEONE SAVED MY LIFE TONIGHT
Producer: Gus Dudgeon
Album: Captain Fantastic and the Red Dirt Cowboy
Record Label: MCA
Songwriters: Elton John, Bernie Taupin

1976

DON'T GO BREAKING MY HEART
Producer: Gus Dudgeon
Album: Elton John's Greatest Hits (Vol. II)
Record Label: Rocket
Songwriters: Elton John, Bernie Taupin

His biggest all-time hit save his latter-day Disney-era Pop ballads, a duet with Kiki Dee.

SORRY SEEMS TO BE THE HARDEST WORD
Producer: Gus Dudgeon
Album: Blue Moves
Record Label: Rocket
Songwriters: Elton John, Bernie Taupin

Nearly getting down to self-examination. Suggested segue: "I'm Sorry" by John Denver.

1977

MAMA CAN'T BUY YOU LOVE
Producer: Thom Bell
Album: The Thom Bell Sessions
Record Label: MCA
Songwriters: Elton John, Bernie Taupin

Elton visits a Soul guru.

1980

LITTLE JEANNIE
Producers: Clive Franks, Elton John
Album: 21 at 33
Record Label: MCA
Songwriters: Gary Osborne, Elton John

Elton at mid-life crisis.

1982

EMPTY GARDEN (HEY HEY JOHNNY)
Album: Jump Up
Record Label: Geffen
Songwriters: Elton John, Bernie Taupin

1983

I GUESS THAT'S WHY THEY CALL IT THE BLUES
Producer: Chris Thomas
Album: Too Low for Zero
Record Label: Geffen
Songwriters: Elton John, Bernie Taupin

Approaching a second heyday.

I'M STILL STANDING
Producer: Chris Thomas
Album: Elton John's Greatest Hits
Record Label: Geffen
Songwriters: Elton John, Bernie Taupin

A credo for benchless piano men everywhere. Jerry Lee Lewis approved.

1984

SAD SONGS (SAY SO MUCH)
Producer: Chris Thomas
Album: Breaking Hearts
Record Label: Geffen
Songwriters: Elton John, Bernie Taupin

Sequel to "I Guess That's Why They Call It the Blues."

1986

NIKITA
Producer: Gus Dudgeon
Album: Ice on Fire
Record Label: Warner Brothers
Songwriters: Elton John, Bernie Taupin

Suggested segues: "Leningrad" by Billy Joel; "Russians" by Sting, "Back in the U.S.S.R." by the Beatles.

1992

THE ONE
Album: The One
Record Label: MCA
Songwriters: Elton John, Bernie Taupin

SIMPLE LIFE
Producer: Chris Thomas
Album: The One
Record Label: MCA
Songwriters: Elton John, Bernie Taupin, Chris Thomas

LITTLE WILLIE JOHN
1956

FEVER
Producer: Henry Glover
Album: Fever
Record Label: King
Songwriters: Otis Blackwell (John Davenport), Joe Seneca (Eddie Cooley)

Top-selling and much-revered #1 R&B/Top-30 R&R standard. Covered by Peggy Lee (Capitol, '58), Elvis Presley (RCA, '60) and the McCoys (Bang, '65).

NEED YOUR LOVE SO BAD
Producer: Henry Glover
Album: Little Willie John
Record Label: King
Songwriter: Willie John

His second Top-10 R&B hit, covered by Irma Thomas (Imperial, '64) and Fleetwood Mac (Sire, '67).

1958

TALK TO ME, TALK TO ME
Producer: Henry Glover
Album: There Is Someone in This World for Me
Record Label: King
Songwriter: Joe Seneca

His biggest crossover hit of the '50s; Top-10 R&B/Top-20 R&R. Covered by Sunny & the Sunglows (Tear Drop, '63).

THERE IS SOMEONE IN THIS WORLD FOR ME
Producer: Henry Glover
Album: There Is Someone in This World for Me
Record Label: King
Songwriter: Darlynn Bonner

One of his best performances.

1959

LEAVE MY KITTEN ALONE
Record Label: King
Songwriters: Willie John, Titus Turner, J. McDougal

R&B/R&R crossover. Covered by the Final Gear (Pye, '64). Performed by the Beatles early in their career; released (Capital, '96).

LET THEM TALK
Producer: Henry Glover
Record Label: King
Songwriters: Sonny Thompson, Henry Glover

More tortured Soul from the original king of pain.

1960

SLEEP
Producer: Henry Glover
Record Label: King
Songwriters: Eric Burtnett, Adam Giebel

His biggest hit; Top-10 R&B/Top-15 R&R.

ROBERT JOHN
1979

SAD EYES
Producer: George Tobin
Album: Robert John
Record Label: EMI-America
Songwriter: Robert John

Frankie Vallie-esque falsetto.

SAMMY JOHNS
1975

CHEVY VAN
Album: Sammy Johns
Record Label: GRC
Songwriter: Sammy Johns

#1 C&W/Top-10 R&R crossover for the first anti-classic car song. Suggested segues: "Convoy" by C. W. McCall, "Like a Rock" by Bob Seger.

JOHNNIE AND JACKEY
1961

SOMEDAY WE'LL BE TOGETHER
Record Label: Tri-Phi
Songwriters: Johnnie Bristol, Jackey Beavers, Harvey Fuqua

Epitomizing the patent insincerity of the latter-day Supremes, their farewell single was neither especially written for the occasion nor actually sung by the Supremes. Diana and a pair of stand-in Supremes sang this nine-year-old tune, first immortalized by Bristol in a duet with Jackey Beavers that went nowhere on the charts. It was the Supremes' fifth #1 R&B/#1 R&R crossover.

JOHNNIE AND JOE
1957

OVER THE MOUNTAIN, ACROSS THE SEA
Record Label: Chess
Songwriter: Rex Garvin

Essential group harmony ode, wistful and symbolic.

JOHNNY & THE HURRICANES
1959

RED RIVER ROCK
Record Label: Warwick
Songwriters: Tom King, Ira Mack, Fred Mendelsohn

Big winner in the post Duane Eddy twangy guitar goldrush.

JOHNNY HATES JAZZ
1988

SHATTERED DREAMS
Producers: Calvin Hayes, Mike Nocito
Album: Turn Back the Clock
Record Label: Virgin
Songwriter: Clark Datchler

Top-10 U.S. a year after it was Top-10 U.K.

ERIC JOHNSON
1991

CLIFFS OF DOVER
Album: Ah Via Musicom
Record Label: Capitol
Songwriter: Eric Johnson

New guitar virtuoso performance.

JESSE JOHNSON
1985

BE YOUR MAN
Producer: Jesse Johnson
Album: Jesse Johnson's Revue
Record Label: A&M
Songwriter: Jesse Johnson

Former guitarist for the Time.

KEVIN JOHNSON

1986

CRAZAY

Producer: Jesse Johnson
Album: Shockadelica
Record Label: A&M
Songwriter: Jesse Johnson

Former guitarist with Prince's first band finds a kindred spirit in this collaboration with Sly Stone.

KEVIN JOHNSON

1973

(ROCK 'N' ROLL I GAVE YOU) THE BEST YEARS OF MY LIFE

Record Label: Mainstream
Songwriter: Kevin Johnson

Dismally poignant picture of the perennial Rock and Roll scuffler. Suggested segue: "Lodi" by Creedence Clearwater Revival. Ironically, Mac Davis' cover (Columbia, '75) was nearly a hit.

LONNIE JOHNSON

1948

TOMORROW NIGHT

Record Label: King
Songwriters: Sam Coslow, Will Grosz

Swing standard introduced by Horace Heidt (Columbia, '39) became, in the hands of Johnson, an electric guitar classic. Covered by LaVern Baker, Charles Brown, Big Joe Turner, Etta Jones, Elvis Presley. #1 R&B/Top-20 R&R.

LOU JOHNSON

1964

(THERE'S) ALWAYS SOMETHING THERE TO REMIND ME

Record Label: Big Hill
Songwriters: Burt Bacharach, Hal David

Covered by Naked Eyes (EMI-America, '83).

KENTUCKY BLUEBIRD

Record Label: Big Hill
Songwriters: Burt Bacharach, Hal David

Covered by Dionne Warwick as "Take a Message to Michael" (Scepter, '66).

MARV JOHNSON

1958

COME TO ME

Album: Marvelous Marv Johnson
Record Label: United Artists
Songwriters: Marvin Johnson, Berry Gordy Jr.

Early echoes of the coming Detroit sound of Motown, the first release on Berry's Gordy label which was then licensed to United Artists.

1959

I LOVE THE WAY YOU LOVE

Album: Marvelous Marv Johnson
Record Label: United Artists
Songwriters: Berry Gordy Jr., Mikaljohn

His biggest hit; Top-5 R&B/Top-10 R&R.

YOU GOT WHAT IT TAKES

Album: Marvelous Marv Johnson
Record Label: United Artists
Songwriters: Berry Gordy Jr., Roquel Davis (Tyran Carlo), Gwen Gordy

Swinging past Motown straight into soul, with a Top-10 R&B/R&R crossover.

SYL JOHNSON

1969

IS IT BECAUSE I'M BLACK?

Record Label: Twinight
Songwriters: Jimmie Jones, Glenn Watts

His biggest R&B hit.

1973

WE DID IT

Producer: Willie Mitchell
Album: Back for a Taste of Your Love
Record Label: Hi
Songwriter: Charles E. McCormick

From the Al Green stable.

FREEDY JOHNSTON

1994

BAD REPUTATION

Producer: Butch Vig
Album: Perfect World
Record Label: Elektra
Songwriter: Freedy Johnston

Prime Midwestern Folk Rock; the sound of the '90s college campus.

EDDIE "GUITAR SLIM" JONES

1954

THINGS THAT I USED TO DO

Producer: Ray Charles
Record Label: Specialty
Songwriter: Eddie "Guitar Slim" Jones

Classic #1 R&B Blues track, covered by James Brown (Kent, '64), Chuck Berry (Chess, '64), Jimi Hendrix (Reprise, '69) and Stevie Ray Vaughan (Epic, '84).

GEORGE JONES

1959

WHITE LIGHTNING

Record Label: Mercury
Songwriter: J. P. Richardson

First Pop hit for the former Rockabilly singer turned archetypal Country crooner is a #1 C&W/Bottom-40 R&R crossover.

GLORIA JONES

1964

TAINTED LOVE

Record Label: Champion
Songwriter: Ed Cobb

Moody R&B gem, covered by Soft Cell (Sire, '81).

GRACE JONES

1981

PULL UP TO THE BUMPER

Producers: Sly Dunton, Robbie Shakespeare
Album: Nightclubbing
Record Label: Island
Songwriters: Sly Dunton, Robbie Shakespeare, Dan Manno

Mondo-bizarro model turned Disco singer delivers her ultimate manifesto.

HOWARD JONES

1985

THINGS CAN ONLY GET BETTER

Producers: Phil Collins, Hugh Padgham
Album: Things Can Only Get Better
Record Label: Elektra
Songwriter: Howard Jones

Riding the wave of British Synth Pop.

1986

NO ONE IS TO BLAME
    Producer: Phil Collins
    Album: Action Replay
    Record Label: Elektra
    Songwriter: Howard Jones
His biggest hit.

JIMMY JONES
1960

GOOD TIMIN'
    Producer: Otis Blackwell
    Album: Good Timin'
    Record Label: Cub
    Songwriters: Clint Ballard Jr., Fred
      Tobias
*Frankie Lymon-inspired Top-10 R&B/R&R
crossover.*

HANDY MAN
    Producer: Otis Blackwell
    Record Label: Cub
    Songwriters: Otis Blackwell, Jimmy
      Jones
*His biggest hit. Covered by James Taylor
(Columbia, '77).*

JOE JONES
1960

YOU TALK TOO MUCH
    Album: You Talk Too Much
    Record Label: Roulette
    Songwriters: Joe Jones, Reginald
      Hall
*Top-10 R&B/R&R crossover from New
Orleans.*

ORAN "JUICE" JONES
1986

THE RAIN
    Album: Juice
    Record Label: Columbia
    Songwriter: Vince Bell

PAUL JONES
1967

SET ME FREE (PRIVILEGE)
    Album: *Privilege* Soundtrack
    Record Label: Uni
    Songwriters: Mike Leander, Mark
      London
From the influential Rock movie Privilege, *by
the lead singer of Manfred Mann. Covered
by the Patti Smith Group (Arista, '78).*

QUINCY JONES
1978

STUFF LIKE THAT
    Producer: Quincy Jones
    Album: Sounds . . . and Stuff Like
      That
    Record Label: A&M
    Songwriters: Nick Ashford, Valerie
      Simpson, Quincy Jones, Steve Gadd,
      Eric Gale, Richard Tee, Ralph
      Macdonald
*The cream of session high society give
Quincy a #1 R&B/Top-30 R&R hit.*

1981

JUST ONCE
    Producer: Quincy Jones
    Album: The Dude
    Record Label: A&M
    Songwriters: Barry Mann, Cynthia
      Weil
*The ultimate adult R&B ballad, with James
Ingram on vocals.*

ONE HUNDRED WAYS
    Producer: Quincy Jones
    Album: The Dude
    Record Label: A&M
    Songwriters: Kathy Wakefield,
      Benjamin Wright, Tony Coleman
More sophisticated R&B.

1989

THE SECRET GARDEN
(SWEET SEDUCTION SUITE)
    Producer: Quincy Joncs
    Album: Back on the Block
    Record Label: Warner Brothers
    Songwriters: Rod Temperton, Snuff
      Garrett, Quincy Jones, El DeBarge
*Another all-star jam, featuring Al B. Sure,
goes #1 R&B/Top-40 R&R.*

TOMORROW (A BETTER YOU, A
BETTER ME)
    Producer: Quincy Jones
    Album: Back on the Block
    Record Label: Warner Brothers
    Songwriters: George Johnson,
      Lewis Johnson, Snuff Garrett
*#1 R&B/Bottom-40 crossover with new
protege Tevin Campbell, who some considered a Jackson 5-era Michael throwback.*

RICKIE LEE JONES
1979

CHUCK E.'S IN LOVE
    Producers: Russ Titelman, Lenny
      Waronker
    Album: Rickie Lee Jones
    Record Label: Warner Brothers
    Songwriter: Rickie Lee Jones
Bohemian Be-Bop goes Top-5 R&R.

1981

WE BELONG TOGETHER
    Album: Pirates
    Record Label: Warner Brothers
    Songwriter: Rickie Lee Jones
Hippie street theatrics.

1982

LIVING IT UP
    Album: Pirates
    Record Label: Warner Brothers
    Songwriter: Rickie Lee Jones
Female Tom Waits in waiting.

1989

HORSES
    Producer: Walter Becker
    Album: Flying Cowboys
    Record Label: Geffen
    Songwriters: Rickie Lee Jones,
      Walter Becker
A meeting of Rock's hipster elite.

TOM JONES
1965

IT'S NOT UNUSUAL
    Album: It's Not Unusual
    Record Label: Parrot
    Songwriters: Les Reed, Gordon
      Mills
*Pop Rock belter from the Woody Allen film
What's New Pussycat?*

JANIS JOPLIN
1962

WHAT GOOD CAN DRINKING DO?
    Producer: John Riney
    Record Label: Sony Legacy
    Songwriter: Janis Joplin
*Just sitting around the house with some
friends in Texas, sipping Southern Comfort,
Janis Joplin realized she could sing. This
was an early demo, collected on a posthumous anthology.*

1969

KOSMIC BLUES

Producer: Gabriel Mekler
Album: I Got Dem Ol' Kosmic Blues Again Mama
Record Label: Columbia
Songwriters: Gabriel Mekler, Janis Joplin

Her first chart hit after leaving Big Brother and the Holding Company—an impassioned, imprisoned lament.

1970

HALF MOON

Producer: Paul Rothchild
Album: Pearl
Record Label: Columbia
Songwriter: John Hall

MERCEDES BENZ

Producer: Paul Rothchild
Album: Pearl
Record Label: Columbia
Songwriters: Janis Joplin, Bobby Neuwirth, Mike McClure

The mother of all classic car songs—classic car: the Mercedes Benz. Eventually used in a Mercedes Benz commercial in '95.

MOVE OVER

Producer: Paul Rothchild
Album: Pearl
Record Label: Columbia
Songwriter: Janis Joplin

LOUIS JORDAN AND HIS TYMPANI FIVE

1944

IS YOU IS OR IS YOU AIN'T MY BABY?

Producer: Milt Gabler
Record Label: Decca
Songwriters: Louis Jordan, Billy Austin

Incredible #1 C&W/R&B/#2 Pop crossover from the Marlene Dietrich movie Follow the Boys, was the B-side of "G.I. Jive" and launched Jordan as a triple threat grits and boogie man. Covered by Buster Brown (Fire, '60) and Joe Jackson (A&M, '81).

1946

AIN'T NOBODY HERE BUT US CHICKENS

Producer: Milt Gabler
Record Label: Decca

Songwriters: Joan Whitney, Alex Kramer

#1 R&B/Top-10 R&R crossover.

CHOO CHOO CH'BOOGIE

Producer: Milt Gabler
Record Label: Decca
Songwriters: Vaughan Horton, Denver Darling, Milt Gabler

One of the biggest #1 R&B hits of all time, and a Top-10 R&R crossover.

LET THE GOOD TIMES ROLL

Producer: Milt Gabler
Record Label: Decca
Songwriters: Louis Jordan, Claude Demetrius

Pioneering Jump Blues artist and track. Covered by Ray Charles (Atlantic, '60). Jordan had the attitude and the spirit of Rock and Roll, as well as the wit, the wisdom, the hipster's jive, and the willingness to commercialize. Some thirty years down the line, his material would beat Leiber & Stoller's to the Broadway stage in Five Guys Named Moe.

1947

JACK YOU'RE DEAD

Producer: Milt Gabler
Record Label: Decca
Songwriters: Richard Miles, Walter Bishop

Hipster treatise on the art of Jive. Covered by Joe Jackson (A&M, '81).

1949

AIN'T THAT JUST LIKE A WOMAN?

Producer: Milt Gabler
Record Label: Decca
Songwriters: Fleecie Moore, Claude Demetrius

Another funky, cheeky rolling Blues rocker. Covered by a big Jordan fan, Fats Domino (Imperial, '61). Suggested segue: Chuck Berry's guitar intro to "Johnny B. Goode."

SATURDAY NIGHT FISH FRY

Producer: Milt Gabler
Record Label: Decca
Songwriters: Louis Jordan, Ellis Walsh

Wine, women, song, plus a visit from the police, a perfect #1 R&B/Top-30 R&R recipe for the upcoming Rock and Roll rebellion.

JOURNEY

1978

WHEEL IN THE SKY

Producer: Roy Thomas Baker
Album: Infinity
Record Label: Columbia
Songwriters: Neal Schon, Robert Fleischman, Diane Valory

San Francisco hard Rock, with mystical overtones.

1980

ANY WAY YOU WANT IT

Producers: Geoff Workman, Kevin Elson
Album: Departure
Record Label: Columbia
Songwriters: Steve Perry, Neil Schon

Defining their Arena Power Pop.

1981

DON'T STOP BELIEVIN'

Producers: Mike Stone, Kevin Elson
Album: Escape
Record Label: Columbia
Songwriters: Steve Perry, Neal Schon, Jonathon Cain

Paving the way for Lite Metal.

WHO'S CRYING NOW

Producers: Mike Stone, Kevin Elson
Album: Escape
Record Label: Columbia
Songwriters: Steve Perry, Jonathan Cain

Their first big hit, on the strength of Perry's soaring vocal chords.

1982

OPEN ARMS

Producers: Mike Stone, Kevin Elson
Album: Escape
Record Label: Columbia
Songwriters: Steve Perry, Jonathan Cain

Their biggest hit.

1983

SEPARATE WAYS (WORLDS APART)

Producers: Mike Stone, Kevin Elson
Album: Frontiers
Record Label: Columbia
Songwriters: Steve Perry, Jonathan Cain

Tear-jerking Metal ballad.

1986

BE GOOD TO YOURSELF
Producer: Steve Perry
Album: Raised on Radio
Record Label: Columbia
Songwriters: Steve Perry, Jonathan Cain, Neal Schon

JOY DIVISION
1980

LOVE WILL TEAR US APART
Producer: Martin Hannett
Album: Substance
Record Label: Factory/Qwest
Songwriters: Ian Curtis, Joy Division

Acidic Punk Metal lament became legendary when Curtis committed suicide just before the band's first American tour. After his death the group reformed as the technologically correct New Order.

SHE'S LOST CONTROL
Producer: Martin Hannett
Album: Unknown Pleasures
Record Label: Factory
Songwriter: Joy Division

Manchester during the war.

JUDAS PRIEST
1979

GREEN MANILISHI (WITH THE TWO PRONGED CROWN)
Producer: James Guthrie
Album: Hell Bent for Leather
Record Label: Columbia
Songwriter: Peter Green

Where the British extremes of Blues and Heavy Metal meet at ex-Fleetwood Mac guitarist Peter Green.

1981

YOU'VE GOT ANOTHER THING COMIN'
Producer: Tom Allom
Album: Screaming for Vengeance
Record Label: Columbia
Songwriters: Rob Halford, Kenneth Downing, Glenn Tipton

Their Metal anthem.

JUMP 'N THE SADDLE
1983

THE CURLY SHUFFLE
Record Label: Atlantic
Songwriter: Peter Quinn

Suggested segue: Aerosmith's ode to the Three Stooges, "Walk This Way."

BILL JUSTIS
1957

RAUNCHY
Album: Cloud Nine
Record Label: Phillips-International
Songwriters: Bill Justis Jr., Sidney Manker

Perfectly named instrumental: Justis on sax, Sid Manker on guitar: Duane Eddy, Link Wray, Dick Dale waiting in the wings to explode.

K

ERNIE K-DOE
1961

A CERTAIN GIRL
Producer: Allen Toussaint
Record Label: Minit
Songwriter: Allen Toussaint (Naomi Neville)

New Orleans classic. Covered by the Final Gear (Pye, '64) (produced by Jimmy Page), the Yardbirds (Epic, '65) as the B-side of "I Wish You Would," and Warren Zevon (Asylum, '80).

MOTHER-IN-LAW
Producer: Allen Toussaint
Album: Mother-in-Law
Record Label: Minit
Songwriter: Allen Toussaint

A #1 R&B/R&R New Orleans crossover, establishing Toussaint as the Boss of Bourbon Street.

TONIO K.
1986

PERFECT WORLD
Album: Romeo Unchained
Record Label: What/A&M
Songwriters: Glen Burnick, Steve Krikorian (Tonio K.)

Caustic singer/songwriter at his most chipper. Covered by co-writer Burnick (A&M, '86). Also in the '92 movies Don't Tell Mom the Babysitter's Dead and Son-in-Law.

K. C. & THE SUNSHINE BAND
1975

GET DOWN TONIGHT
Producers: Harry Casey, Richard Finch
Album: K. C. and the Sunshine Band
Record Label: TK
Songwriters: Harry Casey, Richard Finch

#1 R&B/R&R crossover; first #1 R&B song by a white-led band since Jimmy Gilmer's "Sugar Shack" in '63.

THAT'S THE WAY (I LIKE IT)
Producers: Harry Casey, Richard Finch
Album: K. C. and the Sunshine Band
Record Label: TK
Songwriters: Harry Casey, Richard Finch

Their second straight #1 R&B/R&R crossover.

1976

(SHAKE, SHAKE, SHAKE) SHAKE YOUR BOOTY
Producers: Harry Casey, Richard Finch
Album: Part 3
Record Label: TK
Songwriters: Harry Casey, Richard Finch

Yet another #1 R&B/R&R crossover. When you add their five #1 hits to the fact that Casey and Finch also produced "Rock Your Baby" by George McCrae, you can see why they, and not John Travolta or the Bee Gees, should be known as the undisputed kings of Disco, though they preferred to think of it as Rhythm and Blues.

1977

I'M YOUR BOOGIE MAN
Producers: Harry Casey, Richard Finch
Album: Part 3
Record Label: TK
Songwriters: Harry Casey, Richard Finch

Milking the perfect '70s dance groove.

KEEP IT COMIN', LOVE
Producers: Harry Casey, Richard Finch
Album: Part 3
Record Label: TK

Songwriters: Harry Casey, Richard Finch

#1 R&B/Top-10 R&R.

1979

PLEASE DON'T GO

Producers: Harry Casey, Richard Finch

Album: Do You Wanna Go Party

Record Label: TK

Songwriters: Harry Casey, Richard Finch

Their last #1, a ballad.

JOSHUA KADISON

1993

JESSIE

Producers: Rod Argent, Peter Van Hooke

Album: Painted Desert Seranade

Record Label: SBK

Songwriter: Joshua Kadison

Neo-Elton John Pop rocker.

BRENDA KAHN

1992

MINT JULEPS AND NEEDLES

Producer: Brenda Kahn

Album: Epiphany in Brooklyn

Record Label: Chaos

Songwriter: Brenda Kahn

Dylan-esque portrait of '90s womanhood.

SHE'S IN LOVE

Producer: David Kahne

Album: Epiphany in Brooklyn

Record Label: Chaos

Songwriter: Brenda Kahn

Post-Bangles waif toughs it out on the streets of anti-Folk Rock.

KAJAGOOGOO

1983

TOO SHY

Producer: Nick Rhodes

Album: White Feathers

Record Label: Capitol

Songwriters: Chris Hamill (Limahl), Nick Beggs

Synth-wave surfers.

KALEIDOSCOPE

1968

BEACON FROM MARS

Album: A Beacon from Mars

Record Label: Epic

Songwriter: Kaleidoscope

Mega Middle Eastern Rock extravaganza for David Linley's psychedelic unit. Led Zeppelin and Camper Van Beethoven would profit from the experience.

THE KALIN TWINS

1958

WHEN

Album: Kalin Twins

Record Label: Decca

Songwriter: Paul Evans

Irresistible Calpyso-flavored ditty.

INI KAMOSE

1994

HERE COMES THE HOTSTEPPER

Producer: S. Remi

Album: *Pret à Porter* Soundtrack

Record Label: Columbia

Songwriters: Ini Kamose, Salaam Gibbs, Chris Kenner, Kenton Nix Domino, A. Kinley

Prominence in the Altman high-fashion film boosted this vintage Reggae gem to #1 R&R.

BIG DADDY KANE

1988

LONG LIVE THE KANE

Album: Long Live the Kane

Record Label: Cold Chillin'

Songwriter: Antonio Hardy (Big Daddy Kane)

Self-promotional Rap.

KANSAS

1976

CARRY ON WAYWARD SON

Producer: Jeff Glixman

Album: Leftoverture

Record Label: Kirshner

Songwriter: Kerry Livgren

Inspirational Arena Folk Metal anthem was their first hit.

1977

DUST IN THE WIND

Producer: Jeff Glixman

Album: Point of Know Return

Record Label: Kirshner

Songwriter: Kerry Livgren

Delicate acoustic dirge. Suggested segue: "(Don't Fear) the Reaper" by Blue Oyster Cult.

THOMAS JEFFERSON KAYE

1974

AMERICAN LOVERS

Producer: Gary Katz

Album: First Grade

Record Label: ABC/Dunhill

Songwriters: Donald Fagen, Walter Becker

The great lost Steely Dan track.

KEITH

1966

98.6

Producer: Jerry Ross

Album: 98.6/Ain't Gonna Lie

Record Label: Mercury

Songwriters: Tony Powers, George Fischoff

Basic AM radio reassurance in the midst of the nascent Rock revolution.

JERRY KELLER

1959

HERE COMES SUMMER

Album: Here Comes Jerry Keller

Record Label: Kapp

Songwriter: Jerry Keller

Back when summer songs were an art and a science.

R. KELLY

1992

DEDICATED

Producer: Robert Kelly

Album: Born into the '90s

Record Label: Jive

Songwriter: Robert Kelly

The advent of a new bedroom R&B crooner.

HONEY LOVE

Producer: Robert Kelly

Album: Born into the '90s

Record Label: Jive

Songwriter: Robert Kelly

Evoking the sweet salacious grind of Clyde McPhatter.

SLOW DANCE (HEY MR. DJ)
Producer: Robert Kelly
Album: Born into the '90s
Record Label: Jive
Songwriter: Robert Kelly

1994

BUMP AND GRIND
Producer: Robert Kelly
Album: 12 Play
Record Label: Jive
Songwriter: Robert Kelly

#1 R&B/R&R come-on leads into his most fertile period.

JOHNNY KEMP

1988

JUST GOT PAID
Producers: Teddy Riley, Johnny Kemp
Album: Secrets of Flying
Record Label: Columbia
Songwriters: Johnny Kemp, Gene Griffin

#1 R&B/Top-10 R&R crossover.

1989

BIRTHDAY SUIT
Album: *Sing* Soundtrack
Record Label: Columbia
Songwriters: Rhett Lawrence, Dean Pitchford

TARA KEMP

1991

HOLD YOU TIGHT
Producer: Jake Smith
Album: Tara Kemp
Record Label: Giant
Songwriters: William Hammond, Tuhin Roy, Jake Smith

New Pop dance one-shot.

EDDIE KENDRICKS

1972

GIRL YOU NEED A CHANGE OF MIND (PART I)
Album: People . . . Hold On
Record Label: Tamla
Songwriters: Leonard Caston, Anita Poree

Often cited as the first real Disco record.

1973

KEEP ON TRUCKIN'
Producers: Frank Wilson, Leonard Caston
Album: Eddie Kendricks
Record Label: Tamla
Songwriters: Frank Wilson, Leonard Caston, Anita Poree

#1 R&B/R&R pre-Disco/Disco hit for the former Temptations frontman.

1974

BOOGIE DOWN!
Producers: Frank Wilson, Leonard Caston
Album: Boogie Down!
Record Label: Tamla
Songwriters: Anita Poree, Frank Wilson, Leonard Caston

#1 R&B/Top-10 R&R crossover.

1975

SHOESHINE BOY
Album: For You
Record Label: Tamla
Songwriters: Harry Booker, Linda Allen

#1 R&B/Top-20 R&R crossover.

CHRIS KENNER

1957

SICK AND TIRED
Producer: Dave Bartholemew
Record Label: Imperial
Songwriters: Dave Bartholomew, Chris Kenner

Early work from the itinerant New Orleans wunderkind. Covered by Fats Domino (Imperial, '58).

1961

I LIKE IT LIKE THAT
Producer: Allen Toussaint
Record Label: Instant
Songwriters: Chris Kenner, Allen Toussaint

Crescent City Soul goes national with this choogling #2 R&B/R&R crossover. Covered by the Dave Clark Five (Epic, '65).

1963

LAND OF A THOUSAND DANCES
Producer: Allen Toussaint
Album: Land of a Thousand Dances
Record Label: Instant
Songwriter: Chris Kenner

A New Orleans classic. Covered by Fats

Domino (Imperial, '63), Cannibal and the Headhunters (Rampart, '65) and Wilson Pickett (Atlantic, '66).

CHAKA KHAN

1978

I'M EVERY WOMAN
Producer: Arif Mardin
Album: Chaka
Record Label: Warner Brothers
Songwriters: Nick Ashford, Valerie Simpson

Her signature declaration; #1 R&B/Top-30 R&R crossover. Covered by Whitney Houston in the movie The Bodyguard *(Arista, '92).*

1981

WHAT CHA' GONNA DO FOR ME
Album: What Cha' Gonna Do for Me
Record Label: Warner Brothers
Songwriters: James Stuart, Ned Doheny

#1 R&B/Top-60 R&R crossover.

KID CREOLE AND THE COCONUTS

1981

IN THE JUNGLE
Producer: August Darnell
Album: Fresh Fruit in Foreign Places
Record Label: Sire/Ze
Songwriter: August Darnell

Dr. Buzzard co-founder's parody of the Odyssey, *optioned by theatre impressario Joseph Papp.*

1982

ANNIE, I'M NOT YOUR DADDY
Producer: August Darnell
Album: Wise Guy
Record Label: Sire/Ze
Songwriter: August Darnell

A poignant Disco-era lost classic that hit it big in England.

JOHNNY KIDD AND THE PIRATES

1960

SHAKIN' ALL OVER
Record Label: HMV
Songwriter: Fred Heath (Johnny Kidd)

Presley-esque rocker. Covered by Guess Who (Scepter, '65).

KID 'N PLAY
1990

FUNHOUSE
Album: Kid 'N Play's Funhouse
Record Label: Select
Songwriters: Christopher Reid, Christopher Martin

Featured in their Hip-Hop film House Party.

THE GREG KIHN BAND
1983

JEOPARDY
Producer: Matthew King Kaufman
Album: With the Naked Eye
Record Label: Beserkley
Songwriters: Greg Kihn, Steven Wright

Loopy West Coast rocker's biggest hit.

1987

THE BREAKUP SONG (THEY DON'T WRITE 'EM)
Producer: Matthew King Kaufman
Album: Rockihnroll
Record Label: Beserkley
Songwriters: Greg Kihn, Steven Wright, Gary Philips

Jonathan Richman's labelmates show a knack for the power Pop move.

KILLING JOKE
1985

LOVE LIKE BLOOD
Producer: Chris Kimsey
Album: Night Time
Record Label: EG
Songwriter: Killing Joke

Metal mashers at their most accessible; a hit in England.

ANDY KIM
1974

ROCK ME GENTLY
Producer: Michael Omartian
Album: Andy Kim
Record Label: Capitol
Songwriter: Andy Youachim (Andy Kim)

The essence of Lite Rock.

KING CRIMSON
1969

21ST CENTURY SCHIZOID MAN
Producer: King Crimson
Album: In the Court of the Crimson King
Record Label: Atlantic
Songwriters: Robert Fripp, Ian MacDonald, Greg Lake, Mike Giles, Pete Sinfield

Progressive supergroup at its most paranormal.

COURT OF THE CRIMSON KING
Producer: King Crimson
Album: In the Court of the Crimson King
Record Label: Atlantic
Songwriters: Pete Sinfield, Ian McDonald

Their promethean signature epic, opening the gates for the only English Rock invasion not inspired by any form of Rhythm and Blues.

KING CURTIS
1962

SOUL TWIST
Album: Soul Serenade
Record Label: Enjoy/Capitol
Songwriter: Curtis Ousley (King Curtis)

#1 R&B/Top-20 R&R crossover for the sax giant.

KING FLOYD
1970

GROOVE ME BABY
Record Label: Chimneyville
Songwriter: King Floyd

#1 R&B/Top-10 R&R crossover.

KING HARVEST
1973

DANCING IN THE MOONLIGHT
Producer: Berjot Robinson
Album: Dancing in the Moonlight
Record Label: Perception
Songwriter: Sherman Kelly

Music for an eerie tribal ritual, reminiscent of the Band's "King Harvest (Has Surely Come)."

ALBERT KING
1967

BORN UNDER A BAD SIGN
Producer: Jim Stewart
Album: King of the Blues Guitar
Record Label: Stax
Songwriters: Booker T. Jones, William Bell

Soul Blues standard, Covered by Booker T. and the MGs (Stax, '68), the Paul Butterfield Blues Band (Elektra, '68) and Cream (RSO, '68).

1969

AS THE YEARS GO PASSING BY
Record Label: Atlantic
Songwriter: Deadric Malone

Classic Soul Blues, covered by the Animals (MGM, '69), George Thorogood (EMI-America, '82), Gary Moore (Charisma, '90).

B. B. KING
1951

3 O'CLOCK BLUES
Record Label: RPM
Songwriter: Lowell Fulson

The legendary Blues guitarist's first appearance on the R&B chart, a #1.

1952

BE CAREFUL WITH A FOOL
Record Label: RPM
Songwriters: B. B. King, Jules Taub

Hit R&R charts in '57. Covered by Johnny Winter (Columbia, '69).

YOU KNOW I LOVE YOU
Record Label: R.P.M.
Songwriters: B. B. King, Jules Taub

His second straight #1 R&B.

1952

PLEASE LOVE ME
Record Label: RPM
Songwriters: B. B. King, Jules Taub

1954

YOU UPSET ME, BABY
Album: Live at the Regal
Record Label: RPM
Songwriters: Maxwell Davis, Joe Josea

Classic cut from one of the most important electric guitar albums of the era, revered a decade later by Jerry Garcia, Jimi Hendrix, and Michael Bloomfield, and a generation of Englishmen.

1961

SWEET SIXTEEN
Album: Live in Cook County Jail
Record Label: Kent
Songwriters: B. B. King, Joe Josea
His biggest R&B hit of the '60s.

1962

HOW BLUE CAN YOU GET
Record Label: Kent
Songwriters: B. B. King, Joe Josea
His and Lucille's enduring signature.

1964

ROCK ME BABY
Producer: Jules Bihari
Record Label: Kent
Songwriters: B. B. King, Jules Bihari
Grandfathering the age of Blues Rock.

1969

THE THRILL IS GONE
Producer: Bill Szymczyk
Album: Completely Well
Record Label: Bluesway
Songwriters: Lew Brown, Ray Henderson
A belated reward for his Hall of Fame career; a Top-10 R&B/Top-20 R&R hit with this '31 evergreen.

BEN E. KING

1961

SPANISH HARLEM
Producers: Jerry Leiber, Mike Stoller
Album: Spanish Harlem
Record Label: Atco
Songwriters: Jerry Leiber, Phil Spector
The Brill Building sound of the city personified. Covered by Aretha Franklin (Atlantic, '71) and Laura Nyro (Columbia, '71). Suggested segue: "Spanish Harlem Incident" by Bob Dylan.

STAND BY ME
Producers: Jerry Leiber, Mike Stoller
Album: Ben E. King's Greatest Hits
Record Label: Atco
Songwriters: Jerry Leiber, Mike Stoller, Ben E. King
#1 R&B/Top-10 R&R crossover. Based on the spiritual "Lord, Stand by Me." Revived in the '86 movie Stand by Me.

1962

DON'T PLAY THAT SONG (YOU LIED)
Producers: Jerry Wexler, Ahmet Ertegun
Album: Ben E. King's Greatest Hits
Record Label: Atco
Songwriters: Ahmet Ertegun, Betty Nelson
Covered by Aretha Franklin (Atlantic, '70).

1963

I (WHO HAVE NOTHING)
Producers: Jerry Leiber, Mike Stoller
Album: Ben E. King's Greatest Hits
Record Label: Atco
Songwriters: Jerry Leiber, Mike Stoller, Donita Mogol
Benny reaches for a dramatic Italian ballad: The Elvis/Jackie Wilson move.

1975

SUPERNATURAL THING (PART I)
Producers: Tony Silvester, Bert Coteaux
Album: Supernatural
Record Label: Atlantic
Songwriters: Gwen Guthrie, Patrick Grant
A #1 R&B/Top-10 R&R Disco-era comeback.

CAROLE KING

1962

IT MIGHT AS WELL RAIN UNTIL SEPTEMBER
Producer: Carole King
Record Label: Dimension
Songwriters: Gerry Goffin, Carole King
Parlaying a hot '61 and '62, publisher Don Kirshner's prize writer achieves her first chart record (rejected by Bobby Vee), after years of singing demos. That nasal tone would return several years later as the voice of another decade.

1963

HE'S A BAD BOY
Producer: Carole King
Record Label: Dimension
Songwriters: Gerry Goffin, Carole King
Her biggest stiff.

1971

CHILD OF MINE
Producer: John Fischbach
Album: Carole King: Writer

Record Label: Ode
Songwriter: Carole King
Preparing for the keyboard playing singer/songwriter era she (Billy Joel and Elton John) would usher in.

I FEEL THE EARTH MOVE
Producer: Lou Adler
Album: Tapestry
Record Label: Ode
Songwriter: Carole King
Ode to California living is the B-side of "It's Too Late."

IT'S TOO LATE
Producer: Lou Adler
Album: Tapestry
Record Label: Ode
Songwriters: Toni Stern, Carole King
Her only solo #1.

SO FAR AWAY
Producer: Lou Adler
Album: Tapestry
Record Label: Ode
Songwriter: Carole King

SWEET SEASONS
Producer: Lou Adler
Album: Carol King: Music
Record Label: Ode
Songwriters: Carole King, Toni Stern

TAPESTRY
Producer: Lou Adler
Album: Tapestry
Record Label: Ode
Songwriter: Carole King
Title tune from her landmark album of homemade Brooklyn Soul.

YOU'VE GOT A FRIEND
Producer: Lou Adler
Album: Tapestry
Record Label: Ode
Songwriter: Carole King
Covered by James Taylor (Warner Brothers, '71). The laid-back mellow L.A. singer/ songwriter middle-of-the-dirt-road Folk Rock sound of the '70s, defined by a couple of nasal East coast transplants. The payback for "Woodstock."

1974

JAZZMAN
Producer: Lou Adler
Album: Wrap Around Joy
Record Label: Ode

Songwriters: Carole King, Donald Palmer

Her second biggest solo hit.

NIGHTINGALE

Producer: Lou Adler
Album: Wrap Around Joy
Record Label: Ode
Songwriters: Carole King, David Palmer

1975

REALLY ROSIE

Producer: Lou Adler
Album: Really Rosie
Record Label: Ode
Songwriters: Maurice Sendak, Carole King

Plucky title tune from the musical special she wrote with the renowned children's book author Sendak.

EVELYN CHAMPAGNE KING

1978

SHAME

Producer: T. Life
Album: Smooth Talk
Record Label: RCA
Songwriters: John Fitch, Reuben Cross

Her biggest R&R hit.

1981

I'M IN LOVE

Producer: Kashif
Album: I'm in Love
Record Label: RCA
Songwriter: Kashif

#1 R&B/Top-40 R&R crossover.

1982

LOVE COME DOWN

Producer: Kashif
Album: Get Loose
Record Label: RCA
Songwriter: Kashif

#1 R&B/Top-20 R&R crossover.

FREDDIE KING

1961

HIDE AWAY

Producer: Sonny Thompson
Album: Let's Hide Away and Dance Away
Record Label: Federal

Songwriters: Sonny Thompson, Freddie King

Top-10 R&B/Top-30 R&R crossover by a master of the Blues guitar; covered by Eric Clapton, with John Mayall's Bluesbreakers (London, '65).

I'M TORE DOWN

Producer: Sonny Thompson
Album: Freddie King Sings the Blues
Record Label: Federal
Songwriter: Sonny Thompson

One of six Blues sides the guitarist placed on the R&B charts of '61, and the second to be covered by Eric Clapton (Warner Brothers, '94).

1962

HAVE YOU EVER LOVED A WOMAN

Producer: Sonny Thompson
Album: Let's Hide Away and Dance Away
Record Label: Federal
Songwriter: Billy Myles

Another Freddie King classic covered by Clapton, this time in Derek and the Dominos (Atco, '70).

JONATHAN KING

1965

EVERYONE'S GONE TO THE MOON

Album: Jonathan King or Then Again
Record Label: Parrot
Songwriter: Kenneth King

One-shot commentary by the noted English scenemaker.

THE KINGSMEN

1965

JOLLY GREEN GIANT

Album: The Kingsmen (Vol. III)
Record Label: Wand
Songwriters: Don Harris, Dewey Terry, Lynn Easton

Another Don and Dewey classic-turned-Frat-Rock-perennial by the Oregon house band. From the same album that contains their version of the Olympia, WA Wailers's "Tall Cool One." Their ineffable (and basically intelligible) "Louie Louie" is on their first album The Kingsmen in Person.

THE KINGSTON TRIO

1958

TOM DOOLEY

Producer: Voile Gillmore
Album: The Kingston Trio

Record Label: Capitol
Songwriter: Dave Guard (Arranged)

This altered traditional Blue Ridge Mountain Folk ballad is credited with launching not only the career of Capitol's largest-selling act until the Beatles, but the Folk boom of the '60s as well. Actually, what the Kingston Trio launched was the upscale collegiate answer to Doo-Wop, the current Rock and Roll sound dressed up in a cardigan sweater and covering a different strain of obscure black music. It was the reaction to this sound that produced the Folk scare rebels of the early '60s, like Bob Dylan and Phil Ochs.

1963

GREENBACK DOLLAR

Producer: Voile Gillmore
Album: New Frontier
Record Label: Capitol
Songwriters: Hoyt Axton, Ken Ramsey

Essential Folk sentiments that would later be taken to the level of lifestyle.

THE REVEREND MR. BLACK

Producer: Voile Gillmore
Album: Kingston Trio #16
Record Label: Capitol
Songwriters: Billy Edd Wheeler, Jed Peters

Based on an old Carter Family Folk tune.

SEASONS IN THE SUN

Producer: Voile Gillmore
Album: Time to Think
Record Label: Capitol
Songwriters: Rod McKuen, Jacques Brel

Folky adaptation of the Brel classic by Rock poet manqué Rod McKuen. Covered by Terry Jacks (Bell, '74).

THE KINKS

1964

ALL DAY AND ALL OF THE NIGHT

Producer: Shel Talmy
Album: Kinks Size
Record Label: Reprise
Songwriter: Ray Davies

The British invasion, Music Hall division. Feisty, rollicking, and slightly risqué Ray.

STOP YOUR SOBBING

Producer: Shel Talmy
Album: You Really Got Me

Record Label: Reprise
Songwriter: Ray Davies

Covered by the Pretenders (Sire, '80).

YOU REALLY GOT ME

Producer: Shel Talmy
Album: You Really Got Me
Record Label: Reprise
Songwriter: Ray Davies

Their second biggest hit. Cover by Van Halen was their first single (Warner Brothers, '78).

1965

TIRED OF WAITING FOR YOU

Producer: Shel Talmy
Album: Kinks Size
Record Label: Reprise
Songwriter: Ray Davies

Their biggest hit.

A WELL-RESPECTED MAN

Producer: Shel Talmy
Album: Kinks Kinkdom
Record Label: Reprise
Songwriter: Ray Davies

Revealing a Dickensian curmudgeon beneath the Music Hall shell.

WHO'LL BE THE NEXT IN LINE

Producer: Shel Talmy
Album: Kinks Kinkdom
Record Label: Reprise
Songwriter: Ray Davies

One of Ray's fiercest rockers.

1966

DEDICATED FOLLOWER OF FASHION

Producer: Shel Talmy
Album: Kinks Kinkdom
Record Label: Reprise
Songwriter: Ray Davies

Answering his own "Dandy."

I'M NOT LIKE EVERYBODY ELSE

Producer: Shel Talmy
Record Label: Reprise
Songwriter: Ray Davies

B-side of "Waterloo Sunset."

SEE MY FRIENDS

Producer: Shel Talmy
Album: Kinks Kinkdom
Record Label: Reprise
Songwriter: Ray Davies

Suggested segue: "Positively 4th Street" by Bob Dylan.

SUNNY AFTERNOON

Producer: Shel Talmy
Album: Face to Face
Record Label: Reprise
Songwriter: Ray Davies

Happy-go-lucky Ray, on the edge of doom. Suggested segue: "Taxman" by the Beatles.

1967

DEAD END STREET

Producer: Shel Talmy
Album: Kinks Kronicles
Record Label: Reprise
Songwriter: Ray Davies

Mr. Davies' favorite neighborhood.

WATERLOO SUNSET

Producer: Shel Talmy
Album: Something Else by the Kinks
Record Label: Reprise
Songwriter: Ray Davies

Originally called "Liverpool Sunset." One of his loveliest watercolors; tranquil, spacious, translucent. Suggested segue: "Daydream" by the Lovin' Spoonful.

1968

DAVID WATTS

Producer: Shel Talmy
Album: Something Else by the Kinks
Record Label: Reprise
Songwriter: Ray Davies

Covered by the Jam (Polydor, '78).

1970

APEMAN

Producer: Ray Davies
Album: Lola vs. the Powerman and the Moneygoround (Part I)
Record Label: Reprise
Songwriter: Ray Davies

The monkey motif at the next level. Suggested segue: "Monkey Man" by the Rolling Stones.

VICTORIA

Producer: Ray Davies
Album: Arthur (or the Decline and Fall of the British Empire)
Record Label: Reprise
Songwriter: Ray Davies

Ray's attempted opus; but Arthur was no Tommy.

1971

LOLA

Producer: Ray Davies
Album: Lola vs. the Powerman and the Moneygoround (Part I)
Record Label: Reprise
Songwriter: Ray Davies

Nailing the zeitgeist of the sexually indecisive Glitter generation. Covered by the Raincoats (Rough Trade, '79). Blur was listening.

1972

CELLULOID HEROES

Producer: Ray Davies
Album: Everybody's in Showbiz, Everybody's a Star
Record Label: RCA
Songwriter: Ray Davies

Suggested segue: "Candle in the Wind" by Elton John.

1977

A ROCK 'N ROLL FANTASY

Producer: Ray Davies
Album: Misfits
Record Label: Arista
Songwriter: Ray Davies

Back in a dance hall daze.

1981

DESTROYER

Album: Give the People What They Want
Record Label: Arista
Songwriter: Ray Davies

Detailing his personal battle with the modern killer, Paranoia.

1983

COME DANCING

Producer: Ray Davies
Album: State of Confusion
Record Label: Arista
Songwriter: Ray Davies

Tearing the dance hall down; the Kinks' biggest hit in nearly twenty years.

KISS

1974

DEUCE

Producers: Kenny Kerner, Richie Wise
Album: Kiss
Record Label: Casablanca

Songwriters: Stanley Eisen (Paul Stanley), Gene Simmons

Where their immediate predecessors, the New York Dolls, might have wanted to be the Rolling Stones, Kiss started out in life covering Bobby Rydell's "Kissing Time." This essential track was produced by a pair of bubblegum converts.

STRUTTER

Producers: Kenny Kerner, Richie Wise
Album: Kiss
Record Label: Casablanca
Songwriter: Gene Simmons

Glittery arena anthem for the masked band, featured on a live album, and two greatest hits collections; re-recorded in '78.

1975

ROCK AND ROLL ALL NIGHT

Producers: Neil Bogart, Kiss
Album: Dressed to Kill
Record Label: Casablanca
Songwriters: Stanley Eisen (Paul Stanley), Gene Simmons

Following up "Kissing Time" with a more appropriately metallic rocker.

1976

BETH

Producer: Bob Ezrin
Album: Destroyer
Record Label: Casablanca
Songwriters: Peter Criscuola (Peter Criss), Stanley Penridge, Bob Ezrin

Assaying the traditional arena route to the Top-10, the dreaded Rock ballad. Suggested Segue: "Dream On" by Aerosmith, "More Than a Feeling" by Boston, "Love Hurts" by Nazareth, et al.

CALLING DR. LOVE

Producer: Eddie Kramer
Album: Rock and Roll Over
Record Label: Casablanca
Songwriter: Gene Simmons

Pandering to Simmons' penchant for the lewd double entendre.

DETROIT ROCK CITY

Producer: Bob Ezrin
Album: Destroyer
Record Label: Casablanca
Songwriters: Stanley Elsen (Paul Stanley), Bob Ezrin

One of their best rocking efforts; the B-side of "Beth."

HARD LUCK WOMAN

Producer: Eddie Kramer
Album: Rock and Roll Over
Record Label: Casablanca
Songwriter: Stanley Elsen (Paul Stanley

Covered by Garth Brooks (Polygram, '94).

1977

CHRISTINE SIXTEEN

Producers: Eddie Kramer, Kiss
Album: Love Gun
Record Label: Casablanca
Songwriter: Gene Simmons

Typical slavering Gene. Suggested segue: "Stray Cat Blues" by the Rolling Stones, "Hot Blooded" by Foreigner.

LOVE GUN

Producers: Eddie Kramer, Kiss
Album: Love Gun
Record Label: Casablanca
Songwriter: Stanley Eisen (Paul Stanley)

Paul in Gene territory.

1979

I WAS MADE FOR LOVING YOU

Producer: Vini Poncia
Album: Dynasty
Record Label: Casablanca
Songwriters: Stanley Eisen (Paul Stanley), Desmond Child, Vini Poncia

1982

A WORLD WITHOUT HEROES

Producer: Bob Ezrin
Album: Music from the Elder
Record Label: Casablanca
Songwriters: Stanley Elsen (Paul Stanley), Gene Simmons, Bob Ezrin, Lou Reed

Guest starring a neighborhood contemporary, Lou Reed.

1983

LICK IT UP

Producers: Gene Simmons, M. Jackson
Album: Lick It Up
Record Label: Mercury
Songwriters: Stanley Eisen (Paul Stanley), Vinnie Vincent

Kiss unmasked as middling middle-aged Metal mongers.

1989

FOREVER

Album: Hot in the Shade
Record Label: Mercury
Songwriters: Stanley Eisen (Paul Stanley), Michael Bolton

Their second biggest hit, another ballad.

KLAATU

1977

CALLING OCCUPANTS OF INTERPLANETARY CRAFT

Producer: Klaatu
Album: Klaatu
Record Label: Capitol
Songwriters: Terry Draper, John Woloschuk

Semi-notorious Beatle hoax netted this obscure Canadian band a cover by the Carpenters (A&M, '77).

THE KLF

1991

3 A.M. ETERNAL

Producer: KLF
Album: The White Room
Record Label: Arista
Songwriters: Jimi Cauty, Bill Drummond, T. Thorpe

Spacey U.K. dance track by the Scottish merry prankster, Drummond, and his group, formerly known as the Justified Ancients of Mu Mu. Group named thier indie label Kopyright Liberation Front. Went Top-10 R&R in the U.S.

JUSTIFIED AND ANCIENT

Producer: KLF
Album: The White Room
Record Label: Arista
Songwriters: Jimi Cauty, Bill Drummond

An inspired marriage of techno and schmaltz, with the voice of Country thrush Tammy Wynette.

KLYMAXX

1985

I MISS YOU

Producers: Lynn Malsby, Klymaxx
Album: Meeting in the Ladies Room
Record Label: Constellation
Songwriter: Lynn Malsby

First and biggest hit for the influential R&B band. TLC and SWV were listening.

1986

MAN SIZE LOVE
Producer: Fenderella
Album: Klymaxx
Record Label: Constellation
Songwriter: Rod Temperton
Introduced in the film Running Scared.
Salt-n-Pepa were listening.

1987

I'D STILL SAY YES
Producer: Fenderella
Album: Klymaxx
Record Label: Constellation
Songwriters: Kenny Edmunds
   (Babyface), Gary Scelsa, Joyce
   Fenderella Irby
Their last Top-20 hit.

THE KNACK

1979

MY SHARONA
Producer: Mike Chapman
Album: Get the Knack
Record Label: Capitol
Songwriters: Berton Averre, Douglas
   Fieger
*The male Blondie. But Doug was no Debbie.
And the power Pop one-shot band proved
too calculated to sustain their momentum.
Revived in the '94 film* Reality Bites.

THE KNICKERBOCKERS

1965

LIES (ARE BREAKIN' MY HEART)
Producer: Jerry Fuller
Album: Lies Are Breakin' My Heart
Record Label: Challenge
Songwriters: Buddy Randell, Beau
   Charles
Angst-ridden Garage Band standard.

GLADYS KNIGHT AND THE PIPS

1962

LETTER FULL OF TEARS
Record Label: Fury
Songwriter: Don Covay
*Their first big hit together; Top-10
R&B/Top-20 R&R crossover.*

1970

IF I WERE YOUR WOMAN
Producer: Clay McMurray
Album: If I Were Your Woman

Record Label: Soul
Songwriters: Pam Sawyer, Gloria
   Jones, Clay McMurray
#1 R&B/Top-10 R&R crossover.

1971

I DON'T WANT TO DO WRONG
Producer: Johnny Bristol
Album: If I Were Your Woman
Record Label: Soul
Songwriters: Johnny Bristol,
   Catherine Shaffner, William Guest,
   Gladys Knight, Merald Knight Jr.,
   Walter Jones
*In-concert perennial, establishing their
down-home, common-sense persona.*

MAKE ME THE WOMAN THAT YOU COME HOME TO
Producer: Clay McMurray
Album: Standing Ovation
Record Label: Soul
Songwriter: Clay McMurray
*Cozy come-on epitomizes Gladys's position
as the soul of monogamy.*

1973

BEST THING THAT EVER HAPPENED TO ME
Producer: Tony Camillo
Album: Imagination
Record Label: Buddah
Songwriter: Jim Weatherly
*#1 R&B/Top-10 R&R anthem of a Soul
surivivor.*

I'VE GOT TO USE MY IMAGINATION
Producer: Tony Camillo
Album: Imagination
Record Label: Buddah
Songwriters: Gerry Goffin, Barry
   Goldberg
*New label, new songwriting partnership, as
Gladys continues a major roll on the R&R
charts, with #1 R&B/Top-10 R&R
crossover from their best-selling album.*

NEITHER ONE OF US (WANTS TO BE THE FIRST TO SAY GOODBYE)
Producer: Joe Porter
Album: Neither One of Us
Record Label: Soul
Songwriter: Jim Weatherly
*Saying goodbye to Motown (and hello to a
Grammy award) with their first peek into the
Jim Weatherly catalogue; a #1 R&B/Top-
10 R&R crossover. Their next peek was a
cover of a song Jim released first on Amos,*

*called "Midnight Plane to Houston." It
would be their biggest hit under the title
"Midnight Train to Georgia" (Buddah, '73).*

1974

I FEEL A SONG (IN MY HEART)
Producer: Tony Camillo
Album: I Feel a Song
Record Label: Buddah
Songwriters: Tony Camillo, Pam
   Sawyer
#1 R&B/Top-30 R&R crossover.

ON AND ON
Producer: Curtis Mayfield
Album: Claudine
Record Label: Buddah
Songwriter: Curtis Mayfield
From the movie Claudine.

1983

SAVE THE OVERTIME FOR ME
Album: Visions
Record Label: Columbia
Songwriters: Sam Dees, Ricky
   Smith, Merald Bubba Knight, Gladys
   Knight, Joey Gallo
#1 R&B/Bottom-40 R&R crossover.

1987

LOVE OVERBOARD
Album: All Our Love
Record Label: MCA
Songwriter: Reggie Calloway
*Gladys's ninth (the Pips's tenth) and last to
date #1 R&B. Top-20 R&R crossover.*

JEAN KNIGHT

1971

MR. BIG STUFF
Producer: Wardell Quezerque
Album: Mr. Big Stuff
Record Label: Stax
Songwriters: Joe Broussard, Ralph
   Williams, Carrol Washington
*R&B protest of a personal sort; #1
R&B/Top-10 R&R crossover.*

1985

MY TOOT TOOT
Producer: I. Bolden
Album: My Toot Toot
Record Label: Mirage
Songwriter: Sidney Simien
A touch of classic New Orleans.

ROBERT KNIGHT
1967

EVERLASTING LOVE
Record Label: Rising Sons
Songwriters: James Cason, Mac Gayden

Long-lasting Country Soul standard. Covered by Carl Carlton (Backbeat, '74) and Rex Smith (Columbia, '81).

BUDDY KNOX
1957

HULA LOVE
Producer: Norman Petty
Record Label: Roulette
Songwriter: Buddy Knox

Second attempt to follow up "Party Doll" made it to the Top-10. Don Ho and Gaby Pianuli were poised for stardom. Instead it was Robin Luke who broke through, briefly.

PARTY DOLL
Producer: Norman Petty
Album: Buddy Knox and Jimmy Bowen
Record Label: Roulette
Songwriters: Jimmy Bowen, Buddy Knox

Norman Petty's pre-Buddy Holly calling card. This double A-sided smash (along with "I'm Stickin' with You" by Jimmy Bowen) gave the Rhythm Orchids all the impetus they needed to break up into two separate solo acts. Proving its Rock-and-Roll credibility, this tune crossed over Top-5 R&B not Country (as did Buddy Holly's records). The Pop cover by Steve Lawrence (Coral, '57) charted lower than Knox's version. The R&B covers by Wingy Manone (Decca, '57) and Roy Brown (Imperial, '57) were bombs.

KOOL & THE GANG
1973

HOLLYWOOD SWINGING
Producer: Kool & the Gang
Album: Wild and Peaceful
Record Label: De-Lite
Songwriters: Robert Bell, Ricky West, Charles Smith, George Brown, Ronald Bell, Robert Mickens, Dennis Thomas

#1 R&B/Top-10 R&R crossover; sax-driven Disco Funk standard.

JUNGLE BOOGIE
Producer: Kool & the Gang
Album: Wild and Peaceful

Record Label: De-Lite
Songwriters: Robert Bell, Kool & the Gang

Funk-and-Roll, Disco-age standard bearer became their first Top-10 R&R crossover after ten R&B hits.

1974

HIGHER PLANE
Album: Light of Worlds
Record Label: De-Lite
Songwriters: Robert Bell, Kool & the Gang

Their first #1 R&B/Bottom-20 R&R crossover; Jazz Funk.

1975

SPIRIT OF THE BOOGIE
Album: Spirit of the Boogie
Record Label: De-Lite
Songwriters: Robert Bell, Kool & the Gang

#1 R&B/Top-40 R&R crossover.

1979

LADIES NIGHT
Producer: Eumir Deodato
Album: Ladies Night
Record Label: De-Lite
Songwriters: Robert Bell, Kool & the Gang

#1 R&B/Top-10 R&R crossover.

TOO HOT
Producer: Eumir Deodato
Album: Ladies Night
Record Label: De-Lite
Songwriter: George Brown

1980

CELEBRATION
Producer: Eumir Deodato
Album: Celebrate
Record Label: De-Lite
Songwriters: Robert Bell, Kool & the Gang, Eumir Deodato

Their only #1 R&B/R&R crossover; Disco is dead, long live Funk.

1981

GET DOWN ON IT
Producers: Eumir Deodato, Kool & the Gang
Album: Something Special
Record Label: De-Lite
Songwriters: Robert Bell, Kool & the Gang, Eumir Deodato

TAKE MY HEART
Producers: Eumir Deodato, Kool & the Gang
Album: Something Special
Record Label: De-Lite
Songwriters: James Taylor, Charles Smith, George Brown, Eumir Deodato

#1 R&B/Top-20 R&R crossover.

1983

JOANNA
Producers: Ronald Bell, Kool & the Gang, James Bonneford
Album: In the Heart
Record Label: De-Lite
Songwriters: Robert Bell, Kool & the Gang, James Bonneford

#1 R&B/Top-10 R&R crossover.

1984

CHERISH
Producers: Ronald Bell, Kool & the Gang, James Bonneford
Album: Emergency
Record Label: De-Lite
Songwriters: Ronald Bell, Kool & the Gang, James Bonneford

#1 R&B/Top-10 R&R crossover.

FRESH
Producers: Ronald Bell, Kool & the Gang, James Bonneford
Album: Emergency
Record Label: De-Lite
Songwriters: Ronald Bell, Kool & the Gang, James Bonneford

#1 R&B/Top-10 R&R crossover.

MISLED
Producers: Ronald Bell, Kool & the Gang, James Bonneford
Album: Emergency
Record Label: De-Lite
Songwriters: Ronald Bell, Kool & the Gang, James Bonneford

1986

STONE LOVE
Producers: Ronald Bell, Kool & the Gang, I.B.M.C.
Album: Forever
Record Label: De-Lite
Songwriters: Charles Smith, Kool & the Gang, James Taylor

Their twelfth and last #10 R&R.

VICTORY
Producers: Ronald Bell, Kool & the Gang, I.B.M.C.
Album: Forever
Record Label: De-lite
Songwriters: Ronald Bell, James Taylor

AL KOOPER
1968

YOU DON'T LOVE ME
Album: Supersession
Record Label: Columbia
Songwriter: W. Cobbs

All-purpose Blues track featured in Al Kooper's super one-off with guitarist Mike Bloomfield and Stephen Stills. Covered by Booker T. (Stax, '68), Kaleidoscope (Epic, '68), and the Allman Brothers (Capricorn, '71).

1971

NEW YORK CITY (YOU'RE A WOMAN)
Album: New York City (You're a Woman)
Record Label: Columbia
Songwriter: Al Kooper

Suggested segue: "American City Suite" by Cashman and West.

LEO KOTTKE
1974

PAMELA BROWN
Album: Ice Water
Record Label: Capitol
Songwriter: Tom T. Hall

Best vocal performance by the virtuoso acoustic guitar stylist.

1989

JACK GETS UP
Producer: T-Bone Burnette
Album: My Father's Face
Record Label: Private Music
Songwriter: Leo Kottke

A woebegone gem.

KRAFTWERK
1975

AUTOBAHN
Producers: Ralf Hutter, Florian Schneider
Album: Autobahn
Record Label: Vertigo

Songwriters: Ralf Hutter, Florean Schneider

Introducing the industrialized sound of the new German dancehall.

1977

TRANS EUROPE EXPRESS
Producers: Ralf Hutter, Florian Schneider
Album: Trans Europe Express
Record Label: Capitol
Songwriters: Ralf Hutter, Florian Schneider

The new romantics in England—the Jesus and Mary Chain, My Bloody Valentine, and the Cocteau Twins—were listening; so were the Hip-Hop DJs in America.

BILLY J. KRAMER AND THE DAKOTAS
1963

BAD TO ME
Producer: George Martin
Album: Bad to Me
Record Label: Imperial
Songwriters: John Lennon, Paul McCartney

#1 in the U.K., Top-10 in the U.S. a year later for another of manager Brian Epstein's bands.

1964

LITTLE CHILDREN
Producer: George Martin
Album: Little Children
Record Label: Imperial
Songwriters: J. Leslie McFarland, Mort Shuman

Their biggest hit; #1 U.K./#6 U.S.

LENNIE KRAVITZ
1991

IT AIN'T OVER TILL IT'S OVER
Producer: Lenny Kravitz
Album: Mama Said
Record Label: Virgin
Songwriter: Lenny Kravitz

His biggest hit.

1993

ARE YOU GONNA GO MY WAY
Producer: Lenny Kravitz
Album: Are You Gonna Go My Way
Record Label: Virgin
Songwriters: Lenny Kravitz, Craig Ross

KRISS KROSS
1992

JUMP
Producer: Jermaine Dupri
Album: Totally Krossed Out
Record Label: Ruffhouse/Columbia
Songwriter: Jermaine Dupri

Exhuberant teenybop Hip-Hop #1 R&R debut. Suggested segue: "Hat 2 Da Back" by TLC.

KRIS KRISTOFFERSON
1969

FOR THE GOOD TIMES
Producer: Fred Foster
Album: Kris Kristofferson
Record Label: Monument
Songwriter: Kris Kristofferson

Best new Country singer/songwriter since Mickey Newbury. A #1 C&W/#11 R&R crossover for Ray Price (Columbia, '70).

HELP ME MAKE IT THROUGH THE NIGHT
Producer: Fred Foster
Album: Kris Kristofferson
Record Label: Monument
Songwriter: Kris Kristofferson

#1 C&W/Top-10 R&R crossover for Sammi Smith (Mega, '70). Suggested segue: "Whatever Gets You through the Night" by John Lennon.

SUNDAY MORNIN' COMING DOWN
Producer: Fred Foster
Album: Kris Kristofferson
Record Label: Monument
Songwriter: Kris Kristofferson

Down and out on the streets of Nashville, but at least he had "Me and Bobby McGee" in the bank. A #1 C&W/Top-50 R&R crossover by Johnny Cash (Columbia, '70).

1972

WHY ME
Album: Jesus Was a Capricorn
Record Label: Monument
Songwriter: Kris Kristofferson

His first #1 C&W/Top-20 R&R crossover as an artist.

KROKUS
1983

EAT THE RICH
Album: Headhunter
Record Label: Arista

Songwriters: Christian Rohr, Fernando Von Arb, Marc Storace, Butch Stone

An essential Germanic Heavy Metal philosophy also espoused by Motorhead and Aerosmith in different songs with the same title.

JIM KWESKIN AND THE JUG BAND

1965

I'M A WOMAN
Album: Jug Band Music
Record Label: Vanguard
Songwriters: Jerry Leiber, Mike Stoller

Introducing Maria Muldaur's in-concert seduction number. When she did her own solo version it went Top-20 (Reprise, '75). The definitive Pop rendition is by Peggy Lee (Capitol, '63).

L

L. L. COOL J

1985

I CAN'T LIVE WITHOUT MY RADIO
Producer: Rick Rubin
Album: Radio
Record Label: Def Jam
Songwriters: James Todd Smith, Rick Rubin

Impressive new Rap artist expresses timeless Rock and Roll sentiments. Suggested segue: "Please Don't Take My Air Jordans" by Reg E. Gaines.

I WANT YOU
Producer: Rick Rubin
Album: Radio
Record Label: Def Jam
Songwriters: James Todd Smith, Rick Rubin

The Street Rap equivalent of the Arena Rock ballad.

1987

GOING BACK TO CALI
Producer: Rick Rubin
Album: *Less Than Zero* Soundtrack
Record Label: Def Jam
Songwriters: James Todd Smith, Rick Rubin

Rap and Metal conflagration.

I NEED LOVE
Producers: L. L. Cool J, L.A. Posse
Album: Bigger and Deffer
Record Label: Def Jam
Songwriters: James Todd Smith, B. Erving, Darrell Pierce, Dwayne Simon, S. Etts

#1 R&B/Top-20 R&R chart breakthrough.

1989

I'M THAT TYPE OF GUY
Producer: L. L. Cool J
Album: Walking with a Panther
Record Label: Def Jam
Songwriters: James Todd Smith, Dwayne Simon

1990

AROUND THE WAY GIRL
Producer: Marley Marl
Album: Mama Said Knock You Out
Record Label: Def Jam
Songwriters: James Todd Smith, Marlon Williams, Rick James

With samples from Funk superstar Rick James, this was his biggest hit.

1991

MAMA SAID KNOCK YOU OUT
Producer: Marley Marl
Album: Mama Said Knock You Out
Record Label: Def Jam
Songwriters: James Todd Smith, Marlon Williams

L.T.D.

1976

LOVE BALLAD
Album: Love to the World
Record Label: A&M
Songwriter: Skip Scarborough

#1 R&B/Top-20 R&R crossover. Covered by George Benson (Warner Brothers, '79).

1977

(EVERY TIME I TURN AROUND) BACK IN LOVE AGAIN
Producer: Bobby Martin
Album: Something to Love
Record Label: A&M
Songwriters: Len Hanks, Zane Grey

Funk monster; #1 R&B/Top-10 R&R crossover.

1978

HOLDING ON WHEN LOVE IS GONE
Album: Togetherness
Record Label: A&M

Songwriters: John McGhee, Jeffrey Osborne

#1 R&B/Top-50 R&R crossover.

DAVID LA FLAMME

1976

WHITE BIRD
Producer: David La Flame
Album: White Bird
Record Label: Amherst
Songwriters: David La Flamme, Linda La Flamme

Violin-driven progressive Rock-era perennial.

LA TOUR

1991

PEOPLE ARE STILL HAVING SEX
Producers: La Tour, Mark Picchiotti
Album: La Tour
Record Label: Smash
Songwriter: William LaTour

Primal Top-40 reassurance, Hip-Hop style.

THE L.A.'S

1991

THERE SHE GOES
Album: The L.A.'s
Record Label: London
Songwriter: Lee Mavers

Ineffable trifle, writ large in the Mike Myers movie So I Married an Axe Murderer, as is a version by the Boo Radleys (Chaos/Columbia, '93).

LABELLE

1974

LADY MARMELADE
Producer: Allen Toussaint
Album: Nightbirds
Record Label: Epic
Songwriters: Bob Crewe, Kenny Nolan Helfman

Philadlephia meets New Orleans on a track previously recorded by its authors as Eleventh Hour (20th Century, '74). LaBelle's biggest hit, a #1 R&B/R&R crossover.

PATTI LABELLE AND MICHAEL MCDONALD

1984

IF ONLY YOU KNEW
Album: I'm in Love Again
Record Label: Philadelphia International

Songwriters: Kenny Gamble, Dexter Wansel, Cynthia Biggs

#1 R&B/Top-50 R&R crossover.

1986

ON MY OWN
Album: Winner in You
Record Label: MCA
Songwriters: Burt Bacharach, Carole Bayer Sager

Smash Pop ballad went #1 R&B/R&R; true to its title, each artist recorded separately.

LAKESIDE
1981

FANTASTIC VOYAGE
Producer: Dick Griffey
Album: Fantastic Voyage
Record Label: Solar
Songwriters: Fred Alexander, Otis Stokes, Artis Ivey, Brian Dobbs, Norman Beavers, Marvin Craig, Tiemeyer McCain, Thomas Shelby

Legendary Funk track, covered by Coolio (Tommy Boy, '94).

MAJOR LANCE
1963

THE MONKEY TIME
Producer: Curtis Mayfield
Album: The Monkey Time
Record Label: Okeh
Songwriter: Curtis Mayfield

D.C./Carolina's beach music classic by Curtis Mayfield protege; Top-5 R&B/Top-10 R&R crossover. This tune, along with others, like "Mickey's Monkey," "One Monkey Don't Stop No Show," "Monkey Man," and "Can Your Monkey Do the Dog," helped to establish the monkey as the ultimate Rock-and-Roll party animal. Covered by the Tubes (Capitol, '68).

UM UM UM UM UM UM
Producer: Carl Davis
Album: Um, Um, Um, Um, Um, Um/The Best of Major Lance
Record Label: Okeh
Songwriter: Curtis Mayfield

His biggest R&R hit. Suggested segues: "Fa-Fa-Fa-Fa-Fa (Sad Song)" by Otis Redding, "De Do Do Do De Da Da Da" by the Police, and "Doo Doo Doo Doo Doo (Heartbreaker)" by the Rolling Stones.

k.d. LANG
1992

CONSTANT CRAVING
Producers: Greg Penny, Ben Mink, k.d. lang
Album: Ingenue
Record Label: Sire
Songwriters: Kathryn Dawn Lang, Ben Mink

Patsy Cline reincarnated as Hank Williams.

PATTY LARKIN
1991

USED TO BE
Producers: Patty Larkin, Will Ackerman
Album: Tango
Record Label: High Street
Songwriter: Patty Larkin

In the Joni Mitchell acoustic Folk tradition, but a decade wiser.

THE LARKS
1964

THE JERK
Producer: A. C. Scott
Album: The Jerk
Record Label: Money
Songwriter: Don Julian

New dance gyration written by the former Meadowlark.

DENISE LASALLE
1971

NOW RUN AND TELL THAT
Producer: Denise LaSalle
Album: Trapped by a Thing Called Love
Record Label: Westbound
Songwriter: Denise O. Jones

Rough and raunchy Soul shouter.

TRAPPED BY A THING CALLED LOVE
Producer: Denise LaSalle
Album: Trapped by a Thing Called Love
Record Label: Westbound
Songwriter: Denise O. Jones

#1 R&B/Top-20 R&R crossover; her biggest hit.

THE LAST POETS
1971

THE REVOLUTION WILL NOT BE TELEVISED
Album: The Revolution Will Not Be Televised
Record Label: Douglas
Songwriter: Gil Scott-Heron

Early example of Rap or late example of beat Jazz poetry, this lyrically explicit rant moved with a powerful rhythmic force through the entire black community. Covered by LaBelle (Epic, '73), Gil Scott-Heron & the Flying Dutchman (Arista, '74).

LATIMORE
1974

LET'S STRAIGHTEN IT OUT
Producer: Steve Alaimo
Album: More More More of Benny Latimore
Record Label: Glades
Songwriter: Benny Latimore

Blues-edged #1 R&B/Top-40 R&R crossover by the T.K. sideman.

CYNDI LAUPER
1984

ALL THROUGH THE NIGHT
Producer: Rick Chertoff
Album: She's So Unusual
Record Label: Portrait
Songwriter: Jules Shear

Second-generation Brenda Lee pipes, with second-generation Jimmy Webb material.

SHE BOP
Producer: Rick Chertoff
Album: She's So Unusual
Record Label: Portrait
Songwriters: Cyndi Lauper, Stephen Lunt, Gary Corbett, Rick Chertoff

Suggested segues: "I Touch Myself" by the Divinyls and "Secret" by Madonna.

TIME AFTER TIME
Producer: Rick Chertoff
Album: She's So Unusual
Record Label: Portrait
Songwriters: Cyndi Lauper, Rob Hyman

This three-hankie ballad was her first #1.

1985

THE GOONIES 'R GOOD ENOUGH
Album: *The Goonies* Soundtrack
Record Label: Portrait

Songwriters: Cyndi Lauper, Stephen Lunt, Arthur Stead

From the film soundtrack.

1986

CHANGE OF HEART

Producers: Lenny Petze, Cyndi Lauper
Album: True Colors
Record Label: Portrait
Songwriter: Essra Mohawk

The former Zappa chorus girl, aka Uncle Meat, achieves a long-awaited songwriting mini-epiphany, nearly equal to when the Shangri-Las recorded her "I'll Never Learn" (Mercury, '66).

TRUE COLORS

Producers: Lenny Petze, Cyndi Lauper
Album: True Colors
Record Label: Portrait
Songwriters: Billy Steinberg, Tom Kelly

Corporate Pop Rock at its finest. Suggested segues: "Kodachrome" by Paul Simon and "The Times of Your Life" by Paul Anka.

1989

I DROVE ALL NIGHT

Album: A Night to Remember
Record Label: Epic
Songwriters: Billy Steinberg, Tom Kelly

ANNIE LAURIE

1947

SINCE I FELL FOR YOU

Record Label: De Luxe
Songwriter: Buddy Johnson

Top-5 R&B/Top-20 R&R crossover ballad, with Paul Gayton's band. Covered by Lenny Welch (Cadence, '63).

LINDA LAURIE

1959

AMBROSE (PART V)

Record Label: Glory
Songwriter: Linda Gertz (Linda Laurie)

Perhaps the oddest novelty record to ever crack the Bottom-40, by the Cyndi Lauper of her era, and the author of the Helen Reddy hit "Leave Me Alone (Ruby Red Dress)," which explains a lot.

CHRISTINE LAVIN

1990

SENSITIVE NEW AGE GUYS

Album: Attainable Love
Record Label: Philo
Songwriters: Christine Lavin, John Gorka

A folkie anthem lampooning the ultimate male folkie role model, Alan Alda.

VICKIE LAWRENCE

1973

THE NIGHT THE LIGHTS WENT OUT IN GEORGIA

Producer: Snuff Garrett
Album: The Night the Lights Went out in Georgia
Record Label: Bell
Songwriter: Bobby Russell

Faulknerian #1 C&W/R&R crossover story-song and future TV movie. Suggested TV movie/record segues: "Harper Valley PTA" by Jeannie C. Riley, "Ode to Billie Joe" by Bobbie Gentry, and "The Gambler" by Kenny Rogers.

THE LEAVES

1965

HEY JOE

Producer: Norm Ratner
Album: Hey Joe
Record Label: Mira
Songwriter: Dino Valenti (Billy Roberts)

The Garage Punk standard. Covered by Love (Elektra, '66), Cher (Imperial, '67), Jimi Hendrix as his first U.K. single and subsequently on at least eight different albums (Reprise, '67).

LEADBELLY

1942

ROCK ISLAND LINE

Record Label: Library of Congress
Songwriter: Huddie Ledbetter (Leadbelly)

Introduced by Leadbelly in 1937. Covered by Lonnie Donnegan in '53; hit version in '56 on Decca.

LED ZEPPELIN

1969

BLACK MOUNTAIN SIDE

Producer: Jimmy Page
Album: Led Zeppelin

Record Label: Atlantic
Songwriter: Jimmy Page

Adapted from the British Folk guitarist Davey Graham's "She Moved Through the Fair." Suggested segue: "White Summer," Page's Yardbirds's instrumental.

DAZED AND CONFUSED

Producer: Jimmy Page
Album: Led Zeppelin
Record Label: Atlantic
Songwriter: Jimmy Page

Amps on ten, the new Yardbirds offer their dazed and confused fusion of the Delta Blues and teenybop Metal.

GOOD TIMES, BAD TIMES

Producer: Jimmy Page
Album: Led Zeppelin
Record Label: Atlantic
Songwriters: Jimmy Page, John Bonham, John Paul Jones

Their first chart single in an era that would soon make chart singles all but obsolete.

HEARTBREAKER

Producer: Jimmy Page
Album: Led Zeppelin II
Record Label: Atlantic
Songwriters: Jimmy Page, Robert Plant, John Paul Jones, John Bonham

FM radio staple that would be echoed by a generation of Arena Rock bands.

HOW MANY MORE TIMES

Producer: Jimmy Page
Album: Led Zeppelin
Record Label: Atlantic
Songwriters: Jimmy Page, John Bonham, John Paul Jones

Suggested segue: "How Many More Years" by Howlin' Wolf.

THE LEMON SONG

Producer: Jimmy Page
Album: Led Zeppelin II
Record Label: Atlantic
Songwriters: Jimmy Page, Robert Plant, John Paul Jones, John Bonham

Plant's horny Blues howl that would haunt FM radio for the next two decades.

LIVING LOVING MAID (SHE'S JUST A WOMAN)

Producer: Jimmy Page
Album: Led Zeppelin II

Record Label: Atlantic
Songwriters: Jimmy Page, Robert Plant

B-side of "Whole Lotta Love."

TRAVELING RIVERSIDE BLUES
Producer: John Walters
Record Label: Atlantic
Songwriters: Jimmy Page, Robert Plant, Robert Johnson

Written and recorded in '36 by Robert Johnson. This performance first heard over BBC radio.

WHOLE LOTTA LOVE
Producer: Jimmy Page
Album: Led Zeppelin II
Record Label: Atlantic
Songwriters: Jimmy Page, Robert Plant, John Paul Jones, John Bonham

Their only Top-10 single. Suggested segue: "You Need Love" by Muddy Waters (Chess, '62).

1970

BRON Y' AUR STOMP
Producer: Jimmy Page
Album: Led Zeppelin III
Record Label: Atlantic
Songwriters: Jimmy Page, Robert Plant, John Paul Jones, John Bonham

Revealing their jug-band sympathies.

GALLOWS POLE
Producer: Jimmy Page
Album: Led Zeppelin III
Record Label: Atlantic
Songwriter: Traditional

A Leadbelly tune, revived by the reunited Page and Plant (Atlantic, '94).

IMMIGRANT SONG
Producer: Jimmy Page
Album: Led Zeppelin III
Record Label: Atlantic
Songwriters: Jimmy Page, Robert Plant

One of their rare hit singles.

TANGERINE
Producer: Jimmy Page
Album: Led Zeppelin III
Record Label: Atlantic
Songwriter: Jimmy Page

Page on steel guitar, mapping out the master plan for "Stairway to Heaven."

1971

BLACK DOG
Producer: Jimmy Page
Album: Led Zeppelin IV (Untitled)
Record Label: Atlantic
Songwriters: Jimmy Page, Robert Plant, John Paul Jones

Top-20 R&R single.

GOING TO CALIFORNIA
Producer: Jimmy Page
Album: Led Zeppelin IV (Untitled)
Record Label: Atlantic
Songwriters: Jimmy Page, Robert Plant

Unplugged.

ROCK AND ROLL
Producer: Jimmy Page
Album: Led Zeppelin IV (Untitled)
Record Label: Atlantic
Songwriters: Jimmy Page, Robert Plant, John Paul Jones, John Bonham

One of the classic riffs, found embedded in the far wall at Detroit's Cobo Arena. Or else something they played once at a sound-check somewhere else.

STAIRWAY TO HEAVEN
Producer: Jimmy Page
Album: Led Zeppelin IV (Untitled)
Record Label: Atlantic
Songwriters: Jimmy Page, Robert Plant

Plant and Page write their wedding song: the marriage of Elizabethan imagery and Heavy Metal alchemy, ceremoniously replayed over FM radio every hour on the hour ever since. The #1 Rock track until otherwise advised.

WHEN THE LEVEE BREAKS
Producer: Jimmy Page
Album: Led Zeppelin IV (Untitled)
Record Label: Atlantic
Songwriters: Jimmy Page, Robert Plant, John Paul Jones, John Bonham, Memphis Minnie

Successfully transmogrifying Country Blues, with a credit for the source, Memphis Minnie.

1973

THE CRUNGE
Producer: Jimmy Page
Album: Houses of the Holy
Record Label: Atlantic

Songwriters: Jimmy Page, Robert Plant, John Paul Jones, John Bonham

Their mock Funk homage to James Brown.

DANCING DAYS
Producer: Jimmy Page
Album: Houses of the Holy
Record Label: Atlantic
Songwriters: Jimmy Page, Robert Plant

B-side of "Over the Hills and Far Away" is their answer to the Lovin' Spoonful.

D'YER MAKER
Producer: Jimmy Page
Album: Houses of the Holy
Record Label: Atlantic
Songwriters: John Paul Jones, Robert Plant, John Bonham

Heavy Reggae.

NO QUARTER
Producer: Jimmy Page
Album: Houses of the Holy
Record Label: Atlantic
Songwriters: Jimmy Page, Robert Plant, John Paul Jones

Revived by Plant and Page on their '94 reunion album, along with "The Battle of Evermore" and "Kashmir."

THE OCEAN
Producer: Jimmy Page
Album: Houses of the Holy
Record Label: Atlantic
Songwriters: Jimmy Page, Robert Plant, John Paul Jones, John Bonham

A tribute to their faces.

OVER THE HILLS AND FAR AWAY
Producer: Jimmy Page
Album: Houses of the Holy
Record Label: Atlantic
Songwriters: Jimmy Page, Robert Plant

Perfecting the classic acoustic to electric Rock ballad form.

THE SONG REMAINS THE SAME
Producer: Jimmy Page
Album: Houses of the Holy
Record Label: Atlantic
Songwriters: Jimmy Page, Robert Plant

Reappears as the title song of their '76 Rockumentary.

1975

KASHMIR
Producer: Jimmy Page
Album: Physical Graffiti
Record Label: Atlantic
Songwriters: Jimmy Page, Robert Plant, John Bonham

Page's magnum Eastern opus was always one of the band's favorites, taking up where even the Yardbirds dared not go. Suggested segue: "East-West" by the Paul Butterfield Blues Band.

TRAMPLED UNDER FOOT
Producer: Jimmy Page
Album: Physical Graffiti
Record Label: Swan Song
Songwriters: Jimmy Page, Robert Plant, John Paul Jones

1976

ACHILLES LAST STAND
Producer: Jimmy Page
Album: Led Zeppelin
Record Label: Atlantic
Songwriters: Jimmy Page, Robert Plant, John Paul Jones, John Bonham

Landmark ten-minute performance opus.

1979

ALL MY LOVE
Producer: Jimmy Page
Album: In through the Out Door
Record Label: Swan Song
Songwriters: John Paul Jones, Robert Plant

Plant at his most mock-anguished.

FOOL IN THE RAIN
Producer: Jimmy Page
Album: In through the Out Door
Record Label: Swan Song
Songwriters: Jimmy Page, Robert Plant, John Paul Jones

Answering "Silhouettes on the Shade." You knew then they were running out of gas.

BRENDA LEE

1956

BIGELOW 6-200
Producer: Paul Cohen
Record Label: Decca
Songwriters: Don Woody, Paul Simmons

Brenda's smokin' Rockabilly debut was the B-side of her first single, "Jambalaya."

1957

DYNAMITE
Producer: Paul Cohen
Album: Brenda Lee
Record Label: Decca
Songwriters: Mort Carson, Tom Glazer

Spawning a nickname and a career for the little lady of Rockabilly. Covered by Dave Edmunds (Swan Song, '79).

ONE STEP AT A TIME
Producer: Milt Gabler
Record Label: Decca
Songwriter: Hugh Ashley

Her first Country hit; she wouldn't return to this chart for twelve years, during which time she'd account for approximately 50 singles on the R&R charts (and a half dozen R&B). Stevie Nicks and Cyndi Lauper were listening.

1960

I WANT TO BE WANTED
Producer: Owen Bradley
Album: This Is . . . Brenda
Record Label: Decca
Songwriters: Kim Gannon, Pino Spotti, A. Testa

Softening her image with a ballad from Italy.

I'M SORRY
Producer: Owen Bradley
Album: Brenda Lee
Record Label: Decca
Songwriters: Ronnie Self, Dub Allbritten

Original B-side of "That's All You Gotta Do" became Brenda's biggest hit.

ROCKIN' AROUND THE CHRISTMAS TREE
Producer: Owen Bradley
Record Label: Decca
Songwriter: Johnny Marks

Her all-time Christmas carol.

SWEET NOTHIN'S
Producer: Owen Bradley
Album: Brenda Lee
Record Label: Decca
Songwriter: Ronnie Self

The Rockabilly is still intact on her first Top-10 hit.

THAT'S ALL YOU GOTTA DO
Producer: Owen Bradley
Album: Brenda Lee
Record Label: Decca

Songwriter: Jerry Reed

A-side of "I'm Sorry" enabled Country wild man Reed to eventually get hot himself.

1961

BREAK IT TO ME GENTLY
Producer: Owen Bradley
Album: Let Me Sing!
Record Label: Decca
Songwriters: Diane Lampert, Joe Seneca

Ballad hit.

DUM DUM
Producer: Owen Bradley
Album: All the Way
Record Label: Decca
Songwriters: Jackie DeShannon, Sharon Sheeley

Rockabilly flavor by DeShannon, the West Coast leatherette Carole King.

EMOTIONS
Producer: Owen Bradley
Album: Emotions
Record Label: Decca
Songwriters: Mel Tillis, Ramsey Kearney

Country pedigree by Tillis, but no Country crossover.

FOOL NUMBER 1
Producer: Owen Bradley
Album: Brenda, That's All
Record Label: Decca
Songwriter: Kathryn R. Fulton

YOU CAN DEPEND ON ME
Producer: Owen Bradley
Album: Brenda, That's All
Record Label: Decca
Songwriters: Charles Carpenter, Lois Dunlap, Earl Hines

Introduced by Louie Armstrong (Columbia, '32).

1962

ALL ALONE AM I
Producer: Owen Bradley
Album: All Alone Am I
Record Label: Decca
Songwriters: Arthur Altman, Manos Hadjidakis, Jean Ioannidis

Brenda's post-Rockabilly balladeering peak. Imported from Greece.

EVERYBODY LOVES ME BUT YOU
Producer: Owen Bradley
Record Label: Decca
Songwriter: Ronnie Self

1963

LOSIN' YOU
Producer: Owen Bradley
Album: Let Me Sing
Record Label: Decca
Songwriters: Carl Sigman, Jean Renard, Pierre Havet
Her last Top-10 was originally from France.

1966

COMING ON STRONG
Producer: Owen Bradley
Album: Coming on Strong
Record Label: Decca
Songwriter: David Wilkins
Latter-day, state-fair concert opener.

CURTIS LEE
1961

PRETTY LITTLE ANGEL EYES
Producer: Phil Spector
Record Label: Dunes
Songwriters: Tommy Boyce, Curtis Lee
Brill-Building Soul reaches Spectorian perfection.

UNDER THE MOON OF LOVE
Producer: Phil Spector
Record Label: Dunes
Songwriters: Tommy Boyce, Curtis Lee
Follow up to "Pretty Little Angel Eyes." Cover by Showaddywaddy went to #1 in the U.K. (Bell, '76). A couple of years later they also revived "Pretty Little Angel Eyes."

DICKEY LEE
1962

PATCHES
Album: The Tale of Patches
Record Label: Smash
Songwriters: Barry Mann, Larry Kolber
Classic Country Rock class struggle. Suggested segue: "Poor Side of Town" by Johnny Rivers, "Dawn (Go Away)" by the Four Seasons.

JOHNNY LEE
1980

LOOKIN' FOR LOVE
Album: Lookin' for Love
Record Label: Asylum

Songwriters: Wanda Mallette, Patti Ryan, Bob Morrison
#1 C&W/Top-10 R&R, from the movie Urban Cowboy.

LAURA LEE
1971

WOMEN'S LOVE RIGHTS
Producer: William Weatherspoon
Album: Women's Love Rights
Record Label: Hot Wax
Songwriters: Angelo Bond, William Weatherspoon
Feisty feminist-leaning dance-hall diatribe.

1972

THE RIP OFF
Producer: William Weatherspoon
Album: Laura Lee
Record Label: Hot Wax
Songwriters: Angelo Bond, William Weatherspoon
Taking up where even "Women's Love Rights" feared to tread.

PEGGY LEE
1989

IS THAT ALL THERE IS
Producers: Jerry Leiber, Mike Stoller
Album: Mirrors
Record Label: A&M
Songwriters: Jerry Leiber, Mike Stoller
Once she had the fever; now she couldn't care less.

THE LEFT BANKE
1966

WALK AWAY RENEE
Producers: Harry Lookofsky, Steve Jerome, Bill Jerome
Album: Walk Away Renee/Pretty Ballerina
Record Label: Smash
Songwriters: Michael Brown, Bob Calilli, Tony Sansone
A New-York post-Brill valentine. Covered by the Four Tops (Motown, '68), Orpheus (MGM, '68), and Rickie Lee Jones (Warner Brothers, '83).

1967

PRETTY BALLERINA
Producers: Harry Lookofsky, Bill Jerome, Steve Jerome

Album: Walk Away Renee/Pretty Ballerina
Record Label: Smash
Songwriter: Michael Brown
Art-Pop perfection, the result of too much hanging out at the ASCAP building, right across the street from Lincoln Center.

THE LEMON PIPERS
1967

GREEN TAMBOURINE
Producer: Paul Leka
Album: Green Tambourine
Record Label: Buddah
Songwriters: Shelley Pinz, Paul Leka
Psychedelic bubblegum.

THE LEMONHEADS
1992

IT'S A SHAME ABOUT RAY
Producers: The Robb Brothers, Evan Dando
Album: It's a Shame About Ray
Record Label: Atlantic
Songwriters: Evan Dando, Tom Morgan
College track of the year.

JOHN LENNON
1969

COLD TURKEY
Producers: Phil Spector, John Lennon, Yoko Ono
Album: The Plastic Ono Band, Live Peace in Toronto 1969
Record Label: Apple
Songwriter: John Lennon
Coming down from the Beatles, the first stage, with the Plastic Ono Band.

GIVE PEACE A CHANCE
Producers: John Lennon, Yoko Ono
Album: The Plastic Ono Band, Live Peace in Toronto 1969
Record Label: Apple
Songwriters: John Lennon, Paul McCartney
Lennon's first non-Beatles hit; Yoko-inspired performance art, recorded during a "Bed-in" for peace at their hotel room in Montreal in June, with a backup band consisting of, among others, Dr. Timothy Leary and Tommy Smothers. Sung by Pete Seeger at the Washington Monument during a peace march later in the year.

1970

GOD

Producer: Phil Spector
Album: John Lennon/Plastic Ono Band
Record Label: Apple
Songwriter: John Lennon

Coming down from the Beatles, the second stage: the anti-"Imagine."

INSTANT KARMA (WE ALL SHINE ON)

Producer: Phil Spector
Album: Shaved Fish
Record Label: Apple
Songwriter: John Lennon

Primed by Lennon's fabulous neuroticism, Spector would move on to Leonard Cohen.

MOTHER

Producer: Phil Spector
Album: John Lennon/Plastic Ono Band
Record Label: Apple
Songwriter: John Lennon

Primal scream therapy. Covered by Barbra Streisand (Columbia, '71).

POWER TO THE PEOPLE

Producer: Phil Spector
Album: Shaved Fish
Record Label: Apple
Songwriter: John Lennon

A classic marching song, nearing the end of the era of marches.

WORKING CLASS HERO

Album: John Lennon/Plastic Ono Band
Record Label: Apple
Songwriter: John Lennon

One of his most searching, searing gems. Covered by Marianne Faithfull (Island, '79).

1971

CRIPPLED INSIDE

Producer: John Lennon
Album: Imagine
Record Label: Apple
Songwriter: John Lennon

Rock Therapy.

GIMME SOME TRUTH

Producer: John Lennon
Album: Imagine
Record Label: Apple
Songwriter: John Lennon

Setting a model that verbose rockers from R.E.M. to Billy Joel would use when they wanted to let it all hang out. Suggested segue: "Subterranean Homesick Blues" by Bob Dylan.

HOW DO YOU SLEEP

Producer: John Lennon
Album: Imagine
Record Label: Apple
Songwriter: John Lennon

Post-Beatles post-mortem; giving the bass player some.

IMAGINE

Producers: John Lennon, Yoko Ono, Phil Spector
Album: Imagine
Record Label: Apple
Songwriter: John Lennon

His belated flower-child anthem.

JEALOUS GUY

Producer: John Lennon
Album: Imagine
Record Label: Apple
Songwriter: John Lennon

An emotional breakthrough. Covered by Bryan Ferry (Reprise, '89).

OH YOKO

Producer: John Lennon
Album: Imagine
Record Label: Apple
Songwriter: John Lennon

An ode to his sweetheart. Suggested segues: "An Innocent Man" by Billy Joel, "Fountain of Sorrow" by Jackson Brown, "My Old Man" by Joni Mitchell, "Be My Yoko Ono" by the Bare Naked Ladies.

1973

MIND GAMES

Producer: John Lennon
Album: Mind Games
Record Label: Apple
Songwriter: John Lennon

Problems with his sweetheart.

1974

#9 DREAM

Producer: John Lennon
Album: Walls and Bridges
Record Label: Apple
Songwriter: John Lennon

WHATEVER GETS YOU THRU THE NIGHT

Producer: John Lennon
Album: Walls and Bridges

Record Label: Apple
Songwriter: John Lennon

His first solo #1 single.

1980

(JUST LIKE) STARTING OVER

Producers: John Lennon, Yoko Ono, Jack Douglas
Album: Double Fantasy
Record Label: Geffen
Songwriter: John Lennon

His second and last #1 solo single.

1981

WATCHING THE WHEELS

Producers: John Lennon, Yoko Ono, Jack Douglas
Album: Double Fantasy
Record Label: Geffen
Songwriter: John Lennon

Achieving peace at last. His first posthumous release.

WOMAN

Producers: John Lennon, Yoko Ono, John Douglas
Album: Double Fantasy
Record Label: Geffen
Songwriter: John Lennon

This song, "Imagine," and "(Just Like) Starting Over" all reached #1 in the U.K. in the two months after Lennon was shot and killed.

1984

I'M STEPPING OUT

Album: Milk and Honey
Record Label: Polydor
Songwriter: John Lennon

Posthumous out-take from the "Double Fantasy" sessions.

NOBODY TOLD ME

Album: Milk and Honey
Record Label: Polydor
Songwriter: John Lennon

His last Top-10 R&R hit for a decade.

1988

REAL LOVE

Album: *Imagine* Soundtrack
Record Label: Apple/Capitol
Songwriter: John Lennon

The work tape of a "new" Lennon song, used in the biopic Imagine. It would resurface in '95, with the voices of Paul, George and Ringo added, along with "Free as a Bird," another track from the same era, as the first two new Beatles songs since '70. The video for "Free as a Bird" was a killer.

JULIAN LENNON
1984

VALOTTE
Producer: Phil Ramone
Album: Valotte
Record Label: Atlantic
Songwriters: Julian Lennon, Justin Clayton, Carlton Morales
Obla-de, obla-da.

1985

TOO LATE FOR GOODBYES
Producer: Phil Ramone
Album: Valotte
Record Label: Atlantic
Songwriter: Julian Lennon
Suggested segues: "All Those Years Ago" by George Harrison, "Here Today" by Paul McCartney.

ANNIE LENNOX
1992

WALKING ON BROKEN GLASS
Album: Diva
Record Label: Arista
Songwriter: Annie Lennox
The former member of the Eurythmics exhibits prime dancehall pipes.

KETTY LESTER
1962

LOVE LETTERS
Record Label: Era
Songwriters: Edward Heyman, Victor Young
Soulful version of the title song from the '45 film of the same name was a Top-5 R&B/R&R crossover. Covered by Elvis Presley (RCA, '66).

LET'S ACTIVE
1988

EVERY DOG HAS HIS DAY
Producer: Mitch Easter
Album: Every Dog Has His Day
Record Label: I.R.S.
Songwriter: Mitch Easter
R.E.M. mentor with a cult favorite.

LEVEL 42
1986

SOMETHING ABOUT YOU
Producers: Wally Badarou, Level 42
Album: World Machine
Record Label: Polygram
Songwriters: Mark Lindup, Phil Gould, Boon Gould, Mark King, Wally Badarou

LEVERT
1987

CASANOVA
Album: The Big Throwdown
Record Label: Atlantic
Songwriter: Reggie Calloway
#1 R&B/Top-10 R&R crossover for the second generation O'Jays.

MY FOREVER LOVE
Producers: Gerald Levert, Marc Gordon
Album: The Big Throwdown
Record Label: Atlantic
Songwriters: Gerald Levert, Marc Gordon

1992

BABY HOLD ONTO ME
Album: Private Line
Record Label: East/West
Songwriters: Gerald Levert, Edwin Nicholas
#1 R&B/Top-40 R&R crossover.

BARBARA LEWIS
1963

BABY I'M YOURS
Producer: Ollie McLaughlin
Album: Baby I'm Yours
Record Label: Atlantic
Songwriter: Van McCoy
Warm and comforting Soul in the Warwick mold.

HELLO STRANGER
Producer: Ollie McLaughlin
Album: Baby I'm Yours
Record Label: Atlantic
Songwriter: Barbara Lewis
#1 R&B/Top-5 R&R crossover was her biggest hit.

1965

MAKE ME YOUR BABY
Producers: Ollie Mclaughlin, Bert Berns

Record Label: Atlantic
Songwriters: Roger Atkins, Helen Miller
One of her finest efforts.

BOBBY LEWIS
1961

ONE TRACK MIND
Producer: Joe Rene
Album: Tossin' and Turnin'
Record Label: Beltone
Songwriters: Malou Rene, Bobby Lewis
Covered by Gary Lewis and the Playboys (Liberty, '66).

TOSSIN' AND TURNIN'
Producer: Joe Rene
Album: Tossin' and Turnin'
Record Label: Beltone
Songwriters: Malou Rene, Ritchie Adams
#1 R&B/R&R crossover; the biggest hit of the year.

GARY LEWIS AND THE PLAYBOYS
1964

THIS DIAMOND RING
Producer: Snuff Garrett
Album: This Diamond Ring
Record Label: Liberty
Songwriters: Irwin Levine, Al Kooper, Bob Brass
Rejected by Bobby Vee. Performed briefly by Gary in his father Jerry's '65 film The Family Jewels. Covered by Al Kooper (United Artists, '77).

1965

COUNT ME IN
Producer: Snuff Garrett
Album: A Session with Gary Lewis and the Playboys
Record Label: Liberty
Songwriter: Glen D. Hardin
In the waning days of AM radio.

SHE'S JUST MY STYLE
Producer: Snuff Garrett
Album: She's Just My Style
Record Label: Liberty
Songwriters: Leon Russell, Gary Lewis, Thomas Lesslie, Al Capps
Post-surf L.A. studio Pop Rock.

1966

GREEN GRASS
Producer: Dave Pell
Album: Hits Again!
Record Label: Liberty
Songwriters: Tommy Boyce, Roger Atkins

His last big hit.

SURE GONNA MISS HER
Producer: Snuff Garrett
Album: A Session with Gary Lewis and the Playboys
Record Label: Liberty
Songwriter: Bobby Russell

HUEY LEWIS AND THE NEWS

1982

DO YOU BELIEVE IN LOVE
Producer: Huey Lewis & the News
Album: Picture This
Record Label: Chrysalis
Songwriter: Robert John "Mutt" Lange

Rootsy bar-band rocker, from the versatile Mutt.

1983

HEART AND SOUL
Producer: Huey Lewis & the News
Album: Sports
Record Label: Chrysalis
Songwriters: Mike Chapman, Nicky Chinn

Tailor made for Top-40.

1984

THE HEART OF ROCK AND ROLL
Producer: Huey Lewis & the News
Album: Sports
Record Label: Chrysalis
Songwriters: Johnny Colla, Huey Lewis

Stumping for Cleveland, future site of the Rock and Roll Hall of Fame.

I WANT A NEW DRUG
Producer: Huey Lewis & the News
Album: Sports
Record Label: Chrysalis
Songwriters: Chris Hayes, Huey Lewis

Funk Lite.

IF THIS IS IT
Producer: Huey Lewis & the News
Album: Sports

Record Label: Chrysalis
Songwriters: John Colla, Huey Lewis

1985

THE POWER OF LOVE
Producer: Huey Lewis & the News
Album: *Back to the Future* Soundtrack
Record Label: Chrysalis
Songwriters: Chris Hayes, Huey Lewis, Johnny Colla

Their first #1, from the classic film Back to the Future.

1986

DOING IT ALL FOR MY BABY
Producer: Huey Lewis & the News
Album: Fore!
Record Label: Chrysalis
Songwriters: Phil Feliciato (Phil Cody), M. Duke

HIP TO BE SQUARE
Producer: Huey Lewis & the News
Album: Fore!
Record Label: Chrysalis
Songwriters: Bill Gibson, Huey Lewis, Sean Hopper

New Nerd anthem.

I KNOW WHAT I LIKE
Producer: Huey Lewis & the News
Album: Fore!
Record Label: Chrysalis
Songwriters: Chris Hayes, Huey Lewis

JACOB'S LADDER
Producer: Huey Lewis & the News
Album: Fore!
Record Label: Chrysalis
Songwriters: Bruce Hornsby, John Hornsby

Benefitting from the burgeoning career of the southern Rock jazzbo, Hornsby, whose "The Way It Is" hit the Top-10 a few months before, this tune became their third #1.

STUCK WITH YOU
Producer: Huey Lewis & the News
Album: Fore!
Record Label: Chrysalis
Songwriters: Chris Hayes, Huey Lewis

Evoking the classic hooks of Top-40s heyday.

1988

PERFECT WORLD
Producer: Huey Lewis & the News
Album: Perfect World
Record Label: Chrysalis
Songwriter: Alex Call

Their last automatic add.

JERRY LEE LEWIS

1956

CRAZY ARMS
Producer: Sam Phillips
Record Label: Sun
Songwriters: Ralphy Mooney, Charlie Seals

For his first Sun venture, Jerry Lee modestly tackled the top Country song of the year, introduced by Ray Price (Columbia, '56).

END OF THE ROAD
Producer: Sam Phillips
Record Label: Sun
Songwriters: Allyson Khent, Luther Dixon

B-side of "Crazy Arms."

1957

GREAT BALLS OF FIRE
Producer: Sam Phillips
Album: Jerry Lee's Greatest Hits
Record Label: Sun
Songwriters: Otis Blackwell, Jack Hammer

Proving that his first hit, the #1 C&W/R&B/Top-5 R&R cover of Roy Hall's (and Big Maybelle's) "Whole Lotta Shakin'" was no fluke, Jerry Lee gets another triple crossover, #1 C&W/Top-5 R&B/R&R. Covered by Tiny Tim (Reprise, '69).

1958

BREATHLESS
Producer: Sam Phillips
Record Label: Sun
Songwriter: Otis Blackwell

With his keyboard chops from Ike Turner and his Gospel fervor from his cousin Jimmy Swaggart, Jerry Lee reaches his pumping peak with his third and final triple Top-10 crossover. Covered by X in the '84 remake of the Godard movie Breathless.

HIGH SCHOOL CONFIDENTIAL
Producer: Sam Phillips
Album: High School Confidential
Record Label: Sun
Songwriters: Ron Hargrave, Jerry Lee Lewis

As seen opening the Mamie Van Doren/Russ Tamblyn teen exploitation flick High School Confidential. The same year Jerry Lee would be appearing in the confidential magazines himself, for the sin of marrying his thirteen-year-old cousin.

1968

SHE STILL COMES AROUND (TO LOVE WHAT'S LEFT OF ME)
Album: She Still Comes Around (to Love What's Left of Me)
Record Label: Smash
Songwriter: Glenn Sutton
Continuing his Country comeback.

WHAT'S MADE MILWAUKEE FAMOUS (HAS MADE A LOSER OUT OF ME)
Producer: Jerry Kennedy
Album: Another Place, Another Time
Record Label: Smash
Songwriter: Glenn Sutton
Ravaged, repentant, Jerry Lee is welcomed back to the country charts; Top-5 C&W/Bottom-10 R&R.

1970

SHE EVEN WOKE ME UP TO SAY GOODBYE
Album: She Even Woke Me up to Say Goodbye
Record Label: Smash
Songwriters: Mickey Newbury, Douglas Gilmore

SMILEY LEWIS
1955

I HEAR YOU KNOCKING
Album: I Hear You Knocking
Record Label: Imperial
Songwriters: Dave Bartholomew, Pearl King
Top-5 R&B hit. Cover by Gale Storm (Dot, '55) went Top-5 R&R. Also covered by Dave Edmunds (MAM, '71).

ONE NIGHT (OF SIN)
Record Label: Okeh
Songwriters: Dave Bartholomew, Pearl King
Considered so risqué in '55 that Lewis didn't even make the R&B charts with it. The landscape had changed considerably by the time it was covered by Elvis Presley (RCA, '58). So had the words, from "one night of sin" to "one night with you."

JOHN LEYTON
1961

JOHNNY REMEMBER ME
Producer: Joe Meek
Record Label: Top Rank
Songwriter: Geoffrey Goddard
#1 U.K. hit from the TV show "Harper's West One." Covered by the Bronski Beat with Marc Almond as part of a medley with "Love to Love You Baby" under the title of "I Feel Love" (MCA, '85).

LORI LIEBERMAN
1972

KILLING ME SOFTLY WITH HIS SONG
Record Label: RCA
Songwriters: Norman Gimbel, Charles Fox
Deifying the Folk Rock singer/songwriter Don McLean. Covered by Roberta Flack (Atlantic, '72), the Fugees (Columbia, '96).

JOE LIGGINS
1945

THE HONEYDRIPPER
Producer: Art Rupe
Record Label: Speciality
Songwriter: Joe Liggins
Sexually oriented Jump Blues, the #1 R&B record of the '4Us, suggests a pathway to Rock and Roll for the Dominoes to exploit at Alan Freed's pioneering Cleveland dances. Covered by Roosevelt Sykes (RCA, '46). Suggested segue: "Honeydripper Blues" by Edith Johnson (Paramount, '29).

GORDON LIGHTFOOT
1970

IF YOU COULD READ MY MIND
Producers: Lenny Waronker, Joe Wissert
Album: Sit down Young Stranger
Record Label: Reprise
Songwriter: Gordon Lightfoot
Canadian easy listening Folk Rock. Ian and Sylvia without the chill.

1974

CAREFREE HIGHWAY
Producer: Lenny Waronker
Album: Sundown
Record Label: Reprise
Songwriter: Gordon Lightfoot
Middle-of-the-road rambling song.

SUNDOWN
Producer: Lenny Waronker
Album: Sundown
Record Label: Reprise
Songwriter:·   Gordon Lightfoot
Mellow folk/rocker is his biggest hit.

1976

THE WRECK OF THE EDMUND FITZGERALD
Producers: Lenny Waronker, Gordon Lightfoot
Album: Summertime Dream
Record Label: Reprise
Songwriter: Gordon Lightfoot
Just previous to the dawn of Disco, a modern-day sea shanty could still make the Top-10. Suggested segue: "The Sloop John B." by the Beach Boys.

THE LIMELITERS
1962

THOSE WERE THE DAYS
Album: Folk Matinee
Record Label: RCA
Songwriter: Gene Raskin
Updated Russian Folk tune. Covered by Mary Hopkin (Apple, '68).

BOB LIND
1965

ELUSIVE BUTTERFLY
Producer: Richard Bock
Album: Don't Be Concerned
Record Label: World Pacific
Songwriter: Bob Lind
The effusive downfall of Folk Rock.

KATHY LINDEN
1958

BILLY
Record Label: Felsted
Songwriters: James Kendis, Joe Goodwin, Herman Paley
Revamping a 1911 tune from the American Quartet.

MARK LINDSAY
1969

ARIZONA
Producer: Jerry Fuller
Album: Arizona
Record Label: Columbia
Songwriter: Kenny Young

What Gale Garnett hath wrought: another commitment-phobic female. Suggested segues: "Suzanne" by Leonard Cohen and "Windy" by the Association.

LINEAR
1990

SENDING ALL MY LOVE
Producer: Tolga Katas
Album: Linear
Record Label: Atlantic
Songwriters: Tolga Katas, Charlie Pennachio

Miami dance mix.

BUZZY LINHART
1970

FRIENDS
Record Label: Buddah
Songwriters: Mark Klingman, Buzzy Linhart

Greenwich Village party song. Covered by Bette Midler (Atlantic, '70).

LIPPS, INC.
1979

FUNKYTOWN
Producer: Steve Greenberg
Album: Mouth to Mouth
Record Label: Casablanca
Songwriter: Steve Greenberg

Minneapolis dance track. Covered by Pseudo Echo (RCA, '86).

LISA LISA AND CULT JAM
1985

ALL CRIED OUT
Producer: Full Force
Album: Lisa Lisa and Cult Jam with Full Force
Record Label: Columbia
Songwriter: Full Force

Completing the trip from the street to the stage with a #1 R&B/Top-10 R&R crossover.

I WONDER IF I TAKE YOU HOME
Producer: Full Force
Album: Lisa Lisa and Cult Jam with Full Force
Record Label: Columbia
Songwriter: Full Force

Introducing the candystore evangelist Lisa Velez, with the uptown production team of Full Force.

1987

HEAD TO TOE
Producer: Full Force
Album: Spanish Fly
Record Label: Columbia
Songwriter: Chick Rains

Her crowning groove; a #1 R&B/R&R crossover.

LOST IN EMOTION
Producer: Full Force
Album: Spanish Fly
Record Label: Columbia
Songwriter: Full Force

Their mainstream main chance, a #1 R&B/R&R ballad.

1989

LITTLE JACKIE WANTS TO BE A STAR
Producer: Full Force
Album: Straight to the Sky
Record Label: Columbia
Songwriter: Full Force

1991

LET THE BEAT HIT 'EM
Producer: Rob Clivilles
Album: Straight outa Hell's Kitchen
Record Label: Columbia
Songwriters: Rob Clivilles, David Cole, Alan Friedman, Duran Ramos

Back to the dance floor; back to the #1 R&B/R&R groove.

LITTLE ANTHONY AND THE IMPERIALS
1958

TEARS ON MY PILLOW
Producer: George Goldner
Album: We Are Little Anthony & the Imperials
Record Label: End
Songwriters: Sylvester Bradford, Al Lewis

Echoes of a golden age, the last song of the Rock and Roll era, according to Bob Dylan.

1959

SHIMMY, SHIMMY KO-KO BOP
Producer: George Goldner
Album: We Are Little Anthony & the Imperials
Record Label: End
Songwriter: Bob Smith

Alan Freed's farewell song over 1010 WINS in New York City.

1964

GOIN' OUT OF MY HEAD
Producer: Teddy Randazzo
Album: I'm on the Outside (Looking In)
Record Label: DCP
Songwriters: Teddy Randazzo, Bobby Weinstein

Their biggest hit after "Tears on My Pillow," a precursor to the crooning style that would add years to their career in Las Vegas.

I'M ON THE OUTSIDE (LOOKING IN)
Producer: Teddy Randazzo
Album: I'm on the Outside (Looking In)
Record Label: DCP
Songwriters: Teddy Randazzo, Bobby Weinstein

Doo-Wop goes Middle-of-the-Road.

1965

HURT SO BAD
Producer: Teddy Randazzo
Album: Goin' out of My Head
Record Label: DCP
Songwriters: Teddy Randazzo, Bobby Hart, Bobby Weinstein (Bobby Wilding)

Lounge Rock, covered by Linda Ronstadt (Asylum, '80).

LITTLE CAESAR AND THE ROMANS
1961

THOSE OLDIES BUT GOODIES (REMIND ME OF YOU)
Album: Memories of Those Oldies but Goodies
Record Label: Del-Fi
Songwriters: Paul Politti, Nick Curinga

The end of the Doo-Wop era.

LITTLE EVA
1962

KEEP YOUR HANDS OFF MY BABY
Producer: Gerry Goffin
Album: Llllloco-Motion
Record Label: Dimension
Songwriters: Gerry Goffin, Carole King

In a repressive era for women, a positive Rock and Roll model for expressing agression.

THE LOCO-MOTION

Producer: Gerry Goffin
Album: Lillloco-Motion
Record Label: Dimension
Songwriters: Gerry Goffin, Carole King

With one of their more mindless ditties, Goffin, King, and their babysitter create a long-lasting annuity, attesting once again to the timeless, recurring, curative power of the groove. Covered by Grand Funk (Capitol, '74) and Kylie Minogue (Geffen, '87).

LITTLE FEAT

1970

WILLING

Producer: Russ Titelman
Album: Little Feat
Record Label: Warner Brothers
Songwriter: Lowell George

Their most famous downtown R&B classic.

1974

OH ATLANTA

Producers: Van Dyke Parks, Lowell George
Album: Feats Don't Fail Me Now
Record Label: Warner Brothers
Songwriter: Billy Payne

Country Funk.

1977

ROCKET IN MY POCKET

Producer: Ted Templeman
Album: Time Loves a Hero
Record Label: Warner Brothers
Songwriter: Lowell George

George's signature.

1978

ALL THAT YOU DREAM

Producer: Lowell George
Album: Waiting for Columbus
Record Label: Warner Brothers
Songwriters: Billy Payne, Paul Barrere

Covered by Linda Ronstadt (Asylum, '78).

1988

HANGIN' ON TO THE GOOD TIMES

Producers: Billy Payne, George Massenburg
Album: Let It Roll
Record Label: Warner Brothers
Songwriters: Bill Payne, Paul Barrere, Fred Tacket, Craig Fuller

Poignant reunion song. Suggested

segues:"Back Where It All Begins" by the Allman Brothers and "It's Been a Long Time" by Southside Johnny & the Asbury Jukes.

LITTLE JOE AND THE THRILLERS

1957

PEANUTS

Producer: Leroy Kirkland
Record Label: Okeh
Songwriter: Joe Cook

Falsetto to die for.

LITTLE RICHARD

1951

TAXI BLUES

Record Label: Camden
Songwriter: Leonard Feather

His first R&B effort, before he learned to speed it up, written by a noted Jazz commentator.

1955

TRUE FINE MAMA

Producer: Art Rupe
Album: Here's Little Richard
Record Label: Specialty
Songwriter: Richard Penniman (Little Richard)

Emerging from the limits of R&B as a rocker unrestrained.

TUTTI FRUTTI

Producer: Bumps Blackwell
Album: Here's Little Richard
Record Label: Specialty
Songwriters: Richard Penniman (Little Richard), Robert Blackwell, Dorothy LaBostrie

Arguably the first pure Rock and Roll performance on record, a New Orleans collaboration. Covered by Elvis Presley (RCA, '56).

1956

THE GIRL CAN'T HELP IT

Producer: Art Rupe
Album: Little Richard
Record Label: Specialty
Songwriter: Bobby Troup

Little Richard's coming out party, as seen in the Jayne Mansfield movie The Girl Can't Help It; revived in 1981 by Divine in the camp classic film Polyester.

HEEBY JEEBIES

Producer: Bumps Blackwell
Album: Little Richard
Record Label: Specialty
Songwriters: John Marascalco, Maybelle Wade Jackson

JENNY JENNY

Producer: Art Rupe
Album: Here's Little Richard
Record Label: Specialty
Songwriters: Richard Penniman (Little Richard), Enotris Johnson

LONG TALL SALLY

Producer: Bumps Blackwell
Album: Here's Little Richard
Record Label: Specialty
Songwriters: Enotris Johnson, Richard Penniman, Robert Blackwell

His biggest hit; #1 R&B/Top-10 R&R. Covered by Jerry Lee Lewis (Smash, '64).

READY TEDDY

Producer: Bumps Blackwell
Album: Here's Little Richard
Record Label: Specialty
Songwriters: John Marascalco, Robert Blackwell

B-side of "Rip It Up." Heard in the movie La Dolce Vita by a Little Richard impersonator. Covered by Elvis Presley (RCA, '56) and John Lennon (Apple, '75).

RIP IT UP

Producer: Bumps Blackwell
Album: Here's Little Richard
Record Label: Specialty
Songwriters: John Marascalco, Robert Blackwell

His biggest R&B hit: #1 R&B/Top-20 R&R. Covered by Bill Haley and the Comets (Decca, '56), Elvis Presley (RCA, '57), and the Everly Brothers (Cadence, '60).

SLIPPIN' AND SLIDIN'

Producer: Bumps Blackwell
Album: Here's Little Richard
Record Label: Specialty
Songwriters: Richard Penniman (Little Richard), Albert Collins, Edwin Bocage, James Smith

B-side of "Long Tall Sally."

1957

KEEP A-KNOCKIN'

Producers: Art Rupe, Little Richard
Album: Little Richard
Record Label: Specialty

Songwriter: Richard Penniman
(Little Richard)

His most compelling rocker. Top-5 R&B/Top-10 R&R crossover, featured in the movie Mr. Rock and Roll. Covered by the Everly Brothers (Warner Brothers, '65), the Flamin' Groovies (Buddah, '72), Suzi Quatro (Bell, '74), Mott the Hoople (Atlantic, '74), and the Blasters (Slash, '82).

LUCILLE

Producer: Bumps Blackwell
Album: Little Richard
Record Label: Specialty
Songwriters: Richard Penniman
(Little Richard), Albert Collins

His third #1 R&B/Top-20 crossover. Possibly one Bluesman's ode to another's guitar.

MISS ANN

Producer: Art Rupe
Album: Here's Little Richard
Record Label: Specialty
Songwriters: Richard Penniman
(Little Richard), Enotris Johnson

B-side of "Jenny Jenny."

OOOH! MY SOUL

Producers: Art Rupe, Little Richard
Album: Little Richard
Record Label: Specialty
Songwriter: Richard Penniman
(Little Richard)

SEND ME SOME LOVIN'

Producer: Art Rupe
Album: Little Richard
Record Label: Specialty
Songwriters: John Marascalco, Leo
Price

B-side of "Lucille."

1958

GOOD GOLLY, MISS MOLLY

Producer: Bumps Blackwell
Record Label: Speciality
Songwriters: John Marascalco,
Robert Blackwell

His last gasp on the Top-10, covered by Mitch Ryder (New Voice, '66) in a medley with "Devil with the Blue Dress On," Creedence Clearwater Revival (Fantasy, '69), and the Meat Puppets (SST, '86).

1965

I DON'T KNOW WHAT YOU'VE GOT (BUT IT'S GOT ME)

Producer: J. W. Alexander
Record Label: Vee Jay

Songwriters: Don Covay, Horace
Hall

Cited as one of the all-time-great Soul performances, putting Richard Penniman squarely in the line from James Brown back through Jackie Wilson.

1986

GREAT GOSH A MIGHTY

Producers: Dan Hartman, Billy
Preston
Album: Lifetime Friend
Record Label: Warner Brothers
Songwriters: Richard Penniman
(Little Richard), Billy Preston

Comeback track from the soundtrack of Down and Out in Beverly Hills.

LITTLE RIVER BAND

1978

LONESOME LOSER

Producers: John Boylan, Little River
Band
Album: Sleeper Catcher
Record Label: Harvest
Songwriter: David Briggs

Making the world safe for Air Supply.

REMINISCING

Producers: John Boylan, Little River
Band
Album: Sleeper Catcher
Record Label: Harvest
Songwriter: Graham Goble

Australian Middle-of-the-Road. Men at Work were working on it.

1979

COOL CHANGE

Albu,: Fire under the Wire
Record Label: Capitol
Songwriter: Graham Goble

1981

THE NIGHT OWLS

Album: Time Exposure
Record Label: Capitol
Songwriter: Graham Goble

LITTLE STEVEN AND THE DISCIPLES OF SOUL

1984

I AM A PATRIOT

Producer: Little Steven
Album: Voice of America
Record Label: EMI-America
Songwriter: Steve Van Zandt

Two years after organizing the Sun City Protest Chorus, more impassioned Rock from the Boss' former employer.

LITTLE WALTER

1952

JUKE

Record Label: Checker
Songwriter: Walter Jacobs

#1 R&B hit, furthering the evolution of the Blues harp. Sonny Terry, Junior Parker, Charlie Musselwhite, John Hammond, John Sebastian, John Lennon, Stevie Wonder all took note.

1955

MY BABE

Record Label: Chess
Songwriter: Willie Dixon

First #1 R&B hit for the legendary Chicago songwriter; second for the legendary Blues-harp stylist.

DEETTA LITTLE AND NELSON PIGFORD

1976

GONNA FLY NOW (THEME FROM ROCKY)

Producer: Bill Conti
Album: *Rocky* Soundtrack
Record Label: United Artists
Songwriters: Ayn Robbins, Bill
Conti, Carol Connors

They sang it in the movie. Bill Conti had the hit single (United Artists, '76).

LITTLE WILLIE LITTLEFIELD

1952

K. C. LOVIN'

Producers: Jerry Leiber, Mike Stoller
Record Label: Fury
Songwriters: Jerry Leiber, Mike
Stoller

A couple of white wiseguys invade the urban scene with one of their ultimate classics, steelier than Steely Dan and just as sophisticated. When this was remade as "Kansas City" by Wilbert Harrison (Fury, '59), Leiber and Stoller were already ensconced as the hottest songwriting duo on two coasts. In England, Lennon and McCartney were listening, reading the tiny print under the titles on the singles and album jackets.

LIVE
1994

I ALONE
Producer: Jerry Harrison
Album: Throwing Copper
Record Label: Radioactive/MCA
Songwriters: Edward Kowalcyzk, Patrick Dahlheimer, Chad Gracey, Chad Taylor

Mega Grunge power ballad of the nervous '90s.

LIGHTNING CRASHES
Producer: Jerry Harrison
Album: Throwing Copper
Record Label: Radioactive/MCA
Songwriters: Edward Kowalcyzk, Patrick Dahlheimer, Chad Gracey, Chad Taylor

Their biggest hit, moody and moving in a Hendrixian way.

SELLING THE DRAMA
Producer: Jerry Harrison
Album: Throwing Copper
Record Label: Radioactive/MCA
Songwriters: Edward Kowalcyzk, Patrick Dahlheimer, Chad Gracey, Chad Taylor

Their overground breakthrough.

LIVING COLOUR
1988

GLAMOUR BOYS
Producer: Mick Jagger
Album: Vivid
Record Label: Epic
Songwriter: Vernon Reid

Breaking the tacit black-Metal-color barrier, with the help of a prime imitator.

OPEN LETTER (TO A LANDLORD)
Producer: Ed Stasium
Album: Vivid
Record Label: Epic
Songwriters: Vernon Reid, T. Morris

WHICH WAY TO AMERICA
Producer: Ed Stasium
Album: Vivid
Record Label: Epic
Songwriter: Vernon Reid

1989

CULT OF PERSONALITY
Producer: Ed Stasium
Album: Vivid

Record Label: Epic
Songwriters: Vernon Reid, Will Calhoun, Cary Glover, Muzz Skillings

Their biggest hit, driven by Reid's avant guitar.

1990

ELVIS IS DEAD
Producer: Ed Stasium
Album: Time's Up
Record Label: Epic
Songwriter: Vernon Reid

Suggested segues: "Elvis Is Everywhere" by Mojo Nixon and Skid Roper, and "Calling Elvis" by Dire Straits.

RICHARD LLOYD
1978

ALCHEMY
Album: Alchemy
Record Label: Elektra
Songwriter: Richard Lloyd

Title song from the first solo effort by the co-founder of Television.

LO-KEY?
1992

I GOT A THANG 4 YA!
Album: Where Dey At
Record Label: Perspective
Songwriters: Lance Alexander, Tony Tolbert

#1 R&B/Top-30 R&R crossover.

LOBO
1971

ME AND YOU AND A DOG NAMED BOO
Producer: Phil Gernhard
Album: Introducing Lobo
Record Label: Big Tree
Songwriter: Kent Lavoie

The easy-listening Folk Rock formula of the '70s.

1972

I'D LOVE YOU TO WANT ME
Producer: Phil Gernhard
Album: Of a Simple Man
Record Label: Big Tree
Songwriter: Kent Lavoie

Lavoie's biggest hit.

1973

DON'T EXPECT ME TO BE YOUR FRIEND
Producer: Phil Gernhard
Album: Of a Simple Man
Record Label: Big Tree
Songwriter: Kent Lavoie

HANK LOCKLIN
1960

PLEASE HELP ME I'M FALLING
Album: Please Help Me I'm Falling
Record Label: RCA
Songwriters: Don Robertson, Hal Blair

#1 C&W/Top-10 R&R crossover.

LISA LOEB AND NINE STORIES
1994

STAY (I MISSED YOU)
Producer: J. Patino
Album: *Reality Bites* Soundtrack
Record Label: RCA
Songwriter: Lisa Loeb

Nerd Rock's finest hour: Janis Ian was proud, to say nothing of Gilbert O'Sullivan.

NILS LOFGREN
1977

I CAME TO DANCE
Album Title: I Came to Dance
Record Label: A&M
Songwriter: Nils Lofgren

Ultimate statement of purpose from the itinerant Neil Young and Bruce Springsteen sideman.

LOGGINS AND MESSINA
1971

DANNY'S SONG
Producer: Jim Messina
Album: Sittin' In
Record Label: Columbia
Songwriter: Kenny Loggins

Family-oriented Folk Rock. Covered by Anne Murray (Capitol, '73).

VAHEVELA
Producer: Jim Messina
Album: Sittin' In
Record Label: Columbia
Songwriters: Danny Loggins, Daniel Lottermoser

Familiar FM chant.

1972

ANGRY EYES
Producer: Jim Messina
Album: Loggins and Messina
Record Label: Columbia
Songwriters: Jim Messina, Kenny Loggins

Prime Folk Rock harmonies.

YOUR MAMA DON'T DANCE
Producer: Jim Messina
Album: Loggins and Messina
Record Label: Columbia
Songwriters: Kenny Loggins, Jim Messina

Their biggest hit. Covered by Poison (Enigma, '88).

DAVE LOGGINS
1974

PLEASE COME TO BOSTON
Producer: J. Crutchfield
Album: Apprentice in a Musical Workshop
Record Label: Epic
Songwriter: Dave Loggins

The first anti-rambling Rock song, qualifying it as a middle-of-the-dirt-road classic.

KENNY LOGGINS
1978

WHENEVER I CALL YOU "FRIEND"
Producer: Bob James
Album: Nightwatch
Record Label: Columbia
Songwriters: Kenny Loggins, Melissa Manchester

Adult but not contemporary, a duet with Melissa Manchester.

1980

I'M ALRIGHT
Producers: Bruce Botnick, Kenny Loggins
Album: *Caddyshack* Soundtrack
Record Label: Columbia
Songwriter: Kenny Loggins

Taking over Steven Bishop's Animal House function.

1984

FOOTLOOSE
Producers: Kenny Loggins, Lee DeCarlo
Album: *Footloose* Soundtrack

Record Label: Columbia
Songwriters: Dean Pitchford, Kenny Loggins

Wherein Kevin Bacon makes his dancing debut. But he was no John Travolta (although you could get from Travolta to Bacon in two movies: Travolta starred with Christian Slater in Broken Arrow; *Slater defended Bacon in* Murder in the First*).*

1986

DANGER ZONE
Producer: Giorgio Moroder
Album: *Top Gun* Soundtrack
Record Label: Columbia
Songwriters: Giorgio Moroder, Tom Whitlock

From the Tom Cruise film Top Gun.

1988

NOBODY'S FOOL (THEME FROM *CADDYSHACK II*)
Producer: Dennis Lambert
Album: Back to Avalon
Record Label: Columbia
Songwriters: Kenny Loggins, Michael Towers

LOLITA
1960

SAILOR (YOUR HOME IS THE SEA)
Record Label: Kapp
Songwriters: Alan Holt, Fini Busch, Werner Schaffenberger

Suggested segues: "Schock den Affen" by Peter Gabriel, "99 Luftbalons" by Nena, "Lucky Number" by Lene Lovich.

LAURIE LONDON
1957

HE'S GOT THE WHOLE WORLD IN HIS HANDS
Album: Laurie London
Record Label: Capitol
Songwriter: Geoff Love

One-record British invasion that pictured the English as prep-school wimps. That image would soon change.

LONDONBEAT
1991

I'VE BEEN THINKING ABOUT YOU
Producer: Martyn Phillips
Album: In the Blood
Record Label: Radioactive

Songwriters: George Chandler, William Henshall, Jimmy Chambers, Jimmy Helms

The new rave in England.

LONE JUSTICE
1985

WAYS TO BE WICKED
Producer: Jimmy Iovine
Album: Lone Justice
Record Label: Geffen
Songwriters: Tom Petty, Mike Campbell

Maria McKee's breakout vehicle, stalled in the passing lane.

LONESOME VAL
1990

TO BE YOUNG
Album: Lonesome Val
Record Label: Restless/Bar None
Songwriter: Val Haymes

Reinviting Katrina and the Waves as a New York power Punk band.

SHORTY LONG
1964

DEVIL WITH A BLUE DRESS ON
Producer: William Stevenson
Record Label: Soul
Songwriters: Shorty Long, William Stevenson

First release on the new Motown subsidiary, Soul, defined it. Covered by Mitch Ryder & the Detroit Wheels in a medley with "Good Golly, Miss Molly" (New Voice, '66).

1968

HERE COMES THE JUDGE
Record Label: Soul
Songwriters: Billie Jean Brown, Suzanne DePasse, Frederick Long

His biggest hit; Top-5 R&B/Top-10 R&R. DePasse took this songwriting credit all the way to a top front office position at Motown.

LOOKING GLASS
1972

BRANDY (YOU'RE A FINE GIRL)
Producers: Mike Gershman, Bob Lifton, Looking Glass
Album: Looking Glass

Record Label: Epic
Songwriter: Elliot Lurie

Lilting AM seafaring throwback. Suggested segue: "A Taste of Honey" by Bobby Scott.

A'ME LORAIN

1990

WHOLE WIDE WORLD

Producer: Elliott Wolff
Album: *True Love* Soundtrack
Record Label: RCA
Songwriters: Elliott Wolff, Arnie Roman

Breathy Hip-Hop in the Adbul mode.

LOS BRAVOS

1966

BLACK IS BLACK

Producer: Ivor Ramonde
Album: Black Is Black
Record Label: Parrot
Songwriters: Tony Hayes, Steve Wadey, M. Grainger

Pitney-esque garage Rock one-shot.

LOS DEL RIOS

1995

MACARENA (BAYSIDE BOYS MIX)

Producers: Carlos DeYarza, Mike Triay
Album: Macarena Non Stop
Record Label: Ariola
Songwriters: A. Romero Monge, R. Ruiz

Aided and abetted by the all-girl giggling chorus, second-generation Ronettes (or cousins of the Triplets), this Dance/Chant/Mix became the successor to "Whoof! (There It Is)" and The Wave in the arenas, dance halls, soccer stadiums (and probably bull rings) of the world.

LOS LOBOS

1985

WILL THE WOLF SURVIVE

Producers: T-Bone Burnette, Steve Berlin
Album: Will the Wolf Survive
Record Label: Slash
Songwriters: David Hidalgo, Louie Perez

East L.A. Rockabilly with an ecological perspective.

1987

THE HARDEST TIME

Producer: T-Bone Burnette
Album: By the Light of the Moon
Record Label: Slash
Songwriters: David Hidalgo, Louie Perez

Ineffable Tex-Mex Soul.

ONE TIME ONE NIGHT

Producer: T-Bone Burnette
Album: By the Light of the Moon
Record Label: Slash
Songwriters: David Hidalgo, Louie Perez

Neo-Rootsian bar-band classic.

1992

BEAUTIFUL MARIA OF MY SOUL

Album: *The Mambo Kings* Soundtrack
Record Label: Elektra
Songwriters: Robert Kraft, Arne Glimcher

The Punk Mariachi answer to the question of whether they sold out with their #1 cover of "La Bamba."

LOUD SUGAR

1991

INSTANT KARMA COFFEE HOUSE

Producer: Eric Westfall
Album: Loud Sugar
Record Label: SBK
Songwriter: David Grover

Moralistic Power Pop.

LOVE

1966

7 AND 7 IS

Producer: Jac Holtzman
Album: Da Capo
Record Label: Elektra
Songwriter: Arthur Lee

Biggest hit for the critically favored psychedelic Soul band.

SHE COMES IN COLORS

Producer: Jac Holzman
Album: Da Capo
Record Label: Elektra
Songwriter: Arthur Lee

A post-acid flashback, ignored by the charts.

1967

ALONE AGAIN OR

Producers: Bruce Botnick, Arthur Lee
Album: Forever Changes
Record Label: Elektra
Songwriter: Arthur Lee

A forgotten gem of psychedelic intensity.

YOU SET THE SCENE

Producers: Bruce Botnick, Arthur Love
Album: Forever Changes
Record Label: Elektra
Songwriter: Arthur Lee

Classic psychedelia.

LOVE AND KISSES

1978

THANK GOD IT'S FRIDAY

Producer: Robert Costandinos
Album: *Thank God It's Friday* Soundtrack
Record Label: Casablanca
Songwriter: Robert Costandinos

Disco self-promotion. But it was no Saturday Night Fever.

LOVE AND ROCKETS

1985

IF THERE'S A HEAVEN ABOVE

Producers: John A. Rivers, Love and Rockets
Album: Seventh Dream of Teenage Heaven
Record Label: Beggar's Banquet/RCA
Songwriters: David J., Daniel Ash, Kevin Haskins

An ethereal British dancehall epiphany.

1989

SO ALIVE

Producers: Jon Fryer, Love and Rockets
Album: Love and Rockets
Record Label: RCA
Songwriters: Daniel Ash, Love and Rockets

Moving into teenybop-T-Rex territory for their first and only hit.

LOVE SCULPTURE
1968

SABRE DANCE
Producer: Dave Edmunds
Album: Form and Feeling
Record Label: Parlaphone
Songwriter: Aram Khachaturian

Dave Edmunds begins his archetypically loopy career with a U.K. hit cover of the classical evergreen.

LOVE SPIT LOVE
1994

AM I WRONG
Producer: Dave Jerden
Album: Love Spit Love
Record Label: Imago
Songwriters: Richard Butler, Tom Butler

Remnants of the Psychedelic Furs in mid-tempo, mid-chart, neo-Folk rocker.

LOVE UNLIMITED
1973

LOVE'S THEME
Producer: Barry White
Album: Under the Influence Of
Record Label: 20th Century
Songwriter: Barry White

Instrumental interpretation of the Love Man's eternal Soul message.

1974

I BELONG TO YOU
Producer: Barry White
Album: In Heat
Record Label: 20th Century
Songwriter: Barry White

The Barry White studio singers; #1 R&B/Top-30 R&R.

DARLENE LOVE
1963

CHRISTMAS (BABY PLEASE COME HOME)
Producer: Phil Spector
Album: A Christmas Gift for You
Record Label: Philles
Songwriters: Jeff Barry, Ellie Greenwich, Phil Spector

Covered by U2 (A&M, '87).

A FINE FINE BOY
Producer: Phil Spector
Record Label: Philles

Songwriters: Jeff Barry, Ellie Greenwich, Phil Spector

TODAY I MET THE BOY I'M GONNA MARRY
Producer: Phil Spector
Record Label: Philles
Songwriters: Tony Powers, Ellie Greenwich, Phil Spector

Last gasp of Brill-styled R&B romanticized relationships. Covered by a mid-life crisis Ellie Greenwich (Verve, '73).

WAIT 'TIL MY BOBBY GETS HOME
Producer: Phil Spector
Record Label: Philles
Songwriters: Jeff Barry, Ellie Greenwich, Phil Spector

Biggest solo hit for the legendary Spector back-up singer.

1992

ALL ALONE ON CHRISTMAS
Producer: Steve Van Zandt
Album: *Home Alone II* Soundtrack
Record Label: Fox
Songwriter: Steve Van Zandt

Reviving the heyday of the Christmas Soul rocker.

H P LOVECRAFT
1967

I'VE BEEN WRONG BEFORE
Album: H P Lovecraft
Record Label: Phillips 67
Songwriter: Randy Newman

Previewing the work of L.A.'s favorite cynic, in a lazy, hazy setting.

LOVERBOY
1982

WORKING FOR THE WEEKEND
Producers: Bruce Fairbairn, Paul Dean
Album: Get Lucky
Record Label: Columbia
Songwriters: Paul Dean, Mike Reno, Matthew Frenette

Standard Arena anthem-mode working-class chant. Suggested segue: "Friday on My Mind" by the Easybeats.

1983

HOT GIRLS IN LOVE
Producer: Bruce Fairbairn
Album: Keep It Up
Record Label: Columbia

Songwriters: Paul Dean, Bruce Fairbairn

Lite Metal lite beer fantasy.

1985

LOVIN' EVERY MINUTE OF IT
Producer: Mutt Lange
Album: Lovin' Every Minute of It
Record Label: Columbia
Songwriter: Robert John "Mutt" Lange

Their biggest hit.

THIS COULD BE THE NIGHT
Producer: Mutt Lange
Album: Lovin' Every Minute of It
Record Label: Columbia
Songwriters: Paul Dean, Jonathan Cain, Mike Reno, Bill Wray

Foreigner, Jr.

LYLE LOVETT
1987

L.A. COUNTY
Producers: Tony Brown, Lyle Lovett
Album: Pontiac
Record Label: MCA/Curb
Songwriter: Lyle Lovett

The twisted face of new Country.

SHE'S NO LADY
Producers: Tony Brown, Lyle Lovett
Album: Pontiac
Record Label: MCA/Curb
Songwriter: Lyle Lovett

LENE LOVICH
1979

LUCKY NUMBER
Album: Stateless
Record Label: Stiff
Songwriters: Lene Lovich, Les Chappell

The original twisted sister, along with Exene Cervenka, Poly Styrene, Ivy Rorschach, Lydia Lunch, and Nina Hagen. Courtney Love was taking notes.

THE LOVIN' SPOONFUL
1965

DID YOU EVER HAVE TO MAKE UP YOUR MIND
Producer: Erik Jacobsen
Album: Do You Believe in Magic
Record Label: Kama Sutra
Songwriter: John Sebastian

Armed with his autoharp and harmonica belt, John Sebastian reigns briefly as the king of Hip.

DO YOU BELIEVE IN MAGIC
Producer: Erik Jacobsen
Album: Do You Believe in Magic
Record Label: Kama Sutra
Songwriter: John Sebastian

Epitomizing the good-time Country Blues essence of jug-band music, the Spoonful put Greenwich Village Rock and Roll (Folk Rock) on the map with this single.

THE OTHER SIDE OF THIS LIFE
Producer: Erik Jacobsen
Album: Do You Believe in Magic
Record Label: Kama Sutra
Songwriter: Fred Neil

Folk/Rock rambling standard. Covered by the Jefferson Airplane (RCA, '65), Peter, Paul and Mary (Warner Brothers, '66). Fred Neil's version was on Capitol ('66).

YOUNGER GIRL
Producer: Erik Jacobson
Album: Do You Believe in Magic
Record Label: Kama Sutra
Songwriter: John Sebastian

A West Village anthem (all the other Rock groups lived in the East Village). Covered by the Critters, who came from New Jersey (Kapp, '65).

1966

COCONUT GROVE
Producer: Erik Jacobsen
Album: Hums of the Lovin' Spoonful
Record Label: Kama Sutra
Songwriters: John Sebastian, Zal Yanovsky

Tribute to the mellow essence of Freddy Neil's southern hideaway.

DAYDREAM
Producer: Erik Jacobsen
Album: Daydream
Record Label: Kama Sutra
Songwriter: John Sebastian

Street music for the new denizens of the daylight hours, your average middle-class college dropout.

NASHVILLE CATS
Producer: Erik Jacobsen
Album: Hums of the Lovin' Spoonful
Record Label: Kama Sutra
Songwriter: John Sebastian

Tweaking the Country music business. Their

seventh successive Top-10 single out of seven releases. They would never have another one.

RAIN ON THE ROOF
Producer: Erik Jacobsen
Album: Hums of the Lovin' Spoonful
Record Label: Kama Sutra
Songwriter: John Sebastian

Effete ballad.

SUMMER IN THE CITY
Producer: Erik Jacobsen
Album: Hums of the Lovin' Spoonful
Record Label: Kama Sutra
Songwriters: John Sebastian, Mark Sebastian, Steve Boone

Their biggest hit, complete with jack hammer.

YOU DIDN'T HAVE TO BE SO NICE
Producer: Erik Jacobsen
Album: Daydream
Record Label: Kama Sutra
Songwriters: John Sebastian, Steve Boone

As infernally joyful as Folk Rock gets.

1967

DARLING BE HOME SOON
Producer: Erik Jacobsen
Album: You're a Big Boy Now
Record Label: Kama Sutra
Songwriter: John Sebastian

From Francis Ford Coppola's coming-of-age movie You're a Big Boy Now.

SIX O'CLOCK
Producers: Joe Wissert, The Lovin' Spoonful
Album: Everything's Playing
Record Label: Kama Sutra
Songwriter: John Sebastian

Their last big hit.

YOUNGER GENERATION
Producers: Joe Wissert, the Lovin' Spoonful
Album: Everything's Playing
Record Label: Kama Sutra
Songwriter: John Sebastian

The anxieties of expectant fatherhood.

YOU'RE A BIG BOY NOW
Producer: Erik Jacobsen
Album: You're a Big Boy Now
Record Label: Kama Sutra
Songwriter: John Sebastian

Title tune. After writing "She's a Lady" for the theatre (Jimmy Shine), Sebastian's next title tune would be for TV ("Welcome Back, Kotter").

JIM LOWE
1956

THE GREEN DOOR
Album: Songs Behind the Green Door
Record Label: Dot
Songwriters: Bob Davie, Marvin Moore

Suggested segue: "Party Lights" by Claudine Clark.

NICK LOWE
1978

(I LOVE THE SOUND OF) BREAKING GLASS
Producer: Nick Lowe
Album: Pure Pop for Now People
Record Label: Columbia
Songwriters: Nick Lowe, Andrew Bodnar, Steve Goulding

Biggest U.K. hit for this multi-faceted, many-hatted, retro-kitchy rockologist.

HEART OF THE CITY
Producer: Nick Lowe
Album: Pure Pop for Now People
Record Label: Columbia
Songwriter: Nick Lowe

B-side of "So It Goes," from an album entitled Jesus of Cool when it was released in England; this track was done live.

SO IT GOES
Producer: Nick Lowe
Album: Pure Pop for Now People
Record Label: Columbia
Songwriter: Nick Lowe

First release for the notorious English label Stiff, future home of Elvis Costello.

CRUEL TO BE KIND
Producer: Nick Lowe
Album: Labour of Lust
Record Label: Columbia
Songwriters: Nick Lowe, Robert Ian Gomm

His biggest U.S. hit.

1985

I KNEW THE BRIDE WHEN SHE USED TO ROCK AND ROLL
Producer: Huey Lewis & the News

Album: The Rose of England
Record Label: Columbia
Songwriter: Nick Lowe

Remake of earlier track was his last chart hit.

ROBIN LUKE

1958

SUSIE DARLIN'
Record Label: Dot
Songwriter: Robin Luke

Hawaiian Rockabilly.

LULU

1964

HERE COMES THE NIGHT
Record Label: Decca
Songwriter: Bert Berns

Covered by Them (Parrot, '65).

1967

TO SIR, WITH LOVE
Producer: Mickie Most
Album: Lulu Sings
Record Label: Epic
Songwriters: Don Black, Marc London

Title song from the film was the top Rock ballad of the year. Originally the B-side of "Let's Pretend." Covered by Natalie Merchant and Michael Stipe (Elektra, '94).

1970

OH ME OH MY (I'M A FOOL FOR YOU, BABY)
Producers: Tom Dowd, Jerry Wexler, Arif Mardin
Album: Lulu Sings
Record Label: Atco
Songwriter: Jim Doris

The producers next offered it to Aretha Franklin, who didn't do as well with it (Atlantic, '71).

VICTOR LUNDBERG

1967

AN OPEN LETTER TO MY TEENAGE SON
Record Label: Sun
Songwriter: Robert Thompson

At the height of the rebellious '60s, the reaction sets in. A big AM radio hit.

LUSCIOUS JACKSON

1994

DEEP SHAG
Producers: Jill Coniff, Gabrielle Glaser
Album: Natural Ingredients
Record Label: MCA
Songwriters: Jill Coniff, Gabrielle Glaser, Tom Mangurion

Heavy MTV rotation.

FRANKIE LYMON AND THE TEENAGERS

1956

THE A.B.C.'S OF LOVE
Producer: George Goldner
Album: The Teenagers
Record Label: Gee
Songwriters: George Goldner, Richard Barrett

Original sub-teen hearthrobs of Doo-Wop. A generation later the Jackson Five would sing "ABC" (Motown, '70).

I WANT YOU TO BE MY GIRL
Producer: George Goldner
Album: The Teenagers
Record Label: Gee
Songwriters: George Goldner, Richard Barrett

Their second crossover hit, scripted by the twin powers of New York Doo-Wop.

WHY DO FOOLS FALL IN LOVE
Producer: George Goldner
Album: The Teenagers
Record Label: Gee
Songwriters: Frankie Lymon, George Goldner, Herman Santiago

New York Doo-Wop classic of uncertain lineage. What's certain is that it marked the thirteen-year-old Lymon's meteoric rise to falsetto fame. Little Anthony benefitted, Nolan Strong didn't. Covered by the Diamonds (Mercury, '56), Gale Storm (Dot, '56), and Diana Ross (RCA, '81).

1957

GOODY GOODY
Producer: George Goldner
Album: Rock and Roll
Record Label: Gee
Songwriters: Johnny Mercer, Matt Melneck

Exercising the Doo-Wop reverse-cover perogative, they lift one from the catalogue of no-less-an-urban demigod than Frank Sinatra. The beginning and the end of Frankie's (Lymon that is) solo career.

I'M NOT A JUVENILE DELINQUENT
Producer: George Goldner
Album: Rock and Roll
Record Label: Gee
Songwriter: Frankie Lymon

Frankie's plaintive Doo-Wop quest for acceptance, as showcased in the seminal Tuesday Weld teen exploitation classic Rock, Rock, Rock of 1957.

BARBARA LYNN

1962

YOU'LL LOSE A GOOD THING
Producer: Huey Meaux
Album: You'll Lose a Good Thing
Record Label: Jamie
Songwriter: Barbara Lynn Ozen

Simmering New Orleans Soul.

1966

YOU LEFT THE WATER RUNNING
Record Label: Tribe
Songwriters: Dan Penn, Rick Hall, Oscar Franks

Memphis Soul classic, covered by Otis Redding (Stax, '67), Wilson Pickett (Atlantic, '67) and Maurice and Mac (Checker, '67).

CHERYL LYNN

1978

GOT TO BE REAL
Album: Cheryl Lynn
Record Label: Columbia
Songwriters: David Foster, Cheryl Lynn, David Paich

#1 R&B/Top-20 R&R crossover for a graduate of The Gong Show.

1989

ENCORE
Producers: Jimmy Jam, Terry Lewis
Album: Preppie
Record Label: Columbia
Songwriters: James Harris III, Terry Lewis

#1 R&B/Bottom-40 crossover.

LORETTA LYNN

1970

COAL MINER'S DAUGHTER
Album: Coal Miner's Daughter
Record Label: Decca
Songwriter: Loretta Lynn

#1 C&W/Bottom-20 R&R crossover. Title tune from the '80 biopic of the queen of Country Music.

LYNYRD SKYNYRD
1973

FREE BIRD
Producer: Al Kooper
Album: Lynyrd Skynyrd (pronounced leh-nerd skin-nerd)
Record Label: MCA/Sounds of the South
Songwriters: Ronnie Van Zant, Allen Collins

Dedicated to Southern soulmate Duane Allman. The '76 live version became an FM radio anthem.

GIMME THREE STEPS
Producer: Al Kooper
Album: Lynyrd Skynyrd (pronounced leh-nerd skin-nerd)
Record Label: MCA/Sounds of the South
Songwriters: Ronnie Van Zant, Allen Collins

Sophisticated Southern shuffle.

SWEET HOME ALABAMA
Producer: Al Kooper
Album: Second Helping
Record Label: MCA
Songwriters: Ronnie Van Zant, Edward King, Gary Rossington

In answer to Neil Young's "Southern Man."

1975

SATURDAY NIGHT SPECIAL
Producer: Tom Dowd
Album: Nuthin' Fancy
Record Label: MCA
Songwriters: Ronnie Van Zant, Edward King

Smokin' groove.

1977

I KNOW A LITTLE
Producer: Lynyrd Skynyrd
Album: Street Survivors
Record Label: MCA
Songwriter: Steve Gaines

Previewing the two-step.

THAT SMELL
Producer: Lynyrd Skynyrd
Album: Street Survivors
Record Label: MCA
Songwriters: Ronnie Van Zant, Allen Collins

Compelling anti-drug lyric. Suggested segue: "The Pusher" by Steppenwolf, "Codeine" by Quicksilver Messenger Service, "Suicide Solution" by Ozzie Osbourne.

WHAT'S YOUR NAME
Producer: Lynyrd Skynyrd
Album: Street Survivors
Record Label: MCA
Songwriters: Ronnie Van Zant, Gary Rossington

Suggested segues: "Stray Cat" by the Rolling Stones, and "Hot Blooded" by Foreigner.

YOU GOT THAT RIGHT
Producer: Lynyrd Skynyrd
Album: Street Survivors
Record Label: MCA
Songwriters: Ronnie Van Zant, Steve Gaines

Defining Southern Rock briefly before both Gaines and Van Zant were killed in a plane crash.

MC LYTE
1989

CAPPUCINO
Album: Eyes on This
Record Label: First Priority
Songwriters: MC Lyte, Aquil Davidson, Markel Riley, Walter Scott

Spunky Brooklyn rapper visits the next world.

1993

RUFFNECK
Album: Ain't No Other
Record Label: First Priority
Songwriter: MC Lyte

M

M
1979

POP MUZIK
Producer: M
Album: New York-London-Paris-Munich
Record Label: Sire
Songwriter: Robin Scott

Trans-Atlantic dance sensation.

M PEOPLE
1994

MOVING ON UP
Producer: M People
Album: Elegant Slumming
Record Label: Epic
Songwriters: Mike Pickering, Paul Heard

Big in the '90s Euro-Disco.

M.A.R.R.S.
1988

PUMP UP THE VOLUME
Record Label: 4th and Broadway
Songwriters: Steve Young, Andrew Biggs

Epitomizing the dance Pop revolution in the U.S. and London.

WILLIE MABON
1952

I DON'T KNOW
Record Label: Chess
Songwriters: Willie Mabon, Joe Thomas

Establishing the Chicago label's Blues crossover credentials with a massive #1 R&B tune.

1953

I'M MAD
Record Label: Chess
Songwriter: Willie Mabon

#1 R&B followup. Covered by Buddy Johnson (Mercury, '54).

KIRSTY MACCOLL
1979

THEY DON'T KNOW
Record Label: Stiff
Songwriter: Kirsty MacColl

Her debut stiff on Stiff. Covered by Tracy Ullman (MCA, '84).

1981

THERE'S A GUY WORKS DOWN THE CHIP SHOP SWEARS HE'S ELVIS
Producer: Bazza
Album: Desperate Character
Record Label: Polydor
Songwriters: Kirsty MacColl, Philip Rambow

Local color, British style.

1991

WALKING DOWN MADISON

Producer: Steve Lillywhite
Album: Electric Landlady
Record Label: Charisma
Songwriters: Kirsty MacColl, Johnny Marr

One of the best New York Cityscapes since her own ineffable "Fairtytale of New York," with the Pogues.

MARY MACGREGGOR

1977

TORN BETWEEN TWO LOVERS

Producers: Barry Beckett, Peter Yarrow
Album: Torn Between Two Lovers
Record Label: Ariola
Songwriters: Phil Jarrell, Peter Yarrow

In the delicate Folk Pop tradition of "We'll Sing in the Sunshine," a truly unsettling proposition.

CRAIG MACK

1994

FLAVA IN YA EAR

Producer: Easy Mo Bee
Album: Project: Funk the World
Record Label: Bad Boy/Arista
Songwriter: Craig Mack

The irresistible pulse of the street.

LONNIE MACK

1963

THE WHAM

Album: The Wham of That Memphis Man
Record Label: Fraternity
Songwriter: Lonnie Mack

Scintillating guitar track, coveted and covered by Stevie Ray Vaughan (Epic, '91).

MADNESS

1983

OUR HOUSE

Producers: Clive Langer, Alan Winstanley
Album: Madness
Record Label: Geffen
Songwriters: Charles Smyth, Christopher Foreman

Ska with a sense of humor, Monty Python-esque, of course.

MADONNA

1983

BORDERLINE

Producers: Reggie Lucas, Jellybean Benitez
Album: Madonna
Record Label: Sire
Songwriter: Reggie Lucas

First hit single for the displaced Detroit dancehall diva, a compelling return to girl-group yearning, spiced up with interracial innuendo for the jaded '80s.

LUCKY STAR

Producer: Reggie Lucas
Album: Madonna
Record Label: Sire
Songwriter: Madonna Ciccone

As girlishly innocent as Kathy Young, but with a devilish master plan.

1984

ANGEL

Producer: Nile Rodgers
Album: Like a Virgin
Record Label: Warner Brothers
Songwriters: Steve Bray, Madonna Ciccone

Her sixth of eleven Top-10 singles in a row, demonstrating her undeniable grip on the hot button of an adolescent subculture.

DRESS YOU UP

Producer: Nile Rodgers
Album: Like a Virgin
Record Label: Sire
Songwriters: Peggy Stanziale, Andrea LaRusso

LIKE A VIRGIN

Producer: Nile Rodgers
Album: Like a Virgin
Record Label: Sire
Songwriters: Billy Steinberg, Tom Kelly

First use of the word "virgin" in a Rock song since Laura Nyro's "The Confession," and Madonna didn't even write it. But she certainly took it all the way to the bank, selling it even to the R&B market for her only Top-10 R&B crossover. Steinberg and Kelly would go on to write "Eternal Flame" for Susannah Hoffs of the Bangles. Now there was virgin-like.

MATERIAL GIRL

Producer: Nile Rodgers
Album: Like a Virgin
Record Label: Sire
Songwriters: Peter Brown, Robert Rans

Materialistic, certainly. But even more apropos, she was proving herself amazingly deft and subtle when it came to choosing the perfect material, from stage costumes, to salty one-liners, to dance Rock classics by outside writers.

1985

CRAZY FOR YOU

Producer: Jellybean Benitez
Album: Vision Quest Soundtrack
Record Label: Geffen
Songwriters: John Bettis, Jon Lind

Her second #1 hit, from the inspirational wrestling movie that also spawned "Only the Young" for Journey and Patty Smyth and Scandal.

1986

INTO THE GROOVE

Producers: Steve Bray, Madonna
Album: Desperately Seeking Susan Soundtrack
Record Label: Reprise
Songwriters: Steve Bray, Madonna Ciccone

Like that of Elvis, the Beatles, Jo-ann Campbell, and Blondie, Madonna's Pop success and sex-appeal spawns a movie debut, replete with this suggestive dance track, released in England as a single, where it went to #1.

LA ISLA BONITA

Producers: Patrick Leonard, Madonna
Album: True Blue
Record Label: Sire
Songwriters: Patrick Leonard, Madonna Ciccone, Bruce Gaitsch

LIVE TO TELL

Producers: Patrick Leonard, Madonna
Album: True Blue
Record Label: Sire
Songwriters: Patrick Leonard, Madonna Ciccone

Her #1 ballad move, from the movie At Close Range with her then-husband, Sean Penn. But they were no Sonny and Cher.

OPEN YOUR HEART

Producers: Patrick Leonard, Madonna
Album: True Blue
Record Label: Sire
Songwriters: Patrick Leonard, Madonna Ciccone Peter Rafelson

The album's third #1 song.

PAPA DON'T PREACH
Producers: Steve Bray, Madonna
Album: True Blue
Record Label: Sire
Songwriters: Brian Elliott, Madonna Ciccone, Brian Elliot

Updating Frank Loesser's "Papa Don't Preach to Me," as sung by Betty Hutton in the 1947 movie The Perils of Pauline. *Interestingly, Wanda Jackson also covered a Betty Hutton tune: "Hot Dog, That Made Him Mad." (Capitol, '57).*

TRUE BLUE
Producers: Steve Bray, Madonna
Album: True Blue
Record Label: Sire
Songwriters: Steve Bray, Madonna Ciccone

WHERE'S THE PARTY
Producers: Steve Bray, Madonna
Album: True Blue
Record Label: Sire
Songwriters: Steve Bray, Madonna Ciccone, Patrick Leonard

Returning to the dance fold.

1987

CAUSING A COMMOTION
Producers: Steve Bray, Madonna
Album: Who's That Girl Soundtrack
Record Label: Sirc
Songwriters: Steve Bray, Madonna Ciccone

WHO'S THAT GIRL
Producers: Patrick Leonard, Madonna
Album: Who's That Girl? Soundtrack
Record Label: Sire
Songwriters: Patrick Leonard, Madonna Ciccone

Her sixth #1 R&R.

1989

CHERISH
Producers: Patrick Leonard, Madonna
Album: Like a Prayer
Record Label: Sire
Songwriters: Patrick Leonard, Madonna Ciccone

No relation to the Association tune.

EXPRESS YOURSELF
Producers: Steve Bray, Madonna
Album: Like a Prayer
Record Label: Sire

Songwriters: Steve Bray, Madonna Ciccone

Suggested segues: "Respect Yourself" by the Staple Singers, "Tell Him" by the Exciters.

KEEP IT TOGETHER
Producers: Steve Bray, Madonna
Album: Like a Prayer
Record Label: Sire
Songwriters: Steve Bray, Madonna Ciccone

LIKE A PRAYER
Producers: Patrick Leonard, Madonna
Album: Like a Prayer
Record Label: Sire
Songwriters: Patrick Leonard, Madonna Ciccone

Pretentious video.

VOGUE
Producers: Shep Pettibone, Madonna
Album: Like a Prayer
Record Label: Sire
Songwriters: Shep Pettibone, Madonna Ciccone

Dance groove with a sense of Hollywood history. Suggested segues: "Candle in the Wind" by Elton John, and "Celluloid Heroes" by the Kinks.

1990

HANKY PANKY
Producers: Patrick Leonard, Madonna
Album: I'm Breathless
Record Label: Sire
Songwriters: Patrick Leonard, Madonna Ciccone

No relation to the Tommy James track.

JUSTIFY MY LOVE
Producers: Lenny Kravitz, Andre Betts
Album: The Immaculate Collection
Record Label: Sire
Songwriters: Lenny Kravitz, Madonna Ciccone

Suggested segue: "Security of the First World" by Public Enemy.

RESCUE ME
Producers: Shep Pettibone, Madonna
Album: The Immaculate Collection
Record Label: Sire
Songwriters: Shep Pettibone, Madonna Ciccone

No relation to the Fontella Bass song.

SOONER OR LATER (I ALWAYS GET MY MAN)
Producers: Madonna, Patrick Leonard
Album: I'm Breathless
Record Label: Sire
Songwriter: Stephen Sondheim

Featured in the movie Dick Tracy, *and the most successful of her three collaborations with the noted theater songwriter Sondheim ("More" and "What Can You Lose" were the others) this single won the Oscar for Best Song. But Madonna on Broadway in "Speed the Plow" was a "fiasco at the Belasco."*

1992

BAD GIRL
Producers: Shep Pettibone, Madonna
Album: Erotica
Record Label: Maverick/Sire
Songwriters: Shep Pettibone, Madonna Ciccone

Unable to sell Sex, *her book of erotica, Madonna returns to the safety of post-pubescent dance Rock. No relation to the Smokey Robinson ballad.*

DEEPER AND DEEPER
Producers: Shep Pettibone, Madonna
Album: Erotica
Record Label: Maverick/Sire
Songwriters: Shep Pettibone, Madonna Ciccone, Tony Shimkin

Her answer to "More, More, More" by fellow porn-merchant Andrea True. No relation to the Aretha Franklin quasi-spiritual from Sister Act, Part Two.

EROTICA
Producers: Shep Pettibone, Madonna Ciccone
Album: Erotica
Record Label: Maverick/Sire
Songwriters: Shep Pettibone, Madonna Ciccone

THIS USED TO BE MY PLAYGROUND
Producers: Shep Pettibone, Madonna
Album: Barcelona Gold
Record Label: Warner Brothers
Songwriters: Shep Pettibone, Madonna Ciccone

Oscar-caliber ballad, from the movie A League of Their Own *moves Madonna up to a new, rarified level of schmaltz.*

GOODBYE TO INNOCENCE
1994

Producers: Shep Pettibone, Madonna
Album: Just Say Roe
Record Label: Sire
Songwriters: Shep Pettibone, Madonna Ciccone

Contributed to the pro-choice benefit record.

I'LL REMEMBER
Producers: Patrick Leonard, Madonna
Album: *With Honors* Soundtrack
Record Label: Maverick/Sire
Songwriters: Patrick Leonard, Madonna Ciccone, Richard Page

Obsessed with the big movie ballad, this time she nails one, from the otherwise mediocre film With Honors.

SECRET
Producers: Dallas Austin, Madonna
Album: Bedtime Stories
Record Label: Maverick/Sire
Songwriters: Dallas Austin, Madonna Ciccone

No longer a Virgin, now Madonna is more like the Virgin Mary. Suggested segue: "I Touch Myself" by the Divinyls.

TAKE A BOW
Producers: Madonna, Babyface
Album: Bedtime Stories
Record Label: Maverick/Sire
Songwriters: Kenny Edmunds (Babyface), Madonna Ciccone

The hits keep coming.

MAGAZINE
1979

SHOT BY BOTH SIDES
Album: Real Life
Record Label: Virgin
Songwriter: Howard DeVoto

Post-Buzzcocks one-shot.

THE MAGICIANS
1966

INVITATION TO CRY
Record Label: Columbia
Songwriters: Alan Gordon, J. Woods

Underground Greenwich Village Rock nugget.

MAHAVISHNU ORCHESTRA
1971

THE NOONWARD RACE
Album: The Inner Mounting Flame
Record Label: Columbia
Songwriter: John McLaughlin

Former Miles Davis and Tony Williams Lifetime guitarist moves on to spearhead the Jazz Rock fusion movement with this mini-rave up.

THE MAIN INGREDIENT
1972

EVERYBODY PLAYS THE FOOL
Producers: Luther Simmons, Tony Sylvester
Album: Bitter Sweet
Record Label: RCA
Songwriters: Kenneth Williams, Rudy Clark, Jim Bailey

Mainstream R&B philosophy.

THE MAJORS
1962

A WONDERFUL DREAM
Producer: Jerry Ragovoy
Record Label: Imperial
Songwriter: Norman Margolies

Notable Doo-Wop swansong, featuring falsetto of Ricky Cordo.

YNGWIE MALMSTEEN
1985

BLACK STAR
Album: Rising Force
Record Label: Polydor
Songwriter: Yngwie Malmsteen

Swedish Metal guitar God no longer in waiting.

MALO
1972

SUAVECITO
Producer: David Rubinson
Album: Malo
Record Label: Warner Brothers
Songwriters: Richard Bean, Abel Zarate, Pablo Tellez

Compellingly Santana-esque.

THE MAMAS AND THE PAPAS
1966

CALIFORNIA DREAMIN'
Producer: Lou Adler
Album: If You Can Believe Your Eyes and Ears
Record Label: Dunhill
Songwriters: John Phillips, Michelle Gilliam

Written in New York City, pondering a Westward move. Almost recorded by Barry McGuire as the follow up to "Eve of Destruction."

GO WHERE YOU WANNA GO
Producer: Lou Adler
Album: If You Can Believe Your Eyes and Ears
Record Label: Dunhill
Songwriter: John Phillips

Irresistible harmonies. Cover by the Fifth Dimension (Soul City, '67) was their first hit.

I SAW HER AGAIN LAST NIGHT
Producer: Lou Adler
Album: The Mamas and the Papas
Record Label: Dunhill
Songwriters: John Phillips, Dennis Doherty

MONDAY, MONDAY
Producer: Lou Adler
Album: If You Can Believe Your Eyes and Ears
Record Label: Dunhill
Songwriter: John Phillips

Their biggest hit.

WORDS OF LOVE
Producer: Lou Adler
Album: The Mamas and the Papas
Record Label: Dunhill
Songwriter: John Phillips

Answering Buddy Holly's more idealistic sentiments.

1967

CREEQUE ALLEY
Producer: Lou Adler
Album: Deliver
Record Label: Dunhill
Songwriters: John Phillips, Michelle Gilliam

And then they sang their autobiography.

TWELVE-THIRTY (YOUNG GIRLS ARE COMING TO THE CANYON)

Producer: Lou Adler
Album: Farewell to the First Golden Era
Record Label: Dunhill
Songwriter: John Phillips

The prologue to "Life in the Fast Lane" by the Eagles.

MELISSA MANCHESTER

1975

MIDNIGHT BLUE

Producer: Vini Poncia
Album: Melissa
Record Label: Arista
Songwriters: Melissa Manchester, Carole Bayer Sager

Midler protege, Midler throwaway.

1978

DON'T CRY OUT LOUD

Album: Don't Cry out Loud
Record Label: Arista
Songwriters: Peter Allen, Carole Bayer Sager

Superlative Broadway ballad, written by a couple of showbiz mensches, one of them married to Liza Minnelli, the other to Marvin Hamlisch, though not at the time.

1982

YOU SHOULD HEAR HOW SHE TALKS ABOUT YOU

Album: Hey Ricky
Record Label: Arista
Songwriters: Tom Snow, Dean Pitchford

Nightclub rocker was her biggest hit.

MANFRED MANN

1965

COME TOMORROW

Album: Five Faces of Manfred Mann
Record Label: Ascot
Songwriters: Bob Elgin, Frank Augustus, Dolores Phillips

Anti-war rocker.

IF YOU GOTTA GO, GO NOW (OR ELSE YOU GOT TO STAY ALL NIGHT)

Record Label: HMV
Songwriter: Bob Dylan

#2 U.K. hit. This brilliant folkie seduction number was an early performing highlight for Dylan, not released by him until '91.

MY LITTLE RED BOOK (ALL I DO IS TALK ABOUT YOU)

Album: *What's New Pussycat?* Soundtrack
Record Label: United Artists
Songwriters: Burt Bacharach, Hal David

New bar stool anthem, introduced in the Woody Allen movie What's New Pussycat? *Covered by Love (Elektra, '66).*

1966

PRETTY FLAMINGO

Producer: John Burgess
Album: Pretty Flamingo
Record Label: United Artists
Songwriter: Mark Barkan

In a league with the Kinks' "Waterloo Sunset." Covered by Tommy Roe (ABC/Paramount, '66) and Rod Stewart (Warner Brothers, '76).

1968

THE MIGHTY QUINN (QUINN, THE ESKIMO)

Album: The Mighty Quinn
Record Label: Mercury
Songwriter: Bob Dylan

*Mann's cover of the best track on Dylan's worst album (*Self Portrait*) went to #1 in the U.K. and Top-10 U.S. Mann also covered Dylan's "Just Like a Woman," in '66; "Please Mrs. Henry" (from* The Basement Tapes*) in '72; and "Father of Day, Father of Night" (from* New Morning*) in '74, before moving on to Bruce Springsteen covers.*

THE MANHATTANS

1976

KISS AND SAY GOODBYE

Producer: Bobby Martin
Album: The Manhattans
Record Label: Columbia
Songwriter: Winfred Lovett

Their first and biggest hit; a 1 R&B/Top-10 R&R crossover.

1980

SHINING STAR

Producer: Leo Graham
Album: After Midnight
Record Label: Columbia
Songwriters: Leo Graham Jr., Paul Richmond

BARRY MANILOW

1976

LOOKS LIKE WE MADE IT

Producers: Ron Dante, Barry Manilow
Album: This One's for You
Record Label: Arista
Songwriters: Barry Manilow, Bruce Sussman, Jack Feldman

His third and last #1.

COPACABANA (AT THE COPA)

Producers: Ron Dante, Barry Manilow
Album: Even Now
Record Label: Arista
Songwriters: Barry Manilow, Bruce Sussman, Jack Feldman

Bette Midler's former keyboard player and arranger finds his Disco niche.

BARRY MANN

1961

WHO PUT THE BOMP (IN THE BOMP BA BOMP BA BOMP)

Producers: Al Nevins, Don Kirshner
Album: Who Put the Bomp (in the Bomp Ba Bomp Ba Bomp)
Record Label: ABC-Paramount
Songwriters: Barry Mann, Gerry Goffin

The veteran songwriter's only solo hit. But it was no match for his "The Princess and the Punk" (Arista, '76).

MAR-KEYS

1961

LAST NIGHT

Producer: Chips Moman
Album: Back to Back
Record Label: Satellite
Songwriters: Chips Moman, Jerry Lee Smith, Charles Axton

This band contained Steve Cropper and Duck Dunn, who would go on to form Booker T. and the MGs, the future house band at Stax.

THE MARATHONS

1961

PEANUT BUTTER

Producers: Fred Smith, Cliff Goldsmith
Album: Peanut Butter
Record Label: Arvee

Songwriters: Martin J. Cooper, H. P. Barnum, Clifford Smith, Fred Goldsmith

One of the great falsetto leads. Suggested Segue: "Blue Moon" by the Marcels.

THE MARCELS
1961

BLUE MOON
Producer: Stu Phillips
Album: Blue Moon
Record Label: Colpix
Songwriters: Richard Rodgers, Lorenz Hart

The 1934 standard was covered by Elvis Presley on The Sun Sessions *(RCA, '56). But it was the Marcels perfect Doo-Wop #1 R&B/R&R crossover—aided and abetted by New York DJ, Murray the K—that really had the fathers of ASCAP quaking in their shoes. Suggested Segue: "Zoom Zoom Zoom" by the Collegians.*

HEARTACHES
Producer: Stu Phillips
Record Label: Colpix
Songwriters: Al Hoffman, John Klenner

Their classic Doo-Wop assault on a '32 Guy Lombardo tune wore a little thin.

LITTLE PEGGY MARCH
1963

I WILL FOLLOW HIM (CHARIOT)
Producer: Hugo and Luigi
Album: I Will Follow Him
Record Label: RCA Victor
Songwriters: Jacques Plante, J. W. Stole, Norman Gimble, Arthur Altman

A hit in France for Petula Clark. The adapted American lyrics were a natural for Little Peggy (Battavio) from Pennsylvania, given the prevailing dependent girl-group attitudes of '63. The song is more important for the fact that it topped not only the R&R charts, but crossed over to #1 R&B as well, thus eroding the credibility of that once peerless indicator of Rock and Roll hipness to an extent unapproached since Paul Anka's "Diana." An overhaul was in the offing.

BENNY MARDONES
1980

INTO THE NIGHT
Producer: Barry Mraz
Album: Never Run, Never Hide
Record Label: Polydor

Songwriters: Benny Mardones, Robert Tepper

Dramatic anthem had another chart run in '89.

ERNIE MARESCA
1962

SHOUT! SHOUT! KNOCK YOURSELF OUT!
Album: Shout! Shout! Knock Yourself Out
Record Label: Seville
Songwriters: Ernie Maresca, Thomas Bogdany

Dion's producer and pal jumps into the dance fray. But it was hardly "The Magestic."

THE MARKETTS
1962

SURFER'S STOMP
Record Label: Liberty
Songwriters: Joe Saraceno, Michael Daughtry

May have been the first surf music hit, beating the Beach Boys to the Top-40. But Dick Dale had broken the ground a few months before this release, with "Let's Go Trippin'," which peaked late in '61.

1963

OUT OF LIMITS!
Producer: Joe Saraceno
Album: Out of Limits!
Record Label: Warner Brothers
Songwriter: Michael Z. Gordon

Their biggest hit.

1966

BATMAN'S THEME
Producer: Dick Glaser
Album: Out of Limits!
Record Label: Warner Brothers
Songwriter: Neil Hefti

Cover of the TV theme song is their enduring legacy.

MARKY MARK AND THE FUNKY BUNCH
1991

GOOD VIBRATIONS
Producers: Donnie Wahlberg, Spice
Album: Music for the People
Record Label: Interscope
Songwriters: Donnie Wahlberg, Spice, Mark Walhberg

New Kids on the Block's younger brother. No threat to the legacy of Andy Gibb. Went on to model underwear.

BOB MARLEY & THE WAILERS
1963

EXODUS
Record Label: Island
Songwriter: Bob Marley

In 1977 this became their biggest R&B hit.

1965

ONE LOVE
Producer: Clement Dodd
Record Label: Island
Songwriters: Bob Marley, Bunny Livingston

First two-track recording ever made by the Wailers, espousing what Bob Marley would later turn into his personal philosophy. Wailers later performed this with the Impressions' tune "People Get Ready."

1968

STIR IT UP
Record Label: Trojan
Songwriter: Bob Marley

Covered by Johnny Nash, who had a hit in England with it (CBS, '71) and in the U.S. (Epic, '72). Re-recorded by Marley & the Wailers (Island, '75).

1969

FOUR HUNDRED YEARS
Producer: Lee Perry
Record Label: Island
Songwriter: Winston MacKintosh (Peter Tosh)

The Third-World beat sound of Reggae arrives on these shores, with an outrage and a patience long missing on the American Rock scene.

1971

STOP THAT TRAIN
Record Label: Summit
Songwriter: Bob Marley

TRENCHTOWN ROCK
Producer: Lee Perry
Record Label: Island
Songwriter: Bob Marley

Eloquent and authentic survival anthem.

1972

LIVELY UP YOURSELF
Producer: Bob Marley & the Wailers
Record Label: Green Door
Songwriter: Bob Marley

They updated this old Wailers classic on their album Natty Dread *(Island, '75).*

GET UP, STAND UP
Producers: Chris Blackwell, the Wailers
Album: Burnin'
Record Label: Island
Songwriter: Bob Marley

I SHOT THE SHERIFF
Producers: Chris Blackwell, the Wailers
Album: Burnin'
Record Label: Island
Songwriter: Bob Marley

Covered by Eric Clapton (RSO, '74).

NO MORE TROUBLE
Producers: Chris Blackwell, the Wailers
Album: Catch a Fire
Record Label: Island
Songwriter: Bob Marley

1974

NO WOMAN, NO CRY
Producers: Chris Blackwell, the Wailers
Album: Natty Dread
Record Label: Island
Songwriter: Bob Marley

One of the all-time Reggae standards.

1976

ROOTS, ROCK, REGGAE
Producer: Bob Marley & the Wailers
Album: Rastaman Vibrations
Record Label: Island
Songwriter: Vincent Ford

Their only American chart appearance.

1977

JAMMING
Producer: Bob Marley & the Wailers
Album: Exodus
Record Label: Island
Songwriter: Bob Marley

First U.K. hit single. Suggested segue: "Master Blaster (Jammin')" by Stevie Wonder.

1978

IS THIS LOVE
Producer: Bob Marley & the Wailers
Album: Kaya
Record Label: Island
Songwriter: Bob Marley

Another big U.K. hit.

1980

REDEMPTION SONG
Producer: Bob Marley & the Wailers
Album: Uprising
Record Label: Island
Songwriters: Bob Marley & the Wailers, Chris Blackwell

ZIGGY MARLEY

1988

TUMBLING DOWN
Producers: Jerry Harrison, Chris Frantz
Album: Conscious Party
Record Label: Virgin
Songwriters: Ziggy Marley, Tyrone Downe

Second generation #1 R&B/Reggae crossover.

MARMALADE

1970

REFLECTIONS OF MY LIFE
Producer: Marmalade
Album: Reflections of My Life
Record Label: London
Songwriters: William Campbell, Thomas McAleese

Hit #1 in the U.K.

THE MARSHALL TUCKER BAND

1977

HEARD IT IN A LOVE SONG
Producer: Paul Hornsby
Album: Carolina Dreams
Record Label: Capricorn
Songwriter: Toy Caldwell

Biggest hit for the southern rockers, a lilting cowboy ballad.

MARTHA AND THE VANDELLAS

1963

COME AND GET THESE MEMORIES
Producers: Brian Holland, Lamont Dozier
Album: Come and Get These Memories
Record Label: Gordy
Songwriters: Eddie Holland, Lamont Dozier, Brian Holland

First hit for Motown's hungriest-sounding group.

HEAT WAVE
Producers: Brian Holland, Lamont Dozier
Album: Heat Wave
Record Label: Gordy
Songwriters: Eddie Holland, Lamont Dozier, Brian Holland

Motown's most prolific writers anticipate the long hot summers of the mid-'60s, in Detroit, Newark, Watts, and elsewhere, with a #1 R&B/Top-10 R&R crossover.

QUICKSAND
Producers: Brian Holland, Lamont Dozier
Album: Greatest Hits
Record Label: Gordy
Songwriters: Eddie Holland, Lamont Dozier, Brian Holland

Emphasizing the Martha Reeves/Motown penchant for romantic disaster.

1964

DANCING IN THE STREET
Producer: William Stevenson
Album: Dance Party
Record Label: Gordy
Songwriters: Marvin Gaye, William Stevenson, Ivy Hunter

Their biggest hit. Covered by the Mamas & the Papas (Dunhill, '67). Suggested Segues: "Street Fighting Man" by the Rolling Stones and "Racing in the Streets" by Bruce Springsteen.

1965

NOWHERE TO RUN
Producers: Brian Holland, Lamont Dozier
Album: Dance Party
Record Label: Gordy
Songwriters: Eddie Holland, Lamont Dozier, Brian Holland

Echoing the drastic turmoil of their emotional twin brothers, the Four Tops.

1966

I'M READY FOR LOVE
Producers: Brian Holland, Lamont Dozier
Album: Watchout!
Record Label: Gordy
Songwriters: Eddie Holland, Lamont Dozier, Brian Holland

Top-10 R&B/R&R crossover.

1967

HONEY CHILE
Producer: Richard Morris
Album: Ridin' High

Record Label: Gordy
Songwriters: Sylvia Moy, Richard Morris

JIMMY MACK

Producers: Brian Holland, Lamont Dozier
Album: Watchout!
Record Label: Gordy
Songwriters: Eddie Holland, Lamont Dozier, Brian Holland

#1 R&B/Top-10 R&R crossover.

MARTIKA

1989

TOY SOLDIERS

Producer: Michael Jay
Album: Martika
Record Label: Columbia
Songwriters: Martika Marrero, Michael Jay

Hidden in the Bubble Pop was a protest song not unlike "Which Way You Goin' Billy."

MARTIN AND NEIL

1965

I KNOW YOU RIDER

Album: Tear Down the Walls
Record Label: Elektra
Songwriter: Traditional

A basic Folk Rock repertoire requirement. Covered by the Grateful Dead (Sunflower, '66).

I'M A DRIFTER

Album: Tear Down the Walls
Record Label: Elektra
Songwriter: Fred Neil

Epitome of the rambling genre. Covered by Bobby Goldsboro (United Artists, '69).

DEAN MARTIN

1953

THAT'S AMORE

Record Label: Capitol
Songwriters: Jack Brooks, Harry Warren

There's no discounting Martin's influence on the early—as well as the later—Elvis Presley.

STEVE MARTIN & THE TOOTS UNCOMMONS

1978

KING TUT

Producer: Bill McKuen
Album: A Wild and Crazy Guy
Record Label: Warner Brothers
Songwriter: Steve Martin

His hit single. But not as funny as "What I Believe" (Warner Brothers, '81).

THE MARVELETTES

1961

PLEASE MR. POSTMAN

Producers: Brian Holland, Robert Bateman
Album: Please Mr. Postman
Record Label: Tamla
Songwriters: Freddie Gorman, William Garrett, Brian Holland, Georgia Dobbins

First and biggest hit for Motown's best girl-group, a #1 R&B/R&R crossover. Covered by the Beatles (Capitol, '64). The Carpenters brought it to #1 again (A&M, '75).

1962

BEECHWOOD 4-5789

Producer: William Stevenson
Album: Playboy
Record Label: Tamla
Songwriters: Marvin Gaye, Berry Gordy Jr., William Stevenson

Having taken on the post office in their first hit, the Marvelettes move on to the phone company.

PLAYBOY

Producer: Brianbert
Album: Playboy
Record Label: Tamla
Songwriters: Robert Bateman, William Stevenson, Brian Holland

Their second biggest hit.

STRANGE I KNOW

Producers: Brian Holland, Robert Bateman
Album: Marvelous Marvelettes
Record Label: Tamla
Songwriters: Freddie Gorman, Lamont Dozier, Brian Holland

The song stiffed, but with the addition of Lamont Dozier, two-thirds of Motown's most famous songwriting aggregate was now in place.

1963

LOCKING UP MY HEART

Producer: Lamont Dozier
Album: Marvelous Marvelettes
Record Label: Tamla
Songwriters: Eddie Holland, Brian Holland

The advent of the Holland-Dozier-Holland imprint, fine quality, craftsmanship, and durability of songwriting and production.

1966

DON'T MESS WITH BILL

Producer: Smokey Robinson
Album: Greatest Hits
Record Label: Tamla
Songwriter: Smokey Robinson

Smokey's touch returns them to Top-10 R&B/R&R status.

1967

THE HUNTER GETS CAPTURED BY THE GAME

Producer: Smokey Robinson
Album: The Marvelettes
Record Label: Tamla
Songwriter: Smokey Robinson

Their biggest R&B hit since "Please Mr. Postman."

MY BABY MUST BE A MAGICIAN

Producer: Smokey Robinson
Album: Sophisticated Soul
Record Label: Tamla
Songwriter: Smokey Robinson

Their last big hit.

THE MARVELOWS

1965

I DO

Record Label: ABC-Paramount
Songwriters: Jesse Smith, Johnny Paden, Frank Paden, Willie Stephenson, Melvin Mason

Top-10 R&B. Covered by the J. Geils Band (Atlantic, '77).

MARVIN AND JOHNNY

1954

CHERRY PIE

Producer: Art Rupe
Record Label: Modern
Songwriters: Marvin Phillips, Joe Josea

Doo-Wop classic, covered by Skip and Flip (Brent, '60). The B-side of "Tick Tock."

RICHARD MARX
1987

DON'T MEAN NOTHIN'
Producers: David Cole, Richard Marx
Album: Richard Marx
Record Label: Manhattan
Songwriters: Richard Marx, Bruce Gaitsch
Inheriting the David Gates Soft Rock mantle.

SHOULD'VE KNOWN BETTER
Producer: H. Gatica
Album: Richard Marx
Record Label: EMI-Manhattan
Songwriter: Richard Marx
Casting more of his bread upon the waters of '87.

1988

ENDLESS SUMMER NIGHTS
Producer: H. Gatica
Album: Richard Marx
Record Label: EMI-Manhattan
Songwriter: Richard Marx
Briefly reviving the art of the Summer song.

HOLD ON TO THE NIGHTS
Producer: Richard Marx
Album: Richard Marx
Record Label: Chrysalis
Songwriters: David Cole, Richard Marx
Fourth and biggest hit on the album, reaching #1 after two #3s and a #2.

1989

ANGELIA
Producers: David Cole, Richard Marx
Album: Repeat Offender
Record Label: EMI
Songwriter: RIchard Marx
His seventh straight Top-5 single.

CHILDREN OF THE NIGHT
Producers: David Cole, Richard Marx
Album: Repeat Offender
Record Label: EMI
Songwriter: Richard Marx
Proceeds donated to help end child prostitution. Suggested segues: "Runaway" by Del Shannon, "Runaway" by Bon Jovi.

RIGHT HERE WAITING
Producers: David Cole, Richard Marx
Album: Repeat Offender

Record Label: EMI
Songwriters: Richard Marx, David Cole
His third straight and biggest #1 single.

SATISFIED
Producers: David Cole, Richard Marx
Album: Repeat Offender
Record Label: EMI
Songwriters: Richard Marx, David Cole
And no wonder.

1991

HAZARD
Producer: Richard Marx
Album: Rush Street
Record Label: Capitol
Songwriter: Richard Marx

1994

NOW AND FOREVER
Producers: Terry Thomas, Richard Marx
Album: Paid Vacation
Record Label: Capitol
Songwriter: Richard Marx
Featured in the movie The Getaway.

MARY JANE GIRLS
1985

IN MY HOUSE
Album: Only Four You
Record Label: Gordy
Songwriter: Rick James
Funky dance track.

CAROLYNE MAS
1979

STILL SANE
Producer: Steve Burgh
Album: Carolyne Mas
Record Label: Mercury
Songwriter: Carolyne Mas
Post-Nyro New York confessional rocker.

HUGH MASEKELA
1968

GRAZING IN THE GRASS
Producer: Stewart Levine
Album: The Promise of a Future
Record Label: Uni
Songwriters: Harry Elston, Philemon Hou
#1 R&B/R&R crossover instrumental by the South African trumpeter. Vocal version

by the Friends of Distinction (RCA, '69) was a Top-10 R&B/R&R crossover, with tongue-twisting lyrics by group member Elston.

BARBARA MASON
1965

YES, I'M READY
Producer: Weldon MacDougal
Album: Yes, I'm Ready
Record Label: Arctic
Songwriter: Barbara Mason
The girl-group sound, deflowered by Philadelphia's finest. Covered by Teri DeSario with K. C. (TK, '80).

BONNIE JO MASON
1964

RINGO, I LOVE YOU
Record Label: Annette
Songwriters: Peter Anders, Vini Poncia
Cher, in an earlier, more malleable, period.

DAVE MASON
1970

ONLY YOU KNOW AND I KNOW
Producers: Tommy LiPuma, Dave Mason
Album: Alone Together
Record Label: Blue Thumb
Songwriter: Dave Mason
First solo single from the Traffic co-founder; an FM mini-hit.

SHOULDN'T HAVE TOOK MORE THAN YOU GAVE
Producers: Tommy LiPuma, Dave Mason
Album: Alone Together
Record Label: Blue Thumb
Songwriter: Dave Mason
Prototypically anxious Folk/Rock.

1977

WE JUST DISAGREE
Producer: Jim Kreuger
Album: Let It Flow
Record Label: Columbia
Songwriter: Jim Krueger
His biggest hit.

JOHNNY MATHIS
1957

WONDERFUL, WONDERFUL
Album: Johnny Mathis' Greatest Hits
Record Label: Columbia

Songwriters: Ben Raleigh, Sherman Edwards

Out of his primarily Pop repertoire came several of the all-time classic make-out ballads of the Rock and Roll era, this atmospheric epic the first and the best. His greatest hits album lasted on the charts for about eight years, longer than most of the relationships his mercurial baby boom audience would ever have.

THE DAVE MATTHEWS BAND

1994

WHAT WOULD YOU SAY

Producer: Steve Lillywhite
Album: Under the Table and Dreaming
Record Label: RCA
Songwriter: Dave Matthews

Helping to define the new collegiate sensibility with a loping post-modern Deadhead drawl.

JOHN MAYALL'S BLUESBREAKERS

1967

HAVE YOU HEARD

Producer: Mike Vernon
Album: John Mayall's Bluesbreakers
Record Label: London
Songwriter: John Mayall

Noted British Blues maven and bandleader gives Eric Clapton his first major guitar showcase.

PARCHMAN FARM

Producer: Mike Vernon
Album: John Mayall's Bluesbreakers
Record Label: London
Songwriter: Mose Allison

Erudite Blues classic. Covered by Blue Cheer (Phillips, '68).

STEPPIN' OUT

Producer: Mike Vernon
Album: John Mayall's Bluesbreakers
Record Label: London
Songwriter: James Bracken

Another early Clapton highlight.

1969

ROOM TO MOVE

Album: The Turning Point
Record Label: Polydor
Songwriter: John Mayall

With Jon Mark and Johnny Almond, a new era.

CURTIS MAYFIELD

1970

DON'T WORRY (IF THERE'S A HELL BELOW WE'RE ALL GONNA GO)

Producer: Curtis Mayfield
Album: Curtis
Record Label: Curtom
Songwriter: Curtis Mayfield

Still preaching the Gospel of Soul; a Top-5 R&B/Top-40 R&R crossover for the former leader of the Impressions.

1972

FREDDY'S DEAD (THEME FROM *SUPERFLY*)

Producer: Curtis Mayfield
Album: *Superfly* Soundtrack
Record Label: Curtom
Songwriter: Curtis Mayfield

His biggest hit; from the blaxploitation film, a perfect street-level R&B anthem.

PUSHERMAN

Producer: Curtis Mayfield
Album: *Superfly* Soundtrack
Record Label: Curtom
Songwriter: Curtis Mayfield

Gangsta Rap, without the rap. Suggested segue: "Home Is Where the Hatred Is" by Gil Scott-Heron.

SUPERFLY

Producer: Curtis Mayfield
Album: *Superfly* Soundtrack
Record Label: Curtom
Songwriter: Curtis Mayfield

Completing the trilogy that makes Superfly the best black music soundtrack this side of The Harder They Come.

PERCY MAYFIELD

1951

PLEASE SEND ME SOMEONE TO LOVE

Producer: Art Rupe
Album: Poet of the Blues
Record Label: Specialty
Songwriter: Percy Mayfield

L.A. Bluesman's most famous effort. Covered by the Moonglows (Chess, '57), Irma Thomas (Imperial, '64), B.B. King (Bluesway, '68), Solomon Burke (Bell, '69), Esther Phillips (Atlantic, '71), Paul Butterfield's Better Days (Bearsville, '73).

MAZE

1985

BACK IN STRIDE

Album: Can't Stop the Love
Record Label: Capitol
Songwriter: Frankie Beverly

#1 R&B/Bottom-20 R&R crossover.

MAZZY STAR

1994

FADE INTO YOU

Producer: David Roback
Album: So Tonight That I Might See
Record Label: Capitol
Songwriters: David Roback, Hope Sandoval

In the neo-heyday of the wispy British thrush, one of the wispier of the genre.

THE MC5

1969

KICK OUT THE JAMS

Producers: Bruce Botnick, Jac Holtzman
Album: Kick out the Jams
Record Label: Elektra
Songwriter: The MC5

Revolutionary punk noise tract from Detroit. Suggested segue from San Francisco: "Volunteers of America" by the Jefferson Airplane; from New York: "White Light, White Heat" by the Velvet Underground.

C. W. MCCALL

1975

CONVOY

Producers: Don Sears, Chip Davis
Album: Black Bear Road
Record Label: MGM
Songwriters: William Fries, Louis Davis

#1 C&W/R&R truckstop crossover.

LES MCCANN AND EDDIE HARRIS

1970

COMPARED TO WHAT

Producers: Neshui Ertegun, Joel Dorn
Album: Swiss Movement
Record Label: Atlantic
Songwriter: Gene McDaniels

Fierce Jazz/R&B groove and philosophy.

PETER McCANN
1977

DO YOU WANNA MAKE LOVE
Producer: Hal Yoegler
Album: Peter McCann
Record Label: 20th Century
Songwriter: Peter McCann

The year's most rhetorical musical question.

PAUL McCARTNEY AND LINDA McCARTNEY
1970

MAYBE I'M AMAZED
Producer: Paul McCartney
Album: McCartney
Record Label: Apple
Songwriter: Paul McCartney

Picking up where the Beatles left off, in the middle-of-the-Rock-and-Roll-road. Song became a hit single in '77.

1971

MONKBERRY MOON DELIGHT
Producer: Paul McCartney
Album: Ram
Record Label: Capitol
Songwriters: Paul McCartney, Linda McCartney

While Lennon screams, Paul basks in the lush folds of his country home/studio with his lovely wife Linda.

UNCLE ALBERT/ADMIRAL HALSEY
Producers: Paul McCartney, Linda McCartney
Album: Ram
Record Label: Apple
Songwriters: Paul McCartney, Linda McCartney

Extolling the simple pleasures of post-Beatlemania, with his wife in the John Lennon role, Paul gains his first semi-solo #1.

PAUL McCARTNEY AND WINGS
1971

ANOTHER DAY
Producers: Paul McCartney, Linda McCartney
Album: Wings' Greatest
Record Label: Apple
Songwriters: Paul McCartney, Linda McCartney

Another era. Paul has his first post-Beatles hit with another band.

1972

HI HI HI
Producer: Paul McCartney
Album: Wings over America
Record Label: Apple
Songwriters: Paul McCartney, Linda McCartney

The former cute Beatle at his cutest.

1973

HELEN WHEELS
Producer: Paul McCartney
Album: Band on the Run
Record Label: Apple
Songwriters: Paul McCartney, Linda McCartney

One of his best post-Beatles rockers.

LIVE AND LET DIE
Producer: Paul McCartney
Album: Wings over America
Record Label: Capitol
Songwriters: Paul McCartney, Linda McCartney

Teaming up with Britain's second most famous artistic creation, James Bond. Covered by Guns N' Roses (Geffen, '91).

MY LOVE
Producer: Paul McCartney
Album: Red Rose Speedway
Record Label: Apple
Songwriters: Paul McCartney, Linda McCartney

A straight love song . . . as opposed to a silly one.

1974

BAND ON THE RUN
Producer: Paul McCartney
Album: Band on the Run
Record Label: Apple
Songwriters: Paul McCartney, Linda McCartney

Pretty authentic rocker. Suggested segue: "Homeward Bound" by Simon and Garfunkel, "Leaving on a Jet Plane" by Peter, Paul and Mary.

JET
Producer: Paul McCartney
Album: Band on the Run
Record Label: Apple
Songwriters: Paul McCartney, Linda McCartney

One of his best Rock songs.

JUNIOR'S FARM
Producer: Paul McCartney
Album: Wings' Greatest
Record Label: Apple
Songwriters: Paul McCartney, Linda McCartney

Suggested segue: "Maggie's Farm" by Bob Dylan.

1975

LISTEN TO WHAT THE MAN SAID
Producer: Paul McCartney
Album: Venus and Mars Rock Show
Record Label: Capitol
Songwriters: Paul McCartney, Linda McCartney

1976

LET 'EM IN
Producer: Paul McCartney
Album: Wings at the Speed of Sound
Record Label: Capitol
Songwriter: Paul McCartney

MULL OF KINTYRE
Producer: Paul McCartney
Album: Wings' Greatest
Record Label: Capitol
Songwriter: Paul McCartney

His biggest U.K. hit; not released as a single in the U.S.

SILLY LOVE SONGS
Producer: Paul McCartney
Album: Wings at the Speed of Sound
Record Label: Capitol
Songwriter: Paul McCartney

His ultimate latter-day statement of purpose is his first solo songwriting hit.

WITH A LITTLE LUCK
Producer: Paul McCartney
Album: London Town
Record Label: Capitol
Songwriters: Paul McCartney, Linda McCartney

His fifth and last solo #1 single.

1979

GOODNIGHT TONIGHT
Producer: Paul McCartney
Album: All the Best
Record Label: Capitol
Songwriters: Paul McCartney, Linda McCartney

PAUL MCCARTNEY AND STEVIE WONDER

1982

EBONY AND IVORY
Producer: George Martin
Album: Tug of War
Record Label: Columbia
Songwriter: Paul McCartney

Two Pop prodigies offer their plan for world harmony.

PAUL MCCARTNEY AND MICHAEL JACKSON

1983

SAY SAY SAY
Producer: George Martin
Album: Pipes of Peace
Record Label: Columbia
Songwriters: Paul McCartney, Michael Jackson

A mega-merger between the artist and his publisher gives McCartney his 28th and final #1.

PAUL MCCARTNEY

1980

COMING UP
Producer: Paul McCartney
Album: McCartney II
Record Label: Columbia
Songwriter: Paul McCartney

Recorded live at Glasgow with Wings.

1982

HERE TODAY
Producer: George Martin
Album: Tug of War
Songwriter: Paul McCartney

Dedicated to John Lennon.

TAKE IT AWAY
Producer: George Martin
Album: Tug of War
Record Label: Columbia
Songwriter: Paul McCartney

Reuniting with the former Beatle-producer Martin for another visit to the Top-10.

1984

NO MORE LONELY NIGHTS
Producer: George Martin
Album: *Give My Regards to Broad Street* Soundtrack
Record Label: Columbia
Songwriter: Paul McCartney

It wasn't Tommy.

1986

SPIES LIKE US
Producer: Paul McCartney
Album: *Spies Like Us* Soundtrack
Record Label: Capitol
Songwriter: Paul McCartney

1993

HOPE OF DELIVERANCE
Producer: Paul McCartney
Album: Off the Ground
Record Label: Capitol
Songwriter: Paul McCartney

OFF THE GROUND
Producer: Paul McCartney
Album: Off the Ground
Record Label: Capitol
Songwriter: Paul McCartney

MARILYN MCCOO AND BILLY DAVIS JR.

1976

YOU DON'T HAVE TO BE A STAR (TO BE IN MY SHOW)
Producer: Don Davis
Album: I Hope We Get to Love in Time
Record Label: ABC
Songwriters: James Dean, John Henry Glover

Uplifting #1 R&B/R&R crossover.

1985

SAVING ALL MY LOVE FOR YOU
Album: Marilyn and Billy
Record Label: Columbia
Songwriters: Michael Masser, Gerry Goffin

Cover by Whitney Houston was her first #1 R&B/#1 R&R crossover (Arista, '85).

VAN MCCOY & THE SOUL CITY SYMPHONY

1975

THE HUSTLE
Producer: Hugo and Luigi
Album: Disco Baby
Record Label: Avco
Songwriter: Van McCoy

Disco hits the mainstream as producer McCoy scores a #1 R&B/R&R crossover.

JIMMY MCCRACKLIN

1958

THE WALK
Record Label: Checker
Songwriter: Jimmy McCracklin

A new dance craze, but no Twist . . . or Hucklebuck.

GEORGE MCCRAE

1974

ROCK YOUR BABY
Producer: Harry Casey
Album: Rock Your Baby
Record Label: T.K.
Songwriters: Harry Casey, Richard Finch

Sunshine groove mavens Casey and Finch pave the way for Disco's dominance, with a #1 R&B/R&R crossover.

GWEN MCCRAE

1975

ROCKIN' CHAIR
Producers: Steve Alaimo, Walter Clark, Clarence Read
Album: Rockin' Chair
Record Label: Cat
Songwriters: Clarence Read, Walter Clark

Fierce #1 R&B/Top-10 R&R crossover, with former duet partner, husband George, on backups.

IAN MCCULLOUGH

1989

PROUD TO FALL
Album: Candleland
Record Label: Sire/Reprise
Songwriter: Ian McCullough

Solo hit for the Echo & the Bunnymen lead singer.

GENE MCDANIELS

1961

A HUNDRED POUNDS OF CLAY
Producer: Snuff Garrett
Album: A Hundred Pounds
Record Label: Liberty
Songwriters: Bob Elgin, Kay Rogers, Luther Dixon

Semi-Biblical novelty rocker.

CHIP CHIP
Producer: Snuff Garrett
Record Label: Liberty

Songwriters: Jeff Barry, Artie Resnick, Cliff Crawford

TOWER OF STRENGTH

Producer: Snuff Garrett
Album: Tower of Strength
Record Label: Liberty
Songwriters: Burt Bacharach, Bob Hilliard

MICHAEL MCDONALD
1982

I KEEP FORGETTIN' (EVERY TIME YOU'RE NEAR)

Producers: Ted Templeman, Lenny Waronker
Album: If That's What It Takes
Songwriters: Jerry Leiber, Mike Stoller, Michael McDonald, Ed Sanford

Straying too near Leiber and Stoller's "I Keep Forgettin'" (Chuck Jackson; Wand, '62), McDonald was forced to share writer credit.

1986

SWEET FREEDOM

Album: *Running Scared* Soundtrack
Record Label: MCA
Songwriter: Rod Temperton

From the movie Running Scared.

MCFADDEN AND WHITEHEAD
1979

AIN'T NO STOPPIN' US NOW

Album: McFadden and Whitehead
Record Label: Philadelphia International
Songwriters: Gene McFadden, John Whitehead

#1 R&B/Top-20 R&R crossover from Philly.

BOBBY MCFERRIN
1987

DON'T WORRY, BE HAPPY

Album: *Cocktail* Soundtrack
Record Label: EMI-Manhattan
Songwriter: Bobby McFerrin

Jazz-flavored #1 a-cappella jingle perfectly epitomized the sanitized if not etherized '80s.

KATE AND ANNA MCGARRIGLE
1975

(TALK TO ME OF) MENDOCINO

Producers: Joe Boyd, Greg Prestopino
Album: Kate and Anna McGarrigle
Record Label: Warner Brothers
Songwriter: Kate McGarrigle

One of the rare female rambling classics. Covered by Linda Ronstadt (Asylum, '82).

1977

WALKING SONG

Producer: Joe Boyd
Album: Dancer with Bruised Knees
Record Label: Warner Brothers
Songwriter: Kate McGarrigle

Rambling again, but at a slower pace.

1990

HEARTBEATS ACCELERATING

Producer: Peter Marchand
Album: Heartbeats Accelerating
Record Label: Private Music
Songwriter: Anna McGarrigle

Covered by Linda Ronstadt (Elektra, '94).

STICK MCGHEE
1949

DRINKING WINE SPO-DEE O-DEE

Record Label: Atlantic
Songwriters: Stick McGhee, Mayo Williams

Atlantic records enters the marketplace with a Top-10 R&B hit. The mythic drinking song was covered by Wynonie Harris (King, '49) and Jerry Lee Lewis (Sun, '59; Mercury, '73).

ROGER MCGUINN
1990

KING OF THE HILL

Album: Back from Rio
Record Label: Arista
Songwriters: Roger McGuinn, Tom Petty

McGuinn makes a succesful comeback (from Florida, not Rio) with a Dylan-esque rocker.

BARRY MCGUIRE
1965

EVE OF DESTRUCTION

Producer: Lou Adler
Album: Eve of Destruction

Record Label: Dunhill
Songwriters: Steve Barri, P. F. Sloan

Heavy-handed and second-handed West Coast protest. Nevertheless it topped the charts. Covered by the Turtles (White Whale, '65).

BOB AND DOUG MCKENZIE
1982

TAKE OFF

Producer: Marc Giacommelli
Album: Great White North
Record Label: Mercury
Songwriters: Kerry Crawford, Jonathan Goldsmith, Mark Giacommelli, Rick Moranis, Dave Thomas

Canadian novelty by the "SCTV" geeks Moranis and Thomas.

SCOTT MCKENZIE
1967

SAN FRANCISCO (BE SURE TO WEAR SOME FLOWERS IN YOUR HAIR)

Producer: John Phillips
Album: The Voice of Scott McKenzie
Record Label: Ode
Songwriter: John Phillips

Reducing the Summer of Love to a hippie theme park in San Francisco, written by the man who did the same for Monterey.

SARAH MCLACHLAN
1992

INTO THE FIRE

Producer: Pierre Marchand
Album: Solace
Record Label: Arista
Songwriters: Sarah McLachlan, Pierre Marchand

Joni Mitchell-inspired Canadian singer/songwriter.

1994

WAIT

Album: Fumbling Toward Ecstacy
Record Label: Arista
Songwriter: Sarah McLachlan

Mitchell-esque poetry in emotion.

DON MCLEAN
1971

AMERICAN PIE

Producer: Ed Freeman
Album: American Pie

Record Label: United Artists
Songwriter: Don McLean

Celebrating either Rock's death or its continued resilience, this Folk Rock epic effectively defined and confined McLean's Pop career.

JAMES MCMURTRY
1989

I'M NOT FROM HERE
Producer: John Mellencamp
Album: Too Long in the Wasteland
Record Label: Columbia
Songwriter: James McMurtry

The rambling song to end all rambling songs, by the son of author Larry.

BIG JAY MCNEELY
1957

THERE IS SOMETHING ON YOUR MIND
Record Label: Swingin'
Songwriter: Big Jay McNeely

McNeely on sax, vocals by Little Sonny. Covered by New Orleans crossdressing crossover Soul man Bobby Marchan (Fire, '60) on which he inserted the classic spoken part, detailing how, in "Hey Joe" terms, he shot his woman down. Suggested segue: "Here Comes the Judge" by Shorty Long.

CLYDE MCPHATTER
1956

SEVEN DAYS
Producers: Ahmet Ertegun, Jerry Wexler
Album: Clyde McPhatter and the Drifters
Record Label: Atlantic
Songwriters: Willis Carroll, Carmen Taylor

Honey-voiced lead singer of the Drifters goes solo with a Top-10 R&B/Top-50 R&R classic.

TREASURE OF LOVE
Producers: Ahmet Ertegun, Jerry Wexler
Album: Clyde McPhatter and the Drifters
Record Label: Atlantic
Songwriters: Joe Shapiro, Lou Stallman

Timeless ballad; Top-10 R&B/Top-20 R&R crossover.

1957

WITHOUT LOVE (THERE IS NOTHING)
Producers: Ahmet Ertegun, Jerry Wexler
Record Label: Atlantic
Songwriter: Danny Small

At his soulful best, with another Top-10 R&B/Top-20 R&R crossover. Covered by Ray Charles (ABC, '63) and Tom Jones (Parrot, '70).

1958

A LOVER'S QUESTION
Producers: Ahmet Ertegun, Jerry Wexler
Album: Clyde
Record Label: Atlantic
Songwriters: Brook Benton, Jimmy Williams

Clyde's biggest hit; his first and only #1 R&B (Top-10 R&R crossover).

1961

LOVER, PLEASE
Album: Greatest Hits
Record Label: Mercury
Songwriter: Bill Swan

Clyde's second biggest hit was written by Rockabilly crooner Swan, who would reach the charts with "I Can Help" in '74.

RALPH MCTELL
1971

STREETS OF LONDON
Producer: Gus Dudgeon
Album: You Well-Meaning Brought Me Here
Record Label: Paramount
Songwriter: Ralph McTell

Traditional-sounding Folk elegy that found its way into the hands of Elton John's hot producer and then onto FM play lists. Richard Thompson took heart. Suggested segue: "Dirty Old Town" by Rod Stewart.

CHRISTINE MCVIE
1984

GOT A HOLD ON ME
Producer: Russ Titelman
Album: Christine McVie
Record Label: Warner Brothers
Songwriters: Christine McVie, Todd Sharp

Post-Fleetwood Mac solo turn.

1957

MEADOWLARKS
1955

HEAVEN AND PARADISE
Record Label: Dooto
Songwriter: Don Julian

Early Doo-Wop ethereal classic.

MEAT LOAF
1975

HOT PATOOTIE, BLESS MY SOUL
Album: The Rocky Horror Picture Show Cast Album
Record Label: Ode
Songwriter: Richard O'Brien

Exposing his theatrical roots, Marvin Lee Aday aka Meat Loaf partakes of the era's greatest musical phenomenon.

1977

PARADISE BY THE DASHBOARD LIGHT
Producer: Jim Steinman
Album: Bat out of Hell
Record Label: Epic
Songwriter: Jim Steinman

Co-starring Ellen Foley—later of "Night Court" and a lamentable recording career—and the ineffable Yankee announcer, Phil "The Scooter" Rizzuto, whose words would go on to inspire an entire book of poetry, this primally horny backseat psychodrama took teenage angst way past Springsteenian license.

TWO OUT OF THREE AIN'T BAD
Producer: Jim Steinman
Album: Bat out of Hell
Record Label: Cleveland International
Songwriter: Jim Steinman

Verbose rocker just missed Top-10.

1978

YOU TOOK THE WORDS RIGHT OUT OF MY MOUTH
Producer: Jim Steinman
Album: Bat out of Hell
Record Label: Epic
Songwriter: Jim Steinman

With Steinman writing and producing the effusive Loaf, that's a Promethean task.

1993

I'D DO ANYTHING FOR LOVE (BUT I WON'T DO THAT)
Producer: Jim Steinman
Album: Bat out of Hell II: Back into Hell

Record Label: MCA
Songwriter: Jim Steinman

Long-winded comeback results in his biggest hit.

MEAT PUPPETS

1982

LAKE OF FIRE
Producers: Spot, Meat Puppets
Album: Meat Puppets II
Record Label: SST
Songwriter: Curt Kirkwood

One of the three tracks on this legendary Arizona Punk band's second album covered by the unplugged Nirvana (DGC, '94). The others were "Oh Me" and "Plateau."

1991

SAM
Producer: Pete Anderson
Album: Forbidden Places
Record Label: London
Songwriter: Curt Kirkwood

A decade later the Soft Punk pioneers were still at it, producing the wordiest song to gain radio airplay since Meat Loaf.

1994

BACKWATER
Producers: Paul Lang, Meat Puppets
Album: Too High to Die
Record Label: London
Songwriter: Curt Kirkwood

Their long-awaited breakthrough hit single brought simultaneous cries of "At last!" and "Sellout!": every cult band's eternal dilemma.

MECO

1977

STAR WARS THEME
Producers: M. Monardo, H. Wheeler, Tony Bonglovi
Album: Star Wars and Other Galactic Funk
Record Label: Millenium
Songwriter: John Williams

Space age Disco.

GLENN MEDEIROS

1990

SHE AIN'T WORTH IT
Producers: Ian Prince, Denny Diante
Album: Glenn Medeiros
Record Label: MCA
Songwriters: Bobby Brown, Antonia Armato, Ian Prince

Featuring Bobby Brown; a #1 R&R/Top-50 R&B crossover.

BILL MEDLEY AND JENNIFER WARNES

1987

(I'VE HAD) THE TIME OF MY LIFE
Producer: Michael Lloyd
Album: Dirty Dancing Soundtrack
Record Label: RCA
Songwriters: Franke Previte, John DeNicola, Donald Markowitz

From the retro movie about perfect love in the Catskills, a knockout ballad.

MEGADETH

1988

IN MY DARKEST HOUR
Album: The Decline and Fall of Western Civilization (Part II): The Metal Years Soundtrack
Record Label: Capitol
Songwriters: Dave Mustaine, Dave Ellefson

Second-generation Rock protest from the former Metallica guitarist: louder, faster, heavier than the bomb.

1991

HANGAR 18
Album: Maximum Megadeth
Record Label: Capitol
Songwriter: Dave Mustaine

Supposedly, where the U.S. government keeps its aliens buried.

1992

SYMPHONY OF DESTRUCTION
Album: Countdown to Extinction
Record Label: Capitol
Songwriter: Dave Mustaine

Their signature sound and message.

THE MEKONS

1989

EMPIRE OF THE SENSELESS
Album: The Mekons Rock and Roll
Record Label: A&M
Songwriter: The Mekons

This critically revered Sex Pistols-era English Punk band achieves partial redemption here.

MEL AND TIM

1969

BACKFIELD IN MOTION
Producer: Gene Chandler
Record Label: Bamboo

Songwriters: Herbert T. McPherson, Melvin Harden

Kiddie Soul novelty; Top-10 R&B/R&R crossover.

MELANIE

1969

BEAUTIFUL PEOPLE
Producer: Peter Schekeryk
Album: Melanie
Record Label: Buddah
Songwriter: Melanie Safka

The Edith Piaf of Brooklyn gets started with a yearning flower plaint. Covered by the New Seekers (Elektra, '71).

1970

LAY DOWN (CANDLES IN THE RAIN)
Producer: Peter Schekeryk
Album: Candles in the Rain
Record Label: Buddah
Songwriter: Melanie Safka

A flickering anthem from a wilted flowerchild at the garden of Woodstock.

PEACE WILL COME (ACCORDING TO PLAN)
Producer: Peter Schekeryk
Album: Leftover Wine
Record Label: Buddah
Songwriter: Melanie Safka

Hanging on to the Folk sentiments of the '60s, in the era of reconciliation.

WHAT HAVE THEY DONE TO MY SONG, MA
Producer: Peter Schekeryk
Album: Candles in the Rain
Record Label: Buddah
Songwriter: Melanie Safka

Response to having been typecast as a waif and a flower child, when she wanted to be thought of as a poet and a singer/songwriter. Covered by the New Seekers (Elektra, '70) and Ray Charles (ABC, '72).

1971

BRAND NEW KEY
Producer: Peter Schekeryk
Album: Gather Me
Record Label: Neighborhood
Songwriter: Melanie Safka

Bubblicious #1 hit would stall her efforts to escape a lightweight tag.

JOHN (COUGAR) MELLENCAMP

1979

I NEED A LOVER
Album: John Cougar
Record Label: Riva
Songwriter: John Mellencamp

Indiana rocker updates Dylan's "It Ain't Me Babe."

1981

AIN'T EVEN DONE WITH THE NIGHT
Album: Nothing Matters and What If It Did
Record Label: Riva
Songwriter: John Cougar Mellencamp

In the midst of skinny-tie New Wave, a rootsy, Arena Rock anthem.

1982

HURTS SO GOOD
Album: American Fool
Record Label: Riva
Songwriters: John Cougar Mellencamp, George Michael Green

Through the courtesy of MTV, John Cougar's middle-American macho breaks out of the heartland.

JACK AND DIANE
Producers: Don Gehman, John Mellencamp
Album: American Fool
Record Label: Riva
Songwriter: John Cougar Mellencamp

His biggest hit; Two American kids at #1 R&R. Springsteen would follow Mellencamp into this heartland niche in '84, a niche that he, himself, created in '76 with "Born to Run."

1983

THE AUTHORITY SONG
Producers: Don Gehman, Little Bastard
Album: Uh-Huh
Record Label: Riva
Songwriters: John Cougar Mellencamp, Don Gehman

Not quite "I Fought the Law," but carrying a similar message.

CRUMBLIN' DOWN
Producers: Don Gehman, Little Bastard
Album: Uh-Huh
Record Label: Riva
Songwriters: John Cougar Mellencamp, George Michael Green

PINK HOUSES
Producers: Don Gehman, Little Bastard
Album: Uh-Huh
Record Label: Riva
Songwriter: John Cougar Mellencamp

Updating Malvina Reynolds's "Little Boxes."

1985

LONELY OL' NIGHT
Producers: Don Gehman, Little Bastard
Album: Scarecrow
Record Label: Riva
Songwriter: John Cougar Mellencamp

R-O-C-K IN THE U.S.A. (A SALUTE TO '60S ROCK)
Producers: Don Gehman, Little Bastard
Album: Scarecrow
Record Label: Riva
Songwriter: John Cougar Mellencamp

Homage to Mitch Ryder and James Brown.

SMALL TOWN
Producers: Don Gehman, Little Bastard
Album: Scarecrow
Record Label: Riva
Songwriter: John Cougar Mellencamp

Jack and Diane reminisce again. Suggested Segue: "Glory Days" by Bruce Springsteen.

1987

CHERRY BOMB
Producers: Don Gehman, John Mellencamp
Album: The Lonesome Jubilee
Record Label: Mercury
Songwriter: John Cougar Mellencamp

More heartland nostalgia. Suggested Segue: "Night Moves" by Bob Seger and "Come Dancing" by the Kinks.

PAPER IN FIRE
Producers: Don Gehman, John Mellencamp
Album: The Lonesome Jubilee
Record Label: Mercury
Songwriter: John Mellencamp

1993

WHAT IF I CAME KNOCKING
Album: Human Wheels
Record Label: Mercury
Songwriter: John Mellencamp

Dropping Cougar at last, he writes one of his best songs in years.

THE MELLOW KINGS

1957

TONITE TONITE
Producer: Al Silver
Record Label: Herald
Songwriter: Billy Myles

Doo-wop enters the white neighborhood, where, for a long while, it passed for black. A classic New York oldie, even though it never made the R&B chart.

THE MELODIANS

1970

RIVERS OF BABYLON
Record Label: Mango
Songwriters: Fred Farian, G. Reyam, B. Dowe, F. McNaughton

Traditional African slave tune released in '70 on Trojan and featured on the soundtrack of the Reggae coming-of-age movie classic The Harder They Come. Covered by Linda Ronstadt (Asylum, '76). U.K. song of the year by Boney M. (Sire, '78).

HAROLD MELVIN AND THE BLUENOTES

1972

IF YOU DON'T KNOW ME BY NOW
Producers: Kenny Gamble, Leon Huff
Album: Harold Melvin & the Bluenotes
Record Label: Philadelphia International
Songwriters: Kenny Gamble, Leon Huff

Passionate and poignant Gamble and Huff creation notches #1 R&B/Top-10 R&R. Suggested Segue: "You Don't Know Me" by Ray Charles.

1973

THE LOVE I LOST
Producers: Kenny Gamble, Leon Huff
Album: Black and Blue
Record Label: Philadelphia International
Songwriters: Kenny Gamble, Leon Huff

The unstoppable sound of Philadelphia: #1 R&B/Top-10 R&R ballad.

1975

HOPE THAT WE CAN BE TOGETHER SOON
Producers: Kenny Gamble, Leon Huff
Album: To Be True
Record Label: Philadelphia International
Songwriters: Kenny Gamble, Leon Huff

#1 R&B/Top-50 R&R crossover.

WAKE UP EVERYBODY, PART ONE
Producers: Kenny Gamble, Leon Huff
Album: Wake up Everybody
Record Label: Philadelphia International
Songwriters: Gene McFadden, John Whitehead, Vic Carstarphen

#1 R&B/Top-20 R&R crossover. McFadden and Whitehead would go on to their own Soul careers.

MEN AT WORK
1982

DOWN UNDER
Producer: Peter Mclan
Album: Business as Usual
Record Label: Columbia
Songwriters: Colin Hay, Roy Strykert

Ultimate left field hit from Australia, with a touch of Reggae.

WHO CAN IT BE NOW
Producer: Peter Mclan
Album: Business as Usual
Record Label: Columbia
Songwriter: Colin Hay

Paranoid follow-up.

1983

IT'S A MISTAKE
Producer: Peter Mclan
Album: Cargo

Record Label: Columbia
Songwriter: Colin Hay

OVERKILL
Producer: Peter Mclan
Album: Cargo
Record Label: Columbia
Songwriter: Colin Hay

Aptly titled.

MEN WITHOUT HATS
1983

SAFETY DANCE
Producers: Z. B. Held, Men Without Hats
Album: Rhythm of Youth
Record Label: Backstreet
Songwriter: Ivan Doroschuk

Neo-British Synth invasion one-shot.

NATALIE MERCHANT
1995

CARNIVAL
Producer: Natalie Merchant
Album: Tigerlily
Record Label: Elektra
Songwriter: Natalie Merchant

Nasal nocturnal celebration from the former leader of 10,000 Maniacs is at odds with the earthier, angrier chants issued by many other female singers this year.

MERCY
1969

LOVE (CAN MAKE YOU HAPPY)
Producer: Jamie Guyden
Album: The Mercy and Love (Can Make You Happy)
Record Label: Sundi
Songwriter: Jack Sigler

Soft Rock.

MERRY-GO-ROUND
1967

LIVE
Producer: Larry Marks
Album: The Merry-Go-Round
Record Label: A&M
Songwriter: Emitt Rhodes

The original sound of paisley. Covered by the Bangles (Columbia, '84).

YOU'RE A VERY LOVELY WOMAN
Producer: Larry Marks
Album: The Merry-Go-Round
Record Label: A&M
Songwriter: Emitt Rhodes

Hauntingly McCartney-esque Folk Rock ballad. Covered by Linda Ronstadt (Capitol, '71).

METALLICA
1983

JUMP IN THE FIRE
Producers: Paul Curcio, Mark Whittaker, Metallica
Album: Kill 'Em All
Record Label: Megaforce
Songwriters: James Hetfield, Lars Ulrich, Dave Mustaine

Out of the California sludge, the bastard son of Sabbath emerges.

1984

FADE TO BLACK
Producers: Mark Whittaker, Metallica
Album: Master of Puppets
Record Label: Elektra
Songwriters: James Hetfield, Lars Ulrich, Cliff Burton, Kirk Hammett

A new guitarist, Hammett, the same mission, the heavyweight Metal crown.

FOR WHOM THE BELL TOLLS
Producers: Mark Whittaker, Metallica
Album: Ride the Lightning
Record Label: Megaforce
Songwriters: James Hetfield, Lars Ulrich, Cliff Burton

Essential Burton—the bass beast of the '80s.

1986

MASTER OF PUPPETS
Producers: Fleming Rasmussen, Metallica
Album: Master of Puppets
Record Label: Elektra
Songwriters: James Hetfield, Lars Ulrich, Cliff Burton, Kirk Hammett

Their mega-Metal scrawl.

1988

ONE
Producers: Fleming Rasmussen, Metallica
Album: . . . And Justice for All
Record Label: Elektra

Songwriters: James Hetfield, Lars Ulrich

Metal for the masses of MTV.

1991

ENTER SANDMAN
Producers: Bob Rock, James Hetfield, Lars Ulrich
Album: Metallica
Record Label: Elektra
Songwriters: James Hetfield, Lars Ulrich, Kirk Hammett

Their semi-melodic (commercial) move.

NOTHING ELSE MATTERS
Producers: Bob Rock, James Hetfield, Lars Ulrich
Album: Metallica
Record Label: Elektra
Songwriters: James Hetfield, Lars Ulrich

Sludgifying the Arena Rock ballad.

THE UNFORGIVEN
Producers: Bob Rock, James Hetfield, Lars Ulrich
Album: Metallica
Record Label: Elektra
Songwriters: James Hetfield, Lars Ulrich, Kirk Hammett

Their dark opera anthem.

THE METERS
1969

SOPHISTICATED CISSY
Producers: Allen Toussaint, Marshall Sehorn
Album: The Meters
Record Label: Josie
Songwriters: Arthur Neville, Leo Nocentelli, George Porter, Joseph Modeliste

Introducing their unique brand of pychedelicized New Orleans Funk to the charts; Top-10 R&B/Top-30 R&R. George Clinton was listening.

MFSB
1973

TSOP (THE SOUND OF PHILADELPHIA)
Producers: Kenny Gamble, Leon Huff
Album: Love Is the Message
Record Label: Philadelphia International
Songwriters: Kenny Gamble, Leon Huff

Theme for "Soul Train," TV's landmark black bandstand show, went #1 R&B/R&R, certifying Philadelphia as the teen dance capitol of black America, as it had been a decade and a half ago for white America.

MIAMI SOUND MACHINE
1986

BAD BOY
Producer: Emilio Estefan
Album: Primitive Love
Record Label: Epic
Songwriters: Larry Dermer, Joe Galdo, Rafael Vigil

The unadulterated beat of South Beach.

CONGA
Producer: Emilio Estefan
Album: Primitive Love
Record Label: Epic
Songwriter: Enrique Garcia

Rock and Roll embraces another Gloria, briefly.

1987

RHYTHM IS GONNA GET YOU
Producer: Emilio Estefan
Album: Let It Loose
Record Label: Epic
Songwriters: Gloria Estefan, Enrique Garcia

Gloria takes over the band, the sound, and takes it down 95 to the Fontainbleu.

GEORGE MICHAEL
1987

FAITH
Producer: George Michael
Album: Faith
Record Label: Columbia
Songwriter: George Michael

This second hit from Michael's massive album was the '88 single of the year.

FATHER FIGURE
Producer: George Michael
Album: Faith
Record Label: Columbia
Songwriter: George Michael

Second of four #1 R&R hits from the album. Suggested segues: "Oh Father" by Madonna, "Oh Daddy" by XTC, "Mother" by John Lennon, and "Mommy, Daddy, You and I" by Talking Heads.

I WANT YOUR SEX
Producer: George Michael
Album: Faith
Record Label: Columbia
Songwriter: George Michael

First hit for the teen idol Half of Wham! from the soundtrack of Beverly Hills Cop. In the repressive climate of the late '80s, George would quickly disown this song's sexually provocative video in a classic case of wanting to have one's cake and eating it too.

KISSING A FOOL
Producer: George Michael
Album: Faith
Record Label: Columbia
Songwriter: George Michael

Sixth Top-10 tune from the LP.

ONE MORE TRY
Producer: George Michael
Album: Faith
Record Label: Columbia
Songwriter: George Michael

First #1 R&B/R&R crossover for a white artist since the Four Seasons (if you don't count K.C. and the Sunshine Band).

1988

MONKEY
Producer: George Michael
Album: Faith
Record Label: Columbia
Songwriter: George Michael

Fourth straight #1 tune from Faith invokes the classic monkey motif: see "Mickey's Monkey," "Monkee Man," "One Monkey Don't Stop No Show," et al.

1990

FREEDOM
Producer: George Michael
Album: Listen Without Prejudice (Vol., 1)
Record Label: Columbia
Songwriter: George Michael

His second song with this title. The kind of freedom George was referring to here would be revealed when he sued his record company to get out of his contract.

PRAYING FOR TIME
Producer: George Michael
Album: Listen Without Prejudice (Vol. I)
Record Label: Columbia
Songwriter: George Michael

Having paid the price of fame with critical disdain, George settles for another #1.

1992

TOO FUNKY

Producer: George Michael
Album: Red Hot and Dance
Record Label: Columbia
Songwriter: George Michael

Returning to his long suit as a male model, with his sexiest video yet.

LEE MICHAELS

1971

DO YOU KNOW WHAT I MEAN

Producer: Lee Michaels
Album: 5th
Record Label: A&M
Songwriter: Michael Olson (Lee Michaels)

Overwrought FM perennial.

MICHEL'LE

1990

NO MORE LIES

Album: Michel'le
Record Label: Ruthless
Songwriters: L. A. Dre (Andre Bolton), Laylaw, Michel'le Toussant

Dance action.

MICKEY AND SYLVIA

1957

LOVE IS STRANGE

Producer: Bob Rolontz
Album: New Sounds
Record Label: Vik
Songwriters: Ellas McDaniel (Ethel Smith), Mickey Baker, Sylvia Robinson

Stark guitar-driven exchange of vows, with the guitar provided by session ace Mickey Baker. Covered by such loving couples as the Everly Brothers (Warner Brothers, '65), Sonny and Cher (Reprise, '65), Peaches and Herb (Date, '68), and Paul and Linda McCartney in Wings (Apple, '71). Featured in Mermaids *and* Dirty Dancing. *Suggested segue, "Billy's Blues" by Billy Stewart (Chess, '56). Sylvia Robinson would go on to found the first Rap label, Sugar Hill.*

BETTE MIDLER

1972

DELTA DAWN

Producer: Joel Dorn
Album: The Divine Miss M
Record Label: Atlantic

Songwriters: Alex Harvey, Larry Collins

Rural character portrait, given added character by Bette's suburban swagger. Covered by Tanya Tucker (Columbia, '72) and Helen Reddy (Capitol, '72).

1979

THE ROSE

Producer: Paul Rothchild
Album: *The Rose* Soundtrack
Record Label: Atlantic
Songwriter: Amanda McBroom

The best thing to emerge from the Janis Joplin biopic. Rothchild also produced the generally ineffective Joplin album Pearl.

1983

ALL I NEED TO KNOW (DON'T KNOW MUCH)

Producer: Chuck Plotkin
Album: No Frills
Record Label: Atlantic
Songwriters: Barry Mann, Cynthia Weil, Tom Snow

Mann regains his mid-'60s songwriting chops on this smouldering ballad; best-selling cover as "Don't Know Much" by Linda Ronstadt and Aaron Neville (Elektra, '88).

MIDNIGHT OIL

1987

BEDS ARE BURNING

Producers: Wayne Livesey, Midnight Oil
Album: Diesel and Dust
Record Label: Columbia
Songwriter: Midnight Oil

Biggest U.S. hit for the politically oriented Australian Rock band.

1990

BLUE SKY MINE

Album: Blue Sky Mining
Record Label: Columbia
Songwriter: Midnight Oil

MIDNIGHT STAR

1983

FREAK-A-ZOID

Producer: Reggie Calloway
Album: No Parking on the Dance Floor
Record Label: Solar
Songwriters: Reggie Calloway, Vincent Calloway, William Simmons

Funk number.

1984

OPERATOR

Producer: Reggie Calloway
Album: Planetary Invasion
Record Label: Elektra
Songwriters: Reggie Calloway, Vincent Calloway, Belinda Lipscomb, Boaz Watson

Their biggest hit; #1 R&B/Top-20 crossover.

THE MIDNIGHTERS

1954

ANNIE HAD A BABY

Producer: Henry Glover
Album: The Midnighters
Record Label: Federal
Songwriters: Henry Glover, Syd Nathan (Lois Mann)

Classic R&B sequel to the notorious "Work with Me, Annie," reached #1 R&B four months after the original.

ANNIE'S AUNT FANNY

Producer: Henry Glover
Album: The Midnighters
Record Label: Federal
Songwriter: Hank Ballard

Concluding the Annie trilogy.

SEXY WAYS

Producer: Henry Glover
Album: The Midnighters
Record Label: Federal
Songwriter: Hank Ballard

Continuing the R&B tradition for stretching the boundaries of raunch.

WORK WITH ME, ANNIE

Producer: Henry Glover
Album: The Midnighters
Record Label: Federal
Songwriter: Hank Ballard

Based on the earlier "Get It," which was banned as too dirty for radio, the nominally cleaner saga of Annie hit #1 R&B and launched about a dozen responses, including Etta James' "Roll with Me Henry," which was converted into "Dance with Me Henry," a #1 Pop hit for Georgia Gibbs in '55.

1955

HENRY'S GOT FLAT FEET

Producer: Henry Glover
Album: The Midnighters
Record Label: Federal
Songwriter: Hank Ballard

An answer song to the Etta James hit, "The Wallflower," also known as "Roll with Me Henry," also known as "Dance with Me Henry," the Henry in question not Hank Ballard, but producer Henry Glover.

1959

TEARDROPS ON YOUR LETTER

Producer: Henry Glover
Album: Hank Ballard's Biggest Hits
Record Label: King
Songwriter: Henry Glover

Inspired no covers, ignited no crazes, and lapsed in the Bottom-20, unlike its legendary B-side, "The Twist."

THE TWIST

Producer: Henry Glover
Album: Hank Ballard's Biggest Hits
Record Label: King
Songwriter: Hank Ballard

B-side of "Teardrops on Your Letter." Covered by Dick Clark discovery Chubby Checker (Parkway, '60), "The Twist" ushered in the Baby Boom's first dance era, thus making it by definition headline news; the record made music history as well, returning to #1 sixteen months after leaving that slot, when the Jet Set adopted the dance. Suggested segue: "What'cha Gonna Do" by the Drifters.

1960

FINGER POPPIN' TIME

Album: Hank Ballard's Biggest Hits
Record Label: King
Songwriter: Hank Ballard

Capitalizing on the fallout from "The Twist," Ballard gets his first #1 R&B/Top-10 crossover. He then re-released his original version of "The Twist" a couple of months later, to compete with Chubby Checker.

LET'S GO, LET'S GO, LET'S GO

Album: Hank Ballard's Biggest Hits
Record Label: King
Songwriter: Hank Ballard

Fanning the flames of the dance craze he instigated with "The Twist," Ballard gets his biggest hit, #1 R&B/Top-10 R&R.

MIKE & THE MECHANICS

1985

ALL I NEED IS A MIRACLE

Producer: Christopher Neil
Album: Mike & the Mechanics
Record Label: Atlantic
Songwriters: Mike Rutherford,
   Christopher Neil

Pleasant rocker from the formerly Progressive Mike Rutherford.

SILENT RUNNING (ON DANGEROUS GROUND)

Album: Mike & the Mechanics
Record Label: Atlantic
Songwriters: Mike Rutherford, Brian Robertson

First solo hit for the Genesis guitarist, from the film On Dangerous Ground.

1989

THE LIVING YEARS

Producers: Christopher Neil, Mike Rutherford
Album: Living Years
Record Label: Atlantic
Songwriters: Mike Rutherford, Brian Robertson

Defining adult Rock.

AMOS MILBURN

1948

CHICKEN SHACK BOOGIE

Record Label: Aladdin
Songwriter: Amos Milburn

Defining Adult Rock thirty years earlier, the first #1 R&B hit for the pioneering stylist (reissued in '56). Fats Domino was listening. The Rolling Stones were listening to Milburn's cover of the '40 Don Raye classic, "Down the Road Apiece," which they would cover in '65.

1953

ONE SCOTCH, ONE BOURBON, ONE BEER

Album: Rockin' the Boogie
Record Label: Aladdin
Songwriter: Rudolph Toombs

Detailing the obsession that would prove to be his downfall.

BUDDY MILES

1970

THEM CHANGES

Producer: Robin McBride
Album: Them Changes
Record Label: Mercury
Songwriter: Buddy Miles

Relentless drumming.

ALECK MILLER

1951

ONE WAY OUT

Record Label: Trumpet
Songwriters: Marshall Sehorn, Sonny Boy Williamson (Aleck Miller)

Essential Blues. Covered by the Allman Brothers (Capricorn, '72).

ROGER MILLER

1965

ENGLAND SWINGS

Producer: Jerry Kennedy
Album: Roger Miller's Golden Hits
Record Label: Smash
Songwriter: Roger Miller

A rare Country music acknowledgement of the ebbs and flows of current Rock and Roll.

KING OF THE ROAD

Producer: Jerry Kennedy
Album: The Return of Roger Miller
Record Label: Smash
Songwriter: Roger Miller

#1 C&W/Top-10 R&R crossover. Won Grammys that year for Best Country Song and Best Rock and Roll Performance.

1966

MY UNCLE USED TO LOVE ME BUT SHE DIED

Producer: Jerry Kennedy
Album: Words and Music
Record Label: Smash
Songwriter: Roger Miller

Country/R&R crossover novelty that stiffed on both charts. Covered by the Folk group, Wind in the Willows (Capitol, '68) with Debbie Harry as lead blonde.

1967

ME AND BOBBY MCGEE

Producer: Jerry Kennedy
Album: Roger Miller
Record Label: Smash
Songwriters: Kris Kristofferson, Fred Foster

First appearance of the Country Rock rambling classic went to #12 C&W. Covered by Kristofferson (Monument, '69). The female version was Janis Joplin's only #1 song (Columbia, '71).

THE STEVE MILLER BAND
1968

CHILDREN OF THE FUTURE
Producers: Glyn Johns, Steve Miller
Album: Children of the Future
Record Label: Capitol
Songwriter: Steve Miller

Space-age Blues, by way of San Francisco and Chicago.

DIME A DANCE ROMANCE
Producer: Steve Miller
Album: Sailor
Record Label: Capitol
Songwriter: Boz Scaggs

One of Boz's best.

GANGSTER OF LOVE
Producer: Steve Miller
Album: Sailor
Record Label: Capitol
Songwriter: Johnny Watson

Borrowing the glorious phrase, known only to Rock and Roll addicts, "the pompatus of love," from "The Letter" by the Medallions (Duotone, '54).

LIVING IN THE U.S.A.
Producer: Steve Miller
Album: Sailor
Record Label: Capitol
Songwriter: Steve Miller

In search of a cheeseburger. Jimmy Buffett was listening.

1969

MERCURY BLUES
Producer: Steve Miller
Album: *Revolution* soundtrack.
Record Label: Capitol
Songwriters: K. C. Douglas, Robert Geddins

Classic car song—classic car: the Mercury. Miller covered the work of much-traveled local Bluesman Douglas in the '69 film Revolution. *Covered by David Lindley (Asylum, '81) and Alan Jackson (Arista, '93).*

SPACE COWBOY
Producer: Steve Miller
Album: Brave New World
Record Label: Capitol
Songwriter: Steve Miller

Defining his early psychedelic Blues period. Tracy Nelson was listening.

1973

THE JOKER
Producer: Steve Miller
Album: The Joker
Record Label: Capitol
Songwriters: Steve Miller, Eddie Curtis

#1 breakthrough defines his new Blues Lite period.

1976

FLY LIKE AN EAGLE
Producer: Steve Miller
Album: Fly Like an Eagle
Record Label: Capitol
Songwriter: Steve Miller

San Francisco Blues Rock classic.

ROCK N' ME
Producer: Steve Miller
Album: Fly Like an Eagle
Record Label: Capitol
Songwriter: Steve Miller

#1 boogie.

TAKE THE MONEY AND RUN
Producer: Steve Miller
Album: Fly Like an Eagle
Record Label: Capitol
Songwriter: Steve Miller

1977

JET AIRLINER
Producer: Steve Miller
Album: Book of Dreams
Record Label: Capitol
Songwriter: Paul Pena

One of his toughest rockers.

1982

ABRACADABRA
Producers: Steve Miller, Gary Mallaber
Album: Abracadabra
Record Label: Capitol
Songwriter: Steve Miller

Space cowboy R&B in the video age; his last #1.

1986

I WANT TO MAKE THE WORLD TURN AROUND
Album: Living in the 20th Century
Record Label: Capitol
Songwriter: Steve Miller

And return to 1976.

MILLI VANILLI
1989

ALL OR NOTHING
Producer: Fred Farian
Album: Girl, You Know It's True
Record Label: Arista
Songwriters: Frank Farian, Dietman Kawohl, Harold Baierl

At first all, and then nothing, as the members of the group were stripped of their New Artist Grammy for not actually performing on their hit songs.

BABY DON'T FORGET MY NUMBER
Producer: Fred Farian
Album: Girl, You Know It's True
Record Label: Arista
Songwriters: Frank Farian, Franz Reuter, Brad Howell, Roger Dalton

First #1 single for the fabricated duo.

BLAME IT ON THE RAIN
Producer: Fred Farian
Album: Girl, You Know It's True
Record Label: Arista
Songwriter: Diane Warren

Third of three straight #1s, and Diane Warren didn't have to return any royalties.

GIRL, I'M GONNA MISS YOU
Producer: Fred Farian
Album: Girl, You Know It's True
Record Label: Arista
Songwriters: Frank Farian, Dietman Kawohl, Peter Bischof-Fallenstein

GIRL, YOU KNOW IT'S TRUE
Producer: Fred Farian
Album: Girl, You Know It's True
Record Label: Arista
Songwriters: Frank Farian, Peter Bischof-Fallenstein, Dietman Kawohl

Kicking off a debut album nearly as impressive as George Michael's, no matter who provided the voices.

HAYLEY MILLS
1962

LET'S GET TOGETHER
Producer: Tutti Camarata
Album: *The Parent Trap* Soundtrack
Record Label: Buena Vista
Songwriters: Richard Sherman, Robert Sherman

From the Maureen O'Hara movie The Parent Trap, *by the same team that created Annette Funicello.*

STEPHANIE MILLS

1980

NEVER KNEW LOVE LIKE THIS BEFORE

Album: Sweet Sensation
Record Label: 20th Century
Songwriters: James Mtume, Reggie Lewis

#1 R&B/Top-10 R&R crossover by the girl who played Dorothy on Broadway in "The Wiz."

1987

(YOU'RE PUTTIN') A RUSH ON ME

Album: If I Were Your Woman
Record Label: MCA
Songwriters: Timmy Allen, Paul Laurence

#1 R&B/Bottom-20 R&R crossover.

GARNET MIMMS AND THE ENCHANTERS

1963

CRY BABY

Producer: Jerry Ragovoy
Album: Cry Baby and 11 Other Hits
Record Label: United Artists
Songwriters: Jerry Ragovoy (Norman Meade), Bert Berns (Bert Russell)

#1 R&B/Top-10 R&R crossover. Covered by Janis Joplin (Columbia, '70).

GET IT WHILE YOU CAN

Producer: Jerry Ragovoy
Record Label: United Artists
Songwriters: Jerry Ragovoy (Norman Meade), Mort Shuman

Another legendary Mimms stiff. Covered by Howard Tate (Verve, '66) and Janis Joplin (Columbia, '71).

TRY (JUST A LITTLE BIT HARDER)

Producer: Jerry Ragovoy
Record Label: United Artists
Songwriters: Jerry Ragovoy (Norman Meade), Chip Taylor

As a Ragovoy pipeline to Soul glory, Mimms was again the perfect foil. Covered by Janis Joplin (Columbia, '69).

1967

PIECE OF MY HEART

Producer: Jerry Ragovoy
Record Label: Shout
Songwriters: Bert Berns (Bert Russell), Jerry Ragovoy (Norman Meade)

Another famous stiff by the luckless Mimms. Cover by Erma Franklin (Shout, '67) was a Top-10 R&B/Top-75 R&R crossover. Cover by Janis Joplin (Columbia, '68) went to #12 R&R but did not crossover.

THE MINDBENDERS

1966

A GROOVY KIND OF LOVE

Album: A Groovy Kind of Love
Record Label: Fontana
Songwriters: Toni Wine, Carole Bayer

In the late Brill tradition by two writers who'd achieve considerably more fame collaborating with others. Covered by Phil Collins (Atlantic, '88).

SAL MINEO

1957

START MOVIN'

Album: Sal Mineo
Record Label: Epic
Songwriters: David Hill, Bobby Stevenson

Rebel without a hook.

MINISTRY

1988

LAND OF RAPE AND HONEY

Producers: Alain Jourgensen, Paul Barker
Album: Land of Rape and Honey
Record Label: Sire
Songwriter: Ministry

Fashionably inaccessible industrial strength white British rage.

TONIGHT WE MURDER

Producers: Alain Jourgensen, Paul Barker
Record Label: Sire
Songwriters: Alain Jourgenson, Paul Barker, Nardiello

The hard-to-find non-album B-side.

1992

JESUS BUILT MY HOTROD

Producers: H. Luxa, H. Pan
Album: Psalm 69
Record Label: Sire
Songwriter: Ministry

Commercial breakthrough of a sort, with guest vocal by Gibby Haynes of the Butthole Surfers.

MINK DEVILLE

1977

CADILLAC WALK

Album: Mink DeVille
Record Label: Capitol
Songwriter: John "Moon" Martin

Covered by the writer, John "Moon" Martin (Capitol, '78).

1978

ROLENE

Album: Return to Magenta
Record Label: Capitol
Songwriter: John "Moon" Martin

Post-Roots Revival Rockabilly given the Lower East Side of New York treatment. Covered by the writer (Capitol, '79).

MINOR THREAT

1981

MINOR THREAT

Album: In My Eyes
Record Label: Dischord
Songwriter: Ian MacKaye

Exemplars of the slamming new breed of Hard Core, the white answer to Rap.

MINT CONDITION

1992

BREAKIN' MY HEART (PRETTY BROWN EYES)

Producers: Jellybean Johnson, Mint Condition
Album: Meant to Be Mint
Record Label: Perspective
Songwriters: Larry Waddell, Stokely Williams, Jeffrey Allen

The modern Top-40 groove.

THE MINUTEMEN

1984

HISTORY LESSON (PART II)

Producer: Ethan James
Album: Double Nickels on the Dime
Record Label: SST
Songwriters: Dennes Boon, Mike Watt

Could be Punk Rock's finest moment. Boon becomes his own Bob Dylan to a new generation, who would go on to repeat his tragic history lesson, down to its saddest riff in the world. Suggested Segue: Dylan's "My Back Pages" as covered by the Byrds.

THE MIRACLES

1958

GOT A JOB

Producer: Berry Gordy Jr.
Album: Greatest Hits from the Beginning
Record Label: End
Songwriters: Roquel Davis (Tyran Carlo), Berry Gordy Jr.

A gateway to the Motown era, in which many fine black performers would find employment, none more gainfully than William "Smokey" Robinson.

1959

ALL I WANT IS YOU

Producer: Berry Gordy Jr.
Album: Greatest Hits from the Beginning
Record Label: Chess/Tamla
Songwriter: Smokey Robinson

BAD GIRL

Producer: Berry Gordy Jr.
Album: Greatest Hits from the Beginning
Record Label: Chess/Tamla
Songwriters: Smokey Robinson, Berry Gordy Jr.

Emphasizing their Doo-Wop roots; a tribute to Barrett Strong's cousin Nolan of the seminal Diablos.

1960

WAY OVER THERE

Producer: Berry Gordy Jr.
Album: Hi, We're the Miracles
Record Label: Tamla
Songwriters: Smokey Robinson, Berry Gordy Jr.

Their first release on Tamla, clocking in at #94 R&R.

1961

SHOP AROUND

Producer: Berry Gordy Jr.
Album: Greatest Hits from the Beginning
Record Label: Tamla
Songwriters: Smokey Robinson, Berry Gordy Jr.

Launching the philosophical Soul of Smokey with a #1 R&B/Top-10 R&R crossover.

1962

WHAT'S SO GOOD ABOUT GOODBYE

Producer: Berry Gordy Jr.
Album: I'll Try Something New

Record Label: Tamla
Songwriters: Smokey Robinson, Berry Gordy Jr.

Early example of Smoky-esque wordplay.

1963

A LOVE SHE CAN COUNT ON

Producer: Smokey Robinson
Album: The Fabulous Miracles
Record Label: Tamla
Songwriter: Smokey Robinson

As opposed to Motown's cast of strident sufferers, Smokey Robinson always transcended his condition with hope, common sense, a wistful grace, and phrases that turned on a dime as perfectly as Berry Gordy's patented choreography.

MICKEY'S MONKEY

Producers: Brian Holland, Lamont Dozier
Album: Miracles Doin' Mickey's Monkey
Record Label: Tamla
Songwriters: Eddie Holland, Lamont Dozier, Brian Holland

Helping to establish Rock and Roll's favorite primate with a Top-10 R&B/R&R crossover. A highlight of "The T.A.M.I. Show."

YOU'VE REALLY GOT A HOLD ON ME

Producer: Smokey Robinson
Album: The Fabulous Miracles
Record Label: Tamla
Songwriter: Smokey Robinson

Their second #1 R&B/Top-10 R&R crossover. The generally refined Smokey at his fiercest: "I don't like you . . . but I love you."

1965

GOING TO A GO-GO

Producer: Smokey Robinson
Album: Going to a Go-Go
Record Label: Tamla
Songwriters: Smokey Robinson, Warren Moore, Robert Rogers, Marv Tarplin

Covered by the Rolling Stones (Rolling Stones, '82).

OOH BABY BABY

Producer: Smokey Robinson
Album: Going to a Go-Go
Record Label: Tamla
Songwriters: Smokey Robinson, Warren Moore

Timeless restraint in a typically Smokey ballad. Covered by Linda Ronstadt (Asylum, '78).

THE TRACKS OF MY TEARS

Producer: Smokey Robinson
Album: Going to a Go-Go
Record Label: Tamla
Songwriters: Smokey Robinson, Pete Moore, Marv Tarplin

Motown's literary light strikes again; Top-10 R&B/R&R. Their remaining hits would be recorded as Smokey Robinson and the Miracles. Covered by Aretha Franklin (Atlantic, '69) and Linda Ronstadt (Asylum, '75).

I HEARD IT THROUGH THE GRAPEVINE

Producer: Smokey Robinson
Album: Special Occasion
Record Label: Tamla
Songwriters: Norman Whitfield, Barrett Strong

One of the most powerful efforts in Motown history. Original released by the Miracles stiffed. Marvin Gaye recorded it but didn't release his version until a year after Gladys Knight & The Pips reached #1 R&B/#2 R&R (Soul, '67). Gaye's style was a #1 R&B/R&R crossover (Tamla, '68) and is regarded as one of Rock and Roll's greatest all-time tracks. Also covered by Creedence Clearwater Revival (Fantasy, '70).

1967

I SECOND THAT EMOTION

Producers: Smokey Robinson, Al Cleveland
Album: Greatest Hits (Vol. II)
Record Label: Tamla
Songwriters: Smokey Robinson, Al Cleveland

A #1 R&B/Top-10 R&R crossover inaugurates Smokey's career as the top-billed Miracle; his next promotion would be to Motown V.P.

THE LOVE I SAW IN YOU WAS JUST A MIRAGE

Producer: Smokey Robinson
Album: Make It Happen
Record Label: Tamla
Songwriters: Smokey Robinson, Marv Tarplin

Getting metaphor happy.

MORE LOVE

Producer: Smokey Robinson
Album: Make It Happen
Record Label: Tamla
Songwriter: Smokey Robinson

THE TEARS OF A CLOWN

Producers: Smokey Robinson, Henry Cosby
Album: Make It Happen
Record Label: Tamla
Songwriters: Smokey Robinson, Henry Cosby, Stevie Wonder

Biggest hit for Smokey Robinson and the Miracles, a #1 R&B/R&R crossover, was first released in the U.K., where it also hit #1. The fruition of Smokey's literary Soul aspirations, it was three years old at the time.

1968

IF YOU CAN WANT

Producer: Smokey Robinson
Album: Special Occasion
Record Label: Tamla
Songwriter: Smokey Robinson

One of his more visceral laments.

1969

BABY BABY DON'T CRY

Producers: Smokey Robinson, Al Cleveland, Terry Johnson
Album: Time out for Smokey Robinson and the Miracles
Record Label: Tamla
Songwriters: Smokey Robinson, Pete Moore, Terry Johnson

Their last big hit with Smokey, a Top-10 R&B/R&R crossover.

1970

WHO'S GONNA TAKE THE BLAME

Producers: Nick Ashford, Valerie Simpson
Album: Pocketful of Miracles
Record Label: Tamla
Songwriters: Nick Ashford, Valerie Simpson

Smokey's strongest statement, but one that he was unable to write himself. Even singing it was almost too much for his fragile non-judgmental persona. A year later he came out with "I Don't Blame You at All."

1972

WE'VE COME TOO FAR TO END IT NOW

Producer: Johnny Bristol
Album: Flying High Together
Record Label: Tamla
Songwriters: David Jones, Wade Brown Jr., Johnny Bristol

But clearly the incredible run was over, as this peaked at #46.

1975

LOVE MACHINE (PART I)

Producer: Freddie Perren
Album: City of Angels
Record Label: Tamla
Songwriters: Billy Griffith, Pete Moore

Post-Smokey, the Miracles do Disco, with a Top-10 R&B/R&R crossover.

THE MISFITS

1979

LAST CARESS

Album: Beware the Misfits
Record Label: Cherry Red
Songwriter: Glenn Danzig

The dawning of speedcore Metal malice. Covered by Metallica (Elektra, '87).

1982

MOMMY, CAN I GO OUT AND KILL TONIGHT

Album: Walk Among Us
Record Label: Ruby
Songwriter: Glenn Danzig

Danzig would be back with "Mother." Suggested segue: "The End" by the Doors.

MISSING PERSONS

1982

WORDS

Album: Missing Persons
Record Label: Capitol
Songwriters: Dale Bozzio, Warren Cuccurrillo

Peroxide Blondie.

MISSION OF BURMA

1981

THAT'S WHEN I REACH FOR MY REVOLVER

Album: Signals, Calls and Marches
Record Label: Ace of Hearts
Songwriter: Clint Conley

Critically hailed as their classic.

JONI MITCHELL

1968

I HAD A KING

Producer: David Crosby
Album: Joni Mitchell
Record Label: Reprise
Songwriter: Joni Mitchell

The first lady of Folk Rock poetry pens her opening confession.

MARCIE

Producer: David Crosby
Album: Joni Mitchell
Record Label: Reprise
Songwriter: Joni Mitchell

Influential and quintessential acoustic auto-biography of a post-flower child generation, second among her early works only to the non-album B-side "Urge for Going."

NIGHT IN THE CITY

Producer: David Crosby
Album: Joni Mitchell
Record Label: Reprise
Songwriter: Joni Mitchell

Folk Rock as Creative Writing 101. Mr. Kratzman, her English teacher, would be proud. Paul Simon would be redeemed. Covered by Three Dog Night (Dunhill, '71).

1969

CHELSEA MORNING

Producer: Joni Mitchell
Album: Clouds
Record Label: Reprise
Songwriter: Joni Mitchell

Painterly cityscape. Future favorite song of future President Bill Clinton. Covered by Judy Collins (Elektra, '69).

SONGS TO AGING CHILDREN COME

Producer: Joni Mitchell
Album: Clouds
Record Label: Reprise
Songwriter: Joni Mitchell

Featured in the cult classic film Alice's Restaurant, *where it had much more of an appropriately elegiac flavor than Woodstock.*

THAT SONG ABOUT THE MIDWAY

Producer: Joni Mitchell
Album: Clouds
Record Label: Reprise
Songwriter: Joni Mitchell

Too long at the affair. Covered by Bonnie Raitt (Warner Brothers, '74).

1970

BIG YELLOW TAXI

Producer: Joni Mitchell
Album: Ladies of the Canyon
Record Label: Reprise
Songwriter: Joni Mitchell

Ecological whimsy. B-side is her version of "Woodstock." Suggested Segue: "Nothing But Flowers" by Talking Heads.

BLUE

Producer: Joni Mitchell
Album: Blue
Record Label: Reprise
Songwriter: Joni Mitchell

For a painterly songwriter entering her most vulnerable period, a perfectly appropriate title for this battle report from the aftermath of the sexual revolution. Covered by Sarah McLachlan (Epic, '95).

CAREY

Producer: Joni Mitchell
Album: Blue
Record Label: Reprise
Songwriter: Joni Mitchell

Her uncharactistically lighthearted second single was a bigger stiff than "Big Yellow Taxi."

THE LAST TIME I SAW RICHARD

Producer: Joni Mitchell
Album: Blue
Record Label: Reprise
Songwriter: Joni Mitchell

A bittersweet model for the confessional mode. Even Madonna witnessed it.

RIVER

Producer: Joni Mitchell
Album: Blue
Record Label: Reprise
Songwriter: Joni Mitchell

Celebrating Christmas in the land without snow—or good will toward men. Covered by Sarah McLachlan (Epic, '95).

1972

BLONDE IN THE BLEACHERS

Producer: Joni Mitchell
Album: For the Roses
Record Label: Asylum
Songwriter: Joni Mitchell

COLD BLUE STEEL AND SWEET FIRE

Producer: Joni Mitchell
Album: For the Roses
Record Label: Asylum
Songwriter: Joni Mitchell

Reaching a poetic peak.

FOR THE ROSES

Producer: Joni Mitchell
Album: For the Roses
Record Label: Asylum
Songwriter: Joni Mitchell

Moving out of Folk Rock into Art Rock, through Jazz.

WOMAN OF HEART AND MIND

Producer: Joni Mitchell
Album: For the Roses
Record Label: Asylum
Songwriter: Joni Mitchell

Achieving self-definition.

YOU TURN ME ON, I'M A RADIO

Producer: Joni Mitchell
Album: For the Roses
Record Label: Asylum
Songwriter: Joni Mitchell

Flirting again with the AM radio formula. The B-side is the essential "Urge for Going."

1974

CAR ON A HILL

Producer: Joni Mitchell
Album: Court and Spark
Record Label: Asylum
Songwriter: Joni Mitchell

After-hours cocktail Jazz for survivors of the Folk Rock and sexual revolutions.

FREE MAN IN PARIS

Producer: Joni Mitchell
Album: Court and Spark
Record Label: Asylum
Songwriter: Joni Mitchell

One of her classiest rockers, about dropping out of the musical rat race, released three months after her first and only Top-10 single, "Help Me." Rumored to be about media mogul David Geffen.

HELP ME

Producer: Joni Mitchell
Album: Court and Spark
Record Label: Asylum
Songwriter: Joni Mitchell

Her first and only Top-10 single.

RAISED ON ROBBERY

Producer: Joni Mitchell
Album: Court and Spark
Record Label: Asylum
Songwriter: Joni Mitchell

A three-minute lifetime of complicated relationships.

REAL GOOD FOR FREE

Producer: Joni Mitchell
Album: Miles of Aisles
Record Label: Asylum
Songwriter: Joni Mitchell

A street musician observed.

1976

AMELIA

Producer: Joni Mitchell
Album: Hejira
Record Label: Asylum
Songwriter: Joni Mitchell

Mitchell's most striking metaphor for flight.

1991

COME IN FROM THE COLD

Producers: Joni Mitchell, Larry Klein
Album: Night Ride Home
Record Label: Geffen
Songwriter: Joni Mitchell

Signing with David Geffen's record company, Mitchell finally moves past her distancing Jazz excursions.

RAY'S DAD'S CADILLAC

Producers: Joni Mitchell, Larry Klein
Album: Night Ride Home
Record Label: Geffen
Songwriter: Joni Mitchell

Her most memorable song in over a decade.

MARCIA MITZMAN AND JONATHAN DOKUCHITZ
1993

I BELIEVE MY OWN EYES

Producer: George Martin
Album: *Tommy*
Record Label: RCA
Songwriter: Peter Townshend

Added to the Townshend Rock opera when it reached Broadway, the ultimate end of its twenty-year trail as a musical.

MOBY
1991

GO

Producer: Richard Melville Hall
Record Label: Instinct
Songwriters: Angelo Badalamenti, David Lynch

"Twin Peaks" theme as dancehall rave, by the "Connecticut" Techno geek supreme.

MOBY GRAPE
1967

HEY GRANDMA

Producer: David Rubinson
Album: Moby Grape
Record Label: Columbia

Songwriters: Jerry Miller, Don Stevenson

The great lost San Francisco band's great lost track, an appropriate symbol for a scene, a dream, a moment, a movement, and a revolution down the tubes.

OMAHA

Producer: David Rubinson
Album: Moby Grape
Record Label: Columbia
Songwriter: Skip Spence

The only lasting claim to fame from the great hippie singles band that never was.

MODERN ENGLISH

1982

I MELT WITH YOU

Album: After the Snow
Record Label: Sire
Songwriter: Modern English

Technobabble.

MODERN LOVERS

1970

PABLO PICASSO

Producer: John Cale
Album: The Modern Lovers
Record Label: Beserkley
Songwriter: Jonathan Richman

Could any terminally arrested adolescent have said it better? Low-fi twenty years ahead of its time.

1971

ASTRAL PLANE

Producer: John Cale
Album: The Modern Lovers
Record Label: Beserkley
Songwriter: Jonathan Richman

A Rock original—childlike and childish, charming and charmed—like its unabashed author, lead singer Jonathan Richman. From sessions produced by ex-Velvet Underground co-founder, John Cale, dating back to the '60s.

GIRLFRIEND

Producer: John Cale
Album: The Modern Lovers
Record Label: Beserkley
Songwriter: Jonathan Richman

Unadorned teenage yearning re-invented by an eternal teenager.

ROAD RUNNER

Producer: John Cale
Album: Beserkely Chartbusters
Record Label: Beserkely
Songwriter: Jonathan Richman

Answering James Taylor's New England ode to collegiate rambling, "Sweet Baby James," in the voice of the beknighted high-school dropout. A hit in England in '77. Covered by Joan Jett (CBS/Associated, '86).

SHE CRACKED

Producer: John Cale
Album: The Modern Lovers
Record Label: Beserkley
Songwriter: Jonathan Richman

Pristine, elemental, Rock and Roll purity. The Ramones were listening. The Talking Heads were preparing their pseudo-intellectual response.

1976

IMPORTANT IN YOUR LIFE

Producer: John Cale
Album: Jonathan Richman and the Modern Lovers
Record Label: Beserkley
Songwriter: Jonathan Richman

Last of the early, legendary essentials is Jonathan's tribute to Doo-Wop.

1983

THAT SUMMER FEELING

Producer: Peter Bernstein
Album: Jonathan Richman Sings
Record Label: Sire
Songwriter: Johnathan Richman

A stab at solo greatness finds the inner child still beaming.

DOMENICO MODUGNO

1958

NEL BLU DIPINTO DI BLU (VOLARE)

Producer: Mitchell Parish
Album: Nel Blu Dipinto Di Blu (Volare) and Other Italian Favorites
Record Label: Decca
Songwriters: Mitchell Parish, Domenico Modugno, Franco Migliacci

#1 Italian Pop lovesong, brought into the mainstream Rock lexicon by Bobby Rydell (Cameo, '61) and the Alternative Rock lexicon by Alex Chilton (Big Time, '87). Winner of the first Grammy Award for Song of the Year.

THE MOJO MEN

1966

SIT DOWN I THINK I LOVE YOU

Record Label: Reprise
Songwriter: Stephen Stills

Essential garage band Folk Rock. Covered by Stills' band, Buffalo-Springfield (Atco, '67).

MOLLY HATCHET

1980

FLIRTIN' WITH DISASTER

Producer: Tom Werman
Album: Flirtin' with Disaster
Record Label: Epic
Songwriters: David Lawrence Hludeck, Danny Joe Brown, Banner Harvey Thomas

Taking the hatchet to the memory of Lynyrd Skynyrd.

THE MOMENTS

1970

LOVE ON A TWO-WAY STREET

Producer: Sylvia Robinson
Album: The Moments' Greatest Hits
Record Label: Stang
Songwriters: Sylvia Robinson, Bert Keyes

One of love's stranger comebacks; Sylvia Robinson as writer and producer of this mellow #1 R&B/Top-10 R&R smash.

1975

LOOK AT ME (I'M IN LOVE)

Album: Look at Me
Record Label: Stang
Songwriters: Al Goodman, Harry Ray, Walter Morris

#1 R&B/Top-40 R&R crossover.

EDDIE MONEY

1977

TWO TICKETS TO PARADISE

Producer: Bruce Botnick
Album: Eddie Money
Record Label: Columbia
Songwriter: Edward Mahoney (Eddie Money)

Working-class Rock from San Francisco.

1978

BABY HOLD ON

Producer: Bruce Botnick
Album: Eddie Money

Record Label: Columbia
Songwriters: Eddie Mahoney (Eddie Money), Johnny Lyon

A San Francisco/New Jersey bar-band collaboration

1986

TAKE ME HOME TONIGHT

Producers: Ritchie Zito, Eddie Money
Album: Can't Hold Back
Record Label: Columbia
Songwriters: Mike Leeson, Peter Vale, Jeff Barry, Ellie Greenwich, Phil Spector

For reviving the ineffable voice of Ronnie Spector in "Be My Baby" and not on a sample, either, Money is rewarded with his biggest hit.

1988

WALK ON WATER

Producer: Ritchie Zito
Album: Nothing to Lose
Record Label: Columbia
Songwriter: Jesse Harms

THE MONKEES
1966

I'M A BELIEVER

Producer: Jeff Barry
Album: More of the Monkees
Record Label: Colgems
Songwriter: Neil Diamond

Diamond finally sells a perfect Pop Rock song to publisher Don Kirshner. After it went on to stay at #1 for nearly two months, he would be guaranteed plenty of others, as opposed to the Monkees, who would last only until summer re-runs. Covered by Tin Huey (Warner Brothers, '79), and the Feelies in the '80 movie Something Wild.

LAST TRAIN TO CLARKSVILLE

Producers: Tommy Boyce, Bobby Hart
Album: The Monkees
Record Label: Colgems
Songwriters: Tommy Boyce, Bobby Hart

The first prefabricated hit for the ultimate cartoon band had an anti-war lyric. Reportedly, the Clarksville in question was a heavily traveled jumping off point for Vietnam draftees.

1967

DAYDREAM BELIEVER

Producer: Chip Taylor
Album: The Birds, the Bees and the Monkees

Record Label: Colgems
Songwriter: John Stewart

Their third and final #1 was their finest by far. Covered by the author, the ex-Kingston Trio replacement John Stewart (Warner Brothers, '72) and Anne Murray (Capitol, '79).

A LITTLE BIT ME, A LITTLE BIT YOU

Producer: Jeff Barry
Album: Greatest Hits
Record Label: Colgems
Songwriter: Neil Diamond

And the littlest bit Monkees, all of whom but Davy Jones boycotted this session.

PLEASANT VALLEY SUNDAY

Producer: Douglas Farthing Hatelid
Album: Pisces, Aquarius, Capricorn and Jones
Record Label: Colgems
Songwriters: Gerry Goffin, Carole King

Among the producer's greatest works.

1968

THE PORPOISE SONG

Producer: Gerry Goffin
Album: Head!
Record Label: Colgems
Songwriters: Gerry Goffin, Carole King

Theme from the roundly misunderstood cult classic Head!, *which marked the official demise of the Monkees. Soon Peter Tork would be living in a rented room in the mansion he once owned.*

VALLERI

Producer: The Monkees
Album: The Birds, the Bees, and the Monkees
Record Label: Colgems
Songwriters: Tommy Boyce, Bobby Hart

Legendary guitar part by Louie Shelton.

THE MONOTONES
1957

BOOK OF LOVE

Record Label: Argo
Songwriters: Warren Davis, George Malone, Charles Patrick

The good book, within which is perhaps the missing Tenth Commandment that Harvey and the Moonglows omitted. Inspired, as

were undoubtedly many of the most classic love songs of all time, by a toothpaste commercial, in this case for Pepsodent.

BILL MONROE
1947

BLUE MOON OF KENTUCKY

Record Label: Columbia
Songwriter: Bill Monroe

Country classic was the B-side of Elvis' first single, "That's All Right, Mama."

THE MONROES
1982

WHAT DO ALL THE PEOPLE KNOW

Producer: Bruce Botnick
Album: The Monroes
Record Label: Alfa
Songwriter: Robert Davis

Botnick's career would long outlive this left-field one-shot track and band.

CHRIS MONTEZ
1962

LET'S DANCE

Producer: Jimmy Joe Lee
Album: Let's Dance and Have Some Kinda Fun
Record Label: Monogram
Songwriter: Jim Lee

Among the detritus swept in by "The Twist."

MOODSWINGS
1992

SPIRITUAL HIGH (STATE OF INDEPENDENCE)

Album: Moodfood
Record Label: Arista
Songwriters: Vangelis, Jon Anderson, J. T. F. Hood, Grant Showbiz

Modern English dancehall rush, featuring the voice of Pretender Chrissie Hynde, and heard in the movie Single White Female.

THE MOODY BLUES
1968

NIGHTS IN WHITE SATIN

Producer: Tony Clarke
Album: Days of Future Passed
Record Label: Deram
Songwriter: Justin Hayward

If Montovani had been born during the Baby Boom. Re-released in '72.

RIDE MY SEE SAW

Producer: Tony Clarke
Album: In Search of the Lost Chord
Record Label: Deram
Songwriter: John Lodge

Collected on three different greatest hits albums.

TUESDAY AFTERNOON (FOREVER AFTERNOON)

Producer: Tony Clarke
Album: Days of Future Passed
Record Label: Deram
Songwriter: Justin Hayward

Medley with "Nights in White Satin" could kill an entire day.

1970

QUESTION

Producer: Tony Clarke
Album: A Question of Balance
Record Label: Threshold
Songwriter: Justin Hayward

This first instance of Arena New-Age Rock is their biggest U.K. hit.

1972

I'M JUST A SINGER (IN A ROCK AND ROLL BAND)

Producer: Tony Clarke
Album: A Question of Balance
Record Label: Threshold
Songwriter: John Lodge

The thinking man's version of "Band on the Run."

ISN'T LIFE STRANGE

Producer: Tony Clarke
Album: Seventh Sojourn
Record Label: Threshold
Songwriter: John Lodge

From their best-selling album, a summation of their symphonic progressive Siddharthian Rock.

1981

THE VOICE

Album: Long Distance Voyager
Record Label: Threshold
Songwriter: Justin Hayward

Turning into the Chicago of England.

1986

YOUR WILDEST DREAMS

Producer: Tony Visconti
Album: The Other Side of Life
Record Label: Polygram
Songwriter: Justin Hayward

Their biggest hit since "Nights in White Satin."

1988

I KNOW YOU'RE OUT THERE SOMEWHERE

Producer: Tony Visconti
Album: Sur La Mer
Record Label: Polygram
Songwriter: Justin Hayward

THE MOONGLOWS

1955

SINCERELY

Record Label: Chess
Songwriters: Harvey Fuqua, Alan Freed

First collaboration between two future powers of the Rock and Roll era, a Top-10 R&B/Top-20 R&R crossover. Freed would go on to become a martyred DJ; Fuqua a legendary writer and producer. The tune, meanwhile, merely went on to become a standard, Doo-Wop and otherwise. The Pop cover by the McGuire Sisters (Coral, '55) went to #1.

1958

THE TEN COMMANDMENTS OF LOVE

Record Label: Chess
Songwriter: Marshall Paul

Not just another Top-10 R&B/Top-30 R&R crossover; a cornerstone Doo-Wop philosophical statement, even though they're a commandment short.

JOHNNY MOORE AND THE THREE BLAZERS

1946

DRIFTIN' BLUES

Record Label: Aladdin
Songwriters: Charles Brown, Johnny Moore, Eddie Williams

Charles Brown's down-and-out masterpiece of soulful R&B crooning. Nat Cole, Johnny Ace, Fats Domino, and Jackie Wilson were listening. Sam Cooke (RCA, '63), Ray Charles (ABC/Paramount, '66), Bobby Bland (Duke, '68), and Eric Clapton (RSO, '75) were covering.

1950

ROCK WITH IT

Record Label: RCA
Songwriters: Billy Valentine, B. Goldberg

Seminal pre-Rock Rock and Roll trio's sig-

nature rocker, featuring Moore on guitar, Charles Brown on vocals.

GARRY MOORE

1985

OUT IN THE FIELDS

Album: Run for Cover
Record Label: Mirage
Songwriter: Garry Moore

Burly Bluesy British barroom guitarist hits the singles charts.

JACKIE MOORE

1978

PERSONALLY

Producers: William Bell, Paul Mitchell
Record Label: Columbia
Songwriter: Paul Kelly

His Soul breakthrough. Covered by Karla Bonoff (Columbia, '82).

WILD BILL MOORE

1947

WE'RE GONNA ROCK, WE'RE GONNA ROLL

Producer: Teddy Reig
Record Label: Savoy
Songwriters: Teddy Reig, Bill Moore

Sax-driven, Illinois Jacquet-influenced boogie was a model for Twists to come.

MELI'SA MORGAN

1986

DO ME BABY

Producer: Paul Laurence
Album: Do Me Baby
Record Label: Capitol
Songwriter: Prince Rogers Nelson

Prince in the (erogenous) zone.

ALANIS MORISSETTE

1995

YOU OUGHTA KNOW

Producer: Glen Ballard
Album: Jagged Little Pill
Record Label: Maverick/Reprise
Songwriters: Glen Ballard, Alanis Morissette

Taking up where even Tori Amos (in "Silent All These Years") dared not go—a few years ago, anyway. Now the Fatal Attraction syndrome is not only rampant in Rock, but it wins all the prizes.

THE MORRELLS

1982

THE MAN WHO HAS EVERYTHING
Album: Shake and Push
Record Label: Borrowed
Songwriter: Ben Vaughan

Rootsy rocker. Covered by Ben Vaughan (Enigma, '90).

VAN MORRISON

1967

BROWN EYED GIRL
Producer: Bert Berns
Album: Blowin' Your Mind
Record Label: Bang
Songwriter: Van Morrison

His first hit and one of his most memorable; Dylan-esque, in the effusive, ineffable Dylan Thomas sense. Used in the background of the enema scene in Oliver Stone's Born on the Fourth of July.

1969

CARAVAN
Producer: Lee Merenstein
Album: Astral Weeks
Record Label: Warner Brothers
Songwriter: Van Morrison

A rambling song, for born-again gypsies everywhere.

CYPRESS AVENUE
Producer: Lee Merenstein
Album: Astral Weeks
Record Label: Warner Brothers
Songwriter: Van Morrison

Setting out on Van's metaphorical creative avenue, with guru Bert Burns originally the unlikely spiritual guide. Future '70s and '80s icons Bruce Springsteen and Bono (of U2) were listening.

MADAMME GEORGE
Producer: Lee Merenstein
Album: Astral Weeks
Record Label: Warner Brothers
Songwriter: Van Morrison

Brooding, mystical, Joycean character portrait originally recorded as part of the sessions that produced "Brown Eyed Girl," with Bert Berns in New York in '67.

1970

AND IT STONED ME
Producer: Van Morrison
Album: Moondance
Record Label: Warner Brothers

Songwriter: Van Morrison

Ethereal and earthy, Morrison describes his emotional weather, exquisitely.

CRAZY LOVE
Producer: Van Morrison
Album: Moondance
Record Label: Warner Brothers
Songwriter: Van Morrison

Featured in the '89 film Always.

DOMINO
Producer: Van Morrison
Album: His Band and Street Choir
Record Label: Warner Brothers
Songwriter: Van Morrison

His biggest single.

INTO THE MYSTIC
Producer: Van Morrison
Album: Moondance
Record Label: Warner Brothers
Songwriter: Van Morrison

The centerpiece of his classic album and career, Van's ineffable search for the Holy Grail. Covered by Johnny Rivers (Imperial, '70) without the holiness. Featured in the '71 movie Dusty and Sweets McGee.

MOONDANCE
Producer: Van Morrison
Album: Moondance
Record Label: Warner Brothers
Songwriter: Van Morrison

Van's contribution to the world of dance. Later, Michael Jackson would provide the steps.

1971

BLUE MONEY
Producer: Van Morrison
Album: His Band and Street Choir
Record Label: Warner Brothers
Songwriter: Van Morrison

In the Caledonia Soul groove.

CALL ME UP IN DREAMLAND
Producer: Van Morrison
Album: His Band and Street Choir
Record Label: Warner Brothers
Songwriter: Van Morrison

New Orleans revisited by the mystic Irishman.

TUPELO HONEY
Producers: Van Morrison, Ted Templeman
Album: Tupelo Honey

Record Label: Warner Brothers
Songwriter: Van Morrison

Walking in Memphis years before Marc Cohn.

WILD NIGHT
Producers: Van Morrison, Ted Templeman
Album: Tupelo Honey
Record Label: Warner Brothers
Songwriter: Van Morrison

A Van standard describing the mating habits of the current crop of street habitues, circa downtown L.A. in the '70s. Featured in the '91 movie Thelma and Louise. Covered by John Cougar Mellencamp and Me'shell NdegéOcello (Mercury, '94).

1972

JACKIE WILSON SAID (I'M IN HEAVEN WHEN YOU SMILE)
Producer: Van Morrison
Album: St. Dominic's Preview
Record Label: Warner Brothers
Songwriter: Van Morrison

Combining the sacred and the profane, just like in the days of the Clovers and the Dominoes. Suggested Segue: "When Smokey Sings" by ABC.

LISTENING TO THE LIONS
Producer: Van Morrison
Album: St. Dominic's Preview
Record Label: Warner Brothers
Songwriter: Van Morrison

Confessional Rock at its best, a purging of the soul and spirit.

1986

IN THE GARDEN
Producer: Van Morrison
Album: No Guru, No Method, No Teacher
Record Label: Polygram
Songwriter: Van Morrison

This overwhelming quasi-religious ballad is one of his most moving moments.

1989

HAVE I TOLD YOU LATELY
Producer: Van Morrison
Album: Avalon Sunset
Record Label: Mercury
Songwriter: Van Morrison

Moving from sacred to earthly heaven. Covered by Rod Stewart (Warner Brothers, '93) and Van in a Grammy-winning duet with the Chieftains (RCA, '95).

1991

WHY MUST I ALWAYS EXPLAIN
Album: Hymns to the Silence
Record Label: Polydor
Songwriter: Van Morrison

The other side of Van: mocking his notorious penchant for complaining. Suggested segue: "I Can't Explain" by the Who.

MORRISSEY

1988

EVERYDAY IS LIKE SUNDAY
Album: Viva Hate
Record Label: Sire
Songwriters: Stephen Morrissey, Stephen Street

Covered by the Pretenders in the 1995 film Boys on the Side.

SUEDEHEAD
Album: Viva Hate
Record Label: Sire
Songwriters: Stephen Morrissey, Stephen Street

First U.K. solo single hit for the former head case from the Smiths, an anti-Sinatra to do Bryan Ferry proud.

1989

INTERESTING DRUG
Producer: Stephen Street
Album: Morrissey
Record Label: Sire
Songwriters: Stephen Morrissey, Stephen Street

With the lovely Kirsty MacColl in a supporting role. Suggested Segues: "Love Is the Drug" by Roxy Music, "I Want a New Drug" by Huey Lewis & the News.

1990

LAST OF THE FAMOUS INTERNATIONAL PLAYBOYS
Producers: Clive Langer, Alan Winstanley
Album: Bona Drag
Record Label: Warner Brothers
Songwriters: Stephen Morrissey, Stephen Street

Purportedly written about the gangster brothers, the Crays.

NOVEMBER SPAWNED A MONSTER
Producers: Clive Langer, Alan Winstanley
Album: Bona Drag
Record Label: Warner Brothers

Songwriters: Stephen Morrissey, Clive Langer

1991

DRIVING YOUR GIRLFRIEND HOME
Producers: Clive Langer, Alan Winstantly
Album: Kill Uncle
Record Label: Sire
Songwriters: Stephen Morrissey, Mark Nevin

One of his best tracks.

OUR FRANK
Producers: Clive Langer, Alan Winstanley
Album: Kill Uncle
Record Label: Sire
Songwriters: Stephen Morrissey, Mark Nevin

1992

WE HATE IT WHEN OUR FRIENDS BECOME SUCCESSFUL
Producer: Mick Ronson
Album: Your Arsenal
Record Label: Sire
Songwriters: Stephen Morrissey, Alain Whyte

First U.S. chart hit.

1993

I KNOW IT'S GONNA HAPPEN
Producer: Mick Ronson
Album: Your Arsenal
Record Label: Sire
Songwriter: Stephen Morrissey

1994

MORE YOU IGNORE ME, THE CLOSER I GET
Producer: Steve Lillywhite
Album: Vauxhall and I
Record Label: Sire
Songwriters: Stephen Morrissey, Boz Boorer

His biggest hit.

THE MOTELS

1982

ONLY THE LONELY
Producer: Val Garay
Album: All for One
Record Label: Capitol
Songwriter: Martha Davis

Stone Poneys wannabes rip off an Orbison title.

1983

SUDDENLY LAST SUMMER
Album: Little Robbers
Record Label: Capitol
Songwriter: Martha Davis

A song as turgid as the movie it was named after.

MOTHER EARTH

1968

DOWN SO LOW
Album: Living with the Animals
Record Label: Mercury
Songwriter: Tracy Nelson

Perennially third-billed (to Janis Joplin and Grace Slick) San Francisco Blues Vesuvius, Tracy Nelson, achieved a personal and career epiphany on this gospel-inflected classic. The note she hits on the last "down" is justification, by itself, for the multitude of clinkers that she's lent her precious voice to ever since. Covered by Linda Ronstadt (Asylum, '76). Re-recorded by a solo Tracy Nelson (Atlantic, '73).

THE MOTHERS OF INVENTION

1966

HELP I'M A ROCK
Producer: Tom Wilson
Album: Freak Out
Record Label: Verve
Songwriter: Frank Zappa

Inventing psychedelic Rock.

HUNGRY FREAKS, DADDY
Producer: Tom Wilson
Album: Freak Out
Record Label: Verve
Songwriter: Frank Zappa

Inventing the psychedelic Doo-Wop.

TROUBLE COMIN' EVERY DAY
Producer: Tom Wilson
Album: Freak Out
Record Label: Verve
Songwriter: Frank Zappa

Pre-figuring the kids vs. cops confrontations of L.A. high society. Suggested Segue: "For What It's Worth" by Buffalo Springfield.

WHO ARE THE BRAIN POLICE
Producer: Tom Wilson
Album: Freak Out
Record Label: Verve
Songwriter: Frank Zappa

Symphonic, electronic protest song.

YOU DIDN'T TRY TO CALL ME
Producer: Tom Wilson
Album: Freak Out
Record Label: Verve
Songwriter: Frank Zappa

Zappa's parody/homage to his first love, Doo-Wop. Covered by Zappa as Rueben and the Jets (Verve, '68).

YOU'RE PROBABLY WONDERING WHY I'M HERE
Producer: Tom Wilson
Album: Freak Out
Record Label: Verve
Songwriter: Frank Zappa

Protest of a more personal sort, complete with one of the great Rock and Roll screams.

1967

BROWN SHOES DON'T MAKE IT
Producer: Tom Wilson
Album: Absolutely Free
Record Label: Verve
Songwriter: Frank Zappa

Symphonic social satire. Bach (P.D.Q.) meets Mad Magazine.

DUKE OF PRUNES
Producer: Tom Wilson
Album: Absolutely Free
Record Label: Verve
Songwriter: Frank Zappa

SON OF SUZY CREAMCHEESE
Producer: Tom Wilson
Album: Absolutely Free
Record Label: Verve
Songwriter: Frank Zappa

His most profound character, aside from Uncle Meat, was an L.A. dress designer.

STATUS BACK BABY
Producer: Tom Wilson
Album: Absolutely Free
Record Label: Verve
Songwriter: Frank Zappa

No life after high school.

1968

CONCENTRATION MOON
Producer: Frank Zappa
Album: We're Only in It for the Money
Record Label: Verve
Songwriter: Frank Zappa

Zappa at his most sweetly subversive.

WHO NEEDS THE PEACE CORPS
Producer: Frank Zappa
Album: We're Only in It for the Money
Record Label: Verve
Songwriter: Frank Zappa

Hippie-bashing second-to-none but the Velvet Underground.

1969

CRUISIN' FOR BURGERS
Producer: Frank Zappa
Album: Uncle Meat
Record Label: Bizarre
Songwriter: Frank Zappa

Out of the mire that is Los Angeles, some fast food from the '50s.

1970

MY GUITAR WANTS TO KILL YOUR MAMA
Producer: Frank Zappa
Album: Weasels Ripped My Flesh
Record Label: Bizarre
Songwriter: Frank Zappa

Moving into his post-verbal stage.

1973

MONTANA
Producer: Frank Zappa
Album: Over-nite Sensation
Record Label: DiscReet
Songwriter: Frank Zappa

The rise of a dental-floss magnate coincides with Zappa's emergence as a composer of modern music, which he would do from now on under his own name.

MÖTLEY CRÜE
1987

GIRLS, GIRLS, GIRLS
Producer: Tom Werman
Album: Girls, Girls, Girls
Record Label: Elektra
Songwriters: Tommy Lee, Nikki Sixx, Mick Mars

Meet the new Metal; same as the old Metal.

1989

DR. FEELGOOD
Producer: Bob Rock
Album: Dr. Feelgood
Record Label: Elektra
Songwriters: Mick Mars, Nikki Sixx

An ode to perhaps the same nefarious physician once visited by Aretha Franklin. But a different song.

WITHOUT YOU
Producer: Bob Rock
Album: Dr. Feelgood
Record Label: Elektra
Songwriters: Nikki Sixx, Mick Mars

Anthem for the American Whitesnake.

MOTORHEAD
1977

MOTORHEAD
Producer: Speedy Keen
Album: Motorhead
Record Label: Chiswick
Songwriters: Ian Kilmeister (Lemmy), Philthy Taylor, (Fast) Eddie Clarke

Remake of an old Hawkwind track launches the connoisseur's mega-Metal band.

1979

BOMBER
Producer: Jimmy Miller
Album: Bomber
Record Label: Bronze
Songwriters: Ian Kilmeister (Lemmy), Philthy Taylor, (Fast) Eddie Clarke

England during the blitz was their largest influence.

OVERKILL
Producer: Jimmy Miller
Album: Overkill
Record Label: Bronze
Songwriters: Ian Kilmeister (Lemmy), Philthy Taylor, (Fast) Eddie Clarke

Another monster track.

1980

ACE OF SPADES
Producer: Vic Maile
Album: Ace of Spades
Record Label: Mercury
Songwriters: Ian Kilmeister (Lemmy), Philthy Taylor, (Fast) Eddie Clark

One of their most monumental Metal onslaughts.

WE ARE THE ROAD CREW
Producer: Vic Maile
Album: Ace of Spades
Record Label: Mercury
Songwriters: Ian Kilmeister (Lemmy), Philthy Taylor, (Fast) Eddie Clarke

KILLED BY DEATH

1984

Album: No Remorse
Record Label: Bronze
Songwriters: Ian Kilmeister
(Lemmy), Mick Burston

DEAF FOREVER

1986

Producer: Bill Laswell
Album: Orgasmatron
Record Label: GWR/Profile
Songwriters: Ian Kilmeister
(Lemmy), Mick Burston, Phil
Campbell, Pete Gill

1916

1991

Album: 1916
Record Label: WTG
Songwriter: Ian Kilmeister (Lemmy)

Returning to the Metal wars with a blitzkrieg ballad.

MOTT THE HOOPLE

1972

ALL THE YOUNG DUDES

Producer: David Bowie
Album: All the Young Dudes
Record Label: Columbia
Songwriter: David Bowie

Glam's glitziest moment, with nods to the Velvet Underground, defining, in the waning days of the hippie, the angry opposition, fomenting in England.

ALL THE WAY FROM MEMPHIS

1973

Producers: Ian Hunter, Dave Griffin,
Pete Watts
Album: The Hoople
Record Label: Columbia
Songwriter: Ian Hunter

Searing glam-bam Metal monster, Top-10 in England; in New York City, the Dolls were preparing their response.

GOLDEN AGE OF ROCK 'N' ROLL

1974

Producers: Ian Hunter, Dave Griffin,
Pete Watts
Album: The Hoople
Record Label: Columbia
Songwriter: Ian Hunter

Others opted for '54 with Elvis, Bo Diddley, Chuck Berry, and Fats Domino, or '64 with the Beatles, the Stones, Motown, and Bob Dylan, or '84 with Springsteen, Prince, Michael Jackson, and Madonna, or '94 with Pearl Jam, Hole, Tori Amos, Babyface, and Dinosaur Jr.

BOB MOULD

1989

SEE A LITTLE LIGHT

Producer: Bob Mould
Album: Workbook
Record Label: Virgin
Songwriter: Bob Mould

Richard Thompson-influenced former guitarist of Hüsker Dü writes a song with a Top-40 hook, enjoys it. Later he would form Sugar and go for the Rock mainstream.

MOUNTAIN

1970

FOR YASGUR'S FARM

Producer: Felix Pappalardi
Album: Mountain Climbing
Record Label: Windfall
Songwriters: George Gardes, Corky
Laing, Felix Pappalardi, Gail Collins,
Gary Ship

Rock ballad tribute to the legendary Woodstock host, Max Yasgur.

MISSISSIPPI QUEEN

Producer: Felix Pappalardi
Album: Mountain Climbing
Record Label: Columbia
Songwriters: Leslie West, Corky
Laing, Felix Pappalardi, David Rea

Hard Rock equivalent of "Proud Mary." Suggested Mississippi segue: "Black Water" by the Doobie Brothers.

THEME FOR AN IMAGINARY WESTERN

Producer: Felix Pappalardi
Album: Mountain Climbing
Record Label: Windfall
Songwriters: Jack Bruce, Pete
Brown

Leslie West's guitar epiphany on a typical post-Cream composition.

MOUSE

1966

A PUBLIC EXECUTION

Record Label: Fraternity
Songwriters: Knox Henderson,
Ronny Weiss

Classic garage nugget.

MOUTH AND MACNEAL

1972

HOW DO YOU DO (LET ECHOLS CHECK)

Producer: Hans Van Hemart
Album: How Do You Do
Record Label: Philips
Songwriters: Hans Christan Van
Hemert, Herricas Von Hoof, Ronnie
Ball

Dutch novelty.

THE MOVE

1972

DO YA

Producer: Jeff Lynne
Album: Split Ends
Record Label: United Artists
Songwriter: Jeff Lynne

In some quarters Rock song of the year (of admittedly a relatively mild year). Covered by Lynne in ELO (United Artists, '76) and Ace Frehley (Megaforce, '89).

MR. BIG

1992

TO BE WITH YOU

Producer: Kevin Elson
Album: Lean into It
Record Label: Atlantic
Songwriters: Eric Martin, David
Grahame

The dread Rock ballad produces the dread hit single, anathema for the Metal band that wants to sustain Arena credibility with heavy, axe-wielding tunes like "Addicted to That Rush."

MR. MISTER

1985

BROKEN WINGS

Producer: Mutt Lange
Album: Welcome to the Real World
Record Label: RCA
Songwriters: Richard Page, Steven
George, Robert John "Mutt" Lange

Pop Rock from the Air Supply warehouse.

IS IT LOVE

1986

Producer: Mutt Lange
Album: Welcome to the Real World
Record Label: Warner Brothers

Songwriters: Richard Page, Steven George, Robert John "Mutt" Lange, Pat Mastellotto

The ineffable Mutt Top-40 signature.

KYRIE

Producer: Mutt Lange
Album: Welcome to the Real World
Record Label: RCA
Songwriters: Richard Page, Steven George, Robert John "Mutt" Lange

Utilizing the timeless chant for a #1 follow-up to a #1 ("Broken Wings"). Suggested segue: "Requiem" by the Association, "Sadeness (Part 1)" by Enigma.

MTUME
1983

JUICY FRUIT

Producer: James Mtume
Album: Juicy Fruit
Record Label: Epic
Songwriter: James Mtume

Biggest hit for the Philadelphia Funk band, a #1 R&B.

MUDHONEY
1988

TOUCH ME I'M SICK

Producer: Jack Endino
Album: Superfuzz Bigmuff
Record Label: Sub Pop
Songwriters: Steve Turner, Mark Arm

Key single from the legendary Seattle scenesters later included on Superfuzz Bigmuff (Sub Pop, '88).

MARIA MULDAUR
1973

MAD MAD ME

Producers: Joe Boyd, Lenny Waronker
Album: Maria Muldaur
Record Label: Warner Brothers
Songwriter: Wendy Waldman

Funky Rock confessional launches Waldman, who would have to move to Nashville to achieve further songwriting success.

MIDNIGHT AT THE OASIS

Producers: Joe Boyd, Lenny Waronker
Album: Maria Muldaur

Record Label: Warner Brothers
Songwriter: David Nichtern

Jim Kweskin jugband front-girl steps forward on a loopy, Bob Willsian lovesong, with a great guitar part by Amos Garrett.

MUNGO JERRY
1970

IN THE SUMMERTIME

Producer: Barry Murray
Album: Mungo Jerry
Record Label: Janus
Songwriter: Ray Dorset

Ultimate summer song was top U.K. single of '70.

THE MURMAIDS
1963

POPSICLES AND ICICLES

Producer: Kim Fowley
Record Label: Chattahoochee
Songwriter: David Gates

The Brill Building sound of L.A. Gates would move to Bread, Fowley to the Runaways.

MICHAEL MURPHEY
1975

WILDFIRE

Producer: Bob Johnston
Album: Blue Sky—Night Thunder
Record Label: Epic
Songwriters: Michael Murphey, Larry Cansler

Reviving the lost art of Country Rock.

1982

WHAT'S FOREVER FOR

Album: Michael Martin Murphey
Record Label: Liberty
Songwriter: Rafe Van Hoy

A #1 C&W/Top-20 R&R crossover.

EDDIE MURPHY
1985

PARTY ALL THE TIME

Producer: Rick James
Album: How Could It Be
Record Label: Columbia
Songwriter: Rick James

The comic.

PETER MURPHY
1990

CUTS YOU UP

Producers: Simon Rogers, Peter Murphy
Album: Deep
Record Label: Beggar's Banquet
Songwriters: Peter Murphy, Paul Statham

Bowie-esque.

1992

THE SWEETEST DROP

Producers: Mike Thorne, Peter Murphy
Album: Holy Smoke
Record Label: Beggar's Banquet
Songwriters: Peter Murphy, Paul Statham

Bauhaus founder at his most portentous.

ANNE MURRAY
1970

SNOWBIRD

Producer: Brian Ahern
Album: Snowbird
Record Label: Capitol
Songwriter: Gene Maclellan

A new C&W/R&R crossover from Canada.

PUT YOUR HAND IN THE HAND

Producer: Brian Ahern
Album: Snowbird
Record Label: Capitol
Songwriter: Gene Maclellan

Top-40 Pop-Gospelizing was nearly the follow-up single to "Snowbird." Instead, another Canadian band, Ocean (Kama Sutra, '71) had a Top-10 hit with it.

1975

YOU NEEDED ME

Producer: Jim Ed Norman
Album: Let's Keep It That Way
Record Label: Capitol
Songwriter: Randy Goodrum

#1 R&R/Top-10 C&W crossover ballad.

JUNIOR MURVIN
1976

POLICE AND THIEVES

Producer: Lee Perry
Album: Police and Thieves
Record Label: Mango
Songwriter: Junior Murvin

Subversive Reggae classic. Covered by the Clash (Epic, '79).

THE MUSIC EXPLOSION
1965

LITTLE BIT O' SOUL
Producers: Jerry Kazenetz, Jeff Katz
Album: Little Bit o' Soul
Record Label: Laurie
Songwriters: John Carter, Ken Lewis
Bubble Punk.

THE MUSIC MACHINE
1966

TALK, TALK
Producer: Maurice Bercov
Album: (Turn on) The Music Machine
Record Label: Original Sound
Songwriter: Thomas Sear Bonniwell
L.A. Garage.

MUSICAL YOUTH
1983

PASS THE DUTCHIE
Producer: Peter Collins
Album: The Youth of Today
Record Label: MCA
Songwriters: Jackie Mitoo, Lloyd Ferguson, Fitzroy Simpson
The Jackson Five of Reggae.

MUSIQUE
1978

IN THE BUSH
Producer: Patrick Adams
Album: Keep on Jumpin'
Record Label: Prelude
Songwriters: Patrick Adams, Sandra Cooper
French Disco. Suggested segue: "Je T'aime . . . Moi non plus" by Jane Birkin and Serge Gainsbourg.

MY BLOODY VALENTINE
1991

WHEN YOU SLEEP
Album: Loveless
Record Label: Sire
Songwriter: Kevin Shields
The droning sound of dream Pop arrives; the Cocteau Twins, the Cowboy Junkies, and the Jesus and Mary Chain were all in the same bed.

ALANNAH MYLES
1990

BLACK VELVET
Producer: David Tyson
Album: Alannah Myles
Record Label: Atlantic
Songwriters: David Tyson, Christopher Ward
Elvis-inspired one-shot. Suggested segue: "Walking in Memphis" by Marc Cohn.

THE MYSTICS
1959

HUSHABYE
Record Label: Laurie
Songwriters: Doc Pomus, Mort Shuman
The Elegants never managed to follow up "Little Star," but the Mystics did, in typically magnificent Brill Building fashion.

N

N2DEEP
1993

BACK TO THE HOTEL
Producer: Johnny Z
Album: Back to the Hotel
Record Label: Profile
Songwriters: Johnny Zunino, James Trujillo, Timothy Lyon
Your basic white Rap band on the run.

THE NAILS
1982

88 LINES ABOUT 44 WOMEN
Album: Hotel for Women
Record Label: Jimboco/PVC
Songwriter: David Kaufman
Obscure New York band's masterly couplets about coupling in all its intricate varieties. Later on RCA. Re-rediscovered on EMI in '92. And let's not forget their extravagant "Juanita Juanita" either.

NAPOLEON XIV
1966

THEY'RE COMING TO TAKE ME AWAY, HA-HAAA!
Producer: Jepalana Productions
Album: They're Coming to Take Me Away, Ha-Haaa!

Record Label: Warner Brothers
Songwriter: Rosemary Djivre
A perverse novelty that was banned on some stations, featured on others. Definitely up there with "Ambrose Part V" by Linda Laurie, and the immortal "I Put a Spell on You" by Screaming Jay Hawkins.

GRAHAM NASH
1971

CHICAGO
Producer: Graham Nash
Album: Songs for Beginners
Record Label: Atlantic
Songwriter: Graham Nash
Outside agitating from the former Hollie.

WE CAN CHANGE THE WORLD
Producer: Graham Nash
Album: Songs for Beginners
Record Label: Atlantic
Songwriter: Graham Nash
Voicing sentiments that would remain popular until the McGovern debacle of '72.

JOHNNY NASH
1968

HOLD ME TIGHT
Producers: Johnny Nash, Arthur Jenkins
Album: Hold Me Tight
Record Label: JAD
Songwriter: Johnny Nash
First Top-10 single for the Hawaiian-born Reggae crooner.

1972

I CAN SEE CLEARLY NOW
Producer: Johnny Nash
Album: I Can See Clearly Now
Record Label: Epic
Songwriter: Johnny Nash
First Reggae tune to hit #1 R&R, backed by some of Bob Marley's Wailers.

THE NASHVILLE TEENS
1964

TOBACCO ROAD
Producer: Mickie Most
Album: Possibly
Record Label: London
Songwriter: John D. Loudermilk
English band, Nashville songwriter; U.K./U.S. crossover smash.

NATIONAL LAMPOON
1972

DETERIORATA
Producer: Tony Hendra
Album: Radio Dinner
Record Label: Banana
Songwriters: Christopher Guest, Tony Hendra

Previewing the National Lampoon/ Lemmings satiric sensibility that would dominate TV once "Saturday Night Live" arrived on the air in '75.

NATURAL SELECTION
1991

DO ANYTHING
Album: Natural Selection
Record Label: East/West
Songwriters: Frederick Thomas, Elliot Erickson, Ingrid Chaver

Hip-Hop.

DAVID NAUGHTON
1979

MAKIN' IT
Record Label: RSO
Songwriters: Freddie Perren, Dino Fekaris

TV theme by the "Dr. Pepper guy."

NAUGHTY BY NATURE
1991

O.P.P. (OTHER PEOPLE'S PROPERTY)
Album: Naughty by Nature
Record Label: Tommy Boy
Songwriters: Vinnie Brown, Kier Gist, Anthony Criss, the Corporation

Clever new Hip-Hop sloganeering, with samples from the Jackson Five's "ABC."

1993

HIP-HOP HOORAY
Producer: Naughty by Nature
Album: 19 Naughty III
Record Label: Tommy Boy
Songwriter: Naughty by Nature

Celebrating Hip-Hop's '90s mainstream ascendancy; #1 R&B/Top-10 R&R crossover.

NAZARETH
1975

HAIR OF THE DOG
Album: Hair of the Dog
Record Label: A&M
Songwriter: Nazareth

The Rock and Roll condition, personified. But not as well as on "Love Hurts" from the same album, their best-seller of thirteen that made the charts.

THE NAZZ
1969

HELLO, IT'S ME
Producer: Todd Rundgren
Album: The Nazz
Record Label: SGC
Songwriter: Todd Rundgren

Low-Fi Beatle-mongering. Covered by the group's leader, Todd Rundgren (Bearsville, '72).

ME'SHELL NDEGÉOCELLO
1993

IF THAT'S YOUR BOYFRIEND, HE WASN'T LAST NIGHT
Album: Plantation Lullabies
Record Label: Maverick/Sire
Songwriter: Me'Shell NdegéOcello

Madonna discovery's breakthrough R&B-edged single. Later she would team with John Mellencamp on "Wild Night" (Mercury, '94).

NED'S ATOMIC DUSTBIN
1992

NOT SLEEPING AROUND
Album: Are You Normal
Record Label: Chaos
Songwriter: Ned's Atomic Dustbin

An Alternative hit in the year before Alternative hit.

FRED NEIL
1967

THE DOLPHINS
Producer: Nik Venet
Album: Fred Neil
Record Label: Elektra
Songwriter: Fred Neil

Fred Neil's crowning achievment (aside from playing guitar on "Dream Lover" and "Diana"), swimming with the Dolphins. Covered by Dion (Laurie, '68) and Richie Havens (Stormy Forest, '72).

EVERYBODY'S TALKIN'
Producer: Nik Venet
Album: Fred Neil
Record Label: Elektra
Songwriter: Fred Neil

Explaining himself before taking off for Coconut Grove. Covered by Nilsson (RCA, '67). Nilsson's version became his first Top-10 hit after being featured in the '69 film Midnight Cowboy.

NELSON
1990

(CAN'T LIVE WITHOUT YOUR) LOVE AND AFFECTION
Producers: Marc Tanner, David Thoener
Album: After the Rain
Record Label: Geffen
Songwriters: Matt Nelson, Gunnar Nelson, Marc Tanner

#1 Pop rocker for the sons of the late Rick.

AFTER THE RAIN
Producers: Marc Tanner, David Thoener
Album: After the Rain
Record Label: DCG
Songwriters: Gunnar Nelson, Matt Wilson, Marc Tanner, Rick Wilson

A smash in the same year that produced hits by Wilson Phillips, the scions of California legends Brian Wilson and John Phillips.

RICKY NELSON
1957

BE BOP BABY
Producers: Ricky Nelson, Jimmy Haskell, Ozzie Nelson
Album: Ricky
Record Label: Imperial
Songwriter: Pearl Lendhurst

Early example of the power of TV to move Rock and Roll product to the teens of America. Also, there was Barney Kessel's guitar.

IF YOU CAN'T ROCK ME
Producers: Ricky Nelson, Jimmy Haskell, Ozzie Nelson
Album: Ricky
Record Label: Imperial
Songwriter: Willie Jacobs

One of his best non-hits, released in '63 by Imperial long after Rick had left for Decca. It died after a week on the charts as the B-side of the bomb "Old Enough to Love."

STOOD UP

Producers: Ricky Nelson, Jimmy Haskell, Ozzie Nelson
Album: Ricky
Record Label: Imperial
Songwriters: Dub Dickerson, Erma Herrold

Aided no doubt by his cleancut TV persona, Nelson emulated his idol Elvis's cross-cultural clout by going Top-10 R&R/R&B/C&W with this ditty.

TEENAGER'S ROMANCE

Producers: Ricky Nelson, Jimmy Haskell
Album: Teen Time
Record Label: Verve
Songwriter: Dave Gillam

B-side of his first single, which actually did better than the A-side, "I'm Walking," a cover of the Fats Domino tune.

WAITIN' IN SCHOOL

Producers: Ricky Nelson, Jimmy Haskell, Ozzie Nelson
Album: Ricky
Record Label: Imperial
Songwriters: Johnny Burnette, Dorsey Burnette

B-side of "Stood Up," written by two-thirds of the Rockabilly Trio, Elvis's friends, the Burnette brothers.

1958

BELIEVE WHAT YOU SAY

Producers: Ricky Nelson, Jimmy Haskel, Ozzie Nelson
Album: Ricky Sings Again
Record Label: Imperial
Songwriters: Johnny Burnette, Dorsey Burnette

Rockabilly-esque.

I GOT A FEELING

Producers: Ricky Nelson, Jimmy Haskell, Ozzie Nelson
Album: Ricky Sings Again
Record Label: Imperial
Songwriter: Baker Knight

Clean-cut rocker, B-side of "Lonesome Town." Suggested seque: "Dirty Dirty Feeling" by Elvis Presley.

LONESOME TOWN

Producers: Ricky Nelson, Jimmy Haskell, Ozzie Nelson
Album: Ricky Sings Again
Record Label: Imperial

Songwriter: Baker Knight
Covered by the Cramps (IRS, '79).

POOR LITTLE FOOL

Producer: Ricky Nelson
Album: Ricky Nelson
Record Label: Imperial
Songwriter: Sharon Sheeley

His biggest hit of the '50s, also his biggest C&W/ R&B hit, written by Eddie Cochran's star-crossed girlfriend.

RESTLESS KID

Producers: Ricky Nelson, Jimmy Haskell, Ozzie Nelson
Album: Ricky Sings Again
Record Label: Imperial
Songwriter: Johnny Cash

Title song for the John Wayne movie in which Ricky had his film debut. But he was no Elvis.

1959

IT'S LATE

Producers: Ricky Nelson, Jimmy Haskell, Ozzie Nelson
Album: Ricky Sings Again
Record Label: Imperial
Songwriter: Dorsey Burnette

B-side of "Never Be Anyone Else But You." Ricky's response to "Wake up Little Susie."

JUST A LITTLE TOO MUCH

Producers: Ricky Nelson, Jimmy Haskell, Ozzie Nelson
Album: Songs by Ricky
Record Label: Imperial
Songwriter: Johnny Burnette

B-side of "Sweeter Than You."

NEVER BE ANYONE ELSE BUT YOU

Producers: Ricky Nelson, Jimmy Haskell, Ozzie Nelson
Album: Ricky Sings Again
Record Label: Imperial
Songwriter: Baker Knight

Pleasant ballad.

SWEETER THAN YOU

Producers: Ricky Nelson, Jimmy Haskell, Ozzie Nelson
Album: Songs by Ricky
Record Label: Imperial
Songwriter: Baker Knight

B-side of "Just a Little Too Much" (the first double-B-sided Top-10 single in history).

1961

HELLO MARY LOU

Producer: Rick Nelson
Album: Rick Is 21
Record Label: Imperial
Songwriter: Gene Pitney

After taking a year off to turn 21 and record such stiffs as "I'm Not Afraid," "Yes Sir, That's My Baby," and "Right By My Side," Ricky emerges as Rick, with two of his best sides ever. The A-side was "Travelin' Man."

TRAVELIN' MAN

Producer: Rick Nelson
Album: Rick Is 21
Record Label: Imperial
Songwriter: Jerry Fuller

The fulfillment of his signature Country-Pop-Rock was his biggest all-time hit. Suggested segue: "The Wanderer" by Dion.

1962

IT'S UP TO YOU

Album: It's up to You
Record Label: Imperial
Songwriter: Jerry Fuller

Jerry would move on to Gary Puckett & the Union Gap.

TEENAGE IDOL

Album: It's up to You
Record Label: Imperial
Songwriter: Jack Lewis

Written for a Bobby Vee movie. Suggested segue: "Jukebox Hero" by Foreigner.

YOUNG WORLD

Album: Rick Is 21
Record Label: Imperial
Songwriter: Jerry Fuller

His second biggest hit of the '60s.

1964

FOR YOU

Album: Rick Nelson Sings "For You."
Record Label: Decca
Songwriters: Al Dubin, Joe Burke

1930 hit for Glen Gray.

1972

GARDEN PARTY

Producer: Rick Nelson
Album: Garden Party
Record Label: Decca
Songwriter: Rick Nelson

Snubbing the oldies revival in favor of Country Rock with the Stone Canyon Band.

SANDY NELSON
1959

TEEN BEAT
   Record Label: Original Sound
   Songwriters: Sandy Nelson, Arthur Egnoian
Drum solo.

LET THERE BE DRUMS
   Album: Let There Be Drums
   Record Label: Imperial
   Songwriters: Sandy Nelson, Richard Podolor
Drum solo redux.

TRACY NELSON
1971

SEVEN BRIDGES ROAD
   Album: Bring Me Home
   Record Label: Reprise
   Songwriter: Steve Young
Rock's forgotten diva unearths a Country Rock classic. Covered by Steve Young (Blues Classics, '75) and the Eagles (Asylum, '80).

WILLIE NELSON
1980

ON THE ROAD AGAIN
   Album: *Honeysuckle Rose* Soundtrack
   Record Label: Columbia
   Songwriter: Willie Nelson
The mainstreaming of Outlaw Country; a #1 C&W/Top-20 R&R crossover.

1983

NENA
1984

99 LUFTBALONS (99 RED BALLOONS)
   Album: 99 Luftbalons
   Record Label: Epic
   Songwriters: Joem Fahrenkrog-Petersen, Karlo Karges, Kevin McAlea
The German version was the U.S. hit. Suggested segue: "Shock Den Affen" by Peter Gabriel.

THE NERVES
1976

HANGING ON THE TELEPHONE
   Record Label: Nerves
   Songwriter: Jack Lee
Covered by Blondie (Chrysalis, '79) for their third U.K. hit, which stiffed in the U.S.

NERVOUS NORVUS
1956

TRANSFUSION
   Record Label: Dot
   Songwriter: Jimmy Drake (Nervous Norvus)
Rockabilly novelty, introducing to the teen market the plentious wreck on the highway (or on the railroad tracks) sub-genre.

MICHAEL NESMITH
1970

JOANNE
   Producer: Felton Jarvis
   Album: Magnetic South
   Record Label: RCA
   Songwriter: Michael Nesmith
Returning to his pre-Monkees Folk Rock independence.

ROBBIE NEVIL
1987

C'EST LA VIE
   Album: Robbie Nevil
   Record Label: Manhattan
   Songwriter: Robbie Nevil
In the Richard Marx groove.

WOT'S IT TO YA
   Album: Robbie Nevil
   Record Label: Manhattan
   Songwriters: Robbie Nevil, Brock Walsh

AARON NEVILLE
1966

TELL IT LIKE IT IS
   Producer: George David
   Album: Tell It Like It Is
   Record Label: Par Lo
   Songwriters: Lee Diamond, George Davis
Essential #1 R&B/Top-10 R&R soul crossover for the New Orleans Soul man, Neville.

NEW EDITION
1983

CANDY GIRL
   Producers: Maurice Starr, Michael Jonzun
   Album: Candy Girl
   Record Label: Streetwise
   Songwriters: Larry Johnson (Maurice Starr), Michael Jonzun
#1 U.K./R&B debut for the Boston-based next "Next Jackson Five" wannabes, featuring Bobby Brown, Ralph Tresvant, Ricky Bell, Michael Bivins, and Ronald DeVoe, all future R&B/Hip-Hop legends, including Johnny Gill who replaced Brown in '86.

1984

COOL IT NOW
   Producers: Vincent Brantley, Rick Timas
   Album: New Edition
   Record Label: MCA
   Songwriters: Vincent Brantley, Rick Timas
Their biggest hit.

MR. TELEPHONE MAN
   Producers: Vincent Brantley, Rick Timas
   Album: New Edition
   Record Label: MCA
   Songwriters: Vincent Brantley, Rick Timas
A #1 R&B/Top-20 R&R crossover.

1986

A LITTLE BIT OF LOVE (IS ALL IT TAKES)
   Producer: R. Rudolph
   Album: All for Love
   Record Label: MCA
   Songwriters: Ric Wyatt Jr., Chris Perren
#1 R&B/Top-40 R&R crossover.

1988

BOYS TO MEN
   Producers: Jimmy Jam, Terry Lewis
   Album: Heart Break
   Record Label: MCA
   Songwriters: James Harris III, Terry Lewis
Somewhere in Philly, a neo-Doo-Wop harmony group would be forming around this title. They would have bigger hits than New Edition, but not a bigger influence.

CAN YOU STAND THE RAIN

Producers: Jimmy Jam, Terry Lewis
Album: Heart Break
Record Label: MCA
Songwriters: James Harris III, Terry Lewis

Their collaboration with the hot Minneapolis producers earns them a #1 R&B/Top-50 R&R crossover.

IF IT ISN'T LOVE

Producers: Jimmy Jam, Terry Lewis
Album: Heart Break
Record Label: MCA
Songwriters: James Harris III, Terry Lewis

Back in the R&R Top-10 for the first time since puberty, Johnny Gill standing in for Bobby Brown.

NEW KIDS ON THE BLOCK
1988

COVER GIRL

Producer: Maurice Starr
Album: Hangin' Tough
Record Label: Columbia
Songwriter: Larry Johnson (Maurice Starr)

Cover guys.

HANGIN' TOUGH

Producer: Maurice Starr
Album: Hangin' Tough
Record Label: Columbia
Songwriter: Larry Johnson (Maurice Starr)

Another #1. The B-side was a cover of the Delfonics's "Didn't I Blow Your Mind This Time."

I'LL BE LOVING YOU (FOREVER)

Producers: Maurice Starr, Michael Jonzun
Album: Hangin' Tough
Record Label: Columbia
Songwriter: Larry Johnson (Maurice Starr)

First #1 for the Boston-based "White Jackson Five" created by New Edition Svengali Starr.

PLEASE DON'T GO GIRL

Producer: Maurice Starr
Album: Hangin' Tough
Record Label: Columbia
Songwriter: Larry Johnson (Maurice Starr)

Manufactured white teen idols have their first hit. Kidsmania follows.

YOU GOT IT (THE RIGHT STUFF)

Producers: Maurice Starr, Michael Jonzun
Album: Hangin' Tough
Record Label: Columbia
Songwriter: Larry Johnson (Maurice Starr)

1989

STEP BY STEP

Producer: Maurice Starr
Album: Step by Step
Record Label: Columbia
Songwriter: Larry Johnson (Maurice Starr)

#1 in an era when Tiffany and Debbie Gibson also ruled the charts.

TONIGHT

Producer: Maurice Starr
Album: Step by Step
Record Label: Columbia
Songwriters: Larry Johnson (Maurice Starr), Lancelotti

Last big hit. They would return as NKOTB but, thankfully, to no avail.

NEW ORDER
1982

TEMPTATION

Producer: New Order
Album: 1981–1982
Record Label: Factory
Songwriter: New Order

Out of the ashes of Joy Division, a new British Techno-dance combo emerges.

1983

BLUE MONDAY

Producer: New Order
Album: Power, Corruption and Lies
Record Label: Factory
Songwriter: New Order

This monster 12" topped the U.K. charts. Re-recorded (Qwest, '88).

1985

AGE OF CONSENT

Producer: New Order
Album: Low Life
Record Label: Qwest
Songwriter: New Order

The Bronski Beat named their first album after this.

PERFECT KISS

Producer: New Order
Album: Low Life
Record Label: Qwest
Songwriter: New Order

1986

BIZARRE LOVE TRIANGLE

Producer: New Order
Album: Brotherhood
Record Label: Qwest
Songwriters: Bernard Sumner, Stephen Morris, Peter Hook, Gillian Gilbert

Best of the LP. Covered by Frente (Mammoth, '94).

1993

REGRET

Producer: Stephen Hague
Album: Republic
Record Label: Qwest
Songwriters: Bernard Sumner, Stephen Morris, Peter Hook, Gillian Gilbert, Stephen Hague

NEW RIDERS OF THE PURPLE SAGE
1973

PANAMA RED

Producer: Norbert Putnam
Album: The Adventures of Panama Red
Record Label: Columbia
Songwriter: Peter Rowan

The stuff of Country Folk Rock legend.

THE NEW VAUDEVILLE BAND
1966

WINCHESTER CATHEDRAL

Producer: Geoff Stephens
Album: Winchester Cathedral
Record Label: Fontana
Songwriter: Geoff Stephens

High-camp one-shot.

NEW YORK CITY
1973

I'M DOIN' FINE NOW

Producer: Thom Bell
Album: I'm Doin' Fine Now
Record Label: Chelsea
Songwriters: Thom Bell, Marshall Sherman

Philly Soul East.

NEW YORK DOLLS
1973

LOOKING FOR A KISS
Producer: Todd Rundgren
Album: New York Dolls
Record Label: Mercury
Songwriters: David Johansen, Johnny Thunders

Signature opus of the ultimate critic's Lipstick band. Covered by Jayne County (ESP, '93).

PERSONALITY CRISIS
Producer: Todd Rundgren
Album: New York Dolls
Record Label: Mercury
Songwriters: David Johansen, Johnny Thunders

Their personality crisis: did they want to be Art Rock or Hard Rock; the Velvet Underground or Kiss?

TRASH
Producer: Todd Rundgren
Album: New York Dolls
Record Label: Mercury
Songwriters: David Johansen, Syl Sylvain

Operating out of Andy Warhol's Max's Kansas City, they come up with their defining metaphor.

1974

HUMAN BEING
Producer: Shadow Morton
Album: In Too Much Too Soon
Record Label: Mercury
Songwriters: David Johansen, Johnny Thunders

Johansen would go on to a mainstream career as a cult favorite under the nom de plume Buster Poindexter; Thunders would go on to a legendary cult finale by drinking and drugging himself to an early death, after a number of unsuccessful but legendary solo albums.

THE NEWBEATS
1964

BREAD AND BUTTER
Album: Bread and Butter
Record Label: Hickory
Songwriters: Larry Parks, Jay Turnbow

An awesome falsetto. Suggested segue: "Peanut Butter" by the Marathons.

NEWCLEUS
1984

JAM ON IT
Producers: Joe Webb, Frank Fair
Album: Jam on Revenge
Record Label: Sunnyview
Songwriter: Maurice Cenac

Rap novelty: the black Chipmunks with a beat.

RANDY NEWMAN
1968

COWBOY
Producers: Van Dyke Parks, Russ Titelman, Lenny Waronker
Album: Randy Newman Creates Something New under the Sun
Record Label: Reprise
Songwriter: Randy Newman

Newman exhibits his tender, sentimental side for the first time.

DAVY THE FAT BOY
Producers: Van Dyke Parks, Lenny Waronker
Album: Randy Newman Creates Something New under the Sun
Record Label: Reprise
Songwriter: Randy Newman

After years as a staff songwriter ("Mama Told Me Not to Come") Newman's incomparable twisted signature finally appears on this archetypal character portrait.

LIVING WITHOUT YOU
Producers: Van Dyke Parks, Lenny Waronker
Album: Randy Newman Creates Something New under the Sun
Record Label: Reprise
Songwriter: Randy Newman

Anticipating and lapping the coming singer/songwriter brat pack. Covered by the Nitty Gritty Dirt Band (Liberty, '70), Manfred Mann (Polydor, '72).

SO LONG DAD
Producers: Van Dyke Parks, Lenny Waronker
Album: Randy Newman Creates Something New under the Sun
Record Label: Reprise
Songwriter: Randy Newman

Brief, pointed, droll, and unforgettable reaction to the prolix effusions of the '60s.

1970

GONE DEAD TRAIN
Producer: Jack Nitzsche
Album: Performance Soundtrack
Record Label: Warner Brothers

Searing L.A. Blues by a former Phil Spector studio hand, sung in the movie by Newman. Covered by Crazy Horse (Reprise, '71).

1971

IT'S LONELY AT THE TOP
Producers: Russ Titelman, Lenny Waronker
Album: Randy Newman Live
Record Label: Reprise
Songwriter: Randy Newman

Written for Frank Sinatra. Or was it Tom Jones?

MAYBE I'M DOING IT WRONG
Producers: Russ Titelman, Lenny Waronker
Album: Randy Newman Live
Record Label: Reprise
Songwriter: Randy Newman

A Mose Allison/David Frischberg take on the failure of the sexual revolution.

1972

BURN ON, BIG RIVER
Producers: Russ Titelman, Lenny Waronker
Album: Sail Away
Record Label: Reprise
Songwriter: Randy Newman

Newman on ecology, celebrating Cleveland's polluted Cuyahoga River. Suggested segue: "Cuyahoga" by R.E.M.

GOD'S SONG (THAT'S WHY I LOVE MANKIND)
Producers: Russ Titelman, Lenny Waronker
Album: Sail Away
Record Label: Warner Brothers
Songwriter: Randy Newman

Answering Jesus Christ Superstar. Covered by Etta James (Chess, '72).

HE GIVES US ALL HIS LOVE
Producers: Russ Titelman, Lenny Waronker
Album: Sail Away
Record Label: Reprise
Songwriter: Randy Newman

Became the theme for the movie The Great American Smokeout.

POLITICAL SCIENCE

Producers: Russ Titelman, Lenny Waronker
Album: Sail Away
Record Label: Warner Brothers
Songwriter: Randy Newman

Newman's take on Dr. Strangelove: "Let's drop the big one and see what happens."

SAIL AWAY

Producers: Russ Titelman, Lenny Waronker
Album: Sail Away
Record Label: Warner Brothers
Songwriter: Randy Newman

Newman's own favorite, a treatise on racism.

YOU CAN LEAVE YOUR HAT ON

Producers: Russ Titelman, Lenny Waronker
Album: Sail Away
Record Label: Warner Brothers
Songwriter: Randy Newman

Newman as Woody Allen. Covered by Three Dog Night (ABC, '75). Also covered in its entirety by Joe Cocker during the steamiest moments of the '86 Kim Bassinger/Mickey Rourke steambath, 9 1/2 Weeks, one of the most sardonic moments in the history of Rock in cinema.

1974

LOUISIANA, 1927

Producers: Russ Titelman, Lenny Waronker
Album: Good Old Boys
Record Label: Warner Brothers
Songwriter: Randy Newman

Atmospheric tune from his concept about the Kingfish, Huey Long. Covered by the Neville Brothers (A&M, '91). Used in the film Blaze.

1977

SHORT PEOPLE

Producers: Russ Titelman, Lenny Waronker
Album: Little Criminals
Record Label: Warner Brothers
Songwriter: Randy Newman

Is to Newman's oeuvre what "Dead Skunk" is to Loudon Wainwright's; a hit single that defines him to the masses while not only failing to illuminate the dimension of the artist's on-going talent but obliterating it in a hail of misguided criticism.

1983

I LOVE L.A.

Producers: Russ Titelman, Lenny Waronker
Album: Trouble in Paradise
Record Label: Warner Brothers
Songwriter: Randy Newman

An incipient anthem from the movie Down and Out in Beverly Hills.

MY LIFE IS GOOD

Producers: Russ Titelman, Lenny Waronker
Album: Trouble in Paradise
Record Label: Warner Brothers
Songwriter: Randy Newman

His shining moment of unabashed cynicism.

1988

I WANT YOU TO HURT LIKE I DO

Producers: James Newton Howard, Tommy Lipuma
Album: Land of Dreams
Record Label: Reprise
Songwriter: Randy Newman

Typical of his latter day fall into abject bitterness.

IT'S MONEY THAT MATTERS

Producer: Randy Newman
Album: Land of Dreams
Record Label: Reprise
Songwriter: Randy Newman

From here he would fall into a Rock concept deal with the Devil himself in Randy Newman's Faust (Reprise, '95).

JUICE NEWTON

1975

THE SWEETEST THING I'VE EVER KNOWN

Record Label: RCA
Songwriter: Otha Young

Country Rock ballad. Re-release (Capitol, '81) hit #1 C&W/Top-10 R&R.

OLIVIA NEWTON-JOHN

1973

LET ME BE THERE

Producer: John Farrar
Album: Let Me Be There
Record Label: Mercury
Songwriter: John Rostill

Coy Country Folk Pop from Australia introduces a Debbie Reynolds for a new generation. Written by the former Shadows bass player.

1974

I HONESTLY LOVE YOU

Producer: John Farrar
Album: If You Love Me (Let Me Know)
Record Label: MCA
Songwriters: Jeff Barry, Peter Allen

#1 Grammy winner for Liza Minnelli's ex-husband Peter Allen, who wrote "Quiet Please, There's a Lady on Stage" for his mother-in-law, Judy Garland, and "Tenterfield Saddler" about his grandfather in Australia.

IF YOU LOVE ME (LET ME KNOW)

Producer: John Farrar
Album: If You Love Me Let Me Know
Record Label: MCA
Songwriter: John Rostill

Top-10 C&W/R&R crossover.

1975

HAVE YOU NEVER BEEN MELLOW

Producer: John Farrar
Album: Have You Never Been Mellow
Record Label: MCA
Songwriter: John Farrar

Top-10 C&W/#1 R&R crossover ballad.

PLEASE MR. PLEASE

Producer: John Farrar
Album: Have You Never Been Mellow?
Record Label: MCA
Songwriters: John Rostill, Bruce Welch

Suggested segue: "Don't Play That Song" by Aretha Franklin.

1978

HOPELESSLY DEVOTED TO YOU

Producer: John Farrar
Album: *Grease* (Soundtrack)
Record Label: RSO
Songwriter: John Farrar

From her miscast epic Grease, in which she trades Debbie Reynolds in for Sandra Dee. She wasn't even Doris Day.

YOU'RE THE ONE THAT I WANT

Producer: John Farrar
Album: *Grease* (Soundtrack)
Record Label: RSO
Songwriter: John Farrar

Winsome duet with John Travolta was one of her biggest all-time hits.

A LITTLE MORE LOVE

Producer: John Farrar
Album: Totally Hot
Record Label: MCA
Songwriter: John Farrar

1980

MAGIC

Producer: John Farrar
Album: *Xanadu* Soundtrack
Record Label: MCA
Songwriter: John Farrar

From the film where she conclusively proved that as an actress she was no Debbie Harry. Song went to #1.

XANADU

Producer: Jeff Lynne
Album: *Xanadu* Soundtrack
Record Label: MCA
Songwriter: Jeff Lynne

Her third #1 U.K., courtesy of Xanadu and ELO.

1981

HEART ATTACK

Producer: John Farrar
Album: Physical
Record Label: MCA
Songwriters: Steven Kipner, Paul Bliss

Olivia's new concept: sex kitten.

MAKE A MOVE ON ME

Producer: John Farrar
Album: Physical
Record Label: MCA
Songwriters: John Farrar, Tom Snow

PHYSICAL

Producer: John Farrar
Album: Physical
Record Label: MCA
Songwriters: Stephen Kipner, Terry Shaddick

Olivia in her new workout video: one of the top singles of all-time. Jane Fonda briefly considered a Rock album.

1983

TWIST OF FATE

Producer: John Parrar
Album: *Two of a Kind* Soundtrack
Record Label: MCA
Songwriters: Stephen Kipner, Peter Beckett

Establishing a legacy as the anti-Madonna of the post-sexual revolution.

PAUL NICHOLAS

1977

HEAVEN ON THE SEVENTH FLOOR

Record Label: RSO
Songwriters: Dominic Bugatti, Frank Musker

About what you would expect from a singer who'd appeared in Hair, Grease, Jesus Christ Superstar, and Tommy. Suggested segues: "Knock Three Times" by Dawn, "One Man's Ceiling Is Another Man's Floor" by Paul Simon.

STEVIE NICKS

1981

LEATHER AND LACE

Producer: Jimmy Iovine
Album: Bella Donna
Record Label: Modern
Songwriter: Stephanie Nicks

A Fleetwood Mac member's defining side-venture with Don Henley.

STOP DRAGGIN' MY HEART AROUND

Producers: Jimmy Iovine, Tom Petty
Album: Bella Donna
Record Label: Modern
Songwriters: Tom Petty, Mike Campbell

Dylan-esque rocker with Petty.

EDGE OF SEVENTEEN (JUST LIKE THE WHITE WINGED DOVE)

Producer: Jimmy Iovine
Album: Bella Donna
Record Label: Modern
Songwriter: Stephanie Nicks

Signature FM anthem for Folk Rock's whirling diva. Natalie Merchant was watching her moves.

1983

STAND BACK

Producer: Jimmy Iovine
Album: The Wild Heart
Record Label: Modern
Songwriters: Stephanie Nicks, Rogers Nelson (Prince)

Her best rocker.

TALK TO ME

Producers: Jimmy Iovine, Rick Nowels
Album: Rock a Little
Record Label: Modern
Songwriter: Chas Sandford

Stevie's biggest solo hit. Nowels would move on to ex-Go Go Belinda Carlisle.

NICO

1965

THE LAST MILE

Producer: Jimmy Page
Record Label: Immediate
Songwriters: Jimmy Page, Andrew Loog Oldham

Before Nico fronted the legendary Velvet Underground, before Page invented the legendary Led Zeppelin. 28.5% of Classic Rock on one record.

1967

CHELSEA GIRL

Producer: Tom Wilson
Album: Chelsea Girl
Record Label: Verve
Songwriters: Lou Reed, Sterling Morrison

Title song from the Andy Warhol cult classic film, from which Lou Reed derived a lifetime of material.

EULOGY TO LENNY BRUCE

Producer: Tom Wilson
Album: Chelsea Girl
Record Label: Verve
Songwriter: Tim Hardin

Saying goodbye to a soulmate, the satirist Lenny Bruce. Covered by Tim Hardin (Verve Forcast, '69). Suggested segue: "Lenny Bruce" by Bob Dylan.

I'LL KEEP IT WITH MINE

Producer: Tom Wilson
Album: Chelsea Girl
Record Label: Verve
Songwriter: Bob Dylan

Early Dylan underground gem that Wilson, as Dylan's producer, enticed Nico into interpreting.

LITTLE SISTER

Producer: Tom Wilson
Album: Chelsea Girl
Record Label: Verve
Songwriters: Lou Reed, John Cale

Previewing the Velvet Underground oeuvre.

SOMEWHERE THERE'S A FEATHER
Producer: Tom Wilson
Album: Chelsea Girl
Record Label: Verve
Songwriter: Jackson Browne

Classic from Jackson Browne's Greenwich Village period, which roughly coincided with Joni Mitchell's Greenwich Village period; then they both moved out West to start the laid-back/mellow/L.A./singer-songwriter period that would define the '70s.

THESE DAYS
Producer: Tom Wilson
Album: Chelsea Girl
Record Label: Verve
Songwriter: Jackson Browne

A standard of the Greenwich Village repertoire. Covered by Tom Rush (Elektra, '68), Jackson Browne (Asylum, '72), Gregg Allman (Capricorn, '73), and 10,000 Maniacs (Elektra, '88).

WRAP YOUR TROUBLES IN DREAMS
Producer: Tom Wilson
Album: Chelsea Girl
Record Label: Verve
Songwriter: Lou Reed

Classic pre-Velvet high-fashion emoting.

NIGHT RANGER
1984

SISTER CHRISTIAN
Album: Midnight Madness
Record Label: Camel/MCA
Songwriter: Kelly Keagy

Bread-like Rock ballad hit sank them as an authentic Arena Rock band, after their earlier "(You Can Still) Rock in America" stiffed.

1985

SENTIMENTAL STREET
Album: Seven Wishes
Record Label: MCA
Songwriters: Jack Blades, Frances Fitzgerald

Falling back on the safety of the Arena ballad move. Blades would move on to Damn Yankees, further refining his AOR mastery.

MAXINE NIGHTINGALE
1976

RIGHT BACK WHERE WE STARTED FROM
Producer: Pierre Tubbs
Album: Right Back Where We Started From

Record Label: United Artists
Songwriters: Pierre Tubbs, Vincent Edwards

U.K. Disco Top-10 crossover.

1979

LEAD ME ON
Producer: Denny Diante
Album: Lead Me On
Record Label: Windsong
Songwriters: Allee Willis, David Lasley

Her last dance.

NILSSON
1967

WITHOUT HER
Producer: Rick Jarrard
Album: Pandemonium Shadow Show
Record Label: RCA
Songwriter: Harry Nilsson

Covered by Blood, Sweat and Tears (Columbia, '68).

1968

ONE
Producer: Rick Jarrard
Album: Aeriel Ballet
Record Label: RCA
Songwriter: Harry Nilsson

Living in a parallel universe to Randy Newman on the West coast, Harry Nilsson started off as an East-coast songwriting wunderkind with tunes like this. Covered by Three Dog Night (Dunhill, '69), who took it to the Top-10. A year later they'd bring a Randy Newman cover to #1. Covered by Al Kooper (Columbia, '69).

1969

(I GUESS) THE LORD MUST BE IN NEW YORK CITY
Producer: Nilsson House Productions
Album: Harry
Record Label: RCA
Songwriter: Harry Nilsson

Nilsson starts letting the quirks out.

1970

DAYTON, OHIO 1903
Producer: Nilsson House Productions
Album: Nilsson Sings Newman

Record Label: RCA
Songwriter: Randy Newman

The universes meet.

1971

COCONUT
Producer: Richard Perry
Album: Nilsson Schmilsson
Record Label: RCA
Songwriter: Harry Nilsson

A Reggae-inflected romp.

ME AND MY ARROW
Producer: Harry Nilsson
Album: The Point
Record Label: RCA
Songwriter: Harry Nilsson

From the TV show "The Point," later used as a TV commercial.

YOU'RE BREAKING MY HEART
Producer: Richard Perry
Album: Son of Schmilsson
Record Label: RCA
Songwriter: Harry Nilsson

Terse and hilariously to the point.

1974

REMEMBER (CHRISTMAS)
Producer: Richard Perry
Album: *Son of Dracula* Soundtrack
Record Label: RCA
Songwriter: Harry Nilsson

From the horror movie spoof.

NINE INCH NAILS
1990

HEAD LIKE A HOLE
Producer: Trent Reznor
Album: Pretty Hate Machine
Record Label: TVT
Songwriter: Trent Reznor

Early classic from one of the trailblazing mad scientists of '90s Techno Alternative Rage Rock.

1994

CLOSER
Producers: Trent Reznor, Flood
Album: The Downward Spiral
Record Label: TVT
Songwriter: Trent Reznor

The classic sacred and profane Rock and Roll yin and yang strikes again, in a profoundly disturbing modern setting.

THE 1910 FRUITGUM COMPANY
1968

1, 2, 3, RED LIGHT
Producers: Jerry Kazenetz, Jeff Katz
Album: 1, 2, 3 Red Light
Record Label: Buddah
Songwriters: Sal Trimachi, Bobbi Trimachi

Double Bubble followup to "Simon Says."

SIMON SAYS
Producers: Jerry Kazenetz, Jeff Katz
Album: Simon Says
Record Label: Buddah
Songwriter: Elliot Chiprut

Kazenetz and Katz invent the bubble formula, one part Mother Goose, three parts Joey Levine.

1969

INDIAN GIVER
Producers: Jerry Kazenetz, Jeff Katz
Album: Indian Giver
Record Label: Buddah
Songwriters: Bobby Bloom, Bo Gentry

Bloom would shine on "Montego Bay."

NIRVANA
1988

PAY TO PLAY
Producer: Butch Vig
Album: Nevermind
Record Label: DGC
Songwriter: Kurt Cobain

Demo version of "Stay Away" celebrates their early obscurity in pre-scene Seattle.

1991

ABOUT A GIRL
Producer: Butch Vig
Album: Bleach
Record Label: Sub Pop
Songwriter: Nirvana

Vig at the controls had done wonders with Firetown.

COME AS YOU ARE
Producer: Butch Vig
Album: Nevermind
Record Label: DGC
Songwriters: Kurt Cobain, Krist Novaselic, Dave Grohl

Establishing their punk-with-soul persona.

DRAIN YOU
Producer: Butch Vig
Album: Nevermind
Record Label: DGC
Songwriter: Nirvana

LITHIUM
Producer: Butch Vig
Album: Nevermind
Record Label: DGC
Songwriter: Nirvana

SMELLS LIKE TEEN SPIRIT
Producer: Butch Vig
Album: Nevermind
Record Label: DGC
Songwriters: Kurt Cobain, Krist Novaselic, Dave Grohl

The "Like a Rolling Stone" of its era, a curious little buzzsaw track as unassuming as Dylan's was grandiose, that launched a thousand alternative bands, most of them from or en route to Seattle, along with half the record business of the '90s. Opened the door for guitar bands again, lyrics that cut cryptically to the nub, lead singers who wore flannel instead of spandex and flailed around the stage looking for a place to hide or throw up or both. The Replacements had a replacement at last.

1993

ALL APOLOGIES
Producer: Steve Albini
Album: In Utero
Record Label: DGC
Songwriter: Kurt Cobain

Cobain's posthumous suicide note. As one DJ described it: "The great lie; he did have a gun."

HEART SHAPED BOX
Producer: Steve Albini
Album: In Utero
Record Label: DGC
Songwriter: Nirvana

PENNYROYAL TEA
Producer: Steve Albini
Album: In Utero
Record Label: DGC
Songwriter: Nirvana

RAPE ME
Producer: Nirvana
Album: In Utero
Record Label: DGC
Songwriter: Kurt Cobain

A plea to his devouring fans, unheeded.

NITTY GRITTY DIRT BAND
1970

HOUSE AT POOH CORNER
Producer: Bill McEwen
Album: Uncle Charlie and His Dog Teddy
Record Label: Liberty
Songwriter: Kenny Loggins

Establishing the underexplored Winnie-the-Pooh influence on Rock and Roll. Covered by Loggins and Messina (Columbia, '72).

JACK NITZSCHE
1963

THE LONELY SURFER
Producer: Jimmy Bowen
Record Label: Reprise
Songwriters: Jack Nitzsche, Marty Cooper

Existential surf music.

MOJO NIXON AND SKID ROPER
1987

ELVIS IS EVERYWHERE
Album: Bo-Day-Shus
Record Label: Enigma
Songwriter: Mojo Nixon

Preaching the gospel of Rock to the converted.

1989

DEBBIE GIBSON IS PREGNANT (WITH MY TWO-HEADED LOVE CHILD)
Album: Root Hog or Die
Record Label: Enigma
Songwriter: Mojo Nixon

Responding to the coming of the politically correct '90s.

CLIFF NOBLES & CO.
1968

THE HORSE
Producer: Jesse James
Album: The Horse
Record Label: Phil L.A. of Soul
Songwriter: Jesse James

Top-5 R&B/Top-5 R&R crossover.

KENNY NOLAN
1977

I LIKE DREAMING
Producers: Kenny Nolan, Charlie Callelo

Album: Kenny Nolan
Record Label: 20th Century
Songwriter: Kenny Nolan Helfman

Reward for having written "My Eyes Adored You" and "Lady Marmelade," which succeeded each other at #1, while his own record stalled at #3. A pretty good year, nonetheless.

THE NOTORIOUS B.I.G.
1994

JUICY
Producer: Sean Combs
Album: Ready to Die
Record Label: Bad Boy/Arista
Songwriters: The Notorious B.I.G., Aquil Davidson, Gene Griffin, Teddy Riley, Brandon Mitchell, James Mtume, Markell Riley

Current unsafe street beat. With "Unbelievable" on the B-side.

NRBQ
1974

GET THAT GASOLINE BLUES
Album: Workshop
Record Label: Kama Sutra
Songwriters: Terry Adams, Charlie Craig

Topical tune is the only chart hit for the world's best (or at least oldest) bar band.

NU SHOOZ
1986

I CAN'T WAIT
Producers: John Smith, R. Waritz
Album: Poolside
Record Label: Atlantic
Songwriter: John Smith

As anonymous as its songwriter/producer, John Smith.

TED NUGENT
1975

STRANGLEHOLD
Album: Ted Nugent
Record Label: Epic
Songwriter: Ted Nugent

Motor City guitar madman stalks the wild chord.

1977

CAT SCRATCH FEVER
Producers: Tom Werman, Lew Futterman, Cliff Davies
Album: Cat Scratch Fever

Record Label: Epic
Songwriter: Ted Nugent

Suggested segues: "Stray Cat Blues" by the Rolling Stones, "Hot Blooded" by Foreigner.

1978

YANK ME, CRANK ME
Producers: Tom Werman, Lew Futterman
Album: Double Live Gonzo
Record Label: Epic
Songwriter: Ted Nugent

Essential to the Arena oeuvre.

1980

WANGO TANGO
Producer: Cliff Davies
Album: Scream Dream
Record Label: Epic
Songwriter: Ted Nugent

His defining wang-bar moment. Later, he would cash in on the charts through Damn Yankees.

GARY NUMAN
1979

ARE FRIENDS ELECTRIC
Album: Replicas
Record Label: Atco
Songwriter: Gary Numan

Leading the British synth wave with his first #1 U.K. (with the Tubeway Army).

1980

CARS
Album: The Pleasure Principal
Record Label: Atco
Songwriter: Gary Numan

His lone American hit. The Pet Shop Boys would do it better.

THE NUTMEGS
1955

STORY UNTOLD
Producer: Al Silver
Record Label: Herald
Songwriters: Leroy Griffin, Marty Wilson

An essential Doo-Wop teen romance.

NWA
1988

F--- THA POLICE
Album: Straight Outta Compton
Record Label: Ruthless

Songwriters: M. C. Ren, Ice Cube

Chalk on the sidewalk.

LAURA NYRO
1967

AND WHEN I DIE
Producer: Milt Okun
Album: More Than a New Discovery
Record Label: Verve/Forecast
Songwriter: Laura Nyro

Prime exponent of Nyro's Broadway Soul with a Bronx cheer, covered by Okun's other proteges, Peter, Paul and Mary (Warner Brothers, '66), and turned into a hit by Blood, Sweat, and Tears (Columbia, '69).

STONEY END
Producer: Milt Okun
Album: More Than a New Discovery
Record Label: Verve/Forecast
Songwriter: Laura Nyro

Essential Folk Rock existentialism. Kate Bush and Tori Amos were taking notes. Covered by the Fifth Dimension (Bell, '71) and Barbra Streisand (Columbia, '71).

WEDDING BELL BLUES
Producer: Milt Okun
Album: More Than a New Discovery
Record Label: Verve/Forecast
Songwriter: Laura Nyro

Effusive echoes of subway girl-groups and unrequited high-school passions. Covered by the Fifth Dimension (Soul City, '69).

1968

THE CONFESSION
Producers: Laura Nyro, Charlie Calello
Album: Eli and the Thirteenth Confession
Record Label: Columbia
Songwriter: Laura Nyro

The advent of the confessional mode of Rock songwriting, which would come to fruition with Joni Mitchell, before being demolished by Madonna, only to be resurrected by Tori Amos.

ELI'S COMING
Producers: Laura Nyro, Charlie Calello
Album: Eli and the Thirteenth Confession
Record Label: Columbia
Songwriter: Laura Nyro

Carole King goes to Music and Art instead of 1650 Broadway. Covered by Three Dog Night (Dunhill, '69). Nyro's only appearance on the charts as a performer was with her Bottom-10 cover of Carole's "Up on the Roof" (Columbia, '70).

STONED SOUL PICNIC
Producers: Laura Nyro, Charlie Calello
Album: Eli and the Thirteenth Confession
Record Label: Columbia
Songwriter: Laura Nyro

Laura at Monterey the year before: critically stoned, no picnic. The Fifth Dimension's cover (Soul City, '68) went Top-10 R&B/R&R for a measure of retribution.

SWEET BLINDNESS
Producers: Laura Nyro, Charlie Calello
Album: Eli and the Thirteenth Confession
Record Label: Columbia
Songwriter: Laura Nyro

Celebrating the evil grape. Covered by her favorite clients, the Fifth Dimension (Soul City, '68).

1969

CAPTAIN FOR DARK MORNINGS
Producers: Roy Halee, Laura Nyro
Album: New York Tendaberry
Record Label: Columbia
Songwriter: Laura Nyro

Nyro at the extremes of her melodic, romantic, spaced-out urban Soul.

SAVE THE COUNTRY
Producers: Roy Halee, Laura Nyro
Album: New York Tendaberry
Record Label: Columbia
Songwriter: Laura Nyro

Having conquered the Top-40, Nyro turns to stoopside politics. Covered by the Fifth Dimension (Bell, '70) and Thelma Houston (Dunhill, '70).

TIME AND LOVE
Producers: Roy Halee, Laura Nyro
Album: New York Tendaberry
Record Label: Columbia
Songwriter: Laura Nyro

Covered by her Brooklyn reverse mirror image, Barbra Streisand (Columbia, '71).

1971

BEEN ON A TRAIN
Producers: Arif Mardin, Felix Cavaliere
Album: Christmas and the Beads of Sweat
Record Label: Columbia
Songwriter: Laura Nyro

Laura gets off the Top-40 train for a long and worried journey past confession into torment.

1976

STORMY LOVE
Producers: Laura Nyro, Charlie Calello
Album: Smile
Record Label: Columbia
Songwriter: Laura Nyro

Revealing the ghosts that haunted her five-year silence.

1978

AMERICAN DREAMER
Producers: Laura Nyro, Roscoe Harring
Album: Nested
Record Label: Columbia
Songwriter: Laura Nyro

Returning from the walking wounded of the '60s, Nyro reclaims a bit of her past penchant for unrepentant urban soul.

O

OASIS

1995

WONDERWALL
Producers: D. Morris, Noel Gallagher
Album: What's the Story, Morning Glory
Record Label: Epic
Songwriter: Noel Gallagher

Best of the new British invasion tracks: Waterloo sunset on Penny Lane.

SINEAD O'CONNOR

1988

TROY
Producers: Kevin Maloney, Sinead O'Connor
Album: The Lion and the Cobra
Record Label: Chrysalis

Songwriter: Sinead O'Connor

Joycean epic jump starts the controversial career of this strikingly Irish rebel girl.

1990

EMPEROR'S NEW CLOTHES
Producers: Nellee Hooper, Sinead O'Connor
Album: I Do Not Want What I Haven't Got
Record Label: Ensign/Chrysalis
Songwriter: Sinead O'Connor

After covering Prince's "Nothing Compares to U" as a torchy weeper, O'Connor torches the charts with a Pop rocker. A girl after Elvis Costello's heart, she would next move on to antagonizing the Pope, Frank Sinatra, the cast of "Saturday Night Live," Bob Dylan fans at Madison Square Garden, and the entire Country music audience. Madonna would be challenged to keep up.

ALAN O'DAY

1977

UNDERCOVER ANGEL
Producers: Steve Barri, Michael Omartian
Album: Appetizers
Record Label: Pacific
Songwriter: Alan O'Day

Innocuous chart-topper that further established '77 as the worst year for #1 singles.

THE O'JAYS

1972

BACK STABBERS
Producers: Kenny Gamble, Leon Huff
Album: Back Stabbers
Record Label: Philadelphia International
Songwriters: Kenny Gamble, Leon Huff, John Whitehead

After a variety of stiffs on Neptune, Bell, and Imperial, the O'Jays come home to a theme, a team, and a locale that suits them. The result is a #1 R&B/Top-10 R&R crossover. Featured in the '77 movie Looking for Mr. Goodbar.

LOVE TRAIN
Producers: Kenny Gamble, Leon Huff
Album: Back Stabbers
Record Label: Philadelphia International
Songwriters: Kenny Gamble, Leon Huff

Their biggest hit, a #1 R&B/R&R crossover. Suggested segues: "People Get Ready" by the Impressions, and "Peace Train" by Cat Stevens.

1973

FOR THE LOVE OF MONEY
Producers: Kenny Gamble, Leon Huff
Album: Ship Ahoy
Record Label: Philadelphia International
Songwriters: Kenny Gamble, Leon Huff, Anthony Jackson

More urban philosophizing. Suggested segues: "Money" by Barrett Strong, "It's Money That Matters" by Randy Newman, "Money Honey" by Clyde McPhatter, "Your Cash Ain't Nothin' But Trash" by the Clovers, "Money Changes Everything" by Cyndi Lauper.

NOW THAT WE FOUND LOVE
Producers: Kenny Gamble, Leon Huff
Album: Ship Ahoy
Record Label: Philadelphia International
Songwriters: Kenny Gamble, Leon Huff

Soul classic, covered by Third World (Island, '78) and Heavy D & the Boys (Uptown, '91).

PUT YOUR HANDS TOGETHER
Producers: Kenny Gamble, Leon Huff
Album: Ship Ahoy
Record Label: Philadelphia International
Songwriters: Kenny Gamble, Leon Huff

1975

GIVE THE PEOPLE WHAT THEY WANT
Producers: Kenny Gamble, Leon Huff
Album: Survival
Record Label: Philadelphia International
Songwriters: Kenny Gamble, Leon Huff

First of three #1 R&B hits of '75.

I LOVE MUSIC (PART I)
Producer: Kenny Gamble
Album: Family Reunion
Record Label: Philadelphia International

Songwriters: Kenny Gamble, Leon Huff

Biggest hit from the album; #1 R&B/Top-10 R&R crossover.

LIVING FOR THE WEEKEND
Producer: Kenny Gamble
Album: Family Reunion
Record Label: Philadelphia International
Songwriters: Kenny Gamble, Leon Huff

#1 R&B/Top-20 R&R crossover.

1976

DARLIN' DARLIN' BABY (SWEET TENDER LOVE)
Producers: Kenny Gamble, Leon Huff
Album: Message in Our Music
Record Label: Philadelphia International
Songwriters: Kenny Gamble, Leon Huff

#1 R&B/Bottom-30 R&R crossover.

MESSAGE IN OUR MUSIC
Producer: Kenny Gamble
Album: Message in Our Music
Record Label: Philadelphia International
Songwriters: Kenny Gamble, Leon Huff

#1 R&B/Top-40 R&R crossover.

1977

USE TA BE MY GIRL
Producers: Kenny Gamble, Leon Huff
Album: So Full of Love
Record Label: Philadelphia International
Songwriters: Kenny Gamble, Leon Huff

Top-10 R&R memories of Doo-Wop; their eighth #1 R&B crossover of the '70s.

THE O'KAYSIONS
1968

GIRL WATCHER
Album: Girl Watcher
Record Label: ABC
Songwriter: Ronald Killette (Buck Trail)

Top-10 R&R/R&B one-shot.

DANNY O'KEEFE
1972

GOOD TIME CHARLIE'S GOT THE BLUES
Producer: Arif Mardin
Album: O'Keefe
Record Label: Signpost
Songwriter: Danny O'Keefe

A poignant Country Folk Rock standard, originally recorded on Jerden in '67, and again on Atlantic in '70 (produced by Ahmet Ertegun). Covered by Elvis Presley (RCA, '74).

THE ROAD
Producer: Arif Mardin
Album: O'Keefe
Record Label: Signpost
Songwriter: Danny O'Keefe

Superb picture of Rock and Roll obscurity. Covered by Jackson Browne (Asylum, '78). Suggested segues: "Lodi" by Creedence Clearwater Revival, and "Rock and Roll (I Gave You the Best Years of My Life)" by Kevin Johnson.

ALEXANDER O'NEAL
1987

FAKE
Producers: Jimmy Jam, Terry Lewis
Album: Hearsay
Record Label: Tabu
Songwriters: James Harris III, Terry Lewis

Former Jam and Lewis Minneapolis band-mate in Flyte Tyme gets his biggest U.S. single, a #1 R&B/Top-25 R&R crossover, after four U.K. hits.

SHAQUILLE O'NEAL
1993

(I KNOW I GOT) SKILLZ
Album: Shaq Diesel
Record Label: Jive
Songwriters: Jeff Fortson, Shaquille O'Neal, Meech Wells

No slam dunk.

GILBERT O'SULLIVAN
1972

ALONE AGAIN (NATURALLY)
Producer: Gordon Mills
Album: Gilbert O'Sullivan Himself
Record Label: MAM
Songwriter: Raymond O'Sullivan

Convoluted, most certainly disturbed, seemingly autobiographical tale that invented Nerd Rock.

CLAIR
Producer: Gordon Mills
Album: Back to Front
Record Label: MAM
Songwriter: Raymond O'Sullivan
More from the Irish Jonathan Richman.

1973

GET DOWN
Producer: Gordon Mills
Album: I'm a Writer, Not a Fighter
Record Label: MAM
Songwriter: Raymond O'Sullivan

---

100 PROOF AGED IN SOUL
1970

SOMEBODY'S BEEN SLEEPING IN MY BED
Producer: Greg S. Perry
Album: Somebody's Been Sleeping in My Bed
Record Label: Buddah
Songwriters: Greg S. Perry, General Johnson, Angelo Bond
Processed Soul.

THE OAK RIDGE BOYS
1982

BOBBIE SUE
Album: Bobbie Sue
Record Label: MCA
Songwriters: Wood Newton, Daniel Tyler, Adele Tyler
#1 C&W/Top-20 R&R crossover cutie. But she was no "Elvira."

BILLY OCEAN
1984

CARIBBEAN QUEEN (NO MORE LOVE ON THE RUN)
Producer: Keith Diamond
Album: Suddenly
Record Label: Jive
Songwriters: Keith Diamond, Billy Ocean
From England by way of Trinidad, Ocean crosses several to relaunch his career with a #1 R&B/R&R crossover that was originally called "European Queen."

LOVERBOY
Producer: Keith Diamond
Album: Suddenly

Record Label: Jive
Songwriters: Keith Diamond, Billy Ocean, Robert John "Mutt" Lange, Billy Alessi, Bobby Alessi
Entering the new Jack derby.

SUDDENLY
Producer: Keith Diamond
Album: Suddenly
Record Label: Jive
Songwriters: Keith Diamond, Billy Ocean
Another hit from this year's "love man."

1986

LOVE ZONE
Producer: Mutt Lange
Album: Love Zone
Record Label: Jive
Songwriters: Barry Eastmond, Billy Ocean, Wayne Braithwaite
Third hit from the album; a #1 R&B/Top-10 R&R crossover.

THERE'LL BE SAD SONGS (TO MAKE YOU CRY)
Producer: Mutt Lange
Album: Love Zone
Record Label: Jive
Songwriters: Barry Eastmond, Billy Ocean, Wayne Braithwaite
Sultry ballad is his second #1 R&B/R&R crossover.

WHEN THE GOING GETS TOUGH THE TOUGH GET GOING
Producer: Mutt Lange
Album: Love Zone
Record Label: Jive
Songwriters: Barry Eastmond, Billy Ocean, Robert John "Mutt" Lange, Wayne Braithwaite
#1 R&B/Top-10 R&R crossover from the movie The Jewel of the Nile. Suggested segue: "Ballad of the Green Berets" by Sgt. Barry Sadler.

1988

GET OUTA MY DREAMS, GET INTO MY CAR
Producer: Mutt Lange
Album: Tear Down These Walls
Record Label: Jive
Songwriters: Robert John "Mutt" Lange, Billy Ocean
The title of his massive third #1 R&B/R&R crossover may have been based on a Ringo Starr ad-lib in the outro of his version of "You're Sixteen."

PHIL OCHS
1963

THE POWER AND THE GLORY
Producers: Paul Rothchild, Jac Holzman
Album: All the News That's Fit to Sing
Record Label: Elektra
Songwriter: Phil Ochs
Patriotic protest by the Ohio song journalist, covered in an irony Ochs himself was the first to appreciate, by his natural arch-rival, Anita Bryant (Columbia, '67).

1964

BOUND FOR GLORY
Producers: Paul Rothchild, Jac Holzman
Album: All the News That's Fit to Sing
Record Label: Elektra
Songwriter: Phil Ochs
A tribute to the Folk patron saint, Woody Guthrie, later the title of the Woody biopic.

HERE'S TO THE STATE OF MISSISSIPPI
Producer: Paul Rothchild
Album: I Ain't Marchin' Anymore
Record Label: Elektra
Songwriter: Phil Ochs
Stirring polemic that energized the Civil Rights movement.

I AIN'T MARCHIN' ANYMORE
Producer: Paul Rothchild
Album: I Ain't Marchin' Anymore
Record Label: Elektra
Songwriter: Phil Ochs
First anthem of the draft-dodging counter-culture of the '60s. To Mississippi and Alabama and Washington, DC they would march, but not to Vietnam.

THERE BUT FOR FORTUNE
Producer: Paul Rothchild
Album: I Ain't Marchin' Anymore
Record Label: Elektra
Songwriter: Phil Ochs
Covered by Joan Baez (Vanguard, '65) for her first Folk Rock hit.

1966

CHANGES
Producer: Paul Rothchild
Album: Phil Ochs in Concert
Record Label: Elektra
Songwriter: Phil Ochs

Nailing the generational malaise, and almost getting a hit single. Covered by Crispian St. Peters (Janus, '66) and Jim and Jean (Elektra, '66). Suggested segues: "Urge for Going" by Tom Rush and "Ch-changes" by David Bowie.

LOVE ME, I'M A LIBERAL

Producer: Paul Rothchild
Album: Phil Ochs in Concert
Record Label: Elektra
Songwriter: Phil Ochs

Biting satire of the hands that fed him, book-ending the scathing "Draft Dodger Rag."

1967

OUTSIDE OF A SMALL CIRCLE OF FRIENDS

Album: Pleasures of the Harbor
Record Label: A&M
Songwriter: Phil Ochs

Taking off from the Kitty Genovese killing on a New York street, while her neighbors watched, to make a larger point about the lack of personal involvement.

1968

WHEN IN ROME

Producer: Van Dyke Parks
Album: Tape from California
Record Label: A&M
Songwriter: Phil Ochs

Ochs in California: a small fish out of water, gasping for a final metaphor that wouldn't come.

OCTOBER PROJECT

1993

BURY MY LOVELY

Producer: Glen Rosenstein
Album: October Project
Record Label: Epic
Songwriters: Julie Flanders, Emil Adler

Ethereal Folk Rock, renaissance for the '90s.

OFFSPRING

1994

COME OUT AND PLAY

Producer: Thom Wilson
Album: Smash
Record Label: Epitaph
Songwriters: Dexter Holland, Greg K., Noodles, Ron Welty

Alternative rocker takes on racism and gang warfare.

SELF ESTEEM

Producer: Thom Wilson
Album: Smash
Record Label: Epitaph
Songwriters: Dexter Holland, Greg K., Noodles, Ron Welty

Next they deal with the perennial adolescent trauma of low self-esteem. Definitely a group influenced by everything from punk to Oprah.

OHIO EXPRESS

1968

YUMMY, YUMMY, YUMMY

Producers: Jerry Kazenetz, Jeff Katz
Album: Yummy, Yummy, Yummy
Record Label: Buddah
Songwriters: Artie Resnick, Joey Levine

Perfecting the low art of mass appeal. Joey Levine would be heard from again. And again.

OHIO PLAYERS

1973

FUNKY WORM

Producer: Ohio Players
Album: Pleasure
Record Label: Westbound
Songwriters: Leroy Bonner, Ralph Middlebrooks, Marshall Jones, Walter Morrison, Andrew Noland

First #1 R&B/Top-20 R&R crossover for the Dayton Funk and Roll outfit.

1974

FIRE

Producer: Ohio Players
Album: Fire
Record Label: Mercury
Songwriters: Leroy Bonner, Ralph Middlebrooks, Marshall Jones, William Beck, Marvin Pierce, Jim Williams, Clarence Satchell

Their first #1 R&B/R&R crossover.

1975

LOVE ROLLERCOASTER

Producer: Ohio Players
Album: Honey
Record Label: Mercury
Songwriters: Leroy Bonner, Ralph Middlebrooks, Marshall Jones, William Beck, Marvin Pierce, Jim Williams, Clarence Satchell

Disco classic; #1 R&B/R&R crossover.

SWEET STICKY THING

Producer: Ohio Players
Album: Honey
Record Label: Mercury
Songwriters: Leroy Bonner, Ralph Middlebrooks, Marshall Jones, William Beck, Marvin Pierce, Jim Williams, Clarence Satchell

#1 R&B/Top-40 R&R crossover.

1976

WHO'D SHE COO

Producer: Ohio Players
Album: Contradiction
Record Label: Mercury
Songwriters: Leroy Bonner, Ralph Middlebrooks, Marshall Jones, William Beck, Marvin Pierce, Jim Williams, Clarence Satchell

#1 R&B/Top-20 R&R crossover.

OINGO BOINGO

1985

WEIRD SCIENCE

Album: Dead Man's Party
Record Label: MCA
Songwriter: Danny Elfman

Elfman would move on to scoring pop cultural landmarks like the movie Batman Returns *and the TV series "The Simpsons."*

MIKE OLDFIELD

1974

TUBULAR BELLS

Producer: Mike Oldfield
Album: Tubular Bells
Record Label: Virgin
Songwriter: Mike Oldfield

Virgin Records is launched with the theme from the movie The Exorcist.

OLIVER

1967

GOOD MORNING STARSHINE

Producer: Bob Crewe
Album: Good Morning Starshine
Record Label: Jubilee
Songwriters: James Rado, Gerome Ragni, Galt MacDermot

Performed in the notorious Rock musical Hair! *and on the original cast album by Lynn Kellog, Melba Moore, James Rado, and Gerome Ragni (RCA, '70).*

JEAN

Producer: Bob Crewe
Album: Good Morning Starshine
Record Label: Crewe
Songwriter: Rod McKuen

Unstoppable ballad by the Pop poet, from the movie The Prime of Miss Jean Brodie.

OLLIE AND JERRY
1984

BREAKIN' . . . THERE'S NO STOPPING US

Producer: Ollie Brown
Album: Breakin'
Record Label: Polydor
Songwriters: Ollie E. Brown, Jerry Knight

From the breakdance exploitation film.

THE OLYMPICS
1958

WESTERN MOVIES

Producers: Fred Smith, Cliff Goldsmith
Album: Doin' the Hully Gully
Record Label: Demon
Songwriters: Fred Smith, Cliff Goldsmith

In the novelty mode of the Coasters.

1965

GOOD LOVIN'

Record Label: Loma
Songwriters: Artie Resnick, Rudy Clark

Covered by the Young Rascals (Atlantic, '66).

THE ONLY ONES
1979

ANOTHER GIRL, ANOTHER PLANET

Album: Special View
Record Label: Epic
Songwriter: Peter Perrett

Legendary deep cut, known only to other bands and critics.

YOKO ONO
1981

WALKING ON THIN ICE

Producers: John Lennon, Yoko Ono
Record Label: Geffen
Songwriter: Yoko Ono

Reportedly, Yoko and John were working on

this track the day he was shot. Later, its eerie and affecting video would earn Yoko more critical respect in Rock circles than she previously ever had.

ONYX
1993

SLAM

Album: Bacdafucup
Record Label: JMJ
Songwriters: Chylow Parker, Jason Mizell, T. Taylor, K. Jones, F. Scruggs

Public Enemy without the redeeming social significance.

ROY ORBISON
1956

OOBY DOOBY

Producer: Sam Phillips
Record Label: Sun
Songwriters: Wade Moore, Dick Penner

Coaxing the first few Rockabilly syllables out of the mouth of the reluctant crooner, Roy.

1958

CLAUDETTE

Producer: Sam Phillips
Record Label: Sun
Songwriter: Roy Orbison

Written about Orbison's then-wife, Claudette, who would soon be killed in a motorcycle accident. Covered by the Everly Brothers on the B-side of "All I Have to Do Is Dream" (Cadence, '58).

SWEET AND INNOCENT

Record Label: RCA
Songwriter: Joe South

Early Roy keeper, covered by the Osmonds (MGM, '71).

1960

BLUE ANGEL

Producer: Fred Foster
Album: Roy Orbison's Greatest Hits
Record Label: Monument
Songwriters: Roy Orbison, Joe Melson

ONLY THE LONELY (KNOW THE WAY I FEEL)

Producer: Fred Foster
Album: Roy Orbison's Greatest Hits
Record Label: Monument
Songwriters: Roy Orbison, Joe Melson

His first big hit, setting up a string of tragic pearls.

1961

CANDY MAN

Producer: Fred Foster
Album: Roy Orbison's Greatest Hits
Record Label: Monument
Songwriters: Fred Neil, Beverly Ross

The session guitarist Neil puts a down payment on a condo in Coconut Grove: Unless he sold the rights.

CRYING

Producer: Fred Foster
Album: Crying
Record Label: Monument
Songwriters: Roy Orbison, Joe Melson

An impossibly ecstatic series of closing crescendos define Roy Orbison as Rock's Pagliacci.

RUNNING SCARED

Producer: Fred Foster
Album: Crying
Record Label: Monument
Songwriters: Roy Orbison, Joe Melson

His first #1.

1962

DREAM BABY, HOW LONG MUST I DREAM

Producer: Fred Foster
Album: Roy Orbison's Greatest Hits
Record Label: Monument
Songwriter: Cindy Walker

By the author of "You Don't Know Me" and other Country gems.

1963

BLUE BAYOU

Producer: Fred Foster
Album: In Dreams
Record Label: Monument
Songwriters: Roy Orbison, Joe Melton

B-side of Roy's biggest R&B hit, "Mean Woman Blues." Cover was a million-selling single for Linda Ronstadt (Asylum, '77).

IN DREAMS

Producer: Fred Foster
Album: In Dreams
Record Label: Monument
Songwriter: Roy Orbison

Re-recorded for a scene in the film Blue Velvet.

1964

IT'S OVER

Producer: Fred Foster
Album: More of Roy Orbison's Greatest Hits
Record Label: Monument
Songwriters: Roy Orbison, Bill Dees

Roy at his pained peak.

OH, PRETTY WOMAN

Producer: Fred Foster
Album: Oh, Pretty Woman
Record Label: Monument
Songwriters: Roy Orbison, Bill Dees

Roy gets the girl, albeit only for a short time and possibly by accident. Covered by Van Halen (Warner Brothers, '82). Revived in the movie Pretty Woman, *in which the girl is Julia Roberts who, in a weird Orbisonian twist of irony, was actually gotten in real life by the ungainly, unlikely Orbison-esque Lyle Lovett (albeit only for a short time, and possibly by accident).*

1989

YOU GOT IT

Producer: Jeff Lynne
Album: Mystery Girl
Record Label: Virgin
Songwriters: Jeff Lynne, Roy Orbison, Tom Petty

Going out on a high note, Roy died while in the midst of a comeback, both solo and with the Traveling Wilburys. Covered by Bonnie Raitt in the film Boys on the Side *(Arista, '95).*

ORCHESTRAL MANOEUVRES IN THE DARK (OMD)

1986

IF YOU LEAVE

Producers: Tom Lord-Alge, OMD
Album: *Pretty in Pink* Soundtrack
Record Label: A&M
Songwriter: OMD

Breathless ballad from the U.K. dancemasters.

ORIGINAL CASUALS

1958

SO TOUGH

Record Label: Backbeat
Songwriter: Gary Mears

Resonant '50s pose.

THE ORIGINALS

1969

BABY, I'M FOR REAL

Producer: Marvin Gaye
Album: Baby, I'm for Real
Record Label: Soul
Songwriters: Marvin Gaye, Anna Gaye

#1 R&B/Top-20 R&R crossover, written by Marvin Gaye and his then-wife, Berry Gordy's sister, Anna.

THE ORIOLES

1948

IT'S TOO SOON TO KNOW

Record Label: It's a Natural/Jubilee
Songwriter: Deborah Chessler

Breaking the chains of black music type-casting, Baltimore's Sonny Til & the Orioles create the emotionally charged teen dream of group harmony, otherwise known as Doo-Wop, with this #1 R&B/Top-20 R&R song, the first "race" record to cross over that high on the charts. Pat Boone didn't get around to covering it for a decade (Dot, '58).

1949

TELL ME SO

Record Label: Jubilee
Songwriter: Deborah Chessler

Another #1 R&B classic.

1953

CRYING IN THE CHAPEL

Record Label: Jubilee
Songwriter: Artie Glenn

First known triple crossover by three different artists, presaging the biracial/cultural power of the coming Rock and Roll era. Covered on the Country charts by the author's son, Darrell Glenn (Valley), as well as Rex Allen (Decca). The Orioles had the #1 R&B/Top-20 R&R crossover. June Valli had the Pop hit (RCA). Covered by Elvis Presley (RCA, '65).

TONY ORLANDO

1961

BLESS YOU

Producers: Al Nevins, Don Kirshner
Album: Bless You and 11 Other Hits
Record Label: Epic
Songwriters: Barry Mann, Cynthia Weil

Introducing another pair of Kirshner team-players, Barry and Cynthia. Orlando made his fortune with Dawn.

ORLEANS

1975

DANCE WITH ME

Producer: Chuck Plotkin
Album: Let There Be Music
Record Label: Asylum
Songwriters: John Hall, Johanna Hall

Exemplary Soft Rock.

1976

STILL THE ONE

Producer: Chuck Plotkin
Album: Waking and Dreaming
Record Label: Asylum
Songwriters: John Hall, Johanna Hall

Enduring wedding and anniversary song.

THE ORLONS

1962

THE WAH-WATUSI

Album: The Wah-Watusi
Record Label: Cameo
Songwriters: Kal Mann, Dave Appell

One of approximately seventeen dance tunes to hit the Top-10 in '62. But it was no Twist.

1963

DON'T HANG UP

Album: Not Me
Record Label: Cameo
Songwriter: Dave Appell

Philly dance groove, midway between "American Bandstand" and "Soul Train."

SOUTH STREET

Album: South Street
Record Label: Cameo
Songwriters: Kal Mann, Dave Appell

In Philadelphia hippies walked in pointy-toed Italian dancing shoes, years before donning moccasins in San Francisco.

JOAN OSBORNE

1995

ONE OF US

Producer: Rick Chertoff
Album: Relish
Record Label: Blue Gorilla/Mercury
Songwriter: Eric Bazilian

Major new Folk Rock diva delivers the most unusual lyric to hit the Top-10 in years. Suggested segues: "Dear God" by XTC and "Jesus Is Just Alright with Me" by the Doobie Brothers.

OZZY OSBOURNE
1981

CRAZY TRAIN
Producer: Max Norman
Album: Blizzard of Ozz
Record Label: Jet
Songwriters: Ozzy Osbourne, Randy Rhoads, Bob Daisley, Lee Gary Kerslake

The flamboyant Black Sabbath vocalist creates his own metal legacy, with guitarist Randy Rhoads about to become a legend.

FLYING HIGH AGAIN
Producer: Max Norman
Album: Diary of a Madman
Record Label: Jet
Songwriters: Ozzy Osbourne, Randy Rhoads, Bob Daisley, Lee Gary Kerslake

This would become guitarist Rhoads' epitaph, because he died in a plane crash a few months after the release of the album.

MR. CROWLEY
Producer: Max Norman
Album: Blizzard of Ozz
Record Label: Jet
Songwriters: Ozzy Osbourne, Randy Rhoads, Bob Daisley, Lee Kerslake

Helping to establish the Heavy Metal link to the netherworlds above and below the known with a tribute to Alistair Crowley.

SUICIDE SOLUTION
Producer: Max Norman
Album: Blizzard of Ozz
Record Label: Jet
Songwriters: Ozzy Osbourne, Randy Rhoads, Bob Daisley, Lee Kerslake

Widely misunderstood anti-drug lament.

1986

SHOT IN THE DARK
Producer: Ron Nevison
Album: The Ultimate Sin
Record Label: CBS-Associated
Songwriters: Ozzy Osbourne, Phil Soussan

Best of the post-Rhoads era.

THE OSMONDS
1971

ONE BAD APPLE (DON'T SPOIL THE WHOLE BUNCH)
Producer: Rick Hall
Album: The Osmonds
Record Label: MGM
Songwriter: George Jackson

The white Jackson family. (Or was that the Wilsons?)

YO-YO
Producer: Rick Hall
Album: Phase III
Record Label: MGM
Songwriter: Joe South

Mormon Country soul.

1972

DOWN BY THE LAZY RIVER
Producer: Rick Hall
Album: Phase III
Record Label: MGM
Songwriters: Alan R. Osmond, Merrill Osmond

Defining AM radio's waning days.

DONNY OSMOND
1989

SOLDIER OF LOVE
Producers: Carl Sturken, Evan Rogers
Album: Donny Osmond
Record Label: Capitol
Songwriters: Cal Sturken, Evan Rogers

Year's most unnecessary comeback.

JOHNNY OTIS
1946

HARLEM NOCTURNE
Record Label: Savoy
Songwriters: Earl Hagen, Dick Rogers

Haunting sax instrumental, originated by Randy Brooks in '40. Covered by the Viscounts (Madison, '60).

1950

DOUBLE-CROSSIN' BLUES
Record Label: Savoy
Songwriter: Johnny Otis

Legendary Greek R&B orchestra leader gets his first #1 R&B hit, with Little Esther and the Robins.

MISTRUSTIN' BLUES
Record Label: Savoy
Songwriter: Johnny Otis

Second straight #1 R&B hit, with Little Esther, Mel Walker, and the Robins.

1958

WILLIE AND THE HAND JIVE
Album: The Johnny Otis Show
Record Label: Capitol
Songwriter: Johnny Otis

His most famous single.

THE OUTFIELD
1986

YOUR LOVE
Album: Play Deep
Record Label: Columbia
Songwriter: John Spinks

U.K. Pop Rock one-shot.

THE OUTLAWS
1975

GREEN GRASS AND HIGH TIDES
Album: Outlaws
Record Label: Arista
Songwriter: Hugh Thomasson

Southern Rock guitar extravaganza.

THE OUTSIDERS
1966

TIME WON'T LET ME
Producer: Tom King
Album: Time Won't Let Me
Record Label: Capitol
Songwriters: Chet Kelley, Tom King

Existential Pop Rock passing as Folk Rock.

BUCK OWENS
1963

ACT NATURALLY
Album: The Best of Buck Owens
Record Label: Capitol
Songwriters: Vonie Morrison, Johnny Russell

Buck's first #1 C&W (followed by four more in a row), covered by the Beatles (Capitol, '66).

1965

CRYING TIME
Album: I've Got a Tiger by the Tail
Record Label: Capitol
Songwriter: Buck Owens

In the wake of the Beatles' success with "Act Naturally" came Ray Charles's #1 R&B/Top-10 R&R cover of this Owens tune (ABC/Paramount, '66), recorded by Buck on the B-side of his long-running #1 C&W/Top-30 R&R crossover "I've Got a Tiger by the Tail" (Capitol, '65).

THE OZARK MOUNTAIN DAREDEVILS

1975

JACKIE BLUE
  Producers: Glyn Johns, David Anderle
  Album: It'll Shine When It Shines
  Record Label: A&M
  Songwriters: Larry Lee, Steve Cash

Southern Pop Rock.

P

P.M. DAWN

1991

SET ADRIFT ON MEMORY BLISS
  Producer: P.M. Dawn
  Album: Of the Heart, of the Soul, and of the Cross
  Record Label: Gee Street
  Songwriters: Atrel Cordes, Gary Kemp

Hip-Hop meets Soul at the corner of Doo-Wop and Ashbury.

1992

I'D DIE WITHOUT YOU
  Producer: P.M. Dawn
  Album: *Boomerang* Soundtrack
  Record Label: Gee Street
  Songwriter: Atrel Cordes

From the monster soundtrack album.

1993

LOOKING THROUGH PATIENT EYES
  Producer: P.M. Dawn
  Album: The Bliss Album
  Record Label: Gee Street
  Songwriters: Atrel Cordes, George Michael

The philosopher kings of New-Age Rap network with a bronze God of another era.

PABLO CRUISE

1977

WHATCHA GONNA DO
  Album: A Place in the Sun
  Record Label: A&M
  Songwriters: Cory Lerios, David Jenkins

Their first hit single.

1978

LOVE WILL FIND A WAY
  Producer: Bill Schnee
  Album: World's Away
  Record Label: A&M
  Songwriters: Cory Lerios, David Jenkins

Blue-eyed Soul, minus the soul.

PACIFIC GAS AND ELECTRIC

1970

ARE YOU READY
  Producer: John Hill
  Album: Are You Ready
  Record Label: Columbia
  Songwriters: Charlie Allen, John Hill

R&R/R&B one-shot crossover.

JIMMY PAGE

1988

THE ONLY ONE
  Producer: Jimmy Page
  Album: Outrider
  Record Label: Geffen
  Songwriters: Jimmy Page, Robert Plant

Solo effort from Zeppelin founder reunites him with his recalcitrant ex-lead singer. The real reunion wouldn't take place until '94.

MARTIN PAGE

1994

IN THE HOUSE OF STONE AND LIGHT
  Producer: Martin Page
  Album: In the House of Stone and Light
  Record Label: Mercury
  Songwriter: Martin Page

Adult Rock, as opposed to Adult Alternative.

TOMMY PAGE

1990

I'LL BE YOUR EVERYTHING
  Producers: Jordan Knight, Donnie Wahlberg, Michael Jonzon
  Album: Paintings in My Mind
  Record Label: Warner Brothers
  Songwriters: Jordan Knight, Donnie Wahlberg (Donnie Wood), Tommy Page

What you might expect from a New Kids on the Block protege.

CLARENCE PALMER AND THE JIVE BOMBERS

1956

BAD BOY
  Producer: Fred Mendelsohn
  Record Label: Savoy
  Songwriter: Lil Armstrong

One of the more memorable falsetto performances of Rock and Roll's golden age. Originated by the Blues singer Lil Armstrong.

ROBERT PALMER

1978

YOU'RE GONNA GET WHAT'S COMIN'
  Album: Double Fun
  Record Label: Island
  Songwriter: Robert Palmer

Covered by Bonnie Raitt (Warner Brothers, '79).

1979

BAD CASE OF LOVIN' YOU
  Producer: Robert Palmer
  Album: Secrets
  Record Label: Island
  Songwriter: John Martin

Modern blue-eyed Soul from Britain.

1986

ADDICTED TO LOVE
  Producer: Bernard Edwards
  Album: Riptide
  Record Label: Atlantic
  Songwriter: Robert Palmer

Soundcheck favorite of many a guitar band, from Van Halen to Sonic Youth. Covered by Ciccone Youth (Sonic Youth) (Enigma/Blast First, '89).

1988

SIMPLY IRRESISTIBLE
Producer: Robert Palmer
Album: Irresistible
Record Label: Island
Songwriter: Robert Palmer

Compulsively viewable video featuring several stunning models as his back-up band unintentionally symbolizes the distance between Palmer and the Blues.

PANTERA
1992

MOUTH FOR WAR
Album: A Vulgar Display of Power
Record Label: Atco
Songwriter: Pantera

Metal barrage from underground.

PAPER LACE
1974

THE NIGHT CHICAGO DIED
Producers: Mitch Murray, Peter Callendar
Album: Paper Lace
Record Label: Mercury
Songwriters: Peter Callendar, Lionel Stitcher

The originators of "Billy, Don't Be a Hero" notch another Pop Rock novelty, albeit one with a less lofty theme.

THE PARADONS
1960

DIAMONDS AND PEARLS
Producer: Edward Scott
Record Label: Milestone
Songwriters: West Tyler, Charles Weldon, Bill Myers, William Powers, Edward Scott

Essential Doo-Wop.

PARAGONS
1963

THE TIDE IS HIGH
Record Label: Trojan
Songwriter: John Holt

From the Reggae repertoire of John Holt, Jamaica's top progenitor of Lover's Rock, a tune cherished by the Reggae-influenced Punk bands in England of the mid-'70s and covered by the girl-group-influenced Punk band in New York City, Blondie (Chrysalis, '80). It went on to replace John Lennon's

"Just Like Starting Over" at the top of the charts. And so it was.

THE PARAGONS
1957

FLORENCE
Album: The Paragons Meet the Jesters
Record Label: Winley
Songwriters: Julius McMichaels, Paul Winley

By exploiting the hoodlum image engendered by "Rock Around the Clock" for maximum sales, the Paragons would predate the Rolling Stones by seven years, Snoop Doggy Dogg by more than thirty. Florence was their only musical legacy, however. And she was no "Gloria." Not even "Josephine." More like Blanche.

THE PARIS SISTERS
1961

I LOVE HOW YOU LOVE ME
Producer: Phil Spector
Record Label: Gregmark
Songwriters: Barry Mann, Larry Koller

Fairly tame post-Teddy Bears, pre-Genius, Spectorian balladry.

GRAHAM PARKER
1976

HOLD BACK THE NIGHT
Producer: Mutt Lange
Album: Howlin' Wind
Record Label: Mercury
Songwriter: Graham Parker

One of Britain's angrier young men invades the Pub Rock turf, with his band, the Rumour, led by guitarist Brinsley Schwarz.

FOOL'S GOLD
Producer: Mutt Lange
Album: Heat Treatment
Record Label: Mercury
Songwriter: Graham Parker

The best Stones song of the year.

POURING IT ALL OUT
Producer: Mutt Lange
Album: Heat Treatment
Record Label: Mercury
Songwriter: Graham Parker

His soulful rage finds momentary release.

TURNED UP TOO LATE
Producer: Mutt Lange
Album: Heat Treatment

Record Label: Mercury
Songwriter: Graham Parker

A revenge fantasy toward a fickle public that would never be fulfilled.

1977

SOUL ON ICE
Album: Stick to Me
Record Label: Mercury
Songwriter: Graham Parker

1979

YOU CAN'T BE TOO STRONG
Producer: Jack Nitzsche
Album: Squeezing out Sparks
Record Label: Arista
Songwriter: Graham Parker

1989

SOUL CORRUPTION
Album: Live Alive in America
Record Label: RCA
Songwriter: Graham Parker

JUNIOR PARKER
1953

MYSTERY TRAIN
Producer: Sam Phillips
Record Label: Sun
Songwriters: Herman Parker, Sam Phillips

Seminal rocker—tense, fierce, and elemental—based on a Carter Family Folk song. Covered by Elvis Presley in one of his classic early performances, on the B-side of the #1 C&W "I Forgot to Remember to Forget" (Sun, '56), the Paul Butterfield Blues Band (Elektra, '65), the Band (Capitol, '73), and Neil Young (Reprise, '83).

LITTLE JUNIOR PARKER
1961

DRIVING WHEEL
Record Label: Duke
Songwriter: Roosevelt Sykes

His best since "Mystery Train."

RAY PARKER JR.
1982

THE OTHER WOMAN
Producer: Ray Parker Jr.
Album: The Other Woman
Record Label: Arista
Songwriter: Ray Parker Jr.

Parker leaves Raydio with a #1 R&B/Top-10 R&R crossover.

1984

GHOSTBUSTERS

Producer: Ray Parker Jr.
Album: *Ghostbusters* Soundtrack
Record Label: Arista
Songwriter: Ray Parker Jr.

His biggest hit, from the popular movie, was a #1 R&B/R&R crossover. Suggested segue: "I Want a New Drug" by Huey Lewis and the News.

ROBERT PARKER

1966

BAREFOOTIN'

Producer: Wherly-Burly Productions
Album: Barefootin'
Record Label: Nola
Songwriter: Robert Parker

Only hit for the venerable New Orleans sax man.

VAN DYKE PARKS

1968

VINE STREET

Producer: Van Dyke Parks
Album: Song Cycle
Record Label: Warner Brothers
Songwriter: Randy Newman

Defining the L.A. hippie oeuvre, in one of Randy Newman's earlier gems. Covered by Harry Nilsson (RCA, '70).

PARLIAMENT

1967

(I WANNA) TESTIFY

Producer: George Clinton
Record Label: Revilot
Songwriters: George Clinton, Deron Taylor

The notorious Funkmaster General Clinton enters the Arena as the Parliaments, with a Top-10 R&B/Top-20 R&R crossover.

1974

UP FOR THE DOWN STROKE

Producer: George Clinton
Album: Up for the Down Stroke
Record Label: Casablanca
Songwriters: George Clinton, William "Bootsie" Collins, Bernie Worrell, Fuzzy Haskins

Establishing Funk as the black sound of the '70s.

1976

TEAR THE ROOF OFF THE SUCKER (GIVE UP THE FUNK)

Producer: George Clinton
Album: Mothership Connection
Record Label: Casablanca
Songwriters: George Clinton, William "Bootsie" Collins, Jerome Brailey

Clinton's biggest R&R hit.

1977

BOP GUN (ENDANGERED SPECIES)

Producer: George Clinton
Album: Funkentelechy *vs.* the Placebo Syndrome
Record Label: Casablanca
Songwriters: George Clinton, Gary Shider, Walter Morrison

Updated by Ice Cube as "Bop Gun (One Nation)" (Priority, '94) as a new anthem of the disaffected.

FLASHLIGHT

Producer: George Clinton
Album: Funkentelechy *vs.* the Placebo Syndrome
Record Label: Casablanca
Songwriters: George Clinton, William "Bootsie" Collins, Bernie Worrell

Their first #1 R&B/Top-20 R&R crossover, the deepest Disco groove of the year.

1978

AQUA BOOGIE (A PSYCHOALPHADISCOBETABIOAQUADULOOP)

Producer: George Clinton
Album: Motor Booty Affair
Record Label: Casablanca
Songwriters: George Clinton, William "Bootsie" Collins, Bernie Worrell

#1 R&B/Bottom-20 R&R crossover.

JOHN PARR

1985

ST. ELMO'S FIRE (MAN IN MOTION)

Producer: David Foster
Album: *St. Elmo's Fire* Soundtrack
Record Label: Atlantic
Songwriters: David Foster, John Parr

This emotionally-charged movie ballad marked Parr as the Eddie Money of England.

THE ALAN PARSONS PROJECT

1982

EYE IN THE SKY

Producer: Alan Parsons
Album: Eye in the Sky
Record Label: Arista
Songwriters: Eric Woolfson, Alan Parsons

Biggest hit for the legendary recording engineer (Abbey Road, Dark Side of the Moon). Pie in the Techno-sky.

BILL PARSONS

1958

THE ALL-AMERICAN BOY

Album: Detroit City and 11 Other Hits by Bobby Bare
Record Label: Fraternity
Songwriters: Bill Parsons, Orville Lunsford

Sung by Bobby Bare but credited to the writer, Parsons, who did a lip-sync tour behind it, while Bare was in the service. Bare got the last laugh, however, with a long and prosperous R&R and Country music career; Parsons went on to record "Hot Rod Volkswagon," which stiffed (Starday, '60). Suggested segues: "Johnny B. Goode" by Chuck Berry and "So You Wanna Be a Rock and Roll Star" by the Byrds.

GRAM PARSONS

1971

SHE

Producers: Gram Parsons, Rik Grech
Album: GP
Record Label: A&M
Songwriters: Gram Parsons, Chris Ethridge

Prime Country Folk from the genre's holiest Rock and Roller. Covered by Emmylou Harris (Reprise, '76).

1974

RETURN OF THE GRIEVOUS ANGEL

Producer: Gram Parsons
Album: Grievous Angel
Record Label: Reprise
Songwriter: Gram Parsons

Latter-day signature for the legendary Byrd and Flying Burrito.

DOLLY PARTON
1974

I WILL ALWAYS LOVE YOU
Producer: Bob Ferguson
Album: Jolene
Record Label: RCA
Songwriter: Dolly Parton

Bluegrass-inflected Country yearner with nine lives. Dolly's first recording went #1 C&W. The revival in the movie version of the musical The Best Little Whorehouse in Texas, was a #1 C&W/Bottom-40 R&R crossover (MCA, '82). Covered by X's John Doe and Whitney Houston in separate versions in the movie The Bodyguard, Whitney's record (Arista, '91) went on to be a #1 R&B/#1 R&R crossover, spending the most weeks at the top of the R&R charts of any in history. But was it Rock and Roll?

JOLENE
Producer: Bob Ferguson
Album: Jolene
Record Label: RCA
Songwriter: Dolly Parton

The Bluegrass Country queen's first R&R crossover. The cheatin' classic was a #1 C&W/Bottom-40 R&R and went Top-10 in the U.K.

1981

9 TO 5
Producer: Mike Post
Album: 9 to 5 and Other Odd Jobs
Record Label: RCA
Songwriter: Dolly Parton

Oscar-winning #1 C&W/R&R crossover.

THE PARTRIDGE FAMILY
1970

I THINK I LOVE YOU
Producer: Wes Farrell
Album: The Partridge Family Album
Record Label: Bell
Songwriter: Tony Romeo

#1 hit from the TV show influenced by the Cowsills, with future teen idol David Cassidy and his real-life stepmother Shirley Jones singing.

1971

DOESN'T SOMEBODY WANT TO BE WANTED
Producer: Wes Farrell
Album: Up to Date
Record Label: Bell
Songwriters: Mike Appel, Wes Farrell, Jim Cretecos

Future Springsteen co-producers Appel and Cretecos get a writing credit. Oddly, Springsteen never covered the tune.

I'LL MEET YOU HALFWAY
Producer: Wes Farrell
Album: Up to Date
Record Label: Bell
Songwriters: Gerry Goffin, Wes Farrell

In the Nelsons/Monkees-TV-family instant hit mold. But only got halfway up the Top-20.

THE PASSIONS
1959

JUST TO BE WITH YOU
Record Label: Audicon
Songwriter: Marv Kalfin

The demo of this tune was performed by the Cousins (aka the Co-sines), the dynamic New York duo of Paul Simon and Carol Klein (King).

1960

I ONLY WANT YOU
Record Label: Audicon
Songwriter: Harry Evans

Another certified Doo-Wop classic which didn't make the charts, perhaps because Simon and King weren't involved in the demo.

PATIENCE AND PRUDENCE
1956

TONIGHT YOU BELONG TO ME
Record Label: Liberty
Songwriters: Billy Rose, Billy David

Pre-girl-group, pre-teen standard, introduced by Gene Austin in '27.

PATTY AND THE EMBLEMS
1964

MIXED UP SHOOK UP GIRL
Record Label: Herald
Songwriter: William Borsey

Covered by Mink DeVille (Capitol, '77).

PAUL AND PAULA
1962

HEY, PAULA
Producer: Mayor Bill Smith
Album: Paul and Paula Sing for Young Lovers
Record Label: Philips

Songwriter: Ray Hildebrand

Yearning Pop Country duet from Texas was a #1 R&B/R&R crossover.

1963

YOUNG LOVERS
Album: Paul and Paula Sing for Young Lovers
Record Label: Philips
Songwriters: Ray Hildebrand, Jill Jackson

ALAN PAUL, MARYA SMALL AND CHOIR
1972

BEAUTY SCHOOL DROPOUT
Producer: Arnold Maxin
Album: Grease Original Cast Album
Record Label: MGM
Songwriters: Jim Jacobs, Warren Casey

The only song from the '50s parody that really cuts close to the scalp. "There Are Worse Things I Could Do" is a close second.

BILLY PAUL
1972

ME AND MRS. JONES
Producers: Kenny Gamble, Leon Huff
Album: 360 Degrees of Billy Paul
Record Label: Philadelphia International
Songwriters: Kenny Gamble, Leon Huff, Cary Gilbert

Young adultery hits #1 R&B/R&R.

LES PAUL AND MARY FORD
1951

HOW HIGH THE MOON
Record Label: Capitol
Songwriters: Nancy Hamilton, Morgan Lewis

The definitive version; #1 Pop/#5 R&B. Technically and sonically the nature of the electric guitar took a quantum leap toward Rock and Roll.

1953

I'M SITTIN' ON TOP OF THE WORLD
Record Label: Capitol
Songwriters: Sam Lewis, Joe Young, Ray Henderson

The great guitar inventor, innovator, inspiration, and influence, Les Paul recorded this on one of his signature modified arch-top Gibsons. Covered by Howlin' Wolf (Chess, '66), and the Grateful Dead (Warner Brothers, '67). Originated by Al Jolson in '28, and heard in the '46 movie The Al Jolson Story.

PAVEMENT

1994

CUT YOUR HAIR
Album: Crooked Rain, Crooked Rain
Record Label: Matador
Songwriter: Stephen Malkmus

Low-fi slacker anthem.

TOM PAXTON

1963

BOTTLE OF WINE
Album: Ain't That News
Record Label: Elektra
Songwriter: Tom Paxton

Folk-flavored sing-along drinking song, covered by the Fireballs (Atco, '68).

1964

THE LAST THING ON MY MIND
Album: Ramblin' Boy
Record Label: Elektra
Songwriter: Tom Paxton

Tender folk ballad, covered by Neil Diamond (MCA, '73).

FREDA PAYNE

1970

BAND OF GOLD
Producer: Greg S. Perry
Album: Band of Gold
Record Label: Invictus
Songwriters: Ronald Dunbar, Edyth Wayne

Impassioned pitch for monogamy, from the new home of Motown graduates, Holland-Dozier-Holland.

1971

BRING THE BOYS HOME
Producer: Greg S. Perry
Album: Contact
Record Label: Invictus
Songwriters: Angelo Bond, General Johnson, Greg S. Perry

General Johnson notwithstanding, one of the year's best protest songs. In civilian life, Johnson was the former lead singer of the Showmen ("It Will Stand").

PEACHES AND HERB

1978

REUNITED
Producer: Freddie Perren
Album: 2 Hot!
Record Label: Polydor
Songwriters: Freddie Perren, Dino Fekaris

#1 R&B/R&R crossover.

SHAKE YOUR GROOVE THING
Producer: Freddie Perren
Album: 2 Hot!
Record Label: Polydor
Songwriters: Freddie Perren, Dino Fekaris

Essential Disco groove.

PEARL JAM

1991

ALIVE
Producers: Nick Parashar, Pearl Jam
Album: Ten
Record Label: Epic
Songwriters: Eddie Vedder, Stone Gossard

Early dysfunctional stirrings from the Seattle co-chairmen of Grunge; survivor's guilt that still plagues Eddie Vedder.

BLACK
Producers: Nick Parashar, Pearl Jam
Album: Ten
Record Label: Epic
Songwriter: Pearl Jam

EVEN FLOW
Producers: Nick Parashar, Pearl Jam
Album: Ten
Record Label: Epic
Songwriters: Eddie Vedder, Stone Gossard

JEREMY
Producers: Rick Parashar, Pearl Jam
Album: Ten
Record Label: Epic
Songwriters: Eddie Vedder, Jeff Ament

Portrait of modern-day anomie; their first big video.

1993

DAUGHTER
Producers: Brendan O'Brien, Pearl Jam
Album: Vs
Record Label: Epic
Songwriter: Pearl Jam

Funny, familiar, familial tensions.

DISSIDENT
Producers: Brendan O'Brien, Pearl Jam
Album: Vs
Record Label: Epic
Songwriters: Eddie Vedder, Stone Gossard, Jeff Ament, Mike McCready, Dave Abbruzzese

GO
Producer: Brendan O'Brien
Album: Vs
Record Label: Epic
Songwriters: Brendan O'Brien, Pearl Jam

1994

BETTER MAN
Producers: Brendan O'Brien, Pearl Jam
Album: Vitalogy
Record Label: Epic
Songwriters: Eddie Vedder, Stone Gossard, Jeff Ament, Mike McCready, Dave Abbruzzese

Lives of unquiet desperation, one of his most commercial melodies.

SPIN THE BLACK CIRCLE
Producers: Brendan O'Brien, Pearl Jam
Album: Vitalogy
Record Label: Epic
Songwriters: Eddie Vedder, Stone Gossard, Jeff Ament, Mike McCready, Dave Abbruzzese

A tribute to vinyl.

YELLOW LEDBETTER
Producers: Brendan O'Brien, Pearl Jam
Record Label: Epic
Songwriter: Pearl Jam

Legendary concert-closing B-side of "Jeremy."

PEARLS BEFORE SWINE
1967

PLAYMATE
Producer: Richard Alderson
Album: One Nation Underground
Record Label: ESP
Songwriter: Saxie Dowell
Authentic psychedelic swill.

PEBBLES
1988

GIRLFRIEND
Producers: Babyface, L.A. Reid
Album: Pebbles
Record Label: MCA
Songwriters: Kenny Edmunds
(Babyface), Antonio Reid (L.A. Reid)
#1 R&B/Top-10 R&R progenitor of the '90s Chick-Hop sound.

MERCEDES BOY
Producers: Babyface, L.A. Reid
Album: Pebbles
Record Label: MCA
Songwriter: Perri McKissick
(Pebbles)
Her biggest hit. #1 R&B/Top-10 R&R crossover.

1990

GIVING YOU THE BENEFIT
Producers: Babyface, L.A. Reid
Album: Always
Record Label: MCA
Songwriters: Kenny Edmunds
(Babyface), Antonio Reid (L.A. Reid)
Third #1 R&B/Top-10 R&R crossover for the then-Mrs. Reid.

LOVE MAKES THINGS HAPPEN
Producer: L.A. Reid
Album: Always
Record Label: MCA
Songwriters: Kenny Edmunds
(Babyface), Antonio Reid (L.A. Reid)
#1 R&B/Top-20 R&R crossover.

ANN PEEBLES
1972

I FEEL LIKE BREAKING UP SOMEBODY'S HOME TONIGHT
Producer: Willie Mitchell
Album: Straight from the Heart
Record Label: Hi
Songwriters: Timothy Matthews, Al
Jackson
Primal R&B.

1972

I'M GONNA TEAR YOUR PLAYHOUSE DOWN
Producer: Willie Mitchell
Album: Straight from the Heart
Record Label: Hi
Songwriter: Earl Randle
Rough and ready, like Aretha Franklin, if she hadn't been raised in church.

1973

I CAN'T STAND THE RAIN
Producer: Willie Mitchell
Album: I Can't Stand the Rain
Record Label: Hi
Songwriters: Donald Bryant, Ann
Peebles, Bernard Miller
Her first and last Top-40 R&R.

TEDDY PENDERGRASS
1978

CLOSE THE DOOR
Producers: Kenny Gamble, Leon
Huff
Album: Life Is a Song Worth Singing
Record Label: Philadelphia
International
Songwriters: Kenny Gamble, Leon
Huff
#1 R&B/Top-30 R&R crossover. The ultimate bedroom ballad for the former lead singer of Harold Melvin & the Blue Notes.

1988

JOY
Album: Joy
Record Label: Elektra
Songwriters: Reggie Calloway,
Vincent Calloway, Joel Davis
#1 R&B/Bottom-30 crossover.

THE PENGUINS
1954

EARTH ANGEL (WILL YOU BE MINE)
Producer: Dootsie Williams
Album: The Cool Cool Penguins
Record Label: Dooto
Songwriters: Curtis Williams, Gaynel
Hodge, Jesse Belvin
The B-side of "Hey Senorita" was the first #1 R&B/Top-10 R&R crossover. Deejay and R&B bandleader Johnny Otis may have been the first to flip it (and flip for it). It was the second record after "Sh-Boom" to hit Top-10 R&R. Like "Sh-Boom," it was covered in a higher-charting version by the

Crew Cuts (Mercury, '55). The Crew Cuts never made the R&B charts, however.

1963

MEMORIES OF EL MONTE
Record Label: Original Sound
Songwriters: Frank Zappa, Ray
Collins
Before he took to lovingly satirizing it, Zappa was a Doo-Wop devotee, as evidenced by this obvious dream-come-true situation. His first recorded song stiffed on the charts, but lives deep in the heart of the L.A. streets.

MICHAEL PENN
1989

NO MYTH
Producer: Tony Berg
Album: March
Record Label: RCA
Songwriter: Michael Penn
Clear-eyed Alternative Folk rocker by the brother of Sean.

CE CE PENNISTON
1991

FINALLY
Producer: Felipe Delgado
Album: Finally
Record Label: A&M
Songwriters: Ce Ce Peniston, Felipe
Delgado, E. Linnear
Hip-Hop ballad.

PENTANGLE
1968

LET NO MAN STEAL YOUR THYME
Album: The Pentangle
Record Label: Reprise
Songwriters: Terrence Cox,
Jacqueline Jackson, Bert Jansch,
John Renbourn, Danny Thompson
Influential acoustic Folk lament. Fingerpickers from Paul Simon to Richard Thompson perked up.

PEOPLE'S CHOICE
1975

DO IT ANY WAY YOU WANNA
Album: Boogie Down U.S.A.
Record Label: People's Choice
Songwriter: Leon Huff
#1 R&B/Top-20 R&R Disco crossover.

PERE UBU

1978

30 SECONDS OVER TOKYO
Album: Datapanik in the Year Zero
Record Label: Radar
Songwriter: Peter Laughner

Early exponent of the Akron-based American Punk scene. Collected on Peter Laughner's posthumous album (Coolie, '82).

CODEX
Album: Dub Housing
Record Label: Chrysalis
Songwriters: David Thomas, Allen Ravenstine, Tony Maimone, Scott Krauss, Tom Herman

Personifying the urban, mid-century, white, young, American Blues,with the eerie howl of a heartland Captain Beefheart.

1981

BIRDIES
Producers: Ken Hamann, Pere Ubu
Album: *Urgh! A Music War* Soundtrack
Record Label: A&M
Songwriters: David Thomas, Allen Ravenstine, Tony Maimone, Scott Krauss, Mayo Thompson

Suggested segue: "If You Wanna Be a Bird" by the Holy Modal Rounders.

1988

WE HAVE THE TECHNOLOGY
Producers: Ken Hamann, Pere Ubu
Album: The Tenement Year
Record Label: Enigma
Songwriter: Pere Ubu

The voice of the computer age, a decade ahead of its time.

1991

OH CATHERINE
Producer: Gil Norton
Album: Worlds in Collison
Record Label: Fontana
Songwriters: David Thomas, Jim Jones, Eric Drew Feldman, Tony Maimone, Scott Krauss

A love ballad as aching as it is twisted. One of the best definitions of the life-long Rock and Roll artist and fan: "There's a place in my heart where the years don't go."

PERFECT GENTLEMEN

1990

OOH LA LA (I CAN'T GET OVER YOU)
Album: Rated PG
Record Label: Columbia
Songwriter: Larry Johnson (Maurice Starr)

CARL PERKINS

1955

HONEY DON'T
Producer: Sam Phillips
Album: Dance Album
Record Label: Sun
Songwriter: Carl Perkins

B-side of "Blue Suede Shoes." Covered by the Beatles (Capitol, '65).

1956

BLUE SUEDE SHOES
Producer: Sam Phillips
Album: Dance Album
Record Label: Sun
Songwriter: Carl Perkins

First anthem of the newly-discovered teenage market (i.e., Rock and Roll). The big issues would be style, territory, and attitude. Also the first triple crossover, entering the Country charts two weeks ahead of Elvis's "Heartbreak Hotel," then beating it to the R&B charts by a month in March, and hitting the R&R charts in April to the May arrival of "Heartbreak Hotel." Presley's cover of "Blue Suede Shoes" (RCA, '56) peaked well below Perkins' (and didn't chart R&B or C&W). Oddly enough, and setting the tone for Perkins's later career, the record went to #2 on all three charts. Revived in the classic teen-sex movie Porky's Revenge.

BOPPIN' THE BLUES
Producer: Sam Phillips
Album: Dance Album
Record Label: Sun
Songwriters: Carl Perkins, Howard Griffin

Following up "Blue Suede Shoes" and crossing over C&W/R&R, but with not nearly the same impact.

DIXIE FRIED
Producer: Sam Phillips
Record Label: Sun
Songwriters: Carl Perkins, Herman Parker

Carl's third single was only a C&W hit.

1957

EVERYBODY'S TRYING TO BE MY BABY
Producer: Sam Phillips
Album: Dance Album
Record Label: Sun
Songwriter: Carl Perkins

Covered by the Beatles at the Star Club in Hamburg, Germany, '62, and on Capitol in '65.

MATCHBOX
Producer: Sam Phillips
Album: Dance Album
Record Label: Sun
Songwriter: Blind Lemon Jefferson

Country Blues standard by Blind Lemon Jefferson (Paramount, '27). Covered by the Beatles at the Star Club in Hamburg, Germany, in '62, and on Capitol in '64.

YOUR TRUE LOVE
Producer: Sam Phillips
Record Label: Sun
Songwriter: Carl Perkins

His second biggest crossover hit; Top-20 C&W/Bottom-40 R&R.

STEVE PERRY

1984

OH, SHERRIE
Producer: Steve Perry
Album: Street Talk
Record Label: Columbia
Songwriters: Steve Perry, Randy Goodrum, Bill Cuomo, Craig Krampf

Solo Journeyman's biggest hit.

THE PERSUADERS

1971

THIN LINE BETWEEN LOVE AND HATE
Producers: Richard Poindexter, Robert Poindexter
Album: Thin Line Between Love and Hate
Record Label: Atco
Songwriters: Richard Poindexter, Robert Poindexter, Jackie Members

#1 R&B/Top-20 R&R crossover. Covered by the Pretenders (Sire, '84), and in the movie of the same name by H-town (JAC/MAC/Warner Brothers, '96).

1973

SOME GUYS HAVE ALL THE LUCK
Record Label: Atco
Songwriter: Jeff Fortgang

Covered by Robert Palmer (Island, 82), and Rod Stewart (Warner Brothers, '84).

THE PERSUASIONS

1977

LOOKING FOR AN ECHO

Producer: David Darlev
Album: Chirpin'
Record Label: Elektra
Songwriter: Richard Reicheg

A-cappella commentary on the Doo-Wop lifestyle introduced by Kenny Vance. One of the all-time great "they used to sing on the corner" songs. Featured in the '90 Spike Lee PBS special "Do It A-capella" (Elektra, '90).

PET SHOP BOYS

1986

OPPORTUNITIES (LET'S MAKE LOTS OF MONEY)

Producers: J. J. Jeczalik, N. Froome
Album: Please
Record Label: EMI-American
Songwriters: Neil Tennant, Chris Lowe

Overly clever British Techno-duo's tongue-in-cheek anthem.

WEST END GIRLS

Producer: Stephen Hague
Album: Please
Record Label: EMI-America
Songwriters: Neil Tennant, Chris Lowe

Trans-Atlantic #1 crossover flopped on Epic in '84.

1987

IT'S A SIN

Producer: J. Mendelsohn
Album: Actually
Record Label: EMI-America
Songwriters: Neil Tennant, Chris Lowe

WHAT HAVE I DONE TO DESERVE THIS?

Producer: Stephen Hague
Album: Actually
Record Label: EMI
Songwriters: Neil Tennant, Chris Lowe, Allee Willis

With Dusty Springfield.

1990

HOW CAN YOU EXPECT TO BE TAKEN SERIOUSLY

Album: Behaviour
Record Label: EMI
Songwriters: Neil Tennant, Chris Lowe

1991

DJ CULTURE

Album: Discography: The Complete Singles Collection
Record Label: EMI
Songwriters: Neil Tennant, Chris Lowe

PETER AND GORDON

1964

A WORLD WITHOUT LOVE

Producer: Norman Newell
Album: A World without Love
Record Label: Cameo
Songwriters: John Lennon, Paul McCartney

The Beatle philosophy, cloned. Cover by the anti-Beatle, Bobby Rydell (Cameo, '64) stiffed.

1966

LADY GODIVA

Producer: John Burgess
Album: Lady Godiva
Record Label: Capitol
Songwriters: Mike Leander, Charles Mills

Venturing into Herman & the Hermits territory.

WOMAN

Producer: John Burgess
Album: Woman
Record Label: Capitol
Songwriter: Paul McCartney (Bernard Webb)

Suggested segue: "Woman" by John Lennon.

PETER, PAUL AND MARY

1961

LEMON TREE

Producers: Albert Grossman, Milt Okun
Album: Peter, Paul and Mary
Record Label: Warner Brothers
Songwriter: Will Holt

Putting Greenwich Village on the Folk music

map with their first single, Peter, Paul and Mary would soon do the same for a visitor from Minnesota named Zimmerman.

1963

PUFF (THE MAGIC DRAGON)

Producers: Albert Grossman, Milt Okun
Album: Moving
Record Label: Warner Brothers
Songwriters: Peter Yarrow, Leonard Lipton

The first drug song for children, if you believed the censors.

1964

FOR LOVIN' ME

Producers: Albert Grossman, Milt Okun
Album: A Song Will Rise
Record Label: Warner Brothers
Songwriter: Gordon Lightfoot

Folk reaction to the Beatles philosophy, epitomized in this rambling saga of self-aggrandizing self-destruction.

1967

THE GREAT MANDELLA

Producers: Albert Grossman, Milt Okun
Album: Album 1700
Record Label: Warner Brothers
Songwriter: Peter Yarrow

In the heyday of Indian philoso-babble, a Real Folk Rock gem.

I DIG ROCK AND ROLL MUSIC

Producers: Albert Grossman, Milt Okun
Album: Album 1700
Record Label: Warner Brothers
Songwriters: Paul Stokey, James Mason, Dave Dixon

No one believed it except the radio programmers of America.

LEAVING ON A JET PLANE

Producers: Albert Grossman, Milt Okun
Album: Album 1700
Record Label: Warner Brothers
Songwriter: H. J. Deutschendorf Jr. (John Denver)

Folk Rock classic by classic modern troubadour John Denver; rambling in the space age. Became Peter, Paul and Mary's biggest hit in '69. Covered by John Denver (RCA, '69).

TOO MUCH OF NOTHING
Producers: Albert Grossman, Milt Okun
Album: Late Again
Record Label: Warner Brothers
Songwriter: Bob Dylan

Another product of Dylan's prolific recuperation period with the Band at Big Pink, which would finally surface on The Basement Tapes *(Columbia, '75). This version hit the Top-40 late in '67, adequately detailing the progress of Dylan's convalescent, and yet creatively abundant, state.*

PAUL PETERSON
1962

MY DAD
Producer: Stu Phillips
Album: My Dad
Record Label: Colpix
Songwriters: Barry Mann, Cynthia Weil

Donna Reed's other singing TV offspring (along with Shelly Fabares) sang this on the show.

RAY PETERSON
1959

THE WONDER OF YOU
Producer: Dick Pierce
Album: Tell Laura I Love Her
Record Label: RCA
Songwriter: Baker Knight

Covered by Elvis Presley (RCA, '70).

1960

TELL LAURA I LOVE HER
Producer: Dick Pierce
Album: Tell Laura I Love Her
Record Label: RCA
Songwriters: Jeff Barry, Ben Raleigh

The essential teen disaster epic. The movie rights are still available.

1963

GIVE US YOUR BLESSING
Producers: Jerry Leiber, Mark Stoller
Record Label: Dunes
Songwriters: Jeff Barry, Ellie Greenwich

Covered by America's most tragic girl-group, the Shangri-Las (Red Bird, '65).

TOM PETTY AND THE HEARTBREAKERS
1977

AMERICAN GIRL
Producer: Tom Petty
Album: Tom Petty & the Heartbreakers
Record Label: Shelter
Songwriter: Tom Petty

Rejuvenating the ghost of Folk Rock with a ringing anthem, this ringer for Roger McGuinn wound up garnering a cover version of this tune from his mentor; neither version cracked the charts.

BREAKDOWN
Producer: Tom Petty
Album: Tom Petty & the Heartbreakers
Record Label: Shelter
Songwriter: Tom Petty

Patented tense, taut showstopper became his first Top-40 hit. Covered by Suzi Quatro (RSO, '79).

LISTEN TO HER HEART
Producer: Tom Petty
Album: You're Gonna Get It
Record Label: Shelter
Songwriter: Tom Petty

Venturing into Buddy Holly and the Crickets territory.

1979

DON'T DO ME LIKE THAT
Producers: Jimmy Iovine, Tom Petty
Album: Damn the Torpedoes
Record Label: Backstreet
Songwriter: Tom Petty

His first big hit.

EVEN THE LOSERS
Producers: Jimmy Iovine, Tom Petty
Album: Damn the Torpedoes
Record Label: Backstreet
Songwriter: Tom Petty

Early autobiographical anthem.

HERE COMES MY GIRL
Producers: Jimmy Iovine, Tom Petty
Album: Damn the Torpedoes
Record Label: Backstreet
Songwriters: Tom Petty, Mike Campbell

REFUGEE
Producers: Jimmy Iovine, Tom Petty
Album: Damn the Torpedoes
Record Label: Backstreet
Songwriters: Tom Petty, Mike Campbell

Another gem of coiled tension and release.

1981

THE WAITING
Producer: Jimmy Iovine, Tom Petty
Album: Hard Promises
Record Label: Backstreet
Songwriter: Tom Petty

Wisdom and redemption beyond its Folk Rock changes. Covered by Linda Ronstadt (Elektra, '95).

1983

YOU GOT LUCKY
Producer: Jimmy Iovine
Album: Long After Dark
Record Label: Backstreet
Songwriters: Tom Petty, Mike Campbell

Extracting revenge on all of those who had made him wait.

1987

JAMMIN' ME
Producer: Jeff Lynne
Album: Let Me Up (I've Had Enough)
Record Label: MCA
Songwriters: Tom Petty, Mike Campbell, Bob Dylan

Litany of contemporary woes.

1989

FREE FALLIN'
Producer: Jeff Lynne
Album: Full Moon Fever
Record Label: MCA
Songwriters: Tom Petty, Jeff Lynne

Taking a sabbatical from the Heartbreakers, Tom hires all of the Heartbreakers but the drummer to play on this record.

I WON'T BACK DOWN
Producer: Jeff Lynne
Album: Full Moon Fever
Record Label: MCA
Songwriters: Tom Petty, Jeff Lynne

RUNNIN' DOWN A DREAM
Producer: Jeff Lynne
Album: Full Moon Fever
Record Label: MCA
Songwriters: Tom Petty, Jeff Lynne, Mike Campbell

His essential Folk Rock groove, more timeless than Dylan, more consistent than the Byrds.

1991

INTO THE GREAT WIDE OPEN
Producers: Jeff Lynne, Tom Petty, Mike Campbell
Album: Into the Great Wide Open
Record Label: MCA
Songwriters: Tom Petty, Jeff Lynne

A Rock and Roll parable containing the phrase "a rebel without a clue" and a supporting character called "a roadie named Bart."

LEARNING TO FLY
Producers: Jeff Lynne, Tom Petty, Mike Campbell
Album Title: Into the Great Wide Open
Record Label: MCA
Songwriters: Tom Petty, Jeff Lynne

His essential philosophy: coming down is the hardest thing.

1993

MARY JANE'S LAST DANCE
Producers: Rick Rubin, Tom Petty, Mike Campbell
Album: Greatest Hits
Record Label: MCA
Songwriter: Tom Petty

His biggest hit, a mid-tempo tale of mid-American coming of age.

LIZ PHAIR

1993

FLOWER
Producers: Liz Phair, Brad Wood
Album: Exile in Guyville
Record Label: Matador
Songwriter: Liz Phair

Ushering in the age of female rage, a low-fi Oberlin girl in a Stonesian/Urge Overkill/Alternative Rock world. Suggested segues: "Doll Parts" by Hole and "50 Ft. Queenie" by P. J. Harvey.

GLORY
Producers: Liz Phair, Brad Wood
Album: Exile in Guyville
Record Label: Matador
Songwriter: Liz Phair

Exquisitely moody drone from the Sonic Youth School of Low Art.

HELP ME, MARY
Producer: Liz Phair, Brad Wood
Album: Exile in Guyville
Record Label: Matador

Songwriter: Liz Phair

The critically acclaimed debut album yields another handcrafted tapestry of anguish.

6' 1"
Producers: Liz Phair, Brad Wood
Album: Exile in Guyville
Record Label: Matador
Songwriter: Liz Phair

Janis Ian turns 18, grows several inches over the summer. A new empowering anthem for females of all sizes.

1994

SUPER NOVA
Producer: Liz Phair
Album: Whip Smart
Record Label: Matador
Songwriter: Liz Phair

Sophomore effort gains a Grammy nomination.

ESTHER PHILLIPS

1965

RELEASE ME!
Album: Release Me!
Record Label: Lenox
Songwriters: Eddie Miller, W. S. Stevenson

#1 R&B/Top-10 R&R crossover was originally a Country hit for Jimmy Heaps (Capitol, '54) and Ray Price (Columbia, '54).

1972

HOME IS WHERE THE HATRED IS
Producer: Creed Taylor
Album: From a Whisper to a Scream
Record Label: Kudu
Songwriter: Gil Scott Heron

A Soul Folk standout from the pen of a Lost Poet. Covered by Gil Scott-Heron and Brian Jackson (Arista, '76).

PHIL PHILLIPS

1959

SEA OF LOVE
Producer: Eddie Shuler
Record Label: Mercury
Songwriters: George Khoury, Phil Battiste

#1 R&B/Top-10 R&R crossover, influenced by the timeless depths of the Mississippi. Covered by the Honeydrippers (Esperanza, '84). Suggested segue: "Black Water" by the Doobie Brothers.

SAM PHILLIPS

1991

RAISED ON PROMISES
Producer: T-Bone Burnette
Album: Cruel Inventions
Record Label: Virgin
Songwriter: Sam Phillips

Female Folk rocker with a name taken from Elvis's first mentor and a title taken from the opening line of Tom Petty's "American Girl."

PHISH

1993

BOUNCING AROUND THE ROOM
Producer: Phish
Album: A Live One
Record Label: Elektra
Songwriters: Trey Anastasio, Tom Marshall

Bravura track from the Dead-like New Age jam band.

PHRANC

1991

M.A.R.T.I.N.A.
Producer: Warren Bruleigh
Album: Positively Phranc
Record Label: Island
Songwriter: Phranc

A frank lesbian ode to her role model Navratilova.

BOBBY "BORIS" PICKETT & THE CRYPT KICKERS

1962

MONSTER MASH
Producer: Gary Paxton
Album: The Original Monster Mash
Record Label: Garpax
Songwriters: Bobby Pickett, Leona Capizzi

This Halloween novelty arose from the dead to hit the Top-10 again in '73.

WILSON PICKETT

1963

IF YOU NEED ME
Producer: Wilson Pickett
Record Label: Double-L
Songwriters: Wilson Pickett, Robert Bateman, Sonny Sanders

Covered by Solomon Burke (Atlantic, '63). The early stirrings of Soul.

1965

IN THE MIDNIGHT HOUR

Producers: Tom Dowd, Jerry Wexler, Rick Hall, Jim Stewart, Steve Cropper
Album: In the Midnight Hour
Record Label: Atlantic
Songwriters: Wilson Pickett, Steve Cropper

Future Soul standard, produced by a virtual Soul Hall of Fame Committee, was his first #1 R&B/Top-30 crossover.

1966

634-5789

Producers: Steve Cropper, Jim Stewart
Album: Exciting Wilson Pickett
Record Label: Atlantic
Songwriters: Steve Cropper, Eddie Floyd

His biggest R&B hit; #1 R&B/Top-20 R&R. The Marvelettes were on the party line with "Beechwood 4-5789" (Tamla, '62).

99 AND A HALF

Producers: Steve Cropper, Jim Stewart
Album: The Exciting Wilson Pickett
Record Label: Atlantic
Songwriters: Wilson Pickett, Steve Cropper

One of his greatest performances.

1967

EVERYBODY NEEDS SOMEBODY TO LOVE

Producers: Jerry Wexler, Rick Hall
Album: Wicked Pickett
Record Label: Atlantic
Songwriters: Bert Berns, Solomon Burke, Jerry Wexler

His first of five R&B/R&R crossover hits of '67, only one of which broke Top-20 R&R—"Funky Broadway," originally done by Dyke & the Blazers, which went #1 R&B/Top-10 R&R.

I'M IN LOVE

Producers: Tom Dowd, Tommy Cogbill
Album: I'm in Love
Record Label: Atlantic
Songwriter: Bobby Womack

B-side of "Stag-o-Lee." Cover by Aretha Franklin (Atlantic, '74) was a #1 R&B/Top-20 R&R crossover.

1970

DON'T LET THE GREEN GRASS FOOL YOU

Producer: Marvin Gaye
Album: Wilson Pickett in Philadelphia
Record Label: Atlantic
Songwriters: Jerry Akines, Johnnie Bellmon, Victor Drayton, Reginald Turner

One of his two gold singles.

ENGINE NUMBER 9 (GET ME BACK ON TIME)

Producers: Kenny Gamble, Leon Huff
Album: Wilson Pickett in Philadelphia
Record Label: Atlantic
Songwriters: Kenny Gamble, Leon Huff

1971

DON'T KNOCK MY LOVE

Producers: Brad Shapiro, Dave Crawford
Album: Don't Knock My Love
Record Label: Atlantic
Songwriters: Wilson Pickett, Brad Shapiro

Fifth and last #1 R&B/Top-20 R&R crossover.

PILOT

1975

MAGIC

Producer: Alan Parsons
Album: Pilot
Record Label: EMI
Songwriters: David Payton, William Lyall

PINK FAERIES

1971

DO IT

Album: Never Never Land
Record Label: Polydor
Songwriter: Mick Farren

Covered by Henry Rollins (Texas Hotel, '87).

PINK FLOYD

1967

ARNOLD LAYNE

Producers: Norman Smith, Joe Boyd
Album: Piper at the Gates of Dawn
Record Label: Columbia

Songwriter: Syd Barrett

Tale of a transvestite, told by a basket case.

INTERSTELLAR OVERDRIVE

Producers: Norman Smith, Joe Boyd
Album: Piper at the Gates of Dawn
Record Label: Tower
Songwriters: Roger Waters, Syd Barrett, Nick Mason, Rick Wright

Psychedelia, high-British style. Covered by Camper Van Beethoven (Pitch-a-Tent, '86).

1968

SEE EMILY PLAY

Producer: Norman Smith
Album: Pink Floyd
Record Label: Harvest
Songwriter: Roger Waters

U.K. smash, originally entitled "Games for May." Early psychedelic mood piece for a Tuesday afternoon.

SET THE CONTROLS FOR THE HEART OF THE SUN

Producer: Norman Smith
Album: Saucerful of Secrets
Record Label: Tower
Songwriter: Roger Waters

Moving from rave up to freak out.

1969

COME IN NUMBER-51, YOUR TIME IS UP

Album: Music from the Motion Picture *Zabriskie Point*
Record Label: Columbia
Songwriters: Roger Waters, David Gilmour, Nick Mason, Rick Wright

Psychedelic credibility for Antonioni's counter-cultural dud.

1970

ASTRONOMY DOMINE

Producers: Norman Smith, Pat Peard
Album: Ummagumma
Record Label: Harvest
Songwriter: Syd Barrett

Floyd's (and Barrett's) psychedelic-era swansong, covered by underground Metal contenders, Viovod (Mechanic, '89).

1973

BRAIN DAMAGE

Producer: Pink Floyd
Album: Dark Side of the Moon
Record Label: Harvest
Songwriter: Roger Waters

In which the title phrase is uttered. With "Eclipse," their only Waters vocal.

MONEY

Producer: Pink Floyd
Album: Dark Side of the Moon
Record Label: Harvest
Songwriter: Roger Waters

Breakthrough single from legendary band's most legendary album, one that logged about a decade on the charts. Engineered by Alan Parsons.

TIME

Producer: Pink Floyd
Album: Dark Side of the Moon
Record Label: Harvest
Songwriters: Roger Waters, David Gilmour, Nick Mason, Rick Wright

Reflecting on Thoreau's lives of quiet desperation. Suggested segues: "Does Anybody Really Know What Time It Is" by Chicago, "Old Man" by Neil Young.

US AND THEM

Producer: Pink Floyd
Album: Dark Side of the Moon
Record Label: Harvest
Songwriters: Roger Waters, Rick Wright

Originally written for Zabriskie Point.

1975

HAVE A CIGAR

Album: Wish You Were Here
Record Label: Columbia
Songwriter: Roger Waters

From whence came "Which One's Pink."

SHINE ON, YOU CRAZY DIAMOND

Producer: Pink Floyd
Album: Wish You Were Here
Record Label: Columbia
Songwriter: Roger Waters

A tribute to the lamented, lost Syd Barrett, who reportedly wandered unnoticed into the sessions for the tune.

WISH YOU WERE HERE

Producer: Pink Floyd
Album: Wish You Were Here
Record Label: Columbia
Songwriters: Roger Waters, David Gilmour

Guitarist Gilmour begins to assert himself. Fleetwoodian Blues emerge.

1977

PIGS ON THE WING (PART I)

Producer: Pink Floyd
Album: Animals
Record Label: Columbia

Songwriter: Roger Waters
A love song.

1979

ANOTHER BRICK IN THE WALL

Producers: Roger Waters, David Gilmour, Bob Ezrin
Album: The Wall
Record Label: Columbia
Songwriter: Roger Waters

The voice of the English preppie. All in all, another major statement, as Pink Floyd reinvents itself for the Arena era.

COMFORTABLY NUMB

Producers: Roger Waters, David Gilmour, Bob Ezrin
Album: The Wall
Record Label: Columbia
Songwriters: Roger Waters, David Gilmour

Suggested segue: "I Wanna Be Sedated" by the Ramones.

RUN LIKE HELL

Producers: Roger Waters, David Gilmour, Bob Ezrin
Album: The Wall
Record Label: Columbia
Songwriters: Roger Waters, David Gilmour

1987

ON THE TURNING AWAY

Producer: Bob Ezrin/David Gilmour
Album: A Momentary Lapse of Reason
Record Label: Columbia
Songwriters: David Gilmour, Anthony Moore

Gilmour takes over; a new, mellow-guitar era commences.

1994

KEEP TALKING

Producers: David Gilmour, Bob Ezrin
Album: The Division Bell
Record Label: Columbia
Songwriters: David Gilmour, Polly Samson, Richard Wright

Featuring the voice of kindred-spirit physicist Stephen Hawkings.

PIPKINS

1970

GIMME DAT DING

Album: Gimme Dat Ding
Record Label: Capitol

Songwriters: Albert Hammond, Mike Hazelwood

From "The Benny Hill Show."

GENE PITNEY

1961

EVERY BREATH I TAKE

Producer: Phil Spector
Album: World-Wide Winners
Record Label: Musicor
Songwriters: Gerry Goffin, Carole King

A notable stiff, with Spector at the helm. Pitney would recover to become the East-coast Roy Orbison.

TOWN WITHOUT PITY

Album: World-Wide Winners
Record Label: Musicor
Songwriters: Ned Washington, Dimitri Tiomkin

Title song from the movie, nominated for an Oscar.

1962

THE MAN WHO SHOT LIBERTY VALANCE

Album: Only Love Can Break a Heart
Record Label: Musicor
Songwriters: Hal David, Burt Bacharach

Another movie title tune, in a Country and Eastern twang.

ONLY LOVE CAN BREAK A HEART

Album: Only Love Can Break a Heart
Record Label: Musicor
Songwriters: Burt Bacharach, Hal David

With his biggest hit, Pitney tries out for the Copa, settles for Atlantic City.

1963

MECCA

Album: Gene Pitney Sings Just for You
Record Label: Musicor
Songwriters: Neval Nader, John Gluck Jr.

One of his most dramatic numbers.

1964

I'M GONNA BE STRONG

Album: It Hurts to Be in Love
Record Label: Musicor
Songwriters: Barry Mann, Cynthia Weil

Typically Pitney-esque histrionics.

IT HURTS TO BE IN LOVE

Album: It Hurts to Be in Love
Record Label: Musicor
Songwriters: Howard Greenfield, Helen Miller

The East-coast Orbison gets his third-biggest hit.

THAT GIRL BELONGS TO YESTERDAY

Album: It Hurts to Be in Love
Record Label: Musicor
Songwriters: Mick Jagger, Keith Richards

Big hit in England with this custom-penned early Jagger-Richards gem.

1966

JUST ONE SMILE

Producer: Gene Pitney
Record Label: Musicor
Songwriter: Randy Newman

A U.K. hit by Gene Pitney in '66, six years after it was written. Covered by Blood, Sweat, and Tears (Columbia, '68).

THE PIXIES

1988

BONE MACHINE

Producer: Steve Albini
Album: Surfer Rosa
Record Label: 4AD/Rough Trade
Songwriter: Charles Francis (Black Francis)

By way of the legendary Fort Apache Studio, the noisy beginnings of the Boston alternative sound that would include Dinosaur Jr., Throwing Muses, the Breeders (featuring the Pixies' Kim Deal), and the Lemonheads.

1989

DEBASER

Producer: Gil Norton
Album: Doolittle
Record Label: 4AD/Elektra
Songwriter: Charles Francis (Black Francis)

The East-coast suburban industrial sound of Drudge.

HERE COMES YOUR MAN

Producer: Gil Norton
Album: Doolittle
Record Label: 4AD/Elektra
Songwriter: Charles Francis (Black Francis)

Closest thing to a Pop-hit sound.

MONKEY GONE TO HEAVEN

Producer: Gil Norton
Album: Doolittle
Record Label: 4AD/Elektra
Songwriter: Charles Francis (Black Francis)

Monkey got strings. Suggested segue: "Verdi Cries" by 10,000 Maniacs.

MARY KAY PLACE

1976

BABY BOY

Producer: Brian Ahern
Record Label: Columbia
Songwriter: Mary Kay Place

A #1 C&W/Bottom-40 R&R crossover from the ultra-hip, late-night, Norman Lear soap opera parody "Mary Hartman, Mary Hartman."

ROBERT PLANT

1982

BURNING DOWN ONE SIDE

Album: Pictures at Eleven
Record Label: Swan Song
Songwriters: Jezz Woodruffe, Robert Plant, Robbie Blunt

Led Zeppelin icon carries forward his trademark moan.

1983

BIG LOG

Producer: Pat Moran
Album: The Principle of Moments
Record Label: Es Paranza
Songwriters: Jezz Woodruffe, Robbie Blunt, Robert Plant

His biggest solo hit.

1985

LITTLE BY LITTLE

Album: Shaken 'N' Stirred
Record Label: Es Paranza
Songwriters: Jezz Woodruffe, Robert Plant

Chilly echoes.

1988

TALL COOL ONE

Producers: T. Palmer, Robert Plant, Phil Johnstone
Album: Now and Zen
Record Label: Es Paranza
Songwriters: Phil Johnstone, Robert Plant

With a guitar solo by former Zep-mate Jimmy Page.

1990

HURTING KIND (I'VE GOT MY EYES ON YOU)

Producers: Robert Plant, Phil Johnstone
Album: Manic Nirvana
Record Label: Es Paranza
Songwriters: Phil Johnstone, Robert Plant, Charlie Jones, Chris Blackwell, Doug Boyle

1993

CALLING TO YOU

Album: Fate of Nations
Record Label: Es Paranza/Atlantic
Songwriters: Otis Blackwell, Robert Plant

Teaming up with a crafty old Rock and Roll hand.

THE PLASMATICS

1981

SEX JUNKIE

Producers: Dan Hartman, Rod Swenson
Album: Metal Priestess
Record Label: Stiff America
Songwriters: Rod Swenson, Richie Stotts

This former porno queen's personal philosophy is recommended for true connoisseurs of bad taste. Suggested segue: "More More More" by the Andrea True Connection.

PLASTIC BERTRAND

1978

ÇA PLANE POUR MOI

Producer: Lou Deprijck
Album: Ça Plane Pour Moi
Record Label: Sire
Songwriters: Lou Deprijck, Yves Lacomblez, Alan Ward

Punk Disco novelty from Belgium.

THE PLATTERS

1955

THE GREAT PRETENDER

Producer: Buck Ram
Album: Encore of Golden Hits
Record Label: Mercury
Songwriter: Buck Ram

The quintessential R&B love ballad, under the hand of Buck Ram and the vocal chords of Tony Williams, takes on a rare stately grandeur, gaining, for the Platters, their first

#1 R&B/R&R crossover, and for all their contemporaries, at least a decade's worth of respect.

ONLY YOU
Producer: Buck Ram
Album: Encore of Golden Hits
Record Label: Mercury
Songwriters: Buck Ram, Ande Rand
Their first #1 R&B/Top-10 R&R crossover hit, remade from an earlier failed rendition.

1956

(YOU'VE GOT) THE MAGIC TOUCH
Producer: Buck Ram
Album: Encore of Golden Hits
Record Label: Mercury
Songwriter: Buck Ram
Top-5 R&B/Top-5 R&R crossover.

1958

SMOKE GETS IN YOUR EYES
Producer: Buck Ram
Album: Remember When
Record Label: Mercury
Songwriters: Otto Harbach, Jerome Kern
Introduced in the '33 musical "Roberta"; their fourth and last #1 hit.

TWILIGHT TIME
Producer: Buck Ram
Album: Encore of Golden Hits
Record Label: Mercury
Songwriters: Buck Ram, Morty Nevins, Al Nevins, Artie Dunn
Their third #1 R&B/R&R crossover. Written and introduced by the Three Suns (Victor, '50).

PLAYER
1978

BABY COME BACK
Producers: Dennis Lambert, Brian Potter
Album: Player
Record Label: RSO
Songwriters: Peter Beckett, John Crowley
L.A. studio Soul. Follow-up, "This Time I'm in It for Love," also hit the Top-10.

THE PLAYMATES
1958

BEEP, BEEP
Producer: Hugo and Luigi
Album: At Play with the Playmates

Record Label: Roulette
Songwriters: Donald Claps, Carl Cicchetti
Novelty answer song to "Maybellene" was their biggest hit.

1959

WHAT IS LOVE
Producer: Hugo and Luigi
Album: At Play with the Playmates
Record Label: Roulette
Songwriters: Lee Pockriss, Paul Vance
Celebrating the ponytail as the object of male teenage lust. The authors would next take on the bikini.

THE PLIMSOULS
1981

A MILLION MILES AWAY
Producer: Jeff Eyrich
Album: Valley Girl Soundtrack
Record Label: Bomp
Songwriters: Peter Case, Joey Alkes, Chris Fradkin
Legendary West-coast independent single; unadulterated Folk Rock.

SHELLY PLYMPTON
1967

FRANK MILLS
Producer: Andy Wiswell
Album: Hair! A Tribal Rock Musical
Record Label: RCA
Songwriters: James Rado, Gerome Ragni, Galt MacDermot
Ineffable solo showstopper from the much-maligned Rock musical.

POCO
1970

YOU BETTER THINK TWICE
Producer: Jim Messina
Album: Poco
Record Label: Epic
Songwriter: Jim Messina
Folk Rock city.

THE POGUES
1985

A PAIR OF BROWN EYES
Producer: Elvis Costello
Album: Rum, Sodomy and the Lash
Record Label: MCA
Songwriter: Paddy McGowan

The Irish-pub sound, as poetic and inebriated as Dylan Thomas or Van Morrison.

1988

FAIRYTALE OF NEW YORK
Producer: Steve Lillywhite
Album: If I Should Fall from Grace with God
Record Label: Island
Songwriters: Shane MacGowan, Jem Finer
One of the all-time great Christmas songs, with Mrs. Lillywhite, Kirsty MacColl, on backing vocal.

BUSTER POINDEXTER
1987

HOT! HOT! HOT!
Producer: Hank Medress
Album: Buster Poindexter
Record Label: RCA
Songwriter: Alphonsus Cassell
All dolled up and heading to the disco, Buster commits the party tune of the year.

THE POINTER SISTERS
1973

YES WE CAN CAN
Producer: Richard Perry
Album: The Pointer Sisters
Record Label: Blue Thumb
Songwriter: Allen Toussaint
Strutting to New Orleans.

1975

HOW LONG (BETCHA' GOT A CHICK ON THE SIDE)
Producer: Richard Perry
Album: Steppin'
Record Label: ABC/Blue Thumb
Songwriters: Anita Pointer, Ruth Pointer, June Pointer, Patricia Pointer
First #1 R&B/Top-20 R&R crossover for the best sister act since the Andrews Sisters.

1980

HE'S SO SHY
Producer: Richard Perry
Album: Special Things
Record Label: Planet
Songwriter: Tom Snow
Suggested segues: "Soft-Spoken Guy" by the Chiffons, and "Too Shy" by Kajagoogoo.

1981

SLOW HAND
Producer: Richard Perry
Album: Black and White
Record Label: Planet
Songwriters: John Bettis, Mike Clark

Smouldering bedroom ballad and philosophy; tied for their biggest hit with their 1979 cover of Bruce Springsteen's "Fire."

1982

I'M SO EXCITED
Producer: Richard Perry
Album: So Excited
Record Label: Planet
Songwriters: Anita Pointer, Ruth Pointer, June Pointer, Trevor Lawrence

A bigger hit in '84.

1984

AUTOMATIC
Producer: Richard Perry
Album: Break Out
Record Label: Planet
Songwriters: Brock Walsh, Mark Goldenberg

Dance track of the year.

JUMP (FOR MY LOVE)
Producer: Richard Perry
Album: Break Out
Record Label: Planet
Songwriters: Marti Sharron, Steve Mitchell, Gary Skardina

Third-biggest hit.

NEUTRON DANCE
Producer: Richard Perry
Album: Break Out
Record Label: Planet
Songwriters: Allee Willis, David Sembello

From the soundtrack of Beverly Hills Cop, II.

POISON

1987

TALK DIRTY TO ME
Producer: R. Browde
Album: Look What the Cat Dragged In
Record Label: Enigma
Songwriters: Bobby Dall, C. C. Deville, Brett Michaels, Rikki Rockett

In the wake of Bon Jovi.

1988

EVERY ROSE HAS ITS THORN
Producer: Tom Werman
Album: Open up and Say Ahh
Record Label: Capitol
Songwriters: Bobby Dall, C. C. Deville, Brett Michaels, Rikki Rockett

The prototypical Arena Rock ballad was their biggest hit.

NOTHIN' BUT A GOOD TIME
Producer: Tom Werman
Album: Open up and Say Ahh
Record Label: Capitol
Songwriters: Bobby Dall, C. C. Deville, Brett Michaels, Rikki Rockett

Arena hair at its finest.

1990

SOMETHING TO BELIEVE IN
Album: Flesh and Blood
Record Label: Enigma
Songwriters: Bobby Dall, C. C. Deville, Bret Michaels, Rikki Rockett

UNSKINNY BOP
Album: Flesh and Blood
Record Label: Capitol
Songwriters: Bobby Dall, C. C. Deville, Bret Michaels, Rikki Rockett

Unsubtle Rock metaphor. Kiss would approve.

THE POLICE

1978

CAN'T STAND LOSING YOU
Producer: The Police
Album: Outlandos D'Amour
Record Label: A&M
Songwriter: Gordon Sumner (Sting)

Pop Reggae with a Rock lilt. Was their first U.K. hit when re-released in '79, ushering in New Wave—the measured, intellectual response to Punk.

ROXANNE
Producer: The Police
Album: Outlandos d'Amour
Record Label: A&M
Songwriter: Gordon Sumner (Sting)

Their first U.S. hit. Leonard Cohen's "Suzanne" walks the streets a decade later. Sting does an outstanding acoustic solo version of this on a "Secret Policeman's Other Ball" album (Island, '82).

SO LONELY
Producer: The Police
Album: Outlandos d'Amour
Record Label: A&M
Songwriter: Gordon Sumner (Sting)

1979

MESSAGE IN A BOTTLE
Producers: Nigel Grey, the Police
Album: Reggatta de Blanc
Record Label: A&M
Songwriter: Gordon Sumner (Sting)

Perfection of their early sound and message. Their first of five #1 U.K. hits.

WALKING ON THE MOON
Producers: Nigel Gray, the Police
Album: Regatta De Blanc
Record Label: A&M
Songwriter: Gordon Sumner (Sting)

#1 U.K.

1980

DE DO DO DO, DE DA DA DA
Producers: Nigel Gray, the Police
Album: Zenyatta Mondatta
Record Label: A&M
Songwriter: Gordon Sumner (Sting)

Their first Top-10 hit in the U.S. Suggested segue: "Doo Doo Doo Doo Doo (Heartbreaker)" by the Rolling Stones.

DON'T STAND SO CLOSE TO ME
Producers: Nigel Gray, the Police
Album: Zenyatta Mondatta
Record Label: A&M
Songwriter: Gordon Sumner (Sting)

Sting assumes his most professorial position yet—lusting after a young student.

DRIVEN TO TEARS
Producers: Nigel Gray, the Police
Album: Zenyatta Mondatta
Record Label: A&M
Songwriter: Gordon Sumner (Sting)

1981

EVERY LITTLE THING SHE DOES IS MAGIC
Producers: Hugh Padgham, the Police
Album: Ghost in the Machine
Record Label: A&M
Songwriter: Gordon Sumner (Sting)

Their patented Reggae Lite breaks the U.S. Top-5.

INVISIBLE SUN

Producers: Hugh Padgham, the Police
Album: Ghost in the Machine
Record Label: A&M
Songwriter: Gordon Sumner (Sting)

One of the most haunting early-MTV era videos made this song about the troubles in Northern Ireland even more compelling.

1982

SPIRITS IN THE MATERIAL WORLD

Producers: Hugh Padgham, the Police
Album: Ghost in the Machine
Record Label: A&M
Songwriter: Gordon Sumner (Sting)

A polished nod to George Harrison's "All Things Must Pass." Answered persuasively by Madonna with "Material Girl" in '84.

1983

EVERY BREATH YOU TAKE

Producers: Hugh Padgham, the Police
Album: Synchronicity
Record Label: A&M
Songwriter: Gordon Sumner (Sting)

Peaen to obsessive love was their biggest hit in the U.S. and the U.K.

KING OF PAIN

Producers: Hugh Padgham, the Police
Album: Synchronicity
Record Label: A&M
Songwriter: Gordon Sumner (Sting)

Establishing his permanent persona.

WRAPPED AROUND YOUR FINGER

Producers: Hugh Padgham, the Police
Album: Synchronicity
Record Label: A&M
Songwriter: Gordon Sumner (Sting)

Last big hit; Andy Summers went on to New-Age guitar noodling, Stewart Copeland to worldbeat rhythms, Sting to pretty much of the same.

THE PONI TAILS

1958

BORN TOO LATE

Record Label: ABC Paramount
Songwriters: Fred Tobias, Charles Strouse

Previewing the yearning girl-group sound of the next decade.

IGGY POP

1977

CHINA GIRL

Producer: David Bowie
Album: The Idiot
Record Label: RCA
Songwriter: David Bowie

Covered by David Bowie (EMI-America, '83).

LUST FOR LIFE

Producer: David Bowie
Album: Lust for Life
Record Label: RCA
Songwriters: James Osterberg (Iggy Pop)

Reaching his post-Stooges decadent high (low) point.

THE PASSENGER

Producer: David Bowie
Album: Lust for Life
Record Label: RCA
Songwriters: David Bowie, James Osterberg (Iggy Pop)

Threatening to become the male Nico. Covered by Siouxsie & the Banshees (Geffen, '87).

1990

CANDY

Producer: Don Was
Album: Brick by Brick
Record Label: Virgin
Songwriter: James Osterberg (Iggy Pop)

His Alternative icon status secure, the Popster pops up with kitschy Kate Pierson of the B-52s. Suggested segue: "I Want Candy" by Bow Wow Wow.

THE POPPY FAMILY

1969

WHICH WAY YOU GOIN' BILLY

Producer: Terry Jacks
Album: Which Way You Goin' Billy
Record Label: London
Songwriter: Terry Jacks

An anti-war bubblegum hit. Suggested segue: "Toy Soldiers" by Martika.

PORNO FOR PYROS

1993

PETS

Producers: M. Hyde, Perry Farrell
Album: Porno for Pyros
Record Label: Warner Brothers
Songwriter: Porno for Pyros

Self-conscious Alternative musings.

POSITIVE K

1993

I GOT A MAN

Producer: S. Thomas
Album: Skills Dat Pay Da Bills
Record Label: Island
Songwriter: Positive K

The great debate, started by Mickey and Sylvia in "Love Is Strange," back in '57, continues with high-street style, between K and an unidentified but determinedly resistant female.

THE POWER STATION

1985

SOME LIKE IT HOT

Producer: Bernard Edwards
Album: The Power Station
Record Label: Capitol
Songwriters: Robert Palmer, Andy Taylor, John Taylor

All-star dance Rock one-off.

PRATT AND MCLAIN

1976

HAPPY DAYS

Producers: Steve Barri, Michael Omartian
Album: Pratt and McLain Featuring *Happy Days*
Record Label: Reprise
Songwriters: Norman Gimbel, Charles Fox

Theme from the TV show celebrating the '50s.

ANDY PRATT

1973

AVENGING ANNIE

Producer: John Nagy
Album: Andy Pratt
Record Label: Columbia
Songwriter: Andy Pratt

Smart-mouthed New England Folk Rock one-shot, covered by Roger Daltrey (Atlantic, '77).

PREFAB SPROUT

1985

APPETITE

Producer: Thomas Dolby
Album: Two Wheels Good

Record Label: Epic

Songwriter: Paddy McAloon

Jazzy post-Punk English cabaret charmer.

WHEN LOVE BREAKS DOWN

Producer: Thomas Dolby

Album: Two Wheels

Record Label: Epic

Songwriter: Paddy McAloon

Only Michael Franks could make a living in this vein.

ELVIS PRESLEY

1955

I FORGOT TO REMEMBER TO FORGET

Producer: Sam Phillips

Album: Heartbreak Hotel

Record Label: Sun

Songwriters: Stanley Kesler, Charles Feathers

Legendary, early Elvis Rockabilly classic; #1 C&W hit. "Mystery Train" was on the B-side.

MILKCOW BLUES BOOGIE

Producer: Sam Phillips

Album: A Date with Elvis

Record Label: Sun

Songwriter: Kokomo Arnold

Introduced by Blues-great Kokomo Arnold (RCA, '34). Covered by Ricky Nelson (Imperial, '61).

1956

ANY WAY YOU WANT ME (THAT'S HOW I WILL BE)

Producer: Steve Sholes

Album: Any Way You Want Me

Record Label: RCA

Songwriters: Aaron Schroeder, Cliff Owens

B-side of "Love Me Tender."

DON'T BE CRUEL (TO A HEART THAT'S TRUE)

Producer: Steve Sholes

Album: Real Elvis

Record Label: RCA

Songwriters: Otis Blackwell, Elvis Presley

Accomplishing his first #1 C&W/R&B/R&R crossover, along with co-A-side, the transmogrified, freshly-groomed "Hound Dog." He would do this twice more in his career, both times in '57.

HEARTBREAK HOTEL

Producer: Steve Sholes

Album: Elvis' Golden Records

Record Label: RCA

Songwriters: Mae Boren, Tommy Durden, Elvis Presley

Leading the Rockabilly onslaught of '56 onto the previously highly unattainable upper rung of the Pop ladder, the first Rock and Roll song to hit #1 since Bill Haley's "Rock Around the Clock," nine months before. Although, it should be noted that four other #1s of '55 were white Pop covers of R&B hits: "Sincerely" by the McGuire Sisters, "Hearts of Stone" by the Fontane Sisters, "Dance with Me Henry" by Georgia Gibbs, and "Ain't That a Shame" by Pat Boone. One of the all-time biggest C&W records as well.

I WANT YOU, I NEED YOU, I LOVE YOU

Producer: Steve Sholes

Album: Real Elvis

Record Label: RCA

Songwriters: Maurice Mysels, Ira Kosloff

In the Elvis onlsaught of '56, this spent a mere cup of coffee at #1 C&W/R&R.

I WAS THE ONE

Producer: Steve Sholes

Album: For LP Fans Only

Record Label: RCA

Songwriters: Aaron Schroeder, Claude DeMetrius, Hal Blair, Bill Peppers

B-side of "Heartbreak Hotel."

LOVE ME TENDER

Producer: Steve Sholes

Album: Love Me Tender

Record Label: RCA

Songwriters: Vera Watson, Elvis Presley

His fifth #1 of '56, from his first motion picture, Love Me Tender, with Richard Egan and Debra Paget. Arguably his best movie.

PARALYZED

Producer: Steve Sholes

Album: Elvis

Record Label: RCA

Songwriters: Otis Blackwell, Elvis Presley

Mega-rocking B-side of "Love Me."

1957

(LET ME BE YOUR) TEDDY BEAR

Producer: Steve Sholes

Album: Loving You

Record Label: RCA

Songwriters: Bernie Lowe, Kal Mann

Philadelphia dance Rock songwriters get a leg up on their career with Elvis' second #1 R&R of the year, a #1 C&W crossover as well, from the movie Loving You.

(YOU'RE SO SQUARE) BABY I DON'T CARE

Producer: Steve Sholes

Album: A Date with Elvis

Record Label: RCA

Songwriters: Jerry Leiber, Mike Stoller

Covered by Joni Mitchell (Geffen, '82). Featured in the movie Jailhouse Rock.

ALL SHOOK UP

Producer: Steve Sholes

Album: Just for You

Record Label: RCA

Songwriters: Otis Blackwell, Elvis Presley

Essential shivery rocker, his second of four #1 R&Rs of '57, the number one single of the year (for the second year in a row) and tied for his all-time #1.

JAILHOUSE ROCK

Producer: Steve Sholes, Jerry Leiber, Mike Stoller

Album: Jailhouse Rock

Record Label: RCA

Songwriters: Jerry Leiber, Mike Stoller

Two years after Blackboard Jungle, the image of threatening teens was already fodder for a musical (and not exactly "West Side Story," either). Elvis's last #1 R&B/C&W/R&R crossover. In the film, Mike Stoller plays a piano player in Elvis's band.

LOVING YOU

Producer: Steve Sholes

Album: Elvis

Record Label: RCA

Songwriters: Jerry Leiber, Mike Stoller

B-side of "Teddy Bear," from the movie Loving You.

MEAN WOMAN BLUES

Producer: Steve Sholes

Album: Loving You

Record Label: RCA

Songwriters: Jerry West, Whispering Smith

Covered by Roy Orbison (Monument, '63).

PARTY

Producer: Steve Sholes
Album: Loving You
Record Label: RCA
Songwriters: Jesse Mae Robinson

Cover by the Rockability queen and early Elvis touring partner Wanda Jackson as "Let's Have a Party" as her first chart single (Capitol, '58).

TOO MUCH

Producer: Steve Sholes
Album: Elvis' Golden Records
Record Label: RCA
Songwriters: Bernard Weinman, Lee Rosenberg

Abetted by an appearance on "The Ed Sullivan Show" (albeit only from the waist up), this became Elvis' first #1 of '57. Originated by Bernard Hardison in '54.

TREAT ME NICE

Producers: Steve Sholes, Jerry Leiber, Mike Stoller
Album: Elvis' Golden Records
Record Label: RCA
Songwriters: Jerry Leiber, Mike Stoller

B-side of "Jailhouse Rock."

DANNY

Producer: Steve Sholes
Record Label: RCA
Songwriters: Fred Wise, Ben Weisman

Recorded in '58 for the film King Creole *but never used. Conway Twitty covered it (MGM, '60) as "Lonely Blue Boy" for his second biggest hit. The original finally surfaced on* Elvis: A Legendary Performer, Vol. 3 *(RCA, '79).*

1958

DON'T

Producer: Steve Sholes
Album: Touch of Gold (Vol. I)
Record Label: RCA
Songwriters: Jerry Leiber, Mike Stoller

Early example of sexual harrassment, '50s style. Does he say "kiss" or "kill" in the first verse?

DONCHA THINK IT'S TIME

Producer: Steve Sholes
Album: 50,000,000 Elvis Fans Can't Be Wrong: Elvis' Gold Records (Vol. II)
Record Label: RCA
Songwriters: Clyde Otis, Willie Dixon

B-side of "Wear My Ring."

HARD-HEADED WOMAN

Producer: Steve Sholes
Album: *King Creole*
Record Label: RCA
Songwriter: Claude De Metrius

His first million-selling single, from the Walter Matthau/Carolyn Jones movie King Creole. *De Metrius had formerly collaborated with another legendary mover and shaker, Louis Jordan.*

I BEG OF YOU

Producer: Steve Sholes
Album: Touch of Gold (Vol. I)
Record Label: RCA
Songwriters: Rose Marie McCoy, Kelly Owens

B-side of "Don't."

I GOT STUNG

Producers: Steve Sholes, Chet Atkins
Album: 50,000,000 Elvis Fans Can't Be Wrong: Elvis' Gold Records (Vol. II)
Record Label: RCA
Songwriters: Aaron Schroeder, David Hill

B-side of the Smiley Lewis classic "One Night" (of sin).

WEAR MY RING (AROUND YOUR NECK)

Producer: Steve Sholes
Album: 50,000,000 Elvis Fans Can't Be Wrong: Elvis' Gold Records (Vol. II)
Record Label: RCA
Songwriters: Bert Carroll, Russell Moody

Gone and virtually forgotten in Germany, Elvis's teen fashion/commitment commentary languished at a paltry #2 R&R/#3 C&W/#7 R&B.

1959

(NOW AND THEN THERE'S) A FOOL SUCH AS I

Producers: Steve Sholes, Chet Atkins
Album: 50,000,000 Elvis Fans Can't Be Wrong: Elvis' Gold Records (Vol. II)

Record Label: RCA
Songwriter: Bill Trader

Dramatic ballad was a Country hit for Hank Snow (RCA, '52) and a Pop hit for Jo Stafford (Columbia, '53).

A BIG HUNK O' LOVE

Producers: Steve Sholes, Sid Jaxon, Chet Atkins
Album: 50,000,000 Elvis Fans Can't Be Wrong: Elvis' Gold Records (Vol. II)
Record Label: RCA
Songwriters: Aaron Schroeder, Sid Wyche

His twelfth and last #1 R&R of the '50s, and his only #1 of '59, recorded in Nashville in June of the year, while on leave from the army. By the author of the notorious "Baby Let Me Bang Your Box" by the Toppers.

I NEED YOUR LOVE TONIGHT

Producers: Steve Sholes, Chet Atkins
Album: 50,000,000 Elvis Fans Can't Be Wrong: Elvis' Gold Records (Vol. II)
Record Label: RCA
Songwriters: Sid Wayne, Bix Reichner

B-side of "(Now and Then There's) A Fool Such As I."

MY WISH CAME TRUE

Producer: Steve Sholes
Album: 50,000,000 Elvis Fans Can't Be Wrong: Elvis' Gold Records (Vol. II)
Record Label: RCA
Songwriter: Ivory Joe Hunter

B-side of "A Big Hunk of Love."

1960

ARE YOU LONESOME TONIGHT

Producer: Steve Sholes
Album: Elvis' Golden Records (Vol. III)
Record Label: RCA
Songwriters: Roy Turk, Lou Handman

Taking on a Pop cult soulmate, Al Jolson, who originated this song in '26, Elvis spent six weeks at #1 R&R with it (Top-10 R&B), primarily by virtue of his finely mumbled, near-Shakespearean mid-song recitation, one of the greatest in R&R history. Peaked at #22 C&W, his last appearance on that chart for eight years.

DIRTY DIRTY FEELING

Producers: Jerry Leiber, Mike Stoller
Album: Elvis Is Back
Record Label: RCA
Songwriters: Jerry Leiber, Mike Stoller

From the movie Tickle Me, *Elvis at an all-girl dude ranch!*

FAME AND FORTUNE

Producer: Steve Sholes
Album: Elvis' Golden Records (Vol. III)
Record Label: RCA
Songwriters: Fred Wise, Ben Wiseman

B-side of "Stuck on You." One of his most moving post-army performances.

GIRL OF MY BEST FRIEND

Producer: Steve Sholes
Album: Elvis Is Back
Record Label: RCA
Songwriters: Sam Bobrick, Beverly Ross

Top 10 in England, with "A Mess of Blues" on the B-side (RCA, '60). Covered in the U.S. by Elvis sound-alike Ral Donner (Gore, '61).

I GOTTA KNOW

Producer: Steve Sholes
Album: Elvis' Golden Records (Vol. III)
Record Label: RCA
Songwriters: Paul Evans, Matt Williams

B-side of "Are You Lonesome Tonight."

IT'S NOW OR NEVER

Producer: Steve Sholes
Album: Elvis' Golden Records (Vol. III)
Record Label: RCA
Songwriters: Aaron Schroeder, Wally Gold

Out of the army, Elvis crosses over to the middle-of-the-road for his biggest all-time seller and personal favorite aria. Based on "O Sole Mio."

A MESS O' BLUES

Producer: Steve Sholes
Album: Elvis' Golden Records (Vol. IV)
Record Label: RCA
Songwriters: Doc Pomus, Mort Shuman

Continuing the wildly eclectic nature of his singles, Elvis moves from opera to the Uptown Blues on the B-side of "It's Now or Never."

STUCK ON YOU

Producer: Steve Sholes
Album: Elvis' Golden Records (Vol. IV)
Record Label: RCA
Songwriter: Aaron Schroeder

His first post-army release and his thirteenth #1.

WOODEN HEART

Producer: Steve Sholes
Album: G.I. Blues
Record Label: RCA
Songwriters: Fred Wise, Ben Weisman, Kay Twomey, Bert Kaempfert

One of the more positive results of his experience in Germany. From the movie G.I. Blues. Covered by Joe Dowell (Smash, '61).

1961

(MARIE'S THE NAME) HIS LATEST FLAME

Producer: Steve Sholes
Album: Elvis' Golden Records (Vol. III)
Record Label: RCA
Songwriters: Doc Pomus, Mort Shuman

Double A-side of "Little Sister."

CAN'T HELP FALLING IN LOVE

Producer: Steve Sholes
Album: Blue Hawaii
Record Label: RCA
Songwriters: George Weiss, Luigi Creatore, Hugo Peretti

From Blue Hawaii, *one of his most enduring ballads, covered by UB40 (Virgin, '92) and featured in the film* Sliver. *Also covered by Bono in the Elvis-cover crazy film soundtrack of* Honeymoon in Vegas *(Epic Soundtrax, '92).*

LITTLE SISTER

Producer: Steve Sholes
Album: Elvis' Golden Records (Vol. III)
Record Label: RCA
Songwriters: Doc Pomus, Mort Shuman

Covered by Ry Cooder (Warner Brothers, '79).

SURRENDER

Producer: Steve Sholes
Album: Elvis' Golden Records (Vol. III)
Record Label: RCA
Songwriters: Doc Pomus, Mort Shuman, E. De Curtis, G. B. De Curtis

Based on the aria "Torna a Sorrento," his only #1 of '61.

1962

ANYTHING THAT'S PART OF YOU

Producer: Steve Sholes
Album: Elvis' Golden Records (Vol. III)
Record Label: RCA
Songwriter: Don Robertson

B-side of "Good Luck Charm."

GOOD LUCK CHARM

Producer: Steve Sholes
Album: Elvis' Golden Records (Vol. III)
Record Label: RCA
Songwriters: Aaron Schroeder, Wally Gold

His seventeenth and last #1 until '69.

JUST TELL HER JIM SAID HELLO

Producer: Steve Sholes
Album: Elvis' Golden Records (Vol. IV)
Record Label: RCA
Songwriters: Jerry Leiber, Mike Stoller

B-side of "She's Not You."

RETURN TO SENDER

Producer: Steve Sholes
Album: *Girls! Girls! Girls!*
Record Label: RCA
Songwriters: Otis Blackwell, Winfield Scott

As further psychic, as well as statistical evidence, that a changing of the guard was afoot, this tune spent five weeks at #2 on the charts, kept out of #1 by "He's a Rebel" and then "Big Girls Don't Cry." Not only did it fail to make what would have seemed the obligatory if not honorary final step to #1 (as did "Can't Help Falling in Love" earlier in the year), but it would represent his highest charting item for virtually the remainder of the decade (until "Suspicious Minds" became his last #1 late in '69).

SHE'S NOT YOU

Producer: Steve Sholes
Album: Elvis' Golden Records
(Vol. III)
Record Label: RCA
Songwriters: Jerry Leiber, Mike
Stoller, Doc Pomus

The Brill Building brain-trust follow up Elvis's fifteenth biggest hit five months later with his thirty-second biggest hit.

SUSPICION

Album: Pot Luck
Record Label: RCA
Songwriters: Doc Pomus, Mort
Shuman

Covered by Terry Stafford (Crusader, '64).

1963

(YOU'RE THE) DEVIL IN DISGUISE

Album: Elvis' Golden Records
(Vol. IV)
Record Label: RCA
Songwriters: Bill Giant, Florence
Kaye, Bernie Baum

The forgotten man of '63, with a mere two Top-10s, and one of them was "Bossa Nova Baby." Luckily he had his movies (It Happened at the World's Fair, Fun in Acapulco) to keep him preoccupied.

1964

VIVA LAS VEGAS

Album: *Viva Las Vegas*
Record Label: RCA
Songwriters: Doc Pomus, Mort
Shuman

Saying hello to the future. Covered by ZZ Top in the film Honeymoon in Vegas *(Epic Soundtrax, '92).*

1965

(SUCH AN) EASY QUESTION

Album: Pot Luck
Record Label: RCA
Songwriters: Otis Blackwell, Winfield
Scott

A landmark (or possibly headstone) in Presley's career, his first appearance at #1 on the adult contemporary chart.

1968

IF I CAN DREAM

Album: Elvis
Record Label: RCA
Songwriter: Earl W. Brown

Latter-day inspirational showstopper from his TV special that turned into his first live album.

MEMORIES

Album: Elvis
Record Label: RCA
Songwriters: Mac Davis, Billy
Strange

Hallmark of the later (or fat Elvis) period.

1969

DON'T CRY DADDY

Producers: Chips Moman, Felton
Jarvis, Elvis Presley
Album: Worldwide 50 Gold Award
Hits (Vol. I)
Record Label: RCA
Songwriters: Mac Davis, Billy
Strange

Recorded at his first Memphis session since '55, this was Elvis's biggest hit in Nashville since '58, a Top-20 C&W/Top-10 R&R crossover (Elvis's last appearance on the R&B charts was the above mentioned "Bossa Nova Baby"). Wayne Newton was listening.

IN THE GHETTO (THE VICIOUS CIRCLE)

Producers: Chips Moman, Felton
Jarvis, Elvis Presley
Album: From Elvis in Memphis
Record Label: RCA
Songwriters: Mac Davis, Billy
Strange

In a year of unparalleled interest in all things Country, Elvis returned to his Memphis roots, where he first made the C&W charts. This song of social significance stiffed on the C&W charts, as did Dolly Parton's cover (RCA, '69).

SUSPICIOUS MINDS

Producers: Chips Moman, Felton
Jarvis, Elvis Presley
Album: From Memphis to Vegas
Record Label: RCA
Songwriter: Mark James

Cut in Memphis and introduced at his first live performance since '61, at the Las Vegas Hilton, this was his first #1 since "Good Luck Charm" in '62, eighteenth overall, and last. Covered for the Country market by Waylon Jennings and Jessi Colter (RCA, '70).

1970

KENTUCKY RAIN

Producers: Snuff Garrett, Felton
Jarvis, Elvis Presley
Album: Worldwide 50 Gold Award
Hits (Vol. I)
Record Label: RCA

Songwriters: Eddie Rabbitt, Dick
Heard

From the classic Memphis sessions that produced "Suspicious Minds."

SEPARATE WAYS

Album: Separate Ways
Record Label: RCA
Songwriters: Bobby West, Richard
Mainegra

Las Vegas staple.

ALWAYS ON MY MIND

Album: Separate Ways
Record Label: RCA
Songwriters: Johnny Christopher,
Wayne Carson Thompson, Mark
James

One of his most stirring performances, the B-side of "Separate Ways." Introduced on the Country charts by Brenda Lee (Decca, '72). Number one C&W/Top-10 R&R cover by Willie Nelson (Columbia, '82); #1 U.K./Top-10 R&R cover by the Pet Shop Boys (EMI-Manhattan, '88).

1974

IF YOU TALK IN YOUR SLEEP

Album: Promised Land
Record Label: RCA
Songwriters: Bobby West, Johnny
Christopher

1975

MOODY BLUE

Producers: Felton Jarvis, Elvis
Presley
Album: Moody Blue
Record Label: RCA
Songwriter: Mark James

#1 C&W/Top-40 R&R crossover.

WAY DOWN

Producers: Felton Jarvis, Elvis
Presley
Album: Moody Blue
Record Label: RCA
Songwriter: Layng Martine

Last hit. #1 C&W/Top-20 R&R crossover.

BILLY PRESTON

1971

OUTA-SPACE

Producer: Billy Preston
Album: I Wrote a Simple Song
Record Label: A&M
Songwriters: Billy Preston, Joe
Greene

#1 R&B/#2 R&R instrumental.

1973

SPACE RACE
Producer: Billy Preston
Album: Everybody Likes Some Kind of Music
Record Label: A&M
Songwriter: Billy Preston

Adhering to the year's Soul flavor, this instrumental groove was a #1 R&B/Top-10 R&R crossover.

WILL IT GO ROUND IN CIRCLES
Producer: Billy Preston
Album: Music Is My Life
Record Label: A&M
Songwriters: Billy Preston, Bruce Fisher

His first #1 R&R.

1974

NOTHING FROM NOTHING
Producer: Billy Preston
Album: The Kids and Me
Record Label: A&M
Songwriters: Billy Preston, Bruce Fisher

YOU ARE SO BEAUTIFUL
Producer: Billy Preston
Album: The Kids & Me
Record Label: A&M
Songwriters: Billy Preston, Bruce Fischer

B-side of "Nothing from Nothing." Covered by Joe Cocker (A&M, '75).

1979

WITH YOU I'M BORN AGAIN
Album: *Fast Break* Soundtrack
Record Label: Motown
Songwriters: David Shire, Carol Connor

Duet with Syreeta, for whom Stevie Wonder wrote "Cause We've Ended as Lovers."

JOHNNY PRESTON

1959

RUNNING BEAR
Producer: J. P. Richardson
Album: Running Bear
Record Label: Mercury
Songwriter: J. P. Richardson

Teenage horse opera/soap opera, with the recently departed Richardson (The Big Bopper) on accompanying war-whoops, adding another tragic dimension.

1960

CRADLE OF LOVE
Record Label: Mercury
Songwriters: Jack Fautheree, Wayne Gray

THE PRETENDERS

1980

BRASS IN POCKET (I'M SPECIAL)
Producer: Chris Thomas
Album: The Pretenders
Record Label: Sire
Songwriters: Chrissie Hynde, James Honeyman Scott

#1 U.K. introduction to the tough-minded independent rocker in self-imposed exile from Ohio. As a waitress in the video, she could've been the next Rita Tushingham.

KID
Producer: Chris Thomas
Album: The Pretenders
Record Label: Sire
Songwriter: Chrissie Hynde

Previewing her dominant obsession, aside from Rock and Roll.

MYSTERY ACHIEVEMENT
Producer: Chris Thomas
Album: The Pretenders
Record Label: Sire
Songwriter: Chrissie Hynde

MESSAGE OF LOVE
Producer: Chris Thomas
Album: Pretenders II
Record Label: Sire
Songwriter: Chrissie Hynde

TALK OF THE TOWN
Album: Pretenders II
Record Label: Sire
Songwriter: Chrissie Hynde

One of her best all-time singles.

1984

2000 MILES
Producer: Chris Thomas
Album: Learning to Crawl
Record Label: Sire
Songwriter: Chrissie Hynde

A moving and memorable ode to Ray Davies, at Christmas time, originally the B-side of "Back on the Chain Gang."

BACK ON THE CHAIN GANG
Producer: Chris Thomas
Album: Learning to Crawl
Record Label: Sire
Songwriter: Chrissie Hynde

Her biggest hit was an ode to guitarist James Honeyman Scott, who'd recently died of a drug overdose. Featured in the outstanding soundtrack album to Martin Scorsese's The King of Comedy, with musical direction by Robbie Roberson.

MIDDLE OF THE ROAD
Producer: Chris Thomas
Album: Learning to Crawl
Record Label: Sire
Songwriter: Chrissie Hynde

Passing the big 3-oh with her warmest snarl.

MY CITY WAS GONE
Producer: Chris Thomas
Album: Learning to Crawl
Record Label: Sire
Songwriter: Chrissie Hynde

A melancholy trip back to Ohio. Suggested segues: "Burn on, Big River" by Randy Newman and "Cuyahoga" by R.E.M. A few years later she would write "Downtown (Akron)." A few years after that, she would sing "My City Was Gone" at the concert in Cleveland celebrating the opening of the Rock and Roll Hall of Fame.

1982

SHOW ME
Producer: Chris Thomas
Album: Learning to Crawl
Record Label: Sire
Songwriter: Chrissie Hynde

Trying to present a brave front for the next generation.

TIME THE AVENGER
Producer: Chris Thomas
Album: Learning to Crawl
Record Label: Sire
Songwriter: Chrissie Hynde

Still concerned with aging.

1986

DON'T GET ME WRONG
Producer: Jimmy Iovine
Album: Get Close
Record Label: Sire
Songwriter: Chrissie Hynde

MY BABY
Producer: Jimmy Iovine
Album: Get Close

Record Label: Sire
Songwriter: Chrissie Hynde

Still concerned with babies.

1990

SENSE OF PURPOSE

Album: Packed
Record Label: Sire
Songwriter: Chrissie Hynde

Revived on her acoustic Isle of View *(Warner Brothers, '95).*

1994

I'LL STAND BY YOU

Producer: Ian Stanley
Album: Last of the Independents
Record Label: Sire
Songwriters: Chrissie Hynde, Billy Steinberg, Tom Kelly

Dream assignment for female Rock specialists Steinberg and Kelly (Heart, the Bangles) provides Hynde with a heart (as well as a record) of gold.

NIGHT IN MY VEINS

Producer: Ian Stanley
Album: Last of the Independents
Record Label: Sire
Songwriters: Chrissie Hynde, Billy Steinberg, Tom Kelly

Still rockin' in the free world at forty.

PRETTY POISON

1987

CATCH ME (I'M FALLIN')

Album: Catch Me I'm Falling
Record Label: Virgin
Songwriters: Jade Starling, Whey Cooler

From the movie Hiding Out.

PRETTY THINGS

1964

ROSALYN

Album: The Pretty Things
Record Label: Fontana
Songwriters: Jimmy Duncan, Bill Farley

First U.K. single for the latter-day Stones clones. Covered by David Bowie (RCA, '73). The New York Dolls were listening.

1969

S.F. SORROW IS BORN

Album: S.F. Sorrow
Record Label: Rare Earth

Songwriters: John Alder, Phil May, Jonathan Povey, Richard Taylor, Alan Waller

Purportedly the world's first Rock opera. But it was no "Tommy."

ALAN PRICE

1973

O'LUCKY MAN

Album: O'Lucky Man
Record Label: Warner Brothers
Songwriter: Alan Price

Ponderous progressive Rock staple.

LLOYD PRICE

1952

LAWDY MISS CLAWDY

Producer: Art Rupe
Album: Exciting Lloyd Price
Record Label: Specialty
Songwriter: Lloyd Price

At the tender age of 17, Price attempted to take the New Orleans Soul chalice from Fats Domino, with Fats's band backing him up, at Cosimo Matassa's studio in New Orleans, and with Fats on piano, resulting in a #1 R&B hit. Covered by Elvis Presley (RCA, '57) and the Beatles in the '70 film Let It Be.

1957

JUST BECAUSE

Album: Exciting Lloyd Price
Record Label: ABC-Paramount
Songwriter: Lloyd Price

His first R&R hit. Covered by Larry Williams (Specialty, '57).

1958

STAGGER LEE

Producer: Don Costa
Album: Exciting Lloyd Price
Record Label: ABC-Paramount
Songwriters: Lloyd Price, Harold Logan

New Orleans mythology, updated for a #1 R&B/R&R crossover. See "Stack O Lee Blues," '28. Covered by Fred Waring's Pennsylvanians (Victor, '24) and Mississippi John Hurt (Okeh, '28).

1959

I'M GONNA GET MARRIED

Album: Mr. Personality
Record Label: ABC-Paramount
Songwriters: Lloyd Price, Harold Logan

This proseltyzation for matrimonial bliss earned him a #1 R&B/Top-10 R&R crossover.

WHERE WERE YOU ON OUR WEDDING DAY

Album: Exciting Lloyd Price
Record Label: ABC-Paramount
Songwriters: Lloyd Price, Harold Logan, John Patton

Though it seems Price should have released this tune immediately after (or at least on the flip-side of) "I'm Gonna Get Married," it actually came out five months before it, and was a relative stiff after the #1 success of "Stagger Lee." Ever resilient and persistent, Lloyd righted himself right away by making it to the altar as soon as he feasibly could.

PERSONALITY

Album: Mr. Personality
Record Label: ABC-Paramount
Songwriters: Lloyd Price, Harold Logan

His third #1 R&B/Top-10 R&R crossover.

MAXI PRIEST

1990

CLOSE TO YOU

Album: Bonafide
Record Label: Charisma
Songwriters: Gary Benson, Winston Sela, Max Elliott

#1 Reggae track.

PRIMUS

1991

JERRY WAS A RACE CAR DRIVER

Producer: Primus
Album: Sailing the Seas of Cheese
Record Label: Interscope
Songwriters: Les Claypool, Larry LaLonde, Tim Alexander

Funked-up fun from San Francisco.

PRINCE

1976

SOFT AND WET

Producer: Prince
Album: Prince—For You
Record Label: Warner Brothers
Songwriters: Prince Rogers Nelson, Christopher Moon

The anti-Michael Jackson emerges from Minneapolis.

1979

I FEEL FOR YOU

Producer: Prince
Album: Prince
Record Label: Warner Brothers
Songwriter: Prince Rogers Nelson

Cover by Chaka Cahn (Warner Brothers, '84) was a #1 R&B/Top-40 R&R crossover and the top R&B song of the year.

I WANNA BE YOUR LOVER

Producer: Prince
Album: Prince
Record Label: Warner Brothers
Songwriter: Prince Rogers Nelson

Stating his essential and elemental position, with his first #1 R&B/Top-20 R&R crossover.

1980

PARTYUP

Producer: Prince
Album: Dirty Mind
Record Label: Warner Brothers
Songwriter: Prince Rogers Nelson

WHEN YOU WERE MINE

Producer: Prince
Album: Dirty Mind
Record Label: Warner Brothers
Songwriter: Prince Rogers Nelson

Introducing an important Prince sub-theme, the dysfunctional and/or unconventional man-woman relationship, Prince adds poignance and pathos to his quest for a more perfect union. Cross-gender cover by Cyndi Lauper (Portrait, '84) was even more amazing.

1982

1999

Producer: Prince
Album: 1999
Record Label: Warner Brothers
Songwriter: Prince Rogers Nelson

Party anthem for the ultimate party.

DELIRIOUS

Producer: Prince
Album: 1999
Record Label: Warner Brothers
Songwriter: Prince Rogers Nelson

LITTLE RED CORVETTE

Producer: Prince
Album: 1999
Record Label: Warner Brothers
Songwriter: Prince Rogers Nelson

His first Top-10 R&R, and one of the all-time classic car songs—classic car: the Chevy Corvette.

1984

I WOULD DIE 4 U

Producer: Prince
Album: *Purple Rain* Soundtrack
Record Label: Warner Brothers
Songwriter: Prince Rogers Nelson

Following Elvis and the Beatles to the movies, Prince solidifies his bid for icon-hood with his fourth hit single from the picture. Along the way, he creates a new spelling shorthand that would dominate the '90s.

LET'S GO CRAZY

Producer: Prince
Album: *Purple Rain* Soundtrack
Record Label: Warner Brothers
Songwriter: Prince Rogers Nelson

His second #1 R&B/R&R crossover, from the autobiographical movie.

PURPLE RAIN

Producer: Prince
Album: *Purple Rain* Soundtrack
Record Label: Warner Brothers
Songwriter: Prince Rogers Nelson

Third hit from the biopic.

WHEN DOVES CRY

Producer: Prince
Album: *Purple Rain* Soundtrack
Record Label: Warner Brothers
Songwriter: Prince Rogers Nelson

Showing his sensitive, dysfunctional-relationship side, Prince takes over '84 with the #1 R&B/R&R crossover of the year. His band of the moment: the Revolution.

1985

POP LIFE

Producer: Prince
Album: Around the World in a Day
Record Label: Warner Brothers
Songwriter: Prince Rogers Nelson

RASPBERRY BERET

Producer: Prince
Album: Around the World in a Day
Record Label: Warner Brothers
Songwriter: Prince Rogers Nelson

Suggested segue: "Purple Toupe" by They Might Be Giants.

1986

KISS

Producer: Prince
Album: Parade
Record Label: Warner Brothers
Songwriter: Prince Rogers Nelson

His third #1 R&B/R&R crossover.

1987

BOB GEORGE

Producer: Prince
Album: The Black Album
Record Label: Warner Brothers
Songwriter: Prince Rogers Nelson

From the notorious, much-bootlegged, and primarily X-rated album from '87, finally released in '93.

SIGN 'O' THE TIMES

Producer: Prince
Album: *Sign 'o' the Times* Soundtrack
Record Label: Paisley Park
Songwriter: Prince Rogers Nelson

#1 R&B/Top-10 R&R crossover from his new movie. But it was no Purple Rain.

U GOT THE LOOK

Producer: Prince
Album: *Sign 'o' the Times* Soundtrack
Record Label: Paisley Park
Songwriter: Prince Rogers Nelson

With Sheena Easton, for whom he wrote the salacious "Sugar Walls."

1988

ALPHABET STREET

Producer: Prince
Album: Lovesexy
Record Label: Paisley Park
Songwriter: Prince Rogers Nelson

I COULD NEVER TAKE THE PLACE OF YOUR MAN

Producer: Prince
Album: *Sign 'o' the Times* Soundtrack
Record Label: Paisley Park
Songwriter: Prince Rogers Nelson

One of his more perfect Pop Rock singles, with a tongue-in-cheek hidden message.

1989

BATDANCE

Producer: Prince
Album: *Batman* Soundtrack
Record Label: Warner Brothers

Songwriter: Prince Rogers Nelson

His fourth #1 R&B/R&R crossover.

PARTYMAN
Producer: Prince
Album: *Batman* Soundtrack
Record Label: Warner Brothers
Songwriter: Prince Rogers Nelson

SCANDALOUS
Producer: Prince
Album: *Batman* Soundtrack
Record Label: Warner Brothers
Songwriters: Prince Rogers Nelson,
John Nelson

1990

THIEVES IN THE TEMPLE
Producer: Prince
Album: *Graffiti Bridge* Soundtrack
Record Label: Paisley Park
Songwriter: Prince Rogers Nelson

Another multi-format, multi-media triumph; #1 R&B/Top-10 R&R crossover.

1991

CREAM
Producers: Prince, New Power
Generation
Album: Diamonds and Pearls
Record Label: Paisley Park
Songwriters: Prince Rogers Nelson,
New Power Generation

Introducing his newest back-up band, the New Power Generation.

DIAMONDS AND PEARLS
Producers: Prince, New Power
Generation
Album: Diamonds and Pearls
Record Label: Paisley Park
Songwriters: Prince Rogers Nelson,
New Power Generation

#1 R&B/Top-10 R&R crossover.

MONEY DON'T MATTER TONIGHT
Producers: Prince, New Power
Generation
Album: Diamonds and Pearls
Record Label: Paisley Park
Songwriters: Prince Rogers Nelson,
New Power Generation

Suggested segue: "It's Money That Matters" by Randy Newman.

1993

7
Producer: Prince
Record Label: Paisley Park

Songwriter: Prince Rogers Nelson

Dispensing with the alphabet entirely, Prince, now known by a symbol, writes a mysterious tale about a number.

PINK CASHMERE
Producer: Prince
Album: The Hits/The B Sides
Record Label: Paisley Park
Songwriter: Prince Rogers Nelson

1994

LETITGO
Producer: Prince
Album: Come
Record Label: Warner Brothers
Songwriter: Prince Rogers Nelson

MOST BEAUTIFUL GIRL IN THE WORLD
Producer: Prince
Record Label: Paisley Park
Songwriter: Prince Rogers Nelson

Introduced during the evening gown competion of the Miss U.S.A Beauty Pageant, the artist-formerly-known-as Prince continues his search for the sacred amidst the profane, and vice-versa.

JOHN PRINE
1971

ANGEL FROM MONTGOMERY
Producer: Arif Mardin
Album: John Prine
Record Label: Atlantic
Songwriter: John Prine

Powerful Folk Rock portrait of middle-American emptiness. Covered by Bonnie Raitt (Warner Brothers, '74). Sung by Meg Ryan in the movie Courage under Fire *(1996).*

HELLO IN THERE
Producer: Arif Mardin
Album: John Prine
Record Label: Atlantic
Songwriter: John Prine

An American family portrait by the Ansel Adams of Country Folk Rock. Covered by Bette Midler (Atlantic, '72).

SAM STONE
Producer: Arif Mardin
Album: John Prine
Record Label: Atlantic
Songwriter: John Prine

Nobody's war hero.

1973

DEAR ABBY
Producer: Arif Mardin
Album: Sweet Revenge
Record Label: Atlantic
Songwriter: John Prine

Answering confessional Rock.

1991

TAKE A LOOK AT MY HEART
Album: The Missing Years
Record Label: Oh Boy
Songwriter: John Prine

Beginning a major '90s comeback during which he'd be hailed as the patron Saint of the new hip collegiate Folk Rock radio and album format of the '90s.

THE PRISONAIRES
1953

JUST WALKING IN THE RAIN
Producer: Sam Phillips
Record Label: Sun
Songwriters: Johnny Bragg, Robert
Riley

Covered by Johnny Ray (Columbia, '56).

P. J. PROBY
1966

NIKI HOEKY
Producer: Calvin Carter
Album: Enigma
Record Label: Liberty
Songwriters: Pat Vegas, Lolly
Vegas, Jim Ford

Covered by Aretha Franklin (Atlantic, '68). The Vegases would show up in Redbone.

THE PROCLAIMERS
1989

I'M GONNA BE (500 MILES)
Album: Sunshine on Leith
Record Label: Chrysalis
Songwriters: Craig Reid, Charlie
Reid

Scottish Folk rocker, revived in the movie Benny and Joon *(Chrysalis, '93).*

PROCOL HARUM
1967

CONQUISTADOR
Producer: Chris Thomas
Album: Procol Harum
Record Label: Deram

Songwriters: Gary Brooker, Keith
Reid

Progressive mainstay.

A SALTY DOG
Album: Too Much Between Us
Record Label: A&M
Songwriters: Gary Brooker, Keith
Reid

A WHITER SHADE OF PALE
Producer: Denny Cordell
Album: A Whiter Shade of Pale
Record Label: A&M
Songwriters: Gary Brooker, Keith
Reid

*From Bach to Rock, a chilling precursor of
the classical Euro-Metal sound of
Progressive Rock that would dominate the
early '70s.*

1968

SHINE ON BRIGHTLY
Album: Shine on Brightly
Record Label: A&M
Songwriters: Keith Reid, Gary
Brooker

PROFESSOR LONGHAIR
1950

BALD HEAD
Record Label: Mercury
Songwriter: Henry Roeland Byrd

*Introducing the classic New Orleans Soul
keyboard style of the good professor.
Everyone from Fats Domino to Dr. John was
listening.*

1954

TIPITINA
Record Label: Mercury
Songwriter: Henry Roeland Byrd
(Roy Byrd)

*Ode to the famed New Orleans nightspot
was his signature tune.*

THE PSYCHEDELIC FURS
1981

PRETTY IN PINK
Producer: Steve Lillywhite
Album: Talk Talk Talk
Record Label: Columbia
Songwriters: Richard Butler, Tim
Butler, John Ashton, Vincent Ely,
Roger Morris

*Updated Dylan/Beatle-era Folk rocker, with
a touch of Velvet. Inspired the '86 movie*
Pretty in Pink, *and served as its title track.*

1984

LOVE MY WAY
Producer: Todd Rundgren
Album: Mirror Moves
Record Label: Columbia
Songwriters: Richard Butler, Tim
Butler, John Ashton, Vincent Ely

*Joining the British synth wave for another
hit.*

1987

HEARTBREAK BEAT
Producer: Chris Kimsey
Album: Midnight to Midnight
Record Label: Columbia
Songwriters: Richard Butler, Tim
Butler, John Ashton

*Synth Rock at its most anthemic. The Butler
brothers would next show up in Love Spit
Love.*

PUBLIC ENEMY
1988

BLACK STEEL IN THE HOUR OF CHAOS
Producers: Hank Shocklee, Carl
Ryder
Album: It Takes a Nation of Millions
to Hold Us Back
Record Label: Def Jam
Songwriters: Carlton Ridenhour,
James Boxley, Eric Sadler

*Covered by new Euro-Synth rave Tricky
(Island, '95).*

BRING THE NOISE
Producers: Hank Shocklee, Carl
Ryder
Album: It Takes a Nation of Millions
to Hold Us Back
Record Label: Def Jam
Songwriters: Carlton Ridenhour,
Hank Shocklee, Eric Sadler

*Bringing the threatening nature of R&B up
to date. Featured in the film* Less Than Zero. *Covered by Anthrax (Megaforce, '91).*

DON'T BELIEVE THE HYPE
Producers: Hank Shocklee, Carl
Ryder
Album: It Takes a Nation of Millions
to Hold Us Back
Record Label: Def Jam
Songwriters: Carlton Ridenhour,
Hank Shocklee, Eric Sadler, Charles
Drayton

*Racist, sexist, and visionary Rap, spear-
headed by Ridenhour, a Long Island college
kid, takes collegiate America by storm,
evoking memories of the Black Panthers
and their White Panther sympathizers of the
'60s.*

PARTY FOR YOUR RIGHT TO FIGHT
Producers: Hank Shocklee, Carl
Ryder
Album: It Takes a Nation of Millions
to Hold Us Back
Record Label: Def Jam
Songwriters: Carlton Ridenhour,
Hank Shocklee, Eric Sadler

Answering the Beastie Boys.

SECURITY OF THE 1ST WORLD
Producers: Hank Shocklee, Carl
Ryder
Album: It Takes a Nation of Millions
to Hold Us Back
Record Label: Def Jam
Songwriters: Carlton Ridenhour,
James Boxley, Eric Sadler

*Suggested segue: "Justify My Love" by
Madonna.*

1989

FIGHT THE POWER
Producers: Stuart Roberz, Cerwin
Depper, Gary G. Wiz, the JBL
Album: Fear of a Black Planet
Record Label: Def Jam
Songwriters: Carlton Ridenhour,
Hank Shocklee, Keith Shocklee, Eric
Sadler

*An anthemic polemic featured in Spike
Lee's '89 film* Do the Right Thing.

1990

911 IS A JOKE
Producers: Stuart Robertz, Cerwin
Depper, Gary G. Wiz, the JBL
Album: Fear of a Black Planet
Record Label: Def Jam
Songwriters: Carlton Ridenhour,
Hank Shocklee, Keith Shocklee

Still keeping an ear to the street.

BROTHERS GONNA WORK IT OUT
Producers: Stuart Robertz, Cerwin
Depper, Gary G. Wiz, the JBL
Album: Fear of a Black Planet
Record Label: Def Jam
Songwriters: Charles Ridenhour,
Keith Shocklee, Eric Sadler

Top-20 R&B hit.

FEAR OF A BLACK PLANET

Producers: Stuart Robertz, Cerwin Depper, Gary G. Wiz, the JBL
Album: Fear of a Black Planet
Record Label: Def Jam
Songwriter: Charles Ridenhour

SHUT 'EM DOWN

Producers: Stuart Robertz, Cerwin Depper, Gary G. Wiz, the JBL
Album: Apocalypse '91 . . . The Enemy Strikes Black
Record Label: Def Jam
Songwriter: Charles Ridenhour

1991

CAN'T TRUSS IT

Producers: Stuart Robertz, Cerwin Depper, Gary G. Wiz, the JBL
Album: Apocalypse '91 . . . The Enemy Strikes Black
Record Label: Def Jam
Songwriters: Carlton Ridenhour, Hank Shocklee, Gary Rinaldo

Their biggest hit; Top-10 R&B/Top-50 R&R crossover.

HOW TO KILL A RADIO CONSULTANT

Producers: Stuart Robertz, Cerwin Depper, Gary G. Wiz, the JBL
Album: Apocalypse '91 . . . The Enemy Strikes Black
Record Label: Def Jam
Songwriters: Carlton Ridenhour, Stuart Robertz, Gary G. Wiz, Cerwin Depper

Reacting to their lack of Rock and Roll air play.

1994

GIVE IT UP

Producers: Stuart Robertz, Cerwin Depper, Gary G. Wiz, the JBL
Album: Muse Sick-N-Hour Mess Age
Record Label: Jam/RAL/Island
Songwriters: Charles Ridenhour, Hank Shocklee, Keith Shocklee, Gary Rinaldo, Sean DeVore, Alvertis Isbell, Marvell Thomas

Their second crossover; Top-30 R&B/Top-40 R&R.

PUBLIC IMAGE LTD. (P.I.L.)

1979

THE SUIT

Producer: Public Image Ltd.

Album: Second Edition
Record Label: Warner Brothers
Songwriter: Public Image Ltd.

Almost likeable, in a trancelike way.

1983

THIS IS NOT A LOVE SONG

Producers: John Lydon, Martin Atkins
Album: PiL
Record Label: Virgin
Songwriters: Johnny Lydon, Keith Levine, Martin Atkins

Biggest U.K. hit for Johnny Rotten's post-Sex Pistols bid for Rock and Roll security.

1989

DISAPPOINTED

Producers: Stephen Hague, Eric Thorngren
Album: 9
Record Label: Virgin
Songwriter: Public Image Ltd.

Biggest U.S. hit. But not as big as the Sex Pistols.

GARY PUCKETT AND THE UNION GAP

1967

WOMAN, WOMAN

Producer: Jerry Fuller
Album: The Union Gap
Record Label: Columbia
Songwriters: James W. Glaser, James O. Payne

First hit for the Paul Revere & the Raiders wannabes.

1968

LADY WILLPOWER

Producer: Jerry Fuller
Album: The Union Gap
Record Label: Columbia
Songwriter: Jerry Fuller

Reactionary attitude in the heyday of the sexual revolution strikes a nerve on the Top-10.

OVER YOU

Producer: Jerry Fuller
Album: Incredible
Record Label: Columbia
Songwriter: Jerry Fuller

His fourth straight overbearing Top-10 hit. Neil Diamond was listening. Paul Revere & the Raiders were getting nervous. Lou Christie was calling his manager.

YOUNG GIRL

Producer: Jerry Fuller
Album: Young Girl
Record Label: Columbia
Songwriter: Jerry Fuller

The mainstream male ego strikes back; biggest hit for the lucky Puckett team.

1969

THIS GIRL IS A WOMAN NOW

Producer: Dick Glasser
Album: The New Gary Puckett & the Union Gap
Record Label: Columbia
Songwriters: Victor Millrose, Abe Bernstein

Not so new. His fifth Top-10 R&R performance is basically the same old song, just with a new producer.

PURE PRAIRIE LEAGUE

1975

AMIE

Producer: Robert Alan Ringe
Album: Bustin' Out
Record Label: RCA
Songwriter: Craig Fuller

Folk Rock goes Country; Country Rock goes Pop. A middle-of-the-dirt-road classic.

1980

LET ME LOVE YOU TONIGHT

Album: Firin' Up
Record Label: Casablanca
Songwriters: Jeff Wilson, Dan Greer, Steve Woodward

JAMES AND BOBBY PURIFY

1966

I'M YOUR PUPPET

Producer: Papa Don Schroeder
Record Label: Bell
Songwriters: Spooner Oldham, Dan Penn

In the Sam and Dave mold, with access to most of the same material.

PURSUIT OF HAPPINESS

1988

I'M AN ADULT NOW

Producer: Todd Rundgren
Album: Love Junk
Record Label: Chrysalis
Songwriter: Moe Berg

The Canadian Jonathan Richman/Gordon Gano.

PYLON
1980

COOL
Album: Pylon!!
Record Label: Armageddon
Songwriter: Pylon
R.E.M. contemporaries.

THE PYRAMIDS
1964

PENETRATION
Album: The Original Penetration and Other Favorites
Record Label: Best
Songwriter: Steve Leonard
Early Surf classic.

BIKINI DRAG
Producer: John Hodge
Record Label: Best
Songwriter: Gary Usher
Legendary surf instrumental, featured in the Frankie & Annette film Bikini Beach. *Subsequently covered by neo-Surf diehards the Phantom Surfers, the Finks, and the Boardwalkers.*

Q

? & THE MYSTERIANS
1966

96 TEARS
Producer: Rudy Martinez
Album: 96 Tears
Record Label: Cameo
Songwriter: Rudy Martinez
What Max Crook's musitron hath wrought; the cheesy organ Garage band revolution of the mid-'60s epitomized. Covered by Big Maybelle (Rojac, '67) and Garland Jeffreys (Epic, '81).

QUARTERFLASH
1981

HARDEN MY HEART
Producer: John Boylan
Album: Quarterflash
Record Label: Geffen
Songwriter: Marv Ross

SUZI QUATRO
1973

CAN THE CAN
Producers: Mike Chapman, Nicky Chinn
Album: Suzi Quatro
Record Label: Bell
Songwriters: Mike Chapman, Nicky Chinn
#1 U.K. debut of the petite leather Rock goddess, stiffed in U.S.

1974

DEVIL GATE DRIVE
Producer: Mike Chapman
Album: Quatro
Record Label: Bell
Songwriters: Mike Chapman, Nicky Chinn
#1 U.K.

1978

STUMBLIN' IN
Producer: Mike Chapman
Album: If You Knew Suzi
Record Label: RSO
Songwriters: Mike Chapman, Nicky Chinn
Quatro's nearly Country Rock duet with Chris Norman was her only U.S. hit; by this time she had fallen into self-parody, as Leather Tuscadero on TV's "Happy Days."

QUEEN
1973

KEEP YOURSELF ALIVE
Producers: Roy Thomas Baker, Queen
Album: Queen
Record Label: Elektra
Songwriter: Brian May
The makings of an Arena champion.

1974

KILLER QUEEN
Producers: Roy Thomas Baker, Queen
Album: Sheer Heart Attack
Record Label: Elektra
Songwriter: Freddie Mercury
The charismatic lead singer's heaviest Metal.

STONE COLD CRAZY
Producers: Roy Thomas Baker, Queen
Album: Sheer Heart Attack
Record Label: Elektra
Songwriters: Freddie Mercury, Brian May, Roger Taylor, John Deacon
One of their signature rockers.

1975

BOHEMIAN RHAPSODY
Producer: Roy Thomas Baker
Album: A Night at the Opera
Record Label: Elektra
Songwriter: Freddie Mercury
As befitting their arty record label, Queen exhibits their light operatic leanings in one of the biggest U.K. hits of all time. Lovingly resurrected by Wayne (Mike Myers) and the boys in the movie Wayne's World.

YOU'RE MY BEST FRIEND
Producers: Roy Thomas Baker, Queen
Album: A Night at the Opera
Record Label: Elektra
Songwriter: John Deacon
Having conquered opera, they move to the music hall.

1976

SOMEBODY TO LOVE
Producer: Queen
Album: A Day at the Races
Record Label: Elektra
Songwriter: Freddie Mercury
Back to the Arena.

1977

SHEER HEART ATTACK
Producer: Queen
Album: News of the World
Record Label: Elektra
Songwriter: Roger Taylor

WE ARE THE CHAMPIONS
Producer: Queen
Album: News of the World
Record Label: Elektra
Songwriter: Freddie Mercury
Conquring an Arena of a different sort, this quintessential anthem, especially in its medley form with "We Will Rock You," was adopted in soccer and football stadiums all around the world as a form of taunting the opposition after a victory.

WE WILL ROCK YOU
Producer: Queen
Album: News of the World
Record Label: Elektra
Songwriter: Brian May
Separately or together with "We Are the Champions," their biggest hit of the '70s.

1978

BICYCLE RACE
Producers: Roy Thomas Baker, Queen
Album: Jazz
Record Label: Elektra
Songwriter: Freddie Mercury

Moving onto a sport without an arena; background music for a topless photo op.

1980

ANOTHER ONE BITES THE DUST
Producerss: Queen
Album: The Game
Record Label: Elektra
Songwriter: John Deacon

Back in Deacon's favorite dance hall mode, they achieve their second U.S. #1.

CRAZY LITTLE THING CALLED LOVE
Producers: Mack, Queen
Album: The Game
Record Label: Elektra
Songwriter: Freddie Mercury

Their first #1 and biggest all-time hit.

1982

UNDER PRESSURE
Producers: David Bowie, Queen
Album: Queen's Greatest Hits
Record Label: Elektra
Songwriters: David Bowie, Queen

Techno Rock landmark collaboration with David Bowie, largely for its costly video. Suggested segue: "Ice Ice Baby" by Vanilla Ice.

QUEEN LATIFAH

1989

THE EVIL THAT MEN DO
Producer: KRS-One
Album: All Hail the Queen
Record Label: Tommy Boy
Songwriters: Dana Owens (Queen Latifah), Kris Parker

Strong and positive Rap voice and attitude. A duet with KRS-One.

LADIES FIRST
Producer: D. J. Mark
Album: All Hail the Queen
Record Label: Tommy Boy
Songwriters: Dana Owens (Queen Latifah), Apache, Simone Johnson, Mark James

Landmark feminist Rap, with Monie Love.

Salt-n-Pepa were getting ready to make it commercial.

1991

LATIFAH'S HAD IT UP TO HERE
Producers: Queen Latifah, Sha-Kim
Album: Nature of a Sista
Record Label: Tommy Boy
Songwriters: Dana Owens (Queen Latifah), Vincent Brown, Kier Gist, Anthony Criss

She would soon leave her Rap brothers to their twisted mean streets and join the Fresh Prince with a TV show in L.A.

1993

U.N.I.T.Y.
Album: Black Reign
Record Label: Motown
Songwriters: Dana Owens (Queen Latifah), Joe Sample

Communal Rap anthem.

QUEENSRYCHE

1988

EYES OF A STRANGER
Producer: Peter Collins
Album: Operation: Mindcrime
Record Label: EMI-Manhattan
Songwriters: Chris DeGarmo, Geoff Tate

From their magnum Arena opus.

OPERATION: MINDCRIME
Producer: Peter Collins
Album: Operation: Mindcrime
Record Label: EMI-Manhattan
Songwriters: Chris DeGarmo, Geoff Tate, Michael Wilton

Sequestered Bellevue, Washington, Arena mavens attempt to become the American Queen.

1991

JET CITY WOMAN
Producer: Peter Collins
Album: Empire
Record Label: EMI
Songwriters: Chris DeGarmo, Geoff Tate

SILENT LUCIDITY
Producer: Peter Collins
Album: Empire
Record Label: EMI
Songwriter: Chris DeGarmo

Venturing onto Pink Floydian terrain for their biggest hit.

QUICKSILVER MESSENGER SERVICE

1968

PRIDE OF MAN
Producers: Nick Gravenites, Harvey Brooks
Album: Quicksilver Messenger Service
Record Label: Capitol
Songwriter: Hamilton Camp

Strong Folk rocker, introduced by Bob (Hamilton) Camp becomes a psychedelic staple. Covered by the Washington Squares (Gold Castle, '89).

1970

FRESH AIR
Producer: Quicksilver Messenger Service
Album: Just for Love
Record Label: Capitol
Songwriters: Dino Valenti (Chester Powers), Jesse Farrow

Ecological protest. Suggested segue: "Fresh Garbage" by Spirit.

1971

WHAT ABOUT ME
Producer: Quicksilver Messenger Service
Album: What About Me
Record Label: Capitol
Songwriters: Dino Valenti (Chester Powers)

Proving to be the most activist-minded of the San Francisco bands. Covered by Richie Havens (Stormy Forest, '71).

THE QUINTONES

1958

DOWN THE AISLE OF LOVE
Record Label: Hunt
Songwriter: The Quintones

Essential R&B monogamy.

THE QUOTATIONS

1961

IMAGINATION
Record Label: Verve
Songwriters: Johnny Burke, Jimmy Van Heusen

Doo-Wopping the classics, part XXIV. This tune was introduced by Harry Reser (Columbia, '28).

R

R.E.M.

1980

RADIO FREE EUROPE

Producers: Mitch Easter, Don Dixon
Album: Chronic Town
Record Label: Hibtone
Songwriters: Michael Stipe, Peter Buck, Bill Berry, Mike Mills

Like its historical counterpart, this plucky little tune came whistling out of the static of Reagan-era America, carrying with it the ineffable sound of freedom to a downtrodden generation of Top-40 addled diehards. Taking wing like the Byrds out of ancient Athens, the dreamsound of R.E.M. was borne on the wings of an aching emptiness only a rootsy, poetic, three-chord band could counter. Suggested segues: "Mexican Radio" by Wall of Voodoo, "Mohammed's Radio" by Warren Zevon, "Radio Radio" by Elvis Costello, and "Video Killed the Radio Star" by the Buggles.

1983

(DON'T GO BACK TO) ROCKVILLE

Producers: Don Dixon, Mitch Easter
Album: Reckoning
Record Label: IRS
Songwriters: Michael Stipe, Peter Buck, Bill Berry, Mike Mills

SOUTH CENTRAL RAIN

Producers: Don Dixon, Mitch Easter
Album: Reckoning
Record Label: IRS
Songwriters: Michael Stipe, Peter Buck, Bill Berry, Mike Mills

In the heyday of MTV, with most of the underground still too numb to react against the corporatizing of the aural landscape, the weary beats of R.E.M. provided dreary solace, an instant classic ensuring the enduring jangly essence of the surviving counter culture, chirping in the dead grass like beetles . . . or crickets.

1985

CAN'T GET THERE FROM HERE

Producer: Joe Boyd
Album: Fables of the Reconstruction
Record Label: IRS
Songwriters: Michael Stipe, Peter Buck, Bill Berry, Mike Mills

Evolving into a combo, with their jangly alternative to Van Halen. The Blasters and X on one coast, the Smithereens on the other, and Matthew Sweet somewhere in between

took heart. In Florida, Tom Petty was smiling.

DRIVER 8

Producer: Joe Boyd
Album: Fables of the Reconstruction
Record Label: IRS
Songwriters: Michael Stipe, Peter Buck, Bill Berry, Mike Mills

Perfecting their Rock sound for the Arenas to come.

FALL ON ME

Producer: Don Gehman
Album: Life's Rich Pageant
Record Label: IRS
Songwriters: Michael Stipe, Peter Buck, Bill Berry, Mike Mills

Ready to accept the mantle of Alternative Rock.

1986

CUYAHOGA

Producer: Don Gehman
Album: Life's Rich Pageant
Record Label: IRS
Songwriters: Michael Stipe, Peter Buck, Bill Berry, Mike Mills

Like a good new-generation roots band, their prescription for the future was to start over from the beginning.

FINEST WORKSONG

Producers: Scott Litt, R.E.M.
Album: Document
Record Label: IRS
Songwriters: Michael Stipe, Peter Buck, Bill Berry, Mike Mills

New Folk directive.

IT'S THE END OF THE WORLD AS WE KNOW IT (AND I FEEL FINE)

Producers: Scott Litt, R.E.M.
Album: Document
Record Label: IRS
Songwriters: Michael Stipe, Peter Buck, Bill Berry, Mike Mills

Apocalyptic predictions on the order of Bob's "Subterranean Homesick Blues," Chuck's "Too Much Monkey Business," and Billy's "We Didn't Start the Fire." Suggested segue: "Cuyahoga."

THE ONE I LOVE

Producers: Scott Litt, R.E.M.
Album: Document
Record Label: IRS
Songwriters: Michael Stipe, Peter Buck, Bill Berry, Mike Mills

Love in the ruins; their first Top-10 single.

1988

ORANGE CRUSH

Producers: Scott Litt, R.E.M.
Album: Green
Record Label: Warner Brothers
Songwriters: Michael Stipe, Peter Buck, Bill Berry, Mike Mills

STAND

Producers: Scott Litt, R.E.M.
Album: Green
Record Label: Warner Brothers
Songwriters: Michael Stipe, Peter Buck, Bill Berry, Mike Mills

Counterpart to "Stand" by Sly & the Family Stone.

1991

LOSING MY RELIGION

Producers: Scott Litt, R.E.M.
Album: Out of Time
Record Label: Warner Brothers
Songwriters: Michael Stipe, Peter Buck, Bill Berry, Mike Mills

Wherein Michael Stipe follows Bono Vox to the Godhead, in the process merging with the video generation, most of whom were weaned in part on his music of the '80s.

SHINY HAPPY PEOPLE

Producers: Scott Litt, R.E.M.
Album: Out of Time
Record Label: Warner Brothers
Songwriters: Michael Stipe, Peter Buck, Bill Berry, Mike Mills

A satirical statement. Or was it?

1993

EVERYBODY HURTS

Producers: Scott Litt, R.E.M.
Album: Automatic for the People
Record Label: Warner Brothers
Songwriters: Michael Stipe, Peter Buck, Bill Berry, Mike Mills

Moving into the Dr. Joyce Brothers of his generation mode.

MAN ON THE MOON

Producers: Scott Litt, R.E.M.
Album: Automatic for the People
Record Label: Warner Brothers
Songwriters: Michael Stipe, Peter Buck, Bill Berry, Mike Mills

A tribute to the '70s and '80s and especially to the wrestling comic from "Taxi," Andy Kaufman. Suggested segue: "Back in the Day" by Ahmad.

1994

BANG AND BLAME
Producers: Scott Litt, R.E.M.
Album: Monster
Record Label: Reprise
Songwriters: Michael Stipe, Peter Buck, Bill Berry, Mike Mills

One of their hardest rockers, for the Alternative Arena they now presided over.

WHAT'S THE FREQUENCY, KENNETH
Producers: Scott Litt, R.E.M.
Album: Monster
Record Label: Warner Brothers
Songwriters: Michael Stipe, Peter Buck, Bill Berry, Mike Mills

Updating "It's the End of the World" for the cyber/celebrity age.

EDDIE RABBITT

1980

DRIVING MY LIFE AWAY
Producer: David Malloy
Album: Horizon
Record Label: Elektra
Songwriters: Eddie Rabbitt, Even Stevens, David Malloy

Greeting the new Reagan conservative era with a Country tune; #1 C&W/Top-10 R&R, from the Meat Loaf/Blondie travesty Roadie.

I LOVE A RAINY NIGHT
Producer: David Malloy
Album: Horizon
Record Label: Elektra
Songwriters: Eddie Rabbitt, Even Stevens, David Malloy

#1 C&W/R&R crossover. Nashville awakens to the new prosperity.

1981

STEP BY STEP
Producer: David Malloy
Album: Step by Step
Record Label: Elektra
Songwriters: Eddie Rabbitt, Stevens, Even, Malloy, David

#1 C&W/Top-10 R&R middle-of-the-Country-road crossover.

1982

YOU AND I
Album: Radio Romance
Record Label: Elektra
Songwriter: Frank Myers

#1 C&W/Top-10 R&R crossover with Crystal Gayle.

RADIOHEAD

1993

CREEP
Producers: Sean Slade, Paul Q. Kolderie
Album: Pablo Honey
Record Label: Capitol
Songwriter: Radiohead

Representing the new Beatles-inspired English invasion of the mid-'90s.

GILDA RADNER

1979

HONEY (TOUCH ME WITH MY CLOTHES ON)
Producers: Paul Shaffer, Jerry Wexler
Album: Live in New York
Record Label: Warner Brothers
Songwriters: Gilda Radner, Paul Shaffer

One of the best post-Ronettes Ronettes songs.

GERRY RAFFERTY

1978

BAKER STREET
Producers: Hugh Murphey, Gerry Rafferty
Album: City to City
Record Label: United Artists
Songwriter: Gerry Rafferty

Mellow song of coming home. Great sax part.

RIGHT DOWN THE LINE
Producers: Hugh Murphey, Gerry Rafferty
Album: City to City
Record Label: United Artists
Songwriter: Gerry Rafferty

People were still humming "Baker Street."

RAINBOW

1983

STONE COLD
Producer: Roger Glover
Album: Straight Between the Eyes
Record Label: Mercury
Songwriters: Ritchie Blackmore, Roger Glover, Joe Lynn Turner

Taking the Arena formula straight to the bank. But the bank was closed.

THE RAINCOATS

1981

ONLY LOVED AT NIGHT
Producers: Adam Kidron, the Raincoats
Album: Odyshape
Record Label: Rough Trade
Songwriter: Raincoats

Essential Punk sound, influenced Sonic Youth's Kim Gordon, Nirvana's Kurt Cobain, enough to write liner notes for their first two albums.

THE RAINDROPS

1963

HANKY PANKY
Producers: Jeff Barry, Ellie Greenwich
Album: The Raindrops
Record Label: Jubilee
Songwriters: Jeff Barry, Ellie Greenwich

B-side of the stiff, "That Boy John." Covered by the Shondels (Swap, '63). Re-released by Tommy James & the Shondels (Roulette, '66).

THE KIND OF BOY YOU CAN'T FORGET
Producers: Jeff Barry, Ellie Greenwich
Album: The Raindrops
Record Label: Jubilee
Songwriters: Jeff Barry, Ellie Greenwich

Aka Barry and Greenwich. As good as anything by the Jellybeans, if not the Cookies.

BONNIE RAITT

1972

LOVE HAS NO PRIDE
Producer: Michael Cuscuna
Album: Give It Up
Record Label: Warner Brothers
Songwriters: Eric Kaz, Libby Titus

Folk Rock's groveling standard, upon which Eric Kaz based a minor-legendary career. Covered by Linda Ronstadt (Asylum, '73), Rita Coolidge (A&M, '74), Tracy Nelson (Atlantic, '74), and Kaz's own band, American Flyer (Arista, '76).

LOVE ME LIKE A MAN
Producer: Michael Cuscuna
Album: Give It Up
Record Label: Warner Brothers
Songwriter: Chris Smither

A Bluesy standard that defines the early Raitt's accessibly earthy persona.

1973

GUILTY
Producer: John Hall
Album: Takin' My Time
Record Label: Warner Brothers
Songwriter: Randy Newman

Bonnie turns Newman's neuroticism into a barroom Blues. Covered by Randy Newman (Warner Brothers, '74).

I FEEL THE SAME
Producer: John Hall
Album: Takin' My Time
Record Label: Warner Brothers
Songwriter: Chris Smither

Torchy Blues effectively smoulders. Twenty years later Smither is still writing them this good.

1975

GOOD ENOUGH
Producer: Paul Rothchild
Album: Home Plate
Record Label: Warner Brothers
Songwriters: John Hall, Johanna Hall

Handmade love song, homemade Soul.

SUGAR MAMA
Producer: Paul Rothchild
Album: Home Plate
Record Label: Warner Brothers
Songwriters: Delbert McClinton, Glen Clark

The Country side of the Blues.

1976

I COULD HAVE BEEN YOUR BEST OLD FRIEND
Producers: Bill Payne, George Massenberg
Album: The Glow
Record Label: Warner Brothers
Songwriters: Tracy Nelson, Andy McMahon

Helping to put a down payment on Tracy's Tennessee home.

1977

LOUISE
Producer: Paul Rothchild
Album: Sweet Forgiveness
Record Label: Warner Brothers
Songwriter: Paul Siebel

Down-and-out character portrait was a staple of Raitt's act for years.

1982

ME AND THE BOYS
Producer: Rob Fraboni
Album: Green Light
Record Label: Warner Brothers
Songwriter: Terry Adams

Covered by Dave Edmunds (Columbia, '82). Adams' band, NRBQ, covered it on God Bless Us All (Rounder, '87).

1991

SOMETHING TO TALK ABOUT
Producers: Don Was, Bonnie Raitt
Album: Luck of the Draw
Record Label: Capitol
Songwriter: Shirley Eikhard

Middle-of-the-dirt-road, hit establishes Bonnie as the Queen of the Baby Boom Hop at last.

1994

LOVE SNEAKIN' UP ON YOU
Producers: Don Was, Bonnie Raitt
Album: Longing in Their Hearts
Record Label: Capitol
Songwriters: Tom Snow, Jim Scott

Now just middle-of-the-road.

EDDIE RAMBEAU

1965

CONCRETE AND CLAY
Producer: Bob Crewe
Album: Concrete and Clay
Record Label: Dyno Voice
Songwriters: Tommy Moeller, Brian Parker

THE RAMONES

1976

BEAT ON THE BRAT
Producer: Craig Leon
Album: The Ramones
Record Label: Sire
Songwriters: Douglas Colvin, John Cummings, Jeff Hyman, Thomas Erdelyi

Stellar anti-Folk Rock rant begets a new teen revolution of the working class.

BLITZKRIEG BOP
Producer: Craig Leon
Album: The Ramones
Record Label: Sire

1982

Songwriters: Douglas Colvin, John Cummings, Jeff Hyman, Thomas Erdelyi

A three-chord band anthem to do "Louie Louie" proud.

I WANNA BE YOUR BOYFRIEND
Producer: Craig Leon
Album: The Ramones
Record Label: Sire
Songwriters: Douglas Colvin, John Cummings, Jeff Hyman, Thomas Erdelyi

Joe Perry of Aerosmith described the adolescent condition best when he said it was like being "a hormone in a sneaker." The Ramones wore this costume on stage, lived it off stage, and wrote about it better than anyone.

TEENAGE LOBOTOMY
Producer: Craig Leon
Album: The Ramones
Record Label: Sire
Songwriters: Douglas Colvin, John Cummings, Jeff Hyman, Thomas Erdelyi

A one-joke band, repeating endlessly, endlessly repeatable.

1977

CARBONA NOT GLUE
Producers: Tony Bongiovi, Thomas Erdelyi
Album: Leave Home
Record Label: Sire
Songwriters: Douglas Colvin, John Cummings, Jeff Hyman, Thomas Erdelyi

Reviving the art of sniffing glue. Suggested segue: "Mellow Yellow" by Donovan.

GIMME GIMME SHOCK TREATMENT
Producers: Tony Bongiovi, Thomas Erdelyi
Album: Leave Home
Record Label: Sire
Songwriters: Douglas Colvin, John Cummings, Jeff Hyman, Thomas Erdelyi

Coming a year after "Teenage Lobotomy," an early warning sign that the Ramones might not be able to sustain their brain-draining barrage forever. Nearly twenty years later, however, they would cover Tom Waits' "I Don't Want to Grow Up" as proof that the struggle was still worth the effort.

PINHEAD

Producers: Tony Bongiovi, Thomas Erdelyi
Album: Leave Home
Record Label: Sire
Songwriters: Douglas Colvin, John Cummings, Jeff Hyman, Thomas Erdelyi

Perhaps a tribute to Foudini's dopey TV pal of the '50s. Then again, probably not.

ROCKAWAY BEACH

Producers: Tony Bongiovi, Thomas Erdelyi
Album: Leave Home
Record Label: Sire
Songwriters: Douglas Colvin, John Cummings, Jeff Hyman, Thomas Erdelyi

Shoulda been a contender, but failed to make it out of the Bottom-40.

SHEENA IS A PUNK ROCKER

Producers: Tony Bongiovi, Thomas Erdelyi
Album: Leave Home
Record Label: Sire
Songwriters: Douglas Colvin, John Cummings, Jeff Hyman, Thomas Erdelyi

Their first bid for Top-40 immortality failed miserably.

1978

I WANNA BE SEDATED

Album: Road to Ruin
Record Label: Sire
Songwriters: Douglas Colvin, John Cummings, Jeff Hyman

A future generation-X anthem. Featured in the '80 movie Times Square.

I WANTED EVERYTHING

Album: Road to Ruin
Record Label: Sire
Songwriters: Douglas Colvin, John Cummings, Jeff Hyman

Beginning to succumb to their missed opportunities.

I'M AGAINST IT

Album: Road to Ruin
Record Label: Sire
Songwriters: Douglas Colvin, John Cummings, Jeff Hyman

Staying true to type, at all costs.

1979

DO YOU REMEMBER ROCK AND ROLL RADIO

Producer: Phil Spector
Album: End of the Century
Record Label: Sire
Songwriters: Douglas Colvin, John Cummings, Jeff Hyman

Queens boys protest song, presented in a classic meeting of the titans.

1986

MY BRAIN IS HANGING UPSIDE DOWN (BONZO GOES TO BITBURG)

Producer: Jean Beauvoir
Album: Animal Boy
Record Label: Sire
Songwriters: Douglas Colvin, John Cummings, Jean Beauvoir

Their best protest song since "Do You Remember Rock and Roll Radio," about the time Reagan visited a Nazi cemetery.

TEDDY RANDAZZO

1957

KIDDIO

Record Label: Vik
Songwriters: Brook Benton, Clyde Otis

Introduced by Randazzo in the movie Mr. Rock and Roll. *Cover by Brook Benton (Mercury, '60) was a #1 R&B/Top-10 R&R crossover.*

RANDY AND THE RAINBOWS

1963

DENISE

Producer: The Tokens
Record Label: Rust
Songwriter: Neil Levenson

Essential suburban Doo-Wop. Cover by Blondie, in French (Chrysalis, '78) went to #1 U.K.

RANK AND FILE

1984

LONG GONE DEAD

Album: Long Gone Dead
Record Label: Slash
Songwriters: Chip Kinman, Tony Kinman

In the paisley days of a Folk Rock renaissance inspired by R.E.M. and the Bangles, a droning tribute to the Flying Burritos.

KENNY RANKIN

1972

PEACEFUL

Album: Like a Seed
Record Label: Little David
Songwriter: Kenny Rankin

Laid-back mellow East. Covered by Helen Reddy (Capitol, '73).

RARE EARTH

1971

I JUST WANT TO CELEBRATE

Producers: Tom Baird, Rare Earth
Album: One World
Record Label: Motown
Songwriters: Dino Fekaris, Nick Zesses

Party classic.

THE RASCALS

1965

I AIN'T GONNA EAT OUT MY HEART ANYMORE

Producers: Arif Mardin, the Rascals
Album: The Young Rascals
Record Label: Atlantic
Songwriters: Pam Sawyer, Laurie Burton

Liberated from the discos of 45th Street, the Young Rascals begin their Rock-n-Soul career with their hungriest rocker.

1967

A GIRL LIKE YOU

Producer: The Rascals
Album: Groovin'
Record Label: Atlantic
Songwriters: Felix Cavaliere, Edward Brigati Jr.

They mellow out, as befitting the season, and the marketplace.

GROOVIN'

Producer: The Rascals
Album: Groovin'
Record Label: Atlantic
Songwriters: Felix Cavaliere, Edward Brigati Jr.

The Rascals at their grooviest; this #1 R&R/Top-10 R&B crossover was based on bassist Chuck Rainey's groove, which was in turn, based on a Cuban dance rhythm called baion. Covered by Aretha Franklin (Atlantic, '68).

HOW CAN I BE SURE

Producer: The Rascals
Album: Groovin'
Record Label: Atlantic
Songwriters: Felix Cavaliere, Edward Brigati Jr.

Society on the brink of chaos, Felix Cavaliere on the brink of marriage, this existential Doo-Wop number was popular in certain Italian neighborhoods where time had stopped in 1958.

I'VE BEEN LONELY TOO LONG

Producers: The Rascals, Arif Mardin, Tom Dowd
Album: Rascals Greatest Hits (Time Peace)
Record Label: Atlantic
Songwriters: Felix Cavaliere, Edward Brigati Jr.

First single of '67 attests to Felix's desire to settle down.

1968

A BEAUTIFUL MORNING

Producer: The Rascals
Album: Rascals Greatest Hits (Time Peace)
Record Label: Atlantic
Songwriters: Felix Cavaliere, Edward Brigati Jr.

Blissed-out.

PEOPLE GOT TO BE FREE

Producer: The Rascals
Album: Freedom Suite
Record Label: Atlantic
Songwriters: Felix Cavaliere, Edward Brigati Jr.

Blue-skied Soul.

THE RASPBERRIES

1972

GO ALL THE WAY

Producer: Jimmy Ienner
Album: Raspberries
Record Label: Capitol
Songwriter: Eric Carmen

Frat Rock enters the post-liberated '70s.

1974

OVERNIGHT SENSATION (HIT RECORD)

Producer: Jimmy Ienner
Album: Starting Over
Record Label: Capitol
Songwriter: Eric Carmen

Having dropped out of the frat, Eric Carmen describes his encounter with reality. Eric would find future fame writing for the movies and the discos. Suggested segues: "So You Wanna Be a Rock and Roll Star" by the Byrds, "Rock and Roll I Gave You the Best Years of My Life" by Kevin Johnson.

GENYA RAVAN

1978

JERRY'S PIGEONS

Album: Urban Desire
Record Label: 20th Century
Songwriters: Charles Giordano, Joe Rebaudo, Genya Ravan

Out of Goldie & the Gingerbreads and Ten Wheel Drive, and fresh from producing the Dead Boys, a Rock and Roll lifer named Goldie Yelkowitz continues, a grown-up Shangri-la, if the Shangri-las had lived to grow up.

THE RAVENS

1947

OL' MAN RIVER

Record Label: National
Songwriters: Oscar Hammerstein II, Jerome Kern

From "Showboat," in which it was introduced by Paul Robeson. Covered by such secular luminaries as Aretha Franklin, Ray Charles, Sam Cooke, the Flamingos, and Duane and Greg in the Allman Joys. Influenced by the Mills Brothers, Baltimore's Ravens did the definitive Doo-Wop rendition, selling a couple million copies, and opening the black gateway of the Rock and Roll era to the hallowed halls of Tin Pan Alley. The Monotones were listening. So were the Temptations, and everyone else.

1950

COUNT EVERY STAR

Album: Write Me a Letter
Record Label: National
Songwriters: Bruno Coquatrix, Sammy Gallop

Hugo Winterhalter had the Pop hit (RCA, '50).

1952

ROCK ME ALL NIGHT LONG

Record Label: Mercury
Songwriters: Jimmy Ricks, Bill Sanford

Their biggest R&B hit. Covered by Ella Mae Morse (Capitol, '54).

RAY, GOODMAN AND BROWN

1979

SPECIAL LADY

Producer: Vince Castellano
Album: Ray, Goodman and Brown
Record Label: Polydor
Songwriters: Harold Ray, Al Goodman, L. Walter

#1 R&B/Top-10 R&R crossover.

JAMES RAY

1962

GOT MY MIND SET ON YOU

Record Label: Dynamic Sound
Songwriter: Rudy Clark

Covered by George Harrison (Dark Horse, '88).

IF YOU GOTTA MAKE A FOOL OF SOMEBODY

Producer: Neil Galligan
Record Label: Caprice
Songwriter: Rudy Clark

Top-10 R&B/Top-30 R&R crossover. Covered by Maxine Brown (Wand, '66).

JOHNNY RAY

1951

CRY

Record Label: Okeh
Songwriter: Churchill Kohlman

The #1 Pop record of '52 was the first example of a white song crossing over to the R&B charts (where it was also #1).

1955

YES, TONIGHT JOSEPHINE

Record Label: Okeh
Songwriters: Winfield Scott, Dorothy Goodman

Second only to "Gloria" in the Rock honor roll of girl's names. Ray's song was number one in the U.K., where Jimmy Page might have been listening. The last Yardbirds single was entitled "Goodnight Sweet Josephine."

RAYDIO

1977

JACK AND JILL

Producer: Ray Parker Jr.
Album: Raydio
Record Label: Arista
Songwriter: Ray Parker Jr.

First hit for the Ray Parker-led R&B group, a Top-10 R&B/Top-10 R&R crossover.

1979

YOU CAN'T CHANGE THAT
Producer: Ray Parker Jr.
Album: Rock On
Record Label: Arista
Songwriter: Ray Parker Jr.
Top-10 R&B/Top-10 R&R crossover.

1981

A WOMAN NEEDS LOVE (JUST LIKE YOU DO)
Producer: Ray Parker Jr.
Album: A Woman Needs Love
Record Label: Arista
Songwriter: Ray Parker Jr.
With featured billing, Ray Parker steps out as a new Soul man of the '80s.

THE RAYS
1957

SILHOUETTES
Record Label: Cameo
Songwriters: Frank Slay Jr., Bob Crewe
Teen Doo-Wop classic with the Philadelphia sound. Suggested segue: "Fool in the Rain" by Led Zeppelin.

CHRIS REA
1977

FOOL (IF YOU THINK ITS OVER)
Producer: Gus Dudgeon
Album: Whatever Happened to Benny Santini?
Record Label: Magnet
Songwriter: Chris Rea
Working-class British Rock.

READY FOR THE WORLD
1985

OH SHEILA
Album: Ready for the World
Record Label: MCA
Songwriters: Melvin Riley, Gordon Strozier, Gerald Valentine
#1 R&B/#1 R&R crossover.

1986

LOVE YOU DOWN
Album: Long Time Coming
Record Label: MCA
Songwriters: Melvin Riley, Gordon Strozier, Gerald Valentine
#1 R&B/Top-10 R&R crossover.

REAL MCCOY
1994

ANOTHER NIGHT
Producers: J. Wind, Quickmix, Ojay
Album: Real McCoy
Record Label: Arista
Songwriters: Jai Winding, Patricia Peterson, Olaf Jeglitza
Massive '90s Euro-Disco-groove.

RED CROSS
1980

ANNETTE'S GOT THE HITS
Album: Red Cross
Record Label: Posh Boy
Songwriters: Steve McDonald, Jeff McDonald
Low-fi underground Punk staple of L.A. radio.

I HATE MY SCHOOL
Album: Red Cross
Record Label: Posh Boy
Songwriters: Steve McDonald, Jeff McDonald
The Ramones meet Jonathan Richman at Brian Wilson's house.

1982

CEASE TO EXIST
Album: Born Innocent
Record Label: Smoke 7
Songwriter: Charles Manson
Taking their Los Angelino mythology too far.

RED KROSS
1990

BUBBLEGUM FACTORY
Album: Third Eye
Record Label: Atlantic
Songwriter: Jeff McDonald
Major label debut. To avoid conflict with the real Red Cross, their name has been changed to protect the innocent.

RED HOT CHILI PEPPERS
1985

CATHOLIC SCHOOL GIRLS RULE
Producer: George Clinton
Album: Freaky Styley
Record Label: Enigma/EMI-America
Songwriters: Anthony Kiedis, Michael Balzary (Flea), Hirth Martinez
Getting off to a funking good start, courtesy of their mentor in crime, George Clinton. Suggested segue: "Only the Good Die Young" by Billy Joel.

1991

GIVE IT AWAY
Producer: Rick Rubin
Album: Blood Sugar Sex Majik
Record Label: Warner Brothers
Songwriters: Anthony Kiedis, Michael Balzary (Flea), John Frusciante, Chad Smith
"Summer of Love" sentiments with a '90s snarl.

1991

UNDER THE BRIDGE
Producer: Rick Rubin
Album: Blood Sugar Sex Magik
Record Label: Warner Brothers
Songwriters: Anthony Kiedis, Michael Balzary (Flea), John Frusciante, Chad Smith
Arena Rock recovery ballad breakthrough. Suggested segue: "I Love L.A." by Randy Newman.

1993

SOUL TO SQUEEZE
Album: *The Coneheads* Soundtrack
Record Label: Sire
Songwriters: Anthony Kiedis, Michael Balzary (Flea), John Frusciante, Chad Smith
Cloning their Arena Rock breakthrough ballad.

REDBONE
1974

COME AND GET YOUR LOVE
Producers: Pat Vegas, Lolly Vegas
Album: Wouoka
Record Label: Epic
Songwriter: Lolly Vegas
The '70s AM radio sound.

OTIS REDDING
1963

THESE ARMS OF MINE
Producer: Jim Stewart
Album: The History of Otis Redding
Record Label: Volt
Songwriter: Otis Redding
First R&B/R&R crossover for the John Henry of Soul music, hoisting the scene on his back like a nine-pound hammer.

SECURITY

1964

Producer: Jim Stewart
Album: Pain in My Heart
Record Label: Atco
Songwriter: Otis Redding

Covered by Etta James (Cadet, '68).

1965

I CAN'T TURN YOU LOOSE

Producers: Otis Redding, Jim
Stewart, Steve Cropper
Album: Otis Redding Live in Europe
Record Label: Volt
Songwriters: Otis Redding, Steve
Cropper, McElvoy Robinson

Updating Little Richard for the age of Soul. Originally the B-side of "Just One More Day." Covered by the Chambers Brothers (Columbia, '68).

I'VE BEEN LOVING YOU TOO LONG

Producer: Steve Cropper
Album: The Great Otis Redding
Sings Soul Ballads
Record Label: Volt
Songwriters: Jerry Butler, Otis
Redding

This signature ballad was his second biggest R&B/R&R crossover and one of the more transcendent moments of the Monterey Pop Festival, two years later. Covered by Ike and Tina Turner (Blue Thumb, '69).

MR. PITIFUL

Producer: Steve Cropper
Album: The Great Otis Redding
Sings Soul Ballads
Record Label: Volt
Songwriters: Otis Redding, Steve
Cropper

Diving into a Soul/Blues stereotype.

RESPECT

Producer: Steve Cropper
Album: Otis Blue/Otis Redding Sings
Soul
Record Label: Volt
Songwriter: Otis Redding

An anthem for the downtrodden everywhere. Top-5 R&B/Top-40 R&R crossover. Cover by Aretha Franklin (Atlantic, '67) was a #1 R&B/#1 R&R crossover, springing Otis as well as Aretha nationwide.

THAT'S HOW STRONG MY LOVE IS

Producer: Steve Cropper
Album: The Great Otis Redding
Sings Soul Ballads
Record Label: Volt
Songwriters: O. V. Wright, Roosevelt
Jamison

Wright cut the song, too, a superior ballad, but Otis beat him to the punch.

1966

FA-FA-FA-FA-FA (SAD SONG)

Producers: Otis Redding, Jim
Stewart, Steve Cropper
Album: Dictionary of Soul
Record Label: Volt
Songwriters: Otis Redding, Steve
Cropper

Elemental Soul noodling.

TRY A LITTLE TENDERNESS

Producers: Otis Redding, Jim
Stewart, Steve Cropper
Album: Dictionary of Soul
Record Label: Volt
Songwriters: Harry Woods, Jimmy
Campbell, Reg Connerly

Popularized by Ruth Etting in '32, renovated and rehabilitated by Otis a generation later.

1968

(SITTIN' ON) THE DOCK OF THE BAY

Producer: Steve Cropper
Album: Dock of the Bay
Record Label: Volt
Songwriters: Otis Redding, Steve
Cropper

His mournful poignant farewell, folkish and elegiac; his first and only #1 R&B/#1 R&R crossover, posthumously.

HARD TO HANDLE

Producer: Steve Cropper
Album: Immortal Otis Redding
Record Label: Volt
Songwriters: Otis Redding, Alvertis
Isbell, Booker T. Jones

Intense and rocking B-side of "Amen." Covered by the Black Crowes (Def American, '90). Featured in the '92 movie The Commitments.

I'VE GOT DREAMS TO REMEMBER

Producer: Steve Cropper
Album: Immortal Otis Redding
Record Label: Atco
Songwriters: Otis Redding, Velma
Redding, Joe Rock

Soul ballad heaven.

OLE MAN TROUBLE

Producer: Steve Cropper
Album: Dock of the Bay
Record Label: Volt
Songwriter: Otis Redding

One of his greatest performances.

HELEN REDDY

1972

I AM WOMAN

Producer: Tom Catalano
Album: I Am Woman
Record Label: Capitol
Songwriters: Helen Reddy, Ray
Burton

Women's lib goes to Las Vegas.

1973

LEAVE ME ALONE (RUBY RED DRESS)

Album: Long Hard Climb
Record Label: Capitol
Songwriter: Linda Laurie

By Linda Laurie, the girl who sang "Ambrose Part V."

1974

ANGIE BABY

Producer: Joe Wissert
Album: Free and Easy
Record Label: Capitol
Songwriter: Alan O' Day

She was no "Ruby Red Dress."

JERRY REED

1967

GUITAR MAN

Producer: Chet Atkins
Album: The Unbelievable Guitar and
Voice of Jerry Reed
Record Label: RCA
Songwriters: Jerry Reed

Stiffed on the Country chart, but the cover by Elvis Presley became his last #1 C&W hit.

U.S. MALE

Producer: Chet Atkins
Album: The Unbelievable Guitar and Voice of Jerry Reed
Record Label: RCA
Songwriter: Jerry Reed

Covered by Elvis Presley (RCA, '68).

1971

AMOS MOSES

Album: Georgia Sunshine
Record Label: RCA
Songwriter: Jerry Reed

Cashing in the Elvis chips, with a Top-20 C&W/Top-10 R&R crossover.

WHEN YOU'RE HOT, YOU'RE HOT

Album: When You're Hot, You're Hot
Record Label: RCA
Songwriter: Jerry Reed

On a roll, with a rollicking #1 C&W/Top-10 R&R crossover. Reed would also write "She Got the Goldmine, I Got the Shaft."

JIMMY REED

1955

AIN'T THAT LOVIN' YOU BABY

Record Label: Vee-Jay
Songwriter: Jimmy Reed

Deceptively simple, influential, and hypnotic R&B; Chuck Berry without the irony. Covered by the Youngbloods (RCA, '67) and Elvis Presley (RCA, '68).

1956

YOU GOT ME DIZZY

Record Label: Vee-Jay
Songwriters: Jimmy Reed, Ewart Abner Jr.

1957

HONEST I DO

Record Label: Vee-Jay
Songwriters: Jimmy Reed, Ewart Abner Jr.

His biggest R&R hit.

1960

BABY, WHAT YOU WANT ME TO DO

Album: New Jimmy Reed Album
Record Label: Vee-Jay
Songwriter: Jimmy Reed

His most enduring classic. Covered by the Everly Brothers (Warner Brothers, '60), Etta James (Argo, '64), the Righteous Brothers (Moonglow, '65), Carla Thomas (Stax, '66), Arthur Conley (Atco, '67), Elvis Presley (RCA, '68), the Byrds (Columbia, '69), Ike

and Tina Turner (United Artists, '71), Jerry Lee Lewis (Mercury, '73) and Johnny and Edgar Winter (Blue Sky, '76).

1961

BIG BOSS MAN

Producer: Calvin Carter
Album: New Jimmy Reed Album
Record Label: Vee-Jay
Songwriters: Al Smith, Luther Dixon

One of Reed's grittiest statements. Covered by John Hammond Jr. (Vanguard, '65), Elvis Presley (RCA, '67), and the Grateful Dead (Warner Brothers, '71).

BRIGHT LIGHTS, BIG CITY

Record Label: Vee-Jay
Songwriter: Jimmy Reed

His biggest R&B hit, Covered by the Animals (MGM, '65) and Neil Young (Reprise, '83).

LOU REED

1972

OCEAN

Album: Lou Reed
Record Label: RCA
Songwriter: Lou Reed

An early solo classic.

SATELLITE OF LOVE

Producer: David Bowie
Album: Transformer
Record Label: RCA
Songwriter: Lou Reed

Sincere Lou. Covered by U2 (Island, '92).

VICIOUS

Producer: David Bowie
Album: Transformer
Record Label: RCA
Songwriter: Lou Reed

Putting down the hippies ("You hit me with a flower"), with his version of "Positively 4th Street."

WALK ON THE WILD SIDE

Producers: David Bowie, Lou Reed, Mick Ronson
Album: Transformer
Record Label: RCA
Songwriter: Lou Reed

The clean version of Andy Warhol's mock documentary Chelsea Girls, gives Lou Reed a brief commercial visibility. He would move on from there to become the weathered voice of a lost generation, eventually to get his own Harley spot (or was it Kawasaki?).

1973

BERLIN

Producer: Bob Ezrin
Album: Lou Reed
Record Label: RCA
Songwriter: Lou Reed

Lou visits the spiritual home of Glam Rock on one of his more critically reviled efforts.

1974

KILL YOUR SONS

Producer: Steve Katz
Album: Sally Can't Dance
Record Label: RCA
Songwriter: Lou Reed

Responding to a dose of shock treatment. Suggested segues: "Gimme Gimme Shock Treatment" by the Ramones, "Knockin' Around the Zoo" by James Taylor.

SALLY CAN'T DANCE

Producer: Steve Katz
Album: Sally Can't Dance
Record Label: RCA
Songwriter: Lou Reed

Covered by the Andrea True Connection (Buddah, '77).

1976

CONEY ISLAND BABY

Producer: Lou Reed
Album: Coney Island Baby
Record Label: RCA
Songwriter: Lou Reed

In this tribute to Doo-Wop (and "Coney Island Baby" by the Excellents), Lou stakes his claim as the essential, nasal voice of Long Island, leaving Billy Joel in the dunes off Jones Beach.

1978

DIRT

Producers: Lou Reed, Richard Robinson
Album: Street Hassle
Record Label: Arista
Songwriter: Lou Reed

I WANNA BE BLACK

Producer: Lou Reed
Album: Street Hassle
Record Label: Arista
Songwriter: Lou Reed

Long-time performance highlight. Suggested segue: "Hail Hail Rock and Roll" by Garland Jeffreys.

THE BELLS
1979

Album: The Bells
Record Label: Arista
Songwriter: Lou Reed

One of Reed's personal all-time favorites.

I LOVE YOU, SUZANNE
1984

Album: New Sensations
Record Label: RCA
Songwriter: Lou Reed

Letting down his infamous guard.

NO MONEY DOWN
1986

Producers: Fernando Saunders, Lou Reed
Album: Mistrial
Record Label: RCA
Songwriter: Lou Reed

Answering Chuck Berry with his catchiest tune.

DIRTY BOULEVARD
1989

Producers: Fred Maher, Lou Reed
Album: New York
Record Label: Sire
Songwriter: Lou Reed

Like Springsteen (New Jersey) or the Beach Boys (L.A.), Lou sums up his adopted hometown as well as or better than Neil Diamond (Brooklyn), Dion (the Bronx), or Paul Simon (Queens).

HOLD ON

Producers: Fred Maher, Lou Reed
Album: New York
Record Label: Sire
Songwriter: Lou Reed

Critically acclaimed track from his most critically acclaimed album.

WHAT'S GOOD
1991

Producers: Lou Reed, Mike Rathke
Album: Magic and Loss
Record Label: Sire
Songwriters: Lou Reed, Mike Rathke

One of the most life-affirming death songs; dedicated to the memory of Doc Pomus.

LOU REED AND JOHN CALE

HELLO, IT'S ME
1989

Producers: John Cale, Lou Reed
Album: Songs for Drella
Record Label: Sire
Songwriters: Lou Reed, John Cale

Reuniting fellow Velvets Reed and Cole, this deathbed homage as performance piece debuted at the Brooklyn Academy of Music. Dedicated to the memory of their mentor, Andy Warhol. Tunes in this personal memoir include "Forever Changed," "The Trouble with Classicists," "Smalltown Boy," and "Work."

DELLA REESE

DON'T YOU KNOW
1959

Album: Don't You Know
Record Label: RCA
Songwriter: Bobby Worth

This standard ballad, adapted from "La Bohème," was a #1 R&B/#2 R&R crossover. The following year, labelmate Elvis Presley turned "O Sole Mio" into "It's Now or Never."

JIM REEVES

FOUR WALLS
1957

Producer: Chet Atkins
Album: Four Walls
Record Label: RCA
Songwriters: Marvin Moore, George Campbell

First #1 C&W/Top-20 R&R crossover for the deep-voiced Country Pop crooner.

HE'LL HAVE TO GO
1959

Producer: Chet Atkins
Album: He'll Have to Go
Record Label: RCA
Songwriters: Joe Allison, Audrey Allison

Amidst the year's teen celebrations, a decidedly adult- (not to say mature-) oriented Country ballad. #1 C&W/Top-10 R&R crossover. Answered in "He'll Have to Stay" by Jeanne Black (Capitol, '60). Reeves would remain obsessed with this theme for the rest of his life.

THE REFLECTIONS

(JUST LIKE) ROMEO AND JULIET
1964

Producer: Rob Reeco
Album: (Just Like) Romeo and Juliet
Record Label: Golden World
Songwriters: Bob Hamilton, Freddy Gorman

Teen fantasy. Covered by Sha-Na-Na (Buddah, '74).

THE REGENTS

BARBARA ANN
1961

Producers: Morris Diamond, Lou Cicchetti
Album: Barbara Ann
Record Label: Gee
Songwriter: Fred Fassert

From Dion & the Belmonts' Bronx neighborhood, quintessential white Doo-Wop. Covered on the West coast by the Beach Boys (Capitol, '65).

REGINA

BABY LOVE
1986

Producer: Steve Bray
Album: Curiosity
Record Label: Atlantic
Songwriters: Steve Bray, Regina Richards, Mary Kessler

Bray is better known for his work with Madonna.

THE REMBRANDTS

JUST THE WAY IT IS BABY
1991

Album: The Rembrandts
Record Label: Atco
Songwriters: Phil Solem, Denny Wilde

Solem and Wilde would be better known for performing the hit theme for the TV show "Friends" a few years later.

RENAISSANCE

ASHES ARE BURNING
1973

Album: Ashes Are Burning
Record Label: Sovereign
Songwriters: Michael Dunford, Betty Mary Thatcher

Folk Rock breakthrough for the traditional English Folk sound.

DIANE RENAY
1963

NAVY BLUE
Producer: Bob Crewe
Album: Navy Blue
Record Label: 20th Century-Fox
Songwriters: Bob Crewe, Bud Rehak, Eddie Rambeau

A celebration of sailors, or men in uniform in general. Within a few years that would dramatically change.

RENE AND ANGELA
1985

YOUR SMILE
Album: Street Called Desire
Record Label: Mercury
Songwriters: Angela Winbush, Rene Moore

#1 R&B/Top-40 R&R crossover.

MIKE RENO AND ANN WILSON
1984

ALMOST PARADISE (LOVE THEME FROM *FOOTLOOSE*)
Album: *Footloose* Soundtrack
Record Label: Columbia
Songwriters: Dean Pitchford, Eric Carmen

Big movie ballad, sung by the lead singers of Loverboy and Heart, respectively.

REO SPEEDWAGON
1978

TIME FOR ME TO FLY
Producer: Kevin Cronin
Album: You Can Tune a Piano But You Can't Tuna Fish
Record Label: Epic
Songwriter: Kevin Cronin Jr.

Commercial breakthrough for the Midwestern warhorse road band.

1980

KEEP ON LOVING YOU
Producers: Kevin Cronin Jr., Gary Richrath, Kevin Beamish
Album: Hi Infidelity
Record Label: Epic
Songwriter: Kevin Cronin Jr.

Having gained an inch on the radio, they burst through the door with both shoulders for their first #1 hit. It would take years to get them to leave.

TAKE IT ON THE RUN
Producers: Kevin Cronin Jr., Gary Richrath, Kevin Beamish
Album: Hi Infidelity
Record Label: Epic
Songwriter: Gary Richrath

1982

KEEP THE FIRE BURNIN'
Producers: Kevin Cronin Jr., Gary Richrath, Kevin Beamish, Alan Gratzer
Album: Good Trouble
Record Label: Epic
Songwriter: Kevin Cronin

1985

CAN'T FIGHT THIS FEELING
Producers: Kevin Cronin Jr., Gary Richrath, Alan Gratzer
Album: Wheels Are Turning
Record Label: Epic
Songwriter: Kevin Cronin

Their biggest hit, an Arena ballad, of course.

REPARATA AND THE DELRONS
1964

WHENEVER A TEENAGER CRIES
Producers: Bill Jerome, Steve Jerome
Album: Whenever a Teenager Cries
Record Label: World Artists
Songwriter: Ernie Maresca

Low-rent version of the Shangri-las. Written by the Shadow Morton of the Bronx.

THE REPLACEMENTS
1984

I WILL DARE
Producers: Steve Fjelstad, Paul Westerberg
Album: Let It Be
Record Label: Twin/Tone
Songwriter: Paul Westerberg

Westerberg steps out from his raw Punk beginnings to create the nearest thing to a Minnesota acoustic masterpiece since Bob Zimmerman left Hibbing for Greenwich Village.

UNSATISFIED
Album: Let It Be
Record Label: Twin Tone
Songwriter: Paul Westerberg

Their answer to "(I Can't Get No) Satisfaction" by the Rolling Stones.

1985

HERE COMES A REGULAR
Producer: Tommy Erdelyi
Album: Tim
Record Label: Sire
Songwriter: Paul Westerberg

Honing their sloppy-drunk, sad, rebellious, Alternative image for mass consumption, with the help of a Ramone.

KISS ME ON THE BUS
Producer: Tommy Erdelyi
Album: Tim
Record Label: Sire
Songwriter: Paul Westerberg

The eloquent misery of the teenage condition. Their neighbors, Soul Asylum, were paying attention.

SWINGIN' PARTY
Producer: Tommy Erdelyi
Album: Tim
Record Label: Sire
Songwriter: Paul Westerberg

In Seattle, Kurt Cobain was feeling a similar pain.

1987

ALEX CHILTON
Producer: Jim Dickinson
Album: Pleased to Meet Me
Record Label: Sire
Songwriters: Paul Westerberg, Tom Stinson, Chris Mars

Elegizing a minor deity of Alternative Rock culture, and becoming ones themselves in the process.

CAN'T HARDLY WAIT
Producer: Jim Dickinson
Album: Pleased to Meet Me
Record Label: Sire
Songwriter: Paul Westerberg

1989

ACHIN' TO BE
Producers: Matt Wallace, the Replacements
Album: Don't Tell a Soul
Record Label: Sire
Songwriter: Paul Westerberg

His ultimate Punk Folk ballad—Westerberg achin' to be mainstream.

I'LL BE YOU
Producers: Matt Wallace, the Replacements
Album: Don't Tell a Soul

Record Label: Sire
Songwriter: Paul Westerberg

Their closest thing to a hit single.

TALENT SHOW

Producers: Matt Wallace, the
Replacements
Album: Don't Tell a Soul
Record Label: Sire
Songwriter: Paul Westerberg

Muted anthem for local bands everywhere.

1990

MERRY GO ROUND

Producers: Scott Litt, Paul
Westerberg
Album: All Shook Down
Record Label: Sire
Songwriter: Paul Westerberg

Moving into R.E.M. territory, before the breakup.

RESTLESS HEART

1992

WHEN SHE CRIES

Producers: Josh Leo, Restless Heart
Album: Big Iron Horses
Record Label: RCA
Songwriters: Marc Beeson, Sonny
Lemaire

When Country started crossing over again, this Pop Rock ballad went Top-10 C&W/Top-10 R&R.

REUNION

1974

LIFE IS A ROCK (BUT THE RADIO ROLLED ME)

Record Label: RCA
Songwriters: Norman Dolph, Paul
DiFranco

Twenty years of Top-40 history in two minutes. Covered by Tracy Ullman (MCA, '84). Sung by a man who'd participated in about 19.2% of it, The Golden Throated Joey Levine (The Voice of Bubblegum).

PAUL REVERE & THE RAIDERS

1966

(I'M NOT YOUR) STEPPIN' STONE

Producer: Terry Melcher
Album: Midnight Rider
Record Label: Columbia
Songwriters: Tommy Boyce, Bobby
Hart

This malleable song of personal protest was covered by the Monkees (Colgems, '66) and the Sex Pistols in the film The Great Rock 'n' Roll Swindle *(Warner Brothers, '80).*

KICKS

Producer: Terry Melcher
Album: Midnight Ride
Record Label: Columbia
Songwriters: Barry Mann, Cynthia
Weil

Reacting to the reaction, the staff songwriting mainstream strikes back against the counter-culture. Revere & the Raiders gain their first and biggest hit after many moons of trying.

1967

GOOD THING

Producer: Terry Melcher
Album: The Spirit of '67
Record Label: Columbia
Songwriters: Terry Melcher, Mark
Lindsay, Paul Revere

HIM OR ME, WHAT'S IT GONNA BE

Producer: Terry Melcher
Album: Revolution
Record Label: Columbia
Songwriters: Mark Lindsay, Terry
Melcher

Their fifth Top-10 hit.

HUNGRY

Producer: Terry Melcher
Album: The Spirit of '67
Record Label: Columbia
Songwriters: Barry Mann, Cynthia
Weil

Finally tasting fame after a long apprenticeship.

DEBBIE REYNOLDS

1957

TAMMY

Album: *Tammy and The Bachelor* Soundtrack
Record Label: Coral
Songwriters: Jay Livingston, Ray
Evans

The ultimate wispy, ethereal girlsong: Olivia Newton-John, nine years old, saw her future. Natalie Merchant and Harriet Wheeler, not even born yet, would carry it on. Paul Simon would marry Debbie's daughter, Carrie, briefly.

JODY REYNOLDS

1958

ENDLESS SLEEP

Record Label: Demon
Songwriters: Jody Reynolds,
Dolores Nance

Reynolds' double-suicide dirge inaugurates a new "Bandstand" craze: the dance of death. Suggested segue: "Wall of Death" by Richard and Linda Thompson.

RHYTHM HERITAGE

1975

THEME FROM *S.W.A.T.*

Producers: Steve Barri, Michael
Omartian
Album: Disco-Fied
Record Label: ABC
Songwriter: Barry DeVorzon

Popular ersatz Disco Jazz that would dominate detective show TV soundtracks and especially NBA broadcasts of the Dr. J era.

RHYTHM SYNDICATE

1991

P.A.S.S.I.O.N.

Producers: Carl Sturken, Evan
Rodgers
Album: Rhythm Syndicate
Record Label: Impact
Songwriters: Carl Sturken, Evan
Rogers

Neo-Disco illiteracy.

SIR MACK RICE

1965

MUSTANG SALLY

Record Label: Blue Rock
Songwriter: Bonnie Rice

Car song classic: classic car, the Ford Mustang. Covered by Wilson Pickett (Atlantic, '66) and the Young Rascals (Atlantic, '66).

CHARLIE RICH

1960

LONELY WEEKENDS

Album: Greatest Hits
Record Label: Phillips International
Songwriter: Charlie Rich

His first hit is soft Rockabilly in the Elvis mode, but much more vulnerable. Suggested segue: "Lonely Saturday Night" by Don French.

1965

MOHAIR SAM
Record Label: Smash
Songwriter: Dallas Frazier
Funky follow-up, five years later.

1973

BEHIND CLOSED DOORS
Producer: Billy Sherrill
Album: Behind Closed Doors
Record Label: Epic
Songwriter: Kenny O'Dell
Exemplary Nashville opus gives Rich a long-awaited #1 C&W/Top-10 R&R.

THE MOST BEAUTIFUL GIRL
Producer: Billy Sherrill
Album: Behind Closed Doors
Record Label: Epic
Songwriters: Norro Wilson, Billy Sherrill, Rory Bourke
A rare #1 C&W/R&R crossover for the Sun veteran. Norro Wilson's version (Smash, '68) called "Hey Mister" stiffed.

CLIFF RICHARD

1959

LIVING DOLL
Album: Cliff Sings
Record Label: ABC/Paramount
Songwriter: Lionel Bart
The Elvis of England wasn't even Ricky Nelson over here. He'd be back (more than once), but not before Lionel Bart, who beat him to stardom as the composer of the '63 Broadway musical "Oliver." His backing band, the Drifters, would evolve into the Shadows.

1976

DEVIL WOMAN
Producer: Bruce Welch
Album: I'm Nearly Famous
Record Label: Rocket
Songwriters: Christine Authors, Terry Britten
First big U.S. hit.

1979

WE DON'T TALK ANYMORE
Producer: Bruce Welch
Album: We Don't Talk Anymore
Record Label: EMI-American
Songwriter: Al Tarney
Middle-of-the-road Pop Rock.

1980

DREAMING
Producer: Alan Tarney
Album: I'm No Hero
Record Label: EMI-America
Songwriters: Alan Tarney, Leo Sayer

KEITH RICHARDS

1988

TAKE IT SO HARD
Producers: Steve Jordan, Keith Richards
Album: Talk Is Cheap
Record Label: Virgin
Songwriters: Keith Richards, Steve Jordan
Rare solo effort by the Rolling Stones' lead guitarist/songwriter. Luckily, he never gave up his night job.

LIONEL RICHIE

1981

ENDLESS LOVE
Album: *Endless Love* Soundtrack
Record Label: Motown
Songwriter: Lionel B. Richie
First #1 R&B/R&R crossover for the former leader of the Commodores, sung with Motown princess Diana Ross. This treacly ballad did almost as much to undermine the brilliance of the Scott Spencer novel as the casting, directing, and screenwriting of the movie.

1983

ALL NIGHT LONG (ALL NIGHT)
Producers: Lionel Richie, James Carmichael
Album: Can't Slow Down
Record Label: Motown
Songwriter: Lionel B. Richie
His third #1 R&R, second #1 R&R/#1 R&B crossover was Motown's then-top-selling single of all-time. Sung at the '84 Olympic games in LA.

HELLO
Producers: Lionel Richie, James Carmichael
Album: Can't Slow Down
Record Label: Motown
Songwriter: Lionel B. Richie
#1 R&B/R&R crossover ballad.

RUNNING WITH THE NIGHT
Producers: Lionel Richie, James Carmichael
Album: Can't Slow Down

Record Label: Motown
Songwriter: Lionel B. Richie

1985

DANCING ON THE CEILING
Album: Dancing on the Ceiling
Record Label: Motown
Songwriters: Lionel B. Richie, Carlos Rios

SAY YOU, SAY ME
Album: Dancing on the Ceiling
Record Label: Motown
Songwriter: Lionel B. Richie
#1 R&B/R&R crossover Oscar winner from the movie White Nights.

1992

DO IT TO ME
Album: Back to Front
Record Label: Motown
Songwriter: Lionel B. Richie
#1 R&B/Top-30 R&R crossover.

STAN RIDGWAY

1986

WALKING HOME ALONE
Album: The Big Heat
Record Label: I.R.S.
Songwriter: Stan Ridgway
Solo effort from Wall of Voodoo leader shows promise.

1989

A MISSION IN LIFE
Producers: J. Chiconelli, Stan Ridgway
Album: Mosquitos
Record Label: Geffen
Songwriter: Stan Ridgway
Promise fulfilled, in a big sleazy Raymond-Chandler-in-Hollywood-through-a-shot-glass epic.

RIGHT SAID FRED

1992

I'M TOO SEXY
Producer: Tommy D.
Album: Right Said Fred
Record Label: Charisma
Songwriters: Fred Fairbrass, Richard Fairbrass, Rob Manzoli
Tongue-in-cheek Disco number too close to the truth to be satirical. For instance, main claim to fame of one of the members: he once played the role of the guitar player in a Bob Dylan video.

THE RIGHTEOUS BROTHERS

1963

LITTLE LATIN LUPE LU
Album: Right Now
Record Label: Moonglow
Songwriter: Bill Medley

First hit for the blue-eyed Soul brothers. Covered by an early acolyte, Mitch Ryder and Detroit Wheels (New Voice, '66).

1964

YOU'VE LOST THAT LOVIN' FEELIN'
Producer: Phil Spector
Album: You've Lost That Lovin' Feelin'
Record Label: Philles
Songwriters: Barry Mann, Cynthia Weil, Phil Spector

Phil's epic, tumultuous Dear John letter to the music business was the Righteous Brothers' defining number. See you in Easy Rider, *Phil.*

1965

HUNG ON YOU
Producer: Phil Spector
Album: Back to Back
Record Label: Philles
Songwriters: Gerry Goffin, Carole King, Phil Spector

B-side of "Unchained Melody."

JUST ONCE IN MY LIFE
Producer: Phil Spector
Album: Just Once in My Life
Record Label: Philles
Songwriters: Gerry Goffin, Carole King, Phil Spector

1966

(YOU'RE MY) SOUL AND INSPIRATION
Producer: Bill Medley
Album: Soul and Inspiration
Record Label: Verve
Songwriters: Barry Mann, Cynthia Weil

Kicking off '66 with their biggest hit; Mann and Weil went on a hot streak as well.

1973

ROCK 'N' ROLL HEAVEN
Producers: Dennis Lambert, Brian Potter
Album: Give It to the People
Record Label: Haven

Songwriters: John Stevenson, Alan O'Day
Their third biggest hit.

CHERYL PEPSII RILEY

1988

THANKS FOR MY CHILD
Producer: Full Force
Album: Me, Myself and I
Record Label: Columbia
Songwriter: Full Force

#1 R&B/Top-40 R&R rallying cry for single mothers.

JEANNIE C. RILEY

1968

THE HARPER VALLEY PTA
Producer: Shelby Singleton
Album: The Harper Valley PTA
Record Label: Plantation
Songwriter: Tom T. Hall

The Country music equivalent of "Tommy," becoming a movie in '78 and a TV series in '81. Hall's sudsy classic was also a #1 C&W/#1 R&R crossover, only the second since "Big Bad John" by Jimmy Dean in '61—Bobby Goldsboro having accomplished the same feat with "Honey" barely five months before in April—making '68 the first year since '59 (with "The Three Bells" by the Browns and "The Battle of New Orleans" by Johnny Horton) to produce two such crossovers.

THE RINKY DINKS

1958

EARLY IN THE MORNING
Record Label: Atlantic
Songwriter: Bobby Darin

Recorded pseudonymously by Bobby Darin. Covered by Buddy Holly (Coral, '58).

THE RIP CHORDS

1963

HEY LITTLE COBRA
Producer: Terry Melcher
Album: Hey Little Cobra and Other Red Hot Hits
Record Label: Columbia
Songwriters: Marshal Howard Connors, Carol Connors

Classic car song. Carol Connors is the former Teddy Bear Annette Kleinbard.

MINNIE RIPERTON

1974

LOVIN' YOU
Producer: Stevie Wonder
Album: Perfect Angel
Record Label: Epic
Songwriters: Minnie Riperton, Richard Rudolph

Bravura effort for the gorgeous lead voice of the Rotary Connection.

THE RITCHIE FAMILY

1976

THE BEST DISCO IN TOWN
Producers: Jacques Morali, Ritchie Rome
Album: Arabian Nights
Record Label: Marlin
Songwriters: Henri Belolo, Jacques Morali, Phil Hurtt, Richard Rome

By the people behind The Village People.

JOHNNY RIVERS

1966

POOR SIDE OF TOWN
Producer: Lou Adler
Album: Changes
Record Label: Imperial
Songwriters: Johnny Rivers, Lou Adler

Country Rock in the Dickie Lee "Patches" mold.

SECRET AGENT MAN
Producer: Lou Adler
Album: . . . and I Know You Wanna Dance
Record Label: Imperial
Songwriters: Steve Barri, P. F. Sloan
TV themesong.

1968

SUMMER RAIN
Producer: Lou Adler
Album: Realizations
Record Label: Imperial
Songwriter: James Hendricks
A personal autobiographical peak.

THE RIVIERAS

1964

CALIFORNIA SUN
Album: Let's Have a Party
Record Label: Riviera

Songwriters: Henry Glover, Morris Levy

A couple of the most notorious titans of the early R&B/R&R era acquire writing credits on this essential surf number. Covered by a couple of notorious East coast bands, the Dictators (Epic, '75) and the Ramones (Sire, '77).

THE RIVILERS
1956

A THOUSAND STARS

Record Label: Flyright
Songwriter: Eugene Pearson

Covered by Kathy Young with the Innocents (Indigo, '60) and Billy Fury in the '74 film Stardust.

THE RIVINGTONS
1962

PAPA-OOM-MOW-MOW

Producers: Jack Levy, Adam Ross, Al Frazier
Album: Doing the Bird
Record Label: Liberty
Songwriters: Al Frazier, Turner Wilson Jr., Carl White, John Harris

Noted surf-backup band steps forward with West Coast Doo-Wop surf classic. Follow-up, "Mama-Oom-Mow-Mow" stiffed.

1963

THE BIRD IS THE WORD

Producers: Jack Levy , Adam Ross, Al Frazier
Album: Doing the Bird
Record Label: Liberty
Songwriters: Al Frazier, Turner Wilson Jr., Carl Whlte, John Harris

Frat Rock at its frothiest.

MARTY ROBBINS
1955

SINGING THE BLUES

Record Label: Columbia
Songwriter: Melvin Endsley

#1 C&W/Top-20 R&R crossover, covered by Guy Mitchell (Columbia, '55).

1957

A WHITE SPORT COAT (AND A PINK CARNATION)

Album: Rock N Roll N Robbins
Record Label: Columbia
Songwriter: Marty Robbins

#1 C&W/Top-10 R&R crossover and as close to Rockabilly as he'd ever come.

1959

EL PASO

Producer: Don Law
Album: Gunfighter Ballads and Trail Songs
Record Label: Columbia
Songwriter: Marty Robbins

#1 C&W/#1 R&R crossover. Epic story-song, ending in death.

1961

DON'T WORRY

Record Label: Columbia
Songwriter: Marty Robbins

#1 C&W/Top-10 R&R crossover.

ROBERT AND JOHNNY
1958

WE BELONG TOGETHER

Record Label: Old Town
Songwriters: Johnny Mitchell, Robert Carr, Sam Weiss

Early classic Doo-Wop/R&R crossover.

ROBBIE ROBERTSON
1983

BETWEEN TRAINS

Producer: Robbie Robertson
Album: *The King of Comedy* Soundtrack
Record Label: Warner Brothers
Songwriter: Robbie Robertson

His best post-Band ramblin' song.

1987

BROKEN ARROW

Producers: Robbie Robertson, Daniel Lanois
Album: Robbie Robertson
Record Label: Geffen
Songwriter: Robbie Robertson

Covered by Rod Stewart (Warner Brothers, '92).

SOMEWHERE DOWN THE CRAZY RIVER

Producers: Robbie Robertson, Daniel Lanois
Album: Robbie Robertson
Record Label: Geffen
Songwriter: Robbie Robertson

With Edge and Bono of U2.

THE ROBINS
1954

FRAMED

Producers: Jerry Leiber, Mike Stoller
Record Label: Spark
Songwriters: Jerry Leiber, Mike Stoller

Funky L.A. R&B situation, paving the way for the Coasters.

1954

RIOT IN CELL BLOCK #9

Producers: Jerry Leiber, Mike Stoller
Record Label: Spark
Songwriters: Jerry Leiber, Mike Stoller

Leiber and Stoller landmark, sung by the ubiquitous Richard Berry, author of "Louie Louie." Covered by Dr. Feelgood (Columbia, '76).

1955

SMOKEY JOE'S CAFE

Producers: Jerry Leiber, Mike Stoller
Album: Yakety Yak
Record Label: Spark
Songwriters: Jerry Leiber, Mike Stoller

Another of the songwriting team's epic L.A. story-songs, and the group's only R&B/R&R crossover. Would be moved, forty years later, lock, stock, and bass notes, to Broadway, as the venue for a Leiber and Stoller career review/revue. Covered by Loudon Wainwright (Columbia, '73).

ALVIN ROBINSON
1964

DOWN HOME GIRL

Producers: Jerry Leiber, Mike Stoller
Record Label: Red Bird
Songwriters: Jerry Leiber, Artie Butler

Covered by the Rolling Stones (London, '64).

SOMETHING YOU GOT

Producers: Jerry Leiber, Mike Stoller
Record Label: Tiger
Songwriter: Chris Kenner

Covered by Chuck Jackson and Maxine Brown (Wand, '65).

FENTON ROBINSON

1967

SOMEBODY LOAN ME A DIME

Record Label: Palos
Songwriter: Fenton Robinson

Covered by Boz Scaggs (with Duane Allman on guitar) as "Loan Me a Dime" (Atlantic, '69).

SMOKEY ROBINSON

1973

SWEET HARMONY

Producer: Smokey Robinson
Album: Smokey
Record Label: Tamla
Songwriter: Smokey Robinson

His first solo hit typifies his life's philosophy.

1975

BABY THAT'S BACKATCHA

Producer: Smokey Robinson
Album: Quiet Storm
Record Label: Tamla
Songwriter: Smokey Robinson

#1 R&B/Top-30 R&R crossover.

1976

QUIET STORM

Producer: Smokey Robinson
Album: Quiet Storm
Record Label: Tamla
Songwriters: Smokey Robinson, Rose Ella Jones

Minor impact on the charts, major impact on the course of R&B radio.

1979

CRUISIN'

Producer: Smokey Robinson
Album: Where There's Smoke
Record Label: Tamla
Songwriters: Smokey Robinson, Marvin Tarplin

Biggest hit of the '70s.

1981

BEING WITH YOU

Producer: George Tobin
Album: Being with You
Record Label: Tamla
Songwriter: Smokey Robinson

Biggest solo hit for the Motown veep; #1 R&B/Top-10 R&R crossover.

1987

JUST TO SEE HER

Producers: Pete Bunetta, Rick Chudacoff
Album: One Heartbeat
Record Label: Motown
Songwriters: Jimmy George, Lou Pardini

Hitting his best groove of the '80s; a Top-5 R&B/Top-10 R&R crossover.

ONE HEARTBEAT

Producers: Pete Bunetta, Rick Chudacoff
Album: One Heartbeat
Record Label: Motown
Songwriters: S. Legassick, B. Wray

His last Top-10 R&B/Top-10 R&R crossover to date.

TOM ROBINSON

1978

GLAD TO BE GAY

Producer: Chas Thomas
Album: Power in the Darkness
Record Label: Harvest
Songwriter: Tom Robinson

Anthem of personal protest, originally on the '76 LP Rising Free.

2-4-6-8 MOTORWAY

Producer: Vic Maile
Album: Power in the Darkness
Record Label: Harvest
Songwriter: Tom Robinson

Rousing rocker was a big hit in the U.K.

VICKIE SUE ROBINSON

1976

TURN THE BEAT AROUND (LOVE TO HEAR PERCUSSION)

Producer: Warren Schatz
Album: Never Gonna Let You Go
Record Label: RCA
Songwriters: Peter Jackson, Gerald Jackson

Classic of the Disco age. Covered by Gloria Estefan (Epic, '95).

THE ROCHES

1979

HAMMOND SONG

Producer: Robert Fripp
Album: The Roches
Record Label: Warner Brothers
Songwriter: Maggie Roche

1987

All-Roche harmony trio, artsier than the Fleetwoods (with Maggie in the Gary Troxel role), funnier than the Teddy Bears (with Maggie in the Phil Spector role), achieve critical mass with this litany of parental warnings tied to a sojourn at a Kung Fu temple in Hammond, LA. In Atlanta, the Indigo Girls were listening; in San Francisco, so were the Bangles.

THE MARRIED MEN

Producer: Robert Fripp
Album: The Roches
Record Label: Warner Brothers
Songwriter: Maggie Roche

Greenwich Village abandon tied to Greenwich, CT guilt. Covered by New Jersey's Phoebe Snow (Columbia, '78).

THE TROUBLES

Producer: Robert Fripp
Album: The Roches
Record Label: Warner Brothers
Songwriters: Maggie Roche, Suzzy Roche, Terre Roche

About Northern Ireland. The Cranberries were listening ("Zombie").

1982

ON THE ROAD TO FAIRFAX COUNTY

Producer: Robert Fripp
Album: Keep on Doing
Record Label: Warner Brothers
Songwriter: David Massingill

Neo-Folkie highlight. In Greenwich Village, Suzanne Vega was listening.

1985

LOVE RADIATES AROUND

Producers: Ed Kalehoff, Howard Lindeman
Album: Another World
Record Label: Warner Brothers
Songwriter: Mark Johnson

Sheer, gauzy Folk Rock perfection.

1989

EVERYONE IS GOOD

Producers: Jeffrey Lesser, the Roches
Album: Another World
Record Label: Warner Brothers
Songwriter: Terre Roche

Their most beautiful Folk Rock hymn.

ROCK FOLLIES
1977

O.K.
Album: Rock Follies
Record Label: Polydor
Songwriters: Simon Crampton, Emma James, Louis Smith

Rula Lenska rules; from the PBS Rock serial from England: "Upstairs, Downstairs at the Hard Rock Cafe."

THE ROCK-A-TEENS
1959

WOO-HOO
Album: Woo-Hoo
Record Label: Roulette
Songwriter: George Donald McGraw

What Duane Eddy hath wrought: another guitar instrumental hit of '59.

THE ROCKIN' REBELS
1963

WILD WEEKEND
Album: Wild Weekend
Record Label: Swan
Songwriters: Tom Shannon, Phil Todaro

Surf party instrumental.

ROCKPILE
1980

TEACHER, TEACHER
Producer: Rockpile
Album: Seconds of Pleasure
Record Label: Columbia
Songwriters: Eddie Phillips, Ken Pickett

Only semi-hit from the only album by the Dave Edmunds/Nick Lowe U.K. one-off super/backing group.

ROCKWELL
1984

SOMEBODY'S WATCHING ME
Producers: Curtis Anthony Nolen, Rockwell
Album: Somebody's Watching Me
Record Label: Motown
Songwriter: Rockwell

Suggested paranoid segues: "Who Can It Be Now" by Men At Work, "Paranoia" by the Kinks.

JIMMIE RODGERS
1958

OH, OH, I'M FALLING IN LOVE AGAIN
Producer: Hugo and Luigi
Record Label: Roulette
Songwriters: Al Hoffman, Dick Manning, Hugo Perretti, Luigi Creatore

Top-5 C&W/Top-10 R&R crossover, pre-saging Soft Rock, Adult Rock, M.O.R., etc.

TOMMY ROE
1962

SHEILA
Producer: Felton Jarvis
Album: Sheila
Record Label: ABC
Songwriter: Tommy Roe

His debut single, priming the populace for a true Buddy Holly & the Crickets revival, still a year or so in the offing.

1963

EVERYBODY
Producer: Felton Jarvis
Album: Sweet Pea
Record Label: ABC
Songwriter: Tommy Roe

Buddy Holly-inspired rocker, inspired by Roe's tour with the Beatles. This is the tune that was interrupted on 1010 WINS in New York for the bulletin announcing the assassination of JFK.

1966

HOORAY FOR HAZEL
Producer: Felton Jarvis
Album: Sweet Pea
Record Label: ABC
Songwriter: Tommy Roe

SWEET PEA
Producer: Felton Jarvis
Album: Sweet Pea
Record Label: ABC
Songwriter: Tommy Roe

Paving the way for Bubblegum. Kazenetz and Katz were listening.

1969

DIZZY
Producer: Steve Barri
Album: 12 in a Roe/A Collection of Tommy Roe's Greatest Hits
Record Label: ABC
Songwriters: Tommy Roe, Freddy Weller

Like Elvis, Tommy Roe returned to #1 in '69 for the first time since '62. His biggest hit.

JAM UP AND JELLY TIGHT
Producer: Steve Barri
Album: 12 in a Roe/A Collection of Tommy Roe's Greatest Hits
Record Label: ABC
Songwriters: Tommy Roe, Freddy Weller

His last hit single.

ROGER
1987

I WANT TO BE YOUR MAN
Producers: Roger Troutman
Album: Unlimited
Record Label: Reprise
Songwriter: Larry Troutman

#1 R&B/Top-10 R&R crossover.

KENNY ROGERS
1968

JUST DROPPED IN (TO SEE WHAT CONDITION MY CONDITION WAS IN)
Producer: Mike Post
Album: The First Edition
Record Label: Reprise
Songwriter: Mickey Newbury

Folk rocker with the First Edition was the first hit for the future middle-of-the-road crooner.

1969

RUBY, DON'T TAKE YOUR LOVE TO TOWN
Producer: Jimmy Bowen
Album: The First Edition '69
Record Label: Reprise
Songwriter: Mel Tillis

Anti-war (the Korean War) Country song about a disabled vet, was a Top-40 C&W/Top-10 R&R crossover. Original by Johnny Darrell (United Artists, '67) hit Top-10 C&W.

1976

LUCILLE
Producer: Larry Butler
Album: Kenny Rogers
Record Label: United Artists
Songwriters: Hal Bynum, Roger Bowling

His first solo success is a #1 C&W/Top-10 R&R crossover.

1977

THE GAMBLER
Producer: Larry Butler
Album: The Gambler
Record Label: United Artists
Songwriter: Don Schlitz

#1 C&W/Top-20 R&R crossover spawned a TV movie. The song was better.

1983

ISLANDS IN THE STREAM
Producers: Barry Gibb, Karl Richardson, Albhy Galuten
Album: Eyes That See in the Dark
Record Label: RCA
Songwriters: Barry Gibb, Robin Gibb, Maurice Gibb

#1 C&W/#1 R&R crossover ballad with Dolly Parton.

THE ROLLING STONES

1964

I WANNA BE YOUR MAN
Producer: Andrew Loog-Oldham
Record Label: London
Songwriters: John Lennon, Paul McCartney

B-side of first U.S. single, "Not Fade Away." Covered by the Beatles on their first U.S. album (Capitol, '64). For the remainder of the decade, these two English bands would define American Rock and Roll. Virtually every young band coming up in their wake, would opt to be either the next Beatles or the next Stones. None would succeed. As far as defining American Rock in the '70s and '80s is concerned, only Led Zeppelin, another British band, and to a lesser extent, the Clash, another British band, would challenge them.

TELL ME (YOU'RE COMING BACK)
Producer: Andrew Loog-Oldham
Album: The Rolling Stones
Record Label: London
Songwriters: Mick Jagger, Keith Richards

Introducing the formidable Blues Rock songwriting team of Jagger and Richards. Also introduces Harvey Keitel in the Rock-and-Roll obsessed '73 Martin Scorsese film classic Mean Streets.

1965

GET OFF OF MY CLOUD
Producer: Andrew Loog-Oldham
Album: December's Children (and Everybody's)

Record Label: London
Songwriters: Mick Jagger, Keith Richards

The Stones at their self-absorbed peak.

HEART OF STONE
Producer: Andrew Loog-Oldham
Album: Now
Record Label: London
Songwriters: Mick Jagger, Keith Richards

Their signature sound and image.

(I CAN'T GET NO) SATISFACTION
Producer: Andrew Loog-Oldham
Album: Out of Our Heads
Record Label: London
Songwriters: Mick Jagger, Keith Richards

Fuzz-toned anthem of alienation was their first #1 U.S./#1 U.K. crossover and remains their biggest hit. Covered by the Residents (Ralph, '76) and Devo (Warner Bothers, '79).

I'M FREE
Producer: Andrew Loog-Oldham
Album: December's Children (and Everybody's)
Record Label: London
Songwriters: Mick Jagger, Keith Richards

Covered by the Soup Dragons (Big Time, '90).

THE LAST TIME
Producer: Andrew Loog-Oldham
Album: Out of Our Heads
Record Label: London
Songwriters: Mick Jagger, Keith Richards

Their third #1 U.K. hit, first they'd written. Suggested segue: "Maybe the Last Time" by the Staple Singers.

MOTHER'S LITTLE HELPER
Producer: Andrew Loog-Oldham
Album: December's Children (and Everybody's)
Record Label: London
Songwriters: Mick Jagger, Keith Richards

Invading Country music territory for a morality saga of a pill-popping housewife.

PLAY WITH FIRE
Producer: Andrew Loog-Oldham
Album: Out of Our Heads
Record Label: London

Songwriters: Mick Jagger, Keith Richards, Bill Wyman, Brian Jones, Charlie Watts

For the first and probably only time, the entire group gets credited for this acoustic classic. Phil Spector on acoustic guitar.

UNDER ASSISTANT WEST COAST PROMO MAN
Producer: Andrew Loog-Oldham
Album: Out of Our Heads
Record Label: London
Songwriters: Mick Jagger, Keith Richards

The rare Stonesian sense of humor, tweaking the music business.

1966

19TH NERVOUS BREAKDOWN
Producer: Andrew Loog-Oldham
Album: Big Hits (High Tide and Green Grass)
Record Label: London
Songwriters: Mick Jagger, Keith Richards

Early attempt at Dylan-esque psycho-dramatics.

HAVE YOU SEEN YOUR MOTHER, BABY, STANDING IN THE SHADOW
Producer: Andrew Loog-Oldham
Album: Got Live If You Want It
Record Label: London
Songwriters: Mick Jagger, Keith Richards

LADY JANE
Producer: Andrew Loog-Oldham
Album: Aftermath
Record Label: London
Songwriters: Mick Jagger, Keith Richards

Stones at their most unplugged. B-side of "Mother's Little Helper."

PAINT IT BLACK
Producer: Andrew Loog-Oldham
Album: Aftermath
Record Label: London
Songwriters: Mick Jagger, Keith Richards

UNDER MY THUMB
Producer: Andrew Loog-Oldham
Album: Aftermath
Record Label: London
Songwriters: Mick Jagger, Keith Richards

Previewing the Heavy Metal attitude. Covered by Del Shannon (Liberty, '66).

2,000 LIGHT YEARS FROM HOME
Producer: Andrew Loog-Oldham
Album: Their Satanic Majesties
   Request
Record Label: London
Songwriters: Mick Jagger, Keith
   Richards

A brief and messy fling with psychedelia.

BACK STREET GIRL
Producer: Andrew Loog-Oldham
Album: Flowers
Record Label: London
Songwriters: Mick Jagger, Keith
   Richards

Their version of "Eleanor Rigby." The only song Jagger liked on the album.

DANDELION
Producer: Andrew Loog-Oldham
Album: Through the Past, Darkly
   (Big Hits, Vol. II)
Record Label: London
Songwriters: Mick Jagger, Keith
   Richards

They were never much for flower power.

LET'S SPEND THE NIGHT TOGETHER
Producer: Andrew Loog-Oldham
Album: Between the Buttons
Record Label: London
Songwriters: Mick Jagger, Keith
   Richards

B-side of "Ruby Tuesday," censored on "The Ed Sullivan Show." Covered by David Bowie (RCA, '73). Suggested segue: "All Day and All of the Night" by the Kinks.

RUBY TUESDAY
Producer: Andrew Loog-Oldham
Album: Between the Buttons
Record Label: London
Songwriters: Mick Jagger, Keith
   Richards

Out of the pages of Carnaby Street's trendiest fashion magazine; if Keith had been writing this the next morning it might have been called "Ruby Wednesday."

SHE'S A RAINBOW
Producer: Andrew Loog-Oldham
Album: Their Satanic Majesties
   Request
Record Label: London
Songwriters: Mick Jagger, Keith
   Richards

Another ill-fated attempt to merge with the Zeitgeist.

SOMETHING HAPPENED TO ME YESTERDAY
Producer: Andrew Loog-Oldham
Album: Between the Buttons
Record Label: London
Songwriters: Mick Jagger, Keith
   Richards

The Stones' answer to the Lovin' Spoonful.

WE LOVE YOU
Producer: Andrew Loog-Oldham
Album: More Hot Rocks (Big Hits
   and Fazed Cookies)
Record Label: London
Songwriters: Mick Jagger, Keith
   Richards

B-side of "Dandelion." When taken as a whole single, arguably their creative nadir.

FACTORY GIRL
Producer: Jimmy Miller
Album: Beggars Banquet
Record Label: London
Songwriters: Mick Jagger, Keith
   Richards

With a new producer, they return to their element, the Bluesy working-class old neighborhood.

JUMPIN' JACK FLASH
Producer: Jimmy Miller
Album: Through the Past Darkly (Big
   Hits, Vol. II)
Record Label: London
Songwriters: Mick Jagger, Keith
   Richards

#1 U.K./Top-10 R&R crossover finds them near their rocking peak. Covered by Aretha Franklin (Arista, '86).

NO EXPECTATIONS
Producer: Jimmy Miller
Album: Beggars Banquet
Record Label: London
Songwriters: Mick Jagger, Keith
   Richards

Out of pyschedelia and into Folk Rock.

THE SALT OF THE EARTH
Producer: Jimmy Miller
Album: Beggars Banquet
Record Label: London
Songwriters: Mick Jagger, Keith
   Richards

Out of the clouds and back down to Earth, a biting rocker.

STRAY CAT BLUES
Producer: Jimmy Miller
Album: Beggars Banquet
Record Label: London
Songwriters: Mick Jagger, Keith
   Richards

Mick rewrites "Sweet Little Sixteen" according to his own experience.

STREET FIGHTING MAN
Producer: Jimmy Miller
Album: Beggars Banquet
Record Label: London
Songwriters: Mick Jagger, Keith
   Richard

Answering "All You Need Is Love" and "Why Don't We Do It in the Road" with a remake of "Dancing in the Street," which, in one of the lower moments of Rock and Roll history, Jagger covered with David Bowie (EMI-America, '85).

SYMPATHY FOR THE DEVIL
Producer: Jimmy Miller
Album: Beggars Banquet
Record Label: London
Songwriters: Mick Jagger, Keith
   Richards

At their most intense and focused; recorded the day after Bobby Kennedy was shot in Los Angeles, it features Jagger extemporaneously shouting out who killed the Kennedys. A: It was you and me. Covered by Guns n' Roses in the film Interview with the Vampire *(Geffen, '95).*

YOU GOT THE SILVER
Producer: Jimmy Miller
Album: Let It Bleed
Record Label: London
Songwriters: Mick Jagger, Keith
   Richards

The Stones' answer to the acoustic side of Led Zeppelin, before the question was even asked. Featured in the '70 movie Zabriskie Point.

GIMME SHELTER
Producer: Jimmy Miller
Album: Let It Bleed
Record Label: London
Songwriters: Mick Jagger, Keith
   Richards

Violence and death, a shot away, as evidenced by the chilling documentary named after it. Covered by Merry Clayton (Ode, '70).

HONKY TONK WOMEN

Producer: Jimmy Miller
Album: Through the Past Darkly (Big Hits, Vol. II)
Record Label: London
Songwriters: Mick Jagger, Keith Richards

The Stones on the prowl without Brian Jones. Released the day after his funeral. A classic #1 U.S./#1 U.K. eulogy.

LET IT BLEED

Producer: Jimmy Miller
Album: Let It Bleed
Record Label: London
Songwriters: Mick Jagger, Keith Richards

Perhaps the most eerily-timed event in Rock history, the album Let It Bleed *hitting the charts on December 6th, the day the Stones played their fateful free concert in Altamont, CA, captured in the documentary* Gimme Shelter, *during which a gun-wielding man was stabbed to death by Hell's Angels security guards, to the tune of "Under My Thumb" and "Sympathy for the Devil."*

LOVE IN VAIN

Producer: Jimmy Miller
Album: Let It Bleed
Record Label: London
Songwriters: Mick Jagger, Keith Richards

Drifting with the year's Nashville fever, the Stones go almost Country, delta country that is, with a nod to Robert Johnson.

MIDNIGHT RAMBLER

Producer: Jimmy Miller
Album: Let It Bleed
Record Label: London
Songwriters: Mick Jagger, Keith Richards

Apart from the ironic subtext, a major move in the Stones' journey from Rock and Roll to Rock.

YOU CAN'T ALWAYS GET WHAT YOU WANT

Producer: Jimmy Miller
Album: Let It Bleed
Record Label: London
Songwriters: Mick Jagger, Keith Richards

B-side of "Honky Tonk Women," the Stones at their rational, anti-flower peak. Featured in The Big Chill.

1971

BITCH

Producer: Jimmy Miller
Album: Sticky Fingers
Record Label: Rolling Stones
Songwriters: Mick Jagger, Keith Richards

Stones go Big Band; one of their hornier Rockers.

BROWN SUGAR

Producer: Jimmy Miller
Album: Sticky Fingers
Record Label: Rolling Stones
Songwriters: Mick Jagger, Keith Richards

One of their all-time signature riffs introduce their sixth U.S. #1.

SISTER MORPHINE

Producer: Jimmy Miller
Album: Sticky Fingers
Record Label: Rolling Stones
Songwriters: Mick Jagger, Keith Richards

Druggy dirge, covered by Marianne Faithfull, for whom it was written (Island, '90).

WILD HORSES

Producer: Jimmy Miller
Album: Sticky Fingers
Record Label: Rolling Stones
Songwriters: Mick Jagger, Keith Richards

Their finest acoustic Country rocker. Covered by the Flying Burrito Brothers (Warner Brothers, '74), Melanie (Neighborhood, '74) and the Sundays (DGC, '92).

1972

HAPPY

Producer: Jimmy Miller
Album: Exile on Main Street
Record Label: Rolling Stones
Songwriters: Mick Jagger, Keith Richards

Keith writing against title and type.

TUMBLING DICE

Producer: Jimmy Miller
Album: Exile on Main Street
Record Label: Rolling Stones
Songwriters: Mick Jagger, Keith Richards

Covered by Linda Ronstadt (Asylum, '77).

1973

ANGIE

Producer: Jimmy Miller
Album: Goat's Head Soup
Record Label: Rolling Stones
Songwriters: Mick Jagger, Keith Richards

Jagger at his most convincingly heartfelt, lusting after another man's wife.

DOO DOO DOO DOO DOO (HEARTBREAKER)

Producer: Jimmy Miller
Album: Goat's Head Soup
Record Label: Rolling Stones
Songwriters: Mick Jagger, Keith Richards

Suggested segue: "Baby Talk" by Jan and Dean.

STAR STAR

Producer: Jimmy Miller
Album: Goat's Head Soup
Record Label: Rolling Stones
Songwriters: Mick Jagger, Keith Richards

Previously known as "Star F___er," the companion song to "Stray Cat Blues." Suggested segues: "Sweet Little Sixteen" by Chuck Berry, "Hot Blooded" by Foreigner, "Sexy and Seventeen" by the Stray Cats.

1974

IT'S ONLY ROCK 'N' ROLL (BUT I LIKE IT)

Producer: Glimmer Twins
Album: It's Only Rock 'n' Roll (But I Like It)
Record Label: Rolling Stones
Songwriters: Mick Jagger, Keith Richards

Approaching the philosophical maturity of "You Can't Always Get What You Want."

1976

FOOL TO CRY

Producer: Glimmer Twins
Album: Black and Blue
Record Label: Rolling Stones
Songwriters: Mick Jagger, Keith Richards

One of Jagger's best vocals.

1978

BEAST OF BURDEN

Producer: Glimmer Twins
Album: Some Girls

Record Label: Rolling Stones
Songwriters: Mick Jagger, Keith Richards

Latter-day warhorse. Covered by Bette Midler (Atlantic, '83). A suave Mick appears in the very cool video.

MISS YOU

Producer: Glimmer Twins
Album: Some Girls
Record Label: Rolling Stones
Songwriters: Mick Jagger, Keith Richards

Their eighth and last U.S. #1 to date.

SHATTERED

Producer: Glimmer Twins
Album: Some Girls
Record Label: Rolling Stones
Songwriters: Mick Jagger, Keith Richards

1980

EMOTIONAL RESCUE

Producer: Glimmer Twins
Album: Emotional Rescue
Record Label: Rolling Stones
Songwriters: Mick Jagger, Keith Richards

1981

START ME UP

Producer: Glimmer Twins
Album: Tattoo You
Record Label: Rolling Stones
Songwriters: Mick Jagger, Keith Richards

Another classic riff.

WAITING ON A FRIEND

Producer: Glimmer Twins
Album: Tattoo You
Record Label: Rolling Stones
Songwriters: Mick Jagger, Keith Richards

Like a pitcher who's lost his fastball, the Stones still kill with the change-up and the curve.

1983

UNDERCOVER OF THE NIGHT

Producers: Glimmer Twins, Chris Kimsey
Album: Undercover
Record Label: Rolling Stones
Songwriters: Mick Jagger, Keith Richards

Closest thing to a protest song since "Sympathy for the Devil."

SHE WAS HOT

Producers: Glimmer Twins, Chris Kimsey
Album: Undercover
Record Label: Rolling Stones
Songwriters: Mick Jagger, Keith Richards

Restating their most cogent message.

1989

MIXED EMOTIONS

Producers: Glimmer Twins, Chris Kimsey
Album: Steel Wheels
Record Label: Rolling Stones Records/Columbia
Songwriters: Mick Jagger, Keith Richards

The greatest Rock and Roll band in the world chugs on to their 23rd and last Top-10 hit to date, feeling them all.

ROCK AND A HARD PLACE

Producers: Glimmer Twins, Chris Kimsey
Album: Steel Wheels
Record Label: Rolling Stones Records/Columbia
Songwriters: Mick Jagger, Keith Richards

1994

OUT OF TEARS

Producers: Don Was, Glimmer Twins
Album: Voodoo Lounge
Record Label: Virgin
Songwriters: Mick Jagger, Keith Richards

Like their idols, Muddy and the Wolf, still Rocking at 50.

YOU GOT ME ROCKIN'

Producers: Don Was, Glimmer Twins
Album: Voodoo Lounge
Record Label: Virgin
Songwriters: Mick Jagger, Keith Richards

With a new British invasion afoot, the originals out-rock the baby bands who weren't even born when they first invaded: Blur, Silverchair, Oasis, Sponge, et al., most of them preferring to be the Beatles.

THE ROLLINS BAND

1991

LOW SELF OPINION

Producer: Andy Wallace
Album: The End of Silence
Record Label: Imago
Songwriter: Rollins Band

Suggested segue: "Self Esteem" by Offspring, "Creep" by the Charlatans U.K.

1994

LIAR

Album: Weight
Record Label: Imago
Songwriter: Henry Rollins

Poet Henry gets top billing on this first bravura piece of Heavy Metal Performance Art.

THE ROMANTICS

1980

WHAT I LIKE ABOUT YOU

Producer: Pete Solley
Album: National Breakout
Record Label: Nemperor/Epic
Songwriters: Jimmy Marinos, Wally Palmar, Mike Skill

Latter-day Frat Rock anthem.

1983

TALKING IN YOUR SLEEP

Producer: Pete Solley
Album: In Heat
Record Label: Nemperor
Songwriters: Jimmy Marinos, Wally Palmar, Mike Skill, Coz Canler, Pete Solley

Biggest hit for the skinny-tie '80s band. But it was no "What I Like About You."

ROMEO VOID

1984

A GIRL IN TROUBLE (IS A TEMPORARY THING)

Producer: David Kahne
Album: Instincts
Record Label: Columbia
Songwriters: Debora Iyall, Peter Woods, Frank Zincavage, David Kahne

Alternative nugget.

CHAN ROMERO

1959

HIPPY HIPPY SHAKE
Producer: Bob Keane
Record Label: Del Fi
Songwriter: Chan Romero

In a year of Soft Rock, a blast of energy, prelude to the Garage Band revolution only a British invasion away. Covered by the Swinging Blue Jeans (Imperial, '64) and the Georgia Satellites in the movie Cocktail *(Elektra, '87).*

THE RONETTES

1963

BABY, I LOVE YOU
Producer: Phil Spector
Album: . . . introducing the fabulous Ronettes featuring Ronnie
Record Label: Philles
Songwriters: Jeff Barry, Ellie Greenwich, Phil Spector

Girl-group passion at its most abject and symphonic. Covered by the quintessential dispassionate boy-group, the Ramones (Sire, '80), its irony appreciated only in England.

BE MY BABY
Producer: Phil Spector
Album: . . . introducing the fabulous Ronettes featuring Ronnie
Record Label: Philles
Songwriters: Jeff Barry, Ellie Greenwich, Phil Spector

Spector at his creative and romantic peak, the Ronettes' only Top-10.

1964

WALKING IN THE RAIN
Producer: Phil Spector
Album: . . . introducing the fabulous Ronettes featuring Ronnie
Record Label: Philles
Songwriters: Barry Mann, Cynthia Weil, Phil Spector

And into the sunset.

WHEN I SAW YOU
Producer: Phil Spector
Album: . . . introducing the fabulous Ronettes featuring Ronnie
Record Label: Philles
Songwriter: Phil Spector

Phil's ode to Ronnie, his best since his ode to his father, "To Know Him Is to Love Him."

1966

I CAN HEAR MUSIC
Producer: Phil Spector
Record Label: Philles
Songwriters: Jeff Barry, Ellie Greenwich, Phil Spector

The Ronettes's last chart song, spending a week at number 100, joining such prestigious company as "Sam You Made the Pants Too Long" by Barbra Streisand, "Greetings (This Is Uncle Sam)" by the Monitors, and the Vontastics version of "Day Tripper." Covered by the Beach Boys (Brother, '68).

RONNY AND THE DAYTONAS

1964

G.T.O.
Producer: Bill Justis
Album: G.T.O.
Record Label: Mala
Songwriter: John Wilkin

Car classic: classic car, the Pontiac GTO.

LINDA RONSTADT

1970

LONG LONG TIME
Producer: Elliot Mazur
Album: Silk Purse
Record Label: Capitol
Songwriter: Gary White

Her first solo hit after "Different Drum," with the Stone Poneys in '67.

1974

HEART LIKE A WHEEL
Producer: Peter Asher
Album: Heart Like a Wheel
Record Label: Capitol
Songwriter: Anna McGarrigle

Ronstadt at her earthiest. Covered by Kate and Anna McGarrigle (Reprise, '76). Their version of the song was used in the Joan Didion movie Play It As It Lays.

1975

LOVE IS A ROSE
Producer: Peter Asher
Album: Prisoner in Disguise
Record Label: Asylum
Songwriter: Neil Young

Covered by Neil Young (Reprise, '77).

1976

SOMEONE TO LAY DOWN BESIDE ME
Producer: Peter Asher
Album: Hasten down the Wind
Record Label: Capitol
Songwriter: Karla Bonoff

Anthem of the L.A. singles scene. Covered by Karla Bonoff (Columbia, '77).

1977

HOW DO I MAKE YOU
Producer: Peter Asher
Album: Mad Love
Record Label: Asylum
Songwriter: Billy Steinberg

First Top-10 hit for Ronstadt that is not a classic Rock cover.

1978

WHITE RHYTHM AND BLUES
Producer: Peter Asher
Album: Living in the U.S.A
Record Label: Asylum
Songwriter: John David Souther

Covered by J. D. Souther (Columbia, '79).

1989

CRY LIKE A RAINSTORM
Producer: Peter Asher
Album: Cry Like a Rainstorm, Howl Like the Wind
Record Label: Elektra
Songwriter: Eric Kaz

Kaz's most famous song aside from "Love Has No Pride," which Ronstadt also covered (Asylum, '73).

THE ROOFTOP SINGERS

1963

WALK RIGHT IN
Producers: Erik Darling, Bill Svanoe
Album: Walk Right In
Record Label: Vanguard
Songwriters: Gus Cannon, Harry Woods

American skiffle classic kicks off the Greenwich Village Folk scare on the record charts. Originated by Gus Cannon's Jug Stompers (Victor, '28).

ROSE ROYCE

1977

CAR WASH
Producer: Norman Whitfield
Album: I Wanna Get Next to You

Record Label: MCA
Songwriter: Norman Whitfield
#1 R&B/#1 R&R crossover from the movie Car Wash.

I WANNA GET NEXT TO YOU
Producer: Norman Whitfield
Album: I Wanna Get Next to You
Record Label: MCA
Songwriter: Norman Whitfield
Another hit from Car Wash.

WISHING ON A STAR
Producer: Norman Whitfield
Album: Rose Royce II/In Full Bloom
Record Label: Whitfield
Songwriter: Billy Calvin
Covered by the Cover Girls (Epic, '92).

ROSIE AND THE ORIGINALS
1960

ANGEL BABY
Record Label: Highland
Songwriter: Rose Hamlin
Heavenly echoes of early R&R innocence, after which Rosie Hamlin was lured into a solo career, from which she never emerged.

ANNIE ROSS
1953

TWISTED
Record Label: Prestige
Songwriters: Annie Ross, Wardell Gray
Famous jazz-based tone poem tribute to an analyst was an early classic of vocalese. When Ross formed the legendary Lambert, Hendricks & Ross, it was included on their album Everybody's Boppin' *(Columbia, '59). Covered by Joni Mitchell, who had revered Lambert, Hendricks & Ross since childhood, once referring to them as her* Beatles *(Asylum, '74).*

DIANA ROSS
1970

REACH OUT AND TOUCH (SOMEBODY'S HAND)
Producers: Nick Ashford, Valerie Simpson
Album: Diana Ross
Record Label: Motown
Songwriters: Nick Ashford, Valerie Simpson
Recycling the prevailing communal Zeitgeist on her first solo single, Ross comes up with a future phone company commercial.

1973

YOU'RE A SPECIAL PART OF ME
Producer: Berry Gordy
Album: Diana and Marvin
Record Label: Motown
Songwriters: Gregory Wright, Harold Johnson, Andrew Porter
Duet with Marvin Gaye, but she was no Tammi Terrel.

1975

DO YOU KNOW WHERE YOU'RE GOING TO? (THEME FROM *MAHOGANY*)
Producer: Michael Masser
Album: Diana Ross
Record Label: Motown
Songwriters: Gerry Goffin, Michael Masser
Big movie ballad is her third #1 hit, marking a major return to form for lyricist Goffin.

1976

LOVE HANGOVER
Producer: Hal Davis
Album: Diana Ross
Record Label: Motown
Songwriters: Marilyn McLeod, Pam Sawyer
Diana enters the Disco.

1980

I'M COMING OUT
Producers: Nile Rodgers, Bernard Edwards
Album: Diana
Record Label: Motown
Songwriters: Nile Rodgers, Bernard Edwards
Diana enters the age of sexual revelation.

UPSIDE DOWN
Producers: Nile Rodgers, Bernard Edwards
Album: Diana
Record Label: Motown
Songwriters: Nile Rodgers, Bernard Edwards
Her first solo #1 R&B/#1 R&R crossover since her remake of "Ain't No Mountain High Enough" in 1970.

1981

IT'S MY TURN
Album: To Love Again
Record Label: Motown
Songwriter: Carole Bayer Sager
Her last big hit on Motown is another movie ballad.

MIRROR MIRROR
Album: Why Do Fools Fall in Love?
Record Label: RCA
Songwriter: Michael Sembello

1982

MUSCLES
Producer: Michael Jackson
Album: Silk Electric
Record Label: RCA
Songwriter: Michael Jackson
First collaboration between Michael and Diana since she introduced him to Berry Gordy in 1969.

1984

MISSING YOU
Producer: Lionel Richie
Album: Swept Away
Record Label: RCA
Songwriter: Lionel B. Richie Jr.
A tribute to Marvin Gaye.

DAVID LEE ROTH
1988

DAMN GOOD
Producer: David Lee Roth
Album: Skyscraper
Record Label: Warner Brothers
Songwriters: David Lee Roth, Steve Vai
Acoustic departure from his Pop Metal norm.

JUST LIKE PARADISE
Producer: David Lee Roth
Album: Skyscraper
Record Label: Warner Brothers
Songwriters: David Lee Roth, Brent Tuggle
Biggest hit for the former Van Halen front man.

ROXETTE
1989

LISTEN TO YOUR HEART
Producer: Clarence Ofwerman
Album: Look Sharp!
Record Label: EMI
Songwriter: Per Gessle
Second #1 from the album.

THE LOOK
Producer: Clarence Ofwerman
Album: Look Sharp!
Record Label: EMI
Songwriter: Per Gessle

First big hit for the Abba-esque duo. Ace of Base were listening.

1990

DANGEROUS
Producer: Clarence Ofwerman
Album: Look Sharp
Record Label: EMI
Songwriter: Per Gessel

Perfecting the Swedish penchant for perfect Pop/Rock.

IT MUST HAVE BEEN LOVE
Producer: Clarence Ofwerman
Album: *Pretty Woman* Soundtrack
Record Label: EMI
Songwriter: Per Gessle

As perky and inescapable as Julia Roberts in Pretty Woman.

1991

FADING LIKE A FLOWER
Producer: Clarence Ofwerman
Album: Joyride
Record Label: EMI
Songwriter: Per Gessle

JOYRIDE
Producer: Clarence Ofwerman
Album: Joyride
Record Label: EMI
Songwriter: Per Gessle

Their fourth #1.

ROXY MUSIC

1973

DO THE STRAND
Producers: Chris Thomas, John Astley
Album: For Your Pleasure
Record Label: Warner Brothers
Songwriter: Bryan Ferry

If Frank Sinatra had been a baby boomer he might have created this dance music for late-night sophisticates.

IN EVERY DREAM HOME A HEARTACHE
Producers: Chris Thomas, John Astley, Roxy Music
Album: For Your Pleasure
Record Label: Warner Brothers
Songwriter: Bryan Ferry

The ultimate tortured love song. Stephen Morrissey was listening.

1976

LOVE IS THE DRUG
Producer: Chris Thomas
Album: Siren
Record Label: Atco
Songwriter: Roger Lewis

This cautionary and prophetic Disco-age anthem was their first and biggest U.S. hit.

1979

DANCE AWAY
Producer: Roxy Music
Album: Manifesto
Record Label: Atco
Songwriter: Bryan Ferry

1982

AVALON
Producers: Rhett Davies, Roxy Music
Album: Avalon
Record Label: Warner Brothers
Songwriter: Bryan Ferry

Mood music for the age of decadence.

MORE THAN THIS
Producers: Rhett Davies, Roxy Music
Album: Avalon
Record Label: Warner Brothers
Songwriter: Bryan Ferry

THE ROYAL GUARDSMEN

1966

SNOOPY VERSUS THE RED BARON
Producer: Phil Gernhard
Album: Snoopy vs. the Red Baron
Record Label: Laurie
Songwriters: Phil Gernhard, Richard L. Holler

Novelty hit.

THE ROYAL TEENS

1957

SHORT SHORTS
Record Label: ABC Paramount
Songwriters: Bob Gaudio, Tom Austin, Bill Dalton, Bill Crandall

The white streetcorner sound of the '50s, one part Doo-Wop, one part Folk, two parts voyeurism.

1959

BELIEVE ME
Record Label: Capitol
Songwriters: Joe Villa, Tom Austin

Quintessential suburban Doo-Wop.

BILLY JOE ROYAL

1965

DOWN IN THE BOONDOCKS
Producer: Joe South
Album: Down in the Boondocks
Record Label: Columbia
Songwriter: Joe South

White trash anthem cuts too close to the bone for Country music.

1967

HUSH
Producer: Joe South
Record Label: Columbia
Songwriter: Joe South

Covered by Deep Purple (Tetragrammaton, '68) on their first album, along with "Help" and "Hey Joe," still five years away from "Smoke on the Water" and "Highway Star."

THE ROYALETTES

1965

IT'S GONNA TAKE A MIRACLE
Producer: Teddy Randazzo
Album: It's Gonna Take a Miracle
Record Label: MGM
Songwriters: Teddy Randazzo, Bobby Weinstein, Lou Stallman

Covered with breathless perfection by Laura Nyro (Columbia, '71).

THE ROYALS

1961

EVERY BEAT OF MY HEART
Record Label: Federal
Songwriter: Johnny Otis

A #1 R&B/Top-10 R&R crossover by the Pips (Vee-Jay, '61). Also covered by James Brown (King, '65).

RUBY AND THE ROMANTICS

1963

HEY THERE LONELY BOY
Producer: Allan Stanton
Record Label: Kapp
Songwriters: Earl Shuman, Leon Carr

Covered by Eddie Holman as "Hey There Lonely Girl" (ABC, '69).

OUR DAY WILL COME
Producer: Allen Stanton
Album: Our Day Will Come
Record Label: Kapp

Songwriters: Mort Garson, Bob Hilliard

Ethereal ballad; #1 R&B/R&R crossover.

1964

WHEN YOU'RE YOUNG AND IN LOVE

Producer: Allen Stanton
Record Label: Kapp
Songwriter: Van McCoy

Covered by the Marvelettes (Tamla, '67).

1965

HURTING EACH OTHER

Producer: Allen Stanton
Record Label: Kapp
Songwriters: Gary Geld, Peter Udell

Covered by the Carpenters (A&M, '72).

THE RUDE BOYS

1990

WRITTEN ALL OVER YOUR FACE

Album: Rude Awakenings
Record Label: Atlantic
Songwriter: Larry Marcus

Top Rap track of the year; #1 R&B/Top-20 R&R crossover.

DAVID RUFFIN

1969

MY WHOLE WORLD ENDED (THE MOMENT YOU LEFT ME)

Producers: Johnny Bristol, Harvey Fuqua
Album: My Whole World Ended
Record Label: Motown
Songwriters: Johnny Bristol, Harvey Fuqua, Pam Sawyer, Jimmy Roach

Leaving the Temptations but not the Motown gift for dramatic overstatement.

1975

WALK AWAY FROM LOVE

Producer: Van McCoy
Album: Who I Am
Record Label: Motown
Songwriter: Charles Kipps Jr.

#1 R&B/Top-10 R&R crossover.

JIMMY RUFFIN

1966

WHAT BECOMES OF THE BROKENHEARTED

Producers: Mickey Stevenson, William Weatherspoon
Album: Top Ten
Record Label: Soul

Songwriters: James Dean, Paul Riser, William Weatherspoon

His biggest hit: a Top-10 R&B/Top-10 R&R crossover.

1980

HOLD ON TO MY LOVE

Producer: Robin Gibb
Album: Sunrise
Record Label: RSO
Songwriter: Robin Gibb

RUFUS

1974

TELL ME SOMETHING GOOD

Producers: Rufus, Bob Monaco
Album: Rags to Rufus
Record Label: ABC
Songwriter: Stevie Wonder

Their breakthrough hit, a Top-5 R&B/Top-5 R&R crossover.

YOU GOT THE LOVE

Producers: Rufus, Bob Monaco
Album: Rags to Rufus
Record Label: ABC
Songwriters: Ray Parker Jr., Chaka Khan

Their first #1 R&B/Top-20 R&R crossover introduces two future Soul superstars, Parker and Khan.

1975

ONCE YOU GET STARTED

Producer: Rufus
Album: Rufusized
Record Label: ABC
Songwriter: Gavin Wright

Lead-singer Chaka Khan gains featured billing.

SWEET THING

Producer: Rufus
Album: Rufusized
Record Label: ABC
Songwriters: Tony Maiden, Chaka Khan

#1 R&B/Top-10 R&R crossover for Rufus, featuring Chaka Khan.

1977

AT MIDNIGHT (MY LOVE WILL LIFT YOU UP)

Producer: Rufus
Album: Ask Rufus
Record Label: ABC
Songwriters: Tony Maiden, Lalomie Washburn

#1 R&B/Top-30 R&R crossover.

1979

DO YOU LOVE WHAT YOU FEEL

Producer: Quincy Jones
Album: Masterjam
Record Label: MCA
Songwriter: David Wolinski

#1 R&B/Top-30 R&R crossover.

1983

AIN'T NOBODY

Producer: Russ Titelman
Album: Live—Stompin' at the Savoy
Record Label: Warner Brothers
Songwriter: David Wolinski

#1 R&B/30 R&R crossover.

RUN-D.M.C.

1984

IT'S LIKE THAT

Producers: Russell Simmons, Larry Smith
Album: Run-D.M.C.
Record Label: Profile
Songwriters: Larry Smith, Joseph Simmons, Darryl McDaniels

From Hollis, Queens, the Rap persona moves one giant boast closer to the Rap revolution.

ROCK BOX

Producers: Russell Simmons, Larry Smith
Album: Run-D.M.C.
Record Label: Profile
Songwriters: Larry Smith, Joseph Simmons, Darryl McDaniels

Presaging their Heavy Metal union with Aerosmith on "Walk This Way" a couple of years up the block.

SUCKER MC'S (KRUSH GROOVE)

Producer: Russell Simmons
Album: Run-D.M.C.
Record Label: Profile
Songwriters: Larry Smith, Joseph Simmons, Darryl McDaniels

B-side of "It's Like That."

1985

KING OF ROCK

Album: King of Rock
Record Label: Profile
Songwriters: Larry Smith, Joseph Simmons, Darryl McDaniel

1993

DOWN WITH THE KING

Producer: Pete Rock
Album: Down with the King

Record Label: Profile
Songwriters: Pete Phillips, Joseph Simmons, Darryl McDaniels, John Penn, James Rado, Gerome Ragni, Galt McDermott

Clean and sober and cleared of all charges, the seminal Rap group returns with a kinder and gentler boast, tied to the big ballad from Hair! *"Where Do I Go."*

THE RUNAWAYS

1976

CHERRY BOMB
Producer: Kim Fowley
Album: The Runaways
Record Label: Mercury
Songwriters: Joan Jett, Kim Fowley

Jailbait anthem for the all-girl Metal band featuring future guitar goddesses Joan Jett and Lita Ford. Covered by Joan Jett with L7 (Epic, '95).

TODD RUNDGREN

1972

I SAW THE LIGHT
Producer: Todd Rundgren
Album: Something/Anything
Record Label: Bearsville
Songwriter: Todd Rundgren

Shining moment from the double album by the ubiquitous singer/songwriter/producer/ genius and founder of Runt and the Nazz.

1978

CAN WE STILL BE FRIENDS
Producer: Todd Rundgren
Album: Hermit of Mink Hollow
Record Label: Bearsville
Songwriter: Todd Rundgren

At his most Beatles-esque.

1983

BANG THE DRUM ALL DAY
Producer: Todd Rundgren
Album: The Ever Popular Tortured Artist Effect
Record Label: Bearsville
Songwriter: Todd Rundgren

FM radio standard.

1989

PARALLEL LINES
Producer: Todd Rundgren
Album: Nearly Human
Record Label: Warner Brothers
Songwriter: Todd Rundgren

Going beyond mere Beatlemania, Rundgren originally wrote this for a projected Beatles movie musical called Up Against It, *written by the late Joe Orton. It was finally staged in '89 at the New York Shakespeare Festival, where this tune was sung by Philip Casanov and Alison Fraser.*

RUNT

1970

WE GOTTA GET YOU A WOMAN
Producer: Todd Rundgren
Album: Runt
Record Label: Ampex
Songwriter: Todd Rundgren

Disarming streetcorner Jazz/Rock from Todd in his pre-genius days.

RUSH

1977

CLOSER TO THE HEART
Producers: Terry Brown, Rush
Album: A Farewell to Kings
Record Label: Mercury
Songwriters: Gary Lee Weinrib (Geddy Lee), Alex Zivojinovich (Alex Lifeson), Neil Peart, Peter Talbot

Canadian virtuosic Metal trio produces its first Arena anthem.

1978

LA VILLA STRANGIATA
Producers: Terry Brown, Rush
Album: Hemispheres
Record Label: Mercury
Songwriters: Gary Lee Weinrib (Geddy Lee), Alex Zivojinovich (Alex Lifeson), Neil Peart

Epic that is most often thought of when Lee wins those bass player polls in the musician magazines.

1980

FREEWILL
Producers: Terry Brown, Rush
Album: Permanent Waves
Record Label: Mercury
Songwriters: Gary Lee Weinrib (Geddy Lee), Alex Zivojinovich (Alex Lifeson), Neil Peart

With a nod to novelist Ayn Rand.

THE SPIRIT OF RADIO
Producers: Terry Brown, Rush
Album: Permanent Waves
Record Label: Mercury

Songwriters: Gary Lee Weinrib (Geddy Lee), Alex Zivojinovich (Alex Lifeson), Neil Peart

Their radio breakthrough.

1981

LIMELIGHT
Producers: Terry Brown, Rush
Album: Moving Pictures
Record Label: Mercury
Songwriters: Gary Lee Weinrib (Geddy Lee), Alex Zivojinovich (Alex Lifeson), Neil Peart

The verbose Peart at his most lucid.

TOM SAWYER
Producers: Terry Brown, Rush
Album: Moving Pictures
Record Label: Mercury
Songwriters: Gary Lee Weinrib (Geddy Lee), Alex Zivojinovich (Alex Lifeson), Neil Peart, Pye Dubois

The most novelistic of all Metal bands continues to mine and make classics.

YYZ
Producers: Terry Brown, Rush
Album: Moving Pictures
Record Label: Mercury
Songwriters: Gary Lee Weinrib (Geddy Lee), Alex Zivojinovich (Alex Lifeson), Neil Peart

Geddy Lee at his best.

1982

NEW WORLD MAN
Producers: Terry Brown, Rush
Album: Signals
Record Label: Mercury
Songwriters: Gary Lee Weinrib (Geddy Lee), Alex Zivojinovich (Alex Lifeson)

Closest thing to a hit.

1991

ROLL THE BONES
Producers: Rupert Hine, Rush
Album: Roll the Bones
Record Label: Atlantic
Songwriters: Gary Lee Weinrib (Geddy Lee), Alex Zivojinovich (Alex Lifeson), Neil Peart

After a decade and a half on the boards, looser than ever.

MERRILEE RUSH
1967

ANGEL OF THE MORNING
Producers: Chips Moman, Tommy Cogbill
Album: Angel of the Morning
Record Label: Bell
Songwriter: Chip Taylor

In the late-'60s free-love mode, the one-night stand from the female point of view. Covered by Juice Newton (Capitol, '81), whose version was a big hit in South America, leading to its later use on a car radio in the Oliver Stone movie Salvador. In 1995, Chrissie Hynde covered it for her acting debut on the TV show "Friends." She was no Leather Tuscadero.

OTIS RUSH
1956

I CAN'T QUIT YOU BABY
Producer: Willie Dixon
Record Label: Cobra
Songwriter: Willie Dixon

The crystalline Blues guitar cuts through the pain.

TOM RUSH
1968

NO REGRETS
Producer: Arthur Gordon
Album: The Circle Game
Record Label: Elektra
Songwriter: Tom Rush

Expansive, open D-guitar autobiography by the legendarily tasteful Folkie. Covered in England by the Walker Brothers (GTO, '76), and in America by Emmylou Harris (Reprise, '89).

SOMETHING IN THE WAY SHE MOVES
Producer: Arthur Gordon
Album: The Circle Game
Record Label: Elektra
Songwriter: James Taylor

Bostonion Folk Blues stylist emerged as a revered Folk Rock arbiter with this collection, featuring early works by then barely known future laid-back mainstays James Taylor, Jackson Browne, and Joni Mitchell.

1973

DESPERADOS WAITING FOR A TRAIN
Album: Ladies Love Outlaws
Record Label: Columbia
Songwriter: Guy Clark

Country Rock standard gets the solid Rush treatment.

BRENDA RUSSELL
1988

PIANO IN THE DARK
Producers: A. Fischer, Brenda Russell, Jeff Hull
Album: Get Here
Record Label: A&M
Songwriters: Brenda Russell, Jeff Hull, Scott Cutler

LEON RUSSELL
1970

ROLL AWAY THE STONE
Producer: Denny Cordell
Album: Leon Russell
Record Label: Shelter
Songwriters: Leon Russell, Greg Dempsey

FM hit that established the former Phil Spector session ace.

SONG FOR YOU
Producer: Denny Cordell
Album: Leon Russell
Record Label: Shelter
Songwriter: Leon Russell

One of his most enduring ballads.

1972

THIS MASQUERADE
Producers: Denny Cordell, Leon Russell
Album: Carny
Record Label: Shelter
Songwriter: Leon Russell

The mellow laid-back sound of L.A. in the '70s. Covered by George Benson (Warner Brothers, '76).

TIGHT ROPE
Producers: Denny Cordell, Leon Russell
Album: Carney
Record Label: Shelter
Songwriter: Leon Russell

His best-selling single.

BOBBY RYDELL
1959

KISSIN' TIME
Album: Bobby Sings
Record Label: Cameo
Songwriters: Leonard Frazier, James Frazier

The poor (taste) man's Darin, Rydell was arguably the Bobbiest Bobby of the entire Bobby-Jimmy-Frankie "Bandstand" Era. This tune was not only his chart debut, but it served a similar (in an entirely different context) purpose for Kiss (Casablanca, '74).

WE GOT LOVE
Album: We Got Love
Record Label: Cameo
Songwriters: Kal Mann, Bernie Lowe

His first Top-10 single.

1960

SWINGIN' SCHOOL
Album: Bobby's Biggest Hits
Record Label: Cameo
Songwriters: Kal Mann, Bernie Lowe, Dave Appell

From the Tuesday Weld movie Because They're Young.

WILD ONE
Album: Bobby's Biggest Hits
Record Label: Cameo
Songwriters: Kal Mann, Bernie Lowe, Dave Appell

His biggest hit.

1964

FORGET HIM
Producer: Frank Day
Album: Forget Him
Record Label: Cameo
Songwriter: Tony Hatch

His second biggest hit.

MITCH RYDER AND THE DETROIT WHEELS
1967

SOCK IT TO ME, BABY
Producer: Bob Crewe
Album: Sock It to Me
Record Label: New Voice
Songwriters: Bob Crewe, L. Russell Brown

Blue-eyed, Motor-city Soul. L. Russell Brown would be back with Tony Orlando and Dawn.

S

ROBIN S.
1993

SHOW ME LOVE
Producers: Allen George, Fred McFarlane
Album: Show Me Love
Record Label: Big Beat
Songwriters: Allen George, Fred McFarlane

Top-10 R&B/Top-10 R&R crossover.

S.O.S. BAND
1980

TAKE YOUR TIME (DO IT RIGHT) PART 1
Producers: Jimmy Jam, Terry Lewis
Album: S.O.S.
Record Label: Tabu
Songwriters: Harold Clayton, Sigidi

Top-5 R&B/Top-5 R&R crossover is their first and biggest hit.

1983

JUST BE GOOD TO ME
Producers: Jimmy Jam, Terry Lewis
Album: On the Rise
Record Label: Tabu
Songwriters: James Harris III, Terry Lewis

Coming under the tutelage of Prince proteges Harris and Lewis, the hottest songwriting team of the early '80s.

SADE
1985

SALLY
Producer: R. Millar
Album: Diamond Life
Record Label: Epic
Songwriters: Helen Folesade Adu (Sade), Stuart Matthewman

Decadence, with a mellow international style. Suggested segues: "Seems So Long Ago, Nancy" by Leonard Cohen, and "Chelsea Girls" by Nico.

SMOOTH OPERATOR
Producer: R. Millar
Album: Diamond Life
Record Label: Epic
Songwriters: Helen Folesade Adu (Sade), Raymond St. John

Lanquidly continental Jazz Pop.

1986

SWEETEST TABU
Album: Promise
Record Label: Epic
Songwriters: Helen Folesade Adu (Sade), Martin Ditcham

No relation to the Marquis de, Sade is pronounced "Shah-day."

1988

PARADISE
Producer: Sade
Album: Stronger Than Pride
Record Label: Epic
Songwriters: Helen Folesade Adu (Sade), Stewart Matthewman, Andrew Hale, Paul Denman

#1 R&B/Top-20 R&R crossover.

1992

NO ORDINARY LOVE
Producer: Sade
Album: Love Deluxe
Record Label: Epic
Songwriters: Helen Folesade Adu (Sade), Stuart Matthewman

Crucial in the Robert Redford/Demi Moore movie Indecent Proposal.

STAFF SERGEANT BARRY SADLER
1966

THE BALLAD OF THE GREEN BERETS
Producer: Andy Wiswell
Album: Ballads of the Green Berets
Record Label: RCA
Songwriters: Barry Sadler, Robin Moore

The opposition responds to "Eve of Destruction." Not surprisingly, it was a #1 R&R/C&W smash.

THE SAFARIS
1960

IMAGE OF A GIRL
Record Label: Eldo
Songwriters: Marvin Rosenberg, Richard Clasky

Part of the essential suburban, white Doo-Wop collection, an often overlooked art form, since there were no street corners or elevated train lines to sing on or under (and traffic lights were often miles apart).

BUFFY SAINTE-MARIE
1964

COD'INE
Producer: Elmer Jared Gordon
Album: It's My Way
Record Label: Vanguard
Songwriter: Buffy Sainte-Marie

Striking anti-drug lament made chilling by Sainte-Marie's quaking, quavery voice. Covered by the Charlatans (Kama Sutra, '66) but never released. Covered by Quicksilver Messenger Service, in the movie Revolution (United Artists, '69).

THE UNIVERSAL SOLDIER
Producer: Elmer Jared Gordon
Album: It's My Way
Record Label: Vanguard
Songwriter: Buffy Sainte-Marie

A far cry from the contemporaneous "Soldier Boy" and "Blue Navy Blue," but one that would be getting stronger in the coming years of Folk Rock protest. Covered by Donovan (Hickory, '65).

UNTIL IT'S TIME FOR YOU TO GO
Album: Many a Mile
Record Label: Vanguard
Songwriter: Buffy Sainte-Marie

Earth-mothering Folk ballad answer to Gale Garnett's "We'll Sing in the Sunshine" that found favor among the more macho of Pop Rock belters: i.e., Bobby Darin (Atlantic, '67), Neil Diamond (UNI, '70), Elvis Presley (RCA, '72), and Willie Nelson (Columbia, '84). Covered by Cher (Imperial, '66) and Helen Reddy (Capitol, '73).

1967

THE CIRCLE GAME
Album: Fire and Fleet and Candlelight
Record Label: Vanguard
Songwriter: Joni Mitchell

Written by Mitchell in response to Neil Young's "Sugar Mountain." Covered by Tom Rush (Elektra, '68). Featured in the youth cult movie The Strawberry Statement *(MGM, '70). Mitchell's version is on* Ladies of the Canyon *(Reprise, '70).*

1992

BURY MY HEART AT WOUNDED KNEE
Album: Coincidence & Likely Stories
Record Label: Ensign/Chrysalis
Songwriter: Buffy Sainte-Marie

Of a piece with her other Native American anthem, "My Country 'Tis of Thy People,

You're Dying." Covered by the Indigo Girls (Epic, '95).

THE SAINTS
1987

JUST LIKE FIRE WOULD
Producer: Hugh Jones
Album: All Fool's Day
Record Label: TVT
Songwriter: Chris Bailey

Massive Alternative Arena hook from Australia. The Hoodoo Gurus would have been proud of it. Mott the Hoople might have sued.

KYU SAKAMOTO
1963

SUKIYAKI (MY FIRST LONELY NIGHT)
Producer: Koji Kusano
Album: Sukiyaki and Other Japanese Hits
Record Label: Capitol
Songwriters: Tom Leslie, Buzz Cason, Hachidai Nakamura, Rokusuke Ei

From Japan, where Heavy Metal guitarists go after they die (in the U.S. market), an eternal ethereal ballad. Covered by A Taste of Honey (Capitol, '80) and 4P.M. (Next Plateau/London, '94).

SALT-N-PEPA
1988

PUSH IT
Producer: Herby Luv Bug
Album: Hot, Cool, and Vicious
Record Label: Next Plateau
Songwriter: Herb Azor

First hit for the aggressive female Pop Hip-Hop trio.

1991

LET'S TALK ABOUT SEX
Producer: Herby Luv Bug and the Invincibles
Album: Blacks' Magic
Record Label: Next Plateau
Songwriter: Fingerprints

Ushering in the era of plain talk; on record and daytime TV.

1993

NONE OF YOUR BUSINESS
Producer: S. Azor
Album: Very Necessary

Record Label: Next Plateau
Songwriter: Herb Azor

Answering critics of their rough and realistic approach.

SHOOP
Producers: Mark Sparks, Cheryl James
Album: Very Necessary
Record Label: Next Plateau
Songwriters: Mark Sparks, Cheryl James, Sandy Denton, Otwane Roberts, Nate Turner

Their biggest hit ironically sports a euphemistic hook.

WHATTA MAN
Producers: Mark Sparks, Cheryl James
Album: Very Necessary
Record Label: Next Plateau
Songwriters: Herb Azor, David Crawford, Cheryl James

The temporary supergroup of Salt-n-Pepa and En Vogue depicts the Sensitive New Age Black Guy.

SAM AND DAVE
1966

HOLD ON, I'M COMIN'
Producer: Jim Stewart
Album: Hold on, I'm Comin'
Record Label: Stax
Songwriters: Isaac Hayes, David Porter

A definition of Soul, the FM Rock answer to AM's Motown; #1 R&B/Top-25 R&R crossover.

I TAKE WHAT I WANT
Producer: Jim Stewart
Album: Hold on, I'm Comin'
Record Label: Stax
Songwriters: Isaac Hayes, David Porter, Mabon Hodges

Covered by James and Bobby Purify (Bell, '67).

YOU DON'T KNOW LIKE I KNOW
Producer: Jim Stewart
Album: Hold on I'm Comin'
Record Label: Stax
Songwriters: Isaac Hayes, David Porter

First R&B/R&R crossover for a couple of Soul music's more legendary and prolific couples: Sam and Dave, David and Isaac.

YOU GOT ME HUMMIN'
Producers: Isaac Hayes, David Porter
Album: Double Dynamite
Record Label: Stax
Songwriters: Isaac Hayes, David Porter

Big in Rock circles. Covered by Billy Joel & the Hassles (Vanguard, '67) and Lydia Pense and Cold Blood (San Francisco, '70).

WHEN SOMETHING IS WRONG WITH MY BABY
Producer: Jim Stewart
Album: Double Dynamite
Record Label: Stax
Songwriters: Isaac Hayes, David Porter

Suggested segue: "It Hurts Me Too" by Jr. Wells.

1967

SOUL MAN
Producers: Isaac Hayes, David Porter
Album: Soul Men
Record Label: Stax
Songwriters: Isaac Hayes, David Porter

#1 R&B/Top-10 R&R crossover, in which the legendary exortation "Play it, Steve!" (Cropper) entered the lexicon of Rock and Roll.

1968

I THANK YOU
Producers: Isaac Hayes, David Porter
Album: I Thank You
Record Label: Atlantic
Songwriters: Isaac Hayes, David Porter

Their second biggest hit.

SOUL SISTER, BROWN SUGAR
Producers: Isaac Hayes, David Porter
Record Label: Atlantic
Songwriters: Isaac Hayes, David Porter

WRAP IT UP
Producers: Isaac Hayes, David Porter
Album: I Thank You
Record Label: Atlantic
Songwriters: Isaac Hayes, David Porter

Covered by the Fabulous Thunderbirds (Epic, '86).

SAM THE SHAM AND THE PHARAOHS
1965

WOOLY BULLY
Producer: Stan Kesler
Album: Wooly Bully
Record Label: MGM
Songwriter: Domingo Samudio
Tex-Mex on rye.

1966

LI'L RED RIDING HOOD
Producer: Stan Kessler
Album: Li'l Red Riding Hood
Record Label: MGM
Songwriter: Ronald Blackwell

THE SANDALS
1964

THEME FROM *ENDLESS SUMMER*
Producer: Richard Bock
Album: *The Endless Summer* Soundtrack
Record Label: World Pacific
Songwriters: Gaston Georis, John Blakely

Signing their guitar signature on the celluloid celebration of the surf.

TOMMY SANDS
1957

TEEN AGE CRUSH
Album: Steady Date with Tommy Sands
Record Label: Capitol
Songwriters: Audrey Allison, Joe Allison

Introduced on the TV drama "The Singing Idol." Teen idol Sands would never recover from being verbally ripped to shreds by Bob Dylan on "The Les Crane Show" a few years later.

SANFORD TOWNSHEND BAND
1976

SMOKE FROM A DISTANT FIRE
Producers: Barry Beckett, Jerry Wexler
Album: Sanford Townshend Band
Record Label: Warner Brothers
Songwriters: Ed Sanford, John Townshend, Steven Stewart
L.A. meets Memphis; L.A. wins.

SAMANTHA SANG
1977

EMOTION
Producers: Albey Galutin, Karl Richardson
Album: Emotion
Record Label: Private Stock
Songwriters: Barry Gibb, Robin Gibb
Could'a been the next Olivia Newton-John.

SANTANA
1969

EVIL WAYS
Producers: Brent Dangerfield, Santana
Album: Santana
Record Label: Columbia
Songwriter: Clarence Henry
From San Francisco to Chicago, via Cuba, with Carlos on guitar. Their biggest hit except for their cover of Fleetwood Mac's "Black Magic Woman."

SOUL SACRIFICE
Producers: Brent Dangerfield, Santana
Album: Santana
Record Label: Columbia
Songwriter: Carlos Santana
Latin-flavored percussion extravaganza, showcased at Woodstock.

1971

EVERYBODY'S EVERYTHING (BABY)
Album: Santana III
Record Label: Columbia
Songwriters: Carlos Santana, Milton Brown, Tyrone Moss
With Neal Schon in the band, on his way to Journey, Santana scores its third Top-20 R&R (second Top-40 R&B).

OYE COMO VA (LISTEN HOW IT GOES)
Producers: Fred Catero, Santana
Album: Abraxis
Record Label: Columbia
Songwriter: Tito Puente
Rocking the Latin standard, introduced by Tito Puente in 1963.

SANTO AND JOHNNY
1959

SLEEP WALK
Album: Santo and Johnny
Record Label: Canadian-American

Songwriters: Ann Farina, John Farina, Santo Farina
First #1 appearance for the steel guitar.

SUSAN SARANDON
1975

TOUCHA-TOUCHA-TOUCH ME
Album: *The Rocky Horror Picture Show* Cast Album
Record Label: Ode
Songwriter: Richard O'Brien
A cameo cutie from the classic cult musical.

JOE SATRIANI
1987

ALWAYS WITH ME, ALWAYS WITH YOU
Producers: John Cuniberti, Joe Satriani
Album: Surfing with the Alien
Record Label: Relativity
Songwriter: Joe Satriani
The S.F. guitar teacher (Kirk Hammett, Steve Vai) as hero.

LEO SAYER
1974

THE SHOW MUST GO ON
Record Label: Chrysalis
Songwriters: David Courtney, Leo Sayer
Covered by Three Dog Night (Dunhill, '74).

1975

LONG TALL GLASSES (I CAN DANCE)
Producers: Adam Faith, David Courtney
Album: Just a Boy
Record Label: Warner Brothers
Songwriters: David Courtney, Leo Sayer
Suggested segue: "Judy in Disguise (with Glasses)" by John Fred & the Playboy Band.

1976

YOU MAKE ME FEEL LIKE DANCING
Producer: Richard Perry
Album: Endless Flight
Record Label: Warner Brothers
Songwriters: Vini Poncia, Leo Sayer
Disco-flavored Pop Rock.

1977

WHEN I NEED YOU
Producer: Richard Perry
Album: Endless Flight
Record Label: Warner Brothers
Songwriters: Carole Bayer Sager, Albert Hammond

His biggest hit, here and in England.

BOZ SCAGGS
1976

LIDO SHUFFLE
Producer: Joe Wissert
Album: Silk Degrees
Record Label: Columbia
Songwriters: David Paich, William Scaggs

His defining groove.

LOWDOWN
Producer: Joe Wissert
Album: Silk Degrees
Record Label: Columbia
Songwriters: David Paich, William Scaggs

His biggest hit.

WE'RE ALL ALONE
Producer: Joe Wissert
Album: Silk Degrees
Record Label: Columbia
Songwriter: Boz Scaggs

His breakout barroom ballad. Covered by Rita Coolidge (A&M, '77).

SCANDAL
1983

GOODBYE TO YOU
Producer: Vini Poncia
Album: Scandal
Record Label: Columbia
Songwriter: Zack Smith

Early MTV hit with a do-it-yourself Punk attitude and one of the great New York street girl voices of Rock and Roll history (on this cut, anyway), Patty Smyth. Even Patti Smith would have approved.

LOVE'S GOT A LINE ON YOU
Producer: Vini Poncia
Album: Scandal
Record Label: Columbia
Songwriters: Zack Smith, Kathe Green

Perfect post-Brill Building Power Punk. Cyndi Lauper was listening.

1984

ONLY THE YOUNG
Producer: Mike Chapman
Album: Warrior
Record Label: Columbia
Songwriters: Steve Perry, Neal Schon, Jonathan Cain

Introduced in a feisty rendition by Patty Smyth, in just about her last authentic move. Journey's hit version was featured in the wrestling movie Vision Quest *(Geffen, '85).*

THE WARRIOR
Producer: Mike Chapman
Album: The Warrior
Record Label: Columbia
Songwriters: Holly Knight, Nick Gilder

Patty goes the Rock and Roll equivalent of Hollywood, resulting in a Top-10 hit.

JOEY SCARBURY
1981

BELIEVE IT OR NOT (THEME FROM *THE GREATEST AMERICAN HERO*)
Album: The Greatest American Hero
Record Label: Elektra
Songwriters: Stephen Geyer, Mlke Post

Another Mike Post inescapable TV theme.

THE MICHAEL SCHENKER GROUP
1980

INTO THE ARENA
Album: The Michael Schenker Group
Record Label: Chrysalis
Songwriter: Michael Schenker

Glistening Metal with a Germanic edge, by Rudolf's brother.

PETER SCHILLING
1983

MAJOR TOM (COMING HOME)
Producers: Peter Schilling, Armin Sabol
Album: Error in the System
Record Label: Elektra
Songwriters: Peter Schilling, David Lodge

Answer song to Bowie's "Space Oddity" ten years later. Suggested segues: "Rocket Man" by Elton John, "Ashes to Ashes" by David Bowie.

CLAUDIA SCHMIDT
1983

HARD LOVE
Producers: Claudia Schmidt, Michael Pasfield
Album: New Goodbyes, Old Hellos
Record Label: Flying Fish
Songwriter: Bob Franke

New Folk classic as interpreted by one of the scene's more powerful voices. Joni Mitchell would have loved to have written it. Franke's version, recorded live at a half-empty coffee house, sounds like Phil Ochs with a head cold.

THE SCHOOLBOYS
1957

PLEASE SAY YOU WANT ME
Producer: Leroy Kirkland
Record Label: Okeh
Songwriter: Donald Hayes

On every urban streetcorner in the '50s, another Frankie Lymon, yearning for acceptance and assimilation.

SCHOOLY D
1987

WE GET ILL
Album: Saturday Night (The Album)
Record Label: Schooly D/Jive
Songwriter: Jessie Weaver

The same streetcorner, thirty years later. In your face Rap from Philadelphia that reportedly influenced the Beastie Boys, yearns only for blood.

SCORPIONS
1977

THE SAILS OF CHARON
Producer: Dieter Dirks
Album: Taken by Force
Record Label: RCA
Songwriter: Uli Roth

Mystically inclined legend Uli Roth's showpiece that laid the groundwork for the Heavy Metal guitar excursions of the '80s. Every fleet-fingered aspiring virtuoso, from Randy Rhoads (Ozzy Osbourne) to Yngwie Malmsteen to Jason Becker (David Lee Roth) was listening.

1979

HOLIDAY
Album: Lovedrive
Record Label: Mercury
Songwriters: Rudolf Schenker, Klaus Meine

BOBBY SCOTT

1982

NO ONE LIKE YOU
Producer: Dieter Dirks
Album: Blackout
Record Label: Mercury
Songwriters: Rudolf Schenker, Klaus Meine

Signature riff.

1984

STILL LOVING YOU
Producer: Dieter Dirks
Album: Love at First Sting
Record Label: Mercury
Songwriters: Rudolf Schenker, Klaus Meine

The signature riff strikes again.

ROCK YOU LIKE A HURRICANE
Producer: Dieter Dirks
Album: Love at First Sting
Record Label: Mercury
Songwriters: Rudolf Schenker, Klaus Meine

A good year for Metal; the Scorpions' football chant hits Top-40 (Slade's "Run Runaway" hits Top-20).

1990

WIND OF CHANGE
Producer: Keith Olson
Album: Crazy World
Record Label: Mercury
Songwriter: Klaus Meine

Their biggest hit, inspired by the razing of the Berlin wall.

BOBBY SCOTT

1956

CHAIN GANG
Album: Scott Free
Record Label: ABC Paramount
Songwriters: Sol Quasha, Herb Yakus

Early taste of Jazz Rock.

1960

A TASTE OF HONEY
Album: A Taste of Honey
Songwriters: Ric Marlow, Bobby Scott

Classic Jazz Rock instrumental first performed in the play "A Taste of Honey;" covered by Martin Denny (Liberty, '62), the Beatles (Capitol, '64), and Herb Alpert & the Tijuana Brass (A&M, '65). Used in film version of the play, starring the immortal

Rita Tushingham. Suggested segue: "Brandy (You're a Fine Girl)" by Looking Glass.

FREDDIE SCOTT

1963

HEY, GIRL
Producer: Gerry Goffin
Album: Freddie Scott Sings
Record Label: Colpix
Songwriters: Gerry Goffin, Carole King

Previewing Uptown Soul with Goffin and King.

1967

ARE YOU LONELY FOR ME (BABY)?
Record Label: Shout
Songwriter: Bert Berns

#1 R&B/Top-40 R&R crossover.

JACK SCOTT

1958

MY TRUE LOVE
Producer: Ed Carlton
Album: Jack Scott
Record Label: Carlton
Songwriter: Jack Scott

B-side of "Leroy" was Scott's biggest hit; twangy Rockabilly from Detroit on the brink of Motown. Robert Gordon was listening in the East, Chris Isaac in the West.

1959

GOODBYE BABY
Producer: Ed Carlton
Record Label: Carlton
Songwriter: Jack Scott

THE WAY I WALK
Producer: Ed Carlton
Record Label: Carlton
Songwriter: Jack Scott

Future Rockabilly classic that barely made Top-40. Covered by Dave Edmunds (Swan Song, '77), Robert Gordon (Private Stock, '78), and the Cramps (IRS, '79) as produced by Alex Chilton.

WHAT IN THE WORLD'S COME OVER YOU
Producer: Ed Carlton
Album: What in the World's Come over You
Record Label: Top Rank
Songwriter: Jack Scott

1960

BURNING BRIDGES
Producer: Ed Carlton
Album: Burning Bridges
Songwriter: Melvin Miller

His second-biggest hit.

LINDA SCOTT

1961

DON'T BET MONEY HONEY
Album: Great Scott! Her Greatest Hits
Record Label: Canadian American
Songwriter: Linda Scott

Jack's sister; a voice out of Patience and Prudence, with Lesley Gore's attitude.

I'VE TOLD EVERY LITTLE STAR
Record Label: Canadian-American
Songwriters: Oscar Hammerstein II, Jerome Kern

From the '33 film Music in the Air.

GIL SCOTT-HERON

1975

THE BOTTLE
Album: First Minute of a New Day
Record Label: Arista
Songwriters: Gil Scott-Heron, Brian Jackson

In the great tradition of Amos Milburn ("Bad Bad Whiskey"), a former Lost Poet reclaims his protest turf. Suggested segue: "1 Million Bottlebags" by Public Enemy.

JOHANNESBURG
Album: From South Africa to South Carolina
Record Label: Arista
Songwriter: Gil Scott-Heron

Scott-Heron teams with Brian Jackson to re-invent the genre of Funk Protest, which he invented with "The Revolution Will Not Be Televised."

WINTER IN AMERICA
Album: The First Minute of a New Day
Record Label: Arista
Songwriter: Gil Scott-Heron

1977

WE ALMOST LOST DETROIT
Album: Bridges
Record Label: Arista
Songwriter: Gil Scott-Heron

Envisioning nuclear holocaust.

SCRITTI POLITTI
1985

PERFECT WAY
Producers: Green Strohmeyer-
Gartside, David Gamson
Album: Cupid and Psyche 85
Record Label: Warner Brothers
Songwriters: Green Strohmeyer-
Gartside, David Gamson

Only U.S. hit for the Alternative politicos.

SEAL
1991

CRAZY
Producer: Trevor Horn
Album: Seal
Record Label: Sire
Songwriter: Sealhenry (Seal) Samuel

International dance track, with a Reggae soul.

1994

PRAYER FOR THE DYING
Producer: Trevor Horn
Album: Seal
Record Label: ZTT/Sire
Songwriters: Sealhenry Samuel,
Isidore

Reggae-flavored anti-Gangsta Folk Rock warning.

SEALS AND CROFTS
1971

SUMMER BREEZE
Producer: Louie Shelton
Album: Summer Breeze
Record Label: Warner Brothers
Songwriters: James Seals, Darrell
Crofts

Lilting Folk Rock air. In a statistical quirk that would be more appropriate for a Heavy Metal band, all three of Seals and Crofts' major hits peaked at #6. No wonder they took to the Bahai religion.

1973

DIAMOND GIRL
Producer: Louie Shelton
Album: Diamond Girl
Record Label: Warner Brothers
Songwriters: James Seals, Darrell
Crofts

Everly-esque.

1976

GET CLOSER
Producer: Louie Shelton
Album: Get Closer
Record Label: Warner Brothers
Songwriters: James Seals, Darrell
Crofts

More placid Folk Rock, better known as a toothpaste commercial.

THE SEARCHERS
1964

WHAT HAVE THEY DONE TO THE RAIN
Album: The New Searchers LP
Record Label: Kapp
Songwriter: Malvina Reynolds

Malvina Reynolds' anti-nuke lament hits the Top-40 as Folk Rock.

SEBADOAH
1991

FREED PIG
Album: III
Record Label: Homestead
Songwriter: Lou Barlow

Signature tune for the modern king of low-fi Rock. Barlow's "Natural One" would hit Top-40 in '95 by virtue of its use in the scathing pseudo-documentary Kids.

GIMME INDIE ROCK
Record Label: Homestead
Songwriter: Lou Barlow

Defining the '90s low-fi sound and attitude.

JOHN SEBASTIAN
1969

SHE'S A LADY
Producer: Paul Rothchild
Album: John B. Sebastian
Record Label: Kama Sutra
Songwriter: John B. Sebastian

Written for the Dustin Hoffman musical, "Jimmy Shine." Released as a single just after John left the Spoonful.

1976

WELCOME BACK
Producers: John Sebastian, Steve
Barri
Album: Welcome Back
Record Label: Reprise
Songwriter: John B. Sebastian

Sebastian funds his future jug band with the theme for the TV series "Welcome Back, Kotter."

NEIL SEDAKA
1958

THE DIARY
Producer: Al Nevins
Album: Neil Sedaka
Record Label: RCA Victor
Songwriters: Howard Greenfield,
Neil Sedaka

Rejected by Little Anthony, this tune established Sedaka as a suitable alternate boy soprano.

1959

OH CAROL
Producers: Al Nevins, Don Kirshner
Album: Neil Sedaka Sings His
Greatest Hits
Record Label: RCA
Songwriters: Howard Greenfield,
Neil Sedaka

Sedaka's first Top-10 hit, allegedly written for Brooklyn neighbor, fan, and pizza parlor love object, Carole Klein (King), who responded with "Oh Neil," on Alpine, which, in the Bobby-Jimmy-Teddy "Bandstand" era, was obviously the wrong name at the right time, because even though it stiffed, it not only caught the attention of another neighborhood Neil—Neil Diamond—but also the ear of Don Kirshner, who signed Carole and her husband Gerry (and eventually Neil Diamond as well) to his publishing company, thereby opening the door to several major Brooklyn careers and a jukebox full of classic singles.

1960

STAIRWAY TO HEAVEN
Producers: Al Nevins, Don Kirshner
Album: Neil Sedaka Sings His
Greatest Hits
Record Label: RCA Victor
Songwriters: Howard Greenfield,
Neil Sedaka

Jimmy Page wasn't listening.

1961

CALENDAR GIRL
Producers: Al Nevins, Don Kirshner
Album: Neil Sedaka Sings His
Greatest Hits
Record Label: RCA Victor
Songwriters: Howard Greenfield,
Neil Sedaka

Made into a movie in '94.

HAPPY BIRTHDAY, SWEET SIXTEEN

Producers: Al Nevins, Don Kirshner
Album: Neil Sedaka Sings His Greatest Hits
Record Label: RCA Victor
Songwriters: Howard Greenfield, Neil Sedaka

Quintessential song of the quintessential Rock and Roll age.

1962

BREAKING UP IS HARD TO DO

Producer: Al Nevins
Don Kirshner
Album: Neil Sedaka Sings His Greatest Hits
Record Label: RCA Victor
Songwriters: Howard Greenfield, Neil Sedaka

Reputedly inspired by Rock and Roll classic "It Will Stand" by the Showmen, Sedaka's biggest hit of the '60s. Re-recorded by Sedaka (Rocket, '76).

NEXT DOOR TO AN ANGEL

Producers: Al Nevins, Don Kirshner
Album: Neil Sedaka Sings His Greatest Hits
Record Label: RCA Victor
Songwriters: Howard Greenfield, Neil Sedaka

His sixth and last Top-10 hit of the '60s.

1974

LAUGHTER IN THE RAIN

Producers: Robert Appere, Neil Sedaka
Album: Sedaka's Back
Record Label: Rocket
Songwriters: Phil Cody, Neil Sedaka

Completing his comeback with his first #1.

LOVE WILL KEEP US TOGETHER

Producers: Robert Appere, Neil Sedaka
Album: Sedaka's Back
Record Label: Rocket
Songwriters: Howard Greenfield, Neil Sedaka

Last tune written by the story-writing team before they broke up, Sedaka moving to England. Cover by The Captain and Tennille (A&M, '75). Went to #1 in the U.S. (Top-40 U.K.) and was song of the year. The album Sedaka's Back compiles three albums he made in England.

1975

BAD BLOOD

Producers: Robert Appere, Neil Sedaka
Album: Overnight Success
Record Label: Rocket
Songwriters: Phil Cody, Neil Sedaka

With Elton John on backing vocals, Neil gets his biggest hit.

1980

SHOULD'VE NEVER LET YOU GO

Producers: Robert Appere, Neil Sedaka
Album: In the Pocket
Record Label: Elektra
Songwriters: Phil Cody, Neil Sedaka

With daughter Dara, Sedaka makes another comeback.

SEDUCTION

1989

TWO TO MAKE IT RIGHT

Producer: Rob Clivilles
Album: Nothing Matters without Love
Record Label: Vendetta
Songwriter: David Cole

Nouveau Dance sensation. Clivilles and Cole would be hot in the '90s dance hall.

THE SEEDS

1967

CAN'T SEEM TO MAKE YOU MINE

Producer: Marcus Tybalt
Album: The Seeds
Record Label: GNP-Crescendo
Songwriter: Sky Saxon

Garage band cult favorite. Covered by Big Star (PVC, '68) and the Ramones (Warner Brothers, '94).

PUSHIN' TOO HARD

Producer: Marcus Tybalt
Album: Pushin' Too Hard
Record Label: GNP-Crescendo
Songwriter: Sky Saxon

The ultimate garage anthem, whose place in history was sealed by its inclusion in the Jack Nicholson pre-Easy Rider classic Psyche Out.

PEGGY SEEGER

1962

FIRST TIME EVER I SAW YOUR FACE

Record Label: Folkways
Songwriter: Ewan MacColl

Folk standard, written for Peggy by her husband Ewan and covered by the Kingston Trio (Capitol, '62), and Peter, Paul and Mary (Warner Brothers, '65). It became a hit in '72 after being sung by Roberta Flack in the Clint Eastwood movie Play Misty for Me.

PETE SEEGER

1962

TURN! TURN! TURN! (TO EVERYTHING THERE IS A SEASON)

Producer: John Hammond
Album: The Bitter & the Sweet
Record Label: Columbia
Songwriter: Pete Seeger

From the Bible by way of the prophet Pete Seeger. Covered by the Limeliters (RCA, '62). The Byrds (Columbia, '65) brought it to #1, helping usher in Folk/Rock.

WHERE HAVE ALL THE FLOWERS GONE

Producer: John Hammond
Album: The Bitter & the Sweet
Record Label: Columbia
Songwriter: Pete Seeger

Seeger's classic antiwar song, adapted from the Russian novel And Quietly Flows the Don. Covered by the Kingston Trio (Capitol, '62), Peter, Paul and Mary (Warner Brothers, '62), Johnny Rivers (Imperial, '65).

1964

LITTLE BOXES

Producer: John Hammond
Album: We Shall Overcome
Record Label: Columbia
Songwriter: Malvina Reynolds

Spiritual father of the Folk Rock era, Pete Seeger's only chart appearance of the Rock and Roll era comes with this one minute Malvina Reynolds anti-suburbia gem. Suggested segues: "Big Yellow Taxi" by Joni Mitchell and "Pink Houses" by John (Cougar) Mellencamp.

THE SEEKERS

I'LL NEVER FIND ANOTHER YOU
Producer: Tom Springfield
Album: Best Of
Record Label: Capitol
Songwriter: Tom Springfield
Standard Folk Rock harmonizing.

1966

GEORGY GIRL
Producer: Tom Springfield
Album: Georgy Girl
Record Label: Capitol
Songwriters: Jim Dale, Tom Springfield
Title tune from the movie, co-authored by the Broadway actor Dale.

BOB SEGER

1969

RAMBLIN' GAMBLIN' MAN
Producer: Hideout Product
Album: Ramblin' Gamblin' Man
Record Label: Capitol
Songwriter: Bob Seger
First single for the Hard Rock journeyman and his band, the System, hits Top-20. It would be eight years and many miles before he would better it.

1975

BEAUTIFUL LOSER
Producers: Punch Andrews, Bob Seger
Album: Beautiful Loser
Record Label: Capitol
Songwriter: Bob Seger
His early-years signature, which he must have thought would be his epitaph. Title of Leonard Cohen's first novel.

1976

FIRE DOWN BELOW
Producers: Bob Seger, Jack Richardson
Album: Night Moves
Record Label: Capitol
Songwriter: Bob Seger
Basic sweaty frat-house Rocker.

MAINSTREET
Producers: Jack Richardson, Bob Seger
Album: Night Moves
Record Label: Capitol
Songwriter: Bob Seger

Striving to mythify Michigan the way Springsteen did New Jersey.

NIGHT MOVES
Producers: Jack Richardson, Bob Seger
Album: Night Moves
Record Label: Capitol
Songwriter: Bob Seger
Invading Mellencamp turf with a poignant reminiscence of a Midwestern lost youth.

ROCK AND ROLL NEVER FORGETS
Producers: Jack Richardson, Bob Seger
Album: Night Moves
Record Label: Capitol
Songwriter: Bob Seger
As success beckons, Seger looks back on what brought him here, with his best bar-room rocker.

1977

HOLLYWOOD NIGHTS
Album: Stranger in Town
Record Label: Capitol
Songwriter: Bob Seger
Crediting the Silver Bullet Band, Seger predates Joel and Springsteen as a working-class superstar tempted by a Hollywood cutie.

OLD TIME ROCK AND ROLL
Producers: Punch Andrews, Bob Seger
Album: Stranger in Town
Record Label: Capitol
Songwriters: George Jackson, Harold Jones III
This durable Seger warhorse achieved legendary status when Tom Cruise played air broom to it in the immortal '83 film Risky Business.

STILL THE SAME
Producers: Punch Andrews, Bob Seger
Album: Stranger in Town
Record Label: Capitol
Songwriter: Bob Seger

1979

WE'VE GOT TONIGHT
Producers: Bob Seger, Muscle Shoals Rhythm Section
Album: Stranger in Town
Record Label: Capitol
Songwriter: Bob Seger
Cover by Kenny Rogers and Kim Carnes went #1 C&W/#10 R&R (Liberty, '83).

1980

AGAINST THE WIND
Producer: Bill Szymczyk
Album: Against the Wind
Record Label: Capitol
Songwriter: Bob Seger
Seger returns to his favorite theme, charting his heroic course from Midwestern working-man to superstar and back again.

FIRE LAKE
Producer: Bob Seger
Album: Against the Wind
Record Label: Capitol
Songwriter: Bob Seger
Suggested segue: "Burn On, Big River" by Randy Newman.

1982

SHAME ON THE MOON
Album: The Distance
Record Label: Capitol
Songwriter: Rodney Crowell
With a Country songwriter, Seger gains his second biggest hit single.

1983

MAKIN' THUNDERBIRDS
Album: The Distance
Record Label: Capitol
Songwriter: Bob Seger
Attempting to reclaim his Detroit roots.

1986

LIKE A ROCK
Producers: Punch Andrews, Bob Seger, David Cole
Album: Like a Rock
Record Label: Capitol
Songwriter: Bob Seger
Chevy Metal.

1987

SHAKEDOWN
Producers: Harold Faltermeyer, Keith Forsey
Album: *Beverly Hills Cop II* Soundtrack
Record Label: MCA
Songwriters: Harold Faltermeyer, Keith Forsey, Bob Seger
The last remaining piece of the dream falls into place, when his Hollywood connections pay off with a #1 single.

THE SELECTER
1979

ON MY RADIO
Album: Too Much Pressure
Record Label: Chrysalis
Songwriter: Neol Davis

First and biggest U.K. hit for the influential Ska band. Their instrumental "The Selecter" was the B-side of the Specials' "Gangsters."

MICHAEL SEMBELLO
1983

MANIAC
Producers: Phil Ramone, Michael Sembello
Album: *Flashdance* Soundtrack
Record Label: Casablanca
Songwriters: Michael Sembello, Dennis Matkosky

From a movie that knocked off Saturday Night Fever, with a guitar solo that knocks off Eddie Van Halen's in "Beat It."

THE SENSATIONS
1962

LET ME IN
Producer: Kae Williams
Album: Let Me In
Record Label: Argo
Songwriter: Yvonne Baker

A morality tale of winning and losing in the great party era of the early '60s; the winners went on to star in beach movies, the losers made better records.

THE SERENDIPITY SINGERS
1964

DON'T LET THE RAIN COME DOWN (CROOKED LITTLE MAN)
Producers: Fred Weintraub, Bob Bowers
Album: The Serendipity Singers
Record Label: Philips
Songwriters: Ersel Hickey, Ed Miller

Folk novelty.

DAVID SEVILLE
1958

WITCH DOCTOR
Producer: Ross Bagdasarian
Record Label: Liberty
Songwriter: Ross Bagdasarian

Wholesome family fun with a tape recorder, predating the Chipmunks by about six months.

THE SEX PISTOLS
1977

ANARCHY IN THE U.K.
Producers: Chris Thomas, Bill Price
Album: Never Mind the Bollocks, Here's the Sex Pistols
Record Label: Warner Brothers
Songwriters: Steve Jones, Paul Cook, Glen Matlock, John Lydon (Johnny Rotten)

Launching the good ship Punk Rock in London with a Molotov Cocktail instead of champagne. Every angry young band within earshot on two continents was suitably impressed and influenced.

GOD SAVE THE QUEEN
Producers: Chris Thomas, Bill Price
Album: Never Mind the Bollocks, Here's the Sex Pistols
Record Label: Warner Brothers
Songwriters: Paul Cook, Steve Jones, Glen Matlock, John Lydon (Johnny Rotten)

Their first and biggest U.K. hit, establishing the nihilistic attitude that would make them critics' darlings.

HOLIDAYS IN THE SUN
Producers: Chris Thomas, Bill Price
Album: Never Mind the Bollocks, Here's the Sex Pistols
Record Label: Warner Brothers
Songwriters: Steve Jones, Paul Cook, John Beverly (Sid Vicious), John Lydon (Johnny Rotten)

Suggested segue: "Holidays in Cambodia" by the Dead Kennedys.

PRETTY VACANT
Producers: Chris Thomas, Bill Price
Album: Never Mind the Bollocks, Here's the Sex Pistols
Record Label: Warner Brothers
Songwriters: Steve Jones, Paul Cook, Glen Matlock, John Lydon (Johnny Rotten)

Their lasting credo.

SHA-NA-NA
1971

THE TOP FORTY OF THE LORD
Producer: Erwin Kramer
Album: Sha-Na-Na
Record Label: Buddah

Songwriter: Scott Simon

Ingenious Top-40 show band and TV concept tries its hand at semi-serious spoof; fails.

SHABBA BANKS
1992

MR. LOVERMAN
Album: Rough & Ready, Vol. 1
Record Label: Epic
Songwriters: Rexton Gordon, Mikey Bennett, H. Lindo

Reggae breakthrough, featured in the film Deep Cover.

THE SHADOWS
1960

APACHE
Record Label: Columbia
Songwriter: Jerry Lordan

Legendary #1 U.K. instrumental by Cliff Richard's backing band, the Shadows, with guitar hero Hank Marvin, an early influence on the Ventures, and Mark Knopfler of Dire Straits. U.S. hit by Jorgen Ingmann (Atco, '61). Introduced by the U.K. studio musician Bert Weedon.

THE SHAGGS
1969

MY PAL FOOT FOOT
Album: Philosophy of the World
Record Label: Third World/Red Rooster (80)
Songwriter: Dorothy Wiggins

In the mythology of low-fi, the Shaggs make kindred spirit Jonathan Richman sound like Frank Zappa and Frank Sinatra combined. The album was re-released in '80. The song was re-cut on the Shaggs' Own Thing (Red Rooster, '82). But it still remained awesomely awful.

SHAI
1992

BABY I'M YOURS
Producer: Carl Martin
Album: If I Ever Fall in Love
Record Label: Gasoline Alley/MCA
Songwriters: Carl Martin, Marc Gay

COMFORTER
Producer: Carl Martin
Album: If I Ever Fall in Love
Record Label: Gasoline Alley/MCA
Songwriters: Carl Martin, Marc Gay, Dannel Van Rensalier

IF I EVER FALL IN LOVE
Producer: Carl Martin
Album: If I Ever Fall in Love
Record Label: Gasoline Alley/MCA
Songwriter: Carl Martin

Shades of Doo-Wop past; first and biggest crossover ballad from the D.C. group. All-4-One and Boyz II Men would eventually steal their turf.

SHAKESPEARE'S SISTER
1992
STAY
Album: Hormonally Yours
Record Label: London
Songwriters: Siobhan Fahey, Marcella Levy (Marcella Detroit), Dave Stewart

Bananarama redux.

SHALAMAR
1979
THE SECOND TIME AROUND
Producer: Leon Sylvers
Album: Big Fun
Record Label: Solar
Songwriters: William Shelby, Leon Sylvers

#1 R&B/Top-10 R&R crossover fashion statement from the former "Soul Train" dancers. Jody Watley and Howard Hewitt came from this group.

1984
DANCING IN THE SHEETS
Album: Heartbreak
Record Label: Columbia
Songwriter: Bill Wolfer

Their last big crossover hit, featured in the movie Footloose. *Hewett and Watley left for solo careers.*

THE SHANGRI-LAS
1964
GIVE HIM A GREAT BIG KISS
Producer: Shadow Morton
Album: The Shangri-Las
Record Label: Red Bird
Songwriter: George Morton

Covered by the New York Dolls (Mercury, '74).

LEADER OF THE PACK
Producer: Shadow Morton
Album: The Shangri-Las
Record Label: Red Bird
Songwriters: Jeff Barry, Ellie Greenwich, George Morton

Her Ma said he was bad, but she knew he was sad: This "He's a Rebel"–meets–"Teen Angel," with Long Island's Billy Joel on piano, was their only #1.

REMEMBER (WALKING IN THE SAND)
Producers: Jeff Barry, Ellie Greenwich, Artie Ripp
Album: The Shangri-Las
Record Label: Red Bird
Songwriter: George Morton

Spector's girl-group sound of the Ronettes brought up a dramatic notch to the level of soap opera. First hit for the rebel sisters act (Betty and Mary Weiss, Marge and Mary Ann Ganser) from Queens, New York, was covered by Goffin and King's daughter, Louise, in a sentimental Brill Building tribute (Asylum, '79), and Aerosmith, in an obvious New York Doll's move (Columbia, '80).

1965
I CAN NEVER GO HOME ANYMORE
Producer: Shadow Morton
Album: Past, Present and Future
Record Label: Red Bird
Songwriters: George Morton, Jerry Grimaldi

Their prophetic last hit. Mary and Marge Ganser both died in the '70s.

1966
LONG LIVE OUR LOVE
Producer: Shadow Morton
Album: Past, Present and Future
Record Label: Red Bird
Songwriters: Sidney Barnes, J. J. Jackson

SHANICE
1991
I LOVE YOUR SMILE
Producer: Narada Michael Walden
Album: Inner Child
Record Label: Motown
Songwriters: Shanice Wilson, Narada Michael Walden, Sylvester Jackson, Jarvis La Rue Baker

#1 R&B/Top-10 R&R crossover ballad.

1992
SAVING FOREVER FOR YOU
Producer: David Foster
Album: Beverly Hills 90210 Soundtrack
Record Label: Giant
Songwriter: Diane Warren

Automatic.

SHANNON
1984
LET THE MUSIC PLAY
Album: Let the Music Play
Record Label: Mirage
Songwriters: Chris Barbosa, Ed Chisolm

Big dance track: #1 R&B/Top-10 R&R.

DEL SHANNON
1961
HATS OFF TO LARRY
Producers: Irving Micahnik, Harry Balk
Album: Little Town Flirt
Record Label: Big Top
Songwriter: Del Shannon

His trademark falsetto angst; his second biggest hit.

LITTLE TOWN FLIRT
Producers: Irving Micahnik, Harry Balk
Album: Little Town Flirt
Record Label: Big Top
Songwriters: Del Shannon, Marion McKenzie

Del's major nemesis. Suggested segue: "Runaround Sue" by Dion.

RUNAWAY
Producers: Irving Micahnik, Harry Balk
Album: Little Town Flirt
Record Label: Big Top
Songwriters: Del Shannon, Max Crook

Shannon's first and biggest hit (#1 U.S./U.K.), sported a trademark FarFisa organ sound that would launch a million '60s Garage bands—even though it was actually Max Crook's Musitron.

1964
I GO TO PIECES
Producers: Irving Micahnik, Harry Balk
Record Label: Amy
Songwriter: Del Shannon

Covered by Peter and Gordon (Capitol, '64).

KEEP SEARCHIN' (WE'LL FOLLOW THE SUN)
Producers: Irving Micahnik, Harry Balk
Record Label: Amy
Songwriter: Del Shannon

Last of his eight U.K. Top-10s.

STRANGER IN TOWN
1965

Producers: Irving Micahnik, Harry Balk
Record Label: Amy
Songwriter: Del Shannon

More of a solitary man than Neil Diamond, more of a loner than Neil Young, Del Shannon rides into the sunset.

FEARGAL SHARKEY
1985

A GOOD HEART

Producer: Dave Stewart
Album: Feargal Sharkey
Record Label: A&M/Virgin
Songwriter: Maria McKee

Former Undertones lead singer gets his only #1 U.K., written by former Lone Justice lead singer.

DEE DEE SHARP
1962

MASHED POTATO TIME

Album: It's Mashed Potato Time
Record Label: Cameo
Songwriters: Kal Mann (Jon Sheldon), Harry Land

Her first and her biggest hit, a #1 R&B/Top-10 R&R crossover, co-opted from "(Do the) Mashed Potatoes (Part I)" by Nat Kendrick and the Swans (Dade, '60), and Joey Dee & the Starliters (Roulette, '61). James Brown later verified the step with his own "Mashed Potatoes, U.S.A." (King, '62). But it was no Twist.

RIDE

Record Label: Cameo
Songwriters: Kal Mann (Jon Sheldon), Dave Leon

1963

DO THE BIRD

Album: Do the Bird
Record Label: Cameo
Songwriters: Kal Mann, Dave Appell

A dance later immortalized by the Rivingtons with "The Bird Is the Word."

GRAVY

Album: It's Mashed Potato Time
Record Label: Cameo
Songwriters: Kal Mann, Dave Appell

GEORGIA SHAW
1954

HONEYCOMB

Record Label: Decca
Songwriter: Bob Merrill

Covered by Jimmie Rodgers (Roulette, '57).

SANDIE SHAW
1965

GIRL DON'T COME

Album: Sandie Shaw
Record Label: Reprise
Songwriter: Chris Andrews

Biggest U.S. crossover for the English proto-hippie thrush.

SHEILA E.
1984

THE GLAMOROUS LIFE

Producers: Sheila E., Starr Company
Album: Sheila E. in the Glamourous Life
Record Label: Warner Brothers
Songwriter: Prince Rogers Nelson

First and biggest hit for Prince's drummer and protege.

1986

A LOVE BIZARRE

Producer: Sheila E.
Album: Romance 1600
Record Label: Warner Brothers
Songwriters: Prince Rogers Nelson, Sheila Escovedo

Kiss and Tell.

PETE SHELLEY
1982

HOMOSAPIEN

Album: Homosapien
Record Label: Arista
Songwriter: Pete Shelley

Dance hit for the former leader of the Buzzcocks.

THE SHELLS
1957

BABY OH BABY

Record Label: Johnson
Songwriters: Hiram Johnson, Nathaniel Banknight, Walter Coleman

Classic New York Doo-Wop rescued from obscurity in '61, when it became the group's only hit.

SHEP AND THE LIMELITES
1961

DADDY'S HOME

Album: Our Anniversary
Record Label: Hull
Songwriters: James Sheppard, William Miller

One of the all-time Doo-Wop classics.

SHERIFF
1983

WHEN I'M WITH YOU

Album: Sheriff
Record Label: Capitol
Songwriter: Arnold Lanni

The ultimate one-hit wonder, went to #1 five years after the band broke up.

BOBBY SHERMAN
1969

LA, LA, LA (IF I HAD YOU)

Producer: Jackie Mills
Album: Here Comes Bobby
Record Label: Metromedia
Songwriter: Danny Janssen

Same team, same formula, and nearly the same results as his biggest hit, "Little Woman."

LITTLE WOMAN

Producer: Jackie Mills
Album: Bobby Sherman
Record Label: Metromedia
Songwriter: Danny Janssen

The unlikely teen idol, separated at birth from Barry Manilow.

1970

EASY COME, EASY GO

Producer: Jackie Mills
Album: Here Comes Bobby
Record Label: Metromedia
Songwriters: Diane Hildebrand, Jack Keller

Commentary on Bobby Sherman, the man and the phenomenon.

JULIE, DO YA LOVE ME

Producer: Jackie Mills
Album: Portrait of Bobby
Record Label: Metromedia
Songwriter: Tom Bahler

RICHARD SHINDELL
1992

ARE YOU HAPPY NOW
Album: Sparrow's Flight
Record Label: Philo
Songwriter: Richard Shindell
Witty and biting Folk Rock word play.

SHINEHEAD
1986

WHO THE CAP FITS
Producer: Claude Evans
Album: Rough and Rugged
Record Label: African Love Music
Songwriter: Edmund Aiken
Roots-Rock Reggae Rap, influenced by Bob Marley.

THE SHIRELLES
1958

I MET HIM ON A SUNDAY
Producer: Florence Greenberg
Album: Tonight's the Night
Record Label: Decca
Songwriters: Mickie Harris, Shirley Owens, Beverly Lee, Doris Kenner
Their first song, co-written by the group, a timeless gem of Doo-Wop love and loss. Suggested segue: "Da Doo Ron Ron" by the Crystals (Philles, '63).

1960

BOYS
Producer: Luther Dixon
Album: Tonight's the Night
Record Label: Scepter
Songwriters: Luther Dixon, Wes Farrell
B-side of "Will You Love Me Tomorrow" Covered by the Beatles (Vee-Jay, '64).

TONIGHT'S THE NIGHT
Producer: Luther Dixon
Album: Tonight's the Night
Record Label: Scepter
Songwriters: Luther Dixon, Shirley Owens
Introducing Luther Dixon to the Shirelles; introducing the Shirelles to the national market.

WILL YOU LOVE ME TOMORROW
Producer: Luther Dixon
Album: Greatest Hits
Record Label: Scepter
Songwriters: Gerry Goffin, Carole King

Classic Rock and Roll restatement of the classic teen dilemma. Covered by the Four Seasons (Philips, '68), Linda Ronstadt (Capitol, '70), Melanie (Neighborhood, '73). First of the Shirelles's four #2 R&B hits (no #1s).

1961

BABY, IT'S YOU
Producer: Burt Bacharach
Album: Baby, It's You
Record Label: Scepter
Songwriters: Burt Bacharach, Mack David, Barney Williams
Their abortive Pop move. Covered by the Smith (Dunhill, '69).

MAMA SAID
Producer: Luther Dixon
Album: Greatest Hits
Record Label: Scepter
Songwriters: Luther Dixon, Willie Dennson
Top-10 R&B/R&R crossover. Suggested segue: "Shop Around" by the Miracles.

SOLDIER BOY
Producer: Luther Dixon
Album: Baby, It's You
Record Label: Scepter
Songwriters: Florence Greenburg (Florence Green), Luther Dixon
Their biggest hit; a #2 R&B/#1 R&R crossover.

1962

PUTTY IN YOUR HANDS
Producer: Luther Dixon
Album: Baby, It's You
Record Label: Scepter
Songwriters: John Patton, Edward Snyder
Covered by the Yardbirds (Epic, '65).

1963

FOOLISH LITTLE GIRL
Producer: Luther Dixon
Album: Baby, It's You
Record Label: Scepter
Songwriters: Howard Greenfield, Helen Miller
Their sixth and last Top-10 R&R.

1964

SHA-LA-LA
Producer: Luther Dixon
Record Label: Scepter
Songwriters: Robert Mosley, Robert Taylor
Covered by Manfred Mann (Ascot, '64).

SHIRLEY AND COMPANY
1974

SHAME, SHAME, SHAME
Producer: Sylvia Robinson
Album: Shame, Shame, Shame
Record Label: Vibration
Songwriter: Sylvia Robinson
#1 R&B/Top-20 R&R crossover for Shirley of Shirley and Lee.

SHIRLEY AND LEE
1956

LET THE GOOD TIMES ROLL
Album: Shirley and Lee
Record Label: Aladdin
Songwriter: Lee Leonard
Party classic is one of the ultimate artifacts of New Orleans; Top-10 R&B/Top-20 R&R crossover.

MICHELLE SHOCKED
1988

ANCHORAGE
Producer: Pete Anderson
Album: Short Sharp Shocked
Record Label: Mercury
Songwriter: Michelle Shocked
Austin Folk with a rambling epic.

SHOCKING BLUE
1969

LOVE BUZZ
Producer: Robbie van Leeuwen
Album: This Is the Shocking Blue
Record Label: Colossus
Songwriter: Robbie Van Leeuwen
Covered by Nirvana on the seminal Seattle album Bleach (Sub Pop, '88).

VENUS
Producer: Robbie van Leeuwen
Album: This Is the Shocking Blue
Record Label: Colossus
Songwriter: Robbie Van Leeuwen
Frantic Dutch crossover went to #1 U.S. Cover by England's Bananarama (London, '86) also went to #1 U.S.

THE SHOES
1979

TOMORROW NIGHT
Album: Present Tense
Record Label: Elektra
Songwriters: Jeff Murphy, Gary Klebe

Low-fi super heroes of the Midwest. This is a re-recording of their Bomp single of '78.

TROY SHONDELL

1961

THIS TIME
Producer: Troy Shondell
Record Label: Gold Crest/Liberty
Songwriter: Chips Moman

In the Don French/Rod Bernard Elvis wannabe mold.

SHONEN KNIFE

1990

ICE CREAM CITY
Album: Shonen Knife
Record Label: Gastanka/Giant
Songwriters: Michie Nakatori, Naoko Yamano

The girl-group sound in Japanese. Covered by Christmas (Gastanka Rockville, '90).

SHOW STOPPERS

1968

(AIN'T NOTHING BUT A) HOUSE PARTY
Producer: Del Sharh
Record Label: Heritage
Songwriters: Dell Sharh, Joseph Thomas

Classic Soul shouter, covered by the J. Geils Band (Atlantic, '73).

THE SHOWMEN

1961

IT WILL STAND
Producer: Allen Toussaint
Record Label: Minit
Songwriter: General Johnson

One of Rock and Roll's first anthems. General Johnson went on to lesser things.

JANE SIBERRY

1993

LOVE IS EVERYTHING
Producers: Brian Eno, Jane Siberry, Michael Brooks
Album: When I Was a Boy
Record Label: Reprise
Songwriter: Jane Siberry

Defining moment for the quirky Canadian singer/songwriter: Laurie Anderson via Joni Mitchell.

THE SILENCERS

1990

A BLUES FOR BUDDAH
Producers: Flood, the Silencers
Album: A Blues for Buddah
Record Label: RCA
Songwriter: Jimmie O'Neill

U2-esque plaint from Ireland about the Middle East.

THE SILHOUETTES

1957

GET A JOB
Producer: Kae Williams
Album: Get a Job
Record Label: Ember
Songwriters: Richard Lewis, Howard Biggs

One of the all-time classic one-shots; a #1 R&B/R&R crossover in the Joe Turner mode, its disturbingly realistic content disguised by its nonsense syllables, and marketed to teens via "American Bandstand." Covered by the Mills Brothers (Decca, '57). In response, Smokey Robinson wrote "Got a Job" for the Miracles. In a more delayed but no less appropriate reaction, the '50s parody group Sha-Na-Na named themselves after the song's nonsense syllables.

SILK

1992

FREAK ME
Producers: Keith Sweat, T.H.
Album: Lose Control
Record Label: Keia
Songwriters: Keith Sweat, Roy Murray

#1 R&B/R&R crossover come-on.

THE SILOS

1990

PICTURE OF HELEN
Producers: Pete Moore, Bob Rupe
Album: The Silos
Record Label: RCA
Songwriter: Walter Salas-Humera

The Los Lobos of the East, with a sad lament for their indie past that held so much more promise than their major label present.

SILVER CONVENTION

1975

FLY, ROBIN, FLY
Producer: Michael Kunze
Album: Save Me
Record Label: Midland International
Songwriters: Sylvester Levay, Stephen Prager

#1 R&B/R&R crossover from the discos of Germany.

1976

GET UP AND BOOGIE
Producer: Michael Kunze
Album: Silver Convention
Record Label: Midland International
Songwriters: Sylvester Levay, Stephen Prager

Last dance.

SHEL SILVERSTEIN

1962

BOA CONSTRICTOR
Album: Inside Folk Songs
Record Label: Atlantic
Songwriter: Shel Silverstein

The advent of a twisted talent. As an author, Silverstein has brought endearing quirkiness to the Top-40 with "Cover of the Rolling Stone" for Dr. Hook and the Medicine Show (Columbia, '72) and "I Got Stoned and I Missed It" (Jim Stafford, '75). As a crooner, he makes Tom Waits sound like Johnny Mathis. Covered by Johnny Cash (Columbia, '69).

1969

A BOY NAMED SUE
Producers: Chet Atkins, Felton Jarvis
Album: A Boy Named Sue and His Other Country Songs
Record Label: RCA
Songwriter: Shel Silverstein

Playboy cartoonist strikes again. This Silverstein classic novelty was Johnny Cash's third #1 C&W/#2 R&R crossover of the year (the other two were "Folsom Prison Blues" and "Daddy Sang Bass") and by far his biggest all-time hit (Columbia, '69). Suggested segue: "My Ding-a-Ling" by Chuck Berry (for some career commiseration).

1973

FREAKIN' AT THE FREAKER'S BALL
Album: Freakin' at the Freaker's Ball
Record Label: Columbia
Songwriter: Shel Silverstein

I GOT STONED AND I MISSED IT
Album: Freakin' at the Freaker's Ball
Record Label: Columbia
Songwriter: Shel Silverstein

CARLY SIMON
1971

ANTICIPATION
Producer: Paul Samwell-Smith
Album: Anticipation
Record Label: Elektra
Songwriter: Carly Simon

Stentorian show-Folk Rock-turned-catsup commercial, defining the stopped-up hopes of an impatient generation.

LONG TERM PHYSICAL EFFECTS
Record Label: Decca
Songwriters: Carly Simon, Tim Saunders

Early Carly sings about drugs in a cameo appearance in the Milos Foreman cult film Taking Off.

THAT'S THE WAY I'VE ALWAYS HEARD IT SHOULD BE
Producer: Eddie Kramer
Album: Carly Simon
Record Label: Elektra
Songwriters: Carly Simon, Jacob Brackman

The lament of the privileged white American princess effectively marked the advent of upper middle-class Folk Rock. Performed in an early Rock video by Carly at her Upper West Side New York apartment, in a floor-length pink gown, as broadcast on PBS's lost classic TV series "The Great American Dream Machine."

1972

YOU'RE SO VAIN
Producer: Richard Perry
Album: No Secrets
Record Label: Elektra
Songwriter: Carly Simon

The year's best Pop gossip and her biggest hit. Who was the vain main character of the lyric? Backup singer Mick Jagger? Hubbie James Taylor? Long-shot Warren Beatty? Producer Richard Perry? Carly herself?

1974

HAVEN'T GOT TIME FOR THE PAIN
Producer: Richard Perry
Album: Hotcakes
Record Label: Elektra
Songwriters: Carly Simon, Jacob Brackman

A yuppie credo, penned by Brackman, who'd once defined his generation in Esquire *magazine, short months (or maybe years) before Joyce Maynard defined her generation in the* N.Y. Times Sunday Magazine. *Carly would define her generation by writing songs for Nora Ephron movies.*

1977

NOBODY DOES IT BETTER
Producer: Richard Perry
Album: Greatest Hits Live
Record Label: Elektra
Songwriters: Carole Bayer Sager, Marvin Hamlisch

Title theme for the James Bond film.

1980

JESSE
Album: Come Upstairs
Record Label: Warner Brothers
Songwriters: Carly Simon, Mike Mainieri

A convincing anti-romantic rocker.

1986

COMING AROUND AGAIN
Album: Coming Around Again
Record Label: Arista
Songwriter: Carly Simon

This theme for the Nora Ephron film Heartburn *established Carly as the voice of her newly-divorced Baby Boom generation. A year later she'd put it into a medley with "The Itsy Bitsy Spider."*

1989

LET THE RIVER RUN
Album: *Working Girl* Soundtrack
Record Label: Arista
Songwriter: Carly Simon

Her theme from the Mike Nichols film Working Girl *won an Oscar.*

JOE SIMON
1971

DROWNING IN THE SEA OF LOVE
Producers: Kenny Gamble, Leon Huff
Album: Drowning in the Sea of Love

Record Label: Spring
Songwriters: Kenny Gamble, Leon Huff

Top-5 R&B/Top-20 R&R crossover.

1972

POWER OF LOVE
Producers: Kenny Gamble, Leon Huff
Album: The Power of Joe Simon
Record Label: Spring
Songwriters: Kenny Gamble, Leon Huff, Joe Simon

#1 R&B/Top-20 R&R crossover.

1975

GET DOWN GET DOWN (GET ON THE FLOOR)
Producers: Raeford Gerald, Joe Simon
Album: Get Down
Record Label: Spring
Songwriters: Raeford Gerald, Joe Simon

His biggest hit; #1 R&B/Top-10 R&R crossover.

SIMON AND GARFUNKEL
1964

BLEECKER STREET
Producer: Tom Wilson
Album: Wednesday Morning, 3 A.M.
Record Label: Columbia
Songwriter: Paul Simon

Simon shifts neighborhoods in the mid-'60s, from Tin Pan Alley to Greenwich Village.

HE WAS MY BROTHER
Producer: Tom Wilson
Album: Wednesday Morning 3 A.M.
Record Label: Columbia
Songwriter: Paul Simon (Paul Kane)

Stepping from his teenage role as a R&R entrepreneur, Paul Simon enters adult awareness with his generation, although the tune, about the slain civil rights workers in Mississippi, was written under a pseudonym. Suggested segue: "Michael, Andrew and James" by Dick and Mimi Fariña.

THE SOUNDS OF SILENCE
Producer: Tom Wilson
Album: Wednesday Morning 3 A.M.
Record Label: Columbia
Songwriter: Paul Simon

This obscure acoustic album cut of '64 became an AM radio fave in '65 and the #1

Folk Rock classic of '66, through the magic of the marketplace (and an additional electric backing track).

1966

THE 59TH STREET BRIDGE SONG (FEELIN' GROOVY)

Producer: Bob Johnston
Album: Parsley, Sage, Rosemary and Thyme
Record Label: Columbia
Songwriter: Paul Simon

Atypical Simon at momentary peace. Covered by Harper's Bizarre (Warner Brothers, '67).

7:00 NEWS/SILENT NIGHT

Producer: Bob Johnston
Album: Parsley, Sage, Rosemary and Thyme
Record Label: Columbia
Songwriter: Paul Simon

Anti-war aural collage.

CLOUDY

Producer: Bob Johnston
Album: Parsley, Sage, Rosemary and Thyme
Record Label: Columbia
Songwriter: Paul Simon

Atmospheric Folk Rock, heard in The Graduate.

THE DANGLING CONVERSATION

Producer: Bob Johnston
Album: Parsley, Sage, Rosemary and Thyme
Record Label: Columbia
Songwriter: Paul Simon

Folk Rock goes to college.

FOR EMILY (WHEREVER I MAY FIND HER)

Producer: Bob Johnston
Album: Parsley, Sage, Rosemary and Thyme
Record Label: Columbia
Songwriter: Paul Simon

Simon's most direct love song, released as a single in '72.

HOMEWARD BOUND

Producer: Bob Johnston
Album: Parsley, Sage, Rosemary and Thyme
Record Label: Columbia
Songwriter: Paul Simon

Suggested segues: "Lodi" by Creedence Clearwater Revival and "Band on the Run" by Wings.

I AM A ROCK

Producer: Bob Johnston
Album: Sounds of Silence
Record Label: Columbia
Songwriter: Paul Simon

Folk Rock in denial.

PATTERNS

Producer: Bob Johnston
Album: Parsley, Sage, Rosemary and Thyme
Record Label: Columbia
Songwriter: Paul Simon

Folk Rock goes into psychoanalysis.

SCARBOROUGH FAIR (CANTICLE)

Producer: Bob Johnston
Album: Parsley, Sage, Rosemary and Thyme
Record Label: Columbia
Songwriters: Paul Simon, Art Garfunkel

In the Dylan new tradition: updating an old Elizabethan air.

1968

AMERICA

Producers: Roy Halee, Paul Simon, Art Garfunkel
Album: Bookends
Record Label: Columbia
Songwriter: Paul Simon

Wistful and cloistered as a Greyhound bus heading East, with Kathy out of cigarettes and Mrs. Wagner pies. Covered in a progressive version by England's the Nice (Mercury, '72).

A HAZY SHADE OF WINTER

Producers: Roy Halee, Paul Simon, Art Garfunkel
Album: Bookends
Record Label: Columbia
Songwriter: Paul Simon

Covered by the Bangles in the film Less Than Zero *(Def Jam, '87).*

MRS. ROBINSON

Producers: Roy Halee, Paul Simon, Art Garfunkel
Album: Bookends
Record Label: Columbia
Songwriter: Paul Simon

Boosted by Joe DiMaggio and The Graduate, *these East-Coast anti-revolutionaries achieve a generational epiphany and their second biggest hit.*

1969

THE BOXER

Producers: Roy Halee, Paul Simon, Art Garfunkel
Album: Bridge over Troubled Water
Record Label: Columbia
Songwriter: Paul Simon

Simon moves past his Top-40 Folk Rock adolescense into the progressive FM radio-oriented adulthood called Rock.

BRIDGE OVER TROUBLED WATER

Producers: Roy Halee, Paul Simon, Art Garfunkel
Album: Bridge over Troubled Water
Record Label: Columbia
Songwriter: Paul Simon

Going back to his Rock and Roll roots, with a Gospel-styled single. Cover by Aretha Franklin (Atlantic, '71) was a #1 R&B/Top-10 R&R crossover.

CECILIA

Producers: Roy Halee, Paul Simon, Art Garfunkel
Album: Bridge over Troubled Water
Record Label: Columbia
Songwriter: Paul Simon

A no-account street girl encountered on the stoop. Julio was loitering nearby.

PAUL SIMON

1972

ME AND JULIO DOWN BY THE SCHOOL YARD

Producers: Roy Halee, Paul Simon
Album: Paul Simon
Record Label: Columbia
Songwriter: Paul Simon

Going back to the old neighborhood, where the man at the candystore still calls him Paulie, as if to make amends to Julio for the entire Bobbie-Jimmie-Frankie "Bandstand" era.

MOTHER AND CHILD REUNION

Producers: Roy Halee, Paul Simon
Album: Paul Simon
Record Label: Columbia
Songwriter: Paul Simon

One of the year's best singles, reportedly inspired by a plate of Chinese food.

PEACE LIKE A RIVER

Producers: Roy Halee, Paul Simon
Album: Paul Simon
Record Label: Columbia
Songwriter: Paul Simon

Apart from Garfunkel, Simon enters a new era of expression, independence, productivity, and critical respect.

1973

AMERICAN TUNE
Producer: Paul Samwell-Smith
Album: There Goes Rhymin' Simon
Record Label: Columbia
Songwriter: Paul Simon
Saying goodbye to the counter-culture of the '60s—and good riddance.

KODACHROME
Producer: Paul Samwell-Smith
Album: There Goes Rhymin' Simon
Record Label: Columbia
Songwriter: Paul Simon
Recounting the miserable times of his life.

LOVES ME LIKE A ROCK
Producers: Phil Ramone, Paul Simon
Album: There Goes Rhymin' Simon
Record Label: Columbia
Songwriter: Paul Simon
One of his biggest hits, with the Dixie Hummingbirds, presaging further Roots Rock explorations.

ONE MAN'S CEILING IS ANOTHER MAN'S FLOOR
Producers: Paul Simon, Muscle Shoals Rhythm Section
Album: There Goes Rhymin' Simon
Record Label: Columbia
Songwriter: Paul Simon
One of his finest urban aphorisms.

SOMETHING SO RIGHT
Producers: Phil Ramone, Paul Simon
Album: There Goes Rhymin' Simon
Record Label: Columbia
Songwriter: Paul Simon
Simon at his most Sondheim-esque (or is it Woody Allen-esque?)

1975

FIFTY WAYS TO LEAVE YOUR LOVER
Producers: Phil Ramone, Paul Simon
Album: Still Crazy After All These Years
Record Label: Columbia
Songwriter: Paul Simon
His biggest single and only solo #1.

GONE AT LAST
Producers: Phil Ramone, Paul Simon
Album: Still Crazy After All These Years
Record Label: Columbia
Songwriter: Paul Simon
Queens gospel, sung with New Jersey's Phoebe Snow.

MY LITTLE TOWN
Producers: Paul Simon, Phil Ramone
Album: Still Crazy After All These Years
Record Label: Columbia
Songwriter: Paul Simon
Guest-starring Art Garfunkel, this ripping rocker about escaping from the neighborhood brought them back to the familiar old neighborhood of the Top-10.

STILL CRAZY AFTER ALL THESE YEARS
Producers: Phil Ramone, Paul Simon
Album: Still Crazy After All These Years
Record Label: Columbia
Songwriter: Paul Simon
His defining anthem.

1977

SLIP SLIDIN' AWAY
Producers: Phil Ramone, Paul Simon
Album: Greatest Hits, Etc.
Record Label: Columbia
Songwriter: Paul Simon
More poignance than the Top-10 can usually tolerate.

1980

LATE IN THE EVENING
Producer: Phil Ramone
Album: *One Trick Pony* Soundtrack
Record Label: Warner Brothers
Songwriter: Paul Simon
Best thing to come from the film, inaugurating his fourth decade on the charts.

1982

THE LATE GREAT JOHNNY ACE
Producers: Russ Titelman, Paul Simon
Album: The Concert in Central Park
Record Label: Warner Brothers
Songwriter: Paul Simon
Tribute to a fallen Rock and Roll hero

(Johnny Ace), sung in Central Park within earshot of where another fallen hero (John Lennon) fell; as seen on the video, during the tune a misguided admirer rushed the stage.

1983

ALLERGIES
Producers: Roy Halee, Paul Simon, Russ Titelman
Album: Hearts and Bones
Record Label: Warner Brothers
Songwriter: Paul Simon
Symptomatic of his ingrained urban malaise. Neat solo by Al DiMeola.

RENE AND GEORGETTE MAGRITTE WITH THEIR DOG AFTER THE WAR
Producers: Roy Halee, Paul Simon, Russ Titelman
Album: Hearts and Bones
Record Label: Warner Brothers
Songwriter: Paul Simon
A Sunday afternoon in the recording studio with Paul. Simon's tribute to Doo-Wop.

1986

THE BOY IN THE BUBBLE
Producer: Paul Simon
Album: Graceland
Record Label: Warner Brothers
Songwriter: Paul Simon
Writing from rhythm tracks brought back from Africa, Simon comes up with a free-associative gem of modern-day disassociation.

DIAMONDS ON THE SOLES OF HER SHOES
Producer: Paul Simon
Album: Graceland
Record Label: Warner Brothers
Songwriters: Paul Simon, Joseph Shabalala
The roots of rhythm remain. Written with Shabalala of Ladysmith Black Mambazo.

GRACELAND
Producer: Paul Simon
Album: Graceland
Record Label: Warner Brothers
Songwriter: Paul Simon
Simon achieves a state of Rock and Roll grace, with this father and son rambling song.

YOU CAN CALL ME AL
Producer: Paul Simon
Album: Graceland
Record Label: Warner Brothers

Songwriter: Paul Simon

A shot of Top-40 redemption, with the bass solo of the year by Baghiti Kumalo. Droll video, with a photo opportunity for Chevy Chase, in his last and best performance before becoming a cartoon in a cartoon graveyard.

1990

BORN AT THE RIGHT TIME

Producer: Paul Simon
Album: The Rhythm of the Saints
Record Label: Warner Brothers
Songwriter: Paul Simon

Visiting another port of entry for Rock and Roll, New Orleans, as he prepares for the big 5-0 and the ultimate(?) challenge of Broadway.

SIMPLE MINDS

1981

THEMES FOR GREAT CITIES

Producer: Steve Hillage
Album: Sons and Fascination/Sister Feelings Call
Record Label: Virgin
Songwriter: Simple Minds

Exhilaratingly chaotic mood music for after the apocalypse.

1982

PROMISED YOU A MIRACLE

Album: New Gold Dream (81-82-83-84)
Record Label: A&M/Virgin
Songwriter: Jim Kerr

This Scottish Euro-dance track went Top-10 in Australia.

1985

ALIVE AND KICKING

Producers: Jimmy Iovine, Bob Clearmountain
Album: Once upon a Time
Record Label: A&M
Songwriter: Simple Minds

Symbolizing their Earth-bound, chart-bound incarnation.

DON'T YOU (FORGET ABOUT ME)

Producer: Keith Forsey
Album: *The Breakfast Club* Soundtrack
Record Label: A&M
Songwriters: Keith Forsey, Steve Schiff

Getting a big American boost from its appearance in the proto-Generation-X film.

SANCTIFY YOURSELF

Producers: Jimmy Iovine, Bob Clearmountain
Album: Once upon a Time
Record Label: A&M
Songwriter: Simple Minds

SIMPLY RED

1986

HOLDING BACK THE YEARS

Producer: Steven Levine
Album: Picture Book
Record Label: Elektra
Songwriters: Mick Hucknall, Neil Moss

Blue-eyed English Soul. Originally released by Hucknall's first group, the Frantic Elevators (No Waiting, '83).

BART SIMPSON

1990

DEEP DEEP TROUBLE

Producers: John Boylan, D. J. Jazzy Jeff
Album: The Simpsons Sing the Blues
Record Label: Geffen
Songwriters: Matt Groening, Jeff Townes (D. J. Jazzy Jeff)

Better than Beavis and Butthead's "Come to Butt Head" (Geffen, '93).

FRANK SINATRA

1955

LEARNING THE BLUES

Album: This Is Sinatra!
Record Label: Capitol
Songwriter: Dolores Vicki Silvers

His biggest solo hit (along with "Five Minutes More" from '46). Bobby Darin and Bobby Rydell were listening. In England, so were Bryan Ferry and Stephen Morrissey.

NANCY SINATRA

1966

THESE BOOTS ARE MADE FOR WALKING

Producer: Lee Hazelwood
Album: Boots
Record Label: Reprise
Songwriter: Lee Hazelwood

The liberated housewife moves to Las Vegas. Covered by Sam Phillips in the film Ready to Wear (Columbia, '94).

THE SINGING NUN

1963

DOMINIQUE

Record Label: Phillips
Songwriter: Jeanine Decker (Soeur Sourire)

Soon after singing this Folk lullabye on "The Ed Sullivan Show" Soeur Sourire left the convent to pursue a recording career. While she would remain a one-shot, record-wise, Debbie Reynolds played her in The Singing Nun, *the movie. Soeur Sourire committed suicide in 1985.*

SIOUXSIE AND THE BANSHEES

1978

HONG KONG GARDEN

Producer: Steve Lillywhite
Album: The Scream
Record Label: Polydor
Songwriters: Susan Dallion, Steve Severin, John McKay, Kenny Morris

Debut single for the Sex Pistols-inspired Punk band hit Top-10 U.K.

1988

PEEK-A-BOO

Album: Peepshow
Record Label: Geffen
Songwriters: Susan Dallion, Steven Bailey, Peter Clarke

This hit U.S. dance track re-established them as classic Alternative beacons.

1991

KISS THEM FOR ME

Producer: Stephen Hague
Album: Superstition
Record Label: Geffen
Songwriter: Siouxsie and the Banshees

THE SIR DOUGLAS QUINTET

1965

SHE'S ABOUT A MOVER

Producer: Huey Meaux
Album: She's About a Mover
Record Label: Tribe
Songwriter: Douglas Sahm

A Tex-Mex/Creole gumbo.

1969

MENDOCINO

Producer: Amigas de Music
Album: She's About a Mover
Record Label: Smash
Songwriter: Douglas Sahm

Past Country and into the West. Suggested segue: "Talk to Me of Mendocino" by Kate and Anna McGarrigle.

SIR MIX-A-LOT
1992

BABY GOT BACK

Producer: Sir Mix-a-Lot
Album: Mack Daddy
Record Label: Def American
Songwriter: Anthony Ray (Sir Mix-a-Lot)

Seattle rapper and friend of Public Enemy hits #1 with a backhand tribute to the female anatomy. Suggested segue: "Dunkie Butt" by 12 Gauge.

SISTER SLEDGE
1978

HE'S THE GREATEST DANCER

Producers: Bernard Edwards, Nile Rodgers
Album: We Are Family
Record Label: Cotillion
Songwriters: Bernard Edwards, Nile Rodgers

#1 R&B/Top-10 R&R crossover.

WE ARE FAMILY

Producers: Bernard Edwards, Nile Rodgers
Album: We Are Family
Record Label: Cotillion
Songwriters: Bernard Edwards, Nile Rodgers

This #1 R&B/Top-10 R&R crossover for the Philly group was adopted by the Pittsburgh Pirates as the anthem of their last championship season. Covered by Babes in Toyland (Reprise, '95).

ALL THE MAN I NEED

Album: The Sisters
Record Label: Cotillion
Songwriters: Dean Pitchford, Tom Snow

Another Clive coup: cover by Whitney Houston as "All the Man That I Need" (Arista, '90) was a #1 R&B/R&R crossover.

SISTERS OF MERCY
1988

THIS CORROSION

Producer: Jim Steinman
Album: Floodland
Record Label: Elektra
Songwriter: Andrew Eldritch

The gothic Metal answer to Meat Loaf; their biggest of six U.K. hits.

THE SIX TEENS
1956

A CASUAL LOOK

Record Label: Flip
Songwriter: Ed Wells

Timeless Doo-Wop one-shot.

SKID ROW
1989

EIGHTEEN AND LIFE

Producer: Michael Wagever
Album: Skid Row
Record Label: Atlantic
Songwriters: Dave Sabo, Rachel Bolan

Scathing Metal hit. Suggested segue: "Eighteen" by Alice Cooper.

1990

I REMEMBER YOU

Producer: Michael Wagever
Album: Skid Row
Record Label: Atlantic
Songwriters: Dave Sabo, Rachel Bolan

The obligatory Metal ballad.

SKIP AND FLIP
1959

IT WAS I

Record Label: Brent
Songwriter: Gary Paxton

Everly-esque duo. They also covered Don and Dewey's "Cherry Pie."

SKYLARK
1973

WILDFLOWER

Album: Skylark
Record Label: Capitol
Songwriters: David Richardson, Doug Edwards

Gorgeous ballad by the Canadian one-shot band that produced David Foster. Brought

into the Soul repertoire by New Birth (RCA, '73).

THE SKYLINERS
1959

SINCE I DON'T HAVE YOU

Producer: Joe Rock
Album: The Skyliners
Record Label: Calico
Songwriters: James Beaumont, Janet Vogel, Joseph Verscharen, Wally Lester, John Taylor

First and biggest hit, with the high note of all-time. Was that Janet Vogel or a Stradivarius?

THIS I SWEAR

Producer: Joe Rock
Album: The Skyliners
Record Label: Calico
Songwriters: Jimmy Beaumont, Janet Vogel, Joe Verscharen, Wally Lester, Lennie Martin, Joe Rock, Jack Taylor

No unbelievable high notes, but this was Phil Spector's all-time favorite song.

SKYY
1981

CALL ME

Producer:
Album: Skyy Line
Record Label: Salsoul
Songwriter: Randy Muller

#1 R&B/Top-30 R&R crossover.

1989

REAL LOVE

Producer:
Album: Start of a Romance
Record Label: Atlantic
Songwriter: Solomon Roberts Jr.

#1 R&B/Top-50 R&R crossover.

FREDDIE SLACK AND ELLA MAE MORSE
1946

THE HOUSE OF BLUE LIGHTS

Record Label: Capitol
Songwriters: Freddy Slack, Don Raye

Classic R&B boogie (and Rap) by the author of "Beat Me Daddy, Eight to the Bar" and "Down the Road a Piece" (Raye) and the singer of "Cow Cow Boogie" (Morse with Slack on keyboards). Sung by Morse in the '46 film *How Do You Do.* Watered down crossover Pop hit by Chuck Miller (Mercury, '55). Covered by Chuck Berry (Chess, '74).

SLADE

1972

MAMA WEER ALL CRAZEE NOW
Producer: Chas Chandler
Album: Slayed
Record Label: Polydor
Songwriters: Noddy Holder, Jim Lea
Signature beerhall anthem.

1973

CUM ON FEEL THE NOIZE
Producer: Chas Chandler
Album: Slayed
Record Label: Polydor
Songwriters: Noddy Holder, Jim Lea
Barely literate frat Rock for soccer fans. Entered U.K. charts at #1. Covered by Quiet Riot (Epic, '83).

GUDBYE T'JANE
Producer: Chas Chandler
Album: Slayed
Record Label: Polydor
Songwriters: Noddy Holder, Jim Lea
Worthy of Mott the Hoople.

THE SLADES

1958

YOU CHEATED
Record Label: Domino
Songwriter: Don Burch
The Little Anthony & the Imperials sound transferred to the West Coast. Covered by Jesse Belvin's one-off supergroup, the Shields (Tender/Dot, '58).

SLAVE

1977

SLIDE
Album: Slave
Record Label: Cotillion
Songwriter: Walter Wagner
#1 R&B/Top-40 R&R crossover.

SLAYER

1986

ANGEL OF DEATH
Producer: Rick Rubin
Album: Reign in Blood
Record Label: Def Jam/Geffen
Songwriter: Jeff Hanneman

A staple of the Death Metal repertoire, the soundtrack of the subterranean mall. Sampled by Public Enemy in "She Watches Channel 0" (Def Jam, '88).

PERCY SLEDGE

1966

IT TEARS ME UP
Producers: Quin Ivy, Marlin Greene
Album: Warm and Tender Soul
Record Label: Atlantic
Songwriters: Dan Penn, Spooner Oldham

WHEN A MAN LOVES A WOMAN
Producers: Quin Ivy, Marlin Greene
Album: When a Man Loves a Woman
Record Label: Atlantic
Songwriters: Cameron Lewis, Andrew Wright
One-song definition of Soul; #1 R&B/R&R crossover.

1968

TAKE TIME TO KNOW HER
Producers: Quin Ivy, Marlin Greene
Album: Take Time to Know Her
Record Label: Atlantic
Songwriter: Steve Davis
Sledge in Otis Redding territory.

THE SLICKERS

1972

JOHNNY TOO BAD
Producer: Byron Lee
Album: The Harder They Come Soundtrack
Record Label: Island
Songwriters: Roy Beckford, Derrick Crooks, Winston Bailey, John Martyn
Johnny B. Goode goes bad in the Gangsta Reggae movie The Harder They Come.

THE SLITS

1979

TYPICAL GIRLS
Producer: Dennis Bovell
Album: Cut
Record Label: Antilles
Songwriters: Viv Albertine, Ariane Forster, Paloma McLardy, Teresa Pollitt
The Shaggs a decade later, moved to England and gone on the dole.

SLY AND THE FAMILY STONE

1968

DANCE TO THE MUSIC
Producer: Sly Stone
Album: Dance to the Music
Record Label: Epic
Songwriter: Sylvester Stewart
Injecting the Funk into psychedelic Soul.

1969

DON'T CALL ME NIGGER, WHITEY
Producer: Sly Stone
Album: Stand!
Record Label: Epic
Songwriter: Sylvester Stewart
Message music, ahead of its time.

EVERYDAY PEOPLE
Producer: Sly Stone
Album: Stand!
Record Label: Epic
Songwriter: Sylvester Stewart
Cheery Acid Funk, with a psychedelic Soul chaser was their biggest hit, a #1 R&B/R&R crossover.

HOT FUN IN THE SUMMERTIME
Producer: Sly Stone
Album: Greatest Hits
Record Label: Epic
Songwriter: Sylvester Stewart
Summertime classic. Suggested segues: "In the Summertime" by Mungo Jerry, "Heatwave" by Martha and the Vandellas.

I WANT TO TAKE YOU HIGHER
Producer: Sly Stone
Album: Stand!
Record Label: Epic
Songwriter: Sylvester Stewart
B-side of "Stand" eventually became a Sly staple and personal motto. Covered by Ike and Tina Turner (Liberty, '70).

STAND!
Producer: Sly Stone
Album: Stand!
Record Label: Epic
Songwriter: Sylvester Stewart

1970

EVERYBODY IS A STAR
Producer: Sly Stone
Album: Greatest Hits
Record Label: Epic
Songwriter: Sylvester Stewart

This B-side of "Thank You (Falettingme Be Mice Elf Agin)" reflects the year's pseudo-empowering communal spirit.

THANK YOU (FALETTINGME BE MICE ELF AGIN)
Producer: Sly Stone
Album: Greatest Hits
Record Label: Epic
Songwriter: Sylvester Stewart

Their second #1 R&B/R&R crossover: fashionable, irresistible, irreverent, and bouncy.

1971

(YOU'VE CAUGHT ME) SMILIN'
Producer: Sly Stone
Album: There's a Riot Goin' On
Record Label: Epic
Songwriter: Sylvester Stewart

A rare light moment from a grim album.

FAMILY AFFAIR
Producer: Sly Stone
Album: There's a Riot Goin' On
Record Label: Epic
Songwriter: Sylvester Stewart

Multi-textured, many-leveled, drive-time Funk; #1 R&B/R&R crossover.

RUNNIN' AWAY
Producer: Sly Stone
Album: There's a Riot Goin' On
Record Label: Epic
Songwriter: Sylvester Stewart

Chronicling the despair of the ghetto.

1973

IF YOU WANT ME TO STAY
Producer: Sly Stone
Album: Fresh
Record Label: Epic
Songwriter: Sylvester Stewart

Sly in a psychedelic Funk.

SLY FOX
1986

LET'S GO ALL THE WAY
Album: Let's Go All the Way
Record Label: Capitol
Songwriter: Gary Cooper

Recycling the classic title and concept for the Hip-Hop generation. Suggested segue: "A Fly Girl" by Boogie Boys (Capitol, '85).

THE SMALL FACES
1967

ITCHYCOO PARK
Producers: Steve Marriott, Ronnie Lane
Album: There Are But Four Small Faces
Record Label: Immediate
Songwriters: Steve Marriott, Ronnie Lane

Their answer to "Strawberry Fields."

MILLIE SMALL
1964

MY BOY LOLLIPOP
Producer: Chris Blackwell
Album: My Boy Lollipop
Record Label: Smash,
Songwriters: Johnny Roberts, Morris Levy

The first hit for Island Records was this Jamaican remake from '56, inspired by the Ska-influenced blue-beat sound. Morris Levy displays a heretofore untapped Reggae instinct.

SMASHING PUMPKINS
1991

I AM ONE
Producer: Butch Vig
Album: Tristessa
Record Label: Sub Pop
Songwriters: Billy Corgan, James Iha

Breaking through on the college circuit.

1993

TODAY
Album: Siamese Dream
Record Label: Virgin
Songwriter: Billy Corgan

Anguished rocker defines Chicago band's polished Alternative Metal sound. They'd follow it up in '96 with "Tonight Tonight."

ARTHUR SMITH AND HIS CRACKERJACKS
1946

GUITAR BOOGIE SHUFFLE
Record Label: Superdisc/MGM
Songwriter: Arthur Smith

Covered, in the year of the guitar instrumental, by the Virtues (Hunt, '59). Suggested segue: "Guitar Jamboree" by Chris Spedding (RAK, '76).

FRANKIE SMITH
1981

DOUBLE DUTCH BUS
Album: Children of Tomorrow
Record Label: WMOT
Songwriters: Frankie Smith, William Bloom

#1 R&B/Top-30 R&R crossover; rope-a-dope style for the '80s.

HUEY SMITH
1957

ROCKIN' PNEUMONIA AND THE BOOGIE WOOGIE FLU
Producer: Johnny Vincent
Album: Havin' a Good Time
Record Label: Ace
Songwriter: Huey Smith

B-side of "Rockin' Pneumonia and the Boogie Woogie Flu" (the instrumental) and the first hit for the label.

1958

DON'T YOU JUST KNOW IT
Producer: Johnny Vincent
Album: Havin' a Good Time
Record Label: Ace
Songwriter: Huey Smith

Biggest hit for the New Orleans keyboard man; released just after Mardi Gras, it was a Top-10 R&B/Top-10 R&R crossover.

HURRICANE SMITH
1973

OH BABE, WHAT WOULD YOU SAY
Producer: Norman Smith
Album: Hurricane Smith
Record Label: Capitol
Songwriter: E. B. Smith

Top-10 U.S./U.K. crossover for the 50-year-old deep-voiced record producer.

O. C. SMITH
1968

LITTLE GREEN APPLES
Producer: Jerry Fuller
Album: Hickory Holler Revisited
Record Label: Columbia
Songwriter: Bobby Russell

#2 R&B/R&R crossover was so down homey it should have hit the C&W charts as well. Instead, Roger Miller's Top-10 C&W rendition (Smash, '68) prevented history from being made.

PATTI SMITH

1974

PISS FACTORY

Producer: Lenny Kaye
Record Label: M-R-L
Songwriters: Patti Smith, Richard Sohl

Legendary New York single (with "Hey Joe" on the B-side) from the fair Rock and Roll poet with the great Rock and Roll voice. Later on Great N.Y. Singles *(RDIR, '75).*

1976

GLORIA (IN EXCELSIUS)

Producer: John Cale
Album: Horses
Record Label: Arista
Songwriter: Patti Smith

Patti transforms the girl of Van Morrison's dreams into a raving bohemian demon out of a Lower East Side Rock opera. It would take nearly twenty years before someone finally brought the idea to Broadway in "Rent."

1978

BECAUSE THE NIGHT

Producer: Jimmy Iovine
Album: Easter
Record Label: Arista
Songwriters: Bruce Springsteen, Patti Smith

A meeting of the East Coast titans of poetic romantic angst produces the epic single Phil Spector might have made with Dylan. Covered by 10,000 Maniacs (Elektra, '94).

1988

PATHS THAT CROSS

Producers: Jimmy Iovine, Scott Litt
Album: Dream of Life
Record Label: Arista
Songwriters: Patti Smith, Fred Smith

Her voice is still haunting after all these years.

PEOPLE HAVE THE POWER

Producers: Jimmy Iovine, Scott Litt
Album: Dream of Life
Record Label: Arista
Songwriters: Patti Smith, Fred Smith

The Smiths' version of Lennon and Yoko's "Power to the People." But did they record it in bed?

1996

ABOUT A BOY

Producers: Lenny Kaye, Malcolm Burn
Album: Gone Again
Record Label: Arista
Songwriter: Roger Waters

Patti returns to form after the deaths of her husband and her brother, to eulogize a kindred spirit, Kurt Cobain.

WARREN SMITH

1957

SO LONG I'M GONE

Producer: Sam Phillips
Album: First Country Collection
Record Label: Sun
Songwriters: Roy Orbison, Sam Phillips

Early Roy Orbison Rockabilly was Country star Smith's lone R&R appearance at #72.

THE SMITHEREENS

1982

BEAUTY AND SADNESS

Producer: Don Dixon
Album: Beauty and Sadness
Record Label: D-Tone
Songwriter: Pat DiNizio

Perfect Pop, like perfect love, unrequited.

1986

BEHIND THE WALL OF SLEEP

Producer: Don Dixon
Album: Especially for You
Record Label: Enigma
Songwriter: Pat DiNizio

Brooding post-modern Rockabilly from Hoboken.

BLOOD AND ROSES

Producer: Don Dixon
Album: Especially for You
Record Label: Enigma
Songwriter: Pat DiNizio

Their breakthrough single, from the film Dangerously Close.

1988

SOMETHING NEW

Producer: Don Dixon
Album: Green Thoughts
Record Label: Enigma
Songwriter: Pat DiNizio

Like circa 1965.

THE SMITHS

1984

HAND IN GLOVE

Producer: The Smiths
Album: The Smiths
Record Label: Sire
Songwriters: Stephen Morrissey, Johnny Marr

First single for the British nerd prince of self-pity, Stephen Morrissey and his cohorts. Covered by Sandi Shaw (Rough Trade, '84).

HEAVEN KNOWS I'M MISERABLE NOW

Producer: John Porter
Record Label: Sire
Songwriters: Stephen Morrissey, Johnny Marr

A familiar Morrissey theme provides their first U.K. hit, not released on LP until '87.

THIS CHARMING MAN

Producer: John Porter
Album: The Smiths
Record Label: Sire
Songwriters: Stephen Morrissey, Johnny Marr

Added to the U.S. release.

WHAT DIFFERENCE DOES IT MAKE

Producer: John Porter
Album: The Smiths
Record Label: Sire
Songwriters: Stephen Morrissey, Johnny Marr

1985

HOW SOON IS NOW

Album: Meat Is Murder
Record Label: Sire
Songwriters: Stephen Morrissey, Johnny Marr

Chilling guitar part by Johnny Marr adds real terror to Morrissey's tale of teenage affliction.

1986

BIGMOUTH STRIKES AGAIN

Producers: Stephen Morrissey, Johnny Marr
Album: The Queen Is Dead
Record Label: Sire
Songwriters: Stephen Morrissey, Johnny Marr

Often referred to as their version of "Jumping Jack Flash."

I KNOW IT'S OVER

Producers: Stephen Morrissey,
Johnny Marr
Album: The Queen Is Dead
Record Label: Sire
Songwriters: Stephen Morrissey,
Johnny Marr

Reportedly Marr's favorite Morrissey performance.

THE QUEEN IS DEAD

Producers: Stephen Morrissey,
Johnny Marr
Album: The Queen Is Dead
Record Label: Sire
Songwriters: Stephen Morrissey,
Johnny Marr

Answering "Anarchy in the U.K."

1987

GIRLFRIEND IN A COMA

Producers: Stephen Morrissey,
Johnny Marr
Album: Strangeways Here We Come
Record Label: Sire
Songwriters: Stephen Morrissey,
Johnny Marr

Narcissism as its own reward.

SHOPLIFTERS OF THE WORLD UNITE

Producers: Stephen Morrissey,
Johnny Marr
Album: Louder Than Bombs
Record Label: Sire
Songwriters: Stephen Morrissey,
Johnny Marr

Deifying deviance.

YOU JUST HAVEN'T EARNED IT YET, BABY

Producers: Stephen Morrissey,
Johnny Marr
Album: Louder Than Bombs
Record Label: Sire
Songwriters: Stephen Morrissey,
Johnny Marr

Covered by Kirsty MacColl (Charisma, '90).

PATTY SMYTH

1992

SOMETIMES LOVE JUST AIN'T ENOUGH

Producer: Roy Bittan
Album: Patty Smyth
Record Label: MCA
Songwriters: Patty Smyth, Glen Burtnik

Leaving the candy store and stoop behind for the life of a Hollywood belter.

SNAP

1990

THE POWER

Producer: Snap
Album: World Power
Record Label: Arista
Songwriters: Benito Benites, John Garrett III, Deron Butler, Toni C.

Monster club crossover.

1992

RHYTHM IS A DANCER

Producer: Snap
Album: The Madman's Return
Record Label: Arista
Songwriters: Benito Benites, John Garrett III

Undeniable dance groove.

SNOW

1993

INFORMER

Producer: McShan, John Ficariotta
Album: 12 Inches of Snow
Record Label: Atco East West
Songwriters: Darrin O'Brien, Shawn Moltke, Edmund Leary

Infectious Canadian Reggae.

HANK SNOW

1950

I'M MOVIN' ON

Album: I'm Movin' On
Record Label: RCA
Songwriter: Hank Snow

#1 C&W, with the classic Rock and Roll attitude, and pedigree. Covered by Ray Charles (Atlantic, '59), the Rolling Stones (London, '65), Elvis Presley (RCA, '69), and George Thorogood (EMI, '88).

1952

(NOW AND THEN THERE'S) A FOOL SUCH AS I

Record Label: RCA
Songwriter: Bill Trader

Top-5 C&W hit; covered by Jo Stafford (Columbia, '53). Cover by Elvis Presley (RCA, '59) was a Top-10 R&B/Top-20 R&R crossover.

PHOEBE SNOW

1973

POETRY MAN

Producer: Dino Airali
Album: Phoebe Snow
Record Label: Shelter
Songwriter: Phoebe Snow Laub

Folkie Jazz Pop from the coffee houses of New Jersey.

THE SOFT BOYS

1980

KINGDOM OF LOVE

Album: Underwater Moonlight
Record Label: Armageddon
Songwriter: Robyn Hitchcock

Their best track.

VEGTABLE MAN

Album: Underwater Moonlight
Record Label: Armageddon
Songwriter: Syd Barrett

B-side of "Kingdom of Love."

SOFT MACHINE

1971

MOON IN JUNE

Album: Fourth
Record Label: Columbia
Songwriter: Robert Wyatt

Legendary English progressive Rock band moves on to fusion.

THE SOLITAIRES

1957

WALKING ALONG

Record Label: Argo
Songwriters: Willie Winston, Hy Weiss

JOANIE SOMMERS

1962

JOHNNY GET ANGRY

Album: Johnny Get Angry
Record Label: Warner Brothers
Songwriters: Sherman Edwards, Hal David

Taking up where Shelly Fabares left off in "Johnny Angel."

SONIC YOUTH

1986

EVOL

Producers: Martin Bisi, Sonic Youth
Album: Evol
Record Label: SST
Songwriter: Sonic Youth

Recording since '82 (in at least 82 different guitar tunings), the influential art/noise rockers make their move toward accessibility.

EXPRESSWAY TO YR SKULL

Producers: Martin Bisi, Sonic Youth
Album: Evol
Record Label: SST
Songwriter: Sonic Youth

Suggested segue: "Expressway to Your Heart" by the Soul Survivors.

1987

MASTER DIK

Producer: Sonic Youth
Album: Sister
Record Label: SST

CCD bonus track, with Alternative hero J. Mascis of Dinosaur Jr. guesting on guitar.

1988

SILVER ROCKET

Producers: Nicholas Sansone, Sonic Youth
Album: Daydream Nation
Record Label: Enigma/Blast First
Songwriter: Sonic Youth

Almost Arena-esque.

THE SPRAWL

Producers: Nicholas Sansone, Sonic Youth
Album: Daydream Nation
Record Label: Enigma/Blast First
Songwriter: Sonic Youth

Bassist Kim Gordon inspires a generation of angry women.

TEEN-AGE RIOT

Producers: Nicholas Sansone, Sonic Youth
Album: Daydream Nation
Record Label: Enigma/Blast First
Songwriter: Sonic Youth

Achieving their longed-for guitar drone epiphany. Suggested segue: "Marquee Moon" by Television, from the same neighborhood a decade earlier.

1990

CINDERELLA'S BIG SCORE

Producers: Nicholas Sansone, Sonic Youth
Album: Goo
Record Label: Geffen
Songwriter: Sonic Youth

Major label splash.

1992

100%

Producers: Butch Vig, Edward Douglas
Album: Dirty
Record Label: DGC
Songwriter: Sonic Youth

SONNY

1965

LAUGH AT ME

Producer: Sonny Bono
Album: The Wondrous World of Sonny and Cher
Record Label: Atco
Songwriter: Sonny Bono

West Coast Nerd Rock, originally released before the advent of Sonny and Cher.

SONNY AND CHER

1964

BABY DON'T GO

Producer: Sonny Bono
Album: Baby Don't Go
Record Label: Reprise
Songwriter: Sonny Bono

Taking the quintessential Doo-Wop couplet of the '50s—"I love you so/never let you go"—and turning it mournful, cosmic, and photogenic all at once. Was a West Coast hit (recorded as Caesar and Cleo) before it was re-released after "I Got You Babe."

1965

I GOT YOU BABE

Producer: Sonny Bono
Album: Look at Us
Record Label: Atco
Songwriter: Sonny Bono

Originally the B-side of "It's Gonna Rain." "He's a Rebel" goes to California in suede and leather. Covered by the Dictators (Epic, '75).

1967

THE BEAT GOES ON

Producer: Sonny Bono
Album: In Case You're in Love

Record Label: Atco
Songwriter: Sonny Bono

Sonny's stab at "American Pie."

1971

ALL I EVER NEED IS YOU

Producer: Snuff Garrett
Album: All I Ever Need Is You
Record Label: Kapp
Songwriters: Jimmy Holiday, Eddie Reeves

They would be divorced three years later.

1972

A COWBOY'S WORK IS NEVER DONE

Producer: Snuff Garrett
Album: All I Ever Need Is You
Record Label: Kapp
Songwriter: Sonny Bono

Their fifth and last Top-10 hit.

SOPWITH CAMEL

1966

HELLO, HELLO

Producer: Erik Jacobsen
Album: Sopwith Camel
Record Label: Kama Sutra
Songwriters: Peter Kraemer, Terry MacNeil

West-Coast good-time music, by the producer of the Lovin' Spoonful. Covered by Tiny Tim (Kama Sutra, '66) as the B-side of "Be My Love," the Mario Lanza hit.

SOUL ASYLUM

1988

ENDLESS FAREWELL

Producers: Ed Stasium, Lenny Kaye
Album: Hang Time
Record Label: Twin Tone
Songwriter: Dave Pirner

Little brothers to Minneapolis scenesters Hüsker Dü and the Replacements say goodbye to the Punk era with a tearful ballad (Pirner on keyboards).

1992

RUNAWAY TRAIN

Producer: Michael Beinhorn
Album: Grave Dancers Union
Record Label: Columbia
Songwriter: Dave Pirner

Threatening to become as melodramatic as U2, this wins a Grammy for Rock Song of the Year.

SOMEBODY TO SHOVE

Producer: Michael Beinhorn
Album: Grave Dancers Union
Record Label: Columbia
Songwriter: Dave Pirner

Angry Alternative mainstay.

BLACK GOLD

Producer: Michael Beinhorn
Album: Grave Dancers Union
Record Label: Columbia
Songwriter: Dave Pirner

Powerfully reclaiming their Alternative credibility.

SOUL BROTHERS SIX
1967

(SHE'S) SOME KIND OF WONDERFUL

Record Label: Atlantic
Songwriter: Ralph Ellison

Covered by Grand Funk (Capitol, '75) and Blues legend Buddy Guy (Silvertone, '93).

SOUL II SOUL
1989

BACK TO LIFE

Producers: Nellee Hooper, Jazzie B.
Album: Keep on Movin'
Record Label: Virgin
Songwriter: Romeo

Soulful Reggae, big on the dance floors of England; a #1 R&B/U.K./Top-10 R&R crossover, featuring the voice of Caron Wheeler.

KEEP ON MOVIN'

Producers: Nellee Hooper, Jazzie B.
Album: Keep on Movin'
Record Label: Virgin
Songwriter: Romeo

#1 R&B/Top-20 R&R crossover.

THE SOUL STIRRERS
1956

TOUCH THE HEM OF HIS GARMENT

Producer: Art Rupe
Record Label: Specialty
Songwriter: Sam Cooke

Tapping the Gospel roots of one of Rock's most soulful crooners.

THE SOUL SURVIVORS
1967

EXPRESSWAY TO YOUR HEART

Producers: Kenny Gamble, Leon Huff
Album: When the Whistle Blows Anything Goes
Record Label: Crimson
Songwriters: Kenny Gamble, Leon Huff

Last exit to Philly Soul.

DAVID SOUL
1977

DON'T GIVE UP ON US

Producer: Tony Macaulay
Album: David Soul
Record Label: Private Stock
Songwriter: Tony Macaulay

As singing TV detectives go, Hutch (of "Starsky and Hutch") was more soulful than Don Johnson ("Miami Vice") but not in the same crooning league as Telly Savalas ("Kojak"). He got the only #1 of the bunch, however.

JIMMY SOUL
1963

IF YOU WANNA BE HAPPY

Producer: Frank J. Guida
Album: If You Wanna Be Happy
Record Label: S.P.Q.R.
Songwriters: Frank Guida Jr., Joseph Royster, Carmela Guida

Homespun calypso-based advice to the lovelorn; once quoted by Sam Malone on an episode of "Cheers." #1 R&B/R&R crossover.

SOUNDGARDEN
1994

BLACK HOLE SUN

Producers: Michael Beinhorn, Soundgarden
Album: Superunknown
Record Label: A&M
Songwriter: Chris Cornell

From Seattle, the perfectly gorgeous anti-Beatles rocker. A year later Beatles clones from England would be all over the place.

SPOONMAN

Producers: Michael Beinhorn, Soundgarden
Album: Superunknown
Record Label: A&M
Songwriter: Chris Cornell

Local character.

SOUNDS OF BLACKNESS
1991

OPTIMISTIC

Producers: Jimmy Jam, Terry Lewis
Album: Evolution of Gospel
Record Label: Perspective
Songwriters: James Harris III, Terry Lewis, Gary Hines

Did not make any chart, but it is the producers' favorite song because of the impact it makes on whoever hears it.

SOUP DRAGONS
1992

DIVINE THING

Album: Hot Wired
Record Label: Big Life
Songwriter: Sean Dickson

Marc Bolan lives, from the soundtrack of Hellraiser II.

JOE SOUTH
1969

DON'T IT MAKE YOU WANT TO GO HOME

Producer: Joe South
Album: Don't It Make You Want to Go Home
Record Label: Capitol
Songwriter: Joe South

The essence of Nashville Soul. South's version crossed over to #27 C&W. Cover by Brook Benton (Cotillion, '70) crossed over to #31 R&B. Both hit Top-50 R&B.

GAMES PEOPLE PLAY

Producer: Joe South
Album: Introspect
Record Label: Capitol
Songwriter: Joe South

A typical South C&W/R&R/R&B crossover; South had the R&R hit, Freddie Weller the C&W Top-10 (Columbia, '69), and Donald Height the R&B version (Jubilee, '69). South had the Top-10 U.K. version, and the song won a Grammy.

(I NEVER PROMISED YOU A) ROSE GARDEN

Producer: Joe South
Album: Introspect
Record Label: Capitol
Songwriter: Joe South

Cover by Lynn Anderson was a rare #1 C&W/Top-5 R&R crossover (Columbia, '71). Also covered by Kon Kan as "I Beg Your Pardon" (Atlantic, '89).

1970

WALK A MILE IN MY SHOES
Producer: Joe South
Album: Don't It Make You Want to Go Home
Record Label: Capitol
Songwriter: Joe South

A landmark Country Soul gospel-protest song, and a C&W/R&R crossover. Covered by R&B singer Willie Hightower (Fame, '70).

J. D. SOUTHER

1972

RUN LIKE A THIEF
Album: John David Souther
Record Label: Elektra
Songwriter: John David Souther

The essential Folk/Rock yin and yang, succumbing first to unstoppable lust and then to unendurable guilt. Talking about wanting and having it all. Covered by Bonnie Raitt (Warner Brothers, '75).

1979

YOU'RE ONLY LONELY
Producer: John David Souther
Album: You're Only Lonely
Record Label: Columbia
Songwriter: John David Souther
Laid back, L.A. hit.

SOUTHSIDE JOHNNY AND THE ASBURY JUKES
1976

HE'S GOT THE FEVER
Producer: Steve Van Zandt
Album: I Don't Want to Go Home
Record Label: Epic
Songwriter: Bruce Springsteen

New Jersey bar-band proteges of the Boss deliver the workman-like goods.

I DON'T WANT TO GO HOME
Producer: Steve Van Zandt
Album: I Don't Want to Go Home
Record Label: Epic
Songwriter: Steve Van Zandt
Their enduring party signature.

1991

IT'S BEEN A LONG TIME
Producer: Little Steven
Album: Better Days
Record Label: Impact
Songwriter: Steve Van Zandt

A sentimental reunion. Suggested segues: "No One to Run With" by the Allman Brothers and "Hanging on to the Good Times" by Little Feat.

BOB B. SOXX AND THE BLUE JEANS
1962

ZIP-A-DEE-DOO-DAH
Producer: Phil Spector
Album: Zip-A-Dee-Doo-Dah
Record Label: Philles
Songwriters: Ray Gilbert, Allie Wrubel

From the '45 movie Song of the South. Sung by Darlene Love under yet another nom de guerre.

1963

WHY DO LOVERS BREAK EACH OTHER'S HEARTS
Producer: Phil Spector
Record Label: Philles
Songwriters: Tony Powers, Ellie Greenwich, Phil Spector

SPACEMEN
1959

THE CLOUDS
Record Label: Alton
#1 R&B/Top-50 R&R crossover.

SPANDAU BALLET
1983

TRUE
Album: True
Record Label: Chrysalis
Songwriter: Gary Kemp
Fey balladry in the Roxy Music mode.

THE SPANIELS
1954

GOODNIGHT, SWEETHEART, GOODNIGHT
Album: Goodnight, It's Time to Go
Record Label: Vee-Jay
Songwriters: Calvin Carter, James Hudson
Doo-Wop classic; their biggest R&B hit.

1958

A ROCKING GOOD WAY (TO MESS AROUND AND FALL IN LOVE)
Record Label: Vee-Jay
Songwriters: Brook Benton, Jesus De Luchi, Clyde Otis

#1 R&B/Top-10 R&R crossover for Dinah Washington and Brook Benton (Mercury, '60). Marvin and Tammy were listening.

SPANKY AND OUR GANG
1967

SUNDAY WILL NEVER BE THE SAME
Producer: Jerry Ross
Album: Spanky and Our Gang
Record Label: Mercury
Songwriters: Terry Cashman, Gene Pistilli

Harmony-oriented Folk Rock throwback.

SPARKS AND JANE WIEDLIN
1983

COOL PLACES
Album: Sparks in Outer Space
Record Label: Atlantic
Songwriters: Ron Mael, Russel Mael

Biggest hit for the pets of chic L.A., sung with a Go-Go girl.

THE SPECIALS
1979

GANGSTERS
Producer: Elvis Costello
Album: The Specials
Record Label: 2-Tone/Chrysalis
Songwriter: Jerry Dammers

U.S. single breakthrough launches the British 2-Tone Ska label, paving the way for the Selecter, Madness, the Beat, and eventually Fun Boy Three.

TOO MUCH TOO YOUNG
Producer: Elvis Costello
Album: The Specials
Record Label: 2-Tone/Chrysalis
Songwriter: Jerry Dammers
Their first #1 U.K.

1981

GHOST TOWN
Producer: John Collins
Album: Ghost Town/Why?/Friday Night Saturday Morning

Record Label: 2-Tone/Chrysalis
Songwriter: Jerry Dammers
Their most powerful song; #1 U.K.

1985

FREE NELSON MANDELA
Album: In the Studio
Record Label: Chrysalis
Songwriters: Jerry Dammers, Rhoda Dakar
Another strong political statement.

BENNIE SPELLMAN
1962

LIPSTICK TRACES (ON A CIGARETTE)
Producer: Allen Toussaint
Record Label: Minit
Songwriter: Allen Toussaint (Naomi Neville)
New Orleans Soul. Cover by the O'Jays (Imperial, '65) was their first R&B hit.

SKIP SPENCE
1969

WAR IN PEACE
Album: OAR
Record Label: Columbia
Songwriter: Skip Spence
Solo track from the Moby Grape founder.

TRACIE SPENCER
1991

THIS HOUSE
Producers: Robert Sherrod, Paul Sherrod
Album: Make the Difference
Record Label: Capitol
Songwriters: Matt Sherrod, Paul Sherrod, Sir Spence
Sub-teen thrush, straight outa "Star Search."

THE SPIN DOCTORS
1991

LITTLE MISS CAN'T BE WRONG
Producers: P. Denenberg, Spin Doctors
Album: Pocket Full of Kryptonite
Record Label: Epic
Songwriter: Chris Barron
Previewing the return of the hippie guitar band. Blues Traveler and Phish were already jamming.

1992

TWO PRINCES
Producers: F. Aversa, Spin Doctors
Album: Pocket Full of Kryptonite
Record Label: Epic Associated
Songwriter: Spin Doctors
Post-Love Generation parable; their biggest hit.

SPINAL TAP
1984

STONEHENGE
Album: This Is Spinal Tap Soundtrack
Record Label: Polydor
Songwriters: Christopher Guest, Michael McKean, Harry Shearer, Rob Reiner
From the Rob Reiner movie and the National Lampoon school of parody.

THE SPINNERS
1970

IT'S A SHAME
Producer: Stevie Wonder
Album: 2nd Time Around
Record Label: V.I.P.
Songwriters: Stevie Wonder, Lee Garrett, Syreeta Wright
Breakthrough single for the Philly Soul combo from Detroit after a decade off the R&R charts.

1972

COULD IT BE I'M FALLING IN LOVE
Producer: Thom Bell
Album: The Spinners
Record Label: Atlantic
Songwriters: Melvin Steals, Mervin Steals
#1 R&B/Top-10 R&R crossover: Smokey Robinson transplanted to Philadelphia.

I'LL BE AROUND
Producer: Thom Bell
Album: The Spinners
Record Label: Atlantic
Songwriters: Thom Bell, Phil Hurtt
Defining the dance sound of the early '70s, with a #1 R&B/Top-10 R&R crossover that was originally the B-side of "How Could I Let You Get Away."

ONE OF A KIND (LOVE AFFAIR)
Producer: Thom Bell
Album: The Spinners
Record Label: Atlantic
Songwriter: Joseph Jefferson
#1 R&B/Top-20 R&R crossover.

1973

A MIGHTY LOVE
Producer: Thom Bell
Album: Mighty Love
Record Label: Atlantic
Songwriters: Joseph Jefferson, Bruce Hawes, Charles Simmons
#1 R&B/Top-20 R&R crossover.

1974

THEY JUST CAN'T STOP IT (THE GAMES PEOPLE PLAY)
Producer: Thom Bell
Album: Pick of the Litter
Record Label: Atlantic
Songwriters: Joseph Jefferson, Bruce Hawes, Charles Simmons
#1 R&B/Top-10 R&R crossover.

1976

THE RUBBERBAND MAN
Producer: Thom Bell
Album: Happiness Is Being with the Detroit Spinners
Record Label: Atlantic
Songwriters: Thom Bell, Linda Creed
Reigning Philly Soul songwriting team gives the Spinners their last #1 R&B/Top-10 R&R crossover, their biggest hit (aside from their duet with Dionne Warwick on "Then Came You"), and Phillippe Wynne his defining moment.

SPIRIT
1968

FRESH GARBAGE
Producer: Lou Adler
Album: Spirit
Record Label: Ode
Songwriter: Jay Ferguson
Psychedelic standard. Suggested segue: "Fresh Air" by Quicksilver Messenger Service.

1969

I GOT A LINE ON YOU
Producer: Lou Adler
Album: The Family That Plays Together
Record Label: Ode
Songwriter: Randy California
Their biggest hit.

1970

NATURE'S WAY

Producer: Lou Adler
Album: Twelve Dreams of Dr. Sardonicus
Record Label: Epic
Songwriter: Randy California

Loopy ecological lament. Covered by Victoria Williams (Atlantic, '95).

SPLIT ENZ

1980

I GOT YOU

Producer: David Tickle
Album: True Colours
Record Label: A&M
Songwriter: Neil Finn

Only U.S. hit for the Australian Finn brothers, who would later form Crowded House.

THE SPOKESMEN

1965

DAWN OF CORRECTION

Album: Dawn of Correction
Record Label: Decca
Songwriters: John Madara, David White, Raymond Gilmore

Answer song to "Eve of Destruction."

SPOOKY TOOTH

1969

BETTER BY YOU, BETTER THAN ME

Album: Spooky Two
Record Label: A&M
Songwriter: Gary Wright

Sludge from the moors of England.

DUSTY SPRINGFIELD

1964

I ONLY WANT TO BE WITH YOU

Album: Stay Awhile/I Only Want to Be with You
Record Label: Philips
Songwriters: Mike Hawker, Ivor Raymonde

Blue-eyed Folk Soul from England; her first hit. Covered by the Bay City Rollers (Arista, '76).

1966

GOIN' BACK

Album: Golden Hits
Record Label: Philips
Songwriters: Gerry Goffin, Carole King

Goffin and King master Folk Rock. Top-10 in

England. Covered by the Byrds (Columbia, '67), Carole King (Ode, '71), and Nils Lofgren (A&M, '75). Suggested segue: "Sugar Mountain" by Neil Young.

YOU DON'T HAVE TO SAY YOU LOVE ME

Album: You Don't Have to Say You Love Me
Record Label: Philips
Songwriters: Vicki Wickham, Simon Napier-Bell, V. Pallavicini, P. Donaggio

Italian Soul ballad is her biggest hit. Covered by Elvis Presley (RCA, '70).

1969

NO EASY WAY DOWN

Producers: Tom Dowd, Jerry Wexler, Arif Mardin
Album: Dusty in Memphis
Record Label: Atlantic
Songwriters: Gerry Goffin, Carole King

Another gem from Goffin and King's "bleak" period highlight's Dusty's Memphis revival. Recorded by Carole King (Ode, '71).

SON OF A PREACHER MAN

Producers: Tom Dowd, Jerry Wexler, Arif Mardin
Album: Dusty in Memphis
Record Label: Atlantic
Songwriters: John Hurley, Ronnie Wilkins

Dusty went Top-10 R&R, C&W version by Peggy Little (Dot, '69). R&B version by Aretha Franklin (Atlantic, '70) was the B-side of "Call Me." Revived in the '94 movie Pulp Fiction.

1989

NOTHING HAS BEEN PROVED

Album: Scandal Soundtrack
Record Label: Capitol-EMI
Songwriters: Neil Tennant, Chris Lowe

A comeback courtesy of the Pet Shop Boys and a racy English film.

RICK SPRINGFIELD

1981

JESSIE'S GIRL

Producers: Keith Olson, Rick Springfield
Album: Working Class Dog
Record Label: RCA
Songwriter: Rick Springfield

His biggest rocker benefitted from exposure over the new national video/radio channel, MTV.

1982

DON'T TALK TO STRANGERS

Producers: Keith Olson, Rick Springfield
Album: Success Hasn't Spoiled Me Yet
Record Label: RCA
Songwriter: Rick Springfield

Second-biggest hit for the former soap opera actor.

1983

AFFAIR OF THE HEART

Album: Living in Oz
Record Label: RCA
Songwriters: Rick Springfield, Blaise Tosti, Danny Tate

Showing his Australian roots.

1984

LOVE SOMEBODY

Producers: Bill Drescher, Rick Springfield
Album: *Hard to Hold* Soundtrack
Record Label: RCA
Songwriter: Rick Springfield

Like Madonna, Debbie Harry, Paul Simon, and Neil Diamond, Rick's movie experience was notable primarily for the hit single it spawned.

BRUCE SPRINGSTEEN

1973

4TH OF JULY, ASBURY PARK (SANDY)

Producers: Jim Cretecos, Mike Appel
Album: The Wild, the Innocent and the E Street Shuffle
Record Label: Columbia
Songwriter: Bruce Springsteen

Summer night on the Jersey Shore: the answer to Brooklyn's "Under the Boardwalk."

BLINDED BY THE LIGHT

Producers: Jim Cretecos, Mike Appel
Album: Greetings from Asbury Park
Record Label: Columbia
Songwriter: Bruce Springsteen

First single from the Boss of Asbury Park, after which he was compared in The New York Times to Bob Dylan, Van Morrison, the Band, Allen Ginsberg, the cult movie El Topo, and eventually called the future of Rock and Roll. Most of the comparisons would be justified (immediately and ulti-mately). Brought to #1 by Manfred Mann (Polydor, '73).

FOR YOU

Producers: Jim Cretecos, Mike Appel
Album: Greetings from Asbury Park
Record Label: Columbia
Songwriter: Bruce Springsteen

The emergence of a new white Soul urgency, with all generational bases cov-ered, the jingle jangle rhymes of working class romance, the sheer joy and agony of teenage lust, and Clarence as Daddy Gee on the sax. Covered by Greg Kihn (Beserkley, '77) and Manfred Mann (Warner Brothers, '81).

GROWIN' UP

Producers: Jim Cretecos, Mike Appel
Album: Greetings from Asbury Park
Record Label: Columbia
Songwriter: Bruce Springsteen

An American original strafes his old high school with Dylan-esque word play and Spectorian overstatement.

HEART OF A BALLERINA

Record Label: Columbia
Songwriter: Bruce Springsteen

Sub-titled (or part of a medley with) "Angel from the Inner Lake" (sometimes known as "Thunder Cracks"), this the great lost unreleased Springsteen epic—probably dropped from the repertoire due to its simi-larity to the eventual "Rosalita."

INCIDENT ON 57TH STREET

Producers: Jim Cretecos, Mike Appel
Album: The Wild, the Innocent and the E Street Shuffle
Record Label: Columbia
Songwriter: Bruce Springsteen

10:03 live version was released as the B-side of "Fire" in '87.

LOST IN THE FLOOD

Producers: Jim Cretecos, Mike Appel
Album: Greetings from Asbury Park
Record Label: Columbia
Songwriter: Bruce Springsteen

Tales of the walking wounded of the postwar working class. Suggested segue: "Still in Saigon" by the Charlie Daniels Band.

ROSALITA (COME OUT TONIGHT)

Producers: Jim Cretecos, Mike Appel
Album: The Wild, the Innocent and the E Street Shuffle
Record Label: Columbia
Songwriter: Bruce Springsteen

One of his legendary all-stops-out rollicking rockers. Success as the best revenge on all the girls who snubbed him in high school.

SPIRIT IN THE NIGHT

Producers: Jim Cretecos, Mike Appel
Album: Greetings from Asbury Park
Record Label: Columbia
Songwriter: Bruce Springsteen

Indelible early guided tour through Mr. Springsteen's mythic Rock and Roll neigh-borhood. Covered by Manfred Mann (Warner Brothers, '75).

WILD BILLY'S CIRCUS STORY

Producers: Jim Cretecos, Mike Appel
Album: The Wild, the Innocent and the E Street Shuffle
Record Label: Columbia
Songwriter: Bruce Springsteen

Introducing Danny Federici on accordion.

1975

BACKSTREETS

Producers: Jon Landau, Mike Appel, Bruce Springsteen
Album: Born to Run
Record Label: Columbia
Songwriter: Bruce Springsteen

Expanding his urban mythology stage; New Jersey as the national teenage psyche and all-night parking lot personified.

BORN TO RUN

Producers: Mike Appel, Bruce Springsteen
Album: Born to Run
Record Label: Columbia
Songwriter: Bruce Springsteen

His first Top-40 epic, boiling down his exploding vision into a classic single.

JUNGLELAND

Producers: Jon Landau, Mike Appel, Bruce Springsteen
Album: Born to Run
Record Label: Columbia
Songwriter: Bruce Springsteen

Almost Copland-esque in its majestic sweep and defining American ambition, within

which is embedded a personal history of Rock and Roll.

TENTH AVENUE FREEZE OUT

Producers: Jon Landau, Mike Appel, Bruce Springsteen
Album: Born to Run
Record Label: Columbia
Songwriter: Bruce Springsteen

A new dance of urban despair.

THUNDER ROAD

Producers: Jon Landau, Mike Appel, Bruce Springsteen
Album: Born to Run
Record Label: Columbia
Songwriter: Bruce Springsteen

Orbisonian tragedy, Spectorian romance: a quintessential Springsteenian tale of grow-ing up.

1978

BADLANDS

Producers: Jon Landau, Bruce Springsteen
Album: Darkness on the Edge of Town
Record Label: Columbia
Songwriter: Bruce Springsteen

New Jersey as the Old West.

DARKNESS ON THE EDGE OF TOWN

Producers: Jon Landau, Bruce Springsteen
Album: Darkness on the Edge of Town
Record Label: Columbia
Songwriter: Bruce Springsteen

Leaving the comfortable borders of New Jersey (adolescence) and venturing into the dark unknown (adulthood).

PROVE IT ALL NIGHT

Producers: Jon Landau, Bruce Springsteen
Album: Darkness on the Edge of Town
Record Label: Columbia
Songwriter: Bruce Springsteen

His version of "Sixty Minute Man" and an apt appraisal of his legendary performing prowess.

1980

HUNGRY HEART

Producers: Jon Landau, Bruce Springsteen, Steve Van Zandt
Album: The River

Record Label: Columbia
Songwriter: Bruce Springsteen

One of his most cinematic hits (used prominently in Risky Business*), the teenage outsider grows up to become a rootless adult.*

INDEPENDENCE DAY

Producers: Jon Landau, Bruce Springsteen, Steve Van Zandt
Album: The River
Record Label: Columbia
Songwriter: Bruce Springsteen

Squaring things with the old man. David Mamet was probably listening.

THE RIVER

Producers: Jon Landau, Bruce Springsteen, Steve Van Zandt
Album: The River
Record Label: Columbia
Songwriter: Bruce Springsteen

Aborted dreams of the working class.

1982

ATLANTIC CITY

Producer: Bruce Springsteen
Album: Nebraska
Record Label: Columbia
Songwriter: Bruce Springsteen

Moody film-noir study in desolation and redemption was Springsteen's first (B&W) video. Stands as a companion piece to the Burt Lancaster/Susan Sarandon movie of the same name.

HIGHWAY PATROLMAN

Producer: Bruce Springsteen
Album: Nebraska
Record Label: Columbia
Songwriter: Bruce Springsteen

Armed with an acoustic guitar, Bruce hits the American Road. Covered by Johnny Cash (Columbia, '83).

JOHNNY 99

Producer: Bruce Springsteen
Album: Nebraska
Record Label: Columbia
Songwriter: Bruce Springsteen

Saga of a mass murderer was covered by Johnny Cash (Columbia, '83).

1983

PINK CADILLAC

Record Label: Columbia
Songwriter: Bruce Springsteen

Classic car song; classic car, a big, wide Caddy. B-side of "Dancing in the Dark." Covered by Natalie Cole (Manhattan, '87).

1984

BOBBY JEAN

Producers: Jon Landau, Bruce Springsteen, Steve Van Zandt, Chuck Plotkin
Album: Born in the U.S.A.
Record Label: Columbia
Songwriter: Bruce Springsteen

Tribute to his departed guitarist, Miami Steve.

BORN IN THE U.S.A.

Producers: Jon Landau, Bruce Springsteen, Chuck Plotkin
Album: Born in the U.S.A.
Record Label: Columbia
Songwriter: Bruce Springsteen

His best protest song, co-opted as a campaign slogan by Ronald Reagan. Suggested segue: "Kill for Peace" by the Fugs.

COVER ME

Producers: Jon Landau, Bruce Springsteen, Chuck Plotkin
Album: Born in the U.S.A.
Record Label: Columbia
Songwriter: Bruce Springsteen

Third hit from the album.

DANCING IN THE DARK

Producers: Jon Landau, Bruce Springsteen, Chuck Plotkin
Album: Born in the U.S.A.
Record Label: Columbia
Songwriter: Bruce Springsteen

His biggest hit; Courtney Cox was in the video with a pumped-up Bruce finally having learned how to dance.

GLORY DAYS

Producers: Jon Landau, Bruce Springsteen, Chuck Plotkin
Album: Born in the U.S.A.
Record Label: Columbia
Songwriter: Bruce Springsteen

Fifth of seven Top-10 hits from the album. Suggested segue: "Night Moves" by Bob Seger, "Cherry Bomb" by John Mellencamp.

I'M GOIN' DOWN

Producers: Jon Landau, Bruce Springsteen, Chuck Plotkin
Album: Born in the U.S.A.
Record Label: Columbia
Songwriter: Bruce Springsteen

Heading into the realms of overexposure.

I'M ON FIRE

Producers: Jon Landau, Bruce Springsteen, Chuck Plotkin
Album: Born in the U.S.A.
Record Label: Columbia
Songwriter: Bruce Springsteen

As an actor in his videos, he was better than Dylan and Billy Joel, not as good as Paul Simon or Tom Petty.

MY HOME TOWN

Producers: Jon Landau, Bruce Springsteen, Chuck Plotkin
Album: Born in the U.S.A.
Record Label: Columbia
Songwriter: Bruce Springsteen

Narrowing (and mellowing) his view of mythic New Jersey now that he had accomplished his own escape.

1985

SEEDS

Album: Bruce Springsteen and the E Street Band Live, 1975–1985
Record Label: Columbia
Songwriter: Bruce Springsteen

Entering his Guthrie-esque Folk troubadour phase.

BRILLIANT DISGUISE

Producers: Jon Landau, Bruce Springsteen, Chuck Plotkin
Album: Tunnel of Love
Record Label: Columbia
Songwriter: Bruce Springsteen

All grown up, but hardly settled down.

ONE STEP UP

Producers: Jon Landau, Bruce Springsteen, Chuck Plotkin
Album: Tunnel of Love
Record Label: Columbia
Songwriter: Bruce Springsteen

His best Country song.

TUNNEL OF LOVE

Producers: Jon Landau, Bruce Springsteen, Chuck Plotkin
Album: Tunnel of Love
Record Label: Columbia
Songwriter: Bruce Springsteen

Harrowing vision of love.

WALK LIKE A MAN

Producers: Jon Landau, Bruce Springsteen, Chuck Plotkin
Album: Tunnel of Love
Record Label: Columbia
Songwriter: Bruce Springsteen

Poignant vision of adulthood. Suggested segue: "Uptown Girl" by Billy Joel.

1992

HUMAN TOUCH

Producers: Jon Landau, Bruce Springsteen, Chuck Plotkin
Album: Human Touch
Record Label: Columbia
Songwriter: Bruce Springsteen

Having achieved love and adulthood at last, the Boss finds them not so scary after all.

MY BEAUTIFUL REWARD

Producers: Jon Landau, Bruce Springsteen, Chuck Plotkin
Album: Lucky Town
Record Label: Columbia
Songwriter: Bruce Springsteen

Straightening out his life, but in the process losing a step on the Rock and Roll muse.

1993

STREETS OF PHILADELPHIA

Producers: Chuck Plotkin, Bruce Springsteen
Album: *Philadelphia* Soundtrack
Record Label: Epic Soundtrax
Songwriter: Bruce Springsteen

Entering his soundtrack phase, with five Grammys and a Golden Globe award. Next would be "Dead Man Walking."

1995

YOUNGSTOWN

Producers: Bruce Springsteen, Chuck Plotkin
Album: The Ghost of Tom Joad
Record Label: Columbia
Songwriter: Bruce Springsteen

Entering his second Woody Guthrie phase. Suggested segue: "Allentown" by Billy Joel.

SQUEEZE

1979

COOL FOR CATS

Producers: John Wood, Squeeze
Album: Cool for Cats
Record Label: A&M
Songwriters: Chris Difford, Glenn Tilbrook

First U.K. hit for the singer/songwriters, hailed for their Lennon-esque cleverness and McCartney-esque melodies; derided for their McCartney-esque slightness, Lennon-esque archness.

UP THE JUNCTION

Producers: John Wood, Squeeze
Album: Cool for Cats
Record Label: A&M
Songwriters: Chris Difford, Glenn Tilbrook

Their most affecting rocker.

1980

ANOTHER NAIL IN MY HEART

Album: Argybargy
Record Label: A&M
Songwriters: Chris Difford, Glenn Tilbrook

Pure Progressive Pop.

PULLING MUSSELS (FROM A SHELL)

Album: Argybargy
Record Label: A&M
Songwriters: Chris Difford, Glenn Tilbrook

Defining their parlor-room Soul.

1981

IN QUINTESSENCE

Producers: Elvis Costello, Roger Bechirian
Album: East Side Story
Record Label: A&M
Songwriters: Chris Difford, Glenn Tilbrook

Their most perfect Pop concoction.

TEMPTED

Producers: Elvis Costello, Roger Bechirian
Album: East Side Story
Record Label: A&M
Songwriters: Chris Difford, Glenn Tilbrook

Paul Carrack's best vocal with the band was their first American hit.

1982

BLACK COFFEE IN BED

Album: Sweets from a Stranger
Record Label: A&M
Songwriters: Chris Difford, Glenn Tilbrook

Suggested segue: "Brown Sugar" by the Rolling Stones, "Brother Louie" by Stories.

1987

HOURGLASS

Album: Babylon and On
Record Label: A&M
Songwriters: Chris Difford, Glenn Tilbrook

Comeback single was their biggest hit.

BILLY SQUIER

1981

THE STROKE

Producers: Mack, Billy Squier
Album: Don't Say No
Record Label: Capitol
Songwriter: Billy Squier

Led Zeppelin-inspired rocker, with Kiss-inspired euphemism.

1982

EVERYBODY WANTS YOU

Album: Emotions in Motion
Record Label: Capitol
Songwriter: Billy Squire

Big Arena hit.

1984

ROCK ME TONITE

Album: Signs of Life
Record Label: Capitol
Songwriter: Billy Squier

Possibly the worst video of all-time sends his career into rewind.

STACEY Q

1986

TWO OF HEARTS

Producer: J. St. James
Album: Better Than Heaven
Record Label: Atlantic
Songwriters: John Mitchell, Sue Gatlin, Tim Greene

Dance floor crossover.

JIM STAFFORD

1973

SPIDERS AND SNAKES

Producer: Lobo
Album: Jim Stafford
Record Label: MGM
Songwriters: Jim Stafford, David Bellamy

Country Rock novelty.

WILDWOOD WEED

Producer: Lobo
Album: Jim Stafford
Record Label: MGM
Songwriters: Jim Stafford, Dan Bowman

More pickin' and grinnin'.

THE STAMPEDERS
1971

SWEET CITY WOMAN
Producer: Mel Shaw
Album: Sweet City Woman
Record Label: Bell
Songwriter: Richard Dodson
Canadian crossover.

THE STANDELLS
1965

DIRTY WATER
Producer: Ed Cobb
Album: Dirty Water
Record Label: Tower
Songwriter: Ed Cobb
In the "Coney Island Baby" tradition (where-in a Bronx group portrayed themselves as Brooklyn natives), this Boston garage Rock classic was done by a group from L.A.

LISA STANSFIELD
1990

ALL AROUND THE WORLD
Album: Affection
Record Label: Arista
Songwriters: Lisa Stansfield, Ian Devaney, Andy Morris
Stansfield, with her post-modern Disco Soul and English style, was the first white female to top the R&B charts; tune was also a #1 U.K. crossover.

YOU CAN'T DENY IT
Producers: Ian Devaney, Andy Morris
Album: Affection
Record Label: Arista
Songwriters: Lisa Stansfield, Ian Devaney, Andy Morris
The Soul stylist's second #1 R&B/Top-20 R&R crossover.

1991

ALL WOMAN
Producer: Ian Devaney
Album: Real Love
Record Label: Arista
Songwriters: Lisa Stansfield, Ian Devaney, Andy Morris
#1 R&B/Top-20 R&R crossover.

THE STAPLE SINGERS
1970

HEAVY MAKES YOU HAPPY (SHA-NA-BOOM-BOOM)
Producer: Steve Cropper
Album: The Staple Singers
Record Label: Stax
Songwriters: Jeff Barry, Bobby Bloom
First Top-10 R&B/Top-30 R&R crossover for the family Gospel group.

1971

RESPECT YOURSELF
Producer: Al Bell
Album: Be Altitude: Respect Yourself
Record Label: Stax
Songwriters: Mack Rice, Luther Ingram
Simplified R&B perscription for curing contemporary ills.

1972

I'LL TAKE YOU THERE
Producer: Al Bell
Album: Be Altitude: Respect Yourself
Record Label: Stax
Songwriter: Alvertis Isbell
#1 R&B/R&R follow up to "Respect Yourself." Covered by Bebe and Cece Winans (Capitol, '91).

1973

IF YOU'RE READY (COME GO WITH ME)
Producer: Al Bell
Album: Be What You Are
Record Label: Stax
Songwriters: Homer Banks, Ray Jackson, Carl Hampton
#1 R&B/Top-10 R&R crossover.

1975

LET'S DO IT AGAIN
Producer: Curtis Mayfield
Album: *Let's Do It Again* Soundtrack
Record Label: Curtom
Songwriter: Curtis Mayfield
A long way from their Gospel roots, this titilating title song from the blaxploitation film was a #1 R&B/R&R crossover.

STARBUCK
1975

MOONLIGHT FEELS RIGHT
Producers: Bruce Blackman, Mike Clark
Album: Moonlight Feels Right
Record Label: Private Stock
Songwriter: Michael Bruce Blackman
Easy Folk listening dance track in the Sanford-Townshend/Pablo Cruise/Orleans groove.

STARGARD
1977

THEME SONG FROM *WHICH WAY IS UP*
Album: Stargard
Record Label: MCA, Norman Whitfield
#1 R&B/Top-25 R&R movie theme.

STARLAND VOCAL BAND
1976

AFTERNOON DELIGHT
Producer: Milt Okun
Album: Starland Vocal Band
Record Label: Windsong
Songwriter: Bill Danoff
Harmonious Folk Rock dalliance in the fading heyday of the sunshine era.

EDWIN STARR
1969

25 MILES
Producer: Norman Whitfield
Album: 25 Miles
Record Label: Gordy
Songwriter: Edwin Starr
Top-10 R&B/R&R crossover.

1970

WAR
Producer: Norman Whitfield
Album: War and Peace
Record Label: Gordy
Songwriters: Norman Whitfield, Barrett Strong
Powerful #1 R&R/Top-10 R&B protest song. Covered by Bruce Springsteen (Columbia, '86).

RINGO STARR

1971

IT DON'T COME EASY
   Producer: George Harrison
   Album: Blasts from Your Past
   Record Label: Apple
   Songwriter: Richard Starkey
His first solo hit single.

1972

BACK OFF BOOGALOO
   Producer: George Harrison
   Album: Blasts from Your Past
   Record Label: Apple
   Songwriter: Richard Starkey

1973

PHOTOGRAPH
   Producer: Richard Perry
   Album: Ringo
   Record Label: Apple
   Songwriters: George Harrison,
      Richard Starkey
The luckiest Beatle scores his biggest hit. Covered by Camper Van Beethoven (Pitch-a-Tent, '84). Suggested segue: "Kodachrome" by Paul Simon.

1974

IT'S ALL DOWN TO GOODNIGHT VIENNA
   Producer: Richard Perry
   Album: Goodnight Vienna
   Record Label: Apple
   Songwriter: John Lennon

NO NO SONG
   Producer: Richard Perry
   Album: Goodnight Vienna
   Record Label: Apple
   Songwriters: Hoyt Axton, David
      Jackson Jr.

OH MY MY
   Producer: Richard Perry
   Album: Ringo
   Record Label: Apple
   Songwriters: Richard Starkey, Vini
      Poncia

1975

EARLY 1970
   Producer: Pete Drake
   Album: Blasts from Your Past
   Record Label: Capitol
   Songwriter: Richard Starkey
B-side of his first single, "Beaucoups of Blues."

STARSHIP

1985

SARA
   Producer: Dennis Lambert
   Album: Knee Deep in the Hoopla
   Record Label: Grunt
   Songwriters: Peter Wolf, Ina Wolf
The Jefferson Airplane/Jefferson Starship, stripped of everything but their adopted name, get their second straight #1.

WE BUILT THIS CITY
   Producer: Dennis Lambert
   Album: Knee Deep in the Hoopla
   Record Label: Grunt
   Songwriters: Peter Wolf, Bernie
      Taupin, Martin Page, Dennis Lambert
Anthemic Arena rocker gives the legendary San Francisco band its first #1.

1987

IT'S NOT OVER ('TIL IT'S OVER)
   Producer: Narada Michael Walden
   Album: No Protection
   Record Label: Grunt
   Songwriters: Robbie Nevil, John Van
      Torgeron, Phil Galdston
Epitomizing the Mickey Thomas-era.

NOTHING'S GONNA STOP US NOW
   Producer: Narada Michael Walden
   Album: No Protection
   Record Label: Grunt
   Songwriters: Diane Warren, Albert
      Hammond
From the movie Mannequin, *inspired by Journey.*

THE STATLER BROTHERS

1965

FLOWERS ON THE WALL
   Album: Flowers on the Wall
   Record Label: Columbia
   Songwriter: Lewis DeWitt
#1 C&W/Top-10 R&R crossover.

CANDI STATON

1976

YOUNG HEARTS RUN FREE
   Album: Young Hearts Run Free
   Record Label: Warner Brothers
   Songwriter: Dave Crawford
#1 R&B/U.K./Top-20 R&R crossover.

STATUS QUO

1968

PICTURES OF MATCHSTICK MEN
   Producer: John Schroeder
   Album: Messages from the Status
      Quo
   Record Label: Concept
   Songwriter: Francis Michael Rossi
Psychedelic relic was the first of their twenty-one Top-10 U.K. singles, and the only Top-20 R&R U.S. Covered by Camper Van Beethoven (Virgin, '89).

STEALER'S WHEEL

1973

STUCK IN THE MIDDLE WITH YOU
   Producers: Jerry Leiber, Mike Stoller
   Album: Stealer's Wheel
   Record Label: A&M
   Songwriters: Joe Egan, Gerry
      Rafferty
Bargain-basement Steely Dan. Rafferty would move on to "Baker Street."

STEAM

1969

NA NA, HEY, HEY, KISS HIM GOODBYE
   Producer: Paul Leka
   Album: Na Na, Hey, Hey, Kiss Him
      Goodbye
   Record Label: Fontana
   Songwriters: Gary DeCarlo, Dale
      Frashuer, Paul Leka
Ultimate in-the-studio creation, now an in-the-stadium anthem. Suggested segue: "Whomp, There It Is" by Tag Team.

STEELY DAN

1972

DIRTY WORK
   Producer: Gary Katz
   Album: Can't Buy a Thrill
   Record Label: ABC
   Songwriters: Donald Fagen, Walter
      Becker
Top-40 goes to art college.

DO IT AGAIN
   Producer: Gary Katz
   Album: Can't Buy a Thrill
   Record Label: ABC
   Songwriters: Donald Fagen, Walter
      Becker
The bohemian Jazz ethos, in Top-40 garb; their second biggest hit.

REELING IN THE YEARS
Producer: Gary Katz
Album: Can't Buy a Thrill
Record Label: ABC
Songwriters: Donald Fagen, Walter Becker

1973, when this was released as a single, was one of the great years for wiseguys. Suggested segues: "Kodachrome" by Paul Simon, "You're So Vain" by Carly Simon, "The Cover of Rolling Stone" by Dr. Hook, and "Dead Skin" by Loudon Wainwright III.

1973

BODHISATTVA
Producer: Gary Katz
Album: Countdown to Ecstasy
Record Label: ABC
Songwriters: Donald Fagen, Walter Becker

Artsy collegiate answer to the collected works of George Harrison.

PEARL OF THE QUARTER
Producer: Gary Katz
Album: Countdown to Ecstasy
Record Label: ABC
Songwriters: Donald Fagen, Walter Becker

Transplanted East Coast bohemians visit New Orleans, fall in love.

SHOW BIZ KIDS
Producer: Gary Katz
Album: Countdown to Ecstasy
Record Label: ABC
Songwriters: Donald Fagen, Walter Becker

Venting their laid-back spleen on their adopted L.A.

1974

ANY MAJOR DUDE WILL TELL YOU
Producer: Gary Katz
Album: Pretzel Logic
Record Label: ABC
Songwriters: Donald Fagen, Walter Becker

At the peak of their tongue-in-cheek angst.

CHARLIE FREAK
Producer: Gary Katz
Album: Pretzel Logic
Record Label: ABC
Songwriters: Donald Fagen, Walter Becker

An ode to those who didn't survive the '60s.

RIKKI DON'T LOSE THAT NUMBER
Producer: Gary Katz
Album: Pretzel Logic
Record Label: ABC
Songwriters: Donald Fagen, Walter Becker

Their biggest hit: intricate, swinging, twisted.

1975

ANY WORLD (THAT I'M WELCOME TO)
Producer: Gary Katz
Album: Katy Lied
Record Label: ABC
Songwriters: Donald Fagen, Walter Becker

Swinging at the edge of doom.

BAD SNEAKERS
Producer: Gary Katz
Album: Katy Lied
Record Label: ABC
Songwriters: Donald Fagen, Walter Becker

Mentioning piña colada in a song four years before Rupert Holmes, and in a more properly citified context too.

BLACK FRIDAY
Producer: Gary Katz
Album: Katy Lied
Record Label: ABC
Songwriters: Donald Fagen, Walter Becker

Anticipating the coming crash.

DR. WU
Producer: Gary Katz
Album: Katy Lied
Record Label: ABC
Songwriters: Donald Fagen, Walter Becker

Seeking much needed help.

1976

KID CHARLEMAGNE
Producer: Gary Katz
Album: The Royal Scam
Record Label: ABC
Songwriters: Donald Fagen, Walter Becker

Their ode to the end of the counter culture, with a bravura guitar part by Larry Carlton.

1977

DEACON BLUES
Producer: Gary Katz
Album: Aja
Record Label: ABC
Songwriters: Donald Fagen, Walter Becker

Masterful career retrospective.

PEG
Producer: Gary Katz
Album: Aja
Record Label: ABC
Songwriters: Donald Fagen, Walter Becker

Return to their Top-40 roots.

1980

HEY NINETEEN
Producer: Gary Katz
Album: Gaucho
Record Label: MCA
Songwriters: Walter Becker, Donald Fagen

First Top-10 hit in seven years, but is it worth the effort just to be able to communicate with teenage girls who don't remember Aretha, Queen of Soul?

TIME OUT OF MIND
Producer: Gary Katz
Album: Gaucho
Record Label: MCA
Songwriters: Donald Fagen, Walter Becker

Their last hit.

JIM STEINMAN

1981

ROCK AND ROLL DREAMS COME THROUGH
Album: Bad for Good
Record Label: Cleveland International
Songwriter: Jim Steinman

Covered by Meat Loaf (Epic, '93).

STEPPENWOLF

1968

BORN TO BE WILD
Producer: Gabriel Mekler
Album: Steppenwolf
Record Label: Dunhill
Songwriter: Mars Bonfire

Ultimate biker anthem. Heard the next year in Easy Rider.

MAGIC CARPET RIDE
Producer: Gabriel Mekler
Album: Steppenwolf the Second
Record Label: Dunhill

Songwriters: John Kay, Rushton Moreve

Ultimate biker ballad.

THE PUSHER
Producer: Gabriel Mekler
Album: Steppenwolf
Record Label: Ode
Songwriter: Hoyt Axton

Also featured in Easy Rider. *Suggested segues: "The Needle and the Damage Done" by Neil Young, "That Smell" by Lynyrd Skynyrd, and Steppenwolf's own "Monster."*

1969

ROCK ME
Producer: Gabriel Mekler
Album: At Your Birthday Party
Record Label: Dunhill
Songwriter: John Kay

STEREO MCS
1993

CONNECTED
Album: Connected
Record Label: Gee Street/Island
Songwriters: Rob Birch, Nick Hallan, Harry Casey, Rick Finch

Techno Disco smash, appropriated from K.C. and the Sunshine Band protege Jimmy Bo Horne's R&B hit, "Let Me (Let Me Be Your Lover)" (Sunshinc Sound, '78).

CAT STEVENS
1967

FIRST CUT IS THE DEEPEST
Album: Matthew and Son
Record Label: Deram
Songwriter: Cat Stevens

Hit in England for P. P. Arnold. Covered by Rod Stewart (Warner Brothers, '77).

MATTHEW AND SON
Album: Matthew and Son
Record Label: Deram
Songwriter: Cat Stevens

Donovan, with a beard.

1970

LADY D'ARBANVILLE
Album: Mona Bone Jakon
Record Label: A&M
Songwriter: Cat Stevens

Peter Gabriel on flute.

1971

INTO WHITE
Producer: Paul Samwell-Smith
Album: Tea for the Tillerman
Record Label: A&M
Songwriter: Cat Stevens

Sensitive singer/songwriter disappears into his teacup.

KATMANDU
Producer: Paul Samwell-Smith
Album: Tea for the Tillerman
Record Label: A&M
Songwriter: Cat Stevens

A favorite collegiate summertime hangout in the early '70s. Suggested segues: "Marrakesh Express" by Crosby, Stills and Nash, "Katmandu" by Bob Seger, and "Copenhagen" by Johnny Mathis.

MORNING HAS BROKEN
Producer: Paul Samwell-Smith
Album: Teaser and the Firecat
Record Label: A&M
Songwriters: Cat Stevens, Eleanor Farjeon

His biggest hit.

PEACE TRAIN
Producer: Paul Samwell-Smith
Album: Teaser and the Firecat
Record Label: A&M
Songwriter: Cat Stevens

Answering "People Get Ready" by the Impressions. Covered by 10,000 Maniacs (Elektra, '87).

WILD WORLD
Producer: Paul Samwell-Smith
Album: Tea for the Tillerman
Record Label: A&M
Songwriter: Cat Stevens

Matthew and daughter; the paternalistic Cat.

1974

OH VERY YOUNG
Producer: Paul Samwell-Smith
Album: Buddha and the Chocolate Box
Record Label: A&M
Songwriter: Cat Stevens

Salman Rushdie wasn't listening.

CONNIE STEVENS
1960

SIXTEEN REASONS (WHY I LOVE YOU)
Record Label: Warner Brothers
Songwriters: Bill Post, Doree Post

Hollywood Pop Rock answer to "The Ten Commandments of Love."

DODIE STEVENS
1958

PINK SHOELACES
Album: Dodie Stevens
Record Label: Crystalette
Songwriter: Mickie Grant

Top-40 fashion statement, by the author of the future Broadway musical "Don't Bother Me, I Can't Cope."

RAY STEVENS
1961

JEREMIAH PEABODY'S POLY-UNSATURATED, QUICK DISSOLVING, FAST ACTING, PLEASANT TASTING, GREEN AND PURPLE PILLS
Album: Jeremiah Peabody's Poly-Unsaturated, Quick Dissolving, Fast Acting, Pleasant Tasting, Green and Purple Pills
Record Label: Mercury
Songwriter: Ray Stevens

Tongue-twisting novelty debut.

1962

AHAB THE ARAB
Album: 1,837 Seconds of Humor
Record Label: Mercury
Songwriter: Ray Stevens

Politically incorrect novelty.

1969

GITARZAN
Producers: Fred Foster, Jim Malloy
Album: Gitarzan
Record Label: Monument
Songwriters: Ray Stevens, Bill Everette

1970

EVERYTHING IS BEAUTIFUL
Producer: Ray Stevens
Album: Everything Is Beautiful
Record Label: Barnaby
Songwriter: Ray Stevens

Uncharactertistically rose-colored perspective.

1974

THE STREAK

Producer: Ray Stevens
Album: Boogity Boogity
Record Label: Barnaby
Songwriter: Ray Stevens

Observant Top-10 C&W/#1 R&R crossover, observed most conspicuously that year by David Niven at the Oscar ceremonies.

B. W. STEVENSON

1973

MY MARIA

Producer: David Kershenbaum
Album: My Maria
Record Label: RCA
Songwriters: Daniel Moore, B. W. Stevenson

Texas Pop. England Dan and John Ford Coley were tuned in.

SHAMBALA

Producer: David Kershenbaum
Album: My Maria
Record Label: RCA
Songwriter: Daniel Moore

Good-time Folk Rock. Covered by Three Dog Night (Dunhill, '73).

STEVIE B.

1990

BECAUSE I LOVE YOU (THE POSTMAN SONG)

Producer: Stevie B.
Album: Love and Emotion
Record Label: LMR
Songwriter: W. Allen Brooks

#1 R&R one-shot.

AL STEWART

1977

YEAR OF THE CAT

Producer: Alan Parsons
Album: Year of the Cat
Record Label: Janus
Songwriters: Al Stewart, Peter Wood

Cat Stevens with a Ph.D.

1978

TIME PASSAGES

Producer: Alan Parsons
Album: Time Passages
Record Label: Arista
Songwriters: Al Stewart, Peter White

His biggest hit.

BILLY STEWART

1966

SUMMERTIME

Producer: Billy Davis
Album: Unbelievable
Record Label: Chess
Songwriters: DuBose Heyward, George Gershwin

Jumping remake of the '36 classic from "Porgy and Bess." Covered by Janis Joplin (Columbia, '67).

GARY STEWART

1975

QUITS

Record Label: RCA
Songwriter: Danny O'Keefe

Early classic of Outlaw Country.

JERMAINE STEWART

1986

WE DON'T HAVE TO TAKE OUR CLOTHES OFF

Producer: Narada Michael Walden
Album: Frantic Romantic
Record Label: Arista
Songwriters: Preston Glass, Narada Michael Walden

R&B ballad bucks the prevailing moral Zeitgeist.

JOHN STEWART

1979

GOLD

Album: Bombs Away Dream Baby
Record Label: RSO
Songwriter: John Stewart

Former Kingston Trio lead singer makes a belated leap to Folk Rock.

ROD STEWART

1969

DIRTY OLD TOWN

Producer: Lou Reizner
Album: The Rod Stewart Album
Record Label: Mercury
Songwriter: Ewan MacColl

Rod at his grittiest. Suggested segues: "Streets of London" by Ralph McTell, and "Gilbert Street" by Sweet Thursday.

HANDBAGS AND GLADRAGS

Producer: Lou Reizner
Album: The Rod Stewart Album
Record Label: Mercury

Songwriter: Mike D'Abo

Unsparing Rod, with a classic drizzly Limey epic. Suggested segue: "She's Leaving Home" by the Beatles.

1971

EVERY PICTURE TELLS A STORY

Producer: Tom Dowd
Album: Every Picture Tells a Story
Record Label: Mercury
Songwriters: Rod Stewart, Ron Wood

At his raspin' Rockin' best.

MAGGIE MAY

Producer: Rod Stewart
Album: Every Picture Tells a Story
Record Label: Mercury
Songwriters: Rod Stewart, Martin Quittenton

Rod's ultimate paean to young lust with an older woman was originally the B-side of "Reason to Believe," his first solo single.

MANDOLIN WIND

Producer: Tom Dowd
Album: Every Picture Tells a Story
Record Label: Mercury
Songwriter: Rod Stewart

With Zeppelin-esque eclecticism, Rod stretches the boundaries of Rock. Suggested segue: "Mandolin Rain" by Bruce Hornsby.

1972

YOU WEAR IT WELL

Producer: Rod Stewart
Album: Never a Dull Moment
Record Label: Mercury
Songwriters: Rod Stewart, Martin Quittenton

Rod displays his sensitive side.

1976

TONIGHT'S THE NIGHT (GONNA BE ALL RIGHT)

Producer: Tom Dowd
Album: A Night on the Town
Record Label: Warner Brothers
Songwriter: Rod Stewart

Over-the-top seduction song was his biggest hit.

1977

HOT LEGS

Producer: Tom Dowd
Album: Footloose and Fancy Free
Record Label: Warner Brothers
Songwriter: Rod Stewart

Rod displays his unreconstructedly sexist side, with a landmark music video to boot.

KILLING OF GEORGIE (PARTS I AND II)

Producer: Tom Dowd
Album: A Night on the Town
Record Label: Warner Brothers
Songwriter: Rod Stewart

About the murder of a gay friend.

YOU'RE IN MY HEART (THE FINAL ACCLAIM)

Producer: Tom Dowd
Album: Footloose and Fancy Free
Record Label: Warner Brothers
Songwriter: Rod Stewart

The insecure Rod emerges,

1979

DO YA THINK I'M SEXY

Producer: Tom Dowd
Album: Blondes Have More Fun
Record Label: Warner Brothers
Songwriters: Rod Stewart, Carmine Appice

Rod does Disco.

1980

PASSION

Producers: Rod Stewart Group, Jeremy Andrew Johns, Harry the Hook
Album: Foolish Behaviour
Record Label: Warner Brothers
Songwriters: Rod Stewart, Phil Chen, Jim Cregan, Gary Grainger, Kevin Savigar

1981

YOUNG TURKS

Producers: Rod Stewart, Jim Cregan
Album: Tonight I'm Yours
Record Label: Warner Brothers
Songwriter: Rod Stewart

Joining the MTV-era for a career-boosting rocker.

1982

THAT'S WHAT FRIENDS ARE FOR

Songwriters: Burt Bacharach, Carole Bayer Sager

Introduced by Rod in the film Nightshift. *Cover by Dionne Warwick and friends— Elton John, Gladys Knight, and Stevie Wonder (Arista, '85)—was a #1 R&B/R&R crossover and song of the year Grammy winner, with the proceeds for that recording going to the American Foundation for AIDS Research.*

1983

BABY JANE

Producers: Tom Dowd, Rod Stewart
Album: Body Wishes
Record Label: Warner Brothers
Songwriters: Rod Stewart, Jay Davis

His sixth #1 U.K.

1984

INFATUATION

Producer: Michael Omartian
Album: Camouflage
Record Label: Warner Brothers
Songwriters: Rod Stewart, Wayne Hitchings, W. Robinson

A step down from "Passion," Rod begins his Arena-idol period.

1986

LOVE TOUCH (THEME FROM *LEGAL EAGLES*)

Producer: Mike Chapman
Album: Rod Stewart
Record Label: Warner Brothers
Songwriters: Mike Chapman, Holly Knight, Gene Black

Big movie song.

1988

FOREVER YOUNG

Producers: Rod Stewart, Andy Taylor
Album: Out of Order
Record Label: Warner Brothers
Songwriters: Rod Stewart, Jim Cregan, Kevin Savigar

His version of a Highland hymn.

LOST IN YOU

Producers: Rod Stewart, Andy Taylor
Album: Out of Order
Record Label: Warner Brothers
Songwriters: Rod Stewart, Andy Taylor

His most famous video, Rod as a luckless voyeur.

MY HEART CAN'T TELL YOU NO

Producer: Bernard Edwards
Album: Out of Order
Record Label: Warner Brothers
Songwriters: Simon Climie, Dennis Morgan

1991

THE MOTOWN SONG

Album: Vagabond Heart
Record Label: Warner Brothers
Songwriter: Larry John McNally

Rod revisits the streets of Doo-Wop.

RHYTHM OF MY HEART

Album: Vagabond Heart
Record Label: Warner Brothers
Songwriters: Marc Jordan, John Capek

Rod does M.O.R.

CURTIS STIGERS

1991

I WONDER WHY

Album: Curtis Stigers
Record Label: Arista
Songwriters: Greg Ballard, Curtis Stigers

STEPHEN STILLS

1971

LOVE THE ONE YOU'RE WITH

Producers: Stephen Sills, Bill Halverson
Album: Stephen Stills 2
Record Label: Atlantic
Songwriter: Stephen Stills

Epitomizing the downfall of the sexual revolution, as well as Folk Rock.

STING

1985

FORTRESS AROUND YOUR HEART

Producers: Pete Smith, Sting
Album: The Dream of the Blue Turtles
Record Label: A&M
Songwriter: Gordon Sumner (Sting)

New Age love song.

IF YOU LOVE SOMEBODY SET THEM FREE

Producers: Pete Smith, Sting
Album: The Dream of the Blue Turtles
Record Label: A&M
Songwriter: Gordon Sumner (Sting)

First and biggest solo hit for the ex-Police man establishes his airy Jazz Rock persona.

1987

THEY DANCE ALONE
Producers: Hugh Padgham, Sting
Album: Nothing Like the Sun
Record Label: A&M
Songwriter: Gordon Sumner (Sting)
One of his most haunting songs; "Invisible Sun" for the rebels of South America.

WE'LL BE TOGETHER
Producers: Hugh Padgham, Sting
Album: Nothing Like the Sun
Record Label: A&M
Songwriter: Gordon Sumner (Sting)

1991

ALL THIS TIME
Producers: Hugh Padgham, Sting
Album: The Soul Cages
Record Label: A&M
Songwriter: Gordon Sumner (Sting)

1993

IF I EVER LOSE MY FAITH IN YOU
Producers: Hugh Padgham, Sting
Album: Ten Summoner's Tales
Record Label: A&M
Songwriter: Gordon Sumner (Sting)

THE STONE PONEYS
1965

DIFFERENT DRUM
Producer: Nik Venet
Album: Evergreen (Vol. II)
Record Label: Capitol
Songwriter: Mike Nesmith
The nascent liberated woman, in the adenoidal tones of an Arizona expatriate, written in the parlance of Folk Rock, by the intellectual Monkee.

THE STONE ROSES
1989

FOOL'S GOLD
Producer: John Leckie
Album: The Stone Roses
Record Label: Silvertone/Jive
Songwriters: John Squire, Ian Brown
Top-10 U.K. smash establishes England's droning neo-psychedelic rave scene.

SHE BANGS THE DRUM
Producer: John Leckie
Album: The Stone Roses
Record Label: Silvertone/Jive
Songwriters: John Squire, Ian Brown
Their first U.K. chart single.

1994

LOVE SPREADS
Producer: Simon Dawson
Album: Second Coming
Record Label: Geffen
Songwriter: John Squires
This comeback sound fit squarely with the new Alternative, much of it recycled Beatlemania from England.

STONE TEMPLE PILOTS
1993

PLUSH
Producer: Brendan O'Brien
Album: Core
Record Label: Atlantic
Songwriters: Robert DeLeo, Scott Weiland, Dean DeLeo, Eric Kretz
The Hard Rock side of Alternative.

1994

BIG EMPTY
Producer: Brendan O'Brien
Album: *The Crow* Soundtrack
Record Label: Interscope
Songwriters: Dean DeLeo, Scott Weiland
From the Alternative soundtrack of the year.

INTERSTATE LOVE SONG
Producer: Brendan O'Brien
Album: Purple
Record Label: Atlantic
Songwriters: Robert DeLeo, Scott Weiland, Dean DeLeo, Eric Kretz
The Alternative Sound, but not the feeling.

VASOLINE
Producer: Brendan O'Brien
Album: Purple
Record Label: Atlantic
Songwriters: Robert DeLeo, Scott Weiland, Dean DeLeo, Eric Kretz
Their biggest hit.

THE STOOGES
1969

I WANNA BE YOUR DOG
Producer: John Cale
Album: The Stooges
Record Label: Elektra
Songwriters: James Osterberg, Scott Asheton, Ron Asheton, Dave Alexander
Summing up the nascent Punk three-chord revolution. In New York, the Ramones were pricing Kay guitars.

1970

L.A. BLUES
Producer: Don Gallucci
Album: Fun House
Record Label: Elektra
Songwriter: The Stooges
Punk Rock rears its ugly rear.

1973

RAW POWER
Producer: David Bowie
Album: Raw Power
Record Label: Columbia
Songwriters: James Osterberg, James Williamson
Iggy Pop takes the Stooges to new heights (depths).

SEARCH AND DESTROY
Producer: David Bowie
Album: Raw Power
Record Label: Columbia
Songwriters: James Osterberg, James Williamson
Outlining the Punk philosophy.

PAUL STOOKEY
1971

THE WEDDING SONG
Producers: Jim Mason, Ed Mottau
Album: Paul and
Record Label: Warner Brothers
Songwriter: Noel Paul Stookey
Post-'60s/pre-New Age take on the wedding vows.

STOP THE VIOLENCE
1989

SELF DESTRUCTION
Producers: KRS-One, D-Nice
Album: Self Destruction
Record Label: Jive
Songwriters: Dwight Myers, Doug E. Fresh, MC Lyte, Moe DeWese, Carlton Ridenhour, William Drayton
A gaggle of all-stars address Rap's bad rep.

THE STORY
1993

SO MUCH MINE
Producers: Alain Mallet, Ben Whittman
Album: The Angel in the House
Record Label: Elektra
Songwriter: Jonatha Brooke
Neo-Folk Rock lives.

THE STRANGELOVES
1965

I WANT CANDY
Producers: Bob Feldman, Jerry Goldstein, Richard Gottehrer
Album: I Want Candy
Record Label: Bang
Songwriters: Bob Feldman, Jerry Goldstein, Richard Gottehrer, Bert Berns

The Brill Building goes Garage with this ultimate frat house classic. Covered by Bow Wow Wow (RCA, '82).

THE STRANGLERS
1987

ALWAYS THE SUN
Album: Dreamtime
Record Label: Columbia
Songwriter: The Stranglers

Critical breakthrough of sorts for notorious English punks.

STRAWBERRY ALARM CLOCK
1967

INCENSE AND PEPPERMINTS
Producers: Frank Slay, Bill Holmes
Album: Incense and Peppermints
Record Label: Uni
Songwriters: John Carter, Tim Gilbert

Hippie-esque.

THE STRAWBS
1973

PART OF THE UNION
Album: Bursting at the Seams
Record Label: A&M
Songwriters: Richard Hudson, John Ford

Biggest U.K. hit for Folk Rock relatives of Fairport Convention that at different times featured Sandy Denny, Rick Wakeman, and Dave Cousins in the band.

STRAY CATS
1981

RUNAWAY BOYS
Producer: Dave Edmunds
Album: Stray Cats
Record Label: Arista
Songwriter: Brian Setzer

Rockabilly redux by a Long Island band that broke big in England.

1982

ROCK THIS TOWN
Producer: Dave Edmunds
Album: Built for Speed
Record Label: EMI-America
Songwriter: Brian Setzer

Slickest of the early '80s Roots-Rock revivalists.

STRAY CAT STRUT
Producer: Dave Edmunds
Album: Built for Speed
Record Label: EMI-America
Songwriter: Brian Setzer

Their biggest hit.

1983

(SHE'S) SEXY AND 17
Producer: Dave Edmunds
Album: Rant n' Rave with the Stray Cats
Record Label: EMI-America
Songwriter: Brian Setzer

Suggested segue: "You're Sixteen" by Johnny Barnette.

THE STRINGALONGS
1961

WHEELS
Record Label: Warwick
Songwriters: Jimmy Torres, Richard Stephens

Guitar instrumental.

BARRETT STRONG
1960

MONEY (THAT'S WHAT I WANT)
Producer: Berry Gordy Jr.
Record Label: Anna
Songwriters: Janie Bradford, Berry Gordy Jr.

An apt signature on the blank check that would soon be Motown; more money for black artists in the '60s. Barrett Strong, Nolan's cousin, would be one of the bigger beneficiaries as a songwriter.

THE STUDENTS
1958

I'M SO YOUNG
Record Label: Note
Songwriter: Prez Tyrus

Essential Doo-Wop plaint, revived in '61 on Argo. Covered by the Ronettes (Philles, '64) and the Beach Boys (Capitol, '65).

THE STYLE COUNCIL
1984

MY EVER CHANGING MOODS
Album: My Ever Changing Moods
Record Label: Geffen
Songwriter: Paul Weller

Only Top-40 U.S. single for the former leader of the Jam.

THE STYLISTICS
1971

BETCHA BY GOLLY WOW
Producer: Thom Bell
Album: The Stylistics
Record Label: Avco
Songwriters: Thom Bell, Linda Creed

Doo-Wop enters the Top-10 of the '70s, virtually unscathed.

YOU ARE EVERYTHING
Producer: Thom Bell
Album Title: The Stylistics
Record Label: Avco
Songwriters: Thom Bell, Linda Creed

Introducing a new Philly Soul interracial songwriting team, with a Top-10 R&B/R&R crossover.

1972

BREAK UP TO MAKE UP
Producer: Thom Bell
Album: Round 2: The Stylistics
Record Label: Avco
Songwriters: Thom Bell, Linda Creed, Kenny Gamble

Top-5 R&B/R&R crossover.

I'M STONE IN LOVE WITH YOU
Producer: Thom Bell
Album: Round 2: The Stylistics
Record Label: Avco
Songwriters: Thom Bell, Linda Creed, Anthony Bell

Their third Top-10 R&B/R&R crossover.

1973

ROCKIN' ROLL BABY
Producer: Thom Bell
Album: Rockin' Roll Baby
Record Label: Avco
Songwriters: Thom Bell, Linda Creed

Highlight of their third album; a hit in England, a Top-10 R&B/Top-20 R&R crossover here.

YOU MAKE ME FEEL BRAND NEW
Producer: Thom Bell
Album: Rockin' Roll Baby
Record Label: Avco
Songwriters: Thom Bell, Linda Creed
Their biggest hit, Top-5 R&B/R&R crossover.

STYX

1974

LADY
Producer: Styx
Album: Styx II
Record Label: Wooden Nickel
Songwriter: Dennis DeYoung
Breakthrough Arena ballad.

1977

COME SAIL AWAY
Producer: Styx
Album: The Grand Illusion
Record Label: A&M
Songwriter: Dennis DeYoung
Over-the-top American Pomp Rock theatrics.

1979

BABE
Producer: Styx
Album: Cornerstone
Record Label: A&M
Songwriter: Dennis DeYoung
Their biggest hit.

1981

THE BEST OF TIMES
Producer: Styx
Album: Paradise Theater
Record Label: A&M
Songwriter: Dennis DeYoung
Second-biggest single from their #1 album.

TOO MUCH TIME ON MY HANDS
Producer: Styx
Album: Paradise Theater
Record Label: A&M
Songwriter: Tommy Shaw
Shaw would move on to Damn Yankees in the '90s.

1983

DON'T LET IT END
Producer: Styx
Album: Kilroy Was Here
Record Label: A&M
Songwriter: Dennis DeYoung
Their Top-10 R&R single.

MR. ROBOTO
Producer: Styx
Album: Kilroy Was Here
Record Label: A&M
Songwriter: Dennis DeYoung

1991

SHOW ME THE WAY
Producer: Styx
Album: Edge of the Century
Record Label: A&M
Songwriter: Dennis DeYoung
Adopted by our boys in the Gulf War.

SUEDE

1992

METAL MIKEY
Producer: Ed Buller
Album: Suede
Record Label: Sony
Songwriters: Brett Anderson, Bernard Butler
New English Alternative.

SUGAR

1994

YOUR FAVORITE THING
Album: File under Easy Listening
Record Label: Rykodisc
Songwriter: Bob Mould
The Hüsker Dü guitar man finds a new groove—anything but easy listening.

THE SUGAR HILL GANG

1979

RAPPER'S DELIGHT
Producer: Sylvia Robinson
Record Label: Sugar Hill
Songwriters: Nile Rodgers, Bernard Edwards, Sylvia Robinson, Big Bank Hank Jackson, Wonder Mike Wright, Master Gee O'Brien
Credited as the first Rap record, establishing the rhythm and rhyme of the streetwise urban boasting genre; based on Chic's Disco classic "Good Times."

THE SUGARCUBES

1988

BIRTHDAY
Producers: R. Sholman, P. Burkett
Album: Life's Too Good
Record Label: Elektra
Songwriter: Sugarcubes
First single from the exotic neurotics from Iceland.

1992

HIT
Producer: Paul Fox
Album: Stick Around for Joy
Record Label: Elektra
Songwriter: Sugarcubes
Reaching the college market with a genuine U.S. Alternative hit. Lead singer Björk then left to go solo.

SUGARLOAF

1970

GREEN EYED LADY
Producer: Frank Slay
Album: Sugarloaf
Record Label: Liberty
Songwriters: Jerry Corbetta, J. C. Phillips, David Riordan
Their biggest hit.

1974

DON'T CALL US, WE'LL CALL YOU
Producer: Frank Slay
Album: Don't Call Us, We'll Call You
Record Label: Claridge
Songwriters: Jerry Corbetta, John Canter
Rare instance of Ski Bum Rock. Never caught on like Surf.

SUICIDAL TENDENCIES

1983

INSTITUTIONALIZED
Album: Suicidal Tendencies
Record Label: Frontier
Songwriters: Mike Muir, Amery Smith, Louis Mayorga
Heavy Mental.

SUICIDE

1977

CHEREE
Producers: Craig Leon, Marty Thau
Album: Suicide
Record Label: Red Star
Songwriters: Alan Vega, Martin Rev
Experimental Bowery cult band expands on Lou Reed's bleak Manhattan vision.

DONNA SUMMER

1976

LOVE TO LOVE YOU BABY
Producer: Pete Bellotte
Album: Love to Love You Baby
Record Label: Oasis

Songwriters: Giorgio Moroder, Pete Bellotte, Donna Summer

The first diva of Disco arrives, swooning, from Boston, by way of Germany.

1977

I FEEL LOVE

Producers: Pete Bellotte, Giorgio Moroder
Album: I Remember Yesterday
Record Label: Casablanca
Songwriters: Giorgio Morodor, Pete Bellotte, Donna Summer

#1 U.K. smash typifies Donna's unrelentingly consistent approach.

1978

HEAVEN KNOWS

Producers: Pete Bellotte, Giorgio Moroder
Album: Live and More
Record Label: Casablanca
Songwriters: Giorgio Moroder, Pete Bellotte, Donna Summer, Gregg Mathieson

Another hit, with Brooklyn Dreams.

THE LAST DANCE

Producer: Giorgio Moroder
Album: Live and More
Record Label: Casablanca
Songwriter: Paul Jabara

Oscar winner from the movie Thank God It's Friday, *which was no* Saturday Night Fever.

1979

BAD GIRLS

Producers: Giorgio Moroder, Pete Bellotte
Album: Bad Girls
Record Label: Casablanca
Songwriters: Donna Summer, Bruce Sudano, Joe Esposito, Edward Hokenson

Her first #1 R&B/R&R crossover. Suggested segue: "I'm Livin' in Shame" by the Supremes.

DIM ALL THE LIGHTS

Producers: Giorgio Moroder, Pete Bellotte
Album: Bad Girls
Record Label: Casablanca
Songwriter: Donna Summer

HOT STUFF

Producers: Giorgio Moroder, Pete Bellotte
Album: Bad Girls

Record Label: Casablanca
Songwriters: Pete Bellotte, Harold Faltermeyer, Keith Forsey

Second #1 from the album.

NO MORE TEARS (ENOUGH IS ENOUGH)

Producers: Giorgio Moroder, Pete Bellotte
Album: On the Radio—Greatest Hits (Vols. I and II)
Record Label: Casablanca
Songwriters: Paul Jabara, Bruce Roberts

Dueling divas; her belting duet with Barbra Streisand earns Donna her fourth and last #1 U.S.

ON THE RADIO

Producers: Giorgio Moroder, Pete Bellotte
Album: Greatest Hits (Vols. I and II)
Record Label: Casablanca
Songwriters: Giorgio Moroder, Donna Summer

1980

THE WANDERER

Producers: Giorgio Moroder, Pete Bellotte
Album: The Wanderer
Record Label: Geffen
Songwriters: Giorgio Moroder, Donna Summer

Donna does Rock.

1982

LOVE IS IN CONTROL (FINGER ON THE TRIGGER)

Producer: Quincy Jones
Album: Donna Summer
Record Label: Geffen
Songwriters: Rod Temperton, Quincy Jones, Merria Ross

Donna does Pop.

1983

SHE WORKS HARD FOR THE MONEY

Producer: Michael Omartian
Album: She Works Hard for the Money
Record Label: Mercury
Songwriters: Michael Omartian, Donna Summer

Returning to her Disco roots, with a #1 R&B/Top-10 R&R crossover.

1989

THIS TIME I KNOW IT'S FOR REAL

Producers: Mike Stock, Matt Aitken, Pete Waterman
Album: Another Place and Time
Record Label: Atlantic
Songwriters: Mike Stock, Matt Aitken, Pete Waterman

THE SUNDAYS

1990

HERE'S WHERE THE STORY ENDS

Producers: Ray Shulman, Sundays
Album: Reading, Writing and Arithmetic
Record Label: DGC
Songwriters: David Gavurin, Harriet Wheeler

Ushering in Waif Rock with a captivating U.K. alternative smash. Stevie Nicks was jealous, Natalie Merchant was taking notes.

SUPERCHUNK

1992

SWALLOW THAT

Album: On the Mouth
Record Label: Matador
Songwriters: Jonathan Wurster, James Wilbur, Ralph McLaughan, Laura Ballance

Alternative track, with critical cache.

SUPERTRAMP

1979

THE LOGICAL SONG

Producers: Pete Henderson, Supertramp
Album: Breakfast in America
Record Label: A&M
Songwriters: Richard Davies, Roger Hodgson

Wordy Pomp Rock from England, where Queen did it better.

TAKE THE LONG WAY HOME

Producers: Pete Henderson, Supertramp
Album: Breakfast in America
Record Label: A&M
Songwriters: Richard Davies, Roger Hodgson

THE SUPREMES

1962

YOUR HEART BELONGS TO ME

Producer: Smokey Robinson
Album: Meet the Supremes
Record Label: Motown
Songwriter: Smokey Robinson

A legendary career opens with a solid stiff.

1964

BABY LOVE

Producers: Brian Holland, Lamont Dozier
Album: Where Did Our Love Go
Record Label: Motown
Songwriters: Eddie Holland, Lamont Dozier, Brian Holland

The biggest song of the year, if you discount the Beatles.

COME SEE ABOUT ME

Producers: Brian Holland, Lamont Dozier
Album: Where Did Our Love Go
Record Label: Motown
Songwriters: Eddie Holland, Lamont Dozier, Brian Holland

Perfecting their formula with their third #1 in a row.

WHERE DID OUR LOVE GO

Producers: Brian Holland, Lamont Dozier
Album: Where Did Our Love Go
Record Label: Motown
Songwriters: Eddie Holland, Lamont Dozier, Brian Holland

The Ronettes move to Detroit, go to finishing school, get their first #1 after ten tries. A hot streak of mythic proportions would ensue, thereby delaying the Shirelles entry into the Hall of Fame by a good five years.

1965

BACK IN MY ARMS AGAIN

Producers: Brian Holland, Lamont Dozier
Album: More Hits
Record Label: Motown
Songwriters: Eddie Holland, Lamont Dozier, Brian Holland

Their first #1 R&B/R&R crossover. Only the Beatles had a better year at the top of the charts, and they didn't make the R&B charts at all.

I HEAR A SYMPHONY

Producers: Brian Holland, Lamont Dozier
Album: I Hear a Symphony
Record Label: Motown
Songwriters: Eddie Holland, Lamont Dozier, Brian Holland

NOTHING BUT HEARTACHES

Producers: Brian Holland, Lamont Dozier
Album: More Hits by the Supremes
Record Label: Motown
Songwriters: Eddie Holland, Lamont Dozier, Brian Holland

Breaking a string of five #1s in a row.

STOP! IN THE NAME OF LOVE

Producers: Brian Holland, Lamont Dozier
Album: More Hits by the Supremes
Record Label: Motown
Songwriters: Eddie Holland, Lamont Dozier, Brian Holland

Their biggest hit of the year.

1966

LOVE IS LIKE AN ITCHING IN MY HEART

Producers: Brian Holland, Lamont Dozier
Album: Supremes a Go-Go
Record Label: Motown
Songwriters: Eddie Holland, Lamont Dozier, Brian Holland

One of the most uncomfortable metaphors in R&R/R&B history. Suggested segue: "Poison Ivy" by the Coasters.

MY WORLD IS EMPTY WITHOUT YOU

Producers: Brian Holland, Lamont Dozier
Album: I Hear a Symphony
Record Label: Motown
Songwriters: Eddie Holland, Lamont Dozier, Brian Holland

YOU CAN'T HURRY LOVE

Producers: Brian Holland, Lamont Dozier
Album: Supremes a Go-Go
Record Label: Motown
Songwriters: Eddie Holland, Lamont Dozier, Brian Holland

Their seventh #1 R&R, second #1 R&B/R&R crossover.

YOU KEEP ME HANGIN' ON

Producers: Brian Holland, Lamont Dozier
Album: Sing Holland-Dozier-Holland
Record Label: Motown
Songwriters: Eddie Holland, Lamont Dozier, Brian Holland

#1 R&B/R&R crossover is their closest thing to Rock. Covered by the Vanilla Fudge (Atco, '67), Kim Wild (MCA, '87).

1967

THE HAPPENING

Producers: Brian Holland, Lamont Dozier
Album: Supremes' Greatest Hits
Record Label: Motown
Songwriters: Eddie Holland, Lamont Dozier, Brian Holland

As calculated as the event it exploits. Their tenth #1 R&R hit, and the first as Diana Ross and the Supremes.

IN AND OUT OF LOVE

Producers: Brian Holland, Lamont Dozier
Album: Reflections
Record Label: Motown
Songwriters: Eddie Holland, Lamont Dozier, Brian Holland

LOVE IS HERE AND NOW YOU'RE GONE

Producers: Brian Holland, Lamont Dozier
Album: The Supremes Sing Holland-Dozier-Holland
Record Label: Motown
Songwriters: Eddie Holland, Lamont Dozier, Brian Holland

Their third straight #1 R&B/R&R crossover is their last hit with Florence Ballard in the group.

REFLECTIONS

Producers: Brian Holland, Lamont Dozier
Album: Reflections
Record Label: Motown
Songwriters: Eddie Holland, Lamont Dozier, Brian Holland

Their first single release in sixteen months that didn't hit #1.

1968

LOVE CHILD

Producers: Berry Gordy Jr., Deke Richards, Frank Wilson, Henry Cosby, R. Dean Taylor
Album: Love Child
Record Label: Motown
Songwriters: Pam Sawyer, R. Dean Taylor, Frank Wilson, Deke Richards

Beginning Diana's fabricated Street period; their biggest hit in four years.

1969

I'M LIVIN' IN SHAME

Producer: The Clan
Album: Let the Sunshine In
Record Label: Motown
Songwriters: Pam Sawyer, Berry Gordy Jr., Frank Wilson, R. Dean Taylor, Henry Cosby

Keeping down with the Joneses.

1970

STONED LOVE

Producer: Frank Wilson
Album: New Ways But Love Stays
Record Label: Motown
Songwriters: Frank Wilson, Yennik Samoht

#1 R&B/Top-10 R&R crossover.

UP THE LADDER TO THE ROOF

Producer: Frank Wilson
Album: Right On
Record Label: Motown
Songwriters: Frank Wilson, Vincent Dimirco

The voice of their Street period, Frank Wilson, gives them their last hit. Suggested segue: "Up the Roof" by the Drifters.

AL B. SURE

1988

NITE AND DAY

Producers: Teddy Riley, Al B. Sure
Album: In Effect Mode
Record Label: Warner Brothers
Songwriters: Al B. Sure, Kyle West

Middle-of-the-Street crooner breaks with a #1 R&B/Top-10 R&R crossover.

OFF ON YOUR OWN (GIRL)

Producers: Teddy Riley, Al B. Sure
Album: In Effect Mode
Record Label: Warner Brothers
Songwriters: Al B. Sure, Kyle West

#1 R&B/Top-50 R&R crossover.

1992

MISUNDERSTANDING

Album: Private Times . . . and the Whole 9
Record Label: Warner Brothers
Songwriters: Al B. Sure, D. J. Eddie, F. Nevelle

#1 R&B/Top-50 R&R crossover.

RIGHT NOW

Producers: Kyle West, Al B. Sure
Album: Sexy Versus

Record Label: Warner Brothers
Songwriters: Al B. Sure, Kyle West

#1 R&B/Top-50 R&R crossover.

SURFACE

1987

HAPPY

Producers: Bernard Jackson, David Townshend, David Conley
Album: Surface
Record Label: Columbia
Songwriters: Bernard Jackson, David Townshend, David Conley

Second generation Soul; David is the son of Ed Townshend.

1988

CLOSER THAN FRIENDS

Producers: Bernard Jackson, David Townshend, David Conley
Album: Second Wave
Record Label: Columbia
Songwriters: Bernard Jackson, David Townshend

#1 R&B/Top-60 crossover.

SHOWER ME WITH YOUR LOVE

Producers: Bernard Jackson, David Townshend, David Conley
Album: Second Wave
Record Label: Columbia
Songwriter: Bernard Jackson

Their first #1 R&B/Top-10 R&R crossover.

YOU ARE MY EVERYTHING

Producers: Bernard Jackson, David Townshend, David Conley
Album: Second Wave
Record Label: Columbia
Songwriters: Everett Collins, David Townshend, David Conley, Derrick Cullen

#1 R&B/Bottom-20 R&R crossover.

1990

THE FIRST TIME

Album: 3 Deep
Record Label: Columbia
Songwriters: Bernard Jackson, Brian Simpson

Taking their smooth groove to the max, with a #1 R&B/R&R crossover.

THE SURFARIS

1963

SURFER JOE

Producer: Dale Smallin
Album: Wipe Out

Record Label: Warner Brothers
Songwriters: Al B. Sure, Kyle West

#1 R&B/Top-50 R&R crossover.

Record Label: Dot
Songwriter: Ron Wilson

Where have you gone Murf the Surf?

WIPE OUT

Producer: Dale Smallin
Album: Wipe Out
Record Label: Dot
Songwriters: Ron Wilson, Robert Berryhill, James Fuller, Patrick Connolly

The demented laughter of the title voice would say it all for the surf craze. Suggested segue: "Dead Man's Curve."

SURVIVOR

1982

EYE OF THE TIGER (THE THEME FROM *ROCKY III*)

Producers: Frank Sullivan, Jim Peterik
Album: Eye of the Tiger
Record Label: Scotti Brothers
Songwriters: Frank Sullivan, Jim Peterik

Arena Rock, reduced to accommodate a boxing ring, then expanded to fill a movie screen. Suggested segue: "The Boxer" by Simon and Garfunkel.

1984

HIGH ON YOU

Producer: Ron Nevison
Album: Vital Signs
Record Label: Epic
Songwriters: Frankie Sullivan, Jim Peterik

Arena Rock for the jukebox. Suggested segue: "High Enough" by Damn Yankees.

THE SEARCH IS OVER

Producer: Ron Nevison
Album: Vital Signs
Record Label: Epic
Songwriters: Frankie Sullivan, Jim Peterik

Searching for the lost power chord, a corporate Rock peak worthy of Asia, or even Toto.

1985

BURNING HEART

Producers: Frank Sullivan, Jim Peterik
Album: *Rocky IV* Soundtrack
Record Label: Scotti Brothers
Songwriters: Frankie Sullivan, Jim Peterik

Striking Rocky pay dirt again.

1986

IS THIS LOVE
Producers: Ron Nevison, Frank Sullivan
Album: When Seconds Count
Record Label: Scotti Brothers
Songwriters: Jim Peterik, Frankie Sullivan

SUTHERLAND BROTHERS AND QUIVER

1973

SAILING
Album: Lifeboat
Record Label: Island
Songwriter: Gavin Sutherland

Covered by Rod Stewart (Warner Brothers, '75).

1976

ARMS OF MARY
Producers: Howard Albert, Ron Albert
Album: Reach for the Sky
Record Label: Columbia
Songwriter: Iain Sutherland

Winsome coming of age saga was their commercial and evocative peak. Covered by Chilliwack (Mushroom, '78), the Everly Brothers (Mercury, '86).

BILLY SWAN

1974

I CAN HELP
Producers: Billy Swan, Chip Young
Album: I Can Help
Record Label: Monument
Songwriter: Billy Swan

A rare #1 C&W/R&R crossover for the Rockabilly veteran. Covered by Elvis Presley (RCA, '75).

BETTYE SWANN

1967

MAKE ME YOURS
Record Label: Money
Songwriter: Bettye Jean Champion

Fine Soul ballad; #1 R&B/Top-25 R&R crossover.

THE SWANS

1987

CHILDREN OF GOD
Album: Children of God
Record Label: Caroline

Songwriters: Michael Gira, Jarboe
Peak moment from the experimental New York Art Rock droners.

PATRICK SWAYZE WITH WENDY FRASER

1987

SHE'S LIKE THE WIND
Producer: Michael Lloyd
Album: *Dirty Dancing* Soundtrack
Record Label: RCA
Songwriters: Patrick Swayze, Stacey Widelitz

Hunk Rock.

KEITH SWEAT

1988

I WANT HER
Producer: Teddy Riley
Album: Make It Last Forever
Record Label: Vintertainment
Songwriters: Keith Sweat, Teddy Riley

#1 R&B/Top-10 R&R crossover introduces the '80s version of R&B's perennial bedroom ballad, New Jack Swing. R. Kelly was listening.

1990

I'LL GIVE ALL MY LOVE TO YOU
Album: I'll Give All My Love to You
Record Label: Elektra
Songwriters: Keith Sweat, Bobby Wooten

#1 R&B/Top-10 R&R crossover.

MAKE YOU SWEAT
Album: I'll Give All My Love to You
Record Label: Elektra
Songwriters: Keith Sweat, Bobby Wooten, Timothy Gatling

#1 R&B/Top-20 R&R crossover. Suggested segues: "Gonna Make You Sweat (Everybody Dance Now)" by C&C Music Factory (Columbia, '80), "Sweat (La La La La La Long)" by Inner Circle (Big Beat, '93).

1991

KEEP IT COMIN'
Producers: Keith Sweat, Lionel Job
Album: Keep It Comin'
Record Label: Elektra
Songwriters: Keith Sweat, Lionel Job, Joe Carter, Joseph Sayles, Dew Wyatt, Kev Scott

His fourth #1 R&B/Top-20 R&R crossover.

MATTHEW SWEET

1991

GIRLFRIEND
Producers: Fred Maher, Matthew Sweet
Album: Girlfriend
Record Label: Zoo
Songwriter: Matthew Sweet

Breakthrough track for an Alternative semi-acoustic singer/songwriter.

I'VE BEEN WAITING
Producers: Fred Maher, Matthew Sweet
Album: Girlfriend
Record Label: Zoo
Songwriter: Matthew Sweet

Pure Pop for the '90s.

RACHEL SWEET

1979

STRANGER IN THE HOUSE
Producer: Liam Sternberg
Album: Fool Around
Record Label: Stiff
Songwriter: Elvis Costello

Covered by Elvis Costello (Columbia, '80).

WHO DOES LISA LIKE
Producer: Liam Sternberg
Album: Fool Around
Record Label: Stiff
Songwriter: Liam Sternberg

Brenda Lee as a wasted Midwestern roots rocker; produced and directed by the author of the Bangles' "Walk Like an Egyptian."

1988

HAIRSPRAY
Producer: Kenny Vance
Album: *Hairspray* Soundtrack
Record Label: MCA
Songwriters: Rachel Sweet, Anthony Battaglea, Willa Bassen

Akron's Sweet finds her milieu, a decade too late, in this classic film about Rock and Roll in Baltimore in the early '60s.

THE SWEET

1973

BLOCKBUSTER
Producers: Mike Chapman, Nicky Chinn
Album: The Sweet
Record Label: Bell

Songwriters: Mike Chapman, Nicky Chinn

Their biggest U.K. Kiddie Metal hit, stiffed stateside.

LITTLE WILLY

Producers: Mike Chapman, Nicky Chinn
Album: The Sweet
Record Label: Bell
Songwriter: Mike Day

Top-10 U.S./U.K. crossover was their biggest U.S. hit almost a year after it peaked in England.

1975

BALLROOM BLITZ

Producers: Mike Chapman, Nicky Chinn
Album: Desolation Boulevard
Record Label: Capitol
Songwriters: Mike Chapman, Nicky Chinn

Track's eternal Arena rep was secured when it was featured in the reverently irreverent Rock and Roll fantasy film Wayne's World.

FOX ON THE RUN

Producers: Mike Chapman, Nicky Chinn
Album: Desolation Boulevard
Record Label: Capitol
Songwriters: Brian Connolly, Andrew Scott, Stephen Priest, Michael Tucker

Among the royalty of British Rock.

1977

LOVE IS LIKE OXYGEN

Producers: Mike Chapman, Nicky Chinn
Album: Level Headed
Record Label: Capitol
Songwriters: Trevor Griffin, Andrew Scott

Their last Top-10, after which the group expired.

SWEET SENSATION

1990

IF WISHES CAME TRUE

Album: Love Child
Record Label: Atco
Songwriters: Russell Desalvo, Deena Charles, Bob Steele

#1 R&R Hip-Hop girl-group one-shot. SWV was listening.

SWING OUT SISTER

1987

BREAKOUT

Producers: John McElrath, P. S. O' Duffy
Album: It's Better to Travel
Record Label: Mercury
Songwriter: Swing Out Sister

U.S./U.K. swinging one-shot.

THE SWINGING MEDALLIONS

1966

DOUBLE SHOT (OF MY BABY'S LOVE)

Album: Double Shot (of My Baby's Love)
Record Label: Smash
Songwriters: Don M. Smith, Cyril E. Vetter

Frat-house prequel to "Love Me Two Times" by the Doors.

SWV

1992

RIGHT HERE

Producers: B. A. Morgan, Genard Parker
Album: It's About Time
Record Label: RCA
Songwriter: Brian Alcxander Morgan

Remix of their first hit went #1 R&B/Top-10 R&R, aided by a touch of Michael Jackson's "Human Nature." The B-side "Downtown" scored as well.

1993

I'M SO INTO YOU

Producer: B. A. Morgan
Album: It's About Time
Record Label: RCA
Songwriter: Brian Alexander Morgan

Mining the pre-teen girl-group sound of Hip-Hop.

WEAK

Producer: B. A. Morgan
Album: It's About Time
Record Label: RCA
Songwriter: Brian Alexander Morgan

Celebrating their lack of resistance with a #1 R&B/R&R crossover.

THE SYLVERS

1976

BOOGIE FEVER

Producer: Freddie Perren
Album: Showcase
Record Label: Capitol
Songwriters: Freddie Perren, Keni St. Lewis

#1 R&B/R&R Disco crossover.

1977

HOT LINE

Producer: Freddie Perren
Album: Something Special
Record Label: Capitol
Songwriters: Freddie Perren, Keni St. Lewis

SYLVESTER

1978

DANCE (DISCO HEAT)

Producers: Harvey Fuqua, Sylvester
Album: Step II
Record Label: Fantasy
Songwriters: Victor Orsborn, Eric Robinson

A Disco original. RuPaul was waiting in the wings.

SYLVIA

1973

PILLOW TALK

Producer: Sylvia Robinson
Album: Pillow Talk
Record Label: Vibration
Songwriters: Sylvia Robinson, Michael Burton

Sylvia breaks up with Mickey, goes to the Disco and scores. Rejected by Al Green as being too sexy. But Donna Summer was paying attention in Germany.

SYNCH

1986

WHERE ARE YOU NOW

Album: Don't Fight the Midnight
Record Label: WTG
Songwriters: Jimmy Harnen, R. Congdon

Became a hit in '89.

THE SYNDICATE OF SOUND
1966

LITTLE GIRL
Producer: Gary Thompson
Album: Little Girl
Record Label: Bell
Songwriters: Don Baskin, Bob Gonzalez

Frat house anthem with an Alternative edge. Covered by the Dead Boys (Sire, '77).

SYREETA
1974

CAUSE WE'VE ENDED AS LOVERS
Producer: Stevie Wonder
Album: Stevie Wonder Presents Syreeta
Record Label: Motown
Songwriter: Stevie Wonder

Stevie's heartbreaking farewell to his soon-to-be ex-wife. Covered by Jeff Beck (Epic, '75).

THE SYSTEM
1987

DON'T DISTURB THIS GROOVE
Producer: The System
Album: Don't Disturb This Groove
Record Label: Capitol
Songwriters: Mic Murphy, David Frank

Biggest hit for the synth-based Funk band; #1 R&B/Top-5 R&R crossover.

T

T'PAU
1987

HEART AND SOUL
Producer: Roy Thomas Baker
Album: T'Pau
Record Label: Virgin
Songwriters: Carol Decker, Ronnie Rogers

Top-10 R&R U.K. one-shot.

THE T-BONES
1965

NO MATTER WHAT SHAPE (YOUR STOMACH'S IN)
Producer: Joe Saraceno

Album: No Matter What Shape (Your Stomach's In)
Record Label: Liberty
Songwriter: Sascha Burland

Surf music hits the commercial mainstream.

T. REX
1971

HOT LOVE
Album: Beard of Stars
Record Label: Regal/Zonophone U.K.
Songwriter: Marc Feld (Marc Bolan)

Their biggest U.K. hit. Stalled in the States at a cold #72.

RIDE A WHITE SWAN
Album: T-Rex
Record Label: Reprise
Songwriter: Marc Feld (Marc Bolan)

First big U.K. hit for the Metal Donovan, rode the Bottom-40 here.

1972

BANG A GONG (GET IT ON)
Producer: Tony Visconti
Album: Electric Warrior
Record Label: Reprise
Songwriter: Marc Feld (Marc Bolan)

Lite Metal hit from England, where it was taken more seriously. Suggested segue: "So Alive" by Love and Rockets. Mott the Hoople was listening.

TELEGRAM SAM
Producer: Tony Visconti
Album: The Slider
Record Label: Reprise
Songwriter: Marc Feld (Marc Bolan)

#1 U.K. Covered by Bauhaus (4AD, '81). His biggest U.S. hit, aside from "Bang a Gong," clocking in at #67.

TIMMY T.
1991

ONE MORE TRY
Album: Time After Time
Record Label: Quality
Songwriter: Timmy Torres

In the era of Stevie B., Timmy T. was a kindred Indie spirit.

TACO
1983

PUTTIN' ON THE RITZ
Album: After Eight
Record Label: RCA

Songwriter: Irving Berlin

Eternal Disco novelty. Introduced by Harry Richman (Brunswick, '30). Suggested segue: "Winchester Cathedral" by the New Vaudeville Band.

TAG TEAM
1993

WHOOT! (THERE IT IS)
Producer: Tag Team
Album: Whoot! (There It Is)
Record Label: Life
Songwriter: Tag Team

The Arena chant of the year, as omnipresent as the Wave, spending nearly a year on the charts; a #1 R&B/#2 R&R crossover. Not to be confused with "Whoot, There It Is" by 95 South (Wrap, '93), another Arena chant, restricted to the crowd in the parking lot, waiting for the losers to board their bus home.

TALKING HEADS
1977

PSYCHO KILLER
Producers: Tony Bongiovi, Lance Quinn, Talking Heads
Album: Talking Heads '77
Record Label: Sire
Songwriters: David Byrne, Tina Weymouth, Chris Frantz

The auspicious debut of the artsy, proto-nerd band from the Rhode Island School of Design, a tribute to New York-based serial killer David Berkowitz, with some of the lyrics in French.

1979

LIFE DURING WARTIME
Producer: Brian Eno
Album: Fear of Music
Record Label: Sire
Songwriter: David Byrne

The nervous cousins of the Bowery Punk scene explain why the Disco era is over. Featured in the movie Times Square.

MEMORIES CAN'T WAIT
Producer: Brian Eno
Album: Fear of Music
Record Label: Sire
Songwriters: David Byrne, Jerry Harrison

Covered by Living Colour (Epic, '88).

1981

ONCE IN A LIFETIME
Producer: Brian Eno
Album: Remain in Light
Record Label: Sire
Songwriters: David Byrne, Brian Eno

Byrne legitimizes the video age with this classic treatise on modern anomie and modern dance.

1983

BURNING DOWN THE HOUSE
Producer: Talking Heads
Album: Speaking in Tongues
Record Label: Sire
Songwriters: David Byrne, Chris Frantz, Tina Weymouth, Jerry Harrison

Honing their nerdbeat into a "Bandstand"-worthy hit, their biggest.

1985

AND SHE WAS
Producer: Talking Heads
Album: Little Creatures
Record Label: Sire
Songwriters: David Byrne, Chris Frantz, Tina Weymouth, Jerry Harrison

Steely Dan for the Video Age

ROAD TO NOWHERE
Producer: Talking Heads
Album: Little Creatures
Record Label: Sire
Songwriters: David Byrne, Chris Frantz, Tina Weymouth, Jerry Harrison

Entering the final phase of their exemplary New Wave career, the Heads turn ebullient and garner their fourth biggest hit single.

STAY UP LATE
Producer: Talking Heads
Album: Little Creatures
Record Label: Sire
Songwriters: David Byrne, Chris Frantz, Tina Weymouth, Jerry Harrison

Nerd rockers at home.

1986

WILD, WILD LIFE
Producer: Talking Heads
Album: True Stories
Record Label: Sire
Songwriters: David Byrne, Chris Frantz, Tina Weymouth, Jerry Harrison

Nerd Rock takes on World Beat.

1988

MOMMY DADDY YOU AND I
Album: Naked
Record Label: Sire
Songwriters: David Byrne, Chris Frantz, Tina Weymouth, Jerry Harrison

Rare introspective group family portrait.

NOTHING BUT FLOWERS
Album: Naked
Record Label: Sire
Songwriters: David Byrne, Chris Frantz, Tina Weymouth, Jerry Harrison

Their particular neurosis expanded into a postapocalyptic vision. Suggested segues: "Big Yellow Taxi" by Joni Mitchell, "After the Deluge" by Jackson Browne.

THE TAMS

1964

WHAT KIND OF FOOL
Album: Tams
Record Label: ABC-Paramount
Songwriter: Ray Whitley

NORMA TANEGA

1966

WALKING MY CAT NAMED DOG
Producer: Bob Crewe
Album: Walking My Cat Named Dog
Record Label: New Voice
Songwriter: Norma Tanega

Classic hippie doggerel.

THE TARRIERS

1957

THE BANANA BOAT SONG
Record Label: Glory
Songwriters: Erik Darling, Alan Arkin, Bob Carey

The Folk sound goes Calypso; several trips later this same boat would bring us the infinitely more scintillating sound of Reggae. Harry Belafonte's version of this song was subtitled "Day-O" (RCA, '57).

A TASTE OF HONEY

1978

BOOGIE OOGIE OOGIE
Producer: Fonce Mizell
Album: A Taste of Honey
Record Label: Capitol
Songwriters: Janice Johnson, Perry Kibble, Larry Mizell

A Pop dance groove that peaked at #1 R&B/R&R. Group won a Grammy for Best New Artist.

HOWARD TATE

1966

AIN'T NOBODY HOME
Producer: Jerry Ragovoy
Record Label: Verve
Songwriter: Jerry Ragavoy

His biggest R&B/R&R crossover. Covered by B. B. King (ABC, '72), and Bonnie Raitt (Warner Brothers, '74).

TAVARES

1975

IT ONLY TAKES A MINUTE
Producers: Dennis Lambert, Brian Potter
Album: In the City
Record Label: Capitol
Songwriters: Dennis Lambert, Brian Potter

Latin-flavored #1 R&B/Top-10 R&R crossover.

1977

WHODUNIT
Producer: Freddie Perren
Album: Love Storm
Record Label: Capitol
Songwriters: Freddie Perren, Keni St. Lewis

#1 R&B/Top-25 R&R crossover.

R. DEAN TAYLOR

1970

INDIANA WANTS ME
Producer: R. Dean Taylor
Album: I Think Therefore I Am
Record Label: Rare Earth
Songwriter: R. Dean Taylor

Country-flavored shootout from Motown.

JAMES TAYLOR

1969

CAROLINA IN MY MIND
Producer: Peter Asher
Album: James Taylor
Record Label: Apple
Songwriter: James Taylor

Previewing the laid-back, mellow, middle-of-the-dirt-road sound of the '70s, New

England's Sweet Baby James records in London on the Beatles label with the brother of Paul's old girlfriend Jane producing. Covered by the Everly Brothers (Warner Brothers, '69) and Melanie (Buddah, '70).

KNOCKIN' AROUND THE ZOO

Producer: Peter Asher
Album: James Taylor
Record Label: Apple
Songwriter: James Taylor

About his stay at a high-class sanitarium.

RAINY DAY MAN

Producer: Peter Asher
Album: James Taylor
Record Label: Columbia
Songwriters: James Taylor, Zack Weisner

One of his first acoustic gems. Covered by Bonnie Raitt (Warner Brothers, '74).

SUNSHINE, SUNSHINE

Producer: Peter Asher
Album: James Taylor
Record Label: Apple
Songwriter: James Taylor

Covered by Tom Rush (Elektra, '68).

1970

FIRE AND RAIN

Producer: Peter Asher
Album: Sweet Baby James
Record Label: Warner Brothers
Songwriter: James Taylor

His first hit single charts the depths of his drug problem and the demise of his first band.

STEAMROLLER BLUES

Producer: Peter Asher
Album: Sweet Baby James
Record Label: Warner Brothers
Songwriter: James Taylor

Trademark laid-back Rocker. Covered by Elvis Presley on the triumphant "Aloha from Hawaii Via Satellite" TV special (RCA, '73).

SWEET BABY JAMES

Producer: Peter Asher
Album: Sweet Baby James
Record Label: Warner Brothers
Songwriter: James Taylor

New England cowboy lullabye.

1971

COUNTRY ROAD

Producer: Peter Asher
Album: Sweet Baby James

Record Label: Warner Brothers
Songwriter: James Taylor

Berkshire Country.

1973

DON'T LET ME BE LONELY TONIGHT

Producer: Peter Asher
Album: One Man Dog
Record Label: Warner Brothers
Songwriter: James Taylor

Mid-tempo angst.

1976

SHOWER THE PEOPLE

Producers: Russ Titelman, Lenny Waronker
Album: In the Pocket
Record Label: Warner Brothers
Songwriters: James Taylor

Beatle flashback.

1977

YOUR SMILING FACE

Producer: Peter Asher
Album: JT
Record Label: Columbia
Songwriter: James Taylor

At the peak of his mellowness.

1981

HER TOWN TOO

Producer: Peter Asher
Album: Dad Loves His Work
Record Label: Columbia
Songwriter: James Taylor

Duet with J. D. Souther, about the demise of his mythic marriage to Carly Simon.

1986

ONLY ONE

Producers: Frank Filipotti, James Taylor
Album: That's Why I'm Here
Record Label: Columbia
Songwriter: James Taylor

One of his best love songs.

1988

NEVER DIE YOUNG

Producer: Don Grolnick
Album: Never Die Young
Record Label: Columbia
Songwriter: James Taylor

His Baby Boom anthem.

1991

COPPERLINE

Producer: Don Grolnick
Album: New Moon Shine
Record Label: Columbia
Songwriters: James Taylor, Reynolds Price

Taking on contemporary times, with the help of novelist Price.

JOHNNIE TAYLOR

1968

WHO'S MAKING LOVE

Producer: Don Davis
Album: Who's Making Love
Record Label: Stax
Songwriters: Don Davis, Homer Banks, Bettye Crutcher, Raymond Jackson

First #1 R&B/#Top-10 R&R crossover for the Arkansas Soul stirrer.

1971

JODY'S GOT YOUR GIRL AND GONE

Producer: Don Davis
Album: One Step Beyond
Record Label: Stax
Songwriters: Don Davis, Kent Becker, James Wilson

#1 R&B/Top-30 R&R crossover.

1973

CHEAPER TO KEEP HER

Producer: Don Davis
Album: Taylored in Silk
Record Label: Stax
Songwriter: Mack Rice

I BELIEVE IN YOU (YOU BELIEVE IN ME)

Producer: Don Davis
Album: Taylored in Silk
Record Label: Stax
Songwriter: Don Davis

#1 R&B/#Top-20 R&R crossover.

WE'RE GETTING CARELESS WITH OUR LOVE

Producer: Don Davis
Album: Taylored in Silk
Record Label: Stax
Songwriters: Don Davis, Frank Johnson

Sam Cooke disciple makes his Pop move.

1976

DISCO LADY
Producer: Don Davis
Album: Eargasm
Record Label: Columbia
Songwriters: Don Davis, Harvey Scales, Albert Vance

Defining the Disco era with a #1 R&B/R&R crossover.

LITTLE JOHNNIE TAYLOR
1963

PART-TIME LOVE
Album: Raw Blues
Record Label: Galaxy
Songwriter: Clay Hammond

#1 R&B/Top-20 R&R crossover; covered by Ann Peebles (Hi, '70).

THE TEARDROP EXPLODES
1980

WHEN I DREAM
Producer: Mike Howlett
Album: Kilimanjaro
Record Label: Mercury
Songwriters: Julian Cope, Gary Dwyer, Michael Finkler

Previewing psychedelic Liverpool of the '80s.

TEARS FOR FEARS
1985

EVERYBODY WANTS TO RULE THE WORLD
Producers: Chris Hughes, Roland Orzabel, Ian Stanley
Album: Songs from the Big Chair
Record Label: Mercury
Songwriters: Roland Orzabal, Ian Stanley, Chris Hughes

Philosophical synth jam defines the British Invasion of the '80s.

HEAD OVER HEELS
Producer: Chris Hughes
Album: Songs from the Big Chair
Record Label: Mercury
Songwriters: Roland Orzabal, Ian Stanley, Chris Hughes

SHOUT
Producer: Chris Hughes
Album: Songs from the Big Chair
Record Label: Mercury

Songwriters: Roland Orzabal, Ian Stanley

Released in England before "Everybody," this became the second straight U.S. #1 for the duo; Wham! for closeted intellectuals.

1989

SOWING THE SEEDS OF LOVE
Producer: Tears for Fears
Album: The Seeds of Love
Record Label: Fontana
Songwriters: Roland Orzabel, Curt Smith

1993

BREAK IT DOWN AGAIN
Producers: Tony Palmer, Alan Griffiths, Roland Orzabel
Album: Elemental
Record Label: Mercury
Songwriters: Roland Orzabal, Alan Griffiths

Comeback smash finds Orzabel in Duran Duran territory.

TECHNOTRONIC
1989

GET UP! (BEFORE THE NIGHT IS OVER)
Producer: Jo Bogaert
Album: Pump up the Jam—the Album
Record Label: SBK
Songwriters: Manuella Kamosi, Thomas De Quincey (Jo Bogaert)

Belgian group, big on the international Techno Disco scene.

PUMP UP THE JAM
Producer: Jo Bogaert
Album: Pump up the Jam—the Album
Record Label: Arista
Songwriters: Manuella Kamosi, Thomas De Quincey (Jo Bogaert)

Their first undeniable dancehall smash, featuring the model Felly.

1992

MOVE THIS
Producer: Jo Bogaert
Album: Pump up the Jam—the Album
Record Label: SBK/ERG
Songwriters: Manuella Kamosi, Thomas De Quincy (Jo Bogaert)

Was previously a shampoo commercial.

THE TEDDY BEARS
1958

TO KNOW HIM IS TO LOVE HIM
Producer: Phil Spector
Album: The Teddy Bears Sing
Record Label: Dore
Songwriter: Phil Spector

The neo-girl-group, pre-Fleetwoods, Soft Rock sound of the Teddy Bears shows little of Phil Spector's dramatic production flair, except for its incipient megalomania. The #1 record, originally the B-side of "Don't You Worry My Little Pet," would be all the resume he would need to launch a monster career. Group member Annette Kleinbard became a successful songwriter as well, under the name of Carol Connors.

TEEGARDEN AND VAN WINKLE
1970

GOD, LOVE AND ROCK 'N' ROLL
Record Label: Westbound
Songwriters: Skip Knape, David Teegarden

Summing up the year's major concerns, with a Folk Rock beat, so you couldn't dance to it.

THE TEEN QUEENS
1956

EDDIE, MY LOVE
Album: Eddie My Love
Record Label: RPM
Songwriters: Aaron Collins, Maxwell Davis, Sam Ling

From L.A., girl-group Doo-Wop at its most despairing and compelling, a Top-10 R&B/Top-20 R&R crossover.

TEENA MARIE
1985

LOVERGIRL
Producer: Teena Marie
Album: Starchild
Record Label: Epic
Songwriter: Teena Marie Brockert

Biggest R&R hit for the Rick James discovery, from her sixth album.

1988

OOO LA LA LA
Producer: Teena Marie
Album: Naked to the World
Record Label: Epic

Songwriters: Teena Marie Brockert, Allen McGrier

The only #1 R&B hit for the white Funk anomaly.

TEENAGE FANCLUB
1991

STAR SIGN
Producers: Don Fleming, Paul Chisolm
Album: Bandwagonesque
Record Label: DGC
Songwriter: Gerard Love

Critical favorite from Scotland.

TEENAGE JESUS AND THE JERKS
1979

ORPHANS
Producer: Robert Quine
Album: Teenage Jesus & the Jerks
Record Label: Lust/Unlust
Songwriter: Lydia Lunch

Music only a diehard Punk could love.

TELEVISION
1974

LITTLE JOHNNY JEWEL
Album: Great New York Singles
Record Label: ROIR
Songwriters: Tom Miller (Tom Verlaine), Richard Lloyd

Tune often cited as influential in starting the Bowery Punk scene in New York, along with Patti Smith's "Piss Factory." Covered by Siouxsie & the Banshees (Geffen, '87).

1977

MARQUEE MOON
Producers: Tom Verlaine, Andy Johns
Album: Marquee Moon
Record Label: Elektra
Songwriter: Tom Miller (Tom Verlaine)

The droning apocalyptic New York guitar version of Butterfield/Bloomfield's "East West."

1992

CALL MR. LEE
Album: Television
Record Label: Capitol
Songwriters: Tom Miller (Tom Verlaine), Television

Long-awaited comeback track.

NINO TEMPO AND APRIL STEVENS
1963

DEEP PURPLE
Album: Deep Purple
Record Label: Atco
Songwriters: Mitchell Parrish, Peter De Rose

Doo-Wopping the classics, volume LCIV. Originated by Larry Clinton (RCA, '44).

THE TEMPOS
1959

SEE YOU IN SEPTEMBER
Album: Speaking of the Tempos
Record Label: Climax
Songwriters: Sid Wayne, Sherman Edwards

Classic summertime theme. Covered by the Happenings (B. T. Puppy, '66).

THE TEMPTATIONS
1964

THE WAY YOU DO THE THINGS YOU DO
Producer: Smokey Robinson
Album: Temptations Sing Smokey
Record Label: Gordy
Songwriters: Smokey Robinson, Bobby Rogers

Smokey creates a big brother in his own image. But just a little bit tougher.

1965

IT'S GROWING
Producer: Smokey Robinson
Album: Temptations Sing Smokey
Record Label: Gordy
Songwriters: Smokey Robinson, Warren Moore

Top-10 R&B/Top-20 R&R crossover.

MY GIRL
Producer: Smokey Robinson
Album: The Temptations Sing Smokey
Record Label: Gordy
Songwriters: Smokey Robinson, Ronald White

Their first #1 R&B/R&R crossover; a Smokey Soul classic.

SINCE I LOST MY BABY
Producer: Smokey Robinson
Album: Temptations Sing Smokey
Record Label: Gordy

Songwriters: Smokey Robinson, Warren Moore

Top-10 R&B/Top-20 R&R crossover.

1966

(I KNOW) I'M LOSING YOU
Producer: Norman Whitfield
Album: With a Lot o Soul
Record Label: Gordy
Songwriters: Eddie Holland, Norman Whitfield, Cornelius Grant

Minus Smokey, the Temptations begin to sound more like the Four Tops on this, the last of four straight #1 R&B/Top-10 R&R hits of '66. Covered by Rare Earth (Motown, '70).

AIN'T TOO PROUD TO BEG
Producer: Norman Whitfield
Album: Gettin' Ready
Record Label: Gordy
Songwriters: Eddie Holland, Norman Whitfield

#1 R&B/Top-20 R&R crossover. Seven rooms of Soul-baring intensity.

BEAUTY IS ONLY SKIN DEEP
Producer: Norman Whitfield
Album: Temptations' Greatest Hits
Record Label: Gordy
Songwriters: Eddie Holland, Norman Whitfield

Their biggest hit of '66, a #1 R&B/Top-10 R&R crossover.

GET READY
Producer: Smokey Robinson
Album: Temptations Sing Smokey
Record Label: Gordy
Songwriter: Smokey Robinson

#1 R&B/Top-30 crossover, covered by Rare Earth (Motown, '70).

1967

ALL I NEED
Producer: Norman Whitfield
Album: With a Lot o Soul
Record Label: Gordy
Songwriters: Eddie Holland, Frank Wilson, R. Dean Taylor

Top-10 R&B/R&R crossover.

YOU'RE MY EVERYTHING
Producer: Norman Whitfield
Album: With a Lot o Soul
Record Label: Gordy
Songwriters: Norman Whitfield, Roger Penzabene, Cornelius Grant

Top-5 R&B/Top-10 R&R crossover.

1968

CLOUD NINE

Producer: Norman Whitfield
Album: Cloud Nine
Record Label: Gordy
Songwriters: Norman Whitfield, Barrett Strong

Preaching an anti-drug message.

I COULD NEVER LOVE ANOTHER (AFTER LOVING YOU)

Producer: Norman Whitfield
Album: Wish It Would Rain
Record Label: Gordy
Songwriters: Norman Whitfield, Barrett Strong, Roger Penzabene

#1 R&B/Top-20 R&R crossover.

I WISH IT WOULD RAIN

Producer: Norman Whitfield
Album: I Wish It Would Rain
Record Label: Gordy
Songwriters: Norman Whitfield, Barrett Strong, Roger Penzabene

Hitting their soulful crooning stride; #1 R&B/Top-10 R&R crossover.

1969

DON'T LET THE JONESES GET YOU DOWN

Producer: Norman Whitfield
Album: Puzzle People
Record Label: Gordy
Songwriters: Norman Whitfield, Barrett Strong

I CAN'T GET NEXT TO YOU

Producer: Norman Whitfield
Album: Puzzle People
Record Label: Gordy
Songwriters: Norman Whitfield, Barrett Strong

Their ninth #1 R&B and second #1 R&B/R&R crossover was their biggest hit.

PSYCHEDELIC SHACK

Producer: Norman Whitfield
Album: Psychedelic Shack
Record Label: Gordy
Songwriters: Norman Whitfield, Barrett Strong

Motown visits San Francisco; San Francisco wins.

RUNAWAY CHILD, RUNNING WILD

Producer: Norman Whitfield
Album: Cloud Nine
Record Label: Gordy

Songwriters: Norman Whitfield, Barrett Strong

Their fifth #1 R&B/Top-10 R&R crossover. Suggested segues: "She's Leaving Home" by the Beatles, "Love Child" by the Supremes, "Runaway" by Bon Jovi.

1970

BALL OF CONFUSION (THAT'S WHAT THE WORLD IS TODAY)

Producer: Norman Whitfield
Album: Greatest Hits (Vol. II)
Record Label: Motown
Songwriters: Norman Whitfield, Barrett Strong

Entering their Marvin Gaye phase. Suggested segue: "What's Goin' On" by Marvin Gaye, "War" by Edwin Starr.

1971

JUST MY IMAGINATION (RUNNING AWAY WITH ME)

Producer: Norman Whitfield
Album: Sky's the Limit
Record Label: Gordy
Songwriters: Norman Whitfield, Barrett Strong

Their biggest hit of the '70s, #1 R&B/R&R crossover.

SUPERSTAR, REMEMBER HOW YOU GOT WHERE YOU ARE

Producer: Norman Whitfield
Album: Solid Rock
Record Label: Gordy
Songwriters: Norman Whitfield, Barrett Strong

1972

PAPA WAS A ROLLIN' STONE

Producer: Norman Whitfield
Album: All Directions
Record Label: Gordy
Songwriters: Norman Whitfield, Barrett Strong

Their fourth and last #1 R&R. Suggested segue: "Daddy Could Swear, I Declare" by Gladys Knight and the Pips.

1973

LET YOUR HAIR DOWN

Producer: Norman Whitfield
Album: 1990
Record Label: Gordy
Songwriter: Norman Whitfield

#1 R&B/Top-30 R&R crossover.

MASTERPIECE

Producer: Norman Whitfield
Album: Masterpiece

Songwriters: Norman Whitfield, Barrett Strong

Their fifth #1 R&B/Top-10 R&R crossover. #1 R&B/Top-10 R&R crossover.

1974

HAPPY PEOPLE

Producer: Norman Whitfield
Album: A Song for You
Record Label: Gordy
Songwriters: Lionel B. Richie, Jeffrey Bowen, Donald Baldwin

Their thirteenth and last #1 R&B.

10 C.C.

1973

RUBBER BULLETS

Producer: Strawberry Productions
Album: Rubber Bullets
Record Label: U.K.
Songwriters: Lawrence Creme, Kevin Godley, Graham Gouldman

First big hit, #1 U.K., establishes their brand of satiric Art Rock.

1975

I'M NOT IN LOVE

Producer: 10 c.c.
Album: *The Original* Soundtrack
Record Label: Mercury
Songwriters: Graham Gouldman, Eric Stewart

Their biggest hit; bigger in England.

1977

THE THINGS WE DO FOR LOVE

Producer: 10 c.c.
Album: Deceptive Bends
Record Label: Mercury
Songwriters: Graham Gouldman, Eric Stewart

Suggested segue: "What I Did for Love" from "A Chorus Line."

10,000 MANIACS

1985

MY MOTHER THE WAR

Producer: Joe Boyd
Album: The Wishing Chair
Record Label: Elektra
Songwriters: Natalie Merchant, John Lombardi, Michael Walsh

Introducing upstate New York's leading candidate in the '80s waif-like thrush sweepstakes, Natalie Merchant, her jazzbo band, and their original signature protest anthem.

1987

HEY JACK KEROUAC
Producer: Peter Asher
Album: In My Tribe
Record Label: Elektra
Songwriter: Natalie Merchant

Jazz-flavored Folk Rock with a Beat-generation protagonist. Suggested segues: "Raining down on Bleecker Street" by Devonsquare, "Cassidy" by Bob Weir, "The Persecution and Resurrection of Dean Moriarty (On the Road)" by Aztec Two Step, and "Zen Coan Rides Again" by Dave Van Ronk.

LIKE THE WEATHER
Producer: Peter Asher
Album: In My Tribe
Record Label: Elektra
Songwriter: Natalie Merchant

Breakthrough showcase for Natalie's eloquently tangled locutions is a modern essay on the old ennui.

VERDI CRIES
Producer: Peter Asher
Album: In My Tribe
Record Label: Elektra
Songwriter: Natalie Merchant

A summer song for the privileged class. Suggested segue: "Menemsha" by Carly Simon.

WHAT'S THE MATTER HERE
Producer: Peter Asher
Album: In My Tribe
Record Label: Elektra
Songwriter: Natalie Merchant

Commentary on child-abuse. Suggested segues: "Luka" by Suzanne Vega and "Dear Mr. Jesus" by Powersource.

1989

TROUBLE ME
Producer: Peter Asher
Album: Blind Man's Zoo
Record Label: Elektra
Songwriters: Natalie Merchant, Dennis Drew

1992

THESE ARE DAYS
Producer: Paul Fox
Album: Our Time in Eden
Record Label: Elektra
Songwriters: Natalie Merchant, Peter Buck

One of their more successful post-breakthrough songs.

1993

CANDY EVERYBODY WANTS
Producer: Paul Fox
Album: Our Time in Eden
Record Label: Elektra
Songwriters: Natalie Merchant, Dennis Drew

Sung at the Clinton '92 inaugural along with a Natalie Merchant/Michael Stipe cover of "To Sir, with Love."

TEN YEARS AFTER
1968

I'M GOIN' HOME
Producer: Mike Vernon
Album: Undead
Record Label: Deram
Songwriter: Alvin Lee

Introducing the next great white Blues guitar hope from England, Alvin Lee, with his Woodstock showpiece.

1971

I'D LOVE TO CHANGE THE WORLD
Producer: Ten Years After
Album: A Space in Time
Record Label: Columbia
Songwriter: Alvin Lee

Achieving the Top-40, two years after . . . Woodstock.

TESLA
1989

LOVE SONG
Producers: S. Thompson, M. Barbiero
Album: The Great Radio Controversy
Record Label: Geffen
Songwriters: Frank Hannon, Jeff Keith

Guitar band turns to the Arena ballad for their biggest hit.

JOE TEX
1964

HOLD WHAT YOU'VE GOT
Producer: Buddy Killen
Album: Hold What You Got
Record Label: Dial
Songwriter: Joe Tex

After ten years of trying, the first hit for "Soul Brother No. 2."

1965

I WANT TO DO EVERYTHING FOR YOU
Producer: Buddy Killen
Album: The New Boss
Record Label: Atlantic
Songwriter: Joe Tex

#1 R&B/Top-30 R&R crossover.

1966

PAPA WAS TOO
Producer: Buddy Killen
Album: The Best of Joe Tex
Record Label: Dial
Songwriter: Joe Tex

Suggested segue: "Papa's Got a Brand New Bag" by James Brown, "Papa Was a Rolling Stone" by the Temptations, and "Daddy Could Swear, I Declare" by Gladys Knight and the Pips.

A SWEET WOMAN LIKE YOU
Producer: Buddy Killen
Album: The Love You Save
Record Label: Atlantic
Songwriter: Joe Tex

#1 R&B/Top-30 R&R crossover.

1967

SKINNY LEGS AND ALL
Producer: Buddy Killen
Album: Live and Lively
Record Label: Dial
Songwriter: Joe Tex

Inverse fashion statement was his second biggest hit.

1968

MEN ARE GETTIN' SCARCE
Producer: Buddy Killen
Record Label: Dial
Songwriter: Joe Tex

Oblique Vietnam war-era implications.

1972

I GOTCHA
Producer: Buddy Killen
Album: I Gotcha
Record Label: Dial
Songwriter: Joe Tex

His biggest all-time hit; #1 R&B/Top-10 R&R.

1977

AIN'T GONNA BUMP NO MORE (WITH NO BIG FAT WOMAN)
Producer: Buddy Killen
Album: Bumps and Bruises

Record Label: Epic
Songwriters: Benny Lee McGinty, William Killen

Making a comeback with a variation on his favorite theme.

SISTER ROSETTA THARPE
1948

UP ABOVE MY HEAD, I HEAR MUSIC IN THE AIR
Record Label: Decca
Songwriter: Rosetta Tharpe

Powerful Top-10 R&B hit, influential in the journey of Black music from Gospel to Rock and Roll.

THE THE
1989

THE BEAT(EN) GENERATION
Album: Mind Bomb
Record Label: Epic
Songwriter: Matt Johnson

Suggested segues: "The Blank Generation" by Richard Hell & the Voidoids, "My Generation" by the Who, "My Generation" by Todd Snider, and "I Hate My Generation" by Cracker.

THEM
1965

MYSTIC EYES
Producer: Bert Berns
Album: Them
Record Label: Parrot
Songwriter: Van Morrison

Moving toward their defining sound of Irish Soul.

1966

GLORIA
Producer: Tommy Scott
Album: Here Comes the Night
Record Label: Parrot
Songwriter: Van Morrison

The classic Doo-Wop girlfriend in '60s dress and an Irish brogue. Covered by the Shadows of Knight (Dunwich, '65) and the Doors, at a '69 soundcheck (Elektra, '73). The Patti Smith cover is a whole other story.

THEY MIGHT BE GIANTS
1986

DON'T LET'S START
Album: They Might Be Giants
Record Label: Bar/None

Songwriters: John Flansburgh, John Linnell

As heard over 1–800–SONG (their Brooklyn dial-a-song number); the auspicious beginnings of a prolific career.

1988

ANA NG
Producer: Bill Kraus
Album: Lincoln
Record Label: Restless
Songwriters: John Flansburgh, John Linnell

From a repertoire that defines the Berklee/Berkeley/Beserkley school of collegiate eclectic cross-genre irony, an inspirational modern Rock classic, sped-up, zany, and as inscrutable as the title character.

KISS ME, SON OF GOD
Producer: Bill Kraus
Album: Lincoln
Record Label: Restless
Songwriters: John Flansburgh, John Linnell

A third-world morality tale.

PURPLE TOUPEE
Producer: Bill Kraus
Album: Lincoln
Record Label: Restless
Songwriters: John Flansburgh, John Linnell

Their tribute to Prince and the '60s.

1990

PARTICLE MAN
Producers: Clive Langer, Alan Winstanley, They Might Be Giants
Album: Flood
Record Label: Elektra
Songwriters: John Flansburgh, John Linnell

Their answer to "1999" by Prince.

YOUR RACIST FRIEND
Producers: Clive Langer, Alan Winstanley, They Might Be Giants
Album: Flood
Record Label: Elektra
Songwriters: John Flansburgh, John Linnell

Their best protest song other than their cover of "One More Parade" by Phil Ochs (Elektra, '90).

THIN LIZZY
1976

THE BOYS ARE BACK IN TOWN
Producer: John Alcock
Album: Jailbreak
Record Label: Mercury
Songwriter: Phil Lynott

Springsteen transported to the streets of Ireland.

JAILBREAK
Producer: John Alcock
Album: Jailbreak
Record Label: Mercury
Songwriter: Phil Lynott

Their best guitar moments.

THIRTEENTH FLOOR ELEVATORS
1966

FIRE ENGINE
Producer: Gorbyn Productions
Record Label: International Artists
Songwriter: Roky Erickson

Covered by Television (ROIR, '82).

YOU'RE GONNA MISS ME
Producer: Gorbyn Productions
Album: Best Of the Thirteenth Floor Elevators
Record Label: International Artists
Songwriter: Roky Erickson

Classic Texas Garage Band nugget, written by a certified '60s casualty. Covered by Sir Douglas (Tacoma, '81).

38 SPECIAL
1981

HOLD ON LOOSELY
Producer: Rodney Mills
Album: Wild-Eyed Southern Boys
Record Label: A&M
Songwriters: Jeff Carlisi, Don Barnes, Jim Peterik

Emotionally charged anthem from their early Arena days.

1982

CAUGHT UP IN YOU
Producer: Rodney Mills
Album: Special Forces
Record Label: A&M
Songwriters: Jeff Carlisi, Don Barnes, Jim Peterik, Frankie Sullivan

Mellowing their southern Rock sound. Sullivan and Peterik would move on to Survivor.

B. J. THOMAS

1983

IF I'D BEEN THE ONE
Album: Tour De Force
Record Label: A&M
Songwriters: Jeff Carlisi, Don Barnes, Donnie Van Zant, Larry Steele

Modified Lynyrd Skynyrd.

1989

SECOND CHANCE
Producer: Rodney Mills
Album: Rock and Roll Strategy
Record Label: A&M
Songwriters: Jeff Carlisi, Max Carl, Cal Curtis

Achieving their biggest hit with a Pop Rock formula.

B. J. THOMAS

1968

HOOKED ON A FEELING
Producer: Chips Moman
Album: On My Way
Record Label: Scepter
Songwriter: Mark James

Country Rock from the man who wrote Elvis's "Suspicious Minds."

1970

I JUST CAN'T HELP BELIEVING
Album: Everybody's out of Town
Record Label: Scepter
Songwriters: Barry Mann, Cynthia Weil

Broadway Country Rock Top-10, which missed the country charts.

RAINDROPS KEEP FALLIN' ON MY HEAD
Producers: Burt Bacharach, Hal David
Album: Raindrops Keep Fallin' on My Head
Record Label: Scepter
Songwriters: Burt Bacharach, Hal David

Lilting theme to Butch Cassidy and the Sundance Kid *brings B. J. instant, if brief, hip credibility and a #1 song. Bacharach and David get an Oscar.*

1972

ROCK AND ROLL LULLABYE
Producers: Steve Tyrell, Al Gorgoni
Album: Billy Joe Thomas
Record Label: Scepter

1983

Songwriters: Barry Mann, Cynthia Weil

Duane Eddy on guitar, the Chiffons on backing vocals. Suggested segues: "Three Stars" by Tommy Dee, "Rock and Roll Heaven" by the Righteous Brothers, and "Nightshift" by the Commodores.

1975

(HEY WON'T YOU PLAY) ANOTHER SOMEBODY DONE SOMEBODY WRONG SONG
Producer: Chips Moman
Album: Reunion
Record Label: ABC
Songwriters: Larry Butler, Chips Moman

A rare #1 C&W/R&R crossover.

CARLA THOMAS

1961

GEE WHIZ! (LOOK AT HIS EYES)
Producer: Jim Stewart
Album: Gee Whiz!
Record Label: Atlantic
Songwriter: Carla Thomas

Early example of Memphis Soul is Carla's biggest hit; Top-10 R&B/R&R crossover.

1966

B-A-B-Y
Producers: Isaac Hayes, David Porter
Album: Carla
Record Label: Stax
Songwriters: Isaac Hayes, David Porter

Her biggest R&B hit, a Top-3 R&B/Top-20 R&R crossover.

IRMA THOMAS

1962

IT'S RAINING
Producer: Allen Toussaint
Record Label: Minit
Songwriter: Allen Toussaint (Naomi Neville)

A definitive New Orleans gem, as selected by the Alternative mavens at Spin *Magazine.*

1964

TIME IS ON MY SIDE
Album: Wish Someone Would Care
Record Label: Imperial
Songwriter: Jerry Ragovoy

B-side of "Wish Someone Would Care." Covered by the Rolling Stones (London, '64).

WISH SOMEONE WOULD CARE
Album: Wish Someone Would Care
Record Label: Imperial
Songwriter: Irma Thomas

RUFUS THOMAS

1953

BEAR CAT
Producer: Sam Phillips
Record Label: Sun
Songwriter: Sam Phillips

So blatant a copy of Leiber and Stoller's "Hound Dog" that the author was sued to take it off the market. A year later he would have his revenge.

1963

WALKING THE DOG
Album: Walking the Dog
Record Label: Stax
Songwriter: Rufus Thomas

After l'affaire de "Hound Dog," you would think Rufus would have gotten over his dog fixation. But in '63 it returned. While "the Dog" was just a middling R&B/R&R crossover, the followup became his defining number, a Top-10 R&B/R&R smash. Unsated, he was back in '64 with "Can Your Monkey Do the Dog" (the monkey is the only animal that competes with the dog in the Rock and Roll menagerie), followed a month later by "Somebody Stole My Dog" (his writers were having fun: they'd better, they weren't selling many copies).

1970

DO THE PUSH AND PULL (PART I)
Producers: Al Bell, Thom Nixon
Album: Rufus Thomas Live/Doing the Push and Pull at P. J.'s
Record Label: Stax
Songwriter: Rufus Thomas

A dance for the new post-bliss era is his only #1 R&B hit, a Top-30 R&R crossover. Jules Feiffer might have used it, had "Little Murders" been a musical.

TIMMY THOMAS

1973

WHY CAN'T WE LIVE TOGETHER
Producer: Steve Alaimo
Album: Why Can't We Live Together
Record Label: Glades
Songwriter: Tim Thomas

#1 R&B/Top-10 R&R crossover plea for racial understanding.

THOMPSON TWINS

1983

LOVE ON YOUR SIDE
Producer: Alex Sadkin
Album: Side Kicks
Record Label: Arista
Songwriters: Tom Bailey, Alannah
Currie, Joe Leeway

First U.K. hit for the Synth Rock group from England.

1984

HOLD ME NOW
Producers: Alex Sadkin, Tom Bailey
Album: Into the Gap
Record Label: Arista
Songwriters: Tom Bailey, Alannah
Currie, Joe Leeway

Their biggest hit. But they were no Duran Duran, no Psychedelic Furs. Then again, they weren't twins and they weren't Thompsons either.

1985

LAY YOUR HANDS ON ME
Producers: Alex Sadkin, Nile
Rodgers, Tom Bailey
Album: Here's to Future Days
Record Label: Arista
Songwriters: Tom Bailey, Alannah
Currie, Joe Leeway

1986

KING FOR A DAY
Producers: Nile Rodgers, Tom
Bailey
Album: Here's to Future Days
Record Label: Arista
Songwriters: Tom Bailey, Alannah
Currie, Joe Leeway

Making their crossover dance move.

RICHARD AND LINDA THOMPSON

1974

A HEART NEEDS A HOME
Producers: Simon Nicol, John Wood
Album: Hokey Pokey
Record Label: Island
Songwriter: Richard Thompson

British Folk Rock at its best.

I WANT TO SEE THE BRIGHT LIGHTS TONIGHT
Producers: Richard Thompson,
John Wood
Album: I Want to See the Bright
Lights Tonight
Record Label: Island
Songwriter: Richard Thompson

Introducing the first couple of Post-Elizabethan English Folk music, star-crossed of course.

WHEN I GET TO THE BORDER
Producers: Richard Thompson,
John Wood
Album: I Want to See the Bright
Lights Tonight
Record Label: Island
Songwriter: Richard Thompson

Previewing their death motif.

1975

BEAT THE RETREAT
Producers: Richard Thompson,
John Wood
Album: Pour Down Like Silver
Record Label: Island
Songwriter: Richard Thompson

Obsessed by their death motif.

THE DIMMING OF THE DAY
Producers: Richard Thompson,
John Wood
Album: Pour Down Like Silver
Record Label: Island
Songwriter: Richard Thompson

Covered by Bonnie Raitt (Capitol, '94). Suggested segue: "Sundown" by Gordon Lightfoot.

1982

DID SHE JUMP
Producer: Joe Boyd
Album: Shoot out the Lights
Record Label: Hannibal
Songwriters: Richard and Linda
Thompson

The ex-wife's swan song.

A MAN IN NEED
Producer: Joe Boyd
Album: Shoot out the Lights
Record Label: Hannibal
Songwriter: Richard Thompson

The ex-husband's rationale.

SHOOT OUT THE LIGHTS
Producer: Joe Boyd
Album: Shoot out the Lights
Record Label: Hannibal
Songwriter: Richard Thompson

The final curtain, and incidentally, one of the great guitar parts of the decade.

WALL OF DEATH
Producer: Joe Boyd
Album: Shoot out the Lights
Record Label: Hannibal
Songwriter: Richard Thompson

Hail and farewell to the death motif. Covered by R.E.M. (Capitol, '94).

LINDA THOMPSON

1985

TELLING ME LIES
Producer: Hugh Murphey
Album: One Clear Moment
Record Label: Warner Brothers
Songwriters: Linda Thompson,
Betsy Cook

The more dispassionate half of Richard and Linda Thompson, showcases her smouldering anger, in a pleasant Fleetwood Macian setting. Covered by Dolly Parton, Linda Ronstadt, and Emmylou Harris (as the Trio) (Warner Brothers, '86).

RICHARD THOMPSON

1983

HAND OF KINDNESS
Producer: Joe Boyd
Album: Hand of Kindness
Record Label: Hannibal
Songwriter: Richard Thompson

The more distraught half of Richard and Linda Thompson Rocks out alone.

TEAR STAINED LETTER
Producer: Joe Boyd
Album: Hand of Kindness
Record Label: Hannibal
Songwriter: Richard Thompson

A bitter, beer-hall jig. Covered by Patty Loveless (Epic, '96).

1985

SHE TWISTS THE KNIFE AGAIN
Producer: Joe Boyd
Album: Across a Crowded Room
Record Label: Polygram
Songwriter: Richard Thompson

Showing no mercy, especially on guitar.

WHEN THE SPELL IS BROKEN
Producer: Joe Boyd
Album: Across a Crowded Room
Record Label: Polygram
Songwriter: Richard Thompson

A moody and laconic lament.

1986

NEARLY IN LOVE
Producer: Mitchell Froom
Album: Daring Adventures
Record Label: Polygram
Songwriter: Richard Thompson
He twists the knife again.

VALERIE
Producer: Mitchell Froom
Album: Daring Adventures
Record Label: Polydor
Songwriter: Richard Thompson
Covered by Marshall Crenshaw (Warner Brothers, '89).

1991

1952 VINCENT BLACK LIGHTNING
Producer: Mitchell Froom
Album: Rumor and Sigh
Record Label: Capitol
Songwriter: Richard Thompson
A timeless and compelling modern folk tale, oddly enough, ending in death.

I FEEL SO GOOD
Producer: Mitchell Froom
Album: Rumor and Sigh
Record Label: Capitol
Songwriter: Richard Thompson
Finally whole and ready to rumble, especially on guitar.

I MISUNDERSTOOD
Producer: Mitchell Froom
Album: Rumor and Sigh
Record Label: Capitol
Songwriter: Richard Thompson
His finest ballad, up to that point.

1993

BEESWING
Producer: Mitchell Froom
Album: Mirror Blue
Record Label: Capitol
Songwriter: Richard Thompson
An even finer post-Folk ballad.

SUE THOMPSON

1961

SAD MOVIES ALWAYS MAKE ME CRY
Album: Sue Thompson
Record Label: Hickory
Songwriter: John D. Loudermilk
Even with its songwriting pedigree, and even in a big year for C&W crossovers, this

one went Top-10 R&R, but didn't dent the Country charts.

1962

NORMAN
Album: Sue Thompson
Record Label: Hickory
Songwriter: John D. Loudermilk
Her biggest hit.

BIG MAMA THORNTON

1953

HOUND DOG
Producers: Jerry Leiber, Mike Stoller
Record Label: Peacock
Songwriters: Jerry Leiber, Mike Stoller
Fruition of Leiber and Stoller's lifelong R&B infatuation and a #1 R&B track for Big Mama. Covered in a semi-lewd, semi-novelty version by Elvis Presley (RCA, '56), introduced in a career-enhancing swivel-hipped performance on "The Milton Berle Show" in June. By August it was his second #1 (and his first #1 C&W/R&B/R&R crossover). The Rock and Roll Gold Rush was officially on.

GEORGE THOROGOOD

1982

BAD TO THE BONE
Album: Bad to the Bone
Record Label: EMI-America
Songwriter: George Thorogood
After exhibiting exemplary, if routine, taste in R&R oldies, the Delaware retro-rocker establishes a persona: half-cartoon, half-romance.

1985

I DRINK ALONE
Album: Maverick
Record Label: EMI-America
Songwriter: George Thorogood
The image having fallen through, Thorogood shows an affinity for the true stuff of Rock and Roll legend. Suggested segues: "One Scotch, One Bourbon, One Beer" by Amos Milburn and "Red Red Wine" by UB40.

THE THREE DEGREES

1974

WHEN WILL I SEE YOU AGAIN
Producers: Kenny Gamble, Leon Huff
Album: The Three Degrees
Record Label: Philadelphia International

Songwriters: Kenny Gamble, Leon Huff
#1 U.K./Top-10 U.S. for the Richard Barrett discoveries.

THREE DOG NIGHT

1969

EASY TO BE HARD
Producer: Richard Polodor
Album: Suitable for Framing
Record Label: Dunhill
Songwriters: James Rado, Gerome Ragni, Galt MacDermot
Pop Rock ballad, performed in the musical "Hair!" by Lynn Kellog (RCA, '69).

1970

CELEBRATE
Producer: Gabriel Mekler
Album: Suitable for Framing
Record Label: Dunhill
Songwriters: Garry Bonner, Alan Gordon
One of the all-time frat-party anthems.

1971

JOY TO THE WORLD
Producer: Richard Polodor
Album: Naturally
Record Label: Dunhill
Songwriter: Hoyt Axton
Their biggest hit; a modern day children's song.

NEVER BEEN TO SPAIN
Producer: Richard Polodor
Album: Harmony
Record Label: Dunhill
Songwriter: Hoyt Axton
Another upbeat departure from the Zeitgeist of the era.

AN OLD FASHIONED LOVE SONG
Producer: Gabriel Mekler
Album: Harmony
Record Label: Dunhill
Songwriter: Paul Williams
In the era of the self-contained group, Three Dog Night compared to Judy Collins and Tom Rush for their taste in songwriters. This was their seventh Top-10 R&R hit with an outside song, including Randy Newman's "Mama Told Me Not to Come," Harry Nilsson's "One," Russ Ballard's "Liar," Laura Nyro's "Eli's Coming," as well as "Easy to Be Hard" and "Joy to the World." In this case, the songwriter was the diminutive popster Paul Williams, who wrote "You

and Me Against the World" for Helen Reddy, among others.

1972

BLACK AND WHITE
Producer: Richard Polodor
Album: Seven Separate Fools
Record Label: Dunhill
Songwriters: David Arkin, Earl Robinson

Their third and last #1 R&R was composed in '55 in response to the Supreme Court's decision banning segregation. Introduced in the U.S. by Sammy Davis Jr. and in the U.K. by the U.K. Spinners and covered in the U.K. by Greyhound (Trojan, '71). Robinson also wrote several other American classics, including "Joe Hill," "Ballad for Americans," and "The House I Live In."

1974

SURE AS I'M SITTIN' HERE
Producer: Richard Podolor
Album: Hard Labor
Record Label: Dunhill
Songwriter: John Hiatt

They go out as they came in, introducing another fine songwriter to the industry, with a Top-20 hit. Hiatt would write "Thing Called Love" among many others.

THE THREE FRIENDS
1956

BLANCHE
Record Label: Lido
Songwriters: Frank Stropoli, Anthony Grochowski, Joseph Francavilla (Joe Villa), Nick Cutrone

Celebrating a neighborhood girl, distant cousin of "Sherry."

THE THREE O'CLOCK
1985

MRS. GREEN
Album: Arrive Without Traveling
Record Label: IRS
Songwriter: Michael Quercio

Mrs. Brown's lovely daughter moved to San Francisco to room with the Bangles.

THROWING MUSES
1986

GREEN
Album: Throwing Muses
Record Label: 4AD
Songwriter: Kristen Hersh

The Paisley Underground, Northeast quadrant. Suggested segue: "Mrs. Green."

1992

NOT TOO SOON
Producer: Dennis Herring
Album: The Real Ramona
Record Label: Sire
Songwriter: Tanya Donnelly

Young Tanya, before moving up to Belly. Herring earned his underground credentials with Camper Van Beethoven.

JOHNNY THUNDER
1963

LOOP DE LOOP
Producer: Teddy Vann
Album: Loop De Loop
Record Label: Diamond
Songwriters: Teddy Vann, Joe Dong

Frat Rock ditty. Covered by Harry Nilsson (RCA, '74), with Ringo Starr, Keith Moon, and Jim Keltner on drums!

THUNDERCLAP NEWMAN
1969

SOMETHING IN THE AIR
Producer: Pete Townshend
Album: Hollywood Dream
Record Label: Track
Songwriter: Speedy Keen

#1 U.K. High on Woodstock dreams Thunderclap Newman celebrates the Revolution as if it were a fait accompli, much as Phil Ochs, a few years earlier, declared the Vietnam War over, but that didn't end until 1972, in the middle of a Neil Young concert, at around the same time as the revolution, come to think of it. Featured in the movie The Strawberry Statement *(MGM, '70). Covered by Tom Petty (MCA, '95).*

TICO & THE TRIUMPHS
1961

MOTORCYCLE
Record Label: Madison
Songwriter: Paul Simon

One of Simon's early Brill Building business transactions.

TIFFANY
1987

COULD'VE BEEN
Producer: G. E. Tobin
Album: Tiffany

Record Label: MCA
Songwriter: Lois Blaisch

#1 followup to her #1 debut ("I Think We're Alone Now") established her as the teen queen of the mall.

'TIL TUESDAY
1985

VOICES CARRY
Producer: Mike Thorne
Album: Voices Carry
Record Label: Epic
Songwriters: Aimee Mann, Michael Hausman, Robert Holmes, Joseph Pesce

Introducing Boston's leading candidate in the late-'80s waif-like thrush sweepstakes, Aimee Mann.

JOHNNY TILLOTSON
1960

POETRY IN MOTION
Album: Johnny Tillotsen's Best
Record Label: Cadence
Songwriters: Paul Kaufman, Mike Anthony

Country Rock in the prime Bobby-Johnny-Frankie non-crossover "Bandstand" mode; his biggest hit.

1961

WITHOUT YOU
Album: Johnny Tillotsen's Best
Record Label: Cadence
Songwriter: Johnny Tillotsen

1962

IT KEEPS RIGHT ON A-HURTIN'
Album: It Keeps Right on a-Hurtin'
Record Label: Cadence
Songwriters: Johnny Tillotsen, Lorene Mann

His biggest Country hit, a Top-5 C&W/Top 5 R&R crossover.

1963

TALK BACK TREMBLING LIPS
Producer: Paul Tannen
Album: Talk Back Trembling Lips
Record Label: Cadence
Songwriter: John D. Loudermilk

#1 C&W hit for Ernest Ashworth (Hickory, '63).

TIMBUK 3
1986

THE FUTURE'S SO BRIGHT, I GOTTA WEAR SHADES
Producer: Dennis Herring
Album: Greetings from Timbuk 3
Record Label: IRS
Songwriter: Pat MacDonald

Folk Rock irony from Texas.

JUST ANOTHER MOVIE
Producer: Dennis Herring
Album: Greetings from Timbuk 3
Record Label: IRS
Songwriter: Pat MacDonald

Cogent protest throw-back.

THE TIME
1982

COOL (PART I)
Album: The Time
Record Label: Warner Brothers
Songwriter: Prince Rogers Nelson

Origins of the Minneapolis Funk mafia, presided over by Prince, many of whom were seen in the movie Purple Rain. *Top songwriter/producers James Harris III (Jimmy Jam) and Terry Lewis were graduates.*

1985

JUNGLE LOVE
Producer: Morris Day
Album: Ice Cream Castle
Record Label: Warner Brothers
Songwriters: Prince Rogers Nelson, Jesse Johnson, Morris Day

1990

JERK OUT
Album: Pandemonium
Record Label: Paisley Park
Songwriters: Prince Rogers Nelson, Terry Lewis, James Harris III, Morris Day

The original lineup returns to capture their first #1 R&B/Top-10 R&R crossover.

THE TIMELORDS
1988

DOCTORIN' THE TARDIS
Record Label: KLF
Songwriters: Mike Chapman, Nicky Chinn, Bill Drummond, Jimi Cauty

#1 U.K./Bottom-40 U.S. dance single by members of the Justified Ancients of Mu Mu, who would evolve into the KLF.

TIMEX SOCIAL CLUB
1986

RUMORS
Producers: Denzil Foster, Jay King
Album: Vicious Rumors
Record Label: Danya
Songwriters: Marcus Thompson, Michael Marshall, Alex Hill

#1 R&B/Top-10 R&R crossover.

TIN HUEY
1979

I COULD RULE THE WORLD IF I COULD ONLY GET THE PARTS
Producer: Chris Butler
Album: Contents Dislodged During Shipment
Record Label: Warner Brothers
Songwriter: Chris Butler

Midwestern Frat Punk band that gave birth to an auteur in Chris Butler. Covered by the Waitresses (Polydor, '82).

TINY TIM
1968

TIP TOE THROUGH THE TULIPS
Producer: Richard Perry
Album: God Bless Tiny Tim
Record Label: Reprise
Songwriters: Al Dubin, Joe Burke

Warbling remake of the 1929 standard. Paved the way for Taco, the New Vaudeville Band, and Pee Wee Herman.

TLC
1992

AIN'T 2 PROUD 2 BEG
Producer: Dallas Austin
Album: Ooooooohhh . . . on the TLC Tip
Record Label: LaFace
Songwriters: Dallas Austin, Lisa Lopes

On the new Hip-Hop/R&B girl-group tip.

BABY BABY BABY
Producer: Dallas Austin
Album: Ooooooohhh . . . on the TLC Tip
Record Label: LaFace
Songwriters: Kenny Edmunds (Babyface), Antonio Reid (L.A. Reid), Daryl Simmons

#1 R&B/Top-10 R&R crossover.

HAT 2 DA BACK
Producer: Dallas Austin
Album: Ooooooohhh . . . on the TLC Tip
Record Label: LaFace
Songwriters: Dallas Austin, Lisa Lopes, Kevin Wales

Fashion statement, '90s Hip-Hop style.

WHAT ABOUT YOUR FRIENDS
Producer: Dallas Austin
Album: Ooooooohhh . . . on the TLC Tip
Record Label: LaFace
Songwriters: Dallas Austin, Lisa Lopes

Top-10 R&B/R&R crossover.

1994

CREEP
Producer: Dallas Austin
Album: Crazysexycool
Record Label: LaFace
Songwriter: Dallas Austin

#1 R&B/R&R crossover.

WATERFALLS
Producer: Dallas Austin
Album: Crazysexycool
Record Label: LaFace
Songwriters: Lisa Lopes, Organized Noize, Marqueese Ethridge

Shedding their neo-Supremes image with a cautionary, street-wise tale and great video; Top-10 R&B/#1 R&R crossover.

TOAD THE WET SPROCKET
1992

ALL I WANT
Producer: Gavin Mackillop
Album: Fear
Record Label: Columbia
Songwriters: Dean Dinning, Randy Guss, Todd Nichols, Glen Phillips

Early Pop Rock Alternative chart breakthrough.

TOM AND JERRY
1958

HEY, SCHOOLGIRL
Record Label: Big
Songwriters: Paul Simon, Art Garfunkel

An early "American Bandstand" appearance for the future Simon and Garfunkel propelled this cut to the Top-50.

TOM TOM CLUB
1981

GENIUS OF LOVE
Producer: Tom Tom Club
Album: Tom Tom Club
Record Label: Sire
Songwriters: Tina Weymouth, Chris Frantz, Steven Stanley, Adrian Belew

Influential dance track from the Talking Heads rhythm section.

WORDY RAPPINGHOOD
Producer: Tom Tom Club
Album: Tom Tom Club
Record Label: Sire
Songwriters: Tina Weymouth, Chris Frantz, Steven Stanley, Maria Weymouth

TOMMY TUTONE
1982

867–5309 (JENNY)
Producers: Chuck Plotkin, James Keller, Tommy Tutone
Album: Tommy Tutone 2
Record Label: Columbia
Songwriters: Alex Call, James Keller

Frat Rock in the Romantics mode, but without the skinny tie.

TONE LŌC
1989

FUNKY COLD MEDINA
Producers: Michael Ross, Matt Dike
Album: Lōc-ed After Dark
Record Label: Delicious Vinyl/Island
Songwriters: Marvin Young (Young MC), Michael Ross, Matt Dike

Establishing the distinctive voice of rapper Anthony Smith.

WILD THING
Producers: Michael Ross, Matt Dike
Album: Lōc-ed After Dark
Record Label: Delicious Vinyl/Island
Songwriters: Marvin Young (Young MC), Michael Ross, Matt Dike, Anthony Smith

Rap goes National, with one of the biggest selling singles of all-time. Shortly thereafter, the phrase ("wilding") is pointed to by community leaders to condemn black teenagers as a group, and Rap music en masse, even as TV commercials start springing up to exploit it.

TONY! TONI! TONE!
1988

LITTLE WALTER
Producers: Denzil Foster, Thom McElroy
Album: Who
Record Label: Wing
Songwriters: Denzil Foster, Thom McElroy

From Oakland, the home of Gangsta Rap, a crossover hit in the old style; #1 R&B/Top-50 R&R.

1990

THE BLUES
Producer: Tony! Toni! Tone!
Album: The Revival
Record Label: Polygram
Songwriters: Dwayne Wiggins, Ray Wiggins

#1 R&B/Top-50 R&R crossover.

FEELS GOOD
Producer: Tony! Toni! Tone!
Album: The Revival
Record Label: Wing
Songwriters: Dwayne Wiggins, Ray Wiggins, Timothy Christian, Caron Wheeler

#1 R&B/Top-10 R&R crossover.

IT NEVER RAINS IN SOUTHERN CALIFORNIA
Producer: Tony! Toni! Tone!
Album: The Revival
Record Label: Wing
Songwriters: Timothy Christian, Ray Wiggins

#1 R&B/Top-40 R&R crossover.

WHATEVER YOU WANT
Producer: Tony! Toni! Tone!
Album: The Revival
Record Label: Wing
Songwriters: Dwayne Wiggins, Caron Wheeler

#1 R&B/Top-50 R&R crossover.

1993

ANNIVERSARY
Producer: Tony! Toni! Tone!
Album: Sons of Soul
Record Label: Wing
Songwriters: Raphael Wiggins, Carl Wheeler

#1 R&B/Top-10 R&R crossover.

IF I HAD NO LOOT
Producer: Tony! Toni! Tone!
Album: Sons of Soul
Record Label: Wing
Songwriters: Raphael Wiggins, J. Bautista, Will Harris, O'Shea Jackson

Top-10 R&B/R&R crossover. Suggested segue: "I Wanna Be Rich" by Calloway.

TOOTS AND THE MAYTALS
1970

PRESSURE DROP
Producer: Leslie Kong
Record Label: Trojan
Songwriter: Frederick Toots Hibbert

Reggae classic included on the The Harder They Come Soundtrack. Covered by Robert Palmer (Island, '75), the Clash (Epic, '80), and Izzy Stradlin (Geffen, '92).

1972

54 46 (WAS MY NUMBER)
Producer: Leslie Kong
Album: Toots Live
Record Label: Mango
Songwriter: Frederick Toots Hibbert

Quintessential Reggae lament about a quintessential Reggae situation—being busted for marijuana.

1975

FUNKY KINGSTON
Producers: Chris Blackwell, Warrick Lynn
Album: Funky Kingston
Record Label: Island
Songwriter: Frederick Toots Hibbert

One of the genre's defining moments. From the same album that features their classic cover of John Denver's "Take Me Home Country Roads."

THE TORNADOES
1962

TELSTAR
Producer: Joe Meek
Album: The Original Telstar
Record Label: London
Songwriter: Joe Meek

Soaring British instrumental, clearing the airwaves for the coming invasion.

TOTO

1978

HOLD THE LINE
Producer: Toto
Album: Toto
Record Label: Columbia
Songwriter: David Paich

L.A. studio Soul.

1982

AFRICA
Producer: Toto
Album: Toto IV
Record Label: Columbia
Songwriters: David Paich, Jeff Porcaro

Their biggest hit accomplishes the hitherto improbable feat of fitting Kilimanjaro into the lyric without missing a beat or messing with the meter.

ROSANNA
Producer: Toto
Album: Toto
Record Label: Columbia
Songwriter: David Paich

The epitome of the studio/Arena sound; about actress Rosanna Arquette.

1983

I WON'T HOLD YOU BACK
Producer: Toto
Album: Toto IV
Record Label: Columbia
Songwriter: Steve Lukather

America's answer to Asia.

ALLEN TOUSSAINT

1975

SOUTHERN NIGHTS
Producer: Allen Toussaint
Album: Southern Nights
Record Label: Reprise
Songwriter: Allen Toussaint

What doesn't become a legendary producer most? Singing his own material. Cover by Glen Campbell was a rare #1 C&W/R&R crossover (Capitol, '77).

TOWER OF POWER

1973

SO VERY HARD TO GO
Producer: Tower of Power
Album: Tower of Power
Record Label: Warner Brothers

Songwriters: Emilio Castillo, Stephen Kupka

San Francisco, big-band Funk.

ED TOWNSEND

1958

FOR YOUR LOVE
Record Label: Capitol
Songwriter: Ed Townsend

Classic Doo-Wop, in the Lee Andrews & the Hearts mold.

PETE TOWNSHEND

1972

PURE AND EASY
Album: Who Came First
Record Label: Track
Songwriter: Pete Townshend

Reflecting his newfound contentment.

1977

STREET IN THE CITY
Producer: Glyn Johns
Album: Rough Mix
Record Label: MCA
Songwriter: Pete Townshend

One of his finest songs, from the Ronnie Lane one-off.

MY BABY GIVES IT AWAY
Producer: Glyn Johns
Album: Rough Mix
Record Label: MCA
Songwriter: Pete Townshend

A rocker with former Small Face, Ronnie Lane.

1980

LET MY LOVE OPEN THE DOOR
Producer: Chris Thomas
Album: Empty Glass
Record Label: Atco
Songwriter: Pete Townshend

His first solo album since 1980 finds the lead Who in a mood of rare tranquility.

A LITTLE IS ENOUGH
Producer: Chris Thomas
Album: Empty Glass
Record Label: Atco
Songwriter: Pete Townshend

No longer "fearing maturity," Townshend sees even an empty glass as half full.

ROUGH BOYS
Producer: Chris Thomas
Album: Empty Glass

Record Label: Atco
Songwriter: Pete Townshend

Contemplating his lost Mod youth.

1985

AFTER THE FIRE
Album: Deep End—Live
Record Label: Atlantic
Songwriter: Pete Townshend

Emotionally taut commentary on Northern Ireland; covered by Roger Daltrey (Atlantic, '85). Suggested segues: "Where the Streets Have No Name" by U2, "Zombie" by the Cranberries, "The Troubles" by the Rocks, "Invisible Sun" by Sting.

FACE THE FACE
Producer: Chris Thomas
Album: White City
Record Label: Atco
Songwriter: Pete Townshend

From his album as novel as album.

THE TOYS

1965

A LOVER'S CONCERTO
Producers: Sandy Linzer, Denny Randell
Album: Toys Sing a Lover's Concerto/and Attack
Record Label: Dyno Voice
Songwriters: Sandy Linzer, Denny Randell

Based on a Bach finger exercise.

TRAFFIC

1967

PAPER SUN
Producer: Jimmy Miller
Album: Mr. Fantasy
Record Label: United Artists
Songwriters: Steve Winwood, James Capaldi

First of four chart singles, none of which broke out of the Bottom-40, for Winwood's post-Spencer Davis, Progressive Rock supergroup.

1968

DEAR MR. FANTASY
Producer: Jimmy Miller
Album: Mr. Fantasy
Record Label: United Artists
Songwriters: Steve Winwood, James Capaldi, Chris Wood

Blue-eyed British psychedelic Jazz Rock staple.

FEELIN' ALRIGHT

Producer: Jimmy Miller
Album: Traffic
Record Label: United Artists
Songwriter: David Mason

Covered by Joe Cocker (A&M, '69).

FORTY THOUSAND HEADMEN

Producer: Jimmy Miller
Album: Traffic
Record Label: United Artists
Songwriters: Steve Winwood, James Capaldi

Brooding, funky, acid flashback. Suggested segue: "Under African Skies" by Paul Simon.

YOU CAN ALL JOIN IN

Producer: Jimmy Miller
Album: Traffic
Record Label: United Artists
Songwriter: David Mason

Basic Mason Soul Folk romp.

1969

SHANGHAI NOODLE FACTORY

Album: Last Exit
Record Label: United Artists
Songwriters: Steve Winwood, James Capaldi, Chris Wood

1970

FREEDOM RIDER

Producers: Chris Blackwell, Steve Winwood
Album: John Barleycorn Must Die
Record Label: United Artists
Songwriters: Steve Winwood, James Capaldi

Making their protest move.

1971

THE LOW SPARK OF HIGH HEELED BOYS

Album: The Low Spark of High Heeled Boys
Record Label: Island
Songwriters: Steve Winwood, Jim Capaldi

Making their Bowie–Reed–Mott the Hoople move.

TRAMMPS

1977

DISCO INFERNO

Producer: Norman Harris
Album: Disco Inferno
Record Label: Atlantic

Songwriters: Leroy Green, Ron Kersey

A new context for "Burn Baby Burn." Featured in the landmark Disco epic Saturday Night Fever.

THE TRASHMEN

1963

SURFIN' BIRD

Album: Surfin' Bird
Record Label: Garrett
Songwriters: Al Frazier, John Earl Harris, Carl White, Turner Wilson

Inspired by—and indeed credited to—the Rivingtons, who both sang and wrote the immortal surf nightmare "The Bird's the Word." Covered by neo-Surf Punk rockers the Cramps (IRS, '79).

TRAVELING WILBURYS

1988

HANDLE WITH CARE

Producers: Jeff Lynne, George Harrison
Album: Traveling Wilburys (Vol. I)
Record Label: Wilbury/Warner Brothers
Songwriter: The Traveling Wilburys

Biggest hit for the inspired Country Folk Rock one-off consisting of George Harrison, Bob Dylan, Tom Petty, and Roy Orbison.

1990

7 DEADLY SINS

Producers: Spike Wilbury, Clayton Wilbury
Album: Traveling Wilburys (Vol. III)
Record Label: Wilbury/Warner Brothers
Songwriter: The Traveling Wilburys

Extending the joke to include a takeoff on "The Ten Commandments of Love."

TRAVIS AND BOB

1959

TELL HIM NO

Record Label: Sandy
Songwriter: Travis Pritchett

They were no Skip and Flip.

JOHN TRAVOLTA

1976

LET HER IN

Producer: Bob Reno
Album: John Travolta
Record Label: Midland International

Songwriter: Gary Benson

A quirky stab at teen idolhood.

THE TREMELOES

1967

HERE COMES MY BABY

Producer: Mike Smith
Album: Even the Bad Times Are Good/Silence Is Golden
Record Label: Epic
Songwriter: Cat Stevens

Frat Rock, British style. Stevens would go on to threaten Salman Rushdie.

THE TRENIERS

1952

ROCKIN' IS OUR BUSINESS

Record Label: Okeh
Songwriters: Claude Trenier, Clifton Trenier

The uptempo R&B novelty act performed this crucial number on the Dean Martin and Jerry Lewis "Colgate Comedy Hour," purportedly one of Elvis's favorite TV shows.

RALPH TRESVANT

1991

SENSITIVITY

Producers: Daryl Simmons, Kayo
Album: Ralph Tresvant
Record Label: MCA
Songwriters: James Harris III, Terry Lewis

Formula lite-R&B from a New Edition graduate; #1 R&B/Top-10 R&R crossover.

A TRIBE CALLED QUEST

1990

BONITA APPLEBUM

Producer: A Tribe Called Quest
Album: People's Instinctive Travels and Paths of Rhythm
Record Label: Jive
Songwriters: Jonathan Davis, Ali-Shaheed Muhammed, Malik Taylor

Experimental and invigorating new R&B direction, character.

TRIP SHAKESPEARE

1988

PEARLE

Album: Applehead Man
Record Label: Gark
Songwriter: Matt Wilson

Their defining moment; re-recorded on "Across the Universe" (A&M, '90).

THE TRIPLETS
1991

YOU DON'T HAVE TO GO HOME TONIGHT
Producers: Steve Barri, Tony Peluso
Album: Thicker Than Water
Record Label: Mercury
Songwriters: Eric Lowen, David Navarro, Diana Villegas, Sylvia Villegas, Vicki Villegas

Updated Ronettes, without the attitude.

TRIUMPH
1985

MAGIC POWER
Record Label: RCA
Songwriters: Rik Emmett, Gil Moore, Mike Levine

Canadian Arena Metal breakthrough.

THE TROGGS
1966

WILD THING
Producer: Larry Page
Album: Wild Thing
Record Label: Fontana
Songwriter: Chip Taylor

In the Frat Rock all-time Top-10. Covered by the Jimi Hendrix Experience in a career and Rock defining moment at the Monterey Rock and Pop Festival in '67, released to theaters in '68, and on the album of the event (Warner Brothers, '70). Also covered to significantly different effect, by Senator Bobby (Parkway, '67).

1967

LOVE IS ALL AROUND
Producer: Larry Page
Album: Love Is All Around
Record Label: Fontana
Songwriter: Reg Presley

Repenting from "Wild Thing" with a stand-out ballad. Covered by Wet Wet Wet in the film Four Weddings and a Funeral (Capitol, '94).

TROOP
1990

ALL I DO IS THINK OF YOU
Album: Attitude
Record Label: Atlantic

Songwriters: Michael Lovesmith, Brian Holland

#1 R&B/Top-50 R&R crossover for the Motown veteran Holland, with a Pasadena group discovered by Gerald Levert.

1992

SWEET NOVEMBER
Album: Deepa
Record Label: Atlantic
Songwriter: Kenny (Babyface) Edmunds

#1 R&B/Top-60 R&R crossover.

TROTSKY ICEPICK
1987

BURY MANILOW
Album: Baby
Record Label: SST
Songwriter: Trotsky Icepick

Alternative cynicism. Suggested segue: "Debbie Gibson Is Pregnant with My Two-Headed Love Child" by Mojo Nixon and Skid Roper.

ROBIN TROWER
1974

BRIDGE OF SIGHS
Producer: Matthew Fisher
Album: Bridge of Sighs
Record Label: Chrysalis
Songwriter: Robin Trower

Transcending his Hendrix fixation.

DORIS TROY
1963

JUST ONE LOOK
Producer: Artie Ripp
Album: Just One Look
Record Label: Atlantic
Songwriters: Doris Payne, Gregory Carroll

Top-10 R&B/R&R crossover. Covered by the Hollies (Imperial, '64, '67) and Linda Ronstadt (Asylum, '78).

JOHN TRUDELL
1992

BABY BOOM CHÉ
Producer: Jackson Browne
Album: Aka Graffiti Man
Record Label: Rykodisc
Songwriters: John Trudell, Jesse Ed Davis

Amazing tone poem about the coming of age of the Rock and Roll generation.

ANDREA TRUE
1976

MORE, MORE, MORE (PART I)
Producer: Greg Diamond
Album: More, More, More
Record Label: Buddah
Songwriter: Gregg Diamond

Former porno star exploits her persona in the forgiving Disco Arena.

THE TUBES
1975

WHITE PUNKS ON DOPE
Album: The Tubes
Record Label: A&M
Songwriters: Michael Evans, William Spooner, Roger Steen

San Francisco in the decade after the Summer of Love.

1976

DON'T TOUCH ME THERE
Album: Young and Rich
Record Label: A&M
Songwriters: Ron Nagle, Jane Dornacke

Loopy San Francisco theatrics.

1983

SHE'S A BEAUTY
Producer: David Foster
Album: Outside Inside
Record Label: Capitol
Songwriters: Steve Lukather, David Foster, Fee Waybill

Wacky performance troupe cashes in. The Residents weren't listening.

TOMMY TUCKER
1964

HI-HEEL SNEAKERS
Album: Hi-Heel Sneakers
Record Label: Checker
Songwriter: Robert Higgenbotham

The biggest fashion statement since "Blue Suede Shoes" proved less sociologically important, but more musically malleable. Covered by Jerry Lee Lewis (Smash, '64), Stevie Wonder (Tamla, '65), and José Feliciano (RCA, '68).

THE TUNE WEAVERS
1957

HAPPY, HAPPY BIRTHDAY BABY
Record Label: Checker
Songwriters: Margo Sylvia, Gilbert Lopez

Essential Doo-Wop angst.

THE TURBANS
1955

WHEN YOU DANCE
Record Label: Herald
Songwriters: Andrew Jones, Leroy Kirkland

Major Doo-Wop crossover (in which, possibly for the first time on record, the words "doo-wop" are actually intoned), instigating, or at least benefitting from, the year's parallel mambo craze. Suggested segues: "Mambo Baby" by Ruth Brown, "Papa Loves Mambo" by Perry Como, and "Mambo Rock" by Bill Haley.

IKE AND TINA TURNER
1961

IT'S GONNA WORK OUT FINE
Record Label: Sue
Songwriters: Rose Mary McCoy, Sylvia McKinney

Their only Top-20 R&R song aside from "Proud Mary." Re-recorded in '66 under the thumb of Phil Spector, and released on the River Deep, Mountain High *album (A&M, '69).*

1962

A FOOL IN LOVE
Record Label: Sue
Songwriter: Ike Turner

Their first big hit; a Top-10 R&B/Top-30 R&R crossover.

1966

RIVER DEEP, MOUNTAIN HIGH
Producer: Phil Spector
Album: River Deep, Mountain High
Record Label: Philles
Songwriters: Jeff Barry, Ellie Greenwich, Phil Spector

Their fifteenth biggest hit and purportedly Phil Spector's greatest professional disappointment.

1973

NUTBUSH CITY LIMITS
Album: Nutbush City Limits
Record Label: United Artists

Songwriter: Tina Turner
Covered by Bob Seger (Capitol, '75).

JOE TURNER
1941

CORRINE, CORRINA
Record Label: Decca
Songwriters: Peter Chatman, Mayo J. Williams, Mitchell Parrish

R&B chestnut recorded originally with Art Tatum, revived in '56 by Turner for his first crossover hit; covered by Ray Peterson (Dunes, '61), in Phil Spector's first production after the Teddy Bears.

1951

CHAINS OF LOVE
Record Label: Atlantic
Songwriters: Ahmet Ertegun, Van Walls

Big R&B hit for the honey-throated Kansas City Blues man. Covered by Pat Boone (Dot, '56) and Bobby Bland (Duke, '69).

1954

HONEY HUSH
Producers: Ahmet Ertegun, Jerry Wexler
Album: Joe Turner
Record Label: Atlantic
Songwriter: Joe Turner (Lou Willie Turner)

Top-10 R&B breakthrough; crossed over to R&R in a 1960 reissue, written by Big Joe, under his wife's name.

SHAKE, RATTLE AND ROLL
Producers: Ahmet Ertegun, Jerry Wexler
Album: Joe Turner
Record Label: Atlantic
Songwriter: Jesse Stone (Charles Calhoun)

Anyone who doubts Rock and Roll was originally for adults should listen to this early masterpiece of the form. A cleaned up version by Bill Haley and the Comets (Decca, '55) was deemed more suitable for the new teen audience.

1955

FLIP, FLOP AND FLY
Producers: Ahmet Ertegun, Jerry Wexler
Album: Joe Turner
Record Label: Atlantic
Songwriters: Jesse Stone (Charles Calhoun), Joe Turner (Lou Willie Turner)

Getting more mileage from his previous hit, Turner turns to his favorite collaborator, Jesse Stone.

SAMMY TURNER
1959

LAVENDER BLUE (DILLY DILLY)
Producers: Jerry Leiber, Mike Stoller
Album: Moods or Mods
Record Label: Big Top
Songwriter: Eliot Daniel

Doo-Wopping the classics, part MCIV. This one was popularized by Dinah Shore in '44 in the movie So Dear to My Heart.

TINA TURNER
1984

BETTER BE GOOD TO ME
Producer: Carter
Album: Private Dancer
Record Label: Capitol
Songwriters: Mike Chapman, Nicky Chinn, Holly Knight

Reclaiming her life and career after Ike.

PRIVATE DANCER
Producer: Carter
Album: Private Dancer
Record Label: Capitol
Songwriter: Mark Knopfler

WHAT'S LOVE GOT TO DO WITH IT
Producer: Terry Britten
Album: Private Dancer
Record Label: Capitol
Songwriters: Terry Britten, Graham Lyle

Her defining anthem, later the title of her biopic; her only #1 single.

1985

WE DON'T NEED ANOTHER HERO (THUNDERDOME)
Producer: Terry Britten
Album: *Mad Max Beyond Thunderdome* Soundtrack
Record Label: Capitol
Songwriters: Terry Britten, Graham Lyle

Typecasted as the Black female singing Schwarzenegger.

1986

DON'T TURN AROUND
Producers: Bryan Adams, Bob Clearmountain

Record Label: Capitol

Songwriters: Diane Warren, Albert Hammond

As introduced by Tina Turner on the B-side of "Typical Male," this is an especially powerful rocking farewell to Ike. Cover by the Reggae band Aswad (Mango, '88) was #1 U.K. Ace of Base listened more to the Reggae than the Rock approach; their version went Top-10 R&R (Arista, '94).

TYPICAL MALE

Album: Break Every Rule

Record Label: Capitol

Songwriters: Terry Britten, Graham Lyle

Her second-biggest solo hit.

1993

I DON'T WANNA FIGHT

Producers: Chris Lord-Alge, R. Davies

Album: *What's Love Got to Do with It* Soundtrack

Record Label: Virgin

Songwriters: Steve Duberry, Marie Lawrie (Lulu), Billy Lawrie

A mellow statement of purpose from the movie of her life.

TITUS TURNER
1955

ALL AROUND THE WORLD

Record Label: Wing

Songwriter: Titus Turner

Cover by Little Willie John was his first Top-10 hit (King, '55). Covered by Little Milton as "Grits Ain't Groceries" (Checker, '69).

THE TURTLES
1965

LET ME BE

Producers: Lee Lasseff, Ted Feigin

Album: It Ain't Me Babe

Record Label: White Whale

Songwriter: P. F. Sloan

In the disaffected mode of "It Ain't Me Babe," written by L.A.'s most mysterious songwriter (aside from Phil Spector, or maybe Jack Nitzsche or Van Dyke Parks, or Kim Fowley; Brian Wilson was pretty mysterious; Randy Newman was around by then, too, but he wasn't mysterious, just cantankerous).

1967

HAPPY TOGETHER

Producer: Joe Wissert

Album: Happy Together

Record Label: White Whale

Songwriters: Garry Bonner, Alan Gordon

Their biggest hit; the Lovin' Spoonful go to the beach.

OUTSIDE CHANCE

Producer: Joe Wissert

Album: Turtles Golden Hits

Record Label: White Whale

Songwriter: Warren Zevon

An excitable boy makes an early career move. He also wrote for Jackie DeShannon.

SHE'D RATHER BE WITH ME

Producer: Joe Wissert

Album: Turtles Golden Hits

Record Label: White Whale

Songwriters: Garry Bonner, Alan Gordon

A big year for Bonner and Gordon.

YOU KNOW WHAT I MEAN

Producer: Joe Wissert

Album: Turtles Golden Hits

Record Label: White Whale

Songwriters: Garry Bonner, Alan Gordon

When you're hot, you're hot.

1968

ELENORE

Producer: Chip Douglas

Album: Battle of the Bands

Record Label: White Whale

Songwriters: Howard Kaylan, Mark Volman, Jim Pons, Al Nichol, John Barbata

West-Coast, tongue-in-cheek, post-Doo-Wop neo-Folk Rock at its harmonious peak.

THE STORY OF ROCK AND ROLL

Producer: Chip Douglas

Album: The Turtles, More Golden Hits

Record Label: White Whale

Songwriter: Harry Nilsson

Early Nilsson saga. Suggested segue: "The Story of Bo Diddley" by the Animals (MGM, '65).

2PAC
1993

I GET AROUND

Producer: D. J. Daryl

Album: Strictly 4 My N.I.G.G.A.Z.

Record Label: Interscope

Songwriters: Tupac Shakur, Shock-G, Roger Troutman, Lester Troutman, S. Murdock

KEEP YA HEAD UP

Producer: D. J. Daryl

Album: Strictly 4 My N.I.G.G.A.Z.

Record Label: Interscope

Songwriters: Tupac Shakur, Darrell Anderson, Roger Troutman

A poignant anthem for the urban dispossessed, by the much publicized actor/rapper/gangsta, who was murdered in '96.

TWENTY FINGERS
1994

SHORT DICK MAN

Producer: Charles Babie

Record Label: Zoo

Songwriters: Manfred Mohr, Charles Babie

Moving to new levels of sexual description in the age of the anti-euphemism. The radio version was called "Short Short Man," something of a sell-out.

DWIGHT TWILLEY
1975

I'M ON FIRE

Producers: Mark Smith, Noah Shark, John Hug

Album: Sincerely

Record Label: Shelter

Songwriter: Dwight Twilley

Buddy Holly is alive and horny.

1984

GIRLS

Producer: Oister

Album: Jungle

Record Label: EMI-America

Songwriter: Dwight Twilley

Ten years later, Twilley's gotten older, but the girls have remained the same.

THE TWINTONES
1957

JO-ANN

Record Label: RCA

Songwriters: John Cunningham, James Cunningham

In the Long Island White Doo-Wop Hall of Fame; written about their sister. Covered by the Playmates (Roulette, '57).

CONWAY TWITTY
1958

IT'S ONLY MAKE BELIEVE
Producer: Jim Vinneau
Album: Conway Twitty Sings
Record Label: M-G-M
Songwriters: Conway Twitty, Jack Nance

Future country stalwart Twitty wouldn't have a hit on that chart until he formally renounced Rock and Roll in the mid-'60s. But the R&B chart welcomed "It's Only Make Believe," when this dramatic, Elvis-inspired #1 R&R crossed over to the Top-20. And Broadway gave Twitty even greater creedence (while showing its own ignorance) by naming their prototypical Rock and Roller after him in the anti-Rock musical "Bye Bye Birdie."

THE TYLA GANG
1976

TEXAS CHAINSAW MASSACRE BOOGIE
Album: Hits Greatest Stiffs
Record Label: Stiff
Songwriter: Sean Tyla

Inaugurating the famous Alternative label with a classic teen theme. Tyla would move on to Ducks Deluxe.

TYLER COLLINS
1990

GIRLS NITE OUT
Album: Girls Nite Out
Record Label: RCA
Songwriters: Daryl Ross, Sheri Byers

Propulsive role reversal.

BONNIE TYLER
1977

IT'S A HEARTACHE
Producers: David Mackay, Ronnie Scott, Steve Wolfe
Album: It's a Heartache
Record Label: RCA
Songwriters: Ronnie Scott, Steve Wolfe

Kim Carnes soundalike with a Top-10 C&W/Top-10 R&R hit.

1983

TOTAL ECLIPSE OF THE HEART
Producer: Jim Steinman
Album: Faster Than the Speed of Night

Record Label: Columbia
Songwriter: Jim Steinman

A #1 single, on the grandeur scale halfway between Reparata and the Delrons and Meatloaf.

THE TYMES
1963

SO MUCH IN LOVE
Producer: Billy Jackson
Album: So Much in Love
Record Label: Parkway
Songwriters: William Jackson, Roy Straigis, George Williams

Their first and biggest soft Soul hit. Covered by All-4-One (Atlantic, '94).

U

U.K.
1978

IN THE DEAD OF NIGHT
Album: U.K.
Record Label: Polydor
Songwriters: Eddie Jobson, John Wetton

Chops city, with fusion gods Allan Holdsworth and Bill Bruford.

U.S.A. FOR AFRICA
1985

WE ARE THE WORLD
Producer: Quincy Jones
Album: We Are the World
Record Label: Columbia
Songwriters: Michael Jackson, Lionel Richie Jr.

World-wide all-star charity sing-along went #1 R&B/R&R.

U2
1980

GLORIA
Producer: Steve Lillywhite
Album: October
Record Label: Island
Songwriters: Paul Hewson (Bono), Dave Evans (Edge), Adam Clayton, Larry Mullen

No relation to any of the other Glorias. Although the Irish band was probably familiar with Van Morrison's early squeeze.

INTO THE HEART
Producer: Steve Lillywhite
Album: Boy
Record Label: Island
Songwriters: Paul Hewson (Bono), Dave Evans (Edge), Adam Clayton, Larry Mullen

With "An Cat Dubb" (the Black Cat).

I WILL FOLLOW
Producer: Steve Lillywhite
Album: Boy
Record Label: Island
Songwriters: Paul Hewson (Bono), Dave Evans (Edge), Adam Clayton, Larry Mullen

Best of their early pre-Arena Rockers.

1983

NEW YEAR'S DAY
Producers: Steve Lillywhite, Bill Whelan
Album: War
Record Label: Island
Songwriters: Paul Hewson (Bono), Dave Evans (Edge), Adam Clayton, Larry Mullen

Haunting and powerful dirge, a symbolic and actual renewal for Arena and Alternative Rock.

SUNDAY, BLOODY SUNDAY
Producers: Steve Lillywhite, Bill Whelan
Album: War
Record Label: Island
Songwriters: Paul Hewson (Bono), Dave Evans (Edge), Adam Clayton, Larry Mullen

Bringing their surging Celtic drone to a higher emotional level.

TWO HEARTS BEAT AS ONE
Producers: Steve Lillywhite, Bill Whelan
Album: War
Record Label: Island
Songwriters: Paul Hewson (Bono), Dave Evans (Edge), Adam Clayton, Larry Mullen

1984

PRIDE (IN THE NAME OF LOVE)
Producers: Brian Eno, Daniel Lanois
Album: The Unforgettable Fire
Record Label: Island
Songwriters: Paul Hewson (Bono), Dave Evans (Edge), Adam Clayton, Larry Mullen

Cracking the American Top-40 with a stirring tribute to Martin Luther King Jr.

1987

BULLET THE BLUE SKY

Producers: Brian Eno, Daniel Lanois
Album: The Joshua Tree
Record Label: Island
Songwriters: Paul Hewson (Bono), Dave Evans (Edge), Adam Clayton, Larry Mullen

After a trip to San Salvador. Suggested segue: "They Dance Alone" by Sting.

I STILL HAVEN'T FOUND WHAT I'M LOOKING FOR

Producers: Brian Eno, Daniel Lanois
Album: The Joshua Tree
Record Label: Island
Songwriters: Paul Hewson (Bono), Dave Evans (Edge), Adam Clayton, Larry Mullen

Bono reaches for his anthem; hits #1 a second time.

WHERE THE STREETS HAVE NO NAMES

Producers: Brian Eno, Daniel Lanois
Album: The Joshua Tree
Record Label: Island
Songwriters: Paul Hewson (Bono), Dave Evans (Edge), Adam Clayton, Larry Mullen

Advancing their stature as the first Arena protest band. Suggested segue: "Invisible Sun" by the Police, "Zombie" by the Cranberries.

WITH OR WITHOUT YOU

Producers: Brian Eno, Daniel Lanois
Album: The Joshua Tree
Record Label: Island
Songwriters: Paul Hewson (Bono), Dave Evans (Edge), Adam Clayton, Larry Mullen, Brian Eno

First #1 and biggest hit.

1988

ANGEL OF HARLEM

Producer: Jimmy Iovine
Album: Rattle and Hum
Record Label: Island
Songwriters: Paul Hewson (Bono), Dave Evans (Edge), Adam Clayton, Larry Mullen

Dedicated to Billie Holiday.

DESIRE

Producer: Jimmy Iovine
Album: Rattle and Hum
Record Label: Island
Songwriter: Paul Hewson (Bono)

Their first #1 in the U.K. Suggested segue: "1969" by the Stooges.

1991

MYSTERIOUS WAYS

Producers: Daniel Lanois, Brian Eno
Album: Achtung Baby
Record Label: Island
Songwriter: U2

ONE

Producers: Daniel Lanois, Brian Eno
Album: Achtung Baby
Record Label: Island
Songwriter: U2

Another heart song for the ages and one of Bono's best lyrics. Suggested segue: "He Ain't Heavy, He's My Brother" by the Hollies.

UFO

1977

LIGHTS OUT

Producer: Ron Nevison
Album: Lights Out
Record Label: Chrysalis
Songwriters: Michael Schenker, Phil Mogg, Pete Way, Andy Parker

Metal guitar heroics by Schenker.

UGLY KID JOE

1992

EVERYTHING ABOUT YOU

Producers: Ryan Dorn, Ugly Kid Joe
Album: As Ugly as They Wanna Be
Record Label: Stardog
Songwriters: Klaus Eichstadt, Whitfield Crane

Alternative Bubblegum; featured in Wayne's World.

ULTRAVOX

1977

MY SEX

Producers: Brian Eno, Steve Lillywhite
Album: Ultravox!
Record Label: Island
Songwriter: Billy Currie

U.K. punks invade the Euro-disco.

1980

VIENNA

Producer: Conny Plank
Album: Vienna
Record Label: Chrysalis
Songwriters: Billy Currie, Chris Cross, Warren Cann, Midge Ure

Their biggest #1 U.K. hit.

UNCLE TUPELO

1993

ANODYNE

Producer: Brian Paulson
Album: Anodyne
Record Label: Sire
Songwriters: Jay Farrar, Jeff Tweedy

Edgy latter-day Folk Rock.

THE UNDERTONES

1978

TEENAGE KICKS

Album: Teenage Kicks
Record Label: Good Vibrations
Songwriter: John O'Neill

Irish answer to the Buzzcocks. Influential British DJ John Peel's all-time favorite single.

UNDISPUTED TRUTH

1971

SMILING FACES SOMETIMES

Producer: Norman Whitfield
Album: The Undisputed Truth
Record Label: Gordy
Songwriters: Norman Whitfield, Barrett Strong

Capturing the early '70s penchant for cautionary R&B. Ten years later, all such caution would be thrown to the wind.

PHIL UPCHURCH

1961

YOU CAN'T SIT DOWN

Record Label: Boyd
Songwriters: Dee Clark, Kal Mann, Cornell Muldrow

Twist groove covered by the Dovells (Parkway, '63).

URGE OVERKILL

1993

SISTER HAVANA

Album: Saturation
Record Label: Geffen

Songwriter: Urge Overkill
Early Alternative statement.

URIAH HEAP
1972

EASY LIVIN'
Album: Demons and Wizards
Record Label: Mercury
Songwriter: Ken Hensley
The definition of sludge.

U.S.3
1993

CANTALOOP (FLIP FANTASIA)
Producers: Geoff Wilkinson, Mel
Simpson
Album: Hand on the Torch
Record Label: Blue Note
Songwriters: Herbie Hancock, Geoff
Wilkinson, Mel Simpson
*Nifty Jazz/Rap/Pop concoction, based on
Hancock's Jazz classic "Cantalope Island"
(Columbia, '76).*

THE UTAH SAINTS
1992

SOMETHING GOOD
Producer: The Utah Saints
Album: Something Good
Record Label: London/PLG
Songwriters: Jez Willis, Kate Bush
*Hypnotic British raver updates Bush's clas-
sic "Cloudbusting" (EMI-America, '83).*

UTFO
1985

ROXANNE, ROXANNE
Producer: Full Force
Album: UTFO
Record Label: Select
Songwriters: Curtis Bedeau,
Frederick Reeves, Lucien George,
Hugh Clark, Jeffrey Campbell, Gerard
Charles, Shaun Fequire, Brian
George, Paul George
*The Gloria of Rap, if not the Annie,
"Roxanne" would spawn a year's worth of
rebuttals and revisions, including
"Roxanne's Revenge" by Roxanne Shante
(Lolita Gooden) (Pop Art, '85). The B-side,
originally the A-side, was "The Real
Roxanne." But there was also "Roxanne's
Doctor—The Real Man," "Queen of Rox
(Shante Rox-On)," "Sparky's Turn
(Roxanne You're Thru)," and "Roxanne's a
Man (The Untold Story)."*

UTOPIA
1980

SET ME FREE
Producer: Todd Rundgren
Album: Adventures in Utopia
Record Label: Bearsville
Songwriters: Todd Rundgren, Roger
Powell, Kasim Sultan, John Wilcox
*Todd's house band in Woodstock play their
version of (Catskill) Mountain Music.*

V

STEVE VAI
1990

THE AUDIENCE IS LISTENING
Producer: Steve Vai
Album: Passion and Warfare
Record Label: Relativity
Songwriter: Steve Vai
*Virtuoso guitar from the former Frank Zappa
and David Lee Roth sideman.*

RITCHIE VALENS
1958

COME ON, LET'S GO
Producer: Bob Keane
Album: Richie Valens
Record Label: Del-Fi
Songwriter: Ritchie Valens
*His first hit; a Buddy Holly-inspired, Tex-
Mex rocker.*

DONNA
Producer: Bob Keane
Album: Richie Valens
Record Label: Del-Fi
Songwriter: Ritchie Valens
His biggest hit, a true confession.

LA BAMBA
Producer: Bob Keane
Album: Richie Valens
Record Label: Del-Fi
Songwriter: William Clauson
*This B-side of "Oh Donna," a traditional
Mexican Folk-tune-turned-Rock-and-Roll
classic, was on the charts when Valens died
in the plane crash in Clear Lake, Iowa, along
with Buddy Holly and the Big Bopper in '59.
Has since been covered by half of the
known Rock and Roll, Pop, and marching-
band universe. The Los Lobos version in the*

*movie of Valens' life, La Bamba, went to #1
(Warner Brothers, '87).*

THE VALENTINOS
1962

LOOKIN' FOR A LOVE
Record Label: Sar
Songwriters: James Alexander,
Zelda Samuels
*Top10 R&B/Bottom-30 R&R crossover.
Covered by the J. Geils Band (Atlantic, '71).
Former group member, Bobby Womack,
revived it with a #1 R&B/Top-10 R&R hit
(United Artists, '74).*

1964

IT'S ALL OVER NOW
Record Label: Sar
Songwriters: Bobby Womack, Cecil
Womack
*Essential R&B track spent two weeks in the
Bottom-10. Cover by the Rolling Stones
(London, '64) went to #1 U.K. Also covered
by Rod Stewart (Mercury, '70), Bobby
Womack (United Artists, '75), and Johnny
Winter (Blue Sky, '76).*

FRANKIE VALLI
1965

THE SUN AIN'T GONNA SHINE ANYMORE
Producer: Bob Crewe
Album: Solo
Record Label: Phillips
Songwriters: Bob Gaudio, Bob
Crewe
*Cover by the Walker Brothers (Smash, '66)
was a U.S./U.K. hit.*

1967

CAN'T TAKE MY EYES OFF YOU
Producer: Bob Crewe
Album: Solo
Record Label: Phillips
Songwriter: Frankie Valli
*Frankie's early solo one-off puts him in
supper-club heaven.*

1974

MY EYES ADORED YOU
Producer: Bob Crewe
Album: Closeup
Record Label: Private Stock
Songwriters: Bob Crewe, Kenny
Nolan Helfman
*One of the ultimate Rock ballads of unre-
quited love. His first solo #1.*

1975

SWEARIN' TO GOD

Producer: Bob Crewe
Album: Closeup
Record Label: Private Stock
Songwriters: Bob Crewe, Denny Randell

Frankie reverts to Catholic guilt.

1978

GREASE

Producers: Barry Gibb, Albhy Galuten, Karl Richardson
Album: *Grease* The Original Soundtrack
Record Label: RSO
Songwriter: Barry Gibb

With the title tune from the movie version of the '50s parody, Valli hits a personal singles peak.

LEROY VAN DYKE

1961

WALK ON BY

Record Label: Mercury
Songwriters: Burt Bacharach, Hal David

One of the biggest Country hits of the last thirty years; a #1 C&W/Top-10 R&R crossover. Covered by Dionne Warwick (Scepter, '64).

VAN HALEN

1978

AIN'T TALKIN' 'BOUT LOVE

Producer: Ted Templeman
Album: Van Halen
Record Label: Warner Brothers
Songwriters: Eddie Van Halen, Alex Van Halen, Michael Anthony, David Lee Roth

Early Metal musings from the Pasadena titans's monster debut album; with Eddie on hyper guitar.

ERUPTION

Producer: Ted Templeman
Album: Van Halen
Record Label: Warner Brothers
Songwriters: Eddie Van Halen, Alex Van Halen, Michael Anthony, David Lee Roth

Early signature guitar solo had a profound effect on the nature of Rock guitar playing for the next decade.

JAMIE'S CRYIN'

Producer: Ted Templeman
Album: Van Halen
Record Label: Warner Brothers
Songwriters: Eddie Van Halen, Alex Van Halen, Michael Anthony, David Lee Roth

Becoming the Metal "hair" apparent.

RUNNIN' WITH THE DEVIL

Producer: Ted Templeman
Album: Van Halen
Record Label: Warner Brothers
Songwriters: Eddie Van Halen, Alex Van Halen, Michael Anthony, David Lee Roth

Follow up to "You Really Got Me" stiffed on the charts.

1979

DANCE THE NIGHT AWAY

Producer: Ted Templeman
Album: Van Halen II
Record Label: Warner Brothers
Songwriters: Eddie Van Halen, Alex Van Halen, Michael Anthony, David Lee Roth

First Top-20 single.

1980

AND THE CRADLE WILL ROCK

Producer: Ted Templeman
Album: Women and Children First
Record Label: Warner Brothers
Songwriters: Eddie Van Halen, Alex Van Halen, Michael Anthony, David Lee Roth

Ferocious Metal showpiece.

1982

LITTLE GUITARS

Producer: Ted Templeman
Album: Diver Down
Record Label: Warner Brothers
Songwriters: Eddie Van Halen, Alex Van Halen, Michael Anthony, David Lee Roth

For chops devotees.

1984

HOT FOR TEACHER

Producer: Ted Templeman
Album: 1984
Record Label: Warner Brothers
Songwriters: Eddie Van Halen, Alex Van Halen, Michael Anthony, David Lee Roth

Perfecting their eternal adolescent bad-boy image for the age of MTV.

I'LL WAIT

Producer: Ted Templeman
Album: 1984
Record Label: Warner Brothers
Songwriters: Eddie Van Halen, Alex Van Halen, Michael Anthony, David Lee Roth, Michael H. McDonald

Making their commercial move.

JUMP

Producer: Ted Templeman
Album: 1984
Record Label: Warner Brothers
Songwriters: Eddie Van Halen, Alex Van Halen, Michael Anthony, David Lee Roth

Their only #1, with Eddie on synthesizer as well as guitar, to some an accession to the modern Rock sound of the '80s, to others a masterful triumph over it.

PANAMA

Producer: Ted Templeman
Album: 1984
Record Label: Warner Brothers
Songwriters: Eddie Van Halen, Alex Van Halen, Michael Anthony, David Lee Roth

Squarely into the new groove.

1986

DREAMS

Producers: Van Halen, Don Landee, Mick Jones
Album: 5150
Record Label: Warner Brothers
Songwriters: Eddie Van Halen, Alex Van Halen, Michael Anthony, Sammy Hagar

The epitome of high-gloss '80s corporate Arena Rock, co-authored by the new frontman, Sammy "The Red Rocker" Hagar, dubbed by Roth as just as exciting as "the new Darren on 'Bewitched'."

LOVE WALKS IN

Producers: Van Halen, Don Landee, Mick Jones
Album: 5150
Record Label: Warner Brothers
Songwriters: Eddie Van Halen, Alex Van Halen, Michael Anthony, Sammy Hagar

WHY CAN'T THIS BE LOVE

Producers: Van Halen, Don Landee, Mick Jones
Album: 5150
Record Label: Warner Brothers

Songwriters: Eddie Van Halen, Alex Van Halen, Michael Anthony, Sammy Hagar

Biggest hit after "Jump."

1988

BLACK AND BLUE
Producers: Van Halen, Don Landee
Album: OU812
Record Label: Warner Brothers
Songwriters: Eddie Van Halen, Alex Van Halen, Michael Anthony, Sammy Hagar

Rocking harder, enjoying it less.

FINISH WHAT YA STARTED
Producers: Van Halen, Don Landee
Album: OU812
Record Label: Warner Brothers
Songwriters: Eddie Van Halen, Alex Van Halen, Michael Anthony, Sammy Hagar

No easy task; only the Stones could handle it.

WHEN IT'S LOVE
Producers: Van Halen, Don Landee
Album: OU812
Record Label: Warner Brothers
Songwriters: Eddie Van Halen, Alex Van Halen, Michael Anthony, Sammy Hagar

That slick Top-10 sheen.

1991

RIGHT NOW
Producers: Ted Templeman, Andy Johns, Van Halen
Album: For Unlawful Carnal Knowledge
Record Label: Warner Brothers
Songwriters: Eddie Van Halen, Alex Van Halen, Michael Anthony, Sammy Hagar

Hip video. Same old sound.

TOP OF THE WORLD
Producers: Ted Templeman, Andy Johns, Van Halen
Album: For Unlawful Carnal Knowledge
Record Label: Warner Brothers
Songwriters: Eddie Van Halen, Alex Van Halen, Michael Anthony, Sammy Hagar

Riding an aging Arena warhorse into the new Alternative age.

DAVE VAN RONK AND THE HUDSON DUSTERS
1968

ROMPING THROUGH THE SWAMP
Album: Dave Van Ronk & the Hudson Dusters
Record Label: Verve
Songwriter: Peter Stampfel

With completely bizarre material like this, it's no wonder Van Ronk's attempt to crossover from Folk to Folk Rock cost him his entire bank account. Covered by Stamfel with the Holy Modal Rounders (Rounder, '77).

RANDY VAN WARMER
1979

JUST WHEN I NEEDED YOU MOST
Producer: Dell Newman
Album: Warmer
Record Label: Bearsville
Songwriter: Randy Van Warmer

Folk Rock Lite.

TOWNES VAN ZANDT
1972

PANCHO AND LEFTY
Album: The Late Great Townes Van Zandt
Record Label: Tomato
Songwriter: Townes Van Zabdt

The blueprint for Outlaw Country. Covered by Emmylou Harris (Reprise, '77); #1 C&W. Cover by Willie Nelson and Merle Haggard (Columbia, '83). Guy Clark, Joe Ely, Jerry Jeff Walker, Jimmy Dale Gilmore, Nanci Griffith, John Prine, and all their Alternative Country ilk were listening.

LUTHER VANDROSS
1981

NEVER TOO MUCH
Producer: Luther Vandross
Album: Never Too Much
Record Label: Epic
Songwriter: Luther Vandross

Self-produced demo became the soul balladeer's first #1 R&B/Top-40 crossover.

1987

STOP TO LOVE
Producers: Luther Vandross, Marcus Miller
Album: Give Me the Reason
Record Label: Epic

Songwriters: Luther Vandross, Nat Adderley Jr.

#1 R&B/Top-20 R&R crossover.

1988

ANY LOVE
Producers: Luther Vandross, Marcus Miller
Album: Any Love
Record Label: Epic
Songwriters: Luther Vandross, Marcus Miller

#1 R&B/Top-50 crossover.

1989

HERE AND NOW
Producers: Luther Vandross, Marcus Miller
Album: The Best of Love
Record Label: Epic
Songwriters: Terry Steele, David L. Elliot

His biggest hit, a #1 R&B/Top-10 R&R crossover.

1991

DON'T WANT TO BE A FOOL
Album: Power of Love
Record Label: Epic
Songwriters: Luther Vandross, Marcus Miller

Top-10 R&B/R&R crossover.

POWER OF LOVE/LOVE POWER
Producers: Luther Vandross, Marcus Miller
Album: Power of Love
Record Label: Epic
Songwriters: Luther Vandross, Marcus Miller, Theodore Williams (Teddy Vann)

Grammy-winning medley with Teddy Vann's "Love Power," a tune introduced by the Sandpebbles (Calla, '67).

VANILLA ICE
1990

ICE ICE BABY
Album: To the Extreme
Record Label: SBK
Songwriters: Robbie Van Winkle (Vanilla Ice), Earthquake, David Bowie, Queen

Based on Bowie and Queen's "Under Pressure" (Elektra, '77).

VANITY FAIR

1970

HITCHIN' A RIDE
Record Label: Page One
Songwriters: Peter Callendar, Mitch Murray

GINO VANNELLI

1978

I JUST WANNA STOP
Producers: Gino Vannelli, Joe Vannelli
Album: Brother to Brother
Record Label: A&M
Songwriter: Ross Vannelli

A rare example of Canadian overstatement.

1981

LIVING INSIDE MYSELF
Album: Nightwalker
Record Label: Arista
Songwriter: Gino Vannelli

THE VAPORS

1981

TURNING JAPANESE
Producer: Vic Coppersmith Heaven
Album: New Clear Days
Record Label: United Artists
Songwriter: David Fenton

Covered by Liz Phair, in her early-'90s, pre-discovery days (Matador, '95).

STEVIE RAY VAUGHAN

1983

LOVE STRUCK BABY
Producers: Stevie Ray Vaughan, Double Trouble, Richard Mullen
Album: Texas Flood
Record Label: Epic
Songwriter: Stevie Ray Vaughan

A new Hendrixian Blues guitar god rises in Austin.

PRIDE AND JOY
Producers: Stevie Ray Vaughan, Double Trouble, Richard Mullen
Album: Texas Flood
Record Label: Epic
Songwriter: Stevie Ray Vaughan

An early defining classic.

1984

COULDN'T STAND THE WEATHER
Album: Couldn't Stand the Weather
Record Label: Epic
Songwriter: Stevie Ray Vaughan

TIN PAN ALLEY
Album: Couldn't Stand the Weather
Record Label: Epic
Songwriter: Les Reed

His extended signature Blues blast.

1989

WALL OF DENIAL
Album: In Step
Record Label: Epic
Songwriters: Stevie Ray Vaughan, Doyle Bramhall

This recovery anthem was one of Vaughan's last pieces.

1990

BROTHERS
Producer: Nile Rodgers
Album: Family Style
Record Label: Epic
Songwriters: Stevie Ray Vaughan, Jimmie Vaughan

The long-awaited duet by the brothers, released posthumously.

BOBBY VEE

1960

THE NIGHT HAS A THOUSAND EYES
Producer: Snuff Garrett
Album: The Night Has a Thousand Eyes
Record Label: Liberty
Songwriters: Buddy Bernier, Jerry Brainin

Title song from the 1948 movie was covered by Vee in the 1960 movie Just for Fun.

RUBBER BALL
Producer: Snuff Garrett
Album: Bobby Vee
Record Label: Liberty
Songwriters: Aaron Schroeder, Anne Orlowski

Suggested segue: "Red Rubber Ball" by the Cyrcle.

1961

RUN TO HIM
Producer: Snuff Garrett
Album: Take Good Care of My Baby
Record Label: Liberty
Songwriters: Gerry Goffin, Jack Keller

Follow-up to his only #1, "Take Good Care of My Baby," peaks at #2.

1966

COME BACK WHEN YOU GROW UP
Producer: Snuff Garrett
Album: Come Back When You Grow Up
Record Label: Liberty
Songwriter: Martha Sharp

Suggested segue: "Born Too Late" by The Poni Tails.

ALAN VEGA AND MARTIN REV

1980

DREAM BABY DREAM
Producer: Ric Ocasek
Record Label: Ze
Songwriters: Alan Vega, Martin Rev

Legendary 12" single, by the provocative Lower East Side N.Y. duo otherwise known as Suicide.

SUZANNE VEGA

1985

MARLENE ON THE WALL
Producers: Lenny Kaye, Steve Addabbo
Album: Suzanne Vega
Record Label: A&M
Songwriter: Suzanne Vega

Modern Folk Rock tribute to Marlene Dietrich was a hit in England and in Greenwich Village. Natalie Merchant was listening.

1986

LEFT OF CENTER
Album: *Pretty in Pink* Soundtrack
Record Label: A&M
Songwriters: Suzanne Vega, Steve Addabbo

Duet with Joe Jackson, featured in the cult film Pretty in Pink.

1987

GYPSY
Producers: Lenny Kaye, Steve Addabbo
Album: Solitude Standing
Record Label: A&M
Songwriter: Suzanne Vega

A Washington Square acoustic throw-back in '80s dress.

LUKA

Producers: Lenny Kaye, Steve Addabbo
Album: Solitude Standing
Record Label: A&M
Songwriter: Suzanne Vega

Top-5 Folk Rock fluke on child abuse makes Vega the household name previous protege, Patti Smith, never was.

TOM'S DINER

Producers: Lenny Kaye, Steve Addabbo
Album: Solitude Standing
Record Label: A&M
Songwriter: Suzanne Vega

Spoken cityscape reverie; Vega as a Rock and Roll Sylvia Plath. Revived in a souped-up dancehall version by the DNA production team (A&M, '90).

1992

BAD WISDOM

Producer: Mitchell Froom
Abum Title: 99.9F
Record Label: A&M
Songwriter: Suzanne Vega

Pregnant with hidden meanings.

THE VELVELETTES

1965

HE WAS REALLY SAYING SOMETHING

Producer: Norman Whitfield
Record Label: V.I.P.
Songwriters: Norman Whitfield, Mickey Stevenson, Eddie Holland

This low-charted R&B/R&R gem was a Motown throwaway. Covered by Bananarama (London, '83).

VELVETS

1961

TONIGHT (COULD BE THE NIGHT)

Record Label: Monument
Songwriter: Virgil Johnson

A farewell to Doo-Wop's golden age, written by lead singer, Johnson.

THE VELVET UNDERGROUND

1967

BLACK ANGEL'S DEATH SONG

Producer: Andy Warhol
Album: The Velvet Underground and Nico
Record Label: Verve
Songwriter: Lou Reed

Laying waste to Beatlemania, and putting a torch to Dylan's garbage pail, the Velvet Underground would be the most influential band of the '70s, save Led Zeppelin, who did pretty much the same thing, with a whole other set of power chords.

ALL TOMORROW'S PARTIES

Producer: Andy Warhol
Album: The Velvet Underground and Nico
Record Label: Verve
Songwriter: Lou Reed

The former Long Island staff songwriter derides the fashionably chic, while in the process becoming fashionably chic himself.

EUROPEAN SON:
TO DELMORE SCHWARTZ

Producer: Andy Warhol
Album: The Velvet Underground and Nico
Record Label: Verve
Songwriter: Lou Reed

Like the Fugs, whom they replaced at the Dom, the Velvet Underground were inspired by poets like Delmore Schwartz. Eventually Lou Reed would have his poems published in the Harvard Review. *Unlike the Fugs, the Velvet Underground embraced Rock and Roll as a musical means to saving a few lives. Among those clinging to their lifeline were Alex Chilton of the Box Tops and Paul Westerberg of the Replacements.*

FEMME FATALE

Producer: Andy Warhol
Album: The Velvet Underground and Nico
Record Label: Verve
Songwriter: Lou Reed

At the epicenter of Glam: a moody, suppressed, eyewitness account of the rise and fall of Andy Warhol's Factory.

HEROIN

Producer: Andy Warhol
Album: The Velvet Underground and Nico
Record Label: Verve
Songwriter: Lou Reed

The antidote to the "Summer of Love"; the next evolutionary step on the downward spiral.

I'LL BE YOUR MIRROR

Producer: Andy Warhol
Album: The Velvet Underground and Nico
Record Label: Verve
Songwriter: Lou Reed

Acid Pop, almost decadent in its simplicity.

I'M WAITING FOR THE MAN

Producer: Andy Warhol
Album: The Velvet Underground and Nico
Record Label: Verve
Songwriter: Lou Reed

Long Island hippies on the hunt for drugs. Visionary Rock and Roll for the next two decades of revisionism.

SUNDAY MORNING

Producer: Tom Wilson
Album: The Velvet Underground and Nico
Record Label: Verve
Songwriter: Lou Reed

Hangover music for the morning after.

1968

I HEARD HER CALL MY NAME

Producer: Andy Warhol
Album: White Light/White Heat
Record Label: Verve
Songwriter: Lou Reed

Collected on Reed's Rock & Roll Diary *(Arista, '80).*

SISTER RAY

Producer: Andy Warhol
Album: White Light/White Heat
Record Label: Verve
Songwriter: Lou Reed

Ending the good-vibrations era of "acid, incense, and balloons" with the ultimate, 17-minute (bad) trip. Covered by Joy Division (Factory, '81).

WHITE LIGHT/WHITE HEAT

Producer: Andy Warhol
Album: White Light/White Heat
Record Label: Verve
Songwriter: Lou Reed

Unafraid of the dark side, embracing the dark side, embraced by the dark side. A nerve-jingle-jangling ride.

1969

FOGGY NOTION

Record Label: Verve
Songwriters: Lou Reed, Maureen Tucker, Sterling Morrison, Doug Yule, Weiss Hy

Covered by Jonathan Richman and the Modern Lovers (Rounder, '94).

PALE BLUE EYES

Album: The Velvet Underground
Record Label: MGM
Songwriter: Lou Reed

Covered by Maureen Tucker (50 Skidillun Watts, '80) and Lou Reed (Arista, '80).

1970

ROCK AND ROLL

Producer: The Velvet Underground
Album: Loaded
Record Label: Cotillion
Songwriter: Lou Reed

Their lives were saved by Rock and Roll; they saved Rock and Roll in the process, with this heavy anthem. Covered by a solo Lou Reed (RCA, '74).

SWEET JANE

Producer: The Velvet Underground
Album: Loaded
Record Label: Cotillion
Songwriter: Lou Reed

Lou takes on the protest kids with a gleeful snarl (especially on the word clerk). Classic guitar part by Steve Hunter. Covered by Mott the Hoople (Columbia, '70), Lou Reed (RCA, '74), and the Cowboy Junkies (RCA, '88), whose cowboys-on-Librium version was used in the '94 film Natural Born Killers.

THE VENTURES

1969

HAWAII 5-O

Producer: Joe Saraceno
Album: Hawaii 5-O
Record Label: Liberty
Songwriter: Mort Stevens

Twangy TV theme returns the legendary surf guitar band to the Top-10 after five years.

TOM VERLAINE

1979

KINGDOM COME

Album: Tom Verlaine
Record Label: Elektra
Songwriter: Tom Miller (Tom Verlaine)

Covered by David Bowie (RCA, '79).

LARRY VERNE

1960

MISTER CUSTER

Album: Mr. Larry Verne
Record Label: Era

Songwriters: Fred Darian, Joseph Van Winkle, Al De Lory

Country novelty that never made the Country charts.

VERUCA SALT

1994

SEETHER

Producer: Brad Wood
Album: American Thighs
Record Label: Minty Fresh/DGC
Songwriter: Nina Gordon

Edgy girl-group sound of the '90s.

THE VIBRATIONS

1964

MY GIRL SLOOPY

Album: Shout
Record Label: Atlantic
Songwriters: Bert Berns (Bert Russell), Wes Farrell

Frat Rock meets R&B in the bad part of town. A Top-30 tune, covered by the McCoys (Bang, '65) as "Hang on Sloopy" and by the Yardbirds as "My Girl Sloopy" (Epic, '65), featuring Jeff Beck on guitar.

THE VIDEOS

1958

TRICKLE TRICKLE

Record Label: Casino
Songwriter: Clarence Bassett Jr.

Where Doo-Wop merges with Scat. Covered by Manhattan Transfer (Atlantic, '80).

THE VILLAGE PEOPLE

1977

SAN FRANCISCO (YOU'VE GOT ME)

Producer: Henri Belolo
Album: Village People
Record Label: Casablanca
Songwriters: Henri Belolo, Jacques Morali, Phil Hurtt, Peter Whitehead

Long-lasting dance anthem of the chic Disco set, from Sausalito to Fire Island.

1978

MACHO MAN

Producer: Henri Belolo
Album: Macho Man
Record Label: Casablanca
Songwriters: Henri Belolo, Jacques Morali, Victor Willis, Peter Whitehead

Tongue-in-chic pose of the Disco age.

1979

IN THE NAVY

Producer: Jacques Morali
Album: Go West
Record Label: Casablanca
Songwriters: Henri Belolo, Jacques Morali, Victor Willis

The one-joke band strikes again.

Y.M.C.A.

Producer: Jacques Morali
Album: Cruisin'
Record Label: Casablanca
Songwriters: Henri Belolo, Jacques Morali, Victor Willis

The one-joke band becomes immortal on the dance floors of middle America.

GENE VINCENT

1956

BE-BOP-A-LULA

Producer: Ken Nelson
Record Label: Capitol
Songwriters: Gene Vincent, Sheriff Tex Davis

Introducing another crack Rockabilly guitar band, from Norfolk, Virginia, the Blue Caps, featuring Galluping Cliff Gallup on lead, Wee Willie Williams on rhythm, Jumping Jack Neal on bass, and Gene Vincent handling the vocals and songwriting. Originally the B-side of "Woman Love," this echoing epic went Top-5 C&W/Top-10 R&R.

RACE WITH THE DEVIL

Producer: Ken Nelson
Record Label: Capitol
Songwriters: Gene Vincent, Sheriff Tex Davis

Covered by the Stray Cats (EMI, '86).

1957

DANCE TO THE BOP

Producer: Ken Nelson
Record Label: Capitol
Songwriters: Gene Vincent, Sheriff Tex Davis

LOTTA LOVIN'

Producer: Ken Nelson
Record Label: Capitol
Songwriter: Bernice Bedwell

His second biggest R&R; his only R&B hit.

WEAR MY RING

Producer: Ken Nelson
Record Label: Capitol
Songwriters: Don Kirshner, Bobby Darin

B-side of "Lotta Lovin'." Darin and Kirshner would go on to greater things, but not together.

BOBBY VINTON
1961

ROSES ARE RED (MY LOVE)
Producer: Bob Morgan
Album: Roses Are Red
Record Label: Epic
Songwriters: Al Byron, Paul Evans

Paying the tab at the Turf Cafe for another year or so with the year's biggest graduation/wedding ballad.

VIOLENT FEMMES
1982

BLISTER IN THE SUN
Producer: Mark Van Hecke
Album: Violent Femmes
Record Label: Slash
Songwriter: Gordon Gano

Trademark angst from Minneapolis, with a nasal accent.

KISS OFF
Producer: Mark Van Hecke
Album: Violent Femmes
Record Label: Slash
Songwriter: Gordon Gano

Internalizing the Velvet Underground over a junior-high-school squabble.

1991

AMERICAN MUSIC
Album: Why Do Birds Sing
Record Label: Slash
Songwriter: Gordon Gano

Perennial staple on Los Angeles Rock radio.

VIOVOD
1989

MISSING SEQUENCES
Album: Nothingface
Record Label: Mechanic
Songwriters: Denis Belanger, Denis D'amour, Michel Langevin, Jean Theriault

Scary Metal.

THE VOGUES
1965

FIVE O'CLOCK WORLD
Producer: Dick Glasser
Album: Five O'Clock World

Record Label: Co & Ce
Songwriter: Allen Reynolds

Their biggest hit. Suggested segue: "Friday on My Mind" by the Easybeats.

THE VOLUMES
1962

I LOVE YOU
Record Label: Chex
Songwriters: Willie Ewing, Ernest Newson

Lead singer Ed Vince's showcase Doo-Wop swan song.

W

WADSWORTH MANSION
1971

SWEET MARY
Album: Wadsworth Mansion
Record Label: Sussex
Songwriter: Steve Jablecki

WAILERS
1959

TALL COOL ONE
Album: The Fabulous Wailers
Record Label: Golden Crest
Songwriters: Kent Morrill, John Greek, Rich Dangel

Out of Olympia, Washington, a "Harlem Nocturne" of the Northwest. Covered by the Kingsmen (Wand, '65).

LOUDON WAINWRIGHT III
1971

CAREFUL THERE'S A BABY IN THE HOUSE
Album: Album II
Record Label: Atlantic
Songwriter: Loudon Wainwright III

The James Thurber of Folk/Rock, knocking around the house of domesticity.

MOTEL BLUES
Album: Album II
Record Label: Atlantic
Songwriter: Loudon Wainwright III

The marriage having not panned out, LW takes to the groupie scene, unsuccessfully. Suggested segue: "Hot Blooded" by Foreigner, to see how the other half of Rock and Roll lives.

1972

DEAD SKUNK
Producer: Thomas Jefferson Kaye
Album: Album III
Record Label: Columbia
Songwriter: Loudon Wainwright III

His one and only hit; a middle-of-the-dirt-road smash.

RED GUITAR
Producer: Thomas Jefferson Kaye
Album: Album III
Record Label: Columbia
Songwriter: Loudon Wainwright III

A classic modern Folk morality tale.

1973

THE SWIMMING SONG
Album: Attempted Moustache
Record Label: Columbia
Songwriter: Loudon Wainwright III

Returning to his suburban roots in Cheeverland.

1978

WATCH ME ROCK, I'M OVER THIRTY
Album: Final Exam
Record Label: Arista
Songwriter: Loudon Wainwright III

As age begins to creep into his comic's mug, Wainwright deflects it with a joke. A few years later, he'd be a lot more bitter, in "How Old Are You" (Columbia, '85) and "Harry's Wall" (Silvertone, '89).

1987

THE BACK NINE
Album: More Love Songs
Record Label: Rounder
Songwriter: Loudon Wainwright III

A bogey in the game of life.

1989

ME AND ALL THE OTHER MOTHERS
Album: Therapy
Record Label: Silvertone
Songwriter: Loudon Wainwright III

Updating his earlier domestic efforts, with a new, improved persona.

JOHN WAITE
1984

MISSING YOU
Producers: John Waite, David Thoener, Gary Gersh

Album: No Brakes
Record Label: EMI-America
Songwriters: John Waite, Chas Sandford, Mark Leonard

Leo Sayer with a glower; the former Baby's only solo #1.

THE WAITRESSES

1981

CHRISTMAS WRAPPING
Producer: Chris Butler
Album: I Could Rule the World If I Could Only Get the Parts
Record Label: Polydor
Songwriter: Chris Butler

Ex-Tin Huey maven Butler goes shopping for a record deal with the voice of Patty Donohue as his charge card. Suggested segue: "Wordy Rappinghood" by Tom Tom Club.

1982

I KNOW WHAT BOYS LIKE
Producer: Chris Butler
Album: Wasn't Tomorrow Wonderful?
Record Label: Polydor
Songwriter: Chris Butler

Living in the Post-Blondie material world.

NO GUILT
Producer: Chris Butler
Album: Wasn't Tomorrow Wonderful
Record Label: Polygram
Songwriter: Chris Butler

1983

SQUARE PEGS
Producer: Christopher Butler
Album: I Could Rule the World If I Could Only Get the Parts
Record Label: Polydor
Songwriters: Chris Butler, Daniel Klayman, Marc Williams, Tracy Wormworth, Patty Donahue, William Ficca

Landing the American dream of a TV theme song. Everyone split the credits, but the show didn't last the season.

TOM WAITS

1973

OL' 55
Producer: Jerry Yester
Album: Closing Time
Record Label: Asylum

Songwriter: Tom Waits

The voice of Beefheart with the soul of Ferlinghetti; the neo-bohemian Folk Rock troubadour creates the first car song from Rent-a-Wreck. Covered by the Eagles (Asylum, '74), Sarah McLachlan (Arista, '95).

1974

SAN DIEGO SERENADE
Producer: Bones Howe
Album: The Heart of Saturday Night
Record Label: Asylum
Songwriter: Tom Waits

Ultimate beatnik tribute to the morning after. Covered by Juice Newton (Capitol, '80), Dion (Arista, '89), Nanci Griffith (MCA, '91).

1976

TOM TRAUBERT'S BLUES
Producer: Bones Howe
Album: Small Change
Record Label: Asylum
Songwriter: Tom Waits

Covered by Rod Stewart (Warner Brothers, '94).

1978

ROMEO IS BLEEDING
Producer: Bones Howe
Album: Blue Valentine
Record Label: Elektra
Songwriter: Tom Waits

One of the rare L.A. street songs. Suggested segues: "Romeo and Juliet" by Dire Straits, "Lost in the Flood" by Bruce Springsteen.

WRONG SIDE OF THE ROAD
Producer: Bones Howe
Album: Blue Valentine
Record Label: Elektra
Songwriter: Tom Waits

1980

JERSEY GIRL
Producer: Bones Howe
Album: Heartattack and Vine
Record Label: Asylum
Songwriter: Tom Waits

Tom goes to the carnival, meets Sandy. Covered by Bruce Springsteen (Columbia, '84).

ON THE NICKEL
Producer: Bones Howe
Album: Heartattack and Vine
Record Label: Asylum
Songwriter: Tom Waits

From the indie movie.

1983

GIN-SOAKED BOY
Producer: Tom Waits
Album: Swordfishtrombones
Record Label: Island
Songwriter: Tom Waits

The glorious results of a misspent life.

1985

DOWNTOWN TRAIN
Producer: Tom Waits
Album: Rain Dogs
Record Label: Island
Songwriter: Tom Waits

Tom consorts with Brooklyn girls, never recovers. From the movie Down by Law. Covered by Mary Chapin-Carpenter (Columbia '86), Patty Smyth (Columbia, '87), Rod Stewart (Warner Brothers, '90).

1987

HANG ON ST. CHRISTOPHER
Producer: Tom Waits
Album: Frank's Wild Years
Record Label: Island
Songwriter: Tom Waits

INNOCENT WHEN YOU DREAM (BAR ROOM)
Producer: Tom Waits
Album: Frank's Wild Years
Record Label: Island
Songwriter: Tom Waits

Prominently and poignantly featured in the '95 movie Smoke.

1992

I DON'T WANNA GROW UP
Producer: Tom Waits
Album: Bone Machine
Record Label: Island
Songwriter: Tom Waits

Perhaps his defining anthem. Covered by the Ramones (Rykodisc, '95) as theirs.

WHISTLE DOWN THE WIND
Producer: Tom Waits
Album: Bone Machine
Record Label: Island
Songwriter: Tom Waits

Powerfully moving Waitsian study of inertia. Dedicated to the memory of Tom Jans.

WENDY WALDMAN

1973

VAUDEVILLE MAN
Album: Love Has Got Me
Record Label: Warner Brothers

Songwriter: Wendy Waldman

Infectious Folk Rock charmer, covered by Maria Muldaur (Reprise, '73). Waldman went on to success in Nashville as a songwriter/producer.

JERRY JEFF WALKER
1968

MR. BOJANGLES
Producers: Tom Dowd, Dan Elliot
Album: Jerry Jeff Walker
Record Label: Atco
Songwriter: Jerry Jeff Walker

Greenwich Village underground Folk classic. Covered by the Nitty Gritty Dirt Band (United Artists, '72).

1973

L.A. FREEWAY
Producer: Free Flow Productions
Album: A Man Must Carry On
Record Label: MCA
Songwriter: Guy Clark

One of the all-time great Country/Rock leaving songs, chiefly about the inability to leave.

JR. WALKER AND THE ALL-STARS
1965

(I'M A) ROAD RUNNER
Producers: Brian Holland, Lamont Dozier
Album: (I'm a) Road Runner
Record Label: Soul
Songwriter: Eddie Holland, Lamont Dozier, Brian Holland

B-side of "Shotgun" was a Top-5 R&B/Top-20 R&R crossover a year later.

SHOTGUN
Producer: Berry Gordy
Lawrence Horn
Album: Shotgun
Record Label: Soul
Songwriter: Autry DeWalt

Uptown Soul with horns. A #1 R&B/Top-10 R&R crossover.

1969

WHAT DOES IT TAKE (TO WIN YOUR LOVE)
Album: Home Cookin'
Record Label: Soul
Songwriters: Johnny Bristol, Harvey Fuqua, Vernon Bullock

His biggest hit, #1 R&B/Top-10 R&R crossover.

1970

GOTTA HOLD ON TO THIS FEELING
Album: What Does It Take to Win Your Love
Record Label: Soul
Songwriter: Pam Sawyer, Johnny Bristol, Joe Hinton

Motown horn man's most compelling riff.

T-BONE WALKER
1947

CALL IT STORMY MONDAY
Producer: Ralph Bass
Record Label: Black & White
Songwriter: T-Bone Walker

Monumental guitar influence on Jimi Hendrix and the rest of the Electric Blues aristocracy (Clapton, Beck, Page, Bloomfield, Allman, et al). Covered by the Allman Brothers—with Duane Allman (Capricorn, '71).

WALL OF VOODOO
1982

MEXICAN RADIO
Producer: Richard Mazda
Album: Call of the West
Record Label: IRS/Illegal
Songwriters: Stan Ridgway, Mark Moreland, Oliver Nanini, Charles Gray

Early L.A. Roots-Rock anthem, presaging the Alternative Rock scare of the '80s. Of a piece with R.E.M.'s "Radio Free Europe" and a reaction to Elvis Costello's "Radio Radio." Radio wasn't listening.

JERRY WALLACE
1958

PRIMROSE LANE
Record Label: Challenge
Songwriters: George Callender, Wayne Shanklin

A Top-10 R&R/Top-20 R&B crossover; Wallace would make his future living on the Country charts.

JOE WALSH
1973

ROCKY MOUNTAIN WAY
Producers: Bill Szymczyk, Joe Walsh

Album: The Smoker You Drink, the Player You Get
Record Label: Dunhill
Songwriters: Joe Walsh, Kenny Passarelli, Joey Vitale, Roche Grace

His post-James Gang rock guitar classic.

1978

LIFE'S BEEN GOOD
Producer: Bill Szymczyk
Album: But Seriously, Folks
Record Label: Asylum
Songwriter: Joe Walsh

One of the great answers to "So You Wanna Be a Rock and Roll Star."

1981

LIFE OF ILLUSION
Album: There Goes the Neighborhood
Record Label: Asylum
Songwriters: Joe Walsh, Kenny Passarelli

The sometime-Eagles guitarist sums it up.

WANG CHUNG
1984

DANCE HALL DAYS
Producers: Chris Hughes, Ross Cullum
Album: Points on the Curve
Record Label: Geffen
Songwriter: Jack Hues

Biggest U.K. hit for the U.K. Techno dance band.

1986

EVERYBODY HAVE FUN TONIGHT
Producer: Peter Wolf
Album: Mosaic
Record Label: Geffen
Songwriters: Peter Wolf, Wang Chung

Completing their U.S. crossover with a Top-10 hit.

1987

LET'S GO
Producer: Peter Wolf
Album: Mosaic
Record Label: Geffen
Songwriter: Wang Chung

Their last hit single.

ERIC BURDEN AND WAR
1970

SPILL THE WINE
Producer: Jerry Goldstein
Album: Eric Burdon Declares War
Record Label: MGM
Songwriters: Sylvester Allen, Lee Oscar Levitin, Morris Dickerson, Leroy "Lonnie" Jordan, Howard Scott, Charles W. Miller, Harold R. Brown

The former Animal's last big blue-eyed Soul hit comes with a Black backing band, who would go on to a significant Funk career on their own.

WAR
1972

CISCO KID
Producer: Jerry Goldstein
Album: The World Is a Ghetto
Record Label: United Artists
Songwriters: Sylvester Allen, Lee Oscar Levitin, Morris Dickerson, Leroy "Lonnie" Jordan, Howard Scott, Charles W. Miller, Harold R. Brown

Top-10 R&B/R&R crossover is their biggest R&R hit.

THE WORLD IS A GHETTO
Producer: Jerry Goldstein
Album: The World Is a Ghetto
Record Label: United Artists
Songwriters: Sylvester Allen, Lee Oscar Levitin, Morris Dickerson, Leroy "Lonnie" Jordan, Howard Scott, Charles W. Miller, Harold R. Brown

Typifying Black protest of the early '70s.

1973

GYPSY MAN
Producer: Jerry Goldstein
Album: Deliver the Word
Record Label: United Artists
Songwriters: Sylvester Allen, Lee Oscar Levitin, Morris Dickerson, Leroy "Lonnie" Jordan, Howard Scott, Charles W. Miller, Harold R. Brown

Top-10 R&B/R&R crossover.

1975

LOW RIDER
Producer: Jerry Goldstein
Album: Why Can't We Be Friends
Record Label: United Artists

Songwriters: Sylvester Allen, Lee Oscar Levitin, Morris Dickerson, Leroy "Lonnie" Jordan, Howard Scott, Charles W. Miller, Harold R. Brown

The funk committee puts forth their first #1 R&B/Top-10 R&R crossover.

WHY CAN'T WE BE FRIENDS
Producer: Jerry Goldstein
Album: Why Can't We Be Friends
Record Label: United Artists
Songwriters: Sylvester Allen, Lee Oscar Levitin, Morris Dickerson, Leroy "Lonnie" Jordan, Howard Scott, Charles W. Miller, Harold R. Brown, Gerald Goldstein

1976

SUMMER
Producer: Jerry Goldstein
Album: Greatest Hits
Record Label: United Artists
Songwriters: Sylvester Allen, Lee Oscar Levitin, Morris Dickerson, Leroy "Lonnie" Jordan, Howard Scott, Charles W. Miller, Harold R. Brown, Gerald Goldstein

Solidifying their position as the Chicago of Funk with their sixth Top-10 R&B/R&R crossover.

ANITA WARD
1979

RING MY BELL
Producer: Frederick Knight
Album: Songs of Love
Record Label: Juana
Songwriter: Frederick Knight

#1 R&B/R&R standard bearer of the Disco age.

ROBIN WARD
1963

A WONDERFUL SUMMER
Record Label: Dot
Songwriters: Gil Garfield, Perry Botkin Jr.

Wispy, girl-group styled ephemera.

JENNIFER WARNES
1976

THE RIGHT TIME OF THE NIGHT
Producer: Jim Ed Norman
Album: Jennifer Warnes
Record Label: Arista
Songwriter: Peter McCann

Former backup singer sheds her glasses to discover Linda Ronstadt's pipes, if not over-weening ambition.

WARRANT
1989

HEAVEN
Producer: Beau Hill
Album: Dirty Rotten Filthy Stinkin' Rich
Record Label: Columbia
Songwriter: Jani Lane

Modern Arena Rock ballad.

1990

CHERRY PIE
Producer: Beau Hill
Album: Cherry Pie
Record Label: Columbia
Songwriter: Jani Lane

From the Kiss School of Euphemism. In the R&B arena they'd already dispensed with this sort of thing.

I SAW RED
Producer: Beau Hill
Album: Cherry Pie
Record Label: Columbia
Songwriter: Jani Lane

WARREN G.
1994

REGULATE
Producer: Warren Griffin
Album: Above the Rim Soundtrack
Record Label: Death Row/Interscope
Songwriters: Warren Griffin, Nate Dogg

Urban rap with a gangsta edge on the jazz tip. With Nate Dogg.

THIS D.J.
Producer: Warren Griffin
Album: Regulate . . . the G Funk Era
Record Label: Violator/Ral/Island
Songwriter: Warren Griffin

Strong solo followup.

DEE DEE WARWICK
1967

I'M GONNA MAKE YOU LOVE ME
Producer: Jerry Ross
Record Label: Mercury
Songwriters: Kenny Gamble, Jerry Ross, Jerry A. Williams

Compelling soul ballad by Dionne's sister. Covered by Madeline Bell (Philips, '68), Diana Ross & the Supremes, and the Temptations (Motown, '68).

DIONNE WARWICK

1963

(THEY LONG TO BE) CLOSE TO YOU

Producers: Burt Bacharach, Hal David
Album: Make Way for Dionne Warwick
Record Label: Scepter
Songwriters: Burt Bacharach, Hal David

Gossamer pop/rock ballad, covered by Dusty Springfield (Atlantic, '67), the Carpenters (A&M, '70).

DON'T MAKE ME OVER

Producers: Burt Bacharach, Hal David
Album: Dionne Warwick's Golden Hits, Part One
Record Label: Scepter
Songwriters: Burt Bacharach, Hal David

Despite her obvious proclivity for a Tin Pan Alley ballad, occasionally Warwick's past as a stand-in Shirelle shines through, especially her independent attitude here, which resulted in her first R&R hit, and a Top-5 R&B crossover. Covered by Jennifer Warnes (Arista ,'79).

WISHIN' AND HOPIN'

Producers: Burt Bacharach, Hal David
Album: Make Way for Dionne Warwick
Record Label: Scepter
Songwriters: Burt Bacharach, Hal David

Covered by Dusty Springfield (Philips, '64).

1964

ANYONE WHO HAD A HEART

Producers: Burt Bacharach, Hal David
Album: Dionne Warwick's Greatest Hits, Part One
Record Label: Scepter
Songwriters: Burt Bacharach, Hal David

Supper-club Soul. Whitney Houston was listening.

1967

THE WINDOWS OF THE WORLD

Producers: Burt Bacharach, Hal David
Album: The Windows of the World
Record Label: Scepter
Songwriters: Burt Bacharach, Hal David

Caught up in the year's penchant for Pop protest.

1968

DO YOU KNOW THE WAY TO SAN JOSE

Producers: Burt Bacharach, Hal David
Album: Valley of the Dolls
Record Label: Scepter
Songwriters: Burt Bacharach, Hal David

Suggested segue: "Midnight Train to Georgia" by Gladys Knight and the Pips.

1974

THEN CAME YOU

Producer: Thom Bell
Album: Then Came You
Record Label: Atlantic
Songwriters: Sherman Marshall, Phillip Pugh

Her biggest hit, with the Spinners, a #1 R&B/#1 R&R crossover.

1979

I'LL NEVER LOVE THIS WAY AGAIN

Producer: Barry Manilow
Album: Dionne
Record Label: Arista
Songwriters: Will Jennings, Richard Kerr

One of her Pop peaks.

WAS (NOT WAS)

1981

OUT COME THE FREAKS

Producers: Don Was, David Was
Album: Was (Not Was)
Record Label: Ze
Songwriters: David Weiss (David Was), Donald Fagenson (Don Was)

Early statement of their soul purpose. Re-covered on What up, Dog *(Chrysalis, '88).*

1983

ZAZ TURNED BLUE

Producers: Don Was, David Was
Album: Born to Laugh at Tornadoes

Record Label: Warner Brothers
Songwriters: David Weiss (David Was), Donald Fagenson (Don Was)

A story-song, with guest vocal by Mel Tormé.

1988

DAD I'M IN JAIL

Producers: Don Was, David Was
Album: What up, Dog
Record Label: Chrysalis
Songwriters: David Weiss (David Was), Donald Fagenson (Don Was)

Every parent's worst nightmare. Suggested segue: "Liar" by the Henry Rollins Band.

SPY IN THE HOUSE OF LOVE

Producer: Paul Stavely O'Duffy
Album: What up, Dog
Record Label: Chrysalis
Songwriters: David Weiss (David Was), Donald Fagenson (Don Was)

Twisted blue-eyed Soul in the Steely Dan mode.

WALK THE DINOSAUR

Producers: Don Was, David Was
Album: What up, Dog
Record Label: Chrysalis
Songwriters: David Weiss (David Was), Donald Fagenson (Don Was), Randall Jacobs

Their biggest hit, a dancehall fave, especially in rooms with rubber walls.

DINAH WASHINGTON

1949

BABY GET LOST

Record Label: Mercury
Songwriter: Billy Moore Jr.

This Billie Holiday tune was the first #1 R&B hit for the Queen of the Harlem Blues.

1959

WHAT A DIFF'RENCE A DAY MAKES

Album: What a Diff'rence a Day Makes
Record Label: Mercury
Songwriters: Stanley Adams, Maria Grever

Dinah's biggest hit; a Top-5 R&B/Top-10 R&R crossover, was introduced by the Dorsey Brothers Orchestra (Decca, '34), with Bob Crosby singing vocals.

1960

THIS BITTER EARTH
    Album: Unforgettable
    Record Label: Mercury
    Songwriter: Clyde Otis
#1 R&B/Top-30 R&R crossover.

GROVER WASHINGTON, JR.

1981

JUST THE TWO OF US
    Producers: Grover Washington, Ralph MacDonald
    Album: Winelight
    Record Label: Elektra
    Songwriters: Bill Withers, William Salter, Ralph MacDonald
Adult Pop/R&B at its finest, a duet with Bill Withers.

KEITH WASHINGTON

1991

KISSING YOU
    Album: Make Time for Love
    Record Label: Qwest
    Songwriters: Keith Washington, Marsha Jenkins, Rodney Shelton
#1 R&B/Top-40 R&R crossover.

THE WATERBOYS

1985

WHOLE OF THE MOON
    Producer: Mike Scott
    Album: This Is the Sea
    Record Label: Chrysalis
    Songwriter: Mike Scott
Bouyant tale of personal discovery is an Irish Rock anthem. Covered by Jennifer Warnes (Private, '94).

1988

FISHERMAN'S BLUES
    Album: Fisherman's Blues
    Record Label: Chrysalis
    Songwriters: Mike Scott, Steve Wickham
Irish Rock at its Dylan-esque peak.

CRYSTAL WATERS

1991

GYPSY WOMAN (SHE'S HOMELESS)
    Producers: The Basement Boys
    Album: Surprise
    Record Label: Mercury

    Songwriters: Crystal Waters, Neil Conway
Urban scenario tied to a Hip-Hop beat was a Top-10 R&B/R&R crossover.

1994

100% PURE LOVE
    Producers: The Basement Boys
    Album: Storyteller
    Record Label: Mercury
    Songwriters: Crystal Waters, Teddy Douglas, Jay Steinhour, Tommy Davis
Madonna-esque dance-hall fantasy; Top-10 R&B/R&R crossover.

MUDDY WATERS

1948

I CAN'T BE SATISFIED
    Producer: Leonard Chess
    Record Label: Aristocrat
    Songwriter: McKinley Morganfield (Muddy Waters)

1950

ROLLIN' STONE
    Album: Best of Muddy Waters
    Record Label: Chess
    Songwriter: McKinley Morganfield (Muddy Waters)
An essential Blues drawing board for Rock and Roll, that also served as the basis of a legendary group, a monumental Dylan title, and a groundbreaking magazine of the counter-culture. Beyond all that, it launched the Chess label from the plucky Aristocrat in 1950.

1954

I JUST WANNA MAKE LOVE TO YOU
    Record Label: Chess
    Songwriter: Willie Dixon
Initially entitled "Just Make Love to Me," this was Muddy's biggest R&B hit, with a harp solo by Little Walter. Covered by Chuck Berry (Chess, '63), the Rolling Stones (London, '64), the Righteous Brothers (Moonglow, '65), B.B. King (ABC, '77).

I'M READY
    Record Label: Chess
    Songwriter: Willie Dixon
From Chicago, the Blues get the royal rocking treatment from Muddy, Willie, and Walter.

I'M YOUR HOOCHIE COOCHIE MAN
    Record Label: Chess
    Songwriter: Willie Dixon

The ultimate R&B boast. Obviously too potent to cross over to R&R.

1955

MANNISH BOY
    Producer: Leonard Chess
    Record Label: Chess
    Songwriter: Willie Dixon
Muddy's answer to Bo Diddley's "I'm a Man." Tom Cruise's answer to Rebecca De Mornay in the epic train scene in Risky Business, *segueing out of "In the Air Tonight" by Phil Collins.*

1956

GOT MY MOJO WORKING
    Album: Trouble No More
    Record Label: Chess
    Songwriter: Preston Foster
Symbolizing the magical power of Rock and Roll, the mojo makes its first appearance, obtained by Muddy down in Louisiana, probably New Orleans. Covered by Manfred Mann (Ascot, '64), the Paul Butterfield Blues Band (Elektra, '64), Elvis Presley (RCA, '71).

ROCK ME
    Album: Trouble No More
    Record Label: Chess
    Songwriter: McKinley Morganfield (Muddy Waters)

1962

YOU SHOOK ME
    Record Label: Chess
    Songwriters: Willie Dixon, J.B. Lenoir
Essential primordial Blues. Covered by the Jeff Beck Group (Epic, '68), Led Zeppelin (Atlantic, '69).

ROGER WATERS

1987

RADIO WAVES
    Album: K.A.O.S.
    Record Label: Columbia
    Songwriter: Roger Waters
Solo Floyd, same message.

1992

WHAT GOD WANTS, PART I
    Producers: Roger Waters, Patrick Leonard
    Album: Amused to Death
    Record Label: Columbia
    Songwriter: Roger Waters

JODY WATLEY
1987

DON'T YOU WANT ME
Producer: Bernard Edwards
Album: Jody Watley
Record Label: MCA
Songwriters: Franne Golde, Jody Watley, D. Bryant

Watley's first hit, post Shalamar.

LOOKING FOR A NEW LOVE
Producers: Andre Cymone, David Z.
Album: Jody Watley
Record Label: MCA
Songwriters: Andre Cymone, Jody Watley

#1 R&B/Top-10 R&R crossover.

1988

SOME KIND OF LOVER
Producers: Andre Cymone, David Z.
Album: Jody Watley
Record Label: MCA
Songwriters: Andre Cymone, Jody Watley

1989

EVERYTHING
Producer: Andre Cymone
Album: Larger Than Life
Record Label: MCA
Songwriters: Gardner Cole, James Newton Howard

#1 R&B/Top-10 R&R crossover.

FRIENDS
Producer: Andre Cymone
Album: Larger Than Life
Record Label: MCA
Songwriters: Andre Cymone, Jody Watley

Accompanied by Eric B. and Rakim.

REAL LOVE
Producer: Andre Cymone
Album: Larger Than Life
Record Label: MCA
Songwriters: Andre Cymone, Jody Watley

#1 R&B/Top-10 R&R crossover.

THE WATTS 103RD STREET RHYTHM BAND
1970

EXPRESS YOURSELF
Producer: Charles Wright
Album: Express Yourself

Record Label: Warner Bros.
Songwriter: Charles Wright

Top-10 R&B/Top-20 R&R crossover.

THOMAS WAYNE
1959

TRAGEDY
Producer: Scotty Moore
Record Label: Fernwood
Songwriters: Gerald Nelson, Fred Burch

Prescient gloom-and-doom sentiments from an Elvis classmate, protege of Scotty Moore. Released a week or so before The Day the Music Died.

THE WEATHER GIRLS
1983

IT'S RAINING MEN
Producer: Paul Jabara
Album: Success
Record Label: Columbia
Songwriters: Paul Jabara, Paul Shaffer

Hot dance track, big on the Disco circuit, introduces the world to Martha Wash, the Darlene Love of the '80s.

WEATHER REPORT
1977

BIRDLAND
Producers: Joe Zawinul, Jaco Pastorius
Album: Heavy Weather
Record Label: Columbia
Songwriter: Joe Zawinul

Biggest track from the biggest album by the definers and defenders of the short-lived Jazz/Rock "fusion" genre. Covered by Manhattan Transfer (Atlantic, '79).

TEEN TOWN
Producers: Joe Zawinul, Jaco Pastorius
Album: Heavy Weather
Record Label: Columbia
Songwriter: Jaco Pastorius

A Jaco bass workout.

THE WE FIVE
1965

GET TOGETHER
Album: Make Someone Happy
Record Label: A&M
Songwriter: Dino Valenti (Chester Powers)

San Francisco peace anthem has a career as checkered as its writer, noted beat rocker Dino Valenti, aka Billy Roberts, aka Chester Powers. After folkie Hamilton (Bob) Camp introduced it, the We Five recorded it as a follow up to "You Were on My Mind" (A&M, '65), which stiffed. It was then covered by the San Francisco scenesters, the Jefferson Airplane (RCA, '66). Their San Francisco neighbors, HP Lovecraft, put it on their first album (Philips, '67). The East coast rag and roll contingent, the Youngbloods, next released it as a single (RCA, '67), at which time it stiffed again. In '69, after its initial idealistic communal intent had been all but subverted by its use in a public service announcement for the United Conference of Christians and Jews, it was re-released by the Youngbloods (RCA, '69) to become a Top-10 hit at last. Valenti, meanwhile, was either in jail, at sea, on drugs, contemplating a variety of lawsuits or all of the above. He would turn up in Quicksilver Messenger Service, another San Francisco band, and they would cover another Hamilton Camp tune, "Pride of Man." It was no "Get Together," however.

JIM WEATHERLY
1971

MIDNIGHT PLANE TO HOUSTON
Record Label: Amos
Songwriter: Jim Weatherly

Covered by Cissy Houston as "Midnight Train to Georgia" (Janus, '71). Cover by Gladys Knight & the Pips (Buddah, '73) was a #1 R&B/R&R crossover.

THE WEAVERS
1949

IF I HAD A HAMMER
Record Label: Charter
Songwriters: Pete Seeger, Lee Hayes

Campfire classic was one of the Weavers' earliest Folk hits—Seeger's hammer— from there the Folk Revival became a psychic inevitability. Popularized by Peter, Paul and Mary (Warner Brothers, '62), Trini Lopez (Reprise, '63).

1950

GOODNIGHT IRENE
Producer: Milt Gabler
Record Label: Decca
Songwriters: Huddie Ledbetter, John Lomax

Performed in prison by Leadbelly in 1933, the B-side of the Weavers' first hit, "Tzena

Tzena Tzena," outdid the A-side by reaching #1. Through the '50s, several Leadbelly tunes would achieve visibility through the pioneering work of the Weavers; in the '60s he'd become a generational hero, along with Weavers leader Pete Seeger.

WRECK OF THE JOHN B.
Producer: Milt Gabler
Record Label: Decca
Songwriter: Traditional

B-side of "The Roving Kind." Covered by the Beach Boys as "The Sloop John B." (Capitol, '66).

1951

KISSES SWEETER THAN WINE
Producer: Milt Gabler
Record Label: Decca
Songwriters: Huddie Ledbetter (Paul Campell), Pete Seeger, Lee Hays, Fred Hellerman, Ronnie Gilbert

Covered by Jimmie Rodgers (Roulette, '57).

SO LONG IT'S BEEN GOOD TO KNOW YOU (DUSTY OLD DUST)
Producer: Milt Gabler
Record Label: Decca
Songwriter: Woody Guthrie

One of Woody Guthrie's earliest tunes, this dust bowl ballad was written circa 1935.

WIMOWEH (THE LION SLEEPS TONIGHT)
Producer: Milt Gabler
Record Label: Decca
Songwriters: The Weavers (Paul Campell), Solomon Linda, Roy Ilene, Hugo Perretti, Luigi Creatore, George Weiss, Albert Stanton

Adapted from South African traditional material made famous by the South African group Solomon Linda. New version entitled "The Lion Sleeps Tonight" became a Folk Pop hit by the Tokens (RCA, '61).

1952

MIDNIGHT SPECIAL
Producer: Milt Gabler
Record Label: Decca
Songwriter: Huddie Ledbetter

Polishing another Folk perennial. Covered by Paul Evans (Guaranteed, '60), and Johnny Rivers (Imperial, '65).

1956

MICHAEL, ROW THE BOAT ASHORE
Album: The Weavers on Tour
Record Label: Vanguard
Songwriters: Traditional

Traditional slave song was covered by the Highwaymen (United Artists, '61) as one of the early rash of Folk songs to hit the charts in the wake of the Kingston Trio.

THIS LAND IS YOUR LAND
Album: The Weavers at Home
Record Label: Vanguard
Songwriter: Woody Guthrie

Beatific and bountiful Folk classic would soon be adopted as a national anthem by a new generation at the edge of a New Frontier. Covered by the New Christy Minstrels (Columbia, '63), Bobb B. Soxx & the Blue Jeans (Philles, '64).

1958

GOTTA TRAVEL ON
Album: Travelin' on with the Weavers
Record Label: Vanguard
Songwriters: Pete Seeger, Lee Hayes, Fred Hellerman, Dave Lazar, Ronnie Gilbert, Paul Clayton, Larry Ehrlich

Essential rambling classic. Covered by Billy Grammar (Monument, '58), who had a rare Top-5 R&R/C&W/Top-20 R&B triple crossover.

HOUSE OF THE RISING SUN
Album: Travelin' on with the Weavers
Record Label: Vanguard
Songwriter: Traditional

The legendary American folk classic was performed by Bob Dylan on his first album (Columbia, '61). The Animals covered it in a Folk Rock landmark (MGM, '64).

1963

GUANTANAMERA
Album: Reunion at Carnegie Hall
Record Label: Vanguard
Songwriters: Pete Seeger, Hector Angelo, Jose Marti

A freedom song, translated by the major voice of the '60s generational conscience, Pete Seeger, and presented in a rousing concert of triumph, by his first group, the Weavers. Covered by the Sandpipers (A&M, '66).

JIMMY WEBB
1970

P.F. SLOAN
Album: Words & Music
Record Label: Reprise
Songwriter: Jimmy Webb

A West Coast songwriter searches for his

hero (P.F. Sloan of Barri & Sloan, authors of "Eve of Destruction," and many hits for the Grass Roots and the Turtles, etc.) in a haunting Pop Rock gem that is equal to Sloan at his best. Covered by the Association (Warner Brothers, '71), re-recorded by Webb (Atlantic, '77). Sloan, meanwhile, turned up with an album entitled Serenade of the Seven Sisters, released only in Japan (Pioneer, '94).

THE WEDDING PRESENT
1991

NIAGARA
Album: Sea Monster
Record Label: First Warning
Songwriter: David Gedge

Alternative angst from England.

WEEN
1993

PUSH TH' LITTLE DAISIES
Album: Pure Guava
Record Label: Elektra
Songwriters: Aaron Freeman, Michael Melchiardo

Nerd Rock with a knife.

WEEZER
1994

BUDDY HOLLY
Producer: Ric Ocasek
Album: Weezer
Record Label: DGC
Songwriter: Rivers Cuomo

Alternative on the kitschy Pop tip, aided by "Happy Days"'s own Al Molinaro in the video.

UNDONE (THE SWEATER SONG)
Producer: Ric Ocasek
Album: Weezer
Record Label: DGC
Songwriter: Rivers Cuomo

Suggested segue: "The Sweater" by Meryn Cadell (Warner Brothers, '93).

BOB WEIR
1971

PLAYING IN THE BAND
Album: Ace
Record Label: Warner Brothers
Songwriters: Robert Hunter, Bob Weir, Mickey Hart

Rhythm guitarist's cheerfully Dead-like anthem.

1972

CASSIDY
Album: Ace
Record Label: Warner Brothers
Songwriter: John Barlow

Suggested segues: "On the Road" by Aztec Two-Step, "Hey Jack Kerouac" by 10,000 Maniacs.

ERIC WEISSBERG AND STEVE MANDEL
1972

DUELING BANJOS
Producer: Eric Weisberg
Album: Dueling Banjos
Record Label: Warner Brothers
Songwriter: Arthur Smith

Three decades worth of banjo in the Top-10 on one tune from the movie Deliverance. Answered in the Bottom-10 by Martin Mull with "Dueling Tubas" (Capricorn, '73).

PAUL WELLER
1981

SET THE HOUSE ABLAZE
Album: Sound Affects
Record Label: Polydor
Songwriter: Paul Weller

Biggest solo hit for the founder of the Style Council.

JUNIOR WELLS
1966

IT HURTS ME TOO
Album: Chicago/The Blues Today
Record Label: Vanguard
Songwriter: Elmore James

A Chicago Blues guitar/harp standard, with Buddy Guy supplying the fierce guitar to Junior's bittersweet harp. Briefly, a college generation picked up on this sort of Southside Blues, among them Mike Bloomfield, Paul Butterfield, Tracy Nelson, and Steve Miller, before Eric Clapton and Cream, Jimi Hendrix and the Experience, and Led Zeppelin arrived to bury them under ten thousand amplifiers.

KITTY WELLS
1952

IT WASN'T GOD WHO MADE HONKY TONK ANGELS
Producer: Owen Bradley
Record Label: Decca
Songwriter: J.D. Miller

Monster #1 C&W hit for the Queen of Country Music; the answer to Hank Thompson's "Wild Side of Life" and Marie Adams' "I'm Gonna Play the Honky Tonks."

1954

THOU SHALT NOT STEAL
Record Label: Decca
Songwriter: John D. Loudermilk

Country classic, covered by John D. Loudermilk (RCA, '62), Dick and Dee Dee (Warner Brothers, '65).

MARY WELLS
1961

BYE BYE BABY
Producer: Smokey Robinson
Record Label: Motown
Songwriter: Mary Wells

Mary's audition tune, written for Jackie Wilson, became her first single (Motown 1003), a Top-10 R&B/Top-50 R&R crossover. Motown 1001 was the immortal "My Beloved" by the Sanitones.

1962

THE ONE WHO REALLY LOVES YOU
Producer: Smokey Robinson
Album: One Who Really Loves You
Record Label: Motown
Songwriter: Smokey Robinson

The first lady of Motown gets her first Top-10/R&B/R&R crossover.

TWO LOVERS
Producer: Smokey Robinson
Album: Two Lovers
Record Label: Motown
Songwriter: Smokey Robinson

Essential Mary; quintessential Smokey; a #1 R&B/Top-10 R&R crossover.

YOU BEAT ME TO THE PUNCH
Producer: Smokey Robinson
Album: One Who Really Loves You
Record Label: Motown
Songwriters: Smokey Robinson, Ronald White

As Dionne was to Bacharach & David and Annette to Anka, Mary becomes Smokey's perfect voice: another #1 R&B/Top-10 R&R crossover.

1964

MY GUY
Producer: Smokey Robinson
Album: Mary Wells Sings My Guy
Record Label: Motown

Songwriter: Smokey Robinson
Mary's only #1 R&R hit.

PAUL WESTERBERG
1992

DYSLEXIC HEART
Producers: Scott Litt, Paul Westerberg
Album: *Singles* Soundtrack
Record Label: Epic Soundtrax
Songwriter: Paul Westerberg

From the Cameron Crowe epic immortalizing Seattle, a Minneapolis Replacement.

1993

WORLD CLASS FAD
Producers: Matt Wallace, Paul Westerberg
Album: 14 Songs
Record Label: Sire
Songwriter: Paul Westerberg

Re-establishing his solo Alternative presence with a fierce rocker.

KIM WESTON
1965

TAKE ME IN YOUR ARMS (ROCK ME A LITTLE WHILE)
Producers: Brian Holland, Lamont Dozier
Record Label: Gordy
Songwriters: Eddie Holland, Lamont Dozier, Brian Holland

Simmering Soul ballad was a Top-10 R&B/Top-50 R&R crossover.

WET WILLIE
1974

KEEP ON SMILIN'
Producer: Tom Dowd
Album: Keep on Smilin'
Record Label: Capricorn
Songwriters: Jack Hall, Maurice Hirsch, Lewis Ross, John Anthony, James Hall

Only Top-10 hit for the Southern Rock contingent.

WHAM!
1984

CARELESS WHISPER
Producer: George Michael
Album: Make It Big
Record Label: Columbia

Songwriters: George Michael, Andrew Ridgeley

Listed as Wham! on the label in the U.S., George Michael in the U.K.

EVERYTHING SHE WANTS

Producer: George Michael
Album: Make It Big
Record Label: Columbia
Songwriter: George Michael

#1 followup to a #1 establishes Michael and Ridgeley as the London teen faves of the month, if not the year.

FREEDOM

Producer: George Michael
Album: Make It Big
Record Label: Columbia
Songwriter: George Michael

Another hit from the massive album.

WAKE ME UP BEFORE YOU GO-GO

Producer: George Michael
Album: Make It Big
Record Label: Columbia
Songwriter: George Michael

First American hit for the British Disco dandies, a #1 U.S./U.K. crossover. In the U.S., the New Kids on the Block were listening.

1986

A DIFFERENT CORNER

Producer: George Michael
Album: Music from the Edge of Heaven
Record Label: Columbia
Songwriter: George Michael

Their last #1 U.K./Top-10 U.S.: George would have one more #1 U.K./#1 U.S. with Aretha Franklin on "I Know You Were Waiting (for Me)."

THE EDGE OF HEAVEN

Producer: George Michael
Album: Music from the Edge of Heaven
Record Label: Columbia
Songwriter: George Michael

#1 U.K./Top-10 U.S., 1986.

I'M YOUR MAN

Producer: George Michael
Album: Music from the Edge of Heaven
Record Label: Columbia
Songwriter: George Michael

#1 U.K./Top-5 U.S.

BILLY EDD WHEELER
1962

COAL TATTOO

Producers: Jerry Leiber, Mike Stoller
Album: A New Bag of Songs
Record Label: Kapp
Songwriter: Billy Edd Wheeler

Country Folk crossover. Covered by Judy Collins (Elektra, '64).

THE WHISPERS
1979

AND THE BEAT GOES ON

Album: The Whispers
Record Label: Solar
Songwriters: Leon Sylvers, Stephen Shockley, William Shelby

#1 R&B/Top-20 R&R crossover; also a big hit in the U.K.

1987

ROCK STEADY

Producers: Babyface, L.A. Reid
Album: Just Gets Better with Time
Record Label: Solar
Songwriters: Kenny Edmunds (Babyface), D. Ladd, Boaz Watson

Biggest hit for the twenty-five year old group; #1 R&B/Top-10 R&R crossover.

IAN WHITCOMB
1965

YOU TURN ME ON (THE TURN ON SONG)

Producer: Jerry Dennon
Album: You Turn Me On
Record Label: Tower
Songwriter: Ian Whitcomb

Paving the way for Gilbert O'Sullivan.

WHITE LION
1987

WAIT

Producer: Michael Wagener
Album: Pride
Record Label: Atlantic
Songwriters: Vito Bratta, Mike Tramp

Arena Rock with a New York accent.

WHEN THE CHILDREN CRY

Producer: Michael Wagener
Album: Pride
Record Label: Atlantic
Songwriters: Vito Bratta, Mike Tramp

The obligatory Arena ballad strikes again, and with it go the remains of the band's Rock credibility.

WHITE ZOMBIE
1994

THUNDER KISS

Producers: Rob Date, White Zombie
Album: La Sexorcisto: Devil Music, Vol. 1
Record Label: Geffen
Songwriters: Rob Straker (Rob Zombie), White Zombie

Brings new meaning to the term metal onslaught; the musical equivalent of a Monster Truck rally.

BARRY WHITE
1973

I'M GONNA LOVE YOU JUST A LITTLE MORE BABE

Producer: Barry White
Album: I've Got So Much to Give
Record Label: 20th Century
Songwriter: Barry White

In the deep-toned Isaac Hayes bedside tradition, heavy Barry's first #1 R&B/Top-10 R&R crossover.

NEVER, NEVER GONNA GIVE YA UP

Producer: Barry White
Album: Stone Gon'
Record Label: 20th Century
Songwriter: Barry White

1974

CAN'T GET ENOUGH OF YOUR LOVE, BABE

Producer: Barry White
Album: Can't Get Enough
Record Label: 20th Century
Songwriter: Barry White

His biggest boudoir hit; a #1 R&B/#1 R&R crossover.

YOU'RE THE FIRST, THE LAST, MY EVERYTHING

Producer: Barry White
Album: Can't Get Enough
Record Label: 20th Century
Songwriters: Barry White, Tony Sepe, Peter Radcliffe

#1 R&B/Top-10 R&R crossover.

1975

WHAT AM I GONNA DO WITH YOU

Producer: Barry White
Album: Just Another Way to Say I Love You

Record Label: 20th Century
Songwriter: Barry White

1977

IT'S ECSTASY WHEN YOU LAY DOWN NEXT TO ME

Producer: Barry White
Album: Barry White Sings for Someone You Love
Record Label: 20th Century
Songwriters: Nelson Pigford, Ekundayo Paris

Paris' first hit since "Sooner or Later" by the Grass Roots (Dunhill, '71).

1994

PRACTICE WHAT YOU PREACH

Producers: James Harris III, Terry Lewis, Barry White
Album: Practice What You Preach
Record Label: Atlantic
Songwriters: Barry White, Gerald Levert, Eddie Nicholas

His message and his act, like his physique, unchanged by time, White returns with a #1 R&B/Top-20 R&R crossover.

KARYN WHITE

1988

LOVE SAW IT

Producers: Babyface, L.A. Reid
Album: Karyn White
Record Label: Warner Brothers
Songwriter: Kenny Edmunds (Babyface), Antonio Reed (L.A. Reid), Daryl Simmons

Debuting with a #1 R&B hit.

SECRET RENDEZVOUS

Producers: Babyface, L.A. Reid
Album: Karyn White
Record Label: Warner Brothers
Songwriters: Kenny Edmunds (Babyface), Antonio Reed (L.A. Reid), Daryl Simmons

#1 R&B/Top-10 R&R crossover.

SUPERWOMAN

Producers: Babyface, L.A. Reid
Album: Karyn White
Record Label: Warner Brothers
Songwriters: Kenny Edmunds (Babyface), Antonio Reed (L.A. Reid), Daryl Simmons

#1 R&B/Top-10 R&R crossover; Top R&B song of the year.

THE WAY YOU LOVE ME

Producers: Babyface, L.A. Reid
Album: Karyn White
Record Label: Warner Brothers
Songwriters: Kenny Edmunds (Babyface), Antonio Reed (L.A. Reid), Daryl Simmons

#1 R&B/Top-10 R&R is the first crossover hit for the year's most dynamic debut artist.

1991

ROMANTIC

Producers: Jimmy Jam, Terry Lewis
Album: Ritual of Love
Record Label: Warner Brothers
Songwriters: James Harris III, Terry Lewis, Karyn White

New producers, even better results; a #1 R&B/#1 R&R crossover.

TONY JOE WHITE

1969

POLK SALAD ANNIE

Producer: Billy Swan
Album: Black and White
Record Label: Monument
Songwriter: Tony Joe White

Tall Country/Rock tale by the author of "A Rainy Night in Georgia."

WILLIE AND LAURA MAE JONES

Producer: Billy Swan
Album: Black and White
Record Label: Monument
Songwriter: Tony Joe White

Compelling character portrait. Covered by Dusty Springfield (Atlantic, '69), the Persuasions (Elektra, '77).

WHITESNAKE

1987

HERE I GO AGAIN

Producer: Keith Olsen
Album: Whitesnake
Record Label: Geffen
Songwriters: David Coverdale, Bernie Marsden

Their biggest U.S. hit stiffed in England in '82 in another version.

IS THIS LOVE

Producers: Mike Stone, Keith Olsen
Album: Whitesnake
Record Label: Geffen
Songwriters: David Coverdale, John Sykes

STILL OF THE NIGHT

Producer: Keith Olsen
Album: Whitesnake
Record Label: Geffen
Songwriters: David Coverdale, John Sykes

Former Deep Purple frontman comes up with a standard issue Led Zeppelin tune, leading the wave of '80s hair bands to a '90s cul-de-sac.

CHRIS WHITLEY

1991

LIVING WITH THE LAW

Producer: Malcolm Burn
Album: Living with the Law
Record Label: Columbia
Songwriter: Chris Whitley

Gangsta Folk.

THE WHO

1965

I CAN'T EXPLAIN

Producer: Kit Lambert
Album: Meaty, Beaty, Big, and Bouncy
Record Label: Decca
Songwriter: Pete Townshend

Townshend's first success at songwriting, the most significant Bottom-10 song of the year; he'd go on to become one of Rock's great explainers.

MY GENERATION

Producer: Kit Lambert
Album: The Who Sing My Generation
Record Label: Decca
Songwriter: Pete Townshend

With two hits under his belt, Pete was ready for a larger statement; inspired by living under the shadow of the bomb, three chords, a stutter, and a big booming sound, he got it.

1966

ANYWAY, ANYHOW, ANYWHERE

Producer: Kit Lambert
Album: The Who Sing My Generation
Record Label: Decca
Songwriters: Pete Townshend, Roger Daltrey

Following up "I Can't Explain," this tune was, according to Townshend, an attempt to explain in three words how jazzman Charlie Parker plays the sax. It became the theme for the influential U.K. dance show, "Ready, Steady, Go." Note the rare Daltrey credit.

THE KIDS ARE ALRIGHT
Producer: Kit Lambert
Album: The Who Sing My Generation
Record Label: Decca
Songwriter: Pete Townshend

Pre-Arena Rock anthem; setting the stage for all other classic rock solidarity statements of the '70s.

SUBSTITUTE
Producer: The Who
Record Label: Decca
Songwriter: Pete Townshend

Keith Moon at his best. Not available on an album until it appeared on Live at Leeds in 1970.

1967

HAPPY JACK
Producer: Kit Lambert
Album: Happy Jack
Record Label: Decca
Songwriter: Pete Townshend

Creating a semi-folk hero.

I CAN SEE FOR MILES
Producer: Kit Lambert
Album: The Who Sell Out
Record Label: Decca
Songwriter: Townshend, Peter

Their only Top-10 R&R single; one of the major travesties of the chart system. Suggested segue: "Eight Miles High" by the Byrds (written to explain how John Coltrane plays the sax).

PICTURES OF LILY
Producer: Kit Lambert
Album: Magic Bus/The Who on Tour
Record Label: Decca
Songwriter: Pete Townshend

Quintessential adolescent fantasy. Suggested segue: "She Bop" by Cyndi Lauper.

A QUICK ONE WHILE HE'S AWAY
Producer: Kit Lambert
Album: Happy Jack
Record Label: Decca
Songwriter: Pete Townshend

Practicing for "Tommy" with a ten-minute mini rock-opera. It was better than the Pretty Things' SF Sorrow.

1968

MAGIC BUS
Producer: Kit Lambert
Album: Magic Bus
Record Label: Decca
Songwriter: Pete Townshend

Suggested segues: "Yellow Submarine" by the Beatles, "Purple Haze" by Jimi Hendrix, "Eight Miles High" by the Byrds, "Along Comes Mary" by the Association, "Mellow Yellow" by Donovan, "Puff the Magic Dragon" by Peter, Paul and Mary.

1969

ACID QUEEN
Producer: Kit Lambert
Album: Tommy
Record Label: Decca
Songwriter: Pete Townshend

From the all-purpose deaf, dumb & blind boy pinball epic, remade in the movie as a camp masterpiece by Tina Turner (Polydor, '76).

AMAZING JOURNEY
Producer: Kit Lambert
Album: Tommy
Record Label: Decca
Songwriter: Pete Townshend

Marking the beginning of one of rock's more amazing journeys from rock opera to movie to ballet, to hit album, finally and ultimately, twenty years later, to Broadway itself.

I'M FREE
Producer: Kit Lambert
Album: Tommy
Record Label: Decca
Songwriter: Pete Townshend

Daltrey's "Tommy" showcase. From here he'd go on to play Liszt, in the movie Lisztomania in 1975.

PINBALL WIZARD
Producer: Kit Lambert
Album: Tommy
Record Label: Decca
Songwriter: Pete Townshend

The title tune and first single (Top-20 U.S./#4 U.K.), leaving unanswered only one question: Did Townshend ever play pinball? (Did the Beach Boys know how to surf?)

SEE ME, FEEL ME
Producer: Kit Lambert
Album: Tommy

Record Label: Decca
Songwriter: Pete Townshend

The biggest Tommy single, peaking in the U.S. at #12.

WE'RE NOT GONNA TAKE IT
Producer: Kit Lambert
Album: Tommy
Record Label: Decca
Songwriter: Pete Townshend

Tommy's FM radio anthem.

1970

YOUNG MAN BLUES
Producer: The Who
Album: Live at Leeds
Record Label: Decca
Songwriter: Mose Allison

Something in common with the Yardbirds, a love for the quintessential Long Island Bluesman, Mose Allison. A "Summertime Blues" for the over-21 set.

1971

BABA O'RILEY
Producer: The Who
Album: Who's Next
Record Label: Decca
Songwriter: Pete Townshend

The seeker and the seekee find each other. This was reputedly an early performance milestone for the young Madonna.

BARGAIN
Producer: The Who
Album: Who's Next
Record Label: Decca
Songwriter: Pete Townshend

A ripping rocker.

BEHIND BLUE EYES
Producer: The Who
Album: Who's Next
Record Label: Decca
Songwriter: Pete Townshend

One of Townshend's most haunting ballads.

GOIN' MOBILE
Producer: The Who
Album: Who's Next
Record Label: Decca
Songwriter: Pete Townshend

Known primarily for his slashing rhythm (and the occasional trashing of a stage guitar), this tale of a "hippie gypsy" is enhanced by Townshend's use of an envelope follower on his guitar.

I'M A BOY

Producer: Kit Lambert
Album: Meaty Beaty Big and Bouncy
Record Label: Decca
Songwriter: Pete Townshend

THE SEEKER

Producer: Kit Lambert
Album: Meaty Beaty Big and Bouncy
Record Label: Decca
Songwriter: Pete Townshend

Meier Baba was listening.

THE SONG IS OVER

Producer: The Who
Album: Who's Next
Record Label: Decca
Songwriter: Pete Townshend

WON'T GET FOOLED AGAIN

Producer: The Who
Album: Who's Next
Record Label: Decca
Songwriter: Pete Townshend

Arena anthem and youth culture rallying cry.

1972

JOIN TOGETHER

Producer: The Who
Album: The Kids Are Alright
Record Label: MCA
Songwriter: Pete Townshend

One of their biggest rockers. Featured in the '79 film The Kids Are Alright.

1973

5:15

Producer: John Entwistle
Album: *Quadrophenia*
Record Label: MCA
Songwriter: Pete Townshend

From Townshend's other rock opera.

LOVE, REIGN O'ER ME

Producer: The Who
Album: *Quadrophenia*
Record Label: Track
Songwriter: Pete Townshend

His great sprawling rainy epic.

THE REAL ME

Producer: The Who
Album: *Quadrophenia*
Record Label: Track
Songwriter: Pete Townshend

Returning to his roots among the Mods, Townshend writes his most convincing rocker.

1975

SLIP KID

Producer: Glyn Johns
Album: The Who by Numbers
Record Label: MCA
Songwriter: Pete Townshend

Powerful Townshend; from whence came: "No easy way to be free."

SQUEEZE BOX

Producer: Glyn Johns
Album: The Who by Numbers
Record Label: MCA
Songwriter: Pete Townshend

Returning to the dancehall whimsey of "Happy Jack."

1978

GUITAR AND PEN

Producers: Glyn Johns, Jon Astley
Album: Who Are You
Record Label: MCA
Songwriter: Pete Townshend

At his most eloquent.

WHO ARE YOU

Producers: Glyn Johns, Jon Astley
Album: Who Are You
Record Label: MCA
Songwriter: Pete Townshend

One of his angriest performances.

1981

DON'T LET GO THE COAT

Producer: Bill Szymczyk
Album: Face Dances
Record Label: Warner Brothers
Songwriter: Pete Townshend

In a more mystical frame of mind.

YOU BETTER, YOU BET

Producer: Bill Szymczyk
Album: Face Dances
Record Label: Warner Brothers
Songwriter: Pete Townshend

JANE WIEDLIN

1988

RUSH HOUR

Producer: Stephen Hague
Album: Fur
Record Label: EMI-Manhattan
Songwriters: Jane Wiedlin, Peter Rafelson

Former Go-Go goes solo.

WILD CHERRY

1976

PLAY THAT FUNKY MUSIC

Producer: Robert Parissi
Album: Wild Cherry
Record Label: Epic
Songwriter: Robert Parissi

One-shot Disco era #1 R&B/#1 R&R crossover.

EUGENE WILDE

1976

DON'T SAY NO TONIGHT

Album: Serenade
Record Label: Philly World
Songwriters: Ronnie Broomfield, McKinley Horton

1985

GOTTA GET YOU HOME TONIGHT

Album: Eugene Wilde
Record Label: Atlantic
Songwriters: Ronnie Broomfield, McKinley Horton

#1 R&B/Bottom-20 R&R crossover.

KIM WILDE

1982

KIDS IN AMERICA

Producer: Ricky Wilde
Album: Kim Wilde
Record Label: EMI-America
Songwriters: Ricky Wilde, Marty Wilde

Leading the new British Techno Alternative wave; co-written by her father Marty, an Elvis-styled '50s rocker.

MATTHEW WILDER

1983

BREAK MY STRIDE

Producers: Pete Bunetta, Rick Chudacoff, Bill Elliott
Album: I Don't Speak the Language
Record Label: Private
Songwriters: Matthew Wilder, Greg Prestopino

Pleasant, pulsing Pop/Rock one-shot.

DENIECE WILLIAMS

1984

LET'S HEAR IT FOR THE BOY

Album: *Footloose* Soundtrack
Record Label: Columbia

Songwriters: Dean Pitchford, Tom Snow

Cinematic dance groove, a #1 R&B/#1 R&R celluloid crossover. The boy was Kevin Bacon.

HANK WILLIAMS
1947

MOVE IT ON OVER
Record Label: MGM
Songwriter: Hank Williams

First single release for country music's lonesomest cowboy and an early blueprint for Rockabilly. Covered by Hank Williams Jr. (MGM, '65), George Thorogood & the Delaware Destroyers (Rounder, '78).

1949

I'M SO LONESOME I COULD CRY
Record Label: MGM
Songwriter: Hank Williams

Covered by B.J. Thomas (Scepter, '66).

LOVESICK BLUES
Record Label: MGM
Songwriter: Hank Williams

Originally released in 1922. Hank's first #1 C&W/Top-30 R&R crossover, spending 42 weeks on the charts. Also crossed over to England, where it was a #1 U.K. hit for Frank Ifield (Columbia, '62)/Top-50 U.S. (Vee-Jay, '63). Bob Dylan was listening here, the Beatles there.

1951

COLD, COLD HEART
Record Label: MGM
Songwriter: Hank Williams

Turning his specific Audrey-inspired pain into the stuff of a major career move. Mitch Miller appropriated the tune for a Tony Bennett #1 Pop cover (Columbia, '51).

HEY GOOD LOOKIN'
Record Label: MGM
Songwriter: Hank Williams

Second biggest of his seven Top-10 C&W singles of '51. Country boasting as powerful an aphrodisiac as any R&B.

1952

I'LL NEVER GET OUT OF THIS WORLD ALIVE
Record Label: MGM
Songwriters: Hank Williams, Fred Rose

Prophetic preview of blue-eyed Soul.

JAMBALAYA (ON THE BAYOU)
Record Label: MGM
Songwriter: Hank Williams

New Orleans tribute, #1 C&W/Top-30 R&R; covered by Brenda Lee (Decca, '57), Fats Domino (Imperial, '61).

YOUR CHEATIN' HEART
Record Label: MGM
Songwriter: Hank Williams

Covered by Ray Charles (ABC/Paramount, '62).

1953

TAKE THESE CHAINS FROM MY HEART
Record Label: MGM
Songwriters: Fred Rose, Hy Heath

Hank's 7th and last #1 Country hit. Covered by Ray Charles (ABC/Paramount, '63).

JERRY LYN WILLIAMS
1979

GIVING IT UP FOR YOUR LOVE
Album: Gone
Record Label: Columbia
Songwriter: Jerry Lyn Williams

Covered by Delbert McClinton (Capitol, '80).

LARRY WILLIAMS
1957

BONY MORONIE
Producer: Artie Rupe
Record Label: Specialty
Songwriter: Larry Williams

Learning his rhyming lessons from Little Richard.

SHORT FAT FANNIE
Producers: Blackwell, Bumps
Record Label: Specialty
Songwriter: Larry Williams

First hit for Lloyd Price's former chauffeur; a Top-5 R&B/Top-10 R&R crossover, in the Little Richard mode.

SLOW DOWN
Producer: Art Rupe
Record Label: Specialty
Songwriter: Larry Williams

B-side of "Dizzy Miss Lizzy," covered by the Beatles (Capitol, '64).

1958

SHE SAID YEAH
Producer: Sonny Bono
Record Label: Specialty

Songwriters: Sonny Bono, George Jackson

Sonny Bono gets a leg up in the business. Covered by the Rolling Stones (London, '64).

LUCINDA WILLIAMS
1988

PASSIONATE KISSES
Album: Lucinda Williams
Record Label: Rough Trade
Songwriter: Lucinda Williams

New generation Folk/Rock at its finest. Covered by Mary Chapin Carpenter (Columbia, '93).

1993

SWEET OLD WORLD
Producer: Gurf Morlix
Album: Sweet Old World
Record Label: Chameleon
Songwriter: Lucinda Williams

Eulogy for a friend. Covered by Emmylou Harris (Reprise, '95). Suggested segue: "What's Good" by Lou Reed.

MASON WILLIAMS
1968

CLASSICAL GAS
Producer: Mike Post
Album: Mason Williams' Phonograph Record
Record Label: Warner Brothers
Songwriter: Mason Williams

Guitar showpiece, as heard on "The Smothers Brothers Comedy Hour."

MAURICE WILLIAMS AND THE ZODIACS
1960

STAY
Producers: Phil Gernhard, Johnny McCullough
Album: Stay
Record Label: Herald
Songwriter: Maurice Williams

The author of "Little Darlin'" breaks through with a Top-5 R&B/#1 R&R crossover, covered by the Four Seasons (Vee-Jay, '64), Jackson Browne (Asylum, '77).

OTIS WILLIAMS AND THE CHARMS

1956

IVORY TOWER
Record Label: Deluxe
Songwriters: Jack Fulton, Lois Steele

Top-10 R&B/Top-20 R&R crossover. Covered by Gale Storm (Dot, '56), Cathy Carr (Fraternity, '56).

PAUL WILLIAMS

1949

THE HUCKLEBUCK
Producer: Teddy Reig
Record Label: Savoy
Songwriters: Roy Alfred, Andy Gibson

The honking sax call of the wild introduces a generation to "The Twist" of its era, a #1 R&B (12 weeks)/Top-10 R&R crossover, covered by Roy Milton (Specialty, '49), Tommy Dorsey (RCA, '49), Frank Sinatra (Columbia, '49), and, of course, Chubby Checker (Parkway, '61).

VANESSA WILLIAMS

1988

DREAMIN'
Album: The Right Stuff
Record Label: Wing
Songwriters: Lisa Montgomary, Geneva Paschal, Michael Forte

Unstoppable actress, model, and beauty queen conquers the Pop arena, with a #1 R&B/Top-10 R&R crossover.

1992

RUNNING BACK TO YOU
Album: The Comfort Zone
Record Label: Wing
Songwriters: Kenni Hairston, Trevor Gale

#1 R&B/Top-20 R&R crossover.

SAVING THE BEST FOR LAST
Album: The Comfort Zone
Record Label: Wing
Songwriters: Wendy Waldman, Phil Galdston, Jon Lind

Answering the question whatever happened to Wendy Waldman, this #1 R&B/#1 R&R crossover moved the songwriter one small step closer to Diane Warren territory.

1993

LOVE IS
Album: Beverly Hills 90210 Soundtrack
Record Label: Giant
Songwriter: Steve Krikorian (Tonio K.)

With crooner Brian McKnight, a remarkably straightforward and uplifting ballad from the pen of the usually twisted and cryptic writer.

VICTORIA WILLIAMS

1990

SUMMER OF DRUGS
Album: Swing the Statue
Record Label: Rough Trade
Songwriter: Victoria Williams

Harrowing response to the "Summer of Love," 25 years later. Covered by Soul Asylum (Thirsty Ear/Chaos, '93).

1994

CRAZY MARY
Album: Loose
Record Label: Atlantic
Songwriter: Victoria Williams

Character portrait of the year. Covered by Pearl Jam (Chaos/Columbia, '93).

SONNY BOY WILLIAMSON

1951

EYESIGHT TO THE BLIND
Record Label: Trumpet
Songwriter: Aleck Miller (Sonny Boy Williamson)

First modern genius of the blues harp, paved the way for Junior Wells and Paul Butterfield. Covered by the Larks (Apollo, '51) and by the Who in Tommy *(Decca, '69).*

WILLIE & RUTH

1954

LOVE ME
Record Label: Spark
Songwriters: Jerry Leiber, Mike Stoller

Cover by Elvis Presley (RCA, '56), was not released as a single yet made #2 on the R&R charts.

CHUCK WILLIS

1952

MY STORY
Record Label: Okeh
Songwriter: Chuck Willis

First R&B hit for the mellow singer/songwriter.

1954

I FEEL SO BAD
Producer: Zenas "Big Daddy" Sears
Record Label: Okeh
Songwriter: Chuck Willis

Like a ballgame on a rainy day. Covered by Elvis Presley (RCA, '61).

YOU'RE STILL MY BABY
Producer: Zenas "Big Daddy" Sears
Record Label: Atlantic
Songwriter: Chuck Willis

1956

IT'S TOO LATE
Producer: Zenas "Big Daddy" Sears
Record Label: Atlantic
Songwriter: Chuck Willis

Country flavored R&B classic. Covered by Buddy Holly & the Crickets (Coral, '58), Derek & Dominoes (Atlantic, '70).

1957

C.C. RIDER
Producers: Ahmet Ertegun, Jerry Wexler
Record Label: Atlantic
Songwriters: Ma Rainey, Chuck Willis

First crossover hit for the influential R&B singer/songwriter/King of the Stroll. Originated by Blues legend Ma Rainey. Covered by the Animals (MGM, '64).

1958

BETTY AND DUPREE
Producers: Ahmet Ertegun, Jerry Wexler
Album: King of the Stroll
Record Label: Atlantic
Songwriter: Chuck Willis

Tackling the "Frankie & Johnny" myth.

HANG UP MY ROCK AND ROLL SHOES
Producer: Zenas "Big Daddy" Sears
Record Label: Atlantic
Songwriter: Chuck Willis

B-side of "What Am I Living For." Not the first rocker to contemplate the choice of selling-out, buying in, or going your own way. Would die before he'd get the chance to make that decision.

WHAT AM I LIVING FOR
Producer: Zenas "Big Daddy" Sears
Record Label: Atlantic
Songwriter: Chuck Willis
His biggest hit, a Top-10 R&B/Top-10 R&R crossover, on the charts the day he died.

THE WILLOWS
1956

CHURCH BELLS MAY RING
Record Label: Melba
Songwriters: Tony Middleton, Richard Davis, Ralph Martin, Joe Martin, Marty Craft
Perfectly embodying the eternal harmony and bliss of Doo-Wop, the anti-Blues.

BOB WILLS AND HIS TEXAS PLAYBOYS
1940

SAN ANTONIO ROSE
Record Label: Okeh
Songwriter: Bob Wills
Their most famous Texas Swing tune. Covered by Floyd Cramer (RCA, '61).

WILSON PHILLIPS
1990

HOLD ON
Producer: Glen Ballard
Album: Wilson Phillips
Record Label: SBK
Songwriters: Glen Ballard, Chynna Phillips, Carnie Wilson
Scions of Beach Boy Brian (Wilson) and Papa John (Phillips) produce second generation ephemeral Pop/Rock.

IMPULSIVE
Producer: Glen Ballard
Album: Wilson Phillips
Record Label: SBK
Songwriters: Steve Kipner, Cliff Magness

RELEASE ME
Producer: Glen Ballard
Album: Wilson Phillips
Record Label: SBK
Songwriters: Wilson Phillips
Where have you gone, Olivia Newton-John?

YOU'RE IN LOVE
Producer: Glen Ballard
Album: Wilson Phillips
Record Label: SBK

Songwriter: Glen Ballard, Wilson Phillips
Third #1 from album. Ace of Base would soon arrive to fill this slot. Ballard would move onto the more outspoken Alanis Morissette.

AL WILSON
1973

SHOW AND TELL
Producer: Jerry Fuller
Album: Show and Tell
Record Label: Rocky Road
Songwriter: Jerry Fuller
His biggest hit and only #1 was originally the B-side of "Queen of the Ghetto."

BRIAN WILSON
1988

LOVE AND MERCY
Producers: Brian Wilson, Russ Titelman
Album: Brian Wilson
Record Label: Reprise
Songwriters: Brian Wilson, Eugene Landy
With Warner Brothers royalty at the board and Wilson's therapist in the credits, a poignant statement of purpose nonetheless.

RIO GRANDE
Producers: Brian Wilson, Lenny Waronker, Andy Paley
Album: Brian Wilson
Record Label: Reprise
Songwriters: Brian Wilson, Andy Paley
Getting back to work on "Surf's Up." In another seven years there would be Orange Crate Art, *with Van Dyke Parks.*

JACKIE WILSON
1957

REET PETITE
Producer: Dick Jacobs
Album: He's So Fine
Record Label: Brunswick
Songwriters: Roquel Davis (Tyran Carlo), Berry Gordy Jr.
With a title borrowed from Louis Jordan, the careers of two former Detroit boxers move from Golden Gloves that much closer to gold records.

1958

LONELY TEARDROPS
Producers: Dick Jacobs, Nat Tarnopol

Album: Lonely Teardrops
Record Label: Brunswick
Songwriters: Roquel Davis (Tyran Carlo), Berry Gordy Jr., Gwen Gordy
First #1 R&B/Top-10 crossover for the magnificently gifted R&B crooner. Also the song he was singing when a heart attack on stage put him into a coma from which he'd never emerge.

TO BE LOVED
Producer: Milton DeLugg
Album: He's So Fine
Record Label: Brunswick
Songwriter: Berry Gordy Jr.
One of the great voices of the R&B/Doo-Wop age breaks out of Detroit with his first big soulful, operatic R&B/R&R crossover.

1959

I'LL BE SATISFIED
Producers: Dick Jacobs, Nat Tarnopol
Record Label: Brunswick
Songwriters: Roquel Davis (Tyran Carlo), Berry Gordy, Jr., Gwen Gordy
Your basic R&B, uptempo; a Top-10 R&B/Top-20 R&R crossover.

THAT'S WHY
Producers: Dick Jacobs, Nat Tarnopol
Record Label: Brunswick
Songwriters: Roquel Davis (Tyran Carlo), Berry Gordy, Jr., Gwen Gordy
Padding the coffers for Detroit's musical legacy in the making, Gordy's Motown edifice. Wilson, however, its spiritual heir, would never be part of it.

YOU BETTER KNOW IT
Producers: Dick Jacobs, Nat Tarnopol
Record Label: Brunswick
Songwriters: Jackie Wilson, Norm Henry
#1 R&B/Top-40 R&R crossover.

1960

ALONE AT LAST
Producer: MDL
Record Label: Brunswick
Songwriter: Johnny Lehmann (words & adaptation of music)
Based on the 1st Movement of Tchaikovsky's Piano Concerto in B-flat minor.

DOGGIN' AROUND
Producers: Dick Jacobs, Nat Tarnopol
Album: Jackie Sings the Blues

Record Label: Brunswick
Songwriter: Lena Agree

One of his bluesiest; #1 R&B/Top-20 R&R crossover. B-side of "Night."

NIGHT

Producer: MDL
Record Label: Brunswick
Songwriters: Johnny Lehman, Herb Miller

Another operatic flight, his biggest R&R hit; a Top-5 R&B/R&R crossover.

A WOMAN, A LOVER, A FRIEND

Producers: Dick Jacobs, Nat Tarnopol
Record Label: Brunswick
Songwriter: Sid Wyche

#1 R&B/Top-20 R&R crossover.

1961

MY EMPTY ARMS

Record Label: Brunswick
Songwriters: Al Kasha, Hank Hunter

Less than six months after Elvis had a hit with "O Sole Mio," Jackie responded with this tune, based on "Vesti La Giubba."

1963

BABY, WORKOUT

Album: Baby, Workout
Record Label: Brunswick
Songwriters: Jackie Wilson, Alonzo Tucker

His biggest rocker, a #1 R&B/Top-5 R&R crossover.

1967

(YOUR LOVE KEEPS LIFTING ME) HIGHER AND HIGHER

Producer: Carl Davis
Album: Higher and Higher
Record Label: Brunswick
Songwriters: Gary L. Jackson, Carl Smith, Raynard Miner, Roquel Davis (Tyran Carlo)

The definitive, enduring Jackie. His first #1 R&B/Top-10 R&R crossover in four years and his last.

JESSE WINCHESTER
1971

YANKEE LADY

Producer: Robbie Robertson
Album: Jesse Winchester
Record Label: Ampex
Songwriter: Jessie Winchester

The laconic signature tune of a man twice exiled, from his native South, and his native U.S. Covered by Brewer & Shipley (Kama Sutra, '73).

BEATRICE WINDE
1971

TENTH AND GREENWICH

Album: *Ain't Supposed to Die a Natural Death* Original Cast Album
Record Label: A&M
Songwriter: Melvin Van Peebles

Haunting ode to the Women's House of Detention, introduced in Van Peebles' classic musical prelude to the blaxploitation heyday of '70s Soul.

WINGER
1989

HEADED FOR A HEARTBREAK

Producer: Beau Hill
Album: Winger
Record Label: Atlantic
Songwriter: Kip Winger

Hair guitar.

PETE WINGFIELD
1975

EIGHTEEN WITH A BULLET

Producers: Pete Wingfield, Barry Hammond
Album: Breakfast Special
Record Label: Island
Songwriters: Barry Hammond, William Wingfield

Retro-Doo Wop novelty from England.

THE WINSTONS
1969

COLOR HIM FATHER

Producer: Don Carroll
Album: Color Him Father
Record Label: Metromedia
Songwriter: Richard Spencer

Pop/Soul; Top-10 R&B/R&R crossover.

EDGAR WINTER GROUP
1972

FRANKENSTEIN

Producer: Rick Derringer
Album: They Only Come out at Night
Record Label: Epic
Songwriter: Edgar Winter

Monster instrumental.

FREE RIDE

Producer: Rick Derringer
Album: They Only Come out at Night
Record Label: Epic
Songwriter: Dan Hartman

Southern rock, from Texas, with a touch of Glam.

JOHNNY WINTER
1974

ROCK AND ROLL HOOCHIE KOO

Producer: Rick Derringer
Album: Johnny Winter And
Record Label: Columbia
Songwriter: Rick Derringer

Party down anthem, covered by a million struggling American bar bands through the '70s. Derringer released his own version (Blue Sky, '74).

STEVE WINWOOD
1981

WHILE YOU SEE A CHANCE

Producer: Steve Winwood
Album: Arc of a Diver
Record Label: Island
Songwriters: Steve Winwood, Will Jennings

Former English Blues/Rock prodigy (Spencer Davis Group, Traffic) returns to the singles charts with a lilting adult ballad.

1986

BACK IN THE HIGH LIFE AGAIN

Producers: Steve Winwood, Russ Titleman
Album: Back in the High Life
Record Label: Island
Songwriters: Steve Winwood, Will Jennings

The best beer commercial he never made. Fellow pubstalkers, Eric Clapton and the men of Genesis, took note.

THE FINER THINGS

Producers: Steve Winwood, Russ Titleman
Album: Back in the High Life
Record Label: Island
Songwriters: Steve Winwood, Will Jennings

Winwood scores again with the ladies who lunch.

HIGHER LOVE

Producers: Steve Winwood, Russ Titleman
Album: Back in the High Life

Record Label: Island
Songwriter: Steve Winwood, Will Jennings

With Jennings as his Bernie Taupin, Winwood achieves his first U.S. #1.

1988

DON'T YOU KNOW WHAT THE NIGHT CAN DO

Producers: Steve Winwood, Tom Lord-Alge
Album: Roll with It
Record Label: Virgin
Songwriters: Steve Winwood, Will Jennings

ROLL WITH IT

Producers: Steve Winwood, Tom Lord-Alge
Album: Roll with It
Record Label: Virgin
Songwriters: Steve Winwood, Will Jennings

His biggest single.

WIRE
1977

106 BEATS THAT

Producer: Mike Thorne
Album: Pink Flag
Record Label: Harvest
Songwriters: Colin Newman, Graham Lewis

Staccato signals and constant information. Art school punk minimalism from abroad that would reach American Rock critics, and some influential bands, here and there, R.E.M., the Cure, and U2 among them.

FRAGILE

Producer: Mike Thorne
Album: Pink Flag
Record Label: Harvest
Songwriters: Colin Newman, Graham Lewis

Their anti-Arena Rock ballad.

I AM THE FLY

Producer: Mike Thorne
Album: Pink Flag
Record Label: Harvest
Songwriter: Colin Newman, Graham Lewis

From their landmark album, even terser than the Ramones.

REUTERS

Producer: Mike Thorne
Album: Pink Flag
Record Label: Harvest

Songwriters: Colin Newman, Graham Lewis

STRANGE

Producer: Mike Thorne
Album: Pink Flag
Record Label: Harvest
Songwriters: Colin Newman, Graham Lewis, Bruce Gilbert, Robert Gotobed

Covered by R.E.M. (IRS, '87).

WISH (FEATURING FONDA RAE)
1985

TOUCH ME (ALL NIGHT LONG)

Record Label: Personal
Songwriters: Delyle Carmichael, Patrick Adams

Covered by Cathy Dennis (Polydor, '90).

BILL WITHERS
1971

AIN'T NO SUNSHINE

Producer: Bill Withers
Album: Just As I Am
Record Label: Sussex
Songwriter: Bill Withers

Pop flavored Top-10 R&B/R&R crossover.

1972

LEAN ON ME

Producer: Bill Withers
Album: Still Bill
Record Label: Sussex
Songwriter: Bill Withers

#1 R&B/R&R crossover, covered by Club Nouveau (Tommy Boy, '87). Inspired a movie.

USE ME

Producer: Bill Withers
Album: Still Bill
Record Label: Sussex
Songwriter: Bill Withers

#1 R&B/Top-10 R&R follow up to "Lean on Me." Rock for adults.

PETER WOLF
1984

LIGHTS OUT

Producers: Peter Wolf, Michael Jonzun
Album: Lights Out
Record Label: EMI-America
Songwriters: Peter Wolf, Don Covay

Former leader of the J. Geils Band has a solo flight, having just married Faye Dunaway. Billy Joel empathized.

BOBBY WOMACK
1972

WOMAN'S GOTTA HAVE IT

Album: Understanding
Record Label: United Artists
Songwriters: Bobby Womack, Linda Cooke, Darryl Carter

Critically revered R&B journeyman with his biggest post-Valentinos hit; #1 R&B/Bottom-40 R&R crossover, written with his wife, Sam Cooke's daughter.

STEVIE WONDER
1962

FINGERTIPS

Producer: Berry Gordy, Jr.
Album: The Jazz Soul of Little Stevie
Record Label: Tamla
Songwriters: Henry Cosby, Clarence Paul

Adopting Ray Charles as his honorary Uncle, (Little) Stevie would prove to be more than kin to that blind genius of the Rock and R&B keyboard. His fourth release on Tamla would be his first #1 R&B/R&R crossover, even if he didn't know what key to play it in.

1966

A PLACE IN THE SUN

Producer: Clarence Paul
Album: Down to Earth
Record Label: Tamla
Songwriters: Ronald Miller, Bryan Wells

UPTIGHT (EVERYTHING'S ALRIGHT)

Producers: Henry Cosby, William Stevenson
Album: Uptight
Record Label: Tamla
Songwriters: Stevie Wonder, Sylvia Moy, Henry Cosby

His second #1 R&B/Top-10 R&R crossover.

1967

I WAS MADE TO LOVE HER

Producer: Henry Cosby
Album: I Was Made to Love Her
Record Label: Tamla
Songwriters: Stevie Wonder, Henry Cosby, Lula Mae Hardaway

Somewhere between Franklie Lymon and

Michael Jackson (and Johnny Puleo); another #1 R&B/Top-10 R&R crossover.

1968

FOR ONCE IN MY LIFE
Producer: Henry Cosby
Album: For Once in My Life
Record Label: Columbia
Songwriters: Ronald Miller, Orlando Murden

The original by Tony Bennett (Columbia, '67), stiffed.

SHOO-BE-DOO-BE-DOO-DAY
Producer: Henry Cosby
Album: For Once in My Life
Record Label: Tamla
Songwriters: Stevie Wonder, Henry Cosby, Sylvia Moy

#1 R&B/Top-10 R&R crossover.

1969

MY CHERIE AMOUR
Producer: Henry Cosby
Album: My Cherie Amour
Record Label: Tamla
Songwriters: Stevie Wonder, Henry Cosby, Sylvia Moy

Going after Smokey Robinson's mid-tempo crown. Suggested segue: "Michelle" by the Beatles.

YESTER-ME YESTER-YOU YESTERDAY
Producer: Johnny Bristol
Album: My Cherie Amour
Record Label: Tamla
Songwriters: Ronald Miller, Bryan Wells

Middle-of-the-Soul road.

1970

HEAVEN HELP US ALL
Producers: Ronald Miller, Tom Baird
Album: Signed, Sealed, Delivered
Record Label: Tamla
Songwriter: Ronald Miller

Invoking the religious spirit of the troubled era. Suggested segues: "Instant Karma" by John Lennon, "Put Your Hand in the Hand" by Ocean, "Jesus Is Just All Right" by the Byrds, "Spirit in the Sky" by Norman Greenbaum.

IF YOU REALLY LOVE ME
Producer: Stevie Wonder
Album: Where I'm Coming From
Record Label: Tamla
Songwriters: Stevie Wonder, Syreeta Wright

Like Goffin & King and Barry & Greenwich, the married songwriting team of Syreeta & Stevie was doomed to break up—with only a year's worth of success to show for it before the painful divorce. Suggested segue: Jeff Beck's version of Wonder's tune for Syreeta, "Cause We've Ended As Lovers."

SIGNED, SEALED, DELIVERED I'M YOURS
Producer: Stevie Wonder
Album: Signed, Sealed, Delivered
Record Label: Tamla
Songwriters: Stevie Wonder, Lee Garrett, Lula Mae Hardaway, Syreeta Wright

The entire Wonder family celebrates his new contract with a #1 R&B/Top-10 R&R crossover.

1972

SUPERSTITION
Producer: Stevie Wonder
Album: Talking Book
Record Label: Tamla
Songwriter: Stevie Wonder

Taking over his own writing and production reigns, Stevie finds a new soulful voice, adult perspective, rocking attitude, and his first #1 R&B/R&R crossover in nearly a decade, with a song he wrote for Jeff Beck.

SUPERWOMAN (WHERE WERE YOU WHEN I NEEDED YOU)
Producer: Stevie Wonder
Album: Music of My Mind
Record Label: Tamla
Songwriter: Stevie Wonder

Bye-bye Syreeta.

YOU ARE THE SUNSHINE OF MY LIFE
Producer: Stevie Wonder
Album: Talking Book
Record Label: Tamla
Songwriter: Stevie Wonder

Smokey Wonder.

1973

HIGHER GROUND
Producer: Stevie Wonder
Album: Innervisions
Record Label: Tamla
Songwriter: Stevie Wonder

Secular R&B gospel, a #1 R&B/Top-10 R&R crossover. Covered by Red Hot Chili Peppers (EMI, '89).

LIVIN' FOR THE CITY
Producer: Stevie Wonder
Album: Innervisions

Record Label: Tamla
Songwriter: Stevie Wonder

From the windows of his mind, Stevie creates an urban anthem; #1 R&B/Top-10 R&R crossover. Suggested segue: "Up on the Roof" and "Under the Boardwalk" by the Drifters.

1974

BOOGIE ON REGGAE WOMAN
Producer: Stevie Wonder
Album: Fulfillingness First Finale
Record Label: Tamla
Songwriter: Stevie Wonder

#1 R&B/Top-10 R&R crossover.

YOU HAVEN'T DONE NOTHIN'
Producer: Stevie Wonder
Album: Fulfillingness First Finale
Record Label: Tamla
Songwriter: Stevie Wonder

His fourth #1 R&B/R&R crossover.

1976

I WISH
Producer: Stevie Wonder
Album: Songs in the Key of Life
Record Label: Tamla
Songwriter: Stevie Wonder

#1 R&B/R&R crossover.

ISN'T SHE LOVELY
Producer: Stevie Wonder
Album: Songs in the Key of Life
Record Label: Tamla
Songwriter: Stevie Wonder

Giving birth to another classic.

PASTIME PARADISE
Producer: Stevie Wonder
Album: Songs in the Key of Life
Record Label: Tamla
Songwriter: Stevie Wonder

This tune had a featured role in the modern R&B classic "Gangsta's Paradise," introduced by Coolio in the film Dangerous Minds (MCA, '95).

SIR DUKE
Producer: Stevie Wonder
Album: Songs in the Key of Life
Record Label: Tamla
Songwriter: Stevie Wonder

Another #1 R&B/R&R crossover, and his biggest hit.

1979

SEND ONE YOUR LOVE
Producer: Stevie Wonder
Album: Journey Through the Secret Life of Plants
Record Label: Tamla
Songwriter: Stevie Wonder

1980

I AIN'T GONNA STAND FOR IT
Producer: Stevie Wonder
Album: Hotter Than July
Record Label: Tamla
Songwriter: Stevie Wonder

LATELY
Producer: Stevie Wonder
Album: Hotter Than July
Record Label: Tamla
Songwriter: Stevie Wonder
Covered by Jodeci (Uptown, '93).

MASTER BLASTER (JAMMIN')
Producer: Stevie Wonder
Album: Hotter Than July
Record Label: Tamla
Songwriter: Stevie Wonder
#1 R&B/Top-10 R&R crossover.

1982

DO I DO
Producer: Stevie Wonder
Album: Stevie Wonder's Original Musicquarium
Record Label: Tamla
Songwriter: Stevie Wonder

THAT GIRL
Producer: Stevie Wonder
Album: Stevie Wonder's Original Musiquarium
Record Label: Tamla
Songwriter: Stevie Wonder
#1 R&B/Top-10 R&R crossover.

1984

I JUST CALLED TO SAY I LOVE YOU
Producer: Stevie Wonder
Album: *The Woman in Red* Soundtrack
Record Label: Motown
Songwriter: Stevie Wonder
His big movie ballad is a #1 R&B/R&R crossover.

1985

PART-TIME LOVER
Producer: Stevie Wonder
Album: In Square Circle
Record Label: Motown
Songwriter: Stevie Wonder
His 8th #1 R&B/R&R crossover. Only Michael Jackson has more (if you count his five with the Jackson 5).

1986

GO HOME
Producer: Stevie Wonder
Album: In Square Circle
Record Label: Motown
Songwriter: Stevie Wonder

1987

SKELETONS
Producer: Stevie Wonder
Album: Characters
Record Label: Motown
Songwriter: Stevie Wonder
#1 R&B/Top-20 R&R crossover.

YOU WILL KNOW
Producer: Stevie Wonder
Album: Characters
Record Label: Motown
Songwriter: Stevie Wonder
His 16th #1 R&B hit.

1991

JUNGLE FEVER
Album: *Jungle Fever* Soundtrack
Record Label: Motown
Songwriter: Stevie Wonder
Theme from the Spike Lee movie launches Wonder's 4th decade on the charts. In 1995 he'd win another Grammy.

BRENTON WOOD

1967

GIMME LITTLE SIGN
Producers: Joseph Hooven, Jerry Winn
Album: Oogum Boogum
Record Label: Double Shot
Songwriters: Alfred Smith, Joseph Hooven, Jerry Winn
Mid-tempo soul in the Brook Benton mold. Robert Cray was listening when he wasn't practicing guitar.

SHEB WOOLEY

1958

THE PURPLE PEOPLE EATER
Producer: Neeley Plumb
Album: Sheb Wooley
Record Label: M-G-M
Songwriter: Sheb Wooley
Novelty hit.

WORLD PARTY

1986

ALL COME TRUE
Producer: Karl Wallinger
Album: Private Revolution
Record Label: Chrysalis
Songwriter: Karl Wallinger
Ex-Waterboy Wallinger's debut hit with his own band echoes the Stones.

1990

WAY DOWN NOW
Producer: Karl Wallinger
Album: Goodbye Jumbo
Record Label: Chrysalis
Songwriter: Karl Wallinger
Four years later, still echoing the Stones, but adding traces of the Beatles and Dylan. A few years later, new-generation Beatle bands would be cloning up all over England.

LINK WRAY

1958

RUMBLE
Producer: Milt Grant
Record Label: Cadence
Songwriter: Link Wray
Instrumental version of teen gang warfare, à la "West Side Story" and Wray's trusty Dan Electro Longhorn. So effective it was banned on New York radio.

1959

RAWHIDE
Producer: Milt Grant
Record Label: Epic
Songwriters: Milt Grant, Link Wray
Instrumentally tackling the roots of gang violence, Dodge City style.

WRECKLESS ERIC

1978

WHOLE WIDE WORLD
Producer: Lowe, Nick
Album: Wreckless Eric

Record Label: Stiff
Songwriter: Eric Goulden
(Wreckless Eric)
Legendary Stiff single, stiffed.

WRECKX-N-EFFECT
1992

RUMP SHAKER
Album: Hard or Smooth
Record Label: MCA
Songwriters: Aquil Davidson, David Wynn, Markell Riley, Teddy Riley, Anton Hollins
Modern R&B move.

THE WRENS
1955

(WILL YOU) COME BACK MY LOVE
Producer: George Goldner
Record Label: Rama
Songwriter: Bobby Mansfield
Seminal classic of the Doo-Wop era. Covered by the Cardinals (Atlantic, '55).

BETTY WRIGHT
1971

CLEAN UP WOMAN
Producers: Willie Clarke, Clarence Reid
Album: I Love the Way You Love
Record Label: Alston
Songwriters: Willie Clarke, Clarence Reid
Before Helen Reddy sang "I Am Woman," 19-year-old Betty, from Miami, could already see right through it.

GARY WRIGHT
1976

DREAM WEAVER
Producer: Gary Wright
Album: Dream Weaver
Record Label: Warner Brothers
Songwriter: Gary Wright
Moody blahs.

LOVE IS ALIVE
Producer: Gary Wright
Album: Dream Weaver
Record Label: Warner Brothers
Songwriter: Gary Wright
Spooky toothless.

O.V. WRIGHT
1965

YOU'RE GONNA MAKE ME CRY
Album: O.V. Wright
Record Label: Back Beat
Songwriter: Deadric Malone
Memphis link between Otis Redding and Al Green. Covered by the Staple Singers (Stax, '70).

1967

EIGHT MEN AND FOUR WOMEN
Producer: Willie Mitchell
Album: Eight Men and Four Women
Record Label: Back Beat
Songwriter: Deadric Malone
His biggest R&B hit. Suggested segue: "There Is Something on Your Mind (Part 2)" by Bobby Marchan.

1970

ACE OF SPADE
Producer: Willie Mitchell
Album: A Nickel and a Nail/Ace of Spades
Record Label: Backbeat
Songwriter: Deadric Malone
His biggest R&R hit.

TAMMY WYNETTE
1968

STAND BY YOUR MAN
Producer: Billy Sherrill
Album: Stand by Your Man
Record Label: Epic
Songwriters: Tammy Wynette, Billy Sherrill
Two years before "Clean up Woman," Tammy got a #1 C&W/#1 U.K./Top-20 R&R crossover with these mainstream sentiments in the face of the counter-culture.

X

X
1980

LOS ANGELES
Producer: Ray Manzarek
Album: Los Angeles
Record Label: Slash
Songwriters: John Doe, Exene Cervenka
The slashing and burning of L.A.

WHITE GIRL
Producer: Ray Manzarek
Album: Los Angeles
Record Label: Slash
Songwriters: John Doe, Exene Cervenka
Lawrence Ferlinghetti's Coney Island of the Mind goes west and south to meet the downtrodden masses.

1981

WE'RE DESPERATE
Producer: Ray Manzarek
Album: Wild Gift
Record Label: Slash
Songwriters: John Doe, Exene Cervenka
Ground-breaking Rockabilly Punk track from L.A., featured in the '81 documentary The Decline of Western Civilization.

1982

HUNGRY WOLF
Producer: Ray Manzarek
Album: Under the Big Black Sun
Record Label: Elektra
Songwriters: John Doe, Exene Cervenka
Suggested segue: "Will the Wolf Survive" by Los Lobos.

RIDING WITH MARY
Producer: Ray Manzarek
Album: Under the Big Black Sun
Record Label: Elektra
Songwriters: John Doe, Exene Cervenka
One of their most powerful efforts.

UNDER THE BIG BLACK SUN
Producer: Ray Manzarek
Album: Under the Big Black Sun
Record Label: Elektra
Songwriters: John Doe, Exene Cervenka
Suggested segue: "Black Hole Sun" by Soundgarden.

X-RAY SPECS
1978

OH BONDAGE, UP YOURS!
Producer: Fallon Street
Album: Germ-Free Adolescents
Record Label: EMI
Songwriter: Poly Syrene
Proto girl-group performance highlight of the '78 film Punk Rock Movie, and the '81 film DOA: A Rite of Passage.

XSCAPE
1993

JUST KICKIN' IT
Producer: Jermaine Dupri
Album: Hummin' Comin' at Cha'
Record Label: So So Def/Columbia
Songwriters: Jermaine Dupri,
   Manuel Seals

Hip-Hop groove.

UNDERSTANDING
Producer: Jermaine Dupri
Album: Hummin' Comin' at 'Cha
Record Label: So So Def/Columbia
Songwriter: Manuel Seal

In the decade of the crossover, a #1 R&B/Top-10 R&R ditty.

XTC
1979

THIS IS POP
Producer: Mutt Lange
Album: White Music
Record Label: Virgin
Songwriter: Andy Partridge

Archetypal English art band's impure indulgence for Pop people.

1980

LIVING THROUGH ANOTHER CUBA
Producer: Steve Lillywhite
Album: Black Sea
Record Label: Virgin
Songwriter: Andy Partridge

In a rare power-protest mode.

1982

MAKING PLANS FOR NIGEL
Producer: Steve Lillywhite
Album: Drums and Wires
Record Label: Virgin/Epic
Songwriter: Andy Partridge

Art Rock goes to Oxford, in Oxford shoes. Covered by Primus (Interscope, '93).

SENSES WORKING OVERTIME
Producers: Hugh Padgham, XTC
Album: English Settlement
Record Label: Epic
Songwriter: Andy Partridge

Entering their lush Beatles-esque phase; their biggest hit in the U.K.

1987

DEAR GOD
Producer: Todd Rundgren
Album: Skylarking
Record Label: Geffen
Songwriter: Andy Partridge

Atheist anthem. Suggested segue: "One of Us" by Joan Osborne.

EARN ENOUGH FOR US
Producer: Todd Rundgren
Album: Skylarking
Record Label: Geffen
Songwriter: Andy Partridge

A glorious anomaly: Working-class Pop Rock.

SUMMER'S CAULDRON
Producer: Todd Rundgren
Album: Skylarking
Record Label: Geffen
Songwriter: Andy Partridge

"One Summer Night" in England.

1989

GARDEN OF EARTHLY DELIGHTS
Producer: Paul Fox
Album: Oranges and Lemons
Record Label: Geffen
Songwriter: Andy Partridge

Perfecting their Beatles-esque worldview.

HOLD ME DADDY
Producer: Paul Fox
Album: Oranges and Lemons
Record Label: Geffen
Songwriter: Andy Partridge

The angst-written wordaholic confesses. Suggested segue: "Mother" by John Lennon.

MAYOR OF SIMPLETON
Producer: Paul Fox
Album: Oranges and Lemons
Record Label: Geffen
Songwriter: Andy Partridge

Their biggest U.S. hit.

1992

BALLAD OF PETER PUMPKINHEAD
Producer: Gus Dudgeon
Album: Nonsuch
Record Label: Geffen
Songwriter: Andy Partridge

Covered by Crash Test Dummies in the movie Dumb and Dumber (RCA, '94).

Y

Y & T
1985

SUMMERTIME GIRLS
Album: Open Fire
Record Label: A&M
Songwriter: Y & T

San Francisco work-horse rockers attempt Top-40.

YARBROUGH AND PEOPLES
1981

DON'T STOP THE MUSIC
Producers: Lonnie Simmons, Jonah
   Ellis
Album: The Two of Us
Record Label: Mercury
Songwriters: Lonnie Simmons,
   Jonah Ellis, Alisa Peoples

Soul goes to the Disco; their biggest hit, a #1 R&B/Top-20 R&R crossover.

1984

DON'T WASTE YOUR TIME
Album: Be a Winner
Record Label: Total Experience
Songwriter: Jonah Ellis

#1 R&B/Top-50 R&R crossover.

THE YARDBIRDS
1964

I WISH YOU WOULD
Producer: Giorgio Gomelsky
Album: For Your Love
Record Label: Epic
Songwriter: Billy Boy Arnold

Prototypical Chicago Blues raver was a Marquee Club show-stopper and their first single release, with Allen Toussaint's "A Certain Girl" on the B-side. The Rolling Stones were watching. Covered by the Blasters (Rolling Rock, '80).

1965

EVIL HEARTED YOU
Producer: Paul Samwell-Smith
Album: Having a Rave up with the
   Yardbirds
Record Label: Epic
Songwriter: Graham Gouldman

Big hit in the U.K.

FOR YOUR LOVE

Producer: Paul Samwell-Smith
Album: For Your Love
Record Label: Epic
Songwriter: Graham Gouldman

First trans-Atlantic Top-10 crossover for England's original Heavy Metal band. Guitar god Eric Clapton quit the band before this tune was released. Jeff Beck replaced him.

HEART FULL OF SOUL

Producer: Paul Samwell-Smith
Album: Having a Rave up with the Yardbirds
Record Label: Epic
Songwriter: Graham Gouldman

On their second and last Top-10 hit, Beck imitates a sitar on his fuzz box. Covered by Chris Isaak (Reprise, '87).

I AIN'T DONE WRONG

Producer: Giorgio Gomelsky
Album: For Your Love
Record Label: Epic
Songwriter: Keith Relf

I'M NOT TALKING

Producer: Giorgio Gomelsky
Album: For Your Love
Record Label: Epic
Songwriter: Mose Allison

Appreciating the subtle genius of Blues scholar Mose Allison. The Who were listening.

STILL I'M SAD

Producer: Paul Samwell-Smith
Album: Having a Rave up with the Yardbirds
Record Label: Epic
Songwriters: James McCarty, Paul Samwell-Smith

B-side of "Evil Hearted You" continues their early Indian-music-inspired psychedelic experimentations.

YOU'RE A BETTER MAN THAN I

Producer: Sam Phillips
Album: Having a Rave up with the Yardbirds
Record Label: Epic
Songwriters: Brian Hugg, Michael Hug

Recorded in Memphis at the same session that produced their immortal rendition of "Train Kept a-Rollin'" (later co-opted by Aerosmith), this track features Jeff Beck's bravura and possibly landmark use of a variety of electric guitar effects that would
become standard to the guitar hero repertoire in the years to come.

1966

HAPPENINGS TEN YEARS TIME AGO

Producer: Simon Napier-Bell
Album: Yardbirds' Greatest Hits
Record Label: Epic
Songwriters: Keith Relf, James McCarty, Jeff Beck, Jimmy Page

Beck and Page in a rare collaboration.

JEFF'S BOOGIE

Producers: Paul Samwell-Smith, Simon Napier-Bell
Album: Over Under Sideways Down
Record Label: Columbia
Songwriter: Jeff Beck

Beck would mine this vein further in the Jeff Beck Group, with Rod Stewart as his vocalist.

OVER UNDER SIDEWAYS DOWN

Producers: Paul Samwell-Smith, Simon Napier-Bell
Album: Over Under Sideways Down
Record Label: Epic
Songwriters: Keith Relf, James McCarty, Jeff Beck, Paul Samwell-Smith, Chris Dreja

Their last U.K. hit.

SHAPES OF THINGS

Producer: Giorgio Gomelsky
Album: Yardbirds' Greatest Hits
Record Label: Epic
Songwriters: Keith Relf, James McCarty, Paul Samwell-Smith

1967

LITTLE GAMES

Producer: Mickie Most
Album: Little Games
Record Label: Epic
Songwriters: Harold Spiro, Phil Wainman

STROLL ON

Producer: Peter Spargo
Album: *Blow Up* Soundtrack
Record Label: MGM
Songwriters: Keith Relf, James McCarty, Jeff Beck, Chris Dreja

As seen in the fashionable film Blow Up, *while they bash their guitars à la Townshend.*

1968

GOODNIGHT SWEET JOSEPHINE

Record Label: Epic
Songwriter: Anthony Hazard

Their last single.

WHITE SUMMER

Producer: Mickie Most
Album: Little Games
Record Label: Epic
Songwriter: Jimmy Page

Suggested segues: "She Moves Through the Fair," by Davey Graham; "Black Mountain Side" by Led Zeppelin.

YAZOO

1982

ONLY YOU

Producers: Yazoo, Eric Radcliffe
Album: Upstairs at Eric's
Record Label: Sire
Songwriter: Vince Clarke

First trans-Atlantic hit for the dance Rock stylist Clarke after leaving Depeche Mode on the way to Erasure.

YES

1971

YOURS IS NO DISGRACE

Producers: Eddie Offord, Yes
Album: The Yes Album
Record Label: Atlantic
Songwriters: Jon Anderson, Chris Squire, Bill Bruford, Steve Howe, Tony Kaye

The epitome of British Progressive Rock, the sound of the American FM '70s.

1972

AND YOU AND I

Producers: Eddie Offord, Yes
Album: Close to the Edge
Record Label: Atlantic
Songwriters: Jon Anderson, Chris Squire, Bill Bruford, Steve Howe

Early magnum opus.

CLOSE TO THE EDGE

Producer: Eddie Offord
Album: Close to the Edge
Record Label: Atlantic
Songwriters: Jon Anderson, Steve Howe, Yes

Bach and roll bacchanal.

HEART OF THE SUNRISE
Producers: Eddie Offord, Yes
Album: Fragile
Record Label: Atlantic
Songwriters: Jon Anderson, Chris Squire, Bill Bruford

LONG DISTANCE RUNAROUND
Producers: Eddie Offord, Yes
Album: Fragile
Record Label: Atlantic
Songwriter: Jon Anderson

ROUNDABOUT
Producers: Eddie Offord, Yes
Album: Fragile
Record Label: Atlantic
Songwriters: Jon Anderson, Steve Howe

Their signature opus and biggest hit of the '70s.

1983

OWNER OF A LONELY HEART
Producer: Trevor Horn
Album: 90125
Record Label: Atco
Songwriters: Trevor Rabin, Jon Anderson, Chris Squire, Trevor Horn

Watering down their sound for a Top-40 comeback.

YO LA TENGO
1993

NOWHERE NEAR
Producers: Roger Moutenot, Fred Brockman
Album: Painful
Record Label: Matador
Songwriters: Ira Kaplan, Georgia Hubley

Low-fi drone raver, in the Sonic Youth mode.

YOUNG JESSIE
1955

MARY LOU
Record Label: Modern
Songwriters: Ron Hawkins, Jacqueline Magill

Covered by Ronnie Hawkins (Roulette, '59).

JESSE COLIN YOUNG
1964

FOUR IN THE MORNING
Album: Soul of a City Boy
Record Label: Capitol

Songwriter: Jesse Colin Young
Folk Blues staple of the Jerry White radio show. Covered by Jesse's Folk Rock group, the Youngbloods (RCA, '67).

YOUNG M.C.
1989

BUST A MOVE
Producers: Michael Ross, Matt Dike
Album: Stone Cold Rhymin'
Record Label: Delicious
Songwriters: Marvin Young (Young M.C.), Matt Dike, Michael Ross

Crossover Rap track—street-smart, but not dangerous.

JOHN PAUL YOUNG
1978

LOVE IS IN THE AIR
Producers: Harry Vanda, George Young
Album: Love Is in the Air
Record Label: Scotti Brothers
Songwriters: Harry Vanda, George Young

Fluffy Pop Rock. Vanda and Young wrote "Friday on My Mind" for the Easybeats.

NEIL YOUNG
1969

COWGIRL IN THE SAND
Producers: David Briggs, Neil Young
Album: Everybody Knows This Is Nowhere
Record Label: Reprise
Songwriter: Neil Young

Young finds his muse.

DOWN BY THE RIVER
Producers: David Briggs, Neil Young
Album: Everybody Knows This Is Nowhere
Record Label: Reprise
Songwriter: Neil Young

Epic neo-west Folk Rock answer to "Hey Joe." Covered by Buddy Miles (Mercury, '70) and the Brooklyn Bridge (Buddah, '70). Featured in the '69 film The Strawberry Statement.

I'VE LOVED HER SO LONG
Producer: Jack Nitzsche
Album: Neil Young
Record Label: Reprise
Songwriter: Neil Young

Unrequited Neil.

LAST TRIP TO TULSA
Producer: Jack Nitzsche
Album: Neil Young
Record Label: Reprise
Songwriter: Neil Young

Extended metaphorical explorations. Suggested segue: "The History of Utah" by Camper Van Beethoven.

THE LONER
Producer: Jack Nitzsche
Album: Neil Young
Record Label: Reprise
Songwriter: Neil Young

Stating Young's theme and credo.

1970

AFTER THE GOLDRUSH
Producers: David Briggs, Neil Young, Kendall Pacios
Album: After the Goldrush
Record Label: Reprise
Songwriter: Neil Young

A loner again after a stint with Crosby, Stills and Nash, Young hits his solo stride with this classic history of San Francisco.

CINNAMON GIRL
Producers: David Briggs, Neil Young
Album: Everybody Knows This Is Nowhere
Record Label: Reprise
Songwriter: Neil Young

Classic Neil, with Crazy Horse. Contains the notable pre-Grunge spastic guitar part that the entire city of Seattle was probably weaned on.

DON'T LET IT BRING YOU DOWN
Producers: David Briggs, Neil Young, Kendall Pacios
Album: After the Goldrush
Record Label: Reprise
Songwriter: Neil Young

Prescription for the pervasive post-Woodstock malaise of a generation.

ONLY LOVE CAN BREAK YOUR HEART
Producers: David Briggs, Neil Young, Kendall Pacios
Album: After the Goldrush
Record Label: Reprise
Songwriter: Neil Young

Mournful Top-10 wannabe. But Neil was no Gene Pitney, thankfully.

SOUTHERN MAN

Producers: David Briggs, Neil Young, Kendall Pacios
Album: After the Goldrush
Record Label: Reprise
Songwriter: Neil Young

Relocating his political rage from Ohio to Alabama.

WHEN YOU DANCE (I CAN REALLY LOVE)

Producers: David Briggs, Neil Young, Kendall Pacios
Album: After the Gold Rush
Record Label: Reprise
Songwriter: Neil Young

A homage to the Turbans.

1972

HEART OF GOLD

Producers: Elliot Mazur, Neil Young
Album: Harvest
Record Label: Reprise
Songwriter: Neil Young

In search of a simple rhyme and a simpler time, Neil loses his heart, but gains his only #1 single.

THE NEEDLE AND THE DAMAGE DONE

Producers: Elliot Mazur, Neil Young
Album: Harvest
Record Label: Reprise
Songwriter: Neil Young

The unraveling of a drug-soaked era, written for his late pal Danny Whitten, about whom Nils Lofgren wrote "Beggar's Day."

OLD MAN

Producers: Elliot Mazur, Neil Young
Album: Harvest
Record Label: Reprise
Songwriter: Neil Young

Suggested segue: "Bookends" by Simon and Garfunkel.

1976

LONG MAY YOU RUN

Album: Long May You Run
Record Label: Reprise
Songwriter: Neil Young

With buddy Stephen Stills as the Stills Young Band. Their run was very short, thankfully.

1977

LIKE A HURRICANE

Album: American Stars and Bars
Record Label: Reprise
Songwriter: Neil Young

Fierce rocker.

SUGAR MOUNTAIN

Album: Decade
Record Label: Reprise
Songwriter: Neil Young

Neil's epic farewell to childhood, written in the '60s. Joni Mitchell heard it and wrote "The Circle Game." Used in his film Rust Never Sleeps.

1978

COMES A TIME

Producers: David Briggs, Neil Young, Jim Mulligan, Ben Keith
Album: Comes a Time
Record Label: Reprise
Songwriter: Neil Young

Moving back to Folk Rock.

LOTTA LOVE

Album: Comes a Time
Record Label: Reprise
Songwriter: Neil Young

Covered by Nicolette Larson (Warner Brothers, '79).

1979

RUST NEVER SLEEPS (HEY HEY MY MY INTO THE BLACK)

Producers: Neil Young, David Briggs, Tim Mulligan
Album: Rust Never Sleeps
Record Label: Reprise
Songwriter: Neil Young

From whence came the maxim: "It's better to burn out than to fade away."

1988

THIS NOTE'S FOR YOU

Album: This Note's for You
Record Label: Reprise
Songwriter: Neil Young

Anti-commerce diatribe with the Bluenotes: Young's answer to "Money for Nothing" by Dire Straits.

1989

ROCKIN' IN THE FREE WORLD

Producers: Nico Bolas, Neil Young
Album: Freedom
Record Label: Reprise
Songwriter: Neil Young

The '80s are over. A flannel anthem for the new world from the forever-inflammable Young.

1992

HARVEST MOON

Producers: David Briggs, Neil Young
Album: Harvest Moon

Record Label: Reprise
Songwriter: Neil Young

Answering his own earlier acoustic album, Harvest (Reprise, '72).

PHILADELPHIA

Album: *Philadelphia* Soundtrack
Record Label: Epic Soundtrax
Songwriter: Neil Young

The other great song from the soundtrack.

1994

CHANGE YOUR MIND

Producers: David Briggs, Neil Young
Album: Sleeps with Angels
Record Label: Reprise
Songwriter: Neil Young

Reunited with Crazy Horse, Neil dedicated this tune to his surrogate Rock and Roll heir, the late Kurt Cobain of Nirvana.

PIECE OF CRAP

Producers: David Briggs, Neil Young
Album: Sleeps with Angels
Record Label: Reprise
Songwriter: Neil Young

One of his funniest and truest laments.

SLEEPS WITH ANGELS

Producers: David Briggs, Neil Young
Album: Sleeps with Angels
Record Label: Reprise
Songwriter: Neil Young

Neil's next collaboration would be with Cobain's staunchest competitor, Eddie Vedder of Pearl Jam.

YOUTH OF TODAY

1988

FLAME STILL BURNS

Album: We're Not in This Alone
Record Label: Revelation
Songwriter: Ray Cappo

Positive Rap by a future devotee of Hari Krishna.

TIMI YURO

1962

WHAT'S A MATTER BABY (IS IT HURTING YOU)

Record Label: Liberty
Songwriter: Clyde Otis

One of the more aggressive female voices of the pre-Joplin '60s.

Z

JOHN ZACHERLE
1958

DINNER WITH DRAC
Album: Spook Along with Z
Record Label: Cameo
Songwriter: John Zacherle

Halloween novelty from the DJ/horror-movie host.

ZAGER AND EVANS
1969

IN THE YEAR 2525 (EXORDIUM AND TERMINUS)
Producers: Denny Zager, Rick Evans
Album: In the Year 2525 (Exordium and Terminus)
Record Label: RCA
Songwriter: Rick Evans

From Lincoln, Nebraska into the 26th century. The #1 one-shot of one-shots.

FRANK ZAPPA
1969

PEACHES EN REGALIA
Producer: Frank Zappa
Album: Hot Rats
Record Label: Bizarre
Songwriter: Frank Zappa

One of his classic guitar extravaganzas.

WILLIE THE PIMP (PARTS I AND II)
Producer: Frank Zappa
Album: Hot Rats
Record Label: Bizarre
Songwriter: Frank Zappa

Zappa in Beefheart territory. Tom Waits was eavesdropping.

1971

DANCE OF THE ROCK AND ROLL INTERVIEWERS
Producer: Frank Zappa
Album: *Frank Zappa's 200 Motels* Soundtrack
Record Label: United Artists
Songwriter: Frank Zappa

From Zappa's Rock documentary 200 Motels, with the Royal Philharmonic Orchestra.

1974

DON'T EAT THE YELLOW SNOW
Producer: Frank Zappa
Album: Apostrophe

Record Label: DiscReet
Songwriter: Frank Zappa

One of his three chart singles.

PENGUIN IN BONDAGE
Producer: Frank Zappa
Album: Roxy and Elsewhere
Record Label: DiscReet
Songwriter: Frank Zappa

1979

DANCIN' FOOL
Producer: Frank Zappa
Album: Sheik Yerbouti
Record Label: Zappa
Songwriter: Frank Zappa

Zappa invades the disco for his biggest single. But it was no "Last Dance."

JOE'S GARAGE
Producer: Frank Zappa
Album: Joe's Garage, Act I
Record Label: Zappa
Songwriter: Frank Zappa

One of the more personal memoirs of his funky beginnings.

1982

VALLEY GIRL
Producer: Frank Zappa
Album: Ship arriving too late to save a drowning witch
Record Label: Barking Pumpkin
Songwriters: Frank Zappa, Moon Zappa

With daughter Moon, Zappa's penchant if not compulsion for satire remains undimmed.

WARREN ZEVON
1976

CARMELITA
Producer: Jackson Browne
Album: Warren Zevon
Record Label: Asylum
Songwriter: Warren Zevon

Covered by Linda Ronstadt (Asylum, '77).

EXCITABLE BOY
Producers: Jackson Browne, Waddy Wachtel
Album: Excitable Boy
Record Label: Asylum
Songwriters: Warren Zevon, Leroy Marinell

A defining gem of the L.A. singer/songwriter school of the '70s.

POOR POOR PITIFUL ME
Producer: Jackson Browne
Album: Warren Zevon
Record Label: Asylum
Songwriter: Warren Zevon

Covered by Linda Ronstadt (Asylum, '77). Suggested segues: "White Rhythm and Blues" by Linda Ronstadt, "Mr. Pitiful" by Otis Redding.

1978

LAWYERS, GUNS AND MONEY
Producers: Jackson Browne, Waddy Wachtel
Album: Excitable Boy
Record Label: Asylum
Songwriter: Warren Zevon

Later, Browne would answer this with his own "Lawyers in Love."

WEREWOLVES OF LONDON
Producers: Jackson Browne, Waddy Wachtel
Album: Excitable Boy
Record Label: Asylum
Songwriters: Warren Zevon, Robert Wachtel, Leroy Marinell

His signature Hollywood name-dropping anthem, co-starring James Taylor, Jackson Browne, and Brian De Palma. Featured in the '86 movie The Color of Money and sung on his appearance on "The Larry Sanders Show" in '93.

1987

DETOX MANSION
Producers: Warren Zevon, Andrew Slater
Album: Sentimental Hygiene
Record Label: Virgin
Songwriters: Warren Zevon, Jorge Calderon

Confessions of a substance abuser.

EVEN A DOG CAN SHAKE HANDS
Album: Sentimental Hygiene
Record Label: Virgin
Songwriters: Warren Zevon, Peter Buck, Bill Berry, Mike Mills

Taking over the Stipe role in R.E.M.

1990

SEARCHING FOR A HEART
Album: *Love at Large* Soundtrack
Record Label: Movie Music
Songwriter: Warren Zevon

Used even more powerfully in the Lawrence Kasdan epic of baby-boom generational malaise Grand Canyon (Milan, '92).

1991

RENEGADE
Producer: Waddy Wachtel
Album: Mr. Bad Example
Record Label: Giant
Songwriter: Warren Zevon

One of his Folk Rock peaks, comparing an alternate-culture reprobate to a surviving Civil War soldier.

ZHANE

1993

HEY MR. DJ
Producer: Naughty by Nature
Album: Roll with the Flava
Record Label: Motown
Songwriters: Renee Neufville, Kier Gist, Vincent Brown, Anthony Criss, Leon Ware, Zane Grey, Arthur Bahr

Reinventing the Marvelettes.

THE ZOMBIES

1964

SHE'S NOT THERE
Producer: Ken Jones
Album: The Zombies
Record Label: Parrot
Songwriter: Rod Argent

Their first classic hit, the male version of the Jaynetts's "Sally Go Round the Roses." Covered by Santana (Columbia, '77).

TELL HER NO
Producer: Ken Jones
Album: The Zombies
Record Label: Parrot
Songwriter: Rod Argent

1967

TIME OF THE SEASON
Producers: Rod Argent, Chris White
Album: Odyssey and Oracle
Record Label: Date
Songwriter: Rod Argent

Enduring Jazz-flavored mystic rocker. Traffic would further mine this groove.

ZZ TOP

1973

LA GRANGE
Producer: Bill Ham
Album: Tres Hombres
Record Label: London
Songwriters: Billy Gibbons, Dusty Hill, Frank Beard

Texas Hard Rock boogie celebrating the best little whorehouse in Texas. Carol Hall would use the same inspiration for the off-Broadway play (and later on, Broadway) "The Best Little Whorehouse in Texas," which opened in 1977.

1975

TUSH
Producer: Bill Ham
Album: Fandango
Record Label: London
Songwriters: Billy Gibbons, Dusty Hill, Frank Beard

What you're apt to see a lot of in the best little whorehouse in Texas. Also their biggest hit of the '70s. Featured in the '82 film An Officer and a Gentleman.

1983

GIMME ALL YOUR LOVIN'
Producer: Bill Ham
Album: Eliminator
Record Label: Warner Brothers
Songwriters: Billy Gibbons, Dusty Hill, Frank Beard

Rebirth of the boogie.

SHARP DRESSED MAN
Producer: Bill Ham
Album: Eliminator
Record Label: Warner Brothers
Songwriters: Billy Gibbons, Dusty Hill, Frank Beard

Epitomizing the new, hip, made-for-MTV ZZ Top era.

1984

LEGS
Producer: Bill Ham
Album: Eliminator
Record Label: Warner Brothers
Songwriters: Billy Gibbons, Dusty Hill, Frank Beard

One of their two Top-10 R&R singles. Suggested segue: "Hot Legs" by Rod Stewart.

1985

SLEEPING BAG
Producer: Bill Ham
Album: Afterburner
Record Label: Warner Brothers
Songwriters: Billy Gibbons, Dusty Hill, Frank Beard

Their other Top-10 R&R single.

Bibliography

ASCAP. *ASCAP Index of Performed Compositions.* New York: American Society of Composers, Authors and Publishers, 1978.

Betrock, Alan. *Girl Groups: The Story of a Sound.* New York: Delilah Press, 1982.

Bronson, Fred. *Billboard Book of Number One Hits.* New York: Billboard Publications, 1985.

Christgau, Robert. *Christgau's Record Guide, the 70's.* New Haven, CT: Ticknor & Fields, 1981.

Christgau, Robert. *Christgau's Record Guide, the 80's.* New York: Pantheon Books, 1990.

Clark, Al. *The Rock Yearbook, 1984.* New York: St. Martin's Press, 1983.

Coupe, Stuart and Glenn A. Baker. *The New Rock and Roll: The A–Z of Rock in the 80s.* New York: St. Martin's Press, 1983.

Cranna, Ian. *The Rock Yearbook, 1986.* New York: St. Martin's Press, 1985.

Crenshaw, Marshall. *Hollywood Rock.* New York: Harper Perennial, 1994.

Denisoff, R. Serge and Richard Peterson. *The Sounds of Social Change.* Chicago, IL: Rand McNally, 1972.

Dudley, Bonnie. *Phonlog Reports.* San Diego, CA: Trade Service Corporation.

Ehrenstein, David and Bill Reed. *Rock on Film.* New York: Delilah Press, 1982.

Erlewine, Michael and Scott Bultman. *The All Music Guide.* San Francisco: Miller Freeman, 1992.

Escott, Colin. *Tattooed on Their Tongues.* New York: Schirmer Books, 1996.

Escott, Colin and Martin Hawkins. *Good Rockin' Tonight: Sun Records and the Birth of Rock and Roll.* New York: St. Martin's Press, 1991.

George, Nelson. *Where Did Our Love Go: The Rise and Fall of the Motown Sound.* New York: St. Martin's Press, 1986.

Gilbert, Bob and Theroux, Gary. *The Top Ten, 1956–Present.* New York: Fireside Books, 1982.

Gillette, Charlie. *The Sound of the City: The Rise of Rock & Roll.* New York: Outerbridge and Dienstfrey, 1970.

Groia, Philip. *They All Sang on the Corner.* West Hempstead, NY: Phillie Dee Enterprises Inc., 1983.

Guralnick, Peter. *Feel Like Going Home: Portraits in the Blues and Rock and Roll.* New York: Outerbridge and Dienstfrey, 1971.

Guralnick, Peter. *Sweet Soul Music.* New York: Harper & Row, 1986

Helander, Brock. *The Rock Who's Who,* 2nd ed. New York: Schirmer Books, 1996.

Hibbert, Tom. *The Rock Yearbook, 1987.* New York: St. Martin's Press, 1986.

Hirshey, Gerry. *Nowhere to Run: The Story of Soul Music.* New York: Times Books, 1984.

Jackson, John A. *Big Beat Heat: Alan Freed and the Early Years of Rock and Roll.* New York: Schirmer Books, 1991.

Jancik, Wayne and Tad Lathrop. *Cult Rockers.* New York: Fireside Books, 1995.

Larson, Glen. *The Guinness Encyclopedia of Popular Music.* London: Guinness, 1995.

Lax, Roger and Frederick Smith. *The Great Song Thesaurus.* New York: Oxford University Press, 1984.

McAleer, Dave. *British and American Hit Singles, 1960–1990.* London, New York: Omnibus, 1990.

Marcus, Greil. *Stranded: Rock and Roll for a Desert Island.* New York: Alfred A. Knopf, 1979.

Marsh, Dave. *The Heart of Rock & Soul: The 1001 Best Singles Ever Made.* New York: Plume Books, 1989.

Marsh, Dave and John Swenson. *The Rolling Stone Record Guide.* New York: Random House, 1979.

Marsh, Dave and John Swenson. *The New Rolling Stone Record Guide.* New York: Random House, 1983.

Murrels, Joseph. *Million Selling Records from the 1900s to the 1980s.* New York: Arco, 1985.

Nite, Norm N. *Rock On: The Illustrated Encyclopedia of Rock N' Roll.* New York: Popular Library, 1974.

Palmer, Robert. *Baby That Was Rock and Roll: The Legendary Leiber & Stoller.* New York: Harcourt Brace Jovanovich, 1978.

Palmer, Robert. *Deep Blues.* New York: Penguin, 1982.

Pollock, Bruce. *In Their Own Words: Lyrics and Lyricists, 1955–1974.* New York: Macmillan, 1975

Pollock, Bruce. *When Rock Was Young.* New York: Holt, Rinehart & Winston, 1981.

Pollock, Bruce. *When the Music Mattered.* New York: Holt, Rinehart & Winston, 1983.

Pollock, Bruce. *Interviews with Great Songwriters.* Port Chester, NY: Cherry Lane Books, 1986

Pollock, Bruce. *Hipper than Our Kids.* New York: Schirmer Books, 1993.

Pollock, Bruce. *Popular Music: An Anotated Index of American Popular Songs, 1980–1995.* Detroit, MI: Gale Research Co, 1980–1995.

Quirin, Jim and Barry Cohen. *Rock 100.* Covington, LA: Chartmaster, 1976.

Rhode, H. Kandy. *The Gold of Rock and Roll, 1955–1967.* New York: Arbor House, 1970/

Robbins, Ira. *Trouser Press Record Guide,* 4th ed. New York: Collier/Macmillan, 1991.

Romanowski, Patricia and Holly George-Warren. *Rolling Stone Encyclopedia of Rock & Roll.* New York: Fireside Press, 1996.

Roxon, Lillian. *Roxon's Rock Encyclopedia.* New York: Workman Publishing, 1976.

Santelli, Robert. *The Sixties: A Listener's Guide.* Chicago, IL: Contemporary Books, 1985.

Shannon, Bob and John Javna. *Behind the Hits.* New York: Warner Books, 1986.

Shapiro, Nat and Bruce Pollock. *Popular Music: An Anotated Index of American Popular Songs, 1920–1979.* Detroit, MI: Gale Research Co., 1983.

Tosches, Nick. *Unsung Heroes of Rock 'n' Roll.* New York: Harmony Books, 1991.

Various. *Sun Records: The Discography.* Hambergen, Germany: Bear Family Books, 1987.

Various. *The Rolling Stone Record Review.* New York: Pocket Books, 1971.

Whitburn, Joel. *Bubbling Under, 1959–1981.* Menomonee Falls, WI: Record Research, Inc., 1982.

Whitburn, Joel. *Top Pop Albums, 1955–1992.* Menomonee Falls, WI: Record Research, Inc., 1993.

Whitburn, Joel. *Top Country Hits, 1944–1993.* Menomonee Falls, WI: Record Research, Inc., 1994.

Whitburn, Joel. *Top Pop Singles, 1955–1993.* Menomonee Falls, WI: Record Research, Inc., 1994.

Whitburn, Joel. *Pop Annual, 1955–1994.* Menomonee Falls, WI: Record Research, Inc., 1995.

Whitburn, Joel. *Rock Tracks.* Menomonee Falls, WI: Record Research, Inc., 1995.

Whitburn, Joel. *Top R&B Hits, 1942–1995.* Menomonee Falls, WI: Record Research, Inc., 1996.

Williams, Paul. *Rock and Roll: The Best 100 Singles.* New York: Carroll & Graf, 1993.

SELECTED BOX SET BOOKLETS

Cohen, Norm. *Folk Song America.* Washington, DC: Smithsonian Recordings, 1990.

Guterman, Jimmy. *Sun Records Collection.* Santa Monica, CA: Rhino Records, 1984.

Hyde, Bob. *Doo Wop.* Los Angeles, California: Rhino Records, 1993.

McNeil, W. K. *The Blues.* Washington, DC: Smithsonian Recordings, 1993.

Mansfield, Cary and Robert Simms. *Hitsville USA: The Motown Singles Collection.* Los Angeles: Motown Records, 1992.

Marshall, James. *The Okeh Rhythm & Blues Story, 1949–1957.* New York: Sony Legacy, 1993.

Shaw, Greg and Dawn Eden. *The Brill Building Sound.* Plymouth, MN: K-Tel International, 1993.

Vera, Billy. *The Specialty Story.* Berkeley, CA: Specialty Records, 1994.

Song Index

SONG	ARTIST	YEAR	SONG	ARTIST	YEAR
All Alone on Christmas	Love, Darlene	'92	All Those Years Ago	Harrison, George	'81
All Along the Watchtower	Dylan, Bob	'68	All Through the Night	Lauper, Cyndi	'84
All Apologies	Nirvana	'93	All Together Now	Beatles, The	'68
All Around the World (Grits Ain't Groceries)	Stansfield, Lisa	'90	All Tomorrow's Parties	Velvet Underground, The	'67
			All Woman	Stansfield, Lisa	'91
All Around the World	Turner, Titus	'55	All You Need Is Love	Beatles, The	'67
All By Myself	Carmen, Eric	'75	All-American Boy, The	Parsons, Bill	'58
All Come True	World Party	'86	Allentown	Joel, Billy	'82
All Cried Out	Lisa Lisa & Cult Jam	'85	Allergies	Simon, Paul	'83
All Day and All of the Night	Kinks, The	'64	Alley Cat	Fabric, Bent	'62
All for Love	Adams, Bryan, Rod Stewart, Sting	'93	Alley Oop	Hollywood Argyles, The	'60
			Almost Grown	Berry, Chuck	'59
All Grown Up	Crystals, The	'64	Almost Paradise (Love Theme from *Footloose*)	Reno, Mike and Ann Wilson	'84
All Her Favorite Fruit	Camper Van Beethoven	'89			
All I Could Do Was Cry	James, Etta	'60	Almost Saturday Night	Fogerty, John	'75
All I Do Is Think of You	Troop	'90	Alone	Heart	'87
All I Ever Need Is You	Sonny and Cher	'71	Alone Again (Naturally)	O'Sullivan, Gilbert	'72
All I Have to Do Is Dream	Everly Brothers, The	'58	Alone Again Or	Love	'67
All I Know	Garfunkel, Art	'73	Alone at Last	Wilson, Jackie	'60
All I Know Right Now	Crenshaw, Marshall	'85	Alone with You	Campbell, Tevin	'92
All I Need	Temptations, The	'67	Along Came Jones	Coasters, The	'59
All I Need Is a Miracle	Mike & the Mechanics	'85	Along Comes Mary	Association, The	'66
All I Need to Know (Don't Know Much)	Midler, Bette	'83	Alphabet Street	Prince	'88
			Already Gone	Eagles, The	'74
All I Really Want to Do	Dylan, Bob	'64	Alright	Jackson, Janet	'89
All I Wanna Do	Crow, Sheryl	'94	Always	Atlantic Starr	'87
All I Wanna Do Is Make Love to You	Heart	'90	Always	Bon Jovi	'94
			Always on My Mind	Presley, Elvis	'70
All I Want	Toad the Wet Sprocket	'92	Always the Sun	Stranglers, The	'87
All I Want Is You	Miracles, The	'59	Always with Me, Always with You	Satriani, Joe	'87
All in My Mind	Brown, Maxine	'61	Am I Wrong	Love Spit Love	'94
All Is Loneliness	Big Brother & the Holding Company	'68	Amanda	Boston	'86
			Amazing	Aerosmith	'93
All My Love	Led Zeppelin	'79	Amazing Journey	Who, The	'69
All My Loving	Beatles, The	'64	Ambrose, Part V	Laurie, Linda	'59
All Night Long (All Night)	Richie, Lionel	'83	Amelia	Mitchell, Joni	'76
(All of a Sudden) My Heart Sings	Anka, Paul	'58	Amen	Impressions, The	'64
All or Nothing	Milli Vanilli	'89	America	Simon and Garfunkel	'68
All Right Now	Free	'70	American Beat	Fleshtones, The	'79
All She Wants to Do Is Dance	Henley, Don	'85	American City Suite	Cashman and West	'72
All She Wants to Do Is Rock	Harris, Wynonie	'49	American Dreamer	Nyro, Laura	'78
All Shook Up	Presley, Elvis	'57	American Girl	Petty, Tom & the Heartbreakers	'77
All Summer Long	Beach Boys, The	'64			
All That Jazz	Echo & the Bunnymen	'80	American Lovers	Kaye, Thomas Jefferson	'74
All That She Wants	Ace of Base	'93	American Music	Blasters, The	'80
All That You Dream	Little Feat	'78	American Music	Violent Femmes, The	'91
All the King's Horses	Firm, The	'86	American Pie	McLean, Don	'71
All the Man I Need	Sister Sledge	'82	American Tune	Simon, Paul	'73
All the Way from Memphis	Mott the Hoople	'73	American Woman	Guess Who, The	'70
All the Young Dudes	Mott the Hoople	'72	Amie	Pure Prairie League	'75
All This Time	Sting	'91	Amos Moses	Reed, Jerry	'71

SONG	ARTIST	YEAR
Ana Ng	They Might Be Giants	'88
Anarchy in the U.K.	Sex Pistols, The	'77
Anchorage	Michelle Shocked	'88
And I Love Her	Beatles, The	'64
And I'm Telling You I'm Not Going	Holliday, Jennifer	'82
And It Stoned Me	Morrison, Van	'70
And She Was	Talking Heads	'85
And the Beat Goes On	Whispers, The	'79
And the Cradle Will Rock	Van Halen	'80
And When I Die	Nyro, Laura	'67
And You and I	Yes	'72
Angel	Aerosmith	'87
Angel	Franklin, Aretha	'73
Angel	Madonna	'84
Angel Baby	Rosie & the Originals	'60
Angel Eyes	Healey, Jeff Band, The	'89
Angel from Montgomery	Prine, John	'71
Angel in Your Arms	Hot	'77
Angel of Death	Slayer	'86
Angel of Harlem	U2	'88
Angel of the Morning	Rush, Merrilee	'67
Angelia	Marx, Richard	'89
Angels Listened In, The	Crests, The	'59
(Angels Wanna Wear My) Red Shoes	Costello, Elvis	'77
Angie	Rolling Stones, The	'73
Angie Baby	Reddy, Helen	'74
Angry Eyes	Loggins & Messina	'72
Anji	Jansch, Bert	'65
Anna (Go to Him)	Alexander, Arthur	'63
Annette's Got the Hits	Red Cross	'80
Annie Had a Baby	Midnighters, The	'54
Annie, I'm Not Your Daddy	Kid Creole & the Coconuts	'82
Annie's Aunt Fanny	Midnighters, The	'54
Annie's Song	Denver, John	'74
Anniversary	Tony! Toni! Tone!	'93
Anodyne	Uncle Tupelo	'93
Another Brick in the Wall	Pink Floyd	'79
Another Day	McCartney, Paul and Wings	'71
Another Day in Paradise	Collins, Phil	'89
Another Girl	Beatles, The	'65
Another Girl, Another Planet	Only Ones, The	'79
Another Nail in My Heart	Squeeze	'80
Another Night	Real McCoy	'94
Another One Bites the Dust	Queen	'80
Another Part of Me	Jackson, Michael	'87
Another Sad Love Song	Braxton, Toni	'93
Another Saturday Night	Cooke, Sam	'63
Anthrax	Gang of Four	'80
Anticipation	Simon, Carly	'71

SONG	ARTIST	YEAR
Any Day Now	Jackson, Chuck	'62
Any Love	Vandross, Luther	'88
Any Major Dude Will Tell You	Steely Dan	'74
Any Time at All	Beatles, The	'64
Any Way You Want It	Journey	'80
Any Way You Want Me (That's How I Will Be)	Presley, Elvis	'56
Any World (That I'm Welcome To)	Steely Dan	'75
Anyone Who Had a Heart	Warwick, Dionne	'64
Anything That's Part of You	Presley, Elvis	'62
Anytime, Any Place	Jackson, Janet	'93
Anyway, Anyhow, Anywhere	Who, The	'66
Apache	Shadows, The	'60
Apeman	Kinks, The	'70
Appetite	Prefab Sprout	'85
Apples, Peaches, Pumpkin Pie (Ready or Not)	Jay & the Techniques	'67
Aqua Boogie	Parliament	'78
Aqualung	Jethro Tull	'71
Aquarius	5th Dimension, The	'69
Are Friends Electric	Numan, Gary	'79
Are You a Boy or Are You a Girl	Barbarians, The	'65
Are You Experienced	Hendrix, Jimi	'67
Are You Gonna Go My Way	Kravitz, Lenny	'93
Are You Happy Now	Shindell, Richard	'92
Are You Lonely for Me (Baby)	Scott, Freddie	'67
Are You Lonesome Tonight	Presley, Elvis	'60
Are You Ready	Pacific Gas & Electric	'70
Are You Sure Hank Done It This Way	Jennings, Waylon	'75
Ariel	Friedman, Dean	'77
Arizona	Lindsay, Mark	'69
Armegeddon It	Def Leppard	'87
Arms of Mary	Sutherland Brothers and Quiver	'76
Arnold Layne	Pink Floyd	'67
Around and Around	Berry, Chuck	'59
Around the Way Girl	L.L. Cool J	'90
Arthur's Theme (Best That You Can Do)	Cross, Christopher	'81
As Tears Go By	Faithfull, Marianne	'64
As the Years Go Passing By	King, Albert	'69
Ashes Are Burning	Renaissance	'73
Ashes to Ashes	Bowie, David	'80
Astral Plane	Modern Lovers, The	'71
Astronomy Domine	Pink Floyd	'70
At Last	James, Etta	'61
At Midnight (My Love Will Lift You Up)	Rufus	'77
At My Front Door (Crazy Little Mama Song)	El Dorados, The	'55

SONG	ARTIST	YEAR
At Seventeen	Ian, Janis	'75
(At) The End (of a Rainbow)	Grant, Earl	'58
At the Hop	Danny & the Juniors	'57
At This Moment	Billy & the Beaters	'81
At Your Best (You Are Love)	Isley Brothers, The	'76
Atlantic City	Springsteen, Bruce	'82
Atlantis	Donovan	'69
Atomic Dog	Clinton, George	'83
Attics of My Life	Grateful Dead, The	'70
Audience Is Listening, The	Vai, Steve	'90
Authority Song, The	Mellencamp, John Cougar	'83
Autobahn	Kraftwerk	'75
Automatic	Pointer Sisters, The	'84
Avalon	Roxy Music	'82
Avenging Annie	Pratt, Andy	'73
Away	Feelies, The	'88

B

SONG	ARTIST	YEAR
B-A-B-Y	Thomas, Carla	'66
Baba O'Riley	Who, The	'71
Babalu's Wedding Day	Eternals, The	'59
Babe	Styx	'79
Babe, I'm Gonna Leave You	Baez, Joan	'62
Babooshka	Bush, Kate	'80
Baby Baby Baby	TLC	'92
Baby, Baby Don't Cry	Miracles, The	'69
Baby Blue	Echoes, The	'61
Baby Boom Ché	Trudell, John	'92
Baby Boy	Place, Mary Kay	'76
Baby Come Back	Player	'78
Baby Come to Me	Austin, Patti and James Ingram	'81
Baby, Come to Me	Belle, Regina	'89
Baby, Don't Do It	5 Royales, The	'53
Baby Don't Forget My Number	Milli Vanilli	'89
Baby Don't Get Hooked on Me	Davis, Mac	'72
Baby Don't Go	Sonny and Cher	'64
Baby Don't You Do It	Gaye, Marvin	'64
Baby Fall Down	Burnette, T-Bone	'83
Baby Get Lost	Washington, Dinah	'49
Baby Got Back	Sir Mix-a-Lot	'92
Baby Hold On	Money, Eddie	'78
Baby Hold onto Me	Levert, Gerald	'92
Baby I Love You	Franklin, Aretha	'67
Baby, I Love You	Ronettes, The	'63
Baby I Love Your Way	Frampton, Peter	'75
Baby, I Need Your Loving	Four Tops, The	'64
Baby I'm a-Want You	Bread	'71
Baby, I'm for Real	Originals, The	'69

SONG	ARTIST	YEAR
Baby I'm Hooked (Right into Your Love)	Con Funk Shun	'83
Baby I'm Yours	Lewis, Barbara	'63
Baby I'm Yours	Shai	'92
Baby, It's You	Shirelles, The	'61
Baby Jane	Stewart, Rod	'83
Baby Let Me Follow You Down	Dylan, Bob	'62
Baby Let's Play House	Gunter, Arthur	'54
Baby Love	Regina	'86
Baby Love	Supremes, The	'64
Baby, Now That I've Found You	Foundations, The	'67
Baby Oh Baby	Shells, The	'57
Baby Plays Around	Costello, Elvis	'89
Baby, Scratch My Back	Harpo, Slim	'66
Baby Sittin' Boogie	Clifford, Buzz	'61
Baby Stop Crying	Dylan, Bob	'78
Baby Talk	Jan and Dean	'58
Baby That's Backatcha	Robinson, Smokey	'75
Baby, What a Big Surprise	Chicago	'77
Baby, What You Want Me to Do	Reed, Jimmy	'60
Baby, Workout	Wilson, Jackie	'63
Baby, You're a Rich Man	Beatles, The	'67
Baby You're Right	Brown, James & the Famous Flames	'61
Baby (You've Got What It Takes)	Benton, Brook and Dinah Washington	'60
Babydoll	Hole	'91
Baby's in Black	Beatles, The	'65
Back & Forth	Aaliyah	'94
Back and Forth	Cameo	'86
Back Home Again	Denver, John	'74
Back in Black	AC/DC	'80
Back in My Arms Again	Supremes, The	'65
Back in Stride	Maze	'85
Back in the Day	Ahmad	'94
Back in the High Life Again	Winwood, Steve	'86
Back in the Saddle	Aerosmith	'76
Back in the U.S.A.	Berry, Chuck	'59
Back Nine, The	Wainwright, Loudon	'87
Back of a Car	Big Star	'74
Back off Boogaloo	Starr, Ringo	'72
Back on the Chain Gang	Pretenders, The	'84
Back Stabbers	O'Jays, The	'72
Back Street Girl	Rolling Stones, The	'67
Back to Life	Soul II Soul	'89
Back to the Hotel	N2Deep	'93
Back up, Train	Green, Al	'67
Backfield in Motion	Mel and Tim	'69
Backstreets	Springsteen, Bruce	'75
Backwater	Meat Puppets	'94

SONG	ARTIST	YEAR	SONG	ARTIST	YEAR
Bad	Jackson, Michael	'87	Barbara Ann	Regents, The	'61
Bad Blood	Sedaka, Neil	'75	Barefootin'	Parker, Robert	'66
Bad Boy	Miami Sound Machine	'86	Bargain	Who, The	'71
Bad Boy	Palmer, Clarence & the Jive Bombers	'56	Barracuda	Heart	'77
Bad Boys	Inner Circle	'93	Basket Case	Green Day	'94
Bad Case of Lovin' You	Palmer, Robert	'79	Batdance (from *Batman*)	Prince	'89
Bad Girl	Madonna	'92	Battle Hymn of Lieutenant Calley	C. Company featuring Nelson, Terry	'71
Bad Girl	Miracles, The	'59	Battle of New Orleans, The	Horton, Johnny	'59
Bad Girls	Summer, Donna	'79	Be Bop Baby	Nelson, Ricky	'57
Bad Influence	Cray, Robert	'83	Be Careful with a Fool	King, B.B.	'52
Bad Love	Clapton, Eric	'89	Be Good to Yourself	Journey	'86
Bad Medicine	Bon Jovi	'88	Be My Baby	Ronettes, The	'63
Bad Moon Rising	Creedence Clearwater Revival	'69	Be My Guest	Domino, Fats	'59
Bad Reputation	Jett, Joan	'80	Be My Yoko Ono	Barenaked Ladies	'92
Bad Reputation	Johnston, Freedy	'94	Be Near Me	ABC	'85
Bad Sneakers	Steely Dan	'75	Be Thankful for What You Got	De Vaughn, William	'74
Bad Time	Grand Funk Railroad	'75	Be True to Your School	Beach Boys, The	'63
Bad to Me	Kramer, Billy J. & the Dakotas	'63	Beach Baby	Hutton, Danny	'66
Bad to the Bone	Thorogood, George	'82	Beacon from Mars	Kaleidoscope	'68
Bad Trip	Camper Van Beethoven	'85	Bear Cat	Thomas, Rufus	'53
Bad Wisdom	Vega, Suzanne	'92	Beast of Burden	Rolling Stones, The	'78
Bad, Bad Leroy Brown	Croce, Jim	'73	Beat Goes On, The	Sonny and Cher	'67
Badge	Cream	'69	Beat It	Jackson, Michael	'83
Badlands	Springsteen, Bruce	'78	Beat on the Brat	Ramones, The	'76
Baker Street	Rafferty, Gerry	'78	Beat Surrender	Jam, The	'82
Bald Head	Professor Longhair	'50	Beat the Retreat	Thompson, Richard and Linda	'75
Ball and Chain	Big Brother & the Holding Company	'68	Beat(en) Generation, The	The, The	'89
Ball of Confusion (That's What the World Is Today)	Temptations, The	'70	Beatstreet	Grandmaster Flash & The Furious 5 with Mr. Ness and Cowboy	'84
Ballad of a Teenage Queen	Cash, Johnny	'58	Beautiful Delilah	Berry, Chuck	'58
Ballad of a Thin Man	Dylan, Bob	'65	Beautiful Loser	Seger, Bob	'75
Ballad of Bonnie and Clyde	Fame, Georgie	'68	Beautiful Maria of My Soul	Los Lobos	'92
Ballad of Easy Rider	Byrds, The	'69	Beautiful Morning, A	Rascals, The	'68
Ballad of Ira Hayes	Cash, Johnny	'64	Beautiful People	Melanie	'69
Ballad of John and Yoko, The	Beatles, The	'69	Beauty & Sadness	Smithereens, The	'82
Ballad of Lucy Jordan	Faithfull, Marianne	'80	Beauty Is Only Skin Deep	Temptations, The	'66
Ballad of Peter Pumpkinhead	XTC	'92	Beauty School Dropout	Paul, Alan, Marya Small and Choir	'72
Ballad of the Green Berets, The	Staff Sgt. Sadler, Barry	'66	Be-Bop-a-Lula	Vincent, Gene	'56
Ballroom Blitz	Sweet, The	'75	Because	Beatles, The	'69
Banana Boat Song, The	Tarriers, The	'57	Because	Clark, Dave Five, The	'64
Band of Gold	Payne, Freda	'70	Because I Love You	Stevie B.	'90
Band on the Run	McCartney, Paul & Wings	'74	Because of Love	Jackson, Janet	'93
Bang a Gong (Get It On)	T. Rex	'72	Because of Love	Smith, Patti	'78
Bang and Blame	R.E.M.	'94	Because the Night	Smith, Patti	'78
Bang Bang (My Baby Shot Me Down)	Cher	'66	Because They're Young	Eddy, Duane	'60
Bang the Drum All Day	Rundgren, Todd	'83	Bed of Roses	Bon Jovi	'92
Bangla-Desh	Harrison, George	'71	Beds Are Burning	Midnight Oil	'87
Bank Robber	Clash, The	'80	Beechwood 4-5789	Marvelettes, The	'62
			Been Caught Stealing	Jane's Addiction	'91

SONG	ARTIST	YEAR	SONG	ARTIST	YEAR
Been on a Train	Nyro, Laura	'71	Big Hunk o' Love, A	Presley, Elvis	'59
Beep a Freak	Gap Band, The	'85	Big Hurt, The	Fischer, Miss Toni	'59
Beep, Beep	Playmates, The	'58	Big Log	Plant, Robert	'83
Beeswing	Thompson, Richard	'93	Big Love	Fleetwood Mac	'87
Before I Let You Go	Blackstreet	'94	Big Man	Four Preps, The	'58
Before the Deluge	Browne, Jackson	'74	Big Man in Town	Four Seasons, The	'64
Before You Accuse Me	Diddley, Bo	'57	Big Man on Mulberry Street	Joel, Billy	'86
Beggar's Day	Crazy Horse	'71	Big Shot	Joel, Billy	'78
Beginnings	Chicago	'69	Big Sky, The	Bush, Kate	'85
Behind Blue Eyes	Who, The	'71	Big Time	Gabriel, Peter	'86
Behind Closed Doors	Rich, Charlie	'73	Big Train from Memphis	Fogerty, John	'85
Behind the Wall	Chapman, Tracy	'88	Big Yellow Taxi	Mitchell, Joni	'70
Behind the Wall of Sleep	Smithereens, The	'86	Bigelow 6-200	Lee, Brenda	'56
Being for the Benefit of Mr. Kite	Beatles, The	'67	Biggest Part of Me	Ambrosia	'80
Being with You	Robinson, Smokey	'81	Bigmouth Strikes Again	Smiths, The	'86
Bela Lugosi's Dead	Bauhaus	'79	Bikini Drag	Pyramids, The	'64
Believe Me	Royal Teens, The	'59	Biko	Gabriel, Peter	'80
Believe What You Say	Nelson, Ricky	'58	Billie Jean	Jackson, Michael	'83
Bell Bottom Blues	Derek & the Dominoes	'70	Billy	Linden, Kathy	'58
Belle	Green, Al	'77	Billy, Don't Be a Hero	Donaldson, Bo & the Heywoods	'74
Bells, The	Reed, Lou	'79			
Ben	Jackson, Michael	'72	Bird Dog	Everly Brothers, The	'58
Bend Me, Shape Me	American Breed	'67	Bird Is the Word, The	Rivingtons, The	'63
Bennie and the Jets	John, Elton	'73	Bird on the Wire	Collins, Judy	'68
Berlin	Reed, Lou	'73	Birdies	Pere Ubu	'81
Bernadette	Four Tops, The	'67	Birdland	Weather Report	'77
Best Disco in Town, The	Ritchie Family, The	'76	Birds and the Bees, The	Akens, Jewel	'64
Best of My Love	Eagles, The	'74	Birmingham Bounce	Gunter, Hardrock & the Pebbles	'50
Best of My Love	Emotions, The	'77			
Best of Times, The	Styx	'81	Birmingham Sunday	Baez, Joan	'64
Best Thing That Ever Happened to Me, The	Knight, Gladys & the Pips	'73	Birth, School, Work, Death	Godfathers, The	'88
			Birthday	Beatles, The	'68
Best Things in Life Are Free, The	Jackson, Janet	'92	Birthday	Sugarcubes	'88
Betcha by Golly Wow	Stylistics, The	'71	Birthday Suit	Kemp, Johnny	'89
Beth	Kiss	'76	Bitch	Rolling Stones, The	'71
Bette Davis Eyes	DeShannon, Jackie	'75	Bitch Is Back, The	John, Elton	'74
Better Be Good to Me	Turner, Tina	'84	Bits and Pieces	Clark, Dave Five, The	'64
Better by You, Better Than Me	Spooky Tooth	'69	Bitterest Pill (I Ever Had to Swallow), The	Jam, The	'82
Better Man	Pearl Jam	'94			
Betty and Dupree	Willis, Chuck	'58	Bizarre Love Triangle	New Order	'86
Between Trains	Robertson, Robbie	'83	Black	Pearl Jam	'91
Beyond the Sea	Darin, Bobby	'59	Black & White	Three Dog Night	'72
Bicycle Race	Queen	'78	Black and Blue	Van Halen	'88
Big Bad John	Dean, Jimmy	'61	Black Angel's Death Song	Velvet Underground	'67
Big Beat, The	Domino, Fats	'58	Black Cat	Jackson, Janet	'89
Big Boss Man	Reed, Jimmy	'61	Black Coffee in Bed	Squeeze	'82
Big Boy Pete	Don and Dewey	'59	Black Denim Trousers and Motorcycle Boots	Cheers, The	'55
Big Empty	Stone Temple Pilots	'94			
Big Eyed Beans from Venus	Captain Beefheart	'72	Black Dog	Led Zeppelin	'71
Big Girls Don't Cry	Four Seasons, The	'62	Black Friday	Steely Dan	'75
			Black Gold	Soul Asylum	'93

SONG	ARTIST	YEAR
Black Hole Sun	Soundgarden	'94
Black Is Black	Los Bravos	'66
Black Magic Woman	Fleetwood Mac	'69
Black Mountain Side	Led Zeppelin	'69
Black Night	Brown, Charles	'51
Black or White	Jackson, Michael	'91
Black Pearl	Charles, Sonny & the Checkmates, Ltd.	'69
Black Sabbath	Black Sabbath	'71
Black Slacks	Bennett, Joe & the Sparkletones	'57
Black Star	Malmsteen, Yngwie	'85
Black Steel in the Hour of Chaos	Public Enemy	'88
Black Velvet	Myles, Alannah	'90
Black Water	Doobie Brothers, The	'74
Blackbird	Beatles, The	'68
Blame It on the Rain	Milli Vanilli	'89
Blanche	Three Friends, The	'56
Blank Generation	Hell, Richard and the Voidoids	'76
Blaze of Glory	Bon Jovi, Jon	'90
Bleecker Street	Simon and Garfunkel	'64
Bless You	Orlando, Tony	'61
Blinded by the Light	Springsteen, Bruce	'73
Blister in the Sun	Violent Femmes	'82
Blitzkrieg Bop	Ramones, The	'76
Blockbuster	Sweet, The	'73
Blonde in the Bleachers	Mitchell, Joni	'72
Blood and Roses	Smithereens, The	'86
Blowing in the Wind	Dylan, Bob	'63
Blue	Mitchell, Joni	'71
Blue Angel	Orbison, Roy	'60
Blue Bayou	Orbison, Roy	'63
Blue Hotel	Isaak, Chris	'87
Blue Jay Way	Beatles, The	'67
Blue Jean	Bowie, David	'84
Blue Monday	Domino, Fats	'57
Blue Monday	New Order	'83
Blue Money	Morrison, Van	'71
Blue Moon	Marcels, The	'61
Blue Moon of Kentucky	Monroe, Bill	'47
Blue Shadows	Fulson, Lowell	'50
Blue Sky	Allman Brothers, The	'72
Blue Sky Mine	Midnight Oil	'90
Blue Suede Shoes	Perkins, Carl	'56
Blue Velvet	Clovers, The	'55
Blueberry Hill	Domino, Fats	'56
Bluebird	Buffalo Springfield	'67
Blues for Buddah, A	Silencers, The	'90
Blues Power	Clapton, Eric	'80
Blues, The	Tony! Toni! Tone!	'90
Bo Diddley	Diddley, Bo	'55

SONG	ARTIST	YEAR
Boa Constrictor	Silverstein, Shel	'62
Bob George	Prince	'87
Bobbie Sue	Oak Ridge Boys	'82
Bobby Jean	Springsteen, Bruce	'84
Bobby Sox to Stockings	Avalon, Frankie	'59
Bobby's Girl	Blane, Marcie	'62
Bodhisattva	Steely Dan	'73
Bohemian Rhapsody	Queen	'75
Bomber	Motorhead	'79
Bone Machine	Pixies, The	'88
Bong Bong I Love You Madly	Castro, Vince	'58
Bongo Rock	Epps, Preston	'59
Bonita Applebum	Tribe Called Quest, A	'90
Bony Moronie	Williams, Larry	'57
Boobs a Lot	Fugs, The	'65
Boogaloo down Broadway	Fantastic Johnny C.	'67
Boogie Chillen	Hooker, John Lee	'49
Boogie Down	Kendricks, Eddie	'74
Boogie Fever	Sylvers, The	'76
Boogie Nights	Heatwave	'77
Boogie on Reggae Woman	Wonder, Stevie	'74
Boogie Oogie Oogie	Taste of Honey, A	'78
Boogie Wonderland	Earth, Wind & Fire	'79
Book of Love	Monotones, The	'57
Boom Boom	Hooker, John Lee	'62
Boot Em Up	Du Droppers, The	'54
Boots of Spanish Leather	Dylan, Bob	'63
Bootzilla	Bootsy's Rubber Band	'78
Bop Gun (Endangered Species)	Parliament	'77
Bop-Ting-a-Ling	Baker, LaVern	'55
Boppin' the Blues	Perkins, Carl	'56
Border Radio	Blasters, The	'81
Border Song (Holy Moses)	John, Elton	'70
Borderline	Camper Van Beethoven	'89
Borderline	Madonna	'83
Born at the Right Time	Simon, Paul	'90
Born in Chicago	Butterfield, Paul Blues Band	'65
Born in the U.S.A.	Springsteen, Bruce	'84
Born on the Bayou	Creedence Clearwater Revival	'69
Born to Be My Baby	Bon Jovi	'89
Born to Be Wild	Steppenwolf	'68
Born to Lose	Heartbreakers, The	'77
Born to Run	Springsteen, Bruce	'75
Born Too Late	Poni Tails, The	'58
Born under a Bad Sign	King, Albert	'67
Both Sides Now	Collins, Judy	'68
Both Sides of the Story	Collins, Phil	'93
Bottle of Wine	Paxton, Tom	'63
Bottle, The	Scott-Heron, Gil	'75
Bouncing Around the Room	Phish	'95

SONG	ARTIST	YEAR
Bound for Glory	Ochs, Phil	'64
Box of Rain	Grateful Dead, The	'70
Boxcars	Ely, Joe	'78
Boxer, The	Simon and Garfunkel	'69
Boy from New York City, The	Ad Libs, The	'64
Boy in the Bubble, The	Simon, Paul	'86
Boy Named Sue, A	Silverstein, Shel	'69
Boy with a Problem	Costello, Elvis	'82
Boys	Shirelles, The	'60
Boys Are Back in Town, The	Thin Lizzy	'76
Boys Don't Cry	Cure, The	'79
Boys of Summer, The	Henley, Don	'85
Boys to Men	New Edition	'88
Brain Damage	Pink Floyd	'73
Brand New Key	Melanie	'71
Brand New Lover	Dead or Alive	'86
Brandy (Mandy)	English, Scott	'72
Brandy (You're a Fine Girl)	Looking Glass	'72
Brass in Pocket (I'm Special)	Pretenders, The	'80
Brass Monkey	Beastie Boys, The	'86
Bread and Butter	Newbeats, The	'64
Break It down Again	Tears for Fears	'93
Break It to Me Gently	Franklin, Aretha	'77
Break It to Me Gently	Lee, Brenda	'61
Break My Mind	Box Tops, The	'67
Break My Stride	Wilder, Matthew	'83
Break on Through	Doors, The	'67
Break up to Make Up	Stylistics, The	'72
Breakdance	Cara, Irene	'84
Breakdown	Buzzcocks, The	'78
Breakdown	Petty, Tom & the Heartbreakers	'77
Breakin' My Heart (Pretty Brown Eyes)	Mint Condition	'92
Breakin'...There's No Stopping Us	Ollie and Jerry	'84
Breaking in a Brand New Broken Heart	Francis, Connie	'62
Breaking up Is Hard to Do	Sedaka, Neil	'62
Breakout	Swing Out Sister	'87
Breaks, The	Blow, Kurtis	'80
Breakup Song (They Don't Write 'Em), The	Kihn, Greg Band, The	'87
Breathe Again	Braxton, Toni	'93
Breathing	Bush, Kate	'80
Breathless	Lewis, Jerry Lee	'58
Brian Wilson	Barenaked Ladies	'92
Brick House	Commodores, The	'77
Bridge of Sighs	Trower, Robin	'74
Bridge over Troubled Water	Simon and Garfunkel	'69
Bright Lights, Big City	Reed, Jimmy	'61
Brilliant Disguise	Springsteen, Bruce	'87

SONG	ARTIST	YEAR
Bring It on Home to Me	Cooke, Sam	'62
Bring the Boys Home	Payne, Freda	'71
Bring the Noise	Public Enemy	'88
Bringin' on the Heartbreak	Def Leppard	'81
Bristol Stomp, The	Dovells, The	'61
Broken Arrow	Buffalo Springfield	'67
Broken Arrow	Robertson, Robbie	'87
Broken Wings	Mr. Mister	'85
Bron Y' Aur Stomp	Led Zeppelin	'70
Brother Louie	Hot Chocolate	'73
Brother Love's Traveling Salvation Show	Diamond, Neil	'69
Brothers	Vaughan, Stevie Ray and Jimmie	'90
Brothers Gonna Work It Out	Public Enemy	'90
Brothers in Arms	Dire Straits	'85
Brown Eyed Girl	Morrison, Van	'67
Brown Eyed Handsome Man	Berry, Chuck	'57
Brown Shoes Don't Make It	Mothers of Invention, The	'67
Brown Sugar	Rolling Stones, The	'71
Brownsville Girl	Dylan, Bob	'86
Bruised Violet	Babes in Toyland	'90
Bubblegum	Fowley, Kim	'69
Bubblegum Factory	Red Kross	'90
Buddy Holly	Weezer	'94
Buffalo Soldier	Flamingos, The	'70
Buffalo Stance	Cherry, Neneh	'89
Build Me up, Buttercup	Foundations, The	'69
Bullet the Blue Sky	U2	'87
Bump and Grind	Kelly, R.	'94
Bungle in the Jungle	Jethro Tull	'74
Burn	Deep Purple	'74
Burn on, Big River	Newman, Randy	'72
Burn Rubber on Me (Why You Wanna Hurt Me)	Gap Band, The	'82
Burn That Candle	Haley, Bill & His Comets	'55
Burnin' for You	Blue Oyster Cult	'81
Burning Bridges	Scott, Jack	'60
Burning down One Side	Plant, Robert	'82
Burning down the House	Talking Heads	'83
Burning Heart	Survivor	'85
Burning Love	Alexander, Arthur	'69
Bury Manilow	Trotsky Icepick	'87
Bury My Heart at Wounded Knee	Sainte-Marie, Buffy	'92
Bury My Lovely	October Project	'93
Bus Stop	Hollies, The	'66
Bust a Move	Young M.C.	'89
Busted	Cash, Johnny	'63
Bustin' Loose, Pt. I	Booker, Chuckii	'89
Bustin' Out	James, Rick	'79
But I Do	Henry, Clarence "Frogman"	'60

SONG	ARTIST	YEAR	SONG	ARTIST	YEAR
Butterfly	Gracie, Charlie	'57	Can't Get It out of My Head	Electric Light Orchestra	'74
Buzz Buzz Buzz	Hollywood Flames, The	'57	Can't Get There from Here	R.E.M.	'85
Buzzin' Fly	Buckley, Tim	'69	Can't Hardly Wait	Replacements, The	'87
By the Time I Get to Phoenix	Campbell, Glen	'67	Can't Help Falling in Love	Presley, Elvis	'61
Bye Bye Baby	Big Brother & the Holding Company	'68	(Can't Live Without Your) Love and Affection	Nelson	'90
Bye Bye Baby	Wells, Mary	'61	Can't Seem to Make You Mine	Seeds, The	'67
Bye Bye Johnny	Berry, Chuck	'60	Can't Stand Losing You	Police, The	'78
Bye Bye Love	Everly Brothers, The	'57	Can't Stop	After 7	'89
			Can't Stop This Thing We Started	Adams, Bryan	'91
C			Can't Take My Eyes off You	Valli, Frankie	'67
			Can't Truss It	Public Enemy	'91
C.C. Rider	Willis, Chuck	'57	Can't We Be Sweethearts	Cleftones, The	'56
Ca Plane Pour Moi	Plastic Bertrand	'78	Can't We Try	Hill, Dan	'87
Cadillac Walk	Mink DeVille	'77	Can't You Hear My Heartbeat	Herman's Hermits	'65
Cajun Girl	Fairport Convention	'69	Can't You See That She's Mine	Clark, Dave Five, The	'64
Calendar Girl	Sedaka, Neil	'61	Candida	Dawn	'70
California Dreamin'	Mamas and the Papas, The	'66	Candle in the Wind	John, Elton	'73
California Girls	Beach Boys, The	'64	Candy	Cameo	'86
California Saga (Big Sur)	Beach Boys, The	'73	Candy	Pop, Iggy	'90
California Sun	Rivieras, The	'64	Candy Everybody Wants	10,000 Maniacs	'93
California Über Alles	Dead Kennedys, The	'80	Candy Girl	Four Seasons, The	'63
Call It Stormy Monday	Walker, T-Bone	'47	Candy Girl	New Edition	'83
Call Me	Blondie	'80	Candy Man	Orbison, Roy	'61
Call Me	Franklin, Aretha	'69	Cannonball	Breeders, The	'93
Call Me	Skyy	'81	Cannonball	Eddy, Duane	'58
Call Me (Come Back Home)	Green, Al	'73	Cantaloop (Flip Fantasia)	US3	'93
Call Me the Breeze	Cale, J.J.	'72	Cappucino	Lyte, MC	'89
Call Me up in Dreamland	Morrison, Van	'71	Captain for Dark Mornings	Nyro, Laura	'69
Call Mr. Lee	Television	'92	Captain Jack	Joel, Billy	'71
Call on Me	Chicago	'74	Car on a Hill	Mitchell, Joni	'74
Calling Dr. Love	Kiss	'76	Car Wash	Rose Royce	'77
Calling Occupants of Interplanetary Craft	Klaatu	'77	Cara Mia	Jay & the Americans	'65
Calling to You	Plant, Robert	'93	Caravan	Morrison, Van	'69
Camellia	Hall and Oates	'75	Caravan of Love	Isley/Jasper/Isley	'85
Can I Change My Mind	Davis, Tyrone	'68	Carbona Not Glue	Ramones, The	'77
Can I Get a Witness	Gaye, Marvin	'63	Carefree Highway	Lightfoot, Gordon	'74
Can the Can	Quatro, Suzi	'73	Careful There's a Baby in the House	Wainwright, Loudon	'71
Can We Still Be Friends	Rundgren, Todd	'78	Careless Whisper	Wham!	'84
Can We Talk	Campbell, Tevin	'93	Carey	Mitchell, Joni	'71
Can You Please Crawl out Your Window	Dylan, Bob	'65	Caribbean Queen (No More Love on the Run)	Ocean, Billy	'84
Can You Stand the Rain	New Edition	'88	Carmelita	Zevon, Warren	'76
Can You Stop the Rain	Bryson, Peabo	'91	Carnival	Merchant, Natalie	'95
Can't Buy Me Love	Beatles, The	'64	Carol	Berry, Chuck	'58
Can't Fight This Feeling	REO Speedwagon	'85	Carolina in My Mind	Taylor, James	'69
Can't Find My Way Home	Blind Faith	'69	Caroline No	Beach Boys, The	'66
Can't Get Enough	Bad Company	'74	Carrie	Europe	'86
Can't Get Enough of Your Love, Babe	White, Barry	'74	Carrie-Anne	Hollies, The	'67
			Carry It On	Collins, Judy	'65

SONG	ARTIST	YEAR	SONG	ARTIST	YEAR
Carry on Wayward Son	Kansas	'76	Check Yo Self	Ice Cube	'93
Carry That Weight	Beatles, The	'69	Cheeseburger in Paradise	Buffett, Jimmy	'78
Cars	Numan, Gary	'80	Chelsea Girl	Nico	'67
Casanova	Levert	'87	Chelsea Hotel #2	Cohen, Leonard	'74
Casey Jones	Grateful Dead, The	'70	Chelsea Morning	Mitchell, Joni	'69
Cassidy	Weir, Bob	'72	Cheree	Suicide	'77
Cast Your Fate to the Wind	Guaraldi, Vince, Trio	'62	Cherish	Association, The	'66
Castles Made of Sand	Hendrix, Jimi	'68	Cherish	Kool & the Gang	'84
Casual Look, A	Six Teens, The	'56	Cherish	Madonna	'89
Cat Scratch Fever	Nugent, Ted	'77	Cherry Bomb	Mellencamp, John Cougar	'87
Cat's in the Cradle	Chapin, Harry	'74	Cherry Bomb	Runaways, The	'76
Catch Me (I'm Fallin')	Pretty Poison	'87	Cherry Oh Baby	Donaldson, Eric	'71
Catch the Wind	Donovan	'65	Cherry Pie	Marvin and Johnny	'54
Catch Us If You Can	Clark, Dave Five, The	'65	Cherry Pie	Warrant	'90
Catfish	Cocker, Joe	'76	Cherry, Cherry	Diamond, Neil	'66
Catholic School Girls Rule	Red Hot Chili Peppers	'85	Cherry-Coloured Funk	Cocteau Twins	'90
Cathy's Clown	Everly Brothers, The	'60	Chest Fever	Band, The	'68
Caught up in the Rapture	Baker, Anita	'86	Chestnut Mare	Byrds, The	'70
Caught up in You	38 Special	'82	Chevy Van	Johns, Sammy	'75
Cause We've Ended as Lovers	Syreeta	'74	Cheyenne	Del Lords, The	'88
Causing a Commotion	Madonna	'87	Chicago	Nash, Graham	'71
Cease to Exist	Red Cross	'82	Chick-a-Boom	Daddy Dewdrop	'71
Cecilia	Simon and Garfunkel	'69	Chicken Shack Boogie	Milburn, Amos	'48
Celebrate	Three Dog Night	'70	Child of Mine	King, Carole	'71
Celebrated Summer	Hüsker Dü	'85	Children of God	Swans, The	'87
Celebration	Kool & the Gang	'80	Children of the Future	Miller, Steve Band, The	'68
Celluloid Heroes	Kinks, The	'72	Children of the Grave	Black Sabbath	'71
Centerfield	Fogerty, John	'85	Children of the Night	Marx, Richard	'89
Centerfold	Geils J. Band, The	'82	Chimes of Freedom	Dylan, Bob	'64
Certain Girl, A	K-Doe, Ernie	'61	China Cat Sunflower	Grateful Dead, The	'69
C'est La Vie	Nevil, Robbie	'87	China Girl	Pop, Iggy	'77
C'est La Vie (You Never Can Tell)	Berry, Chuck	'64	China Grove	Doobie Brothers, The	'73
Chain Gang	Scott, Bobby	'56	Chinese Rocks	Heartbreakers, The	'77
Chain of Fools	Franklin, Aretha	'67	Chip Chip	McDaniels, Gene	'61
Chain, The	Fleetwood Mac	'77	Chocolate Cake	Crowded House	'91
Chains	Cookies, The	'62	Choice of Colors	Impressions, The	'69
Chains of Love	Erasure	'88	Chokin' Kind, The	Jennings, Waylon	'67
Chains of Love	Turner, Joe	'51	Choo Choo Ch'Boogie	Jordan, Louis & His Tympani Five	'46
Change Is Gonna Come, A	Cooke, Sam	'65			
Change of Heart	Lauper, Cyndi	'86	Choo Choo Train	Box Tops, The	'69
Change Your Mind	Young, Neil	'94	Christine Sixteen	Kiss	'77
Changes	Bowie, David	'71	Christmas (Baby Please Come Home)	Love, Darlene	'63
Changes	Ochs, Phil	'66			
Chantilly Lace	Big Bopper	'58	Christmas Wrapping	Waitresses, The	'81
Chapel of Love	Dixie Cups, The	'64	Christo Redemptor	Byrd, Donald	'63
Charity Ball	Fanny	'71	Chuck E.'s in Love	Jones, Rickie Lee	'79
Charlie Brown	Coasters, The	'59	Church Bells May Ring	Willows, The	'56
Charlie Freak	Steely Dan	'74	Church of the Poison Mind	Culture Club	'83
Chattahoochie	Jackson, Alan	'93	Cinderella's Big Score	Sonic Youth	'90
Cheating in the Next Room	Hill, Z.Z.	'82	Cindy Incidentally	Faces, The	'73
			Cindy Tells Me	Eno, Brian	'77

SONG	ARTIST	YEAR	SONG	ARTIST	YEAR
Cindy's Birthday	Crawford, Johnny	'62	Cod'ine	Sainte-Marie, Buffy	'64
Cinema Show	Genesis	'73	Cold As Ice	Foreigner	'77
Cinnamon Girl	Young, Neil	'70	Cold Blooded	James, Rick	'83
Circle	Brickell, Edie & New Bohemians	'88	Cold Blue Steel and Sweet Fire	Mitchell, Joni	'72
			Cold, Cold Heart	Williams, Hank	'51
Circle Game, The	Sainte-Marie, Buffy	'67	Cold-Hearted	Abdul, Paula	'88
Circle in the Sand	Carlisle, Belinda	'88	Color Him Father	Winstons, The	'69
Cisco Kid	War	'72	Cold Sweat	Brown, James & the Famous Flames	'67
Cities on Flame with Rock and Roll	Blue Oyster Cult	'72			
City of New Orleans, The	Goodman, Steve	'71	Cold Turkey	Lennon, John	'69
Civil War	Guns N' Roses	'91	Colorado	Chase, Chevy	'73
Clair	O'Sullivan, Gilbert	'72	Colorado	Flying Burrito Brothers, The	'71
Clap for the Wolfman	Guess Who, The	'74	Colors	Ice-T	'88
Clapping Song (Clap Pat Clap Slap), The	Ellis, Shirley	'65	Combination of the Two	Big Brother & the Holding Company	'68
Clash City Rockers	Clash, The	'77	Come a Little Bit Closer	Jay & the Americans	'64
Classical Gas	Williams, Mason	'68	Come and Get It	Badfinger	'69
Claudette	Orbison, Roy	'58	Come and Get These Memories	Martha & the Vandellas	'63
Clean up Woman	Wright, Betty	'71	Come and Get Your Love	Redbone	'74
Cleveland Rocks	Hunter, Ian	'79	Come and Stay with Me	Faithfull, Marianne	'65
Cliffs of Dover	Johnson, Eric	'91	Come and Talk to Me	Jodeci	'91
Clock, The	Ace, Johnny	'53	Come as You Are	Nirvana	'91
Close My Eyes Forever	Ford, Lita (with Ozzy Osbourne)	'89	Come Back Baby	Charles, Ray	'54
			Come Back to Me	Jackson, Janet	'89
Close the Door	Pendergrass, Teddy	'78	Come Back When You Grow Up	Vee, Bobby	'66
Close to the Edge	Yes	'72	Come Dancing	Kinks, The	'83
Close to You	Maxi Priest	'90	Come Go with Me	Del Vikings, The	'57
Close Your Eyes	Five Keys, The	'55	Come Go with Me	Expose	'87
Closer	Nine Inch Nails	'94	Come in from the Cold	Mitchell, Joni	'91
Closer Than Friends	Surface	'88	Come in Number-51, Your Time Is Up	Pink Floyd	'69
Closer to Fine	Indigo Girls, The	'89			
Closer to Home	Grand Funk	'70	Come Inside	Intro	'93
Closer to the Heart	Rush	'77	Come Monday	Buffett, Jimmy	'74
Closer You Are, The	Channels, The	'56	Come On	Berry, Chuck	'61
Closest Thing to Perfect	Jackson, Jermaine	'85	Come on down to My Boat	Every Mother's Son	'66
Closing Time	Cohen, Leonard	'92	Come on Eileen	Dexy's Midnight Runners	'83
Cloud Nine	Temptations, The	'68	Come on, Baby	Campbell, Jo-Ann	'57
Cloudbusting	Bush, Kate	'85	Come on, Let's Go	Valens, Ritchie	'58
Clouds, The	Spacemen	'59	Come out and Play	Offspring	'94
Cloudy	Simon and Garfunkel	'66	Come Sail Away	Styx	'77
C'mon & Get My Love	Dennis, Cathy	'90	Come See About Me	Supremes, The	'64
C'mon and Swim	Freeman, Bobby	'64	Come Softly to Me	Fleetwoods, The	'59
C'mon Everybody	Cochran, Eddie	'58	Come to Butt-Head	Beavis and Butt-Head	'93
C'mon Marianne	Four Seasons, The	'67	Come to Me	Johnson, Marv	'58
Coal Miner's Daughter	Lynn, Loretta	'70	Come to My Window	Etheridge, Melissa	'93
Coal Tattoo	Wheeler, Billy Edd	'62	Come to the Sunshine	Harper's Bizarre	'66
Coca Cola Douche	Fugs, The	'65	Come Together	Beatles, The	'69
Cocaine	Clapton, Eric	'77	Come Tomorrow	Manfred Mann	'65
Coconut	Nilsson	'71	Come Undone	Duran Duran	'93
Coconut Grove	Lovin' Spoonful, The	'66	Comes a Time	Young, Neil	'78
Codex	Pere Ubu	'78	Comfortably Numb	Pink Floyd	'79

SONG	ARTIST	YEAR	SONG	ARTIST	YEAR
Comforter	Shai	'92	Cover Girl	New Kids on the Block	'88
Coming Around Again	Simon, Carly	'86	Cover Me	Springsteen, Bruce	'84
Coming into Los Angeles	Guthrie, Arlo	'69	Cover of the *Rolling Stone*	Dr. Hook	'73
Coming on Strong	Lee, Brenda	'66	Cowboy	Newman, Randy	'68
Coming out of the Dark	Estefan, Gloria	'91	Cowboy's Work Is Never Done, A	Sonny and Cher	'72
Coming Up	McCartney, Paul	'80	Cowboys to Girls	Intruders, The	'68
Commercial Rain	Inspiral Carpets	'90	Cowgirl in the Sand	Young, Neil	'69
Common Man	Blasters, The	'85	Crackerbox Palace	Harrison, George	'76
Compared to What	McCann, Les and Eddie Harris	'70	Crackin' Up	Diddley, Bo	'59
Complete Control	Clash, The	'77	Cracklin' Rosie	Diamond, Neil	'70
Concentration Moon	Mothers of Invention, The	'68	Cradle of Love	Idol, Billy	'90
Concrete and Clay	Rambeau, Eddie	'65	Cradle of Love	Preston, Johnny	'60
Coney Island Baby	Excellents, The	'62	Crazay	Johnson, Jesse	'86
Coney Island Baby	Reed, Lou	'76	Crazy	Boys, The	'90
Confession, The	Nyro, Laura	'68	Crazy	Cline, Patsy	'61
Conga	Miami Sound Machine	'86	Crazy	Seal	'91
Connected	Stereo MCs	'93	Crazy Arms	Lewis, Jerry Lee	'56
Conquistador	Procol Harum	'67	Crazy for You	Madonna	'85
Constant Craving	lang, k.d.	'92	Crazy Little Thing Called Love	Queen	'80
Continuing Story of Bungalow Bill, The	Beatles, The	'68	Crazy Love	Morrison, Van	'70
			Crazy Mama	Cale, J.J.	'72
Contort Yourself	Chance, James	'79	Crazy Man, Crazy	Haley, Bill & the Comets	'53
Convoy	McCall, C.W.	'75	Crazy Man Michael	Fairport Convention	'69
Coo Coo	Big Brother & the Holding Company	'68	Crazy Mary	Williams, Victoria	'94
			Crazy on You	Heart	'76
Cool	Pylon	'80	Crazy Train	Osbourne, Ozzy	'81
Cool Change	Little River Band	'79	Cream	Prince	'91
Cool down Boy	Jeffreys, Garland	'77	Creep	Radiohead	'93
Cool for Cats	Squeeze	'79	Creep	TLC	'94
Cool It Now	New Edition	'84	Creeque Alley	Mamas and the Papas, The	'67
Cool Jerk	Capitols, The	'66	Crimson and Clover	James, Tommy & the Shondells	'69
Cool Metro	Johansen, David	'78			
Cool Part I	Time, The	'82	Crippled Inside	Lennon, John	'71
Cool Places	Sparks and Jane Wiedlin	'83	Crocodile Rock	John, Elton	'73
Cop Killer	Body Count	'92	Cross My Broken Heart	Jets, The	'87
Copacabana (at the Copa)	Manilow, Barry	'77	Cross-Eyed Mary	Jethro Tull	'71
Copperhead Road	Earle, Steve	'88	Crossroads	Cream	'68
Copperline	Taylor, James	'91	Crosstown Traffic	Hendrix, Jimi	'68
Corrine, Corrina	Turner, Joe	'41	Crucify	Amos, Tori	'92
Cosmic Slop	Funkadelic	'73	Cruel Little Number	Healey, Jeff Band, The	'92
Cottonfields	Highwaymen, The	'61	Cruel Summer	Bananarama	'84
Could It Be I'm Falling in Love	Spinners, The	'72	Cruel to Be Kind	Lowe, Nick	'78
Could This Be Magic	Dubs, The	'57	Cruisin'	Robinson, Smokey	'79
Could've Been	Tiffany	'87	Cruisin' for Burgers	Mothers of Invention, The	'69
Couldn't Get It Right	Climax Blues Band	'77	Crumblin' Down	Mellencamp, John Cougar	'83
Couldn't Stand the Weather	Vaughan, Stevie Ray	'84	Crunge, The	Led Zeppelin	'73
Count Every Star	Ravens, The	'50	Crush on You	Jets, The	'86
Count Me In	Lewis, Gary and the Playboys	'65	Cry	Godley and Creme	'85
Count on Me	Jefferson Starship, The	'78	Cry	Ray, Johnny	'51
Country Road	Taylor, James	'71	Cry Baby	Mimms, Garnet & the Enchanters	'63
Court of the Crimson King	King Crimson	'69			

SONG	ARTIST	YEAR
Cry Baby Cry	Beatles, The	'68
Cry for Help	Astley, Rick	'91
Cry for You	Jodeci	'93
Cry Like a Baby	Box Tops, The	'68
Cry Like a Rainstorm	Ronstadt, Linda	'89
Cry to Me	Burke, Solomon	'61
Cryin'	Aerosmith	'93
Crying	Orbison, Roy	'61
Crying Game, The	Berry, Dave	'65
Crying in the Chapel	Orioles, The	'53
Crying in the Rain	Everly Brothers, The	'62
Crying Time	Owens, Buck	'65
Crystal Blue Persuasion	James, Tommy & the Shondells	'69
Crystal Ship	Doors, The	'67
Cult of Personality	Living Colour	'89
Cum on Feel the Noize	Slade	'73
Cupid	Cooke, Sam	'61
Curly Shuffle, The	Jump 'n the Saddle	'83
Cut Across Shorty	Cochran, Eddie	'58
Cut the Cake	Average White Band, The	'75
Cut Your Hair	Pavement	'94
Cuts Like a Knife	Adams, Bryan	'83
Cuts You Up	Murphy, Peter	'90
Cuyahoga	R.E.M.	'86
Cynical Girl	Crenshaw, Marshall	'82
Cypress Avenue	Morrison, Van	'69

D

SONG	ARTIST	YEAR
Da Butt	E.U.	'88
Da Doo Ron Ron	Crystals, The	'63
Dad I'm in Jail	Was (Not Was)	'88
Daddy's Home	Shep & the Limelites	'61
Damn Good	Roth, David Lee	'88
Damn, I Wish I Was Your Lover	Hawkins, Sophie B.	'92
Dance (Disco Heat)	Sylvester	'78
Dance Away	Roxy Music	'79
Dance Hall Days	Wang Chung	'84
Dance Little Sister	D'Arby, Terence Trent	'87
Dance of the Rock & Roll Interviewers	Zappa, Frank	'71
Dance the Night Away	Van Halen	'79
Dance This Mess Around	B-52's, The	'79
Dance to the Bop	Vincent, Gene & His Blue Caps	'57
Dance to the Music	Sly & the Family Stone	'68
Dance with Me	Brown, Peter & Betty Wright	'77
Dance with Me	Drifters, The	'59
Dance with Me	Orleans	'75
Dance with Me Henry (The Wallflower)	James, Etta	'55

SONG	ARTIST	YEAR
Dance, Dance, Dance	Beach Boys, The	'64
Dance, Dance, Dance (Yowsah, Yowsah, Yowsah)	Chic	'77
Dancin' Fool	Zappa, Frank	'79
Dancing Days	Led Zeppelin	'73
Dancing in the Dark	Springsteen, Bruce	'84
Dancing in the Moonlight	King Harvest	'73
Dancing in the Sheets	Shalamar	'84
Dancing in the Street	Martha & the Vandellas	'64
Dancing Machine	Jackson 5, The	'74
Dancing on the Ceiling	Richie, Lionel	'85
Dancing Queen	Abba	'77
Dancing with Myself	Idol, Billy	'81
Dandelion	Rolling Stones, The	'67
Dandy	Herman's Hermits	'66
Danger Zone	Loggins, Kenny	'86
Dangerous	Roxette	'90
Dangling Conversation, The	Simon and Garfunkel	'66
Daniel	John, Elton	'72
Danny	Presley, Elvis	'58
Danny's Song	Loggins & Messina	'71
Dark End of the Street, The	Carr, James	'67
Dark Lady	Cher	'74
Dark Star	Grateful Dead, The	'68
Darkness on the Edge of Town	Springsteen, Bruce	'78
Darlin'	Beach Boys, The	'67
Darlin' Darlin' Baby (Sweet Tender Love)	O'Jays, The	'76
Darling Be Home Soon	Lovin' Spoonful, The	'67
Daughter	Pearl Jam	'93
David Watts	Kinks, The	'68
Davy the Fat Boy	Newman, Randy	'68
Dawn (Go Away)	Four Seasons, The	'64
Dawn of Correction	Spokesmen, The	'65
Day After Day	Badfinger	'71
Day by Day	Godspell, Cast of	'71
Day Dreaming	Franklin, Aretha	'72
Day in the Life, A	Beatles, The	'67
Day in—Day Out	Bowie, David	'87
Day of the Locusts	Dylan, Bob	'70
Day Tripper	Beatles, The	'65
Daydream	Lovin' Spoonful, The	'66
Daydream Believer	Monkees, The	'67
Days Between	Grateful Dead, The	'95
Dayton, Ohio 1903	Nilsson	'70
Dazed and Confused	Led Zeppelin	'69
Dazz	Brick	'77
De Do Do Do, De Da Da Da	Police, The	'80
Deacon Blues	Steely Dan	'77
Dead End Street	Kinks, The	'67
Dead Man's Curve	Jan and Dean	'64

SONG	ARTIST	YEAR
Dead Skunk	Wainwright, Loudon	'72
Deaf Forever	Motorhead	'86
Dear Abby	Prine, John	'73
Dear God	XTC	'87
Dear Lady Twist	Bonds, Gary U.S.	'61
Dear Landlord	Dylan, Bob	'68
Dear Mr. Fantasy	Traffic	'68
Dear One	Finnegan, Larry	'62
Dear Prudence	Beatles, The	'68
Debaser	Pixies, The	'89
Debbie Gibson Is Pregnant (with My Two-Headed Love Child)	Nixon, Mojo & Skid Roper	'89
December 1963 (Oh What a Night)	Four Seasons, The	'75
Dede Dinah	Avalon, Frankie	'58
Dedicated	Kelly, R.	'92
Dedicated Follower of Fashion	Kinks, The	'66
Dedicated to the One I Love	5 Royales, The	'58
Deep Dark Truthful Mirror	Costello, Elvis	'89
Deep Deep Trouble	Simpson, Bart	'90
Deep Purple	Tempo, Nino and April Stevens	'63
Deep Shag	Luscious Jackson	'94
Deeper and Deeper	Madonna	'92
Defrost Your Heart	Feathers, Charlie	'55
Delirious	Prince	'82
Delta Dawn	Midler, Bette	'72
Delta Lady	Cocker, Joe	'69
Denise	Randy & the Rainbows	'63
Deportees (the Plane Wreck at Los Gatos)	Guthrie, Arlo	'69
Der Kommissar	After the Fire	'83
Deserie	Charts, The	'57
Desert Moon	De Young, Dennis	'84
Desire	U2	'88
Desolation Row	Dylan, Bob	'65
Desperado	Eagles, The	'73
Desperados Waiting for a Train	Rush, Tom	'73
Destroyer	Kinks, The	'81
Deteriorata	National Lampoon	'72
Detox Mansion	Zevon, Warren	'87
Detroit City	Bare, Bobby	'63
Detroit Rock City	Kiss	'76
Deuce	Kiss	'74
Devil Gate Drive	Quatro, Suzi	'74
Devil in His Heart	Donays, The	'62
Devil Inside	Inxs	'87
Devil or Angel	Clovers, The	'55
Devil Went down to Georgia	Daniels, Charlie Band, The	'79
Devil with a Blue Dress On	Long, Shorty	'64
Devil Woman	Richard, Cliff	'76
Devil You Know, The	Jesus Jones	'93

SONG	ARTIST	YEAR
Devoted to You	Everly Brothers, The	'58
Dial My Heart	Boys, The	'88
Diamond Girl	Seals and Crofts	'73
Diamonds and Pearls	Paradons	'60
Diamonds and Pearls	Prince	'91
Diamonds and Rust	Baez, Joan	'75
Diamonds on the Soles of Her Shoes	Simon, Paul	'86
Diana	Anka, Paul	'57
Diary, The	Sedaka, Neil	'58
Did It in a Minute	Hall and Oates	'81
Did She Jump	Thompson, Richard and Linda	'82
Did You Ever Have to Make up Your Mind	Lovin' Spoonful, The	'65
Diddey Wah Diddey	Diddley, Bo	'57
Diddley Daddy	Diddley, Bo	'55
Didn't I (Blow Your Mind This Time)	Delfonics, The	'70
Different Corner, A	Wham!	'86
Different Drum	Stone Poneys, The	'65
Dim All the Lights	Summer, Donna	'79
Dim, Dim the Lights (I Want Some Atmosphere)	Haley, Bill & the Comets	'54
Dime a Dance Romance	Miller, Steve Band, The	'68
Dimming of the Day, The	Thompson, Richard and Linda	'75
Dinner with Drac	Zacherle, John	'58
Dirt	Reed, Lou	'78
Dirty Boulevard	Reed, Lou	'89
Dirty Deeds Done Dirt Cheap	AC/DC	'81
Dirty Diana	Jackson, Michael	'87
Dirty Dirty Feeling	Presley, Elvis	'60
Dirty Laundry	Henley, Don	'82
Dirty Old Town	Stewart, Rod	'69
Dirty Water	Standells, The	'65
Dirty Work	Steely Dan	'72
Disappear	Inxs	'90
Disappointed	Public Image Ltd.	'89
Disco Inferno	Trammps	'77
Disco Lady	Taylor, Johnnie	'76
Disco Nights (Rock Freak)	GQ	'79
Dissident	Pearl Jam	'93
Divine Thing	Soup Dragons	'92
Dixie Fried	Perkins, Carl	'56
Dizz Knee Land	dada	'92
Dizzy	Roe, Tommy	'69
DJ Culture	Pet Shop Boys	'91
Do Anything	Natural Selection	'91
Do Fries Go with That Shake	Clinton, George	'86
Do I Do	Wonder, Stevie	'82
Do It	Pink Faeries	'71

SONG	ARTIST	YEAR
Do It ('Til You're Satisfied)	B.T. Express	'74
Do It Again	Beach Boys, The	'68
Do It Again	Steely Dan	'72
Do It Any Way You Wanna	People's Choice	'75
Do It to Me	Richie, Lionel	'92
Do Me Baby	Morgan, Meli'sa	'86
Do Me!	Bell Biv Devoe	'90
Do Right Woman, Do Right Man	Franklin, Aretha	'67
Do the Bird	Sharp, Dee Dee	'63
Do the Push & Pull, Pt. 1	Thomas, Rufus	'70
Do the Strand	Roxy Music	'73
Do They Know It's Christmas	Band-Aid	'84
Do Wah Diddy (Diddy)	Exciters, The	'63
Do Ya	Move, The	'72
Do Ya Think I'm Sexy	Stewart, Rod	'79
Do You Believe in Love	Lewis, Huey & the News	'82
Do You Believe in Magic	Lovin' Spoonful, The	'65
Do You Feel Like We Do	Frampton, Peter	'76
Do You Know the Way to San Jose	Warwick, Dionne	'68
Do You Know What I Mean	Michaels, Lee	'71
Do You Know Where You're Going To (Theme from *Mahogany*)	Ross, Diana	'75
Do You Love Me	Contours, The	'62
Do You Love What You Feel	Rufus	'79
Do You Really Want to Hurt Me	Culture Club	'83
Do You Remember	Collins, Phil	'90
Do You Remember Rock and Roll Radio	Ramones, The	'79
Do You Wanna Make Love	McCann, Peter	'77
Do You Wanna Touch Me	Glitter, Gary	'73
Do You Want to Dance	Freeman, Bobby	'58
Do You Want to Know a Secret	Beatles, The	'63
Doctor My Eyes	Browne, Jackson	'72
Doctor, The	Doobie Brothers, The	'89
Doctorin' the Tardis	Timelords, The	'88
Does Anybody Really Know What Time It Is	Chicago	'70
Does Your Chewing Gum Lose It's Flavor on the Bedpost Overnight	Donegan, Lonnie	'59
Doesn't Somebody Want to Be Wanted	Partridge Family, The	'71
Doggin' Around	Wilson, Jackie	'60
Doin' It to Death	JB's	'73
Doin' the New Continental	Dovells, The	'62
Doing It All for My Baby	Lewis, Huey & the News	'86
Doll Parts	Hole	'94
Dolly Dagger	Hendrix, Jimi	'71
Dolphins, The	Neil, Fred	'67
Dominique	Singing Nun, The	'63
Domino	Morrison, Van	'70

SONG	ARTIST	YEAR
Don't	Presley, Elvis	'58
Don't Ask Me to Be Friends	Everly Brothers, The	'62
Don't Ask Me to Be Lonely	Dubs, The	'57
Don't Be a Drop-Out	Brown, James & the Famous Flames	'66
Don't Be Afraid	Hall, Aaron	'91
Don't Be Cruel	Brown, Bobby	'88
Don't Be Cruel (to a Heart That's True)	Presley, Elvis	'56
Don't Believe the Hype	Public Enemy	'88
Don't Bet Money Honey	Scott, Linda	'61
Don't Bogart Me (Don't Bogart That Joint)	Fraternity of Man	'68
Don't Bother Me	Beatles, The	'64
Don't Break the Heart That Loves You	Francis, Connie	'62
Don't Bring Me Down	Animals, The	'66
Don't Bring Me Down	Electric Light Orchestra	'79
Don't Call Me Nigger, Whitey	Sly & the Family Stone	'69
Don't Call Us, We'll Call You	Sugarloaf	'74
Don't Cry	Guns N' Roses	'91
Don't Cry Daddy	Presley, Elvis	'69
Don't Cry out Loud	Manchester, Melissa	'78
Don't Disturb This Groove	System, The	'87
Don't Do Me Like That	Petty, Tom & the Heartbreakers	'79
Don't Dream It's Over	Crowded House	'87
Don't Eat the Yellow Snow	Zappa, Frank	'74
Don't Expect Me to Be Your Friend	Lobo	'73
Don't Fall Apart on Me Tonight	Dylan, Bob	'83
(Don't Fear) Reaper, The	Blue Oyster Cult	'76
Don't Forbid Me	Boone, Pat	'56
Don't Forget Me (When I'm Gone)	Glass Tiger	'86
Don't Get Me Wrong	Pretenders, The	'86
Don't Give Up	Gabriel, Peter	'86
Don't Give up on Us	Soul, David	'77
(Don't Go Back to) Rockville	R.E.M.	'83
Don't Go Breaking My Heart	John, Elton and Kiki Dee	'76
Don't Go Home with Your Hard On	Cohen, Leonard	'77
Don't Hang Up	Orlons, The	'63
Don't It Make My Brown Eyes Blue	Gayle, Crystal	'77
Don't It Make You Want to Go Home	South, Joe	'69
Don't Just Stand There (What's on Your Mind)	Duke, Patty	'64
Don't Knock My Love	Pickett, Wilson	'71
Don't Leave Me This Way	Houston, Thelma	'77
Don't Let Go	Hamilton, Roy	'58
Don't Let Go the Coat	Who, The	'81
Don't Let It Bring You Down	Young, Neil	'70
Don't Let It End	Styx	'83

SONG	ARTIST	YEAR
Don't Let Me Be Lonely Tonight	Taylor, James	'73
Don't Let Me Be Misunderstood	Animals, The	'65
Don't Let Me Down	Beatles, The	'69
Don't Let the Green Grass Fool You	Pickett, Wilson	'70
Don't Let the Joneses Get You Down	Temptations, The	'69
Don't Let the Rain Come Down (Crooked Little Man)	Serendipity Singers, The	'64
Don't Let the Sun Catch You Crying	Gerry & the Pacemakers	'64
Don't Let the Sun Go down on Me	John, Elton	'74
Don't Let's Start	They Might Be Giants	'86
Don't Lie to Me	Big Star	'72
Don't Look Back	Boston	'78
Don't Look Back	Fine Young Cannibals	'89
Don't Lose My Number	Collins, Phil	'85
Don't Make Me Over	Warwick, Dionne	'63
Don't Mean Nothin'	Marx, Richard	'87
Don't Mess with Bill	Marvelettes, The	'66
Don't Mind Rockin' Tonight	Ducks Deluxe	'74
Don't Pass Me By	Beatles, The	'68
Don't Pay the Ferryman	DeBurgh, Chris	'83
Don't Play That Song (You Lied)	King, Ben E.	'62
Don't Pull Your Love	Hamilton, Joe Frank & Reynolds	'71
Don't Push It Don't Force It	Haywood, Leon	'80
Don't Run Wild	Del Fuegos, The	'85
Don't Say Goodnight (It's Time for Love)-Parts 1 & 2	Isley Brothers, The	'80
Don't Say No Tonight	Wilde, Eugene	'76
Don't Say Nothin' Bad (About My Baby)	Cookies, The	'63
Don't Shake Me Lucifer	Erickson, Roky & the Aliens	'82
Don't Shed a Tear	Carrack, Paul	'88
Don't Stand So Close to Me	Police, The	'80
Don't Stop	Fleetwood Mac	'77
Don't Stop 'Til You Get Enough	Jackson, Michael	'79
Don't Stop Believin'	Journey	'81
Don't Stop the Music	Yarbrough and Peoples	'81
Don't Talk to Strangers	Springfield, Rick	'82
Don't Tell Me Lies	Breathe	'86
Don't Think Twice, It's All Right	Dylan, Bob	'63
Don't Touch Me There	Tubes, The	'76
Don't Try to Lay No Boogie Woogie on the King of Rock and Roll	Baldry, Long John	'71
Don't Turn Around	Turner, Tina	'86
Don't Walk Away	Jade	'93
Don't Wanna Fall in Love	Child, Jane	'90
Don't Want to Be a Fool	Vandross, Luther	'91
Don't Waste Your Time	Yarbrough and Peoples	'84
Don't Worry	Robbins, Marty	'61
Don't Worry (If There's a Hell Below We're All Gonna Go)	Mayfield, Curtis	'70

SONG	ARTIST	YEAR
Don't Worry Baby	Beach Boys, The	'64
Don't Worry, Be Happy	McFerrin, Bobby	'87
Don't You (Forget About Me)	Simple Minds	'85
Don't You Care	Buckinghams, The	'67
Don't You Just Know It	Smith, Huey	'58
Don't You Know	Charles, Ray	'54
Don't You Know	Reese, Della	'59
Don't You Know I Love You	Clovers, The	'51
Don't You Know What the Night Can Do	Winwood, Steve	'88
Don't You Want Me	Human League	'82
Don't You Want Me	Watley, Jody	'87
Don't You Worry 'Bout a Thing	Wonder, Stevie	'73
Doncha' Think It's Time	Presley, Elvis	'58
Donna	Valens, Ritchie	'58
Donna the Prima Donna	Dion	'63
Doo Doo Doo Doo Doo (Heartbreaker)	Rolling Stones, The	'73
Door Is Still Open to My Heart, The	Cardinals, The	'55
Double Dare Ya	Bikini Kill	'92
Double Dutch Bus	Smith, Frankie	'81
Double Shot (of My Baby's Love)	Swinging Medallions, The	'66
Double Vision	Foreigner	'78
Double-Crossin' Blues	Otis, Johnny	'50
(Down at) Poppa Joe's	Dixiebelles, The	'63
Down by the Lazy River	Osmonds, The	'72
Down by the River	Young, Neil	'69
Down by the Water	Harvey, P.J.	'95
Down Home Blues	Z.Z. Hill	'81
Down Home Girl	Robinson, Alvin	'64
Down in Mexico	Coasters, The	'56
Down in the Boondocks	Royal, Billy Joe	'65
Down in the Bottom	Howling Wolf	'50
Down in the Flood	Dylan, Bob	'72
(Down in) New Orleans	Bonds, Gary U.S.	'60
Down on Me	Big Brother & the Holding Company	'68
Down on the Corner	Creedence Clearwater Revival	'69
Down River	Ackles, David	'68
Down So Low	Mother Earth	'68
Down the Aisle of Love	Quintones, The	'58
Down Under	Men at Work	'82
Down with the King	Run-D.M.C.	'93
Downtown	Clark, Petula	'64
Downtown Train	Waits, Tom	'85
Dr. Feelgood	Motley Crue	'89
Dr. Wu	Steely Dan	'75
Drag City	Jan and Dean	'63
Draggin' the Line	James, Tommy	'71
Drain You	Nirvana	'91
Dre Day	Dr. Dre	'92
Dream Baby Dream	Vega, Alan and Martin Rev	'80

SONG	ARTIST	YEAR
Dream Baby, How Long Must I Dream?	Orbison, Roy	'62
Dream Lover	Darin, Bobby	'59
Dream On	Aerosmith	'73
Dream Weaver	Wright, Gary	'76
Dreamin'	Burnette, Johnny	'60
Dreamin'	Williams, Vanessa	'88
Dreaming	Blondie	'79
Dreaming	Richard, Cliff	'80
Dreaming, The	Bush, Kate	'82
Dreams	Cranberries, The	'93
Dreams	Fleetwood Mac	'77
Dreams	Van Halen	'86
Dreamtime	Hall, Daryl	'86
Dress	Harvey, P.J.	'92
Dress Rehearsal Rag	Collins, Judy	'66
Dress You Up	Madonna	'84
Drift Away	Gray, Dobie	'73
Driftin' Blues	Moore's, Johnny Three Blazers	'46
Drinking Wine Spo-Dee O-Dee	McGhee, Stick	'49
Drip Drop	Drifters, The	'58
Drive	Cars, The	'84
Drive My Car	Beatles, The	'65
Drive South	Hiatt, John	'88
Drive-in Show	Cochran, Eddie	'57
Driven to Tears	Police, The	'80
Driver 8	R.E.M.	'85
Driving My Life Away	Rabbitt, Eddie	'80
Driving Wheel	Little Junior Parker	'61
Driving Your Girlfriend Home	Morrissey	'91
Drown in My Tears	Charles, Ray	'56
Drowning in the Sea of Love	Simon, Joe	'71
Drug Store Truck Drivin' Man	Byrds, The	'69
Dude (Looks Like a Lady)	Aerosmith	'87
Dueling Banjos	Weissberg, Eric & Mandel, Steve	'72
Duke of Earl	Chandler, Gene	'61
Duke of Prunes	Mothers of Invention, The	'67
Dum Dum	Lee, Brenda	'61
Dust in the Wind	Kansas	'77
Dutchman, The	Goodman, Steve	'70
D'Yer Maker	Led Zeppelin	'73
Dynamite	Lee, Brenda	'57
Dyslexic Heart	Westerberg, Paul	'92

E

SONG	ARTIST	YEAR
Early 1970	Starr, Ringo	'70
Early in the Morning	Gap Band, The	'82
Early in the Morning	Rinky Dinks, The	'58

SONG	ARTIST	YEAR
Early Morning Rain	Collins, Judy	'65
Earn Enough for Us	XTC	'87
Earth Angel (Will You Be Mine)	Penguins, The	'54
Easier Said Than Done	Essex, The	'63
East West	Butterfield, Paul, Blues Band	'66
Easy	Commodores, The	'77
Easy Come, Easy Go	Sherman, Bobby	'70
Easy Livin'	Uriah Heap	'72
Easy Lover	Bailey, Philip	'85
Easy to Be Hard	Three Dog Night	'69
Eat the Rich	Krokus	'83
Ebb Tide	Hamilton, Roy	'54
Ebony and Ivory	McCartney, Paul & Stevie Wonder	'82
Ebony Eyes	Everly Brothers, The	'61
Echoes of Love	Doobie Brothers, The	'77
Eddie, My Love	Teen-Queens, The	'56
Edge of Heaven, The	Wham!	'86
Edge of Seventeen	Nicks, Stevie	'82
Effigy	Creedence Clearwater Revival	'69
Efflouresce and Deliquesce	Chills, The	'90
Egg Plant (That Ate Chicago), The	Dr. West's Medicine Show and Junk Band	'66
Eight Days a Week	Beatles, The	'65
Eight Men and Four Women	Wright, O.V.	'67
Eight Miles High	Byrds, The	'66
Eighteen	Cooper, Alice	'71
Eighteen and Life	Skid Row	'89
Eighteen with a Bullet	Wingfield, Pete	'75
Einstein on the Beach (for an Eggman)	Counting Crows	'94
El Paso	Robbins, Marty	'59
Eleanor Rigby	Beatles, The	'66
Elected	Cooper, Alice	'72
Election Day	Arcadia	'85
Electric Avenue	Grant, Eddy	'83
Electric Blue	Icehouse	'88
Elenore	Turtles, The	'68
Eli's Coming	Nyro, Laura	'68
Elusive Butterfly	Lind, Bob	'65
Elvira	Frazier, Dallas	'66
Elvis Is Dead	Living Colour	'90
Elvis Is Everywhere	Nixon, Mojo & Skid Roper	'87
Embryonic Journey	Jefferson Airplane, The	'67
Emma	Hot Chocolate	'75
Emotion	Sang, Samantha	'77
Emotional Rescue	Rolling Stones, The	'80
Emotionally Yours	Dylan, Bob	'85
Emotions	Carey, Mariah	'91
Emotions	Lee, Brenda	'61
Emperor's New Clothes	O'Connor, Sinead	'90

SONG	ARTIST	YEAR
Empire of the Senseless	Mekons, The	'89
Empty Arms	Hunter, Ivory Joe	'57
Empty Cup (and a Broken Date), An	Crickets, The	'57
Empty Garden (Hey Hey Johnny)	John, Elton	'82
Encore	Lynn, Cheryl	'89
End of the Innocence, The	Henley, Don	'89
End of the Road	Boyz II Men	'92
End of the Road	Lewis, Jerry Lee	'56
End of the World, The	Davis, Skeeter	'63
End, The	Beatles, The	'69
End, The	Doors, The	'67
Endless Farewell	Soul Asylum	'88
Endless Love	Richie, Lionel and Diana Ross	'81
Endless Sleep	Reynolds, Jody	'58
Endless Summer Nights	Marx, Richard	'88
Endlessly	Benton, Brook	'59
Engine Number 9 (Get Me Back on Time)	Pickett, Wilson	'70
England Swings	Miller, Roger	'65
Enjoy the Silence	Depeche Mode	'90
Enjoy Yourself	Jacksons, The	'76
Enter Sandman	Metallica	'91
Entertainer, The	Joel, Billy	'74
Epic	Faith No More	'90
Erotica	Madonna	'92
Eruption	Van Halen	'78
Escapade	Jackson, Janet	'89
Escape (the Pina Colada Song)	Holmes, Rupert	'79
Eternal Flame	Bangles, The	'89
Eton Rifles	Jam, The	'79
Eulogy to Lenny Bruce	Nico	'67
Euphoria	Holy Modal Rounders, The	'67
European Son: To Delmore Schwartz	Velvet Underground, The	'67
Eve of Destruction	McGuire, Barry	'65
Even a Dog Can Shake Hands	Zevon, Warren	'87
Even Flow	Pearl Jam	'91
Even It Up	Heart	'80
Even the Losers	Petty, Tom & the Heartbreakers	'79
Ever Fallen in Love (with Someone You Shouldn't Have Fallen in Love With)	Buzzcocks, The	'78
Everlasting Love	Knight, Robert	'67
Everlasting Love, An	Gibb, Andy	'78
Every 1's a Winner	Hot Chocolate	'79
Every Beat of My Heart	Royals, The	'61
Every Breath I Take	Pitney, Gene	'61
Every Breath You Take	Police, The	'83
Every Day I Have the Blues	Fulson, Lowell	'50
Every Day I Write the Book	Costello, Elvis	'83

SONG	ARTIST	YEAR
Every Dog Has His Day	Let's Active	'88
Every Grain of Sand	Dylan, Bob	'81
Every Little Kiss	Hornsby, Bruce & the Range	'86
Every Little Step	Brown, Bobby	'89
Every Little Thing	Beatles, The	'65
Every Little Thing She Does Is Magic	Police, The	'81
Every Picture Tells a Story	Stewart, Rod	'71
Every Rose Has Its Thorn	Poison	'88
(Every Time I Turn Around) Back in Love Again	L.T.D.	'77
Every Time You Go Away	Hall and Oates	'85
Everybody	Roe, Tommy	'63
Everybody Everybody	Black Box	'90
Everybody Have Fun Tonight	Wang Chung	'86
Everybody Hurts	R.E.M.	'93
Everybody Is a Star	Sly & the Family Stone	'70
Everybody Loves Me But You	Lee, Brenda	'62
Everybody Needs Somebody to Love	Pickett, Wilson	'67
Everybody Plays the Fool	Main Ingredient, The	'72
Everybody Wants to Rule the World	Tears for Fears	'85
Everybody Wants You	Squier, Billy	'82
Everybody's Been Burned	Byrds, The	'67
Everybody's Everything (Baby)	Santana	'71
Everybody's Got Something to Hide except Me and My Monkey	Beatles, The	'68
Everybody's Happy Nowadays	Buzzcocks, The	'79
Everybody's Somebody's Fool	Francis, Connie	'60
Everybody's Talkin'	Neil, Fred	'67
Everybody's Trying to Be My Baby	Perkins, Carl	'57
Everyday	Collins, Phil	'93
Everyday	Holly, Buddy	'58
Everyday Is Like Sunday	Morrissey	'88
Everyday People	Sly & the Family Stone	'69
Everyone Is Good	Roches, The	'89
Everyone's Gone to the Moon	King, Jonathan	'65
Everything	Watley, Jody	'89
Everything About You	Ugly Kid Joe	'92
(Everything I Do) I Do It for You	Adams, Bryan	'91
Everything I Miss at Home	Cherrelle	'88
Everything I Own	Bread	'72
Everything Is Beautiful	Stevens, Ray	'70
Everything Is Broken	Dylan, Bob	'89
Everything She Wants	Wham!	'84
Everything Your Heart Desires	Hall and Oates	'88
Everything Zen	Bush	'94
Everything's Alright	Elliman, Yvonne	'71
Evil	Howling Wolf	'54
Evil Eye	Alcatrazz	'84
Evil Hearted You	Yardbirds, The	'65

SONG	ARTIST	YEAR
Evil That Men Do, The	Queen Latifah	'89
Evil Ways	Santana	'69
Evil Woman	Electric Light Orchestra	'75
Evol	Sonic Youth	'86
Excitable Boy	Zevon, Warren	'78
Exodus	Marley, Bob & the Wailers	'63
Exorcising the Evil Spirits from the Pentagon, Oct. 21, 1967	Fugs, The	'68
Expecting to Fly	Buffalo Springfield	'67
Express	B.T. Express	'74
Express Yourself	Madonna	'89
Express Yourself	Watts 103rd Street Rhythm Band, The	'70
Expressway to Your Heart	Soul Survivors, The	'67
Expressway to Yr Skull	Sonic Youth	'86
Eye in the Sky	Parsons, Alan Project, The	'82
Eye of Fatima (Parts 1 and 2)	Camper Van Beethoven	'88
Eye of the Tiger (The Theme from *Rocky III*)	Survivor	'82
Eyes of a New York Woman	Insect Trust	'70
Eyes of a Stranger	Queensryche	'88
Eyes Without a Face	Idol, Billy	'84
Eyesight to the Blind	Williamson, Sonny Boy	'51

F

SONG	ARTIST	YEAR
Fa-Fa-Fa-Fa-Fa (Sad Song)	Redding, Otis	'66
Face the Face	Townshend, Pete	'85
Factory Girl	Rolling Stones, The	'68
Fade into You	Mazzy Star	'94
Fade to Black	Metallica	'84
Fading Like a Flower	Roxette	'91
Fairytale of New York	Pogues, The	'88
Faith	Michael, George	'87
Fake	O'Neal, Alexander	'87
Fall on Me	R.E.M.	'85
Fallin' in Love (Again)	Hamilton, Joe Frank & Reynolds	'75
Falling	Cruise, Julee	'90
Fame	Bowie, David	'75
Fame	Cara, Irene	'80
Fame and Fortune	Presley, Elvis	'60
Family Affair	Sly & the Family Stone	'71
Family Man	Hall and Oates	'83
Famous Blue Raincoat	Cohen, Leonard	'71
Fannie Mae	Brown, Buster	'60
Fantastic Voyage	Lakeside	'81
Far Behind	Candlebox	'93
Farewell Angelina	Baez, Joan	'65
Farewell Song	Big Brother & the Holding Company	'68
Farm Yard Connection, The	Fun Boy Three	'83

SONG	ARTIST	YEAR
Farmer John	Don and Dewey	'59
Farmer's Daughter	Beach Boys, The	'63
Farther up the Road	Bland, Bobby	'57
Fashion	Bowie, David	'80
Fast Car	Chapman, Tracy	'88
Fast Times at Ridgemont High	Hagar, Sammy	'82
Fat Man, The	Domino, Fats	'50
Father Figure	Michael, George	'87
Fear Is a Man's Best Friend	Cale, John	'74
Fear of a Black Planet	Public Enemy	'90
Feed the Tree	Belly	'93
Feel Like Makin' Love	Flack, Roberta and Donnie Hathaway	'74
Feel Like Making Love	Bad Company	'75
Feel the Pain	Dinosaur Jr.	'94
Feelin' Alright?	Traffic	'68
Feels Good	Tony! Toni! Tone!	'90
Feels Like the First Time	Foreigner	'77
Femme Fatale	Velvet Underground, The	'67
Ferry Cross the Mersey	Gerry & the Pacemakers	'64
Fever	John, Little Willie	'56
Ffun	Con Funk Shun	'77
Fields of Fire	Big Country	'84
Fifty Ways to Leave Your Lover	Simon, Paul	'75
Fight the Power	Public Enemy	'89
Fight the Power, Pt. I	Isley Brothers, The	'75
Final Countdown, The	Europe	'86
Finally	Penniston, Ce Ce	'91
Finally Got Myself Together (I'm a Changed Man)	Impressions, The	'74
Fine Fine Boy, A	Love, Darlene	'63
Fine Fine Day, A	Carey, Tony	'84
Finer Things, The	Winwood, Steve	'86
Finest Worksong	R.E.M.	'86
Finger Poppin' Time	Midnighters, The	'60
Fingertips	Wonder, Little Stevie	'62
Finish What Ya Started	Van Halen	'88
Fire!	Brown, Arthur (The Crazy World of)	'68
Fire	Gordon, Robert	'78
Fire	Hendrix, Jimi	'67
Fire	Ohio Players, The	'74
Fire and Rain	Taylor, James	'70
Fire and Water	Free	'70
Fire Down Below	Seger, Bob	'76
Fire Engine	Thirteenth Floor Elevators	'66
Fire Lake	Seger, Bob	'80
First Cut Is the Deepest	Stevens, Cat	'67
First Girl I Loved, The	Incredible String Band, The	'67
First I Look at the Purse	Contours, The	'65
First Time Ever I Saw Your Face	Seeger, Peggy	'62

SONG	ARTIST	YEAR	SONG	ARTIST	YEAR
First Time, The	Surface	'90	For Everyman	Browne, Jackson	'73
Fisherman's Blues	Waterboys, The	'88	(For God's Sake) Give More Power to the People	Chi-Lites, The	'71
Fishnet	Day, Morris	'88			
Five "D" (Fifth Dimension)	Byrds, The	'66	For Lovin' Me	Peter, Paul & Mary	'64
Five Feet High and Rising	Cash, Johnny	'59	For No One	Beatles, The	'66
Five Long Years	Boyd, Eddie	'52	For Once in My Life	Wonder, Stevie	'68
Five O'Clock World	Vogues, The	'65	For the Good Times	Kristofferson, Kris	'69
Five to One	Doors, The	'68	For the Love of Money	O'Jays, The	'73
Fixing a Hole	Beatles, The	'67	For the Love of You (Parts 1 & 2)	Isley Brothers, The	'75
Flag Day	Housemartins, The	'86	For the Roses	Mitchell, Joni	'72
Flame Still Burns	Youth of Today	'88	For Those About to Rock (We Salute You)	AC/DC	'81
Flame, The	Cheap Trick	'88			
Flashdance...What a Feeling	Cara, Irene	'83	For What It's Worth	Buffalo Springfield	'67
Flashlight	Parliament	'77	For Whom the Bell Tolls	Metallica	'84
Flava in Ya Ear	Mack, Craig	'94	For Yasgur's Farm	Mountain	'70
Flip, Flop and Fly	Turner, Joe	'55	For You	Nelson, Rick	'64
Flirtin' with Disaster	Molly Hatchet	'80	For You	Springsteen, Bruce	'73
Float On	Floaters, The	'77	For You Blue	Beatles, The	'70
Florence	Paragons, The	'57	For Your Eyes Only	Easton, Sheena	'81
Flower	Phair, Liz	'93	For Your Love	Townsend, Ed	'58
Flowers on the Wall	Statler Brothers, The	'65	For Your Love	Yardbirds, The	'65
Fly Like an Eagle	Miller, Steve Band, The	'76	For Your Precious Love	Butler, Jerry & the Impressions	'58
Fly, Robin, Fly	Silver Convention	'75			
Fly, The	Checker, Chubby	'61	Forever	Kiss	'89
Flyin' the Flannel	fIREHOSE	'91	Forever Man	Clapton, Eric	'85
Flying High Again	Osbourne, Ozzy	'81	Forever Young	Dylan, Bob	'73
Flying Saucer, The	Goodman, Dickie	'56	Forever Young	Stewart, Rod	'88
Foggy Notion	Velvet Underground, The	'69	Forever Young (the Wild Ones)	BoDeans, The	'87
Follow	Havens, Richie	'67	Forever Your Girl	Abdul, Paula	'88
Follow You Follow Me	Genesis	'78	Forget Him	Rydell, Bobby	'64
Folsom Prison Blues	Cash, Johnny	'56	Fortress Around Your Heart	Sting	'85
Fool (If You Think Its Over)	Rea, Chris	'77	Fortunate Son	Creedence Clearwater Revival	'69
Fool for You, A	Charles, Ray	'55	Forty Days	Hawkins, Ronnie	'59
Fool in Love, A	Turner, Ike and Tina	'62	Forty Miles of Bad Road	Eddy, Duane	'59
Fool in the Rain	Led Zeppelin	'79	Forty Thousand Headmen	Traffic	'68
Fool Number 1	Lee, Brenda	'61	Found out About You	Gin Blossoms	'92
Fool on the Hill, The	Beatles, The	'67	Fountain of Sorrow	Browne, Jackson	'74
Fool to Cry	Rolling Stones, The	'76	Four Days Gone	Buffalo Springfield	'68
Fool's Gold	Parker, Graham	'76	Four Hundred Years	Marley, Bob & the Wailers	'69
Fool's Gold	Stone Roses, The	'89	Four in the Morning	Young, Jessie Colin	'64
Fool, Fool, Fool	Clovers, The	'51	Four Strong Winds	Ian and Sylvia	'64
Fool, The	Clark, Sanford	'56	Four Walls	Reeves, Jim	'57
Fooled Around and Fell in Love	Bishop, Elvin	'76	Fourth of July	Alvin, Dave	'87
Foolin'	Def Leppard	'83	Fox on the Run	Sweet, The	'75
Foolish Beat	Gibson, Debbie	'87	Foxy Lady	Hendrix, Jimi	'67
Foolish Little Girl	Shirelles, The	'63	Fragile	Wire	'77
Footloose	Loggins, Kenny	'84	Framed	Robins, The	'54
For a Dancer	Browne, Jackson	'74	Frank Mills	Plympton, Shelly	'67
For All We Know	Carpenters, The	'71	Frankenstein	Winter, Edgar Group	'72
For Emily (Wherever I May Find Her)	Simon and Garfunkel	'66	Frankie	Francis, Connie	'59
			Franklin's Tower	Grateful Dead, The	'75

SONG	ARTIST	YEAR
Freak Me	Silk	'92
Freak Scene	Dinosaur Jr.	'87
Freak-a-Zoid	Midnight Star	'83
Freakin' at the Freaker's Ball	Shel Silverstein	'73
Freakshow on the Dancefloor	Bar-Kays, The	'84
Freaky Dancin'	Cameo	'81
Freddy's Dead (Theme from Superfly)	Mayfield, Curtis	'72
Free Bird	Lynyrd Skynyrd	'73
Free Fallin'	Petty, Tom	'89
Free Man in Paris	Mitchell, Joni	'74
Free Nelson Mandela	Special AKA	'85
Free Ride	Winter, Edgar Group	'72
Free the People	Delaney and Bonnie	'70
Free Your Mind	En Vogue	'92
Freed Pig	Sebadoah	'91
Freedom	Havens, Richie	'70
Freedom	Hendrix, Jimi	'71
Freedom	Michael, George	'90
Freedom	Wham!	'84
Freedom Rider	Traffic	'70
Freeway Jam	Beck, Jeff	'76
Freeway of Love	Franklin, Aretha	'85
Freewill	Rush	'80
Freeze-Frame	Geils J. Band, The	'82
Freight Train	Draper, Rusty	'57
Frenchette	Johansen, David	'77
Frenzy	Fugs, The	'65
Fresh	Kool & the Gang	'84
Fresh Air	Quicksilver Messenger Service	'70
Fresh Garbage	Spirit	'68
Friday I'm in Love	Cure, The	'92
Friday on My Mind	Easybeats, The	'66
Friend of the Devil	Grateful Dead, The	'70
Friends	Linhart, Buzzy	'70
Friends	Watley, Jody	'89
From a Buick 6	Dylan, Bob	'65
From a Distance	Griffith, Nanci	'87
From Me to You	Beatles, The	'63
From Small Things (Big Things One Day Come)	Edmunds, Dave	'82
From the Beginning	Emerson, Lake & Palmer	'72
F___ Tha Police	NWA	'88
Fujiyama Mama	Allen, Annisteen	'55
Full of Fire	Green, Al	'75
Fun Fun Fun	Beach Boys, The	'64
Funhouse	Kid 'N Play	'90
Funk #49	James Gang, The	'70
Funkdafied	Da Brat	'94
Funky Broadway (Part 1)	Dyke & the Blazers	'67

SONG	ARTIST	YEAR
Funky But Chic	Johansen, David	'77
Funky Ceili (Bridie's Song)	Black 47	'92
Funky Cold Medina	Tone Loc	'89
Funky Kingston	Toots & the Maytals	'75
Funky Worm	Ohio Players, The	'73
Funkytown	Lipps, Inc.	'79
Funny (How Time Slips Away)	Elledge, Jimmy	'61
Fuse, The	Browne, Jackson	'76
Future's So Bright, I Gotta Wear Shades	Timbuk 3	'86

G

SONG	ARTIST	YEAR
G.T.O.	Ronny & the Daytonas	'64
Galileo	Indigo Girls, The	'92
Gallows Pole	Led Zeppelin	'70
Galveston	Campbell, Glen	'69
Gambler, The	Rogers, Kenny	'77
Game of Love, The	Fontana, Wayne and the Mindbenders	'64
Games	Booker, Chuckii	'92
Games People Play	South, Joe	'69
Games Without Frontiers	Gabriel, Peter	'80
Gangsta Lean	D.R.S.	'93
Gangster of Love	Miller, Steve Band, The	'68
Gangsters	Specials, The	'79
Garden of Earthly Delights	XTC	'89
Garden Party	Nelson, Rick	'72
Gates of Eden	Dylan, Bob	'65
Gee Baby, Ain't I Good to You	Cole, Nat King	'44
Gee Whiz! (Look at His Eyes)	Thomas, Carla	'61
Gee!	Crows, The	'54
Genius of Love	Tom Tom Club	'81
Gentle on My Mind	Hartford, John	'67
George Jackson	Dylan, Bob	'71
Georgia on My Mind	Charles, Ray	'60
Georgy Girl	Seekers, The	'66
Get a Job	Silhouettes, The	'57
Get Back	Beatles, The	'69
Get Closer	Seals and Crofts	'76
Get Dancin'	Disco Tex & the Sex-O-Lettes	'74
Get Down	O'Sullivan, Gilbert	'73
Get Down Get Down (Get on the Floor)	Simon, Joe	'75
Get Down on It	Kool & the Gang	'81
Get Down Tonight	K.C. & the Sunshine Band	'75
Get Here	Adams, Oleta	'91
Get It Right	Franklin, Aretha	'83
Get It While You Can	Mimms, Garnet & the Enchanters	'63
Get Off	Foxy	'78

SONG	ARTIST	YEAR	SONG	ARTIST	YEAR
Get off of My Cloud	Rolling Stones, The	'65	Girl, You'll Be a Woman Soon	Diamond, Neil	'67
Get off This	Cracker	'93	Girlfriend	Brown, Bobby	'86
Get on the Good Foot, Pt. 1	Brown, James	'72	Girlfriend	Modern Lovers, The	'71
Get on Up	Esquires, The	'67	Girlfriend	Pebbles	'88
Get out of Control	Ash, Daniel	'92	Girlfriend	Sweet, Matthew	'91
Get out of My Life Woman	Dorsey, Lee	'65	Girlfriend in a Coma	Smiths, The	'87
Get outa My Dreams, Get into My Car	Ocean, Billy	'88	Girls	Twilley, Dwight	'84
			Girls and Boys	Blur	'94
Get Ready	Temptations, The	'66	Girls Just Want to Have Fun	Hazard, Robert	'82
Get That Gasoline Blues	NRBQ	'74	Girls Nite Out	Tyler Collins	'90
Get Together	We Five, The	'65	Girls on Film	Duran Duran	'81
Get up and Boogie	Silver Convention	'76	Girls Talk	Costello, Elvis	'80
Get up Stand Up	Marley, Bob & the Wailers	'73	Girls, Girls, Girls	Motley Crue	'87
Get Up! (Before the Night Is Over)	Technotronic	'89	Gitarzan	Stevens, Ray	'69
(Get Your Kicks on) Route 66	Cole, Nat King	'46	Give Him a Great Big Kiss	Shangri-Las, The	'64
Getaway	Earth, Wind & Fire	'76	Give It Away	Red Hot Chili Peppers	'91
Getting Better	Beatles, The	'67	Give It to Me	Geils J. Band, The	'73
Getto Jam	Domino	'93	Give It to Me Baby	James, Rick	'81
Ghetto Heaven	Family Stand, The	'90	Give It Up	Public Enemy	'94
Ghost Town	Specials, The	'81	Give It up or Turn It Loose	Brown, James	'69
Ghostbusters	Parker, Ray Jr.	'84	Give Me Just a Little More Time	Chairmen of the Board, The	'70
Ghosts upon the Road	Andersen, Eric	'89	Give Me Love (Give Me Peace on Earth)	Harrison, George	'73
Gimme All Your Lovin'	ZZ Top	'83			
Gimme Dat Ding	Pipkins	'70	Give Me the Night	Benson, George	'80
Gimme Gimme Shock Treatment	Ramones, The	'77	Give Peace a Chance	Plastic Ono Band, The	'69
Gimme Indie Rock	Sebadoah	'91	Give the People What They Want	O'Jays, The	'75
Gimme Little Sign	Wood, Brenton	'67	Give Us Your Blessing	Peterson, Ray	'63
Gimme Shelter	Rolling Stones, The	'69	Giving It All Away	Daltrey, Roger	'73
Gimme Some Lovin'	Davis, Spencer Group	'67	Giving It up for Your Love	Williams, Jerry	'79
Gimme Some Truth	Lennon, John	'71	Giving You the Benefit	Pebbles	'90
Gimme Three Steps	Lynyrd Skynyrd	'73	Giving You the Best That I Got	Baker, Anita	'88
Gimme Your Love	Franklin, Aretha and James Brown	'89	Glad All Over	Clark, Dave Five, The	'64
			Glad to Be Gay	Robinson, Tom	'78
Gin & Juice	Dogg, Snoop Doggy	'93	Glamorous Life, The	Sheila E.	'84
Gin-Soaked Boy	Waits, Tom	'83	Glamour Boys	Living Colour	'88
Gingerbread	Avalon, Frankie	'58	Glass Onion	Beatles, The	'68
Girl	Beatles, The	'65	Gloria	Branigan, Laura	'82
Girl Can't Help It, The	Little Richard	'56	Gloria	Brown, Charles	'47
Girl Don't Come	Shaw, Sandie	'65	Gloria	Cadillacs, The	'54
Girl from the North Country	Dylan, Bob	'63	Gloria	Them	'66
Girl, I Got My Eyes on You	Today	'89	Gloria	U2	'80
Girl, I'm Gonna Miss You	Milli Vanilli	'89	Gloria (in Excelsius)	Smith, Patti	'76
Girl in Trouble (Is a Temporary Thing), A	Romeo Void	'84	Glory	Phair, Liz	'93
			Glory Days	Springsteen, Bruce	'84
Girl Is Mine, The	Jackson, Michael	'82	Glory of Love (Theme from The Karate Kid, Part 2)	Cetera, Peter	'86
Girl Like You, A	Rascals, The	'67			
Girl of My Best Friend	Presley, Elvis	'60	Glory of Love, The	Five Keys, The	'51
Girl Watcher	O'Kaysions, The	'68	Go	Moby	'91
Girl, You Know It's True	Milli Vanilli	'89	Go	Pearl Jam	'93
Girl You Need a Change of Mind (Part 1)	Kendricks, Eddie	'72	Go All the Way	Raspberries, The	'72
			Go Home	Wonder, Stevie	'86

SONG	ARTIST	YEAR
Go, Jimmy, Go	Clanton, Jimmy	'59
Go Now	Banks, Bessie	'63
Go See the Doctor	Dee, Kool Moe	'87
Go Where You Wanna Go	Mamas and the Papas, The	'66
Go Your Own Way	Fleetwood Mac	'77
God	Amos, Tori	'94
God	Plastic Ono Band, The	'70
God Gave Rock and Roll to You	Argent	'73
God, Love and Rock 'n' Roll	Teegarden and Van Winkle	'70
God Only Knows	Beach Boys, The	'66
God Save the Queen	Sex Pistols, The	'77
God's Comic	Costello, Elvis	'89
God's Song (That's Why I Love Mankind)	Newman, Randy	'72
Godzilla	Blue Oyster Cult	'77
Goin' Back	Springfield, Dusty	'66
Goin' Down to Laurel	Forbert, Steve	'79
Goin' Down to Liverpool	Bangles, The	'84
Goin' Home	Domino, Fats	'52
Goin' Mobile	Who, The	'71
Goin' out of My Head	Little Anthony and the Imperials	'64
Goin' to the River	Domino, Fats	'53
Going Back to Cali	L.L. Cool J	'87
Going in Circles	Friends of Distinction	'69
Going to a Go-Go	Miracles, The	'65
Going to California	Led Zeppelin	'71
Going Underground	Jam, The	'79
Going up the Country	Canned Heat	'68
Gold	Stewart, John	'79
Golden Age of Rock 'n' Roll	Mott the Hoople	'74
Golden Slumbers	Beatles, The	'69
Golden Years	Bowie, David	'76
Gone at Last	Simon, Paul	'75
Gone Dead Train	Newman, Randy	'70
Gonna Fly Now (Theme from *Rocky*)	Little, DeEtta, and Nelson Pigford	'76
Gonna Make You Sweat	C&C Music Factory	'91
Goo Goo Muck	Cramps, The	'81
Good Day Sunshine	Beatles, The	'66
Good Enough	Brown, Bobby	'92
Good Enough	Raitt, Bonnie	'75
Good Golly, Miss Molly	Little Richard	'58
Good Heart, A	Sharkey, Feargal	'85
Good Hearted Woman, A	Jennings, Waylon and Willie Nelson	'75
Good Life, The	Firetown	'89
Good Lovin'	Clovers, The	'53
Good Lovin'	Olympics, The	'65
Good Lovin' Ain't Easy to Come By	Gaye, Marvin and Tammi Terrell	'69

SONG	ARTIST	YEAR
Good Luck Charm	Presley, Elvis	'62
Good Morning Starshine	Oliver	'67
Good Morning, Good Morning	Beatles, The	'67
Good Morning, Little School Girl	Grateful Dead, The	'67
Good News	Cooke, Sam	'64
Good Old Rock and Roll	Cat Mother & the All Night Newsboys	'69
Good Rockin' Tonight	Brown, Roy	'47
Good Thing	Fine Young Cannibals	'89
Good Thing	Revere, Paul & the Raiders	'67
Good Time Charlie's Got the Blues	O'Keefe, Danny	'72
Good Times	Chic	'79
Good Times, Bad Times	Led Zeppelin	'69
Good Times Roll	Cars, The	'78
Good Timin'	Jones, Jimmy	'60
Good Vibrations	Beach Boys, The	'66
Good Vibrations	Marky Mark & the Funky Bunch	'91
Goodbye and Hello	Buckley, Tim	'67
Goodbye Baby	Scott, Jack	'59
Goodbye Cruel World	Darren, James	'63
Goodbye Pork Pie Hat	Beck, Jeff	'76
Goodbye to Innocence	Madonna	'94
Goodbye to Love	Carpenters, The	'72
Goodbye to You	Scandal	'83
Goodbye Yellow Brick Road	John, Elton	'73
Goodnight Irene	Weavers, The	'50
Goodnight My Love	Belvin, Jesse	'51
Goodnight Saigon	Joel, Billy	'82
Goodnight Sweet Josephine	Yardbirds, The	'68
Goodnight Tonight	McCartney, Paul & Wings	'79
Goodnight, Sweetheart, Goodnight	Spaniels, The	'54
Goody Goody	Lymon, Frankie and the Teenagers	'57
Goody Two Shoes	Ant, Adam	'82
Goonies 'R Good Enough	Lauper, Cyndi	'85
Got a Hold on Me	McVie, Christine	'84
Got a Job	Miracles, The	'58
Got Me Waiting	Heavy D & the Boys	'94
Got My Mind Set on You	Ray, James	'62
Got My Mojo Working	Waters, Muddy	'56
Got to Be Real	Lynn, Cheryl	'78
Got to Be There	Jackson, Michael	'71
Got to Get You into My Life	Beatles, The	'66
Got to Get You off My Mind	Burke, Solomon	'65
Got to Give It Up (Part 1)	Gaye, Marvin	'77
Got to Move	Fleetwood Mac	'68
Gotta Get You Home Tonight	Wilde, Eugene	'85
Gotta Hold on to This Feeling	Walker, Jr. & the All-Stars	'70
Gotta Serve Somebody	Dylan, Bob	'79
Gotta Travel On (Done Laid Around)	Weavers, The	'58

SONG	ARTIST	YEAR	SONG	ARTIST	YEAR
Graceland	Simon, Paul	'86	Gypsy, The	Ink Spots, The	'46
Graduation Day	Four Freshmen, The	'56			
Gravy	Sharp, Dee Dee	'63	**H**		
Grazing in the Grass	Masekela, Hugh	'68			
Grease	Valli, Frankie	'78	Had a Dream About You, Baby	Dylan, Bob	'87
Greasy Heart	Jefferson Airplane, The	'68	Hail, Hail Rock 'n' Roll	Jeffreys, Garland	'91
Great Balls of Fire	Lewis, Jerry Lee	'57	Hair of the Dog	Nazareth	'75
Great Gosh a Mighty	Little Richard	'86	Hair!	Cowsills, The	'69
Great Mandella, The	Peter, Paul & Mary	'67	Hairspray	Sweet, Rachel	'88
Great Pretender, The	Platters, The	'55	Half a Mind	Holy Modal Rounders, The	'65
Greatest Love of All, The	Benson, George	'77	Half Moon	Joplin, Janis	'70
Green	Throwing Muses	'86	Half-Breed	Cher	'73
Green Day	Green Day	'91	Hallelujah, I Love Her So	Charles, Ray	'56
Green Door, The	Lowe, Jim	'56	Hammond Song	Roches, The	'79
Green Eyed Lady	Sugarloaf	'70	Hand in Glove	Smiths, The	'84
Green Grass	Lewis, Gary and the Playboys	'66	Hand of Kindness	Thompson, Richard	'83
Green Grass and High Tides	Outlaws, The	'75	Handbags and Gladrags	Stewart, Rod	'69
Green Manilishi (with the Two Pronged Head)	Judas Priest	'79	Handle with Care	Traveling Wilburys	'88
			Hands to Heaven	Breathe	'88
Green Onions	Booker T. & the MG's	'62	Handsome Johnny	Havens, Richie	'67
Green River	Creedence Clearwater Revival	'69	Handy Man	Jones, Jimmy	'60
Green Tambourine	Lemon Pipers, The	'67	Hang Em High	Booker T. & the MG's	'68
Greenback Dollar	Kingston Trio, The	'63	Hang on in There Baby	Bristol, Johnny	'74
Greenfields	Brothers Four, The	'60	Hang on St. Christopher	Waits, Tom	'87
Groom's Still Waiting at the Altar, The	Dylan, Bob	'81	Hang up My Rock and Roll Shoes	Willis, Chuck	'58
			Hangar 18	Megadeth	'91
Groove Is in the Heart	Deee-Lite	'90	Hangin' on to the Good Times	Little Feat	'88
Groove Line, The	Heatwave	'78	Hangin' Tough	New Kids on the Block	'88
Groove Me Baby	King Floyd	'70	Hanging on the Telephone	Nerves, The	'76
Groovin'	Rascals, The	'67	Hanky Panky	Madonna	'90
Groovin' Is Easy	Electric Flag	'68	Hanky Panky	Raindrops, The	'63
Groovy Kind of Love, A	Mindbenders, The	'66	Happening, The	Supremes, The	'67
Group Sex	Circle Jerks, The	'80	Happenings Ten Years Time Ago	Yardbirds, The	'66
Growin' Up	Springsteen, Bruce	'73	Happiness Is a Warm Gun	Beatles, The	'68
Growin' up in the Hood	Compton's Most Wanted	'91	Happy	Rolling Stones, The	'72
Guantanamera	Weavers, The	'63	Happy	Surface	'87
Gudbye T'Jane	Slade	'73	Happy Birthday	Altered Images	'81
Guess Things Happen That Way	Cash, Johnny	'58	Happy Birthday, Sweet Sixteen	Sedaka, Neil	'61
Guilty	Raitt, Bonnie	'73	Happy Days	Pratt and McLain	'76
Guitar and Pen	Who, The	'78	Happy Go Lucky Me	Evans, Paul	'60
Guitar Boogie Shuffle	Smith, Arthur & His Crackerjacks	'46	Happy, Happy Birthday Baby	Tune Weavers, The	'57
			Happy Hour	Housemartins, The	'86
Guitar Man	Reed, Jerry	'67	Happy Jack	Who, The	'67
Guitar Town	Earle, Steve	'86	Happy Organ, The	Cortez, Dave "Baby"	'59
Gulf Coast Highway	Griffith, Nanci	'88	Happy People	Temptations, The	'74
Gypsies, Tramps and Thieves	Cher	'71	Happy Together	Turtles, The	'67
Gypsy	Vega, Suzanne	'87	Happy When It Rains	Jesus and Mary Chain, The	'87
Gypsy Life, The	Gorka, John	'92	Hard Day's Night, A	Beatles, The	'64
Gypsy Man	War	'73	Hard Habit to Break	Chicago	'84
Gypsy Woman	Impressions, The	'61	Hard-Headed Woman	Presley, Elvis	'58
Gypsy Woman (She's Homeless)	Waters, Crystal	'91	Hard Love	Schmidt, Claudia	'83

SONG	ARTIST	YEAR
Hard Lovin' Loser	Farina, Dick and Mimi	'66
Hard Luck Woman	Kiss	'76
Hard Rain's a-Gonna Fall, A	Dylan, Bob	'63
Hard to Handle	Redding, Otis	'68
Hard to Say	Fogelberg, Dan	'81
Hard to Say I'm Sorry	Chicago	'82
Harden My Heart	Quarterflash	'81
Harder They Come, The	Cliff, Jimmy	'72
Hardest Time, The	Los Lobos	'87
Harlem Nocturne	Otis, Johnny	'46
Harlem Shuffle	Bob and Earl	'64
Harper Valley PTA, The	Riley, Jeannie C.	'68
Harvest Moon	Young, Neil	'92
Hat 2 Da Back	TLC	'92
Hats off to Larry	Shannon, Del	'61
Haunted House	Fuller, Johnny	'59
Have a Cigar	Pink Floyd	'75
Have I the Right	Honeycombs, The	'65
Have I Told You Lately	Morrison, Van	'89
Have Mercy Baby	Dominoes, The	'52
Have Mercy Judge	Berry, Chuck	'70
Have You Ever Loved a Woman	King, Freddie	'62
Have You Ever Loved Somebody	Jackson, Freddie	'86
Have You Ever Seen the Rain	Creedence Clearwater Revival	'70
Have You Heard	Mayall's, John, Bluesbreakers	'67
Have You Never Been Mellow	Newton-John, Olivia	'75
Have You Seen Her	Chi-Lites, The	'71
Have You Seen Her Face	Byrds, The	'66
Have You Seen the Saucers	Jefferson Airplane, The	'69
Have You Seen Your Mother, Baby, Standing in the Shadow	Rolling Stones, The	'66
Haven't Got Time for the Pain	Simon, Carly	'74
Having a Party	Cooke, Sam	'62
Hawaii 5-Oh	Ventures, The	'69
Hawk (El Gavilan), The	Faithfull, Marianne	'86
Hazard	Marx, Richard	'91
Hazy Shade of Winter, A	Simon and Garfunkel	'68
He Ain't Heavy...He's My Brother	Cocker, Joe	'69
He Gives Us All His Love	Newman, Randy	'72
He Hit Me (and It Felt Like a Kiss)	Crystals, The	'63
He Was a Friend of Mine	Dylan, Bob	'63
He Was My Brother	Simon and Garfunkel	'64
He Was Really Saying Something	Velvelettes, The	'65
He Will Break Your Heart	Butler, Jerry	'60
He'll Have to Go	Reeves, Jim	'59
He's a Bad Boy	King, Carole	'63
He's a Rebel	Crystals, The	'62
He's Gone	Chantels, The	'57
He's Got the Fever	Southside Johnny & the Asbury Jukes	'76
He's Got the Whole World	London, Laurie	'57

SONG	ARTIST	YEAR
in His Hands		
He's So Fine	Chiffons, The	'63
He's So Shy	Pointer Sisters, The	'80
He's Sure the Boy I Love	Crystals, The	'62
He's the Greatest Dancer	Sister Sledge	'78
Head Games	Foreigner	'79
Head Like a Hole	Nine Inch Nails	'90
Head over Heels	Tears for Fears	'85
Head to Toe	Lisa Lisa & Cult Jam	'87
Headed for a Heartbreak	Winger	'89
Hear My Train a-Coming	Hendrix, Jimi	'71
Heard It in a Love Song	Marshall Tucker Band, The	'77
Heart and Soul	Cleftones, The	'61
Heart and Soul	Lewis, Huey & the News	'83
Heart and Soul	T'Pau	'87
Heart Attack	Newton-John, Olivia	'81
Heart Country	Firetown	'87
Heart Full of Soul	Yardbirds, The	'65
Heart Like a Wheel	Ronstadt, Linda	'74
Heart Needs a Home, A	Thompson, Richard and Linda	'74
Heart of a Ballerina	Springsteen, Bruce	'73
Heart of Glass	Blondie	'78
Heart of Gold	Young, Neil	'72
Heart of Rock and Roll, The	Lewis, Huey & the News	'84
Heart of Stone	Rolling Stones, The	'65
Heart of the City	Lowe, Nick	'78
Heart of the Matter	Henley, Don	'89
Heart of the Sunrise	Yes	'72
Heart Shaped Box	Nirvana	'93
Heartache Tonight	Eagles, The	'79
Heartaches	Marcels, The	'61
Heartbeat	Holly, Buddy	'59
Heartbeat-It's a Lovebeat	DeFranco Family, The	'73
Heartbeats Accelerating	McGarrigle, Kate and Anna	'90
Heartbreak Beat	Psychedelic Furs, The	'87
Heartbreak Hotel	Jacksons, The	'80
Heartbreak Hotel	Presley, Elvis	'56
Heartbreaker	Charles, Ray	'54
Heartbreaker	Led Zeppelin	'69
Hearts	Balin, Marty	'81
Hearts of Stone	Charms, The	'54
Heat Is On, The	Frey, Glenn	'85
Heat of the Moment	Asia	'82
Heat of the Night	Adams, Bryan	'87
Heat Wave	Martha & the Vandellas	'63
Heaven	Adams, Bryan	'84
Heaven	Warrant	'89
Heaven and Paradise	Meadowlarks	'55
Heaven Help Me	Estus, Deon	'89
Heaven Help Us All	Wonder, Stevie	'70

SONG	ARTIST	YEAR	SONG	ARTIST	YEAR
Heaven Is a Place on Earth	Carlisle, Belinda	'87	Here Today	McCartney, Paul	'82
Heaven Knows	Summer, Donna	'78	Here We Go	C&C Music Factory	'91
Heaven Knows I'm Miserable Now	Smiths, The	'84	Here's to the State of Mississippi	Ochs, Phil	'64
Heaven on the Seventh Floor	Nicholas, Paul	'77	Here's Where the Story Ends	Sundays, The	'90
Heavy Makes You Happy (Sha-Na-Boom-Boom)	Staple Singers, The	'71	Hero	Carey, Mariah	'93
			Heroes	Bowie, David	'77
Heeby Jeebies	Little Richard	'56	Heroes and Villains	Beach Boys, The	'67
Helen Wheels	McCartney, Paul & Wings	'73	Heroin	Velvet Underground, The	'67
Hell's Bells	AC/DC	'80	Hey! Baby	Channel, Bruce	'62
Hello	Richie, Lionel	'83	Hey Bo Diddley	Diddley, Bo	'57
Hello, Goodbye	Beatles, The	'67	Hey Bulldog	Beatles, The	'69
Hello, Hello	Sopwith Camel	'66	Hey Deannie	Cassidy, Shaun	'78
Hello, I Love You	Doors, The	'68	Hey, Girl	Scott, Freddie	'63
Hello in There	Prine, John	'71	Hey Good Lookin'	Williams, Hank	'51
Hello, It's Me	Nazz, The	'69	Hey Grandma	Moby Grape	'67
Hello, It's Me	Reed, Lou & John Cale	'89	Hey Jack Kerouac	10,000 Maniacs	'87
Hello Mary Lou	Nelson, Rick	'61	Hey Jealousy	Gin Blossoms	'92
Hello Stranger	Faithfull, Marianne	'87	Hey Joe	Leaves, The	'65
Hello Stranger	Lewis, Barbara	'63	Hey Jude	Beatles, The	'68
Help!	Beatles, The	'65	Hey Ladies	Beastie Boys, The	'89
Help I'm a Rock	Mothers of Invention	'66	Hey Little Cobra	Rip Chords, The	'63
Help Me	Mitchell, Joni	'74	Hey, Little Girl	Clark, Dee	'59
Help Me Make It Through the Night	Kristofferson, Kris	'69	Hey Mr. DJ	Zhane	'93
Help Me, Mary	Phair, Liz	'93	Hey Nineteen	Steely Dan	'80
Help Me, Rhonda	Beach Boys, The	'65	Hey, Paula	Paul and Paula	'62
Help Me Somebody	5 Royales, The	'53	Hey, Schoolgirl	Tom and Jerry	'58
Helpless	Crosby, Stills, Nash & Young	'70	Hey, That's No Way to Say Goodbye	Cohen, Leonard	'68
Helter Skelter	Beatles, The	'68			
Henry's Got Flat Feet	Midnighters, The	'55	Hey There Lonely Boy	Ruby & the Romantics	'63
Her Royal Majesty	Darren, James	'63	Hey, Western Union Man	Butler, Jerry	'68
Her Town Too	Taylor, James	'81	(Hey Won't You Play) Another Somebody Done Somebody Wrong Song	Thomas, B.J.	'75
Here 'Tis	Diddley, Bo	'55			
Here and Now	Vandross, Luther	'89			
Here Come Those Tears Again	Browne, Jackson	'76	Hi Hi Hi	McCartney, Paul & Wings	'72
Here Comes a Regular	Replacements, The	'85	Hi-Heel Sneakers	Tucker, Tommy	'64
Here Comes My Baby	Tremeloes, The	'67	Hickory Wind	Byrds, The	'68
Here Comes My Girl	Petty, Tom & the Heartbreakers	'79	Hidden Love	Case, Peter	'89
			Hide Away	King, Freddie	'61
Here Comes Summer	Keller, Jerry	'59	High Coin	Harper's Bizarre	'67
Here Comes That Rainy Day Feeling Again	Fortunes, The	'71	High Enough	Damn Yankees	'90
			High Flying Bird	Havens, Richie	'67
Here Comes the Hotstepper	Kamose, Ini	'94	High on You	Survivor	'84
Here Comes the Judge	Long, Shorty	'68	High on Your Love Suite	James, Rick	'79
Here Comes the Night	Lulu	'64	High School Confidential	Lewis, Jerry Lee	'58
Here Comes the Rain Again	Eurythmics	'84	High School Nights	Edmunds, Dave	'85
Here Comes the Sun	Beatles, The	'69	High School U.S.A.	Facenda, Tommy	'59
Here Comes Your Man	Pixies, The	'89	High Time We Went	Cocker, Joe	'71
Here I Am (Come and Take Me)	Green, Al	'73	Higher Ground	Wonder, Stevie	'73
Here I Go Again	Whitesnake	'87	Higher Love	Winwood, Steve	'86
Here, There and Everywhere	Beatles, The	'66	Higher Plane	Kool & the Gang	'74
(Here They Come) From All over the World	Jan and Dean	'65	Highway 61 Revisited	Dylan, Bob	'65

SONG	ARTIST	YEAR	SONG	ARTIST	YEAR
Highway Patrolman	Springsteen, Bruce	'82	Homecoming Queen's Got a Gun, The	Brown, Julie	'87
Highway Star	Deep Purple	'72	Homeward Bound	Simon and Garfunkel	'66
Highway to Hell	AC/DC	'79	Homosapien	Shelley, Pete	'82
Highway Toes	Guest, Christopher	'73	Honest I Do	Reed, Jimmy	'57
Him	Holmes, Rupert	'79	Honey	Goldsboro, Bobby	'68
Him or Me, What's It Gonna Be	Revere, Paul & the Raiders	'67	Honey Chile	Martha & the Vandellas	'67
Hip Hop Hooray	Naughty by Nature	'93	Honey Don't	Perkins, Carl	'55
Hip to Be Square	Lewis, Huey & the News	'86	Honey Hush	Turner, Joe	'54
Hippy Hippy Shake	Romero, Chan	'59	Honey Love	Drifters, The	'54
His Lips Got in the Way	Castro, Bernadette	'64	Honey Love	Kelly, R.	'92
History Lesson (Part Two)	Minutemen, The	'84	Honey Pie	Beatles, The	'68
History of Utah	Camper Van Beethoven	'86	Honey (Touch Me with My Clothes On)	Radner, Gilda	'79
Hit	Sugarcubes	'92	Honeycomb	Rodgers, Jimmie	'57
Hit Me with Your Best Shot	Benatar, Pat	'80	Honeydripper, The	Liggins, Joe	'45
Hit Me with Your Rhythm Stick	Dury, Ian & the Blockheads	'79	Hong Kong Garden	Siouxsie & the Banshees	'78
Hit the Road, Jack	Charles, Ray	'61	Honky Cat	John, Elton	'72
Hitch Hike	Gaye, Marvin	'64	Honky Tonk	Doggett, Bill	'56
Hitchin' a Ride	Vanity Fair	'70	Honky Tonk Man	Horton, Johnny	'56
Hocus Pocus	Focus	'73	Honky Tonk Masquerade	Ely, Joe	'78
Hold Back the Night	Parker, Graham	'76	Honky Tonk Women	Rolling Stones, The	'69
Hold Me	Fleetwood Mac	'82	Hooked on a Feeling	Thomas, B.J.	'68
Hold Me Daddy	XTC	'89	Hooray for Hazel	Roe, Tommy	'66
Hold Me Now	Thompson Twins, The	'84	Hoover Factory	Costello, Elvis	'80
Hold Me Tight	Nash, Johnny	'68	Hope of Deliverance	McCartney, Paul	'93
Hold My Hand	Hootie and the Blowfish	'94	Hope That We Can Be Together Soon	Melvin, Harold & the Bluenotes	'75
Hold On	En Vogue	'90	Hopelessly Devoted to You	Newton-John, Olivia	'78
Hold On	Reed, Lou	'89	Horse, The	Nobles, Cliff & Co.	'68
Hold On	Wilson Phillips	'90	Horse with No Name	America	'72
Hold on Loosely	38-Special	'81	Horses	Jones, Rickie Lee	'89
Hold on Tight	Electric Light Orchestra	'81	Hot Blooded	Foreigner	'78
Hold on to My Love	Ruffin, Jimmy	'80	Hot Burrito #1	Flying Burrito Brothers, The	'69
Hold on to the Nights	Marx, Richard	'88	Hot Child in the City	Gilder, Nick	'78
Hold on, I'm Comin'	Sam and Dave	'66	Hot for Teacher	Van Halen	'84
Hold the Line	Toto	'78	Hot Fun in the Summertime	Sly & the Family Stone	'69
Hold What You've Got	Tex, Joe	'64	Hot Girls in Love	Loverboy	'83
Hold You Tight	Kemp, Tara	'91	Hot! Hot! Hot!	Poindexter, Buster	'87
Hold Your Head Up	Argent	'72	Hot in the City	Idol, Billy	'82
Holding Back the Years	Simply Red	'86	Hot Legs	Stewart, Rod	'77
Holding on When Love Is Gone	L.T.D.	'78	Hot Line	Sylvers, The	'77
Hole Hearted	Extreme	'90	Hot Love	T. Rex	'71
Holiday	Scorpions, The	'79	Hot N' Nasty	Humble Pie	'72
Holiday in Cambodia	Dead Kennedys, The	'80	Hot Pants (She Got to Use What She Got to Get What She Wants)	Brown, James	'71
Holidays in the Sun	Sex Pistols, The	'77	Hot Pastrami	Dartells, The	'63
Holly Holy	Diamond, Neil	'69	Hot Patootie—Bless My Soul	Meat Loaf	'74
Hollywood Nights	Seger, Bob	'77	Hot Rod Hearts	Dupree, Robbie	'80
Hollywood Swinging	Kool & the Gang	'73	Hot Rod Lincoln	Bond, Johnny	'55
Holocaust	Big Star	'78	Hot Stuff	Summer, Donna	'79
Home Is Anywhere You Hang Your Head	Costello, Elvis	'86			
Home Is Where the Hatred Is	Phillips, Esther	'72			

SONG	ARTIST	YEAR	SONG	ARTIST	YEAR
Hotel California	Eagles, The	'77	Humpin' Around	Brown, Bobby	'92
Hotel Happiness	Benton, Brook	'63	Humpty Dance, The	Digital Underground	'90
Hound Dog	Thornton, Big Mama	'53	Hundred Pounds of Clay, A	McDaniels, Gene	'61
Hound Dog Man	Fabian	'59	Hung on You	Righteous Brothers, The	'65
Hourglass	Squeeze	'87	Hungry	Revere, Paul & the Raiders	'66
House at Pooh Corner	Nitty Gritty Dirt Band	'70	Hungry Eyes	Carmen, Eric	'87
House of Blue Lights, The	Slack, Freddie and Ella Mae Morse	'46	Hungry Freaks, Daddy	Mothers of Invention	'67
			Hungry Heart	Springsteen, Bruce	'80
House of the Rising Sun, The	Weavers, The	'58	Hungry Like the Wolf	Duran Duran	'83
House That Jack Built, The	Franklin, Aretha	'68	Hungry Wolf	X	'82
How 'bout Us	Champaign	'81	Hunter Gets Captured by the Game, The	Marvelettes, The	'67
How Am I Supposed to Live Without You	Branigan, Laura	'83	Hurdy Gurdy Man	Donovan	'68
How Blue Can You Get	King, B.B.	'62	Hurricane (Part I)	Dylan, Bob	'75
How Can I Be Sure	Rascals, The	'67	Hurt	Hamilton, Roy	'54
How Can I Ease the Pain	Fischer, Lisa	'91	Hurt So Bad	Little Anthony and the Imperials	'65
How Can I Fall	Breathe	'88			
How Can I Meet Her	Everly Brothers, The	'62	Hurting Each Other	Ruby & the Romantics	'65
How Can I Refuse	Heart	'83	Hurting Kind (I've Got My Eyes on You)	Plant, Robert	'90
How Can We Be Lovers	Bolton, Michael	'90			
How Can You Expect to Be Taken Seriously	Pet Shop Boys	'90	Hurts Me to My Heart	Adams, Faye	'54
			Hurts So Good	Mellencamp, John Cougar	'82
How Can You Mend a Broken Heart	Bee Gees, The	'71	Hush	Royal, Billy Joe	'67
How Deep Is Your Love	Bee Gees, The	'77	Hushabye	Mystics, The	'59
How Do I Make You	Ronstadt, Linda	'77	Hustle, The	McCoy, Van	'75
How Do You Do It	Gerry & the Pacemakers	'64	Hypnotized	Drifters, The	'57
How Do You Do (Let Echols Check)	Mouth and MacNeal	'72	Hysteria	Def Leppard	'87
How Do You Sleep	Lennon, John	'71	**I**		
How Do You Talk to an Angel	Heights, The	'92			
How High the Moon	Paul, Les and Mary Ford	'51	I Adore Him	Angels, The	'63
How Long	Ace	'75	I Adore Mi Amor	Color Me Badd	'91
How Long (Betcha' Got a Chick on the Side)	Pointer Sisters, The	'75	I Ain't Done Wrong	Yardbirds, The	'65
			I Ain't Goin' out Like That	Cypress Hill	'93
How Many More Times	Led Zeppelin	'69	I Ain't Gonna Eat out My Heart Anymore	Rascals, The	'65
How Many More Years	Howling Wolf	'51			
How Much I Feel	Ambrosia	'78	I Ain't Gonna Stand for It	Wonder, Stevie	'80
How Soon Is Now	Smiths, The	'85	I Ain't Marchin' Anymore	Ochs, Phil	'64
How Sweet It Is (to Be Loved by You)	Gaye, Marvin	'64	I Ain't Superstitious	Howling Wolf	'62
			I Almost Had a Weakness	Costello, Elvis and the Brodsky Quartet	'93
How to Kill a Radio Consultant	Public Enemy	'91			
How Will I Know	Houston, Whitney	'85	I Almost Lost My Mind	Hunter, Ivory Joe	'50
Hucklebuck, The	Williams, Paul	'49	I Alone	Live	'94
Hula Love	Knox, Buddy	'57	I Am a Child	Buffalo Springfield	'68
Human	Human League	'86	I Am a Patriot	Little Steven & the Disciples of Soul	'84
Human Behaviour	Bjork	'93			
Human Being	New York Dolls	'74	I Am a Rock	Simon and Garfunkel	'66
Human Fly	Cramps, The	'79	I Am a Scientist	Guided by Voices	'94
Human Nature	Jackson, Michael	'83	I Am a Town	Carpenter, Mary Chapin	'92
Human Touch	Springsteen, Bruce	'92	I Am...I Said	Diamond, Neil	'71
Humbled in Love	Cohen, Leonard	'79	I Am One	Smashing Pumpkins	'91
			I Am the Fly	Wire	'77

SONG	ARTIST	YEAR
I Am the Walrus	Beatles, The	'67
I Am Woman	Reddy, Helen	'72
I Beg of You	Presley, Elvis	'58
I Believe	Buzzcocks, The	'79
I Believe I'll Dust My Broom	James, Elmore	'52
I Believe in You (You Believe in Me)	Taylor, Johnnie	'73
I Believe My Own Eyes	Mitzman, Marcia and Jonathan Dokuchitz	'93
I Belong to You	Love Unlimited Orchestra	'74
I Came to Dance	Lofgren, Nils	'77
I Can Dream About You	Hartman, Dan	'84
I Can Hear Music	Ronettes, The	'66
I Can Help	Swan, Billy	'74
I Can Never Go Home Anymore	Shangri-Las, The	'65
I Can See Clearly Now	Nash, Johnny	'72
I Can See for Miles	Who, The	'67
I Can't Be Satisfied	Waters, Muddy	'48
I Can't Dance	Genesis	'91
I Can't Drive 55	Hagar, Sammy	'84
I Can't Explain	Who, The	'65
I Can't Get Next to You	Temptations, The	'69
(I Can't Get No) Satisfaction	Rolling Stones, The	'65
I Can't Go for That (No Can Do)	Hall and Oates	'81
I Can't Help Myself (Sugar Pie, Honey Bunch)	Four Tops, The	'65
I Can't Hold On	Bonoff, Karla	'77
I Can't Let Go	Hollies, The	'66
I Can't Live without My Radio	L.L. Cool J	'85
I Can't Quit Her	Blood, Sweat & Tears	'68
I Can't Quit You Baby	Rush, Otis	'56
I Can't Stand It	Clapton, Eric	'81
I Can't Stand the Rain	Peebles, Ann	'73
I Can't Stay Mad at You	Davis, Skeeter	'63
I Can't Stop Dancing	Bell, Archie & the Drells	'68
I Can't Stop Loving You	Gibson, Don	'58
I Can't Tell You Why	Eagles, The	'79
I Can't Turn You Loose	Redding, Otis	'65
I Can't Wait	Nu Shooz	'86
I Can't Wait Another Minute	Hi-Five	'91
I Could Have Been Your Best Old Friend	Raitt, Bonnie	'76
I Could Never Love Another (After Loving You)	Temptations, The	'68
I Could Never Take the Place of Your Man	Prince	'88
I Could Rule the World If I Could Only Get the Parts	Tin Huey	'79
I Couldn't Get High	Fugs, The	'65
I Count the Tears	Drifters, The	'61
I Cried a Tear	Baker, LaVern	'59
I Didn't Mean to Turn You On	Cherrelle	'84

SONG	ARTIST	YEAR
I Dig Rock and Roll Music	Peter, Paul & Mary	'67
I Do	Marvelows, The	'65
I Do the Rock	Curry, Tim	'79
I Don't Believe You (She Acts Like We Never Have Met)	Dylan, Bob	'64
I Don't Care Anymore	Collins, Phil	'82
I Don't Have the Heart	Ingram, James	'90
I Don't Know	Mabon, Willie	'52
I Don't Know How to Love Him	Elliman, Yvonne	'71
I Don't Know What You've Got (But It's Got Me)	Little Richard	'65
I Don't Like Mondays	Boomtown Rats, The	'79
I Don't Live Today	Hendrix, Jimi	'67
I Don't Need No Doctor	Charles, Ray	'66
I Don't Think So	Dinosaur Jr.	'94
I Don't Wanna Fight	Turner, Tina	'93
I Don't Wanna Go on with You Like That	John, Elton	'88
I Don't Wanna Live without Your Love	Chicago	'88
I Don't Want to Do Wrong	Knight, Gladys & the Pips	'71
I Don't Want to Go Home	Southside Johnny & the Asbury Jukes	'76
(I Don't Want to Go to) Chelsea	Costello, Elvis	'80
I Don't Want to Grow Up	Waits, Tom	'92
I Don't Want to Live without You	Foreigner	'88
I Don't Want to Spoil the Party	Beatles, The	'65
I Don't Want to Talk About It	Crazy Horse	'71
I Don't Want Your Love	Duran Duran	'88
I Drink Alone	Thorogood, George	'85
I Drove All Night	Lauper, Cyndi	'89
I Fall to Pieces	Cline, Patsy	'61
I Feel a Song (in My Heart)	Knight, Gladys & the Pips	'74
I Feel Fine	Beatles, The	'64
I Feel for You	Prince	'79
I Feel Free	Cream	'67
I Feel Good	Green, Al	'77
I Feel Like a Bullet (in the Gun of Robert Ford)	John, Elton	'76
I Feel Like Breaking up Somebody's Home Tonight	Peebles, Ann	'72
I-Feel-Like-I'm-Fixin'-to-Die Rag	Country Joe and The Fish	'67
I Feel Love	Summer, Donna	'77
I Feel So Bad	Willis, Chuck	'54
I Feel So Good	Thompson, Richard	'91
I Feel the Earth Move	King, Carole	'71
I Feel the Same	Raitt, Bonnie	'73
I Forgot to Be Your Lover	Bell, William	'68
I Forgot to Remember to Forget	Presley, Elvis	'55
I Fought the Law	Crickets, The	'59
I Found a Love	Falcons, The	'62

SONG	ARTIST	YEAR
I Found a Love, Oh What a Love	Jo-Ann and Troy	'65
I Found Someone	Cher	'87
I Found That Essence Rare	Gang of Four	'80
I Get Around	Beach Boys, The	'64
I Get Around	2Pac	'93
I Get So Excited	Hunter, Ian	'75
I Get Weak	Carlisle, Belinda	'88
I Go Crazy	Davis, Paul	'78
I Go Crazy	Flesh for Lulu	'87
I Go to Extremes	Joel, Billy	'89
I Go to Pieces	Shannon, Del	'64
I Got a Feeling	Nelson, Ricky	'58
I Got a Line on You	Spirit	'69
I Got a Man	Positive K	'93
I Got a Name	Croce, Jim	'73
I Got a Thang 4 Ya!	Lo-Key	'92
I Got a Woman (I Got a Sweetie)	Charles, Ray	'55
I Got Loaded	Harris, Peppermint	'51
I Got Love on My Mind	Cole, Natalie	'76
I Got My Mind Made Up (You Can Get It Girl)	Instant Funk	'79
I Got No Answers	Jett, Joan & the Blackhearts	'84
I Got Stoned and I Missed It	Shel Silverstein	'73
I Got Stung	Presley, Elvis	'58
I Got the Feelin'	Brown, James & the Famous Flames	'68
I Got You	Split Enz	'80
I Got You Babe	Sonny and Cher	'65
I Got You (I Feel Good)	Brown, James & the Famous Flames	'65
I Gotcha	Tex, Joe	'72
I Gotta Know	Presley, Elvis	'60
I Guess I Showed Her	Cray, Robert	'86
I Guess That's Why They Call It the Blues	John, Elton	'83
(I Guess) The Lord Must Be in New York City	Nilsson	'69
I Had a King	Mitchell, Joni	'68
I Had Too Much to Dream (Last Night)	Electric Prunes	'67
I Hate My School	Red Cross	'80
I Hate Myself for Loving You	Jett, Joan & the Blackhearts	'88
I Hear a Symphony	Supremes, The	'65
I Hear You Knocking	Lewis, Smiley	'55
I Heard a Rumour	Bananarama	'87
I Heard Her Call My Name	Velvet Underground, The	'68
I Heard It Through the Grapevine	Miracles, The	'67
I Honestly Love You	Newton-John, Olivia	'74
I Just Called to Say I Love You	Wonder, Stevie	'84
I Just Can't Help Believing	Thomas, B.J.	'70
I Just Can't Stop Loving You	Jackson, Michael	'87

SONG	ARTIST	YEAR
(I Just) Died in Your Arms	Cutting Crew	'87
I Just Wanna Make Love to You	Waters, Muddy	'54
I Just Wanna Stop	Vannelli, Gino	'78
I Just Want to Be Your Everything	Gibb, Andy	'77
I Just Want to Celebrate	Rare Earth	'71
I Just Wasn't Made for These Times	Beach Boys, The	'66
I Keep Forgettin' (Every Time You're Near)	McDonald, Michael	'82
I Knew the Bride When She Used to Rock and Roll	Lowe, Nick	'85
I Knew You Were Waiting (for Me)	Franklin, Aretha	'87
I Know (You Don't Love Me No More)	George, Barbara	'61
I Know a Little	Lynyrd Skynyrd	'77
I Know a Place	Clark, Petula	'65
(I Know I Got) Skillz	O'Neal, Shaquille	'93
I Know I'll Never Love This Way Again	Warwick, Dionne	'79
I Know It's Gonna Happen	Morrissey	'93
I Know It's Over	Smiths, The	'86
I Know What Boys Like	Waitresses, The	'82
I Know What I Like	Lewis, Huey & the News	'86
I Know You Rider	Martin and Neil	'65
I Know You're out There Somewhere	Moody Blues, The	'88
I Know Your Little Secret	Afghan Whigs	'90
(I Know) I'm Losing You	Temptations, The	'66
I Like	Guy	'88
I Like Dreaming	Nolan, Kenny	'77
I Like It	Dino	'89
I Like It Like That	Kenner, Chris	'61
I Like the Way (the Kissing Game)	Hi-Five	'90
I Live for Cars and Girls	Dictators, The	'75
I Love a Rainy Night	Rabbitt, Eddie	'80
I Love How You Love Me	Paris Sisters, The	'61
I Love L.A.	Newman, Randy	'83
I Love Music (Part 1)	O'Jays, The	'75
I Love Rock and Roll	Jett, Joan & the Blackhearts	'82
I Love the Nightlife (Disco Round)	Bridges, Alicia	'77
(I Love the Sound of) Breaking Glass	Lowe, Nick	'78
I Love the Way You Love	Johnson, Marv	'60
I Love You	Climax	'81
I Love You	Volumes, The	'62
(I Love You) For Sentimental Reasons	Cole, Nat King	'47
I Love You More Than You'll Ever Know	Blood, Sweat & Tears	'68
(I Love You) Still	Anderson, Bill	'63
I Love You, Suzanne	Reed, Lou	'82
I Love Your Smile	Shanice	'91

SONG	ARTIST	YEAR
I May Not Be Your Kind	Jeffreys, Garland	'77
I Melt with You	Modern English	'82
I Met Her in Church	Box Tops, The	'68
I Met Him on a Sunday	Shirelles, The	'58
I Miss You	Klymaxx	'85
I Missed Again	Collins, Phil	'81
I Misunderstood	Thompson, Richard	'91
I Need a Lover	Mellencamp, John Cougar	'79
I Need Love	L.L. Cool J	'87
I Need You	America	'72
I Need You	Beatles, The	'65
I Need Your Love Tonight	Presley, Elvis	'59
I Never Cry	Cooper, Alice	'76
I Never Loved a Man (the Way I Love You)	Franklin, Aretha	'67
I Only Have Eyes for You	Flamingos, The	'59
I Only Want to Be with You	Springfield, Dusty	'64
I Only Want You	Passions, The	'60
I Pity the Fool	Bland, Bobby	'61
I Put a Spell on You	Hawkins, Screaming Jay	'56
I Ran	Flock of Seagulls, A	'82
I Remember Holding You	Boys Club	'88
I Remember You	Ifield, Frank	'62
I Remember You	Skid Row	'90
I Saw Her Again Last Night	Mamas and the Papas, The	'66
I Saw Her Standing There	Beatles, The	'63
I Saw Red	Warrant	'90
I Saw the Best Minds of My Generation Rot	Fugs, The	'65
I Saw the Light	Rundgren, Todd	'72
I Second That Emotion	Miracles, The	'67
I Shall Be Released	Band, The	'68
I Shot the Sheriff	Marley, Bob & the Wailers	'73
I Should Have Known Better	Beatles, The	'64
I Sold My Heart to the Junkman	Bluebelles, The	'62
I Started a Joke	Bee Gees, The	'68
I Still Haven't Found What I'm Looking For	U2	'87
I Swear	All-4-One	'94
I Take What I Want	Sam and Dave	'66
I Thank You	Sam and Dave	'68
I Think I Love You	Partridge Family, The	'70
I Think It's Gonna Rain Today	Collins, Judy	'66
I Think We're Alone Now	James, Tommy & the Shondells	'67
I Touch Myself	Divinyls	'91
I Understand Just How You Feel	Four Tunes, The	'54
I Walk on Gilded Splinters	Dr. John	'68
I Walk the Line	Cash, Johnny	'56
I Wanna Be a Lifeguard	Blotto	'80
I Wanna Be Black	Reed, Lou	'78

SONG	ARTIST	YEAR
I Wanna Be Down	Brandy	'94
I Wanna Be Rich	Calloway	'90
I Wanna Be Sedated	Ramones, The	'78
I Wanna Be Your Boyfriend	Ramones, The	'76
I Wanna Be Your Dog	Stooges, The	'69
I Wanna Be Your Lover	Prince	'79
I Wanna Be Your Man	Rolling Stones, The	'64
I Wanna Dance Wit' Choo (Doo Dat Dance) Part I	Disco Tex & the Sex-O-Lettes	'75
I Wanna Dance with Somebody (Who Loves Me)	Houston, Whitney	'87
I Wanna Get Next to You	Rose Royce	'77
I Wanna Have Some Fun	Fox, Samantha	'89
I Wanna Love Him So Bad	Jelly Beans, The	'64
I Wanna Sex You Up	Color Me Badd	'91
(I Wanna) Testify	Parliaments, The	'67
I Want a New Drug	Lewis, Huey & the News	'84
I Want Candy	Strangeloves, The	'65
I Want Her	Sweat, Keith	'88
I Want to Be Wanted	Lee, Brenda	'60
I Want to Be Your Man	Roger	'87
I Want to do Everything for You	Tex, Joe	'65
I Want to Hold Your Hand	Beatles, The	'63
I Want to Know What Love Is	Foreigner	'84
I Want to Make the World Turn Around	Miller, Steve Band, The	'86
I Want to See the Bright Lights Tonight	Thompson, Richard and Linda	'74
I Want to Take You Higher	Sly & the Family Stone	'69
I Want to Tell You	Beatles, The	'66
I Want to Walk You Home	Domino, Fats	'59
I Want You	Dylan, Bob	'66
I Want You	Gaye, Marvin	'76
I Want You	L.L. Cool J	'85
I Want You Back	Jackson 5, The	'69
I Want You (She's So Heavy)	Beatles, The	'69
I Want You to Be My Baby	Briggs, Lillian	'56
I Want You to Be My Girl	Lymon, Frankie and the Teenagers	'56
I Want You to Hurt Like I Do	Newman, Randy	'88
I Want You to Want Me	Cheap Trick	'77
I Want You, I Need You, I Love You	Presley, Elvis	'56
I Want Your Love	Chic	'78
I Want Your Sex	Michael, George	'87
I Want'a Do Something Freaky to You	Haywood, Leon	'75
I Wanted Everything	Ramones, The	'78
I Was Made for Dancin'	Garrett, Leif	'79
I Was Made for Loving You	Kiss	'79
I Was Made to Love Her	Wonder, Stevie	'67
I Was the One	Presley, Elvis	'56

SONG	ARTIST	YEAR	SONG	ARTIST	YEAR
I Wasn't Born to Follow	Byrds, The	'68	If I Fell	Beatles, The	'64
I (Who Have Nothing)	King, Ben E.	'63	If I Had a Hammer	Weavers, The	'49
I Will	Beatles, The	'68	If I Had a Rocket Launcher	Cockburn, Bruce	'85
I Will Always Love You	Parton, Dolly	'74	If I Had No Loot	Tony! Toni! Tone!	'93
I Will Dare	Replacements, The	'84	If I Needed Someone	Beatles, The	'65
I Will Follow	U2	'82	If I Were a Carpenter	Hardin, Tim	'67
I Will Follow Him (Chariot)	March, Little Peggy	'63	If I Were Your Woman	Knight, Gladys & the Pips	'70
I Will Survive	Gaynor, Gloria	'78	If I'd Been the One	38-Special	'83
I Wish	Wonder, Stevie	'76	If It Isn't Love	New Edition	'88
I Wish I Knew (How It Would Feel to Be Free)	Burke, Solomon	'68	If Loving You Is Wrong I Don't Want to Be Right	Ingram, Luther	'71
I Wish It Would Rain	Temptations, The	'68	If Not for You	Dylan, Bob	'70
I Wish It Would Rain Down	Collins, Phil	'89	If Only You Knew	Labelle, Patti	'84
I Wish You Would	Yardbirds, The	'64	If She Knew What She Wants	Bangles, The	'86
I Won't Back Down	Petty, Tom	'89	If That's Your Boyfriend, He Wasn't Last Night	NdegeOcello, Me'Shell	'93
I Won't Hold You Back	Toto	'83	If There's a Heaven Above	Love and Rockets	'85
I Wonder If I Care as Much	Everly Brothers, The	'57	If This Is It	Lewis, Huey & the News	'84
I Wonder If I Take You Home	Lisa Lisa & Cult Jam	'85	I'll Always Love My Mama	Intruders, The	'73
I Wonder What She's Doing Tonight?	Boyce, Tommy & Bobby Hart	'67	I'll Be Around	Spinners, The	'72
I Wonder Why	Dion & the Belmonts	'58	I'll Be Doggone	Gaye, Marvin	'65
I Wonder Why	Stigers, Curtis	'91	I'll Be Good to You	Brothers Johnson, The	'76
I Would Die 4 U	Prince	'84	I'll Be Home	Flamingos, The	'56
I Write the Songs	Captain and Tennille, The	'75	I'll Be Loving You (Forever)	New Kids on the Block	'88
I.G.Y. (What a Beautiful World)	Fagen, Donald	'82	I'll Be Satisfied	Wilson, Jackie	'59
Ice Cream City	Shonen Knife	'90	I'll Be There	Escape Club, The	'91
Ice Cream for Crow	Captain Beefheart	'82	I'll Be There	Jackson 5, The	'70
Ice Ice Baby	Vanilla Ice	'90	I'll Be There for You	Bon Jovi	'89
I'd Die Without You	P.M. Dawn	'92	I'll Be You	Replacements, The	'89
I'd Do Anything for Love (But I Won't Do That)	Meat Loaf	'93	I'll Be Your Baby Tonight	Dylan, Bob	'68
			I'll Be Your Everything	Page, Tommy	'90
I'd Love to Change the World	Ten Years After	'71	I'll Be Your Mirror	Velvet Underground, The	'67
I'd Love You to Want Me	Lobo	'72	I'll Come Running Back to You	Cooke, Sam	'57
I'd Really Love to See You Tonight	England Dan & John Ford Coley	'75	I'll Cry Instead	Beatles, The	'64
			I'll Feel a Whole Lot Better	Byrds, The	'65
I'd Still Say Yes	Klymaxx	'87	I'll Follow the Sun	Beatles, The	'65
Ideal World	Christians, The	'88	I'll Get You	Beatles, The	'63
Idiot Wind	Dylan, Bob	'74	I'll Give All My Love to You	Sweat, Keith	'90
Iesha	Another Bad Creation	'91	I'll Have to Say I Love You in a Song	Croce, Jim	'73
If	Bread	'71			
If	Jackson, Janet	'93	I'll Keep It with Mine	Dylan, Bob	'66
If 6 Was 9	Hendrix, Jimi	'68	I'll Make Love to You	Boyz II Men	'94
If Ever You're in My Arms Again	Bryson, Peabo	'84	I'll Meet You Halfway	Partridge Family, The	'71
If He's Ever Near	Bonoff, Karla	'77	I'll Never Find Another You	Seekers, The	'65
If I Can Dream	Presley, Elvis	'68	I'll Never Get out of This World Alive	Williams, Hank	'52
If I Can't Have You	Elliman, Yvonne	'77			
If I Could Build My Whole World Around You	Gaye, Marvin and Tammi Terrell	'67	I'll Never Get over You (Getting over Me)	Expose	'93
If I Could Turn Back Time	Cher	'89	I'll Remember	Madonna	'94
If I Ever Fall in Love	Shai	'92	I'll Remember (in the Still of the Night)	Five Satins, The	'56
If I Ever Lose My Faith in You	Sting	'93			

SONG	ARTIST	YEAR	SONG	ARTIST	YEAR
I'll Rise	Harper, Ben	'93	I'm Just a Singer (in a Rock and Roll Band)	Moody Blues, The	'72
I'll Stand by You	Pretenders, The	'94	I'm Leaving It up to You	Don and Dewey	'57
I'll Stick Around	Foo Fighters	'95	I'm Livin' in Shame	Supremes, The	'69
I'll Take Care of You	Bland, Bobby	'60	I'm Looking for Someone to Love	Crickets, The	'57
I'll Take You There	Staple Singers, The	'72	I'm Looking through You	Beatles, The	'65
I'll Tumble 4 Ya	Culture Club	'83	I'm Mad	Mabon, Willie	'53
I'll Wait	Van Halen	'84	I'm Movin' On	Snow, Hank	'50
I'm a Believer	Monkees, The	'66	I'm Not a Juvenile Delinquent	Lymon, Frankie and the Teenagers	'57
I'm a Boy	Who, The	'71	I'm Not from Here	McMurtry, James	'89
I'm a Drifter	Martin and Neil	'65	I'm Not Gonna Let It Bother Me Tonight	Atlanta Rhythm Section	'78
I'm a Happy Man	Jive Five, The	'65	I'm Not in Love	10 c.c.	'75
I'm a King Bee	Harpo, Slim	'57	I'm Not Like Everybody Else	Kinks, The	'66
I'm a Loser	Beatles, The	'65	I'm Not Talking	Yardbirds, The	'65
I'm a Man	Davis, Spencer Group, The	'67	(I'm Not Your) Steppin' Stone	Revere, Paul & the Raiders	'66
I'm a Man	Diddley, Bo	'55	I'm on Fire	Springsteen, Bruce	'84
I'm a Man	Fabian	'58	I'm on Fire	Twilley, Dwight	'75
I'm a Mover	Free	'70	I'm on the Outside (Looking In)	Little Anthony and the Imperials	'64
I'm a Woman	Kweskin, Jim & the Jug Band	'65	I'm Ready	Domino, Fats	'59
(I'm a) Road Runner	Walker, Jr. & the All-Stars	'65	I'm Ready	Waters, Muddy	'54
I'm Against It	Ramones, The	'78	I'm Ready for Love	Martha & the Vandellas	'66
I'm Allowed	Buffalo Tom	'94	I'm Sittin' on Top of the World	Paul, Les and Mary Ford	'53
I'm Alright	Loggins, Kenny	'80	I'm So Bored with the USA	Clash, The	'77
I'm an Adult Now	Pursuit of Happiness	'88	I'm So Excited	Pointer Sisters, The	'82
I'm Blue (the Gong Gong Song)	Ikettes, The	'61	I'm So Glad	Cream	'67
I'm Coming Out	Ross, Diana	'80	I'm So into You	SWV	'93
I'm Doin Fine Now	New York City	'73	I'm So Lonesome I Could Cry	Williams, Hank	'49
I'm Easy	Carradine, Keith	'75	I'm So Proud	Impressions, The	'64
I'm Every Woman	Khan, Chaka	'78	I'm So Young	Students, The	'58
I'm Free	Rolling Stones, The	'65	I'm Sorry	Denver, John	'75
I'm Free	Who, The	'69	I'm Sorry	Lee, Brenda	'60
I'm Goin' Down	Springsteen, Bruce	'84	I'm Sorry (but So Is Brenda Lee)	Crenshaw, Marshall	'85
I'm Goin' Home	Ten Years After	'68	I'm Stepping Out	Lennon, John	'84
I'm Gonna Be (500 Miles)	Proclaimers, The	'89	I'm Stickin' with You	Bowen, Jimmy	'57
I'm Gonna Be a Wheel Someday	Domino, Fats	'59	I'm Still in Love with You	Green, Al	'72
I'm Gonna Be Strong	Pitney, Gene	'64	I'm Still Standing	John, Elton	'83
I'm Gonna Get Married	Price, Lloyd	'59	I'm Stone in Love with You	Stylistics, The	'72
I'm Gonna Love You Just a Little More Babe	White, Barry	'73	I'm Talking About You	Berry, Chuck	'61
I'm Gonna Love You Too	Holly, Buddy	'58	I'm Telling You Now	Freddie & the Dreamers	'65
I'm Gonna Make You Love Me	Warwick, Dee Dee	'67	I'm That Type of Guy	L.L. Cool J	'89
I'm Gonna Play the Honky Tonks	Adams, Marie	'52	I'm the Only One	Etheridge, Melissa	'93
I'm Gonna Tear Your Playhouse Down	Peebles, Ann	'72	I'm Too Sexy	Right Said Fred	'92
I'm Happy Just to Dance with You	Beatles, The	'64	I'm Tore Down	King, Freddie	'61
I'm Henry VIII, I Am	Herman's Hermits	'65	I'm Tore Up	Gayles, Billy with Ike Turner's Rhythm Rockers	'56
I'm in Love	King, Evelyn Champagne	'81	I'm Waiting for the Man	Velvet Underground, The	'67
I'm in Love	Pickett, Wilson	'67	I'm Walkin'	Domino, Fats	'57
I'm in Love Again	Domino, Fats	'56	I'm Your Baby Tonight	Houston, Whitney	'90
I'm in the Mood	Hooker, John Lee	'51			
I'm in You	Frampton, Peter	'77			
I'm into Something Good	Earl-Jean	'64			

SONG	ARTIST	YEAR
I'm Your Boogie Man	K.C. & the Sunshine Band	'77
I'm Your Hoochie Coochie Man	Waters, Muddy	'54
I'm Your Man	Cohen, Leonard	'88
I'm Your Man	Wham!	'86
I'm Your Puppet	Purify, James and Bobby	'66
Innocent Man, An	Joel, Billy	'83
It Was a Good Day	Ice Cube	'95
It's Not Over ('Til It's Over)	Starship	'87
I've Been in Love Before	Cutting Crew	'87
I've Been Lonely Too Long	Rascals, The	'67
I've Been Loving You Too Long	Redding, Otis	'65
I've Been Thinking About You	Londonbeat	'91
I've Been Waiting	Sweet, Matthew	'91
I've Been Wrong Before	Lovecraft, H.P.	'67
(I've Been) Searchin' So Long	Chicago	'74
I've Found Someone of My Own	Free Movement	'71
I've Got a Rock and Roll Heart	Clapton, Eric	'83
I've Got Dreams to Remember	Redding, Otis	'68
I've Got the Music in Me	Dee, Kiki	'74
I've Got to Get a Message to You	Bee Gees, The	'68
I've Got to Use My Imagination	Knight, Gladys & the Pips	'73
I've Had It	Bell Notes, The	'58
(I've Had) The Time of My Life	Medley, Bill & Jennifer Warnes	'87
I've Just Seen a Face	Beatles, The	'65
I've Loved Her So Long	Young, Neil	'69
I've Told Every Little Star	Scott, Linda	'61

J

SONG	ARTIST	YEAR
Jack and Diane	Mellencamp, John Cougar	'82
Jack and Jill	Raydio	'77
Jack Gets Up	Kottke, Leo	'89
Jack You're Dead	Jordan, Louis & His Tympani Five	'47
Jackie Blue	Ozark Mountain Daredevils, The	'75
Jackie Wilson Said (I'm in Heaven When You Smile)	Morrison, Van	'72
Jacob's Ladder	Lewis, Huey & the News	'86
Jailbreak	Thin Lizzy	'76
Jailhouse Rap	Fat Boys, The	'85
Jailhouse Rock	Presley, Elvis	'57
Jam on It	Newcleus	'84
Jam Tonight	Jackson, Freddie	'86
Jam up and Jelly Tight	Roe, Tommy	'69
Jambalaya (on the Bayou)	Williams, Hank	'52
James	Bangles, The	'84
James Dean	Eagles, The	'74
Jamie	Holland, Eddie	'61
Jamie's Cryin'	Van Halen	'78

SONG	ARTIST	YEAR
Jammin' Me	Petty, Tom & the Heartbreakers	'87
Jamming	Marley, Bob & the Wailers	'77
Jane	Jefferson Starship, The	'80
Janie's Got a Gun	Aerosmith	'89
Janis	Country Joe and the Fish	'67
Jazz Thing	Gang Starr	'90
Jazzman	King, Carole	'74
Je T'Aime...Moi Non Plus	Birkin, Jane and Serge Gainsbourg	'70
Jealous Guy	Lennon, John	'71
Jealous Kind	Cocker, Joe	'76
Jean	Oliver	'67
Jean Genie	Bowie, David	'72
Jeff's Boogie	Yardbirds, The	'66
Jenny Jenny	Little Richard	'56
Jenny-Lee	Jan and Arnie	'58
Jeopardy	Kihn, Greg Band, The	'83
Jeremiah Peabody's Poly-Unsaturated, Quick Dissolving, Fast Acting, Pleasant Tasting, Green and Purple Pills	Stevens, Ray	'61
Jeremy	Pearl Jam	'91
Jerk Out	Time, The	'90
Jerk, The	Larks, The	'64
Jerry Was a Race Car Driver	Primus	'91
Jerry's Pigeons	Ravan, Genya	'78
Jersey Girl	Waits, Tom	'80
Jesse	Simon, Carly	'80
Jessica	Allman Brothers, The	'73
Jessie	Kadison, Joshua	'93
Jessie's Girl	Springfield, Rick	'81
Jesus Built My Hotrod	Ministry	'91
Jesus Christ Superstar	Head, Murray	'70
Jesus Is Just Alright	Byrds, The	'70
Jet	McCartney, Paul & Wings	'74
Jet Airliner	Miller, Steve Band, The	'77
Jet City Woman	Queensryche	'91
Jim Dandy	Baker, LaVern	'57
Jim Dandy Got Married	Baker, LaVern	'57
Jimmy Lee	Franklin, Aretha	'86
Jimmy Mack	Martha & the Vandellas	'67
Jingle-Bell Rock	Helms, Bobby	'57
Jive Talkin'	Bee Gees, The	'75
Jo Jo Gunne	Berry, Chuck	'59
Jo-Ann	Twintones, The	'57
Joan Crawford	Blue Oyster Cult	'81
Joanna	Kool & the Gang	'83
Joanne	Nesmith, Michael	'70
Jody's Got Your Girl and Gone	Taylor, Johnnie	'71
Joe Stalin's Cadillac	Camper Van Beethoven	'86

SONG	ARTIST	YEAR	SONG	ARTIST	YEAR
Joe's Garage	Zappa, Frank	'79	Just a Song Before I Go	Crosby, Stills & Nash	'77
Joey	Dylan, Bob	'75	Just About Glad	Costello, Elvis	'94
Johannesburg	Scott-Heron, Gil	'75	Just Another Dream	Dennis, Cathy	'91
John Wesley Harding	Dylan, Bob	'68	Just Another Movie	Timbuk 3	'86
Johnny 99	Springsteen, Bruce	'82	Just Another Night	Jagger, Mick	'85
Johnny Angel	Fabares, Shelley	'62	Just Ask Your Heart	Avalon, Frankie	'59
Johnny Are You Queer	Cotton, Josie	'81	Just Be Good to Me	S.O.S. Band, The	'83
Johnny B. Goode	Berry, Chuck	'58	Just Because	Baker, Anita	'88
Johnny Get Angry	Sommers, Joannie	'62	Just Because	Price, Lloyd	'57
Johnny Remember Me	Leyton, John	'61	Just Between You and Me	Gramm, Lou	'90
Johnny Too Bad	Slickers, The	'72	Just Can't Get Enough	Depeche Mode	'81
Join Together	Who, The	'72	Just Coolin'	Levert	'88
Joker, The	Miller, Steve Band, The	'73	Just Don't Want to Be Lonely Tonight	Dyson, Ronnie	'73
Jokerman	Dylan, Bob	'83			
Jolene	Parton, Dolly	'74	Just Dropped In (to See What Condition My Condition Was In)	Rogers, Kenny	'68
Jolly Green Giant	Kingsmen, The	'65			
Journey to the Center of the Mind	Amboy Dukes, The	'68	Just Got Paid	Kemp, Johnny	'88
Joy	Pendergrass, Teddy	'88	Just Kickin' It	Xscape	'93
Joy to the World	Three Dog Night	'71	Just Like a Woman	Dylan, Bob	'66
Joyride	Roxette	'91	Just Like Fire Would	Saints, The	'87
Judy in Disguise (with Glasses)	Fred, John & His Playboy Band	'67	Just Like Heaven	Cure, The	'87
			Just Like Honey	Jesus and Mary Chain, The	'86
Judy's Turn to Cry	Gore, Lesley	'63	Just Like Jesse James	Cher	'89
Juicy	Notorious B.I.G., The	'94	Just Like Paradise	Roth, David Lee	'88
Juicy Fruit	Mtume	'83	(Just Like) Romeo and Juliet	Reflections, The	'64
Juke	Little Walter & His Nightcats	'52	(Just Like) Starting Over	Lennon, John	'80
Juke Box Hero	Foreigner	'82	Just Like Tom Thumb's Blues	Dylan, Bob	'65
Julia	Beatles, The	'68	Just My Imagination (Running Away with Me)	Temptations, The	'71
Julie, Do Ya Love Me	Sherman, Bobby	'70			
Julie's in the Drug Squad	Clash, The	'78	Just Once	Jones, Quincy	'81
Jump	Kriss Kross	'92	Just Once in My Life	Righteous Brothers, The	'65
Jump	Van Halen	'84	Just One Look	Troy, Doris	'63
Jump (for My Love)	Pointer Sisters, The	'84	Just One Smile	Pitney, Gene	'66
Jump Around	House of Pain	'92	Just out of Reach (of My Two Open Arms)	Burke, Solomon	'61
Jump in the Fire	Metallica	'83			
Jump to It	Franklin, Aretha	'82	Just Perfect	All	'88
Jumpin' Jack Flash	Rolling Stones, The	'68	Just Tell Her Jim Said Hello	Presley, Elvis	'62
Jumping Someone Else's Train	Cure, The	'79	Just the Two of Us	Washington, Grover Jr.	'81
Jungle Boogie	Kool & the Gang	'73	Just the Way It Is Baby	Rembrandts, The	'91
Jungle Fever	Wonder, Stevie	'91	Just the Way You Are	Joel, Billy	'78
Jungle Love	Time, The	'85	Just to Be Close to You	Commodores, The	'76
Jungleland	Springsteen, Bruce	'75	Just to Be with You	Passions, The	'59
Junior's Bar	Iron City House Rockers, The	'80	Just to See Her	Robinson, Smokey	'87
Junior's Farm	McCartney, Paul & Wings	'74	Just Walking in the Rain	Prisonaires, The	'53
Junk Food Junkie	Groce, Larry	'76	Just What I Needed	Cars, The	'78
Just a Dream	Clanton, Jimmy	'58	Just When I Needed You Most	Van Warmer, Randy	'79
Just a Friend	Biz Markie	'89	Just You 'n' Me	Chicago	'73
Just a Little	Beau Brummels	'65	Justified and Ancient	KLF, The	'91
Just a Little Bit Better	Herman's Hermits	'65	Justify My Love	Madonna	'90
Just a Little Too Much	Nelson, Ricky	'59	Justine	Don and Dewey	'58

SONG	ARTIST	YEAR	SONG	ARTIST	YEAR
K			Kind of a Drag	Buckinghams, The	'66
K.C. Lovin'	Littlefield, Little Willie	'52	Kind of Boy You Can't Forget, The	Raindrops, The	'63
Karma Chameleon	Culture Club	'83	Kind Woman	Buffalo Springfield	'68
Karn Evil 9 (1st Impression, Pt. 2)	Emerson, Lake & Palmer	'73	Kingdom Come	Verlaine, Tom	'79
Kashmir	Led Zeppelin	'75	King for a Day	Thompson Twins, The	'86
Katmandu	Stevens, Cat	'71	King Harvest (Has Surely Come)	Band, The	'68
Keep A-Knockin'	Little Richard	'57	King of Pain	Police, The	'83
(Keep Feeling) Fascination	Human League	'83	King of Rock	Run-D.M.C.	'85
Keep It Comin'	Sweat, Keith	'91	King of the Hill	McGuinn, Roger	'90
Keep It Comin, Love	K.C. & the Sunshine Band	'77	King of the New York Streets	Dion	'89
Keep It Together	Madonna	'89	King of the Road	Miller, Roger	'65
Keep on Dancing	Gentrys, The	'65	King of Wishful Thinking	Go West	'90
Keep on Loving You	REO Speedwagon	'80	King Tut	Martin, Steve and the Toots Uncommons	'78
Keep on Movin'	Soul II Soul	'89	Kingdom of Love	Soft Boys, The	'80
Keep on Pushing	Impressions, The	'64	Kiss	Prince	'86
Keep on Smilin'	Wet Willie	'74	Kiss and Say Goodbye	Manhattans, The	'76
Keep on Truckin'	Kendricks, Eddie	'73	Kiss Me Deadly	Ford, Lita	'88
Keep Searchin' (We'll Follow the Sun)	Shannon, Del	'64	Kiss Me on the Bus	Replacements, The	'85
Keep Talking	Pink Floyd	'94	Kiss Me, Son of God	They Might Be Giants	'88
Keep the Fire Burnin'	REO Speedwagon	'82	Kiss Off	Violent Femmes	'82
Keep Ya Head Up	2Pac	'93	Kiss on My List	Hall and Oates	'81
Keep Your Hands off My Baby	Little Eva	'62	Kiss Them for Me	Siouxsie & the Banshees	'91
Keep Your Hands to Yourself	Georgia Satellites	'86	Kiss This Thing Goodbye	Del Amitri	'90
Keep Yourself Alive	Queen	'73	Kiss You All Over	Exile	'78
Keeper of the Castle	Four Tops, The	'72	Kisses on the Wind	Cherry, Neneh	'89
Kentucky Bluebird	Johnson, Lou	'64	Kisses Sweeter Than Wine	Weavers, The	'51
Kentucky Rain	Presley, Elvis	'70	Kissin' Time	Rydell, Bobby	'59
Kentucky Woman	Diamond, Neil	'67	Kissing a Fool	Michael, George	'87
Kerosene	Big Black	'86	Kissing You	Washington, Keith	'91
Key Largo	Higgins, Bertie	'82	Klan, The	Havens, Richie	'68
Kick in the Eye	Bauhaus	'81	Knock on Wood	Floyd, Eddie	'66
Kick out the Jams	MC5, The	'69	Knock Three Times	Dawn	'70
Kicks	Revere, Paul & the Raiders	'66	Knockin' Around the Zoo	Taylor, James	'69
Kid	Pretenders, The	'80	Knockin' Boots	Candyman	'90
Kid About It	Costello, Elvis	'82	Knockin' Da Boots	H-Town	'93
Kid Charlemagne	Steely Dan	'76	Knockin' on Heaven's Door	Dylan, Bob	'73
Kiddio	Randazzo, Teddy	'57	Knocking at Your Back Door	Deep Purple	'85
Kids Are Alright, The	Who, The	'66	Knowing Me, Knowing You	Abba	'77
Kids in America	Wilde, Kim	'82	Knowledge Is King	Dee, Kool Moe	'89
Kill for Peace	Fugs, The	'65	Ko Ko Mo (I Love You So)	Gene and Eunice	'55
Kill Your Sons	Reed, Lou	'74	Kodachrome	Simon, Paul	'73
Killboy Powerhead	Didjets	'90	Koko Joe	Don and Dewey	'58
Killed by Death	Motorhead	'84	Kokomo	Beach Boys, The	'88
Killer Queen	Queen	'74	Kookie Little Paradise, A	Campbell, Jo Ann	'60
Killing an Arab	Cure, The	'79	Kookie, Kookie, Lend Me Your Comb	Byrnes, Edward and Connie Stevens	'59
Killing Floor	Howling Wolf	'66	Kosmic Blues	Joplin, Janis	'69
Killing Me Softly with His Song	Lieberman, Lori	'72	Kung Fu Fighting	Douglas, Carl	'74
Killing of Georgie (Part 1 & 2), The	Stewart, Rod	'77	Kyrie	Mr. Mister	'86

SONG	ARTIST	YEAR
L		
L.A. Blues	Stooges, The	'70
L.A. County	Lovett, Lyle	'87
L.A. Freeway	Walker, Jerry Jeff	'73
L.A. Woman	Doors, The	'71
L-O-V-E (Love)	Green, Al	'75
La Bamba	Valens, Ritchie	'58
La Dee Dah	Billy and Lillie	'58
La Grange	ZZ Top	'73
La Isla Bonita	Madonna	'86
La, La, La (If I Had You)	Sherman, Bobby	'69
La La La (Means I Love You)	Delfonics, The	'68
La Villa Strangiata	Rush	'78
Ladies First	Queen Latifah	'89
Ladies Night	Kool & the Gang	'79
Lady	Styx	'74
Lady Came from Baltimore, The	Hardin, Tim	'67
Lady D'Arbanville	Stevens, Cat	'70
Lady Friend	Byrds, The	'68
Lady Godiva	Peter and Gordon	'66
Lady in Red, The	DeBurgh, Chris	'86
Lady Jane	Rolling Stones, The	'66
Lady Madonna	Beatles, The	'68
Lady Marmelade	Labelle	'74
Lady Willpower	Puckett, Gary & the Union Gap	'68
Lady You Bring Me Up	Commodores, The	'81
Laid	James	'94
Lake of Fire	Meat Puppets	'82
Lamb Lies down on Broadway	Genesis	'74
(Lament of the Cherokee) Indian Reservation, The	Fardon, Don	'68
Land of a Thousand Dances	Kenner, Chris	'63
Land of Confusion	Genesis	'86
Land of Rape and Honey	Ministry	'88
Landslide	Fleetwood Mac	'75
Language of Violence	Disposable Heroes of Hiphoprisy	'92
Last Caress	Misfits, The	'79
Last Child	Aerosmith	'76
Last Cigarette	Dramarama	'89
Last Dance, The	Summer, Donna	'78
Last Date	Cramer, Floyd	'60
Last Goodbye	Buckley, Jeff	'94
Last in Line, The	Dio	'84
Last Kiss	Cochran, Wayne	'61
Last Mile, The	Nico	'65
Last Night	Mar-Keys	'61
Last of the Famous International Playboys	Morrissey	'89

SONG	ARTIST	YEAR
Last Song	Edward Bear	'73
Last Thing on My Mind, The	Paxton, Tom	'64
Last Time, The	Rolling Stones, The	'65
Last Time I Saw Richard, The	Mitchell, Joni	'71
Last Train to Clarksville	Monkees, The	'66
Last Trip to Tulsa	Young, Neil	'69
Late Great Johnny Ace, The	Simon and Garfunkel	'82
Late in the Evening	Simon, Paul	'80
Lately	Wonder, Stevie	'80
Lather	Jefferson Airplane, The	'68
Latifah's Had It up to Here	Queen Latifah	'91
Laugh at Me	Sonny	'65
Laugh, Laugh	Beau Brummels	'64
Laughing	Guess Who, The	'69
Laughter in the Rain	Sedaka, Neil	'74
Lavendar Blue (Dilly Dilly)	Turner, Sammy	'59
Lawdy Miss Clawdy	Price, Lloyd	'52
Lawyers in Love	Browne, Jackson	'83
Lawyers, Guns and Money	Zevon, Warren	'78
Lay Down (Candles in the Rain)	Melanie	'70
Lay Down Sally	Clapton, Eric	'77
Lay down Your Weary Tune	Dylan, Bob	'64
Lay Your Hands on Me	Thompson Twins	'85
Lay, Lady, Lay	Dylan, Bob	'69
Layla	Derek & the Dominos	'70
Le Freak	Chic	'78
Lead Me On	Nightingale, Maxine	'79
Leader of the Band	Fogelberg, Dan	'81
Leader of the Pack	Shangri-Las, The	'64
Lean on Me	Withers, Bill	'72
Leaning on the Lamp Post	Herman's Hermits	'66
Learning How to Love You	Hiatt, John	'87
Learning the Blues	Sinatra, Frank	'55
Learning to Fly	Petty, Tom & the Heartbreakers	'91
Leather and Lace	Nicks, Stevie	'81
Leave Me Alone (Ruby Red Dress)	Reddy, Helen	'73
Leave My Kitten Alone	John, Little Willie	'59
Leave My Woman Alone	Charles, Ray	'58
Leavin' Me	Independents, The	'73
Leaving Las Vegas	Crow, Sheryl	'94
Leaving on a Jet Plane	Peter, Paul & Mary	'67
Left of Center	Vega, Suzanne	'86
Legs	ZZ Top	'84
Lemon Song, The	Led Zeppelin	'69
Lemon Tree	Peter, Paul & Mary	'61
Leningrad	Joel, Billy	'89
Lenny Bruce	Dylan, Bob	'81
Leopard-Skin Pill-Box Hat	Dylan, Bob	'66
Less Than Zero	Costello, Elvis	'77

SONG	ARTIST	YEAR	SONG	ARTIST	YEAR
Let 'Em In	McCartney, Paul & Wings	'76	Let's Stay Together	Green, Al	'72
Let Her Cry	Hootie & the Blowfish	'94	Let's Straighten It Out	Latimore	'74
Let Her In	Travolta, John	'76	Let's Talk About Girls	Chocolate Watchband	'66
Let It Be	Beatles, The	'70	Let's Talk About Sex	Salt-n-Pepa	'91
Let It Be Me	Atkins, Chet	'59	Let's Twist Again	Checker, Chubby	'61
Let It Bleed	Rolling Stones, The	'69	Let's Wait Awhile	Jackson, Janet	'86
Let It Out (Let It All Hang Out)	Hombres, The	'67	Let's Work Together	Harrison, Wilbert	'69
Let It Rain	Clapton, Eric	'70	Letitgo	Prince	'94
Let It Rock	Berry, Chuck	'60	Letter Full of Tears	Knight, Gladys & the Pips	'62
Let It Whip	Dazz Band, The	'82	Letter, The	Box Tops, The	'67
Let Me Be	Turtles, The	'65	Letter, The	Don and Dewey	'58
Let Me Be the One	Exposé	'87	Levon	John, Elton	'71
Let Me Be There	Newton-John, Olivia	'73	Liar	Argent	'69
(Let Me Be Your) Teddy Bear	Presley, Elvis	'57	Liar	Rollins, Henry Band, The	'94
Let Me Die in My Footsteps	Dylan, Bob	'63	Liar, Liar	Castaways, The	'65
Let Me In	Sensations, The	'62	Lick It Up	Kiss	'83
Let Me Love You Tonight	Pure Prairie League	'80	Lido Shuffle	Scaggs, Boz	'76
Let Me Ride	Dr. Dre	'93	Lies	En Vogue	'90
Let My Love Open the Door	Townshend, Pete	'80	Lies (Are Breakin' My Heart)	Knickerbockers, The	'65
Let No Man Steal Your Thyme	Pentangle	'68	Life During Wartime	Talking Heads	'79
Let the Beat Hit 'Em	Lisa Lisa & Cult Jam	'91	Life in a Northern Town	Dream Academy, The	'85
Let the Four Winds Blow	Brown, Roy	'57	Life in the Fast Lane	Eagles, The	'77
Let the Good Times Roll	Jordan, Louis & His Tympani Five	'46	Life Is a Carnival	Band, The	'71
			Life Is a Highway	Cochrane, Tom	'92
Let the Good Times Roll	Shirley and Lee	'56	Life Is a Rock (but the Radio Rolled Me)	Reunion	'74
Let the Little Girl Dance	Bland, Billy	'60			
Let the Music Play	Shannon	'84	Life Is But a Dream	Harptones, The	'54
Let the River Run	Simon, Carly	'89	Life of Illusion	Walsh, Joe	'81
Let Them Talk	John, Little Willie	'56	Life's Been Good	Walsh, Joe	'78
Let There Be Drums	Nelson, Sandy	'61	Light My Fire	Doors, The	'67
Let Your Hair Down	Temptations, The	'73	Light of Day	Barbusters, The	'87
Let's Dance	Bowie, David	'83	Lightnin' Strikes	Christie, Lou	'66
Let's Dance	Montez, Chris	'62	Lightning Crashes	Live	'94
Let's Do It Again	Staple Singers, The	'75	Lights Out	Byrne, Jerry	'58
Let's Get It On	Gaye, Marvin	'73	Lights Out	UFO	'77
Let's Get Serious	Jackson, Jermaine	'80	Lights Out	Wolf, Peter	'84
Let's Get Together	Mills, Hayley	'62	(Lights Went Out in) Massachussettes, The	Bee Gees, The	'67
Let's Go	Cars, The	'79			
Let's Go	Wang Chung	'87	Like a Hurricane	Young, Neil	'77
Let's Go All the Way	Sly Fox	'86	Like a Prayer	Madonna	'89
Let's Go Crazy	Prince	'84	Like a Rock	Seger, Bob	'86
Let's Go Get Stoned	Charles, Ray	'66	Like a Rolling Stone	Dylan, Bob	'65
Let's Go to Bed	Cure, The	'83	Like a Virgin	Madonna	'84
Let's Go Tripping	Dale, Dick & the Deltones	'61	Like Strangers	Everly Brothers, The	'60
Let's Go, Let's Go, Let's Go	Midnighters, The	'60	Like the Way I Do	Etheridge, Melissa	'88
Let's Groove	Earth, Wind & Fire	'81	Like the Weather	10,000 Maniacs	'87
Let's Hang On (to What We've Got)	Four Seasons, The	'65	Lil Red Riding Hood	Sam the Sham and the Pharoahs	'66
Let's Hear It for the Boy	Williams, Deniece	'84			
Let's Live for Today	Grass Roots	'67	Limbo Rock	Champs, The	'62
Let's Spend the Night Together	Rolling Stones, The	'67	Limelight	Rush	'81
			Ling Ting Tong	Five Keys, The	'54

SONG	ARTIST	YEAR
Linger	Cranberries, The	'93
Lipstick on Your Collar	Francis, Connie	'59
Lipstick Traces (on a Cigarette)	Spellman, Bennie	'62
Lipstick Vogue	Costello, Elvis	'78
Listen People	Herman's Hermits	'66
Listen to Her Heart	Petty, Tom & the Heartbreakers	'77
Listen to the Music	Doobie Brothers, The	'72
Listen to What the Man Said	McCartney, Paul & Wings	'75
Listen to Your Heart	Roxette	'89
Listening to the Lions	Morrison, Van	'72
Lithium	Nirvana	'91
Little Bit Me, a Little Bit You, A	Monkees, The	'67
Little Bit o' Soul	Music Explosion, The	'65
Little Bit of Soap, A	Jarmels, The	'61
Little Bitty Pretty One	Day, Bobby	'57
Little Boxes	Seeger, Pete	'64
Little by Little	Plant, Robert	'85
Little Children	Kramer, Billy J. & the Dakotas	'64
Little Darlin'	Gladiolas, The	'57
Little Diane	Dion	'62
Little Egypt	Coasters, The	'61
Little Games	Yardbirds, The	'67
Little Girl	Syndicate of Sound, The	'66
Little Girl of Mine	Cleftones, The	'56
Little Green Apples	Smith, O.C.	'68
Little Guitars	Van Halen	'82
Little Honda	Hondells, The	'64
Little Is Enough, A	Townshend, Pete	'80
Little Jackie Wants to Be a Star	Lisa Lisa & Cult Jam	'89
Little Jeannie	John, Elton	'80
Little Johnny Jewel	Television	'74
Little Latin Lupe Lu	Righteous Brothers, The	'63
Little Lies	Fleetwood Mac	'87
Little Marie	Berry, Chuck	'64
Little Martha	Allman Brothers, The	'72
Little Miss Can't Be Wrong	Spin Doctors, The	'91
Little More Love, A	Newton-John, Olivia	'79
Little Old Lady (from Pasadena), The	Jan and Dean	'64
Little Ole Man (Uptight Everything's Alright)	Cosby, Bill	'67
Little Queenie	Berry, Chuck	'59
Little Red Corvette	Prince	'82
Little Red Rooster	Howling Wolf	'61
Little Respect, A	Erasure	'89
Little Sister	Nico	'67
Little Sister	Presley, Elvis	'61
Little Star	Elegants, The	'58
Little Town Flirt	Shannon, Del	'61
Little Walter	Tony! Toni! Tone!	'88

SONG	ARTIST	YEAR
Little Wild One (No. 5)	Crenshaw, Marshall	'85
Little Willy	Sweet, The	'73
Little Wing	Hendrix, Jimi	'68
Little Woman	Sherman, Bobby	'69
Live	Merry-Go-Round	'67
Live and Learn	Joe Public	'92
Live and Let Die	McCartney, Paul & Wings	'73
Live to Tell	Madonna	'86
Lively up Yourself	Marley, Bob & the Wailers	'72
Liverpool Drive	Berry, Chuck	'64
Lives in the Balance	Browne, Jackson	'86
Livin' for the City	Wonder, Stevie	'73
Livin' for the Weekend	O'Jays, The	'75
Livin' for You	Green, Al	'73
Livin' on a Prayer	Bon Jovi	'87
Livin' on the Edge	Aerosmith	'93
Livin' Thing	Electric Light Orchestra	'76
Living a Lie	dBs, The	'81
Living a Little, Laughing a Little	Hiatt, John	'85
Living Doll	Richard, Cliff	'59
Living in America	Brown, James	'86
Living in the Past	Jethro Tull	'72
Living in the U.S.A.	Miller, Steve Band, The	'68
Living inside Myself	Vannelli, Gino	'81
Living It Up	Jones, Rickie Lee	'82
Living Loving Maid (She's Just a Woman)	Led Zeppelin	'69
Living through Another Cuba	XTC	'80
Living with the Law	Whitley, Chris	'91
Living without You	Newman, Randy	'68
Living Years, The	Mike & the Mechanics	'89
Load Out, The	Browne, Jackson	'77
Locking up My Heart	Marvelettes, The	'63
Loco de Amor (Crazy for Love)	Byrne, David & Celia Cruz	'86
Loco-Motion, The	Little Eva	'62
Lodi	Creedence Clearwater Revival	'69
Logical Song, The	Supertramp	'79
Lola	Kinks, The	'71
London Calling	Clash, The	'79
London's Burning	Clash, The	'77
Lonely at the Bottom	Belushi, John	'73
Lonely at the Top	Newman, Randy	'71
Lonely Avenue	Charles, Ray	'56
Lonely Boy	Anka, Paul	'59
Lonely Boy	Gold, Andrew	'77
Lonely Days	Bee Gees, The	'70
Lonely Island	Cooke, Sam	'57
Lonely Nights	Hearts, The	'55
Lonely Ol' Night	Mellencamp, John Cougar	'85
Lonely People	America	'74

SONG	ARTIST	YEAR
Lonely Surfer, The	Nitzsche, Jack	'63
Lonely Teardrops	Wilson, Jackie	'58
Lonely Teenager	Dion	'60
Lonely Weekends	Rich, Charlie	'60
Loner, The	Young, Neil	'69
Lonesome Loser	Little River Band	'78
Lonesome Town	Nelson, Ricky	'58
Long and Winding Road, The	Beatles, The	'70
Long as I Can See the Light	Creedence Clearwater Revival	'70
Long Cool Woman (in a Black Dress)	Hollies, The	'72
Long Distance Runaround	Yes	'72
Long Gone Dead	Rank and File	'84
Long Honeymoon, The	Costello, Elvis	'82
Long Live Our Love	Shangri-Las, The	'66
Long Live the Kane	Kane, Big Daddy	'88
Long Lonely Nights	Andrews, Lee & the Hearts	'57
Long Long Time	Ronstadt, Linda	'70
Long Tall Glasses (I Can Dance)	Sayer, Leo	'75
Long Tall Sally	Little Richard	'56
Long Term Physical Effects	Simon, Carly	'71
Long Time	Boston	'76
Long Train Running	Doobie Brothers, The	'73
Long White Cadillac	Blasters, The	'83
Longer	Fogelberg, Dan	'79
Longest Time, The	Joel, Billy	'83
Longfellow Serenade	Diamond, Neil	'74
Longview	Green Day	'94
Look at Me (I'm in Love)	Moments, The	'75
Look Away	Chicago	'88
Look in My Eyes	Chantels, The	'61
Look of Love	Gore, Lesley	'64
Look of Love (Part One)	ABC	'82
Look What You Done for Me	Green, Al	'72
Look, The	Roxette	'89
Lookin' for a Love	Valentinos, The	'62
Lookin' for Love	Lee, Johnny	'80
Lookin' out My Back Door	Creedence Clearwater Revival	'70
Looking for a Kiss	New York Dolls	'73
Looking for a New Love	Watley, Jody	'87
Looking for an Echo	Persuasions, The	'77
Looking for the Perfect Beat	Bambaataa, Afrika & Soulsonic Force	'86
Looking Through Patient Eyes	P.M. Dawn	'93
Looks Like We Made It	Manilow, Barry	'76
Loop De Loop	Thunder, Johnny	'63
Loosey's Rap	James, Rick	'88
Los Angeles	X	'80
Loser	Beck	'93
Losin' You	Lee, Brenda	'63
Losing My Religion	R.E.M.	'91

SONG	ARTIST	YEAR
Lost in Emotion	Lisa Lisa & Cult Jam	'87
Lost in the Flood	Springsteen, Bruce	'73
Lost in the Supermarket	Clash, The	'79
Lost in You	Stewart, Rod	'88
Lost in Your Eyes	Gibson, Debbie	'89
Lost Johnny	Hawkwind	'74
Lost Without Your Love	Bread	'76
Lotta Love	Young, Neil	'78
Lotta Lovin'	Vincent, Gene & His Blue Caps	'57
Louie Louie	Berry, Richard	'56
Louis Quatorze	Bow Wow Wow	'80
Louise	Raitt, Bonnie	'77
Louisiana, 1927	Newman, Randy	'74
Lovable	Costello, Elvis	'86
Love (Can Make You Happy)	Mercy	'69
Love Again	Cochran, Eddie	'58
Love and Affection	Armatrading, Joan	'76
Love and Anger	Bush, Kate	'89
Love and Mercy	Wilson, Brian	'88
Love Ballad	L.T.D.	'76
Love Bites	Def Leppard	'87
Love Bizarre, A	Sheila E.	'86
Love Buzz	Shocking Blue	'69
Love Came to Me	Dion	'62
Love Child	Supremes, The	'68
Love Come Down	King, Evelyn Champagne	'82
Love Grows (Where My Rosemary Goes)	Edison Lighthouse	'70
Love Gun	Kiss	'77
Love Hangover	Ross, Diana	'76
Love Has No Pride	Raitt, Bonnie	'72
Love Her Madly	Doors, The	'71
Love Hurts	Everly Brothers, The	'60
Love I Lost, The	Melvin, Harold & the Bluenotes	'73
Love I Saw in You Was Just a Mirage, The	Miracles, The	'67
Love in an Elevator	Aerosmith	'89
Love in the First Degree	Alabama	'81
Love in Vain	Rolling Stones, The	'69
Love Is	Williams, Vanessa and Brian McKnight	'93
Love Is a Battlefield	Benatar, Pat	'83
Love Is a House	Force M.D.'s, The	'87
Love Is a Rose	Ronstadt, Linda	'75
Love Is a Wonderful Thing	Bolton, Michael	'91
Love Is Alive	Wright, Gary	'76
Love Is All Around	Troggs, The	'67
Love Is Everything	Siberry, Jane	'93
Love Is for Lovers	dBs, The	'84

SONG	ARTIST	YEAR	SONG	ARTIST	YEAR
Love Is Here and Now You're Gone	Supremes, The	'67	Love Train	O'Jays, The	'72
Love Is in Control (Finger on the Trigger)	Summer, Donna	'82	Love Walks In	Van Halen	'86
			Love Will Find a Way	Pablo Cruise	'78
Love Is in the Air	Young, John Paul	'78	Love Will Keep Us Together	Sedaka, Neil	'74
Love Is Just a Four-Letter Word	Baez, Joan	'67	Love Will Never Do Without You	Jackson, Janet	'89
Love Is Like an Itching in My Heart	Supremes, The	'66	Love Will Tear Us Apart	Joy Division	'80
Love Is Like Oxygen	Sweet, The	'77	Love Won't Let Me Wait	Harris, Major	'75
Love Is Strange	Mickey and Sylvia	'57	Love You Down	Ready for the World	'86
Love Is the Drug	Roxy Music	'76	Love You Inside Out	Bee Gees, The	'79
(Love Is) Thicker Than Water	Gibb, Andy	'79	Love You Save, The	Jackson 5, The	'70
Love Letters	Lester, Ketty	'62	Love You So	Holden, Ron	'60
Love Lies Bleeding	John, Elton	'73	Love Zone	Ocean, Billy	'85
Love Like Blood	Killing Joke	'85	Love's Got a Line on You	Scandal	'83
Love Machine (Part 1)	Miracles, The	'75	Love's Made a Fool of You	Crickets, The	'59
Love Makes a Woman	Acklin, Barbara	'68	Love's Theme	Love Unlimited Orchestra	'73
Love Makes Things Happen	Pebbles	'90	Love, Love, Love	Clovers, The	'56
Love Me	Willie and Ruth	'54	Love, Reign O'er Me	Who, The	'72
Love Me Do	Beatles, The	'63	Lovely Rita	Beatles, The	'67
Love Me Like a Man	Raitt, Bonnie	'72	Lover's Concerto, A	Toys, The	'65
Love Me Tender	Presley, Elvis	'56	Lover's Question, A	McPhatter, Clyde	'58
Love Me Two Times	Doors, The	'67	Lover, Please	McPhatter, Clyde	'61
Love Me, I'm a Liberal	Ochs, Phil	'66	Loverboy	Ocean, Billy	'84
Love Minus Zero/No Limit	Dylan, Bob	'65	Lovergirl	Teena Marie	'85
Love My Way	Psychedelic Furs, The	'84	Lovers Never Say Goodbye	Flamingos, The	'59
Love of a Lifetime	Firehouse	'91	Lovers Who Wander	Dion	'62
Love on a Two-Way Street	Moments, The	'70	Loves Me Like a Rock	Simon, Paul	'73
Love on the Rocks	Diamond, Neil	'81	Lovesick Blues	Williams, Hank	'49
Love on Your Side	Thompson Twins	'83	Lovey Dovey	Clovers, The	'55
Love or Let Me Be Lonely	Friends of Distinction, The	'70	Lovin' Every Minute of It	Loverboy	'85
Love Overboard	Knight, Gladys & the Pips	'87	Lovin' You	Ripperton, Minnie	'74
Love Potion Number Nine	Clovers, The	'59	Loving the Sinner, Hating the Sin	Dream Syndicate	'88
Love Radiates Around	Roches, The	'85	Loving You	Presley, Elvis	'57
Love Rollercoaster	Ohio Players, The	'75	Low	Cracker	'93
Love Saw It	White, Karyn	'88	Low Rider	War	'75
Love Shack	B-52's, The	'89	Low Self Opinion	Rollins Band, The	'91
Love She Can Count On, A	Miracles, The	'63	Low Spark of High Heeled Boys, The	Traffic	'71
Love Sneakin' up on You	Raitt, Bonnie	'94			
Love So Right	Bee Gees, The	'76	Lowdown	Scaggs, Boz	'76
Love Somebody	Springfield, Rick	'84	Lucille	Little Richard	'57
Love Song	Cure, The	'89	Lucille	Rogers, Kenny	'76
Love Song	Tesla	'89	Lucky Charm	Boys, The	'88
Love Spreads	Stone Roses, The	'94	Lucky Lips	Brown, Ruth	'57
Love Stinks	Geils J. Band, The	'79	Lucky Man	Emerson, Lake & Palmer	'71
Love Struck Baby	Vaughan, Stevie Ray	'83	Lucky Number	Lovich, Lene	'79
Love Takes Time	Carey, Mariah	'90	Lucky Star	Madonna	'83
Love That Burns	Fleetwood Mac	'69	Lucy in the Sky with Diamonds	Beatles, The	'67
Love the One You're With	Stills, Stephen	'71	Luka	Vega, Suzanne	'87
Love to Love You Baby	Summer, Donna	'76	Lullabye	Cure, The	'89
Love Touch (Theme from Legal Eagles)	Stewart, Rod	'86	Lust for Life	Iggy Pop	'77
			Lyin' Eyes	Eagles, The	'75

SONG	ARTIST	YEAR
M		
M.A.R.T.I.N.A.	Phranc	'91
M.T.A., The	Holt, Will	'57
Macarena (Bayside Boys Mix)	Los Del Rio	'95
MacArthur Park	Harris, Richard	'68
Machine Gun	Commodores, The	'74
Macho Man	Village People, The	'78
Mack the Knife	Armstrong, Louis	'56
Mad About You	Carlisle, Belinda	'86
Mad Mad Me	Muldaur, Maria	'73
Madamme George	Morrison, Van	'69
Madonna of the Wasps	Hitchcock, Robyn and the Egyptians	'89
Maggie May	Stewart, Rod	'71
Maggie's Farm	Dylan, Bob	'65
Maggot Brain	Funkadelic	'71
Magic	Newton-John, Olivia	'80
Magic	Pilot	'75
Magic Bus	Who, The	'68
Magic Carpet Ride	Steppenwolf	'68
Magic Man	Heart	'76
Magic Power	Triumph	'81
Magical Mystery Tour	Beatles, The	'67
Magnet and Steel	Egan, Walter	'77
Mainline Prosperity Blues	Farina, Dick and Mimi	'66
Mainstreet	Seger, Bob	'76
Major Tom (Coming Home)	Schilling, Peter	'83
Make a Move on Me	Newton-John, Olivia	'81
Make It Easy on Yourself	Butler, Jerry	'62
Make It Funky (Part 1)	Brown, James	'71
Make It Like It Was	Belle, Regina	'89
Make It Real	Jets, The	'87
Make It with You	Bread	'70
Make Me Lose Control	Carmen, Eric	'88
Make Me Smile	Chicago	'70
Make Me the Woman That You Come Home To	Knight, Gladys & the Pips	'71
Make Me Your Baby	Lewis, Barbara	'65
Make Me Yours	Swann, Bettye	'67
Make You Sweat	Sweat, Keith	'90
Makin' It	Naughton, David	'79
Makin' Thunderbirds	Seger, Bob	'83
Making Love out of Nothing at All	Air Supply	'83
Making Our Dreams Come True	Grecco, Cyndi	'76
Making Plans for Nigel	XTC	'82
Mama (He Treats Your Daughter Mean)	Brown, Ruth	'53
Mama Can't Buy You Love	John, Elton	'77
Mama Didn't Lie	Bradley, Jan	'63
Mama Kin	Aerosmith	'73

SONG	ARTIST	YEAR
Mama Said	Shirelles, The	'61
Mama Said Knock You Out	L.L. Cool J	'91
Mama Told Me Not to Come	Animals, The	'66
Mama Weer All Crazee Now	Slade	'72
Mama You Been on My Mind	Dylan, Bob	'64
Mama's Pearl	Jackson 5, The	'70
Mambo Baby	Brown, Ruth	'54
Man in Need, A	Thompson, Richard and Linda	'82
Man in the Mirror	Jackson, Michael	'87
Man on the Moon	R.E.M.	'93
Man Size Love	Klymaxx	'86
Man Who Has Everything, The	Morrells, The	'82
Man Who Shot Liberty Valance, The	Pitney, Gene	'62
Man Who Sold the World, The	Bowie, David	'70
Man with the Child in His Eyes, The	Bush, Kate	'78
Mandolin Rain	Hornsby, Bruce & the Range	'86
Mandolin Wind	Stewart, Rod	'71
Maneater	Hall and Oates	'82
Maniac	Sembello, Michael	'83
Manic Depression	Hendrix, Jimi	'67
Manic Monday	Bangles, The	'86
Manimal	Germs, The	'80
Mannish Boy	Waters, Muddy	'55
Many Rivers to Cross	Cliff, Jimmy	'70
Marcie	Mitchell, Joni	'68
Margaritaville	Buffett, Jimmy	'77
Marie Marie	Blasters, The	'80
(Marie's the Name) His Latest Flame	Presley, Elvis	'61
Marlene on the Wall	Vega, Suzanne	'85
Marmendy Mill	Flo and Eddie	'71
Marquee Moon	Television	'77
Marrakesh Express	Crosby, Stills & Nash	'69
Married Men, The	Roches, The	'79
Martha My Dear	Beatles, The	'68
Mary Jane's Last Dance	Petty, Tom & the Heartbreakers	'93
Mary Lou	Young Jessie	'55
Mashed Potato Time	Sharp, Dee Dee	'62
Master and Servant	Depeche Mode	'85
Master Blaster (Jammin')	Wonder, Stevie	'80
Master Dik	Sonic Youth	'87
Master of Puppets	Metallica	'86
Masterpiece	Atlantic Starr	'92
Masterpiece	Temptations, The	'73
Masters of War	Dylan, Bob	'63
Matchbox	Perkins, Carl	'57
Material Girl	Madonna	'84
Matter of Trust, A	Joel, Billy	'86
Matthew and Son	Stevens, Cat	'67

SONG	ARTIST	YEAR	SONG	ARTIST	YEAR
Maxwell's Silver Hammer	Beatles, The	'69	Method of Modern Love	Hall and Oates	'85
May This Be Love	Hendrix, Jimi	'67	Mexican Radio	Wall of Voodoo	'82
Maybe	Chantels, The	'58	Mexico	Jefferson Airplane, The	'69
Maybe Baby	Crickets, The	'57	Miami 2017 (Seen the Lights Go out on Broadway)	Joel, Billy	'76
Maybe I Know	Gore, Lesley	'64			
Maybe I'm Amazed	McCartney, Paul	'71	Miami Vice Theme	Hammer, Jan	'85
Maybe I'm Doing It Wrong	Newman, Randy	'71	Michael (Row the Boat Ashore)	Weavers, The	'56
Maybellene	Berry, Chuck	'55	Michael the Lover	Jackson Five, The	'67
Mayor of Simpleton	XTC	'89	Michael, Andrew and James	Farina, Dick and Mimi	'65
Me and a Gun	Amos, Tori	'92	Michelle	Beatles, The	'65
Me and All the Other Mothers	Wainwright, Loudon	'89	Mickey	Basil, Toni	'82
Me and Bobby McGee	Miller, Roger	'67	Mickey's Monkey	Miracles, The	'63
Me and Julio Down by the School Yard	Simon, Paul	'72	Middle of the Road	Pretenders, The	'84
			Midlife Crisis	Faith No More	'92
Me and Mrs. Jones	Paul, Billy	'72	Midnight at the Oasis	Muldaur, Maria	'73
Me and My Arrow	Nilsson	'71	Midnight Blue	Gramm, Lou	'87
Me and My Uncle	Collins, Judy	'65	Midnight Blue	Manchester, Melissa	'75
Me and the Boys	Raitt, Bonnie	'82	Midnight Confessions	Grass Roots	'67
Me and You and a Dog Named Boo	Lobo	'71	Midnight Plane to Houston	Weatherly, Jim	'71
Me Myself and I	De La Soul	'89	Midnight Rambler	Rolling Stones, The	'69
Mean Mr. Mustard	Beatles, The	'69	Midnight Rider	Allman Brothers, The	'70
Mean Woman Blues	Presley, Elvis	'57	Midnight Special	Weavers, The	'52
Mecca	Pitney, Gene	'63	Mighty Love, A	Spinners, The	'73
Meet on the Ledge	Fairport Convention	'68	Mighty Quinn (Quinn, the Eskimo), The	Manfred Mann	'68
Melissa	Allman Brothers, The	'72			
Mellow Yellow	Donovan	'66	Milkcow Blues Boogie	Presley, Elvis	'55
Memo from Turner	Jagger, Mick	'70	Million Dollar Bash	Dylan, Bob	'75
Memories	Presley, Elvis	'68	Million Miles Away, A	Plimsouls, The	'81
Memories Can't Wait	Talking Heads	'79	Million to One, A	Charles, Jimmy	'60
Memories of El Monte	Penguins, The	'63	Mind Games	Lennon, John	'73
Memphis	Berry, Chuck	'59	Minor Threat	Minor Threat	'81
Men Are Gettin' Scarce	Tex, Joe	'68	Mint Juleps and Needles	Kahn, Brenda	'92
Men's Room L.A.	Friedman, Kinky	'76	Minute by Minute	Doobie Brothers, The	'78
Mendocino	Sir Douglas Quintet, The	'69	Miracles	Jefferson Starship, The	'75
Mercedes Benz	Joplin, Janis	'70	Mirage	James, Tommy & the Shondells	'67
Mercedes Boy	Pebbles	'88			
Mercury Blues	Miller, Steve Band, The	'69	Mirror Mirror	Ross, Diana	'81
Mercy Mercy Me (the Ecology)	Gaye, Marvin	'71	Miserlou	Dale, Dick and the Deltones	'61
Mercy Street	Gabriel, Peter	'86	Misled	Kool & the Gang	'84
Mercy, Mercy, Mercy	Adderly, Cannonball	'67	Miss Ann	Little Richard	'57
Merry Christmas Baby	Berry, Chuck	'58	Miss Me Blind	Culture Club	'84
Merry Go Round	Replacements, The	'90	Miss World	Hole	'94
Mess Around	Charles, Ray	'54	Miss You	Rolling Stones, The	'78
Mess o' Blues, A	Presley, Elvis	'60	Miss You Like Crazy	Cole, Natalie	'89
Message in a Bottle	Police, The	'79	Miss You Much	Jackson, Janet	'89
Message in Our Music	O'Jays, The	'76	Missing Sequences	Viovod	'89
Message of Love	Pretenders, The	'82	Missing You	Ross, Diana	'84
Message, The	Grandmaster Flash and the Furious 5	'82	Missing You	Waite, John	'84
			Mission Bell	Brooks, Donnie	'60
Messiah Will Come Again, The	Buchanon, Roy	'72	Mission in Life, A	Ridgway, Stan	'89
Metal Mikey	Suede	'92	Missionary Man	Eurythmics	'86

SONG	ARTIST	YEAR	SONG	ARTIST	YEAR
Mississippi Queen	Mountain	'70	More Than a Feeling	Boston	'76
Missunderstanding	Sure, Al B.	'92	More Than I Can Say	Crickets, The	'60
Mister Custer	Verne, Larry	'60	More Than This	Roxy Music	'82
Mistrustin' Blues	Otis, Johnny	'50	More Than Words	Extreme	'90
Misty Blue	Burgess, Wilma	'67	More Than Words Can Say	Alias	'90
Misunderstanding	Genesis	'80	More You Ignore Me, the Closer I Get	Morrissey	'94
Mixed Emotions	Rolling Stones, The	'89	More, More, More (Part 1)	True, Andrea	'76
Mixed up Shook up Girl	Patty & the Emblems	'64	Morning Dew	Dobson, Bonnie	'63
Mmm Mmm Mmm Mmm	Crash Test Dummies	'94	Morning Has Broken	Stevens, Cat	'71
Mockingbird	Foxx, Inez	'63	Morning Morning	Fugs, The	'65
Modern Love	Bowie, David	'83	Morning Train	Easton, Sheena	'81
Modern Woman (from Ruthless People)	Joel, Billy	'86	Most Beautiful Girl in the World	Prince	'94
Mohair Sam	Rich, Charlie	'65	Most Beautiful Girl, The	Rich, Charlie	'73
Mommy Daddy You and I	Talking Heads	'88	Most Likely You Go Your Way (and I'll Go Mine)	Dylan, Bob	'66
Mommy, Can I Go out and Kill Tonight	Misfits, The	'82	Motel Blues	Wainwright, Loudon	'71
Mona	Diddley, Bo	'57	Mother	Danzig	'88
Mona Lisa	Cole, Nat King	'51	Mother	Lennon, John	'70
Monday, Monday	Mamas and the Papas, The	'66	Mother and Child Reunion	Simon, Paul	'72
Money	Pink Floyd	'73	Mother Nature's Son	Beatles, The	'68
Money (That's What I Want)	Strong, Barrett	'60	Mother Popcorn (You Got to Have a Mother for Me) (Part 1)	Brown, James	'69
Money Changes Everything	Brains, The	'80	Mother's Little Helper	Rolling Stones, The	'65
Money Don't Matter Tonight	Prince	'91	Mother-in-Law	K-Doe, Ernie	'61
Money for Nothing	Dire Straits	'85	Motorcycle	Tico & the Triumphs	'61
Money Honey	Bay City Rollers, The	'75	Motorhead	Motorhead	'77
Money Honey	Drifters, The	'53	Motown Song, The	Stewart, Rod	'91
Moneytalks	AC/DC	'90	Motownphilly	Boyz II Men	'91
Mongoloid	Devo	'78	Moulty	Barbarians, The	'66
Monkberry Moon Delight	McCartney, Paul & Wings	'71	Mountain of Love	Dorman, Harold	'60
Monkey	Michael, George	'88	Mountain's High, The	Dick and Deedee	'61
Monkey Gone to Heaven	Pixies, The	'89	Mountains O' Things	Chapman, Tracy	'88
Monkey Time, The	Lance, Major	'63	Mouth for War	Pantera	'92
Monster Mash	Pickett, Bobby "Boris" and the Crypt Kickers	'62	Move Away	Culture Club	'86
Montana	Mothers of Invention, The	'73	Move It on Over	Williams, Hank	'47
Montego Bay	Bloom, Bobby	'70	Move Over	Joplin, Janis	'70
Monterey	Animals, The	'67	Move This	Technotronic	'92
Mony Mony	James, Tommy & the Shondells	'68	Movin'	Brass Construction	'76
Moody Blue	Presley, Elvis	'75	Movin' 'N Groovin'	Eddy, Duane	'58
Moody River	Boone, Pat	'61	Movin' On	Bad Company	'74
Moon Dawg	Gamblers, The	'59	Moving on Up	M People	'94
Moon in June	Soft Machine, The	'70	Moving Out (Anthony's Song)	Joel, Billy	'79
Moon Is a Harsh Mistress, The	Collins, Judy	'75	Mr. Big Stuff	Knight, Jean	'71
Moon River	Butler, Jerry	'61	Mr. Blue	Fleetwoods, The	'59
Moondance	Morrison, Van	'70	Mr. Bojangles	Walker, Jerry Jeff	'68
Moonlight Drive	Doors, The	'67	Mr. Crowley	Osbourne, Ozzy	'81
Moonlight Feels Right	Starbuck	'75	Mr. Dream Merchant	Butler, Jerry	'67
More and More	Captain Hollywood Project	'93	Mr. Jones	Counting Crows	'93
More Love	Miracles, The	'67	Mr. Lee	Bobbettes, The	'57
			Mr. Loverman	Shabba Ranks	'92

SONG	ARTIST	YEAR
Mr. Pitiful	Redding, Otis	'65
Mr. Roboto	Styx	'83
Mr. Scary	Dokken	'87
Mr. Soul	Buffalo Springfield	'67
Mr. Spaceman	Byrds, The	'66
Mr. Tambourine Man	Dylan, Bob	'65
Mr. Telephone Man	New Edition	'84
Mr. Vain	Culture Beat	'93
Mr. Wendall	Arrested Development	'92
Mrs. Brown, You've Got a Lovely Daughter	Herman's Hermits	'65
Mrs. Green	Three O'Clock, The	'85
Mrs. Robinson	Simon and Garfunkel	'68
Mule Skinner Blues (Blue Yodel #8)	Fendermen, The	'60
Mull of Kintyre	McCartney, Paul & Wings	'76
Murder Was the Case	Dogg, Snoop Doggy	'95
Muscles	Ross, Diana	'82
Must of Got Lost	Geils J. Band, The	'75
Must to Avoid, A	Herman's Hermits	'65
Musta Notta Gotta Lotta	Ely, Joe	'81
Mustang Sally	Rice, Sir Mack	'65
My Babe	Little Walter	'55
My Baby	Pretenders, The	'86
My Baby Gives It Away	Townshend, Pete	'77
My Baby Left Me	Crudup, Arthur Big Boy	'50
My Baby Must Be a Magician	Marvelettes, The	'67
My Baby Thinks He's a Train	Cash, Rosanne	'81
My Back Pages (I'm Younger Than That Now)	Dylan, Bob	'64
My Beautiful Reward	Springsteen, Bruce	'92
My Best Friend's Girl	Cars, The	'78
My Boy Lollipop	Small, Millie	'64
My Boyfriend	Cucumbers, The	'83
My Boyfriend's Back	Angels, The	'63
My Brain Is Hanging Upside Down (Bonzo Goes to Bitburg)	Ramones, The	'86
My Cherie Amour	Wonder, Stevie	'69
My City Was Gone	Pretenders, The	'84
My Dad	Peterson, Paul	'62
My Dearest Darling	James, Etta	'60
My Ding-a-Ling	Berry, Chuck	'72
My Empty Arms	Wilson, Jackie	'61
My Ever Changing Moods	Style Council, The	'84
My Eyes Adored You	Valli, Frankie	'74
My Fantasy	Guy	'88
My Father	Collins, Judy	'68
My Forever Love	Levert	'87
My Generation	Who, The	'65
My Girl	Temptations, The	'65
My Girl Sloopy	Vibrations, The	'64
My Guitar Wants to Kill Your Mama	Mothers of Invention, The	'70

SONG	ARTIST	YEAR
My Guy	Wells, Mary	'64
My Happiness	Francis, Connie	'59
My Heart Can't Tell You No	Stewart, Rod	'88
My Heart Has a Mind of Its Own	Francis, Connie	'60
My Heart Is an Open Book	Dobkins, Carl Jr.	'57
My Home Town	Springsteen, Bruce	'84
My Juanita	Crests, The	'57
My Life	DeMent, Iris	'94
My Life	Joel, Billy	'78
My Life Is Good	Newman, Randy	'83
My Little Red Book (All I Do Is Talk About You)	Manfred Mann	'65
My Little Town	Simon, Paul	'75
My Love	McCartney, Paul & Wings	'73
My Lovin' (You're Never Gonna Get It)	En Vogue	'92
My Maria	Stevenson, B.W.	'73
My Mother the War	10,000 Maniacs	'85
My My My	Gill, Johnny	'90
My Opening Farewell	Browne, Jackson	'72
My Pal Foot Foot	Shaggs, The	'69
My Pledge of Love	Jeffrey, Joe Group, The	'69
My Prayer	Ink Spots, The	'39
My Prerogative	Brown, Bobby	'88
My Sex	Ultravox	'77
My Sharona	Knack, The	'79
My Sister	Hatfield, Juliana Three, The	'93
My Song	Ace, Johnny	'52
My Special Angel	Helms, Bobby	'57
My Story	Willis, Chuck	'52
My Sweet Lord	Harrison, George	'70
My Thang	Brown, James	'74
My Toot Toot	Knight, Jean	'85
My Town	Cucumbers, The	'87
My True Love	Scott, Jack	'58
My True Story	Jive Five, The	'61
My Uncle Used to Love Me But She Died	Miller, Roger	'66
My Whole World Ended (the Moment You Left Me)	Ruffin, David	'69
My Wish Came True	Presley, Elvis	'59
My World Is Empty without You	Supremes, The	'66
Mysterious Ways	U2	'91
Mystery Achievement	Pretenders, The	'80
Mystery Train	Parker, Junior	'53
Mystic Eyes	Them	'65

N

SONG	ARTIST	YEAR
Na Na, Hey, Hey, Kiss Him Goodbye	Steam	'69
Nadine (Is It You?)	Berry, Chuck	'64

SONG	ARTIST	YEAR	SONG	ARTIST	YEAR
Name	Goo Goo Dolls	'95	New York, New York	Grandmaster Flash & the Furious 5	'83
Name Game, The	Ellis, Shirley	'64			
Nashville Cats	Lovin' Spoonful, The	'66	New York State of Mind	Joel, Billy	'76
Nasty	Jackson, Janet	'86	Next Door to an Angel	Sedaka, Neil	'62
Natural High	Bloodstone	'73	Next Time I Fall, The	Cetera, Peter & Amy Grant	'86
Nature's Way	Spirit	'70	Niagara	Wedding Present, The	'91
Naughty Girls Need Love Too	Fox, Samantha	'88	Nice 'N' Slow	Jackson, Freddie	'88
Navy Blue	Renay, Diane	'63	Nice to Be with You	Gallery	'72
Nearly in Love	Thompson, Richard	'86	Nice, Nice, Very Nice	Ambrosia	'75
Need You Tonight	Inxs	'87	Night	Wilson, Jackie	'60
Need Your Love So Bad	John, Little Willie	'56	Night Before, The	Beatles, The	'65
Needle and the Damage Done, The	Young, Neil	'72	Night Bird Flying	Hendrix, Jimi	'71
Needles and Pins	DeShannon, Jackie	'63	Night Chicago Died, The	Paper Lace	'74
Neither One of Us (Wants to Be the First to Say Goodbye)	Knight, Gladys & the Pips	'73	Night Fever	Bee Gees, The	'77
			Night Has a Thousand Eyes, The	Vee, Bobby	'60
Nel Blu Dipinto Di Blu (Volare)	Modugno, Domenico	'58	Night in My Veins	Pretenders, The	'94
Neon Rainbow	Box Tops, The	'67	Night in the City	Mitchell, Joni	'68
Nervous Breakdown	Cochran, Eddie	'61	Night Moves	Seger, Bob	'76
Neutron Dance	Pointer Sisters, The	'84	Night Owls, The	Little River Band	'81
Never	Heart	'85	Night the Lights Went out in Georgia, The	Lawrence, Vickie	'73
Never Be Anyone Else but You	Nelson, Ricky	'59			
Never Been to Spain	Three Dog Night	'71	Night They Drove Old Dixie Down, The	Band, The	'68
Never Can Say Goodbye	Jackson 5, The	'70			
Never Die Young	Taylor, James	'88	(Night Time Is the) Right Time	Charles, Ray	'58
Never Ending Song of Love	Delaney and Bonnie	'71	Night Train	Forrest, Jimmy	'52
Never Gonna Give You Up	Astley, Rick	'87	Nightingale	King, Carole	'74
Never Knew Love Like This Before	Mills, Stephanie	'80	Nightmare on My Street, A	D.J. Jazzy Jeff and the Fresh Prince	'88
Never Lie	Immature	'94			
Never My Love	Association, The	'67	Nights Are Forever Without You	England Dan & John Ford Coley	'76
Never Surrender	Hart, Corey	'85			
Never Tear Us Apart	Inxs	'87	Nights in White Satin	Moody Blues, The	'68
Never Too Much	Vandross, Luther	'81	Nights on Broadway	Bee Gees, The	'75
Never, Never Gonna Give Ya Up	White, Barry	'73	Nightshift	Commodores, The	'85
New Age Girl	Deadeye Dick	'94	Niki Hoeky	Proby, P.J.	'66
New England, A	Bragg, Billy	'83	Nikita	John, Elton	'86
New Girl in School, The	Jan and Dean	'64	Nite and Day	Sure, Al B.	'88
New Jack Hustler (Nino's Theme)	Ice-T	'91	Nite Owl	Allen, Tony	'55
New Kid in Town	Eagles, The	'77	Nitty Gritty, The	Ellis, Shirley	'63
New Life	Depeche Mode	'81	No Chemise, Please!	Granahan, Gerry	'58
New Moon on Monday	Duran Duran	'83	No Easy Way Down	Springfield, Dusty	'69
New Morning	Dylan, Bob	'70	No Excuses	Alice in Chains	'94
New New Minglewood Blues	Grateful Dead, The	'67	No Expectations	Rolling Stones, The	'68
New Rose	Damned, The	'76	No Guilt	Waitresses, The	'82
New Sensation	Inxs	'87	No Matter What	Badfinger	'70
New World Coming	Cass, Mama	'70	No Matter What Shape (Your Stomach's In)	T-Bones, The	'65
New World Man	Rush	'82			
New Year's Day	U2	'83	No Money Down	Berry, Chuck	'57
New York City (You're a Woman)	Kooper, Al	'71	No Money Down	Reed, Lou	'86
New York Groove	Frehley, Ace	'79	No More Lies	Michel'le	'89
New York Mining Disaster 1941 (Have You Seen My Wife Mr. Jones)	Bee Gees, The	'67	No More Lonely Nights	McCartney, Paul	'84
			No More Mr. Nice Guy	Cooper, Alice	'74
			No More Tears (Enough Is Enough)	Summer, Donna	'79

SONG	ARTIST	YEAR
No Myth	Penn, Michael	'89
No No Song	Starr, Ringo	'74
No One Is to Blame	Jones, Howard	'86
No One Knows	Dion & the Belmonts	'58
No One Like You	Scorpions, The	'82
No Ordinary Love	Sade	'92
No Particular Place to Go	Berry, Chuck	'64
No Quarter	Led Zeppelin	'73
No Rain	Blind Melon	'93
No Regrets	Rush, Tom	'68
No Reservations	Hüsker Dü	'87
No Sleep Till Brooklyn	Beastie Boys, The	'86
No Son of Mine	Genesis	'91
No Time	Guess Who, The	'69
No Time Like the Right Time	Blues Project, The	'67
No Woman, No Cry	Marley, Bob & the Wailers	'74
Nobody but Me	Isley Brothers, The	'63
Nobody Does It Better	Simon, Carly	'77
Nobody Told Me	Lennon, John	'84
Nobody's Fool	Cinderella	'87
Nobody's Fool (Theme from Caddyshack II)	Loggins, Kenny	'88
None of Your Business	Salt-n-Pepa	'93
Noonward Race, The	Mahavishnu Orchestra	'71
Norman	Thompson, Sue	'62
North to Alaska	Horton, Johnny	'60
Norwegian Wood (This Bird Has Flown)	Beatles, The	'65
Not Fade Away	Crickets, The	'57
(Not Just) Knee Deep	Funkadelic	'79
Not Sleeping Around	Ned's Atomic Dustbin	'92
Not So Sweet Martha Lorraine	Country Joe and The Fish	'67
Not Too Soon	Throwing Muses	'92
Nothin' at All	Heart	'86
Nothin' but a Good Time	Poison	'88
Nothing but Flowers	Talking Heads	'88
Nothing but Heartaches	Supremes, The	'65
Nothing Compares 2 U	Family, The	'85
Nothing Else Matters	Metallica	'91
Nothing from Nothing	Preston, Billy	'74
Nothing Has Been Proved	Springfield, Dusty	'89
Nothing Was Delivered	Byrds, The	'68
Nothing's Gonna Stop Us Now	Starship	'87
Notorious	Duran Duran	'86
November Rain	Guns N' Roses	'91
November Spawned a Monster	Morrissey	'90
Now and Forever	Marx, Richard	'94
(Now and Then There's) a Fool Such As I	Snow, Hank	'52
Now Run and Tell That	LaSalle, Denise	'71
Now That I Am Dead	French Frith Kaiser Thompson	'90

SONG	ARTIST	YEAR
Now That We Found Love	O'Jays, The	'73
Nowadays Clancy Can't Even Sing	Buffalo Springfield	'67
Nowhere Man	Beatles, The	'65
Nowhere Near	Yo La Tengo	'93
Nowhere to Run	Martha & the Vandellas	'65
Number of the Beast	Iron Maiden	'82
Nut Rocker	B. Bumble and the Stingers	'62
Nutbush City Limits	Turner, Ike and Tina	'73
Nuthin' but a "G" Thang	Dr. Dre	'93
Nuttin' but Love	Heavy D & the Boys	'94

O

SONG	ARTIST	YEAR
O Dio Mio	Annette	'60
O Superman	Anderson, Laurie	'82
O.K.	Rock Follies	'77
O.P.P.	Naughty By Nature	'91
Ob-La-Di, Ob-La-Da	Beatles, The	'68
Obsession	Animotion	'85
Ocean	Reed, Lou	'72
Ocean, The	Led Zeppelin	'73
Octopus's Garden	Beatles, The	'69
Ode to Billie Joe	Gentry, Bobbie	'67
Off on Your Own (Girl)	Sure, Al B.	'88
Off the Ground	McCartney, Paul	'93
Off the Wall	Jackson, Michael	'79
Oh Atlanta	Little Feat	'74
Oh Babe, What Would You Say	Smith, Hurricane	'73
Oh Baby Doll	Berry, Chuck	'58
Oh Bondage, up Yours!	X-Ray Specs	'78
Oh Boy	Crickets, The	'57
Oh Carol	Sedaka, Neil	'59
Oh Catherine	Pere Ubu	'91
Oh! Darling	Beatles, The	'69
Oh England My Lionheart	Bush, Kate	'80
Oh Girl	Chi-Lites, The	'72
Oh Happy Day	Hawkins, Edwin Singers, The	'69
Oh Julie	Crescendos	'58
Oh Lonesome Me	Gibson, Don	'58
Oh Me Oh My (I'm a Fool for You, Baby)	Lulu	'70
Oh My My	Starr, Ringo	'74
Oh No	Commodores, The	'81
Oh! No, Not My Baby	Brown, Maxine	'64
Oh, Pretty Woman	Orbison, Roy	'64
Oh Sheila	Ready for the World	'85
Oh, Sherrie	Perry, Steve	'84
Oh Very Young	Stevens, Cat	'74
Oh Well- Pt.1	Fleetwood Mac	'69
Oh What a Dream	Brown, Ruth	'54
Oh What a Night	Dells, The	'56

SONG	ARTIST	YEAR
Oh Yoko	Lennon, John	'71
Oh-Oh, I'm Falling in Love Again	Rodgers, Jimmie	'58
Ohio	Crosby, Stills, Nash & Young	'70
Okie from Muskogee	Haggard, Merle	'70
Ol' 55	Waits, Tom	'73
Old Days	Chicago	'75
Old Fashioned Love Song, An	Three Dog Night	'71
Old Man	Young, Neil	'72
Old Man down the Road, The	Fogerty, John	'85
Ol' Man River	Ravens, The	'47
Old Time Rock and Roll	Seger, Bob	'77
Ole Man Trouble	Redding, Otis	'68
Oliver's Army	Costello, Elvis	'79
O'Lucky Man	Price, Alan	'73
Omaha	Moby Grape	'67
On a Carousel	Hollies, The	'67
On and On	Knight, Gladys & the Pips	'74
On Bended Knee	Boyz II Men	'94
On Broadway	Drifters, The	'63
On My Own	Labelle, Patti and Michael McDonald	'86
On My Radio	Selecter, The	'79
On Our Own (From *Ghostbusters II*)	Brown, Bobby	'89
On the Dark Side	Cafferty, John & the Beaver Brown Band	'84
On the Nickel	Waits, Tom	'80
On the Radio	Summer, Donna	'79
On the Road Again	Canned Heat	'68
On the Road Again	Nelson, Willie	'80
On the Road to Fairfax County	Roches, The	'82
On the Turning Away	Pink Floyd	'87
On the Way Home	Buffalo Springfield	'68
On the Wings of a Nightingale	Everly Brothers, The	'84
Once Bitten, Twice Shy	Hunter, Ian	'75
Once I Was	Buckley, Tim	'67
Once in a Lifetime	Talking Heads	'81
Once You Get Started	Rufus	'75
One	Bee Gees, The	'89
One	Metallica	'88
One	Nilsson	'68
One	U2	'91
One, The	John, Elton	'92
One and Only, The	Hawkes, Chesney	'91
One Bad Apple (Don't Spoil the Whole Bunch)	Osmonds, The	'71
One Fine Day	Chiffons, The	'63
One Good Woman	Cetera, Peter	'88
One Heartbeat	Robinson, Smokey	'87
One Hundred Ways	Jones, Quincy	'82
One I Love, The	R.E.M.	'86
One in a Million You	Graham, Larry	'80

SONG	ARTIST	YEAR
One Kiss Led to Another	Coasters, The	'56
One Love	Marley, Bob & the Wailers	'65
One Man's Ceiling Is Another Man's Floor	Simon, Paul	'73
One Million Billionth of a Millisecond on a Sunday Morning	Flaming Lips, The	'87
One Mint Julep	Clovers, The	'52
One Monkey Don't Stop No Show	Big Maybelle	'54
One More Night	Collins, Phil	'85
One More Try	Michael, George	'87
One More Try	T., Timmy	'91
One Nation under a Groove	Funkadelic	'78
One Night (of Sin)	Lewis, Smiley	'55
One Nite Stan	Ethel and the Shameless Hussies	'88
One of a Kind (Love Affair)	Spinners, The	'72
One of These Nights	Eagles, The	'75
One of Us	Osborne, Joan	'95
One of us Must Know (Sooner or Later)	Dylan, Bob	'66
One on One	Hall and Oates	'83
One Scotch, One Bourbon, One Beer	Milburn, Amos	'53
One Step at a Time	Lee, Brenda	'57
One Step Up	Springsteen, Bruce	'87
One Summer Night	Danleers, The	'58
One Sweet Day	Carey, Mariah and Boyz II Men	'95
One Thing Leads to Another	Fixx, The	'83
One Time One Night	Los Lobos	'87
One Toke over the Line	Brewer and Shipley	'71
One Too Many Mornings	Dylan, Bob	'64
One Track Mind	Lewis, Bobby	'61
One, Two, Three (1-2-3)	Barry, Len	'65
One Way or Another	Blondie	'78
One Way Out	Miller, Aleck	'51
One Who Really Loves You, The	Wells, Mary	'62
Only a Pawn in Their Game	Dylan, Bob	'64
Only Flame in Town, The	Costello, Elvis	'84
Only in America	Jay & the Americans	'63
Only in My Dreams	Gibson, Debbie	'87
Only Love Can Break a Heart	Pitney, Gene	'62
Only Love Can Break Your Heart	Young, Neil	'70
Only Loved at Night	Raincoats, The	'81
Only One	Taylor, James	'86
Only One, The	Page, Jimmy	'88
Only Sixteen	Cooke, Sam	'59
Only the Good Die Young	Joel, Billy	'77
Only the Lonely	Motels, The	'82
Only the Lonely (Know the Way I Feel)	Orbison, Roy	'60

SONG	ARTIST	YEAR
Only the Strong Survive	Butler, Jerry	'69
Only the Young	Scandal	'84
Only Time Will Tell	Asia	'82
Only Women (Bleed)	Cooper, Alice	'75
Only You	Platters, The	'55
Only You	Yazoo	'82
Only You Know and I Know	Mason, Dave	'70
Ooby Dooby	Orbison, Roy	'56
Ooh Baby Baby	Miracles, The	'65
O-o-h Child	Five Stairsteps, The	'70
Ooh La La (I Can't Get over You)	Perfect Gentlemen	'90
Ooh Poo Pah Doo (Part One)	Hill, Jessie	'60
Ooo La La La	Teena Marie	'88
Oooh! My Soul	Little Richard	'57
Oop Shoop	Gunter, Shirley & the Queens	'54
Open Arms	Journey	'82
Open Letter (to a Landlord)	Living Colour	'88
Open Letter to My Teenage Son, An	Lundberg, Victor	'67
Open Your Heart	Madonna	'86
Opened	Breeders, The	'90
Operation: mindcrime	Queensryche	'88
Operator	Midnight Star	'84
Ophelia	Band, The	'75
Opportunities (Let's Make Lots of Money)	Pet Shop Boys	'86
Opposites Attract	Abdul, Paula	'88
Optimistic	Sounds of Blackness	'91
Orange Crush	R.E.M.	'88
Ordinary World	Duran Duran	'93
Orgasm Addict	Buzzcocks, The	'77
Orinoco Flow (Sail Away)	Enya	'88
Orphans	Teenage Jesus & the Jerks	'79
Other Side of Summer, The	Costello, Elvis	'91
Other Side of This Life, The	Lovin' Spoonful, The	'65
Other Woman, The	Parker, Ray Jr.	'82
Our Day Will Come	Ruby & the Romantics	'63
Our Frank	Morrissey	'91
Our House	Crosby, Stills, Nash & Young	'70
Our House	Madness	'83
Our Lips Are Sealed	Go-Go's, The	'81
Our Love	Cole, Natalie	'77
Out Come the Freaks	Was (Not Was)	'81
Out Here on My Own	Cara, Irene	'80
Out in the Fields	Moore, Garry	'85
Out of Limits	Marketts, The	'63
Out of Tears	Rolling Stones, The	'94
Out of the Blue	Gibson, Debbie	'87
Out of Time	Farlowe, Chris	'66
Out of Touch	Hall and Oates	'84
Out of Work	Bonds, Gary U.S.	'82

SONG	ARTIST	YEAR
Outa-Space	Preston, Billy	'71
Outside Chance	Turtles, The	'67
Outside of a Small Circle of Friends	Ochs, Phil	'67
Outstanding	Gap Band, The	'82
Over and Over	Day, Bobby	'58
Over My Head	Fleetwood Mac	'75
Over the Hills and Far Away	Led Zeppelin	'73
Over the Mountain, across the Sea	Johnnie and Joe	'57
Over Under Sideways Down	Yardbirds, The	'66
Over You	Puckett, Gary & the Union Gap	'68
Overkill	Men at Work	'83
Overkill	Motorhead	'79
Overnight Sensation (Hit Record)	Raspberries, The	'74
Owner of a Lonely Heart	Yes	'83
Oye Come Va (Listen How It Goes)	Santana	'71

P

SONG	ARTIST	YEAR
P.A.S.S.I.O.N.	Rhytm Syndicate	'91
P.F. Sloan	Webb, Jimmy	'70
(P.S.) I Love You	Beatles, The	'63
P.T. 109	Dean, Jimmy	'62
P.Y.T. (Pretty Young Thing)	Jackson, Michael	'83
Pablo Picasso	Modern Lovers, The	'70
Pacific	808 State	'89
Pack up Your Sorrows	Farina, Dick and Mimi	'65
Paint It Black	Rolling Stones, The	'66
Pair of Brown Eyes, A	Pogues, The	'85
Pale Blue Eyes	Velvet Underground, The	'69
Palisades Park	Cannon, Freddy	'62
Pamela Brown	Kottke, Leo	'74
Panama	Van Halen	'84
Panama Red	New Riders of the Purple Sage	'73
Pancho and Lefty	Van Zandt, Townes	'72
Papa Don't Preach	Madonna	'86
Papa Don't Take No Mess	Brown, James	'74
Papa Was a Rollin' Stone	Temptations, The	'72
Papa Was Too	Tex, Joe	'66
Papa's Got a Brand New Bag	Brown, James & the Famous Flames	'65
Papa-Oom-Mow-Mow	Rivingtons, The	'62
Paper in Fire	Mellencamp, John Cougar	'87
Paper Sun	Traffic	'67
Paperback Writer	Beatles, The	'66
Paradise	Sade	'88
Paradise by the Dashboard Light	Meat Loaf	'77
Paradise City	Guns N' Roses	'89
Parallel Lines	Rundgren, Todd	'89
Paralyzed	Presley, Elvis	'56
Paranoid	Black Sabbath	'70
Parchman Farm	Mayall's, John, Bluesbreakers	'67

SONG	ARTIST	YEAR	SONG	ARTIST	YEAR
Parents Just Don't Understand	D.J. Jazzy Jeff and the Fresh Prince	'88	Pennyroyal Tea	Nirvana	'93
			People Are People	Depeche Mode	'84
Part of the Plan	Fogelberg, Dan	'75	People Are Still Having Sex	La Tour	'91
Part of the Union	Strawbs, The	'73	People Are Strange	Doors, The	'67
Part Time Love	Taylor, Little Johnnie	'63	People Everyday	Arrested Development	'92
Part-Time Lover	Wonder, Stevie	'85	People Get Ready	Impressions, The	'65
Particle Man	They Might Be Giants	'90	People Got to Be Free	Rascals, The	'68
Party	Presley, Elvis	'57	People Have the Power	Smith, Patti	'88
Party All the Time	Murphy, Eddie	'85	People Who Died	Carroll, Jim Band, The	'80
Party Doll	Knox, Buddy	'57	Peppermint Twist	Dee, Joey & the Starliters	'61
Party for Your Right to Fight	Public Enemy	'88	Percy's Song	Fairport Convention	'69
Party Lights	Clark, Claudine	'62	Perfect Kiss	New Order	'85
Party out of Bounds	B-52's, The	'80	Perfect Way	Scritti Politti	'85
Partyman	Prince	'89	Perfect World	K., Tonio	'86
Partyup	Prince	'80	Perfect World	Lewis, Huey & the News	'88
Pass the Dutchie	Musical Youth	'83	Persecution and Restoration of Dean Moriarty (On the Road), The	Aztec Two-Step	'72
Pass the Mic	Beastie Boys, The	'92			
Passenger, The	Pop, Iggy	'77	Personal Jesus	Depeche Mode	'90
Passion	Stewart, Rod	'80	Personality	Price, Lloyd	'59
Passionate Kisses	Williams, Lucinda	'88	Personality Crisis	New York Dolls	'73
Pastime Paradise	Wonder, Stevie	'76	Personally	Moore, Jackie	'78
Pastures of Plenty	Guthrie, Woody	'41	Pets	Porno for Pyros	'93
Patches	Lee, Dickey	'62	Philadelphia	Young, Neil	'93
Patches (I'm Depending on You)	Chairmen of the Board, The	'70	Philadelphia Freedom	John, Elton	'75
Paths That Cross	Smith, Patti	'88	Photograph	Def Leppard	'83
Patience	Guns N' Roses	'87	Photograph	Starr, Ringo	'73
Patterns	Simon and Garfunkel	'66	Physical	Newton-John, Olivia	'81
Pay to Cum	Bad Brains	'80	Piano in the Dark	Russell, Brenda	'88
Pay to Play	Nirvana	'88	Piano Man	Joel, Billy	'74
Payback, The	Brown, James	'73	Pick up the Pieces	Average White Band, The	'74
Payoff Mix, The	Double Dee and Steinski	'85	Picture of Helen	Silos, The	'90
Peace in Our Time	Costello, Elvis	'84	Pictures of Lily	Who, The	'67
Peace Like a River	Simon, Paul	'72	Pictures of Matchstick Men	Status Quo	'68
Peace Train	Stevens, Cat	'71	Piece of Crap	Young, Neil	'94
Peace Will Come (According to Plan)	Melanie	'70	Piece of My Heart	Mimms, Garnet & the Enchanters	'67
Peaceful	Rankin, Kenny	'72	Pied Piper, The	Changin' Times	'65
Peaceful Easy Feeling	Eagles, The	'72	Piggies	Beatles, The	'68
Peaches En Regalia	Zappa, Frank	'69	Pigs on the Wing, Pt. 1	Pink Floyd	'77
Peanut Butter	Marathons, The	'61	Pillow Talk	Sylvia	'73
Peanuts	Little Joe & the Thrillers	'57	Pinball Wizard	Who, The	'69
Pearl of the Quarter	Steely Dan	'73	Pinhead	Ramones, The	'77
Pearle	Trip Shakespeare	'88	Pink Bedroom	Hiatt, John	'79
Peek-A-Boo	Siouxsie & the Banshees	'88	Pink Cadillac	Springsteen, Bruce	'83
Peg	Steely Dan	'77	Pink Cashmere	Prince	'93
Peggy Sue	Holly, Buddy	'57	Pink Houses	Mellencamp, John Cougar	'83
Peggy Sue Got Married	Crickets, The	'60	Pink Pegged Slacks	Cochran, Eddie	'56
Pencil Neck Geek	Blassie, Freddie	'77	Pink Shoelaces	Stevens, Dodie	'58
Penetration	Pyramids, The	'64	Pipeline	Chantays, The	'63
Penguin in Bondage	Zappa, Frank	'74	Pirate Looks at Forty	Buffett, Jimmy	'75
Penny Lane	Beatles, The	'67	Piss Factory	Smith, Patti	'74

SONG	ARTIST	YEAR	SONG	ARTIST	YEAR
Place in the Sun, A	Wonder, Stevie	'66	Poor Poor Pitiful Me	Zevon, Warren	'76
Plain Jane	Darin, Bobby	'59	Poor Side of Town	Rivers, Johnny	'66
Planet Rock	Bambaataa, Afrika & Soulsonic Force	'82	Pop Life	Prince	'85
			Pop Muzik	M	'79
Play That Funky Music	Wild Cherry	'76	Popcorn, The	Brown, James	'69
Play with Fire	Rolling Stones, The	'65	Popeye the Hitchhiker	Checker, Chubby	'62
Play with Toys	Basehead	'92	Popsicles and Icicles	Murmaids, The	'63
Playboy	Marvelettes, The	'62	Porpoise Song, The	Monkees, The	'68
Playboys and Playgirls	Dylan, Bob	'63	Positively 4th Street	Dylan, Bob	'65
Playground	Another Bad Creation	'91	Pour Some Sugar on Me	Def Leppard	'88
Playground in My Mind	Holmes, Clint	'73	Pourin' It All Out	Parker, Graham	'76
Playing in the Band	Weir, Bob	'71	Power	Doobie Brothers, John Hall & James Taylor, The	'79
Playmate	Pearls Before Swine	'67			
Plea, The	Chantels, The	'57			
Pleasant Valley Sunday	Monkees, The	'67	Power and the Glory, The	Ochs, Phil	'63
Please Come Home for Christmas	Brown, Charles	'61	Power of Gold	Fogelberg, Dan	'78
Please Come to Boston	Loggins, Dave	'74	Power of Love	Simon, Joe	'72
Please Don't Go	K.C. & the Sunshine Band	'79	Power of Love, The	Lewis, Huey & the News	'85
Please Don't Go Girl	New Kids on the Block	'88	Power of Love/Love Power	Vandross, Luther	'91
Please Don't Take My Air Jordans	Gaines, Reg E.	'93	Power of Two	Indigo Girls, The	'94
Please Forgive Me	Adams, Bryan	'93	Power to the People	Lennon, John	'70
Please Help Me I'm Falling	Locklin, Hank	'60	Power, The	Snap	'90
Please Let Me Wonder	Beach Boys, The	'65	Practice What You Preach	White, Barry	'94
Please Love Me	King, B.B.	'53	Pray	Hammer, M.C.	'90
Please Love Me Forever	Cathy Jean and the Roommates	'61	Prayer for the Dying	Seal	'94
			Praying for Time	Michael, George	'90
Please Mr. Please	Newton-John, Olivia	'75	Precious and Few	Climax	'72
Please Mr. Postman	Marvelettes, The	'61	Presence of the Lord	Blind Faith	'69
Please Please Me	Beatles, The	'63	Pressure Drop	Toots & the Maytals	'70
Please, Please, Please	Brown, James & the Famous Flames	'56	Pretender, The	Browne, Jackson	'77
			Pretty as You Feel	Jefferson Airplane, The	'71
Please Say You Want Me	Schoolboys, The	'57	Pretty Ballerina	Left Banke, The	'67
Please Send Me Someone to Love	Mayfield, Percy	'51	Pretty Boy Floyd	Guthrie, Woody	'42
Pleasure Principle, The	Jackson, Janet	'86	Pretty Flamingo	Manfred Mann	'66
Pledging My Love	Ace, Johnny	'54	Pretty Girls Everywhere	Church, Eugene	'59
Plush	Stone Temple Pilots	'93	Pretty in Pink	Psychedelic Furs, The	'81
Plynth (Water down the Drain)	Beck, Jeff Group, The	'68	Pretty Little Angel Eyes	Lee, Curtis	'61
Poetry in Motion	Tillotson, Johnny	'60	Pretty on the Inside	Hole	'91
Poetry Man	Snow, Phoebe	'73	Pretty Thing	Diddley, Bo	'58
Point of No Return	Expose	'87	Pretty Vacant	Sex Pistols, The	'77
Poison	Bell Biv Devoe	'90	Price of Love	Everly Brothers, The	'65
Poison	Cooper, Alice	'89	Pride (In the Name of Love)	U2	'84
Poison Ivy	Coasters, The	'59	Pride and Joy	Coverdale, David and Jimmy Page	'93
Police and Thieves	Murvin, Junior	'76			
Policy of Truth	Depeche Mode	'90	Pride and Joy	Gaye, Marvin	'63
Political Science	Newman, Randy	'72	Pride and Joy	Vaughan, Stevie Ray	'83
Politician	Cream	'68	Pride of Man	Quicksilver Messenger Service	'68
Polk Salad Annie	White, Tony Joe	'69			
Polythene Pam	Beatles, The	'69	Pride, The (Part 1)	Isley Brothers, The	'77
Pony Time	Covay, Don	'61	Primrose Lane	Wallace, Jerry	'58
Poor Little Fool	Nelson, Ricky	'58	Prisoner of Life	Adams, Johnny	'91

SONG	ARTIST	YEAR	SONG	ARTIST	YEAR
Reach out and Touch (Somebody's Hand)	Ross, Diana	'70	Remember Walking in the Sand	Shangri-Las, The	'64
			Reminiscing	Little River Band	'78
Reach out of the Darkness	Friend and Lover	'68	Rene and Georgette Magritte with Their Dog After the War	Simon, Paul	'83
Reach out, I'll Be There	Four Tops, The	'66			
Ready or Not	After 7	'89	Renegade	Zevon, Warren	'91
Ready or Not	Browne, Jackson	'73	Reno, Nevada	Farina, Dick and Mimi	'65
Ready Teddy	Little Richard	'56	Repeater	Fugazi	'90
Real Good for Free	Mitchell, Joni	'74	Repetition	Fall, The	'77
Real Love	Blige, Mary J.	'92	Reptile	Church, The	'88
Real Love	Doobie Brothers, The	'80	Rescue Me	Bass, Fontella	'65
Real Love	Lennon, John	'88	Rescue Me	Madonna	'90
Real Love	Skyy	'89	Respect	Redding, Otis	'65
Real Love	Watley, Jody	'89	Respect Yourself	Staple Singers, The	'71
Real Me, The	Who, The	'73	Rest in Peace	Extreme	'92
Real Real Real	Jesus Jones	'91	Restless Kid	Nelson, Ricky	'58
Real Wild Child	Ivan (Jerry Allison)	'58	Return of the Grievous Angel	Parsons, Gram	'74
Really Rosie	King, Carole	'75	Return to Innocence	Enigma	'94
Reason to Believe	Hardin, Tim	'66	Return to Sender	Presley, Elvis	'62
Reasons	Earth, Wind & Fire	'75	Reunited	Peaches and Herb	'78
Rebel Rebel	Bowie, David	'74	Reuters	Wire	'77
Rebel Rouser	Eddy, Duane	'58	Reverend Mr. Black, The	Kingston Trio, The	'63
Rebel Yell	Idol, Billy	'84	Revolution	Arrested Development	'92
Rebirth of Slick (Cool Like Dat)	Digable Planets	'93	Revolution (Revolution 1)	Beatles, The	'68
Reconsider Baby	Fulson, Lowell	'54	Revolution 9	Beatles, The	'68
Red Guitar	Wainwright, Loudon	'72	Revolution Will Not Be Televised, The	Last Poets, The	'71
Red Hot	Five Scamps, The	'49			
Red House	Hendrix, Jimi	'69	Rhiannon (Will You Ever Win)	Fleetwood Mac	'75
Red Rain	Gabriel, Peter	'86	Rhythm Is a Dancer	Snap	'92
Red Red Wine	Diamond, Neil	'67	Rhythm Is Gonna Get You	Miami Sound Machine	'87
Red River Rock	Johnny & the Hurricanes	'59	Rhythm Nation	Jackson, Janet	'89
Red Rubber Ball	Cyrcle, The	'66	Rhythm of My Heart	Stewart, Rod	'91
Red Shoes, The	Bush, Kate	'93	Rhythm of the Night	DeBarge	'85
Redemption Song	Marley, Bob & the Wailers	'80	Rhythm of the Night, The	Corona	'94
Redneck Friend	Browne, Jackson	'73	Rhythm of the Rain	Cascades, The	'63
Redsox Are Winning, The	Earth Opera	'69	Rich Girl	Hall and Oates	'76
Reelin' and Rockin'	Berry, Chuck	'58	Rico Suave	Gerardo	'91
Reeling in the Years	Steely Dan	'72	Ride	Sharp, Dee Dee	'62
Reet Petite	Wilson, Jackie	'57	Ride a White Swan	T. Rex	'71
Reflections	Supremes, The	'67	Ride Captain Ride	Blues Image	'70
Reflections of My Life	Marmalade	'70	Ride Like the Wind	Cross, Christopher	'79
Reflex, The	Duran Duran	'83	Ride My See Saw	Moody Blues, The	'68
Refugee	Petty, Tom & the Heartbreakers	'79	Ride on Time	Black Box	'89
			Ride the Wild Surf	Jan and Dean	'64
Regret	New Order	'93	Ride Your Pony	Dorsey, Lee	'65
Regulate	Warren G & Nate Dogg	'94	Riders on the Storm	Doors, The	'71
Relax	Frankie Goes to Hollywood	'84	Riding with Mary	X	'82
Release Me	Phillips, Little Esther	'65	Riding with the King	Hiatt, John	'83
Release Me	Wilson Phillips	'90	Right Back Where We Started From	Nightingale, Maxine	'76
Remember (Christmas)	Nilsson	'74	Right down the Line	Rafferty, Gerry	'78
Remember the Time	Jackson, Michael	'91	Right Here	SWV	'92
Remember Then	Earls, The	'62	Right Here Waiting	Marx, Richard	'89

SONG	ARTIST	YEAR	SONG	ARTIST	YEAR
Right Here, Right Now	Jesus Jones	'91	Rock in the U.S.A. (a Salute to 60's Rock)	Mellencamp, John (Cougar)	'85
Right Now	Sure, Al B.	'92	Rock Island Line	Leadbelly	'42
Right Now	Van Halen	'91	Rock Lobster	B-52's, The	'79
Right on Track	Breakfast Club, The	'87	Rock Me	Steppenwolf	'69
Right Place Wrong Time	Dr. John	'73	Rock Me	Waters, Muddy	'56
Right Side of My Brain	Angry Samoans	'80	Rock Me All Night Long	Ravens, The	'52
Right Time of the Night, The	Warnes, Jennifer	'76	Rock Me Amadeus	Falco	'86
Rikki Don't Lose That Number	Steely Dan	'74	Rock Me Baby	King, B.B.	'64
Ring My Bell	Ward, Anita	'79	Rock Me Gently	Kim, Andy	'74
Ring of Fire	Cash, Johnny	'63	Rock Me on the Water	Browne, Jackson	'72
Ringo, I Love You	Mason, Bonnie Jo	'64	Rock Me Tonight (for Old Times Sake)	Jackson, Freddie	'85
Rio	Duran Duran	'83	Rock Me Tonite	Squier, Billy	'84
Rio Grande	Wilson, Brian	'88	Rock My Plimsoul	Beck, Jeff Group, The	'68
Riot in Cell Block #9	Robins, The	'54	Rock n' Me	Miller, Steve Band, The	'76
Rip It Up	Little Richard	'56	Rock of Ages	Def Leppard	'83
Rip Off, The	Lee, Laura	'72	Rock On	Essex, David	'73
Ripple	Grateful Dead, The	'70	Rock Steady	Franklin, Aretha	'71
Rise Above	Black Flag	'81	Rock Steady	Whispers, The	'87
River	Mitchell, Joni	'71	Rock the Boat	Hues Corporation, The	'74
River Deep, Mountain High	Turner, Ike and Tina	'66	Rock the Casbah	Clash, The	'82
River of Dreams	Joel, Billy	'93	Rock Therapy	Burnette, Johnny & the Rock and Roll Trio	'56
River, The	Springsteen, Bruce	'80	Rock This Town	Stray Cats, The	'82
Rivers of Babylon	Melodians, The	'70	Rock Wit'cha	Brown, Bobby	'88
Road Runner	Modern Lovers, The	'71	Rock with It	Moore's, Johnny Three Blazers	'50
Road to Cairo	Ackles, David	'68	Rock with You	Jackson, Michael	'79
Road to Nowhere	Talking Heads	'85	Rock You Like a Hurricane	Scorpions, The	'84
Road, The	O'Keefe, Danny	'72	Rock Your Baby	McCrae, George	'74
Roadhouse Blues	Doors, The	'70	Rock 'n' Roll Fantasy	Bad Company	'79
Roam	B-52's, The	'89	Rock 'n' Roll Heaven	Righteous Brothers, The	'73
Rock 'n Roll Fantasy, A	Kinks, The	'77	Rockabilly Boogie	Burnette, Johnny & the Rock & Roll Trio	'56
(Rock 'n' Roll I Gave You) The Best Years of My Life	Johnson, Kevin	'73	Rockaway Beach	Ramones, The	'77
Rock 'n' Roll Is King	Electric Light Orchestra	'83	Rocket 2U	Jets, The	'88
Rock a-Beating Boogie	Haley, Bill & the Comets	'52	Rocket 88	Brenston, Jackie & His Delta Cats	'51
Rock and a Hard Place	Rolling Stones, The	'89	Rocket in My Pocket	Little Feat	'77
Rock and Roll	Led Zeppelin	'71	Rocket Man (I Think It's Gonna Be a Long Long Time)	John, Elton	'72
Rock and Roll	Velvet Underground, The	'70	Rockin' All over the World	Fogerty, John	'75
Rock and Roll (Part II)	Glitter, Gary	'72	Rockin' Around the Christmas Tree	Lee, Brenda	'60
Rock and Roll All Night	Kiss	'75	Rockin' at Midnight	Brown, Roy	'49
Rock and Roll Dreams Come Through	Steinman, Jim	'81	Rockin' Chair	McCrae, Gwen	'75
Rock and Roll Girls	Fogerty, John	'85	Rockin' Good Way (to Mess Around and Fall in Love), A	Spaniels, The	'58
Rock and Roll Hoochie Koo	Winter, Johnny	'74	Rockin' in the Free World	Young, Neil	'89
Rock and Roll Is Here to Stay	Danny & the Juniors	'58	Rockin' Is Our Business	Treniers, The	'52
Rock and Roll Love Letter	Bay City Rollers, The	'75	Rockin' Pneumonia & the Boogie Woogie Flu	Smith, Huey	'57
Rock and Roll Lullabye	Thomas, B.J.	'72			
Rock and Roll Music	Berry, Chuck	'57			
Rock and Roll Never Forgets	Seger, Bob	'76			
Rock and Roll Woman	Buffalo Springfield	'67			
Rock Around with Ollie Vee	Holly, Buddy	'56			
Rock Box	Run-D.M.C.	'84			

SONG	ARTIST	YEAR
Rockin' Robin	Day, Bobby	'58
Rockin' Roll Baby	Stylistics, The	'73
Rockit	Hancock, Herbie	'83
Rocky Mountain High	Denver, John	'73
Rocky Mountain Way	Walsh, Joe	'73
Rocky Racoon	Beatles, The	'68
Rolene	Mink DeVille	'78
Roll Away the Stone	Russell, Leon	'70
Roll over Beethoven	Berry, Chuck	'59
Roll the Bones	Rush	'91
Roll with It	Winwood, Steve	'88
Rollin' Stone	Waters, Muddy	'50
Romantic	White, Karyn	'91
Romeo	Dino	'90
Romeo and Juliet	Dire Straits	'80
Romeo Is Bleeding	Waits, Tom	'78
Romeo's Tune	Forbert, Steve	'79
Romping through the Swamp	Van Ronk, Dave & the Hudson Dusters	'68
Roni	Brown, Bobby	'89
Ronnie	Four Seasons, The	'64
Room Full of Mirrors	Hendrix, Jimi	'71
Room to Move	Animotion	'89
Room to Move	Mayall, John	'69
Roots, Rock, Reggae	Marley, Bob & the Wailers	'76
Rosalita (Come out Tonight)	Springsteen, Bruce	'73
Rosalyn	Pretty Things	'64
Rosanna	Toto	'82
Rose and a Baby Ruth, A	Hamilton, George IV	'56
Rose Garden	South, Joe	'69
Rose, The	Midler, Bette	'79
Roses Are Red (My Love)	Vinton, Bobby	'61
Rough Boys	Townshend, Pete	'80
Round Here	Counting Crows	'93
Roundabout	Yes	'72
Roxanne	Police, The	'78
Roxanne, Roxanne	UTFO	'85
Rub You the Right Way	Gill, Johnny	'90
Rubber Ball	Vee, Bobby	'60
Rubber Biscuit	Chips, The	'56
Rubber Bullets	10 c.c.	'73
Rubberband Girl	Bush, Kate	'93
Rubberband Man, The	Spinners, The	'76
Ruby Baby	Drifters, The	'56
Ruby Tuesday	Rolling Stones, The	'67
Ruby, Don't Take Your Love to Town	Rogers, Kenny	'69
Ruffneck	Lyte, MC	'93
Rumble	Wray, Link	'58
Rumors	Timex Social Club	'86
Rump Shaker	Wreckx-N-Effect	'92

SONG	ARTIST	YEAR
Run Around	Blues Traveler	'94
Run for the Roses	Fogelberg, Dan	'82
Run for Your Life	Beatles, The	'65
Run Like a Thief	Souther, J.D.	'72
Run Like Hell	Pink Floyd	'79
Run Rudolph Run	Berry, Chuck	'58
Run Through the Jungle	Creedence Clearwater Revival	'70
Run to Him	Vee, Bobby	'61
Run to the Hills	Iron Maiden	'82
Run to You	Adams, Bryan	'84
Run, Run, Run	Jo Jo Gunne	'72
Runaround Sue	Dion	'61
Runaway	Bon Jovi	'84
Runaway	Shannon, Del	'61
Runaway Boys	Stray Cats, The	'81
Runaway Child, Running Wild	Temptations, The	'69
Runaway Train	Soul Asylum	'92
Runnin' Away	Sly & the Family Stone	'71
Runnin' down a Dream	Petty, Tom	'89
Runnin' with the Devil	Van Halen	'78
Running Back to You	Williams, Vanessa	'92
Running Bear	Preston, Johnny	'59
Running on Empty	Browne, Jackson	'77
Running Scared	Orbison, Roy	'61
Running up That Hill	Bush, Kate	'85
Running with the Night	Richie, Lionel	'83
Rush	Big Audio Dynamite	'91
Rush Hour	Wiedlin, Jane	'88
Rush, Rush	Abdul, Paula	'91
Rust Never Sleeps (Hey Hey My My into the Black)	Young, Neil	'79

S

SONG	ARTIST	YEAR
S.F. Sorrow Is Born	Pretty Things	'69
Sabre Dance	Love Sculpture	'69
Sacred	Castells, The	'61
Sad Eyes	John, Robert	'79
Sad Movies Always Make Me Cry	Thompson, Sue	'61
Sad Songs (Say So Much)	John, Elton	'84
Sad-Eyed Lady of the Lowlands	Dylan, Bob	'66
Sadeness, Part 1	Enigma	'91
Safe European Home	Clash, The	'78
Safety Dance	Men Without Hats	'83
Saigon Bride	Baez, Joan	'67
Sail Away	Newman, Randy	'72
Sail On	Commodores, The	'79
Sail on Sailor	Beach Boys, The	'73
Sailing	Cross, Christopher	'80
Sailing	Sutherland Brothers & Quiver, The	'73

SONG	ARTIST	YEAR
Sailor (Your Home Is the Sea)	Lolita	'60
Sails of Charon, The	Scorpions, The	'75
Saints	Breeders, The	'93
Sally	Sade	'85
Sally Can't Dance	Reed, Lou	'74
Sally Go 'Round the Roses	Jaynettes, The	'63
Salt in My Tears, The	Briley, Martin	'83
Salt of the Earth, The	Rolling Stones, The	'68
Salty Dog, A	Procol Harum	'67
Sam	Meat Puppets	'91
Sam Stone	Prine, John	'71
Same Old Lang Syne	Fogelberg, Dan	'80
San Antonio Rose	Wills, Bob & His Texas Playboys	'40
San Diego Serenade	Waits, Tom	'74
San Franciscan Nights	Animals, The	'67
San Francisco (Be Sure to Wear Some Flowers in Your Hair)	McKenzie, Scott	'67
San Francisco (You've Got Me)	Village People, The	'77
San Francisco Bay Blues	Fuller, Jesse	'54
San Francisco Girls (the Return of the Native)	Fever Tree	'68
Sanctified Lady	Gaye, Marvin	'85
Sanctify Yourself	Simple Minds	'86
Sara	Dylan, Bob	'76
Sara	Fleetwood Mac	'79
Sara	Starship	'85
Sara Smile	Hall and Oates	'75
Saran Wrap	Fugs, The	'65
Sat in Your Lap	Bush, Kate	'82
Satellite of Love	Reed, Lou	'72
Satisfied	Marx, Richard	'89
Saturday in the Park	Chicago	'72
Saturday Night	Bay City Rollers, The	'75
Saturday Night Fish Fry	Jordan, Louis & His Tympani Five	'49
Saturday Night Special	Lynyrd Skynyrd	'75
Saturday Night's Alright (for Fighting)	John, Elton	'72
Sausalito Summernight	Diesel	'81
Save It for Later	English Beat, The	'82
Save It for Me	Four Seasons, The	'64
Save the Country	Nyro, Laura	'69
Save the Last Dance for Me	Drifters, The	'60
Save the Overtime for Me	Knight, Gladys & the Pips	'83
Save Your Heart for Me	Hyland, Brian	'63
Saved	Baker, LaVern	'61
Saving All My Love for You	McCoo, Marilyn and Billy Davis	'85
Saving Forever for You	Shanice	'92
Saving the Best for Last	Williams, Vanessa	'92

SONG	ARTIST	YEAR
Savoy Truffle	Beatles, The	'68
Say Goodbye to Hollywood	Joel, Billy	'76
Say It Isn't So	Hall and Oates	'83
Say It Loud—I'm Black and I'm Proud	Brown, James & the Famous Flames	'68
Say Man	Diddley, Bo	'59
Say Say Say	McCartney, Paul & Michael Jackson	'83
Say You Love Me	Fleetwood Mac	'75
Say You Will	Foreigner	'88
Say You, Say Me	Richie, Lionel	'85
Say, Has Anybody Seen My Sweet Gypsy Rose	Dawn	'73
Scandalous	Prince	'89
Scarborough Fair - Canticle	Simon and Garfunkel	'66
Scenes from an Italian Restaurant	Joel, Billy	'77
School Day	Berry, Chuck	'57
School Is Out	Bonds, Gary U.S.	'61
School's Out	Cooper, Alice	'72
Science Fiction Double Feature	Donnelly, Jamie	'74
Scorpio	Coffey, Dennis	'71
Sea Cruise	Ford, Frankie	'59
Sea of Love	Phillips, Phil	'59
Sealed with a Kiss	Hyland, Brian	'62
Search and Destroy	Stooges, The	'73
Search Is Over, The	Survivor	'84
Searchin'	Coasters, The	'57
Searching for a Heart	Zevon, Warren	'90
Season of the Witch	Donovan	'65
Seasons Change	Expose	'87
Seasons in the Sun	Kingston Trio, The	'63
Seasons of Wither	Aerosmith	'74
Second Chance	38 Special	'89
Second Hand Love	Francis, Connie	'62
Second Time Around, The	Shalamar	'79
Secret	Madonna	'94
Secret Agent Man	Rivers, Johnny	'66
Secret Garden (Sweet Seduction Suite), The	Jones, Quincy	'89
Secret Lovers	Atlantic Starr	'86
Secret Rendezvous	White, Karyn	'89
Secret Sharer	Half Japanese	'84
Security	Redding, Otis	'64
Security of the 1st World	Public Enemy	'88
See a Little Light	Mould, Bob	'89
See Emily Play	Pink Floyd	'68
See Me, Feel Me	Who, The	'69
See My Friends	Kinks, The	'66
See You in September	Tempos, The	'59
See You Later, Alligator	Charles, Bobby	'55
Seeds	Springsteen, Bruce	'85

SONG	ARTIST	YEAR
Seeker, The	Who, The	'70
Seems So Long Ago, Nancy	Cohen, Leonard	'69
Seesaw	Covay, Don	'65
Seether	Veruca Salt	'94
Self Control	Branigan, Laura	'84
Self Destruction	Stop the Violence	'89
Self Esteem	Offspring	'94
Selling the Drama	Live	'94
Send Me Some Lovin'	Little Richard	'57
Send One Your Love	Wonder, Stevie	'79
Sending All My Love	Linear	'90
Sense of Purpose	Pretenders, The	'90
Senses Working Overtime	XTC	'82
Sensitive New Age Guys	Lavin, Christine	'90
Sensitivity	Tresvant, Ralph	'91
Sentimental Lady	Fleetwood Mac	'72
Sentimental Street	Night Ranger	'85
Separate Lives (Love Theme from *White Nights*)	Collins, Phil and Marilyn Michaels	'85
Separate Ways	Presley, Elvis	'70
Separate Ways (World's Apart)	Journey	'83
September	Earth, Wind & Fire	'79
September Gurls	Big Star	'74
Serpentine Fire	Earth, Wind & Fire	'77
Set Adrift on Memory Bliss	P.M. Dawn	'91
Set Me Free	Jones, Paul	'67
Set Me Free	Utopia	'80
Set the Controls for the Heart of the Sun	Pink Floyd	'68
Set the House Ablaze	Weller, Paul	'81
Set You Free This Time	Byrds, The	'65
Seven Bridges Road	Nelson, Tracy	'71
Seven Days	McPhatter, Clyde	'56
Seven Little Girls (Sitting in the Back Seat)	Evans, Paul	'59
Seven Rooms of Gloom	Four Tops, The	'67
Seven Spanish Angels	Charles, Ray with Willie Nelson	'84
Seven Year Ache	Cash, Rosanne	'81
Seven-Day Weekend	Bonds, Gary U.S.	'62
Seventeen	Bennett, Boyd	'55
Seventh Son, The	Allison, Mose	'58
Sex (I'm A)	Berlin	'83
Sex and Drugs and Rock 'n' Roll	Dury, Ian & the Blockheads	'78
Sex Junkie	Plasmatics, The	'81
Sex Machine	Brown, James	'70
Sexual Healing	Gaye, Marvin	'82
Sexuality	Bragg, Billy	'91
Sexy Eyes	Dr. Hook	'79
Sexy Sadie	Beatles, The	'68
Sexy Ways	Midnighters, The	'54

SONG	ARTIST	YEAR
Sgt. Pepper's Lonely Hearts Club Band	Beatles, The	'67
Sh-Boom (Life Could Be a Dream)	Chords, The	'54
Sha-La-La	Shirelles, The	'64
Sha-La-La (Make Me Happy)	Green, Al	'74
Shadow Dancing	Gibb, Andy	'78
Shah Sleeps in Lee Harvey Oswald's Grave, The	Butthole Surfers	'83
Shake	Cooke, Sam	'65
Shake a Hand	Adams, Faye	'53
Shake It Up	Cars, The	'82
Shake Me, Wake Me (When It's Over)	Four Tops, The	'66
Shake Some Action	Flamin' Groovies	'76
Shake You Down	Abbott, Gregory	'86
Shake Your Body (down to the Ground)	Jacksons, The	'78
Shake Your Groove Thing	Peaches and Herb	'78
Shake Your Love	Gibson, Debbie	'87
Shake Your Money Maker	Butterfield, Paul Blues Band	'65
Shake, Rattle and Roll	Turner, Joe	'54
(Shake, Shake, Shake) Shake Your Booty	K.C. & the Sunshine Band	'76
Shakedown	Seger, Bob	'87
Shakin' All Over	Kidd, Johnny & the Pirates	'60
Shambala	Stevenson, B.W.	'73
Shame	King, Evelyn Champagne	'78
Shame on the Moon	Seger, Bob	'82
Shame, Shame, Shame	Shirley & Company	'74
Shanghai Noodle Factory	Traffic	'69
Shannon	Gross, Henry	'76
Shape I'm In, The	Band, The	'70
Shapes of Things	Yardbirds, The	'66
Share the Land	Guess Who, The	'70
Share Your Love with Me	Franklin, Aretha	'69
Sharing the Night Together	Dr. Hook	'78
Sharkey's Day	Anderson, Laurie	'84
Sharp Dressed Man	ZZ Top	'83
Shattered	Rolling Stones, The	'78
Shattered Dreams	Johnny Hates Jazz	'88
She	Parsons, Gram	'71
She Ain't Worth It	Medeiros, Glenn	'90
She Bangs the Drums	Stone Roses, The	'90
She Belongs to Me	Dylan, Bob	'65
She Blinded Me with Science	Dolby, Thomas	'83
She Bop	Lauper, Cyndi	'84
She Came in through the Bathroom Window	Beatles, The	'69
She Comes in Colors	Love	'67
She Cracked	Modern Lovers, The	'71
She Cried	Jay & the Americans	'62

SONG	ARTIST	YEAR	SONG	ARTIST	YEAR
She Drives Me Crazy	Fine Young Cannibals	'89	Shine a Little Love	Electric Light Orchestra	'79
She Even Woke Me up to Say Goodbye	Lewis, Jerry Lee	'70	Shine on Brightly	Procol Harum	'68
			Shine on, You Crazy Diamond	Pink Floyd	'75
She Hates to Go Home	Crenshaw, Marshall	'89	Shining Star	Earth, Wind & Fire	'75
She Loves the Jerk	Hiatt, John	'83	Shining Star	Manhattans, The	'80
She Loves You	Beatles, The	'63	Shiny Happy People	R.E.M.	'91
She Said the Same Things to Me	Hiatt, John	'85	Ship on a Stormy Sea	Clanton, Jimmy	'59
She Said Yeah	Williams, Larry	'58	Shipbuilding	Costello, Elvis	'83
She Sells Sanctuary	Cult, The	'85	Ships	Hunter, Ian	'79
She Still Comes Around (to Love What's Left of Me)	Lewis, Jerry Lee	'68	Shock the Monkey	Gabriel, Peter	'82
			Shoeshine Boy	Kendricks, Eddie	'75
She Talks to Angels	Black Crowes, The	'90	Shoo-Be-Doo-Be-Doo-Day	Wonder, Stevie	'68
She Twists the Knife Again	Thompson, Richard	'85	Shoop	Salt-n-Pepa	'93
She Wants to Dance with Me	Astley, Rick	'89	Shoop, Shoop Song (It's in His Kiss), The	Everett, Betty	'64
She Was Hot	Rolling Stones, The	'84			
She Works Hard for the Money	Summer, Donna	'83	Shoot out the Lights	Thompson, Richard and Linda	'82
She'd Rather Be with Me	Turtles, The	'67	Shop Around	Miracles, The	'61
She's a Bad Mama Jama	Carlton, Carl	'81	Shoplifters of the World Unite	Smiths, The	'87
She's a Beauty	Tubes, The	'83	Shopping for Clothes	Coasters, The	'60
She's a Fool	Gore, Lesley	'63	Short Dick Man	Twenty Fingers	'94
She's a Lady	Sebastian, John	'69	Short Fat Fannie	Williams, Larry	'57
She's a Rainbow	Rolling Stones, The	'67	Short People	Newman, Randy	'77
She's a Woman	Beatles, The	'64	Short Shorts	Royal Teens, The	'57
She's About a Mover	Sir Douglas Quintet, The	'65	Shot by Both Sides	Magazine	'79
She's Always a Woman	Joel, Billy	'77	Shot in the Dark	Osbourne, Ozzy	'86
She's as Beautiful as a Foot	Blue Oyster Cult	'72	Shot of Poison	Ford, Lita	'91
She's Gone	Hall and Oates	'74	Shot of Rhythm and Blues, A	Alexander, Arthur	'62
She's Got You	Cline, Patsy	'62	Shotgun	Walker, Jr. & the All-Stars	'65
She's in Love	Kahn, Brenda	'92	Should I Stay or Should I Go	Clash, The	'82
She's Just My Style	Lewis, Gary & the Playboys	'65	Should We Tell Him	Everly Brothers, The	'58
She's Leaving Home	Beatles, The	'67	Should've Known Better	Marx, Richard	'87
She's Like the Wind	Swayze, Patrick with Wendy Fraser	'87	Should've Never Let You Go	Sedaka, Neil and Dara Sedaka	'80
			Shouldn't Have Took More Than You Gave	Mason, Dave	'70
She's Lost Control	Joy Division	'80			
She's No Lady	Lovett, Lyle	'87	Shout	Tears for Fears	'85
She's Not There	Zombies, The	'64	Shout (Pt. 1)	Isley Brothers, The	'59
She's Not You	Presley, Elvis	'62	Shout! Shout! Knock Yourself Out!	Maresca, Ernie	'62
She's out of My Life	Jackson, Michael	'79	Show and Tell	Wilson, Al	'73
She's Playing Hard to Get	Hi-Five	'92	Show Biz Kids	Steely Dan	'73
She's Strange	Cameo	'84	Show Me	Pretenders, The	'84
(She's) Sexy & 17	Stray Cats, The	'83	Show Me Love	Robin S.	'93
(She's) Some Kind of Wonderful	Soul Brothers Six	'67	Show Me the Way	Frampton, Peter	'75
Sheena Is a Punk Rocker	Ramones, The	'77	Show Me the Way	Styx	'91
Sheer Heart Attack	Queen	'77	Show Must Go On, The	Sayer, Leo	'74
Sheila	Roe, Tommy	'62	Show, The	Fresh, Doug E. and the Get Fresh Crew	'85
Shelter from the Storm	Dylan, Bob	'74			
Sherry	Four Seasons, The	'62	Shower Me with Your Love	Surface	'88
Shilo	Diamond, Neil	'67	Shower the People	Taylor, James	'76
Shimmy, Shimmy Ko-Ko Bop	Little Anthony and the Imperials	'59	Shut 'Em Down	Public Enemy	'91
			Shut Down	Beach Boys, The	'63
Shine	Collective Soul	'94	Sick and Tired	Kenner, Chris	'57

SONG	ARTIST	YEAR
Sideshow	Blue Magic	'74
Sidewalk Talk	Jellybean	'86
Sign 'o' the Times	Prince	'87
Sign on the Window	Dylan, Bob	'70
Sign Your Name	D'Arby, Terence Trent	'87
Sign, The	Ace of Base	'93
Signed, Sealed, Delivered I'm Yours	Wonder, Stevie	'70
Signs	Five Man Electrical Band	'71
Silent All These Years	Amos, Tori	'92
Silent Lucidity	Queensryche	'91
Silent Running (on Dangerous Ground)	Mike & the Mechanics	'85
Silhouettes	Rays, The	'57
Silly Love Songs	McCartney, Paul & Wings	'76
Silver Machine	Hawkwind	'72
Silver Rocket	Sonic Youth	'88
Silver Threads and Golden Needles	Jackson, Wanda	'56
Silvio	Dylan, Bob	'88
Simon Says	1910 Fruitgum Company, The	'68
Simon Smith & His Amazing Dancing Bear	Harper's Bizarre	'67
Simple Life	John, Elton	'92
Simple Twist of Fate	Dylan, Bob	'74
Simply Irresistible	Palmer, Robert	'88
Sin City	Flying Burrito Brothers, The	'69
Since I Don't Have You	Skyliners, The	'59
Since I Fell for You	Laurie, Annie	'47
Since I Lost My Baby	Temptations, The	'65
Since I Met You Baby	Hunter, Ivory Joe	'56
Since You're Gone	Cars, The	'82
Sincerely	Moonglows, The	'55
Sing Me Back Home	Everly Brothers, The	'68
Singasong	Earth, Wind & Fire	'75
Singing the Blues	Robbins, Marty	'55
Single Life, The	Cameo	'85
Sink the Bismarck	Horton, Johnny	'60
Sinner's Prayer	Charles, Ray	'52
Sir Duke	Wonder, Stevie	'76
Sister Christian	Night Ranger	'84
Sister Golden Hair	America	'75
Sister Havana	Urge Overkill	'93
Sister Morphine	Rolling Stones, The	'71
Sister Ray	Velvet Underground, The	'68
Sisters Are Doin' It for Themselves	Eurythmics	'85
Sisters of Mercy	Collins, Judy	'68
Sit Down I Think I Love You	Mojo Men, The	'66
Sittin' in Circles	Electric Flag	'68
Sittin' in the Balcony	Cochran, Eddie	'57
(Sittin' on) the Dock of the Bay	Redding, Otis	'68
Sitting in Limbo	Cliff, Jimmy	'72

SONG	ARTIST	YEAR
Six Days on the Road	Dudley, Dave	'63
Six Nights a Week	Crests, The	'59
Six o'Clock	Lovin' Spoonful, The	'67
Sixteen Reasons (Why I Love You)	Stevens, Connie	'60
Sixty Minute Man	Dominoes, The	'51
Skeletons	Wonder, Stevie	'87
Skinny Legs and All	Tex, Joe	'67
Skinny Minnie	Haley, Bill & the Comets	'58
Sky High	Jigsaw	'75
Sky Is Crying, The	James, Elmore	'60
Sky Pilot	Animals, The	'68
Slam	Onyx	'93
Slave to Love	Ferry, Bryan	'85
Sledgehammer	Gabriel, Peter	'86
Sleep	John, Little Willie	'60
Sleep Walk	Santo and Johnny	'59
Sleeping Bag	ZZ Top	'85
Sleeping Satellite	Archer, Tasmine	'92
Sleeps with Angels	Young, Neil	'94
Slide	Slave	'77
Slip Away	Carter, Clarence	'67
Slip Kid	Who, The	'75
Slip Slidin' Away	Simon, Paul	'77
Slippery When Wet	Commodores, The	'75
Slippin' and Slidin'	Little Richard	'56
Slow Dance (Hey Mr. DJ)	Kelly, R.	'92
Slow Dancing	Funky Kings, The	'75
Slow Death	Flamin' Groovies	'72
Slow Down	Williams, Larry	'57
Slow Hand	Pointer Sisters, The	'81
Slow Ride	Foghat	'76
Slow Twistin'	Checker, Chubby and Dee Dee Sharpe	'62
Slum Goddess	Fugs, The	'65
Small Town	Mellencamp, John (Cougar)	'85
Small Town Boy	Bronski Beat	'85
Small Town Talk	Butterfield's, Paul Better Days	'73
Smells Like Teen Spirit	Nirvana	'91
Smiling Faces Sometimes	Undisputed Truth	'71
Smoke from a Distant Fire	Sanford Townshend Band	'76
Smoke Gets in Your Eyes	Platters, The	'58
Smoke on the Water	Deep Purple	'72
Smokestack Lightning	Howling Wolf	'56
Smokey Joe's Cafe	Robins, The	'55
Smokey Places	Corsairs, The	'61
Smokie—Part 2	Black's, Bill Combo	'59
Smokin' in the Boys Room	Brownsville Station	'73
Smoking Gun	Cray, Robert	'87
Smooth Criminal	Jackson, Michael	'87
Smooth Operator	Sade	'85
Smuggler's Blues	Frey, Glenn	'85

SONG	ARTIST	YEAR	SONG	ARTIST	YEAR
Snap Your Fingers	Henderson, Joe	'62	Somebody's Watching Me	Rockwell	'84
Snatching It Back	Carter, Clarence	'69	Someday Never Comes	Creedence Clearwater Revival	'72
Snoopy Versus the Red Baron	Royal Guardsmen, The	'66	Someday, Someway	Gordon, Robert	'81
Snow Queen	City, The	'68	Someday Soon	Ian and Sylvia	'64
Snowbird	Murray, Anne	'70	Someday We'll All Be Free	Hathaway, Donnie	'73
So Alive	Love and Rockets	'89	Someday We'll Be Together	Johnnie and Jackey	'61
So Far Away	King, Carole	'71	Someone Saved My Life Tonight	John, Elton	'75
So Fine	Fiestas, The	'59	Someone to Lay down Beside Me	Ronstadt, Linda	'76
So in to You	Atlanta Rhythm Section	'76	Someone to Love	Great Society, The	'65
So It Goes	Lowe, Nick	'78	Someplace Where Love Can't Find Me	Crenshaw, Marshall	'89
So Lonely	Police, The	'78			
So Long Dad	Newman, Randy	'68	Somethin' Else	Cochran, Eddie	'59
So Long I'm Gone	Smith, Warren	'57	Something	Beatles, The	'69
So Long It's Been Good to Know You (Dusty Old Dust)	Weavers, The	'51	Something About You	Level 42	'86
			Something Good	Utah Saints, The	'92
So Long, Marianne	Cohen, Leonard	'68	Something Happened on the Way to Heaven	Collins, Phil	'89
So Much in Love	Tymes, The	'63			
So Much Mine	Story, The	'93	Something Happened to Me Yesterday	Rolling Stones, The	'67
So Sad (to Watch Good Love Go Bad)	Everly Brothers, The	'60			
			Something He Can Feel	Franklin, Aretha	'76
So Tough	Original Casuals	'58	Something in the Air	Thunderclap Newman	'69
So Very Hard to Go	Tower of Power	'73	Something in the Way She Moves	Rush, Tom	'68
So What'cha Want	Beastie Boys, The	'92	Something New	Smithereens, The	'88
So You Wanna Be a Rock and Roll Star	Byrds, The	'67	Something So Right	Simon, Paul	'73
			Something So Strong	Crowded House	'87
So You Win Again	Hot Chocolate	'77	Something to Believe In	Poison	'90
Society's Child (Baby, I've Been Thinking)	Ian, Janis	'67	Something to Talk About	Raitt, Bonnie	'91
			Something You Got	Robinson, Alvin	'64
Sock It to Me, Baby	Ryder, Mitch and the Detroit Wheels	'67	Something's Got a Hold on Me	James, Etta	'62
			Sometimes Love Just Ain't Enough	Smyth, Patty	'92
Soft and Wet	Prince	'76	Sometimes When We Touch	Hill, Dan	'77
Sold American	Friedman, Kinky	'73	Somewhere down the Crazy River	Robertson, Robbie	'87
Sold Me down the River	Alarm, The	'89	Somewhere There's a Feather	Nico	'67
Soldier Boy	Shirelles, The	'61	Son of a Preacher Man	Springfield, Dusty	'69
Soldier of Love	Alexander, Arthur	'62	Son of Suzy Creamcheese	Mothers of Invention, The	'67
Soldier of Love	Osmond, Donny	'89	Song for a Future Generation	B-52's, The	'83
Solid	Ashford and Simpson	'84	Song for Adam	Browne, Jackson	'72
Solitaire	Branigan, Laura	'83	Song for the Dreamers	Danny and Dusty	'85
Solitary Man	Diamond, Neil	'66	Song for Whoever	Beautiful South, The	'89
Solo	Denny, Sandy	'74	Song for You	Russell, Leon	'70
Solo Flight	Christian, Charlie	'44	Song Is Over, The	Who, The	'71
Solsbury Hill	Gabriel, Peter	'77	Song Remains the Same, The	Led Zeppelin	'73
Some Guys Have All the Luck	Persuaders, The	'73	Song to Woody	Dylan, Bob	'62
Some Kind a Wonderful	Drifters, The	'61	Songs Sung Blue	Diamond, Neil	'72
Some Kind of Lover	Watley, Jody	'88	Songs to Aging Children Come	Mitchell, Joni	'69
Some Like It Hot	Power Station, The	'85	Sonic Reducer	Dead Boys, The	'77
Somebody Loan Me a Dime	Robinson, Fenton	'67	Sooner or Later	Grass Roots	'71
Somebody to Love	Queen	'76	Sooner or Later (I Always Get My Man)	Madonna	'90
Somebody to Shove	Soul Asylum	'92			
Somebody's Baby	Browne, Jackson	'82	Sophisticated Cissy	Meters, The	'69
Somebody's Been Sleeping in My Bed	100 Proof Aged in Soul	'70	Sorry Seems to Be the Hardest Word	John, Elton	'76

SONG	ARTIST	YEAR	SONG	ARTIST	YEAR
Sorry Somehow	Hüsker Dü	'86	St. Stephen	Grateful Dead, The	'69
Sorry, I Ran All the Way Home	Impalas, The	'59	Stage Fright	Band, The	'70
Soul Corruption	Parker, Graham	'89	Stagger Lee	Price, Lloyd	'58
Soul Deep	Box Tops, The	'69	Stairway to Heaven	Led Zeppelin	'71
Soul Man	Sam and Dave	'67	Stairway to Heaven	Sedaka, Neil	'60
Soul on Fire	Baker, LaVern	'53	Stand	R.E.M.	'88
Soul on Ice	Parker, Graham	'77	Stand Back	Nicks, Stevie	'83
Soul Sacrifice	Santana	'69	Stand by Me	King, Ben E.	'61
Soul Sister, Brown Sugar	Sam and Dave	'68	Stand by Your Man	Wynette, Tammy	'68
Soul to Squeeze	Red Hot Chili Peppers	'93	Stand or Fall	Fixx, The	'82
Soul Twist	King Curtis	'62	Stand Tall	Cummings, Burton	'76
Sounds of Silence, The	Simon and Garfunkel	'64	Stand Up	Ferron	'90
South Central Rain	R.E.M.	'83	Stand Up (Kick Love into Motion)	Def Leppard	'92
South Street	Orlons, The	'63	Stand!	Sly & the Family Stone	'69
Southern Cross	Crosby, Stills & Nash	'82	Standing in the Shadows of Love	Four Tops, The	'66
Southern Man	Young, Neil	'70	Star Sign	Teenage Fanclub	'91
Southern Nights	Toussaint, Allen	'75	Star Star	Rolling Stones, The	'73
Sowing the Seeds of Love	Tears for Fears	'89	Star Wars Theme	Meco	'77
Space Cowboy	Miller, Steve Band, The	'69	Stars	Hear'n'Aid	'86
Space Oddity	Bowie, David	'68	Start Me Up	Rolling Stones, The	'81
Space Race	Preston, Billy	'73	Start Movin'	Mineo, Sal	'57
Space Truckin'	Deep Purple	'72	State of Shock	Jacksons, The	'84
Spanish Harlem	King, Ben E.	'61	Statesboro Blues	Allman Brothers, The	'71
Spanish Harlem Incident	Dylan, Bob	'64	Status Back Baby	Mothers of Invention, The	'67
Special Lady	Ray, Goodman & Brown	'79	Stay	Jodeci	'91
Speed of the Sound of Loneliness	Carnes, Kim	'88	Stay	Shakespeare's Sister	'92
Speedoo	Cadillacs, The	'55	Stay	Williams, Maurice and the Zodiacs	'60
Spiders and Snakes	Stafford, Jim	'73	Stay (I Missed You)	Loeb, Lisa & Nine Stories	'94
Spies Like Us	McCartney, Paul	'86	Stay Awhile	Bells, The	'71
Spill the Wine	War	'70	Stay Free	Clash, The	'78
Spin the Black Circle	Pearl Jam	'94	Stay in My Corner	Dells, The	'65
Spin the Bottle	Hatfield, Juliana Three, The	'93	Stay up Late	Talking Heads	'85
Spinning Wheel	Blood, Sweat & Tears	'69	Stay with Me	Ellison, Lorraine	'66
Spirit in the Dark	Franklin, Aretha	'70	Stay with Me	Faces, The	'72
Spirit in the Night	Springsteen, Bruce	'73	Stayin' Alive	Bee Gees, The	'77
Spirit in the Sky	Greenbaum, Norman	'70	Steal Away	Dupree, Robbie	'79
Spirit of Radio, The	Rush	'80	Steal Away	Hughes, Jimmy	'64
Spirit of the Boogie	Kool & the Gang	'75	Steam	Gabriel, Peter	'92
Spirits in the Material World	Police, The	'82	Steamroller Blues	Taylor, James	'70
Spiritual High (State of Independence)	Moodswings	'92	Step by Step	Crests, The	'60
Splish Splash	Darin, Bobby	'58	Step by Step	New Kids on the Block	'89
Spooky	Classics IV, The	'68	Step by Step	Rabbitt, Eddie	'81
Spoonful	Howling Wolf	'60	Steppin' Out	Jackson, Joe	'82
Spoonman	Soundgarden	'94	Steppin' Out	Mayall's, John Bluesbreakers	'67
Sprawl, The	Sonic Youth	'88	Steppin' Out (Gonna Boogie Tonight)	Dawn	'73
Spy in the House of Love	Was (Not Was)	'88	Stick Up	Honey Cone	'71
Square Pegs	Waitresses, The	'83	Still	Commodores, The	'79
Squeeze Box	Who, The	'75	Still Alive and Well	Hoodoo Rhythm Devils	'72
St. Elmo's Fire (Man in Motion)	Parr, John	'85			

SONG	ARTIST	YEAR	SONG	ARTIST	YEAR
Still Crazy After All These Years	Simon, Paul	'75	Strawberry Letter 23	Brothers Johnson, The	'77
Still I'm Sad	Yardbirds, The	'65	Stray Cat Blues	Rolling Stones, The	'68
Still in Saigon	Daniels, Charlie Band, The	'82	Stray Cat Strut	Stray Cats, The	'82
Still Loving You	Scorpions, The	'84	Streak, The	Stevens, Ray	'74
Still of the Night	Whitesnake	'87	Street Fighting Man	Rolling Stones, The	'68
Still the One	Orleans	'76	Street in the City	Townshend, Pete	'77
Still the Same	Seger, Bob	'77	Street Rock	Blow, Kurtis & Bob Dylan	'86
Still...You Turn Me On	Emerson, Lake & Palmer	'73	Streets of London	McTell, Ralph	'71
Stillsane	Mas, Carolyne	'79	Streets of Philadelphia	Springsteen, Bruce	'93
Stir It Up	Marley, Bob & the Wailers	'68	Strike It Up	Black Box	'90
Stomp	Brothers Johnson, The	'79	Stroke, The	Squier, Billy	'81
Stone Cold	Rainbow	'82	Stroke You Up	Changing Faces	'94
Stone Cold Crazy	Queen	'74	Stroll, The	Diamonds, The	'57
Stone Free	Hendrix, Jimi	'68	Stroll On	Yardbirds, The	'67
Stone Love	Kool & the Gang	'86	Strut	Easton, Sheena	'84
Stoned Love	Supremes, The	'70	Strutter	Kiss	'74
Stoned Soul Picnic	Nyro, Laura	'68	Stubborn Kind of Fellow	Gaye, Marvin	'62
Stonehenge	Spinal Tap	'84	Stuck in the Middle with You	Stealer's Wheel	'73
Stones in the Road	Baez, Joan	'92	Stuck inside of Mobile with the Memphis Blues Again	Dylan, Bob	'66
Stoney End	Nyro, Laura	'67			
Stood Up	Nelson, Ricky	'57	Stuck on You	Presley, Elvis	'60
Stop and Think It Over	Dale and Grace	'64	Stuck with You	Lewis, Huey & the News	'86
Stop Draggin' My Heart Around	Nicks, Stevie	'81	Stuff Like That	Jones, Quincy	'78
Stop! In the Name of Love	Supremes, The	'65	Stumblin' In	Quatro, Suzi & Chris Norman	'78
Stop, Stop, Stop	Hollies, The	'66	Stupid Cupid	Francis, Connie	'58
Stop That Train	Marley, Bob & the Wailers	'71	Suavecito	Malo	'72
Stop the Violence	Boogie Down Productions	'88	Substitute	Who, The	'70
Stop to Love	Vandross, Luther	'87	Subterranean Homesick Blues	Dylan, Bob	'65
Stop Your Sobbing	Kinks, The	'64	Such a Night	Drifters, The	'54
Stories We Could Tell, The	Everly Brothers, The	'72	(Such an) Easy Question	Presley, Elvis	'65
Stormy	Classics IV, The	'68	Sucker MC's (Krush Groove)	Run-D.M.C.	'84
Stormy Love	Nyro, Laura	'76	Suddenly	Ocean, Billy	'84
Story of Rock and Roll, The	Turtles, The	'68	Suddenly Last Summer	Motels, The	'83
Story Untold	Nutmegs, The	'55	Suddenly Seymour	Greene, Ellen & Lee Wilkoff	'82
Straight from the Heart	Adams, Bryan	'83	Suedehead	Morrissey	'88
Straight On	Heart	'78	Suffragette City	Bowie, David	'72
Straight Up	Abdul, Paula	'88	Sugar Daddy	Jackson 5, The	'71
Straighten up and Fly Right	Cole, Nat King	'44	Sugar Magnolia	Grateful Dead, The	'70
Stranded in the Jungle	Cadets, The	'56	Sugar Mama	Raitt, Bonnie	'75
Strange	Wire	'77	Sugar Mountain	Young, Neil	'77
Strange Brew	Cream	'67	Sugar Shack	Gilmer, Jimmy and the Fireballs	'63
Strange Feeling	Buckley, Tim	'69			
Strange I Know	Marvelettes, The	'62	Sugar Sugar	Archies, The	'69
Strange Magic	Electric Light Orchestra	'75	Sugar Walls	Easton, Sheena	'84
Strange Weather	Faithfull, Marianne	'87	Sugaree	Garcia, Jerry	'72
Stranger in the House	Sweet, Rachel	'79	Suicide Blonde	Inxs	'90
Stranger in Town	Shannon, Del	'65	Suicide Solution	Osbourne, Ozzy	'81
Stranger Song	Cohen, Leonard	'68	Suit, The	Public Image Ltd.	'79
Stranglehold	Nugent, Ted	'75	Suite: Judy Blue Eyes	Crosby, Stills & Nash	'69
Strawberry Fields Forever	Beatles, The	'67	Sukiyaki (My First Lonely Night)	Sakamoto, Kyu	'63
			Sultans of Swing	Dire Straits	'79

SONG	ARTIST	YEAR	SONG	ARTIST	YEAR
Summer	War	'76	Supper's Ready	Genesis	'72
Summer Breeze	Seals and Crofts	'71	Sure as I'm Sittin' Here	Three Dog Night	'74
Summer in the City	Lovin' Spoonful, The	'66	Sure Gonna Miss Her	Lewis, Gary and the Playboys	'66
Summer Nights	Demas, Carole and Barry Bostwick	'72	Surf City	Jan and Dean	'63
			Surfer Girl	Beach Boys, The	'63
Summer of '69	Adams, Bryan	'84	Surfer Joe	Surfaris, The	'63
Summer of Drugs	Williams, Victoria	'90	Surfer's Holiday	Dale, Dick	'64
Summer Rain	Rivers, Johnny	'68	Surfer's Stomp	Marketts, The	'62
Summer Song, A	Chad and Jeremy	'66	Surfin'	Beach Boys, The	'61
Summer's Cauldron	XTC	'87	Surfin' Bird	Trashmen, The	'63
Summertime	D.J. Jazzy Jeff & the Fresh Prince	'91	Surfin' Safari	Beach Boys, The	'62
			Surfin' USA	Beach Boys, The	'63
Summertime	Stewart, Billy	'66	Surrender	Cheap Trick	'76
Summertime Blues	Cochran, Eddie	'58	Surrender	Presley, Elvis	'61
Summertime Girls	Y&T	'85	Susie Darlin	Luke, Robin	'58
Summertime, Summertime	Jamies, The	'58	Susie Q	Hawkins, Dale	'57
Sun Ain't Gonna Shine Anymore, The	Valli, Frankie	'65	Suspended in Gaffa	Bush, Kate	'82
			Suspicion	Presley, Elvis	'62
Sun City	Artists United Against Apartheid	'85	Suspicious Minds	Presley, Elvis	'69
			Sussudio	Collins, Phil	'85
Sunday Girl	Blondie	'79	Suzanne	Collins, Judy	'66
Sunday Kind of Love, A	Harptones, The	'53	Swallow That	Superchunk	'92
Sunday Mornin' Coming Down	Kristofferson, Kris	'69	Swearin' to God	Valli, Frankie	'75
Sunday Morning	Velvet Underground, The	'67	Sweater, The	Cadell, Meryn	'92
Sunday Will Never Be the Same	Spanky & Our Gang	'67	Sweet and Innocent	Orbison, Roy	'58
Sunday, Bloody Sunday	U2	'83	Sweet Baby James	Taylor, James	'70
Sundown	Lightfoot, Gordon	'74	Sweet Blindness	Nyro, Laura	'68
Sunglasses at Night	Hart, Corey	'84	Sweet Caroline	Diamond, Neil	'69
Sunny	Hebb, Bobby	'66	Sweet Cherry Wine	James, Tommy & the Shondells	'69
Sunny Afternoon	Kinks, The	'66			
Sunny Goodge Street	Donovan	'65	Sweet Child O' Mine	Guns N' Roses	'88
Sunshine	Edwards, Jonathan	'72	Sweet City Woman	Stampeders, The	'71
Sunshine of Your Love	Cream	'68	Sweet Dreams	Gibson, Don	'60
Sunshine on My Shoulders	Denver, John	'74	Sweet Dreams (Are Made of This)	Eurythmics	'83
Sunshine, Sunshine	Taylor, James	'69	Sweet Emotion	Aerosmith	'75
Sunshine Superman	Donovan	'66	Sweet Freedom	McDonald, Michael	'86
Sunshine, Lollipops and Rainbows	Gore, Lesley	'65	Sweet Gene Vincent	Dury, Ian & the Blockheads	'78
Super Bad	Brown, James	'70	Sweet Harmony	Robinson, Smokey	'73
Super Freak (Part 1)	James, Rick	'81	Sweet Hitch-Hiker	Creedence Clearwater Revival	'71
Super Nova	Phair, Liz	'94	Sweet Home Alabama	Lynyrd Skynyrd	'74
Superfly	Mayfield, Curtis	'72	Sweet Jane	Velvet Underground, The	'70
Supergirl	Fugs, The	'65	Sweet Little Rock and Roller	Berry, Chuck	'59
Superman	Clique, The	'68	Sweet Little Sixteen	Berry, Chuck	'58
Supernatural Thing-Part 1	King, Ben E.	'75	Sweet Love	Baker, Anita	'86
Superstar	Carpenters, The	'71	Sweet Love	Commodores, The	'75
Superstar Remember How You Got Where You Are	Temptations, The	'71	Sweet Lullabye	Deep Forest	'94
			Sweet Mary	Wadsworth Mansion	'71
Superstition	Wonder, Stevie	'72	Sweet Nothin's	Lee, Brenda	'60
Superwoman	White, Karyn	'89	Sweet November	Troop	'92
Superwoman (Where Were You When I Needed You)	Wonder, Stevie	'72	Sweet Old World	Williams, Lucinda	'93

SONG	ARTIST	YEAR
Sweet Pea	Roe, Tommy	'66
Sweet Seasons	King, Carole	'71
Sweet Sixteen	King, B.B.	'61
Sweet Sixteen Bars	Charles, Ray	'58
Sweet Soul Music	Conley, Arthur	'67
Sweet Sticky Thing	Ohio Players, The	'75
Sweet Talkin' Guy	Chiffons, The	'66
Sweet Talkin' Woman	Electric Light Orchestra	'77
Sweet Thing	Rufus	'75
Sweet Woman Like You, A	Tex, Joe	'66
(Sweet, Sweet Baby) Since You've Been Gone	Franklin, Aretha	'67
Sweeter Than You	Nelson, Ricky	'59
Sweetest Drop, The	Murphy, Peter	'92
Sweetest Tabu	Sade	'86
Sweetest Thing I've Ever Known, The	Newton, Juice	'75
Sweetheart	Franke & the Knockouts	'81
Sweethearts	Camper Van Beethoven	'89
Sweets for My Sweet	Drifters, The	'61
Swimming Song, The	Wainwright, Loudon	'73
Swingin' Party	Replacements, The	'85
Swingin' School	Rydell, Bobby	'60
Sylvia's Mother	Dr. Hook	'72
Sympathy for the Devil	Rolling Stones, The	'68
Symphony of Destruction	Megadeth	'92

T

SONG	ARTIST	YEAR
Tainted Love	Jones, Gloria	'64
Take a Bow	Madonna	'94
Take a Chance on Me	Abba	'77
Take a Letter, Maria	Greaves, R.B.	'69
Take a Look at My Heart	Prine, John	'91
Take a Message to Mary	Everly Brothers, The	'59
Take Good Care of My Baby	Dion	'61
Take It Away	McCartney, Paul	'82
Take It Easy	Eagles, The	'72
Take It on the Run	REO Speedwagon	'80
Take It So Hard	Richards, Keith	'88
Take It to the Limit	Eagles, The	'76
Take Me (Just as I Am)	Burke, Solomon	'67
Take Me Home	Collins, Phil	'85
Take Me Home, Country Road	Denver, John	'71
Take Me Home Tonight	Money, Eddie	'86
Take Me in Your Arms (Rock Me a Little While)	Weston, Kim	'65
Take Me to the Pilot	John, Elton	'70
Take Me to the River	Green, Al	'73
Take My Breath Away (Love Theme from *Top Gun*)	Berlin	'86
Take My Heart	Kool & the Gang	'81

SONG	ARTIST	YEAR
Take Off	McKenzie, Bob & Doug	'82
Take on Me	A-Ha	'85
Take the Long Way Home	Supertramp	'79
Take the Money and Run	Miller, Steve Band, The	'76
Take the Skinheads Bowling	Camper Van Beethoven	'85
Take These Chains from My Heart	Williams, Hank	'53
Take This Longing	Cohen, Leonard	'74
Take Time to Know Her	Sledge, Percy	'68
Take Your Time (Do It Right) Part 1	S.O.S. Band, The	'80
Takin' Care of Business	Bachman Turner Overdrive	'73
Takin' It to the Streets	Doobie Brothers, The	'76
Talent Show	Replacements, The	'89
Tales of Brave Ulysses	Cream	'68
Talk Back Trembling Lips	Tillotson, Johnny	'63
Talk Dirty to Me	Poison	'87
Talk of the Town	Pretenders, The	'82
Talk, Talk	Music Machine, The	'66
Talk to Me	Nicks, Stevie	'86
(Talk to Me of) Mendocino	McGarrigle, Kate and Anna	'75
Talk to Me, Talk to Me	John, Little Willie	'58
Talking in the Dark	Costello, Elvis	'80
Talking in Your Sleep	Romantics, The	'83
Talking Loud & Sayin' Nothing, Pt. II	Brown, James	'72
Tall Cool One	Plant, Robert	'88
Tall Cool One	Wailers	'59
Tall Paul	Annette	'59
Tallahassee Lassie	Cannon, Freddy	'59
Tammy	Reynolds, Debbie	'57
Tangerine	Led Zeppelin	'70
Tangled up in Blue	Dylan, Bob	'74
Tapestry	King, Carole	'71
Tarzan Boy	Baltimora	'86
Taste of Honey, A	Scott, Bobby	'60
Tasty Love	Jackson, Freddie	'86
Taxi	Chapin, Harry	'72
Taxi Blues	Little Richard	'51
Taxman	Beatles, The	'66
Teach Your Children	Crosby, Stills, Nash & Young	'70
Teacher, Teacher	Rockpile	'80
Teahouse on the Tracks	Fagen, Donald	'93
Tear It Up	Burnette, Johnny & the Rock and Roll Trio	'56
Tear Stained Letter	Thompson, Richard	'83
Tear the Roof off the Sucker (Give up the Funk)	Parliament	'76
Teardrops	Andrews, Lee & the Hearts	'57
Teardrops from My Eyes	Brown, Ruth	'50
Teardrops on Your Letter	Midnighters, The	'59
Teardrops Will Fall	Doo, Dickey & the Don'ts	'59
Tears in Heaven	Clapton, Eric	'91

SONG	ARTIST	YEAR	SONG	ARTIST	YEAR
Tears of a Clown, The	Miracles, The	'67	Tenth Avenue Freeze Out	Springsteen, Bruce	'75
Tears of Rage	Band, The	'68	Tequila	Champs, The	'58
Tears on My Pillow	Little Anthony and the Imperials	'58	Tequila Sunrise	Eagles, The	'73
Teddy	Francis, Connie	'60	Terrapin	Barrett, Syd	'74
Teen Age Crush	Sands, Tommy	'57	Terrifying Love	Crenshaw, Marshall	'85
Teen Angel	Dinning, Mark	'59	Texas Chainsaw Massacre Boogie	Tyla Gang, The	'76
Teen Angst (What the World Needs Now)	Cracker	'91	Thank God I'm a Country Boy	Denver, John	'74
Teen Beat	Nelson, Sandy	'59	Thank God Its Friday	Love and Kisses	'78
Teen Town	Weather Report	'77	Thank You (Falettingme Be Mice Elf Agin)	Sly & the Family Stone	'70
Teen-Age Riot	Sonic Youth	'88	Thank You and Goodnight	Angels, The	'63
Teenage Head	Flamin' Groovies	'71	Thank You for Being a Friend	Gold, Andrew	'78
Teenage Heaven	Cochran, Eddie	'59	Thank You Girl	Beatles, The	'63
Teenage Idol	Nelson, Rick	'62	Thank You John	Chilton, Alex	'85
Teenage Kicks	Undertones, The	'78	Thank You, Pretty Baby	Benton, Brook	'59
Teenage Lobotomy	Ramones, The	'76	Thank You World	World Party	'90
Teenage Suicide (Don't Do It)	Big Fun	'89	Thanks for My Child	Riley, Cheryl "Pepsii"	'88
Teenager in Love, A	Dion & the Belmonts	'59	That Girl	Wonder, Stevie	'82
Teenager's Romance	Nelson, Ricky	'57	That Girl Belongs to Yesterday	Pitney, Gene	'64
Telegram Sam	T. Rex	'72	That Is Rock and Roll	Coasters, The	'59
Telephone Line	Electric Light Orchestra	'76	That Lady	Isley Brothers, The	'73
Tell Her About It	Joel, Billy	'83	That Old Sweet Roll	City, The	'68
Tell Her No	Zombies, The	'64	That Smell	Lynyrd Skynyrd	'77
Tell Him	Exciters, The	'63	That Song About the Midway	Mitchell, Joni	'69
Tell Him No	Travis and Bob	'59	That Summer Feeling	Modern Lovers, The	'83
Tell It Like It Is	Neville, Aaron	'66	That'll Be the Day	Crickets, The	'57
Tell It to the Rain	Four Seasons, The	'66	That's All	Genesis	'83
Tell Laura I Love Her	Peterson, Ray	'60	That's All Right, Mama	Crudup, Arthur Big Boy	'47
Tell Mama	James, Etta	'67	That's All You Gotta Do	Lee, Brenda	'60
Tell Me (You're Coming Back)	Rolling Stones, The	'64	That's Amore	Martin, Dean	'53
Tell Me So	Orioles, The	'49	That's How Strong My Love Is	Redding, Otis	'65
Tell Me Something Good	Rufus	'74	That's Old Fashioned	Everly Brothers, The	'62
Tell Me What You Want Me to Do	Campbell, Tevin	'92	That's Rock 'N' Roll	Cassidy, Shaun	'77
Tell Me Why	Beatles, The	'64	That's the Way (I Like It)	K.C. & the Sunshine Band	'75
Tell Me Why	Expose	'89	That's the Way I've Always Heard It Should Be	Simon, Carly	'71
Tell Me Why	Fox, Norman & the Rob Roys	'57	That's the Way Love Goes	Jackson, Janet	'93
Tell That Girl to Shut Up	Holly & the Italians	'81	That's the Way Love Is	Bland, Bobby	'63
Tell the Truth	Five Royals, The	'57	That's the Way Love Is	Gaye, Marvin	'69
Telling Me Lies	Thompson, Linda	'85	That's the Way of the World	Earth, Wind & Fire	'75
Telstar	Tornadoes, The	'62	That's What Friends Are For	Stewart, Rod	'82
Temptation	Corrina	'91	That's When I Reach for My Revolver	Mission of Burma	'81
Temptation	Heaven 17	'82	That's Why	Wilson, Jackie	'59
Temptation	New Order	'82	Them Changes	Miles, Buddy	'70
Tempted	Squeeze	'81	Them Heavy People	Bush, Kate	'78
Ten Commandments of Love, The	Moonglows, The	'57	Theme for an Imaginary Western	Mountain	'70
Tender Love	Force M.D.'s, The	'86	Theme from *Batman*	Marketts, The	'66
Tender Lover	Babyface	'89	Theme from *Endless Summer*	Sandals, The	'64
Tennessee	Arrested Development	'92	Theme from *S.W.A.T.*	Rhythm Heritage	'75
Tennessee Flat-Top Box	Cash, Johnny	'61	Theme from *Shaft* (Who Shaft Where)	Hayes, Isaac	'71
Tenth and Greenwich	Winde, Beatrice	'71			

SONG	ARTIST	YEAR	SONG	ARTIST	YEAR
Theme from the *Greatest American Hero* (Believe It or Not)	Scarbury, Joey	'81	Think	5 Royales, The	'57
Theme from *Trouble Man*	Gaye, Marvin	'72	Think	Franklin, Aretha	'68
Theme Song from *Which Way Is Up*	Stargard	'77	Think for Yourself	Beatles, The	'65
Themes for Great Cities	Simple Minds	'81	Think It Over	Crickets, The	'58
Then Came You	Warwick, Dionne	'74	Third Week at the Chelsea	Jefferson Airplane, The	'71
Then He Kissed Me	Crystals, The	'63	Thirsty Boots	Collins, Judy	'65
Then You Can Tell Me Goodbye	Casinos, The	'67	Thirteen Steps Lead Down	Costello, Elvis	'94
There but for Fortune	Ochs, Phil	'64	Thirty Days	Berry, Chuck	'55
There Goes My Baby	Drifters, The	'59	This Bitter Earth	Washington, Dinah	'60
There Is a Mountain	Donovan	'67	This Boy (Ringo's Theme)	Beatles, The	'64
There Is Someone in This World for Me	John, Little Willie	'58	This Charming Man	Smiths, The	'84
There Is Something on Your Mind	McNeely, Big Jay	'57	This Corrosion	Sisters of Mercy	'87
There She Goes	LA's, The	'91	This Could Be the Night	Loverboy	'85
There'll Be Sad Songs (to Make You Cry)	Ocean, Billy	'85	This D.J.	Warren G.	'94
			This Diamond Ring	Lewis, Gary & the Playboys	'64
There's a Guy Works down the Chip Shop Swears He's Elvis	MacColl, Kirsty	'81	This Girl Is a Woman Now	Puckett, Gary & the Union Gap	'69
There's a Kind of Hush (All over the World)	Herman's Hermits	'67	This House	Spencer, Tracie	'91
There's a Moon out Tonight	Capris, The	'61	This I Swear	Skyliners, The	'59
There's a Place	Beatles, The	'63	This Is My Country	Impressions, The	'68
There's Gonna Be a Showdown	Bell, Archie and the Drells	'69	This Is Not a Love Song	Public Image Ltd	'83
There's No Other	Crystals, The	'61	This Is Pop	XTC	'79
(There's) Always Something There to Remind Me	Johnson, Lou	'64	This Is the Time	Joel, Billy	'86
			This Land Is Your Land	Weavers, The	'56
These 23 Days in September	Blue, David	'68	This Little Bird	Faithfull, Marianne	'65
These Are Days	10,000 Maniacs	'92	This Little Girl	Bonds, Gary U.S.	'81
These Arms of Mine	Redding, Otis	'63	This Little Girl of Mine	Charles, Ray	'55
These Boots Are Made for Walking	Sinatra, Nancy	'66	This Little Girl's Gone Rockin'	Brown, Ruth	'58
These Days	Nico	'67	This Magic Moment	Drifters, The	'60
These Dreams	Heart	'86	This Masquerade	Russell, Leon	'72
These Eyes	Guess Who, The	'69	This Note's for You	Young, Neil	'88
They Dance Alone	Sting	'87	This Old Heart of Mine (Is Weak for You)	Isley Brothers, The	'66
They Don't Know	MacColl, Kirsty	'79	This Song	Harrison, George	'76
(They Long to Be) Close to You	Warwick, Dionne	'63	This Time	Shondell, Troy	'61
They Want Money	Dee, Kool Moe	'89	This Time I Know It's for Real	Summer, Donna	'89
They're Coming to Take Me Away, Ha-Haaa!	Napoleon XIV	'66	This Used to Be My Playground	Madonna	'92
			This Wheel's on Fire	Band, The	'68
Thick as a Brick	Jethro Tull	'72	This Will Be (an Everlasting Love)	Cole, Natalie	'75
Thieves in the Temple	Prince	'90	This Woman's Work	Bush, Kate	'88
Thin Line Between Love and Hate	Persuaders, The	'71	Those Oldies but Goodies (Remind Me of You)	Little Caesar and the Romans	'61
Thing Called Love	Hiatt, John	'87	Those Were the Days	Limeliters, The	'62
Things	Darin, Bobby	'62	Thou Shalt Not Steal	Wells, Kitty	'54
Things Can Only Get Better	Jones, Howard	'85	Thousand Miles Away, A	Heartbeats, The	'56
Things Could Turn Around	fIREHOSE	'86	Thousand Stars, A	Rivilers, The	'56
Things That I Used to Do	Jones, Eddie "Guitar Slim"	'54	Three Bells, The	Browns, The	'59
Things That Make You Go Hmmmm	C&C Music Factory featuring Freedom Williams	'91	Three Flights Up	Christian, Frank	'88
			Three Little Pigs	Green Jelly	'93
Things We Do for Love, The	10 c.c.	'77	Three Stars	Cochran, Eddie	'59
Things We Said Today	Beatles, The	'64	Three Steps to Heaven	Cochran, Eddie	'60

SONG	ARTIST	YEAR	SONG	ARTIST	YEAR
Three Times a Lady	Commodores, The	'78	To Be Young, Gifted and Black	Franklin, Aretha	'71
Three Times in Love	James, Tommy	'80	To Each His Own (That's My Philosophy)	Faith, Hope & Charity	'75
Thrill Is Gone, The	King, B.B.	'69	To Hell with Poverty	Gang of Four	'82
Thriller	Jackson, Michael	'83	To Kingdom Come	Band, The	'68
Through Being Cool	Devo	'81	To Know Him Is to Love Him	Teddy Bears, The	'58
Through the Storm	Franklin, Aretha	'89	To Love Somebody	Bee Gees, The	'67
Through Your Hands	Hiatt, John	'90	To Sing for You	Donovan	'65
Throwing It All Away	Genesis	'86	To Sir, with Love	Lulu	'67
Thunder Island	Ferguson, Jay	'77	To the Aisle	Five Satins, The	'57
Thunder Kiss	White Zombie	'94	Toad	Cream	'67
Thunder Road	Springsteen, Bruce	'75	Tobacco Road	Nashville Teens, The	'64
Ticket to Ride	Beatles, The	'65	Today	Smashing Pumpkins	'93
Tide Is High, The	Paragons	'63	Today I Met the Boy I'm Gonna Marry	Love, Darlene	'63
Tie a Yellow Ribbon Round the Old Oak Tree	Dawn	'73			
Tiger	Fabian	'59	Together Forever	Astley, Rick	'88
Tight Connection to My Heart (Has Anybody Seen My Love)	Dylan, Bob	'85	Tom Dooley	Kingston Trio, The	'58
			Tom Sawyer	Rush	'81
Tight Rope	Russell, Leon	'72	Tom Traubert's Blues	Waits, Tom	'76
Tighten Up	Bell, Archie and the Drells	'68	Tom's Diner	Vega, Suzanne	'87
Tighter Tighter	Alive and Kicking	'70	Tommy Gun	Clash, The	'78
Time	Pink Floyd	'73	Tomorrow (a Better You, a Better Me)	Jones, Quincy	'89
Time (Clock of the Heart)	Culture Club	'83			
Time After Time	Lauper, Cyndi	'84	Tomorrow Is a Long Time	Dylan, Bob	'62
Time and Love	Nyro, Laura	'69	Tomorrow Never Knows	Beatles, The	'66
Time for Me to Fly	REO Speedwagon	'78	Tomorrow Night	Johnson, Lonnie	'48
Time Has Come Today	Chambers Brothers, The	'67	Tomorrow Night	Shoes, The	'79
Time in a Bottle	Croce, Jim	'72	Tonight	New Kids on the Block	'89
Time Is on My Side	Thomas, Irma	'64	Tonight (Could Be the Night)	Velvets	'61
Time Is Tight	Booker T. & the MG's	'69	Tonight I Think I'm Gonna Go Downtown	Gilmore, Jimmie Dale & the Flatlanders	'72
Time of the Season	Zombies, The	'67			
Time out of Mind	Steely Dan	'80	Tonight I'll Be Staying Here with You	Dylan, Bob	'69
Time Passages	Stewart, Al	'78			
Time Passes Slowly	Dylan, Bob	'70	Tonight Is What It Means to Be Young	Fire, Inc.	'84
Time the Avenger	Pretenders, The	'84			
Time Will Reveal	DeBarge	'83	Tonight She Comes	Cars, The	'85
Time Won't Let Me	Outsiders, The	'66	Tonight We Murder	Ministry	'88
Times of Your Life	Anka, Paul	'76	Tonight You Belong to Me	Patience and Prudence	'56
Times They Are A-Changin', The	Dylan, Bob	'64	Tonight's the Night	Burke, Solomon	'65
Tin Can Alley	Andersen, Eric	'68	Tonight's the Night	Shirelles, The	'60
Tin Man	America	'74	Tonight's the Night (Gonna Be All Right)	Stewart, Rod	'76
Tin Pan Alley	Vaughan, Stevie Ray	'84			
Ting-a-Ling	Clovers, The	'52	Tonight, Tonight, Tonight	Genesis	'87
Tip Toe through the Tulips	Tiny Tim	'68	Tonite, Tonite	Mellow Kings, The	'57
Tipitina	Professor Longhair	'54	Too Busy Thinking About My Baby	Gaye, Marvin	'69
Tired of Being Alone	Green, Al	'71	Too Funky	Michael, George	'92
Tired of Toein' the Line	Burnette, Rocky	'80	Too Hot	Kool & the Gang	'79
Tired of Waiting for You	Kinks, The	'65	Too Hot ta Trot	Commodores, The	'77
To Be Loved	Wilson, Jackie	'58	Too Late for Goodbyes	Lennon, Julian	'85
To Be with You	Mr. Big	'92	Too Late to Turn Back Now	Cornelius Brothers and Sister Rose, The	'72
To Be Young	Lonesome Val	'90			
			Too Many Walls	Dennis, Cathy	'91

SONG	ARTIST	YEAR	SONG	ARTIST	YEAR
Too Much	Presley, Elvis	'57	Treat Her Right	Head, Roy	'65
Too Much Heaven	Bee Gees, The	'78	Treat Me Nice	Presley, Elvis	'57
Too Much Monkey Business	Berry, Chuck	'57	Trenchtown Rock	Marley, Bob & the Wailers	'71
Too Much of Nothing	Peter, Paul & Mary	'67	Triad	Byrds, The	'67
Too Much Time on My Hands	Styx	'81	Tribute to a King	Bell, William	'68
Too Much Too Young	Specials, The	'79	Trickle Trickle	Videos, The	'58
Too Old to Rock 'n' Roll: Too Young to Die	Jethro Tull	'76	Troglodyte (Cave Man)	Castor, Jimmy, Bunch, The	'72
			Trooper, The	Iron Maiden	'83
Too Pooped to Pop	Berry, Chuck	'60	Trouble	Buckingham, Lindsay	'82
Too Shy	Kajagoogoo	'83	Trouble Blues	Brown, Charles	'49
Too Tight	Con Funk Shun	'81	Trouble Comin' Every Day	Mothers of Invention, The	'66
Too Weak to Fight	Carter, Clarence	'69	Trouble Me	10,000 Maniacs	'89
Too Young	Cole, Nat King	'51	Troubles, The	Roches, The	'79
Top Forty of the Lord, The	Sha-Na-Na	'71	Troy	O'Connor, Sinead	'88
Top of the World	Carpenters, The	'73	Truckin'	Grateful Dead, The	'70
Top of the World	Van Halen	'91	True	Spandau Ballet	'83
Topsy, Pt. II	Cole, Cozy	'58	True Blue	Madonna	'86
Torn Between Two Lovers	MacGreggor, Mary	'77	True Colors	Lauper, Cyndi	'86
Tossin' and Turnin'	Lewis, Bobby	'61	True Fine Mama	Little Richard	'55
Total Eclipse of the Heart	Tyler, Bonnie	'83	True Love Ways	Holly, Buddy	'58
Touch Me	Doors, The	'69	Try (Just a Little Bit Harder)	Mimms, Garnet & the Enchanters	'63
Touch Me (All Night Long)	Wish, featuring Fonda Rae	'85			
Touch Me (I Want Your Body)	Fox, Samantha	'87	Try a Little Tenderness	Redding, Otis	'66
Touch Me I'm Sick	Mudhoney	'88	Try Me	Brown, James & the Famous Flames	'58
Touch of Grey	Grateful Dead, The	'87			
Touch the Hem of His Garment	Soul Stirrers, The	'56	Tryin' to Love Two	Bell, William	'77
Toucha-Toucha-Toucha Me	Sarandon, Susan	'74	Trying to Hold on to My Woman	Dozier, Lamont	'74
Tower of Song	Cohen, Leonard	'88	Trying to Live My Life without You	Clay, Otis	'72
Tower of Strength	McDaniels, Gene	'61	TSOP (The Sound of Philadelphia)	MFSB	'73
Town without Pity	Pitney, Gene	'61	Tubular Bells	Oldfield, Mike	'74
Toy Soldiers	Martika	'89	Tuesday Afternoon (Forever Afternoon)	Moody Blues, The	'68
Traces	Classics IV, The	'69			
Tracks of My Tears, The	Miracles, The	'65	Tuff	Cannon, Ace	'61
Tracy	Cuff Links, The	'69	Tuff Enuff	Fabulous Thunderbirds, The	'86
Tragedy	Bee Gees, The	'78	Tulane	Berry, Chuck	'70
Tragedy	Wayne, Thomas	'59	Tulsa Time	Clapton, Eric	'78
Train in Vain (Stand by Me)	Clash, The	'79	Tumbling Dice	Rolling Stones, The	'72
Train Kept a-Rollin', The	Burnette, Johnny & the Rock and Roll Trio	'56	Tumbling Down	Marley, Ziggy	'88
			Tunnel of Love	Dire Straits	'80
Tramp	Fulson, Lowell	'67	Tunnel of Love	Springsteen, Bruce	'87
Trampled under Foot	Led Zeppelin	'75	Tupelo Honey	Morrison, Van	'71
Trans Europe Express	Kraftwerk	'77	Turn Back the Hands of Time	Davis, Tyrone	'70
Transfusion	Nervous Norvus	'56	Turn Me Loose	Fabian	'59
Trapped by a Thing Called Love	LaSalle, Denise	'71	Turn on the News	Hüsker Dü	'84
Trash	New York Dolls	'73	Turn on Your Love Light	Bland, Bobby	'61
Travelin' Band	Creedence Clearwater Revival	'70	Turn the Beat Around (Love to Hear Percussion)	Robinson, Vickie Sue	'76
Travelin' Man	Nelson, Rick	'61			
Traveling Riverside Blues	Led Zeppelin	'69	Turn to Stone	Electric Light Orchestra	'77
Treasure of Love	McPhatter, Clyde	'56	Turn! Turn! Turn! (To Everything There's a Season)	Seeger, Pete	'62
Treat Her Like a Lady	Cornelius Brothers and Sister Rose, The	'71			
			Turned up Too Late	Parker, Graham	'76

SONG	ARTIST	YEAR
Turning Japanese	Vapors, The	'81
Turquoise	Donovan	'66
Tush	ZZ Top	'75
Tusk	Fleetwood Mac	'79
Tutti Frutti	Little Richard	'55
TV Party	Black Flag	'81
TVC 15	Bowie, David	'76
Tweedlee Dee	Baker, LaVern	'54
Twelve-Thirty (Young Girls Are Coming to the Canyon)	Mamas and the Papas, The	'67
Twenty Flight Rock	Cochran, Eddie	'56
Twiggs Approved	Dixie Dregs, The	'80
Twilight Time	Platters, The	'58
Twilight Zone	Golden Earring	'83
Twine Time	Cash, Alvin & the Crawlers	'65
Twist and Crawl	English Beat, The	'80
Twist and Shout	Isley Brothers, The	'62
Twist of Fate	Newton-John, Olivia	'83
Twist, The	Midnighters, The	'59
Twist, Twist Senora	Bonds, Gary U.S.	'62
Twisted	Ross, Annie	'53
Twistin' the Night Away	Cooke, Sam	'62
Two Faces Have I	Christie, Lou	'63
Two Hearts	Collins, Phil	'88
Two Hearts Beat as One	U2	'83
Two Lovers	Wells, Mary	'62
Two Occasions	Deele, The	'87
Two of Hearts	Stacey Q	'86
Two out of Three Ain't Bad	Meat Loaf	'77
Two Princes	Spin Doctors, The	'92
Two Tickets to Paradise	Money, Eddie	'77
Two to Make It Right	Seduction	'89
Two Tribes	Frankie Goes to Hollywood	'84
Two Tub Man	Dictators, The	'75
Typical Girls	Slits, The	'79
Typical Male	Turner, Tina	'86

U

SONG	ARTIST	YEAR
U Can't Touch This	Hammer, M.C.	'90
U Got the Look	Prince	'87
U.N.I.T.Y.	Queen Latifah	'93
U.S. Male	Reed, Jerry	'67
Uhh Ahh	Boyz II Men	'91
Um Um Um Um Um Um	Lance, Major	'63
Unbelievable	EMF	'91
Unchain My Heart	Charles, Ray	'60
Unchained Melody	Hamilton, Roy	'55
Uncle Albert/Admiral Halsey	McCartney, Paul & Wings	'71
Uncle John's Band	Grateful Dead, The	'70
Under a Raging Moon	Daltrey, Roger	'85

SONG	ARTIST	YEAR
Under Assistant West Coast Promo Man	Rolling Stones, The	'65
Under My Thumb	Rolling Stones, The	'66
Under Pressure	Queen and David Bowie	'82
Under the Big Black Sun	X	'82
Under the Boardwalk	Drifters, The	'64
Under the Bridge	Red Hot Chili Peppers	'91
Under the Milky Way	Church, The	'88
Under the Moon of Love	Lee, Curtis	'61
Under Your Spell	Dylan, Bob	'86
Undercover Angel	O'Day, Alan	'77
Undercover of the Night	Rolling Stones, The	'83
Understand Your Man	Cash, Johnny	'64
Understanding	Xscape	'93
Undone (the Sweater Song)	Weezer	'94
Uneasy Rider	Daniels, Charlie Band, The	'73
Unforgiven, The	Metallica	'91
Unicorn, The	Irish Rovers, The	'68
Union of the Snake	Duran Duran	'83
United We Stand	Brotherhood of Man	'70
Universal Soldier, The	Sainte-Marie, Buffy	'63
Unknown Soldier	Doors, The	'68
Unsatisfied	Replacements, The	'84
Unskinny Bop	Poison	'90
Unsung	Helmet	'92
Until It's Time for You to Go	Sainte-Marie, Buffy	'64
Until You Come Back to Me (That's What I'm Gonna Do)	Franklin, Aretha	'73
Up Above My Head, I Hear Music in the Air	Tharpe, Sister Rosetta	'48
Up Around the Bend	Creedence Clearwater Revival	'70
Up for the down Stroke	Parliament	'74
Up on Cripple Creek	Band, The	'68
Up on the Roof	Drifters, The	'62
Up the Junction	Squeeze	'79
Up the Ladder to the Roof	Supremes, The	'70
Up Where We Belong	Cocker, Joe and Jennifer Warnes	'82
Up—Up and Away	5th Dimension, The	'67
Upside Down	Jesus and Mary Chain, The	'84
Upside Down	Ross, Diana	'80
Uptight (Everything's Alright)	Wonder, Stevie	'66
Uptown	Crystals, The	'62
Uptown Girl	Joel, Billy	'83
Urge for Going	Hamilton, George IV	'67
Urgent	Foreigner	'81
Us and Them	Pink Floyd	'73
Use Me	Withers, Bill	'72
Use ta Be My Girl	O'Jays, The	'77
Used to Be	Larkin, Patty	'91
Usual, The	Hiatt, John	'85

SONG	ARTIST	YEAR
V		
V	Farina, Dick and Mimi	'65
V-a-c-a-t-i-o-n	Francis, Connie	'62
Vacation	Go-Go's, The	'82
Vahevela	Loggins and Messina	'71
Valentine Melody	Buckley, Tim	'68
Valerie	Thompson, Richard	'86
Valleri	Monkees, The	'68
Valley Girl	Zappa, Frank and Moon Unit	'82
Valley Road, The	Hornsby, Bruce & the Range	'88
Valotte	Lennon, Julian	'84
Vanilla Olay	DeShannon, Jackie	'72
Vasoline	Stone Temple Pilots	'94
Vaudeville Man	Waldman, Wendy	'73
Vegtable Man	Soft Boys, The	'80
Vehicle	Ides of March, The	'70
Ventura Highway	America	'72
Venus	Avalon, Frankie	'59
Venus	Shocking Blue	'69
Venus in Blue Jeans	Clanton, Jimmy	'61
Verdi Cries	10,000 Maniacs	'87
Veronica	Costello, Elvis	'89
Vicious	Reed, Lou	'72
Victim of the Ghetto	College Boyz, The	'92
Victor Jara	Guthrie, Arlo	'76
Victoria	Kinks, The	'70
Victory	Kool & the Gang	'86
Video Killed the Radio Star	Buggles, The	'79
Vienna	Ultravox	'80
Viet Nam	Cliff, Jimmy	'70
View to a Kill, A	Duran Duran	'85
Vine Street	Parks, Van Dyke	'68
Violet	Hole	'94
Violets of Dawn	Blues Project, The	'66
Vision of Love	Carey, Mariah	'90
Visions of Johanna	Dylan, Bob	'66
Viva Las Vegas	Presley, Elvis	'64
Vogue	Madonna	'89
Voice, The	Moody Blues, The	'81
Voices Carry	Til Tuesday	'85
Voodoo Chile (Slight Return)	Hendrix, Jimi	'68
Vow, The	Flamingos, The	'56
W		
Wah-Watusi, The	Orlons, The	'62
Wait	McLachlan, Sarah	'94
Wait	White Lion	'87
Wait 'Til My Bobby Gets Home	Love, Darlene	'63
Waitin' in School	Nelson, Ricky	'57

SONG	ARTIST	YEAR
Waiting, The	Petty, Tom & the Heartbreakers	'81
Waiting for a Girl Like You	Foreigner	'81
Waiting for a Star to Fall	Boy Meets Girl	'88
Waiting on a Friend	Rolling Stones, The	'81
Waiting Room	Fugazi	'88
Wake Me up Before You Go-Go	Wham!	'84
Wake Me, Shake Me	Blues Project, The	'67
Wake up Everybody, Part One	Melvin, Harold & the Bluenotes	'75
Wake up, Little Susie	Everly Brothers, The	'57
Walk a Mile in My Shoes	South, Joe	'70
Walk Away from Love	Ruffin, David	'75
Walk Away Renee	Left Banke, The	'66
Walk, Don't Run	Atkins, Chet	'57
Walk Like a Man	Four Seasons, The	'63
Walk Like a Man	Springsteen, Bruce	'87
Walk Like an Egyptian	Bangles, The	'86
Walk of Life	Dire Straits	'85
Walk on By	Van Dyke, Leroy	'61
Walk on the Wild Side	Reed, Lou	'72
Walk on Water	Money, Eddie	'88
Walk Right Back	Everly Brothers, The	'60
Walk Right In	Rooftop Singers, The	'63
Walk the Dinosaur	Was (Not Was)	'88
Walk This Way	Aerosmith	'73
Walk, The	McCracklin, Jimmy	'58
Walking After Midnight	Cline, Patsy	'56
Walking Along	Solitaires, The	'57
Walking Away	Information Society	'88
Walking down Madison	MacColl, Kirsty	'91
Walking down Your Street	Bangles, The	'86
Walking Home Alone	Ridgway, Stan	'86
Walking in Memphis	Cohn, Marc	'91
Walking in Rhythm	Blackbyrds	'75
Walking in the Rain	Ronettes, The	'64
Walking My Cat Named Dog	Tanega, Norma	'66
Walking on Broken Glass	Lennox, Annie	'92
Walking on Sunshine	Grant, Eddy	'79
Walking on the Moon	Police, The	'79
Walking on Thin Ice	Ono, Yoko	'81
Walking Song	McGarrigle, Kate and Anna	'77
Walking the Dog	Thomas, Rufus	'63
Walking to New Orleans	Domino, Fats	'60
Wall of Death	Thompson, Richard and Linda	'82
Wall of Denial	Vaughan, Stevie Ray	'89
Wanderer, The	Dion	'62
Wanderer, The	Summer, Donna	'80
Wango Tango	Nugent, Ted	'80
Wanna Be Startin' Something	Jackson, Michael	'83
Want-Ads	Honey Cone	'71

SONG	ARTIST	YEAR	SONG	ARTIST	YEAR
Wanted Dead or Alive	Bon Jovi	'87	We Don't Talk Anymore	Richard, Cliff	'79
Wanted Man	Cash, Johnny	'69	We Get Ill	Schooly D	'87
War	Starr, Edwin	'70	We Got Love	Rydell, Bobby	'59
War in Peace	Spence, Skip	'69	We Got the Beat	Go-Go's, The	'82
Warmth of the Sun, The	Beach Boys, The	'64	We Gotta Get You a Woman	Runt	'70
Warrior, The	Scandal	'84	We Gotta Get outa This Place	Animals, The	'65
Wasted	Black Flag	'78	We Hate It When Our Friends Become Successful	Morrissey	'92
Wasted on the Way	Crosby, Stills and Nash	'82			
Watch Me Rock, I'm over Thirty	Wainwright, Loudon	'78	We Have the Technology	Pere Ubu	'88
Watching the Detectives	Costello, Elvis	'77	We Just Disagree	Mason, Dave	'77
Watching the River Flow	Dylan, Bob	'71	We Live So Fast	Heaven 17	'82
Watching the Wheels	Lennon, John	'80	We Love You	Rolling Stones, The	'67
Waterfalls	TLC	'94	We Will Rock You	Queen	'77
Waterloo	Abba	'74	We'll Be Together	Sting	'87
Waterloo	Jackson, Stonewall	'59	We'll Never Have to Say Goodbye Again	England Dan and John Ford Coley	'78
Waterloo Sunset	Kinks, The	'67			
Way Down	Presley, Elvis	'77	We'll Sing in the Sunshine	Garnett, Gale	'64
Way down Yonder in New Orleans	Cannon, Freddy	'60	We're a Winner	Impressions, The	'67
Way I Walk, The	Scott, Jack	'59	We're All Alone	Scaggs, Boz	'76
Way It Is, The	Hornsby, Bruce & the Range	'86	We're an American Band	Grand Funk Railroad	'73
Way over There	Miracles, The	'60	We're Desperate	X	'80
Way to Blue	Drake, Nick	'69	We're Getting Careless with Our Love	Taylor, Johnnie	'73
Way We Make a Broken Heart, The	Cash, Rosanne	'87			
			We're Gonna Make It	Little Milton	'65
Way You Do the Things You Do, The	Temptations, The	'64	We're Gonna Make It (After All)	Greenwich, Ellie	'85
			We're Gonna Rock, We're Gonna Roll	Moore, Wild Bill	'47
Way You Love Me, The	White, Karyn	'89			
Way You Make Me Feel, The	Jackson, Michael	'87	(We're Gonna) Rock around the Clock	Haley, Bill & the Comets	'53
Ways to Be Wicked	Lone Justice	'85			
We Ain't Got Nothing Yet	Blues Magoos, The	'66	We're Not Gonna Take It	Who, The	'69
We All Sleep Alone	Cher	'88	We're Ready	Boston	'86
We Almost Lost Detroit	Scott-Heron, Gil	'77	We've Come Too Far to End It Now	Miracles, The	'72
We Are Family	Sister Sledge	'78	We've Got Tonight	Seger, Bob	'77
We Are the Champions	Queen	'77	We've Only Just Begun	Carpenters, The	'70
We Are the Normal	Goo Goo Dolls	'93	Weak	SWV	'93
We Are the Road Crew	Motorhead	'80	Wear My Ring	Vincent, Gene & His Blue Caps	'57
We Are the World	U.S.A. for Africa	'85			
We Belong	Benatar, Pat	'84	Wear My Ring (around Your Neck)	Presley, Elvis	'58
We Belong Together	Jones, Rickie Lee	'81	Wear Your Love Like Heaven	Donovan	'67
We Belong Together	Robert and Johnny	'58	Wedding Bell Blues	Nyro, Laura	'67
We Built This City	Starship	'85	Wedding Song, The	Stookey, Paul	'71
We Can Be Together/Volunteers	Jefferson Airplane, The	'69	Wednesday Week	Costello, Elvis	'80
We Can Change the World	Nash, Graham	'71	Wee Wee Hours	Berry, Chuck	'57
We Can Work It Out	Beatles, The	'65	Weight, The	Band, The	'68
We Can't Go Wrong	Cover Girls, The	'89	Weird Science	Oingo Boingo	'85
We Did It	Johnson, Syl	'73	Weirdo	Charlatans U.K., The	'92
We Didn't Start the Fire	Joel, Billy	'89	Welcome Back	Sebastian, John	'76
We Don't Have to Take Our Clothes Off	Stewart, Jermaine	'86	Welcome to My Nightmare	Cooper, Alice	'75
			Welcome to Paradise	Green Day	'92
We Don't Need Another Hero (Thunderdome)	Turner, Tina	'85	Welcome to the Boomtown	David and David	'86
			Welcome to the Jungle	Guns N' Roses	'87

SONG	ARTIST	YEAR
Welcome to the Pleasure Dome	Frankie Goes to Hollywood	'85
Welcome to the Working Week	Costello, Elvis	'77
Well	Captain Beefheart	'69
Well All Right	Crickets, The	'58
Well-Respected Man, A	Kinks, The	'65
Wendy	Beach Boys, The	'64
Went to See the Gypsy	Dylan, Bob	'70
Werewolf	Holy Modal Rounders, The	'65
Werewolves of London	Zevon, Warren	'78
West End Girls	Pet Shop Boys	'86
Western Movies	Olympics, The	'58
Western Union	Five Americans, The	'67
Wham, The	Mack, Lonnie	'63
What a Fool Believes	Doobie Brothers, The	'79
(What a) Wonderful World	Cooke, Sam	'60
What About Love?	Heart	'85
What About Me	Quicksilver Messenger Service	'71
What About Us	Coasters, The	'59
What About Your Friends	TLC	'92
What Am I Gonna Do with You	White, Barry	'75
What Am I Living For	Willis, Chuck	'58
What Becomes of the Brokenhearted	Ruffin, Jimmy	'66
What Cha' Gonna Do for Me	Khan, Chaka	'81
What Difference Does It Make	Smiths, The	'84
What Do All the People Know	Monroes, The	'82
What Does It Take (to Win Your Love)	Walker, Jr. & the All-Stars	'69
What God Wants, Part I	Waters, Roger	'92
What Good Can Drinking Do	Joplin, Janis	'62
What Have I Done to Deserve This	Pet Shop Boys	'87
What Have They Done to My Song, Ma	Melanie	'70
What Have They Done to the Rain	Searchers, The	'64
What Have You Done for Me Lately	Jackson, Janet	'86
What I Am	Brickell, Edie & New Bohemians	'88
What I Like About You	Romantics, The	'80
What If I Came Knocking	Mellencamp, John Cougar	'93
What in the World's Come over You	Scott, Jack	'59
What Is Life	Harrison, George	'70
What Is Love	Haddaway	'93
What Is Love	Playmates, The	'59
What It Takes	Aerosmith	'89
What Kind of Fool	Tams, The	'64
What Kind of Man Would I Be	Chicago	'89
What Made Milwaukee Famous (Has Made a Loser out of Me)	Lewis, Jerry Lee	'68
What the World Needs Now Is Love	DeShannon, Jackie	'65
What Would You Say	Matthews, Dave, Band, The	'94

SONG	ARTIST	YEAR
What You Don't Know	Expose	'89
What You Need	Inxs	'86
What You Won't Do for Love	Caldwell, Bobby	'78
What'd I Say	Charles, Ray	'59
What's a Matter Baby (Is It Hurting You)	Yuro, Timi	'62
What's Forever For	Murphey, Michael Martin	'82
What's Goin' On	Gaye, Marvin	'71
What's Good	Reed, Lou	'91
What's Love Got to Do with It	Turner, Tina	'84
What's My Name	Dogg, Snoop Doggy	'93
What's My Scene	Hoodoo Gurus, The	'87
What's on Your Mind (Pure Energy)	Information Society	'88
(What's So Funny 'Bout) Peace, Love and Understanding	Brinzley Schwarz	'74
What's So Good About Goodbye	Miracles, The	'62
What's the Frequency, Kenneth	R.E.M.	'94
What's the Matter Here	10,000 Maniacs	'87
What's Up	4 Non Blondes	'93
What's up Doc? (Can We Rock)	Fu-Schnickens with Shaquille O'Neal	'93
What's Your Name	Lynyrd Skynyrd	'77
What's Your Name	Don and Juan	'61
Whatcha Gonna Do	Drifters, The	'53
Whatcha Gonna Do	Pablo Cruise	'77
Whatcha See Is What You Get	Dramatics, The	'71
Whatever Gets You thru the Night	Lennon, John	'74
Whatever You Want	Tony! Toni! Tone!	'90
Whatta Man	Salt-n-Pepa featuring En Vogue	'93
Wheel in the Sky	Journey	'78
Wheel of Fortune	Four Flames, The	'52
Wheels	Stringalongs, The	'61
When	Kalin Twins, The	'58
When a Man Loves a Woman	Sledge, Percy	'66
When Can I See You	Babyface	'94
When Doves Cry	Prince	'84
When I Come Around	Green Day	'94
When I Dream	Teardrop Explodes, The	'80
When I Get to the Border	Thompson, Richard and Linda	'74
When I Grow up to Be a Man	Beach Boys, The	'64
When I Look in Your Eyes	Firehouse	'92
When I Need You	Sayer, Leo	'77
When I Paint My Masterpiece	Dylan, Bob	'71
When I Saw You	Ronettes, The	'64
When I See You Smile	Bad English	'89
When I Think of You	Jackson, Janet	'86
When I Win the Lottery	Camper Van Beethoven	'89
When I'm Gone	Holloway, Brenda	'64
When I'm Sixty-four	Beatles, The	'67
When I'm with You	Sheriff	'83

SONG	ARTIST	YEAR
When in Rome	Ochs, Phil	'68
When It's Love	Van Halen	'88
When Love Breaks Down	Prefab Sprout	'85
When She Cries	Restless Heart	'92
(When She Wants Good Lovin) My Baby Comes to Me	Coasters, The	'57
When She Was My Girl	Four Tops, The	'81
When Smokey Sings	ABC	'87
When Something Is Wrong with My Baby	Sam and Dave	'66
When the Children Cry	White Lion	'87
When the Going Gets Tough the Tough Get Going	Ocean, Billy	'85
When the Levee Breaks	Led Zeppelin	'71
When the Music's Over	Doors, The	'67
When the Ship Comes In	Dylan, Bob	'64
When the Spell Is Broken	Thompson, Richard	'85
When We Get Married	Dreamlovers, The	'61
When We Ran	Hiatt, John	'85
When We Was Fab	Harrison, George	'87
When Will I Be Loved	Everly Brothers, The	'60
When Will I See You Again	Three Degrees, The	'74
When You Dance	Turbans, The	'55
When You Dance (I Can Really Love)	Young, Neil	'70
When You Gonna Wake Up	Dylan, Bob	'79
When You Sleep	My Bloody Valentine	'91
When You Walk in the Room	DeShannon, Jackie	'64
When You Were Mine	Prince	'80
When You're Hot You're Hot	Reed, Jerry	'71
When You're in Love with a Beautiful Woman	Dr. Hook	'79
When You're Young and in Love	Ruby & the Romantics	'64
When Your Heart Is Weak	Cock Robin	'85
Whenever a Teenager Cries	Reparata & the Delrons	'64
Whenever I Call You 'Friend'	Loggins, Kenny	'78
Whenever You're on My Mind	Crenshaw, Marshall	'83
Where Are You Now?	Synch	'86
Where Are You Tonight	Dylan, Bob	'78
Where Did Our Love Go	Supremes, The	'64
Where Do the Children Go	Hooters, The	'85
Where Have All the Flowers Gone	Seeger, Pete	'62
Where I'm From	Digable Planets	'93
Where Is the Love	Flack, Roberta and Donnie Hathaway	'72
Where or When	Dion & the Belmonts	'60
Where the Boys Are	Francis, Connie	'61
Where the Streets Have No Names	U2	'87
Where Were You on Our Wedding Day	Price, Lloyd	'59
Where's the Party	Madonna	'86

SONG	ARTIST	YEAR
Which Way to America	Living Colour	'88
Which Way You Goin' Billy	Poppy Family, The	'69
While My Guitar Gently Weeps	Beatles, The	'68
While You See a Chance	Winwood, Steve	'81
Whip Appeal	Babyface	'89
Whip It	Devo	'80
Whipping Post	Allman Brothers, The	'70
Whiskey and Women and Money to Burn	Ely, Joe	'94
Whispering Bells	Del Vikings, The	'57
Whispering/Cherchez La Femme/ C'est Si Bon	Dr. Buzzard's Original Savannah Band	'76
Whistle down the Wind	Waits, Tom	'92
White Bird	La Flamme, David	'76
White Christmas	Drifters, The	'55
White Girl	X	'80
White Light/White Heat	Velvet Underground, The	'68
White Lightning	Jones, George	'59
White Lines (Don't Do It)	Grandmaster Flash and Melle Mel	'83
White Man in Hammersmith Palais	Clash, The	'78
White Punks on Dope	Tubes, The	'75
White Rabbit	Great Society, The	'65
White Rhythm and Blues	Ronstadt, Linda	'78
White Riot	Clash, The	'77
White Room	Cream	'68
White Sport Coat (and a Pink Carnation), A	Robbins, Marty	'57
White Summer	Yardbirds, The	'68
White Wedding	Idol, Billy	'83
Whiter Shade of Pale, A	Procol Harum	'67
Who Are the Brain Police	Mothers of Invention, The	'66
Who Are You	Who, The	'78
Who Can It Be Now	Men at Work	'82
Who Do You Love	Diddley, Bo	'55
Who Does Lisa Like	Sweet, Rachel	'79
Who Knows Where the Time Goes	Fairport Convention	'69
Who Loves You	Four Seasons, The	'75
Who Made Who	AC/DC	'86
Who Needs the Peace Corps	Mothers of Invention, The	'68
Who Put the Bomp (in the Bomp Ba Bomp Ba Bomp)	Mann, Barry	'61
Who the Cap Fits	Shinehead	'86
Who Was in My Room Last Night	Butthole Surfers	'93
Who Will You Run To	Heart	'87
Who'd She Coo	Ohio Players, The	'76
Who'll Be the Next in Line	Kinks, The	'65
Who'll Stop the Rain	Creedence Clearwater Revival	'70
Who's Crying Now	Journey	'81
Who's Gonna Take the Blame	Miracles, The	'70
Who's Holding Donna Now	DeBarge	'85

SONG	ARTIST	YEAR	SONG	ARTIST	YEAR
Who's Johnny	Debarge, El	'86	Wildflower	Skylark	'73
Who's Making Love	Taylor, Johnnie	'68	Wildwood Weed	Stafford, Jim	'73
Who's Sorry Now	Francis, Connie	'58	Will It Go Round in Circles	Preston, Billy	'73
Who's That Girl	Madonna	'87	Will the Wolf Survive	Los Lobos	'85
Who's That Knocking	Genies, The	'58	Will You Be There	Jackson, Michael	'91
Who's Zoomin' Who	Franklin, Aretha	'85	Will You Love Me Tomorrow	Shirelles, The	'60
Whodunit	Tavares	'77	Will You Still Love Me	Chicago	'87
Whole Lotta Love	Led Zeppelin	'69	(Will You) Come Back My Love	Wrens, The	'55
Whole Lotta Loving	Domino, Fats	'58	Willie and the Hand Jive	Otis, Johnny	'58
Whole Lotta Rosie	AC/DC	'77	Willie the Pimp, Parts One & Two	Zappa, Frank	'69
Whole Lotta Shakin' Goin' On	Big Maybelle	'55	Willing	Little Feat	'70
Whole of the Moon	Waterboys, The	'85	Wimoweh (The Lion Sleeps Tonight)	Weavers, The	'51
Whole Wide World	Lorain, A'me	'90			
Whole Wide World	Wreckless Eric	'78	Win Your Love for Me	Cooke, Sam	'58
Whoot! (There It Is)	Tag Team	'93	Winchester Cathedral	New Vaudeville Band, The	'66
Why	Avalon, Frankie	'59	Wind	Circus Maximus	'67
Why Can't I Be You	Cure, The	'87	Wind Cries Mary, The	Hendrix, Jimi	'67
Why Can't This Be Love	Van Halen	'86	Wind of Change	Scorpions, The	'90
Why Can't We Be Friends	War	'75	Wind, The	Diablos, The	'54
Why Can't We Live Together	Thomas, Timmy	'73	Windows of the World, The	Warwick, Dionne	'67
Why Do Fools Fall in Love	Lymon, Frankie and the Teenagers	'56	Windy	Association, The	'67
			Winner Takes It All	Abba	'80
Why Do Lovers Break Each Other's Hearts	Soxx, Bob B. & the Blue Jeans	'63	Winter	Amos, Tori	'92
			Winter in America	Scott-Heron, Gil	'75
Why Does Love Got to Be So Sad	Derek & the Dominoes	'70	Winter Lady	Cohen, Leonard	'68
Why Don't They Understand	Hamilton, George IV	'57	Wipe Out	Surfaris, The	'63
Why Don't We Do It in the Road	Beatles, The	'68	Wish Someone Would Care	Thomas, Irma	'64
Why Don't You Write Me	Jacks, The	'55	Wish You Were Here	Pink Floyd	'75
Why Me	Kristofferson, Kris	'72	Wishful, Sinful	Doors, The	'69
Why Must I Always Explain	Morrison, Van	'91	Wishin' and Hopin'	Warwick, Dionne	'63
Why Worry	Dire Straits	'85	Wishing on a Star	Rose Royce	'77
Why You Treat Me So Bad	Club Nouveau	'87	Wishing Well	D'Arby, Terence Trent	'87
Wichita Lineman	Campbell, Glen	'68	Witch Doctor	Seville, David	'58
Wicked Game	Isaak, Chris	'89	Witchi-Tai-To	Everything Is Everything	'69
Wild Billy's Circus Story	Springsteen, Bruce	'73	Witchy Woman	Eagles, The	'72
Wild Boys, The	Duran Duran	'84	With a Little Help from My Friends	Beatles, The	'67
Wild Honey Pie	Beatles, The	'68	With a Little Luck	McCartney, Paul & Wings	'78
Wild Horses	Rolling Stones, The	'71	With God on Our Side	Dylan, Bob	'63
Wild in the Streets	Jeffreys, Garland	'77	With or Without You	U2	'87
Wild Life	Captain Beefheart	'69	With You I'm Born Again	Preston, Billy and Syreeta	'79
Wild Night	Morrison, Van	'71	Within You, Without You	Beatles, The	'67
Wild One	Rydell, Bobby	'60	Without Her	Nilsson	'67
Wild Thing	Tone Loc	'89	Without Love (There Is Nothing)	McPhatter, Clyde	'57
Wild Thing	Troggs, The	'66	Without You	Motley Crue	'89
Wild Weekend	Rockin' Rebels, The	'63	Without You	Badfinger	'70
Wild, Wild Life	Talking Heads	'86	Without You	Tillotson, Johnny	'61
Wild, Wild West	Escape Club, The	'88	Woman	Lennon, John	'80
Wild Wild West	Dee, Kool Moe	'87	Woman	Peter and Gordon	'66
Wild, Wild Young Men	Brown, Ruth	'55	Woman from Tokyo	Deep Purple	'73
Wild World	Stevens, Cat	'71	Woman Needs Love (Just Like You Do), A	Raydio	'81
Wildfire	Murphey, Michael	'75			

SONG	ARTIST	YEAR
Woman of Heart and Mind	Mitchell, Joni	'72
Woman to Woman	Brown, Shirley	'74
Woman's Got Soul	Impressions, The	'65
Woman's Gotta Have It	Womack, Bobby	'72
Woman, a Lover, a Friend, A	Wilson, Jackie	'60
Woman, Woman	Puckett, Gary & the Union Gap	'67
Women Is Losers	Big Brother & the Holding Company	'68
Women's Love Rights	Lee, Laura	'71
Won't Get Fooled Again	Who, The	'71
Won't You Try/Saturday Afternoon	Jefferson Airplane, The	'68
Wonder of You, The	Peterson, Ray	'59
Wonderful Dream, A	Majors, The	'62
Wonderful Summer, A	Ward, Robin	'63
Wonderful Tonight	Clapton, Eric	'77
Wonderful World, Beautiful People	Cliff, Jimmy	'70
Wonderful, Wonderful	Mathis, Johnny	'57
Wondering Where the Lions Are	Cockburn, Bruce	'79
Wonderwall	Oasis	'95
Woo-Hoo	Rock-a-Teens, The	'59
Wooden Heart	Presley, Elvis	'60
Wooden Ships	Crosby, Stills & Nash	'69
Woodstock	Crosby, Stills, Nash & Young	'70
Wooly Bully	Sam the Sham and the Pharaohs	'65
Word to the Badd	Jackson, Jermaine	'91
Word, The	Beatles, The	'65
Word Up	Cameo	'86
Words	Missing Persons	'82
Words of Love	Holly, Buddy	'58
Words of Love	Mamas & the Papas, The	'66
Wordy Rappinghood	Tom Tom Club	'81
Work for Food	Dramarama	'93
Work to Do	Isley Brothers, The	'72
Work with Me Annie	Midnighters, The	'54
Workin' My Way Back to You	Four Seasons, The	'66
Working Class Hero	Lennon, John	'70
Working for the Weekend	Loverboy	'82
Working in the Coal Mine	Dorsey, Lee	'65
World Class Fad	Westerberg, Paul	'93
World Is a Ghetto, The	War	'72
World Without Heroes, A	Kiss	'82
World without Love, A	Peter and Gordon	'64
Worst That Could Happen	5th Dimension, The	'67
Wot's It to Ya	Nevil, Robbie	'87
Would	Alice in Chains	'92
Would I Lie to You	Charles & Eddie	'92
Would I Lie to You	Eurythmics	'85
Wouldn't It Be Nice	Beach Boys, The	'66
Wow	Bush, Kate	'80

SONG	ARTIST	YEAR
WPLJ	Four Deuces, The	'55
Wrap It Up	Sam and Dave	'68
Wrap My Body Tight	Gill, Johnny	'91
Wrap Your Troubles in Dreams	Nico	'67
Wrapped Around Your Finger	Police, The	'83
Wrathchild	Iron Maiden	'81
Wreck of the Edmund Fitzgerald, The	Lightfoot, Gordon	'76
Wreck of the John B.	Weavers, The	'50
Written All over Your Face	Rude Boys, The	'90
Wrong 'Em Boyo	Clash, The	'79
Wrong Side of the Road	Waits, Tom	'78
Wuthering Heights	Bush, Kate	'78

X

SONG	ARTIST	YEAR
X-Offender	Blondie	76
Xanadu	Electric Light Orchestra and Olivia Newton-John	'80

Y

SONG	ARTIST	YEAR
Y.M.C.A.	Village People, The	'79
Ya Ya	Dorsey, Lee	'61
Yah Mo B There	Ingram, James	'84
Yakety Yak	Coasters, The	'58
Yank Me, Crank Me	Nugent, Ted	'78
Yankee Lady	Winchester, Jesse	'71
Year of the Cat	Stewart, Al	'77
Year That Clayton Delaney Died, The	Hall, Tom T.	'71
Yellow Brick Road	Captain Beefheart	'66
Yellow Ledbetter	Pearl Jam	'94
Yellow Submarine	Beatles, The	'66
Yer Blues	Beatles, The	'68
Yes, I'm Ready	Mason, Barbara	'65
Yes It Is	Beatles, The	'65
Yes, Tonight Josephine	Ray, Johnny	'55
Yes We Can Can	Pointer Sisters, The	'73
Yesterday	Beatles, The	'65
Yesterday's Songs	Diamond, Neil	'81
Yester-Me Yester-You Yesterday	Wonder, Stevie	'69
Yo-Yo	Osmonds, The	'71
Yogi	Ivy Three, The	'60
You	Aquatones, The	'58
You Ain't Goin' Nowhere	Byrds, The	'68
You Ain't Seen Nothin' Yet	Bachman Turner Overdrive	'74
You and I	James, Rick	'78
You and I	Rabbitt, Eddie	'82
You and Me	Cooper, Alice	'77
You Angel You	Dylan, Bob	'74
You Are Everything	Stylistics, The	'71

SONG	ARTIST	YEAR	SONG	ARTIST	YEAR
You Are My Destiny	Anka, Paul	'58	You Don't Miss Your Water	Bell, William	'62
You Are My Everything	Surface	'88	You Don't Own Me	Gore, Lesley	'63
You Are My Lady	Jackson, Freddie	'85	You Dropped a Bomb on Me	Gap Band, The	'82
You Are So Beautiful	Preston, Billy	'74	You Give Good Love	Houston, Whitney	'85
You Are the Sunshine of My Life	Wonder, Stevie	'72	You Give Love a Bad Name	Bon Jovi	'86
You Are the Woman	Firefall	'76	You Got It	Orbison, Roy	'89
You Beat Me to the Punch	Wells, Mary	'62	You Got It (the Right Stuff)	New Kids on the Block	'88
You Belong to Me	Doobie Brothers, The	'77	You Got It All	Jets, The	'87
You Belong to the City	Frey, Glenn	'85	You Got Lucky	Petty, Tom & the Heartbreakers	'83
You Better Know It	Wilson, Jackie	'59			
You Better Move On	Alexander, Arthur	'62	You Got Me Dizzy	Reed, Jimmy	'56
You Better Sit down Kids	Cher	'67	You Got Me Floatin'	Hendrix, Jimi	'68
You Better Think Twice	Poco	'70	You Got Me Hummin'	Sam and Dave	'66
You Better, You Bet	Who, The	'81	You Got Me Rockin'	Rolling Stones, The	'94
You Can All Join In	Traffic	'68	You Got That Right	Lynyrd Skynyrd	'77
You Can Call Me Al	Simon, Paul	'86	You Got the Love	Rufus	'74
You Can Depend on Me	Lee, Brenda	'61	You Got the Silver	Rolling Stones, The	'68
You Can Do Magic	America	'82	You Got What It Takes	Johnson, Marv	'59
You Can Get It If You Really Want	Dekker, Desmond	'70	You Gotta Be	Des'ree	'94
You Can Have Her	Hamilton, Roy	'61	(You Gotta) Fight for Your Right to Party	Beastie Boys, The	'86
You Can Leave Your Hat On	Newman, Randy	'72			
You Can't Always Get What You Want	Rolling Stones, The	'69	You Haven't Done Nothin'	Wonder, Stevie	'74
You Can't Be Too Strong	Parker, Graham	'79	You Just Haven't Earned It Yet, Baby	Smiths, The	'87
You Can't Catch Me	Berry, Chuck	'67	You Keep Me Hangin' On	Supremes, The	'66
You Can't Change That	Raydio	'79	You Know I Love You	King, B.B.	'52
You Can't Deny It	Stansfield, Lisa	'90	You Know What I Mean	Turtles, The	'67
You Can't Do That	Beatles, The	'64	You Left the Water Running	Lynn, Barbara	'66
You Can't Get What You Want (Till You Know What You Want)	Jackson, Joe	'84	You Look Mahvelous	Crystal, Billy	'85
			You Made This Love a Teardrop	Griffith, Nanci	'89
You Can't Hurry Love	Supremes, The	'66	You Make Loving Fun	Fleetwood Mac	'77
You Can't Judge a Book by Looking at the Cover	Diddley, Bo	'55	You Make Me Feel Brand New	Stylistics, The	'73
			You Make Me Feel Like Dancing	Sayer, Leo	'76
You Can't Sit Down	Upchurch, Phil	'61	(You Make Me Feel Like) A Natural Woman	Franklin, Aretha	'67
You Can't Turn Me Off (in the Middle of Turning Me On)	High Inergy	'77			
			You Make My Dreams	Hall and Oates	'81
You Cheated	Slades, The	'58	You May Be Right	Joel, Billy	'79
You Didn't Have to Be So Nice	Lovin' Spoonful, The	'66	You Mean the World to Me	Braxton, Toni	'93
You Didn't Try to Call Me	Mothers of Invention, The	'66	You Might Think	Cars, The	'84
You Don't Have to Be a Star (to Be in My Show)	McCoo, Marilyn & Billy Davis, Jr.	'76	You Needed Me	Murray, Anne	'75
			You Never Even Called Me By My Name	Goodman, Steve	'70
You Don't Have to Go Home Tonight	Triplets, The	'91			
			You Never Give Me Your Money	Beatles, The	'69
You Don't Have to Say You Love Me	Springfield, Dusty	'66	You Oughta Be with Me	Green, Al	'72
			You Oughta Know	Morissette, Alanis	'95
You Don't Have to Worry	En Vogue	'90	You Really Got Me	Kinks, The	'64
You Don't Know Like I Know	Sam and Dave	'66	You Remind Me	Blige, Mary J.	'92
You Don't Know Me	Charles, Ray	'62	You Say You Don't Love Me	Buzzcocks, The	'79
You Don't Know What You've Got (Until You Lose It)	Donner, Ral	'61	You Send Me	Cooke, Sam	'57
			You Set the Scene	Love	'67
You Don't Love Me	Kooper, Al	'68	You Sexy Thing	Hot Chocolate	'75
You Don't Mess Around with Jim	Croce, Jim	'72			

SONG	ARTIST	YEAR	SONG	ARTIST	YEAR
You Shook Me	Waters, Muddy	'62	(You're Puttin') A Rush on Me	Mills, Stephanie	'87
You Shook Me All Night Long	AC/DC	'80	You're Sixteen, You're Beautiful and You're Mine	Burnette, Johnny	'60
You Should Be Dancing	Bee Gees, The	'76	You're So Fine	Falcons, The	'59
You Should Hear How She Talks About You	Manchester, Melissa	'82	(You're So Square) Baby I Don't Care	Presley, Elvis	'57
You Shoulda Been There	Crenshaw, Marshall	'89	You're So Vain	Simon, Carly	'72
You Showed Me	Byrds, The	'69	You're Still My Baby	Willis, Chuck	'54
You Spin Me Round (Like a Record)	Dead or Alive	'85	You're the First, the Last, My Everything	White, Barry	'74
You Talk Too Much	Jones, Joe	'60	You're the Inspiration	Chicago	'85
You Took the Words Right out of My Mouth	Meat Loaf	'77	You're the One	Clark, Petula	'65
You Turn Me On (the Turn on Song)	Whitcomb, Ian	'65	You're the One That I Want	Newton-John, Olivia and John Travolta	'78
You Turn Me on, I'm a Radio	Mitchell, Joni	'72	You're the Only One	Geils J. Band, The	'77
You Upset Me, Baby	King, B.B.	'54	You're the Reason I'm Living	Darin, Bobby	'63
You Want This	Jackson, Janet	'93	(You're the) Devil in Disguise	Presley, Elvis	'63
You Wear It Well	DeBarge, El with DeBarge	'85	(You've Caught Me) Smilin'	Sly & the Family Stone	'71
You Wear It Well	Stewart, Rod	'72	You've Got a Friend	King, Carole	'71
You Were Mine	Fireflies, The	'59	You've Got Another Thing Comin'	Judas Priest	'81
You Were on My Mind	Ian and Sylvia	'64	You've Got to Hide Your Love Away	Beatles, The	'65
You Will Know	Wonder, Stevie	'87	You've Got Your Troubles	Fortunes, The	'65
You Won't See Me	Beatles, The	'65	(You've Got) The Magic Touch	Platters, The	'56
You'll Lose a Good Thing	Lynn, Barbara	'62	You've Lost That Lovin' Feelin'	Righteous Brothers, The	'64
You're a Better Man Than I	Yardbirds, The	'65	You've Made Me So Very Happy	Holloway, Brenda	'67
You're a Big Boy Now	Lovin' Spoonful, The	'67	You've Really Got a Hold on Me	Miracles, The	'63
You're a Special Part of Me	Ross, Diana	'73	Young Americans	Bowie, David	'75
You're a Very Lovely Woman	Merry-Go-Round	'67	Young Blood	Coasters, The	'57
You're a Wonderful One	Gaye, Marvin	'64	Young Girl	Puckett, Gary & the Union Gap	'68
You're All I Need to Get By	Gaye, Marvin and Tammi Terrell	'68	Young Hearts Run Free	Staton, Candi	'76
You're All I've Got Tonight	Cars, The	'78	Young Love	James, Sonny	'56
You're Breaking My Heart	Nilsson	'72	Young Lovers	Paul and Paula	'63
You're Gonna Get What's Comin'	Palmer, Robert	'78	Young Man Blues	Who, The	'70
You're Gonna Lose That Girl	Beatles, The	'65	Young Turks	Stewart, Rod	'81
You're Gonna Make Me Cry	Wright, O.V.	'65	Young World	Nelson, Rick	'62
You're Gonna Miss Me	Thirteenth Floor Elevators	'66	Younger Generation	Lovin' Spoonful, The	'68
You're in Love	Wilson Phillips	'90	Younger Girl, A	Lovin' Spoonful, The	'65
You're in My Heart (the Final Acclaim)	Stewart, Rod	'77	Youngstown	Springsteen, Bruce	'95
You're Living All over Me	Dinosaur Jr.	'87	Your Cash Ain't Nothin' but Trash	Clovers, The	'54
You're My Best Friend	Queen	'75	Your Cheatin' Heart	Williams, Hank	'52
You're My Everything	Temptations, The	'67	Your Favorite Thing	Sugar	'94
You're My Favorite Waste of Time	Crenshaw, Marshall	'82	Your Generation	Generation X	'78
You're My Love Interest	Hiatt, John	'79	Your Heart Belongs to Me	Supremes, The	'62
(You're My) Soul and Inspiration	Righteous Brothers, The	'66	Your Love	Graham Central Station	'75
You're No Good	Everett, Betty	'63	Your Love	Outfield, The	'86
You're Not Alone	Chicago	'89	Your Love Is Driving Me Crazy	Hagar, Sammy	'83
You're Only Human (Second Wind)	Joel, Billy	'85	(Your Love Keeps Lifting Me) Higher and Higher	Wilson, Jackie	'67
You're Only Lonely	Souther, J.D.	'79	Your Ma Said You Cried in Your Sleep Last Night	Dino, Kenny	'61
You're Probably Wondering Why I'm Here	Mothers of Invention, The	'66	Your Mama Don't Dance	Loggins and Messina	'72

SONG	ARTIST	YEAR
Your Mother Should Know	Beatles, The	'67
Your Own Back Yard	Dion	'70
Your Own Special Way	Genesis	'77
Your Precious Love	Gaye, Marvin and Tammi Terrell	'67
Your Racist Friend	They Might Be Giants	'90
Your Smile	Rene and Angela	'85
Your Smiling Face	Taylor, James	'77
Your Song	John, Elton	'70
Your True Love	Perkins, Carl	'57
Your Wildest Dreams	Moody Blues, The	'86
Yours Is No Disgrace	Yes	'71

SONG	ARTIST	YEAR
Yummy, Yummy, Yummy	Ohio Express	'68
Yvonne	Crenshaw, Marshall	'85
YYZ	Rush	'81

Z

SONG	ARTIST	YEAR
Zanz Can't Dance (Vanz Can't Dance)	Fogerty, John	'85
Zaz Turned Blue	Was (Not Was)	83
Zip-a-Dee-Doo-Dah	Soxx, Bob B. & the Blue Jeans	'62
Zombie	Cranberries, The	94